THE FREE WORLD

THE
FREE WORLD

Art and Thought in the Cold War

LOUIS MENAND

Farrar, Straus and Giroux
New York

Farrar, Straus and Giroux
120 Broadway, New York 10271

Library of Congress Cataloging-in-Publication Data
Names: Menand, Louis, author.
Title: The free world : art and thought in the Cold War / Louis Menand.
Other titles: Art and thought in the Cold War
Description: First edition. | New York : Farrar, Straus and Giroux,
    2021. | Includes bibliographical references and index.
Identifiers: LCCN 2020050736 | ISBN 9780374158453 (hardcover)
Subjects: LCSH: United States—Civilization—1945– | United States—
    Intellectual life—20th century. | Popular culture—United States—
    History—20th century. | Political culture—United States—
    History—20th century. | Cold War—Social aspects.
Classification: LCC E169.12 .M454 2021 | DDC 306.0973/0904—dc23
LC record available at https://lccn.loc.gov/2020050736

Our books may be purchased in bulk for promotional, educational, or business
use. Please contact your local bookseller or the Macmillan Corporate and
Premium Sales Department at 1-800-221-7945, extension 5442, or by email at
MacmillanSpecialMarkets@macmillan.com.

www.fsgbooks.com
www.twitter.com/fsgbooks • www.facebook.com/fsgbooks

1   3   5   7   9   10   8   6   4   2

In memory of my father

Louis Menand III
(1923–2008)

civil libertarian, environmentalist, anti-anti-Communist

We are free to the extent that we know what we are about.

—TOM HAYDEN

How can my pursuit of happiness work if yours is in the way? What am I willing to give up for you too to be free?

—WYNTON MARSALIS

Many a man thinks he is making something when he's only changing things around.

—ZORA NEALE HURSTON

CONTENTS

PREFACE

This book is about a time when the United States was actively engaged with the rest of the world. In the twenty years after the end of the Second World War, the United States invested in the economic recovery of Japan and Western Europe and extended loans to other countries around the world. With the United Kingdom, it created the World Bank and the International Monetary Fund to support global political stability and international trade. It hosted the new United Nations. Through its government, its philanthropic foundations, its universities, and its cultural institutions, it established exchange programs for writers and scholars, distributed literature around the globe, and sent art from American collections and music by American composers and performers abroad. Its entertainment culture was enjoyed almost everywhere. And it welcomed and adapted art, ideas, and entertainment from other countries. Works of literature and philosophy from all over the world were published in affordable translations. Foreign movies were imported and distributed across the country.

The number of Americans attending college increased exponentially. Book sales, record sales, and museum attendance soared. Laws were rewritten to permit works of art and literature to use virtually any language and to represent virtually any subject, and to protect almost any kind of speech. American industry doubled its output. Consumer choice expanded dramatically. The income and wealth gap between top earners and the middle class was the smallest in history. The ideological differences between the two major political parties were minor, enabling the federal government to invest in social programs. The legal basis for the social and political equality of Americans of African ancestry was established and economic opportunities were opened up for women. And around the world, colonial empires collapsed, and in their place rose new independent states.

As conditions changed, so did art and ideas. The expansion of the university, of book publishing, of the music business, and of the art world, along with new technologies of reproduction and distribution, speeded up the rate of innovation. Most striking was the nature of the audience: people cared. Ideas mattered. Painting mattered. Movies mattered. Poetry mattered. The way people judged and interpreted paintings, movies, and poems mattered. People believed in liberty, and thought it really meant something. They believed in authenticity, and thought it really meant something. They believed in democracy and (with some blind spots) in the common humanity of everyone on the planet. They had lived through a worldwide depression that lasted almost ten years and a world war that lasted almost six. They were eager for a fresh start.

In the same period, American citizens were persecuted and sometimes prosecuted for their political views. Agencies of the government spied on Americans and covertly manipulated nongovernmental cultural and political organizations. Immigration policies remained highly restrictive. The United States used its financial leverage to push American goods on foreign markets. It established military bases around the globe and intervened in the internal political affairs of other states, rigging elections, endorsing coups, enabling assassinations, and supporting the extermination of insurgents. A cold war rhetoric, much of it opportunistic and fear-mongering, was allowed to permeate public life. And the nation invested in a massive and expensive military buildup that was out of all proportion to any threat.

A fifth of the population lived in poverty. The enfranchisement of Black Americans and the opening of economic opportunity to women did little to lessen the dominance in virtually every sphere of life of white men. A spirit of American exceptionalism was widespread, as was a quasi-official belief in something called "the American way of life," based on an image of normativity that was (to put it mildly) not inclusive.

The culture industries, as they expanded, absorbed and commercialized independent and offbeat culture-makers, and the university, as it expanded, swallowed up the worlds of creative writing and dissident political opinion. At the end of this period, the country plunged into a foreign war of national independence from which it could not extricate itself for eight years. When it finally did, in the 1970s, growth leveled off, the economy entered a painful period of adjustment, ideological differences sharpened, and the income gap began rapidly increasing. The United States grew wary of foreign commitments, and other countries grew wary of the United States.

And yet, something had happened. An enormous change in America's relations with the rest of the world had taken place. In 1945, there was widespread skepticism, even among Americans, about the value and sophistication of American art and ideas, and widespread respect for the motives and intentions of the American government. After 1965, those attitudes were reversed. The United States lost political credibility, but it had moved from the periphery to the center of an increasing international artistic and intellectual life.

Cultures get transformed not deliberately or programmatically but by the unpredictable effects of social, political, and technological change, and by random acts of cross-pollination. *Ars longa* is the ancient proverb, but actually, art making is short-term. It is a response to changes in the immediate environment and the consequence of serendipitous street-level interactions. Between 1945 and 1965, the rate of serendipity increased, and the environment changed dramatically. So did art and thought.

The transformation of American culture after 1945 was not accomplished entirely by Americans. It came about through exchanges with thinkers and artists from around the world, from the British Isles, France, Germany, and Italy, from Mexico, Canada, and the Caribbean, from decolonizing states in Africa and Asia, from India and Japan. Some of these people were émigrés and exiles (in one case, a fugitive), and some never visited. Many of the American artists and writers were themselves the children of immigrants. Even in an era of restrictive immigration policies and geopolitical tensions, art and ideas got around. The artistic and intellectual culture that emerged in the United States after the Second World War was not an American product. It was the product of the Free World.

This is not a book about the "cultural Cold War" (the use of cultural diplomacy as an instrument of foreign policy), and it is not a book about "Cold War culture" (art and ideas as reflections of Cold War ideology and conditions). It is about an exceptionally rapid and exciting period of cultural change in which the existence of the Cold War was a constant, but only one of many contexts.[1]

I had two reasons for writing the book. The first was the historiographic challenge: how to tell a story of change on this scale. I tried to take into account three dimensions: the underlying social forces—economic, geopolitical, demographic, technological—that created the conditions for the possibility of certain kinds of art and ideas; what was happening "on the street," how X ran into Y, which led to Z; and what was going on in people's heads, what they understood it meant to make a painting or address an injustice or interpret a poem in those years.

To do this, I made a series of vertical cross-sections rather than a survey. And I focused on the headliners, the artists and thinkers who became widely known. I do not think their stories are the only interesting ones, but one of the things I was trying to understand is why certain figures became emblematic. Although this meant leaving a lot out, there is a horizontal through-line. The book I ended up writing is a little like a novel with a hundred characters. But the dots do connect.

The other reason I wrote it is personal. As you have probably guessed, this is the period I grew up in. I was born in 1952. My parents were intellectuals who were mainly interested in politics and whose tastes were not avant-garde, but they were knowledgeable about what was going on in literature and the arts, and I heard all of these names, or almost all of them, when I was a kid. But I had only a vague idea who those people really were, what they actually did, or what made them important such that people like my parents knew about them. Writing this book was a way of filling in the blanks in my own story. It was (as all history writing ultimately is) a way of understanding my own subjectivity.

If you asked me when I was growing up what the most important good in life was, I would have said "freedom." Now I can see that freedom was the slogan of the times. The word was invoked to justify everything. As I got older, I started to wonder just what freedom is, or what it can realistically mean. I wrote this book to help myself, and maybe you, figure that out.

THE FREE WORLD

INTRODUCTION: WHAT THE COLD WAR MEANT

Red Army soldiers Alyosha Kovalyov and Abdulkhakim Ismailov raising the Soviet flag on the roof of the Reichstag building in Berlin, May 2, 1945. A flag had been raised there on the night of April 30. The picture, by Yevgeny Khaldei, is of a reenactment. This is the altered version; one of the two watches on Ismailov's wrists—evidence of looting—has been edited out. Khaldei was inspired by Joe Rosenthal's photograph (also of a reenactment) of marines raising the American flag on Mount Suribachi on the island of Iwo Jima, February 23, 1945. Khaldei's image was iconic because it was evidence for the claim that it was the Communists who had defeated fascism in Europe. (*Tass / Getty Images*)

The wartime alliance between the United States and the Soviet Union was a union of necessity. The war against Nazi Germany had to be a two-front war. The United Kingdom and the United States needed the Red Army to engage the Wehrmacht in the east, and the Red Army did its job. Between June 22, 1941, the day Germany invaded Russia, and June 6, 1944, D-Day, 93 percent of German military casualties, 4.2 million missing, wounded, or killed, were inflicted by Soviet forces.[1] And Stalin needed (and complained that he was slow to get) British and American forces to attack Germany from the west. The Allied coalition was held together, in the end, by one common goal: the total defeat of Nazi Germany.

As long as the fighting continued, few people thought it prudent to speculate publicly about future animosity between the United States and the Soviet Union. Many officials in the Roosevelt administration, although they were realistic about the matters that divided the two countries and were frequently exasperated by Soviet behavior, operated in the hope that the United States and the Soviet Union would be cooperative partners in world affairs after the war was over. These included, besides Roosevelt himself, his two secretaries of state, Cordell Hull and Edward Stettinius, and, more important, since Roosevelt paid relatively little attention to the State Department, his secretary of war, Henry Stimson, and his longtime consigliere, Harry Hopkins.[2]

Roosevelt died on April 12, 1945. On May 8, Germany surrendered, ending the war in Europe. Less than three months later, the United States dropped atomic bombs on Hiroshima and Nagasaki, and on August 15, Japan surrendered. The defeat of the Axis powers meant that the Allies had to reach agreements about the future of Japan, Italy, and Germany, but it also put the fate of a vast amount of territory into play. And much of that territory—Poland, Czechoslovakia, Hungary, and Romania in the west; Turkey and Iran in the south; and Manchuria, Korea, and the Kuril Islands in the east—lay on the borders of the Soviet Union. With their enemies defeated and their armies no longer in the field, the United States and the Soviet Union could disagree openly about the design of the postwar map. And they did.

This was not surprising. The Americans and the Soviets had different national security interests; they had different understandings of international relations; they had very different political, economic, and diplomatic principles. For eighteen months, each government tested the resolve and goodwill of the other and was duly disappointed. Then, on March 12, 1947, in a speech before a joint session of Congress, Harry S. Truman relieved the situation of ambiguity.

"At the present moment in world history," Truman said, "nearly every nation must choose between alternative ways of life."

> One way of life is based upon the will of the majority, and is distinguished by free institutions, representative government, free elections, guarantees of individual liberty, freedom of speech and

religion, and freedom from political oppression. The second way of life is based upon the will of a minority forcibly imposed upon the majority. It relies upon terror and oppression, a controlled press and radio, fixed elections, and the suppression of personal freedoms.

"I believe that it must be the policy of the United States," he said, "to support free peoples who are resisting attempted subjugation by armed minorities or by outside pressures."[3] Truman did not mention the Soviet Union in his speech, but everyone who heard him understood that "armed minorities" referred to Communist insurgents and that "outside pressures" referred to the Kremlin. This became known, almost immediately, as the "Truman Doctrine." The speech was, effectively, the declaration of the Cold War. It would last forty-four years.

During those years, each nation accused the other of cynicism and hypocrisy. Each claimed that the other was seeking to advance its own power and influence in the name of some grand civilizing mission. But each nation also honestly believed that history was on its side and that the other was headed down a dead end.[4] This meant that the outcome of their rivalry could not properly be decided by military superiority alone, since the matter was not finally about brute strength. It was about ideas, and ideas in the broadest sense—about economic and political doctrines, civic and personal values, modes of expression, philosophies of history, theories of human nature, the meaning of truth.

Truman called his speech "the turning point in America's foreign policy," and many in his administration thought the same thing.[5] Its image of a world divided between irreconcilable systems had a powerful effect on policy. Among other things, it killed any chance for a revival of prewar isolationism. It underwrote an enormous buildup of American military capacity. In 1947, the national defense budget was $12.8 billion, or 5.4 percent of GDP; in 1952, Truman's last year in office, it was $46.1 billion, 12.9 percent of GDP. In 1953, even though the Korean War had ended, $53 billion of the nation's $76 billion budget was spent on defense, and the defense budget remained around 10 percent of GDP for the rest of the decade.[6] And Truman's dichotomy—if you are not with us, you are against us—drew the United States into conflicts around the world in which disputes that appeared to be indigenous and parochial could be reframed as battles in the struggle between liberal democracy and totalitarianism.

Totalitarianism, not Communism specifically, was the threat Truman identified in his speech, and Truman thought that all totalitarian systems are essentially police states and essentially the same.[7] In the United States during the Cold War, anti-Communism was just one variety of a politics that was close to universal: anti-totalitarianism. For some Americans who worried about these matters, the future toward which things might be headed was "Communistic"; for others, it was "fascistic." But the imagined futures—whether evoked by allusions to the Brown Shirts or the Bolsheviks, the gas chambers or the Gulag, the Gestapo or the KGB—were fundamentally the same. American anti-Communists were anti-totalitarian, and so were American anti-anti-Communists. The anxiety that the liberal democracies could be sliding toward totalitarianism was shared by people who otherwise shared little. It was equally a left-wing anxiety, a right-wing anxiety, a mainstream anxiety, and a countercultural anxiety.

But what is totalitarianism? How does it arise? Why are people drawn to it? Most important: Could it happen here? People disagreed about how to answer the first three questions, and this made the last question an urgent one. Anything might potentially be a step in the wrong direction. Truman's dichotomy therefore had the same effect on art and thought as it did on government policy: it transformed intramural disputes into global ones. It made questions about value and taste, form and expression, theory and method into questions that bore on the choice between "alternative ways of life." It suggested that whatever did not conduce to liberal democracy might conduce to its opposite. Was consumerism the road to serfdom? Was higher education manufacturing soulless technocrats? Was commercial culture a mode of indoctrination? How could racial and gender inequities be compatible with democratic principles? Which was more important, liberty or equality? Freedom of expression or national security? Artistic form or political content? Was dissent a sign of strength or subversion? Was that a national liberation movement or was it Communist aggression?

In the first two decades of the Cold War, many people therefore believed that art and ideas were an important battleground in the struggle to achieve and maintain a free society. Artistic and philosophical choices carried implications for the way one lived one's life and for the kind of polity in which one wished to live it. The Cold War charged the atmosphere. It raised the stakes.

I

AN EMPTY SKY

Passport photograph of George Kennan, May 1924, when he
was a student at Princeton. (*Courtesy of Joan Kennan*)

1.

When George Kennan composed the documents that would be received
as the rationale for American Cold War foreign policy—the Long Telegram, written in Moscow in February 1946, and "The Sources of Soviet
Conduct," the so-called X Article, published in *Foreign Affairs* in July
1947—he did not imagine he was prescribing a new attitude for a new
time. He was stating what he thought the American attitude toward the
Soviet Union should always have been. He was saying something that
he had been trying to say for years but that he felt few people wanted to
hear. He produced those documents out of exasperation, not inspiration.

Kennan never understood why people talked about the Cold War as
something that began at the end of the Second World War.[1] He thought
that Stalin was a particularly brutal and cunning dictator, but that

Soviet paranoia and insecurity were not products of the Russian Revolution and had, at bottom, nothing to do with Communism. They had to do with Russia's peculiar relation to the West, which had its roots in the eighteenth century. That Russian power would someday present a problem to the rest of Europe and the United States was always, as he put it, "in the cards."[2] He therefore devoted enormous diligence and eloquence to the business of persuading the American government to de-ideologize its differences with the Soviet Union. He did not have much success. This did not surprise him. He was always dubious about the ability of democratically elected politicians to run a sensible foreign policy.

Kennan is sometimes taken to be a member of what was eventually known as the Establishment, or (a term that similarly mixed respect with mild sarcasm) the Wise Men. These were the pragmatic and largely nonpartisan internationalists who played a major role in the running of American foreign policy in the first two thirds of the twentieth century. It was a clan-like group. Most were graduates of Yale, and most had successful careers as Wall Street bankers and lawyers. They believed in something that a later generation would regard as a hypocritical oxymoron: the altruistic use of American power. They wanted the United States to promote its interests abroad; but they also believed that this was for the world's good. They did not conspire to open foreign markets to American business and "the American way of life," because there was nothing conspiratorial about them. They were just what they seemed to be: representatives of an American conception of prosperity and an American sense of global responsibility.

The line can be traced back to the time the United States became an imperial power, during the presidencies of William McKinley and Theodore Roosevelt.* A founding figure was Elihu Root, secretary of war under McKinley and Roosevelt and secretary of state under Roosevelt, a creator of the Council on Foreign Relations, and the winner, in 1912, of the Nobel Peace Prize. Root's protégé Henry Stimson (Andover, Yale, and a partner in the Wall Street firm Root and Clark, founded by Elihu Root's son) was secretary of war under William Howard Taft, secretary of state under Herbert Hoover, and secretary of war again under Franklin D. Roosevelt. Stimson's protégé Robert Lovett

---

* Leaving aside the conquest of Native lands.

(Hill School, Yale, Brown Brothers Harriman) was Truman's secretary of defense; another protégé, John J. McCloy (Peddie, Amherst, Cravath and Cadwalader, Wickersham and Taft), was assistant secretary of war under Roosevelt and Truman, president of the World Bank, and high commissioner for Germany. Others in the mold include two men Kennan worked closely with: Averell Harriman (Groton, Yale, Brown Brothers Harriman), who was made ambassador to the Soviet Union by Roosevelt, and Dean Acheson (Groton, Yale, Covington & Burling), who became Truman's secretary of state.[3]

Kennan had affinities with these men and he was comfortable around them. He had a patrician temperament. But he was not a lawyer or a banker, and he did not get called to public service through connections formed in school. He was a professional diplomat, a lifetime civil servant with practical experience in the field of foreign affairs. He was unlike the others in another, more significant, way, too. He did not believe in the virtues of Americanization.

For one of the peculiar things about Kennan, a man not short on peculiarities, is that he had little love for the country whose fortunes he devoted his life to safeguarding. He realized very early in his career that his loyalty to the United States "would be a loyalty *despite*, not a loyalty *because*, a loyalty of principle, not of identification."[4] What Kennan admired about the United States was the value it placed on the freedom of thought—the supreme good for Cold War intellectuals. Toward American life generally, though, he had the attitude of the typical midcentury European: he thought that Americans were shallow, materialistic, and self-centered. He was firmly anti-majoritarian, not only in foreign affairs, where he considered public opinion a menace, but also in governmental decision-making generally.

In the draft of a book begun in 1938, when he was thirty-four, he advocated restricting the vote to white males and other measures designed to create government by an elite.[5] Even after the war, and in his most widely read books—*American Diplomacy*, published in 1951, and the first volume of his *Memoirs*, which came out in 1967 and won a Pulitzer Prize—he was frank about his estrangement from American life and his problem with democracy. He believed that the form of government has little to do with a nation's quality of life, and he admired conservative autocracies, such as prewar Austria and Portugal under António Salazar.[6] "Democracy, as Americans understand it, is not necessarily the future of all mankind," he wrote in 1985, when he was eighty-one, "nor is it the duty of the U.S. government to assure that it becomes that."[7]

To make the irony complete, the country he felt closest to was Russia. "Russia had been in my blood," he says in the *Memoirs*. "There was some mysterious affinity which I could not explain even to myself."[8] He liked to imagine that he had lived in St. Petersburg in a previous life.[9] When he visited Tolstoy's estate, Yasnaya Polyana, it made him feel, he said, "close to a world to which, I always thought, I could really have belonged, had circumstances permitted."[10]*

He had no sympathy for, or much interest in, Marxism, and he had no illusions about Stalin. He despised the whole Soviet apparat, in part because its minions prevented him from associating with ordinary Russians when he worked at the American embassy in Moscow. Still, he thought that even under Communism, Russians maintained a resilience of character that was disappearing in the West. When he imagined the day the Iron Curtain was lifted, a day his own policy recommendations were intended to bring about, he dreaded what would happen to the Russians once they were exposed to "the wind of material plenty" and "its debilitating and insidious breath."[11] Though he had advocated the reunification of Germany, he took little satisfaction when, in 1990, it finally occurred. It was just the result, he thought, of agitation by young East Germans motivated "by the hope of getting better jobs, making more money, and bathing in the fleshpots of the West." He wondered whether that was what the United States had really wanted when it set out, more than forty years before, to wage a cold war.[12]

2.

Kennan's father was a Minneapolis tax attorney who was fifty-two when his son was born, in 1904. Kennan's mother died of peritonitis from a ruptured appendix when he was two months old. (There is a story that the doctor refused to operate without permission from the husband, who was away on a fishing trip.)[13] He went to St. John's Military Academy, in Wisconsin, and then to Princeton, where he landed squarely in

---

* "Tolstoy would have approved of him," Isaiah Berlin once said of Kennan. "He'd have had a good time with Tolstoy." (John Lewis Gaddis, *George F. Kennan* [New York: Penguin, 2011], 562.)

the role of outsider, a role that was partly cultivated and partly thrust upon him.

Kennan had read *This Side of Paradise* in high school, but preppie-dom was a foreign land. "[M]y college career bore little resemblance to Fitzgerald's," as he put it in the *Memoirs*.[14] He told of being left behind while his classmates all went off to the Yale game. In desperation, he hitched a ride to New Haven, but since he didn't have a ticket, he couldn't get into the stadium, and he returned to Princeton as solitary as when he left it.[15] In his freshman year, he had an attack of scarlet fever, which set him back socially and seems to have triggered a lifelong susceptibility to illness.

He was not an outstanding student, but he had ambition. He joined the Foreign Service in 1926, a year after graduating from Princeton, with an initial posting to Hamburg by way of Geneva. Two years later, he was quick to take advantage of a State Department offer to pay the way for any member of the Foreign Service who wanted to achieve fluency in Chinese, Japanese, Arabic, or Russian. In 1928, the United States did not recognize the government of the Soviet Union and there were no diplomatic relations between the countries. But there were Americans who did business in the Soviet Union—Averell Harriman, for example, owned a manganese concession in the Caucasus in the 1920s—and Kennan saw that the freeze could not last forever. He felt destiny operating as well in the form of a distant cousin, also named George Kennan, who had written an important book on Siberia and the exile system under the tsars.[16]

It was in the language-training program that Kennan discovered his special feeling for Russian life. He was one of just seven men chosen to learn Russian in the ten years the program ran, from 1926 to 1936. His studies were supervised by the head of the State Department's Division of Eastern European Affairs, Robert Kelley. Kelley was a formidable figure, and his attitude toward the Soviet Union almost certainly influenced the views of many of the officers who passed through the program, including Kennan and the man, also a Soviet specialist, who became Kennan's closest friend in the Foreign Service, Charles (Chip) Bohlen.

Kelley had spent a year after college at Harvard working on his Russian at the École Nationale des Langues Orientales Vivantes in Paris, then returned to Harvard to begin work on a PhD. He joined the State Department in 1922.[17] Kelley understood that Communism was a subject that stirred up passions, and he was scrupulous about thoroughness and objectivity in running his division. The reports his office produced were noted for their scholarly rigor.[18] But he took a legalistic view of Soviet behavior. He regarded the government as an outlaw regime whose word could not be trusted, dangerous to its neighbors and a defaulter on its debts. And he took a hard line on recognition.[19] Even in 1933, when it was clear that Roosevelt, a man with little patience for legalism, intended to open diplomatic relations with Moscow, Kelley, though only a junior official in the State Department, delivered combative testimony before the Senate Foreign Relations Committee on the matter and composed a vigorous opposing brief, which was duly transmitted to the president.[20]

To begin his language training, in 1928, Kennan was sent to Tallinn, in Estonia, for a preliminary tryout in the consulate (and "to make sure that we could cope with the local liquor and the local girls," he later said), and then, briefly, to Riga, in Latvia.[21] Since he was already fluent in German, he chose Berlin to study in. (Five of the other trainees went to Paris; one went to Prague.)[22] In 1929, his first year there, he took Russian-language classes at the Seminar für Orientalische Sprachen, a school established by Bismarck for training diplomats, and with private tutors. He also took courses on Russian subjects at the Hochschule für Politik, a private academy created to support democracy and the Weimar Republic. He spent his second year as a student at the Friedrich-Wilhelms-Universität (now Humboldt-Universität zu Berlin, also long referred to as the University of Berlin).[23] And he met the woman he married, Annelise Sørensen, who was Norwegian.

Kennan's tutors in Berlin were Russian émigrés. They read Russian classics together, and he became friendly with some of them.[24] His studies entirely avoided Marxism, Communism, and the Russian Revolution. This was by Kelley's design. It happened that excellent courses on subjects such as Soviet finance and Soviet political structure were offered at the university, and Kennan wrote to Kelley to ask if he should take them. Kelley said no, he wanted him to get the same education that a Russian who attended one of the tsarist universities before the Revolution would have had.[25] "It was wise direction, for which I have been always grateful," Kennan wrote in his *Memoirs*.[26] What all of this meant, of course, was that he was acculturated into the pre-Revolution Russian world that the Bolsheviks had overthrown.

Kennan's views on the Soviet Union were more supple than Kelley's.[27] Kennan was not disposed to be legalistic in analyzing international relations, and he discounted the ideological pretensions of Soviet policy declarations. He thought that subversion and talk of world revolution were things to be taken seriously, but he was not alarmed by them. He shared with Kelley a conviction that Soviet leadership was perfectly untrustworthy, and he opposed opening diplomatic relations. "The present system of Soviet Russia is unalterably opposed to our traditional system," he wrote to a friend in 1931. This means that "there can be no possible middle ground or compromise between the two . . . that the two systems cannot even exist together in the same world unless an economic cordon is put around one or the other of them, and that within twenty or thirty years either Russia will be capitalist or we shall be communist."[28] When he wrote those words, Kennan had never been to the Soviet Union and he had met only a handful of Soviet officials.[29] But "[n]ever," he wrote in the *Memoirs*, "—neither then nor at any later date—did I consider the Soviet Union a fit ally or associate, actual or potential, for this country."[30]

After two years in Berlin, Kennan was posted to the American legation in Riga, which was used by the State Department as a listening post for intelligence about the Soviet Union.[31] In 1933, Roosevelt opened diplomatic relations, and Kennan and Bohlen were assigned to accompany the American ambassador, William Bullitt, to Moscow, where Kennan helped set up the new embassy.[32]

Bullitt began his ambassadorship with enthusiasm, but regular dealings with the Kremlin quickly soured him on the Soviet experiment. In 1936, he quit, and was appointed ambassador to France by Roosevelt.* Bullitt's successor, Joseph Davies, also started out with friendly feelings, and although he attended, with Kennan translating for him, the last of the Moscow show trials—the trials, with their forced confessions, that Stalin used to exterminate his rivals among the old Bolsheviks—Davies elected not to be disabused.[33] During Davies's term, the Division of Eastern European Affairs was shut down and Kelley was reassigned to the American embassy in Ankara, where he remained until the end of the war. Kennan was transferred to Washington. He spent a year

---

* They were old friends, although they would break later on when Bullitt essentially used blackmail, involving alleged homosexual propositions, to get another Roosevelt intimate, Sumner Welles, fired from the State Department. Welles *was* fired, but Roosevelt saw to it that Bullitt's career was ruined.

manning the new Russia desk in the State Department, and then was dispatched to Prague.

He arrived there on September 29, 1938, the day Neville Chamberlain, the British prime minister, announced the Munich Agreement, handing to Hitler the part of Czechoslovakia the Germans called the Sudetenland. Kennan was in Wenceslas Square when the agreement was announced. "[O]ne of my first impressions of the post-Munich Prague," he later wrote, "was thus the sight of crowds of people weeping, unabashedly, in the streets at this death knell of the independence their country had enjoyed for a brief twenty years."[34] Within six months, the German army had occupied the rest of Czechoslovakia.

When Germany invaded Poland, in September 1939, Kennan was transferred to Berlin. He had little contact with Nazi officials, and he thought that most Berliners seemed detached from the country's military adventures.[35] On December 11, 1941, four days after the attack on Pearl Harbor, Germany declared war on the United States, and the American legation was taken from Berlin by sealed train to the town of Bad Nauheim, where it was interned, incommunicado, under the supervision of the Gestapo. Kennan was in charge of the hundred and thirty Americans. Kennan recalled the Bad Nauheim quarantine with distaste. "The details of this ordeal would alone make a book," he wrote in the *Memoirs*.[36] He was not referring to the Gestapo; he was referring to the Americans, who he thought behaved like spoiled children. When everyone was released, after five and a half months, he wrote a satirical poem about his fellow inmates.

His next posting was to Lisbon, where he negotiated with the prime minister, António Salazar, for the use of bases in the Azores by Allied aircraft. In January 1944, with the end of the war in sight, Kennan served as political adviser to the American ambassador to the United Kingdom, John G. Winant, at meetings of the European Advisory Commission in London, set up to discuss the political problems of postwar Europe.[37] Bohlen, who had been in Tokyo when Pearl Harbor was attacked and was interned for six months, remembered Kennan returning to Washington from the meetings "appalled by the behavior of American soldiers—their reading of comic books, their foul language, and their obsession with sex, among other things. He wondered whether the United States was capable of being a world power."[38]

Back in Washington, Kennan got his first major break. It was completely unexpected. As a hard-liner on Soviet relations and a protégé of the warehoused Kelley, he had every reason to assume that he would never see Moscow as an American diplomat again. But Bohlen was now chief of the State Department's Soviet Section, and Roosevelt had made Harriman his ambassador to the Soviet Union. Bohlen introduced Kennan to Harriman, who, it turned out, had read the elder George Kennan's books on the Siberian prison system.[39] (It happened that that Kennan had also written a biography of Harriman's father, E. H. Harriman, the railroad executive who ran the Union Pacific.) Harriman offered Kennan the position of minister-counselor—essentially, second-in-command. Kennan arrived in Moscow on July 1, 1944, just in time to witness an endgame he had long anticipated: the liberation of Eastern Europe by the Red Army.

3.

Although Stalin had ordered a special translation for himself of *Mein Kampf* and had underlined the passages in which Hitler laid out his vision of expansion into Russia and the destruction of Bolshevism, he seems to have been blindsided by Germany's invasion of the Soviet Union.[40] It began on June 22, 1941, twenty-two months after the two nations had signed a nonaggression pact, splitting up Poland—the start of the Second World War. By the middle of November, German troops were within forty miles of Moscow. Parts of the Soviet government, including the foreign ministry, were evacuated to Kuybyshev, on the east bank of the Volga, six hundred miles to the east.[41]

Then, in a strategic miscalculation, Hitler delayed his advance on Moscow and the German army was caught in a Russian winter for which it was unprepared. Temperatures fell to −45°F. At the cost of more than six hundred thousand lives, the Soviets were able to stop the German advance and save Moscow.[42] After an extraordinary mobilization that produced, in a nation of 170 million people, a total force of more than 34 million, the Soviets began to push the Germans out. The counteroffensive at Stalingrad in the winter of 1942–1943 and the German defeat in the epic tank battle at Kursk in July 1943 turned the tide of the war in Europe.[43] The Soviets rolled the Germans back through western Russia, Moldova, Ukraine, Belorussia, and the Baltic states and into the German-occupied nations of Eastern Europe. By the time Kennan arrived in Moscow in the summer of 1944, the Red Army had crossed into Poland and was within a hundred miles of Warsaw.[44]

Kennan flew in via Stalingrad. The battle there had lasted two hundred days, and from the air, everything but the airport building seemed to have been destroyed. He could see dumping grounds filled with wrecked planes and tanks.[45] The damage in the war between Germany and the Soviet Union was staggering. Hitler's wars in Western Europe were militarily conventional affairs aimed at the capitulation, always swift, of the enemy government. The war in the east was different. Hitler was not trying to knock the Soviet Union out in order to protect his conquests in Western Europe; he had made those conquests precisely so that he would not be distracted from the main goal of his foreign policy: ethnic cleansing, the enslavement of the Slavs, and the creation of *Lebensraum* in the east.[46]

The war in Russia was therefore a *Vernichtungskrieg*—a war of extermination—and, once the Soviets saw what the Germans were doing, that is how both sides fought it. Prisoners were starved, shot, or sent to slave labor camps. When the main fighting in a region was over, the two armies' political units, the NKVD and the *Einsatzgruppen*, rounded up local leaders, who might someday form resistance movements, and executed them or sent them to camps. The Soviets killed prisoners of war and deported "anti-Soviet elements"; the Germans wiped out Jewish communities on the spot and transported captured Jews to the death camps in the former Poland.[47] In retreat, both armies pursued a scorched earth policy. What could not be expropriated was sabotaged or demolished. In the USSR alone, more than 1,700 towns, 70,000 villages, 32,000 industrial plants, and 65,000 kilometers of railroad track were destroyed. Total Soviet deaths, military and civilian, are estimated to have exceeded 26 million, 15 percent of the population.[48]

The defeat of the Wehrmacht in the east is what made the liberation of Western Europe possible. Roosevelt and Churchill understood the military logic from the moment the Soviet Union was invaded, and they did not hesitate to ally themselves with Stalin—a man who, less than two years earlier, had made an agreement with Hitler to divide up Poland. Roosevelt liked to quote a Balkan proverb: "It is permitted you in time of grave danger to walk with the devil until you have crossed the bridge."[49] Both nations immediately undertook to provide the Soviets with enormous quantities of matériel, even though the United States was not yet a combatant.[50]

From the start of what Churchill called the "Grand Alliance," the question was what the price would be. Stalin's own view was uncomplicated. "This war is not as in the past; whoever occupies a territory also imposes on it his own social system," he explained to a group of Communist officials when the Red Army was bearing down on Berlin. "Everyone imposes his own system as far as his army can reach. It cannot be otherwise."[51] That is exactly how Kennan thought the Soviets understood the matter, and he regarded Soviet intentions in Eastern Europe as the toad in the Allied garden. As long as the Soviets needed the Americans and the British in order to destroy the Third Reich, Stalin would act the statesman. Once Germany was defeated, the Kremlin would revert to prewar form and the United States would have very little leverage. But Kennan felt that he could not get anyone to acknowledge that the toad was there.

When they split up Poland in 1939, the Germans and the Soviets had taken measures to eliminate nationalistic threats, imprisoning or executing tens of thousands of Poles. But a hundred thousand Poles managed to evade capture, and they formed the core of the Polish Home Army, the Armija Krajowa—the second-largest national resistance movement, after Josip Broz Tito's Yugoslav Partisans, in Europe. The Polish government-in-exile, which directed the actions of the Armija Krajowa, was based in London. Stalin therefore knew, as his army approached Warsaw in the summer of 1944, that the job of eliminating nationalistic elements in Poland was not finished. On July 27, he recognized the Polish Committee of National Liberation, based in Chelm, near Lublin, as the true representatives of the Polish people. The Committee was a collection of political figures willing to accept Soviet authority. The production of the Lublin Poles was effectively an announcement that after the Germans were driven out, the Soviet Union did not intend to recognize the claims of the Poles in London.[52]

At the American embassy in Moscow, in conversation with a diplomat who suggested that Stalin might be willing to compromise on this matter in the interest of good relations among the Allies, Kennan was caustic. "The Russians have a long-term consistent policy," as he recorded his comments in his diary. "We have—and they know we have—a fluctuating policy reflecting only the momentary fancies of public opinion in the United States. We are incapable of conceiving and executing a long-term consistent policy. The Russians know from this that if they only wait long enough they can always find, sooner or later, a situation in which they can get what they want from us . . . In their opinion, as one of them recently told me, nothing is impossible."[53]

Stalin did not compromise, and the denouement was more terrible than even Kennan could have imagined. On August 1, with Soviet troops now on the outskirts of Warsaw, the Armija Krajowa, led by General Tadeusz Bór-Komorowski, staged an uprising against the city's German occupiers.* Taken by surprise, the Germans found themselves in a pitched battle with the Polish fighters, but within a week, the counterattack began. Hitler, who had barely survived an assassination attempt less than two weeks earlier, put Heinrich Himmler in charge; the operation was carried out by the SS under the command of Erich von dem Bach-Zelewski, a specialist in anti-partisan warfare who had supervised, for Himmler, the extermination of Jews in Belorussia. The SS massacred populations in the suburbs they captured; hospitals were burned down; partisans seeking to flee in the sewers were killed with gas grenades; citizens were thrown out the windows of their apartment buildings; wounded men and women were soaked with gasoline and burned to death.[54]

From the first days of the insurrection, the London Poles pleaded with the Soviets for the Red Army, sections of which were encamped just across the Vistula River to the east, to enter Warsaw. But the Soviets did nothing. The British and the Americans asked Stalin to air-drop supplies to the partisans. He refused. The uprising, he told Churchill, was "a reckless and fearful gamble . . . Soviet headquarters have decided that they must dissociate themselves from the Warsaw adventure since they cannot assume either direct or indirect responsibility for it."[55]

Harriman met with Andrei Vyshinsky, a subordinate of Vyacheslav Molotov, the foreign minister, who informed him that the Soviet Union wished to have no hand in the Warsaw revolt, and that the American request to refuel in Soviet air bases after air-dropping supplies to the insurgents was denied. Harriman pressed his case and was given an

---

* This 1945 insurrection, sometimes referred to as the Warsaw Rising, is distinct from the Warsaw Ghetto Uprising, which took place in 1943.

audience with Molotov, who explained, again, that the Soviet Union could do nothing to save the Home Army and the London Poles from their own folly.[56] "For the first time since coming to Moscow I am gravely concerned by the attitude of the Soviet Government in its refusal to permit us to assist the Poles in Warsaw as well as in its own policy of apparent inactivity," Harriman wrote to the secretary of state, Cordell Hull.[57] But Roosevelt was annoyed with the Poles, who had not notified the Allies in advance of their plans and who were now driving a wedge into the Alliance, and he declined to make a personal appeal on the matter to Stalin.[58]

On September 13, Soviet aircraft began dropping matériel into Warsaw, though the drops were made without parachutes, damaging some of the supplies.[59] American planes were permitted to use Soviet bases for supply runs over Warsaw. But it was too late. On October 3, Bór-Komorowski surrendered. After sixty-two days of fighting, 15,000 Polish partisans and some 200,000 civilians had been killed. The delay of the Soviet advance allowed Himmler to ship almost all of the 67,000 Jews held in the ghetto in Łódź to Auschwitz, the last remaining death camp, where most were killed.[60] When the fighting was over, half a million Warsaw Poles were sent to concentration camps. The rest were deported to do forced labor in Germany. On Hitler's orders, the city was razed. Warsaw had had the largest concentration of Jews of any city in Europe.[61] When the Red Army finally entered it, in January 1945, the streets were filled with dead bodies. Not a single living person, Jew or Gentile, remained.[62]

The Warsaw uprising was a bad miscalculation, but for the plan to have worked at all, the timing would have had to have been exquisite. The Poles needed the Soviets to apply just enough pressure on the German forces in the city to make their own job successful, but not enough to make it unnecessary. The rising was intended to set up a confrontation with Stalin over the future leadership of Poland. The Home Army hoped to present Stalin with a fait accompli.[63] Stalin's order to his army to halt at the banks of the Vistula and wait for the uprising to play itself out was mainly a political decision.[64] And he timed carefully the aid he eventually did extend to ensure that it would be ineffective. As Churchill put it, the Soviets "wished to have the non-Communist Poles destroyed to the full, but also to keep alive the idea that they were going to their rescue."[65]

This was the game into which Roosevelt refused to be drawn. But Kennan thought that the United States should have forced the Soviets to show their hand. "I was personally not present at this fateful meeting with Stalin and Molotov," he wrote in the *Memoirs* (Stalin did not, in fact, meet with Harriman on this issue); "but I can recall the appearance of the ambassador and General Deane [John R. Deane, head of the military mission] as they returned, in the wee hours of the night, shattered by the experience. There was no doubt in any of our minds as to the implications of the position the Soviet leaders had taken. This was a gauntlet thrown down, in a spirit of malicious glee, before the Western powers."[66]

For the rest of his life, Kennan cited the Warsaw crisis as the moment when Soviet leaders "should have been confronted with the choice between changing their policy completely and agreeing to collaborate in the establishment of truly independent countries in Eastern Europe or forfeiting Western-Allied support and sponsorship for the remaining phases of their war effort."[67] Kennan didn't think that calling the Kremlin out would have stopped Stalin; he considered the creation of a Soviet "sphere of influence" inevitable. But he thought that it would have ended the impression of American acquiescence to Soviet designs on Eastern Europe and possibly served as a check on Soviet expansion elsewhere.

The Warsaw disaster inspired Kennan to produce his first major treatise on the nature of Soviet society and Soviet power, an essay entitled "Russia—Seven Years Later." (The seven years referred to the time between Kennan's two Moscow postings.) He handed the essay to Harriman in September 1944, who took it with him to Washington later that fall. Kennan never heard from Harriman about it, but Harriman seems to have read it and to have given a copy to Harry Hopkins, the man closest to Roosevelt.[68] Harriman must have realized that Kennan had something to say that the president needed to hear but that he did not want to tell Roosevelt himself. Seventeen months later, though, Harriman gave Kennan his big chance to speak directly to Washington.

4.

Even though the Warsaw crisis had momentarily shaken his confidence, Harriman believed that he could talk turkey with Stalin. Kennan emphatically did not believe in personal diplomacy, and he thought the idea that Stalin was someone the United States could cut reasonable deals with was delusional. In some ways, this made for a productive relationship. Harriman was happy to let Kennan write his opinionated and sometimes unsolicited reports, since if they didn't interest him, he simply ignored them. He didn't care if Kennan's views diverged from official policy, either, because he didn't negotiate strictly from policy anyway. He flew by the seat of his pants. Although he affected brusqueness—he was known as the Crocodile: somnolent until provoked—he admired Kennan and respected his intellect. "I've never been able to work with anyone as closely as I did with him," he said many years later.[69]

Kennan didn't just disapprove of diplomacy by intuition and of idealistic policy talk; he deeply loathed them. Declarations about the self-determination of peoples or international economic cooperation—the things Roosevelt and Churchill announced as Allied war aims in the Atlantic Charter—seemed to him not only utopian and unenforceable but also dangerous restrictions on a government's scope of action. The Polish question was a perfect example. The United States did not want to jeopardize the fight against Germany in order to decide which group of partisans should form the government of a liberated Poland. The fate of Poland was not something that affected the national interests of the United States. In Kennan's view, it was better to be frank about this and stop pretending that the United States was fighting for a democratic Poland, or that Moscow and Washington had the same goals and values. But the American government wants to appear virtuous for domestic political reasons, Kennan thought, so it continued to say that self-determination was its goal and to call the Soviets comrades and allies, even as those allies were preparing to walk all over the Atlantic Charter.

Kennan put all of this in a long letter to Bohlen in January 1945. The United States, he argued, should abandon Eastern Europe to the Soviets, accept the division of Germany, and give up plans for the United Nations, which he considered a classic case of political wishful thinking. When he received the letter, Bohlen was busy at the Yalta Conference, where the Allies were negotiating the future of Europe, and his reply to Kennan was curt. "Foreign policy of that kind cannot be made in a democracy," he said.[70]

A year later, on February 9, 1946, Stalin delivered an election speech, broadcast from the Bolshoi Theatre in Moscow. (Stalin was "running" for deputy to the Supreme Soviet, a powerless body.) In it, he described the Second World War as the "inevitable result of the development of the world economic and political forces on the basis of monopoly capitalism."[71] The statement was perfectly doctrinal: that capitalist countries will always go to war was a basic tenet of Marxism-Leninism, and saying so was unusual only in the context of the brief period of the wartime alliance, which was now, for all intents and purposes, at an end. Kennan didn't think the speech was worth more than a summary in his regular report. He called Stalin's remarks about the causes of the Second World War a "[s]traight Marxist interpretation," though "more militant and oratorical in tone" than customary.[72]

But in Washington, Stalin's words were read with alarm. The secretary of state, James Byrnes, asked the embassy in Moscow for an analysis. Harriman had finished his appointment as ambassador and was leaving Moscow for good, so he gave Kennan his blessing to reply as he saw fit. Kennan seized the day. "They had asked for it," as he put it in the *Memoirs*. "Now, by God, they would have it."[73] The result was reputedly the longest telegram in State Department history, 5,500 words in five numbered parts. Not uncharacteristically, Kennan was ill and lying in bed when he dictated it.

The Long Telegram was Kennan unbound. Yes, he said, American capitalism and Soviet Communism were incompatible systems; Washington shouldn't have been surprised to hear Stalin say so. But Stalin's speech had more to do with the nature of Russia than with the nature of Communism. Russian foreign policy had always been motivated by fear of the outside world, and Marxism gave the current regime an ideological fig leaf for its insecurity and paranoia. What the world was seeing was simply "the steady advance of uneasy Russian nationalism, a centuries old movement in which conceptions of offense and defense are inextricably confused. But in new guise of international Marxism, with its honeyed promises to a desperate and war torn outside world, it is more dangerous and insidious than ever before."[74] Whatever it might say, the Soviet Union would always seek to undermine the West. That was just Russian nature.

Still, Kennan suggested, the Soviet Union was weak. It had suffered catastrophic damage; it was territorially overstretched; and it did not want a war. It only wanted to take advantage of opportunities to extend its power. The policy of the United States, therefore, should be vigilance against allowing such opportunities to arise. "Soviet power, unlike that of Hitlerite Germany, is neither schematic nor adventuristic," Kennan explained. "It does not work by fixed plans. It does not take unnecessary risks. Impervious to logic of reason, and it is highly sensitive to logic of force."[75] If the United States showed resolve whenever Moscow made threatening noises, if it extended aid to the European democracies so that they would know who their friends were, and if it otherwise tended its own garden, there was no reason to expect World War Three.

Byrnes was pleased with Kennan's telegram. Harriman, back in Washington, found it "a little bit slow reading in spots," but showed it to James Forrestal, the secretary of the navy—and this turned out, for better or worse, to be the key to Kennan's postwar fortunes.[76]

Forrestal (Princeton; Dillon, Read) was a dedicated anti-Communist.[77] Paul Nitze (Hotchkiss; Harvard; Dillon, Read), whom Forrestal had brought into the government from Dillon, Read and was now a mid-level official in the State Department, had come to the Pentagon to warn Forrestal that Stalin's February 9 speech amounted to a "delayed declaration of war on the U.S."[78] Forrestal later claimed that Supreme Court Associate Justice William O. Douglas had called the speech "the Declaration of World War III."[79]

In fact, there was nothing in Stalin's speech suggesting a declaration of war. His prediction, entirely theoretical, was of a war between capitalist powers, which he thought would present a danger to the Soviet Union. But Forrestal interpreted Kennan's telegram as a confirmation of his own reading of Soviet intentions. He had the telegram mimeographed and circulated to members of the cabinet and senior military officials. Whether Truman read it is unknown, but the telegram took the capital by storm. Within weeks, Kennan was recalled to Washington and installed, with Forrestal's help, at the new National War College with the title Deputy Commandant for Foreign Affairs.[80] His job was to give lectures on international relations to military, State Department, and Foreign Service officials. The State Department also dispatched him on a speaking tour to instruct the public on the true nature of the Soviet threat. "I seem to have hit the jackpot as a 'Russian expert,'" Kennan wrote to one of his sisters, Jeanette. "You'd be amazed, what seems to be coming my way."[81]

In the beginning of his presidency, Truman, too, had imagined that he could talk turkey with Stalin, who he said reminded him of Tom Pendergast, the Kansas City political boss who was his patron back in Missouri.[82] Truman's theory was the same as Harriman's: wise guys keep their word. But his confidence did not last much beyond the end of the war. The Soviet Union was slow to withdraw its troops from northern Iran, in defiance of earlier agreements; in January 1946, it refused to join the newly established World Bank and the International Monetary Fund, set up at the Bretton Woods conference.[83] And in February, the American public learned of a major Soviet spy ring in Canada, which had been exposed the previous fall by a defector named Igor Gouzenko.[84] The spies had been stealing atomic secrets.

In a meeting on the same day as his election speech, Stalin assured listeners that Soviet scientists would soon be able to create atomic weapons. (The remarks were reported in *Pravda* and may have been on Kennan's mind when he wrote the Long Telegram.)[85] The comity of the Grand Alliance was unraveling, but there was no consensus in Washington about how a Soviet policy should be constructed. In this context, Kennan's telegram looked like a blueprint.

Forrestal was a classic anti-Communist: he believed that Stalin's actions could be explained by Marxist philosophy and that the goal of Soviet foreign policy was world revolution. He took the ideology seriously, in other words—just the view that Kennan had taken pains to debunk. But Forrestal must have felt when he read the telegram that he had finally found someone in the State Department who was willing to take a hard line on the Soviet Union.

In December 1945, Forrestal asked one of his consultants, a Smith College professor named Edward Willett, to prepare an analysis of Marxist theory. Willett knew nothing about Marxism, and the paper he produced, on his third try, "Dialectical Materialism and Russian Objectives," did not entirely satisfy Forrestal. Forrestal asked Kennan to rework the paper. Kennan was not particularly interested in Marxism himself, and he did not believe that Soviet behavior had anything to do with dialectical materialism. But in January 1947, he handed Forrestal an essay of his own called "Psychological Background of Soviet Foreign Policy."

"Soviet pressure against the free institutions of the western world," Kennan explained, "is something that can be contained by the adroit and vigilant application of counter-force at a series of constantly shifting geographical and political points, corresponding to the shifts and maneuvers of Soviet policy, but which cannot be charmed or talked out of existence." This was the doctrine of containment. Containment need not be a stalemate, Kennan said; for "the possibility remains (and in the opinion of this writer it is a strong one) that Soviet power, like the capitalist world of its conception, bears within it the seeds of its own decay, and that the sprouting of these seeds is well advanced."[86] Forrestal was pleased with the paper and sent it to the secretary of state, George Marshall. When the editor of *Foreign Affairs*, Hamilton Fish Armstrong, asked Kennan for a contribution to his journal, Kennan requested permission to publish his paper. It was agreed that since Kennan was a State Department official, it would be published pseudonymously. This was the X Article, "The Sources of Soviet Conduct."[87] It came out in July, three months after Truman delivered his "alternative ways of life" speech.

In the X Article, Kennan suggested that Marxism presented itself to the Soviets as "a highly convenient rationalization for their own instinctive desires," and that it continued to justify measures—hostility toward the outside world, for example, and the retention of the dictatorship—that were consistent with the behavior of the Russian state in the time of the tsars.[88] After that, the article was a restatement of the Long Telegram: it stressed the Soviet Union's present weakness, the likelihood of its eventual internal collapse, and the unlikelihood of military aggression against the West.

The Marxist-Leninist belief in the inevitability of world socialism provided Kennan with his key metaphor. The Soviet Union was in no hurry to reach that consummation, since, according to the theory, the work is being done by history. The Soviets only needed to keep the pressure on, to act as "a fluid stream which moves constantly, wherever it is permitted to move, toward a given goal." The policy of the United States must therefore be one of "long-term, patient but firm and vigilant containment of Russian expansive tendencies."[89] In the long run, the Soviets might not smash up the car, but they would go broke paying the tickets. The aim was to keep Communism in its box until that happened. That is what "containment" boils down to.

When the X Article appeared, Kennan had started in what would be his most influential government post. Marshall had appointed him chief of the new Policy Planning Staff, created in an effort to think ahead in the area of international relations—not something the United States had had much practice with. The Staff became the principal source of policy ideas for Marshall, and thus for the president. Kennan dominated the meetings, did most of the writing, and worked in the office next to Marshall's. For two years, he essentially formulated American foreign policy.*

The circulation of *Foreign Affairs* was under twenty thousand. But on July 8, United Press identified Kennan as the author of the X Article, and thirteen days later, *Newsweek*, a vigorously anti-Communist publication with a circulation of half a million, published a lead story on Kennan. The X Article, *Newsweek* said, illuminated "the reasons behind the Truman Doctrine," and its publication represented the triumph of the State Department's Soviet experts who, having managed to survive "the appeasement and war years," had been trained back in the 1930s by Robert Kelley.[90] The hard-liners had won.

In September, Kennan was attacked in the *New York Herald Tribune* by the political columnist Walter Lippmann.† In a series of twelve columns, Lippman, too, identified the article as the rationale for the Truman Doctrine, and he criticized Kennan for failing to recognize the Soviet Union's genuine national security interests in Eastern Europe. The policy of containment, Lippmann said, called for an impractical deployment of military forces; it handed the Soviets the advantage of picking the sites of confrontation; and it forced the United States to devote resources to areas of minor importance on the periphery of the Soviet Union rather than to its allies in Western Europe. He called the policy a "strategic monstrosity."[91]

Kennan was appalled. He believed that he had proposed a policy of selective diplomatic and economic confrontation, an asymmetrical response to Soviet actions, not a state of global military preparedness.[92] He wrote a letter to Lippmann explaining that he had been misinterpreted but he could not bring himself to send it.[93]

Nor did he wish to be identified with the Truman Doctrine. He had been shown a draft of Truman's speech, written by Dean Acheson, and had objected to the conversion of a policy recommendation to provide aid to Greece and Turkey (the ostensible purpose of the speech) into an anti-Communist crusade.[94] The first report Kennan wrote for the Policy Planning Staff, two months later, included a request that steps be taken

---

* Kennan's successor was Paul Nitze, a major figure in the production, in 1950, of the secret protocol known as NSC-68 that laid the groundwork for the militarization of the Cold War.
† There may have been some bad blood in this, too. Lippmann had been banished from the pages of *Foreign Affairs* because Armstrong's wife had left him for Lippmann in 1938.

to make it clear that the Truman Doctrine was not a "blank check."[95] Steps were not taken. Kennan was now suddenly on the other side of the anti-Communist issue. He had gone from being a little too hard to being a little too soft.

The Long Telegram and "The Sources of Soviet Conduct" had similar contents but dissimilar contexts. The Long Telegram could not have been read as an intellectual peg for the Truman administration to hang its policy hat on because when Kennan wrote it, the White House did not really have a policy toward the Soviet Union and Eastern Europe. There were hard-liners in the administration, like Forrestal, but there were also accommodationists, like Henry Wallace, the secretary of commerce. Kennan's telegram provided Washington with a middle path, a way to be anti-Communist without going to war. Kennan didn't say that the Soviets were reasonable or democratic or decent in any way; he did say that the United States did not need to drop the bomb on them.[96]

When the X Article appeared, almost a year and a half later, the United States did have a policy, and it was well on its way down a non-accommodationist road. On March 21, 1947, nine days after his speech, Truman signed an executive order establishing the Federal Employees Loyalty Program, which assigned the FBI and other agencies to undertake investigations of government workers suspected of disloyalty.[97] Between 1947 and 1953, 4,765,705 federal employees filled out forms initiating loyalty investigations; 26,236 were referred for further scrutiny and 560 (proportionately a small haul) were fired or not hired. Some 1,700 cases were left pending when the program expired. The loyalty program had a chilling effect on federal employees who remained in government and who identified themselves with the tradition of New Deal progressivism. The program discovered no espionage.[98]*

On June 5, in a commencement speech at Harvard, Marshall announced the European Recovery Program—the Marshall Plan, which Kennan had been instrumental in designing.[99] Marshall's speech, drafted by Bohlen, was short, just under eleven minutes, and it was interrupted by applause twice, both times in response to lines implicitly criticizing the Soviet Union.[100] At Kennan's suggestion, Marshall aid was open to all countries, including the nations of Eastern Europe and the

---

* The Soviet Union's first successful deployment of an atomic bomb, August 29, 1949, is probably a reason for the persistence of these loyalty tests.

Soviet Union. Kennan knew that Stalin would refuse the aid and would compel his satellites to refuse it as well—which he did, thereby assuming some of the blame for the Cold War division of Europe.[101]

On July 26, Truman signed the National Security Act, establishing the CIA, the National Security Council, and the Joint Chiefs of Staff. On September 17, Forrestal became secretary of defense. And on October 20, 1947, the House Un-American Activities Committee began its investigation into Communists in Hollywood. In the context of these events, the X Article read not as a wake-up call but as a gloss on existing policy. Washington was already awake.

Faithful to the choreography of Cold War geopolitics, Moscow's steps were virtually synchronous. On March 28, 1947, seven days after Truman ordered the loyalty program for federal employees, the Central Committee of the Communist Party established a Court of Honor charged with investigating Western influences on Soviet art and science. This was an institutionalization of Zhdanovshchina, the Zhdanov Doctrine, a campaign against artistic formalism and other evidence of creeping Westernization that had been implemented in 1946 by the Kremlin's chief ideologist, Andrei Zhdanov.

On September 22, 1947, the first meeting of the Communist Information Bureau—Cominform—was held in the resort town of Skłarska Poręba in Polish Silesia, a region from which hundreds of thousands of ethnic Germans had recently been deported. The Cominform was Stalin's response to the Marshall Plan. Delegates were told that the goal of the meeting was to organize resistance to "attempts by American imperialism to enslave economically the countries of Europe."[102] "A new alignment of political forces has arisen," Zhdanov told representatives of the Communist Parties of France, Italy, the Soviet Union, and six Eastern European nations. "The more the war recedes into the past, the more distinct become two major trends in post-war international policy, corresponding to the division of the political forces operating on the international arena into two major camps: the imperialist and anti-democratic camp"—led by the United States—"on the one hand, and the anti-imperialist and democratic camp, on the other."[103]

It was the Truman Doctrine in a mirror. European Communists interpreted Zhdanov's speech as a command to exchange the policy of national unity for one of confrontation and subversion.[104] The United States responded in turn by designing its own program of covert psychological warfare run out of the CIA—a time bomb that would explode twenty years later.[105] In November 1947, Lippmann collected the columns he had written on Kennan and containment and published them as a book. He called it *The Cold War*. Lippmann was correct. It had begun.

5.

Kennan was not in the habit of citing his contemporaries in his work.[106] The impression he gave, that he was simply describing things the way they struck an intelligent and unsentimental observer, was one reason for his effectiveness as a writer. But Kennan did not form his views in an intellectual vacuum. He was an eloquent and exceptionally well-placed exponent of the theory of international relations known as realism.

A realist is someone who thinks that a nation's foreign policy should be guided by a cold consideration of its own interests, not by some set of legal or moral principles. This is because although in domestic politics conflicts can be adjudicated by a supreme law of the land, in international politics, no such law exists. When Germany invaded Poland, Poland could not take Germany to court. The essential condition of international politics is anarchy. There are just a lot of nations out there, each one attempting to secure and, if possible, extend its own power. That is what nations do. It's their nature. Establishing courts of international justice, or outlawing wars of aggression, or making pacts of collective security are simply attempts, dressed up in the language of human rights and self-determination, by the stronger powers to lock in the status quo. They instantiate winner's normativity.

What makes this complicated, and, to a non-realist, confusing, is that nations ordinarily justify what they are doing, and object to what other nations are doing, in legal and moral terms. On one level, they do this in order to win popular support at home and respect in the eyes of the world. But it's more than that. For nations tend to believe their own stories. Hitler believed that the punitiveness of the Treaty of Versailles entitled Germany to violate agreements about rearmament and territorial expansion. Stalin believed that the Soviet Union had historical precedent and legitimate national security reasons to install puppet governments in Eastern Europe.

In the international sphere, in other words, morality and legality are relative. Many Americans (not to mention many Eastern Europeans) considered Soviet justifications for interfering in the affairs of countries on their borders to be transparent fictions, but the Soviets felt similarly about, for example, the Marshall Plan. From the American point of view, the plan was the humanitarian act of a generous nation that had the best interests of its beneficiaries at heart; from the Soviet point of view, it was a means of buying loyalty, of opening markets to American business, and of suppressing a rival economic system, socialism. From the realist point of view, both nations, the United States when it offered the aid and the Soviet Union when it refused it, were only doing what they thought was in their own national interest.

Two books were responsible for helping people see the world this way, and both benefited from timing. The first was *The Twenty Years' Crisis*, by the British historian E. H. Carr, published in September 1939, just as the United Kingdom and France were declaring war on Germany. The second was *Politics Among Nations*, by the émigré academic Hans Morgenthau, which was published nine years later, after the Cold War had begun. Both were theories of realism, and both had a major influence on the understanding of international relations among American academics and intellectuals.

Technically, Morgenthau was not a refugee, since he had been living outside Germany—in Geneva, Madrid, and Paris—before he immigrated to the United States in 1937. But the reason he had been teaching and writing abroad—his field was international law—was that as a Jew, he had no future in German academia. The United States was his choice of almost last resort. (He did turn down a job in Venezuela.) His English was poor, and when he disembarked, he had no prospect of work. After five months, during which he was told at an agency for émigré scholars that he might have luck looking for a position as an elevator operator, he managed to get a temporary teaching appointment at Brooklyn College.[107]

In 1939, he moved to the University of Kansas City, and in 1943, he accepted a six-month replacement position at the University of Chicago. When the professor he was filling in for, Quincy Wright, who had gone to Washington to serve as a consultant in the State Department, stayed away longer than expected, Morgenthau was given a regular appointment.[108] He made the most of it. Between 1946 and 1951, he brought out three major books, including *Politics Among Nations*; he edited or co-edited three more books, among them an important textbook, *Principles and Problems of International Politics*; and he published thirty-four articles. Within a year of its publication, *Politics Among Nations* had been adopted as an introductory text at Harvard, Columbia, Yale, Princeton, and ninety other colleges. Within four years, it was being used by more instructors in North American universities than all other international relations textbooks combined.[109] By 1954, the year of the second edition, Morgenthau was the preeminent figure in the field.

The key term in Morgenthau's theory was "power." "Man's aspiration for power is not an accident of history," he wrote in an essay a year before the big book appeared; "it is not a temporary deviation from a normal state of freedom; it is an all-permeating fact which is of the very essence of human existence."[110] Liberal internationalists, or "idealists," such as Woodrow Wilson, think that war and conflict are aberrations, consequences of bad governments, and that human nature can be improved or overcome by democracy, rational policies, and goodwill. They think that nations share "a harmony of interests"—that they understand that what is bad for one nation is for all nations. Morgenthau's Chicago colleague Quincy Wright's major work, for example, was *A Study of War* (1942), two massive volumes ending with a chapter called "Toward a Warless World." Morgenthau thought this was a fantasy. "[T]he struggle for power is universal in time and space and is an undeniable fact of experience," he wrote in *Politics Among Nations*. "The desire to dominate, in particular, is a constitutive element of all human associations."[111]

The term "realism" did not appear in the first edition of *Politics Among Nations*. It was with the second edition, six years later, that Morgenthau positioned his book as both the foundation for an academic field and a primer for policy makers—a double identity that has always characterized the field of international relations. The new edition opened with a section entitled "Six Principles of Political Realism," along with a map showing resources for the manufacture of nuclear bombs in Communist and non-Communist areas of the world, and it incorporated new references to containment and the Cold War.

Although Morgenthau characterized the conflict between idealism and realism as "the great debate," there does not seem to have been much of a debate.[112] After Hitler and Hiroshima, the notion that what every nation really wants is peace did not have much purchase. So by the mid-1950s, the discipline of international relations had acquired a new profile: it was understood to operate with a realist paradigm, to be dominated by American academics whose interests responded to the changing state of American foreign relations, and to be a European import.[113] As Arnold Wolfers, a professor of international relations at Yale who had emigrated from Germany in 1933, put it: an Anglo-American "philosophy of moral choice," which assumes that nations are free to pursue their goals and moral convictions, was in conflict with a European "philosophy of necessity," which assumes that nations pursue their interests.[114]

This was something of a caricature. There had been realist thinkers in the United States since the late nineteenth century, even, arguably, since the time of Alexander Hamilton and the Federalists.[115] Lippmann's criticism of Kennan was not a criticism of realism; on the contrary, it was a realist's attack on what Lippmann took to be an expression of the crusader mentality. Still, Cold War realism presented itself as a European chastening of American naïveté. That was part of its attraction. The term derives, after all, from *Realpolitik*, and the modern statesman who personified European *Realpolitik* was Otto von Bismarck. Kennan's first exposure to a realist way of thinking about foreign relations came in Berlin, at the Seminar für Orientalische Sprachen, Bismarck's creation, when he studied there as a young man in 1929–1930.[116]

Kennan met Morgenthau during a visit to the University of Chicago in 1948; a year later, when he was director of policy planning, he invited Morgenthau and Wolfers to a conference with administration officials and other public figures at the State Department to discuss the desirability of a reduction of American presence in Western Europe (a suggestion the consultants rejected).[117] Morgenthau returned the favor by arranging for Kennan to give the Charles R. Walgreen Foundation Lectures at the University of Chicago. Kennan delivered these in the spring of 1951, and they were published that fall as *American Diplomacy, 1900–1950*. The jacket carried a reading title: "And the challenge of Soviet power." The X Article was included as an appendix.

Does realism have moral content? Value relativism seems built into the theory. As Morgenthau put it, nations "meet under an empty sky from which the gods have departed."[118] Criticism of other nations' political behavior reflects only the contingent biases of the nation that criticizes. "German aggression and lawlessness were not morally obnoxious to France and Great Britain as long as they were directed against

Russia," Morgenthau pointed out in 1946. He was writing about the Nuremberg Trials, where German aggression (natural state behavior) was made a crime (a violation of legal and moral principles). He considered the trials "a symptom of the moral and intellectual confusion of our times."[119] The Second World War "was a war for survival, undertaken by individual nations in their own national interest, not the punitive war of a morally united humanity for the purpose of making eternal justice prevail."[120] Kennan, too, regarded the Nuremberg Trials with "horror."[121] He thought the United States had no moral standing to judge what Germany had done in the East. In the single allusion to the Holocaust in the two volumes of his *Memoirs*, he says that it was not America's business.

So is "the national interest" a morally empty category? Morgenthau was aware of this problem. In an otherwise admiring essay on Carr's work, he complained that *The Twenty Years' Crisis* "leads of necessity to a relativistic, instrumentalist conception of morality." With no transcendent position from which to judge politics among nations, "the political moralist transforms himself into a utopian of power."[122] Still, Morgenthau was hard pressed to define the proper transcendent position. He worried that such a position would become the justification for a crusade. A moralist, he said, is someone who thinks that "[w]hat is good for the crusading country is by definition good for all mankind, and if the rest of mankind refuses to accept such claims to universal recognition, it must be converted with fire and sword."[123] Wilson's mission to make the world safe for a democracy was such a crusade; Bolshevism's aspiration to world revolution was such a crusade. And so, Morgenthau implied, was a policy designed to free the world from Communism. This was always Kennan's worry, too—that the great danger for the United States in the Cold War was the temptation to combine power politics with a moral mission, to turn containment from a pragmatic foreign policy into an anti-Communist crusade backed by nuclear bombs.

The realist version of "the harmony of interests" is "the balance of power." Realism is a Great Power theory of international relations. Smaller states, what George Orwell called "comic opera states," don't matter.[124] The goal is to keep the major powers happy enough with what they have and sufficiently intimidated by the other major powers that they don't start going after weaker states—not because that would violate the sovereignty of weaker states, but because it would upset the balance of power. Carr thought that Chamberlain did the right thing at Munich when he handed the Sudetenland over to Hitler. He was acting as a realist: he exchanged part of Czechoslovakia for what he called "peace for our time."* Kennan thought, similarly, that the only way to have prevented the Soviet occupation of Eastern Europe would have been for the American army to get there first. Great powers such as Germany and Russia have always had "spheres of influence." It is unrealistic to pretend that states within those spheres have an absolute right to self-determination, or that, if they do, it is the business of the United States to secure it.

"Power always thinks it has a great Soul," John Adams wrote to Thomas Jefferson.[125] After Europe destroyed itself in the Second World War, the United States had power over other nations to a degree unprecedented in its history, possibly in the world's history, and it was natural for Americans to conclude that they deserved it—that their good fortune had moral validation. Kennan worried that such a belief could become a high-minded justification for interference in the affairs of other nations. He thought that Americans needed to be realists because they could not trust themselves to be moralists.

---

* In the 1946 edition of *The Twenty Years' Crisis*, Carr removed the passages in which he defended the appeasement of Hitler.

2

THE OBJECT OF POWER

The view from Orwell's bedroom at Barnhill, on the island
of Jura, in Scotland, where he finished *Nineteen Eighty-Four*.
(*Photograph courtesy of Damaris Fletcher*)

1.

Although it was Walter Lippmann who gave the term currency, the
first writer to use "Cold War" to describe postwar international relations was George Orwell.[1] Orwell did not advocate a Cold War; on the
contrary, he dreaded the prospect. He thought it would mean a world
dominated by totalitarian monsters locked in an interminable and unwinnable struggle. All possible futures considered, he preferred a hot
war, a nuclear exchange that wiped out most of the race and sent the
planet back to the Bronze Age, where humanity could begin again with
a clean slate.[2]

Yet after his death from tuberculosis in January 1950, at the age of
forty-six, Orwell became an iconic figure not to pacifists or to people
who believed that the Cold War was avoidable, but to Cold Warriors

from virtually every point on the political compass. Ex-Communists, socialists, liberals, neoliberals, neoconservatives, conservatives, libertarians, and the far-right anti-Communist John Birch Society all identified with Orwell.[3]* His name was turned into a description of the kind of future these people wanted the West mobilized to prevent: Orwellian. Even though his great contribution to the twentieth-century political imaginary, *Nineteen Eighty-Four*, published in 1949, was intended as a warning about what a Cold War might turn the world into, it was evoked for forty years as a warning of what the world might become without one.

Nineteen Eighty-Four belongs to the midcentury literature on totalitarianism, a powerful agent in shaping postwar thought. Some of these books were based on personal experience: Victor Kravchenko's *I Chose Freedom* (1946), Margarete Buber-Neumann's *Under Two Dictators* (1948), Czeslaw Milosz's *The Captive Mind* (1953). Some were philosophical, such as Karl Popper's *The Open Society and Its Enemies* (1945) or academic, like Carl Friedrich and Zbigniew Brzezinski's *Totalitarian Dictatorship and Autocracy* (1956), a standard text in academic political science. Many were polemical: Friedrich Hayek's *The Road to Serfdom* (1944), Arthur Schlesinger, Jr.'s, *The Vital Center* (1949), Raymond Aron's *The Opium of the Intellectuals* (1955). And a few, including Arthur Koestler's *Darkness at Noon* (1940) (an influence on *Nineteen Eighty-Four*: Koestler and Orwell were friends) and Ray Bradbury's *Fahrenheit 451* (1953), were fictional. These books were not read simply as reports on totalitarian life, or attempts to explain recent history, or fictional imaginings of a possible future. They were used to gauge the health of nontotalitarian states and to identify traits and tendencies that might lead to totalitarian conditions in liberal democracies like the United Kingdom, France, and the United States. They became instruments of diagnosis and analysis. They were looked to for ways to answer the question: Could it happen here?

Initially, there were three problems to untangle. The first was whether totalitarianism is just another form of dictatorship, which is an ancient and recurrent type of political regime, or a phenomenon unique to the twentieth century. Very quickly, the balance of opinion swung to

---

* The John Birch Society used 1984 as the last four digits of the phone number in its Washington office.

the second position. Most people who wrote about totalitarianism analyzed it as a product, or a disease, of modernity. They also understood it, more specifically, not merely as a consequence of political and economic developments since the Enlightenment (or the French Revolution, or the rise of industrial capitalism), but as a response to the existential condition of twentieth-century human beings.

A second problem was whether the same term could be used to classify both Nazi Germany and Stalinist Russia. Public opinion on this matter tended to follow events, and events, as is their way, were unhelpful. Although in the 1930s the American press often treated Nazi Germany and the Soviet Union as comparable regimes, ideologically they were antagonistic.[4] Anti-Bolshevism was a basic component of Nazism from the start, and the Popular Front, which Stalin created in 1935 through the offices of the Communist International, defined itself as a coalition of anti-fascist parties.

The Nonaggression Pact in August 1939 threw this alignment into confusion and led some people to claim that Stalin's Soviet Union had revealed itself to be the Nazi-like regime it really was. Less than two years later, however, after Germany invaded the Soviet Union and Stalin became a member of the Grand Alliance, "anti-fascist" made a comeback in Kremlin rhetoric, and the word "totalitarian" started appearing less frequently in American newspapers. But after the war was over, it was soon customary to talk about fascism and Communism as taxonomically identical.[5] "There isn't any difference in totalitarian states," Harry S. Truman said in 1947. "I don't care what you call them—you call them Nazi, Communist or Fascist, or Franco, or anything else—they are all alike."[6] This remained the view of the American public. People referred to "Red Fascists" without any sense of contradiction.[7]

This had been the view of a growing number of both Marxist and non-Marxist intellectuals since 1934 as well. And after 1945, most Marxists in the United States (this was less the case in Europe, where the differences were more robustly defended until 1956) gave up trying to preserve a distinction between Stalinism and Nazism as regime types.[8] "Totalitarianism" thus became a phenomenon that floated free of specific ideologies or political leaders or historical and geopolitical circumstances. Functionally, Nazi racial doctrine and the Soviet goal of the classless society could be considered interchangeable—chiliastic ends that justified criminal means. Hitler and Stalin, too, were treated as effectively the same: supreme figureheads who were nevertheless replaceable, and who could almost be a fiction, the face on a million posters—*Nineteen Eighty-Four*'s Big Brother or *Darkness at Noon*'s No. 1. And analytically, writers did not distinguish between a major industrial power that felt emasculated by a punitive peace treaty (Germany) and a developmentally backward nation that believed it was encircled by imperialist enemies (Russia)—just as one does not distinguish medically between a king and a peasant when they both have the flu. Totalitarianism was a disease that threatened all.

This led to a third question: Was totalitarianism, in some form, the direction in which history was headed, an inevitable consequence of modernization, of high-tech economies and mass publics? Or was it an antibody within modernity, a backlash against enlightenment, a nihilism marking the outer pale of liberal tolerance? The first view was the prevalent view. People worried that totalitarianism was latent in the organization of modern society, and, if this was so, that it was contagious, which meant that it had to be quarantined and, ultimately, eradicated. The policy of containment therefore had two faces. One looked outward to identify threats to democratic self-determination around the world; the other looked within, to detect dangerous trends and vulnerabilities within the liberal polity. "Much depends on health and vigor of our own society," George Kennan wrote in the Long Telegram. "World communism is like a malignant parasite which feeds only on diseased tissue. This is a point at which domestic and foreign policies meet."[9]

The midcentury writers on totalitarianism reached a large number of readers; Koestler and Hayek, in particular, reached a very large number. But none had as many readers as Orwell. Between 1949 and 1956, the peak years of Cold War tensions, *Nineteen Eighty-Four* sold more than two million copies. *Nineteen Eighty-Four* and *Animal Farm*, Orwell's satire of Bolshevism, were eventually translated into more than sixty languages, and by 1989, the year the Berlin Wall came down and the Soviet Union entered its death spiral, the two books had sold forty million copies.[10] Relatively few of the people who read those books had much knowledge of totalitarianism other than what they got from Orwell.

2.

Orwell knew that he was dying before he finished *Nineteen Eighty-Four*, that it would almost certainly be his last book.[11] Its key character, and the reason Orwell wrote the novel, is not Winston, the skeptical apparatchik whose brief escape from official surveillance turns out to be illusory and leads to his destruction. The key figure is the commissar who devises Winston's entrapment, explains to him why it was necessary, "cures" him of his deviationism, and then has him shot—O'Brien. O'Brien was the diagnosis of a mentality Orwell thought he knew well. O'Brien was the product of a lifetime spent observing left-wing intellectuals.

Orwell was a left-wing intellectual, too. For much of his life, in fact, he was a revolutionary socialist. But he was also a contrary man. He was a socialist whose abuse of socialists—"all that dreary tribe of high-minded women and sandal-wearers and bearded fruit-juice drinkers who come flocking towards the smell of 'progress' like bluebottles to a dead cat," he described one type—could be as vicious as any Tory's.[12] His friends and colleagues admired his integrity but they also found him a little unfeeling. "Writing was the one great thing in his life," remembered a friend, Brenda Salkeld, who had known Orwell since he was a young man. "Nothing—not even people—got in the way of that."[13] Orwell might not have disagreed. He was a confessed graphomaniac. "[A]s soon as a book is finished, I begin, actually from the next day, worrying because the next one is not begun," he wrote near the end of his life.[14] By then, he had published nine books and hundreds of articles and essays. He said that he couldn't escape the feeling that he had wasted too much time not writing.

Orwell was born in 1903 in Motihari, in British India, where his father was a subdeputy agent in the Opium Department of the Indian Civil Service, which supervised the legal opium trade with China. He went to England when he was a year old and was raised there by his mother. (The family name was Blair; Orwell's given name was Eric.) Orwell's father visited the family for three months in 1907, attending to domestic matters with sufficient diligence to leave his wife pregnant, and did not return until 1912. By then, Orwell was boarding as a scholarship student at St. Cyprian's, the school he wrote about, many years later, in the essay "Such, Such Were the Joys." He studied hard and won a scholarship to Eton, and it was there that a pattern of self-denial began. He deliberately slacked off, earning a reputation as an indifferent student. Instead of taking the exams for university, he joined the Imperial Police and went to Burma. (Two much-anthologized essays came from his time there: "A Hanging" and "Shooting an Elephant.") In 1927, after five years in Burma, while on leave in England and with no employment prospects, he resigned. He spent the next five years as a tramp and itinerant worker, experiences that became the basis for his first book, *Down and Out in Paris and London*, published under his new pen name, George Orwell, in 1933. He taught school briefly, worked in a bookstore (the subject of the essay "Bookshop Memories"), and spent two months in the industrial districts in the north of England gathering material for *The Road to Wigan Pier*, which came out in 1937.[15]

That was the year Orwell went to Spain, where he fought with the Loyalists against Francisco Franco's fascists. He joined the militia of the Partido Obrero de Unificación Marxista (Workers' Party of Marxist Unification, or POUM) and fought for almost six months, until he was shot in the throat by a fascist sniper.[16] He witnessed the brutal suppression by the Moscow Communists of independent socialist parties like POUM in the Republican alliance. His account of those experiences, *Homage to Catalonia*, was published in 1938. Although it did not sell many copies (six hundred in twelve years) until it was republished after the war, the book established him in the position he would occupy for the rest of his life: the leading anti-Stalinist intellectual of the British left.[17]

During the Second World War, Orwell worked in the Eastern Service of the BBC, where he produced and, along with T. S. Eliot, William Empson, and other well-known writers, delivered radio talks, mostly on literary subjects, aimed at rallying Indian support for the British war effort. For the first time since 1927, he received the salary he had enjoyed as a policeman in Burma, but he disliked the work, which he regarded as propaganda. Room 101, the torture chamber in *Nineteen Eighty-Four*, was the name of the room where the Eastern Service held its compulsory committee meetings.[18]

In 1943, Orwell quit the BBC and became literary editor of *Tribune*, a socialist weekly edited by Aneurin Bevan, a leader of the Labour Party and a man whose politics and person Orwell respected. Between December 1943 and April 1947, Orwell wrote eighty weekly columns for

Tribune called "As I Please." After the financial success of *Animal Farm*, which, after being turned down by five publishing houses in England, appeared in the last month of the war, Orwell removed himself to a rented farmhouse on Jura, a climatologically challenged island in the Inner Hebrides, off the west coast of Scotland. And that was where, when he was not too sick to type, he wrote *Nineteen Eighty-Four.*[19]

There is no great mystery behind the life choices Orwell made: he wanted to de-class himself. From his days at St. Cyprian's, possibly even earlier, he saw the class system as a system of oppression, and nothing but a system of oppression. He didn't merely take adventures in class crossing. He turned his life into an experiment in classlessness. His commitment to the experiment was the main reason for his attachment to socialism, and it was also the reason friends and colleagues occasionally found him perverse and exasperating. His insistence on living in uncomfortable conditions, his refusal (despite his bad lungs) to wear a hat and coat in winter, his habit of pouring his tea into the saucer and slurping it (in the working-class manner) struck people not as colorful eccentricities, but as reproaches directed at their own bourgeois addiction to comfort and decorum.[20] Which they were. Orwell was a brilliant and cultured man, with an Eton accent and an anomalous, vaguely French mustache, who wore the same beat-up tweed jacket nearly every day, made his own furniture, and lived, most of the time, one step up from squalor. He read Joyce and kept a goat in the backyard. He was authentic and inauthentic at the same time, a writer who believed in honesty above all things and who published under a made-up name.

The guilt that Orwell felt about his own position as a member of the white imperialist bourgeoisie preceded his interest in politics as such. He thought that Englishmen who boasted of liberty and prosperity while India was still a colony were hypocrites. "Under the capitalist system, in order that England may live in comparative comfort, a hundred million Indians must live on the verge of starvation—an evil state of affairs, but you acquiesce in it every time you step into a taxi or eat a plate of strawberries and cream," he wrote in *The Road to Wigan Pier.*[21] He hoped that there would be a socialist revolution in England, and if violence was necessary, he condoned it. "I dare say the London gutters will have to run with blood," he wrote in 1940. "All right, let them, if it is necessary."[22]

A year later, in a little book called *The Lion and the Unicorn: Socialism and the English Genius*, he wrote: "It is only by revolution that the native genius of the English people can be set free . . . Whether it happens with or without bloodshed is largely an accident of time and place."[23] Like many people, he had concluded long before that capitalism had failed. He thought that Hitler's military success on the Continent proved the superiority of a planned economy. "What this war has demonstrated is that private capitalism . . . *does not work*. It cannot deliver the goods," he wrote. ". . . It is not certain that Socialism is in all ways superior to capitalism, but it is certain that, unlike capitalism, it can solve the problems of production and consumption . . . The State simply calculates what goods will be needed and does its best to produce them."[24]

Near the end of his life, Orwell listed *The Lion and the Unicorn* as one of the works he did not want reprinted.[25] He had moderated some of his views, particularly about the virtues of a centrally planned economy, but the book was also uncharacteristically programmatic. Apart from the commitment to equality, there was not much about socialist theory that was important to Orwell. His ideas about economics were rudimentary, and he had little patience for the temporizing that ordinary politics requires. In 1945, after Germany surrendered, Winston Churchill and the Conservatives were voted out and a Labour government came in with Aneurin Bevan as minister of health. Within less than a year, Orwell was complaining that the new government had taken no steps to abolish the House of Lords.[26]

A great deal of Orwell's journalism was therefore directed at his fellow leftists. He wrote to promote his own version of socialist ideals against the views of other socialists, especially, after 1938, against the tendency to excuse or justify the behavior of the Soviet Union. So when he wrote, for example, about the 1944 Warsaw uprising, he was less interested in what was actually going on in Poland—about which, as he admitted, he did not have much information—than he was in the attitude of the British left. He dismissed as pro-Soviet propaganda the charge that the London Poles had planned the uprising as a way of stealing a step on Stalin in the establishment of a postwar government, and he dismissed as anti-Soviet propaganda the charge that Stalin was deliberately letting the Germans wipe out the Home Army. (Both of those charges now seem to have been justified.) But his principal targets were the Soviet apologists in the British press. "Their attitude towards Russian foreign policy is not 'Is this policy right or wrong?' but 'This is Russian policy: how can we make it appear right?'" he complained. "And this attitude is defended, if at all, solely on grounds of power. The Russians are powerful in Eastern Europe, we are not: therefore we must not oppose them. This involves the principle, of its nature alien to Socialism, that you must not protest against an evil which you cannot prevent."[27]

This type of infighting is a feature of most political journalism, and the mid-twentieth-century left in particular was obsessed with internal deviationism, an obsession inherited from one of the most merciless political infighters of all time, Karl Marx. Most of these doctrinal disputes led to sectarianism, to the splintering of parties and movements, and, ultimately, to obsolescence. Occasionally, though, they produced theoretical novelties. *Nineteen Eighty-Four* was a product of one of those novelties.

3.

Many intellectuals changed their politics between the time of the Great Depression and the time of the Cold War, but James Burnham was unusual: he went from revolutionary Marxism and Trotskyism to right-wing anti-Communism without passing through anything resembling liberalism. In 1939, he was condemning reformist leftists for putting intellectual freedom ahead of revolution; by 1947, he was advocating a preemptive nuclear strike against the Soviet Union.[28] From 1949 to 1953, Burnham worked as an adviser on anti-Communist political warfare in the CIA's Office of Policy Coordination, a covert operations group devised by Kennan's State Department Office of Policy Planning.[29] After Burnham left the CIA, he helped found the conservative *National Review*, which began publishing in 1955. For twenty-three years, he wrote a column for the magazine called at first "The Third World War," and then, when that failed to materialize, "The Protracted Conflict." After Burnham died, in 1987, the *National Review*'s first and longtime editor, William F. Buckley, called him "[b]eyond any question . . . the dominant intellectual influence in the development of this journal."[30]

From Trotsky to Buckley, there was one constant for Burnham. "Burnham hated liberalism," as the democratic socialist Irving Howe put it. "He thought it was soft."[31] Burnham was a realist, but a different kind of realist from Morgenthau and Kennan. For them, realism was a theory of international relations designed to avoid conflict by acknowledging it. For Burnham, the logical consequence of acknowledging conflict was to take the upper hand. Realism made him a hawk.

Burnham came to Marxism from the wrong side—which is to say, the right side—of the tracks. He was born into a well-off Catholic family. His father, a British immigrant, was vice president of a railroad company; his brother Philip would become co-editor of the Catholic journal *Commonweal*. Burnham finished at the top of his class at Princeton. His interest was literature; T. S. Eliot was his hero. He pursued his studies at Balliol College, Oxford, where he was taught by (among others) J. R. R. Tolkien, and received a degree in 1929.* That fall, he accepted a position in the philosophy department at New York University, where he became a colleague of Sidney Hook, who was then a Marxist and fellow traveler. In 1930, he founded and edited, with his friend the poet Philip Wheelwright, *Symposium*, a literary and philosophical journal that attracted a range of distinguished contributors, from John Dewey to William Carlos Williams.

Burnham's big book, *The Managerial Revolution: What Is Happening in the World*, was published in 1941, less than a year after his break with socialism. A dozen publishers had turned it down; Hook intervened with his own publisher, Richard Fleming at the John Day Company, which printed it. Fleming did not think the book would sell even a thousand copies, but it was a sensation. *Time* named it one of the top six books of 1941 (along with *Darkness at Noon*); a reviewer at *The New York Times* listed it as one of the year's best (also along with *Darkness at Noon*). A hundred thousand copies were sold in the United States and the United Kingdom and a paperback edition did even better. After the war, the book was translated into fourteen languages.[32]

In the book, Burnham claimed that the world was undergoing a transition to a managerial society. Control over the means of production was now in the hands of a new elite: the managers, executives, financiers, and stockholders who owned and ran corporations, and the government administrators who regulated them. This new elite emerged, he explained, for a Marxist reason: in a world of advanced technology and mass markets, the class of managers and administrators, people who know how the system works, is more productive than the class of bourgeois capitalists.†

---

* *The Hobbit*, Tolkien's first Middle Earth book, did not come out until 1937. The *Lord of the Rings* trilogy was published in 1954–1955.
† The general idea had precursors, such as *The Modern Corporation and Private Property* (1932),

That was how Marx thought class relations change. Burnham already considered Roosevelt's New Deal to be a means of "preparing the United States for the comparatively smooth transition to Fascism," and he folded the United States easily into his picture of a world headed toward managerialism.[33] He thought that the nations that were farthest along that road were Russia, Germany, and Italy, and this suggested to him that totalitarian dictatorship was managerialism's natural political form.[34]

Burnham predicted the emergence of "a comparatively small number of great nations, or 'super-states,' which will divide the world among them." Burnham imagined three of these, centered in the areas where advanced industry was already concentrated: the United States, Japan, and north-central Europe.[35] Wars of the future (Burnham thought there would always be wars: war is how human beings settle their differences) would be struggles among these super-states for world control. But they would be unwinnable. "[I]t does not seem possible for any one of these to conquer the others," he wrote; "and even two of them in coalition could not win a decisive and lasting victory over the third."[36]

In 1943, Burnham published *The Machiavellians: Defenders of Freedom*, in which he laid out his version of realism. The Machiavellians (that is, the realists) are the only people who understand the truth about power: that "the primary object, in practice, of all rulers is to serve their own interest, to maintain their own power and privilege. There are no exceptions." Burnham did not state this as desirable; he stated it as fact. Hardheaded acknowledgment of this (as opposed to liberal, or idealist, denials of it) leads to the realization that the only way to constrain the power of the powerful is to permit public opposition to them: "Only power restrains power."[37] Realism is thus the proper and unsentimental basis for the defense of political liberty.

The Machiavellians was less widely read than *The Managerial Revolution*, and it attracted some negative reviews—one of them by the theologian Reinhold Niebuhr, a friend of Hans Morgenthau's and a realist himself, who complained about the book's cynicism.[38] One person who was fascinated by Burnham's books was George Orwell.

---

by the New Dealers Adolf Berle and Gardiner Means. And the identification of a "new class" or "elite" of trained experts had a long postwar history, from the Yugoslavian Communist Milovan Đilas's *The New Class: An Analysis of the Communist System* (1957), Barbara Ehrenreich and John Ehrenreich's "The Professional-Managerial Class" (1977), and Alvin Gouldner's *The Future of Intellectuals and the Rise of the New Class* (1979) to Daniel Markovits's *The Meritocracy Trap* (2019).

4.

Orwell mentioned *The Managerial Revolution* in his *Tribune* column in 1944, which was the year his plans for *Nineteen Eighty-Four* were taking shape.[39] He agreed with Burnham that the world seemed to be dividing itself up into "several great power blocks," that a managerial class might take control, and that its rule could be totalitarian.[40] But he objected to the suggestion of inevitability. He thought that Burnham was too readily convinced of the superior efficiency of totalitarian systems. He pointed out that Nazi Germany had pretty much destroyed itself in little more than a decade, and that the Soviet Union was likely to self-destruct as well.

But in the winter of 1945, at the time of the Yalta Conference, where the Allied powers met to discuss the future of Europe, Orwell told a somewhat surprised Isaac Deutscher (a recent Polish émigré and good friend of E. H. Carr, who would become Trotsky's biographer) that Roosevelt, Churchill, and Stalin were colluding in the tripartite division of the postwar world.[41] In his column, Orwell wrote,

> Already, quite visibly and more or less with the acquiescence of all of us, the world is splitting up into the two or three huge super-states forecast in James Burnham's *Managerial Revolution*. One cannot draw their exact boundaries as yet, but one can see more or less what areas they will comprise. And if the world does settle down into this pattern, it is likely that these vast states will be permanently at war with one another.[42]

Eight months later, after the atomic bombing of Japan ended the Second World War, he declared,

> Burnham's geographical picture of the new world has turned out to be correct . . . We may be heading not for general breakdown but for an epoch as horribly stable as the slave empires of antiquity. James Burnham's theory has been much discussed, but few people have yet considered its ideological implications—that is, the kind of world-view, the kind of beliefs, and the social structure that would probably prevail in a State which was at once *unconquerable* and in a permanent state of "cold war" with its neighbours.[43]

But Orwell was worried that Burnham displayed an unhealthy attraction to power, and in 1946, he produced a reconsideration. In a pamphlet published by the Socialist Book Centre, *James Burnham and the Managerial Revolution*, Orwell said that the reason Burnham believed that a totalitarian future was inevitable was because he was seduced by power. "Power-worship blurs political judgment," Orwell wrote, "because it leads, almost unavoidably, to the belief that present trends will continue . . . [S]o long as they were winning, Burnham seems to have seen nothing wrong with the methods of the Nazis."* He attributed what he mistakenly interpreted as Burnham's "new-found admiration for Stalinism" to this basic amorality in his theory of politics.[44]

A few years later, Orwell was still worried about the Burnhamian future. The existence of the atomic bomb, he wrote in the summer of 1947, could mean (since everyone would be afraid to use it)

> the division of the world among two or three vast super-states, unable to conquer one another and unable to be overthrown by any internal rebellion. In all probability their structure would be hierarchic, with a semidivine caste at the top and outright slavery at the bottom, and the crushing out of liberty would exceed anything that the world has yet seen. Within each state the necessary psychological atmosphere would be kept up by complete severance from the outer world, and by a continuous phony war against rival states. Civilizations of this type might remain static for thousands of years.[45]

This was the world that Burnham had predicted. And it became the world of the novel that Orwell was busy writing.

Almost as soon as it appeared, in June 1949, *Nineteen Eighty-Four* was interpreted as an attack on socialism and the Labour Party. (In the novel, the regime of Big Brother is said to have derived from the principles of "Ingsoc," that is, English Socialism.) Orwell was distressed enough to issue a statement through his publisher explaining his

---

* Burnham had published an encomium to Stalin's greatness, called "Lenin's Heir." It was actually a satire, but many readers, including Orwell, thought he meant it.

intentions. "I do not believe that the kind of society I describe necessarily *will* arrive," he said,

> but I believe (allowing of course for the fact that the book is a satire) that something resembling it *could* arrive. I believe also that totalitarian ideas have taken root in the minds of intellectuals everywhere, and I have tried to draw these ideas out to their logical consequences. The scene of the book is laid in Britain in order to emphasize that the English-speaking races are not innately better than anyone else, and that totalitarianism, *if not fought against*, could triumph anywhere.[46]

One of the intellectuals Orwell had in mind, of course, was Burnham. The book that O'Brien gives to Winston Smith and Julia, *The Theory and Practice of Oligarchical Collectivism*, is an analysis of Big Brother's regime by the novel's Trotsky figure, Emmanuel Goldstein.* The imaginary book's real-life analogue is Trotsky's attack on Stalinism, *The Revolution Betrayed*, published in 1936. But *The Theory and Practice of Oligarchical Collectivism* is also a parody of *The Managerial Revolution*. The description of the "splitting-up of the world into three great super-states" (Oceania, Eurasia, and Eastasia), the facts that "[n]one of the three super-states could be definitely conquered even by the other two in combination" and that the new aristocracy was "made up for the most part of bureaucrats, scientists, technicians, trade-union organisers, publicity experts, sociologists, teachers, journalists, and professional politicians" are all taken directly from Burnham's book.[47]

Winston is not appalled by the book O'Brien has given him; on the contrary, he is fascinated. "It was the product of a mind similar to his own, but enormously more powerful, more systematic, less fear-ridden," he thinks. "You must read it," he tells Julia, when they are lying in bed together after making love. She has him read it aloud to her.[48] The book makes sense of things that Winston was aware of but could never explain—with one exception. Winston cannot make sense of the book's nihilism. And that nihilism becomes the subject of the novel's torture scenes. Like the interrogation scenes between the Old Bolshevik Rubashov and the Stalinist Gletkin in *Darkness at Noon*, those scenes are

---

* A phonic allusion to Trotsky's real name, Lev Bronstein.

efforts to understand imaginatively one of the mysteries of Stalinism: the confessions of the defendants to absurd charges in the Moscow Trials.*

"Why should we want power?" O'Brien asks Winston. "You are ruling over us for our own good" is Winston's answer. O'Brien pulls the lever on the torture machine. "That was stupid, Winston, stupid!" he says. "You should know better than to say a thing like that." He will tell him the correct answer, O'Brien says.

> "It is this. The Party seeks power entirely for its own sake. We are not interested in the good of others; we are interested solely in power . . . We are different from all the oligarchies of the past, in that we know what we are doing . . . We know that no one ever seizes power with the intention of relinquishing it. Power is not a means, it is an end. One does not establish a dictatorship in order to safeguard a revolution; one makes the revolution in order to establish the dictatorship. The object of persecution is persecution. The object of torture is torture. The object of power is power."[49]

By this point we can recognize who O'Brien is. He is the intellectual who has been seduced by the idea of power. O'Brien's famous image, uttered at the climax of his ideological catechism of Winston, is Orwell's satirical *reductio* of Burnhamese: "If you want a picture of the future, imagine a boot stamping on a human face—for ever."[50] It is also the nightmare version of Orwell's personal political obsession: permanently asymmetrical power relations.

Orwell's novel gave expression—satirical in the novel, but not in its nonfiction analogues—to the belief that people have a natural susceptibility to totalitarian ideologies, that those ideologies appeal to an inherent sadism in human nature. "There is a Hitler, a Stalin in every breast," Arthur Schlesinger, Jr., wrote in his liberal manifesto, *The Vital Center*, in 1949.[51] This belief that totalitarianism has a psychological basis appeared in many forms. In 1941, *Time* described "the triumphant emergence of a new human type, totalitarian man—superbly armed, deliberately destructive and dominant—at the very heart of what had been Europe's cultural sanctuaries."[52] Totalitarianism was associated

---

* It was eventually revealed that the defendants were tortured, but at the time, their confessions seemed evidence of totalitarianism's brainwashing power.

with certain personality types, with post-Christian angst, and with the anomic character of modern life.[53]

Orwell saw that in Burnham's politics, like O'Brien's politics, there is no ground for truth. If politics is only the struggle to acquire and hold on to power, then everything else is a lie. And if everything else is a lie, then language is only an instrument of power. There is nothing paradoxical in *Nineteen Eighty-Four* about the fact that the Ministry of Truth is the propaganda bureau. Truth is what the ruling class decides it is.

O'Brien's proof that two plus two equals five, and Newspeak, the manufactured language of Oceania, were Orwell's special contributions to the literature on totalitarianism. Orwell made jargon, formula, elision, obfuscation, and cliché the enemies of liberty and democracy and the symptoms of creeping totalitarianism. In *Nineteen Eighty-Four* and the essay "Politics and the English Language" (1946), he put language on the slippery slope. His warnings had an appeal to a class of persons whose livelihood is intimately connected to the use of language: intellectuals. By his writing and his example, Orwell gave these intellectuals a mission: they were the monitors of the well-being of the polity. They could recognize in the distortions of political discourse the symptoms of incipient totalitarianism and warn politicians (too concerned with gaining or retaining power) and the public (susceptible to convenient untruths) before it was too late.

Nineteen Eighty-Four popularized the convergence theory of totalitarianism. This was the view—Burnham's view—that all mass societies with advanced economies, whatever their ostensive ideological differences, are evolving in the same direction: toward a regime type variously characterized by a dominant technocratic or managerial class, a planned economy, increased state control over civic and private life, more or less overt forms of censorship, a propagandistic entertainment culture, secretive domestic intelligence agencies, excessive levels of military preparedness, and perpetual "cold war" tensions fueled by alarmist political rhetoric. This convergence theory lay behind many influential analyses of postwar American life.

The convergence theory also helped to create a Cold War within the Cold War. An official anti-totalitarianism directed at Communist states (Cold War I) was replicated by an unofficial anti-totalitarianism directed at tendencies within the liberal democracies (Cold War II). And this had been Orwell's intention. *Nineteen Eighty-Four* is, after all, a futurist novel. Its purpose was not to anatomize Stalinism; Orwell had already done that in *Animal Farm*. Its purpose was to warn about totalitarian tendencies everywhere, and to describe a future to which those tendencies might lead. Most liberal anti-Communists were Cold Warriors in both senses, I and II: they looked within as well as without. For them, Orwell's title became the alarm clock of Cold War II: "How close are we to 1984?"

5.

In 1942, a critique of *The Managerial Revolution* appeared in the scholarly journal *Ethics*. It had two authors: a twenty-five-year-old graduate student and a German émigré who was registered as an enemy alien. The authors argued that although managers and bureaucrats might be said to constitute a "new middle class" vital to the functioning of the modern state, it did not follow that they have power. Power resides where it had always resided: the state, with its monopoly on violence, and property owners, whose hold on wealth can be preserved through inheritance.

Burnham's idea that the managerial class was a revolutionary class was a fantasy, the writers said. Soviet technicians had no leverage against the Soviet state; German managers were employees of industry owners. Experts tended to be clueless about power and how it was exercised. "[J]ust as a rather petty species of executive manager in the Peloponnesian states became for Plato the World-builder," they wrote, "so Burnham Platonizes and imputes an irresistible movement toward power to the production expert and administrative executive."[54]

The émigré was Hans Gerth, who had been educated at Heidelberg, where he knew Hannah Arendt, who was writing her doctoral dissertation there, and Frankfurt, where he knew Arendt's first husband, Günther Stern, who was writing *his* thesis, and where he attended seminars led by Theodor Adorno, Max Horkheimer, and other members of the Institut für Sozialforschung—the Institute for Social Research, later known as the Frankfurt School. Gerth was a Gentile. He arrived in the United States, via Denmark and England, in 1938. He bounced around briefly, and ended up in the sociology department at the University of Wisconsin at Madison.

When the United States entered the war, in December 1941, Gerth, as an enemy alien, was not allowed to leave the vicinity of Madison or to own a radio. He decided to pass the time, and improve his English, by translating the work of Max Weber, the writer who had first got him excited about sociology. He employed graduate students to correct his English grammar and syntax; one of them was the co-author of the piece on Burnham, C. Wright Mills.[55]

Charles Wright Mills was a Texan. He was born in Waco in 1916 and attended Texas A&M, transferring after a year to the University of Texas at Austin. He was a large (over two hundred pounds) and energetic man; he was also disciplined, organized, and prolific. By the time he died, of a heart attack at the age of forty-five, he had written seven books.*

Mills entered the University of Wisconsin as a graduate student in 1939. Gerth joined the department the following year as an assistant professor, and he and Mills became lifelong correspondents and collaborators, a relationship not without tension.[56] The Weber translations were eventually published with a seventy-four-page introduction in 1946 as *From Max Weber*, with Gerth and Mills listed as co-translators, -editors, and -authors. The volume was paperbacked in 1958 and it introduced generations of American students to Weber. It is still in print. By the time it came out, Mills was at Columbia, where he would spend the rest of his career.

Mills was interested in the problem that Burnham and Orwell were interested in: power. And he came to feel that there had been a change in power relations in the United States since 1941. The change was caused, he believed, by what he called "the new international position of the United States"—that is, the Cold War. He presented his theory in 1956 in what would be his most influential work, *The Power Elite*.

Power, Mills argued, was now in the hands of three "institutions": "the political directorate," "the corporate rich," and the military. The power of the first group, the politicians, had waned relative to the power of the other two (he called them "corporate chieftains" and "professional warlords"), but the significant thing was that the three groups did not have rival interests. Groups with rival interests serve as a check on power. But in the postwar United States, the military, the government,

* It was his fourth heart attack. Mills's heart condition had been diagnosed in 1942, when he was classified 4-F by the selective service.

and the wealthy constituted a single homogeneous ruling class, whose members, virtually all white male Protestants, circulated from one institution to another interchangeably. (The Wise Men would be a case in point, and, of course, the president was a former general.) "What I am asserting," as Mills summed it up,

> is that in this particular epoch a conjunction of historical circumstances has led to the rise of an elite of power; that the men of the circles composing this elite, severally and collectively, now make such key decisions as are made; and that, given the enlargement and the centralization of the means of power now available, the decisions that they make and fail to make carry more consequences for more people than has ever been the case in the world history of mankind.[57]

Exactly what the interests of the power elite were, just what their ideology was, Mills never explained, a failure remarked on by his critics, notably his Columbia colleague Daniel Bell, who called *The Power Elite* "a book which discusses power but rarely politics."[58] As it was for Orwell and Burnham, the object of power for Mills seems to have been power. A more glaring failure, not mentioned by Bell, is the absence in a book on power relations of any reference to race or white supremacy. The issue was hardly remote for Mills. He had spent the first twenty-three years of his life in a Jim Crow state. For that matter, there is no mention of patriarchy, or, for another, heteronormativity.

But ideology was not what Mills was interested in. He had written his dissertation on pragmatism. The leading American pragmatist, John Dewey, was still at Columbia when Mills arrived there, and Mills believed, as Dewey believed, that democratic participation is constitutive of self-realization, whatever decisions are collectively arrived at. The only goal of the democratic experiment is to keep the experiment going. And he concluded that democracy in the United States was broken. "The rise of the power elite," he argued, ". . . rests upon, and in some ways is part of, the transformation of the publics of America into a mass society."[59]

> The powers of ordinary men are circumscribed by the everyday world in which they live, yet even in these rounds of job, family, and neighborhood they often seem driven by forces they can

neither understand nor govern. "Great changes" are beyond their control, but affect their conduct and outlook none the less. The very framework of modern society confines them to projects not their own, but from every side, such changes now press upon the men and women of the mass society who accordingly feel that they are without purpose in an epoch in which they are without power.[60]

"[W]e have moved a considerable distance along the road to the mass society," Mills warned. "At the end of that road there is totalitarianism."[61] That was Orwell's warning, too.

3

FREEDOM AND NOTHINGNESS

Simone de Beauvoir in her Paris apartment, 1949. Photograph by Elliott Erwitt.
(*Elliott Erwitt / Magnum Photos*)

1.

When Allied forces landed in France on June 6, 1944, D-Day, the liberation of Paris was not a priority. The city had no military significance, and the prospect of pitched battles in narrow streets, tying down troops that could be advancing on Berlin, persuaded Dwight Eisenhower, Supreme Allied Commander in Europe and the man in charge of Operation Overlord, to direct forces elsewhere. They would soon be having enough trouble dealing with the *bocage*—the hedgerows—of Normandy.[1]

Paris had enormous political significance, however. Charles de Gaulle, the commander of the Free French Forces and head of France's de facto government-in-exile, had the same concern that the London Poles were having at the same time about the liberation of Warsaw: that whatever group displaced the Germans in the capital would install itself as the presumptive postwar government. De Gaulle had some reason to worry that the collaborationist Vichy regime—which had charged him with desertion and sentenced him to death, and whose chief of state, Philippe Pétain, was, remarkably, still popular—might try to establish itself in power once the Germans were gone. His main apprehension, though, had to do with the French Communist Party—the PCF.[2]

The Communists had played a prominent role in the Resistance (whose numbers swelled rapidly after D-Day).[3] Like Communists and socialists in many European countries, including the countries of Eastern Europe, they interpreted the war as a final judgment on capitalism. The PCF had amassed much goodwill during the Occupation. Operating independently of Moscow (it was explained that Stalin did not want to complicate relations with the Allies), the PCF had pursued a policy of unity, and it expected to be the majority political party in France after the war.[4] De Gaulle had no sympathy with socialism, and he was anxious to get his people on the ground inside Paris as quickly as possible. He saw civil war as a serious possibility if he did not. It was in his interest to liberate Paris sooner rather than later.

For a small group of people, however, Paris was significant for an entirely different reason. It represented a set of values that had supreme status in midcentury art and thought: it was capital of the modern. For a hundred years, Paris was where advanced Western culture—especially painting, sculpture, literature, dance, film, and photography, but also fashion, cuisine, and sexual mores—was believed to be created, accredited, and transmitted. "Paris was where the twentieth century was," Gertrude Stein wrote in 1940, the year France fell.[5] "The laboratory of the twentieth century has been shut down," the critic Harold Rosenberg wrote in the same year. ". . . [U]p to the day of the occupation, Paris had been the Holy Place of our time. The only one."[6]

In this context, Paris did not mean France, a country where most people were, like de Gaulle himself, conservative and bourgeois. It did not even mean all of Paris, a city that housed plenty of academicians and reactionaries. It meant, essentially, a handful of neighborhoods: Montmartre, Montparnasse, the Latin Quarter, Saint-Germain-des-Prés, and the rue du Faubourg Saint-Honoré, the street of the great fashion houses.

Paris did not mean only Parisians, either. After the First World War,

Paris became one of the most cosmopolitan cities in the world. By the mid-1920s, of the fewer than three million people living in the city, nearly half a million were foreigners.[7] "Paris represented the International of culture," Rosenberg wrote. ". . . Because Paris was the opposite of the national in art, the art of every nation increased through Paris."[8] People went to Paris to transform themselves from regional or national figures into citizens of the world republic of art. Paris was the crossroads. Paris was where Henry James met Ivan Turgenev, where Pablo Picasso met Gertrude Stein, where Vladimir Nabokov met James Joyce. Amedeo Modigliani, Piet Mondrian, Wassily Kandinsky, Alexander Calder, Constantin Brancusi, Max Ernst, Alberto Giacometti, Juan Gris, and Joan Miró all lived in Paris. Oscar Wilde's *Salomé* and Igor Stravinsky's *Le Sacre du printemps* were first performed there. Paris was where Luis Buñuel made *L'Âge d'or*, where Picasso painted *Les Demoiselles d'Avignon*, where Isadora Duncan and Vaslav Nijinsky danced and Josephine Baker performed. Ernest Hemingway's *The Sun Also Rises*, Joyce's *Finnegans Wake*, and Henry Miller's *Tropic of Cancer* were all written in Paris. Ezra Pound edited "The Waste Land" there. *Ulysses* was published there. Paris was the birthplace of Cubism and Surrealism; it was the home of Dada and the musical modernists known as Les Six. The world's first cinema opened in Paris.

As events unfolded, the city was liberated quickly. On August 15, the Paris police unexpectedly went on strike (they were hoping to dissociate themselves from their wartime collaboration), triggering an insurgency inside the city.[9] Citizens and members of the Forces Françaises de l'Intérieur (FFI) launched a haphazard but heroic insurrection. They were aware of what was happening at that very moment to the insurgents in Warsaw: if Allied forces bypassed Paris, they knew what they could expect from the Germans. That this motley and poorly armed uprising was not immediately crushed made it clear to Allied commanders that the Germans were not interested in putting up a fight. The city was ripe for the taking, and, since taking it would constitute a moral victory, the Allies decided to move in.

Allied commanders acceded to de Gaulle's request that a unit of the Free French Forces be the first to enter the city. It seems to have been important to everyone concerned, the Americans and the British as well as de Gaulle, that the troops be white. Because many of their soldiers were recruited from French colonies in Africa, most of the Free French divisions were majority nonwhite. One exception was the Second Armored Division, commanded by Philippe Leclerc, which was 75 percent white. It was chosen to lead the advance.[10]*

After beating back German resistance in the suburbs, French tanks entered Paris in the evening of August 24, followed, a few hours later, by the U.S. Fourth Infantry Division. Although German sniper fire persisted, tens of thousands of Parisians flooded the streets to welcome the troops. De Gaulle had arrived by a secret route on August 20 and managed to install his followers in key positions in the ministries. On August 25, he delivered an impassioned extemporaneous address from the balcony of the Hôtel de Ville. "Paris outragé! Paris brisé! Paris martyrisé! mais Paris libéré! libéré par lui-même, libéré par son peuple," he cried—"Paris liberated by its people."[11] Though it was undoubtedly far from his mind, de Gaulle's words echoed Karl Marx's mythologizing of another episode in the city's history, the Commune of 1871: "Working, thinking, fighting, bleeding Paris—almost forgetful, in its incubation of a new society, of the cannibals at its gates—radiant in the enthusiasm of its historic initiative!"[12] The German commander, General Dietrich von Choltitz, once known as "the smasher of cities," surrendered that afternoon. He had ignored Hitler's order that Paris be burned to the ground.[13]

When French and American troops arrived in the city, the press rode in along with them: Ernest Hemingway, writing for *Collier's*; A. J. Liebling and Irwin Shaw, from *The New Yorker*; the legendary war correspondent Ernie Pyle of the Scripps-Howard newspapers; Robert Capa and Ralph Morse, photographers for *Life*. It was the ideal journalistic occasion: the weather was good, the city was beautiful, casualties were light, and the outcome was righteous.

Life described the Liberation as the lifting of a curse. "Paris is like a magic sword in a fairy tale—a shining power in those hands to which it rightly belongs, in other hands tinsel and lead," its editorial began. "Whenever the City of Light changes hands, Western civilization shifts its political balance. So it has been for seven centuries; so it was in 1940; so it was last week . . . The civilized world went wild with joy when Paris was freed. Paris is the second capital of every nation."[14] A week later,

---

* More than a hundred soldiers in the Second Division were Spanish, members of a unit formed in North Africa called La Nueve. The last surviving member of La Nueve, Rafael Gómez Nieto, died in Spain in 2020 of Covid-19, the coronavirus. He was ninety-nine.

Life ran fourteen pages of coverage of the Liberation. Like most of the press, the magazine embraced the interpretation advanced by Charles de Gaulle on the balcony of the Hôtel de Ville: Paris had been liberated "by her own people." "Before Allied troops reached the city Parisians were fighting and rioting against the enemy, as they had always fought and rioted against oppressors," the magazine explained, adding the surprising thought that "there was even something Parisian in the way collaborators started shooting from housetops when de Gaulle passed."[15]

"It has been six days now since the troops came in," wrote Time Inc.'s London bureau chief, Charles Wertenbaker, who was one of the first Americans to enter the city, accompanying Philippe Leclerc and the French Second Armored Division, "four days since the shooting stopped and today, after two days of rain, the sun shines warm on the domes and on the boulevards, and people crowd the Café de la Paix drinking *demi-blondes* . . . Paris again is Paris."[16] "For the first time in my life and probably the last, I have lived for a week in a great city where everybody is happy," Liebling wrote in a *New Yorker* column dated September 1. "The city is resuming normal life with a speed I would never have believed possible."[17]

Fewer than three thousand Parisians died during the Liberation. By the standards of Warsaw, or any other place where partisans took arms against German occupiers, those were minor casualties. Paris was liberated because the German army threw in its cards and conceded the city. But de Gaulle's declaration that Paris had liberated itself would become a crucial piece of postwar French self-understanding.

During the war, Paris was treated differently from other capitals the Germans occupied. In Vienna, Prague, and Budapest, the cultural elite either managed to escape before the Germans arrived or suffered censorship, imprisonment, deportation, and execution once the Nazis were in charge. The same was true in Berlin, which artists and intellectuals had been fleeing since 1933. But to a remarkable extent, and excepting the Jews, the cultural life of Paris went on in a way that was superficially close to normal.

The man initially given charge of the city, Otto Abetz, the head of the German embassy, was a Francophile and was married to a Frenchwoman, Susanne de Bruyker. During the Liberation, he would help Choltitz by tricking Berlin into believing that Hitler's orders to destroy Paris were being obeyed.[18] Other officials in key positions were also

Francophiles—notably Sonderführer Gerhard Heller, the chief literature censor, and Major Frank Hensel, director of cinema for the German army.[19] These men were not disloyal to Hitler. They simply wanted
what everyone wanted from Paris: to demonstrate to the world their
worldliness. A lively Paris was an advertisement for Nazi tolerance and,
even, Nazi taste. The Germans didn't close the theaters, the nightclubs,
the museums, the restaurants, and the art galleries; they wanted to enjoy
them. Patronizing French culture was German policy.

It was, of course, entirely show tolerance. The boundaries were plainly
marked; the threat of terror was always there. The Germans purged the
culture industries of Jews, and they censored and burned hundreds of
books. Outside the Jeu de Paume, where they stored plundered art, they
publicly destroyed paintings by Fernand Léger, Francis Picabia, Ernst,
Miró, and Picasso.[20] And as they did with all the professions, they arrested artists and intellectuals who fell under suspicion and sent them
to jail, to the camps, or to death. Many people in literature and the
arts fled to the south of France in 1940, and a number managed to
immigrate to the United States. Joyce, who had been living in Paris
since 1920, barely escaped. His application for an entrance visa to Switzerland was held up because Swiss authorities apparently believed that
he was Jewish.* He finally got to Zurich in December 1940, leaving his
daughter, Lucia, behind. He died less than a month later, at the age of
fifty-eight.[21] And, as the German position in Europe deteriorated, the
danger of living in Paris, from which there was no longer any way out,
only increased.

Although the Nazi presence was clearly marked by flags, swastikas,
German-language signage, and the constant sight of uniformed officers and soldiers in public places, there was an active underground. This
included a new press, Les Éditions de Minuit, which was co-founded by
Jean Marcel Bruller and which published, under his nom de guerre, Vercors, Bruller's novel Le Silence de la mer, the most famous underground
work of the Occupation. More than a thousand clandestine newspapers
and journals were published. And there was a black market in banned
cultural goods, including American fiction in French translation.[22]

But active resistance in Paris, as in France as a whole, was minimal.
After the war, the government ministry deputed to award certificates

---

* "There's a remarkable discovery," was his reaction.

and determine pensions calculated that over the four years of the Occupation, out of a population of 2.5 million, 29,817 Parisians had been *résistants*.[23] In the entire country, the figure was probably fewer than 200,000 in a population of 35 million. In four years, approximately 30,000 French civilians (nondeportees) were executed by the Germans.[24]

France was policed mainly by the French.* The Germans had only about 7,500 of their own police and administrative personnel in the entire country. (German soldiers, most of whom were stationed on the coast, did not have security duties.)[25] It was the French themselves who began deporting Jews. Between 1942 and 1944, 4,000 French Jews died in captivity and 75,000 were sent to the East. Fewer than 2,700 returned.[26] And the Germans found plenty of collaborators—writers, journalists, filmmakers, actors, musicians, artists, and publishers who were content to have a place in Hitler's New Europe.

Most Parisians were neither collaborators nor resisters. They were *attentistes*: they waited. They were fully aware of the hollowness of appearances and the fragility of normal life, but they discovered that it was possible to coexist, and even, occasionally, to fraternize with the Germans and still go about their business without feeling that they had sacrificed too much moral or political self-respect. Almost every Surrealist painter fled, since Surrealism was a target of the Nazi crusade against degenerate art. But Picasso remained throughout the war. The poet Paul Valéry lectured at the Collège de France. Georges Braque exhibited his paintings. Jean Cocteau continued his work without interruption. So did Christian Dior, who outfitted Nazi wives. Coco Chanel closed up shop but seems to have become a German agent. Maurice Chevalier and Édith Piaf sang and Alfred Cortot played to mixed French and German audiences. The career of the actor and director Jean-Louis Barrault was launched at the Comédie-Française during the Occupation. The film industry, under Nazi supervision and purged of Jews, continued to produce movies. The great restaurants stayed open, unchanged. And, despite Joseph Goebbels's directive that Berlin be made the fashion capital of Europe, the fashion houses remained and, allowing for material shortages, the industry thrived.[27]

After permitting the Germans to purge his backlist of anti-Nazi

---

* Until 1942, the country was divided between German-occupied France and Vichy France, or the "Free Zone," run as a client state of Germany.

works and books by Jews, Gaston Gallimard ran his publishing house. (The list of banned books, put into effect in September 1940, was known as the "Otto List," after Abetz.) Gallimard obliged the Germans by firing the only well-known Jew working at the house, Jacques Schiffrin, who had created the Pléiade collection of classic French writers and brought it to Gallimard in 1936.[28]* Gallimard also published the prestigious *Nouvelle Revue Française*. He was obliged to replace its editor, the underground *résistant* Jean Paulhan, who had run the journal for fifteen years, with the French fascist Pierre Drieu La Rochelle. But he kept Paulhan on as an editorial adviser in an office just down the hall from Drieu's. When Paulhan was arrested, in 1941, Drieu intervened to have him released. (After the war, Drieu committed suicide, and the *NRF* was banned for a year for collaboration. But then Paulhan returned and served for another twenty-two years as its editor.)[29]

Nightclub and café business boomed. More than half of the two hundred cabarets in wartime central Paris opened after 1940.[30] The scene now included German officers, but it was otherwise undisturbed. It even flourished, since one way to cope with the curfew was to drink all night. As a gesture of resistance, some writers refused to publish during the Occupation on grounds that journals such as the *NRF* and the publishing houses were under German control; a few writers published books hostile to the occupiers and were sent to the camps or executed.[31] But most continued their careers.[32] Georges Bataille, Paul Éluard, François Mauriac, Jacques Prévert, Raymond Queneau, Jean Anouilh, Colette, and Marguerite Duras worked in Paris during the Occupation. Camus published *L'Étranger* and *Le Mythe de Sisyphe* (after acceding to Gallimard's request that he remove an essay on Kafka, since Jews could not be mentioned in books published in German-occupied territory). He also produced two plays. Simone de Beauvoir published her first novel, *L'Invitée* (translated as *She Came to Stay*). Georges Clouzot directed *Le Corbeau* (*The Raven*). Marcel Carné directed *Les Enfants du paradis*. Olivier Messiaen composed much of *Quatuor pour la fin du temps* in a concentration camp in Görlitz, in eastern Germany, where the piece had its premiere in 1941. He was released later that year and

---

* Schriffrin had fled Russia when the Bolsheviks came to power. He would leave France and come to New York City, where he co-founded, with Kurt and Helen Wolff, Pantheon Books. Schiffrin's son André was involved in the formation of Students for a Democratic Society. He took over as executive editor at Pantheon after Random House bought the company in 1961.

lived in Paris for the rest of the war, working as an organist, composer, and professor at the Conservatoire de Paris.[33]

Paris was bombed by British and American aircraft during the war (and by a German plane at the very end), but unlike Berlin, Rome, London, and many other French cities, it did not suffer massive damage. The city was conquered, occupied, and liberated almost without a fight. The physical plant of galleries, publishing houses, fashion houses, theaters, movie studios, nightclubs, restaurants, and cafés remained largely intact, as did their administrative infrastructures. The *épuration*— the purge of collaborators—that followed the Liberation targeted individual actors, directors, artists, and writers but for the most part ignored the businessmen who published the books, sold the art, owned the restaurants, and exhibited the films. Cultural life recovered quickly after the Liberation because it had never been effectively suppressed.

Still, the Occupation was a page it was in everyone's interest to turn quickly. For those who had resisted and for those who had waited, and even for some of those who had collaborated, the Liberation represented the chance for a fresh start. The stage had not been dismantled. Everything was set for a new culture hero to walk onto it. As if on cue, one did.

2.

Jean-Paul Sartre's philosophy and his person constituted a unitary phenomenon. He was famous for who he was and how he lived as much as for what he wrote. The phenomenon was so well suited to the postwar moment in France that it might have seemed calculated or opportunistic. In fact, Sartre's philosophical views and style of life were products of more than a decade of reflection and self-cultivation.

For much of that time, he had no public aims in mind. Until the war broke out, he had little interest in politics. He was nominally a socialist, but he couldn't understand how some of his friends could spend time and energy on the mundane business of political action. "The political aspirations [*prétensions*] of left-wing intellectuals made him shrug his shoulders," his lifelong partner, Simone de Beauvoir, wrote in her memoir *La Force de l'âge* (*The Prime of Life*). ". . . Talk, declamations, manifestoes, propaganda—what a lot of pointless fuss!"[34] She and Sartre didn't even vote.

The war changed that. On September 3, 1939, two days after the invasion of Poland, France declared war on Germany and Sartre was mobilized. (France had a treaty obliging it to come to Poland's defense.) He was assigned to the meteorological unit in an artillery division: he was a weatherman.* For more than eight months—the so-called phony war, or *drôle de guerre*—France waited, and nothing happened. Then, on May 10, Hitler struck. The Wehrmacht invaded Belgium, the Netherlands, Luxembourg, and France. The great French Army, over a hundred divisions, collapsed—an inexplicable event for many people at the time—and by June 14, the Germans were in Paris.[35] Eight days later, on June 22, France surrendered. Sartre and the rest of his unit had been taken prisoner the day before, after being abandoned by their officers. It was his thirty-fifth birthday.

The Germans took 1.8 million French prisoners of war. About 330,000 were either set free or repatriated for medical reasons in 1940 and 1941, and some 16,000 escaped. Most of the rest spent the war in prison camps or doing forced labor in Germany.[36] Sartre was a prisoner for nine months, the last seven in Stalag XII D in the city of Trier, inside Germany.†

Life in the camps was, at bottom, brutal. There were no ethical boundaries, even implicit ones, between those with power and those without it. Prisoners had no protections. But for Sartre, conditions were not unusually onerous. He had published two works of fiction to some acclaim before the war began: his first novel, *La Nausée*, in April 1938, and *Le Mur*, a collection of stories, in January 1939. The Germans seem to have understood him to be an important writer and he was allowed to pursue his work. He studied Martin Heidegger's *Sein und Zeit* (*Being and Time*), using a copy smuggled in by a friendly priest, and he began writing his first major philosophical work, whose title alludes to Heidegger's, *L'Être et le néant* (*Being and Nothingness*), in captivity.

Sartre got himself released in March 1941, evidently by using a faked medical certificate—although the Germans may have preferred the publicity of a distinguished writer producing books in Nazi-occupied Paris to the publicity of one being held in a concentration camp. In any event, they do not seem to have looked on Sartre as a political threat.

---

* In the meaningless coincidence department: Martin Heidegger served in a meteorological unit in the First World War.
† Also meaningless: Trier was the birthplace of Karl Marx. Engels used to call him "the black fellow from Trier."

He returned to Paris, where, reunited with Beauvoir, he spent the rest of the war.[37]

The Germans were wrong. Sartre had changed his mind about politics. In February 1940, while on leave during the phony war, he had spent a week with Beauvoir and had presented her with his new view. "Sartre was thinking a good deal about the postwar period; he had firmly made up his mind to hold aloof from politics no longer," she recalled in La Force de l'âge. "His new morality was based on the notion of 'genuineness' [authenticité], and he was determined to make a practical application of it to himself. It required every man to shoulder the responsibility of his situation in life; and the only way in which he could do so was to transcend that situation by engaging upon some course of action. Any other attitude was mere escapist pretense, a masquerade based upon insincerity [mauvaise foi: bad faith]. It will be clear that a radical change had taken place in him."[38]

Sartre's first act after his release by the Germans was to organize a group, Socialisme et Liberté, dedicated to resisting the Nazi Occupation and planning for a socialist postwar France. He and Beauvoir were joined by a friend, the philosopher Maurice Merleau-Ponty, but the initiative did not get far. Sartre's attempt to recruit two of the biggest names in French letters, André Gide and André Malraux, was fruitless. Both writers were living in the south of France, where he and Beauvoir visited them, and neither saw much promise in Sartre's idea. Gide was over seventy and considered himself hors de combat; he would soon move to North Africa for the duration of the war. Malraux told Sartre that French resistance was futile and that the war could be won only by American planes and Russian tanks. (Much later, Malraux would join the Resistance and be captured, briefly, by the Gestapo.)[39] Later that summer, after two people associated with Socialisme et Liberté were arrested and deported, Sartre dropped the project. "Born in enthusiasm, our little unit caught a fever and died a year later, for want of knowing what to do," is how he put it many years later. The deportees were never seen again.[40]

Apart from writing articles for the underground press and, in 1943, joining the Comité National des Écrivains (CNE), a large group of writers organized by the PCF, that was pretty much the sum of Sartre's resistance activities. He published L'Être et le néant in 1943 and had two plays approved by the censor and produced: Les Mouches (The Flies), in

1943, and *Huis clos* (*No Exit*), a major success, in 1944. In some respects, his behavior looks self-protective. He did not protest the dismissal of Jews from the French academic system, for instance. He even took over the teaching position of one of them, Henri Dreyfus-Le Foyer (a nephew of Alfred Dreyfus), at the Lycée Condorcet.[41] He contributed two articles to a collaborationist journal, *Comœdia*—though neither was collaborationist in content or spirit.[42]

Sartre did not fight in the uprising of August 1944 (apart from joining a group dispatched to protect the Comédie-Française, which was not attacked). He covered the Liberation as a reporter for the underground paper *Combat*, edited by his friend Albert Camus. This put him in danger, but it was no different from the danger faced by everyone who worked in the underground press. Nevertheless, after the Liberation, Sartre was frequently identified in the American press as a hero of the Resistance.

The first piece by Sartre to appear in the United States came out in *The Atlantic Monthly* in December 1944. The magazine described him as "a French dramatist and poet [Sartre wrote no poetry] who distinguished himself as one of the military leaders of the FFI through the long years of German domination."[43] Seven months later, an editor's note accompanying an article by Sartre in *Vogue* referred to him as "a man of the Resistance," someone who might have been seen "on the barricades."[44] In a collection of writings about the Resistance published in the United States in 1946, he was described as having been "fearless and active in the underground."[45] *Life* reported that "he risked a concentration camp or the execution squad by playing an active role in the Communist-dominated resistance organization, Front National."[46] A profile in *Harper's Bazaar* informed readers that Sartre had played "an active part in the resistance movement."[47] (That profile was written by Beauvoir. The phrase about the Resistance was inserted by the editors.)[48]

Sartre never made false claims about his role in the Resistance himself, but he didn't go out of his way to correct misperceptions about it, either. To have scruples about those misperceptions, he explained, would be self-centered.[49] He likely had two other reasons for acceding to the mistake. One is that he thought of writing—of any kind: novels, plays, philosophy—as a form of action, to be judged as such. This is not because he thought writing was a privileged activity, but because he thought it wasn't. The writer is the same as anyone—the soldier, the politician, the teacher, the lover, in some sense the person crossing the street. He or she is undertaking an action and is therefore making a choice. All we can ask (though for Sartre, this was everything) is that the choice be free, and that it be made in the name of freedom. That is what he meant by *authenticité*. And a free act made in the name of freedom, whatever the act is and whoever makes it, is by its nature an act of resistance. It is a refusal to be controlled by one's situation—in this case, by the occupier. As a free writer, he was in effect a *résistant*.

The other reason it made sense for Sartre to allow exaggerated claims about his role during the Occupation to pass is because he made exaggerated claims about everyone's role. He did this in order to make a point about the human condition. "Every second, we lived to the full the meaning of that banal little phrase: 'Man is mortal!'" he wrote about life during the Occupation in one of his most frequently reprinted pieces, "La République du silence." (This was the piece, translated by Lincoln Kirstein, that appeared in *The Atlantic Monthly* in 1944.)

> And the choice each of us made of his life and being was an authentic choice, since it was made in the presence of death, since it could always have been expressed in the form: "Better dead than . . ." . . . [I]n the shadows and in blood, the strongest of Republics was forged. Each of its citizens knew he had an obligation to all and that he had to rely on himself alone. Each, in the most total abandonment, fulfilled his role in history. Each, standing against the oppressors, made the effort to be himself irremediably. And by choosing himself in freedom, he chose freedom for all.[50]

Sartre dismissed de Gaulle's assertion that Paris had liberated itself. The eviction of the Germans, he wrote on the first anniversary of the Liberation, was the work of the Allied armies (as Malraux had predicted it must be). The uprising was not even necessary, in fact, since the Germans were already leaving the city. And if the Germans had not evacuated Paris, and if the insurgents had acted alone, without Allied help, the fighters would have accomplished nothing. They would simply have been wiped out, like the Warsaw Poles. But none of that was a reason not to rise up, because none of that mattered. What mattered was that Parisians acted *in the name of* freedom.

> Whether the retreating divisions fell on Paris and made another Warsaw of our city did not depend on them. But what did depend on them was to bear witness by their actions—regardless of the outcome of the unequal struggle they had undertaken—to the will of the French people . . . This accounts for that other aspect of the Paris uprising, the festive air it never ceased to have. Whole sections of the city dressed up in their Sunday best. And if I ask myself just what they were celebrating, I see that it was man and his powers.[51]

Sartre turned France's wartime experience into a metaphor for a philosophical position he had formulated before the war began. He troped the Occupation.

The intellectual path Sartre took to that position was, in a word, un-French. It arose out of his encounters with two realms of achievement not frequently associated: German philosophy and American fiction. That Sartre transformed those influences into, first, a philosophy of resistance to the German occupation, and, later on, a philosophy of resistance to American power—that he fashioned them into a worldview that seemed to many people quintessentially French—is not perverse. It is what happens when styles and ideas shift contexts. Sartre's command of German was limited—he read it with effort and could never speak it—and he did not understand English.[52] But this only made the transformation of his German and American influences more effective. In the business of cultural exchange, misprision is often the key to transmission.

3.

Sartre followed the prescribed French route to intellectual stardom. He was a *normalien*. He entered the École Normale Supérieure (ENS) in Paris in 1924, when he was nineteen. Though he was regarded as a brilliant student, he failed in his first attempt at the *agrégation*, the highly competitive examination for careers in the French school system, possibly by trying too hard to be original. This unanticipated contingency is, appropriately, what led, in 1929, to his meeting with Beauvoir.

She was twenty-one, a philosophy student at the Sorbonne (the ENS did not officially admit female students), and she, too, was studying for the *agrégation*.[53] She was a handsome woman, and she had a boyfriend, René Maheu (who gave her the permanent nickname *le Castor*—the Beaver). But after she got over the physical impression Sartre made, she fell in love with him. Their relationship, the object of much legend building (and, after their deaths, debunking), was not just a prominent aspect of their public personae. It was the lens through which many people read their work and interpreted their thought.

Sartre was five feet two inches tall. He had lost almost all the sight in his right eye from a cold he caught when he was three or four—hence his strabismus, which made him wall-eyed. He dressed in oversized and flamboyant clothes, with no sense of fashion, and he was indifferent to hygiene. He was conscious of his ugliness—he often talked about it—but it was the kind of aggressive male ugliness that can be charismatic, and he wisely refrained from disguising it. He simply, as a matter of principle and well past ordinary standards of neglect and abuse, ignored his body. By the time he reached his late sixties, he was almost completely broken down.

He was also smart, generous, mild-mannered, extremely funny, and a great talker. After the war, when he had acquired a reputation as a formidable intellectual, strangers were often amazed by his affability. Sartre liked other people to like him—which, in social situations, can be almost as good as liking other people. He was a gifted mimic, he looked surprisingly good in drag, and he did a great Donald Duck impression. He enjoyed drinking and talking all night, and so did Beauvoir.[54] He liked pretty women, because (he said) he didn't have to talk with them about ideas. Beauvoir, he thought, was different: she had, he said, "a man's intelligence . . . and a woman's sensitivity."[55]

Sartre had already been working on what he called a "theory of contingency," and he proposed to Beauvoir to apply it to their relationship. Their love did not require marriage for its consummation, he told her. As Beauvoir later explained it:

> The comradeship that welded our lives together made a superfluous mockery of any other bond we might have forged for ourselves. What, for instance, was the point of living under the same roof when the whole world was our common property? Why fear to set great distances between us when we could never truly be parted? One single aim fired us, the urge to embrace all experience, and

to bear witness concerning it. At times this meant that we had to follow diverse paths—though without concealing even the least of our discoveries from one another. When we were together we bent our wills so firmly to the requirements of this common task that even at the moment of parting we still thought as one. That which bound us freed us; and in this freedom we found ourselves bound as closely as possible.[56]

This was the famous "pact": they could have affairs, but they were required to tell each other everything. As Sartre put it to her: "What *we* have is an *essential* love [*un amour nécessaire*]; but it is a good idea for us also to experience *contingent* love affairs."[57]

Beauvoir's life to that point had been an effort to escape the culture of her family. Her mother had been raised in a convent; her father was a conservative Paris lawyer of diminished means who, although he was proud of her mind ("Simone has a man's brain; she thinks like a man; she *is* a man," he would say), discouraged his daughter's interest in philosophy and would probably have discouraged her pursuit of any career if he had been able to provide her with a dowry.[58] She had already set herself on defying bourgeois norms before she met Sartre, and she was excited by the affront to conventional notions of domesticity that his arrangement posed. She shared their friends' high opinion of Sartre's mind. She probably also saw that the pact bound to her for life a man she knew would never be faithful. It closed off the normal exit.

Sartre and Beauvoir both passed the *agrégation* in 1929. Sartre took first place. There is evidence that Beauvoir gave the stronger performance—but he was a *normalien*, it was his second try, and she was a woman.[59] (Maheu failed. At the Sorbonne, Beauvoir had graduated second in philosophy, behind Simone Weil.)[60] Sartre's first teaching job was in Le Havre (the model for Bouville in his novel *La Nausée*); hers was in Marseille, but after a year, she was transferred to a school in Rouen much closer to his.

Their schedules gave them a lot of time to be together. One weekend, probably in the winter or spring of 1933, they met Sartre's ENS classmate Raymond Aron in Paris for drinks—according to Beauvoir, at the Bec de Gaz in Montparnasse. Aron had finished first in the *agrégation* that Sartre failed, and he was studying at the Maison Académique

Française in Berlin, where he had become interested in the phenomenology of Edmund Husserl. They were drinking apricot cocktails, a house specialty and a favorite of Beauvoir's, and Aron pointed to the glass and said to Sartre, "If you are a phenomenologist, you can talk about this cocktail and make a philosophy out of it!"

Beauvoir said that Sartre "turned pale with emotion." This was what he had been looking for: a way to do philosophy and take account of everyday life at the same time.[61] Sartre already knew something about Husserl and phenomenology, but he had evidently never grasped the implications so dramatically.[62] (Those implications were purely abstract: Sartre later remembered that the drink Aron pointed to was beer.)[63] He arranged with Aron to swap positions for a year, and in the fall of 1933, he went to Berlin as a resident at the Maison Académique Française and Aron spent the year in Le Havre.

Hitler had been in power for nine months when Sartre arrived in Berlin. But unlike Aron (who was Jewish, although, since his hair was blond and his eyes were blue, he passed for Aryan), Sartre seems to have made no observations about political developments in Germany.[64] (Aron, for his part, helped Jews in Berlin trying to emigrate.)[65] He worked on *La Nausée* and wrote two essays on Husserl.

Heidegger was Husserl's student, and Sartre came to Heidegger later. He had read a French translation by the philosopher Henry Corbin of Heidegger's 1929 lecture "Was Ist Metaphysik?" ("What Is Metaphysics?") in 1931. This was the first French translation of anything by Heidegger; it appeared in the same issue of a journal, *Bifur*, that contained one of Sartre's own early articles.[66] Sartre had trouble understanding it, though. He bought a copy of *Sein und Zeit* in Berlin in 1933 but decided that one German philosopher was enough and stuck to Husserl.[67] It was not until 1939 that he began to read Heidegger systematically—no doubt helped by Corbin's translation of a selection of Heidegger's works, including "Was Ist Metaphysik?" and excerpts from *Sein und Zeit*, published in 1938. This doesn't mean, of course, that Sartre didn't pick up Heideggerian concepts along the way.[68] When he told Beauvoir, in their conversation in 1940, during the phony war, about his notion of a morality based on "authenticity," he was using a key term of Heidegger's.

Heidegger's project in *Sein und Zeit* is the meaning of being. In discussions of Heidegger's thought, emphasis is usually placed on the "being" part, and understandably, since his major claim is that the question of what it means for something to be had been neglected in Western philosophy since Plato. But the crucial piece is the meaning part.

There is no meaning on Mars. There would be no meaning on Earth, either, if there were no human beings on the planet. It is because there are people that the question of what things mean arises—what raising my hand means, what a poem or a sunset or a red light means, why I keep a rabbit's foot in my pocket. Absent human beings, a rabbit's foot is just an object without a name. Objects and animals, tables and elephants, are beings, but they do not (we assume) think about what it means to be a table or an elephant. Human beings are different, because they can ask what it means to be what they are. Humans, Heidegger says, are "[t]hat entity which in its Being has this very Being as an issue."[69]

It follows that we can talk about "tableness" or "elephantness" but not about some essential humanness. Human life is unfixed; we are always consciously and provisionally coping with our past, with our present situation, and with our possible future. We are always looking for ways to be. Heidegger's term for this kind of existence is *Dasein* (as opposed to *Sein*, "being" in the elephant sense), which Corbin translated as *réalité-humaine*. (He cleared this translation with Heidegger himself, but it led French readers to think of *Dasein* in terms of the individual human being, rather than as something more like a way of life shared by humans, like a language.)[70] And he connected *Dasein*, in "Was Ist Metaphysik?," with the concept of *das Nichts*, which Corbin translated as *néant*, the term Sartre used—nothingness.

Nothingness is the state of affairs on Mars. It is what the world would be like if it were stripped of meaning. In everyday life, we experience the world fully clothed with the meanings that we assign to things, including other people. That's a table, that's an elephant, that's my mother-in-law, love is more important than money, the virus caused the disease. These meanings are not capriciously added on to a more primordial atomistic apprehension of the world. Although we alter old meanings and learn new ones all the time, from the beginning of consciousness we perceive the world as a meaningful constellation of things. In his famously mesmerizing lectures at the University of Marburg at the start of his career, Heidegger would analyze the experience of seeing the lectern at which he was speaking.[71]

We can relate to things pragmatically, in terms of their usefulness to us (as I relate to my rabbit's foot), or we can relate to them scientifically, without regard to their human uses (as a zoologist relates to a rabbit's foot). But Heidegger thought that in order to apprehend pure being we need to drop, or transcend, these ordinary ways of understanding the meaning of things, and this means encountering *das Nichts.* "We release ourselves into the nothing, which is to say that we liberate ourselves from those idols everyone has and to which they are wont to go cringing," he wrote in "Was Ist Metaphysik?"[72] Only then can a human being be *Dasein*, the entity for which being is a question.

Heidegger associated the experience of nothingness with the feeling of anxiety. "The nothing reveals itself in anxiety [*der Angst*]," he wrote.[73] Another name for the nothing is "the absurd." An apprehension of the absurdity of the world, what Heidegger called "the total strangeness of beings," produces a sensation of anxiety or (a better translation of *Angst*) of dread.[74] A familiar example is the experience of staring into the night sky and having a vertiginous sensation of contingency and homelessness. This glimpse into nothingness or absurdity can put us into a third kind of relation to the world, can reveal a third kind of meaning, not pragmatic or scientific, but one in which we become aware of the truth of being—or, as Heidegger preferred to put it, one in which being reveals itself. "Human existence can relate to beings only if it holds itself out into the nothing," he wrote.[75] And this experience also reveals us to ourselves: "Without the original revelation of the nothing, no selfhood and no freedom."[76]

Being as such did not interest Sartre. What interested him was the idea that the essence of being a human being lies in what we choose (or choose not) to do, rather than in what we simply are. "*The essence of Dasein lies in its existence*," Heidegger wrote in *Sein und Zeit*.[77] Sartre gave a name to this condition: freedom. "Man does not exist *first* in order to be free *subsequently*," he says in *L'Être et le néant*; "there is no difference between the being of man and his *being-free*."[78] No predetermined concept of humanness constrains us.

For Sartre, there is nothing nonhuman about nothingness. Humans bring nothingness into the world. Consciousness is a nothingness. Faced with a choice, free people feel anxiety because they know that there is nothing either "in here" or "out there," in the nature of the universe or in the nature of being human, that dictates what that choice should be, nothing that validates a priori that their choice is the right choice. Anxiety is a symptom that tells us that the choice is being made freely. "[M]y freedom is the unique foundation of values," Sartre argued, "and . . . *nothing*, absolutely nothing, justifies me in adopting this or that particular value, this or that particular scale of values. As a being by whom values exist, I am unjustifiable. My freedom is anguished at being the foundation of values while itself without foundation."[79] Because humans have no essence, they have an essence: freedom.

Sartre called a being that does not experience this anxiety and that is not free an *être-en-soi* (being-in-itself); he called a being that chooses freely an *être-pour-soi* (being-for-itself). People who allow their situation to determine their actions, or who allow other people or even their own emotions to decide for them, are like tables and elephants. They remain within their own immanence, "in themselves." People who choose freely transcend what they already are; they are beings "for themselves." And humans are the only beings that can be "for themselves." In Sartre's formulation, human beings are not what they are and they are what they are not. "I am condemned to exist forever beyond my essence, beyond the causes and motives of my act," he wrote in *L'Être et le néant*; "I am condemned to be free."[80]

Human beings consequently have a strong desire to escape from freedom. Allowing one's circumstances or one's feelings to determine one's choices is a way of avoiding anxiety. The term Sartre gave to this mode of being was *mauvaise foi*—bad faith. "To the extent that the for-itself wishes to hide its own nothingness from itself and to incorporate the in-itself as its true mode of being, it is trying also to hide its freedom from itself," he instructed. ". . . Human-reality [*réalité-humaine*] is free because it is *not enough* . . . Freedom is precisely the nothingness which is *made-to-be* [*est été*] at the heart of man and which forces human-reality to *make itself* instead of *to be* . . . [F]or human reality, to be is to *choose oneself*."[81]

Leaving aside the atheism, Sartre's definition of freedom is consistent with the German philosophical tradition. It is the definition used by Kant, Schiller, Hegel, and Marx: freedom is transparency (understanding one's situation without mystification) and self-mastery. You may choose to submit to external authority—to be religiously observant or patriotic, for example—and still be free so long as you not do so blindly. Your actions should be choices, not reactions. You should think for yourself.

Still, there is nothing quite like Sartre's idea of freedom in Husserl or Heidegger. For Heidegger, the end of thinking is a state whose features are not entirely clear, but that could be called quasi-mystical. *Gelassenheit*—release, serenity, a "letting be"—is a term he eventually chose for this state.[82] The aim is to achieve an awareness of things; it is not to change them. For Sartre, the aim is not contemplation. It is action. Philosophy proper falls by the wayside, one more false promise to back up our choices for us. This part of Sartre's thought took some of its inspiration from a completely different mode of expression, American fiction.

4.

A classic instance of the Paris effect—the transformation of a regional writer into a global one—is the case of William Faulkner.[83] And a tiny but crucial role in that transformation was played by James Burnham. One of Burnham's professors at Princeton was a French émigré named Maurice-Edgar Coindreau. Coindreau had begun his career in Madrid, teaching at a lycée and translating Spanish plays into French. In 1922, when he was thirty years old, he took a position as an instructor of modern languages at Princeton.[84] He did not know a word of English.[85]

While he was in Madrid, Coindreau had met John Dos Passos. (They were introduced by a common friend, José [Pepe] Robles, who would be murdered, possibly by agents of the Kremlin, during the Spanish Civil War.)[86] When Dos Passos's novel *Manhattan Transfer* was published, in 1925, Coindreau, now at Princeton, decided to translate it into French. He thought it might be a useful exercise for improving his English. Dos Passos, then in a leftist phase, was living in New York City, and every two weeks or so, Coindreau went in from Princeton to see him. It was during Prohibition, and they met in a speakeasy, where the beer, as Coindreau later remembered it, "prenait saveur de péché"—took on the flavor of sin.[87] Coindreau would show Dos Passos what he had done and Dos Passos, whose French was excellent, would correct mistakes and help Coindreau with idiomatic terms.

When they finished the first chapter, Coindreau asked Dos Passos if he could see whether a French publisher might be interested. Dos Passos consented, and Coindreau sent the chapter to Gaston Gallimard. Gallimard liked it and commissioned the rest, and in 1928, Coindreau's translation of *Manhattan Transfer* came out in two volumes in France. It was a sensation. *Ulysses*, although it had been set by French printers and published in Paris in 1922, had not yet been translated into French. *Manhattan Transfer*'s kaleidoscopic form—Dos Passos's juxtaposition of multiple narratives, somewhat as Joyce had done in parts of *Ulysses*—seemed to French readers a thrilling and original way to represent the modern city as a palimpsest of simultaneous but discontinuous experiences.[88]

Gallimard decided that he had a good thing in Maurice-Edgar Coindreau and he encouraged him to continue to find ways of improving his English.[89] Coindreau saw that what was wanted was avant-garde fiction, and he asked his Princeton colleagues for contemporary American authors to translate. Their recommendations—Booth Tarkington, Willa Cather—seemed unsuitable, so he solicited Burnham's advice. Burnham was then teaching at New York University. He recommended Faulkner, who, at the time, was neither well known nor well regarded. *The Sound and the Fury* (1929) and *As I Lay Dying* (1930) had been largely disparaged or ignored. The first edition of *The Sound and the Fury* sold only five hundred copies.[90] Coindreau read those novels, then he read *Sanctuary* (1931).[91] It was the beginning of a lifelong love affair.

Coindreau wrote to Faulkner to arrange for Gallimard to buy the rights to the French translations, and he wrote an essay on Faulkner that his friend Jean Paulhan published in the *Nouvelle Revue Française* in 1931, the first article on Faulkner in France and one of the first anywhere. (Burnham had published a similarly prescient essay on Faulkner in his own journal, *Symposium*, earlier that year. "If every American novelist were to bring out a book tomorrow and I could have only one I should take William Faulkner's," Burnham said.)[92]

Gallimard arranged for *Sanctuary*, Faulkner's first commercial success in the United States but regarded by many people as a scandalous book, to be translated by René Raimbault and Henri Delgove.[93] Their translation appeared in 1933; Coindreau's translation of *As I Lay Dying* (*Tandis que j'agonise*) came out a year later.[94] Both were big hits. The actor Jean-Louis Barrault was obsessed by *Tandis que j'agonise*. He spent six months studying it, and, in 1935, created a stage adaptation, a pantomime called *Autour d'une mère*. It was his first production, and featured Antonin Artaud.[95]

The Faulkner translations appeared in a series that Gallimard started up called *Du Monde Entier*—foreign novels with prefaces by well-known French writers. The preface to *Sanctuary* was written by Malraux, who had just published the hugely popular *La Condition humaine* (*Man's Fate*). The preface to *As I Lay Dying* was by Valery Larbaud, a friend of Joyce's and the man who supervised the French translation of *Ulysses*. Gallimard had already requested, and Coindreau had supplied, translations of Hemingway's *A Farewell to Arms*, published in 1932 with a preface by Drieu La Rochelle, and *The Sun Also Rises*, which appeared in 1933 with a preface by the journalist Jean Prévost.[96]*

Coindreau went on to translate many more American novels—thirty-five in all—including *Light in August* (1935) and *The Sound and the Fury* (1938), Erskine Caldwell's *God's Little Acre* (1936) and *Tobacco Road* (1937), and John Steinbeck's *Of Mice and Men* (1939). The war put an official end to the distribution of American fiction in occupied France (though there was a black market for the books in Paris). But after the war was over, Coindreau picked up where he left off, and translated, among other American writers, Flannery O'Connor, Truman Capote, Reynolds Price, William Goyen, Shelby Foote, and William Styron.

Other French publishers responded to the demand for American fiction. Grasset published a translation of Dos Passos's *The 42nd Parallel* in 1933; a translation of *1919* was published by Éditions Sociales Internationales in 1937. (The third volume of Dos Passos's *U.S.A.* trilogy, *The Big Money*, was not published in France until 1946.) Faulkner, Dos Passos, Steinbeck, Caldwell, and Hemingway became known as *les cinq grands*.[97]

Coindreau was a canon-maker. The effect of his work was enormous, not only on the Americans he translated, particularly Faulkner, whose French reception was almost certainly crucial to his receiving the Nobel Prize in 1949, but also on French literary culture itself.[98] The 1930s became known as "the age of the American novel." "The appearance in French translation of *Manhattan Transfer*, *Farewell to Arms*, and *Sanctuary* was a revelation to the entire French reading public," Beauvoir wrote after the war.[99] "The greatest literary development in France between 1929

* Prévost had once enjoyed the mixed fortune of boxing with Hemingway, who cheated. He later joined the Resistance and was killed during the Liberation.

and 1939," wrote Sartre, "was the discovery of Faulkner, Dos Passos, Hemingway, Caldwell, Steinbeck."[100]

The French had their own way of reading American fiction and their own understanding of what it was about. That understanding was partly an effect of translation and partly the consequence of a received idea of Americans. Almost none of the French writers who were influenced by American fiction had ever been to the United States. Their knowledge of the American character derived from translated novels and Hollywood movies. (But: misprision is part of transmission.)

Coindreau taught at Princeton until his retirement, in 1961, but he was, quite self-consciously, a Frenchman. His own politics were reactionary. He was from a town called La Roche-sur-Yon, which is in the Vendée, in western France, once the heart of royalist and clerical opposition to the French Revolution and Napoléon. Despite their friendship and the success of *Manhattan Transfer*, Coindreau declined to translate Dos Passos's *U.S.A.*, because he didn't like its left-wing politics. The reason he translated so many Southerners was because he identified with them as rebels against the modern liberal state.[101]

Coindreau's reference points as a translator were the major French authors—Rabelais, Montaigne, Flaubert, Gide. What interested him in American writing was the technique, not the Americana. He called the problem of translating dialect, for example, "a detail of slight importance." The country people in Faulkner's novels "speak above all as country people do," he explained, "and nothing else matters. The same reasoning may be applied to Negroes." What matters about Dilsey, "the admirable 'mammy' of the Compson family in *The Sound and the Fury*," is not the color of her skin. "All men of my generation in France have known in the homes of their parents and their grandparents white counterparts of Dilsey. We know how they spoke and this is the only thing that concerns us."[102] He advised French readers that the Grand-Guignol plots in Faulkner's novels—along with the idiocy, murder, rape, incest, racism, and general depravity—could be ignored. "In the works of William Faulkner the subject is only a pretext for a display of technique," he wrote in his *NRF* article. ". . . To be fair to Faulkner one must forget his themes and consider only the way he deals with them."[103]

Gallimard's translators therefore regarded dialect as something they were not obliged to reproduce. "The patois might interest the English-language reader," Larbaud explained in his preface to *Tandis que j'agonise*, ". . . but it is no more than a degraded English, spoiled by negligence and bad habits, that for us is more impenetrable than colorful."[104] In one respect, Larbaud and Coindreau were making a virtue of necessity. For how *do* you translate American vernacular prose, and particularly American colloquial speech, which is predominantly Anglo-Saxon, into a Romance language like French? "Dat's de troof," says Job, the old Black man who works in Jason Compson's shop in *The Sound and the Fury*. Coindreau's rendering: "Ça, c'est bien vrai, dit-il." It's not the same.[105]

This meant that French translations of American novels largely bleached out markers of race, region, and class. The effect was to classicize. Malraux described *Sanctuary* as "the eruptions of Greek tragedy into a detective story"; Larbaud called *As I Lay Dying* "Homeric." These phrases from the prefaces were parroted in the reviews, and they became the basis for the French reception of contemporary American fiction.[106] Discounting the plot and universalizing the themes threw the focus onto the technique, which is exactly where Coindreau wanted it to be thrown.

What did the French find so modern and exciting about American literary technique? First, they thought that writers such as Faulkner and Dos Passos had solved a problem with the representation of time. Time is a traditional French preoccupation. Marcel Proust's novel is a monument to that fascination, which is also behind the celebrity of the philosopher Henri Bergson, whose distinction between clock time and experienced time, which he called *la durée*, was the basis of his first book, *Essai sur les donées immédiates de la conscience* (translated as *Time and Free Will*), in 1889. The French thought that Faulkner had achieved a powerful representation of lived time by radically subjectivizing the narration and by collapsing the distinction between percept and memory. In the opening section of *The Sound and the Fury*, for example, Benjy's stream of consciousness alternates between present perceptions and remembered perceptions without obvious textual signaling (which is the reason many readers have trouble making sense of it).

Faulkner and Dos Passos showed French novelists that you could organize a narrative nonlinearly and nonchronologically. "Faulkner had contrived to give his narrative *durée* even though he annihilated normal-time sequence," as Beauvoir put it.[107] Coindreau thought that for Faulkner, the concept of a past, present, and future is only "a convenient illusion in our brains."[108] Another French critic proposed that Faulkner had gone beyond Joyce and Virginia Woolf by abandoning the factitious coherence of the stream of consciousness—the *I*—and had reproduced "the incongruous multiplicity [*la multiplicité hétéroclite*] of the elementary sensations of selfhood."[109]

The other thing about American fiction that fascinated the French was what they took to be the elimination of psychology. "Hemingway never enters inside his characters," Sartre wrote. "He describes them always from the outside . . . The heroes of Hemingway and Caldwell never explain themselves. They act only."[110] Sartre thought that Faulkner was his kind of phenomenologist: he showed the inside only to confirm that there is nothing there. Thought in Faulkner is simply the sum of one's intentions and character the sum of one's actions. The American novel seemed to have completely rejected what the modern French novel, and Proust's novel paradigmatically, had made its specialty: introspection and analysis.[111]

Although the French talked in a general way about *l'école d'outre-atlantique* and *le style américain*, different French novelists responded to different American writers. Jules Romains admired Dos Passos, whom he thought had discovered a narrative technique for representing collectivity, for making the spirit of the city the protagonist of a novel.[112] Beauvoir said that although she borrowed formal elements from Dos Passos for *L'Invitée*, the most obvious influence on her writing was Hemingway (some of whose stories she read in English).[113] Camus (who did not know English) said that he wrote *L'Étranger* in an American style, which Sartre identified as Hemingway's.[114] Sartre published influential essays on Faulkner, but in the end found him too fatalistic. "I love his art," he wrote; "I do not believe in his metaphysics."[115] But he called Dos Passos "the greatest writer of our time" and the crisscrossing narrative of his own trilogy *Les Chemins de la liberté* (*The Roads to Freedom*) was modeled on *U.S.A.* (or at least the two volumes Sartre was able to read in French).[116]

A myth of primitivism figured in the French reception of American culture. In his preface to *A Farewell to Arms*, Drieu wrote excitedly about the brutality and rawness of Hemingway's writing. When the Harvard professor Perry Miller toured European universities lecturing on American literature after the war, he reported enthusiasm wherever he went for American writing—provided it was violent. "As long as a book flaunted the stigmata of American violence, it was accepted uncritically as the real thing," Miller reported. ". . . Almost anything which pretends to be 'tough' will be read."[117] He found that he could not get Europeans excited about the Henry James revival.

The French thought that American fiction was raw and direct because that was the way Americans are. In American novels, Camus said in 1947, "[m]an is described but never explained"; the stories are universal, but "only at the level of the elementary."[118] Sartre thought that *le style américain* was uncalculated and unreflective, a spontaneous outburst, and that American writers expressed themselves that way because they couldn't help it. "When Hemingway writes his short, disjointed sentences, he is only obeying his temperament," Sartre explained. "He writes what he sees . . . If Faulkner breaks the chronological order of his story, it is because he cannot do otherwise. He sees time jumping about in disordered leaps."[119] Of course, Faulkner didn't show time jumping about in disordered leaps because he couldn't help it. He showed time that way because he had read Bergson.[120]

French critics had an explanation for the absence of explanation in American fiction: they thought that American writers were imitating the movies. The argument was made in the most important critical study in France of American fiction (there were several), Claude-Edmonde Magny's *L'Âge du roman américain* (*The Age of the American Novel*), published in 1948 but composed of articles originally published in 1944 and 1945.[121] Magny argued that the techniques in American fiction were literary adaptations of cinema. She said a lot about montage and ellipsis, but at the most basic level, the French thought that the influence of film could be seen in the paratactic atomization of action— the *and then, and then, and then* narration—of writers like Hemingway and Dos Passos. What we are presented with is a sequence of actions without commentary, like a scene in a film.[122]

Sartre and Beauvoir's enthusiasm for American fiction went hand in hand with their enthusiasm for American popular culture generally and American movies in particular. They read Dashiell Hammett; they were devoted to American folk music—spirituals, working songs, the blues. They loved Hollywood Westerns and gangster pictures. When they launched their own journal after the war as a replacement for the suspended *NRF,* they named it after a Charlie Chaplin movie, *Modern Times.* They hated French films and French fiction. "[W]e loathed the whole idea of *la vie intérieure,*" said Beauvoir.[123]

During his time in the army, Sartre recorded in his diary a fantasy of becoming a man of unreflective action. Such a man, he wrote, would be

> handsome, hesitant, obscure, slow and upright in his thoughts; [he would] not have had any acquired grace, but only a silent, spontaneous kind: I saw him, for some reason, as a worker and hobo in the Eastern USA. How I should like to feel uncertain ideas slowly, patiently forming within me! How I should have liked to boil with great, obscure rages; faint from great, motiveless outpourings of tenderness! My American worker (who resembled Gary Cooper) could do and feel all that. I pictured him sitting on a railway embankment, tired and dusty; he'd be waiting for the cattle-truck [*le wagon à bestiaux*], into which he'd jump unseen— and I should have liked to be *him* . . . [a man] who thought little, spoke little and always did the right thing.[124]

Sartre seems to have confused the eastern and western parts of the United States, and it is entertaining to imagine him as Gary Cooper jumping into a cattle truck whatever that is. He was plainly taking his idea of America and the American from the movies. But it made sense for him to do this, because he was trying to analyze his way out of a culture of analysis. In a sense, he was trying to do philosophy in *le style américain*.

5.

At first, Sartre avoided the term "existentialism." This may have been partly because of its associations with *Existenzphilosophie*—that is, with German philosophy—and partly because "existentialism" was already being used by Christian thinkers influenced by Kierkegaard, such as the French philosopher Gabriel Marcel. Mainly, though, it was because Sartre didn't want to foreclose an alliance with the Communists, with whom he had had patchy relations during the Occupation. After the Liberation, the Communist press began attacking existentialists, including Sartre and writers associated with him, such as Camus.

This was not something to ignore. The PCF had substantial media power. It controlled twelve daily newspapers and forty-seven weeklies in France plus another seventeen weeklies operated by parties in its

National Front coalition. *Les Lettres Françaises*, a Resistance paper the Communists took over after the Liberation, had a circulation of a hundred thousand.[125] So on December 29, 1944, Sartre published "À propos de l'existentialisme: mise au point" ("About Existentialism: A More Precise Explanation") in the Communist paper *Action*. It was the first time he used the term "existentialism" in print.

The editors of *Action* had invited Sartre's contribution, and as his title suggests, he imagined it as a clarification preliminary to a rapprochement. He dismissed the charges that existentialism was infected by Nazism by virtue of its connection with Heidegger (who had joined the Nazi Party), and that it was a philosophy of pessimism and despair—attacks, he said, that seemed "inspired by bad faith and ignorance." On the key question, he argued that existentialism is compatible with Marxism. "Is it not a fact," he asked, "that Marx would accept *this motto of ours for man: make, and in making make yourself, and be nothing but what you have made of yourself?*" All that existentialism does, he explained, is to clarify that although the worker is, by historical circumstance, a member of an oppressed class, he or she still has a choice: to be dictated to by that circumstance or to take action to end it—"to be the man who refuses to let destitution be man's lot."[126] There is a difference, in other words, between the working class "in-itself" and a working class "for-itself." Consciousness of one's situation is the first step toward transcending it.

On January 11, 1945, two weeks after his article came out, Sartre left for the United States. Camus had invited him to represent *Combat* on a tour for French journalists organized by the American Office of War Information and intended to promote the war effort—and in particular, to smooth American relations with de Gaulle. There were eight French journalists on the trip, and it was a serious tour. Sartre spent four months in the United States and Canada, traveling to, among other places, New York City, Baltimore, Chicago, Pittsburgh, the Grand Canyon (their pilot flew the plane inside the canyon), Hollywood (where he saw *Citizen Kane* and *Casablanca*, movies that had not been seen in occupied Europe), and the South. The group met with President Roosevelt in the White House. Sartre wrote thirty-two articles during his visit, twenty-one for *Combat* and eleven for *Le Figaro*, most of them short but well-reported stories about conditions, especially labor and race relations, in the United States.[127]

When Sartre got back to Paris in May 1945, the city had changed.

The nonpartisan spirit of the Resistance and the euphoria of the Liberation had already begun to dissipate toward the end of 1944, and the winter of 1944–1945 was one of the worst of the century. The *épuration* was under way; some suspected collaborators were arrested and tried and many others were persecuted or assassinated by vigilantes. And the country was out of money. Living conditions after the Liberation were not significantly better than living conditions in wartime.

In April, Parisians saw newsreels and photographs of Dachau and Belsen for the first time. In May, the surviving deportees (more than 200,000 had died in captivity) began returning from forced labor in Germany and from the concentration camps. They were processed through the Gare d'Orsay—broken, emaciated, visibly traumatized. Six thousand died soon after their arrival.[128] There had been rumors about the camps, but when the deportees returned, Beauvoir wrote, "we discovered that we had known nothing . . . I was ashamed to be alive."[129] People who came out to greet their loved ones wept. These images, as much as the myth of the Resistance, became ingrained in the postwar imagination.

But intellectual life was robust. Ideas mattered again. They were no longer thoughts in a vacuum or circulated underground; consequences seemed possible. Only two thousand copies of *L'Être et le néant* had been printed when it came out in the summer of 1943, and it received little critical attention. But by the time Sartre returned from his American trip, the book had become, along with Camus's *Le Mythe de Sisyphe*, one of the prime exhibits in what Merleau-Ponty called *la querelle de l'existentialisme*—the quarrel over existentialism.[130]

In June, *Action* published a reply to Sartre's "Mise au point" by the Marxist sociologist Henri Lefebvre. Lefebvre had been critical of Heidegger since the early 1930s, and he saw in *L'Être et le néant* the same contemplative intellectualism he disliked in Heidegger's philosophy.[131] He accused Sartre of idealism, narcissism, and obscurantism. "La réalité humaine" is "une réalité historique," he wrote, and he called existentialism a "theoretical war machine against Marxism."[132] In short, Sartre's offer of a rapprochement was declined.

By the summer, existentialism was being talked about everywhere. In France, the philosopher Jean Beaufret, a former *normalien* whose interest in Heidegger and Husserl had been provoked by Sartre's early writings, published a multipart study of existentialism in the humanist journal *Confluences*.[133] In the United Kingdom, the logical positivist A. J. Ayer wrote a two-part critique of *L'Être et le néant* for *Horizon*.[134] Unsurprisingly, it was not friendly. "[A] mass of often very subtle, but desperately wrong-headed, ratiocination" is how he described Sartre's discussion of time.[135]

In the United States, *Partisan Review*'s Paris correspondent, Harold Kaplan, referred to Sartre, Camus, and Beauvoir as "the liveliest literary movement in France," and devoted half of his "Paris Letter" in the fall 1945 issue to a discussion of French existentialism, chiefly Sartre's.[136] Albert Guerard, a Harvard professor serving in France in the Army Psychological Warfare unit, reported in *Harper's* that intellectual Paris had two obsessions: the American novel and the philosophy of Sartre. American novels were popular, he suggested, because they were understood as fictional expressions of existential philosophy.[137] Sartre himself published widely—in *Vogue*, "New Writing in France" (promoting Camus), and in *Horizon* and *Partisan Review*, "The Case for Responsible Literature."[138]

The concept of the writer's responsibility might have meant many things to Sartre's American and British readers, but it meant something specific in France. It was an allusion to the *épuration*. It was an implicit answer to the question of whether writers who collaborated should be punished. Why should the writer who collaborated be treated differently from the industrialist? Vercors had asked in February, when Sartre was in the United States. Because the writer is responsible not only for his own thoughts but also for the thoughts of all the people he has influenced. "To compare the industrialist to the writer," Vercors wrote, "is like comparing Cain to the devil. Cain's crime ends with Abel. The danger of the devil is without limit."[139]

What Beauvoir called "the existentialist offensive" began in the fall of 1945.[140] In September, Sartre published the first two volumes of *Les Chemins de la liberté* and Beauvoir published her second novel, *Le Sang des autres* (*The Blood of Others*). On October 1, the first issue of *Les Temps Modernes* appeared. An editorial statement calling for a literature of engagement was an expanded version of the article on "responsible literature" that Sartre had published in *Horizon* and *Partisan Review*. With that statement, Sartre effectively adapted the legal and ethical standard of the postwar purges to peacetime. Writers must always be held responsible for the political effects of what they write.

Sartre's and Beauvoir's novels and the new journal received much attention in the French press, so it was only a little surprising that on the evening of October 29, when Sartre showed up to deliver a public lecture in a room on the rue Jean Goujon, so many people were trying to get inside to hear him that he could barely enter himself. At first, he thought that the Communists had turned out to protest. The next day, *Combat* printed a colorful description of an overheated room with four hundred in the audience, broken furniture, people fainting, and the speaker struggling for fifteen minutes to reach the platform.[141]

Combat was then promoting everything that Sartre and Beauvoir did, so it would be possible to suspect some tongue-in-cheek hyperbole. But every paper that carried a story reported a tremendous crush.[142] Sartre had delivered a lecture on the same topic a few days earlier in Brussels and a large crowd had turned out there, too.[143] In Paris, Gaston Gallimard was in the audience; Gabriel Marcel, who had been invited by the organizers and who arrived twenty minutes early, couldn't get in. "Imagine a Métro station, Opéra or Châtelet, after a one-hour delay, and that will give you a feeble idea of the crowd trying to enter," he described it.[144]

Sartre's title, "L'existentialisme est un humanisme," had been decided on at the last minute in consultation with the event's organizers, and the whole affair had an improvised character. Sartre spoke extemporaneously, his hands in his pockets, for an hour, then left. A planned discussion was canceled because of the lateness of the hour. The next day, Sartre discovered that he had become famous. His lecture was the cultural event of 1945.[145]

Its fame was so great that Louis Nagel, a publisher who was also Sartre's dramatic agent, persuaded Sartre to write down what he could remember of the talk.* An editor padded out the volume with a staged "discussion," in which Sartre responded to questions from Pierre Naville, a former Trotskyist, and an anonymous interlocutor. The book came out in Paris in February 1946 as *Existentialisme est un humanisme*; an English translation was published the following year by the Philosophical Library, titled, simply, *Existentialism*. Since a complete English translation of *L'Être et le néant* did not appear until 1956—and, even

---

* Sartre omitted a claim, reported in the *Combat* story, that T. E. Lawrence—Lawrence of Arabia—was an existentialist.

then, most nonphilosophers found the book fairly impenetrable—the result was that, to Sartre's dismay, this popular lecture became the most widely known of all his philosophical writings.[146]

Existentialism, Sartre explains in the little book, is nothing but "an attempt to draw all the consequences of a coherent atheistic position." The existentialist finds it distressing that God does not exist, because the disappearance of God means that, as Dostoyevsky's Ivan Karamazov says, everything is possible. But, Sartre goes on, this is "the very starting point of existentialism." It means that every decision is a free one and that we, and only we, are responsible for it. Every choice is therefore a moral gamble. Once we have chosen, then we have to live in such a way as to make that choice the right choice. Nothing outside the act can validate it. As Sartre puts it: "[I]n the bright realm of values, we have no excuse behind us, nor justification before us. We are alone, with no excuses."[147]

Sartre liked to draw illustrations from literature and to create his own fictional characters and vignettes—such as the waiter in *L'Être et le néant* whose internalization of the persona of "the waiter" exemplifies the concept of bad faith.* (This use of fictional illustration is a feature of existentialist writing, which owes so much of its sense of character to literature.)[148] In *Existentialisme est un humanisme*, Sartre made some of his points using incidents taken from *The Mill on the Floss* and *La Chartreuse de Parme*. But the key story in the book is the one known as "the student's dilemma."

During the war, Sartre says, a student came to ask his advice. His brother has been killed by the Germans; his father has collaborationist tendencies. The student is the only source of solace left to his mother. His dilemma is whether he should join the Free French Forces in Britain, avenging his brother and fighting for France, or stay home to tend to his mother, who, if he were killed, would be desolated. It is a dilemma because good reasons can be given for either choice. There is no ideal solution. What is the student to do? "I had," Sartre concludes, "only one answer to give: 'You're free, choose; that is, invent.' No general ethics

---

* In *The Presentation of Self in Everyday Life*, first published in 1956, the Canadian sociologist (he taught in the United States) Erving Goffman quoted happily Sartre's description of the waiter, although for Goffman, people performing their roles is just how society works. "All the world is not, of course, a stage," Goffman wrote, "but the crucial ways in which it isn't are not easy to specify." (Garden City: Doubleday, 1959, 72.)

can show you what is to be done; there are no omens [*il n'y a pas de signe*] in the world."[149]

It cannot be that all ethical systems are indeterminate regarding the dilemma the student faces. Sartre's point is that no choice dictated by a priori principles can be a free choice, but any choice made in the name of freedom is by definition the right choice. And—Sartre is explicit about this—the identical choice made unfreely is always the wrong choice. There is no credit for lucking out. One has to get out over the abyss before one can say that one has acted freely, and after one has acted, there is no longer a need to explain. "The heroes of Hemingway and Caldwell never explain themselves. They act only."

It is not known whether Sartre invented the student's dilemma, but it is recognizable as a version of the final scene in *Casablanca*, when Humphrey Bogart chooses to join the Free French rather than fly off with Ingrid Bergman. (*The Maltese Falcon*, which Sartre might also have seen on his visit to Hollywood, ends the same way, when Bogart decides to turn Mary Astor over to the law.) It is a choice between love and duty; each time, duty wins. How do we know that duty is the right choice? Because Bogart might, with our approval, have chosen love instead. He weighs the merits of each option, but his decision is not made on the merits. The end of his analysis—the end of all analysis—is: Who knows? The thing is simply to jump into the cattle truck.

This does not seem to provide much sustenance for a politics, but for many people, that was precisely existentialism's appeal. At a time when the damage caused by commitment to ideology was everywhere visible, Sartrean existentialism was anti-ideological. It was a philosophy of engagement, but it did not dictate any *particular* engagement. In a Cold War context, this could be liberating. Confronted with the choice between East and West, existentialism said only: Choose; that is, invent. But take responsibility for your choice.*

"With despair, true optimism begins," Sartre had written in the article in *Action*.[150] He meant that it is only when we realize that the world we want will not come into being simply by our hoping for it that we are ready to take responsibility for our actions—that we are ready to join the Free French (as, we assume, the hypothetical student does). But our

---

* This last part of the argument seems to be a way of grounding free choice in some realm of values that are not merely personal. What those values might be is a persistent problem in moral philosophy.

commitment is always to the unrealized. We are faithful to an ideal that lies somewhere over the horizon of the present. The strange consequence of this is that, in the end, it *is* the vagaries of the present situation that dictate our choices. We have nothing else to orient us.[151] No morality is implied by existentialism, Beauvoir told Dominique Aury in an interview a month after Sartre's lecture. "For my part," she said, "I am looking to identify one."[152]

6.

For the next twenty years, Sartre struggled to work out a modus vivendi between existentialism and Marxism—specifically, Marxism in its twentieth-century instantiation, the Soviet Union. In the course of that struggle, never straightforward, he lost the friendship of most of his contemporaries, including Aron, Merleau-Ponty, and, in the most public and painful break, Camus. He lost much of his audience in the United States and Britain as well.

But for three years after the lecture that became *Existentialisme est un humanisme*, existentialism was almost an obsession in France, the United Kingdom, and the United States. *Partisan Review, Horizon*, and Dwight Macdonald's little magazine *Politics* all published special French issues devoted largely to existentialist writers. *Les Temps Modernes* returned the compliment with a special American issue that included essays on comic books, Negro spirituals, the music of New Orleans, and Santa Monica Boulevard. Existentialism was the topic of an influential issue of *Yale French Studies*. Small arts magazines with an existentialist flavor sprouted up in New York City: *Possibilities* (1947), *Instead* (1948), *Tiger's Eye* (1948).[153] The existentialists themselves—that is, almost exclusively, Sartre, Beauvoir, and, though he tried to dissociate himself from the philosophy, Camus—were objects of fascination in the press. Some of the coverage was caricatural and satirical, but that is one of the ways the press pays homage to success.[154]

A dozen books on existentialism, from the introductory to the scholarly and polemical, were published in France and the United States. Among the more significant were the *Partisan Review* editor William Barrett's *What Is Existentialism?* (1947) and the Hungarian critic Georg Lukács's *Existentialisme ou marxisme?* (1948), a semiofficial repudiation of Sartre by the dean of European Marxists. Lukács called the whole tradition of *Existentialphilosophie*, from Husserl to Sartre, a "permanent carnival of fetishized inwardness."[155] The official repudiation was delivered in Wrocław, Poland, in 1948, at the Soviet-sponsored Congress of Intellectuals for World Peace, organized by Andrei Zhdanov, where the chairman of the Union of Soviet Writers, Alexander Fadeyev, referred to writers like Sartre as "jackals who learned how to type, hyenas who know how to use a pen."[156] The same year, the Holy Office of the Vatican placed all of Sartre's works on the Index of prohibited books.[157]*

Existentialism had little effect on academic philosophy outside France. Its influence was registered in other realms—but there were many of them. In the United States, existentialism was taken to have something to do with avant-garde literature and painting, with jazz, with questions of meaning and value, with the possibility or impossibility of religious faith, with the mores of private life. French existentialism also appealed because it was Parisian: it came from the heart of the modern. And almost the most common thing said about existentialism in the United States was how European it was. "It was a triumph for French culture to make 57th Street talk philosophy," Barrett wrote. (Fifty-Seventh was the street of the midtown art galleries in New York.) "Existential philosophy had acquired the voice of French eloquence, and it was something to be assimilated along with French painting, millinery, and literature, endowed with the charms of Gallic taste and *finesse*."[158]

Beauvoir had a similar theory. "The City of Light had gone dark," she has Henri, the Camus figure, think to himself in her roman à clef about postwar Paris, *Les Mandarins* (1954). "If one day it should glitter again, the splendor of Paris would be that of other fallen world capitals—Venice, Prague, long-dead Bruges. Not the same streets, not the same city, not the same world."[159] Beauvoir interpreted the vogue of existentialism as a sort of compensation for this loss of genuine international influence. "[N]ow a second-class power," she wrote in her memoirs, "France was exalting her most characteristic national products with an eye on the export market: *haute couture* and literature . . . Other countries were affected by the racket and seemed only too happy to make it even louder."[160]

And interest in French existentialism *did* coincide with an interest in French fashion. In March 1945, a spectacular fashion exhibition with

---

* The Holy Office did not see fit to put *Mein Kampf* on the Index.

mannequins, called *Le Théâtre de la Mode*, was mounted at the Louvre. It then embarked on a world tour, traveling to London, where the queen had a private viewing; Leeds, the capital of the Yorkshire textile industry; Barcelona; New York City, where it was covered closely by industry journals like *Women's Wear Daily*; and San Francisco. It reminded the world that French fashion was still alive.[161] Then, in February 1947, Christian Dior unveiled his "New Look" in women's apparel. His show was avidly covered by American fashion magazines, notably *Harper's Bazaar*, which had already had a special "Paris issue" in 1946. In fact the term "New Look" was originally a phrase used by the editor of *Harper's Bazaar*, Carmel Snow.* There was a stampede of fashionable women from Britain and the United States to the Avenue Montaigne, where Dior had his atelier.[162]

Existentialism became something more than a philosophy. It became a fashion, a mode of thought—even the name for a way of life. It flooded the cultural field. Existentialism gave postwar life a Sartrean vocabulary: anxiety, authenticity, bad faith. It got linked to terms that derived principally from Camus: the absurd, the outsider, the rebel. More amorphously, and more profoundly, existentialism provided art and thought with an image of "man." It is the image found in a painting by Jean Dubuffet or a sculpture by Alberto Giacometti or a play by Samuel Beckett: emptied out, unprotected, in extremis, but, therefore, purely human—"just a long, indistinct silhouette walking across the horizon," as Sartre described a Giacometti sculpture.[163] This figure was the antihero of midcentury fiction, the stranger, the unnamable, the dangling man.[164] But it was still "man," still the creature that possesses one thing that distinguishes it from the rest of existence: the power to choose. It's obvious who this figure was. This French export, the end product of a long chain of cross-cultural appropriations and misinterpretations, was the image of the postwar European—the exile, the *résistant*, the survivor of the camps.

---

* *Harper's Bazaar* is where Richard Avedon got his start as a fashion photographer. He photographed the Dior collection in 1947.

4

OUTSIDE THE LAW

Hannah Arendt in Paris, 1936, after she and her mother fled Berlin, arriving by way of Prague and Geneva. Arendt was twenty-nine. (*Courtesy of the Hannah Arendt Bluecher Literary Trust / Art Resource, NY*)

1.

The First World War broke up four empires: the German, the Russian, the Ottoman, and the Austro-Hungarian. When the fighting was over, a series of treaties—Versailles (1919), Saint Germain (1919), Neuilly (1919), Trianon (1920), Sèvres (1920), and Lausanne (1923)—carved up large portions of those former empires' territories into states organized according to a principle the United States had entered the war to establish: self-determination.

A chief aim of the victorious powers was the creation of a *cordon sanitaire* (a medical term adopted during the Versailles peace conference by the French prime minister, Georges Clemenceau) between Germany and Russia. But the new borders were drawn to circumscribe existing ethnic populations. The authors of the treaties seem to have imagined nations as ethnically homogeneous sovereignties, and to have believed that they were stabilizing a potentially volatile region by imposing on it a Western European model of statehood.

In fact, Western European nations were by no means ethnically homogeneous, and in any case, from a realist point of view, self-determination is an unsound basis for nation building. For it is always a question of which selves are doing the determining. Central and Eastern Europe was an ethnically mixed, cosmopolitan region; and so, almost everywhere, by identifying the state with its ethnic majority, the postwar treaties relegated much of the population to minority status. By definition, the number of people in the new dispensation who were governed by people ethnically like themselves was greater than the number of people who were not, but the second number was enormous. In an area with a population of 90 million, some 30 million people became, officially, minorities within their own countries.[1] One million ethnic Germans were living in Poland, for example; 3.2 million were living in Czechoslovakia. These people, the *Volksdeutsche*, would provide Adolf Hitler with his justification for annexing the Sudetenland in 1938 and invading Poland in 1939.[2]

Although the new states were compelled to sign minority protection treaties, these were resented as limitations on sovereignty, and ethnic majorities quickly assumed control of governments and branded national cultures with their identities. When ethnic minorities were suppressed, the Western powers did little to help them. The impotence of the League of Nations, which had been designed as the supranational defender of minorities, left millions without political representation or legal rights.

These people were known as *les apatrides* or *die Staatenlosen*—stateless persons. Already in 1922, in what would become the predominant English-language poem in the interwar period, "The Waste Land," T. S. Eliot could use them as a hallucinatory image of collapse.

> Who are those hooded hordes swarming
> Over endless plains, stumbling in cracked earth
> Ringed by the flat horizon only
> What is the city over the mountains
> Cracks and reforms and bursts in the violet air
> Falling towers

Jerusalem Athens Alexandria
Vienna London
Unreal[3]

Eliot had originally written, in the second line, "Over Polish plains."[4] The poem's note to the lines is a quotation from Hermann Hesse's essay *"Die Brüder Karamasoff* oder der Untergang Europas" (*"The Brothers Karamazov* or the Downfall of Europe)": "Schon ist halb Europa, schon ist zumindest der halbe Osten Europas auf dem Wege zum Chaos, fährt betrunken im heiligen Wahn am Abgrund entlang und singt dazu"— "Half of Europe, at least half of Eastern Europe is already on the road to chaos, moving in a drunken state in holy delusion along the abyss."[5]

Hitler's (perfectly legal) ascendance to the chancellorship of Germany on January 30, 1933, put almost the entire continent in motion. Jews and political opponents of Hitler's regime began fleeing Germany. As Germany annexed and occupied neighboring countries, they were followed by Austrians, Belgians, Hungarians—by the potential targets of Nazism all across Europe. A small number went into hiding and internal exile; a number that was probably not much larger managed, often after surmounting formidable barriers, to escape overseas. Many were captured and interned. Millions died in concentration camps and performing slave labor or were killed in the extermination camps and killing fields in the east.

The refugees were stateless, too. Wherever they went, they were metics, resident aliens, uncitizens. They were known as *les hors-la-loi* and "the scum of the earth"—people who had fallen outside the protection of the state. In France, a Frenchman arrested for a crime had more rights than a German seeking refuge from Hitler. The stateless persons—the ethnic minorities, refugees, émigrés, and exiles—were the real-life corollaries of existentialism's outsiders. They were, literally, *déracinés*, uprooted, political dangling men. They had suffered a civic death. If these people had a perception of contingency, of homelessness, and of existence without philosophical backup, they arrived at it not by means of philosophical reflection but through a physical and often terrifying ordeal.

Hannah Arendt was once a stateless person. Her experience and her reflections on its causes and implications became the basis for the work she began writing after she arrived in the United States in 1941, at the end of an eight-year flight from Nazi Germany. Arendt was seven when the First World War broke out, in the summer of 1914. Her hometown (also Immanuel Kant's hometown) was Königsberg, the capital of East Prussia, less than a hundred miles from Russia. On August 7, 1914, the Russian First and Second Armies invaded East Prussia. Arendt and her mother, Martha (her father had died of syphilis the year before), joined a crowd of panicked citizens, soldiers, and farmers from the east escaping the Russian advance and fled by train to Berlin. But the German army defeated the Russians at the Battle of Tannenberg and drove them out of East Prussia before they could get to Königsberg. After ten weeks in Berlin, Arendt and her mother returned.[6] It was Arendt's first encounter with dislocation.

Arendt was precocious. By the time she entered the University of Marburg, in 1924, when she was seventeen, she had read Kierkegaard (theology was her first interest), Kant's *Kritik der reinen Vernunft* (*Critique of Pure Reason*), and Karl Jaspers's formidable *Psychologie der Weltanschauungen* (*Psychology of Worldviews*), as well as a wide variety of literature, particularly poetry, much of which she knew by heart. She could read Greek and Latin. She was sometimes shy when she was young, but she was always independent. At Marburg, she cut a figure, with short hair and modish clothes. Students called her "the green one," after an emerald-green dress she liked to wear. She had intense features—particularly her eyes, which are mentioned in almost every description of her—and an intense intellect. She lived in an attic near the university, where friends gathered to discuss literature and philosophy. The attic is where she began her affair with Martin Heidegger.[7]

Although he had published little, Heidegger's lectures had made him a legend in German academic circles. Students were drawn to Marburg by, as Arendt later described it, "the rumor of the hidden [*heimlichen*: secret] king."[8] He was a charismatic lecturer, nicknamed "the little magician from Messkirch" (the small town in southern Germany he came from). "The power of fascination that emanated from him was partly based on his impenetrable nature," one of his students described the experience: "nobody knew where they were with him."[9] His students already included people who would become major figures in twentieth-century intellectual life: Leo Strauss, Hans-Georg Gadamer, Hans Jonas.[10] He was thirty-five and married, and had two sons.

Heidegger picked Arendt out at his lectures and invited her to visit him in his office. She was demure and passive when they met but the spark was lit. He sent her an ardent letter—"I will never be able to make you mine, but from now on you will belong in my life, and it shall grow with you"—and asked to be allowed to visit her that evening. Soon after, sometime in February 1925, the affair began.[11] Heidegger insisted on the strictest secrecy, and Arendt quickly understood that he was not going to change his life for her. (It is not clear that this was something she wanted, either. Despite her youth, she was no ingénue.) In 1926, she left Marburg to study for a semester at the University of Freiburg with Heidegger's teacher and mentor, Edmund Husserl, and then went to the University of Heidelberg to write her doctoral dissertation, on Augustine's concept of love, under Jaspers.

For several years, though, the trysts continued, and it was during their relationship that Heidegger wrote *Sein und Zeit*. The book was published in April 1927, dedicated to Husserl; a year later, Heidegger was appointed to the chair at Freiburg opened by Husserl's retirement, and he broke off the affair. She accepted the new arrangement. "I love you as I did on the first day—you know that, and I have always known it," she wrote to him. ". . . I would lose my right to live if I lost my love for you, but I would lose this love and its *reality* if I shirked the responsibility it forces on me."[12]

Arendt and Heidegger shared a passion for philosophy and poetry—for the high culture of *Bildung*. But almost everything else about their relationship is mysterious. Though she came from a highly assimilated family, Arendt had a distinct sense of herself as a Jew. There is a story that when she arrived in Marburg and was being interviewed by the theologian Rudolph Bultmann for admission to his class on the New Testament, she informed him that "there must be no anti-Semitic remarks." (Bultmann reassured her.)[13] Heidegger's wife, Elfride, was an overt anti-Semite. Heidegger's own anti-Semitism was more calculated. He had Jewish students, and he was the protégé of a Jewish philosopher, Husserl; but he privately disparaged Jews on nationalist (not biological) grounds, and after the Nazis came to power, an event he welcomed enthusiastically as newly appointed rector at Freiburg, he aggressively oversaw the *Gleichschaltung*—the forced coordination—of the university with Nazism, and largely cut off his Jewish students and former colleagues. He personally signed the dismissal of Husserl from the university and removed the dedication from *Sein und Zeit*. He was a member of the Nazi Party until the end of the war and he never expressed regret about that, or about what the Nazis had done to the Jews, to Germany, and to Europe.[14]

A few years after their breakup, Arendt wrote to Heidegger to ask about rumors she had heard concerning his treatment of Jews at the university. Heidegger responded with a defensive letter, adopting an offended tone that she must have known was a bluff, and for the next seventeen years, there was no communication between them.[15] In 1950, though, Arendt returned to Europe as the executive director of Jewish Cultural Reconstruction, an agency dedicated to recovering Jewish artifacts looted by the Nazis, and they met again, on her initiative. Heidegger was in disgrace, stripped of his license to teach, desperate for admiration and support. She was appalled and somewhat sorry for him, but also partially reenchanted and, ultimately, loyal. She seems to have decided that Heidegger was part of her life, for good or bad, and they remained on generally friendly terms until her death, in December 1975.[16] (Heidegger died six months later.) Arendt knew that Heidegger lied about many things, including his past, and there was much about his life and thought during the Nazi period of which she was ignorant. Still, the friendship between the Nazi admirer of Hitler and the Jewish analyst of totalitarianism was incongruous.

What is almost as peculiar is how little interest Heidegger showed in Arendt as a writer and thinker. They seem to have carried on a one-sided conversation—all about his work. Heidegger figured Arendt as a source of solace and stimulation, the personification of some principle of femininity. He set the terms in his very first letter to her. "Someday you will understand and be grateful—not to me—that this visit to my 'office hour' was the decisive step back from the path toward the terrible solitude of academic research, which only man can endure," he wrote. Her role, he explained in his next letter, was to inspire him: "May masculine inquiry learn what respect is from simple devotion; may one-sided activity learn breadth from the original unity of womanly Being."[17] (This language-on-stilts is characteristic of their correspondence.)

In short, he treated Arendt as an *être-en-soi*. And the irony is not that Arendt was a fierce enemy of essentialist and instrumentalist ways of regarding human beings, although she was. It's that anti-essentialism and anti-instrumentalism were positions she had learned from *Existenzphilosophie*—from Kierkegaard, from Jaspers, and from

Heidegger himself. They are the very bones of existentialism. She complained a little about the way Heidegger treated her, but she tolerated it from him, and from no one else.

When Heidegger ended their affair, Arendt had already been seeing a fellow student at Heidelberg, a man named Benno von Weise. In January 1929, at a masked ball in Berlin to which she came dressed as an Arab harem girl, she encountered Günther Stern, a young philosopher, also Jewish, who had been a student of Husserl and of Heidegger. They were married in September. They moved first to Frankfurt, where Stern worked, fruitlessly, on his *Habilitationsschrift* (the thesis required for a university post). His subject was the philosophy of music; Theodor Adorno was one of his readers and found the work unsatisfactory—the beginning of Arendt's lifelong dislike of Adorno.[18]*

When Hitler came to power, Arendt and Stern were living in Berlin. He associated with Communists; she associated with Zionists. These were not groups it was prudent to be in the company of, and the Reichstag fire, on February 27, 1933, which was almost certainly set by a Dutch Communist named Marinus van der Lubbe and which led to the suspension of civil liberties and a roundup of German Communists, convinced them that they were not safe. Many Germans had the same realization: Nazism was not going to be a temporary phenomenon. That year, more than 53,000 people fled Germany; 37,000 of them were Jews.[19] Arendt said that this was when she became political.[20]

At first, the government did not cancel passports—the Nazis were happy to see their political opponents go—and Stern left almost immediately for Paris. Arendt stayed behind and turned her apartment into a kind of underground railroad station for Communists and others seeking to escape. Soon, though, she was arrested while on an assignment from the German Zionist Organization to collect samples of anti-Semitic remarks in the Prussian State Library. The policeman who took her into custody seemed unsure what to do with her. She lied to him about her connections and managed to charm him into releasing her. But she had spent eight days in jail, and she knew she had been fortunate.

By then, concerned that the émigrés might agitate from abroad, the

---

* As these things sometimes go, in 1983, fourteen years after Adorno's death, Stern, who changed his name to Günther Anders, won the Adorno Prize.

government had stopped allowing people to leave.[21] In August, without proper papers, Arendt and her mother fled through the Erzgebirge range, south of Berlin, to Prague, which had become a haven for German refugees. She moved from there to Geneva, and then, in the fall, to Paris, where she was reunited with Stern. She shared a place with him, but they had grown apart, and the marriage was at an end.

In the 1930s, France was by far the most popular destination for refugees from Germany and the countries it occupied.[22] Many of these were ordinary people who required relief, but some were accomplished artists, writers, and intellectuals, and there was a significant German-language émigré community in Paris. Arendt also became friendly with French intellectuals such as Sartre's former classmate Raymond Aron, and, thanks to Aron, she attended sessions of a legendary seminar on Hegel, run by Alexandre Kojève, at the École Pratique des Hautes Études.* In 1936, she met Heinrich Blücher, a German Communist (but about to leave the Party), married (but separated), and a Gentile. Blücher was an autodidact, a blocked writer but a great talker. They were married in January 1940, after they had obtained their divorces. It was the time of the phony war.[23]

In May, worried about a fifth column inside France, the government ordered the internment of all German refugees as "enemy aliens." Arendt was incarcerated in a covered sports stadium, the Vélodrome d'Hiver. (A little more than two years later, French police would round up seven thousand Jews and hold them in the Vélodrome, under punishing conditions, for deportation, ultimately to Auschwitz.)[24] From the Vélodrome, she was taken to an internment camp for women, Gurs, one of what would eventually be more than thirty camps set up by the Vichy regime in the south of France.[25]

Five weeks after Arendt arrived, the defeat of France briefly threw administrative matters into chaos. She seized the chance and secured papers allowing her to leave the camp. She walked and hitched rides to Montauban, two hundred kilometers to the northeast, a city that refugees believed was safe, and found Blücher there. (He had also been rounded up, but he escaped from a forced march when the line was strafed by German planes.)[26] In October, when Jews were ordered to

---

* A Russian émigré, Kojève had been a student of Jaspers; he received his doctorate in 1926, leaving Heidelberg just as Arendt was arriving. His interpretation of Hegel was a major influence on Francis Fukuyama's "end of history" thesis at the end of the Cold War.

register with local officials, Arendt and Blücher fled to Marseille, the main gathering point for refugees trying to get out of Europe. They obtained emergency visas—two of just two hundred and thirty-eight issued by the United States between August and December 1940—thanks to the intervention of Stern's family, which was already in the United States, and, possibly, Aron.[27] Arendt's mother got a visa a little later. When Arendt and Blücher picked up their visas in Marseille they were spotted by police and escaped only after Arendt created a distraction by making a scene at their hotel.

Again, the door opened just a crack. In January the Vichy government made it briefly easier to get exit permits, and Arendt and Blücher were able to leave France and travel by train to Lisbon. They waited there for three months until they could get a boat to New York. Their tickets were paid for by the HIAS (the Hebrew Immigrant Aid Society, a venerable American charitable organization). Just after they arrived in the United States, in May 1941, the State Department stiffened its policy, already highly restrictive, for admitting refugees. Arendt had squeezed through a series of collapsing boxes in which many were trapped and crushed. Suicide was not an uncommon end for German refugees.[28]

One of the German émigrés Arendt met in Paris was the critic Walter Benjamin, who also fled to Marseille. He was a distant cousin of Stern and he became, Arendt later said, her and Blücher's "best friend in Paris."[29] In Marseille, he gave them a manuscript and asked them, if they made it to the United States, to deliver it to Adorno, who had moved, along with most of the rest of the Institute for Social Research, to New York.[30] Benjamin then tried to escape from France without an exit visa through Spain, but the border was closed. Suffering from depression and a heart condition, he took a large quantity of morphine tablets he had brought with him. He died in a small hotel in the fishing village of Port Bou. The border was reopened the next day.[31]

When Arendt and Blücher landed in New York, they had twenty-five dollars in their pockets plus the promise of seventy dollars a month from the Zionist Organization of America. They knew almost no English. (They had taken a few lessons, joined by Benjamin, shortly before the German invasion, in 1940. As part of his effort to learn the language, Benjamin read Faulkner's *Light in August* in French translation.)[32] They rented a two-room furnished apartment with no kitchen on the Upper West Side, where they lived with Martha Arendt. They would remain in that apartment for nine years.

In 1942, Arendt and Blücher began reading reports of the extermination program that the Nazis called *die Endlösung der Judenfrage*—the final solution of the Jewish question. In December, an American German-language weekly, *Aufbau*, to which Arendt was contributing, ran an eyewitness report by a French clergyman of the deportation of the inmates at Gurs. The paper printed the names of many of the deportees; almost all of them were refugees from Germany and Poland. Among the deportees were six thousand Jews who had been smuggled into Gurs from outside France by Adolf Eichmann.

They were taken first to Drancy, a Nazi camp in a suburb of Paris where conditions were notorious, and then to the death camp at Auschwitz, in the former Poland.[33] The news shook Arendt and Blücher, and not only for personal reasons. "It was really as if an abyss had opened," as Arendt said later. "Because we had the idea that amends could be somehow made for everything else, as amends can be made for just about everything at some point in politics. But not for this. *This ought not to have happened.*"[34] It was then that she began planning the book that would make her famous, *The Origins of Totalitarianism*.

2.

"This ought not to have happened" was not an ethical judgment. It was a logical judgment. The extermination policy—which, although mass killings were already being carried out, was officially implemented following the Wannsee Conference in January 1942—made no political or military sense. With its army engaged in a protracted and deadly war on the eastern front and with the United States now an official combatant, the Third Reich chose to commit valuable resources to a large-scale and increasingly frantic effort to exterminate millions of people none of whom posed the slightest threat to the regime. For Arendt, this showed that totalitarianism was not simply an unusually ruthless form of dictatorship. It was something new. She thought that new things are rare in politics, and she set out to explain where this one came from.

The Origins of Totalitarianism, which was published in 1951, is a historical account of what Arendt saw as the train wreck of the European political order in the fifty years leading to the rise of Hitler. At the same time, it is a work of moral and political thought. The book is densely documented, and the documents are also actors in an intellectual drama. There are few books quite like it, and even people who disagreed with it found it fascinating. "The mixture of German metaphysics, subtle sociology, and moral vituperations ends up exaggerating the qualities and the faults of men and of regimes," wrote Aron, who was one such reader, ". . . substituting for real history a history that is at every moment ironic or tragic."[35]

The book also appears to be confusingly organized. That is partly because Arendt changed course two thirds of the way through. She originally intended it to be a book about imperialism. In the fall of 1946, in a letter to her editor at Houghton Mifflin, she referred to the project as "the imperialism-book," and proposed as possible titles "The Elements of Shame. Anti-Semitism–Imperialism–Racism" and "The Three Pillars of Hell. Anti-Semitism–Imperialism–Racism." In her letter and in a five-page outline she enclosed with it, the word "totalitarianism" does not appear.[36]

A year later, she changed her mind. Writing to Jaspers, she explained that the third and final section of the book would be an analysis of totalitarianism and that it would deal with the Soviet Union as well as Nazi Germany.[37] By then, she had gotten involved with writers and editors at *Partisan Review*, for whom Stalinism was a far more pressing issue than imperialism. By then, too, Truman had given his "alternative ways of life" speech, and the Cold War was under way.

The shift obliged Arendt to take what she had already written as an explanation for Nazism and use it as an explanation for Stalinism as well. This obviously made for some problems, which she tried to finesse by suggesting that Stalin had created artificially the political and psychological conditions that Western European history had handed to Hitler.[38] When the book came out, several reviewers questioned the legitimacy of this move. E. H. Carr, in *The New York Times*, complained about "a certain lack of historical perspective."[39] In the end, though, he was not really bothered, and neither were most readers. For they were much more interested in the book's anatomy of totalitarianism than they were in the history.

So was Arendt. The main reason the book is confusing is because Arendt rejected conventional historiographic methods. The manuscript that Benjamin handed to her and Blücher in Marseille was called "Über den Begriff der Geschichte" ("On the Concept of History," translated as "Theses on the Philosophy of History"). It was the last essay Benjamin wrote. Arendt and Blücher read it in Lisbon while they were waiting for passage to the United States, and when, in 1968, Arendt edited the collection of Benjamin's essays that introduced him to English-language readers, *Illuminations*, she included it as the last in the book.*

"Über den Begriff der Geschichte" is a manifesto against detachment and objectivity. "To articulate the past historically does not mean to recognize it 'the way it really was,'" Benjamin wrote.† "It means to seize hold of a memory as it flashes up at a moment of danger."[40] Conventional history, Benjamin explained,

> contents itself with establishing a causal connection between various moments in history. But no fact that is a cause is for that very reason historical. It became historical posthumously, as it were, through events that may be separated from it by thousands of years. A historian who takes this as his point of departure stops telling the sequence of events like the beads of a rosary. Instead, he grasps the constellation which his own era has formed with a definite earlier one.[41]

"It became historical posthumously": this is the principle of historicist hermeneutics, a rejection of the assumption that we can attain an objective understanding of a prior moment, on the grounds that we are ourselves, as subjects, products of that moment. But our present experience of the past is not something that needs to be overcome. Our present experience is precisely what gives the past its significance. History is not facts, but the meaning of facts.

This means that the reference to "origins" in Arendt's title is misleading. When a revised edition came out, in 1958, she confessed, in her publisher's newsletter: "What does bother me is that the title suggests, however faintly, a belief in historical causality which I did not

---

* The essay contains one of the most famous passages in Benjamin's work, the description of the "Angel of History," based on a painting by Paul Klee (which Benjamin owned). It is hard to realize that this essay came very close to being lost.

† In the English translation, Arendt added, in parentheses, "Ranke," to attribute this view to the nineteenth-century historian Leopold von Ranke, the champion of empirical research.

hold when I wrote the book and in which I believe even less today." It was not a historical book, she explained; it was a political book. "[T]he 'origins' . . . became origins only after the event had taken place."[42]

Arendt was hostile to causal and empirical interpretations, and she was hostile to theoretical interpretations as well—for example, Marxist interpretations. She thought that they blind us to the meaning of what happened. "What is the subject of our thought? Experience! Nothing else!" she insisted at a conference on her work toward the end of her life. "And if we lose the ground of experience then we get into all kinds of theories. When the political theorist begins to build his systems he is also usually dealing with abstraction."[43] Not the lectern and the apricot cocktail but the *experience* of the lectern and the cocktail is the proper object of understanding. It is a phenomenological approach to history.

Arendt thought of history writing as storytelling—or, in a metaphor she used to describe Benjamin's method, pearl diving.[44] This is why *The Origins of Totalitarianism* is a kind of evil fairy tale, a lurid animation of the underside of European history. Some readers complained that Arendt's long expositions on anti-Semitism and imperialism didn't add up to an explanation for totalitarianism. But that was, quite self-consciously, not her intention. "The main stylistic task of this study," she explained to her editor, ". . . is to avoid the inherent law of all historiography which is preservation and justification and praise; and to present its result in such a way that it serves the opposite and intrinsically unhistoric purpose of destruction. The elements which should be eliminated from Western tradition and thought are prepared in the form of historical cross-sections. The author never aims at presenting history as a whole."[45]

The Origins of Totalitarianism is therefore what one skeptical reviewer, the sociologist Philip Rieff, described as "a massive prophecy of hindsight."[46]* Arendt by no means believed that the defeat of National Socialism had ended the threat of totalitarianism. On the contrary: she thought that the conditions that had made Hitler possible were still present, and that the West needed to be reborn. The European tradition had destroyed itself. "The whole of nearly three thousand years of Western civilization with all its implied beliefs,

---

* Some of Rieff's publications in this period of his career were ghostwritten by his wife, Susan Sontag.

traditions, and standards of judgment has come toppling down over our heads," she wrote.[47]

Like *Nineteen Eighty-Four*, *The Origins of Totalitarianism* was a book about the postwar world. Arendt wrote it to help people grasp what she called, in 1948, "the most essential political criterion for judging the events of our time: Will it lead to totalitarian rule or will it not?"[48] The book's epigraph, from Jaspers's *Von der Wahrheit* (*Of the Truth*), made the intention clear: "Weder dem Vergangenen anheimfallen noch dem Zukünftigen. Es kommt darauf an, ganz gegenwärtig zu sein"—"To succumb neither to the past nor the future. What matters is to be entirely present."[49]

Nazism arose in two countries, Germany and Austria, that had produced some of the preeminent achievements of Western civilization, not only in philosophy, literature, and the arts but also in scholarship and scientific research—in *Wissenschaft*. Many people commented on the paradox; it was intimately real for Arendt. She had started out, in the city in which Kant spent his entire life, as a lover of poetry, philosophy, and theology; she had been a favored student of the most eminent philosophers in Europe and the author of a book on Augustine. Then, at the age of thirty-five, she found herself living on charity in two furnished rooms in a nation whose culture she did not know or care for and whose language she could barely speak.

And she was lucky. Less than twelve months before, she had been confined in a concentration camp with thousands of people who would be deported and gassed en masse. Most of those people were Germans, and it was mostly Germans who killed them. By the time she was finishing *The Origins of Totalitarianism*, Königsberg was no more; it had become the Soviet city Kaliningrad. When Arendt wrote that the whole of Western culture "has come toppling down over our heads," she meant it literally. Hers was one of the heads.

Arendt thought that the First World War, which had briefly driven her and her mother from their home, marked the breakdown of the European political order. "The real significance of the First World War," she explained to her editor, "was that it either mortally endangered or actually destroyed all political structures which for decades had been allowed to vegetate because in an era of expanding economy and progressing welfare nobody was much interested in them. The resulting vacuum made room for all subterranean streams of European history"—racism, anti-Semitism, imperialism—"which the Nazis made flow together."[50]

The stateless people therefore constituted "the most symptomatic group in contemporary politics."[51] For those people were not criminals. They had done nothing wrong. They were victims simply of who they were. They could change their behavior and they could change their loyalty, but they could not change that. "Once they had left their homeland they remained homeless," Arendt wrote; "once they had left their state they became stateless; once they had been deprived of their human rights they were rightless, the scum of the earth. Nothing which was being done, no matter how stupid, no matter how many people knew and foretold the consequences, could be undone or prevented. Every event had the finality of a last judgment, a judgment that was passed neither by God nor by the devil, but looked rather like the expression of some unredeemably stupid fatality."[52] They were living under an empty sky.

The Jews were the prototypical stateless people. Legally and politically, they were nothing but Jews, a condition they could not alter even by conversion. As Arendt put it in an article in the *Menorah Journal* soon after she learned about the Gurs deportations: "If we should start telling the truth that we are nothing but Jews, it would mean that we expose ourselves to the fate of human beings who, unprotected by any specific law or political convention, are nothing but human beings."[53]

The breakdown of the nation-state and the class system also cut people loose from bonds of social obligation and produced "the masses." "The fall of protecting class walls," Arendt explained, "transformed the slumbering majorities behind all parties into one great unorganized, structureless mass of furious individuals who had nothing in common except their vague apprehension that the hopes of party members were doomed, that, consequently, the most respected, articulate and representative members of the community were fools and that all the powers that be were not so much evil as they were equally stupid and fraudulent." It was then that "the psychology of the European mass man developed."[54]

The breakdown of social classes produced a second group, which Arendt called "the mob." The mob was made up of the refuse of every class: disempowered aristocrats, disillusioned intellectuals, gangsters, denizens of the underworld. They were people who believed that the respectable world was a conspiracy to deny them what they were owed; they were embodiments of the politics of resentment. Arendt thought that the leadership of totalitarian movements came from this group.

Mass man can achieve a "sense of having a place in the world only from his belonging to a movement, or from his membership in the party," Arendt said. Totalitarian movements are simply "mass organizations of atomized, isolated individuals."[55] Totalitarian ideology explains everything by means of a superhuman law—that is its appeal to the atomized individual. In Nazi Germany, this was a law of nature; in the Soviet Union, it was a law of history. And it was the superhuman laws that made the individual—even the totalitarian leader himself—superfluous. Those laws are the wind from the future. Nothing can resist the blast.

Absurd claims were made in the name of these laws because to the mob, everything is a lie anyway. It didn't matter that the charges to which the defendants in the Moscow Trials confessed were transparently bogus, or that the *Protocols of the Elders of Zion* and the documents used in the case against Alfred Dreyfus were forgeries. All that mattered was the movement, and the movement was locked onto an inexorable transhistorical force. Totalitarianism was the perverse union of the belief that there is a supreme and unappeasable law of historical development with the belief that nothing is true and therefore everything is possible. "Totalitarianism became this century's curse," Arendt warned, "only because it so terrifyingly took care of its problems."[56]

Arendt thought that the camps were what made totalitarianism a new thing in the world. And the key to the camps was the fact that the people sent to them had done nothing. "A fundamental difference between modern dictatorships and all other tyrannies of the past is that terror is no longer used as a means to exterminate and frighten opponents, but as an instrument to rule masses of people who are perfectly obedient," she wrote. "Terror as we know it today strikes without any preliminary provocation, its victims are innocent even from the point of view of the persecutor."[57]

Since for Arendt the camps represented what totalitarianism was all about, the parallels in the accounts of Nazi camps on the one hand and the Communist Gulag on the other sustained her contention that Stalinism and Nazism were twin manifestations of the same phenomenon. And what mattered about the camp inmates was not that they were punished or even that they were killed. It was that they were, like Winston Smith, psychologically destroyed. They were made to understand that they were worth nothing. In existentialist terms, they were turned from whos into whats, from agents into objects.* "Men insofar as they are more than animal reaction and fulfillment of functions are entirely superfluous to totalitarian regimes," Arendt wrote. "Totalitarianism strives not toward despotic rule over men, but toward a system in which men are superfluous."[58]

Arendt thought that totalitarianism was therefore, in theory, always global. She did not subscribe to Orwell's prediction of several super-states. "The full aspirations of totalitarian governments could not be achieved even if the earth were divided between several totalitarian governments, for totalitarianism allows for no diversification," she wrote. "Only when no competitor, no country of physical refuge, and no human being whose understanding may offer a spiritual refuge, are left can the process of total domination and the change of the nature of man begin in earnest."[59]

3.

Houghton Mifflin rejected *The Origins of Totalitarianism*. The press sent the manuscript out for review to a Harvard professor (whose name is not known), who advised against publication. As she had done when she lived in Marburg and Paris, Arendt had formed an intellectual circle, convening first in the rooms on West Ninety-Fifth Street and later in her apartment on Morningside Drive. One of the most devoted of the new friends was the literary critic Alfred Kazin, whose first book, *On Native Grounds*, had come out in 1942, when he was twenty-seven. Kazin helped edit Arendt's book in order to (as he put it) "de-Teutonize" the prose. (She reciprocated by correcting the Yiddish, which she found "very confused," in Kazin's memoir *A Walker in the City* [1951].)[60] After Houghton Mifflin turned Arendt's book down, Kazin showed it to an editor at Harcourt Brace, Robert Giroux. Giroux is supposed to have read the manuscript overnight; he told Kazin the next morning that it was a great book, and Harcourt published it in 1951.[61]

The timing was good. By 1951, Eastern Europe had been colonized by the Soviet Union, both sides in the Cold War had nuclear weapons, China was a Communist state, and Stalin was still alive. Probably most

---

* This is the burden of Simone Weil's "*L'Iliad* ou le poème de la force," published in France in 1940 and in Dwight Macdonald's *Politics* in 1945, in a translation by Mary McCarthy. War makes people into things.

important, the Korean War, which some people thought could be the start of the Third World War, was under way, and it was not going well. Arendt's conviction that the death of Hitler did not mean the death of totalitarianism did not seem outdated.

People had been theorizing about totalitarianism since the rise of Mussolini in the 1920s, which is when the term was coined.[62] Arendt was not the first Central European émigré—she was actually among the last—to write on the subject.* Most of these writers shared certain premises with Arendt. They thought that totalitarianism signaled a new phase in Western history; that it had something to do with "the masses"; and that it was associated with the appearance of a new personality type. None of them thought that European totalitarianism was a backlash, or an anomalous irruption, in modern life. They thought that it was the portent of a very possible future.

What was striking about the émigré writers on totalitarianism was what they did not do: they did not explain totalitarianism as a national phenomenon. They did not situate it in German or Russian political history.[63] They explained it as a product of modernity. Arendt, too, denationalized totalitarianism. She picked her examples from all over Europe. She devoted a long section of her book, for example, to the Dreyfus Affair. The Dreyfus Affair took place in France. There was widespread anti-Semitism in France; France was an imperial power; there were French fascists and French collaborators. But totalitarianism did not emerge in France. Arendt's chapters on imperialism were filled with Britons: Cecil Rhodes, Rudyard Kipling, Benjamin Disraeli, T. E. Lawrence. (Sartre had figured Lawrence as an existentialist; Arendt saw him as a man on the borderline of fanaticism.) Yet Britain, the epitome of the industrialist, imperialist, bourgeois capitalist state in the nineteenth century, was never close to a totalitarian takeover.

These were areas where Benjamin's "history by constellation"—or history by isomorphism: x has a structural resemblance to y—camouflaged a lot of loose ends. History is filled with resemblances, but history never repeats itself. The appearance of one or more elements of

---

* Émigré works include Peter Drucker's *The End of Economic Man: A Study of the New Totalitarianism* (1939), Emil Lederer's *The State of the Masses: The Threat of the Classless Society* (1940), Erich Fromm's *Escape from Freedom* (1941), Sigmund Neumann's *Permanent Revolution: The Total State in a World at War* (1942), and Ludwig von Mises's *Omnipotent Government: The Rise of the Total State and Total War* (1944).

the totalitarian "constellation" somewhere has not meant that totalitarianism was imminent. Arendt herself warned frequently against
prediction: predicting is what people who believe in superhuman laws
do. Like Sartre, Arendt thought that belief in such forces is a limitation
on the supreme good of human freedom.[64] But by teasing out distinct
elements of the totalitarian regime, she encouraged the tendency to
find, potentially everywhere, a slippery slope.

The Origins of Totalitarianism added the weight of an unusually ab-
sorbing study by a writer respected in New York intellectual circles to what
was already a consensus view. Arendt later acquired a reputation as the
person who linked Nazi Germany and the Soviet Union as similar regime
types. Her book certainly reinforced belief in that equation, but there was
nothing new about it. Except for writers like Carr, who was sympathetic
to Bolshevism, and in venues like the Trotskyist Max Shachtman's journal,
the *New International*, where her book was scornfully received, reviewers
did not mention the link between Communism and fascism as especially
significant.[65] No one seems to have considered it a novel idea.[66]

What was unusual about Arendt's book were two distinctions she
drew. One was a distinction between ideas and ideology. Even though
it was written by someone trained as a philosopher, *The Origins of Totalitarianism* is a work of political, not intellectual, history. It does not explain totalitarianism by means of a story about Western thought, which
has always been a popular way to come to grips with the subject—as
Karl Popper did in *The Open Society and Its Enemies*, as the Polish émigré
Jacob Talmon did in *The Origins of Totalitarian Democracy*, published in
Britain a year after Arendt's book, and as the Oxford philosopher Isaiah Berlin, a Russian émigré, who detested Arendt's work, would do in
many lectures and essays.

Arendt thought that politics and philosophy were separate activities. This was because philosophy—that is, thinking—is done in solitude, and politics is practiced with others.[67] Politics concerns action.
Philosophy concerns truth, and truth is an absolute. It is not a safe criterion to use to guide political choices. What modern politicians discovered, Arendt believed, was the use not of ideas, but of ideology. In an
essay called "Ideology and Terror," published in 1953 and then included
in the paperback edition of *The Origins of Totalitarianism* in 1958, she
defined ideology as (a little confusingly) "the logic of an idea. Its subject
matter is history, to which the 'idea' is applied."[68] Ideology is what turns

an idea into an instrument, into something that can be used to override human freedom.

There were always philosophers who brought their ideas into the public square. Plato was one. Heidegger was another. For Arendt, this was a category mistake. In an essay written on the occasion of Heidegger's eightieth birthday, she illustrated the point with a story about the pre-Socratic philosopher Thales, who, out studying the stars one night, fell down a well.[69] The horror of the *Gleichschaltung* for Arendt was watching thinkers like Heidegger fall down a well. Their ideas blinded them to what any ordinary person could plainly see. Her first reaction to the news about German academics' embrace of Nazism, she told an interviewer, was: "Never again! I shall never again get involved in any kind of intellectual business. I want nothing to do with that lot . . . The worst thing was that some people really believed in Nazism! . . . I found that grotesque. Today I would say that they were trapped by their own ideas."[70]

Arendt preferred to call herself a political theorist, not a philosopher.[71] Heidegger was a philosopher, and philosophy was the higher calling. This was why she was able, after the war, to forgive him. He had made a wrong turn and, she believed (or wanted to believe), he had realized his error. It is "striking and perhaps exasperating that Plato and Heidegger, when they entered into human affairs, turned to tyrants and Führers," she conceded in the essay written for Heidegger's birthday. But this was merely a *déformation professionelle.* "With these few it does not finally matter where the storms of their century may have driven them. For the wind that blows through Heidegger's thinking—like that which still sweeps toward us after thousands of years from the work of Plato—does not spring from the century he happens to live in. It comes from the primeval, and what it leaves behind is something perfect."[72]* The belief that when ideas enter politics they can become ideologies, and that ideologies are the enemies of freedom and the public good, would have a lot of resonance in the United States in the next decade. That belief did not depend on Arendt's work, but her work helped to make it persuasive.

The second distinction is one that Arendt developed more fully in

---

* As Heidegger had taught: "Regarding the personality of a philosopher, our only interest is that he was born at a certain time, that he worked, and that he died." (*Basic Concepts of Aristotelian Philosophy*, lectures at Marburg, 1924.)

her next book, *The Human Condition*, which came out in 1958. This was a distinction between the political and the social. The difference was extremely important to Arendt, which does not mean that she did a good job explaining it.[73] What is distinctive about human beings is what Arendt called "plurality." Human beings share a species membership; in that sense, we are all alike. But a condition of membership in our species is that each human being is different from every other human being who has ever lived. Other animal species don't (so far as we can tell) have plurality in that sense. There are differences among nonhuman organisms, but those organisms cannot express those differences. People *can* express their differences, because they can express more than just what they have in common with everyone else, such as hunger and fear.[74] To become "nothing but a human being," therefore, means to be reduced to the condition of a being that is identical to every other animal being: hungry and afraid. That was the purpose of the camps. That was the goal of totalitarianism.

Plurality, for Arendt, is the essential condition of freedom; it is what makes the human mode of being, Heidegger's *Dasein*, different from the being of a rutabaga or (hypothetically) an elephant. The "social," in her idiosyncratic definition, is where people suppress individual differences in order to meet the demands of others. Society is the realm of conformity. Arendt thought that society derived from the household, and that the household is a hierarchically organized micro-unit whose purpose is to do what every animal has to do: find the means to survive.

The political realm, the polis, is not hierarchical, it is not driven by necessity, and it is where human differences are displayed. Politics is a realm in which people engage as equals in discussion and debate and make value choices about their future together. The goal of politics is not survival, and it is certainly not a utilitarian principle like the greatest happiness of the greatest number, since that formula is merely a bargain with necessity. The goal of politics—the concept comes from Arendt's understanding of Machiavelli and the ancient Greeks—is glory (*kleos*).[75] In the arena of life on this planet, the only things that become immortal are great deeds. There is nothing outside the realm of human existence to validate those deeds or to whose principles they must answer. They are ends in themselves.

The political realm was important for another reason, too, having to do with the stateless people. The leaders of the French Revolution had proclaimed the Universal Rights of Man. Arendt thought that the aftermath of First World War exposed the limitations of that concept. It became clear that the source of rights is not the universe or natural law. Rights are political goods acquired through citizenship in a nation. "Man, it turns out, can lose all so-called Rights of Man without losing his essential quality as man, his human dignity," Arendt wrote in 1949. "Only the loss of a polity itself expels him from humanity."[76]

Arendt believed that political participation was the single safeguard against the kind of disaster that happened in Europe after 1914. It was because the nineteenth-century British bourgeoisie, through the Reform Laws, which extended the franchise, participated in politics that Britain was preserved from totalitarianism. It was because the Central European bourgeoisie took no interest in political affairs that Nazism took hold there. And it was because European Jews lacked a political sense that they bore some responsibility for the fate that befell them. This was the view that, when Arendt published her book about the trial of Adolf Eichmann in 1963, would make her, then and for many years after her death, a figure of controversy.[77] But what she wrote there was, for her, a logical consequence of her theoretical position. If you do not engage in political life, you are vulnerable to bad actors.

Arendt's distinction between the social and the political was highly notional and unstable, and few readers did not have trouble with it. But it translated into a view that was embraced by many intellectuals after the war. This was the view that the American political system was a protector of liberty, but American society was a dangerous realm of conformity. Arendt adopted this view soon after she arrived in the United States. She was placed for several weeks with a family in Massachusetts in order to give her an opportunity to learn English. She considered the family to be small-town bourgeois, with provincial tastes and hopelessly uncosmopolitan. They were vegetarians; she was allowed to smoke only in her room; and so on. She was astonished, therefore, when these people responded to news of the removal of Japanese-Americans on the West Coast to camps by writing to their own congressman. They had never laid eyes on a Japanese-American; the relocation order had no effect on them or anyone they knew. Yet they felt a responsibility to register their opinion.[78]

"There is so much I could say about America," she wrote to Jaspers five years later, in one of the first letters she sent him when they renewed contact after the war. (American troops arrived in Heidelberg just two weeks before Jaspers and his Jewish wife were scheduled to be deported.)[79] "There really is such a thing as freedom here and a strong feeling among many people that one cannot live without freedom," she told him. ". . . [P]eople here feel themselves responsible for public life to an extent I have never seen in any European country." American political life was healthy. But, she continued, there was also a great evil: the social pressure to be like everyone else. "The fundamental contradiction in this country," she told Jaspers, "is the coexistence of political freedom and social oppression."[80]

Tocqueville, of course, had made the same observation a century before, and (apart from the Marxists in the Institute for Social Research) this was almost unanimously the view adopted by the émigrés who stayed in the United States after the war, as a large percentage of Central European refugees did. And it became a feature of American intellectual culture. American democracy preserves freedom; American society fosters conformity. The book that came to stand as the expression of that view, David Riesman's *The Lonely Crowd*, was written while its author was reading the manuscript of *The Origins of Totalitarianism*.

4.

The Lonely Crowd came out in 1950. By 1995, it had sold more than a million copies, far more than any other book by an American sociologist to that point.[81] The public understanding of works of serious nonfiction reaching that level of sales is often oversimplified or reduced to a one-sentence takeaway. In the case of *The Lonely Crowd*, though, the message was not oversimplified. It was misinterpreted.[82] Part of this is the fault of the title, which would be a great title if it did not suggest something like "individual anomie within mass society," which is not what the book is about.* But part of the responsibility is Riesman's.

Riesman's basic intuition was that people are more independent and resourceful than most social and political concepts suggest. This led him to question many of the terms of intellectual debate in the postwar period, terms such as "totalitarianism," "consumerism," and "mass

---

* The title was a last-minute inspiration of the publisher—as was the title of Sloan Wilson's novel *The Man in the Gray Flannel Suit* (1955), another book that is not about what people think it's about.

culture." James Burnham's and C. Wright Mills's preoccupation with "power," for example, seemed to him just such a case of misplaced concreteness. "The grabbing for power makes people feel—even if they are far from power—that there must be somebody, somewhere at the wheel," he wrote to one of his collaborators on *The Lonely Crowd* about Mills. "Actually things roll along under their own logics and hold together much in the same way that companies turn out goods—because nobody seriously tries to stop them, certainly not because there is real efficiency or leadership."[83]

This cast of mind made it hard for Riesman to write a book that advanced two such over-explanatory concepts, "inner-directed" and "outer-directed" personality types, without continually tweaking his own arguments and turning them inside out. When Riesman's friend Lionel Trilling read *The Lonely Crowd*, he told Riesman that it was like reading a realist novel—meaning that it seemed to capture social life in all its density. "I felt all the time I was reading that I was getting now what I used to get or think I was getting from novels," Trilling told him.[84] On the other hand, Trilling, too, misunderstood what Riesman was saying.

Riesman was not, professionally, a sociologist. His undergraduate degree, from Harvard College, was in biochemistry; his only graduate degree was a JD from Harvard Law School. The first social science course he ever took was the first social science course he taught as a visiting assistant professor at the University of Chicago in 1946, fifteen years after graduating from college. The major figures in the development of his thinking were German immigrants: Carl Friedrich, who was a tutor in Riesman's undergraduate house at Harvard and later a friend, and Erich Fromm, who was Riesman's psychoanalyst.

"I owe my introduction to the social sciences to Friedrich," Riesman said.[85] Friedrich's field was political theory. (He would publish, with his student Zbigniew Brzezinski, *Totalitarian Dictatorship and Autocracy* in 1956.) Friedrich introduced Riesman to public opinion polls. Polling fascinated Riesman because it provides a window on what is going on down on the ground, what people really think as opposed to what political or social theory says they must be thinking. He was also interested in the level below that, what people don't think but tell pollsters they do. He wondered, for example, why so few survey respondents answer "Don't know," even on issues they have no way of forming an intelligent opinion about. He concluded that if you are an American, you are supposed to have an opinion—which opens the question of what people's survey answers are really worth, a question that would lead to studies of voting behavior in the 1950s showing that on political issues, most people don't know what they're talking about.* They squirm out from under the social scientist's microscope. Riesman liked that. Typically, he also argued that this kind of political apathy, which writers like Arendt took to be a symptom of creeping totalitarianism, might be a virtue in a democracy.†

Riesman met Fromm through his mother, Eleanor. She was in analysis in New York with Karen Horney. At the time Eleanor Riesman was seeing her, Horney was in a romantic relationship with Fromm. At his mother's request, Riesman met with Horney, who pronounced him (in Riesman's words) a "very resigned young man" and referred him to Fromm. Riesman was then teaching in Buffalo, and he came down to New York City every other weekend for two two-hour sessions with Fromm.[86]

Fromm, like Horney, was a German émigré. He did his training analysis at the Berliner Psychoanalytisches Institut with Hanns Sachs, an orthodox Freudian. Around 1929, he became involved with the Institut für Sozialforschung. He shared its members' interest in Freud and Marx (an unlikely couple with completely divergent theories of virtually everything, whose thought was subjected to numerous efforts at synthesis in the twentieth century). And after Hitler came to power, Fromm, on a trip to the United States, helped arrange the migration of the Institute to Morningside Heights, under the auspices of Columbia University. When this happened, in 1935, Fromm and Horney were already settled in New York City.[87]

Fromm's first book in English, *Escape from Freedom*, came out in 1941. (It would sell 5 million copies, not as many as his book *The Art of Loving* [1956], which sold 25 million.) The book is an attempt to solve the problem Arendt and many other people were trying to solve: why people are attracted to totalitarianism. Fromm's theory was that in modern society, freedom produces anxiety, and totalitarian ideology

---

* The classic study, growing out of research at the University of Michigan in the 1950s, is Philip E. Converse's "The Nature of Belief Systems in Mass Publics" (1964). Converse concluded that only around 10 percent of voters have an "ideology," by which he meant a coherent and consistent set of views. This was, in a way, Lionel Trilling's point in *The Liberal Imagination*: people's political choices are shaped by what is essentially cultural conditioning.
† Apathy was the original subject of Riesman's book. At one point he was considering "Passionless Existence in America" as a title. It is hard to see that one becoming a bestseller.

promises an "escape" from that anxiety. Before the modern era, freedom was something people fought for, but in modern societies, it is a condition of life without evident value in itself. It produces not commitment but aimlessness.

This kind of argument—that people are passive pawns of other people's ideas—would not have appealed to Riesman. But he was inspired by Fromm's next book, which came out in 1947, *Man for Himself.* There, Fromm identified various social-character types, one of which he said was peculiar to modern societies and which he called "the marketing orientation." A marketing orientation describes people who experience themselves as commodities, and their personal value as exchange value. People with a "marketing orientation" are goods for sale, Fromm said—like "handbags on a counter, for instance, could they feel and think."[88] Fromm proposed that this character type had arisen in the American urban middle class and, through its example, had affected the entire population. This figure became *The Lonely Crowd*'s "other-directed" person.

Riesman first got in touch with Arendt in February 1947, when he was teaching at Chicago. He had been reading her articles in *Partisan Review,* he told her, but his colleague Daniel Bell had given him some work of hers that he had not seen.[89] He was writing to ask for more. That summer, Riesman accepted an offer from the Yale Committee on National Policy of a two-year fellowship to work on any project he chose. That was when he began *The Lonely Crowd.*

Riesman always imagined his book as collaborative, and he began trying to recruit Arendt. He had secured funding from Yale, he told her, "to permit you to write an historical chapter, dealing with the problems of tracing changing character structure in the Western world."[90] She put him off. Nine months later, in February 1949, he was still writing to her of "the need for collaboration with you."[91] But she was absorbed by *The Origins of Totalitarianism.* She began sending her manuscript-in-progress to Riesman, and he responded enthusiastically. "I want to say at once what a simply exciting and enlivening work it is," he told her after he had read just one and a half chapters. ". . . Your really brilliant point is completely sound, namely, that these movements are entirely different from dictatorship and that the difference lies in part in the destruction of classes and other nucleated groups in the society."[92] After reading the chapter on the masses and the mob: "I am simply overwhelmed by your vision . . . I think now that you really touched genius."[93] After finishing the manuscript: "your work haunts me . . . I think of it all the time."[94]

Riesman did make his usual suggestion, however: Might Arendt be mistaking the ideology of totalitarianism for the lived reality? Might she be imagining that totalitarian systems are more coherent and all-powerful than they really are? "I think you tend . . . to assume that Stalin and Hitler are more calculating than I think is the case," he told her in one letter. In another: "I think you may underestimate the element of accident in a large bureaucratic setup."[95] Riesman thought that the existence of corruption and black markets in places like the Soviet Union, which he had visited after graduating from college and found to be replete with incompetence and confusion—"Order socialist or otherwise, was the last thing we ourselves experienced," he remembered—means that everyone knows the system isn't doing what is being claimed for it, that it is largely a pretense.[96]

Arendt therefore should probably not have been surprised when Riesman repeated these criticisms when he reviewed *The Origins of Totalitarianism* in *Commentary*. (Why he or his editors thought the assignment was appropriate is another question.) The book was "extraordinarily penetrating," he said, but he thought it betrayed on Arendt's part "a certain amount of fanaticism." "*The Origins of Totalitarianism*," he wrote, "must be placed on that small shelf of truly seminal works whose very errors, exaggerations, and over-systemizations so often turn out, in the unpredictable history of ideas, to be liberating and fructifying for thought." Arendt, he went on, "overinterprets specific actions in terms of long-range goals, and does not allow for any more or less accidental concatenations of bureaucratic forces, slip-ups, careerisms, as explanatory factors . . . [E]ven the Soviet MVD [Ministerstvo Vnutrennikh Del: Ministry of Internal Affairs] can make mistakes; the kind of balefully brilliant scrutiny of the hero recounted in *Nineteen Eighty-Four* may be less frequent than a flat-footed brutality and incompetence."[97]

Riesman had sent a draft of his review to Arendt for corrections, and he made a few after hearing from her. But Arendt did not take well to being called a fanatic. Riesman's suggestion that, underneath the ideological swagger, the Soviet Union was a klutzy bureaucracy run by thugs was just the kind of inability to take totalitarianism seriously that she had written her book to warn against. The review seems to have marked, apart from a few cordial but perfunctory exchanges, the end of her correspondence with David Riesman.

In the end, Riesman did have two co-authors on *The Lonely Crowd*: Reuel Denney, a high school teacher Riesman met in Buffalo, and Nathan Glazer, a graduate student at Columbia whose column "The Study of Man" in *Commentary*, a monthly roundup of work in the social sciences, had impressed Riesman. Although Riesman credited them as "collaborators," Denney and Glazer were essentially researchers. Denney studied popular culture, including children's books, and Glazer assisted Riesman in interviewing and in analyzing interviews collected by the National Opinion Research Center, founded at the University of Chicago in 1941. Glazer also had access to the raw interviews Mills conducted for his first book, *White Collar*. Riesman later said that they found Mills had distorted the material to make his subjects sound more discontented than they had actually reported themselves to be.[98]

The Lonely Crowd was published on October 4, 1950. Reception among social scientists was mixed. The book has a somewhat off-the-cuff manner, as though written from the armchair. "[I]t seems to me essentially 'Dave Riesman on contemporary America," Friedrich told Riesman, "—to me a very worthwhile and significant job, and one that will stand up to fairly searching critical evaluation. What it is not is 'science.'"[99] Among a wider readership, however, the book took off. The first print run at Yale University Press was three thousand copies, and the Press had to go back for thirteen more printings before the book came out in paperback from Anchor Books in 1953 and reached a wider readership still.[100]

The Anchor edition is a somewhat different book. Riesman marked it as "abridged," and it is shorter than the 1950 edition, but he also rewrote parts to give more point to the argument. "This is a book about social character," the new edition begins. ". . . More particularly, it is about the way in which one kind of social character, which dominated America in the nineteenth century, is gradually being replaced by a social character of quite a different sort."[101] There is nothing like this in the opening pages of the first edition, which dilate somewhat speculatively on the concept of "social character" itself. It is as though—it must be the case that—Riesman learned from its reception precisely what his book was about, and what made nonspecialists, an audience he had hoped to reach, want to read it.

The two types of social character are the "inner-directed," defined as direction "implanted early in life by the elders and directed toward generalized but nonetheless inescapably destined goals," and the "other-directed," a person who takes direction from peers, "either those known to him or those with whom he is indirectly acquainted, through friends and through the mass media."[102] Riesman's metaphor for the inner-directed character was the gyroscope, for the other-directed, the radar dish.* Inner-directed and other-directed are both modern types; people in pre-modern societies Riesman called "tradition-directed."

It is not difficult to see why many readers, and readers at second hand, of *The Lonely Crowd* took the book to be an indictment of conformism on a "new man" model familiar from books on totalitarianism. Even if the gyroscope was implanted by parents and teachers, life for the inner-directed is *experienced* as meaningful. People who are radar dishes are only the sum total of other people's projections. They have no core being. The inner-directed seem independent and self-sufficient; the outer-directed cannot survive without the approval of the herd. They might be ripe for totalitarian ideologies.

Riesman *was* concerned about conformity and about threats to autonomy. But what he was analyzing was really the effects of a shift from an economy centered on production to one centered on consumption. Those economic systems call for, and reward, different kinds of personalities. The distinction had been drawn attention to by a member of the transplanted Institute, Leo Löwenthal, who in 1944 noted a shift in popular biography from what he called "idols of production" to "idols of consumption"—such as athletes and entertainers.[103]

On a Marxist account, the change in personality types would reflect change in the means of production. The workplace sends signals about what kind of worker will succeed, and people adapt. But Riesman believed that Marx was no longer relevant for understanding life in postwar America, and that hopes for a working-class revolution in the United States were absurd. Marx had not anticipated a key development in modern societies: the commodification of leisure. Character was no longer formed for work; it was formed for leisure and consumption, and "both leisure and means of consumption are widely distributed."[104]

---

* Riesman acknowledged that he was describing a white-collar and upper-middle-class phenomenon. In subsequent books, notably *Faces in the Crowd*, written with Glazer and published in 1952, he would give more attention to social character in marginalized groups.

Riesman believed in autonomy (a rather alien concept for a sociologist). He just wanted to make the case for its possibility within consumer capitalism.

Autonomous individuals are rare in twentieth-century America, he admitted, but they do exist. Their characters are defined neither by the news and entertainment media nor by their peers. Of course, individuals cannot transcend the forces of socialization, but they can play them off against one another and thereby achieve a degree of independence. "We must acknowledge our debt to the entertainment world," Riesman wrote, "and defend its freedom to find new leisure patterns against the fears of the censor . . . The entertainers, in their media, out of their media, and in the never-never land between, exert a constant pressure on the accepted peer-groups and suggest new modes of escape from them."[105]

This is an argument that Hannah Arendt, who saw entertainment as a consumable, like food, could not have made. She thought that a society that produces only for consumption, as she believed mass societies like the United States increasingly do, loses the "public worldly space whose existence is independent of and outside the sphere of its life processes"—that is, the realm of politics.[106] For sociologists like Riesman and Glazer, though, politics is just a bunch of people, who are no more "independent of . . . the sphere of life processes" than any other bunch.

In fact, Riesman was claiming for commercial culture something like a role long assigned to literature and the fine arts, that of giving people alternative visions of the good life. Within fifteen years, this would become the core faith of American youth culture and its critical adherents. It is probably unnecessary to say that that was a culture Riesman found distasteful. But that is the thing about social history, as Riesman of all people should have known. The screw always takes another turn.

5

THE ICE BREAKERS

Peggy Guggenheim and Jackson Pollock in front of *Mural*, in the entrance hall at 155 East Sixty-First Street, New York City, probably March 19, 1946, when Guggenheim threw a party to show off the painting. The sculpture in the foreground is by David Hare, who had been editor of the surrealist journal *VVV*. He married the artist Jacqueline Lamba, ex-wife of André Breton, in 1946. Photograph by George Karger. (*Pollock-Krasner Foundation / Artists Rights Society / Solomon Guggenheim Museum Foundation*)

1.

Jackson Pollock met Clement Greenberg on Varick Street in New York City in the winter of 1942. As Greenberg remembered afterward, because he said he never saw him do it again, Pollock was wearing a hat. They were introduced by Lee Krasner, who was a friend of Greenberg's and who had just started seeing Pollock.[1]

Pollock was turning thirty. He was desperately ambitious, but although he had devoted himself to making art since his student days at

Manual Arts High School in Los Angeles and had lived in New York since 1930, he was almost unknown. Krasner met him at a party in 1936, but they didn't get together until the fall of 1941, when an art-world figure named John Graham—a somewhat mythomaniacal Russian émigré, born Ivan Gratianovitch Dombrowski in Kiev—put together an exhibition called *American and French Paintings* and invited Krasner and Pollock to be in the show. It opened at the McMillen Gallery in mid-town on January 20, 1942, and failed to make a stir. It was around the time of that show that Krasner and Pollock ran into Greenberg.[2]

Greenberg had just turned thirty-three. His career as a critic was only three years old. He had started out as a traveling salesman for his father, a businessman in the wholesale necktie trade, wrote poetry on the side, and then took jobs in government agencies, including the Veterans Administration. In 1940, after publishing two pieces there, one a short book review, he became an editor at *Partisan Review*. The magazine had begun as an organ of the Communist John Reed Club but was relaunched in 1937 as a journal friendly to both socialism and modernist art and literature—the banes of Stalinism and Zhdanovism. It then had no more than eight hundred subscribers, and Greenberg kept his day job as an appraiser for the Department of Wines and Liquors in the United States Customs Service. He worked in a building on the corner of Varick and Houston.

Krasner knew a lot of people in the downtown art world. In the early 1930s, she had worked as a waitress in a café called Sam Johnson's on West Third Street, where she met Harold Rosenberg, a poet and critic with a law degree who liked to draw. For a while, she and her partner, Igor Pantuhoff, another, only slightly less fantastic Russian émigré, shared an apartment on West Fourteenth Street with Rosenberg and his wife, May Tabak, who ran a shop that sold run-down "antiques."

Krasner met Greenberg through the Rosenbergs. (Greenberg knew them because his cousin Sonia lived in the Village and was a friend of May's.) Greenberg was interested in learning about the art scene, so Krasner introduced him to Arshile Gorky and Willem de Kooning, then obscure and struggling painters. Krasner was also a student at a school run by Hans Hofmann, a German émigré who had studied in Paris and who brought the theories and techniques of modern painting to New York when he moved there in 1932. She took Greenberg to meet Hofmann, and Greenberg attended some of his lectures. Apart from a few life drawing classes, that was the only formal instruction in art that Greenberg ever had.[3]

Together, Greenberg, Krasner, and Pollock changed the course of modern art and art criticism. Pollock and Greenberg were the ones who became famous, but Krasner was the glue. She created the conditions that allowed Pollock to produce the works that conferred authority on Greenberg's ideas. She also probably gave Greenberg some of those ideas. And, against tough odds and at some interim cost to her own career as a painter, she was the manager of Pollock's public image and commercial fortunes.

In 1945, Krasner and Pollock married and moved out of Manhattan to Springs, a hamlet in the town of East Hampton where the Rosenbergs also owned a house. Greenberg, who had become the art critic for *The Nation* (he quit his job at Customs not long after meeting Pollock), was a frequent guest. When Greenberg visited, the talk was mostly between Greenberg and Krasner. They talked for hours.[4] It was in Springs that Pollock had the remarkable three-and-a-half-year run, from the spring or summer of 1947 to November 1950, that produced the drip paintings—works that, although they seemed to many people to require no special talent, turned out to be inimitable.

Looking backward, it could be said that Greenberg solved a problem in art criticism and Pollock solved a problem in painting. That doesn't mean Greenberg and Pollock were originals or iconoclasts. Everyone in the American art world understood, more or less, what needed to be done; Greenberg and Pollock were the ones who struck people as having done it. As often happens in cases of cultural change, they jettisoned certain commitments—political, philosophical, formal—that had previously seemed sacrosanct or indispensable and showed that life would go on without them. They produced things (art criticism and paintings) that worked partly by abandoning things that no longer worked. They made certain styles of painting and certain ways of thinking about art obsolete, or retrievable only in quotation marks.

"Jackson has finally broken the ice," de Kooning is supposed to have remarked at the crowded opening of Pollock's solo show at the Betty Parsons Gallery in November 1949—the only commercially successful show Pollock had in his lifetime. De Kooning reprised the metaphor seven years later at a symposium held shortly after Pollock's death, and it was eventually integrated into a standard story about postwar American art.[5]

De Kooning might have meant that Pollock was the first American abstractionist to break into the mainstream art world, or he might have meant that Pollock had broken through a stylistic logjam that American painters felt blocked by. De Kooning was a bit of a riddler—it's one of the things people found charming about him—and he probably meant both things, for mainstream recognition can be a ratification of artistic accomplishment. American painters of Pollock's generation—and Pollock especially—didn't always know what to do with recognition once they had it, but that doesn't mean they didn't want it.

Greenberg was annoyed by de Kooning's remark about ice-breaking. He thought that it reduced Pollock to a transitional figure. But all figures are transitional. Not every figure, however, is a hinge, someone who represents a moment when one mode of practice swings over to another. After Pollock, people painted differently. After Greenberg, people thought about painting differently. These people (or most of them) didn't become disciples or imitators. They were just living in a post-Pollock and post-Greenberg world. There was no going back.

2.

In the 1960s, Greenberg would become associated with something called (not his phrase) "the triumph of American painting."[6] In the 1970s, this association would turn into a reputational liability. Greenberg was far from being the first person to predict that New York City would supplant Paris as the capital of modern art.[7] But because he was so closely identified, as both their champion and their theorist, with the first group of American artists to receive international attention, the Abstract Expressionists, he was assigned a leading role in a narrative in which the promotion of American cultural goods such as fine-art paintings was interpreted as an instrument of Cold War foreign policy, as capitalist propaganda.[8] So it is interesting that what inspired Greenberg to pursue his career as an art critic was an essay written in Moscow by a Hungarian Communist.

The essay was about the nineteenth-century poet Heinrich Heine, and it appeared in 1937 in *Internationale Literatur/Deutsche Blätter*, the literary organ of Communists who had fled Germany for the Soviet Union after the rise of Nazism. The author of the essay was one of those exiles, Georg Lukács.[9] Lukács (who, eleven years later, would deliver the Marxist repudiation of existentialism) was a Stalinist, and *Internatio-nale Literatur* was a Stalinist journal.[10] Greenberg, like virtually everyone in his intellectual and artistic circles, was a Trotskyist, and therefore anti-Stalinist.[11] The fact that he was reading a journal like *Internationale Liter-atur* reveals something important about him, which is that although he acquired a reputation as pugnacious and dogmatic, the kind of person who turns cocktail-party disagreements into fistfights, Greenberg was widely read and had enormous curiosity. Beyond the college level, he was largely self-taught, something that was true of many of the literary and politi-cal intellectuals in his world, particularly the ones who were Jewish, since there was virtually no place for them in university humanities depart-ments. They turned into journalists instead and ended up having a greater impact on literary and intellectual life than most academics ever do.

Greenberg's parents were Jews who came to the United States around the turn of the century from eastern Poland, inside the Pale of Settle-ment. They spoke Yiddish at home and had socialist sympathies. Green-berg used to say that when he was little, he thought "socialist" meant "Jewish."[12] The family started with very little and became reasonably well off. Greenberg went to Syracuse University, where he learned Ger-man and Italian (he had taken French and Latin in high school) and taught himself Greek. He graduated in 1930, and then, for the rest of the decade, he seemed to drift.

He got married in San Francisco in 1934 and moved in with his wife's parents, had a son in 1935, moved back to his own parents' apart-ment on Ocean Parkway in Brooklyn, got divorced in 1936. All along, he pursued his interest in languages, acquiring a reading knowledge of Italian and Portuguese (later useful in his Customs work). His German was good enough to get him a few jobs as a translator. He had advanced tastes. He went to art museums; Bertolt Brecht and T. S. Eliot were special enthusiasms. He owned a copy of the banned Shakespeare and Company edition of *Ulysses*.[13]

Greenberg pictured himself as a poet and a fiction writer, possibly a painter. There is no sign that he aspired to be an art critic.[14] Toward the end of 1938, he was introduced by Rosenberg and another friend, Lionel Abel, to Dwight Macdonald at *Partisan Review* as someone who could write about literature. Greenberg showed Macdonald an essay he had written on Brecht; Macdonald promised to take it under consider-ation. Meanwhile, he asked Greenberg (or Greenberg offered) to review an English translation of Brecht's novelization of *Die Dreigroschenoper* (*The Threepenny Opera*). The review came out in the winter 1939 issue of *Partisan Review*. It was the first piece of criticism Greenberg published.[15] His previous publications had all been poems. He had just turned thirty. That issue also contained the final installment of a three-part article by Macdonald on Soviet cinema.

For Macdonald, *Partisan Review* was a stop on his personal journey from Ivy League mandarin (at Yale) to *Fortune* writer to Trotskyist to *New Yorker* writer to his ultimate destination, anarchist. Movies were always an interest of Macdonald's. His father had served on the boards of several film companies and had lectured at Yale on the movie industry.[16] In the 1920s, some of the most innovative movies in the world were coming out of the Soviet Union, silent films by Dziga Vertov, Vsevolod Pudovkin, Aleksandr Dovzhenko, and Sergei Eisenstein. "Those were the years when one went to the 'little' movie houses which showed Russian films as one might visit a celebrated cathedral or museum—reverently, expectantly," Macdonald wrote.

> One joined a congregation of *avant-garde* illuminati, sharing an exhilarating consciousness of experiencing a new art form—many, including myself, felt it was *the* great modern art. In the darkened auditorium of the theatre, one came into a deep and dynamic contact with twentieth century life.[17]

But, Macdonald complained, the Soviet avant-garde had been killed off by official demands for a doctrinaire product and official hostility to formal experimentation. Soviet film under Stalin, Macdonald wrote, had become "something that more and more closely approaches the output of Hollywood."[18]

Greenberg read the article with some irritation: he felt that Macdonald had lifted ideas from his as-yet-unpublished essay on Brecht. He decided to vent his annoyance in a letter to Macdonald in which he nevertheless carefully suppressed his suspicions about the theft of intellectual property. The letter was eight pages long, but it mainly took issue with an assertion Macdonald had made that the reason a Russian peasant prefers the paintings of Ilya Repin (a nineteenth-century Russian realist) to Picasso's was because the Soviet state had failed to educate them otherwise.

This explanation, Greenberg informed Macdonald, was insufficiently Marxist. Artistic taste has nothing to do with top-down things like education; it is a function of the worker's relationship to the means of production. As long as the mass of people live without genuine socialism, as long as the economic order deprives them of the leisure necessary to cultivate an appreciation of fine art, they will prefer *Kitsch*—"a wonderful German word that covers all this crap"—to modern art.[19]

Macdonald was (this was characteristic) delighted to have provoked criticism, even and especially criticism that presumed to out-Marx him, and he invited Greenberg to turn his letter into an article for *Partisan Review*. Greenberg was happy to do so. He wrote an essay and sent it in. Macdonald called to say that it needed work, and that he and his wife, Nancy, would come over to Greenberg's place to discuss it. Greenberg was leaving town in two days for Europe, so revision was postponed.[20]

Greenberg spent two months traveling. The continent was on the brink of war. Through a correspondent for *Time* and *Life*, Sherry Mangan, whom he met on the boat going over, he was able to arrange a meeting with Jean-Paul Sartre. Sartre had not yet written *L'Être et le néant*; Greenberg knew him only as the author of *La Nausée*, which he admired. They discussed American fiction, disagreeing about the merits of Dos Passos (Greenberg dissenting), agreeing about Faulkner (both men affirming).[21] When Greenberg got back, he learned that *Partisan Review* was demanding a lot of work on his essay, "because," as he explained in a letter to his college friend Harold Lazarus, "of its unsupported & large generalizations."[22]

Macdonald offered to help. Macdonald was a lively writer; Greenberg was not and knew it. In a letter to Lazarus, he unhappily but not unjustly compared his prose to the notoriously wooden writing of John Dewey and Thorstein Veblen.[23] Also, he had never written a theoretical essay before. Theoretical and historical generalization was not Macdonald's strong suit, either, but they worked on the piece together over the summer, Greenberg at one point tearing up what he had written and starting over. The essay that emerged from this process was therefore to some extent a collaboration. (Many years later, Macdonald would claim that he had "invented" Clement Greenberg. "I'm in the position of Frankenstein, you know," he told an interviewer, Diana Trilling.)[24] "Avant-Garde and Kitsch" appeared in *Partisan Review* in the fall of

1939. By the time it came out, the Second World War was under way. The essay was the second piece of critical prose that Greenberg published, and it became one of the most widely known and imitated essays in postwar intellectual life.

3.

"I must never forget that Georg Lukacez's [*sic*] article on Heine, in the *Internationale Blätter* in 1938 (I think) set me off on 'Avant-Garde and Kitsch' & other things," Greenberg wrote in his journal in 1951.[25] The article is called "Heinrich Heine als Nationaler Dichter"("Heinrich Heine as National Poet"), and the problem Lukács addresses is Heine's relationship to German Romanticism, a bourgeois literary mode. In an orthodox Marxist, or Zhdanovian, assessment, Heine's concessions to Romantic styles and tropes, his persistent if conflicted attachment to them, infect his work with subjectivism, with sentimental ideas about the unity of man and nature, and with similar reactionary attributes. In defending Heine, Lukács did not defend Romanticism as such. Instead, he argued that Heine was what he called "a *borderline* phenomenon," caught between the rise and the decline of the bourgeoisie. (It is not difficult to understand why Lukács felt a duty to solve the "problem" of Heine in Moscow in 1938: Heine was much admired by Karl Marx. They met in Paris, both exiles, in 1844, and became close friends.)[26]

When Heine was born, in 1797, the bourgeoisie was still what Marxists call "an objectively revolutionary class." The French Revolution and industrial capitalism were historically necessary. They destroyed an obsolete social and economic order, feudalism, and created a new means of production and a new class of owners that maximized productive capacity. Inevitably, of course, capitalism, too, was fated to be undone by its contradictions. Heine lived to see and understand the crisis (he died in 1856), but not what would succeed it. Hence his ironic relation to Romanticism is precisely what his situation called for. He was not merely a symptom or index of that situation. He was both its victim and its analyst. Like the novels of Honoré de Balzac, also admired by Marx and Engels, Heine's work was "historically fully justified."[27] It represented a stage of history between a dying social order and a coming order not yet apprehensible.

In a stunning move that had nothing to do with Macdonald's

article on Soviet film or his own letter to Macdonald about it, Greenberg applied this line of reasoning to modern art and literature—the "avant-garde" of his essay's title. Avant-gardism sprang from the same crisis as Heine's poetry. When a society "becomes less and less able . . . to justify the inevitability of its particular forms," Greenberg said, the artist loses contact with the audience. In earlier periods of historical crisis, artists responded with Alexandrianism, a retreat to technical virtuosity and creative stasis. But in the nineteenth century, the response produced something new and unprecedented: the avant-garde.

The reason avant-gardism appeared instead of Alexandrianism, Greenberg believed, was because nineteenth-century artists had "a superior consciousness of history." That is, they saw that the creation and destruction of social formations is how history works, that all structures of assumptions and expectations are temporary. That's exactly what Marx saw—"all that is solid melts into air," in the words of *The Communist Manifesto* in 1848—and Greenberg thought it was therefore no accident that avant-garde art appeared at the same time as "scientific revolutionary thought"—that is, socialism—in the second half of the nineteenth century.

This left artists with a problem: What was their subject matter? Art can't be arbitrary; it has to be created in obedience to some external constraint. Previously, that constraint had been "the world of common, extroverted experience" (aka reality), which artists and writers represented—in Plato and Aristotle's term, "imitated"—with greater or lesser success. Mimesis was the paradigm. Now that this external world was no longer available, now that it was undergoing destruction preparatory to a new birth, avant-garde artists and writers turned to the method of imitation, to the "processes or disciplines" of art and literature, as their subject matter.

The avant-garde's subject matter was art-making itself. Modern artists—Greenberg named Picasso, Braque, Mondrian, Miró, Kandinsky, Brancusi, Klee, Matisse, and Cézanne—derived "their chief inspiration from the medium they work in." And modern poets—Rimbaud, Mallarmé, Valéry, Éluard, Pound, Hart Crane, Stevens, Rilke, and Yeats—focused on "the effort to create poetry and on the 'moments' themselves of poetic conversion, rather than on experience to be converted into poetry." In short, he concluded, modern art and literature is "the imitation of imitat*ing*." Painting had turned nonobjective or abstract; poetry had become self-reflexive.

"That avant-garde culture is the imitation of imitating—the fact itself—calls for neither approval nor disapproval," Greenberg wrote, and he would later claim that his own taste was for representational art. The point was that abstract art was (as Lukács said of Heine) historically fully justified: "by no other means is it possible today to create art and literature of a high order." In its very commitment to artistic autonomy, modern art registered the crisis of the times and its own imperiled status. It represented reality by refusing to represent. The crucial, affective element was the silent gesture toward what was no longer possible.[28]

This was the avant-garde portion of Greenberg's argument. The kitsch portion was an expanded version of what he had said in the letter to Macdonald. Greenberg defined kitsch as "popular, commercial art and literature with their chromeotypes, magazine covers, illustrations, ads, slick and pulp fiction, comics, Tin Pan Alley music, tap dancing, Hollywood movies, etc., etc." And he proposed that kitsch was a product of the same historical moment that led to avant-gardism: the industrial revolution. Urbanization and mass literacy created a new market; to meet the demand, "a new commodity was devised, ersatz culture, kitsch, destined for those who, insensible to the values of genuine culture, are hungry nevertheless for the diversion that only culture of some sort can provide." This manufactured, formulaic, for-profit culture drove out folk art, an authentic popular culture, and replaced it with what were essentially commodities. Macdonald, Greenberg wrote, had shown how Stalin turned Soviet cinema into kitsch. The same thing was happening to the arts in Germany and Italy under Hitler and Mussolini. Kitsch was a way for dictators to ingratiate themselves with the masses.

This was a warning to the liberal democracies. For "[c]apitalism in decline finds that whatever of quality it is still capable of producing becomes almost invariably a threat to its own existence. Advances in culture, no less than advances in science and industry, corrode the very society under whose aegis they are made possible." A desperate capitalism will devour its own best art. Socialism was necessary not only for the creation of a new culture but also "for the preservation of whatever living culture we have right now."[29] In his diary, he put it this way: "Kitsch is equivalent in culture of bourgeois democracy in politics."[30]

"My piece has been a 'success,'" Greenberg wrote to Lazarus in November 1939. ". . . James Burnham says it's one of the best articles they've published. Van Wyck Brooks wrote a note to say he thought it very fine. Louise Bogan likes it. Delmore Schwartz thinks it's a 'wonderful piece of work' and should be printed in italics, and so forth . . . Now, the PR wants me to write more articles for them, and I feel very warm and gratified." Six months later, his essay was reprinted in the British journal *Horizon*, just started by the critic Cyril Connolly. Greenberg reported to Lazarus that Harold Rosenberg had told Macdonald that he liked the essay, "with reservations," but that he never mentioned it to Greenberg himself. "What an egoism," Greenberg wrote, "that can't afford to give me the little salve of a compliment."[31] It was the start of a lifelong animosity.

Greenberg turned immediately to his next essay, a theoretical extension of the argument of "Avant-Garde and Kitsch." This the editors at *Partisan Review* were considerably less enthusiastic about. It was heavily edited, and they sat on it for nine months.[32] It finally appeared in the July–August issue in 1940 as "Towards a Newer Laocoon." The immediate impact was small, but the essay articulated a position that Greenberg would make well known through his subsequent work an art critic: medium specificity.

"Towards a Newer Laocoon" argues backward from the "present supremacy" of abstract art to the principles upon which such an art must be based. Greenberg decided that these had to do with what he called "purity." The abstract artist is committed to keeping painting within the boundaries of its own medium. Painting is experienced visually and synchronically, and is therefore not like literature, which is experienced cognitively and diachronically. Literature tells a story; painting should not. Painting is two-dimensional, and therefore not like sculpture. Neither painting nor poetry is about ideas, which belong to non-aesthetic media. Greenberg thought that achieving this purity was the project of modern art and literature, and that by 1940, that project had succeeded. "The arts lie safe, now, each within its 'legitimate' boundaries, and free trade has been replaced by autarchy," he wrote. "Purity in art consists in the acceptance, willing acceptance, of the limitations of the medium of the specific art . . . It is by virtue of its medium that each art is unique and strictly itself."[33]

Greenberg had met the literary editor of *The Nation*, Margaret

Marshall, at a party at Macdonald's in the fall of 1940. In March 1942, she offered him a job as the magazine's regular art critic. *The Nation* paid much better than *Partisan Review*, which is why he was able to quit his job at Customs. Around the time that "Avant-Garde and Kitsch" came out, Greenberg had met and begun a relationship with Cyril Connolly's American wife, Jean Bakewell. The two were living independent lives. She left Connolly, and her affair with Greenberg was still going on when he was drafted, in February 1943. Jean filled in for him at *The Nation*.[34]

Greenberg hated army life—one of his jobs was guarding German prisoners of war in Oklahoma—and he had a breakdown. He seems to have been overwhelmed by forced intimacy with hundreds of men with whom he felt nothing in common. The "horror," he wrote Macdonald in June, "is not in what you experience so much as in what you contemplate, the idea of your own life presented to you with all its waste and emptiness."[35] "The very sight of the base," he wrote to Jean in a letter that he never sent, "poured awful blackness into me, awful, awful."[36] She visited him during the summer, then wrote to break off the relationship. His depression deepened. In August, he was diagnosed with "adult maladjustment," and in September he received an honorable discharge.[37] When he picked up his *Nation* column again, Jackson Pollock was just arriving on the New York art scene.

4.

Pollock's moment was made possible by an improbable dynamo in the midcentury art world, Peggy Guggenheim. And Peggy Guggenheim was a financial supporter and personal and professional intimate of an art movement whose theory and practice contradicted nearly every claim that Greenberg had made about the avant-garde, Surrealism. From its emergence as a movement in Paris in 1924, Surrealism had a politics and it had a subject matter. The politics was revolutionary, and the subject matter was the realm beyond or beneath ordinary modes of consciousness. Surrealist artists were formally and technically innovative, but for the purpose of fulfilling their political and representational missions, not for the purpose of exploring the limits of the medium.

The movement's founder and leader, André Breton, was inspired by his experience treating trauma patients (or, as they were then called, victims of shell shock) during the First World War. This led him to an interest in Freudian psychoanalysis and the unconscious.[38] Breton believed that human beings are suffering under what he called, in his first *Manifeste du surréalisme*, "the reign of logic," and he saw Surrealism as a way to express "the actual functioning of thought." Surrealism is "the 'invisible ray' that will one day allow us to triumph over our adversaries."[39] This was not a call for the "imitation of imitating" or medium specificity.

From the start, Breton sought an alliance with the French Communist Party. In 1929, he changed the name of his journal from *La Révolution surréaliste* to *Le Surréalisme au Service de la Révolution*. He did break with the Communists in 1935, however, and became loyal to Trotsky, whose writings he had long admired.[40]

Guggenheim was rich, though not as rich as her uncle Solomon, who would found the Museum of Non-Objective Painting as a gift to his mistress in New York City in 1939—the precursor of the Guggenheim Museum. Peggy Guggenheim received some inheritance in 1919, when she was twenty-one (her father died on the *Titanic*), and then moved to Paris, where she married an expatriate writer and artist named Laurence Vail.[41] Vail was unreliable and unfaithful, so was she, and the marriage didn't last. But it helped get her acquainted with the Parisian avant-garde. At some point, as the marriage was unraveling, she decided she wanted to be a patron of something, and she chose contemporary art.[42]

She started by opening a gallery in London called Guggenheim Jeune, and by collecting art (also, as she would reveal later on in her somewhat scandalous memoir, men). In 1939, she closed the London gallery and went to Paris to buy art, with the idea of opening a museum. Unlike almost everyone else, she was oblivious of the Nazi threat, and she therefore got very good prices.[43] "The day Hitler walked into Norway, I walked into Léger's studio and bought a wonderful 1919 painting from him for one thousand dollars," she wrote in the memoir. "He never got over the fact that I should be buying paintings on such a day."[44] She seems to have amassed her remarkable collection of modern art for less than forty thousand dollars.[45] One of her guides was a friend of Breton's and a leading figure in the Surrealist phenomenon, Marcel Duchamp, who introduced Guggenheim to European artists and advised her on what to collect.

By the fall of 1940, even Guggenheim realized that as a Jewish woman with a large collection of degenerate art, it would be prudent to get out of France.[46] So did the Surrealists. Few of them were Jewish.* But the Nazi exhibition of *Entartete Kunst* (Degenerate Art), held in Munich from July 19 to November 30, 1937, and then sent on tour, was seen by more than three million people.[47] The Surrealists knew they were targets of Nazi persecution. The United States was the last place most of them wanted to end up. A "Surrealist Map of the World," published in 1929, completely omitted the United States: North America consisted of Alaska, Labrador, and Mexico. But for most of the artists, the United States was their best hope.

Getting there was difficult. Between 1933 and 1944, the United States admitted 530,000 immigrants. About half that number were people fleeing Nazi or fascist governments. It was the lowest rate of immigration since records started being kept in the 1820s. Between 1921 and 1930, immigration had been over four million. Between 1901 and 1910, it was close to nine million.[48]

The United States had adopted a per-country quota system in 1924, but the problem in the 1930s wasn't quotas. Every European country in those years was under quota. The problem was a Depression-era regulation that applied restrictions on immigrants "likely to become a public charge"—a provision known as the LPC clause. An additional hurdle was erected after the Germans occupied France and the State Department took control of the visa process in order to protect against the immigration of enemy aliens. A regulation denying a visa to anyone with "close relatives" in occupied Europe—a large set of potential immigrants—went into effect. When the United States entered the war at the end of 1941, American consulates in occupied countries were shut, and that effectively put an end to European immigration to the United States.

The restrictions were not created because of anti-Semitism, although anti-Semitism was a reason they were politically difficult to remove. The Immigration and Nationalization Service did not record immigrants' religious affiliation, but it did use the category "Hebrew." Between January 1933, when Hitler took power, and June 1938, the United States admitted 27,000 Hebrews from Germany.[49] Between 1933 and 1943, it

---

* Méret Oppenheim was an exception, but she was Swiss and, when the war started, was able to return to Switzerland.

admitted, from all countries, 168,128 Hebrews with permanent visas—
about 45 percent of all European immigrants admitted—and 43,944
with temporary visas.[50] That is fewer than a quarter of a million people.
Approximately six million "Hebrews" died in the Shoah.

Europeans seeking an immigration visa were required to supply
documents that people fleeing persecution might not have readily at
hand, including a passport, a birth certificate and marriage certificate,
a photograph, and evidence of assets. Starting in 1940, they also needed
two financial affidavits and two letters of reference from American citizens.[51] This meant finding sponsors, as Hannah Arendt had done when
the Zionist organization she worked for in Paris arranged her emigration, which was paid for by an American charity. The exiled Institute
for Social Research had been Walter Benjamin's sponsor, which is why
when he died, he had a U.S. visa but not a French exit permit.

Many of the Surrealists relied on Varian Fry to get them out. Fry
became a legend for his work securing visas for writers and artists
in 1940 and 1941. After graduating from Harvard, where he majored in
classics, he had worked as a reporter, but in the 1930s, he became increasingly concerned about the fate of European Jews. (Fry was a Gentile.) When war broke out, he became European representative for the
Emergency Rescue Committee, an organization committed to helping
people get out of occupied Europe. And in August 1940, he set up an
office, the Emergency Relief Center (ERC), in Marseille.[52]

The ERC was a nongovernmental organization, operating with
funds raised privately through its office in New York City. In Marseille,
Fry and a small group of associates processed applicants for help securing visas. A key element of the service was negotiating clients past
the LPC clause. Part of the job, therefore, was determining who was
sufficiently talented to find work and not become a public liability. For
applicants who arrived in Marseille unknown to Fry, the procedure
was not complicated. Those claiming to be artists were sent down to
the harbor and requested to make a sketch. An assistant of Fry's with
some training in art history, Miriam Davenport, reviewed the results
and determined which refugees to assist with obtaining visas. People
claiming to be poets were dealt with in a similar manner.[53]

In other words, the ERC was a small-scale version of American immigration policy generally. European émigrés in the Nazi period had
almost no demographic impact on the United States; the numbers were

far too small. But they had an enormous cultural impact because they were chosen from the elite of European art, scholarship, and science. Getting into the United States was like getting into a highly selective college. Those émigrés were cherry-picked.

Fry helped several thousand people escape from occupied Europe before he was thrown out by French police in August 1941, after the United States, which regarded his activities as outside the law, refused to renew his passport. Altogether, through Fry and other means, about 30,000 French refugees reached the United States.[54] They were from many professions, but the most famous of Fry's clients were the painters.[55]

Fry helped Breton and his wife secure passage, paid for by Guggenheim, on a ship to Martinique. Guggenheim's family sent a plane to fetch her. She flew out of Lisbon accompanied by a new lover, the German painter Max Ernst, whom she would marry in New York. Duchamp was one of the last to leave. On May 14, 1942, he took a boat to Casablanca.[56] Altogether, between 1933 and 1944 more than seven hundred European artists came to the United States.[57] Fry was crushed when, after they got to New York, almost all of the artists he had helped to escape shunned him.[58]

The New York art world took notice of the European painters' arrival. It had been prepared by two blockbuster exhibitions in 1936 at the Museum of Modern Art: *Cubism and Abstract Art* in February, and *Fantastic Art, Dada, Surrealism* in December. The second show contained nearly seven hundred works, then the largest exhibition ever mounted by an American museum. It attracted more attention and commentary than any American exhibition since the Armory Show of 1913, where Duchamp had showed *Nude Descending a Staircase, No. 2*. The scandalous piece this time was Méret Oppenheim's *Object*—the fur-covered tea set.[59]

When she arrived in New York, Guggenheim set up a gallery called Art of This Century, above a grocery store on Fifty-Seventh Street. At the suggestion of Howard Putzel, an American art dealer she had met in Paris, she hired Frederick Kiesler, an Austro-Hungarian émigré, to design the interior, which he did with the aim of integrating the art with the architecture. There were four gallery spaces; three displayed Guggenheim's own collection, and the fourth was for temporary exhibitions of works for sale.

In 1943, the gallery announced a Spring Salon for Young Artists. A jury that included Duchamp, Putzel, Alfred Barr, who was the director of the Museum of Modern Art, and Piet Mondrian selected works for the show. Somewhat surprisingly, Mondrian is supposed to have been the juror who picked out a painting by Pollock, *Stenographic Figure*. (It is possible that Mondrian wished to appear broad-minded in order to make the panel more amenable to his own preferred candidate.)[60] Duchamp declined to veto the choice.

This was the first serious recognition Pollock had received. Putzel persuaded Guggenheim to follow up with a visit to Pollock in his studio, on Eighth Street. She made the visit and offered him an allowance of $150 a month so he could devote himself to painting. (He was working as a custodian at the Museum of Non-Objective Painting, which was then, in its first instantiation, in a converted automobile showroom on East Fifty-Fourth Street.) She also commissioned a large painting for the foyer of a town house on East Sixty-First Street where she was renting a duplex apartment on the upper floors.[61] These agreements resulted in Pollock's first solo show, at Art of This Century, on November 9, 1943, and in the work known as *Mural*.

5.

Pollock was not a verbal person. Friends reported that he could talk insightfully about other people's art, but in social settings he was generally diffident (or, when drunk, obstreperous), and he did not have much to say about his own paintings. He didn't even like to think up titles for them. Many of his best-known titles, such as *Lavender Mist*, *Autumn Rhythm*, and *Full Fathom Five*, were supplied by friends.* Pollock's few published statements about his own work—in his failed application for a Guggenheim fellowship in 1947, and in the single-issue journal *Possibilities*, edited by Harold Rosenberg and Robert Motherwell, in 1948—were probably coached, the first by Greenberg and the second by Motherwell.

But many people have talked *about* Pollock as a man with negatively charged charisma. "He was like a trapped animal who never should have left Wyoming," Guggenheim wrote about him years later.[62] "A driven creature," Betty Parsons, his next dealer, called him.[63] A good deal of this reputation is postmortem, though. A mythology grew up around

---

* *Lavender Mist* was supplied by Greenberg, who loved jazz and who may have borrowed the phrase from a Duke Ellington number, "Lady of the Lavender Mist," released on the LP *Mood Ellington* in 1949.

Pollock—that he was violent, that he was a cowboy, that he represented some kind of a masculinist aesthetics. The fact is that he had a medical condition: alcoholism. He had a low threshold for intoxication, and he became abusive and sometimes violent. And he was a binge drinker. "People should have known that he was a radical alcoholic," Greenberg said, "the most radical one I've ever known."[64] Yet, Greenberg went on, "[h]e was really gentle, quiet, warm. He had antennae. His sweetness was in his presence rather than in his actions. He was no good to anybody . . . Yet when I felt bad, no one was sweeter to me than he was."[65] "I knew Pollock well," the dealer Leo Castelli said, "and can say that despite his rough edges, he was a highly sensitive and lovable man."[66]

Pollock made big paintings, but all the painters in his circle, men and women, made big paintings. It is sheer speculation to ascribe human qualities to artworks, but it is hard to see Pollock's drip paintings as aggressive or domineering. The surfaces are astonishingly delicate and layered. He achieved this effect by throwing paint, but he threw it with design. He was not somehow attacking the canvas.

One consequence of the fascination with and desire to talk about Pollock is a large archive of first-person reminiscence and hearsay. This is true of the art world that Pollock belonged to generally. Large portions of midcentury art history are basically oral history—that is, gossip. Stories that were half-true because they were designed to enhance the reputation of the storyteller, or that were simply tall tales or invented memories, got repeated in print so often that they became indistinguishable from fact. The story of *Mural* is a classic case.

What in Pollock's prior experience with art influenced *Mural* and the drip paintings that followed it? The answer seems to be: Everything. "What is interesting about Pollock," George McNeil, a painter who knew him in the 1930s, said, "is that he came from very bad influences like [Thomas Hart] Benton and the Mexican muralists and other anti-painterly influences, and yet, somehow, in a kind of alchemy, he took all the negatives and made them into a positive. It's a mystery."[67]

Pollock was a Westerner. He was born in Cody, Wyoming, and was named after Jackson Lake, in the Grand Tetons. The Pollocks left Wyoming when Jackson was an infant, and he grew up in Arizona and Southern California. He never learned to ride a horse. In fact, he was afraid of horses.[68] Pollock's father, Roy, left the family when Jackson was eight or nine. Roy worked on road crews, and he continued to provide support, but he was mostly absent when Jackson was growing up. Pollock's mother, Stella, had an interest in arts and crafts, and she seems to have been behind the family's gravitation toward painting. There were five boys, and three of them became, or tried to become, painters.

Jackson was the youngest. In 1930, after two years at Manual Arts High School, he followed after his brother Charles and went to New York City, where he began taking classes at the Art Students League, on Fifty-Seventh Street. His teacher was Thomas Hart Benton, a bumptious and opinionated man who was a leading representative of the American Regionalist school of painting. Benton's work was all about sculptural contour—he called it "the hollow and the bump"—and composition. He taught that the canvas, or the mural surface, should be organized rhythmically along rows of verticals.[69] He disliked the left-wing politics of the New York art scene, and he returned to Missouri, his home state, in 1935, taking a job at the Kansas City Art Institute. Benton's replacement at the Art Students League was John Sloan, but Pollock couldn't work with Sloan—Sloan thought Pollock's drawing wasn't good enough—and he quit. In 1935, he got a job with the Federal Arts Project of the Works Progress Administration, an agency that kept many American fine-art painters going until it closed down in 1943.

One of Pollock's favorite works of art was a mural, *Prometheus*, that José Orozco painted for a dining hall at Pomona College in Claremont, California. Pollock went with one of his brothers to see it in 1930, soon after Orozco finished it, and he always spoke of it as a great work of art. He kept a reproduction in his studio.[70] In 1936, another Mexican muralist, David Siqueiros, began holding workshops in a studio on Union Square, and Pollock participated.* Artists at the workshops used industrial paints, lacquer, and sand; they painted on concrete and plywood; they practiced silk screening. Pollock and Siqueiros seem to have had a rapport.

Pollock met John Graham, Krasner's friend, in 1939.[71] Graham hated contour. His teaching was all about flatness—he thought that the invention of chiaroscuro had ruined painting for five hundred years—and he taught Pollock about abstraction. Graham's text was his own book, a combination of art theory and spiritual counsel called *System and Dialectics of Art*, published in 1937.

---

* In May 1940, Siqueiros would lead a failed assassination attempt against Leon Trotsky in a suburb of Mexico City, where Trotsky was living. A subsequent attack, in August, by Ramón Mercader, was successful.

The purpose of art, Graham wrote there, "is to re-establish a lost contact with the unconscious . . . Conscious mind is incapable of creating, it is only a clearing house for the powers of the unconscious."[72] The corollary of this (Surrealist) principle was the abandonment of painterly technique (not a Surrealist principle). "No technical perfection or elegance can produce a work of art," Graham explained. "Cold-blooded calculation and perfect technical execution do not constitute a work of art but a work of industry and it is harmful and criminal before the public, artists, art students and posterity to misrepresent such as works of art." A painting must be

> the immediate, unadorned record of an authentic intellecto-emotional REACTION of the artist set in space . . . This authentic reaction recorded within the measurable space immediately and automatically in terms of brush pressure, saturation, velocity, caress or repulsion, anger or desire which changes and varies in unison with the flow of feeling at the moment, constitutes a work of art.[73]

Graham's hero was Pablo Picasso.[74] Pollock saw Picasso's Spanish Civil War mural-sized painting Guernica when it was hung in the Valentine Dudensing Gallery on Fifty-Seventh Street in January 1939. He returned to look at it more than once and, in November, he visited a major Picasso retrospective at the Museum of Modern Art, where Les Demoiselles d'Avignon seems to have made a great impression.[75] It was around this time that people started paying more attention to Pollock's own painting.

So when the Surrealists arrived in New York, in 1941, Pollock had already been Europeanized. Even in 1944, answering a questionnaire with the assistance of either Putzel or Motherwell, he identified himself (or was willing to be identified) with European art. "American painters have generally missed the point of modern painting from beginning to end," he is quoted as saying. ". . . Thus the fact that good European moderns are now here is very important, for they bring with them an understanding of the problems of modern painting." The idea of "American painting" seemed absurd to him, he said, "just as the idea of creating a purely American mathematics or physics would seem absurd."[76]

Pollock's alcoholism led to a series of psychiatric interventions. His psychiatrists—Joseph Henderson, from 1939 to 1940, and Violet Staub de Laszlo, from 1940 until Pollock started living with Krasner, in 1942—were Jungians.[77] Henderson seems to have encouraged Pollock to use Jungian archetypes in his work.[78] Which he did. *Stenographic Figure*, the painting Mondrian singled out for the Spring Salon at Guggenheim's Art of This Century in 1943, was such a work.[79] So were most of the paintings in Pollock's solo show the next fall. The titles tell the story: *The Moon-Woman Cuts the Circle, The She-Wolf, Guardians of the Secret, Conflict, Male and Female in Search of a Symbol*.

Pollock was trying to cope with the central problem of Surrealism, which is the problem of rendering in visual form things that are supposed to be unconscious and intangible. Breton had defined the movement in the first manifesto: "SURREALISM, n. m. Psychic automatism in its pure state, by which one proposes to express—verbally, by means of the written word, or in any other manner—the actual functioning of thought."[80] "Psychic automatism" was supposed to give artists access to the unconscious, to enable them to achieve Graham's "immediate, unadorned record of an authentic intellecto-emotional REACTION."

Pollock's involvement with the Surrealists came principally through Motherwell. Motherwell was from a wealthy California family. After college at Stanford and graduate work at Harvard, he came to New York in 1940 to study with the Columbia art historian Meyer Schapiro. Because he spoke French and was young, obliging, and unthreatening, Motherwell became one of the few Americans accepted into the circle of Surrealist exiles. In 1942, Motherwell introduced Pollock to the Chilean Surrealist Roberto Matta, who had been in Paris and had fled just before the war broke out. Matta was holding workshops in his studio apartment on Ninth Street in which he discussed automatism, or, as Motherwell called it, "doodling."[81] Pollock's patience with Matta did not last long, but he was exposed to the core technical principle of Surrealist art-making. Automatism did not solve the iconographic problem, however, the problem of what an "authentic intellecto-emotional reaction" is supposed to look like—Jungian? Pre-Columbian? Phantasmagoric? Wouldn't those all be predetermined imageries?

With Guggenheim's commission, *Mural*, Pollock left the iconographic problem behind. *Mural* is not, in fact, a mural. It is a painting on canvas of a mural, designed to fit flush against an entire wall in the lobby of the building where Guggenheim was living. The canvas Pollock stretched for the commission was roughly twenty feet by eight feet; he had to knock a hole in a wall of his apartment to work on it. *Mural* was almost certainly not painted quickly, but it *looks* as though it was painted quickly. It is a work that, when you see it for the first time, gives you the impression that the painter has just left the room. *Mural* was one step short—the step of lifting the brush off the canvas—of the drip paintings.

The story of how the painting was created suits the impression it made a little too well. People who thought they knew that story heard it from Krasner. She told them that the painting was due to be installed in January 1944 in time for a party Guggenheim was throwing, but that after stretching the canvas, Pollock was blocked for weeks. The night before the work was due, Krasner went to sleep with the canvas still blank. By the next morning, Pollock had painted *Mural*.[82]

Guggenheim was the source for much of the rest. She claimed that Duchamp and a workman were on hand when Pollock delivered the canvas, rolled up, to be installed, but the painting was too long. Pollock had mismeasured. According to legend (this part is attributed to a member of the Surrealist circle, David Hare), Duchamp, in a Dada gesture, snipped eight inches off from the sides. Pollock had meanwhile discovered where Guggenheim hid her liquor. He got drunk, Guggenheim said, walked naked into the party, now under way, and urinated in the fireplace.[83]

The story has an unusually high degree of implausibility. The painting is dated, on the back of the canvas, 1943, not 1944. As Pollock wrote to his brother Charles, the work was commissioned for the opening of Pollock's solo show, on November 16, 1943, not for a party the following January.[84] A letter from Guggenheim to a friend, dated November 12, mentions the work as already completed and, in a letter to one of his brothers, Pollock reported that he had painted it over the summer.

The painting was never trimmed. Both edges where the canvas is tacked to the sides of the stretcher are unpainted. And it would have been highly uncharacteristic for Pollock to take his clothes off in front of people he didn't know; there are no other reports of him doing anything like that. There was an unused fireplace in the entrance lobby where the piece was installed; if Pollock urinated somewhere, he probably did it there in the presence of Duchamp and another man.[85] Krasner's and Guggenheim's stories stuck, though, because they were consistent with an image that the public would form of Pollock, after he became famous, as an artist who was spontaneous and uncivilized.

Jean Connolly had reviewed the 1943 Spring Salon show at Art of This Century for *The Nation* when Greenberg was in the army. She noted that "there is a large painting by Jackson Pollack [sic] which, I am told, made the jury starry-eyed."[86] Her source was almost certainly Guggenheim herself, for Connolly and Guggenheim had become friends; at some point, Connolly moved in with her. When Connolly broke off her affair with Greenberg, it was because she had become involved with Guggenheim's ex-husband, Laurence Vail.[87] She and Vail decided to leave New York together (they would eventually marry), and the January party on East Sixty-First Street was their going-away party. Greenberg was invited, too. (Apparently, some sort of emotional maturity was implied in acknowledging these partner swaps.) That is when he saw *Mural*.[88]

Greenberg never referred to that painting in any of his published work—it was not available for public view until March 1945, when visitors to Pollock's second solo show at Art of This Century were invited to walk over to Sixty-First Street to see it—but he made it clear that this was the work that convinced him Pollock was a great painter. "I took one look at it and I thought, 'Now *that's* great art,'" he told Pollock's biographers. "I told Jackson, '*That* is great art,'" he said to another interviewer.[89] In an uncompleted book on Pollock, he wrote: "I was overwhelmed."[90]

Greenberg had included a paragraph on Pollock in a review of the November 1943 Art of This Century show, describing him as a painter of promise. He made his first major critical statement about Pollock in a review of Pollock's second solo show at Art of This Century, in 1945. As with the 1943 show, the paintings featured the same Jungian and Surrealist-influenced iconography, with titles such as *Totem Lesson 1, Totem Lesson 2*, and *Night Magic*. But Greenberg ignored the iconography. He saw the paintings in terms of the impression of Pollock's art he had formed a year before, when he saw *Mural*.[91] He treated Pollock's pre-abstract paintings as though they were already abstractions, and he declared Pollock to be "the strongest painter of his generation and perhaps the greatest one to appear since Miró."[92]

6.

One reader who was not pleased with "Avant-Garde and Kitsch," Greenberg told Lazarus soon after that essay appeared, was Meyer Schapiro—"who says in addition that I borrowed some of his ideas."[93] Arguably, he had.

Schapiro was born in 1904 in Lithuania, then part of the Russian Empire. His family came to New York City when he was three, and he grew up in Brownsville. He was a gifted student, and he entered Columbia College on a Pulitzer scholarship, awarded to a graduate of Brooklyn public schools, when he was sixteen. He received his PhD from Columbia in 1929—his specialty was Romanesque sculpture— and he spent his entire academic career there. In 1933, he moved to the Village and became involved in the contemporary art scene.[94]

Schapiro was a lifelong socialist. He began writing for journals associated with the Communist Party in 1932. He contributed to the Marxist paper *New Masses* under a pseudonym, John Kwait, and in 1936 began writing for *Art Front*, the journal of the Artists Union, an organization that was set up, largely by members of the Communist Party, to represent artists working in the WPA.

The challenge at *Art Front* was the challenge the editors of *Partisan Review* faced: how to embrace modern art in terms consistent with socialist politics. In 1936, Schapiro delivered an address at the First American Artists' Congress against War and Fascism, held over three days at Town Hall and the New School. Siqueiros and Orozco were in the audience as the Mexican delegates. "There are artists and writers for whom the apparent anarchy of modern culture—as an individual affair in which each person seeks his own pleasure—is historically progressive," Schapiro said; but ". . . this freedom of a few individuals is identified largely with consumption and enjoyment; it detaches man from nature, history and society, and although, in doing so, it discovers new qualities and possibilities of feeling and imagination, unknown to older culture, it cannot realize those possibilities of individual development which depend on common productive tasks, on responsibilities, on intelligence and cooperation in dealing with the urgent social issues of the moment."[95] It was the Marxist case against modernism. Schapiro repeated the point in *Art Front*. The artist, he warned, "must combat the illusion that his own insecurity and the wretched state of our culture can be overcome within the framework of our present society."[96]

Then, affected by the news of the Moscow Trials, Schapiro divorced his socialism from his aesthetics. (Rosenberg dissociated himself from the Communist Party not long after.)[97] Suddenly, he was no longer worried that modern painting might be politically irresponsible. In 1937, in "Nature of Abstract Art," published in *Marxist Quarterly*, a journal founded by a group that included James Burnham, Sidney Hook, and Schapiro himself, Schapiro described abstract painting as work in which "the very process of designing and inventing seemed to have been brought on to the canvas; the pure form once masked by an extraneous content was liberated and could now be directly perceived."[98]

This is very like Greenberg's "imitation of imitating," and this was the essay that Schapiro apparently thought Greenberg had cribbed from. It appeared just as *Partisan Review* was making its break with the John Reed Club, and for exactly the same reasons: the turn in Schapiro's thought was part of the general breakup of the American left over the issue of intellectual and artistic freedom. As Greenberg suggested, "Avant-Garde and Kitsch" did not inaugurate that shift. It closed it out. It marked the moment when American socialism dropped its demands on the arts. Art now bore no responsibility to the revolution; it was historically justified as what it was in itself. Greenberg rescued modernist art and literature for leftists by depoliticizing it. In 1961, in a parenthetical remark that became widely quoted, he commented, "[S]ome day it will have to be told how 'anti-Stalinism,' which started out more or less as 'Trotskyism,' turned into art for art's sake, and thereby cleared the way, heroically, for what was to come."[99] He meant that in "Avant-Garde and Kitsch" he had used a Marxist interpretation of history as a ladder to reach an understanding of modern art and literature, and in "Towards a Newer Laocoon," he had kicked the ladder away. For the rest of his career, he found that he could operate as a critic without the politics, and he taught many other people how to do so as well.

Greenberg's ideas about medium specificity were also not new in 1940.* That painting is essentially a two-dimensional medium was one of Hans Hofmann's chief pedagogical points, and it is a central principle in Graham's *System and Dialectics of Art*.[100] "The aim of painting as of any pure art is to exploit its *legitimate assets* which are limitless without encroaching upon the domain of other arts," Graham said. "Thus painting that resorts to literature, sculpture, etc., to improve itself is a decadent art"—almost exactly what Greenberg said in "Towards a Newer Laocoon."[101] Still, Graham also believed that the purpose of art

---

* As Greenberg's title acknowledges, the theory dates from Gottold Ephraim Lessing's *Laokoon, oder Über die Grenzen der Malerei und Poesie* (*Laocoön: On the Limits of Poetry and Painting*), 1766. Lessing's argument was revived by Walter Pater in the third edition, 1888, of *The Renaissance*, and by the Harvard literature professor Irving Babbitt, who was T. S. Eliot's teacher, in *The New Laocoön*, in 1910.

was to "establish a link between humanity and the unknown; to create new values; to put humanity face to face with a new event."[102] This part of his thought belongs to the metaphysics of Surrealism, and that was something Greenberg rejected.

Mural is, from one perspective, an all-over abstraction constructed on Bentonian principles—a row of vertical forms embedded in swirls of shapes.[103] But Pollock replaced sculptural illusion with something specifically painterly: a layered surface. And the layers were applied in an automatist manner, that is, by reiterated movements of the painter's body. The recipe could have come directly from a book published a year earlier by another exile who came over with the Surrealists, Nicolas Calas. In "physiological automatism," Calas wrote,

> one has the impression that the objects have been produced by a rhythmical movement of the arm and hand . . . The shapes . . . are the product of an attention that is used to protect the free development of physiological movement from interruptions and that is why the forms and images thus created look, although they are purely imaginary, as if they were alive. They are *biomorphic*.[104]

This is a good description of what Pollock accomplished for the first time in *Mural* and what he would do again and again once he discovered the method that enabled him to produce the drip paintings.

7.

Soon after the 1945 show that led Greenberg to call Pollock "the strongest painter of his generation," Pollock and Krasner married and moved to Springs. There, for four years, Pollock abandoned figuration almost completely. He did not stop his drinking, but he seems to have moderated it (and he never painted when he was drunk).[105] His first drip works date from 1947.

The term "drip" is controversial—Pollock actually poured or flung paint onto the canvas—but it was a word Pollock used himself. Krasner disliked it. She thought the appropriate term was "aerial": "it was aerial and it landed," was how she put it.[106] Pollock had thrown paint before, in Siqueiros's workshop, for example, and also when playing around while working in the Museum of Non-Objective Art. But the mature drip method seems to have originated when he found that he did not have enough room in the new house to stretch a canvas and so he laid it on the floor. He liked the results, and, after a barn on the property was converted into a studio, he tried it again. Greenberg visited soon after—the period of the drip paintings was also the period of their closest friendship—and he is supposed to have encouraged Pollock to continue painting on the floor.[107]

Pollock's first exhibition of the new work, at the Betty Parsons Gallery in January 1948, was a disaster. *Time* had recently run a quizzical story with the headline "The Best?" (quoting Greenberg's claim about Pollock), and the show was ridiculed in the press. This was *Life*'s take on modern art generally. Later that year, the magazine published a piece on Jean Dubuffet, one of the leading painters in France, and entitled it "Dead End: A Frenchman's Mud-and-Rubble Paintings Reduce Modernism to a Joke."

But then, *Life* shifted its position. This was possibly because of an eight-page letter that John Hay Whitney, chairman of the Board of Trustees at the Museum of Modern Art, and Nelson Rockefeller, president of the museum, sent to Henry Luce criticizing his magazines' art coverage. "If [*Life*] cannot deal with the arts fairly," they told him, "it ought not to treat them editorially."[108] More likely, though, it was because one of *Life*'s young art editors, Dorothy Seiberling, had a sophisticated understanding of modern art.

Seiberling was from Akron; she was a granddaughter of the founder of Goodyear Tire and Rubber. She attended Vassar, graduating in 1943, then began her career at Time, Inc. It took her many years to work her way up the ladder; she eventually became art editor at *Life*.[109] Her uncle, Frank, was a professor of art history at Ohio State University. *Time* continued to be dismissive of abstract painting well into the 1950s, but *Life*, thanks at least in part to Seiberling, began treating contemporary art with more even-handed appreciation.[110]

On August 8, 1949, *Life* ran an article with the headline "Jackson Pollock: Is He the Greatest Living Painter in the United States?" It referred to Pollock as "the shining new phenomenon of American art."[111] This publicity prepared the ground for Pollock's second Betty Parsons show, on November 21. And this time, everyone turned out: collectors, museum directors, artists, and critics. On the advice of Alfred Barr,

Mrs. John D. Rockefeller purchased a painting.[112] This was the evening when de Kooning remarked that Pollock had broken the ice.

Since the days of the WPA, the New York artists had been looking for a way to liberate spontaneity from iconographic and ideological constraints, to achieve "the pure form once masked by an extraneous content," as Schapiro had described it in 1937. The European Surrealists were perceived as a catalyst. Everyone understood this. Motherwell thought that there was a "deep relation between Abstract Expressionism and the Surrealists' theory of 'automatism.'"[113] The art critic Robert Goldwater, who became the editor of the *Magazine of Art* in 1948, thought that the Surrealists gave American painters the license they needed to experiment.[114] Even Greenberg, writing in the special American issue of *Les Temps Modernes* in 1946, noted "the stimulant their [the Surrealists'] presence, if not their art, had in supporting a certain number of abstract painters."[115] To the extent that anyone thought that Abstract Expressionism represented "the triumph of American painting" (a phrase coined twenty years later), it was because American artists had finally produced work that they felt was valid by European standards.

And (like Pop Art fifteen years later) it all happened at once. In 1947, the year Pollock began the drip paintings, Clyfford Still made the first of his monumental color-field paintings and Mark Rothko dropped Surrealist figuration and started producing the works known as the multiform paintings, leading, in 1949, to his signature compositions: the floating boxes of color. In 1948, de Kooning showed black-and-white abstract paintings at the Charles Egan Gallery, his first solo show (praised by Greenberg), and in 1950, he made his major abstract work (maybe his best work), over six feet by eight feet, *Excavation*.[116]

Franz Kline abandoned figuration in 1948 or 1949 and began using a Bell-Opticon overhead projector, borrowed from de Kooning, to enlarge his drawings, which he then painted using a house-painting brush—the method that produced the calligraphic black-and-white canvases. Kline's first solo show, at the Charles Egan Gallery, was in 1950. Motherwell began his *Elegies to the Spanish Republic* paintings in 1948, and Barnett Newman painted *Onement I*, the first of the so-called zip paintings, the same year. Newman had his first solo show at Betty Parsons in January 1950. Critical recognition came quickly for Rothko and de Kooning, somewhat later for Kline and Newman, but the Abstract Expressionists arrived on the scene together—right after the European artists had gone home.

Pollock's drip period came to an abrupt end. He had an alcoholic relapse. There may have been a number of reasons, including a disastrous family reunion in the summer of 1950 and a negative story in *Time* about the Italian reception of Pollock's work, which was being shown at the Venice Biennale. (The *Time* piece was unfair: it quoted selectively from what was in fact a positive review by the Italian critic Bruno Alfieri.)[117] But the immediate cause of Pollock's breakdown was the completion of a short film of him at work.

The filmmaker, Hans Namuth, was a German émigré. Pollock had been suggested to him as a possible subject by Alexy Brodovitch, a Russian émigré who was art director of *Harper's Bazaar*.[118] Initially, Namuth had little interest in Pollock's art, but he liked the challenge of trying to capture an artist at work. Over the summer of 1950, he took some five hundred photographs of Pollock painting in his barn. In the fall, he decided to make a film. To save on the cost of lighting, the painting was done outdoors, which disrupted Pollock's normal work rhythm. He found himself standing around waiting for cues from Namuth when to start and stop, and the result was a distorted representation of his actual practice, which was more studied and discontinuous, less spontaneous, than the impression created by the photographs and the film.[119]

Since Pollock was standing and the canvas was on the ground, Namuth was unable to get painter and painting together in the frame effectively. The solution he arrived at was to film Pollock painting on glass. The inspiration was probably a well-known film of Picasso at work, *Visite à Picasso*, made by the Belgian artist and filmmaker Paul Haesaerts in 1949 and exhibited in 1950. At the end of that film, Haesaerts shot Picasso painting on a glass wall placed between the artist and the camera.[120] So Namuth had a platform erected in Pollock's yard; Pollock stood above a plate of glass, and Namuth filmed him painting from underneath.

It was cold, the takes were long, and Pollock had never painted on glass before and was unhappy with the results. When the shoot was finished, everyone went into the house. Pollock found a bottle and began drinking. Krasner had arranged a dinner party—it was Thanksgiving weekend—but Pollock began to quarrel with Namuth. Becoming enraged, he is supposed to have tipped over the dinner table and sent the dishes crashing to the floor.[121]

That was November 25, 1950. Three days later, Pollock had his fourth show at Betty Parsons, and this one was a commercial disaster. Of thirty-two works, which included the great paintings from the summer of 1950, *Lavender Mist, Autumn Rhythm, Number 32*, and *One: Number 31, 1950*, only *Lavender Mist* was sold. A good friend of the Pollocks, Alfonso Ossorio, bought it for fifteen hundred dollars, paid in installments.[122] (In 1976, after the trustees of the Boston Museum of Fine Arts vetoed the purchase of *Lavender Mist* because they considered it to have deteriorated, Ossorio would sell the painting to the National Gallery for $2 million.)[123]

After that, Pollock mostly stopped making drip paintings. He turned to figuration, then began working in black and white. At the end of 1954, he gave up making art almost altogether. He died in a car accident near his house on Long Island on the night of August 11, 1956. He had been drinking and there were two women in the car with him, Ruth Kligman, with whom he was having an affair, and her friend Edith Metzger. They were headed for a party at Ossorio's house in East Hampton. Pollock drove off the road and the car flipped over. Metzger was crushed to death. Kligman was thrown clear, and, although she suffered serious injuries, survived. Pollock, too, was thrown out of the car. He struck his head on a tree and died instantly. Krasner was in Paris. Greenberg reached her by phone and told her the news.[124]

8.

Were Pollock's abstract works paintings about painting, an "imitation of imitating"? The drip paintings do not ask the question, What is art? Obviously, Pollock's paintings are art. But they do ask a related question: What are the essential attributes of a painting? They pose this question not only about the tradition of easel painting, in which the canvas is imagined as a window on the world—a tradition that Pollock symbolically rejected by the simple act of placing his canvas on the ground. They ask the question about the visual arts in general.

Pollock's paintings resist conventional distinctions between figure and ground, detail and design, accident and method.[125] They alter the expected relation between the parts and the whole.[126] They resist ordinary methods of interpretation and even ordinary methods of description.[127] Pollock freed color and line from their traditional function of defining space and turned them into an "autonomous pictorial element."[128] In *Mural* and many of the drip paintings, "top" and "bottom" become arbitrary designations and the edges often appear to be accidents of the size of the canvas. "There was a reviewer a while back who wrote that my pictures didn't have any beginning or any end," Pollock once commented. "He didn't mean it as a compliment, but it was."[129] The paintings make a persistent and unanswerable question of where the optimal viewing point might be. From a distance, the paintings are color bombs; up close, they reveal a dense profusion of design, a kind of petri dish of microforms.

When people said, My five-year-old could do that, they were referring to a genuine problem, which is that although Pollock's drip paintings are almost impossible to fake, no obvious technical or teachable ability is required to make them. To the extent that serious art is associated with craft and training, a different vocabulary is required to describe their production. From one point of view, they are anti-art. Pollock didn't just put the canvas on the ground. He used house paint and plumber's aluminum paint. He glued objects such as keys, combs, caps from paint tubes, tacks, cigarette butts, and burnt matches to the canvas. It is not irrelevant to say that the canvases look as though the paint had been pissed onto them. There is a kind of extreme materiality, amounting to debasement, in these works, as though they did not want to be anyone's idea of high art.

From another perspective, though, they dematerialize art. For they can be understood as the record of another, primal work that cannot be replicated: the act of their creation. In these terms, the work is not the canvas. The work is the actions Pollock performed when he threw the paint. The paintings are the residua of dancelike performances, documentations (but not representations) of bodily movements that are irretrievable. Pollock stopped just short of abandoning the space of art altogether and turning our relations to everything around us into relations with art.[130] This somewhat conceptual aspect of the drip paintings, particularly the idea that art is essentially performance, is what became their greatest influence on future artists, even artists who did not work primarily with paint. And it is why Namuth's photographs of Pollock working (not the film so much, since it was for many years difficult to see), along with similar photographs by Arnold Newman, some published in *Life*, are crucial ingredients in Pollock's reputation. The idea of a "Pollock painting" includes Pollock painting.

Are the paintings *too* beautiful? The question was posed almost immediately when the photographer Cecil Beaton used *Autumn Rhythm* and *Lavender Mist* as backdrops in a fashion shoot for *Vogue* in March 1951, which raised the further question of whether they belong to the category of the decorative rather than the artistic, whether they are avant-garde art objects or very expensive wallpaper, whether they are noble or vulgar.[131] These are all formalist questions, questions about how the paintings work, not about what they mean. And they are the kind of questions that Greenberg taught critics to ask.

Still, those are not the questions that casual viewers of Pollock's paintings ask. These people are not interested in the formal problems that preoccupied Greenberg. They need another handle on works that defy conventional expectations, a different account of what the work is about. And that account was provided by Harold Rosenberg.

Rosenberg had a reputation as a brilliant intellectual among people who took intellectual brilliance very seriously. The Rosenbergs regarded Greenberg as a "mediocrity."[132] Although the Rosenbergs had a house near the Pollocks in Springs, relations between the couples were rocky. Rosenberg was a talker, and Pollock was not. Rosenberg could hold his liquor, and Pollock could not. After Pollock became famous, with the *Life* article in 1949, there were tensions.

Before 1952, although Rosenberg had written about art for *Art Front* and elsewhere, he was primarily regarded as a literary critic. He had been a contributor, in the early 1930s, to James Burnham's literary journal, *Symposium*. But he had many personal connections to the New York art world, and, unlike Greenberg, he was drawn to Surrealism. In 1948, he co-edited the little magazine *Possibilities* to which Pollock contributed a brief statement, and which was largely devoted to Surrealism. The painter Rosenberg was closest to was de Kooning. De Kooning's charisma was positively charged. Other artists liked him. He was generous with his ideas, convivial, and good-looking. He was admired as a painter's painter, someone who had enormous talent as a draftsman but who had committed himself to the avant-garde.

In 1952, Rosenberg published an essay in the December issue of *ART-news* called "The American Action Painters." It offered an interpretation of avant-garde art that was completely different from Greenberg's. "The American vanguard painter took to the white expanse of the canvas as Melville's Ishmael took to the sea," Rosenberg wrote. The painters threw themselves into the uncreated, the unknown—put themselves out over the abyss. "At a certain moment the canvas began to appear to one American painter after another as an arena in which to act," he said. And: "The act-painting is of the same metaphysical substance as the artist's existence. The new painting has broken down every distinction between art and life."[133]

Rosenberg did not name a single contemporary American artist in his essay, and many readers assumed that the "action painter" he had in mind was Pollock. In the art world, though, the article was recognized immediately as an *attack* on Pollock and Greenberg. On December 14, Clyfford Still wrote to Pollock. "In the last issue of The Art News there is an article by Harold Rosenberg," he told him. "Two paragraphs of the article indulge in some very pointed insults to your work and mine." He enclosed a copy of a letter he was sending to Rosenberg. It said: "I thought any intelligent man would hold to the rigor that when a hatchet-job is undertaken his respect for the most elementary craftsmanship would cause him to carry out his crime with some finesse." But Rosenberg had proven himself "an intellectual lout."[134]

Still was notorious for his fiery letters, and Rosenberg was bemused. On the back of the letter, he scribbled a note: "Actually, there is nothing offensive in 'The American Action Painters,' except for one who interprets himself in a way to be offended. True, there is a lure lying among the water lilies for those looking in innocence. I'm sorry it was you who chose to snap it up."[135] He clearly meant that his intended targets were Pollock and Greenberg. Pollock could read a phrase Rosenberg used, "apocalyptic wallpaper," as an allusion to the *Vogue* photographs and an attack on his paintings and their commercial acceptance.[136] He was right, for the action-artist Rosenberg had in mind was not Pollock. It was de Kooning.

Of the many odd things about Rosenberg's essay, none is odder than the ascription of action painting to de Kooning. Just a year earlier, the editor who published Rosenberg's essay in *ARTnews*, Thomas Hess, had published a book on abstract painting in which he had a long description of de Kooning at work on one of the *Woman* series, the figural paintings that he would begin showing in 1953. "As it is fitted into the visual structure," Hess explained, "each component must undergo tests and transformations as if each were a purely geometrical shape; then again, it must be twisted and balanced to invoke the eloquent poetry of the massive figure. Finally it is settled in the form where the widest range of meaning is offered."[137]

Pollock, too, was a methodical and careful painter. He meditated each stage of composition. Kline traced blowups of drawings. There is nothing "action" based in Newman's zip paintings. The artist Rosenberg's description of the action painter best suits is, strangely, Hofmann. Hofmann painted "from nature"—that is, he took his inspiration from some actual object—but once he started painting, he attacked the canvas with unpremeditated energy and finished quickly.[138]

Rosenberg's essay did not make an impression on artists or professional art critics. But it made an impression on the art world—on dealers, collectors, nonart intellectuals, and the press. It got additional circulation when Rosenberg reprinted it in his first collection, *The Tradition of the New*, published in 1959 with a dust jacket designed by de Kooning. "Action painting" became a popular term for abstract art and the figure of the modern artist was assimilated to the existentialist image of man.

Rosenberg always denied that he had been influenced by French existentialism. He claimed that he had stressed the concept of action long before existentialism became known in the United States, back when he was writing for *Symposium*.[139] But the story is more complicated. For Rosenberg's piece on action painting was originally intended for *Les Temps Modernes*.[140]

Rosenberg met Simone de Beauvoir on her first trip to the United States, in 1947. Beauvoir reported to Sartre that she found Rosenberg brilliant but exhausting.[141] In March 1952, Rosenberg wrote to her with an idea for a piece for *Les Temps Modernes*: "I should also like to write something about painting here—in which the act or gesture on canvas is the dominant tendency of the new movement—resulting for the most part in a total antagonism to thought; indifference to politics, manner or mores (since the only true act is, in any case, the one of painting!); and a revival of the mystique of genius."[142]

That summer, Sartre published "Les Communistes et la paix" in *Les Temps Modernes*, aligning himself, at last, with Communism and the Soviet Union. Rosenberg was annoyed, because he felt (somewhat improbably) that Sartre had stolen some of his ideas. When *Les Temps Modernes* refused to publish a letter from him addressing this issue, he pulled his piece on American art. De Kooning's wife, Elaine, was a regular contributor to *ARTnews*, and she agreed to show the retracted essay to the editors there. Hess accepted it, and, in the process of editing it with Rosenberg, turned the argument inside out. As pitched to *Les Temps Modernes*, "American Action Painters" was to be an attack on American abstract painting in the name of a Sartrean *art engagé*; Hess and Rosenberg transformed it into an encomium on abstraction. The very aspect of American painting that Rosenberg had ridiculed in his letter to Beauvoir—"the only true act is, in any case, the one of painting!"—was now represented as a kind of heroism. By this completely upside-down means, Rosenberg's essay became an existentialist manifesto for advanced American art.

Meanwhile, Peggy Guggenheim had closed Art of This Century and moved to Venice. Before she left, she loaned *Mural* to Yale, but the university was not interested in keeping it. So, with some trouble, Guggenheim managed to get the University of Iowa to take it off her hands. The transaction was finally consummated in 1951, and for many years, *Mural* hung in the studio where Iowa art students worked; it was later displayed in the library. It was finally exhibited to the public when, under the leadership of Frank Seiberling, who had moved to Iowa from Ohio State in 1959, the university built its own art museum, completed in 1969. It had become, needless to say, worth a lot of money. A sale of the painting was explored at least twice by the university, in 1961 and 1974, and debated in the state legislature in 2008 and 2011.[143] But it remains in Iowa, the most valuable work of art owned by any state in America.

6

THE BEST MINDS

Neal Cassady in New York City, 1947, shortly after he met Jack Kerouac and Allen Ginsberg. He is wearing his first suit, purchased in Chinatown. Photograph by Allen Ginsberg. (*CORBIS / Getty Images*)

1.

In 1936, when he was a thirty-year-old PhD student and instructor in the Columbia English department, Lionel Trilling was informed that he was being dismissed from the program. It was felt, he learned from a friend, that he was unhappy at Columbia and that it would be in his best interests to go elsewhere. Happiness mattered little to Trilling generally; he certainly did not see what it had to do with his merits as a student and teacher. In a highly uncharacteristic act of self-assertion, he confronted one by one the faculty he knew best and demanded an account. One by one, they assured him that their own reservations were minor. The case for dismissal had really been pressed by others.

When Trilling asked what, minor or not, their reservations were, they all said the same thing. He had "irritated many freshman students by talking about literature as sociology or psychology," the department chairman told him. Another professor said that there had been complaints about his "emphasis on 'Sociology.'" His dissertation adviser, a scholar of nineteenth-century British literature named Emery Neff, explained that Trilling's "sociological tendencies" had obscured his literary gifts "in the [doctoral] thesis as in the classroom." Neff confided to a friend of Trilling's that Trilling was not a good "fit" at Columbia because he "involved himself with Ideas," also because he was a Jew.[1]

Concerns about "fit" or "happiness" are common rationales for discrimination, and before 1945, institutional anti-Semitism was an issue at universities like Columbia, especially in fields like English.[2] "You weren't born to it," is how the chairman of the English department at Northwestern explained the matter to Saul Bellow when, around the same time that Trilling received his notice of dismissal, Bellow asked him for advice about going to graduate school.[3] Trilling's teachers had always considered him dreamy and somewhat diffident.[4] They seem to have been stunned by his chutzpah, and the decision was reversed. After receiving his PhD in 1938, he was appointed an assistant professor—the first Jewish professor in the history of the Columbia English department.

"My heartiest congratulations for this triple victory over pedants, anti-Semites and malicious rivals," Meyer Schapiro wrote to him. (Schapiro had been made an assistant professor of art history in 1936.) "Lillian and Sidney & other friends also delighted."[5] (Lillian was Lillian Hellman; Sidney was Sidney Hook, who would later claim that it was he who had persuaded Trilling to confront his department over the threat of dismissal.)[6]* To forestall the possibility that the department would balk, Trilling's appointment was made by Columbia's Committees on Education and Finance, "acting for the Trustees under their summer powers" at the behest of the university's president, Nicholas Murray Butler, an autocrat of the old school of university presidents.[7] Soon after, Neff called on Trilling and his wife, Diana, at their apartment to say that he hoped that Trilling would not use his appointment as a wedge to open the department to more Jews.[8]

Neff, a man who showed up for class wearing Lederhosen, was apparently speaking only for himself (and it is hard to imagine why he thought

---

* Hook's memories involving Trilling (at least) seem unreliable. Many years later, in 1976, Diana Trilling publicly disputed Hook's recollections of Trilling's relationship with his college classmate Whittaker Chambers.

having that conversation was a good idea). Although anti-Semitism did not disappear from humanities departments after 1945, with the establishment, at least officially, of meritocracy in higher education, it ceased being institutionally sanctioned.[9] Yale tenured its first Jewish professor, the philosopher Paul Weiss, in 1946.[10] By the mid-1950s, Trilling, Harry Levin (AB Harvard, no PhD) at Harvard, M. H. Abrams (PhD Harvard) at Cornell, Richard Ellmann (PhD Yale) at Northwestern, Leon Edel (PhD Université de Paris) at New York University, and Charles Feidelson (PhD Yale) at Yale, all Jewish, were leading figures in the field of English literature.

The Jewishness of these men had little bearing on their professional identities. "I do not think of myself as a 'Jewish writer,'" Trilling wrote a few years after his appointment. "I do not have it in mind to serve by my writing any Jewish purpose. I should resent it if a critic of my work were to discover in it either faults or virtues which he called Jewish."[11] The complaint about Trilling's "sociological" approach was much more significant than any discomfort with his Jewishness. That was what separated him from the rest of his department. Trilling may have stood up to his professors partly out of panic: he was supporting his parents and was continually short of money. He needed the income. But he also had been developing—possibly the fear of losing his position helped him realize it—a way of writing about literature that had nothing traditionally academic about it, and he rose to defend it.

"Sociological" is the wrong word for what he was doing. Trilling did not write about the institutions of literary production and reception (apart from the classroom); he did not interpret literature as a reflection of social or economic conditions; he had no interest in popular culture. His criticism was, really, political. The word "liberal" in the title of his most famous book, *The Liberal Imagination*, does not mean "free" or "disinterested," the meanings it has in the term "liberal education." It refers to a political ideology: liberalism. Trilling used literary criticism as a way to address the condition of the polity, and he saw the condition of the polity as tied up with the cultural attitudes and tastes of educated people, people like the Trillings and their friends. That emphasis and that audience might seem limited, but who else reads literary criticism? Those were the people Trilling wanted to reach. Most academics write for other academics. They are specialists talking to specialists. Trilling didn't care about other academics, and his teachers could sense it.

The year of Trilling's great (and only) professional crisis, 1936, was also the year when many American intellectuals who had been friendly to Communism started to have second thoughts. Trilling, too, had once been friendly to Communism, and he was one of the intellectuals whose views shifted. After finishing his dissertation, a critical biography of Matthew Arnold, he began writing the essays he would publish in 1950 in *The Liberal Imagination*. Liberalism was a discredited doctrine among left-leaning American intellectuals in the 1930s, but after the war, it was resurrected as the politics of enlightened anti-Communism. When the target went up, Trilling had his arrows ready.

2.

Trilling's parents were immigrants. His father, David, came from a part of Poland then controlled by Russia; his mother, Fannie, came from London, to which her father, Israel Cohen, had emigrated, also from Poland. David Trilling made his living as a men's tailor. When Lionel was born, in 1905, the family was comfortably middle class.* Lionel was bar mitzvahed at the Jewish Theological Seminary in Manhattan. Israel Cohen had two wives and thirteen children, and it was Trilling's mother and her sisters who encouraged his interest in books. "From earliest boyhood Lionel's life had been directed to an intellectual and literary career," Diana wrote in her memoir.[12]

Diana's parents, Sadie and Joseph Rubin, also came from Poland, and she spoke Polish at home as a child. The Rubins were well-off: Joseph owned a factory and the family had a chauffeur. (Joseph Rubin and David Trilling would both lose everything in the Depression.) Diana grew up in Larchmont and New Rochelle. She entered Radcliffe in the same year, 1921, that Lionel entered Columbia. They were both sixteen.[13] After graduating, Lionel spent a year teaching in an experimental college at the University of Wisconsin, then returned to Columbia to get a PhD.

Trilling's sixteen-year career as a Columbia student (he had wanted to go to Yale, but his parents didn't want him to leave the city) coincided almost exactly with a period of institutional anti-Semitism in American higher education. In 1900, 7 percent of Harvard freshmen were Jewish;

---

* Trilling's first name, which he disliked, was an Anglicized form of Lev.

in 1922, the figure was 21 percent. There were comparable increases at Yale and (in smaller numbers) Princeton, and all three schools undertook to reduce the numbers of Jews they admitted. So did Columbia.[14] To address what Columbia's dean, Frederick Keppel, explained was "a social problem," the college began requesting information about applicants' character, requiring photographs as part of the application process, and interviewing candidates.[15]

In 1919, under Keppel's successor, Herbert Hawkes, the college started administering an IQ test called the Thorndike Tests for Mental Alertness, developed by the psychologist Edward Thorndike of Columbia Teachers College (and a former student of William James). The theory was that IQ tests expose overachievers, as some Jewish students were imagined to be—that is, their test results would be lower than their high school grades predicted. Trilling was among the first cohort of applicants to take it. Overall, the changes were effective. Before they were instituted, 40 percent of entering freshmen at Columbia were Jewish. In Trilling's class, the figure was 18 percent.[16]

Still, in a country in which Jews were 3 percent of the population, 18 percent was a lot. In New York City, the institutional anti-Semitism of the 1920s and 1930, part of a national backlash against immigration, confronted a demographic tidal wave. When Trilling applied to college, more than a quarter of New Yorkers were Jewish. Thirty-nine percent of the students at Hunter College (all women), 80 percent of the students at the College of the City of New York (all men), and almost half the students at New York University were Jewish.[17] By the time of the Second World War, there were far more Catholics and Jews than Protestants in New York City. (Just 6 percent of New Yorkers were Black.)[18] The mayor, Fiorello La Guardia, had a Jewish mother and spoke Yiddish. By 1945, more Jews were living in New York City than in Western Europe, South America, and Palestine combined.[19]

The size of the Jewish population in New York made it natural for second-generation Jews to assimilate and for discriminatory barriers to fall.[20] Although some continued to try, it made no sense for schools, employers, and even private associations to exclude a quarter or more of the local population. A notion later grew up that a sense of being socially and culturally marginalized is what drew Jewish intellectuals to the coterie life of radical politics and gave them a critical eye on mainstream culture.[21] None of them ever claimed this. Most of them felt, with the same reservations that any American intellectual might have had, that they were part of mainstream culture. What they rejected was the *Yiddishkeit*, the Jewish-centered provincialism, of their parents.[22] And, of course, the overwhelming majority of second-generation American Jews had nothing to do with radical politics or cultural criticism.

Trilling's intellectual formation had two major inputs, one curricular and the other journalistic, and both were committed to exactly this belief: that in the United States, ethnic difference is something to be not suppressed or transcended but normalized. The people behind those inputs came from very different places. John Erskine was the son of a well-off New Jersey manufacturer and became a lifelong vestryman in the Episcopal Church. He received a PhD in English from Columbia in 1903 and, after several years at Amherst, returned to Columbia and began teaching there in 1909.[23] He is the father of the Columbia College course known as Literature Humanities—the one-year "great books" course required of all freshmen since 1937.*

In 1915, Erskine proposed a course in which students would read and discuss one "great book" a week. The course was intended to be a mechanism for assimilation, one based on the belief that the great books speak to everyone.[24] Opposition from the faculty and from Keppel, followed by the American entry into the First World War, held the proposal up, but in 1920, Erskine launched a two-year course for selected juniors and seniors in which groups of twenty students met once a week with two instructors and discussed classic texts in the Western tradition. The initial syllabus listed fifty-one books, starting with Homer and ending with William James's *Principles of Psychology*, published in 1890. The course was called—not Erskine's choice: he thought the name was elitist—General Honors.[25]

Trilling not only took General Honors; he took it over. In 1925, Erskine published a book called *The Private Life of Helen of Troy*, a somewhat droll novel about an unrepentant Helen after her return from Troy, in which Homer's characters talk in a twentieth-century idiom. The book became an enormous bestseller, ultimately selling over half a million copies, and Erskine resigned from Columbia. He went on to become the president of the Juilliard School.

In 1932, his course was revived by Jacques Barzun, a General

---

* Undergraduates in Columbia Engineering have a separate liberal arts requirement.

Honors alumnus now an assistant professor in the history department. And, in 1934, Barzun invited Trilling, still a graduate student, to teach it with him. They renamed it the Colloquium on Important Books and ended up teaching it together, on and off, for more than thirty years, eventually replacing it with a similar course for graduate students.[26] The course is the spine that runs through Trilling's criticism. His last book, *Sincerity and Authenticity*, published in 1972, is essentially a gloss on the reading list.

In the history of American higher education, General Honors belongs to a brief period of reaction against disciplinary specialization.[27] Research faculty are specialists first, teachers second. That is why there was faculty opposition to the course, which persisted even when Barzun and Trilling were running it. A standard college course on, say, Dante would consist of lectures by a Dante scholar with the text studied in Italian. Trilling was not a Dante scholar and he didn't know Italian. Apart from some rather poor French, he didn't have any languages at all. The idea that he was teaching Dante's *Inferno* in translation and covering the whole text in a single discussion session was a scandal.[28]

When colleagues accused Erskine of dilettantism, his response was that every great book was once read for the first time.[29] What he meant was that those books were not written for scholars, and therefore no special knowledge should be required to understand them. That was the spirit in which General Honors was taught, and it was one of the reasons the English department decided that Trilling was not a good fit. He wasn't interested in conventional scholarly standards. Even when he was awarded his PhD, one professor at his dissertation defense told him that since he had consulted only published sources, what he had written was no doubt a good book, but it was by no means a good dissertation.[30]

The other big influence on Trilling was a man who had given up hope of having an academic career. Elliot Cohen was born in Des Moines and grew up in Mobile, Alabama, where his father, who had been a rabbi in Russia, ran a small clothing store. A prodigy, Elliot entered Yale at fifteen and studied English and philosophy. After graduating in 1917, he seems to have stayed on for a year or two of graduate school but left when he realized that his religion made an academic career impossible. Instead, he became managing editor of the *Menorah Journal*.[31]

The *Menorah Journal*, founded in 1915 by a Harvard alumnus named Henry Hurwitz, was conceived, in part, as a means of raising Jewish self-esteem. Cohen turned out to be a brilliant editor. He cultivated bright Jewish college students such as Trilling, who began writing for it in 1925, at the end of his senior year. Over the next five years, Trilling contributed twenty-four essays, short stories, and reviews, plus two translations, and even worked at the magazine part-time as an editor (an unhappy experience). He stopped writing for it when Hurwitz forced Cohen out in 1931.[32]

Cohen's ambition was to get the magazine's readers (and its contributors) to see, as Trilling put it, "that society was actual and that we were in some relation to it."[33] In other words, Cohen believed that being Jewish was just another way of being in the mix. For Trilling, this was transformative. "The discovery . . . of the Jewish situation had the effect of making society at last available to my imagination," he later wrote. "It made America available to my imagination."[34] After he became an assistant professor, this was his own message to students. "As for Jewish traits of mind or character," he said in a talk to Jewish undergraduates, "I think there are none to be distinguished as inherently Jewish . . . What molds our life is the American culture."[35]

Erskine had a reputation as a charismatic teacher, but Trilling did not have much respect for him. "Had he ever any talent, or even any quality?" he wrote about Erskine in his journal. ". . . Terrible to think that he was regarded by the academic world much as I am—until Helen of Troy quite drew him beyond the academic world."[36] But Trilling never lost his awe of Cohen. "I have long thought of him as the greatest teacher I have ever known," he wrote in 1960, after Cohen died (a suicide). "If I may speak of my own particular case, I would wish to acknowledge him as the *only* great teacher I ever had."

Cohen taught him two things, he said. First, "that no idea was so difficult and complex but that it could be expressed in a way that would make it understood by anyone to whom it might conceivably be of interest." This is the premise of all literary journalism. The second was that culture is a whole. "[T]here are many of us," Trilling wrote, "who, if we live our intellectual lives under the aspect of a complex and vivid idea of culture and society, owe that idea not to the social sciences but to Elliot Cohen. Elliot's own mind was dominated by his sense of the subtle interrelations that exist between the seemingly disparate parts of a culture, and between the commonplaces of daily life and the most highly developed works of the human mind."[37] The books we read are connected to the attitudes, often barely conscious, that lie behind our everyday decisions. If you bring this insight of Cohen's to bear on Erskine's reading list, you get Trilling's literary criticism.

3.

The Trillings were converted to Communism by Sidney Hook. All three were spending the summer of 1931 at Yaddo, the artists' colony in Saratoga Springs, New York, where Hook was writing *Toward the Understanding of Karl Marx*, an influential explication that he published in 1933. Hook believed that Marxism is essentially a philosophy of action and compatible with the pragmatism of his teacher, John Dewey. (Dewey was unpersuaded.) He was a powerful proselytizer, and in 1932, the Trillings joined the National Committee for the Defense of Political Prisoners (NCDPP).

The NCDPP was a Communist front. Theodore Dreiser was chair and Elliot Cohen was executive secretary. Cohen and the Trillings were witting fellow travelers.[38] But the romance was brief. The Trillings worked as low-level administrators, and they were able to see, up close, how the Party did business. They considered it ruthless and cynical, and they soon resigned. By the time of the 1936 Moscow Trials, Trilling was still a socialist, but he had become an anti-Stalinist.

In their cohort of American intellectuals, the Trillings' experience was typical. Many of the writers who emerged after the war as outspoken anti-Communists were disillusioned fellow travelers. A few, like the Trillings' friend and Lionel's Columbia classmate Whittaker Chambers, were disillusioned Party members. Almost none had been to a Communist country. Of course, they could read the newspaper; but they felt that they knew what Communists were like and how Communism worked because they had rubbed up against Communists in the American Party (CPUSA).

That experience also made them feel that Communism was not a remote threat or a problem only for Europe, but was something that "could happen here." Tiny as the American Party was, they had once been close to it or inside it, and movements look much bigger from the inside. "I live with a deep fear of Stalinism at my heart," Trilling wrote in 1946 to Eric Bentley, an English professor at the University of Minnesota who would later join the Columbia department. ". . . I am willing to say that I think of my intellectual life as a struggle, not energetic enough, against all the blindnesses and malign obfuscations of the

Stalinoid mind of our time."[39] Trilling was writing just two weeks after Kennan wrote the Long Telegram—well before the Truman Doctrine, the Berlin blockade, and the Soviet annexation of Eastern Europe. He was already a Cold Warrior.

Bentley wrote back to suggest that an uncompromising anti-Stalinism might risk replicating the mentality Trilling found so objectionable. Trilling was not buying it. "What revolts and disgusts me in the Stalinist grab for power," he replied,

> is the hideous involvement of ideals, feelings, social indignations, exhibitions of martyrdom, self-pity. I expect a quantum of injustice in any imperium, expect contradictions as the price of order—what brings me to the puking-point is the fine feelings. And what brings me to the fighting-point is the increasingly sure sense that Stalinist power aims at the annihilation of anything that does not contribute to power.[40]

In his published writings, Trilling waged this struggle in a much more elliptical manner. He did not go after Stalinists; he went after people who couldn't see that Stalinism was a problem. He called those people liberals, and he referred to them (a subtle touch) as "we." His persona was that of a man critical of liberalism writing from within the liberal camp. This is the authorial voice of *The Liberal Imagination*.

The Liberal Imagination was Trilling's fourth book. He had published his dissertation, on Matthew Arnold, in 1939. It was reviewed by Edmund Wilson in *The New Republic*—a major recognition. Wilson called it "one of the first critical studies of any solidity and scope by an American of his generation."[41] The book was also reviewed by Robert Penn Warren in *The Kenyon Review*. Warren called it "an admirable book, well written, thoughtful, and dispassionate."[42] The British edition was reviewed in the *Times Literary Supplement*, where it was called "the best . . . book on Matthew Arnold that exists."[43] (*TLS* reviewers were then virtually all anonymous; the writer was John Middleton Murry, a friend and critical rival of T. S. Eliot's.) Contrary to what had been predicted at his dissertation defense, *Matthew Arnold* established Trilling's academic reputation. He never felt it necessary to produce another work of scholarship. He had spent twelve years on the dissertation; he wrote his next book, *E. M. Forster*, in six weeks.[44]

The choice of subject was mildly eccentric. Forster had a reputation in the United States as a novelist of manners, but of English manners. Yet Trilling found a way to recruit him to the critique of liberalism. "For all his long commitment to the doctrines of liberalism," he announced, "Forster is at war with the liberal imagination." *E. M. Forster* is a short book, but it was widely reviewed. *Time* devoted almost four columns to it and called the opening chapter "brilliant."[45]

Trilling's next book had a less happy reception. This was his only completed novel, *The Middle of the Journey*, published by Viking in 1947. Trilling's lifelong ambition was to be a novelist. And he didn't want to be a novelist like Forster or Henry James, both writers of what he approvingly called "moral realism."[46] He wanted to be a novelist like Ernest Hemingway. He knew that this was a fantasy. Few men were less like Hemingway; Trilling could barely drive a car. But he was captivated by the idea of a great artist who is indifferent to convention—a peculiar taste for a critic famous for the scrupulosity of his attention to moral obligation.

The Middle of the Journey is composed much more in the style of Forster than of Hemingway. It is an attempt to capture the split between fellow travelers and anti-Stalinists in the late 1930s. It is set in a Connecticut village where a group of writers and professors is spending the summer. The cast of this uncomic pastoral includes a fellow-traveling couple, the Crooms; a Trillingesque liberal, called Laskell; and a man who is desperately looking to break with the Communist Party, but who fears that his life may consequently be in danger. His name is Gifford Maxim, and his character was based on Whittaker Chambers.

Chambers and Trilling knew each other from their time at Columbia College. By 1947, when the novel came out, Chambers had indeed broken with the Communist Party. He had quit in fear for his life in 1938, after six years in the underground, and he had become an editor and writer at the bumptiously anti-Communist *Time* (which may explain the attention the magazine gave to Trilling's book on Forster).[47] In 1933, though, when he was still a Party operative, Chambers had approached Diana Trilling and asked her to serve as a "drop" for clandestine mail relating to Party business. (She said that she declined.)[48] Trilling used that episode in his novel.

The Middle of the Journey was criticized for being idea-driven. But what chilled the book's reception may have been not so much the prominence of the ideas as their anti-Communist implications. Those implications certainly seem to have affected Viking's promotion. The dust jacket promised "a flashing comedy of manners," but as Trilling acknowledged in a letter to Bentley, he did not have an ear for comedy. "I can imagine some wonderfully gifted comic writer who sees the sadness and avoids having to say anything explicitly," he told him.[49] The *New York Times*'s chief book critic, Orville Prescott, called the novel "about as emotionally contagious as the solution to a problem in geometry."[50] Sales were poor.

The book was spectacularly unlucky in its timing. It came out in October 1947. In August 1948, in testimony before the House Un-American Activities Committee, Chambers made the stunning accusation that Alger Hiss, a former high-ranking State Department official, was a Soviet agent. But by then, Trilling's novel was out of the stores and nearly forgotten. If *The Middle of the Journey* had come out ten months later, when everyone knew who Whittaker Chambers was, it would have been one of the most talked about books of its day. Trilling had already started another novel, this one very Jamesian in style and subject matter, but he abandoned it after writing a little more than two hundred pages.[51] After that, he never wrote fiction again.

Chambers and Hiss were iconic figures in anti-Communist versus anti-anti-Communist disagreements for the entire Cold War period, and for years Trilling tried to persuade Viking to reprint his novel and cash in on the notoriety of the Hiss case. But the press declined. The Trillings eventually became convinced that Ben Huebsch, one of the top editors at Viking whom they thought was a fellow traveler, was standing in the way.[52] A paperback edition did come out from Avon in 1966. The hardcover was finally republished by Harcourt Brace in 1975, the last year of Trilling's life. He added an introduction explaining that the character of Gifford Maxim was based on Chambers. In the first six months after publication, the book sold fifty thousand copies.[53]

4.

Trilling was forty-four when *The Liberal Imagination* came out. The book was a publishing phenomenon. It sold seventy thousand copies in hardcover and a hundred thousand in paperback, and it did something that very few books have ever done: it made literary criticism matter to people who were not literary critics.

Although "liberalism" is characterized in various ways in *The Liberal*

Imagination, it is never really defined. And as a matter of political theory, there are very different types of liberalism. There is the classical liberalism of the nineteenth century (free markets and individual rights) and the left liberalism of democratic socialism (public ownership and economic equality). And although he never referred to them as such, Trilling clearly meant to include other types as well: socialists, fellow travelers, and Stalinists. So when, in his preface, he claimed that "[i]n the United States at this time liberalism is not only the dominant but even the sole intellectual tradition," Trilling was indicating that he was treating all liberals alike.[54] How could that be? What did John Stuart Mill have in common with Karl Marx, or Leon Trotsky with John Dewey?

In Trilling's view, the faith that all liberals share is that human betterment is possible, that there is a straight, or reasonably straight, road to health and happiness. A liberal is a person who believes that the right economic system, the right political reforms, the right undergraduate curriculum, the right psychotherapy will do away with, or significantly mitigate, unfairness, snobbery, resentment, prejudice, neurosis, and tragedy. The argument of *The Liberal Imagination* is that literature teaches that life is not so simple—for unfairness, snobbery, resentment, prejudice, neurosis, and tragedy happen to be literature's special subject matter.

A classic example is money, a dominant topic in the literature of moral realism. Contrary to what classical liberalism presumes, human beings just do not behave rationally with respect to money. They hoard it, waste it, envy it, obsess over it, slave for it, marry for it, kill for it. A liberal, in Trilling's conception, is someone who thinks that money can be made not to matter more than it reasonably should. When people behave antisocially or self-destructively around money, or anything else, liberals are the people who ask whether the system is to blame.

Literature, Trilling said, puts beliefs like these "under some degree of pressure." "To the carrying out of the job of criticizing the liberal imagination, literature has a unique relevance," he wrote in a sentence frequently quoted, "not merely because so much of modern literature has explicitly directed itself upon politics, but more importantly because literature is the human activity that takes fullest and most precise account of variousness, possibility, complexity, and difficulty."[55] This is why literary criticism has something to say about politics.

Trilling called liberalism "a large tendency rather than a concise body of doctrine."[56] He was similarly vague in the first chapter of *E. M. Forster*, where he described it as "that loose body of middle class opinion which includes such ideas as progress, collectivism, and humanitarianism."[57] The vagueness might seem a trick to avoid dealing with the prima facie philosophical differences among liberalisms. But a key perception of *The Liberal Imagination* is that most human beings have ideologies, just not in the form of distinct ideas. Trilling's notion of ideology bore some resemblance to Hannah Arendt's. "[I]deology is not acquired by thought," as he put it, "but by breathing the haunted air . . . [It] is a strange submerged life of habit and semihabit in which to ideas we attach strong passions but no very clear awareness of the concrete reality of their consequences."[58]

Trilling believed, in other words, that philosophical coherence is not a notable feature of most people's politics. Their political opinions may be rigid; they are not necessarily rigorous. They tend to float up out of some mix of sentiment, custom, moral aspiration, and aesthetic pleasingness. People hold certain views because it feels good or right to hold them (which is why they have an answer for pollsters even when they have never given an issue serious thought). Trilling thought that this does not make those opinions any less potent. On the contrary, it is unexamined attitudes and assumptions—things people take to be merely matters of manners or taste, and nothing so consequential as political positions—that demand critical attention. "Unless we insist that politics is imagination and mind," he wrote, "we will learn that imagination and mind are politics, and of a kind that we will not like."[59]

The business of criticism is therefore a perilous one. Preferring one writer over another taps into more consequential differences. "Dreiser and James," Trilling warned: "with that juxtaposition we are immediately at the dark and bloody crossroads where literature and politics meet . . . The liberal judgment of Dreiser and James goes back of politics, goes back to the cultural assumptions that make politics."[60] Why, for example, do liberals admire Dreiser and Sherwood Anderson and condescend to Henry James and William Dean Howells? Trilling suggested that it has something to do with their conception of reality. Why do they find the heroines of Austen's *Mansfield Park* and Dickens's *Little Dorrit* unappealing? The answer tells us something about their conception of the will. Why does enjoying Kipling make them feel guilty? It has something to do with changing attitudes toward loyalty and the nation.

Trilling thought that people's literary preferences tell us something about the kind of human beings they wish to be and about the way they wish other human beings to be—that is, something about their morality and their politics. He summed up his methodology in an essay he published in *Partisan Review* in 1961 called "On the Modern Element in Modern Literature." (The title alludes to Arnold's inaugural lecture as Professor of Poetry at Oxford, "On the Modern Element in Literature.") "[M]y own interests," Trilling wrote, "lead me to see literary situations as cultural situations, and cultural situations as great elaborate fights about moral issues, and moral issues as having something to do with gratuitously chosen images of personal being, and images of personal being as having something to with literary style."[61] This was Trilling's "sociology."

Watching over the canon was therefore one of the critic's chief duties. The critic was a kind of public health inspector, and the job was not an easy one, since a book's politics might be quite different from its political effects. "[T]he contemporary authors we most wish to read and most wish to admire for their literary qualities," Trilling said, "demand of us a great agility and ingenuity in coping with their antagonism to our social and political ideals."[62] The critic lets us know which angels are worth wrestling with.

5.

Trilling's most famous student was Allen Ginsberg. This is almost as incongruous as it sounds. Ginsberg entered Columbia on a scholarship in the fall of 1943, when he was seventeen, and took the required literature survey class that descended from Erskine's General Honors, then called Humanities A. Trilling was his teacher. Ginsberg became infatuated with Trilling, and Trilling reciprocated not only by inviting Ginsberg over for tea and by commenting on his poems, but also by intervening twice on Ginsberg's behalf when Ginsberg was in trouble, the first time with the dean, the second with the police. Ginsberg later said he thought it was his Jewishness that made Trilling empathetic.[63]

Boundaries meant nothing to Ginsberg. They meant a great deal to Trilling, and he eventually felt compelled to assert the status difference between them. Ginsberg adjusted—he rarely allowed a useful connection to lapse—and he and Trilling remained on friendly, though sometimes cool, terms for the rest of Trilling's life. But the Trillings always treated Ginsberg as essentially an undergraduate—an interesting, possibly gifted, not fully mature young man desperate for their attention and approval.

The literary movement of which Ginsberg was chief promoter and curator, the Beats, arose out of the intersection of two disparate social circles. Ginsberg and his friends were Ivy Leaguers, young men who had gone to Columbia and Harvard. They were bookish, serious, and, by virtue of their educations, socially advantaged. The people in the other circle were drifters, hustlers, petty criminals, drug users. Some had literary aspirations, but they were effectively outside the class system, persons without cultural capital, social dropouts. They were "beat," carny slang meaning beaten down, destitute, at the bottom of the world. The Ivy Leaguers did have cultural capital, and they troped the condition of beatness. They translated it into a literary concept.

Ginsberg was from Paterson, New Jersey, where his father, Louis, was a schoolteacher and a moderately successful poet. Louis was born in Newark, the child of Russian immigrants. He met Ginsberg's mother, Naomi, in high school. She had emigrated with her family from inside the Pale of Settlement. The Ginsbergs were left-wing—Ginsberg's older brother was named for Eugene Debs, the leader of the Socialist Party—and secular. English was the language at home. (The parents spoke Yiddish with relatives.) Allen did not learn Hebrew, and he was not bar mitzvahed. The family spent two summers at a Communist summer camp, Camp Nicht-Gedaiget (Camp Not-to-Worry), in upstate New York.

Naomi worked for the Communist Party. She was a paranoid schizophrenic, and she began a long and painful life passing in and out of mental institutions when Allen was still young. He was often obliged to be her caretaker and witnessed some potentially traumatizing scenes. But he was an exceptionally cheerful child and an excellent student. Sometime in high school, he realized that he was attracted to boys. It would be his somewhat unhappy fate, as an adult, to fall in love mostly with heterosexual men.

Ginsberg's infatuation with Trilling was not unusual. Ginsberg was frequently infatuated with men. He is supposed to have chosen Columbia because a boy he had a crush on, Paul Roth, was going there.[64] And many students were attracted to Trilling. He was still an assistant professor when Ginsberg met him, but he had already established—by his distinguished appearance, his self-possessed manner, and his style of critical modulation—a mystique.[65]*

In fact, Trilling was deeply neurotic about this persona. He knew its value and he never betrayed it. But he felt it was untrue to both the personality he actually had and the one he wished he had. Trilling's disgust with his public character and ambivalence about the kind of success he achieved was lifelong; after his death, his wife and his son both wrote at length about it.[66] "I am <u>ashamed</u> of being in a university," Trilling wrote in his journal in 1948, the year he was promoted to full professor. "I have one of the great reputations in the academic world. This thought makes me retch."[67] Several years later, he complained to his psychoanalyst, Rudolph Loewenstein, that his success with the Arnold book had coincided with sexual difficulties. The two of them decided, as Trilling put it, that, "superior at this point, I refused to be superior in all."[68]

Ginsberg entered Columbia determined to become a labor lawyer, but he got turned around very quickly. In December of his freshman year, he became friends with another student in Trilling's class, Lucien Carr. Carr was from a well-off St. Louis family and had spent time at Phillips Andover (he was kicked out), Bowdoin (he either walked away or was forced to leave), and the University of Chicago before ending up at Columbia.

Carr was strikingly good-looking in an androgynous, almost exotic way. "[H]e moved like a cat," Jack Kerouac's girlfriend Edie Parker, who met him in a studio art class run by the émigré George Grosz, described him. "His movements were like mercury over rocks. His eyes were slanted, almost oriental, and pure green, so green they dazzled you."[69] He cultivated European literary and musical tastes; his hero was Arthur Rimbaud, whom he associated with libertinage, intoxication, living on the edge. He considered Ginsberg pitifully naïve and teased him. Ginsberg responded by becoming obsessed with Carr. Soon after they met, Carr took Ginsberg to the Village to meet his friend William Burroughs.

---

* Alfred Kazin on meeting Trilling for the first time, in 1942: "With the deep-sunk colored pouches under his eyes, the cigarette always in hand like an intellectual gesture, an air that combined weariness, vanity, and immense caution, he was already a personage. He seemed intent on not diminishing his career by a single word." (*New York Jew* [New York: Knopf, 1978], 43.) The Trillings, for their part, found Kazin somewhat unrefined.

Burroughs, too, was from a well-to-do St. Louis family. He was twelve years older than Ginsberg. After graduating from Harvard in 1936, he had studied medicine in Vienna, where he married a Jewish woman, Ilse Herzfeld, so she could emigrate, then returned to the United States to take courses, mostly in anthropology, at Harvard, Columbia, and Chicago. He had recently come to New York City mainly because Carr and a St. Louis friend of both, David Kammerer, had moved there. Burroughs was living on a two-hundred-dollar monthly allowance from his parents (this would continue for twenty-five years) and he had not decided what to do with his life.[70] But he had already developed his signature manner as a sort of gentleman bomb-thrower. He loved guns, experimented with drugs, read advanced literature and social thought, and was a member of the University Club in midtown, where he took friends to lunch.

In May 1944, Carr introduced Ginsberg to Jack Kerouac. Kerouac was four years older than Ginsberg. He was from a working-class family in the Little Canada section of Lowell, Massachusetts. His parents were French-Canadian immigrants, and the family spoke joual, a Quebec dialect, at home. He had entered Columbia on a football scholarship in 1940—he was a running back—but an injury, followed by a falling-out with the coach, led to his quitting the team and dropping out of Columbia in his sophomore year. After serving in the Merchant Marine and, briefly, the navy, he had returned to Morningside Heights and was living with Edie Parker. Kerouac was exceptionally handsome in a virile way, but shy and vulnerable. Like Carr, he liked to drink and carouse; unlike Carr, he was earnest and unpretentious. Ginsberg became obsessed with him, too.[71]

Three months later, in the early morning of August 14, 1944, Carr stabbed Kammerer almost to death in Riverside Park. He tied rocks to Kammerer's body with strips of clothing and dumped him in the Hudson, where Kammerer drowned, and then sought out Burroughs and Kerouac. Burroughs advised him to get a lawyer and plead self-defense; Kerouac helped him dispose of the knife. Carr turned himself in, and the story ran on the front page of *The New York Times*, which also reported the arrests of Burroughs and Kerouac as material witnesses.[72]

Kammerer was thirty-three, and he had known Carr for five years. The self-defense story that Carr's lawyers proposed was that Kammerer was a homosexual stalker who had made an aggressive advance.

"Kammerer's personality steadily deteriorated during his year in this city, until he was little more than a derelict, barely keeping himself alive by his janitorial work," was the *Times*'s account of Carr's story.[73] Carr attracted the attention of the press by appearing indifferent to the proceedings and carrying a copy of William Butler Yeats's *A Vision* with him into court. This was almost certainly an act. The idea was that Kammerer's persistent attentions had made Carr deranged.[74]

The district attorney's office bought the theory, and Carr was allowed to plead guilty to first-degree manslaughter. He served two years in Elmira Reformatory. Burroughs and Kerouac both posted bond and their cases were dropped. After Carr got out of Elmira, he settled down and had a successful career as a writer and editor at United Press International. In public, he was careful ever after to keep his distance from Ginsberg, Kerouac, and Burroughs, although they remained friends.[75]

The story of the Kammerer murder got embedded in Beat legend. Carr's version became the official version, but although Kammerer was clearly obsessed with Carr, he was not a derelict. He, too, was from a well-off family, and he had a master's degree in English from Washington University.[76] He wrote poetry, read (and possibly introduced Carr to) Rimbaud and other French writers, and was a good friend of Burroughs. Kammerer was stabbed twelve times. The real nature of the relationship is impossible to know.[77]

Once Kammerer was dead, though, the first instinct of Kerouac, Burroughs, and Ginsberg was to protect Carr. They were cautious when discussing Carr's sexuality, since his defense depended on his being traumatized by a homosexual advance. Their second instinct, though, was to turn Kammerer's murder into literature.

Ginsberg began his version, a novel called "The Bloodsong," right after Carr's conviction in the fall of 1944. Word that he was working on the subject for a writing course reached one of the deans, and he was ordered to abandon the project.[78] Kerouac and Burroughs collaborated on their version, a novel they called *And the Hippos Were Boiled in Their Tanks*—a title supposed to have derived from a news report about a fire at a zoo, though there is no record of such a fire—and they managed to work in many literary and cinematic allusions, including five references to Rimbaud.[79] (The parallel between Carr's relationship with Kammerer and Rimbaud's relationship with his lover, Paul Verlaine, who shot him, was obvious to everyone, and irresistible.)

After he and Burroughs were done, Kerouac wrote yet *another* novelization of the affair, which he called "I Wish I Were You," and sent it to an agent. The agent showed the manuscript to the editor in chief at Random House, Robert Linscott; Linscott found the subject repellent.[80] Kerouac and Burroughs submitted *And the Hippos Were Boiled in Their Tanks* to several publishers without luck, until Carr asked them to stop.* But that novel was Burroughs's first adult piece of creative writing. He always credited Kerouac with launching his career.[81] Those early attempts at fictionalization established a core principle of Beat writing, which is that you can make literature by writing about yourself and your friends. Ginsberg's "Howl," published in 1956, and Kerouac's *On the Road*, which came out in 1957, are basically group biographies.

"Allen, as classwork, is writing a novel whose hero is a fictionalized Lucien Carr, a twisted eccentric," Louis Ginsberg complained to one of his sisters in January 1945.[82] In February, Louis wrote to Trilling expressing concern about his son's "undesirable friends." "[H]e is making clever but false verbal rationalizations that the immoralist way of life (à la Gide, I think) is a valid one," he told Trilling. "Allen holds you in high esteem and places great value on your dicta."[83] Trilling seems to have ignored this, but a month later, he had cause to intervene.

As part of a feud with the maid who cleaned (or failed to clean) his dorm room and whom he suspected of being anti-Semitic, Ginsberg had written "Butler Has No Balls" and "Fuck the Jews" in the dust on his windowpane, along with a skull and crossbones and a drawing of a penis. He was duly reported to the same dean who had pulled the plug on "The Bloodsong." At Ginsberg's request, Trilling met with the dean to explain that "Fuck the Jews" was intended to make a political point, but the dean was not mollified, and Ginsberg was suspended for a year. That summer, he joined the U.S. Maritime Service, a training program for sailors joining the Merchant Marine, which counted, during the Second World War, as military service.[84]

Ginsberg wrote to Trilling from shipboard in Sheepshead Bay, off Brooklyn, to ask whether he'd had a chance to read a long poem he had given him. In order to fit in with his shipmates, he reported, he had

---

* It remained unpublished until after Carr's death in 2005. Kerouac did write a lightly fictionalized version of the story in his last novel, *Vanity of Duluoz* (1968).

purchased some Batman comic books—and "I brought here my be-loved Rimbaud."[85]

Trilling commented positively on the poem. "Your mention of Rimbaud," he added, "crystallized my impulse (a slow one) to know more about him and I am now the next name after yours on the library card of the Starkie biography [the Irish writer Enid Starkie's biography of Rimbaud came out in 1938] you so warmly recommended to me. I doubt he will ever be my 'beloved Rimbaud' as he is yours or that I will ever even understand how he can be yours; but if I cannot be affectionate to him I at least need not be ignorant!" He added, "What is <u>Batman</u>?"[86]

Ginsberg was so excited by Trilling's response to his poem that he sent the letter to Kerouac, who was duly impressed. It "represents something I'd like to happen to me someday," he wrote to Ginsberg, "namely, to be liked and admired by someone like him." He asked to keep the letter for a while so he could show it around.[87] Ginsberg composed a long reply to Trilling. "That you are unable to understand why I make so much of Rimbaud, dismays me somewhat," he wrote, and he set out to explain why Rimbaud was his "personal saint."[88] (A good deal of the explanation was derived from Delmore Schwartz's introduction to his translation—notoriously inaccurate: Schwartz's French was not good—of *Une Saison en enfer*, published in 1939.)[89]

Rimbaud did not believe in art for art's sake, Ginsberg told Trilling. He believed in experience for art's sake. Finding that civilization "offers no hope of personal salvation, no vital activity, no way of life within its accepted structure," he broke off completely and went to Africa.

> This was the exodus from society not into the futile exile of the artist, but into living salvation in the land of the primitive, unre-stricted, uninhibited . . . With Rimbaud as catalyst the problems that supposedly beset the sensitive youth of the day are crystal-lized realistically for the first time I think.

"Batman," Ginsberg also informed Trilling, "is second on the bestseller list of semiliterate America."[90]

Trilling wrote back quickly. He had read Starkie's book and conceded that "your interpretation is a just one." Still, he demurred. "You will have to understand about me that I am very largely an old-fashioned humanist, and although the humanist tradition sometimes exasperates me to the point of violence, I pretty much stay with it," he told Ginsberg. "Involved in Rimbaud's attitudes is an absolutism which is foreign to my nature, and which I combat." He thought that the ostentatious rejection of convention implied acceptance of its values: "establishment and 'success' and the power of success." "I know this is an easy way of attack," he added, "but . . . I think it is fair."[91]

This little exchange puts a frame around the difference between Trilling and Ginsberg. Trilling imagined culture—in the anthropological sense—as a Möbius strip. You can invert mainstream values, but it is mainstream values that give the inversion meaning. You're still on the strip. In the case of someone like Rimbaud, Trilling thought that a move to the underside was just another way of achieving the same set of socially constructed goals that everyone else was trying to achieve—only doing it in the name of iconoclasm and rebellion.

Poems like Rimbaud's, or like Ginsberg's in emulation of Rimbaud's, don't come from some place not on the strip. They do not represent an independent alternative to the way things are. They are among the things that are, even when they belong to what Trilling would later call "the adversary culture."[92] The adversarial is part of the system; it helps to hold the other parts in place. This is why, in the sort of phenomenon that fascinated Trilling, responsible liberals feel better adjusted for having an appreciation of art and ideas that are contemptuous of the values of responsible liberals. It validates them in their place because it makes the world seem round. There is, in the end, no right or wrong side of the strip, just different ways of fooling yourself about where you are.

Ginsberg thought that there was a wrong side, or a false side. He was not very coherent, in his letter to Trilling about Rimbaud, about what the alternative looked like. He offered up a list of hard-boiled character types as examples of another way to be: "the Raymond Chandler hero, the sharp-eyed gambler, the dead-pan cardsharp . . . the psychopath who moves in his pattern unaffected by moral compunction."[93] In 1948, though, while (as he told the story) reading William Blake's poetry and masturbating alone in his apartment in East Harlem, he had an experience he described as "a sudden awakening into a totally deeper real universe than I'd been existing in."[94]

The visionary moment was fleeting, but it convinced him that ordinary consciousness is out of touch with the "real universe," and he dedicated himself to finding ways to expand the mind. This became the rainbow Ginsberg forever chased. He would spend much of the 1960s proselytizing with Timothy Leary on behalf of LSD. By then, though, he and Trilling had become each other's cautionary example.

6.

The Beats had a male muse. He was Neal Cassady, the protagonist of both *On the Road*, where he is Dean Moriarty, and "Howl," where he is "N.C., secret hero of these poems, cocksman and Adonis of Denver."[95] Cassady was an uncanny cross between W. C. Fields and James Dean—a screwup with a profile, a stud with an endless supply of goofy gab. He was a serial seducer who lived in the moment. Many people who knew him and liked him thought he was a con man, and some people who knew him, including Burroughs and Carr, disliked and avoided him.[96]

A lot of the Cassady phenomenon had to do with sex. He was, as Kerouac told his friend John Clellon Holmes, "a vast semeny kind of guy."[97] He pursued women obsessively, but he was comfortable having sex with men if other considerations made it worthwhile. Holmes considered him "a psychopath in the traditional and most rigorous sense of the term. That is, he acted out everything that occurred to him."[98] He charmed people to get what he needed, and he did it in the psychopath's way: by concentrating all his attention on the other person and anticipating every thought they had.

"Neal, a tower of unfathomable energy, does not destroy people's natural defenses against him: he leaps over them. He leaves your capacity to judge him intact, but he makes it useless. He moves so quickly that one can only concentrate on trying to keep up," Holmes wrote soon after meeting him. "When he wants something, he displays a tremendous arsenal of weapons of all varieties by which to attain his end. Kindness, thoughtfulness, charm, malice, amoralism: it is all possible with Neal."[99] Cassady's second wife, Carolyn, said the same thing: "He was a master at getting you to think that he knew exactly where you were and what you needed and he could always supply it. Everybody could recognize the brilliance of his mind but you simply couldn't stay with it, your mind couldn't work that fast."[100]

People did find him hard to resist. Most of those people needed something from Cassady, too—sex or companionship or good times.

And Cassady had no material ambitions. His idea for getting rich was a scheme for betting on the horses. Mainly, he was content to get by, and although he had three wives in rapid succession and juggled his attentions between them and assorted girlfriends, he was intermittently serious about all of them. Everything about Cassady was intermittent. He had a kind of sociosexual ADD.

Not surprisingly, Cassady embellished the story of his life, and a good deal of his autobiography, *The First Third*, is fabrication. Most of it made its way into Beat legend anyway.[101] And the underside of his behavior, the damage he left behind by forever moving on, tended to be romanticized. He was a bigamist; he stole from friends and from people who let him stay with them; he abandoned girls he made pregnant. He beat women and he raped his first wife, LuAnne Henderson.* He may have had as many as four illegitimate children before his first marriage. "Neal never enjoyed it unless there was violence," Carolyn said about sex with him. "He couldn't manage it any other way . . . It had to be rape." It is unlikely that all of what "Howl" refers to as his "innumerable lays" were entirely consensual. He was also, for much of his life, a frustrated and unhappy man.[102] That much is clear from *On the Road*: Dean is a priapic pinball. No one would want to be like him.

Cassady grew up on the streets of Denver, where he lived with his father, who was a wino, and he learned to cope by relying on enormous energy, adaptive wit, and movie-star looks. He was a car thief and joyrider, and spent some time in reform school, but he got interested in books and decided he wanted to be a writer. He heard about Ginsberg and Kerouac from a Columbia student who lived in Denver, Haldon (Hal) Chase, and he drove and bussed his way across the country to look them up. He brought along his wife, LuAnne. She was sixteen years old (she was fifteen when they married); he was twenty. They arrived in New York City at Christmastime in 1946 and he stayed until March.

Cassady was made to order for Ginsberg and Kerouac in the same way that the heroes of Hollywood Westerns were made to order for Sartre and Beauvoir. He embodied the unmediated. As Holmes put it, "Neal was enormously attractive to people who sat on their ass most of

---

* "Luanne was covered with discolorations from the beatings he [Cassady] has given her in the last days." John Clellon Holmes, Journal, January 19, 1949. "Neal was known as a woman beater." Carolyn Cassady, interview with Gina Berriault, *Rolling Stone* (October 12, 1972).

the day in a dim room, biting their nails, and typing out shit."[103] By the time Cassady left New York, Kerouac had determined to write a novel about him, and Ginsberg had fallen in love with him. Cassady fixed on Ginsberg as the possible key to his literary ambitions; he saw that Ginsberg was gay and he wasted no time initiating sex. That summer, Ginsberg went to Denver hoping to be with Cassady, and Kerouac followed by bus to Chicago, hitchhiking the rest of the way, the first of the cross-country trips that became the basis of *On the Road*. Cassady added Ginsberg to his sexual juggling act.

In August, Ginsberg reported to Trilling that he was returning to New York via Texas (where Burroughs had moved to start up a marijuana plantation). "Traveling with me will be one of Denver's dissolute young bucks (his name is Neal Cassady) whose education, for the time, I find myself superintending," he wrote. ". . . Dispite [*sic*] a background of bumming and reform schools and living off women he strikes me as the wisest & most powerful personality I have run across, in school or out, among the young."[104] He wondered whether Trilling might be interested in helping out with Cassady's education. (It is hard to imagine what Ginsberg was thinking.) He was also writing, he informed Trilling, to address the "sterility" of their relationship. The last time they talked, he said, he had tried to have an intimate conversation and felt rebuffed by what he called Trilling's "artificiality of conduct."

Trilling took his time responding. "I think our relationship is not intended to be the kind you assume in your letter," he finally wrote. "Its right condition is set by the original connection between us, that of student and teacher, and by the difference in our ages . . . I value highly the relationships that are conditioned by, as it were, function. If you present your life to me in the manner that you have done, I am willing to receive seriously and affectionately what you tell me, but I can do that only as your teacher and older friend; it would be impossible and pointless for me to reciprocate in anything approaching kind."[105] Ginsberg did not renew the subject. By then, he had other reasons for unhappiness. Cassady had broken off with him and he had, in his desolation, taken a boat to Africa.

A few years later, in 1949, Ginsberg needed Trilling again. He had got involved with a friend of Burroughs named Herbert Huncke, a drifter, small-time criminal, and gay hustler who hung out around Times Square. Huncke had introduced Burroughs to heroin, a habit

Burroughs would struggle with for years. He showed up one day at Ginsberg's apartment, starved and penniless, and Ginsberg let him stay; Huncke reciprocated by using the place to stash stolen goods. In April, Ginsberg was in a car conveying some of those goods when police tried to stop it. There was a chase and the car tipped over. Ginsberg ran off, but he was tracked down and arrested. According to the *Times*, he told the police that he was a copy boy for a news service who had become involved with criminals "to obtain 'realism' he needed to write a story."[106] (If we substitute "poet" for copy boy, we get an idea of Ginsberg's real relationship, in his own mind, with the vagrants and dropouts he describes in "Howl.") The police locked him up.

After his father bailed him out, Ginsberg wrote immediately to Trilling. "I suppose that you are aware by this time of what I have let happen to 'me' now," he told him. "I hope the publicity around Columbia is not too widespread."[107] At Trilling's suggestion, he called Meyer Schapiro, with whom he had taken a class. Schapiro was calm and empathetic. "He told me to come over, and sat talking with me about the Universe for 2½ hours," Ginsberg told Kerouac; "also told me about how he was in jail in Europe for being a stateless bum."[108] (That was in 1923, when Schapiro was traveling through Europe with Whittaker Chambers, one of his closest friends.)[109]

Trilling stepped in. He took the Ginsbergs to see Herbert Weschler, a Columbia Law School professor and a high-powered figure who had worked in the Justice Department during the war and had argued before the Supreme Court.* His advice was to plead insanity. Both Lionel and Diana Trilling testified successfully on Ginsberg's behalf at a hearing to determine whether he should be charged, and the university arranged for him to enter the New York Psychiatric Institute, part of Columbia Presbyterian Hospital, in upper Manhattan, where he stayed for seven months.[110] Louis Ginsberg wrote to Trilling to thank him: "Ever since Allen entered college, your name has been a household word with us," he wrote. ". . . Allen looks up to you with something of veneration."[111] Huncke got five years. As he put it later, "I ended up doing a bit. Somebody had to do it." He would spend most of the next decade in prison.[112]

Ginsberg was twenty-three when he entered the Psychiatric Institute,

---

* Weschler later represented *The New York Times* in the landmark libel case *New York Times v. Sullivan*, decided in 1964.

and seven months of treatment is a long time. Two important things happened to him there. On his first day in the wards, he met a fellow patient, two years younger, named Carl Solomon. A "big queer from Greenwich Village," Ginsberg described him to Kerouac, ". . . also a true Rimbaud type."[113] Solomon had been in the Merchant Marine, and in 1947 he had jumped ship in France and gone looking for the existentialists. In Paris, he happened on a reading being given by the actor and director Antonin Artaud. This would have been a famous performance at the Théâtre Vieux-Colombier, in Saint-Germain-des-Prés, billed as *Histoire vécue d'Artaud-Momo*, Artaud's first public appearance after being released from nine years in asylums. The date was January 13, 1947. It was an enormous cultural event in Paris, and Solomon likely did not actually get into the theater or see Artaud (who died a little over a year later). But he was excited by the pandemonium surrounding the reading, and he became fascinated by Surrealism. Solomon gave Ginsberg what he later called "an apocryphal history of my adventures," some of which Ginsberg used in "Howl."[114] That poem is dedicated to Solomon.

The other significant effect institutionalization had on Ginsberg was to convince him to pursue a "normal" life. "A turning point has been reached in that I am not going to have anymore homosexual affairs anymore [*sic*]," he wrote to Kerouac on the day he was released; "my will is free enough now to put this in writing as a final statement."[115] It is an indication of the effectiveness of this pledge that, a few months later, Ginsberg wrote a long letter to Cassady that concluded: "I also finally got to bed with Claude. Strange after all these years. I was impotent. That's even stranger and more true."[116] Cassady would have known who "Claude" was. Back when they were students at Columbia, Ginsberg used to call himself Gillette; Lucien Carr adopted the name Claude de Maubris.[117]

7.

Ginsberg was not confined to the ward while he was in treatment. He spent weekends at his father's house in Paterson. He also met with Trilling. One day, the subject of Kerouac's new novel came up. After the two unpublished Lucien Carr books, Kerouac had started another autobiographically based novel combining stories about his New York friends with memories of his childhood in Lowell. This was *The Town and the City*, published in March 1950.

Ginsberg had read the manuscript, and he spoke highly of it to Trilling, who he hoped might help promote it. Trilling was still recovering from the poor reception of his first novel and the abandonment of his second, and he recorded the conversation in his journal. "We spoke of Kerouac's book," he wrote. "I predicted that it wld not be good & insisted. But later I saw with what bitterness I had made the prediction—not wanting K's book to be good because if the book of an accessory to murder is good, how can one of mine be?—The continuing sense that wickedness—or is it my notion of courage—is essential for real creation."[118]*

About a year later, Trilling spent an evening with David Riesman, and they discussed Trilling's difficulty writing fiction. "[W]ith absolute precision he laid his finger on my literary trouble," Trilling wrote afterward, "although he did not know it the thing that has kept me from writing—my admiration of an [sic] commitment to what I have called the fierce and charismatic writers—as he said, my greater respect for Dostoevsky than Tolstoi. He was enormously perceptive, very brilliant, on the point." Trilling received Riesman's analysis as a "manumission," a release from bondage. "I could not fail to see that my impulse for the fierce and charismatic is connected with all the confused tendencies that I have been discovering in my psn [personality] . . . —the meaning of the sadistic ideal in its character as representative of the superego. My sense that from no [sic] on I could be content to be quiet, that this was my own thing to do."[119]

The "sadistic ideal" is Trilling's own term, but it apparently derives from Freud's concept of the "ego ideal," an internalized image of the self to which the ego aspires—essentially, a feature of the superego—which Freud introduced in "Zur Einführung des Narzißmus" ("On Narcissism") in 1914. Trilling seems to have associated his attraction to "fierce and charismatic" or "wicked" writers—the attraction he had distanced himself from in the correspondence with Ginsberg about Rimbaud—with a sadistic aspiration in his own personality.

In his Marxist phase, Trilling had been hostile to Freud. In 1931, he

---

* In his journals, Kerouac described an episode around this time when Trilling refused to recognize him on the street—"in the most farcical way, because so solemn, as if I'd suddenly acquired leprosy and it was his rational duty to himself as Liberal Enlightener of Intellectuals to repair at a safe distance from the area of my septic running sores." (*Windblown World: The Journals of Jack Kerouac*, ed. Douglas Brinkley [New York: Viking, 2004], 253.)

was asked to review *Civilization and Its Discontents* for the *New Freeman*, a Trotskyist journal. He wrote a piece calling the book absurd. But the *New Freeman* folded, and the review never ran; later on, Trilling wondered what things would have been like for him if that piece had appeared.[120] For by then, he had a major stake in *Civilization and Its Discontents*, and in particular in what Freud called *der Todestrieb*, the death drive. He made *Civilization and Its Discontents* the final text, replacing *The Principles of Psychology*, in the course he taught with Barzun, and the titles of the two essay collections he brought out after *The Liberal Imagination*—*The Opposing Self* in 1955 and *Beyond Culture* in 1965—both allude to the death drive. The concept turns up in the concluding chapter of his last book, *Sincerity and Authenticity*. The death drive is what grounded Trilling's anti-utopianism.

Trilling was in analysis for most of his adult life; he started seeing Loewenstein after the war.[121] Between them, Hitler and Stalin had driven psychoanalysis, which the Nazis called the "Jewish science," out of Europe. Its practitioners—the ones who were not murdered—were forced to immigrate to Britain and the United States (a country Freud held in contempt). The number of psychodynamic psychiatrists who fled to the United States after 1933 was small, probably no more than two hundred and fifty, and only around fifty who were institutionally certified psychoanalysts.[122] But they were preeminent in their field, and they dominated American psychiatry in the 1950s, a decade during which, thanks in part to the founding of the National Institute of Mental Health in 1949, psychiatry underwent a professional boom, and Freudian ideas enjoyed popularization.[123]

Between 1946 and 1956, the number of psychiatric residency programs in the United States doubled. In 1954, 12.5 percent of medical students chose psychiatry as their specialization, an all-time high, and half the patients in American hospitals had been admitted with psychiatric diagnoses. Most psychiatrists in the United States were not analysts, but they used Freudian terminology, and psychoanalysis was the principal science of the mind, the theory taught in medical schools and on which the first two editions, 1952 and 1968, of the *Diagnostic and Statistical Manual of Mental Disorders* (*DSM*) were based.[124] In the 1950s, everyone had heard of penis envy and the Oedipus complex.

Loewenstein was part of the exodus. He was from Poland, and he had been a popular training analyst in Paris; Jacques Lacan was one of his analysands.[125] When the Germans invaded, Loewenstein fled to Marseille and then, in 1942, to New York City, where he quickly established himself. From 1950 to 1952, while Trilling was in treatment with him, he was president of the New York Psychoanalytic Institute. (Diana Trilling disliked Loewenstein intensely, and eventually had her own analyst intervene and persuade Lionel to drop him.)[126]

Along with the émigrés Ernst Kris and Heinz Hartmann, Loewenstein was a leading proponent of ego psychology, which became the most influential school of psychoanalysis in the United States.[127] The idea was that people have the ability, by the exercise of will and reason, to adapt to external conditions. That this was regarded as a novelty is an indication of how inward-looking and pessimistic Freudian psychodynamic theory had become.

The centerpiece of Freudian pessimism was the *Todestrieb*. Among the many peculiarities of the translations in the *Standard Edition* of Freud's works, which was overseen in Britain by James Strachey (brother of Lytton) and Anna Freud, but whose publication was subvented largely by the American Psychoanalytic Association, is the translation of *Trieb* as "instinct."[128] Freud used *Instinkt* to refer to animal behavior. *Trieb* means "drive," something less reflexive and less specific than an instinct, something more like an urge or a persistent impulse. Drives can be (and generally are) displaced, redirected, or repressed, things it does not make sense to say about instincts.

Freud claimed a scientific basis for the death drive, which he first introduced in *Jenseits des Lustprinzips* (*Beyond the Pleasure Principle*), in 1920. He cited biological evidence that all organic impulses are essentially conservative, and that one of these impulses is to return to an inorganic state. Why, then, does every creature fend off threats to its survival instinctively? Because, Freud concluded, "the organism wishes to die only in its own fashion."[129] To spare the self, the death drive can be redirected outward as aggression. "The instinct is then called the destructive instinct [*Destruktionstrieb*], the instinct for mastery, or the will to power," Freud said.[130] Sadism can therefore be understood as a redirection of a more primary impulse, masochism. We hurt others instead of ourselves because we wish to live a little longer, so that we may die on our own terms.

The *Todestrieb* was one of the few Freudian concepts that most of his followers found impossible to accept. "[T]he most bizarre monster of all his gallery of monsters," an English psychiatrist, William McDougall, called it.[131] At first, Freud pretended to regard the concept as speculative and provisional. In fact, he was thrilled with his new idea.[132] It made sense of sadism, masochism, aggression, and other destructive impulses. It explained the repetition compulsion associated with trauma, in which victims cannot stop reliving events they have every reason to wish to forget. It even explained the tendency of analysis to fail due to resistance and negative transference (hostility toward the analyst) on the part of the patient. As Freud concluded in one of his last essays, with the monitory title "Die Endliche und die Unendliche Analyse" ("Analysis Terminable and Interminable"), there must be something within the analysand that makes them prefer to suffer rather than change, and this something he associated with the death drive. The thesis of *Civilization and Its Discontents* is that culture is a by-product of the struggle between two internal drives—Freud called them the "Heavenly powers"—Eros and death.[133] Eros explains why people strive for harmony and unity; the *Todestrieb* explains why they will never get there.

Apart from an allusion to the success of the Nazi Party in the Reichstag elections that Freud added to the second edition, in 1931, the only contemporary reference in *Civilization and Its Discontents* is to communism. That was Freud's example of an Eros-driven project doomed to fail because of the inexorability of the death drive. "The communists believe that they have found the path to deliverance from our evils," he wrote. "According to them, man is wholly good and is well-disposed to his neighbour; but the institution of private property has corrupted his nature. The ownership of wealth gives the individual power, and with it the temptation to ill-treat his neighbour; while the man who is excluded from possession is bound to rebel in hostility against his oppressor."

This was a caricature of Marxist thought, but Freud was treating communism simply as the type of thinking that imagines that social reforms can eliminate aggression and cruelty. "I have no concern with any economic criticisms of the communist system," he went on; "I cannot enquire into whether the abolition of private property is expedient or advantageous. But I am able to recognize that the psychological premises on which the system is based are an untenable illusion . . . Aggressiveness was not created by property . . . [I]t forms the basis of every relation of affection and love among people." Even if we were to abolish property, he went on, there would still be sexual jealousy. And even "[i]f we were to remove this factor, too, by allowing complete freedom of sexual life and thus abolishing the family, the germ-cell of civilization, we cannot, it is true, easily foresee what new paths the development of civilization could take; but one thing we can expect, and that is that this indestructible feature of human nature will follow it there."[134] The death drive is in the biology.

Unhappiness does not arise because human beings become more civilized, in other words; unhappiness is a condition of life per se. Trilling agreed with Freud. The imperviousness of the personality to cultural and social engineering was the position he had taken in the preface to *The Liberal Imagination*. That was what literature shows us. But Trilling also saw a way to put the concept of the death drive to a positive use. The case he picked was McCarthyism.

In 1951, Sidney Hook revived an organization called the Committee for Cultural Freedom that he and Dewey had briefly headed and renamed it the American Committee for Cultural Freedom (ACCF), an organization for liberal anti-Communists. In 1952, Hook issued a pamphlet based on an article he had published in *The New York Times Magazine* a year before called "Heresy, Yes—Conspiracy, No!," in which he laid out the ACCF position on whether Communists were protected by the principle of intellectual freedom. (A book version was published by John Day in 1953.)

"Liberalism in the twentieth century must toughen its fibre, for it is engaged in a fight on many different fronts," Hook wrote.

> It must defend the free market in ideas against the racists, the professional patrioteers, and those spokesmen of the status quo who would freeze the existing inequalities of opportunity and economic power by choking off criticism. It must also be defended against those agents and apologists of Communist totalitarianism who, instead of honestly defending their heresies, resort to conspiratorial methods of anonymity and other techniques of fifth columnists.[135]

Hook's distinction between dissent (protected) and deception (proscribed) was a tricky needle to thread.

Both Trillings joined the ACCF; Diana eventually became a member of the executive board. And in 1953, Lionel had an opportunity to thread Hook's needle when he was asked to chair a four-man Columbia committee charged with formulating the university's position on congressional investigations into the loyalty of professors—in particular, what to do when professors assert their right against self-incrimination and refuse to answer questions.

This was a live issue at Columbia, because the university had recently had to finesse the case of an untenured lecturer in the anthropology department, Gene Weltfish, who had taken the Fifth Amendment before the Senate Internal Security Subcommittee (also known as the McCarran Committee), one of at least a hundred teachers to do so in congressional hearings on Communists in education.[136]* Faced with pressure from some trustees to fire her, Columbia's president, Grayson Kirk, got the board to pass a rule limiting the number of years a lecturer could serve to five. Weltfish had been in the job since 1936; she was let go. She was not able to obtain another academic position until 1961. The university explained that its decision was purely bureaucratic and had had nothing to do with her political views.[137]

When Trilling's committee issued its statement, *The New York Times* reported it as a triumph for civil liberties: "Educators Attack Congress Inquiries: School Red Investigations Are 'Unnecessary and Harmful,' Columbia Group Asserts" was the headline.[138] But Trilling felt that this was not the message his committee had intended to convey, and he wrote a letter to the paper to set it straight. It was true, he wrote, that the committee had stated that "it cannot be made a condition of membership in the teaching profession that a person surrender rights which are guaranteed by the law of the land." However, he went on, "it was the intention of the statement not only to say that a refusal to testify must not be automatically condemned but also to say that a refusal to testify must not be automatically condoned." Some people might claim the Fifth "for purposes of evasion"; others might do so "by reasons of principle and honor."

---

* Weltfish had already attracted the attention of the FBI when she published, with her Columbia colleague Ruth Benedict, a pamphlet for the Army called *The Races of Mankind*, arguing that racial differences are cultural, not biological. A Southern congressman denounced the pamphlet for reporting that Northern Black people outperformed Southern white people on Army IQ tests. Up to 750,000 copies were distributed, however.

This distinction rendered the right otiose, of course, since it meant that it could be honored only in the cases of people who didn't need it, who were just being principled.* In other cases—and Weltfish, whose political views were well known, would have fallen into this category— Trilling thought it was proper to infer that the witness had something to hide. And he reminded the *Times* that the committee's report had concluded that "membership in Communist organizations almost certainly implies a submission to an intellectual control which is entirely at variance with the principles of academic competence as we understand them."[139]

And this was exactly the formula Kirk needed: it was reasonable to interpret taking the Fifth as an attempt to conceal an affiliation "at variance with the principles of academic competence." Weltfish remained fired. Columbia subsequently adopted a policy of procrastination and waited for the wave of anti-Communist anxiety to subside, which, in a few years, it did.

The principle invoked by opponents of congressional inquiries into the views of educators was the principle of academic freedom. Academic freedom does not mean that professors can write or teach anything they like. What it means is that decisions about who gets hired and who gets fired, and why, are made by the faculty, not by politicians, trustees, regents, alumni, coaches, or other nonacademic parties.[140] There was a major test of this principle at the University of California, where, in 1949, the university's Board of Regents required the faculty to sign a loyalty oath. U.C. faculty had been obliged to swear allegiance to federal and state constitutions since 1942; this new oath required them to affirm, in addition, that they were not members of the Communist Party.

The faculty balked—not at excluding Communists from teaching, but at firing professors who refused to sign the oath.† For two years, the faculty battled the Regents, and thirty-one professors were fired. Finally, the faculty agreed to sign an oath that the state legislature had

---

* The reason many witnesses took the Fifth is that it asserts only a personal privilege. Once a witness admits involvement in any organization under scrutiny, they are legally obliged to answer questions asking them to name other people.
† As late as 1943, there was a secret committee of Berkeley faculty that was a Communist Party cell. The physicist J. Robert Oppenheimer belonged to it. Whether he and the others were "card-carrying" members of the CPUSA is uncertain, but that may be a technical distinction.

adopted and required of all state employees. This was evidently not regarded as an abrogation of the principle of faculty self-governance. (In 1952, the California Supreme Court ordered the dismissed faculty reinstated; it was not until 1956 that the American Association of University Professors, essentially the national union for professors, censured the university.)[141]

It is estimated that about six hundred teachers and professors in the United States lost their jobs in the anti-Communist purges, more than half of them in New York City.[142] In a country with 960,000 public school teachers and (by 1955–1956) 300,000 college and university faculty, that was less than a hundredth of a percent.[143]* The chill, however, was substantial. In a national survey of social science professors in 1955, a majority of interviewees agreed that threats to intellectual freedom had increased in the past five years, and a minority reported feelings of apprehension. Still, an overwhelming majority stated that their own work and teaching were unaffected.[144] Although the anti-Communist purge of schools and universities is often called McCarthyism, McCarthy had little interest in educators.† His principal target was Communists in the government, particularly the State Department and the armed services. The educational purge was carried on by other politicians and administrators, and at many levels of government. It was not restricted to Communists, either. Educators were persecuted for associations with any of the "subversive" organizations on the often arbitrary official and unofficial lists. Homosexuals were frequently caught up in these "investigations," on the theory that they were susceptible to blackmail.

Obviously, real spies do not carry cards saying who they are. (Ted Morgan, *Reds: McCarthyism in Twentieth-Century America* [New York: Random House, 2003], 267.)

* The total number whose careers were damaged by "McCarthyism" is hard to estimate. McCarthy's Senate subcommittee itself caused perhaps forty government employees to lose their jobs, and not one was convicted of a crime. But many people resigned rather than be caught up in investigations, and a few committed suicide, although usually for a combination of reasons. Some government agencies, notably the Foreign Service, simply stopped hiring new people or else cleared appointments with McCarthy first. More important were the many local and state anti-Communist groups that pressured employers to not hire or to fire persons suspected of disloyalty. An outside estimate of the number of Americans who lost their jobs in those years (which could be dated 1947 to 1957) is ten thousand. (Larry Tye, *Demagogue: The Life and Long Shadow of Senator Joe McCarthy* [Boston: Houghton Mifflin Harcourt, 2020], 336–39.)

† Which is not to say he had no interest. He was obsessed with Harvard, since its presidents, James Conant and Nathan Pusey, had made public their opposition to his investigations. Pusey had been president of Lawrence University, in Appleton, Wisconsin, McCarthy's hometown, and had endorsed an attack on him in the 1952 Senate race. A lot of McCarthy's crusade was political score-settling.

In 1953, the Group for the Advancement of Psychiatry (GAP), formed in 1946 under the leadership of the psychiatrist William Menninger, met to discuss the psychological effects of loyalty oaths, and the California case was a main topic of discussion. A committee charged with studying the issue reported that loyalty oaths were "only one manifestation in a growing general trend towards enforcement of conformity of thinking and acting." Loyalty oaths cause psychological damage: they endanger the development of the ego by restricting access to "the object world," distort the development of a "workable super-ego" by "emphasizing the external threat at the expense of self-responsibility," and threaten "the ego-ideal appropriate to a free and democratic society by introducing increasingly contradictory ideals and by depreciating the image and model value of the teacher."[145]

Trilling took exception to the GAP report, and two years later, in an address to the New York Psychoanalytic Institute and Society, which he expanded and published as a little book called *Freud and the Crisis of Our Culture*, he made his case. What he disputed was the assumption that cultural conditions—in this case, a repressive political climate—damage individual psychology. He pointed out that Freud had lived in Vienna, where anti-Semitism was virtually the official culture, yet "the cultural circumstance in which he was reared did not, so far as I can make out, impair the functioning of his ego or his super-ego."[146] What enabled the self to resist cultural pressures, Trilling argued, was the death drive. He was in no position, he said, to judge whether Freud's concept stood up "under scientific inquiry." He understood it simply to name an element in the self that is intractable to social conditioning. This idea was "liberating," he said, because "[i]t suggests that there is a residue of human quality beyond the reach of cultural control."[147] That was what he meant by the titles *The Opposing Self* and *Beyond Culture*: they referred to this residual immunity to socialization and acculturation.

Trilling said that the example of Freud's Vienna was "in some degree unfair, for the society of Vienna, although certainly not what we would call free and democratic, was apparently such a mess of a society that one might, without difficulty, escape whatever bad intentions it had; and its tolerance of mess may lead us to conclude that it had certain genial intentions of freedom."[148] American society, however, was dangerously *un*messy. It acculturated by seduction rather than coercion. In liberalism's "free" culture, in which there are no countervailing pressures, the individual has no choice but to conform. In fact (and this turn was characteristic of Trilling), wasn't anti-conformity just another type of conformity? It seemed to him to amount to not much more than "the right to have had some sympathetic connection with Communism ten or twenty years ago." For most liberals, he went on, "our settled antagonism to that instance of reactionary tendency we call McCarthyism is simply the badge of our class . . . Admiring non-conformity and loving community, we have decided that we are all non-conformists together."[149]

In citing Freud's relation to anti-Semitism, Trilling was possibly thinking of his own success in overcoming anti-Semitism at Columbia, an experience that had made him feel empowered rather than damaged. But the Austrian example was ill-chosen. The German annexation of Austria—the *Anschluss*—in March 1938 was welcomed by many Austrians, and the persecution of Jews began as soon as the German army arrived. Edward R. Murrow launched his career at CBS News reporting from Vienna by radio as an eyewitness to the looting of homes of Viennese Jews.[150] Soon after, Anna Freud was picked up and interrogated by the Gestapo, and this finally persuaded Sigmund to flee. He and Anna secured exit visas in June 1938, and went via Paris to London, where, a year and a half later, he died of cancer of the jaw.[151] Freud had five sisters; four of them died in the camps, one at Theresienstadt, the others probably at Auschwitz and Treblinka.[152]

In a century that had showed how easily inchoate paranoia and resentment can be mobilized into a program of oppression and genocide, it was a little strange for Trilling to discount the dangers of political persecution in the United States. And his claim that liberals "cannot really imagine non-conformity" leaves open the question of what genuine nonconformity would have looked like to Trilling. There would be a test very soon. For a few months after Trilling gave his talk on Freud to the New York Psychoanalytic Institute, Allen Ginsberg wrote "Howl."

8.

After his discharge from the New York Psychiatric Institute, Ginsberg remained in New York City attempting to form a heterosexual attachment. In 1954, he moved to San Francisco, planning to go to graduate school at Berkeley. He adopted non-bohemian dress, got a job in market research, and began living on Nob Hill with a woman named Sheila Williams Boucher, who worked as an advertising copywriter and who knew the Bay Area jazz scene.[153]

Ginsberg gave different accounts of what happened next. He was seeing a psychiatrist named Philip Hicks at the Langley-Porter Psychiatric Hospital and Clinic, part of the U.C. Medical School in San Francisco. One day, Hicks asked Ginsberg what he really wanted. Ginsberg said what he really wanted was to live with another person and write poetry. So why don't you? Hicks said. Ginsberg had evidently never got this advice from a psychiatrist before. The conversation seems to have changed his life. Either just before it or soon afterward, he met Peter Orlovsky.[154]

Orlovsky was from a broken family. He was born on the Lower East Side, where his father, a Russian émigré, tried and failed at a business making silk-screened neckties. Orlovsky dropped out of high school at seventeen and began working in a series of menial jobs. In 1953, he was drafted and ended up serving as a medic in a San Francisco army hospital. After he was discharged, he was picked up by a painter named Robert LaVigne, and he was living with him when Ginsberg met him in December 1954. Two months later, Ginsberg and Orlovsky began living together. Like Ginsberg's other major love interests, Orlovsky was primarily heterosexual, but he and Ginsberg worked out a sexual arrangement that kept them together for the rest of Ginsberg's life.[155]

Six months later, Ginsberg produced "Howl." Ginsberg was normally a slow writer, but the first part of the poem ("I saw the best minds of my generation") and the third part ("Carl Solomon! I'm with you in Rockland") were written in a concentrated rush in August 1955. On October 7, at the Six Gallery in North Beach, in a group reading with half a dozen West Coast poets, Ginsberg read Part I of "Howl." There were about a hundred people in the audience—Kerouac was present, passing out wine—and the event became legendary. People remembered it as a breakthrough.[156]

To some extent, this was a retrospective consensus. Michael McClure, one of the poets who participated—it was his first reading; he was twenty-two—later described the reaction to hearing Ginsberg read

"Howl." "In all of our memories no one had been so outspoken in poetry before—we had gone beyond a point of no return," he said in a lecture in 1980. "None of us wanted to go back to the gray, chill, militaristic silence, to the intellective void—to the land without poetry—to the spiritual drabness. We wanted to make it new."[157] Back in 1959, however, McClure told a reporter that when he first heard "Howl," he thought it was "a terrible poem. I was very involved in the French idea of poetry at that time. And then, gradually, it seeped in."[158]

One of the people who saw right away that the poem might become important was Lawrence Ferlinghetti, the founder and owner of City Lights Pocket Book Shop in North Beach. (Like *Les Temps Modernes*, the bookstore was named after a Chaplin movie.) As it happened, Ferlinghetti, too, had studied with Trilling. He was a graduate student at Columbia in 1947 (Ginsberg was still there) before going to Paris to write his dissertation, on the city in modern literature. He, too, became somewhat obsessed with Trilling; he is supposed to have attended all of his classes.[159]

Ferlinghetti had launched a paperback book line that August. After the reading, he went home and wrote to Ginsberg what Ralph Waldo Emerson had written to Walt Whitman after reading *Leaves of Grass*. "I greet you at the beginning of a great career." He added, "When do I get the manuscript."[160] A reprise of the Six Gallery reading was held at Berkeley in the spring, this one attracting press attention. And on May 16, Ginsberg had "Howl" and the other poems he had written in San Francisco, including "America" and (possibly his best poem, written in twenty minutes) "Sunflower Sutra," mimeographed. This was the collection that would be published by City Lights that fall as *Howl and Other Poems*.

Ginsberg dittoed somewhere between twenty-five and fifty copies, and he sent one to Schapiro and another to Trilling. "They are natural developments of the method & practice I was pursuing about 5 years ago," he explained to Trilling in his accompanying letter. "There seems to have been enuf mercy around to get me to heaven anyway, no?" He hoped that Trilling would let him know what he thought, and he added, in a postscript: "If you like these poems see what you can do to have them reviewed because in normal run of things they likely will not be."[161]

Trilling did not mince words. He wrote back:

Dear Allen,

I'm afraid I have to tell you that I don't like the poems at all. I hesitate before saying that they seem to me quite dull, for to say a work which undertakes to be violent and shocking that it is dull is, I am aware, a well known and all too easy device. But perhaps you will believe that I am being sincere when I say they are dull . . . There is no real voice here. As for the doctrinal element of the poems, apart from the fact that I of course reject it, it seems to me that I heard it very long ago and that you give it to me in all its orthodoxy, with nothing new added.

Sincerely yours, Lionel Trilling[162]

Ginsberg also sent a mimeograph to his father. "It has violence; it has life; it has *vitality*," Louis wrote back. ". . . I am glad that you are finding happiness and perhaps some purgative cleansing in your writing poetry. I fervent[ly] hope fame and success will come your way."[163]

7

THE HUMAN SCIENCE

Visitors to *The Family of Man* exhibition in Moscow, 1959. Photograph by Carl Mydans. (*LIFE Picture Collection / Getty Images*)

1.

When the Second World War began, seven European nations—the United Kingdom, France, the Netherlands, Belgium, Spain, Portugal, and Italy—had jurisdiction over some 40 percent of the earth's land area and more than a third of its population.[1] It was the high point in a history of European colonialism that dated back to 1415, when Portugal captured the North African city of Ceuta. Twenty-five years after the Second World War ended, those empires, apart from a few mostly short-lived holdouts, had vanished. Tens of millions of square miles and hundreds of millions of people had been liberated. By 1970, more than eighty former colonies had become independent sovereign states.[2]

The Cold War and decolonization were coterminous.[3] They are the duck-or-rabbit of postwar world history. The Cold War can be explained as ideologically camouflaged imperial rivalry, in which anti-colonial struggles functioned as great-power proxy wars. Or the great-power conflict can be understood as a reaction to the undoing of colonialism, which put a quarter of the globe into motion and drew the United States and the Soviet Union, by trying to manage the outcome, into repeated confrontations.

Those confrontations had some strategic significance (often less than political leaders claimed), but their ideological significance was great. Both the United States and the Soviet Union were officially anti-imperialist; each accused the other of being imperialistic.[4] That capitalist countries inevitably turn imperialist was Communist dogma since the time of Lenin. That Communism is an ideology committed to expansion and even world conquest was a rationale frequently advanced in American foreign policy debates.

It was hardly conceivable that the United States or the Soviet Union would take a disinterested position on decolonization. Of course major powers have a stake in the political alignment of smaller powers: realism dictates that they should. The challenge on both sides was to influence the alignment of the decolonizing regions—or what was called, after the term was coined in France in 1952, "the Third World"—in the name of those states' independence from outside influence.[5] This was not hypocrisy. It was exactly the politically and ethically vexed problem it appears to be.

The two world wars transformed major-power opinion about colonialism. In 1914, European—and by then, American and Japanese—political leadership was pro-imperialist. Creating empires was what major powers did. Thirty-one years later, that way of thinking, for all intents and purposes, was extinct. The European powers in 1945 were financially destitute and could not have sustained their colonial positions even if they had wanted to.

Colonial possessions had been valuable sources of raw materials—in 1939, 94 percent of the world's rubber came from British and Dutch colonies—and trade did follow the flag (which often followed the church). But European nations sold their manufactured goods largely in domestic markets and "developed" countries.[6] In 1910, for example, Germany's colonies—more than a million square miles of territory, all of which would be confiscated after the First World War—accounted for less than 1 percent of Germany's exports.[7] You could take rubber out of Malaya, but you were not going to sell a lot of automobile tires to Malayans.

As a result, the imperial powers ran large trade deficits, importing far more goods and services from their colonies than they exported. But these deficits were—somewhat counterintuitively—quite beneficial. That is because the income from the overseas assets, like the rubber plantations, did not stay in the colonies; it flowed back to Europe along with the raw materials, supporting a high level of consumption by a rentier class.[8] For European countries owned the companies that harvested the rubber and drilled for the oil. They were not paying the "natives" for those goods. They were paying themselves.*

The civilizing mission was not, or not merely, a fig leaf for economic exploitation. It was the rationale for European colonization in the late nineteenth century. That mission and its hollowness is what Joseph Conrad, who spent twenty years in the French, British, and Belgian merchant marine, represented in the character of Kurtz in *Heart of Darkness* in 1899. The book came out in the middle of a huge burst of territorial expansion. Between 1876 and 1915, Europe added 10 million square miles to its empires. Britain acquired 4 million square miles, France 3.5 million. (The United States acquired a little more than 100,000 square miles of territory, most of it in the Philippines.)[9]

Unlike earlier episodes, some of which produced "white-settler colonies" such as South Africa and Australia, late nineteenth-century expansion was explicitly labeled "imperialist," and the nature of the power differential, the only common element in the many varieties of colonial relations, was defined in a new way. In earlier periods, nonwhite peoples were "othered" by Europeans. They were figured as simple and uncorrupted (as in Michel de Montaigne's essay "Des Cannibales" in 1580) or exotic and decadent (as in Eugène Delacroix's painting *La Mort de Sardanapale* in 1827). As caricatural as those representations were, they figured non-Western societies as alternative modes of being human. (On the ground, of course, and in the slave trade, less nuanced understandings of otherness were manifest.)

---

* It's useful to keep in mind that the major beneficiaries of imperial economics constituted a very small fraction of the population. In 1910, the top 10 percent owned 90 percent of the wealth in France and more than 90 percent in Britain, where 1 percent owned 70 percent of the wealth. (Thomas Piketty, *Capital in the Twenty-First Century* [Cambridge, MA: Harvard University Press, 2014], 339–45.)

This changed after 1876. Nonwhite non-Europeans started to be considered on a scale of white European norms and, by that measure, as backward and inferior—the view dramatized in E. M Forster's *A Passage to India* in 1924.[10] Nonwhites, to this way of thinking, were peoples who could not govern themselves. Some, such as the Indians and the Algerians, might acquire European ways, but many, such as peoples in the Pacific islands and sub-Saharan Africa, never would. And what made nonwhite people inferior was their nonwhiteness. It was a biological idea, derived from Lamarckianism, Social Darwinism, eugenics, and physical anthropology. There was widespread belief among white people in a phylogenetic theory according to which the nonwhite races belonged to earlier stages in the evolution of the species.

Racism did not disappear after 1945, but the scientific discourse that supported it shrank dramatically. Physical anthropology was supplanted by cultural anthropology as a way of understanding human difference. Human beings were different because their cultures, not their biologies, were different. Cultural anthropology had its origins in nineteenth-century Germany, but the form that became dominant after the Second World War and influenced thinking across the humanities and social sciences arose out of a meeting between a French exile and a Russian exile in New York City.

2.

The French exile was Claude Lévi-Strauss.[11] In many respects, Lévi-Strauss was a typical Parisian academic. He was formal and aloof—even people who liked and admired him remarked on a certain coldness—disdainful of modern life, and extremely clever.[12] He was elected to both the Collège de France, which was founded in the sixteenth century and has only fifty professors, and the Académie française, which dates from the seventeenth century and has just forty members, known as *les immortels*.

These honors meant a great deal to Lévi-Strauss. He liked the recognition; he also respected the institutions. He made a point of abjuring politics because he believed in the disinterested pursuit of knowledge. He was happy in an ivory tower. Still, he became a public figure. This was partly because academics sometimes do become celebrities in France, and partly because, despite the demurrals, Lévi-Strauss probably enjoyed having an audience. But it was mainly because of a book he wrote hastily during a brief period of professional frustration, *Tristes Tropiques*.

Lévi-Strauss was not a *normalien*. He was born in 1908 in Brussels, where his father, a portrait painter, was working on a commission, and he was raised in Paris's Sixteenth Arrondissement, where he would live most of his life. He was discouraged from applying to the École Normale Supérieure and took a joint degree in law and philosophy at the Sorbonne instead. He disliked both subjects. He met Simone de Beauvoir in 1929 during the pedagogical evaluation stage of the *agrégation*, and he finished third on the oral examination, which he took in 1931, the same year as Simone Weil.

Anthropology was not a well-established discipline in France. It was recommended to Lévi-Strauss by a friend of Jean-Paul Sartre's, Paul Nizan. Around the same time, Lévi-Strauss happened to read *Primitive Society*, by Robert Lowie, an Austrian émigré teaching at the University of California. Ethnography, work on actual human beings, seemed exhilarating after philosophy, a discipline practiced in an armchair. An opportunity to pursue the new enthusiasm came in 1934, when Lévi-Strauss was recruited to join the faculty at the recently opened University of São Paulo. The following February, he and his wife, Dina Dreyfus, also an ethnologist, went to Brazil.[13]

Apart from casual exploration outside São Paulo while he was at the university, Lévi-Strauss made two ethnographic expeditions in Brazil. The first lasted about five months, from November 1935 to March 1936 (the Brazilian summer), when he visited groups known as—to use the names Lévi-Strauss used—the Caduveo and the Bororo. The second, a major undertaking, financed in part by the French government and with supplies requiring the services of thirty oxen, lasted about nine months, from May 1938 to January 1939. On that trip, he encountered three more indigenous groups, remote and quite small: the Nambikwara, the Mundé, and the Tupi-Kawahib.[14]

Subtracting preparation and travel time, Lévi-Strauss spent less than a year with his subjects, and he never stayed more than a few weeks in any one place. Much of that time was devoted to collecting artifacts to bring back to Paris, labor he later regretted as wasted. He knew none of the languages of the people he was studying. In the case of the Mundé, with whom he spent a total of four days, he didn't even have a translator. Except for a week in Pakistan in the 1950s and brief trips to British Columbia in the 1970s, that was all the fieldwork Lévi-Strauss ever did.[15] He learned most of his anthropology in a library.

When Lévi-Strauss returned to Paris, in March 1939, he had no idea what to make of the data he had collected. He started writing a novel, called *Tristes Tropiques*, in the style of Conrad, one of his favorite writers, but abandoned it. When the war began, he served as a liaison officer for the British Expeditionary Force (BEF), a post that turned out to be supererogatory when, less than a month after the Germans invaded, the survivors in the BEF, nearly two hundred thousand men, were evacuated from Dunkirk; Paul Nizan was one of the French casualties. Lévi-Strauss returned to teaching, but in October, he was fired under the Vichy government's Jewish Statute—one of about a thousand French Jews in education to lose their jobs.[16]

Then, unexpectedly, he received an invitation from the Rockefeller Foundation to teach at the New School for Social Research in New York City, where a program to bring in endangered European scholars had been in place since 1933. Lowie had read an article by Lévi-Strauss on the Bororo in the *Journal de la Société des Américainistes*, and he and Alfred Métraux, a Swiss anthropologist whom Lévi-Strauss had met in Brazil and who was teaching at Yale, proposed him. Since there was a job waiting in America, the paperwork was straightforward. It was a matter of finding a ship. Lévi-Strauss invited Dina—they had separated—to come with him. She declined (and would join the Resistance) and, on March 24, 1941, he sailed from Marseille on a boat carrying André Breton and 220 other passengers, including the Trotskyist Victor Serge, who was fleeing France as an undocumented Russian alien with his twenty-year-old son, Vlady Kibalchich.

Lévi-Strauss admired the Surrealists—in France before the war, Surrealists and anthropologists formed semi-overlapping circles—and he and Breton began a friendship that continued in New York, where Lévi-Strauss arrived, via Martinique and Puerto Rico, at the end of May.[17] (Lévi-Strauss got along well with Breton, although he thought him, he said, rather grand.)[18]

He found an apartment on West Eleventh Street, in a building where, he later learned, Claude Shannon, the founder of information theory, was also living. At the New School, he taught under the name Claude L. Strauss in order not to be confused with the blue jeans manufacturer. He met the leading anthropologists in the United States: Lowie, Margaret Mead, Ruth Benedict, Alfred Kroeber, and the teacher of them all, Franz Boas, a German émigré who taught at Columbia.[19] Back before the First World War, Boas had been a leading debunker of claims about racial difference based on physical anthropology, and he was one of the first anthropologists to shift the focus of the discipline to culture.[20] Boas was in his eighties and long retired; Lévi-Strauss was sitting next to him when he died of a heart attack during lunch at the Columbia Faculty Club in 1942.[21]

Along with Breton and other exiles, Lévi-Strauss wrote and delivered French-language radio broadcasts—Allied propaganda—for the U.S. Office of War Information from its office on Fifty-Seventh Street. He became a friend there of a woman with whom Sartre would later fall in love, Dolorès Vanetti.[22] Lévi-Strauss was close to the exiled Surrealists; they shared an interest in pre-Columbian culture. He, Breton, and Max Ernst shopped for Native American artifacts in Third Avenue antique stores.[23] He also discovered the New York Public Library, and for three years he spent every morning there reading in the American Room. "What I know of anthropology I learned during those years," he said.[24]

In 1942, through the efforts of Alvin Johnson, co-founder and director of the New School, the École Libre des Hautes Études was launched. It was designed for French-speaking academic refugees, and was housed on West Twelfth Street, next to the New School itself.[25] That is where Lévi-Strauss was introduced to the Russian exile Roman Jakobson. (The introduction was facilitated by another Russian exile, Alexandre Koyré, who had once studied with Husserl.)[26]

Jakobson was a prodigy and a polymath. He is supposed to have spoken fifteen languages. He was twelve years older than Lévi-Strauss and had already lived in Russia, Czechoslovakia, Denmark, Norway, and Sweden. Not all the stops in that itinerary were freely chosen. In Moscow, where he was born, he was involved in the study of language and folklore and in avant-garde literature and art, specifically, Russian Futurism. The poet Vladimir Mayakovsky and the painter Kazimir Malevich were friends. When he was nineteen, Jakobson founded the Moscow Linguistic Circle. He also participated, in a group that included the literary critic Victor Shklovsky, in the creation in St. Petersburg of the Obščestvo izučenija Poètičeskogo Jazyka (Society for the

Study of Poetic Language, or OPOJAZ). A chief interest of both groups was the nature of poetic language. The school of literary theory known as Russian Formalism arose out of their work.[27]

In 1920, Jakobson went to Czechoslovakia as a translator in a Soviet Red Cross mission to Russians who had been interned in concentration camps there during the war. Disaffected with the mission, he elected to remain in Czechoslovakia. He married a Czech folklorist, Svatava Pírková, and in 1937 he became a Czech citizen. He was a member of the Prague Linguistic Circle, made up mostly of Russian and Czech linguists, and he taught at Masaryk University in Brno.

The Prague linguists, and, in particular, another Russian expatriate and a close collaborator of Jakobson's, Nikolai Trubetzkoy, were anti-Nazi. In 1938, Trubetzkoy died of a heart attack possibly brought on by a Gestapo raid on his house.[28] When the Germans occupied the country after the Munich Agreement, in March 1939, they closed Masaryk University, and friends warned Jakobson, who was Jewish, that he was in danger. He hid in the apartment of his wife's parents in Prague until visas could be obtained, and in April, he and his wife arrived by train (via Berlin, from which Jakobson mailed a postcard to astonished friends) in Denmark.

They soon had to move again, this time to Norway, where they arrived on September 1, the first day of the war. In the spring, the Germans threatened to bomb Oslo, where the Jakobsons were living, and they fled to Sweden, part of the way with Jakobson hiding in a coffin in the back of a hearse and part of the way on skis. They stayed in Sweden a year.

In May 1941, with an invitation from the New School, they were able to get a boat to New York. Two days out at sea, their ship was boarded by Germans checking the identity of the passengers. The Jakobsons managed to pass themselves off as refugees from Russia—then still a German ally. Less than two months later, when Germany and Russia were at war, they would not have been so lucky.[29]

Jakobson was a bon vivant; Lévi-Strauss was not. But their friendship lasted forty years.[30] Each attended the other's lectures, delivered in French, at the École Libre des Hautes Études. Jakobson's were on phonology; Lévi-Strauss's were on kinship. The discovery that the two subjects might be responsive to the same methodology was the birth of postwar structuralism.

3.

Structuralism is anti-empiricist, anti-historicist, and anti-humanist. It rejects a priori almost everything most people believe indispensable to humanistic study: attending to the particularity of cultural objects, interpreting them in light of the circumstances in which they were produced and the intentions of their producers, evaluating their moral and political implications, and regarding them as irreducible to a scientific explanation. Structuralism is a science of culture.

When you look at all the languages, all the kinship systems, or all the poems in the world, what you see on the surface are snowflakes—sheer variety. Each language, kinship system, and poem is different from every other. You can study them by comparing them, or you can study them historically, by tracing their evolution over time. But comparative and historical studies only give you more data. In order to understand languages, kinship systems, and poems—none of which is required by biology, all of which are cultural—you can't just collect information about them. You have to understand why human beings create them, what their function is. Only then are you in a position to discover what Jakobson, in the very first lecture Lévi-Strauss heard him give, in 1942, called "les invariants à travers la variété"—"the invariants across the variety."[31]

When Lévi-Strauss started attending the lectures, he was hoping to get some tips on devising a notation for transcribing the languages of the groups he was studying. Instead, he experienced what he called a "revelation."[32] Jakobson's lectures, he later said, "were stunning . . . His dramatic gift was unequalled; he transported his audience, who had the justifiable impression that they were experiencing a key moment in the history of thought."[33] After just two of the lectures, he reported to his parents on "the remarkable linguistic course of a colleague who provides me with knowledge essential to my work."[34]

The revelatory insight was the concept of invariants. As data, the material Lévi-Strauss brought back from Brazil and the information he was gathering in the New York Public Library were inchoate, just a huge pile of facts. The science of phonetics, Jakobson explained in his lectures, was in the same condition. Phoneticists had accumulated massive amounts of information about the sounds that human beings make when they speak, but they had neglected to ask *why* human beings make those sounds.

The answer is not difficult: in order to communicate. Those sounds mean something, and it follows that they must be organized in a way that enables them to do so. The apparent randomness on the surface implies a system underneath, and that system is the invariant. It underlies all individual speech acts. It is what makes the sounds people utter meaningful, and not just noise, to people in the same language group. Phonology is the study of these systems and was one of the areas the Prague Linguistic Circle worked on. Jakobson appears to have been the first person to call their approach "structuralist."[35]

As Jakobson explained, the phonological theory he laid out in his lectures derived from his own work with Trubetzkoy and from earlier work by the Polish linguist Jan Baudouin de Courtenay and the Swiss linguist Ferdinand de Saussure. Structuralist analysis begins with the basic quantum of spoken language, the phoneme. A phoneme is a vocal sound that has significance. In some languages stress (as in Russian) and pitch (as in Mandarin) are phonemes, in others (as in English) generally not. In some languages /l/ and /r/ are different phonemes (as in French), in others (as in Japanese) generally not.

By definition, phonemes signify. But they don't refer to anything. In English, /b/ before -at signifies something different from /m/ before -at, but /b/ and /m/ mean nothing in themselves. The significant feature of /b/ is that it is not /m/, or any other phoneme that might be in that place. "A phoneme signifies something different from another phoneme in the same position," as Jakobson put it: "this is its sole value."[36]

It's like a deck of playing cards. You can create a virtually limitless number of card games based on how you make rank, suit, and color signify. Rank, suit, and color have no content in themselves and they refer to nothing outside the deck of cards. They are signifiers without signifieds. Their meaning is entirely relational. Jakobson came to believe that there are just twelve binary oppositions in the world's languages—open versus closed, acute versus grave, and so on*—and that each language selects some set of these binaries from which to construct its phonological system.[37]

Lévi-Strauss became convinced that with structural linguistics, the study of culture had become a science. In 1945, in the first issue of a

---

* 1) Vocalic/non-vocalic, 2) consonantal/non-consonantal, 3) interrupted/continuant, 4) checked/unchecked, 5) strident/mellow, 6) voiced/unvoiced, 7) compact/diffuse, 8) grave/acute, 9) flat/plain, 10) sharp/plain, 11) tense/lax, 12) nasal/oral.

new journal, *Word*, that Jakobson helped launch in New York, Lévi-Strauss announced that a revolution had occurred. Structural linguists, he predicted, would "play the same renovating role with respect to the social sciences that nuclear physics, for example, has played for the physical sciences."[38]

The trick was to treat other subjects of social scientific inquiry on the model of language. "Although they belong to *another order of reality*," Lévi-Strauss wrote, "kinship phenomena are *of the same type* as linguistic phenomena."[39] Like phonological systems, kinship systems are symbolic. That is, they are systems in which something always stands for something else. That is what makes them cultural. All sexually reproducing organisms have progenitors and offspring; only humans have uncles, aunts, in-laws, cousins, and so on, *as part of a symbolic system*. A maternal elephant can have a male sibling, but elephants (it is assumed) do not have a concept of the avuncular. And a human is an uncle, hence avuncular, only by virtue of his relation to the other categories in the kinship system.

Lévi-Strauss argued that kinship systems have three essential elements: consanguinity (brother/sister), affinity (relationship by marriage), and descent (parent/child). These are the invariants, the deck of cards, with which each culture operates. Since nature does not require kinship systems, the question about them is the same as the question phonologists ask about phonological systems: What is their function? Lévi-Strauss thought that the purpose of kinship systems is to enable men to exchange women with other men.* Kinship systems mark off available mates from unavailable ones. It's a binary system, like phonics. How do we know this is their purpose? Because of the incest prohibition. Lévi-Strauss thought that the prohibition against incest has nothing to do with an evolutionarily implanted fear that offspring of consanguineous mates may be genetically inferior, or with psychic conflict between filial and erotic emotions (or, as Freud proposed, with the fear of castration). The reason for the incest prohibition is to require people to seek or be assigned their mates from another family, because this strengthens social bonds.

The prohibition, therefore, is universal. It can be highly restricted—to

---

* He adapted the theory of societies as exchange economies, with acknowledgment, from a famous work by the French sociologist Marcel Mauss, *Essai sur le don* (*Essay on the Gift*) (1924).

only younger sisters, for example—but you can't have a society without one. "The primitive and irreducible character of the basic unit of kinship," as Lévi-Strauss put it, ". . . is actually a direct result of the universal presence of an incest taboo [*prohibition de l'inceste*]. This is really saying that in human society a man must obtain a woman from another man who gives him a daughter or a sister."[40] Language exists so that words can be exchanged; kinship systems exist so that women can be exchanged. They are both, in effect, means of communication, or information exchange. They enable human beings, at some cost to autonomy, to form societies. "[L]inguists and sociologists do not merely apply the same methods," Lévi-Strauss later wrote, "but are studying the same thing."[41]

This can seem an ingenious description of marriage practices, just as phonology can seem an ingenious description of speech sounds. And to the extent that language and kinship systems are thought of as the equivalents of playing cards, there is nothing scientific about structuralist analysis. It's just a clever way of making sense of the data. But Lévi-Strauss and Jakobson believed that they were onto something that was scientific. They thought they were making a discovery about the nature of the mind.

They began with the assumption that the human vocal apparatus evolved in concert with the brain. As humans became able to produce more subtly differentiated vocal sounds, their brains had to become better able to process those sounds, to pick out phonetic differences. If language-as-communication is the basic function that the mind evolved to perform, it follows that all other cultural outputs could be organized "like a language"—because that is the way the brain works. It has evolved, through natural selection, to treat binary pairs as related couples, and to manipulate those relationships. The most basic form of human cognition is the binary I/not-I. But all "natural" categories—kin/stranger, nature/culture, *en-soi/pour-soi*, avant-garde/kitsch, or, for that matter, "alternative ways of life"—seem to be perceived as binary oppositions. It's how we cognize the world.

Once we had language, on this theory, we had this capacity—or, once we had this capacity, we had language, and kinship systems, and all the rest of human culture. "[T]here is a direct relationship between what we may know of the structure of the brain and the way in which communication processes operate," Lévi-Strauss announced at a symposium in

1952 at which Jakobson was present. "And, of course, communication is not only a field for linguistics, but it can be said that society is, by itself and as a whole, a very large machine for establishing communication on many different levels between human beings."[42]

All culture is therefore amenable to structuralist analysis. "The customs of a community, taken as a whole, always have a particular style and are reducible to systems," Lévi-Strauss later wrote. "I am of the opinion that the number of such systems is not unlimited and that . . . human societies, like individuals, never create absolutely, but merely choose a certain combination from an ideal repertoire that it should be possible to define"—as Jakobson had argued about languages.[43] So he was always on the lookout for examples of basic binary oppositions in other fields. He was excited to learn from Meyer Schapiro, for example, that all of Renaissance architecture, painting, sculpture, and decoration could be analyzed using just five pairs of polar terms: linear versus picturesque, parallel versus diagonal, closed versus open, composite versus fused, and clear versus unclear.[44] And he was fascinated by developments in genetics, cybernetics, and information theory because they seemed to him to corroborate the structuralist hypothesis about the nature of the mind.[45]

4.

When the war ended, Lévi-Strauss was instrumental in disbanding the École Libre (which led to some hard feelings) and in negotiating with the Rockefeller and Ford Foundations the funding of a new social science division, known as Section VI, in the École Pratique des Hautes Études in Paris. French academics returning from the École Libre formed the core of the new faculty; Lévi-Strauss would eventually teach there himself. (In 1975, Section VI became the École des Hautes Études en Sciences Sociales.)[46] Jakobson, who could not go back to Czechoslovakia, took a position at Columbia. In 1949, he moved to Harvard, where, splitting his time with MIT, he spent the rest of his career.

Lévi-Strauss returned to Paris in January 1945 and reunited with his parents, who had lived in the south of France during the war. The Germans had looted their Paris apartment, and they had lost everything. He quickly returned to New York to serve as cultural attaché in the French consulate, a position whose few responsibilities included chaperoning French visitors, like Albert Camus, around the city. He met Raymond de Saussure, the son of the linguist, who was a psychoanalyst, and, through him, Trilling's analyst, Rudolph Loewenstein, and other émigré psychoanalysts.[47] He had plenty of time left over for the New York Public Library.

In 1948, he turned down an offer from the University of Chicago, the first of several from American universities he declined, and returned to Paris, where, in June, he defended his dissertation, *Les Structures élémentaires de la parenté* (*The Elementary Structures of Kinship*). Virtually all of the dissertation was researched and written in the United States. It was published in 1949 and reviewed in prominent intellectual journals in France. In *Les Temps Modernes*, Beauvoir called it "a stunning revival" of French social science and ended her review with the words *il faut le lire*: it must be read.[48]

In fact, the book was easy neither to read nor to obtain. Only a small number of copies were printed, and although it was appreciated by some British and American anthropologists, it remained untranslated for twenty years.[49] Still, it secured Lévi-Strauss's academic reputation.

But in 1949 and again in 1950, he was defeated for election to the Collège de France, devastating disappointments. He later said he suspected "an element of anti-Semitism."[50] His second marriage, to a woman he had known since childhood, Rose-Marie Ullmo, had broken up, and short of money, he temporarily moved to the Eleventh Arrondissement. Though he got an appointment at the École Pratique des Hautes Études, he seems to have felt at an impasse personally and professionally, and it was in this period that he produced two uncharacteristic works: an intervention on a political issue and a memoir.

The intervention was a pamphlet called *Race and History*, part of a series commissioned by the United Nations Educational, Scientific, and Cultural Organization (UNESCO). The United Nations, which opened for business in October 1945, is the paradoxical face of postimperial international relations. On the one hand, the UN is a resurrected League of Nations and incorporates liberal internationalist principles. The UN protects sovereignty, and it instantiates the belief that world government can be a guarantor of peace.[51] This is the image of the mission projected by one of its two governing bodies, the General Assembly.

The United Nations is also an organ of realism. It helps the great powers lock into place a world order that does not threaten their interests, a function institutionalized in the organization's other governing body, the Security Council. The Security Council gave France, the United Kingdom, the United States, the Soviet Union, and China (the Republic of China, not the Communist People's Republic) veto power. (Soviet objections to the scope of this power almost prevented the UN from coming into existence. Stalin's eventual concession may have been linked to recognition of the Lublin government in Poland. By 1952, the Soviet Union had used the veto forty-four times, the United States zero.)[52] The Security Council serves to check ambitions to major-power status among the world's other nations. This institutional structure is a paradox and not a simple contradiction because it models a great-power world that is at the same time anti-colonial.

On the subject of colonies, the UN Charter is circumlocutionary. Old imperial terms are replaced by talk of "trusts" and "territories." But by organizational design, the major powers serve as protectors of the sovereignty of member states, and as decolonization got under way, these increased from 51 in 1945 to 99 in 1960 to 127 in 1970. The major powers were obliged to speak the language of equality and cooperation, even as they tried to control (or block efforts by others to control) international affairs.

The new rationale in international relations represented an overturning of the race-and-ethnicity-defined view of the world that had prevailed in the imperial powers at the time of the League of Nations. The intellectual challenge was therefore to unlink the human sciences from that old, hierarchical view and to associate them instead with the new, post-racial understanding. This is the project that *Race and History* was part of.

Lévi-Strauss tended to downplay his public activities.[53] But he was involved with the United Nations for most of the 1950s, ultimately serving as secretary-general of the International Social Sciences Research Council of UNESCO. In 1949, he met with social scientists from seven other countries to draft a report on "race problems," which UNESCO published in 1950. The cause of differences among groups, these experts (as they were identified) explained, is not biology; it is culture. "For all practical social purposes, 'race' is not so much a biological phenomenon as a social myth," they wrote. ". . . The unity of mankind from both the biological and social viewpoints is the main thing. To recognize this and to act accordingly is the first requirement of modern man."[54]

Two years later, Lévi-Strauss published a pamphlet called *Race and History*. As Boas had forty years before, Lévi-Strauss attacked what he called "false evolutionism," the notion that the races are at different stages on the evolutionary path of the species. Much of his essay elaborates on points already made in the 1950 experts' declaration.[55] But he also argued against a notion that might be thought implicit in a phrase like "the unity of mankind": the notion of a "world civilization." We don't want a global monoculture, he said, because cultures benefit from contact with cultures that are different. He compared civilization to a game of roulette. Social groups invent cultural systems—languages, marriage laws, cuisine, mythologies—that are, in effect, gambles on survival. The greater the diversity of available systems, the better the odds of winning. The pre-Columbian cultures he studied in Brazil, he said, were virtually destroyed in part because of insufficient cultural heterogeneity. They lacked resources for creating new means of adaptation. It is by "pooling . . . the wins which each culture has scored in the course of its historical development" that civilizations flourish, he said, and "the greater the diversity between the cultures concerned, the more fruitful such a coalition will be."[56] At the end of the essay, he conceded that diversity is a finite resource. Cultures that exchange become more alike, which means that the cost of intercultural contact is an overall reduction in diversity. Three years later, in the memoir *Tristes Tropiques* (he resurrected the title from his abandoned novel), this reservation was amplified into a warning.

Tristes Tropiques was commissioned for a series called Terre Humaine, launched by an anthropologist and geographer, Jean Malaurie, who had recently returned from northern Greenland. "I wrote the book in a kind of rage and impatience," Lévi-Strauss later said. "I also felt some remorse. I thought I should have been writing something else."[57] He believed he was "committing a sin against science."[58] The writing took him a little over four months, October 1954 to March 1955. His method of composition was not unlike the one Jack Kerouac used for *On the Road*—a continuous typescript with no breaks (though on separate sheets of paper). Speed was possible in part because Lévi-Strauss simply pasted in excerpts of previously published scholarly work, of his and his first wife's field notes, and of the abandoned novel, from which he cannibalized the title and a bravura description of a sunset at sea.[59] He claimed that he had not taken pains with the writing, but the book was received as (and is) a classic of French prose.

A key feature of *Tristes Tropiques* is reflexivity. The author is always looking over his own shoulder. The book is a travelogue that begins: "I hate travelling and explorers." It is a memoir that asks: "Why . . . should I give a detailed account of so many trivial circumstances and insignificant happenings?"[60] It is an ethnography that includes, alongside structuralist interpretations of Caduveo face paintings and Bororo housing patterns, first-person accounts of the ethnologist's mistakes and misadventures. And the book is designed to reach its climax with a reflection on the ethical and epistemological dilemmas of anthropology itself.

Tristes Tropiques came out in October 1955. After the publication of *Race and History*, Lévi-Strauss had been charged with being a cultural relativist and a West-basher. In *Tristes Tropiques*, he pled guilty. He did not deny that he was a cultural relativist, if that meant accepting "that each society has made a certain choice, within the range of existing human possibilities, and that the various choices cannot be compared with each other: they are all equally valid."[61] The West, he said, placed its bet on "progress." To use "progress" as a way of judging cultures for whom the concept is meaningless is pure ethnocentrism.

And he did not deny that he was ashamed of Western civilization. "It has sometimes been said that European society is the only one which has produced anthropologists, and that therein lies its greatness," he wrote.* But the anthropologist's "very existence is incomprehensible except as an attempt at redemption: he is the symbol of atonement." Anthropology is not a sign of superiority. It is a sign that a civilization realizes that it has gone terribly off track. Europeans could take some solace, he suggested, in the recognition that there have been other wicked societies—for example, the Aztecs.[62] The sin being atoned for by anthropology was colonialism. European civilization, Lévi-Strauss said, "for a widespread and innocent section of humanity, has amounted to a monstrous and incomprehensible cataclysm."[63] And colonialism is just an extension of a culture that, in the name of progress and enlightenment, damages the lives of Europeans as well.

The writer Lévi-Strauss admired most was Jean-Jacques Rousseau, and he agreed with the argument of Rousseau's spectacular philosophical debut, the *Discours sur les sciences et les arts*, published in 1750:

---

* He was referring to an attack on him in the pages of the *Nouvelle Revue Française* by Roger Caillois, which, along with Lévi-Strauss's riposte, caused a commotion in intellectual Paris.

advances in the arts and sciences that are believed to make life more "civilized" actually rob human beings of virtue. Lévi-Strauss thought that the more civilized, in Rousseau's sense, humans become, the more the species exhausts itself. The fact that we humans create cultures does not confer a privileged place on us.

"The world began without man and will end without him," he wrote in the final chapter of *Tristes Tropiques*. Human creations "will merge into the general chaos, as soon as the human mind has disappeared."

> ... [C]ivilization, taken as a whole, can be described as an extraordinarily complex mechanism, which we might be tempted to see as offering an opportunity of survival for the human world, if its function were not to produce what physicists call entropy, that is inertia. Every verbal exchange, every line printed, establishes communication between people, thus creating an evenness of level, where before there was an information gap and consequently a greater degree of organization. Anthropology could with advantage be changed into "entropology," as the name of the discipline concerned with the study of the highest manifestations of this process of disintegration.[64]

Entropy has been used in contradictory ways ever since the term was invented by the German physicist Rudolph Clausius in the nineteenth century.[65] Lévi-Strauss was thinking of the use of it made in information theory, a field he was introduced to by Jakobson. When Jakobson was at Harvard and Lévi-Strauss was back in Paris, Jakobson mailed him Norbert Wiener's *Cybernetics*, published in 1948. Soon after, he sent along Claude Shannon and Warren Weaver's *The Mathematical Theory of Communication*, published in 1949. Even though they lived in the same building during the war, Lévi-Strauss had never met Shannon. He was thrilled by his book. "I literally devoured it," he wrote to Jakobson. "The immense interest of the book is precisely to give a theory of thought [*théorie de la pensée*] from the point of view of the machine— that is, for what seems to me to be the first time, considered as an object."[66] A year later, Shannon coined the word "bit," short for "digital binary," and his idea that information and communications technology is based on binaries—1/0, yes/no, flip/flop—correlated beautifully with the structuralist and posthumanist understanding of the mind.

Wiener, who was Shannon's teacher at MIT, is the inventor of cybernetics, which is a theory for all self-regulating systems—it grew in part out of Wiener's work on feedback mechanisms for anti-aircraft guns—of which both human biology and society are examples. Wiener and Shannon used entropy differently, though. In Shannon's theory, entropy is a measure of the amount of information in a communication. The greater the number of possible messages, the more "information" and the higher the degree of entropy.[67] Wiener interpreted entropy as a measure of the disorganization, or chaos, in a system, and this must have been the interpretation that Lévi-Strauss had in mind when he used the term in *Tristes Tropiques*.[68] Lévi-Strauss's idea was that the better people understand one another, the more alike they become, but this means that cultural differences, and therefore cultural possibilities, disappear. Culture evens out, becomes homogeneous. It suffers the equivalent of heat death in thermodynamics. Order, which requires difference, gives way to chaos, where everything is on the same level—the same temperature, so to speak—and there are no distinctions.

This was the allegorical meaning of the sunset. Lévi-Strauss returned to that sunset in the final volume of his major scholarly enterprise, *Mythologiques* (literally: myth-logics) in 1971, where he described mythology as "that huge and complex edifice which also glows with a thousand iridescent colors as it builds up before the analyst's gaze, slowly expands to its full extent, then crumbles and fades away in the distance, as if it had never existed."[69] Cultures are created so that people can communicate: that's how and why societies come into being. But communication breaks down the very divisions it is designed to overcome. Monoculture, driven by Western expansion, turns out to be the direction humanity is headed. On this view of the future, politics are irrelevant. "Marxist, Communist, and Totalitarian ideology," Lévi-Strauss said, "is only a stratagem of history to promote the faster Westernization of peoples who until recent times have remained on the periphery."[70] This is why the tropics are sad. They have been co-opted into a self-destructive organism.

Triste Tropiques was a popular book and it introduced many readers to structuralism. *Tristes Tropiques* was also a topical book. France was undergoing violent ruptures with two of its colonies. On May 7, 1954, French forces surrendered to the Viet Minh at Dien Bien Phu in Indochina. Three weeks later, on November 1, in Algeria, the Front de Libération Nationale (FLN) launched a series of revolts throughout the country—the start of the Algerian War, which would last for seven and a half years and which France would lose. In March 1956, Tunisia, a French protectorate since 1881, became an independent state and, in July, a member of the United Nations.

Decolonization had begun. The anxiety in the imperial states was no longer that nonwhite peoples could not govern themselves. It was that they might govern themselves all too well. For the first time in international affairs, majority-nonwhite states were demanding a vote. The British edition of the English translation of *Tristes Tropiques* came out in 1963, while Britain was in the process of (with varying degrees of willingness) granting independence to its African colonies. The title was *World on the Wane*, suggesting a nostalgia for empire that Lévi-Strauss certainly did not intend.

5.

The Museum of Modern Art's blockbuster photography exhibition *The Family of Man*, which opened in January 1955, was a visual expression of the central assertion of UNESCO's "Statement by Experts on Race Problems" that Lévi-Strauss signed in 1950: "The unity of mankind from both the biological and social viewpoints is the main thing. To recognize this and to act accordingly is the first requirement of modern man."

The show was a collection of photographs of people from around the world, some by well-known photographers like Dorothea Lange, Diane Arbus, Gordon Parks, Helen Levitt, Edward Weston, Richard Avedon, Henri Cartier-Bresson, Robert Frank, Irving Penn, and Alfred Eisenstaedt, others by amateurs. The pictures were identified by country and photographer, and arranged thematically to illustrate birth, love, family, work, play, grief, war, faith, death, and, at the end, childhood again. They were intended to demonstrate, in the words of the catalogue, "the essential oneness of mankind throughout the world."[71] The photographs were accompanied by tags from the Bible, folk adages, and sayings by well-known figures: "I know no safe depository of the ultimate powers of society but the people themselves . . . ," Thomas Jefferson. "I still believe that people are really good at heart," Anne Frank. The show was a major international cultural event.

The Family of Man was entirely the inspiration of its curator, Edward

Steichen. He began imagining an exhibition on "Human Relations and Human Rights" in 1949, two years after his appointment as director of the museum's department of photography. Steichen was then seventy years old. He was born in Luxembourg and came to the United States when he was an infant, and he had had major achievements in virtually every genre of photography: art photography (he was a close associate of Alfred Stieglitz early in the century), advertising and fashion photography (he was the photographer for Condé Nast from 1923 to 1938; his 1925 portrait of Marion Morehouse, the wife of the poet E. E. Cummings, in a dress by Lucien Lelong is iconic), aerial photography (for the army during the First World War and the navy during the Second World War), even documentary film.[72] His movie about life on an aircraft carrier, *The Fighting Lady*, won the Academy Award for Best Documentary in 1945. He intended *The Family of Man* to be his crowning achievement.

The story of the show is a story of numbers. That is how it was promoted and how its effect was measured. Steichen, his friend Dorothea Lange, and his assistant, Wayne Miller, spent three years in preparation, and reviewed more than three million photographs. Steichen met with photographers in twenty cities in eleven European countries. The show contained 503 photographs by 273 photographers from 68 countries. It broke attendance records at MoMA, where it was on display for 103 days and attracted a quarter of a million visitors. It traveled to six other American cities, and replicas toured the world for seven years. Attendance numbers were fantastic: 276,000 in Belgrade, 350,000 in Calcutta, 293,000 in Tokyo.[73] In all, the exhibition was seen in eighty-eight venues in thirty-seven countries by nine million people. A catalogue was published in at least four separate formats. The paperback version alone is estimated to have sold more than four million copies.[74] It was designed by Leo Lionni, a European émigré who would shortly afterward publish a popular children's book about racial discrimination, *Little Blue and Little Yellow*.

The photographs ranged in size from eight by ten inches to ten by twenty feet and were mounted, in an installation designed by the architect Paul Rudolph (a student at Harvard of the founder of the Bauhaus, Walter Gropius), mostly on Masonite boards without frames, and were hung unconventionally—from wires or on poles—and grouped in specially designed areas.[75]

This method of exhibition was not new. A show of images two years earlier at the Institute of Contemporary Arts in London, *Parallel of Life and Art*, was hung in the same manner. But *The Family of Man* was an installation: that is, the exhibition, not the individual photographs, was the artwork. Because they were not wall-mounted, it was possible for viewers to see photographs from different areas at the same time. People were rarely seeing just a single image. Visitors followed a path through the thematic sequence, ending in a room containing a six-by-eight-foot color transparency of a hydrogen bomb explosion. All the photographs were intended to be observed in passing. A gruesome picture of a lynching, taken by an anonymous photographer in Mississippi in 1937, was removed early on because viewers stopped to stare at it, disturbing the flow. At the end, there was a smoky mirror in which people could see their own faces, and the space was designed so that those on the way out passed those on the way in and were forced to make eye contact.[76]

Formally, the exhibition was received as an assault on fine-art norms. The artwork was de-aestheticized, not isolated for contemplation; the viewer was de-individualized, made to function as part of a crowd; the art of composition was reduced to an act of selection. The idea that artistic merit could be expressed quantitatively—503 images, 273 photographers, nine million viewers, and so on—was mildly scandalous. This was box-office art. For photographers whose careers had been devoted to securing fine-art status for photography, the show was a betrayal. Minor White, a disciple of Stieglitz and the editor of *Aperture*, complained that Steichen had appropriated the works of individual artists and subordinated them to a spectacle of his own.[77]

The Family of Man was received not only as a betrayal of art photography. It flouted the aesthetic principles laid down by Clement Greenberg, by then the most influential art critic in the country. Greenberg did not review Steichen's exhibition; he had Hilton Kramer do it. Kramer had made a name for himself in 1953, when he was twenty-five, with an attack in *Partisan Review* on Harold Rosenberg's essay "The American Action Painters"—the essay in which he implicitly undercut Greenberg and disparaged Pollock. When Rosenberg described the canvas as "an arena in which to act," Kramer argued, he was no longer talking about art; he was talking about theater.[78] The article naturally caught the attention of Greenberg, who was then an editor at *Commentary*, and Greenberg and Kramer became friends. (It might have helped that Kramer, like Greenberg, was a graduate of Syracuse University.) And in 1955, Greenberg had Kramer write some pieces for the magazine.

The Family of Man wasn't art, Kramer complained; it was journalism. "And as so often happens in our culture when art abandons itself to journalism," he said, "its mode of articulation has a distinct ideological cast—in this instance, a cast which embodies all that is most facile, abstract, sentimental, and rhetorical in liberal ideology."[79] By "liberal ideology," Kramer meant what Lionel Trilling meant: progressivism without irony, the fellow-traveling mentality.

He was not wrong. The message of *The Family of Man*—peace and democracy through tolerance and understanding—was the Soviet line. And so it should not be surprising that no one loved *The Family of Man* more than the left-wing press. The American Communist Party's newspaper, *The Daily Worker*, called it "a stirring ode to all of the earth's people" and promoted the show and its catalogue repeatedly.[80] The show received positive reviews in left-wing journals such as *The New Republic* and *The Progressive*.[81] The progressive (though anti-Communist) United Auto Workers devoted an entire issue of its bulletin, *Ammunition*, to the exhibition. The issue was entitled "UAW–CIO and The Family of Man"; it printed seventeen pages of photographs from the show followed by forty-one pages of photographs of UAW activities.[82]

When the exhibition came to France, in 1956, three months after *Tristes Tropiques* came out, the review in the French Communist Party's newspaper *L'Humanité* was headlined "A Deeply Moving [*bouleversante*] Exhibition." "It is heart-warming to know that this unique collection, which is touring the world, comes to us from the United States, expressing as it does the love of mankind, the brotherhood of this great family which inhabits the earth," wrote the paper's film critic, Samuel Lachize. He called it "a great exhibition that must be seen."[83] (The public affairs official in the American embassy was delighted to send a copy of this review to Washington.)[84] "Un Art qui crie la verité"—"an art that cries out the truth"—was the headline in the Communist-supported *Les Lettres Françaises*. The reviewer, Marcel Cornu, a member of the French Communist Party, called the show "an extraordinary exhibition." He deplored the texts—"a marmalade of sweet and bland words"—but he found the images "vivid and explosive." The exposition, he wrote, was "a marvel."[85]

The show reached Moscow in the summer of 1959 as part of the

American National Exhibition, an enormous spectacle dedicated mainly to consumerism, with displays of American automobiles, color television sets, boats, sporting equipment, farm machinery, computers, food, fashion, books, newspapers, art, and a geodesic dome designed by Buckminster Fuller.* The art included works by Jackson Pollock, Mark Rothko, and Willem de Kooning, and also by Edward Hopper, Andrew Wyeth, Grant Wood, and many other realists.

As was true of virtually every government-sponsored art exhibition since 1946, there were domestic complaints about the style of the art and the politics of the artists whose work was being sent to Moscow. President Eisenhower was asked by a reporter whether the art "truly represents Americans to the Russians." His answer is a classic sample of his ad hoc verbal manner: "I am not going, I assure you, I am not going to be the censor myself for the art that has already gone there. Now I think I might have something to say if we have another exhibit, anywhere, to the responsible officials of the methods they produce, or get the juries and possibly there ought to be one or two people that, like most of us here, say we are not too certain exactly what art is but we know what we like and what America likes—what America likes is after all some of the things that ought to be shown."[86] Twenty-seven paintings, mostly from the nineteenth century, were duly added to the exhibit. No paintings were withdrawn. The most popular painting was an Andrew Wyeth.[87] More than 2.7 million Russians, plus tens of thousands of gate-crashers, attended the exhibit, and they were invited to vote on their favorite attractions. Only a fraction did, but *The Family of Man* was No. 1.[88]

The Family of Man's world tour was run by the United States Information Agency (USIA), not the Museum of Modern Art, and, measured by eyeballs, it was probably the most successful venture in cultural diplomacy in the entire Cold War. The USIA was created by the Eisenhower administration, which explained, persistently, that the agency's mission was not propaganda, but information. It is unlikely that a single person was fooled by this. Eisenhower was a great believer

---

* It was at this exhibition, in the model kitchen of a model ranch house (furnished by Macy's), that Vice President Richard Nixon and the Soviet premier, Nikita Khrushchev, had the exchange about living standards and leadership in technology that became known as the "kitchen debate." The subtext was Khrushchev's recently announced intention to cut off Western access to Berlin, an escalation of tensions.

in propaganda; for one thing, it was a lot cheaper than maintaining a standing army.[89] And cultural diplomacy just *is* propaganda. It puts a national brand on art and ideas.

The Family of Man was sometimes edited according to the venue. In Japan, the transparency of the bomb explosion was replaced by images of Japanese atomic bomb victims.[90] In Moscow, an official Soviet request for the removal of a picture of a Chinese child begging was granted.[91] But the overall design required balance, and the fact that, apart from country and photographer, there was no identifying information about the pictures depoliticized most of the images. Every image was generic—which, of course, was the point.

The original exhibition includes a photograph of young men throwing paving stones at tanks during the 1953 workers' uprising (quickly suppressed) in East Germany, but that is the only allusion to Communism. Apart from the hydrogen bomb transparency and the removed lynching photograph, the major image of political violence is a photograph used at the Nuremberg Trials of Jews being marched out of the burning ruins of the Warsaw Ghetto after the uprising was crushed in 1943. A photograph of Asian women screaming behind barbed wire is, despite appearances, actually a picture of young South Koreans protesting the signing of the armistice that ended the Korean War in 1953. Most of the photographs signifying poverty are of Americans.

The message of the exhibition was not anti-Communism. It was anti-colonialism. The exhibition was used by the American government to signal where the sympathies of the United States should be understood to lie in the coming struggles over decolonization. Since that happened to be the same place where the Soviets wanted their sympathies to be understood to lie, it was a message the Communist press was quick to embrace.

6.

The Family of Man opened in Paris at the Musée National d'Art Moderne in an exhibition mounted by Steichen personally. Sixty thousand people went to see it. In its monthly magazine, UNESCO ran a fifteen-page spread of images from the show accompanied by an essay, by a British scientist, Cyril Bibby, on racist subtexts in ordinary speech.[92] One of the reviewers of the Paris show was Roland Barthes, and his eight-paragraph essay about it is possibly the best-known thing he ever wrote.

Barthes was only seven years younger than Lévi-Strauss, but his career was held up by bouts of tuberculosis. He made his debut in 1953 with a well-received collection of essays, *Le Degré zéro de l'écriture* (*Writing Degree Zero*)—a term he first applied to the style of Albert Camus's *L'Étranger*.

Barthes's essay on Camus had appeared in *Combat*. His editor there was Maurice Nadeau, a literary critic who covered Sartre's "Existentialism Is a Humanism" lecture in 1945, and who was one of the first to write about Samuel Beckett, eliciting grateful letters from Beckett himself.[93] When Nadeau left *Combat* to start up the weekly *France Observateur*, he invited Barthes to write a column for its literary supplement, *Les Lettres Nouvelles*. That column, "Petite Mythologie du mois" ("Little Mythology of the Month"), is where the essay on *The Family of Man* appeared. Barthes would collect those columns in the book called *Mythologies*, which came out in 1957 and made him famous.

Barthes's complaint about *The Family of Man* was that the show ignored the existence of injustice and exploitation in the name of what, for people suffering from those things, amounted to a spurious notion of human commonality. Barthes asked what use the parents of Emmett Till (he misspelled the name, and Till had only one parent: his father was dead), the fourteen-year-old who had been lynched in Mississippi a few months earlier, or North African workers in the immigrant neighborhoods of Paris might have for the concept of "the family of man." (In the *Les Lettres Nouvelles* version, Barthes added "or the black schoolgirl in Alabama," a reference to Autherine Lucy, who had become the first Black student admitted to the University of Alabama just a month before.[94] Photographs of her being mocked by a white mob appeared in the French press.)

This was a perverse misreading of the show, and it suggests that, in fact, Barthes never actually saw it. He may have been reacting simply to the publicity and to reviews like the one in *L'Humanité*. He would have had no reason to know about the removed lynching photograph, but there were many images of suffering and oppression, and the photograph of Jews being led from the Warsaw Ghetto would have been hard to overlook in Paris in 1956, a time when the subject of the Holocaust was still carefully avoided. Alain Resnais's thirty-two-minute documentary about the camps, *Nuit et brouillard* (*Night and Fog*), which was shown at Cannes over the objections of West Germany in April 1956 and which opened in Paris on May 22, was one of the first efforts in France to address the fact of the camps. And *Nuit et brouillard* is also a universalizing enterprise: the word "Jewish" is heard in the movie just once.[95] You would hardly know that the Holocaust was the result of an intention to massacre Jews. (American reviewers seemed not to register the Warsaw photograph, either: "Deliberate evil has been carefully excluded," Phoebe Adams complained in *The Atlantic Monthly*.)[96] But *The Family of Man* was all about eradicating injustice and discrimination in the name of human rights. That was the essence of its progressivism.[97]

Barthes had a philosophical objection as well. The exhibition, he said, relied on "a very old mystification, which consists in always placing Nature at the bottom of History." Viewers were prevented from penetrating "that further zone of human conduct, where historical alienation introduces those 'differences' which we shall here call quite simply injustices."[98] The "natural," Barthes was arguing, is itself a product of history—that is, contingent, not immutable or universal. Exactly the same criticism could be made about structuralist anthropology. The view of mankind in *The Family of Man* is highly sentimentalized, but it is structuralist. In a completely unscientific way, the show suggests that cultural differences are unimportant, that the essence of life is not progress but reproduction, and that humans are, at bottom, just another species temporarily inhabiting the planet. Steichen and everyone else involved in the exhibition would probably have been horrified to be called anti-humanist, but the viewers going out passing the viewers coming in must have had the brief sensation that we are all ants on the same doomed anthill—the argument of *Tristes Tropiques*.

"Le structuralisme n'est pas un humanisme," in other words. If structuralism's break with existentialism was not obvious enough, Lévi-Strauss spelled it out in the final pages of *La Pensée Sauvage* (1962), in which he attacked Sartre for "making historicity the last refuge of a transcendental humanism: as if men could regain the illusion of liberty on the plane of the 'we' merely by giving up the 'I's that are too obviously wanting in consistency."[99] Unlike anthropology and linguistics, he wrote, history has no real-world object. History is like kinship systems: it exists only in people's minds. It is just a cultural mode produced by modern societies—that is, societies that have writing. It is no different from the cultural mode that "primitive" societies produce, which is myths. History is the mythology of the West.

Sartre waited several years to respond to Lévi-Strauss's attack, and that turned out to be too long. By then, the fight was over. Existentialism had been eclipsed. The center of intellectual activity moved to journals such as *L'Homme*, *Communications*, *Poétique*, and *Tel Quel*, places with a much more specialized readership than *Les Temps Modernes*. The scientism of structuralist theory may have had something to do with its appeal, particularly in the academy. But existentialism was born in response to an experience of extremity, and by 1962, France was in the middle of a period of rising affluence and robust economic growth. In times of prosperity, concepts like "freedom" become increasingly abstract, and a philosophy of anxiety and risk no longer seems apropos. It becomes less a necessity than a style.

As for Barthes, in 1958, a year after *Mythologies* came out, he asked Lévi-Strauss to supervise his doctoral thesis, which he proposed to write on fashion. Much to his dismay, Lévi-Strauss turned him down. He did recommend Vladimir Propp's structuralist study *Morphology of the Folktale* (*Morfologiia skazki*), translated by Svatava Pírková, Jakobson's wife, which Jakobson had recently sent him.[100] Barthes read it and, years later, he wrote *Système de la Mode* (*The Fashion System*). But he never wrote a thesis. He seems not to have grasped that although he appropriated the method of structural anthropology in *Mythologies*, in which he analyzed popular culture as myths, and although his writings created an interest in structuralist thinking far outside social-scientific circles, Lévi-Strauss had no taste for his work.[101]

8

THE EMANCIPATION OF DISSONANCE

Merce Cunningham at Black Mountain College, ca. 1952–1953.
Photograph by Hazel Larsen Archer. (*Estate of Hazel Larsen Archer and
Black Mountain College Museum + Arts Center*)

1.

It was not long after France was invaded and émigré artists began arriving in the United States that people started saying that the capital of modern art had moved from Paris to New York. A day after Pearl Harbor, Peyton Boswell, the editor of *Art Digest*, announced, "The first two years of the Hitlerian war shifted the art capital of the world from Paris to New York, making America, in effect, the custodian of Western culture."[1] The same month, *Fortune* published "The Flight of Culture," featuring reproductions of works by French painters, and the art collector Sidney Janis, later Jackson Pollock's dealer, published an essay called "School of Paris Comes to U.S." "New York is supplanting Paris as the art center of the world," he said.[2]

The assumption was not that American-style painting was superior to European-style painting. It was that the Nazi domination of Europe would last much longer than a few years and modern artists would have to expatriate. Neither happened. Most of the painters who fled to the United States after Hitler came to power were never fully integrated into the American art world, and when Paris was liberated, they went back as quickly as they could. By November 1945, Daniel-Henry Kahnweiler, the leading modern art dealer in France, was able to write with evident satisfaction, "It has . . . been suggested that the centre of artistic creation has shifted—the painters who have remained in France are left out of account—and that New York has become a modern Alexandria, an international metropolis of the arts. True, many a painter has sought refuge in America, but so numerous are those who have written to me bewailing their exile (not all of them Frenchmen even) and begging me to hasten their return, that I have not a moment's doubt about the attraction which Paris still holds for them."[3] And, after the war, young American artists resumed going to Paris. European artists, by and large, did not come to New York.

In the spring of 1946, after most of the French artists had left New York, Clement Greenberg ran into John Bernard Myers, then the young managing editor of *View*, later co-founder of the Tibor de Nagy Gallery. They went into the Vanderbilt Hotel on East Thirty-Fourth Street for a drink; Myers recorded the conversation in his journal. "You know," Greenberg said, "Paris has been limping along as the world center of art since 1936." "But what will replace the School of Paris?" Myers asked. "The place where the money is," Greenberg replied. "New York."[4]

It took almost ten years for Greenberg's prediction to be realized, and even then, he was only half-right. New York did become the financial center of the art world, but art itself became international. To the extent that a single artist was the key to this transformation, the artist was Robert Rauschenberg. It was because of Rauschenberg, or, more accurately, because of changes in the art world that Rauschenberg's career was bound up with, that after 1964, people stopped talking about contemporary art in nationalist terms. Artists might be French or

American, but there was no longer a New York School or a School of Paris. Art was global.[5]

Rauschenberg was fearless and prolific, but his art and his influence were enhanced by his association with three other innovative figures who also became internationally renowned: John Cage, Merce Cunningham, and Jasper Johns. Like, probably, most productive collaborations, there was some latent competitiveness there, and for Rauschenberg, the relationships wound down somewhat unhappily. But not before the four of them had changed the game.

2.

Rauschenberg was born in 1925 in Port Arthur, Texas, which, he was later excited to learn, is also the hometown of Janis Joplin. Being excited by serendipity was very Rauschenbergian. He cultivated a catch-as-catch-can, happy-go-lucky manner. He was an enfant terrible who was pure of heart, a troublemaker who couldn't help himself, an iconoclast but not a cynic. He liked to say that he never worked from an art-historical agenda; he simply tried things out. "Nearly everything that I've done was to see what would happen if I did this instead of that," he once explained.[6] "Art shouldn't have a concept," he said on another occasion. "That's the only concept that I've ever been consistent with."[7]

People found it hard not to like Rauschenberg. He was gregarious and he had a big laugh—though not everyone found the ingenuousness entirely ingenuous. As he was perfectly aware, Rauschenberg pushed art in directions that art-historical conditions made possible, and pretending not to have an art-historical agenda was one of those directions. From the beginning of his career—he had his first gallery show in 1951—Rauschenberg made art that looked messy, willful, and arbitrary. His principal champions in the 1960s, the curators William Seitz and Alan Solomon and the critic Leo Steinberg, insisted that what seemed haphazard and prankish actually had formal and iconographic integrity.[8] This did not so much overrate the coherence of Rauschenberg's work as underrate its radicalness. When Rauschenberg said that his only concept was to work without concepts, he was not making a phrase. He was identifying his key problematic. Keeping concepts at bay does not mean relying on intuition, which is what a lot of people assumed that Rauschenberg was doing. On the contrary, it requires constant discipline. It's not just difficult not to have a concept when you are making a work of art. It's impossible. Like Cage's music and Cunningham's choreography, Rauschenberg's art is among the most counterintuitive creative works ever produced. It just looks random.

Rauschenberg's grandfather was a German émigré who settled in Texas and married a Cherokee woman. His father was an employee of the Gulf States Utilities who had no schooling beyond the third grade and whose main interests were fishing and hunting. The Rauschenbergs were Church of Christ fundamentalists; as a boy, Rauschenberg's ambition was to become a preacher. He loved to draw, but he claimed he never realized that there were such things as art and artists until he visited the Huntington Art Gallery, in San Marino, California, while he was on furlough from the navy. He said he recognized two of the paintings because he had seen them on the backs of playing cards. After his discharge—he worked as an aide in military hospitals during the war—he spent a year doing menial jobs in Los Angeles, then enrolled, on the G.I. Bill, in the Kansas City Art Institute (KCAI), where Pollock's teacher Thomas Hart Benton had taught after leaving New York. (By the time Rauschenberg arrived, Benton was no longer on the faculty.)

While he was in Kansas City, Rauschenberg made the decision to call himself Bob (his given name was Milton). He had made a list of the most ordinary names he could think of and decided that of the names on the list, he knew the most Bobs. When people assumed that his real name was Robert, he adopted that.[9] He stayed at KCAI for a year; then, in 1948, having saved up for the trip, he went to Paris, where he enrolled at the Académie Julian, a French art school open to students with G.I. Bill benefits. He lasted about six months. Rauschenberg had no French and he found the classes boring, so he spent his time going to museums and painting on his own. He made friends with another American studying at the Académie, Susan Weil. She was eighteen and had just graduated from the Dalton School in New York City. One of her teachers there recommended Black Mountain College in North Carolina as a place to study painting, and, in the fall of 1948, she and Rauschenberg enrolled.[10]

Black Mountain College is famous for the number of artists and poets, later prominent, who studied or taught there, but it was not an art school. It was a college. It was launched during the Depression by a renegade

Classics professor named John Andrew Rice, who had been fired from Rollins College in Florida, and for twenty-four years, it led a hand-to-mouth existence in the foothills of the Blue Ridge Mountains outside Asheville. In a good year, enrollment was sixty. The college opened in the fall of 1933 with twenty-two students, fourteen of whom, along with four of the faculty, had followed Rice from Rollins. To the extent that finances permitted, and depending on who was available to teach, it offered a full liberal education. Students could take courses in science, mathematics, history, economics, psychology, languages, and literature.

What made Black Mountain different from other colleges was that the center of the curriculum was art-making. Students studied, and faculty taught, whatever they liked, but every student was expected to take a class in some kind of arts practice—painting, sculpture, pottery, weaving, poetry, architecture, design, dance, music, photography. The goal was not to produce painters, poets, and architects. It was to produce citizens. "The democratic man," as Rice explained his philosophy, ". . . must be an artist."[11] Rice thought that people learn best by doing, rather than by reading books or listening to lectures, and he regarded art-making as a form of mental discipline. It instills a habit of making independent choices, which is important in a democracy. This was the pedagogy of progressivism, derived from the educational theories of John Dewey, who visited the college frequently and served on its advisory board.[12]

Dewey wanted to break down what he thought was an invidious distinction between doing and knowing, the distinction that gives philosophers, for example, a higher status than carpenters. We do not pursue knowledge for its own sake, Dewey believed; we pursue it in order to do things, and it is by doing things that we acquire more knowledge. Dewey's student-centered pedagogy of "learning by doing" is the philosophy of progressive education. It had a lasting influence on preschool education, but it was also adopted in high schools and colleges. Dalton, Susan Weil's school, was founded as a progressive school; so was Rollins (although Rice believed that it had betrayed its mission).[13]

This sounds nicely suited to arts education, but in 1933, painting and sculpture were still taught almost everywhere in the academic, or beaux arts, tradition, in which students learn by drawing models and copying famous works—the kind of training that Rauschenberg and Weil found so uninspiring in Paris. Rice needed someone committed to a Deweyan method of teaching, hands-on and experimental. He got lucky. It was

1933; many people were looking for ways to get out of Germany. Two of them were Josef and Anni Albers.

Josef Albers was born in Westphalia, in western Germany, in 1888. His father was a housepainter, something Albers made a point of when discussing his credentials. He began his career as a schoolteacher, which is when, he said, he realized the value of learning by experience.[14] He read Dewey's *The School and Society*, published in 1899 and translated into German in 1904. Dewey's ideas about education would not have been news to German readers; they had their origins in nineteenth-century German-language writers: Johann Herbart, Friedrich Fröbel, and Johann Pestalozzi. Still, Dewey's pragmatism and his commitment to democracy made his book controversial in German educational circles.[15] Albers was on Dewey's side.

In 1919, Albers happened to pick up a leaflet written by the architect Walter Gropius and distributed to art schools throughout Germany announcing the opening of the Bauhaus in Weimar, a school where architecture, design, handcrafts, and the fine arts would be taught in an integrated manner. Albers was thirty-two, but he registered as a student.[16] "That was the best step I made in my life," he later said.[17] Albers's specialty was glasswork. He used to go to the Weimar city dump and collect bottles and cans and use them to create what he called *Scherbenbilder*—shard pictures.[18]

In 1922, he met Anni Fleischmann, who was from a wealthy Berlin family, and he helped her get admitted to the Bauhaus as a student. Her specialty was weaving (a choice she made not because of her gender but because she had a frail physique).[19] They married in 1925. Josef had joined the Bauhaus faculty in 1922; in 1923, he began co-teaching the school's preliminary design course, the *Vorkurs*, with the Hungarian émigré László Moholy-Nagy. Moholy-Nagy left the Bauhaus in 1928; Albers continued to the end. That came in April 1933. The school had moved, first to Dessau, then to Berlin, but it did not last much beyond the coming to power of Adolf Hitler. This was in part because it was associated with styles of art the Nazis labeled "degenerate," in part because it resisted the *Gleichschaltung* and refused to accept Nazis on the faculty. The school closed, and most of its teachers went into diaspora, with significant consequences for American art, architecture, and design.[20]

Josef was from a Catholic family; Anni's parents' families, the Ullsteins and the Fleischmanns, had converted from Judaism to Protestantism a generation before she was born. But this still made her Jewish in, as she put it, "the Hitler sense of the word."[21] The Alberses had no interest in the United States. "[N]o pumpernickel, such red and green drinks in America," is the way Josef described their attitude. "All I knew was Buster Keaton and Henry Ford. I knew no English."[22] But they were happy to get a letter from Rice inviting them to join the faculty at Black Mountain.

Rice had got their names through the efforts of another ex-Rollins professor, Ted Dreier, a Harvard graduate who taught physics and was from a well-off New York family. Dreier's mother put Rice in touch with a woman whose husband was the secretary of the Museum of Modern Art, and she, in turn, put him in touch with Edward Warburg, a wealthy young trustee who was one of the founders of MoMA. Warburg arranged a meeting for Rice with Alfred Barr, the director of the museum, and Philip Johnson, founder and curator of the architecture department.

Barr had visited the Bauhaus in 1929—by then, the school was a site of pilgrimage, accommodating up to 250 visitors every week—and he had met and subsequently corresponded with Josef Albers.[23] Johnson had just returned from Berlin, where he had been impressed by Anni Albers's weavings. (Johnson was also attracted to Hitler and Nazism.) To enter the United States, of course, the Alberses needed a promise of employment. Money was raised for a salary for Josef (normally, Black Mountain faculty received only room and board) and for two first-class steamship tickets. The Alberses landed in New York in November 1933; Johnson greeted them at the dock and took them to Warburg's parents' house on Fifth Avenue. Their arrival was reported in the press.[24] It was a tremendous coup for Black Mountain College.

The Alberses loved Black Mountain, and—atypically for German refugees—they loved America. "[A]merica must be incredibly large," they wrote to their friend and fellow Bauhausler Wassily Kandinsky and his wife a week after arriving in North Carolina. "[W]hat we have seen of it is really interesting, particularly the americans themselves. very, very friendly. it has been a long time since we experienced such kindness. and such youth and vitality and—interest in the arts. new york is wonderfully lively and often reminds us of paris."[25]

The Alberses visited Mexico regularly, often in the company of Diego Rivera, who became a friend, and their work began to reflect the influence of Mesoamerican pottery, architecture, and design.[26] They also developed contacts in New York. Josef had his first show there in 1936; eventually, he was represented by Sidney Janis. In 1949, Anni became the first weaver to have a one-person show at the Museum of Modern Art. They were both thrilled with American form-fits-function mass-market products: laminated countertops (so easy to clean), salad bars (with metal containers to keep the food cool), Heinz ketchup bottles (engineered to fit the hand), drip-dry shirts (why fuss with ironing?).[27]

Albers became the dominant figure at Black Mountain. He offered a course based on the *Vorkurs* (in the beginning, he used a translator in the classroom) and arranged for former Bauhauslers to visit, among them Alexander (Xanti) Schawinsky, an avant-garde theater designer, and Gropius himself, who became head of the Graduate School of Design at Harvard in 1938 and was a frequent lecturer at Black Mountain.[28] Other faculty members sat in on Albers's classes to study his teaching methods. Along with Gropius, Moholy-Nagy, Marcel Breuer, and Ludwig Mies van der Rohe (with whom Philip Johnson would collaborate on the design of the Seagram Building in New York City, completed in 1958), Josef and Anni Albers brought Bauhaus-style teaching and Bauhaus-style art to the United States.[29]

What is Bauhaus-style teaching? Simply put, it was a reaction against the beaux-arts tradition, which dates from the Renaissance.[30] At the Bauhaus, experiment, rather than imitation, was the basis for learning— just as, in the theory of progressive education, making, rather than reading or listening, is the basis for acquiring knowledge. On the Bauhaus model, the central skill is the one that lies at the intersection of art and craft: design.

And what is Bauhaus-style art? The Bauhaus had two slogans, both supplied by Gropius. In the leaflet that motivated Albers to enroll in 1919, Gropius wrote: "wir alle müssen zum Handwerk zurück"—"we must all return to the crafts."[31] Four years later, in a lecture in Weimar, Gropius proclaimed "Kunst und Technik: eine neue Einheit"—"Art and technology: a new unity."[32] As people did not fail to notice, these pronouncements are contradictory.[33] The first allies art with preindustrial artisanship, the second with mass production. It is a consequential difference. In Deweyan terms, though, what Gropius was doing was eliding (not collapsing) the conventional distinction between objects created for appreciation and objects created for use, between what you encounter in a museum and what you encounter in a hardware store, or your kitchen. He was making space for the ketchup bottle.

When Albers was introduced to the faculty and students at Black Mountain, someone asked him what he hoped to accomplish. He answered: "I want to open eyes."[34] This meant getting students to see that any object is subject to artistic treatment and aesthetic consideration. Albers had students scavenge for ordinary materials—wood, straw, cardboard, dirt—and then explore the relations between them.[35] He made art out of dead leaves; Anni made jewelry out of paper clips. It was Anni's weaving—what was called at the Bauhaus *ein Bild aus Wolle*, "a picture out of wool"—that encapsulated the essential Bauhaus challenges: the conversion of everyday materials to artistic purposes and, conversely, the artistic handling of the everyday.[36]

Rauschenberg and Weil took Josef Albers's class in 1948–1949. Rauschenberg was often asked about the experience. His responses varied. In 1995, he called Albers "a negative influence." The only thing he got from Albers, he said, was humiliation. He said that he and his friend Cy Twombly, who also attended Black Mountain, made their art in secret because they knew that Albers wouldn't like it, and that Albers disapproved when Rauschenberg brought his infant son to class in a laundry basket.[37]

But this was all made up. Albers left Black Mountain for good in 1949—in 1950, he was hired to direct a new department of design at Yale, where he spent the rest of his career—and Twombly didn't come to Black Mountain until 1951, which is also the year that Rauschenberg and Weil's son, Christopher, was born. Twombly never knew Albers, and if Christopher was taken to someone's class in a basket, it wasn't Albers's.

In 1969, on the other hand, in a documentary about Albers by Hans Namuth (the man who had filmed Pollock) and Paul Falkenberg, Rauschenberg called Albers "a beautiful teacher but an impossible person . . . I'm still learning what he taught me. What he taught had to do with the whole visual world . . . I consider Albers the most important teacher I ever had, and I'm sure he considered me one of his poorest students."[38] They certainly did not get along. A classmate remembered continuous rivalry.[39] Albers was formal in manner, and he is reported to have found

Rauschenberg frivolous and irritating (not hard to believe).[40] Rauschenberg "never fought with Albers," Weil remembered, "but Albers fought with him . . . Bob was always respectful, but he [Albers] had a chip on his shoulder about Bob, because he thought he had ego, and ego was really not something he could contend with at all."[41]

Still, Rauschenberg was productive. The title of his first mature work, created at Black Mountain, suggests his precocity as a conceptual innovator: *This Is the First Half of a Print Designed to Exist in Passing Time*. The piece consists of fourteen prints made from a single woodblock, with a new line cut into the block for each successive print, so that the image evolves from all-black to half-black and half-white. The title is hand-printed on tracing paper and attached with twine.[42] It may have been the kind of thing Albers found silly, but the piece is quite sophisticated. It's an experiment about representing change in a static medium, and it concludes that this can be accomplished only by verbal description. Without the written attachment, there are just fourteen static images. The allusion might be to silent movies: still pictures sequenced to simulate motion, with titles attached.

At the end of the school year, Rauschenberg and Weil returned to New York and began taking classes in the Art Students' League (Rauschenberg was still using G.I. Bill money) and experimenting with blueprint paper. They had people lie naked on the paper and shined a lamp on them, leaving a shadow-like image. They brought the results to Edward Steichen at MoMA, who liked them and showed one in an exhibition of abstract photography. (Steichen would later buy two photographs Rauschenberg made at Black Mountain for the museum.) In 1950, Rauschenberg and Weil got married. Her parents were concerned about Rauschenberg's homosexuality; she appears to have been somewhat clueless. They were happy together, and she assumed that gay men felt pressure to have heterosexual marriages. Until their wedding night, they had not slept together.[43]

In May 1951, Rauschenberg had his first show, at the Betty Parsons Gallery on East Fifty-Seventh Street—Pollock's gallery. He had walked in with his portfolio on a hunch and was stunned when Parsons offered him a date. Almost all of the seventeen works in that show were lost or destroyed, but they seem, based on reviews and photographs, to have been composed mainly of simple figures (squares, circles, numbers, flowers) arranged in self-consciously whimsical and naïve designs.[44] Only one work was sold, a collage.

Actually, that piece was given away, since the buyer explained that the price didn't matter because he didn't have any money. The buyer, or rather, the giftee, was John Cage.

3.

That was not the only time Cage used that line. He rarely had much money. Early in his career, he made a decision never to hold a job, which sometimes made it necessary for him to beg from his friends. Although he did record his music, he disliked doing it because he thought that records encourage the belief that there is only one way a piece should sound. "[T]hey turn music into an object," he said. Even at the height of his renown, he did not own a phonograph.[45] Cage's performances drew mostly a coterie audience, and they often repelled listeners who had the wrong idea about what to expect. Cage wanted recognition—he was not that unworldly—and he eventually enjoyed a popular-culture celebrity as a zany genius, a part he could play. Like Rauschenberg, he didn't care very much if other people considered him a clown, or, at least, he dealt with it. And he, too, was gregarious and had a big laugh.

Cage was thirteen years older than Rauschenberg, but he recognized Rauschenberg immediately as a kindred spirit. It was "understanding at first sight," he said; they were "born accomplices."[46] Cage said that when he listened to Rauschenberg answer questions about his work, he felt that he would have said exactly the same thing.[47] Rauschenberg recalled Cage telling him, "You know, Bob, it wouldn't have had to be both of us"—meaning that they were making the same contribution to art. He said that Cage "had a fantastic influence on my thinking. He simply gave me permission to go on thinking."[48]

Cage was from Los Angeles. Neither of his parents went to college. His father was a self-taught electrical engineer who made a living as an inventor. Cage graduated from Los Angeles High School in 1928 with the highest academic average in the school's history. The yearbook noted him for "*being radical*."[49] He entered Pomona College, but lost interest in academic pursuits. At the end of his sophomore year—the year José Orozco painted the mural *Prometheus* for the campus dining hall that Jackson Pollock, Cage's contemporary, would visit that summer—he dropped out and hitchhiked to Galveston, where he got a boat to France. He was seventeen.

Cage had some French (though he always spoke it with an undisguised American accent), and he spent just six months in Paris, but he kept busy. He worked for an architect named Ernö Goldfinger, a Hungarian émigré (who would serve, much later, as the model for the character in the James Bond novel); he painted; he studied piano (that is, he took a few lessons) at the Paris Conservatoire. He also had his first gay relationships. One was a brief affair with John Goheen, the son of an American professor. The second was with another American, Don Sample, an artist twelve years older than Cage, who introduced him to current trends in art and literature. Cage and Sample traveled around Europe. They visited the Bauhaus in Dessau, where it was being run by Mies van der Rohe, and when they returned to the United States in the fall of 1931, they brought a collection of books and magazines about Bauhaus aesthetics with them.[50]

Back in Los Angeles, Cage and Sample lived on Kings Road in West Hollywood, where they met Galka Scheyer, a German émigré who was the American agent for the painters who called themselves Die Blauen Vier.* Scheyer took to Cage and introduced him to her Hollywood neighbor Walter Arensberg, a wealthy collector who was Marcel Duchamp's patron and friend. Arensberg had helped Duchamp pick out the urinal he used for *Fountain*, in 1917; he owned *Nude Descending a Staircase, No. 2*.[51]

Deciding that his prospects as a composer might be brighter than his prospects as a painter, Cage made contact with Henry Cowell, a leading American avant-garde composer. Cowell had spent time in Europe and had given a concert at the Bauhaus, and it was through Cowell's connections that Cage ended up studying with Arnold Schoenberg.[52]

Of the quarter of a million refugees admitted to the United States between 1933 and 1944, the Immigration and Naturalization Service classified more than twice as many as musicians (1,501) than as artists (702).[53] Many of those musicians came from Germany and Austria, which meant that they arrived earlier and stayed longer than the painters

---

* The Blue Four: Lyonel Feininger, Wassily Kandinsky, Paul Klee (all Bauhauslers), and Alexej von Jawlensky. This was a successor group to Der Blaue Reiter, formed in Munich in 1911.

who escaped from France, and, as a consequence, they became more integrated into American cultural life. They included conductors (Arturo Toscanini, Erich Leinsdorf, Otto Klemperer), composers (Igor Stravinsky, Darius Milhaud, Kurt Weill), performers (Lotte Lenya, Artur Rubinstein, Wanda Landowska), and musicologists. A number became successful composing for Hollywood movies: Hanns Eisler, Franz Waxman, Friedrich Hollander, and Erich Korngold all received Academy Award nominations.[54] The reaction of the American music world was the same as the reaction of the American art world to the arrival of the Surrealists: people concluded that the Nazis had closed down Vienna as the capital of Western music. "[I]f music is to have a future, it lies in the United States," the composer and critic Roger Sessions wrote in 1938, six weeks after the *Anschluss*.[55]

Schoenberg arrived in the fall of 1933. He was fifty-nine and, along with Stravinsky, who emigrated from Paris in 1939, one of the most famous composers in Europe. He had been raised in modest circumstances—his father was a shopkeeper—in a Jewish family in Vienna. Musically, he was almost entirely self-taught. His great breakthrough as a composer was what he called "die Emanzipation der Dissonanz"—"the emancipation of dissonance."[56]

All music composed in a key (say, C major) has dissonance. A dissonant note (for example, in the case of a C major triad, F) is a sound the ear expects to be "resolved" by a cadence—a return to the original key, or tonic. Until the time of Richard Wagner, virtually all the music that Western listeners call "classical" was composed around a tonic. With Wagner, beginning, spectacularly, with the Prelude to *Tristan und Isolde*, in 1865, composers began pushing the limits of this style by writing music in which the tonic triad (the major or minor chord) gets "lost" for long periods in a kind of chromatic blur.

Schoenberg, along with two of his pupils, Anton Webern and Alban Berg, took the next step. They abandoned the tonic completely, and thereby "emancipated" dissonance from the obligation to be resolved.[57]* Schoenberg published his first work in no key, *Drei Klavierstücke* (*Three Pieces for Piano*), in 1909. By 1923, he had developed *Zwölftonmusik*, the twelve-tone system, in which all of the notes in the chromatic scale

---

* There are precursors—for example, Franz Liszt's *Bagatelle ohne Tonart*—but they are relatively obscure.

(A, A#, B . . . G#) are arranged in a series that forms the basis for the piece. Every note is used; no note is predominant.

Their music was labeled "atonal," even though the term, as Schoenberg complained, is meaningless. Any musical sound is, in relation to other musical sounds, a tone.[58] (It also makes no sense to call something both "twelve-tone" and "atonal.") But the term stuck: music without a tonic just *sounds* atonal, tuneless, to Western ears. In March 1913, a performance of Schoenberg's, Berg's, and Webern's music at the Musikverein in Vienna incited a riot. It became known as the *Skandalkonzert*—the scandalous concert. Two months later, Stravinsky's music (discordant but not "atonal") for the ballet *Le Sacre du printemps*, choreographed by Vaslav Nijinsky, caused a commotion at the Théâtre Champs-Élysées in Paris.[59] When they were both living in the United States, Schoenberg and Stravinsky were perceived as rivals. That is how Theodor Adorno framed the matter in *Philosophie der neuen Musik* (*Philosophy of the New Music*), published in 1949. But Stravinsky is said to have studied *Drei Klavierstücke* when he was composing *Le Sacre du printemps*.[60]

Soon after Hitler came to power, Schoenberg fled with his family first to Paris, then to the United States. (He had converted to Protestantism when he was eighteen; in Paris, he converted back to Judaism.) In 1934, after a year in Boston, he moved to Los Angeles, where the climate was better, and where he joined a German émigré community that came to include Thomas Mann, Bertolt Brecht, and Adorno. He taught music composition both privately and at the University of Southern California and UCLA.

Cage's experience with Schoenberg was like Rauschenberg's with Albers (including the unreliability of their recollections). Cage was a storyteller who tended to repeat, almost verbatim, the same anecdotes in interview after interview, which is a good way of locking in erroneous memories. He also enjoyed open-ended parables. He had no stake in historical accuracy, but, because his theory of art was also a philosophy of life, he had some stake in stories that suited a certain idea of the universe. In 1959, he recorded an album of folktales and autobiographical anecdotes, some about Schoenberg, called *Indeterminacy*—a title that is, among other things, a suggestion about how to understand them.[61]

Appropriately for a composer who avoided continuity, Cage was also extremely unreliable about dates. He misstated the year he met

Schoenberg and he may have exaggerated the amount of time he studied with him. But he did study privately with him, starting in 1935,
and he almost certainly sat in on some of Schoenberg's classes at USC
and UCLA.[62] According to Cage, Schoenberg told Cage he probably
couldn't afford the fee for private lessons and Cage replied that it didn't
matter, since he had no money anyway. Schoenberg said if Cage devoted his life to music, he would teach him for nothing.[63] Whether this
is the way it happened or not, the arrangement was not exceptional.
Schoenberg often took on students gratis.[64]

Like Albers, Schoenberg thought of education as exploration. "Only
action, movement," he wrote in 1922, "produces what could truly be
called education or culture (*Bildung*) . . . Action must start with the
teacher himself; his unrest must infect the pupils. Then they will search
as he does."[65] Still, Schoenberg did not teach the twelve-tone system.
He instructed his students by having them study the masters.[66] Schoenberg, Berg, and Webern were known as the Second Viennese School,
with the implication that they were following on the achievements of
a "First" Viennese school: Haydn, Mozart, Beethoven, and Schubert.
And that is how Schoenberg thought of his work. He was not breaking
with the tradition; he was extending it.

Cage did not find Schoenberg any more supportive than Rauschenberg found Albers. "In all the time I studied with Schoenberg," he said,
"he never once led me to believe that my work was distinguished in any
way. He never praised my compositions, and when I commented on
other students' work in class he held my comments up to ridicule. And
yet I worshipped him like a god."[67] Like Albers, Schoenberg represented
both discipline and iconoclasm. Like Rauschenberg, Cage wanted to
take those things to another level.

Cage had no interest in the tradition, however. He was especially
uninterested in two features of composition that Schoenberg emphasized: variation and harmony. Cage composed pieces using the
twelve-tone system, but he was looking for a way to escape tonality altogether. Schoenberg had broken down conventional distinctions among
tones. Cage decided that he would break down conventional distinctions among musical sounds, noise, and silence. He would treat them as
equals, just as Schoenberg treated the twelve tones as equals. "Whereas,
in the past, the point of disagreement has been between dissonance and
consonance," Cage explained in 1940 in a lecture called "What Next

in American Art?," "it will be, in the immediate future, between noise and so-called musical sounds. The present methods of writing music, principally those which employ harmony and its reference to particular steps in the field of sound, will be inadequate for the composer . . . New methods will be discovered, bearing a definite relation to Schoenberg's twelve-tone system."[68]

Cage needed something *like* the twelve-tone system, some template from which to compose his pieces. He reasoned that of the four fundamental elements of music—pitch, timbre, volume, and duration—the only one that musical sounds, noise, and silence have in common is duration. Duration—"rhythmic structure," he called it—became the foundation of his music.[69] He began composing pieces from what he called "sonorities," rather than tones: music for percussion instruments and "prepared piano"—that is, a piano with objects inserted between some of the strings, so that pressing certain keys produces unexpected sounds. He was also searching for a method that imposed a discipline on the act of composing itself. The one he discovered was composition by chance. By the time he and Rauschenberg became friends, Cage had the method completely worked out. First, though, he met Cunningham.

4.

Mercier Cunningham was born in 1919 in Centralia, Washington, about fifty miles south of Tacoma. His father was a lawyer who chose to practice in a small community. Cunningham always loved to dance. "I didn't *become* a dancer," he said; "I've always danced."[70] Over the course of his career, he almost never missed a performance, and he danced until he was ninety. People who worked with him found him moody and uncommunicative, but they thought that the moment he came onstage, he was transformed.

They also thought that Cunningham was one of the greatest dancers they had ever seen. He had superb technique and he was powerfully athletic, even after he lost his youthful ability to attain extraordinary elevations. He had an unusual body, and he used all of it. He thought that Western dance had failed to explore what he called "the disciplined use of the face," and in photographs of him in performance, the face and the positioning of the head are invariably arresting.[71] Carolyn Brown, who danced with Cunningham for twenty years, described him as "a strange, disturbing mixture of Greek god, panther, and madman."[72]

Cunningham and Cage met in 1938 at the Cornish School, in Seattle. Cornish was a secondary school of the arts; Cunningham went there to study theater, which included classes in dance. Cage had got married, in 1935, to Xenia Andreyevna Kashevaroff, a young artist with exotic features. She had had an affair with the photographer Edward Weston, who used her as a model; her father was a priest in the Eastern Orthodox Greek-Russian Church in Alaska (then a territory).[73] Cage had been hired as an accompanist for the dance classes, and it was at Cornish that, when the assigned space was too small to accommodate an orchestra of percussion instruments, he created his first prepared piano.[74]

In 1939, Cunningham attended the summer session of the Bennington School of Dance, held at Mills College in Oakland. The Cages went, too. Martha Graham, the leading modern dancer in the country, was there. The director of the summer program, Martha Hill, picked Cunningham out the first day. "There was something in the turn of his head—something almost Nijinsky-like," she remembered, and she told Graham to come watch him perform.[75] Graham was impressed, and invited Cunningham to New York. Somewhat to her surprise, he showed up, in September 1939, and became one of the first two male dancers in her company.[76] (The other was Erick Hawkins, whom she married.)

Another visitor at Mills was László Moholy-Nagy. He had left Europe in 1937 to direct, on Gropius's recommendation, a school of design in Chicago to be called the New Bauhaus. For financial reasons, the school had to close after a year, but in 1939 it reopened as the Chicago School of Design, and Moholy-Nagy invited Cage there to teach experimental music.[77] The Cages moved to Chicago in 1941. About a year later, they met Max Ernst, who invited them to come to New York and stay with him and Peggy Guggenheim in her house on East Fifty-First Street, overlooking the East River. The Cages arrived in the summer of 1942.

Cage was thrilled to meet, through Guggenheim, André Breton and many of the émigré painters. He also met Duchamp, who had just escaped from Marseille. Some of Cage's music was performed at the Museum of Modern Art, and the concert was covered in *Time* and *Life*. That broke up his relationship with Guggenheim, who had arranged for Cage to give a concert at Art of This Century and felt upstaged. The Cages stayed on in the city, though. They had reconnected with Cunningham (who played a Caribbean instrument, the marimbula, in the MoMA concert), and this led to a crisis.

"I was, in the forties, in certain ways very confused both in my personal life and in my understanding of what the function of art in the society could be," Cage said later.[78] Xenia knew all about Cage's bisexuality. His relationship with Sample had been an open one (and Philip Johnson claimed to have been one of Cage's partners); before his marriage, he had had affairs with women, notably Pauline Schindler, the ex-wife of the architect Rudolph Schindler, who built a famous concrete-and-glass house on Kings Road in 1922.[79]

Cage is reported to have said (though it was in an interview a few months before his death in 1992) that at first he and Xenia were both attracted to Cunningham and there was a ménage à trois.[80] There is also a story (but there are many such stories involving Peggy Guggenheim) about a sex party at Guggenheim's house that included both Cages and at which Duchamp is supposed to have been present.[81] Whatever the Cages' marital understanding may have been, though, Cunningham was different. He represented an artistic as well as a romantic partnership. The end of the Cages' marriage was painful.[82]

Cage was professionally troubled as well. He could no longer see the point of composing. Schoenberg had already shown that you could write music without a key, and composers had used noise and silence in their music before Cage came along. All those things *could* be done. The question was, Why do them? Cage always said that the answer came from Buddhism. "It was through the study of Buddhism that I became, it seemed to me, less confused," he said.[83] More specifically, he said, this new understanding was "the result of my attending the lectures of Suzuki for three years. I think it was from 1949 to 1951."[84] This is wrong on every count. The dates, as usual, can't be right. And by the time Cage met Suzuki, he had already been introduced to Buddhism.

The major influence on Cage's thinking about Asian culture was not Suzuki. It was a twenty-five-year-old musician named Gita Sarabhai, to whom he was introduced by the artist Isamu Noguchi in August 1946. (Noguchi designed the sets for Cunningham's first ballet, *The Seasons*, in 1947.) Sarabhai belonged to a wealthy Indian family; her father, Ambalal, was a major supporter of Mahatma Gandhi. She came to New York because she was worried that Western music was driving out traditional music in India, and she made a deal with Cage: if he would teach her the twelve-tone system, she would teach him about Indian music.

They met several times a week, and a lot of the conversation was about religion and philosophy. Before she left, in December, Sarabhai gave Cage a copy of *The Gospel of Sri Ramakrishna* (published in English translation in 1942). By his own report and the recollection of friends, Cage carried it with him everywhere for the next twelve months.[85] In 1960, he listed it as one of the ten books having the greatest influence on his thought, along with Ananda Coomaraswamy's *The Transformation of Nature in Art* and Huang-Po's *Doctrine of Universal Mind* ("in the original 75¢ form," published in 1947).[86] But for some reason, Cage preferred to associate this aspect of his thought not with Sarabhai, but with Suzuki.*

Daisetsu Suzuki was a major figure in the popular fascination with Zen Buddhism in the 1950s. He made his first visit to the United States in 1893, when he was twenty-three. He returned in 1907 and remained eleven years, translating Asian philosophical and religious texts into English. (Suzuki knew many languages.) He returned to Japan to teach and write. Many years later, a sailor stationed at Pearl Harbor named Richard De Martino happened to read a paper of Suzuki's in an anthology. After the war, De Martino was serving in the International Military Tribunal in Tokyo, when, by happenstance, he met Suzuki at his home in Kamakura. As many people who encountered Suzuki were, he was captivated.

De Martino accompanied Suzuki on his return to the United States, first to the Claremont Graduate Center, where Suzuki taught in the spring of 1950, and then on a tour of American universities speaking on "Oriental Culture and Thought," funded by the Rockefeller Foundation. They ended up in New York City in the fall of 1950. Suzuki gave some lectures in New York, including three at Columbia in the spring of 1951, but he did not begin teaching the course Cage was referring to until the spring of 1952.[87] By then, Suzuki was eighty-two.

Suzuki's was a regular Columbia University course, offered first in

* As was the case for many Americans (Ginsberg, for example) fascinated by Eastern thought, the books that influenced Cage represented different traditions. Ramakrishna was a Hindu mystic; Coomaraswamy was a scholar and philosopher; Huang-Po was a Chinese master of Zen Buddhism.

the Department of Religion and then in the Philosophy department. It was taught from four to seven on Fridays on the seventh floor of Philosophy Hall in a room containing a photograph of John Dewey. (Dewey had been in the Philosophy department for twenty-six years; he died in June 1952.) A handful of students enrolled, Zen Buddhism not being a field with much professional promise. The students sat around a table; an overflow audience of auditors sat along the walls or stood outside the door. Cage attended the lectures in the spring and fall of 1952 and possibly beyond. (Suzuki retired from teaching in 1957.)

It's unlikely that Cage learned much from the lectures that he didn't already know—he had read some of Suzuki's writings—except from Suzuki's personal example. For Cage, too, found him fascinating: a small, elderly man, dressed like an American academic, who was almost inaudible, avoided arguments and conclusions, and sometimes appeared to have nothing to say. (As a teacher, Dewey was the same: colorless and charismatic.) Suzuki seemed the embodiment of Zen—although probably mainly to people who, like Cage, already got it. This would have been consistent with Suzuki's customary warning in class that the only students who could be enlightened by what he had to say were already enlightened.[88] Nevertheless, people who knew Cage before and after his encounters with Suzuki felt that he had changed from an argumentative and sometimes truculent person to a model of serenity—although, as with Rauschenberg's boyish self-presentation, not everyone found the new Cage entirely persuasive.[89]

Suzuki did not bring Buddhist thought to the United States, of course. It had come with Chinese and Japanese immigrants in the nineteenth century, and non-Asians on the West Coast, such as the poets Philip Whalen and Gary Snyder, had ample access to East Asian art and thought. Allen Ginsberg and Jack Kerouac both got interested in Buddhism before they knew much about Suzuki, and they did not meet him until 1958. (Suzuki was unimpressed.)

Still, Suzuki's presence in New York was one of the reasons for what was soon named the "Zen 'boom.'"[90] He had an international reputation, and his books, particularly *An Introduction to Zen Buddhism*, published in 1934, and *Essays in Zen Buddhism: First Series*, published in 1927, were avidly read by people like Snyder and Cage. In 1956, the New York University philosopher and *Partisan Review* writer William Barrett edited a paperback anthology of Suzuki's writings, *Zen Buddhism*. The enthusiasm for Zen was also promoted by two popular books: *Zen in the Art of Archery*, by Eugen Herrigel, a German philosopher who had studied in Japan, which came out in English, with an introduction by Suzuki, in 1953; and *The Way of Zen*, by the British émigré Alan Watts, published in 1957.

Zen also got a boost from its association with the Beats—Kerouac's *The Dharma Bums* came out in 1958, a year after *On the Road*—and with J. D. Salinger, who knew Suzuki and who may have attended some of his lectures before he went down his rabbit hole and abandoned New York City for Cornish, New Hampshire, in 1953. Salinger used a Zen koan—"What is the sound of one hand clapping?"—as the epigraph to *Nine Stories* in 1953.[91] And his last published stories, "Zooey," in *The New Yorker* in 1957, and "Seymour: An Introduction," in 1959, make allusions to Zen, to Suzuki, and even (explaining Seymour Glass's preternatural skill at marbles) to *Zen in the Art of Archery*.[92] Cage's music and writings helped create the popular interest in Zen; popular interest in Zen helped make Cage a minor celebrity.

For Suzuki, what meditation reveals is the absence of conflict. "The mistake consists in our splitting into two what is really and absolutely one," he wrote.[93] Oppositions—something/nothing, finite/infinite, darkness/enlightenment, life/death, the binaries by which much conscious thought appears to be structured—are figments of the intellect, and therefore cannot be transcended by rational means. Since language is a tool of the intellect, it is impossible to *explain* Zen. This is why Zen teachings are riddles, "indeterminate." Meaning/non-meaning is one more false binary.

This mapped nicely onto Cage's idea about the distinction between sound and silence. But the question of what music is good for remained. A standard answer is that music is a form of personal expression. But Cage felt that when, during the war, he had written pieces intended to express feelings of loneliness and devastation, listeners had completely missed the point.[94] Sarabhai explained to him that personal expression had no place in the Indian conception of music, and this seems to have been the key to Cage's new way of thinking about what he was doing.

Los Angeles High School seniors knew their classmate: *being radical* was a prescient assessment. When Cage abandoned personal expression, he abandoned it utterly. He was no longer even interested in self-expressive work by other people. He thought the whole approach was misconceived and a bad way to listen to music or look at art. "Say Abstract Expressionism really is the expressionism of the artist's feelings through his gesture and art," he once asked, "then isn't he doing it rather poorly?"[95]

But even work that is not explicitly intended to express something can be infected by the personality of the composer. The great musical taboos for Cage were memory (of music the composer already knows) and taste, and he set about devising elaborate protocols to prevent his personal preferences and associations from determining what the listener hears. That was the purpose of chance composition. It locked out the ego. It was a discipline, not unlike putting a scroll of paper in the typewriter or throwing paint on the canvas: it took away a lot of agency. Chance may "emancipate" the sounds; it does not emancipate the composer.

Obviously, a piece of music cannot be itself entirely a product of chance. It has to start with a choice. In Cage's scheme, a composer begins with what Schoenberg called "the Idea."[96] What Schoenberg meant by that term is somewhat obscure, but for Cage it took the form of a question. How would you create a composition for live radios? (*Imaginary Landscape No. 4* [1951].) How about a piece for radio, prepared piano, whistles, water containers, a deck of cards, and a wooden stick? (*Water Music* [1952].) A piece composed entirely of tape-recorded sounds— country sounds, city sounds, electronic sounds, and so on? (*Williams Mix* [1952].) Having decided on the idea, Cage then used chance procedures to organize some or all of the compositional elements: rhythm, pitch, sonority, dynamics.

Cage used various techniques, but the one he liked the best and became most closely associated with was the *I Ching*, the ancient Chinese divination text. Cage had known about the *I Ching* for some time, probably in an 1882 English translation by James Legge, but his use of it to compose began in 1950. That was the year a sixteen-year-old named Christian Wolff knocked on Cage's door and asked if he could study with him. Wolff had been inspired to compose after his parents took him to a concert at Tanglewood featuring the music of Schoenberg, Berg, and Webern, when he was fourteen. Cage agreed to accept him gratis, as Schoenberg had done for Cage, and Wolff quickly became part of Cage's circle.

Wolff was born in Nice in 1934. His parents, Helen and Kurt, had been publishers in Germany—Franz Kafka and Walter Benjamin were among their authors—and had fled Berlin. (Kurt's mother was Jewish, but their association with Jewish writers alone would have put them in jeopardy.) They were interned as enemy aliens, but managed to get to Marseille and, with the help of Varian Fry, to the United States. They had no money; they had to borrow to pay for the passage over.

They arrived in 1941, and soon after, with Jacques Schiffrin, the editor who had been let go at Gallimard as a concession to the Germans, they founded Pantheon Books. Pantheon published the English translation of *Zen in the Art of Archery*. It also produced the Bollingen series, funded by the Mellon Foundation and dedicated principally to the works of Carl Jung. In 1950, Pantheon brought out in the Bollingen series a new English translation of the *I Ching* by Hellmut Wilheim and Cary Baynes. (Wilheim and Baynes actually translated a German translation that had been made by Wilheim's father, Richard, and published with an introduction by Jung emphasizing the role of chance.) Wolff gave a copy to Cage in lieu of a fee.[97] Cage took one look at it and put it to use.

The *I Ching* contains sixty-four numbered hexagrams, diagrams consisting of combinations of six broken or continuous lines, each combination associated with pieces of advice and prediction. A hexagram is traditionally cast, or chosen, by drawing marked straws (or yarrow stalks). Cage tossed coins instead. He drew up a chart with sixty-four different combinations of one of the musical elements to be used in the piece. He then flipped three coins six times to come up with a hexagram, looked up the number of the hexagram in the *I Ching*, and chose the corresponding numbered combination from the chart.[98] This method of composition was not completely new: Mozart had written a piece (or at least the piece is attributed to him) called *Musikalisches Würfelspiel* (*Musical Dice-Game*), for which dice are rolled to indicate the number of the measure to be played. For Cage, though, it wasn't a game.

The craft aspect of the method must have appealed to him, because note by note, it is absurdly labor-intensive. The first piece of Cage's that uses chance for all its elements—pitch, duration, and dynamics—is *Music of Changes*. (The *I Ching* is also known as *The Book of Changes*.) It was composed in 1951 and it took Cage nine months. To economize on time, Cage flipped coins on the subway (leading to interesting conversations with other passengers), and had visitors to his apartment flip them, too.[99] To splice together the pieces of tape that make *Williams Mix*, Cage alone spent nine months, and he had a number of collaborators. The piece itself is less than five minutes long. Suzuki started teaching at Columbia the same year, 1952, but Cage had already resolved his professional crisis.

5.

Cage and Cunningham staged their first collaboration before a small audience in a theater on West Sixteenth Street. It was 1944, the year the Cages separated; Cunningham quit dancing with Martha Graham a year later. Cunningham performed six solo pieces and Cage did the music. "I date my beginning from this concert," Cunningham said.[100]

Back at the Cornish School, Cage had talked about music being "an integral part of the dance."[101] And in the beginning, Cage and Cunningham still composed referential works—music and dance that were "about" a mood or a natural setting. But they soon adopted a different philosophy: the music and the choreography should be independent. This had nothing to do with Zen. Cunningham was reacting against two dance traditions. He wanted to free movement from synchronicity with music, what he called "the 'boom for boom' school," and from the obligation to present characters and tell a story—all attributes of ballet.[102] He also wanted to free dance from the obligation to mean something, from the modern-dance commitment to expression.

"If a dancer dances—which is not the same as having theories about dancing or wishing to dance or trying to dance or remembering in his body someone else's dance—but if the dancer *dances*, everything is there," Cunningham wrote in 1955.[103] "I don't work through images or ideas—I work through the body," he said later. "And I don't ever want a dancer to start thinking that a movement *means* something. That was what I really didn't like about working with Martha Graham."[104] So after deciding on the length of each part of the performance, Cage composed and Cunningham choreographed separately. When he had his own company, Cunningham refused to tell his dancers the significance of the movements he assigned them—the dancers weren't supposed to "express" anything—and the first time they heard the music was the first time they went onstage to perform the work.

In 1948, Cage and Cunningham went on a national tour by car, just the two of them. In April, they spent five days performing (for room and board) at Black Mountain College. For Cage, the Bauhaus atmosphere was familiar and congenial. "I found my ideas were absolutely like two peas in a pod with those of Josef Albers," he said.[105] Albers "combined the strictness of German thinking . . . and the ability to inspire people with the possibility of their own individual freedom."[106] Among the many things they had in common was a distaste for self-expression.[107] Cage and Cunningham enjoyed the visit and agreed to come back that summer to teach.

After 1945, enrollment at Black Mountain swelled, thanks to the G.I. Bill. Seventy-four students attended the 1948 summer session. On Cage's recommendation, Albers invited Willem and Elaine de Kooning and the sculptor Richard Lippold. (De Kooning had just had his first one-person show, at the Charles Egan Gallery, but nothing sold.) Albers asked Buckminster Fuller, who came and erected his first geodesic dome. (As Fuller had forewarned, it collapsed.) Isaac Rosenfeld, a writer who was one of Saul Bellow's closest friends—they produced together a Yiddish translation of "The Love Song of J. Alfred Prufrock"—also visited. (He is supposed to have hated the place.)[108]

With Albers's approval, Cage arranged a summer-long festival of the music of the French composer Erik Satie. The music faculty at Black Mountain was led for years by a German émigré who was one of Schoenberg's first students, Heinrich Jalowetz. Jalowetz died in 1946, but he had been one of the most admired faculty at the college—his widow, Johanna, still lived there—and the musical spirit of Black Mountain remained Viennese. Cage therefore knew what he was getting into when he devoted one of the brief talks Albers asked him to give before performances of Satie's music to explaining what was wrong with Beethoven.

"Beethoven was in error, and his influence, which has been as extensive as it is lamentable, has been deadening to the art of music," Cage said. The error was believing that harmony is the basis for music, when the true basis, of course, is duration. "There can be no right making of music that does not structure itself from the very roots of sound and silence—lengths of time," Cage announced. "In India, rhythmic structure is called Tala. With us, unfortunately, it is called a new idea."[109]

This did not go over well with the émigrés (although the college was accustomed to intellectual food fights). Like Schoenberg, they believed in tradition. To Cage, though, tradition was one more way for memory and taste to determine composition, and that attitude would always separate him from European avant-garde composers. He knew exactly what buttons he was pushing, and he was, naturally, undaunted.

Cage had discovered in the rare books collection of the New York Public Library a short play by Erik Satie called *Le Piège de Méduse* (*The Ruse of Medusa*). He had it translated by Mary Caroline (M. C.) Richards, who taught literature at the college, and performed with a cast that included Cunningham, Rosenfeld, Fuller, and the de Koonings, who also designed the sets. Lippold designed a costume for Cunningham.

The amateurs had some trouble acting, so a twenty-six-year-old student, Arthur Penn, at Black Mountain on the G.I. Bill, was brought in to co-direct with Helen Livingston, a drama teacher. Penn had been reading Konstantin Stanislavski on acting, and he introduced some improvisation into the script, which seems to have relaxed inhibitions. Penn was astonished watching Cunningham onstage. He "really existed up there—in a way that very few people I've ever seen had," he said later.[110] Cage and Cunningham left Black Mountain in August and so missed the arrival of Rauschenberg and Weil that fall.

It's possible that Cage and Rauschenberg met in New York a few years later, around the time of Rauschenberg's show at Betty Parsons, but both dated their friendship from the summer of 1952, when they were again at Black Mountain. Rauschenberg had gone there, alone and uninvited, in July 1951, the month his son was born. He went back and forth to New York, but he returned in the winter and stayed through the summer session. Weil came to join him for the summer, but discovered that he had fallen in love with Twombly and returned to New York. They were divorced in October.[111]

Albers was gone. He was replaced as de facto leader of the college by the poet Charles Olson. Olson was large (six feet seven inches, two hundred and fifty pounds). He was remembered as "maddening and magnanimous . . . oracular, terrifying, a Mexican wool serape magisterially flung over his shoulders, even when he was bare-torsoed on the hottest North Carolina summer day."[112] Olson took a visceral dislike to Rauschenberg—"such an endocrine [hormonal] creature," he called him. He was especially distressed by being summoned one night in January to help rescue Rauschenberg from the middle of the campus lake in freezing temperatures. Olson found Twombly standing in the lake calling

Rauschenberg's name. Whether Rauschenberg swam out as a prank or from more melodramatic motives is unclear, but Olson sensed homosexual overtones and had a panicky reaction. He didn't like Cage much, either.[113]

That did not prevent Cage from producing that summer what would become his two most famous works: the mixed-media event known as *Theatre Piece No. 1* and *4' 33"*, the so-called silent piece for piano. Cage was scheduled to teach composition, but after he announced that class time would be spent helping him compose his piece of sounds for tape recorder, *Williams Mix*, no one enrolled. This left him free to pursue his own projects. *Theatre Piece* was conceived one day in August at lunchtime and performed the same evening. It was cooked up by Cage and the pianist David Tudor.

Tudor was an indispensable figure in postwar avant-garde music because he was one of the few people in the world who could play it. People found him somewhat inscrutable—self-possessed, laconic, a little secretive. He was freakishly gifted: he could sight-read the most complex and unconventional scores ever written. When avant-garde music became electronic, Tudor mastered that medium, too. His ability allowed composers to write music that might otherwise have remained unwritten because it was otherwise unplayable. Composers wrote pieces *for* Tudor. In the 1950s, he became a one-man cultural exchange program, performing new American music in Europe and new European music in the United States.[114]

Tudor was born in Philadelphia and went to Swarthmore, where he studied piano with Irma Wolpe and, later, composition and analysis with her husband, Stefan, both German émigrés. When he met Cage, in 1949, Tudor was twenty-three. Cage was looking for someone to record a piano piece that was too difficult for him to play. They got together again about eight months later when Cage needed someone to play Pierre Boulez's new *Deuxième Sonate pour piano*, a key work in Boulez's career and technically formidable. Tudor ended up playing the American premiere of Boulez's piece in the Carnegie Recital Hall on December 17, 1950, and that performance made his reputation. People were still talking about it ten years later.[115]

Tudor also premiered Cage's first all-chance composition, *Music of Changes*, on New Year's Day, 1952, at the Cherry Lane Theatre in the Village. Cage was madly in love with him.[116] Tudor admired Cage's work, but he did not reciprocate Cage's affections, and he somehow managed to extricate himself from the relationship's amorous implications. He worked with Cage and, after Cage died, with Cunningham for the rest of his life.

Tudor had already been to Black Mountain. He visited in the summer of 1951, and persuaded Olson to hire Stefan Wolpe to head the music faculty. Wolpe was a perfect fit: he had been a student at the Bauhaus in Weimar; he had known Jalowetz and Schoenberg in Berlin; he had studied with Webern. Clement Greenberg was also teaching at Black Mountain, on de Kooning's recommendation; Kenneth Noland was a student in his class.[117] And Tudor met M. C. Richards. She had come to Black Mountain with her husband, a philosopher named Albert (Bill) Levi, in 1945, but they had separated. She had a PhD from Berkeley and had helped recruit Olson. She taught (among other things) the criticism of Georg Lukács, then little known in the United States. She fell in love with Tudor; in this case, he reciprocated. At the end of the summer, she went back to New York with him.[118]

Both returned for the summer session in 1952, along with Cage, Cunningham, and Franz Kline. (Olson invited the Alberses, who declined.) When he was preparing to play the Boulez sonata, Tudor learned that Boulez had been reading Antonin Artaud's essays in *Le Théâtre et son double* (*The Theatre and Its Double*), published in 1938. Tudor worked up his French so he could read Artaud's book, and it helped him with the piece. He got Cage started reading Artaud as well. Very little of Artaud's work had been published in English; Tudor encouraged Richards to make a translation. By the summer of 1952, she had almost finished it, and she read passages aloud to Tudor, Cage, and Cunningham at Black Mountain.[119]

Artaud's book was therefore one of the things Tudor and Cage had in mind when they came up with their idea for a mixed-media event. Artaud wanted to decouple dramatic action from words, from a script. He wanted an avant-garde version of what Wagner called (though he was not the first to use the term) the *Gesamtkunstwerk*, the total work of art. As Artaud put it in an essay on Jean-Louis Barrault's dramatic adaptation of Faulkner's *As I Lay Dying*, in which he acted:

> the theatre, which opens on a physical field, requires that this field
> be filled, that its space be furnished with gestures, that this space

live magically in itself, release within itself an aviary of sounds, and discover there new relations between sound, gesture, and voice.

Artaud wrote of theater as "total spectacle" and "organized anarchy."[120] He was a great admirer of the Marx Brothers.

These ideas all suited *Theatre Piece No. 1*, but there was nothing new about them at Black Mountain in 1952. The college had been putting on mixed-media events for years, starting with a theatrical format that Xanti Schawinsky brought with him from the Bauhaus that he called Spectrodrama, which was followed, after Schawinsky left, by the Light Sound Movement Workshop, with which Richards was involved. *Theatre Piece No. 1* had a spectacular afterlife; but the audience that saw it did not find it so unusual. Although people were taking pictures continually at Black Mountain, there does not seem to be a single extant photograph of *Theatre Piece No. 1*.[121]

This makes it difficult to know what took place. Almost everything about the performance is disputed, from the length of time it took to what really happened.* There was no stage as such. The piece was presented in the dining hall with chairs arranged in four quadrants around an open space, so the performers used the aisles and the audience faced one another. Since Cage was the person who organized it, his account, in an interview thirteen years later, is presumably the most reliable.

> At one end of the rectangular hall, the long end, was a movie and at the other end were slides. I was up on a ladder delivering a lecture which included silences and there was another ladder which M. C. Richards and Charles Olson went up at different times [to read poetry] . . . Robert Rauschenberg was playing an old-fashioned phonograph that had a horn and a dog on the side listening, and David Tudor was playing a piano, and Merce Cunningham and other dancers were moving through the audience and around the audience. Rauschenberg's pictures were suspended above the audience . . . They were suspended at various angles, a canopy of painting above the audience.[122]

---

* The historian Martin Duberman collected three detailed eyewitness accounts; they are almost completely different from one another. (*Black Mountain*, 372–79.)

Greater specificity is elusive. Cage later said that he read a lecture he had written that year to give at the Juilliard School, a lecture in which he refers to Beethoven as "a roll of toilet paper."[123] This suggests that the performance lasted about forty-five minutes.

Theatre Piece No. 1 can sound like a cacophony of simultaneous and unrehearsed independent actions, but there was a program. The sole surviving document from the original event is Cage's instructions to the projectionist:

> Begin at 16 min
> play freely until 23 min
>
> Begin again at 24:30
> play freely until 35:45
>
> Begin at 38:20
> play freely until 44:25[124]

In other words, movies were being projected for only about twenty-five of the forty-five minutes the performance lasted. And the same was true of the readings (Cage's lecture had silences already built into it), the music played on the piano, the records played on the Victrola, and the dancing. Each element was performed for strictly measured segments of time. And those measures were determined by Cage's usual method: by chance.

The seating arrangement was the key to the piece, because it decentered the performance. This was a standard convention of the new music: eliminating the tonic decenters the listening experience. Tudor said that in Boulez's music, "there was nothing leading, nothing on which the music centered itself."[125] It was also a standard practice for Cunningham. He ignored the orientation dictated by the proscenium stage; he thought all directions could be "the front." Dances did not have to be choreographed around a single point.[126] In *Theatre Piece No. 1*, this meant that the experience of each member of the audience was a function of the direction in which they were looking and the actions to which they elected to pay attention. It amused Cage that Johanna Jalowetz arrived early and asked him where the best seat was. There was no best seat.[127] The performance lacked a focal point, which is why accounts of it differ so dramatically. That was the intention.

Although Richards remembered them as Kline's, the paintings that were hung above the audience were from Rauschenberg's series *White Paintings*, which he had made at Black Mountain the previous fall. They are oil on canvas (Rauschenberg used house paint in a matte white), and there are six, each a different size and number of panels, from one panel (48 x 48 inches) to seven (72 x 126 inches).

Rauschenberg initially saw the *White Paintings* as a breakthrough. In a letter to Betty Parsons soon after he made them, he described them as "a group of paintings I consider almost an emergency. They bear the contradictions [Rauschenberg was dyslexic] that deserves them a place with other outstanding art and yet they are not Art because they take you to a place in painting art has not yet been."[128] But that was before Rauschenberg got to know Cage. When he did, he was quick to see the advantages of Cage's more matter-of-fact, What if I try this? mode of explanation, and, in subsequent accounts, he was much less apocalyptic. "I really wanted to see for myself whether there would be anything to look at," he said about the *White Paintings* in 1968. "I did not do it as an extreme logical gesture."[129] "I was so innocently and indulgently excited about the pieces because they worked," he said in 1987. "I did them as an experiment."[130]

The discipline in the *White Paintings* is the uninflected surface. Rauschenberg was insistent about this. If the paintings began to show signs of age, he wanted them repainted. Keeping the artist out of the work required constant vigilance. It also meant that the paintings' significance changes hands. The artist doesn't make the paintings signify; the viewer does. This was a standard idea of Marcel Duchamp's, and it is phenomenological: the art object itself is empty, inert; it is "made" by the spectator—or by what might be called the spectatorial environment (the room, the light, the context). As long as there is a spectator, there is significance.

Rauschenberg knew little about Duchamp in 1951, but Cage had known his work since 1931 or 1932, when he met Arensberg in Los Angeles, and he had known Duchamp himself, of course, since meeting him at Peggy Guggenheim's in 1942. Cage got what was going on in the *White Paintings*. He described them as "airports for the light, shadows, and particles" in the space around them. They proved that "*[a] canvas is never empty*."[131] The art is happening *because* of the canvas, but not *on* the canvas.

Cage said that the *White Paintings* were what inspired him to compose *4′ 33″*, which he did about a week after *Theatre Piece No. 1*. It was performed not at Black Mountain but in the Maverick Concert Hall, an open-air theater in Woodstock, New York, on August 29, 1952. The pianist was Tudor, and there were nine works on the program, all new music, including Boulez's first piano sonata and *The Banshee*, by Cage's old mentor, Henry Cowell, a work played on the open strings of the piano. Tudor determined the order of the pieces by chance; *4′33″* was next to last. It was listed in the program as a piece in three movements, with the times for each movement given, meaning that the audience, which included M. C. Richards and the dancer Carolyn Brown, knew that the silence was not going to last forever.

Tudor began the performance by sitting down at the piano, opening the score, starting a stopwatch, and closing the lid of the keyboard. After thirty seconds, during which he turned the pages of the score, he raised the lid and turned off the stopwatch. He repeated those actions twice more, at intervals lasting two minutes and twenty-three seconds and one minute and forty seconds. This is how Cage described the experience:

> You could hear the wind stirring outside during the first movement. During the second, raindrops began pattering on the roof [which was made of corrugated metal], and during the third the people themselves made all kinds of interesting sounds as they talked or walked out.[132]

The audience, mostly artists, was—Tudor's word—"incensed."[133] It is Cage's signature work. After 1952, people who knew nothing else about Cage knew about the silent piece. More than twenty commercial recordings have been made; in 2004, it was performed in Britain by a symphony orchestra.[134] Cage always said that *4′ 33″* was his best piece and the one he liked the most.

These works—the *White Paintings*, *Theatre Piece No. 1*, and *4′33″*—are at the center of the Rauschenberg-Johns-Cage-Cunningham aesthetic, and they are easily misread. They are not Dada or anti-art, and they do not embrace a philosophy of "anything goes." They are completely committed to a traditional view of art as a transformative experience, and they are highly disciplined. They rule out much more than they permit.

Cage explained that he composed *4' 33"* "note by note" using the same method he had used for *Music of Changes* a year earlier—except, of course, he had to derive only durations; pitch and dynamics were irrelevant. Instead of the *I Ching*, he used marked Tarot cards, which he shuffled and then dealt in a complicated card-spread. The durations were chance-determined. The score was not a dummy: Tudor was actually counting the measures for each movement. Whether the overall length of the piece was predetermined is unknown, though Cage may have had the playing time of a 78-rpm record in mind.[135]

Phenomenologically, there are three stages to the artwork-spectator encounter with the *White Paintings*, the Black Mountain theater piece, and the silent piece. The spectator comes to the work with an everyday perceptual apparatus—with "Where's the best seat?" expectations. Expectations like that are deliberately and programmatically frustrated by the artwork. There is no focal point where a focal point is expected, no shapes or colors where shapes and colors are customary, no designed sounds even though sound is the medium. Yet something is there. And when the spectator returns to the world, it is with new eyes, new ears, and a new sense of the order and disorder in things as they are. "To open eyes."

Sarabhai told Cage that for Indians, the purpose of music is "to season and sober the mind thus making it susceptible to divine influences." He liked her formulation, but he secularized it: "divine influences" became "the environment in which we are." "Our business in living," he said, "is to become fluent with the life we are living, and art can help this."[136] For Cage, Rauschenberg, and Cunningham, the key to helping people see, hear, and feel was to refuse to tell people what they should be seeing, hearing, and feeling. "I don't think that what I do is non-expressive," Cunningham said, "it's just that I don't try to inflict it on anybody."[137]

6.

In 1946, Cage moved into a building on Monroe Street, near the Williamsburg Bridge. The neighborhood was desolate. Christian Wolff, who grew up in the Village, recalled his first visit. "It was one of the only places in New York where I saw rats crossing the street," he said. ". . . The first thing on Monroe Street you'd come across was this sort of burned-out building, which seemed to have been a bread factory. Somehow you could still smell little bits of bread smells . . . The last building on Monroe Street was this really dismal-looking tenement about five stories high, kind of noisy and smelly."[138]

That was Cage's building. He lived on the top floor in a two-room walk-up. He painted the place white and furnished it minimally. The apartment enjoyed spectacular river views, east and south, and the rent was minuscule. Consistent with Cage's flair for publicity, his place was written up in *Junior Bazaar* (a short-lived supplement in *Harper's Bazaar*). "He has launched a trend in living," the magazine said.[139] *Harper's Bazaar* later used the apartment for fashion shoots.

Cage worked and entertained there, and his apartment became a gathering place for artists and musicians in his circle and for visitors, such as Boulez, from Europe. Lippold and his wife, Louise, a dancer, moved in next door. The artist Ray Johnson, who had been Albers's student at Black Mountain, lived in the building. The composer Morton Feldman, who Cage met at a New York Philharmonic concert in 1950, moved in downstairs. Feldman, a large, vociferous man who composed some of the softest and most evanescent music ever recorded, had been a student of Stefan Wolpe's. Feldman, Wolff, and Earle Brown all had pieces on the program at the premiere of *4' 33"*.

Feldman and Wolff (until he entered Harvard in the fall of 1951) were in the apartment almost daily, along with the composer Earle Brown, who had come to New York from Denver with his wife, Carolyn, the dancer, to be around Cage. Cage and his friends called the building the Bozza Mansion (the landlord's name was Bozza), and Cage lived there until 1953, when the building was scheduled to be demolished to make way for the Vladeck Houses, a public housing development. He was not amused when Carolyn Brown suggested that on the Zen principle of nonattachment, he should regard not having the apartment as no different from having the apartment. "Don't you *ever* parrot my words back to me!" he said.[140]

Cage's circle of composers was thoroughly integrated with the downtown art world. When they performed concerts, the audience consisted mostly of artists and writers, not composers and musicians. They also socialized with painters. "John [Cage] and I would drop in at the Cedar Bar [the Cedar Tavern, on University Place, was popular with the Abstract Expressionists] at six in the afternoon and talk until it closed and after it closed," Feldman remembered. "I can say without exaggeration that we did this every day for five years of our lives."[141]

The composers around Cage regarded the painters, and Pollock in particular, as inspirations. Feldman composed the soundtrack for Hans Namuth's movie of Pollock. (Lee Krasner had asked Cage to do it, but Cage found Pollock's behavior offensive and referred her to Feldman.) Feldman later named compositions after de Kooning, Kline, and Rothko. "That's what started me off—the company I kept," he said in 1960. "Pollock, Kline, de Kooning. I'm an expressionist, actually. I try to paint with tones."[142] Earle Brown was inspired by seeing Pollock's art in the *Life* "Is He the Greatest Living Painter?" article in 1949. "It *looked* like what I wanted my music to *sound* like," he said.[143]

Cage's response was more ambivalent. He said that he used to cross the street to avoid Pollock, and he disliked *Mural* when he saw it in Peggy Guggenheim's building because (he thought) it was based on the human body. He also disliked de Kooning's *Woman* paintings. "If that's what art is, it doesn't interest me," he said. This was all part of his general aversion to affective art. "I wanted them to change my way of seeing, not my way of feeling," he said about the Abstract Expressionists. "I'm perfectly happy about my feelings . . . I don't want to spend my life being pushed around by a bunch of artists."[144] But he liked what he called "the overall surface without any center" in de Kooning's black-and-white abstractions and Pollock's drip paintings.[145] There is no "best seat" for looking at those works.

"What was great about the fifties was that for one brief moment—maybe, say, six weeks—nobody understood art. That's why it all happened," Feldman said. Rauschenberg said: "I thought my friends and I were inventing art."[146] The belief that the medium evolved in a linear way—the belief that led Greenberg to champion color-field abstractionists such as Kenneth Noland and Jules Olitski as the next stage in modern art—younger artists and composers like Rauschenberg, Feldman, and Cage found absurd. There are only individual works that are more or less interesting.

It was easier for composers not to appear to be imitating Pollock and de Kooning than it was for painters. In 1952, after their summer at Black Mountain, Rauschenberg and Twombly went to Rome, then to North Africa. They returned in March. Rauschenberg had quit Betty Parsons: he was upset when she told him she had talked Philip Johnson into buying one of his pieces. He felt this was unsupportive.[147] He moved to the Stable Gallery, one of the first galleries in the postwar boom specializing in contemporary American art. It had just opened in what had been a horse stable on Seventh Avenue near Fifty-Eighth Street. The odor of its former inmates remained, and the owner, Eleanor Ward, offered Rauschenberg and Twombly shows in exchange for cleaning the place up.

In the fall, Rauschenberg exhibited two of the *White Paintings* and several from another series of monochromes, all-black paintings, along with some sculptures. Rauschenberg's show was not a success; neither was Twombly's. Ward said she had to remove the guest book "because so many awful things were being written in it." Robert Coates, the *New Yorker's* art critic, walked out. Barnett Newman was reported to have remarked, dismissively, about the *White Paintings* that Rauschenberg "thinks it's easy. The point is to do it with paint."[148]

Rauschenberg took note. One Sunday that fall, he asked Cage to drive his car, a Model A, down to Fulton Street, where Rauschenberg was living in a cold-water loft. (He took baths in the Browns' apartment on Cornelia Street.) Rauschenberg had glued together twenty of the largest sheets of paper he could find, and while he poured black house paint on the pages, he had Cage drive slowly over them. It was a rainy day, but Rauschenberg salvaged the piece. It is twenty-two feet long and he called it *Automobile Tire Print*.

There is a visual resemblance to *This Is the First Half of a Print Designed to Exist in Passing Time*, the early Black Mountain piece, and both works engage with representing motion in a static medium. Essentially, though, *Automobile Tire Print* is Rauschenberg's response to Newman. Newman's painterly signature was the "zip," a vertical line separating large monochrome panels. The zips were notorious in the art world: after Newman had his first one-man show, at Betty Parsons in January 1950, the furniture at the Club—an artists' society on Eighth Street frequented by avant-gardists in every medium—was festooned with strips of tape in his honor, to mimic the zips.[149] Rauschenberg must have asked himself, And what is *not* easy about a zip? Visually, the tire track is a parody of the first of Newman's zip paintings, *Onement 1*, painted in 1948. It is a Bauhaus version of a Newman painting: art meets technology. And it was easy. And he did it with paint.

Around the same time, Rauschenberg called on de Kooning in his studio and asked him for a drawing he could erase. De Kooning was curious but not disagreeable. He took his time to find something that would be hard to erase, a drawing made with grease pencil, ink, and crayon. Rauschenberg said erasing it took him a month. He put it in a gold-leaf frame with a mat.[150] (When Rauschenberg exhibited the work, many years later, de Kooning was extremely annoyed.)[151]

Rauschenberg explained the piece, later known as *Erased de Kooning Drawing*, as a "white drawing," a complement to the *White Paintings*. He said he calculated that to make such a work he had to erase an actual drawing, and it had to be a drawing by an artist. By the fall of 1953, de Kooning had established himself as the painter's painter—his show of the *Woman* paintings the previous spring had been a sensation—and that is why Rauschenberg, with a bottle of Jack Daniels and some trepidation, had approached him.

Automobile Tire Print and *Erased de Kooning Drawing* are not just insider jokes, but they do point down a cul-de-sac. Rauschenberg was trying other kinds of art in the fall of 1953, including painting on fabric, which would become an important technique for him. But he was disheartened by the reaction to his Stable show. Only one piece was sold—to the Browns, who bought one of the black paintings for $26.30, the amount of a rebate check they had just received from the phone company.[152] It wasn't just that buyers weren't interested; it was that artists rejected his work as well.

Rauschenberg would later recall with amusement the days when he was regarded as a jester, but that was a retrospective satisfaction. He had been ridiculed by Albers. He had no money. And he was a competitive man. He must have known that outraging art-world opinion and tweaking or subverting the work of more established artists was not a promising career path. If that is how he was feeling in the fall of 1953, he was rescued, fortuitously, by two collaborators.

The first was Cunningham. Cunningham formed his own company at Black Mountain in the summer of 1953, and Rauschenberg soon began designing costumes, sets, and lighting for their dances. The company operated on the principles Cunningham and Cage had worked out. Each dancer was effectively a soloist, so that there was no central figure in the performance, and Rauschenberg designed the costumes and sets in the same way Cage wrote the music: without knowing the choreography in advance. The dancers found out what they would be wearing and what the set would look like on the day of the performance.

Rauschenberg, Cage, and Cunningham worked together, and traveled the world, in this way for ten years.

Rauschenberg's other collaborator was Jasper Johns.

7.

Johns said of his childhood that it "wasn't specially cheerful."[153] He was born in 1930 in Augusta, Georgia. His parents separated when he was two, and he was sent to live with his grandfather, a farmer, in Allendale, South Carolina, a town of a little more than two thousand people. The grandfather died when Johns was seven, and he went to live with his mother and stepfather and their children. After a year, he was sent off again, this time to an aunt in an isolated area called the Corner, near Lake Murray, where he attended a two-room school. In 1946, he returned to his mother's house, now in Sumter, South Carolina, and a year later graduated from the local high school. By then, he had attended five different schools. He enrolled in the University of South Carolina, where his art teachers encouraged him. After three semesters, he moved to New York City. He was eighteen. "I didn't know artists," he later said, "but at an early age I realized that in order to be one I'd have to be somewhere else."[154]

He studied at the Parsons School of Design, but dropped out after a semester and made a living as a messenger and a shipping clerk. He saw a lot of contemporary art, including Pollock's 1950 show at Betty Parsons, which included *Lavender Mist, One: Number 31, 1950*, and *Autumn Rhythm*, and Newman's second solo show there, in 1951, where he exhibited what would be his best-known work, an eighteen-foot painting with five zips called *Vir Heroicus Sublimis*.

In May 1951, Johns was drafted. He spent two years in the army, the last six months, as the Korean War was winding down, in Japan. Back in New York, in the fall of 1953, he entered Hunter College on the G.I. Bill, but he collapsed on the street after the first day of classes and never returned. He took a job working the night shift at Marboro Books, an art bookstore on Fifty-Seventh Street near Carnegie Hall. And that is when he met Rauschenberg.

Rauschenberg was still working as a janitor around the corner at the Stable Gallery, and one night in late 1953 or early 1954, he and Johns met on the sidewalk. They were introduced by Suzi Gablik, an artist (later art critic and historian) who had spent a summer at Black Mountain. Johns and Rauschenberg met again at a party in the studio of Sari Dienes, a Hungarian émigré who had studied with Fernand Léger in Paris and who was specializing in works she called *Sidewalk Rubbings*, created by rubbing paper laid over manhole covers, subway gratings, and other urban infrastructure. She was a friend of Cage's, and by the end of January 1954, Johns had met Cage, Cunningham, Feldman, and the Browns.

Johns was cool and diffident, quick to shut down—the opposite of Rauschenberg. He had ethereal looks, and Rauschenberg was fascinated by him. So was Rachel Rosenthal. She was an artist and dancer who had fled France with her wealthy parents and settled in New York in 1941. After the war, she returned to Paris, where, in 1949, she met Cage and Cunningham. She came back to New York, and, through them, met Rauschenberg.

Rosenthal and Rauschenberg both started hanging around on Fifty-Seventh Street waiting for Johns to get out of work. "He had skin like moonstone, almost transparent, and silky platinum hair. And huge blue eyes with long lashes. He was very private," Rosenthal said. "I knew he was gay," she later said. "It was obvious he was trying to get away from Bob, who was making a big play for him."[155] She and Johns had a brief affair. After it was over, they decided to move downtown, and found two lofts in a condemned building on Pearl Street on the Lower East Side, near Rauschenberg's place on Fulton. Rosenthal took the top floor, Johns the floor beneath. More than a year later, in the summer of 1955, Rosenthal left for California, where she began a career as a performance artist, and in September, Rauschenberg moved into her loft. Her presence is sometimes elided in accounts of Rauschenberg's and Johns's artistic development, but when they had their breakthroughs, Rosenthal was there.

Johns collaborated with Rauschenberg on some of Cunningham's sets. They also created window displays—backdrops for the mannequins—for Bonwit Teller. They worked for Eugene Moore, who was in charge of window displays at Bonwit and Tiffany's, and who liked supporting young artists. The work was well paid by avant-garde standards, and it allowed Johns to quit his job at Marboro and devote himself to painting. Rauschenberg and Johns sometimes used a pseudonym, Matson Jones, on their window-display work.[156]

They arrived at their mature artistic modes at virtually the same moment. In the summer of 1954, Rauschenberg made his first combine. The term may have come from Johns, who defined it as "painting playing the game of sculpture"; Rauschenberg remembered deriving it from a word Duchamp coined for Alexander Calder's hanging sculptures: mobile.[157] Another definition would be "three-dimensional collage." Combines are assemblages (another term that was used for them, though not by Rauschenberg), usually heavily marked or painted, of found materials, ranging from posters, magazine illustrations, and comic strips to light bulbs, Coca-Cola bottles, mirrors, and stuffed animals. Rauschenberg's first combine, *Untitled*, is seven feet two inches high, made with oil, pencil, and crayon on paper, canvas, and fabric; it incorporates newspapers, photographs, wood, glass, mirror, tin, cork, a found painting, painted leather shoes, dried grass, and a stuffed Plymouth Rock hen.[158]

The inspiration for the combines is almost certainly the work Rauschenberg was doing with Cunningham and Cage. The method of creating the music, sets, and choreography independently had a rationale. When you are walking down the street, there are three elements present: sounds (traffic, voices, sirens, and so on); the visual environment (buildings, trash cans, cars, people around you); the movements of your own body. None of these elements was "created" in conjunction with any of the other elements. They are all independent, yet they exist in the same time and space. We therefore normally never consciously experience them simultaneously; we attend to one or another. Cunningham's dances are designed to force us to attend to exactly that: the coexistence of unrelated stimuli.

A combine works in the same way. The front page of a printed newspaper is a collage. Radically dissimilar stories are juxtaposed: an article about a murder case is printed next to a photo of the winner of a dog show. Again, we habitually edit out the disjunctiveness and attend to one thing at a time. Rauschenberg's combines force us to attend to radical disjunctiveness in the artwork so that we might better attend to it elsewhere in our lives. "Random order" was the term Rauschenberg used to describe this aesthetic.[159]

Johns's development required a rupture. Around the time he met Rauschenberg, he destroyed almost all of his work. (A few items do survive.) "Most of my early attempts at painting consisted of trying to make something like somebody else made, and that never worked," he explained later; he wanted "to avoid repeating what others were doing and to rid myself of a tendency to imitate."[160] Then, in the fall of 1954, he had a dream in which he painted an American flag. He decided to take this as good career advice, and he finished his first flag painting (called *Flag*) in 1955. The work is in encaustic—pigmented wax—a technique he learned about from a book he found at Marboro. (Encaustic dries faster than oils, allowing the artist to repaint quickly.) In *Flag*, the paint is applied on a newspaper collage, which is just visible underneath. Johns went on to create a series of flags, also a series of targets (some with plaster casts mounted on them), of maps, and of numerals.

From the fall of 1955 until the summer of 1961, when the relationship ended, Rauschenberg and Johns were together every day, living until 1958 on Pearl Street and then, when the building was scheduled to be demolished, on Front Street. They were virtual collaborators, sometimes working on each other's pieces in addition to the work they did for Cunningham and Gene Moore. But Johns's art presents very differently from Rauschenberg's: rigorous and austere versus playful and indiscriminate. What did they have in common?

They were both making art that is figural but not representational, anti-illusionist but not abstract. The elements in a combine are not images of things; they *are* things, just as the flag painting *is* a flag, not (only) a picture of a flag. Johns had seen his first show of the work of René Magritte at the Janis Gallery in March 1954—a show that included Magritte's *Ceci n'est pas une pipe*.[161] *Flag* is not a flag, and it is a flag. It adds a new twist to an old paradox. For both Johns and Rauschenberg, the compositional challenge consisted in making an artwork that allows things to be themselves. "Using something that's more familiar some place else," Rauschenberg explained, "its identity has to remain the same. But somehow the context should be able to free it or open it up to thinking about it differently . . . [W]hen you have finished the painting, the glass of water [used in one of his combines] looks as reasonable there as it would any place else you might have it."[162] The glass of water is part of an artwork, but it remains a glass of water.

In the same way, *Flag* is not a found object (like Duchamp's urinal) or a trompe l'oeil. It's a painting, but a painting that does not make its subject a vehicle for a particular meaning or feeling. "Using this design took care of a great deal for me because I didn't have to design it," Johns said about *Flag*. "So I went on to similar things like the targets—things the mind already knows . . . A picture ought to be looked at the same way you look at a radiator."[163] "I never want to free myself from images at all," he said on another occasion; "I want images to free themselves from me . . . I simply want the object to be free."[164]

Rauschenberg once explained that he took inspiration from Leonardo da Vinci's *Annunciation*, a painting of the Virgin Mary, which he saw in the Uffizi in Florence when he was in Italy with Twombly. "In that work," he explained to a skeptical French interviewer in 1961, "the tree, the rock, and the Virgin all have the same importance at the same time. There is no hierarchy: that's what interests me."[165] Few observers would see Leonardo's painting in quite this way (although Rauschenberg's interlocutor seems to have been impressed). But Rauschenberg had already taken his inspiration from Cage. He was describing Leonardo's *Annunciation*, and therefore his own art, in Cage's aesthetic terms.

Avoiding hierarchy required the same discipline that Cage used. In fact, Rauschenberg considered chance procedures, but he told Cage that the result would be too intellectual.[166] So he worked by continually vetoing his own instinctive choices, the same thing Cage was doing when he composed by chance. "I think the largest consideration is that you don't let any single element actually dominate the picture," Rauschenberg said. "So that nothing becomes subservient." That is the logic of twelve-tone composition.[167]

Rauschenberg did not put the elements of his combines together by a process of association, even though that is a natural assumption to make. On the contrary: "If I see any superficial subconscious relationships that I'm familiar with—clichés of association—I change the picture," he said. "I always have a good reason for taking something out but never have one for putting something in. I don't want to—because that means that the picture is being painted predigested."[168]

The work that posed the greatest challenge to these requirements is the stuffed goat with an automobile tire around it, *Monogram*. The goat, an Angora, was a found object: Rauschenberg happened on it in 1955 in an office furniture and supplies store, whose owner had acquired it inadvertently when he purchased an abandoned box in an auction. Rauschenberg paid fifteen dollars on deposit for the goat (the man asked for thirty-five and never saw the other twenty), and then spent four years trying to figure out how to use it in a combine.[169]

The goat was Rauschenberg's Virgin Mary: an exotic object that threatened to become the focal point, the dominant key, center stage of the artwork. He tried many solutions before coming up with the tire. The tire satisfies Rauschenberg's artistic preconditions: it has no association with goats; it is there without a reason; most important, it cancels out the goat as a center of interest. You cannot say that the combine is "about" either a goat or a tire. It is about a goat-with-a-tire. At Johns's suggestion, Rauschenberg mounted this on a painted platform that functions as a pasture, and he had his combine.[170]

8.

Postwar American artists needed an "art world."* That is, they needed critics and reviewers who could understand and would write about their work, dealers who would show it, and curators and collectors who wanted to buy it. Pollock had Peggy Guggenheim, Betty Parsons, and Clement Greenberg; de Kooning had Charles Egan and Harold Rosenberg. Neither painter, in the beginning, had collectors, or dealers who were part of the international art market. Johns and Rauschenberg were lucky. They had Leo Castelli.

Castelli came late to the art business—he was almost fifty when he opened the Leo Castelli Gallery—and he always gave the impression that he was in it for the art, not the business. In fact, Castelli was a shrewd promoter. It also helped that he was infinitely suave. He knew how to lead, not push, collectors to a purchase. But that was the minor part. Castelli also did things no other dealer thought to do: he spent money on public relations; he collaborated, rather than competed, with other art galleries; he worked the art-journal world; above all, he exploited the international market. He saw that for American art to be successful, it needed to be bought by Europeans.

And Castelli knew Europeans. He was a paragon of cosmopolitanism. His father was Hungarian; his mother was Italian. Castelli was her

---

* "A work of art in the classificatory sense is (1) an artifact (2) a set of the aspects of which has had conferred upon it the status of candidate for appreciation by some person or persons acting on behalf of a certain social institution (the artworld)," George Dickie, *Art and the Aesthetic: An Institutional Analysis* (Ithaca: Cornell University Press, 1974), 179–80; "Art worlds consist of all the people whose activities are necessary to the production of the characteristic works which that world, and perhaps others as well, define as art," Howard S. Becker, *Art Worlds* (Berkeley: University of California Press, 1982), 34.

family name; the father's was Krausz. Leo was born in 1907 and raised in Trieste. He spent the war years at school in Vienna. The family was well off: Castelli's mother was an heiress, his father a banker. Castelli went to work for an insurance agency in Bucharest, where he met Ileana Shapira, the daughter of a wealthy Romanian businessman. They married and, in 1934, moved to Paris, where, in 1939, Castelli and René Drouin, an architect and interior designer, opened an art gallery in the Place Vendôme.

They mounted exactly one show, an exhibition of Surrealist works in the spring of 1939. The gallery closed for the summer; the war began in September. When Germany invaded France, Ileana's father was already in New York, and he was able to obtain visas for the couple. They arrived in New York, via Casablanca, Tangier, Spain, and Cuba, in March 1941 and moved into an apartment on East Seventy-Seventh Street. It was in that apartment, sixteen years later, that Castelli opened his gallery.[171]

Castelli had been involved in the arts scene for a long time. He was a habitué of the downtown Club and a force behind what became known as "The Ninth Street Show" in 1951, the first Abstract Expressionist group show. Castelli's first show in his own gallery, in February 1957, featured lesser-known painters who worked in the Abstract Expressionist style.[172] Then he discovered Johns.

Johns and Rauschenberg had been approached through the artist Allan Kaprow about being represented in a show at the Jewish Museum to be called *Artists of the New York School: Second Generation*. The show was being organized by Meyer Schapiro, with whom Kaprow had studied. Johns got into a contentious discussion about his work *Target with Plaster Casts*, which included a cast of a penis that the museum was reluctant to put on display, but he was subsequently visited in his loft by a man whom he remembered talking with him about *Zen in the Art of Archery* and who selected a different painting, *Green Target*, for the show.[173] The Jewish Museum is on Fifth Avenue in what was formerly the Warburg mansion, where the Alberses stayed when they first arrived in New York. Castelli went to the preview, on March 7, 1957, and he saw *Green Target*. He was transfixed. He was also struck by the artist's name: "It seemed almost like an invented name—Jasper Johns," he said.[174]

By chance, the next evening, Morton Feldman brought the Castellis to Rauschenberg's loft to see his work. Cocktails were served, and Rauschenberg said he had to run downstairs to "Jasper's" loft, where the communal refrigerator was, to get some ice. Castelli asked whether this was the Jasper who made *Green Target*, and, learning that it was, asked to meet him. Johns came up, they met, and then everyone went downstairs. Castelli was astonished. He was confronted by a space filled with targets, flags, and alphabet paintings. "There was about a million dollars' worth of paintings that were worth nothing, just there," he later said. He asked Johns if he would like a show.[175]

Johns's show at the Castelli Gallery, from January 20 to February 8, 1958, rocked the art world. The month it opened, Thomas Hess ran a reproduction of *Target with Four Faces*—a work by an artist almost no one had heard of—on the cover of *ARTnews*. Alfred Barr came to the show with Dorothy Miller, the curator of painting and sculpture at MoMA, and bought four works for the museum, including *Flag*. Worried that the trustees might find the work unpatriotic, Barr persuaded Philip Johnson to buy it. He paid nine hundred dollars.* (Interestingly, Johns's *Flag on Orange Field* had appeared in a window display in Bonwit Teller a year earlier and no one had complained: commercial culture was way ahead of institutional culture in 1958.)

Other MoMA trustees bought pieces, and so did several collectors who would become financial mainstays of contemporary American art in the next decade. Every work sold except (possibly because the political meaning was too overt) *White Flag*, which Johns kept, and the troublesome *Target with Plaster Casts*, which Castelli bought. He waived the commission.

It was MoMA's purchases of work by a virtually unknown artist that got the art world's attention. The museum had been famously stingy about acquiring American art. "When Alfred Barr went to the first Jasper Johns exhibition and bought three [*sic*] pictures for MoMA's permanent collection," Hilton Kramer said later, ". . . I don't believe there were three Rothkos in the museum . . . It was like a gunshot. It commanded everybody's attention."[176] Johns's work was received as a new direction for American art. His paintings were neither abstract nor expressionist. But the show was important for another reason as well: it announced the

---

* Johnson did not finally donate it to the museum until 1973, when it was worth a good deal more.

emergence of a New York art world. Johns's art had a gallery (Castelli), a journal (*ARTnews*), a museum (MoMA), and collectors. It would soon have a critic. Johns had done nothing to create this world; the world had discovered him. But in discovering Johns, it had discovered itself.

Rauschenberg was a little peeved that a younger artist who might have been regarded as his protégé was given a show when the Castellis had originally come to Pearl Street to see his work. Partly out of compassion, Castelli gave Rauschenberg his own show. It opened in March, and included several combines that would later become iconic, including *Bed*, made from a quilt a friend had lent Rauschenberg at Black Mountain to cover the hood of his car on cold nights. Only one work sold, and it was quickly returned. Castelli bought *Bed* (which he gave to the Museum of Modern Art twenty years later, when its value was estimated at up to $10 million).[177] Some visitors to the gallery found Rauschenberg's work offensive; not many found it exciting. "This is a very good show," one wrote in the guest book, "but nothing like Jasper Johns."[178] Still, Johns and Rauschenberg now had money. Virtually the first thing they did with it was to produce a retrospective concert of the music of John Cage.

After Cage lost his place on Monroe Street, he had moved to Stony Point, in Rockland County, about fifty miles north of the city. He lived there in a cooperative designed and financed by Paul and Vera Williams, former students at, and benefactors of, Black Mountain College. (Paul Williams was an architect who had come into a large inheritance.) Cage was joined in Stony Point by David Tudor, M. C. Richards, Sari Dienes, and two potters from Black Mountain, Karen and David Weinrib. Cunningham stayed in New York so that he could teach class. Cage would later move back to the city, but Tudor and Dienes remained in Stony Point for the rest of their lives.[179]

Cage, Cunningham, Johns, and Rauschenberg soon met a Rockland County resident named Emile de Antonio, who was living with the third of his six wives, Lois Long, a successful textile designer. (She and Cage would collaborate on a children's book, *The Mud Book*, which they were unable to publish.) De Antonio produced a concert of Cage's music in the auditorium of a local high school in 1955—many people came up from the city to attend—and in 1958, he joined Johns and Rauschenberg in organizing a Cage retrospective. Each man put up a thousand dollars.[180]

"The 25-Year Retrospective Concert of the Music of John Cage" was performed in Town Hall on West Forty-Third Street on May 15, 1958. The event would later be talked about as the final gathering of the first postwar generation of the New York avant-garde. Almost a thousand people attended. The Stable Gallery mounted an accompanying exhibition of Cage's musical scores. The selections for the concert were made by Tudor; Cunningham conducted—that is, kept time in the manner of a metronome.

The high point of the evening was the *Williams Mix*, the piece Cage had been working on at Black Mountain in the summer of 1952. It is named for Paul Williams, who had given Cage money to work on it, and it was created by splicing recorded sounds together, using chance procedures, on magnetic tape. The tape played at fifteen inches a second. Feldman, Tudor, and Brown all helped; at one point, Feldman's instructions required making 1,097 separate sections to fit into a quarter inch of tape—one sixtieth of a second.

Williams Mix is played on eight tape recorders simultaneously. It was next to last in the Town Hall program, and it elicited an ovation of boos and bravos that lasted almost half as long as the work itself. During the final piece of the evening, *Concert for Piano and Orchestra*, a group in the balcony staged a protest with whistles and catcalls. Cheering and shouting went on long after the concert was finished. It was all perfectly in the spirit of avant-garde performance. Town Hall was Cage's *Skandalkonzert.*[181]

9.

Ten weeks later, in Darmstadt, West Germany, Cage delivered a series of lectures that rattled the European musical avant-garde. It was the start of a six-year period during which Cage, Cunningham, Johns, and Rauschenberg took their work across Europe and Asia, from Paris and Stockholm to Bombay and Tokyo, and became catalysts in the globalization of the arts.

It is not as though the world was passively awaiting their appearance. Their reception was determined by local cultural politics and by artistic developments already under way in the places they visited. And they were supported by an international network of patrons, dealers, collectors, critics, government officials, museum directors, record companies, and conference and festival organizers. Cage, Cunningham, Johns, and Rauschenberg became leading actors in a worldwide artistic drama already in progress.

Darmstadt, a city of about a hundred thousand people twenty-five miles south of Frankfurt, was (and remains) the home of the Internationale Ferienkurse für Neue Musik (IFNM)—the International Summer Courses for New Music. The IFNM rose, literally, from the ashes of the Second World War. Darmstadt was the headquarters of Merck, the chemical manufacturer, and on the night of September 11–12, 1944, the Royal Air Force bombed the city. In twenty minutes, nearly 80 percent of the city's buildings were destroyed and tens of thousands of people were made homeless.[182] It was a preview of the firebombing of Dresden five months later.[183]

Yet just a month after the war in Europe ended, the mayor was approached by a music critic named Wolgang Steincke with a proposal to make Darmstadt a center for contemporary culture. As remote from the immediate task of rebuilding as it seemed, Steincke's idea suited the desires of the local government, and it suited the desires of the organization to which that government reported, the Office of Military Government for the United States (OMGUS). In the postwar partition of Germany, Darmstadt was in the American zone.

The Germans referred to 1945 as *Stunde Null*, Zero Hour. The presumption was that beginning anew meant reviving the traditions that had been ruptured by Nazism, and Germans undertook the task of cultural renewal with speed and avidity, particularly in two fields with which Germany was closely identified, philosophy and music.[184] The United States government was fully supportive. It saw that German cultural renewal could be a step toward European integration, which was a priority for American foreign policy planners, who believed that one way of avoiding what was known as "the German problem" was by tying the fate of Germany to the rest of Europe. In 1947, the Joint Chiefs of Staff directed the head of OMGUS, General Lucius Clay, to "encourage German initiative and responsible participation in [the] work of cultural reconstruction and . . . expedite the establishment of these international cultural relations which will overcome the spiritual isolation imposed by National Socialism and further the assimilation of the German people into the world community of nations."[185]

This was to a considerable extent wishful thinking. The example of

Heidegger showed how tricky it was to disentangle German philosophy from Nazism. And the case of music was, if anything, worse, since many distinguished German composers, conductors, and performers flourished under Hitler. Even Steincke had a somewhat sketchy past. Still, it was in everyone's interest to use music as a means of restoring a sense of national identity and cosmopolitan engagement, and Darmstadt came to symbolize this ambition. By August 1945, Steincke had become *Kulturreferent*—culture officer—of the city, and the IFNM offered its first courses a year later.[186]

Steincke was fortunate that the principal figures he had to deal with in OMGUS were trained musicologists. Everett Helm, head of the Theater and Music Branch, had studied at Harvard with Hugo Leichtentritt, a German émigré, and had continued his musical studies in Italy before the war. John Evarts, the branch's local officer, was a member of the founding faculty of Black Mountain College: he translated for Josef Albers in the early days, and taught music there until 1942, when he enlisted. These men understood contemporary European music, and they were generous to Darmstadt. Between 1949 and 1951, about 20 percent of the IFNM's budget came from OMGUS.[187]

When Cage made his appearance in Darmstadt, twelve years after its founding, more than two hundred European musicians were attending the IFNM every year. Cage entered a dispute already under way concerning the future of serialism, the method of composition devised by Schoenberg, Berg, and Webern back before Hitler. By 1958, serialism had evolved to a system known as "multiple serialism," in which all musical elements—in addition to pitch (the only element serialized in Schoenberg's system), dynamics, rhythm, and so on—were subjected to serial methods in the name of the principle that Schoenberg had announced: "emancipation" from traditional musical formulas. The debate was over how much of this process the composer should cede to chance. The principal antagonists were Boulez (more conservative) and the young German composer Karlheinz Stockhausen (more Cagean).

The atmosphere was primed by talks in the two summers before Cage arrived. In 1955, Stefan Wolpe, whose financial situation became precarious when Black Mountain closed, wrote to Steincke to ask about teaching at the IFNM. Steincke invited him to the 1956 session; it was Wolpe's first visit to Germany in more than twenty years. He was accompanied by Tudor, and they presented a survey of recent American music that included the first European performance of Cage's *Music of Changes*, as well as a discussion of jazz and improvisation.[188] Wolpe's message to his European audience was that American composers showed that there was no need to adhere to serialism or any other system. "Everything is possible," he told them. "Everything lies open. That is the historical situation."[189] After Wolpe spoke, Boulez and Stockhausen got into a verbal fight that lasted an hour, Boulez trying to talk Stockhausen out of a Cagean position.[190]

The next year, the Italian composer Luigi Nono, who was married to one of Arnold Schoenberg's daughters, gave a lecture, "Die Entwicklung der Reihentechnik" ("The Development of Serial Technique"), in which he announced the existence of a "school of Darmstadt," which, he said, "could be compared . . . with the Bauhaus of Weimar and Dessau."[191] The phrase caught on. The idea of a "school" alluded not just to the Bauhaus but to the Second Viennese School as well, both victims of Nazism.* It thus captured the postwar spirit of renewal by reconnecting contemporary music with the pre-Hitler past. It also implied a degree of agreement among the participants in the IFNM—specifically, a commitment to serialism—that may have been misplaced.[192]

Whatever agreements may have existed, Cage blew them apart. By 1958, the German economy was robust and American support for cultural events such as the FSNM was no longer necessary. In fact, the balance of trade had tilted in the other direction: Germany was now a source of financial sustenance for avant-garde American musicians, who had few sources of income at home. Steincke could bring people like Cage and Tudor to Darmstadt by offering generous stipends for teaching and performing and by arranging concerts and recording sessions for them in Germany.[193]

Cage gave three lectures in Darmstadt, from September 6 to 9, with Tudor providing musical illustrations. Cage recited Zen parables, and elements of his lectures were chance determined. In one lecture, for example, he was obliged at predetermined points to stop speaking and light a cigarette. The controversial part of the lectures was what Cage called "indeterminacy."

---

* Anton Webern seems to have had Nazi sympathies, but this would not have been known at the time.

Indeterminacy arose out of Cage's desire to "emancipate" music from one last hierarchy: the relationship between composer and performer. Indeterminacy means that the work can be performed in more than one way *at the choice of the performer*. Choices might concern the number of performers, the instruments to be used, pitch, duration, and so forth. Cage explained to his audience that indeterminacy was necessary because chance methods were not enough. Performers were still expected to follow a score. He even renounced *Music of Changes*. "The function of the performer in the case of *Music of Changes*," he said,

> is that of a contractor who, following an architect's blueprint, constructs a building . . . The fact that these things that constitute it, though only sounds, have come together to control a human being, the performer, gives the work the alarming aspect of a Frankenstein monster. This situation is of course characteristic of Western music, the masterpieces of which are its most frightening examples, which when concerned with humane communication only move over from Frankenstein monster to Dictator.[194]

In the third and final lecture, most of which took the form of unanswered questions, Cage cast the distinction between his own practice and "the school of Darmstadt" as a difference between American and European values (evoking Wolpe's 1956 lecture). The problem with European composers, Cage said, is that they refuse to relinquish control over what the performers play and the audience hears. "The difference between the Europeans and the Americans lies in that the latter include more silence in their works . . . When silence, generally speaking, is not in evidence, the will of the composer is. Inherent silence is equivalent to a denial of the will.[195]

In case there was uncertainty about his point, Cage repeated it again a year later in an article he wrote at Steincke's request for the IFNM's journal, *Darmstädter Beiträge*. The European composers' problem, Cage explained, was tradition. Tradition operated as one more a priori. Europeans needed to do what Americans had already done and reject tradition altogether. Cage was sure this would happen. "It will not be easy," he said, ". . . for Europe to give up being Europe. It will, nevertheless, and must: for the world is one world now."[196]

Cage was conveying the sentiments of his own musical circle. He and his friends in New York thought that their European counterparts were committed to a dying paradigm. "The thing that we were beginning to feel pretty soon about this hyperorganized, European/Darmstadt music," Wolff said, "was that it could be just as dead as a doornail. Theoretically it was very exciting and interesting, but somehow it was like machinery. It just didn't swing."[197]

It is not hard to see why Cage's Darmstadt lectures provoked outrage. It's true that Cage was only using Schoenberg's prewar rhetoric of "emancipation," but to talk to German audiences of "dictators" and "the will" after 1945 was a provocation. So was comparing composers to fascists and dismissing "tradition" as one more shackle for music to throw off. Reconnecting with tradition was the very rationale of places like Darmstadt. Tradition represented Europe's hope for resurrection. Cage was associating it with more enslavement. He was never invited back to Darmstadt.

After Cage's article in *Darmstädter Beiträge*, Nono delivered an all-out attack on him at the IFNM. Nono was a member of the Italian Communist Party, and an admirer of Sartre and the Italian Marxist Antonio Gramsci. It was significant, he pointed out, that Cage used Zen parables in defense of his compositional practices. "These apply wonderfully," he said, "if one conveniently forgets that they were designed to glorify the ideology of a dynasty which attempted to stop the clock in order to preserve its own religious and political injustices from the eroding force of progress." Nono ridiculed the equation of serial methods with totalitarianism. He called it "a childish attempt to terrify others." For composers like Cage, he said,

> "liberty" is the oppression which the instinct exerts on the mind; their liberty is a spiritual suicide . . . Our "Aesthetes of Freedom" know nothing of real creative liberty, which presupposes a consciously acquired ability to know what decisions must be taken and how to carry them out . . . Music will always be an historical reality to men who face the process of history and who at every moment make their decisions intuitively and logically.[198]

Nono demanded a politically engaged music, and his talk effectively declared the School of Darmstadt, the very entity he had conjured up just three years before, dead. The European musical avant-garde split off in divergent directions, Boulez one way, Stockhausen another, Nono a third. Which was just what Cage had predicted.[199]

After leaving Darmstadt, Cage and Tudor performed in Cologne, Stockholm, Warsaw, Düsseldorf, Copenhagen, Brussels (at Expo 1958, a World's Fair), Oxford, Hamburg (where they accompanied dances by Cunningham and Carolyn Brown), Milan, Florence, and Padua.[200] In Italy, Cage became a television star. He appeared on a tremendously popular quiz show called *Lascia o Raddoppia?* (*Double or Nothing?*), the Italian equivalent of *The $64,000 Question*, where contestants answered questions on a subject of their choice. Cage's was mushrooms. He had developed a fascination with them after moving to Stony Point, and he sometimes sold mushrooms he gathered locally to restaurants in the city, including the Four Seasons in the new Seagram Building, De Antonio acting as a middleman.

On the Italian program, Cage lasted into the fifth and final week when, with the entire jackpot at stake, he was required to name every white-spored mushroom. There are twenty-four; Cage named them in alphabetical order. He won five million lira—six thousand dollars. He became a celebrity, and was invited to audition for a part in Federico Fellini's *La Dolce Vita*, then being filmed. It was by far the largest amount of money he had ever earned, and when he got back to New York, he used $2,336 of it to buy a Volkswagen bus for Cunningham and his company to tour in.[201]

10.

In New York, Rauschenberg's career was gaining traction. In the spring of 1959, he had a solo show at Castelli where he exhibited *Monogram*, causing a sensation, and where he sold his first work to a public collection. The piece was a combine called *Migration*; the buyer was Alan Solomon, the founder and director of the Andrew Dickson White Museum of Art at Cornell, where he taught art history. Later that year, along with Johns and another Castelli artist, Frank Stella, Rauschenberg appeared in *Sixteen Americans* at the Museum of Modern Art. The exhibition was curated by Dorothy Miller, who had put together an all–Abstract Expressionist *New American Painting* exhibition that toured Europe the year before, and who had helped Barr choose the works for MoMA to buy in Johns's first solo show. Miller had mounted regular exhibitions of contemporary American painting and sculpture since 1942, and the shows attracted press attention (not always favorable).[202] Rauschenberg contributed to the catalogue a few lines that would become eternally attached to him: "Painting relates to both art and life. Neither can be made. (I try to act in that gap between the two.)"[203]

In 1961, Rauschenberg had two combines—one, *Canyon*, featuring a stuffed bald eagle, would become iconic—in another prominent MoMA exhibition called *The Art of Assemblage*, curated by William Seitz. Solomon resigned his position at Cornell that year and moved to New York to become the director of the Jewish Museum, and his first show there, in 1963, was a Rauschenberg retrospective. He followed it a year later with a Johns retrospective. Both shows received major attention.

But the most important events in Rauschenberg's life were two separations. During the summer of 1961, while they were with Cunningham's company in residency at Connecticut College, he and Johns broke up. Rauschenberg's new partner was Steve Paxton, one of Cunningham's dancers. Neither Rauschenberg nor Johns was ever forthcoming about their intimacy. Rauschenberg attributed the breakup to the stress of being an art-world power couple. "What had been tender and sensitive became gossip," he explained many years later when he was asked about the separation. "It was sort of new to the art world that the two most well-known, up-and-coming studs were affectionately involved."[204] The titles of several works Johns painted that fall suggest that other factors may have been involved: *In Memory of My Feelings—for Frank O'Hara*, *Good Time Charley*, *Liar*, and *No*.

The second event was the divorce of Leo and Ileana Castelli. Ileana was seventeen when she married Leo (he was twenty-six), and the marriage was unhappy for various reasons. One day in 1959, she decided she had had enough. She found out that the state of Georgia offered no-fault divorce to landowners. She arranged a purchase of land there, had divorce papers drawn up over the phone, flew to Georgia, signed the papers, sold the property on the way back to the airport, and returned to New York the same day. The next morning she announced to Leo that they were no longer married.[205]

Both parties were relieved. Soon after, Ileana married Michael Sonnabend, a friend of the family (and Dante scholar: he was helping Rauschenberg produce a series of illustrations of the *Inferno*), whom she had met many years earlier taking courses at Columbia. They moved to Paris, and in 1962, she opened the Galerie Ileana Sonnabend on the Quai des Grands Augustins.

She and Leo were now business partners. He gave her exclusive rights to represent his artists in Europe, where she copied his formula by pursuing an aggressive public relations strategy and setting up collaborative arrangements with European museums and galleries. She established contacts in Milan, Rome, Zurich, Munich, Amsterdam, Düsseldorf, and Cologne.[206] She had the same business philosophy Leo did: for American artists to be taken seriously, they needed European sales.

Rauschenberg had caught the attention of the director of the new Moderna Museet in Stockholm, Pontus Hultén. In 1959, Hultén came to New York, where he fell in love with *Monogram*. Robert Scull, one of the new collectors of contemporary American art (he had made his fortune in the taxi business), had offered to buy *Monogram* for the Museum of Modern Art, but the museum declined. Barr was apparently worried that the goat might deteriorate. Hultén got Rauschenberg to promise not to sell it until he could raise the money to buy it for his museum, which he finally did, for fifteen thousand dollars, in December 1964.

In 1961, Hultén put together *Bewogen Beweging* (*Moving Movement*, or *Art in Motion*), an exhibition of more than two hundred works by eighty-three artists from twenty countries that opened at the Stedelijk in Amsterdam. It included works by Rauschenberg and Johns (and broke the attendance record set by *The Family of Man*). In 1962, with Sonnabend's support, the Moderna Museet mounted *Four Americans*, two of whom were Rauschenberg and Johns. The show traveled to Switzerland and the Netherlands. In the catalogue, Hultén wrote, "Artists used to go to Paris to learn to paint and never left the city entirely. But this is not the case anymore . . . After World War II, the greatest adventures in art have played themselves out in America, with the most interesting painting being made in New York."[207]

In February 1964, Rauschenberg's solo show at the Whitechapel Gallery in London—forty combines plus the Dante illustrations—broke attendance records.[208] By that summer, his work had appeared in thirty exhibitions in Europe. The European art world knew all about him. He had been perfectly prepped for the Venice Biennale.

The Biennale is one of the oldest international competitions in the world. It dates from 1895, around the time that the modern Olympic Games (first held in Athens in 1896) and the Nobel Prizes (first awarded in 1901) got started.[209] Those competitions are both globalizing and nationalistic. They are globalizing because in order to compete, people from different nations all have to be playing the same game. What counts as a track and field event or a work of art or a scientific advance in one country has to be the same in every other country; otherwise, the judges are comparing apples to oranges.* They are nationalistic, though, because the prizes go to athletes, artists, writers, and scientists as representatives of their own countries. (In the case of the Olympics and the Biennale, this is explicit. Nobel winners are not identified by country, but that is generally how they are reported.) The competitions are also opportunities for the sponsoring entities (in the case of the Olympics, the host cities) to promote themselves. The Venice Biennale therefore reflected both debates within the Italian art world and the international aspirations of the Italian government.

The artistic debate in Italy was part of a larger European debate, complicated by the importance in Italy's cultural and political life of the Partito Comunista Italiano (PCI). Avant-garde European painting after the war adopted styles similar to (though not under the influence of) the American Abstract Expressionists': Art Informel, Tachisme, Art Autre (all terms made popular by the French critic and collector Michel Tapié), or, more broadly, "gestural" painting. The PCI initially adhered to Zhdanovian doctrine, that is, socialist realism, a position buttressed by the association in Italy (unlike in Germany) of Futurism and modernism with fascism.[210] Nonrepresentational, or gestural, painting was non-socialist-realist and therefore politically problematic.

In 1957, control of the Biennale was assumed by the anti-Communist Democrazia Cristiana (Christian Democratic, or DC) government in Rome, which favored the promotion of gestural painting. The presumption was that gestural art was now the European style, for it was the government's policy to seek increased integration with the rest of Europe. What officials interpreted as its "universalism" made abstract art the appropriate diplomatic vehicle for this ambition.

By 1962, though, abstraction had come to seem a predictable and even anachronistic mode of painting. That year marked the high point

---

* The definition of what counts is, of course, Euro-centered.

of Italy's "economic miracle." Average annual growth of GDP between 1958 and 1963 was 6.6 percent (compared with 4.2 percent in the United States), and Italy was moving rapidly into a consumer economy. Television sets, refrigerators, washing machines, and automobiles were the new emblems of prosperity (and gave filmmakers such as Fellini and Michelangelo Antonioni a subject matter for satire). Advertising, previously nonexistent in Italy, became ubiquitous. Radiotelevisione Italiana (RAI), the public agency that regulated television, required all commercials to be broadcast in a single half-hour program every night called *Carosello*. *Carosello* was launched in 1957; by 1960, it was the most watched television show in the country.[211] Next to the iconography of consumerism, abstract painting was looking old-fashioned.

Castelli and Sonnabend read the possibilities. To the extent that the obstacle to postgestural art was the fear of sliding back into representationalism, Johns and Rauschenberg had the solution: a figural art that was anti-illusionistic. Castelli was drawn more to Johns; in 1963, *Newsweek* called Johns "probably the most influential younger painter in the world."[212] Sonnabend's favorite was Rauschenberg. From a business perspective, of course, it didn't matter. Either client could potentially represent the future of painting at a Biennale.

The Sonnabends spent summers in Italy—after 1961, in Venice— and they were friendly with many people in the Italian art world. Castelli was also well-connected—he was, essentially, Italian himself—and he began promoting Johns and Rauschenberg there in 1961. The first salvo was an essay on Rauschenberg by John Cage called "Robert Rauschenberg, Artist, and His Work," which was published in a new Italian journal called *Metro*, a glossy bilingual international journal of contemporary art with American distribution. This was the essay in which Cage described the *White Paintings* as "airports for the light, shadows, and particles." To make their importance clear, he prefaced his essay with a declaration:

> To Whom it May Concern: The white paintings came first; my silent piece came later.
> J. C.[213]

The essay had been engineered by Castelli. *Metro* was published in Milan; the editor was Bruno Alfieri, who had begun his editorial career in his father's publishing business, Alfieri Edizioni d'Arte di Venezia. The house specialty was printing the catalogues of the Venice Biennale. Alfieri's early enthusiasm was for French art, but in 1950, he saw Pollock's work in an exhibition at Peggy Guggenheim's Venetian villa. He was stunned, and wrote a piece explaining that although the paintings were chaotic and provided no critical point of entry, it was clear that Pollock had surpassed Picasso as the most advanced artist in the world. (This is the review *Time* mentioned but chose to quote only the "chaos" part from, ignoring what meant most to Pollock: the favorable comparison to Picasso.)[214]

Alfieri launched *Metro* in 1960. In January 1961, Castelli offered him a Rauschenberg work for two thousand dollars, "a very special price." Alfieri accepted ("Non è molto," he replied—it's not much). And a little more than two weeks later, Castelli wrote back with "sensational news." He had arranged for an essay about Rauschenberg for *Metro*, to be written by John Cage. It would be ready by February.[215]

A year after Cage's piece appeared, Alfieri published an article on Johns. That article, too, was engineered by Castelli. The author was Leo Steinberg. Steinberg was born in Moscow in 1920. His father was Lenin's commissar of justice, but he and Lenin did not see eye to eye, and his tenure was short-lived. The family was forced into exile in Berlin. After Hitler came to power, they moved again, to England, where Leo studied art at the Slade School in London. The family came to New York after the war. Steinberg had many interests, but he settled on art history and enrolled in a doctoral program at New York University.[216]

Steinberg's modus operandi as a critic was bafflement. Why did the artist do that? He liked puzzles. He met Rauschenberg in 1954, and when he heard about the *Erased de Kooning Drawing*, he phoned him to ask him what the point of it was. Would he have erased a drawing by Wyeth or Rembrandt? Rauschenberg said he did not relate to Wyeth and that a Rembrandt would have been too easy—which Steinberg took to mean that it would just have produced a piece of anti-art. Steinberg found the conceptual aspects of the erased de Kooning intriguing.[217]

Steinberg's essay on Johns was published in *Metro* in 1962, the first major critical analysis of Johns's work. Five years after it appeared, Steinberg was accused of having done the piece on commission from Castelli. He responded indignantly. He had begun writing the article on his own, he said; Castelli had merely offered to help him get it published.[218]

It was only much later, he said, that he learned that Castelli had also helped pay his fee.

Castelli told a different story. In his version, Alfieri approached him and said he wanted to publish an article about one of Castelli's painters. Which artist would Castelli recommend? Castelli replied, Johns. And did Castelli know a good person to write the article? Castelli said he did. Castelli then approached Steinberg and asked him how much money he would need to do a piece. Steinberg said a thousand dollars. "Now, this turned out to be five times more than the magazine could afford to pay," Castelli explained. "So I agreed to put up the other 80 percent."[219]

And Steinberg knew perfectly well who was paying his fee, because Castelli's eight-hundred-dollar supplement took the form of a discount on a work of Johns's called *Shade*, which Steinberg purchased. The sale was finalized in November, shortly after the *Metro* article appeared.[220] No doubt Castelli didn't tell Steinberg what to write, but of course that wasn't necessary. As he had done with Alfieri in the case of the Cage essay, Castelli had made sure that Steinberg had a stake in the reputation of his subject.

Along with Steinberg's essay, abundantly illustrated, Alfieri ran a piece by an Italian art critic, Gillo Dorfles, who argued that Johns's paintings of commonplace objects rescued them from the "serial nature of the industrially produced object, the use of which, in becoming mass use, risks losing all its charm to be converted only into the uninterrupted cycle of an economically directed and controlled production"—a politically approved rationale for the use of commercial imagery in the fine arts.[221] The Biennale pump was being primed.

Steinberg's essay is one of the most influential ever written about Johns's work, and it went right to the heart of the art-critical issue. The "liberating discovery" of Johns's art, Steinberg wrote, is that

> the man-made alone can be made, whereas whatever else that's to be seen in our environment is only imitable by make-believe. The position of esthetic anti-illusionism finds here its logical resting place. The street and the sky—they can only be simulated on canvas; but a flag, a target, a 7—these can be made, and the completed painting will represent no more than what actually is. For no likeness or image of a 7 is paintable, only the thing itself . . . Johns eliminates

a residue of double dealing in modern painting. Since his picture plane is to be flat, nothing is paintable without make-believe but what is flat by nature. And if for some reason he wants something 3-D, let the artist insert the thing, or a cast of it.[222]

Johns generally did not have much use for interpreters of his art, but he later said that he thought Steinberg was one critic who understood it. "He saw the work as something new, and then tried to change himself in relation to it," he said. "I admired that."[223] The year the article came out, Steinberg married Dorothy Seiberling, the editor at *Life* behind the "Is He the Greatest Living Painter?" article on Pollock.

The 1964 Venice Biennale displayed three thousand works by eighty invited artists exhibited in thirty national pavilions.[224] Since the end of the war, the American art at the Biennale had been sponsored by the Museum of Modern Art, alternating with other arts organizations. After the 1962 exhibition, though, MoMA announced that it was not continuing, and the job fell to a government agency, the United States Information Agency (USIA). The director of the USIA was Edward R. Murrow, who took the position after he felt he was being pushed out of CBS News for programming that was too controversial, and who was therefore indisposed to impose political tests on the works the agency disseminated. The chief of the service's fine arts section was Lois Bingham, a graduate of Oberlin and the first woman ever admitted to the Yale School of Architecture. She had been at the USIA since 1955.[225] Bingham asked Alan Solomon to curate the American pavilion, with the Jewish Museum acting as co-sponsor.

Castelli could not have chosen better himself. He and Solomon not only had a professional commitment to the same artists; they also had become friends after Solomon moved to New York, got divorced, and undertook to make over his somewhat academic persona. From the moment Solomon took the job, in November 1963, the plan was clear: it was to produce an American prizewinner. He flew immediately not to Italy but to Paris, to huddle with the Sonnabends. He was in the airport when he learned that President Kennedy had been assassinated. "What will happen to all our schemes now?" he wrote to Castelli. But, he reported, he had met the Sonnabends: "I have brought them up to date."[226]

Solomon organized the American exhibition around two pairs of artists: Rauschenberg and Johns, whose work he mounted, because

of space problems, in the United States Consulate, and Kenneth Noland and Morris Louis, whom he exhibited in the American pavilion
on festival grounds. It was, symbolically, Castelli versus Greenberg,
since Greenberg had let it be known that he considered Johns's work
"easy," and had named Noland and Louis as the cutting edge after Pollock.[227] In the context of the European artistic debate, this meant that
Rauschenberg and Johns would, as nongestural post-abstractionists, be
contrast-gainers.

Solomon was perfectly straightforward about his intention. "At the
present moment Europeans are very much aware of American ascen-
dancy in the arts," he wrote in the catalogue that accompanied the
American exhibition. ". . . The fact that the world art center has shifted
from Paris to New York is acknowledged on every hand."[228]

This kind of bravado was not Castelli's style, and the Sonnabends
were horrified.[229] But Solomon had read the situation correctly. French
artists had dominated the Grand Prize for Painting at the Biennale
since 1948, and this did not sit well with the Italians. And Italian artists were familiar with American art: more American artists were working in Rome in the 1950s than in Paris. Twombly had moved there in
1957 and had married an Italian, Tatiana Franchetti, a painter, whose
brother, Giorgio, was an art collector. (Castelli was Twombly's dealer.)[230]
To the extent that the Biennale was a nationalist competition, the Italians were not competing with the Americans. They were competing
with the French. Solomon gave Italy a chance to break with abstraction
and the School of Paris.

It helped that Rauschenberg was in town. He was still designing
sets, costumes, and lighting for Cunningham, and when it was announced that the company would be touring Europe that summer, Solomon requested that it be allowed to perform at the opening gala of
the Biennale, arguing that that would increase attendance.[231] Officials
were unmoved, but Cunningham was able to reserve Venice's famous
Teatro La Fenice, where, on June 18, two days before the prizes were
scheduled to be announced, the company performed before a crowd
unusually raucous even for them. Rauschenberg had gone all out with
the set, with trap doors opening and closing, stage levels rising and falling, bars of light coming and going, and stagehands "working" in the
background. People were dazzled. The jury took note.

The jury had been divided. It included one American member, Sam

Hunter, who was not partial to Castelli's artists; the others were from Switzerland, Brazil, Poland, and the Netherlands, plus two Italians, Giuseppe Marchiori and Marco Valsecchi, both art critics. The fact that Rauschenberg's paintings were not on the grounds of the Biennale became an issue. A compromise was proposed: give the Grand Prize to Noland. When he learned of this, Solomon announced that he would withdraw all the American artists if Rauschenberg was disqualified on a technicality. To meet the objections about siting, however, he agreed to transport three Rauschenberg combines by gondola from the consulate to the American pavilion. And on June 20, Rauschenberg was awarded the Grand Prize for Painting.[232]

The award was immediately perceived as a scandal—not only in the French and Italian press but in the United States as well.[233] There were insinuations in Italy that the prize had been *"comprato"*—bought.[234] But the main accusation was colonialism. "Venice Colonized by America," was the headline in the French journal *Arts*. Solomon's assertion that the center of the art world had moved to New York was described as "a declaration of war." "Europe Explodes as American Takes the Prize" was the headline in *Life*.[235] Hilton Kramer told people that Rauschenberg's victory was an act of "cultural imperialism" by Castelli.[236] Castelli, naturally, preferred a more genteel explanation. "Alan Solomon is an independent man," he said; "our tastes just happened to coincide. Of course, I didn't talk to the judges . . . [I]t was the most natural thing in the world to win."

But Solomon not only knew what he was about; he also knew more than he should have known. "I told him [Alfred Barr] what actually happened," he informed Castelli after the Biennale was over— "leaving out, of course, the more intimate details."[237] "We might have one [*sic*] it anyway (apart from the question of merit)," he told Lois Bingham, "but we really engineered it."[238] "Marchiori and Santomaso, working together, really swung it," he confided to Calvin Tomkins, who was covering the Biennale for *Harper's*. "Don't say this, tho!"[239] Tomkins did not.

But Giuseppe Santomaso, a prominent Venetian painter who taught in the art college, was not on the jury, so lobbying almost certainly occurred. Although Castelli later insisted, "Of course, I didn't talk to the judges," one of the first things he did after arriving in Venice was to call on Marchiori and Santomaso.[240] On the other hand, lobbying seems to have been a long-standing practice at the Biennale, much as it is in the Academy Awards.* Some of the "shock" about the award was the *Casablanca* variety.[241]

In September following the Biennale, Daniel Cordier, who had given Rauschenberg his first solo show in Paris in 1961, announced that he was closing his gallery. "Americans have taste, curiosity and the means to satisfy them," he explained, "and this is why New York, once merely a market, will soon become a predominant cultural center. We may be headed toward a period in which artistic centers scattered all over the world will reject the supremacy of any single one . . . Be that as it may, Paris's role in this area is now a thing of the past."[242] "There's no 'art world' any more, no capital, here or there," Marcel Duchamp said two years later. "Still, the Americans persist in wanting to smash the Paris hegemony. They are idiots, because there is no hegemony, in Paris or in New York."[243]

When the prize was announced, Santomaso arranged a celebration in the Piazza San Marco, where Rauschenberg was hoisted onto the shoulders of young Italian painters, thrilled to identify with the United States at the expense of France. But Rauschenberg was shocked by the hostility of the French reaction. He had been personally as well as artistically popular in Paris. Soon after, he was seen weeping on the street in Saint-Germain-des-Prés.[244] But Rauschenberg also knew that, overnight, he had become the leading artist in a world now bristling with museums eager to display new art and collectors eager to buy it. His success began to erode his relationship with Cunningham and Johns.

For, even after the prize, Rauschenberg was obliged to continue to work with them every day. He had signed on for a world tour and it had just begun. Cunningham and Cage's initial plan was to travel only as far as India, where they had been invited by Cage's old friend Gita Sarabhai, and Japan. The Japanese invitation had come from Toshi Ichiyanagi on behalf of the Sogetsu Art Center in Tokyo. Ichiyanagi was an avant-garde composer and married to Yoko Ono. He had enrolled in, and she had audited, one of Cage's classes at the New School, and they had already hosted a Cage visit to Japan, with Tudor, in 1962, a thirty-day tour.[245]

---

* Castelli's method of persuasion seems to have been purely rhetorical. There is no evidence in the gallery's records of sales to anyone related to the Biennale.

Cage and Cunningham decided to see whether they could drum up European dates as well (and some money to fund the trip). They did, and the result was a tour lasting six months involving a company of sixteen (ten dancers, two musicians, two stage technicians, and two managers) and seventy performances. It began on June 6, 1964, in Strasbourg and traveled to (among other cities) Paris (where they were pelted with eggs and tomatoes), Bourges, Vienna, Cologne, London (where they were an enormous hit and extended their stay), Stockholm (where Pontus Hultén was their host), Helsinki, Prague, Warsaw, Poznań, Brussels, Antwerp, The Hague, Bombay, Ahmedabad (home of the Sarabhais), Delhi, Bangkok, and, from November 6 to 28, Tokyo. In some venues, the company was luxuriously treated by its hosts (American officials were cautious about associating with them); in some, they lived hand-to-mouth. There was never quite enough money, and the quality of the performance facilities varied enormously, as did the audiences. Audiences in Prague were boisterously divided; audiences in India and Bangkok were difficult to read.

After his success in Venice, Rauschenberg attracted attention everywhere, and Cage and Cunningham began to feel that he considered himself one of the company's stars. As it had always been, Rauschenberg's method was to forage, in every venue, for props, and to provide new ideas at every performance. The Cunningham dance called *Story*, for example, required an "object" to be onstage during the performance. In Vienna, Rauschenberg came on himself as the object, covered in burlap, tree branches, and wooden slats; in Devon, he and his assistant, Alex Hay, spent the performance onstage ironing shirts.[246] He seemed to be making the work about himself. Cunningham was not happy.

By the time the company reached Tokyo, everyone was just waiting for the trip to be over. Much of the problem was exhaustion, but part of it was that, in the tacit rift between Rauschenberg and Cunningham, the dancers tended to side with Rauschenberg. He was affable; Cunningham was aloof.

On the last night in Tokyo, Rauschenberg performed a piece on his own with the Japanese critic Yoshiaki Tono, who had met Johns and Rauschenberg in New York, through Castelli, back in 1959, and had done a great deal to promote their art in Japan. The event was planned as a public interview with the title "Twenty Questions for Bob Rauschenberg," and was staged before a full house at the Sogetsu Art Center.

Rauschenberg appeared in a painter's jumpsuit. A large gold screen had been placed on the stage. With Tono leading, Rauschenberg was asked a series of questions, all of which he ignored, while he, Hay, and Paxton worked on the screen. Rauschenberg splashed paint on it, then added an assortment of items: a speedometer, Coca-Cola bottles, a necktie painted gold, a pair of shoes, an RCA Victor dog. He drank, but he never spoke or responded to the questions. After four hours, he was finished. By then, most of his audience had left.

Including Cage and Cunningham. Cunningham left soon after the event began, because one of his dancers, Viola Farber, was flying out that night and he felt he should be with her at the airport. He returned, but when Cage suggested they both leave, he agreed. The next day, they got a message from Rauschenberg:

> dear john and merce
> i am not going to work with the company anymore. it was so
> nice of you to share the last nite with me in such a friendly way.
> thanks bob

Cage and Cunningham did not appreciate the sarcasm; Cage was angry, but Cunningham was conciliatory. Rauschenberg replied to him.

> dear merce
> my rudness last nite was brought on by over emotion, drink,
> exhaustion. please over look my manner. it has been an honer
> and pleasure to work for you . . . i would very much like to be
> your friend and fan. i hope to look you in the eye with good
> conscince + love, if I haven't screwed that possibility up. thank
> you for this great tour.
> bob[247]

When Cunningham was able to assemble a company again, Rauschenberg was replaced as set designer by Jasper Johns.

The European outcry about the Grand Prize was really an admission of surrender—not to the Americanization of art but to the internationalization of art. That was, in a way, the solution: to recognize the artist, rather than a city or a nation, as the center of significance. The French critic Alain Jouffroy had provided the formula even before Venice:

"Rauschenberg's art is not defined within the limits of a single nation," he wrote in the journal *L'Oeil*. "From the beginning, he has participated in the artistic creation of an international conscience, shared by his generation."[248]

In 1965, a year after the Biennale, the journal *Arts* asked 120 people in the French art world to rank the world's greatest artists under fifty. Rauschenberg came out No. 1.[249] But having reached a degree of renown unimaginable to any of them ten years before, the fabulous foursome was a foursome no more.

9

NORTHERN SONGS

Alan Freed MC-ing one of his rock 'n' roll concerts in Cleveland in the early 1950s. The man on the far right, standing directly behind Freed, is probably Lew Platt, a local promoter. (*Michael Ochs Archive / Getty Images*)

1.

The first person to use the term "youth culture" was a Harvard professor, Talcott Parsons. Parsons was describing the culture of adolescents, the chief characteristic of which he identified as irresponsibility. "One of its dominant notes," he wrote, "is 'having a good time.'" He thought that this had a negative side: "a strong tendency to repudiate interest in adult things and to feel at least a certain recalcitrance to the pressure of adult expectations and discipline."[1] Parsons was a sociologist. He wasn't judging; he was only observing. The year was 1942.

That was also the year clothing manufacturers and department stores began making and marketing clothes specifically for teenage girls. ("Girls" and "boys" are what most people called teenagers at the time.) Two years later, in September 1944, the first issue of *Seventeen* came out. Four hundred thousand copies were printed; the magazine sold out in six days. The first agency to collect and sell data on teenage tastes opened in 1945, and that year, *The New York Times Magazine* ran an article entitled "A 'Teen-Age Bill of Rights." The fifth right was "the right to have fun and companions"; the ninth was "the right to struggle towards his own philosophy of life."

By July 1949, the circulation of *Seventeen* was 2.5 million, more than 40 percent of the teenage female population of the United States—adding in what publishers call pass-alongs, the magazine probably reached at least half a million more—and the term "teenager" had become the name for a distinctive demographic. By 1955, American teenagers were spending between $7 billion and $9 billion a year on fashion, food, and entertainment.[2]

The concept of a "counterculture" was first applied to teenagers in 1960 by another sociologist, Milton Yinger (who borrowed the term from Parsons's major work, *The Social System*, published in 1951). A year later, James Coleman, a sociologist at Johns Hopkins, published *The Adolescent Society: The Social Life of the Teenager and Its Impact on Education*, which concludes: "The adolescent is no longer a child, but will spend his energies in the ways he sees fit."[3]* By then, the notion that teenagers represent a distinct taste group with a quasi-independent culture manifesting "a certain recalcitrance to the pressure of adult expectations and discipline" was well established.

Two things about this phenomenon are notable. The first is that it had nothing to do with the spike in the U.S. birth rate between 1946 and 1964—the baby boom.[4] When Coleman's book came out, in 1961, the oldest person in the postwar generation was fifteen and just beginning sophomore year in high school. The members of its largest cohort, born in 1957, were four.† And until the 1970s, almost all of what was called "youth culture" in the United States was created and performed by people who were born before 1945 (in a period of abnormally low birth

---

* Coleman is best known for the 1966 report *Equality of Educational Opportunity* (aka the Coleman Report), which argued that family background, and not the quality of the schools, accounts for the difference between Black and white student achievement.
† There were 4,254,784 live births in 1957, a number not reached again for fifty years.

rates), and produced and distributed by people who were born before 1940, many of them before 1930.*

In 1969, the year of Woodstock and of the Stonewall riots that launched the Gay Liberation movement, the median age of Americans born between 1946 and 1964 was fourteen. The oldest had just graduated from college; the youngest was five.[5] "Young people" in the 1960s were not that young. On the witness stand at his trial on charges stemming from protests at the 1968 Democratic National Convention, Abbie Hoffman was asked when he was born. "Psychologically, 1960," he said.[6] Hoffman was born in 1936. He went to college at Brandeis, where he was a student of Herbert Marcuse.

A second feature of this history is that although they tended to get written out of the social history of the period, a large proportion of the consumers of youth culture were girls. *Seventeen* is a magazine for girls, and most of the press stories in the 1950s about the teenage market focused on the spending habits of girls. About 25 percent of teenage spending in the 1950s was on clothes and cosmetics. Cars, the principal non-entertainment commodity coveted by boys, were beyond the price range of most teenagers, and the automobile industry largely ignored them.[7] The gender imbalance was by no means restricted to shopping. The audiences at Frank Sinatra's concerts in the 1940s and Elvis Presley's in the 1950s were overwhelmingly female.[8] Many teenage boys wanted to be Elvis Presley; millions of teenage girls wanted to touch him. The latter helps to explain the former.

As Parsons recognized, for a youth culture—in fact, for the category of "teenager" itself—to exist, a socioeconomic space between childhood (dependency) and adulthood (parenting and/or full-time employment) had to open up. As he also recognized, that space was high school. Between 1910 and 1930, high school enrollment in the United States increased by more than 400 percent: those were the people Parsons was writing about. In 1900, just 10.2 percent of fourteen- to seventeen-year-olds were in school; in 1910, 14.5 percent; in 1930, 51.1 percent. Despite

---

* The so-called baby boom began (informally) in July 1946, eleven months after the Japanese surrender, when live births jumped to 286,000, and ended in December 1964, when 331,000 babies were born. That's approximately 76 million people. Generalizations about this demographic are obviously meaningless. Birth rates for non-white people were significantly higher than birth rates for white people, but the baby-boom narrative is almost entirely a middle-class white person's narrative.

the Depression, the trend continued. By 1940, 73 percent of Americans between fourteen and seventeen attended high school.[9]

This growth was the result of a loosely coordinated national movement to get people to stay in school longer, but it also tracked changes in the workforce.[10] In 1910, 21 percent of workers had white-collar jobs; in 1940, 31 percent did. That was a significant change, but a much more dramatic one involved agriculture. In 1900, 38 percent of employed Americans were farm workers; in 1950, 12 percent were. By 1960, it was a little over 6 percent.[11] The statistic that captures these shifts most precisely is the education level of sixteen- and seventeen-year olds, ages when people are, skill sets aside, old enough for full-time employment and no longer legally required to attend school. In 1920, 51 percent of American sixteen-year-olds were in school; in 1950, it was 81 percent. Among seventeen-year-olds, 35 percent were in school in 1920; 68 percent in 1950.[12]

This rate of growth in secondary education was unique to the United States.[13] In 1955, when 84 percent of high-school-age Americans were in school, the figure for Western Europe was 16 percent. In Italy in 1951, only 10 percent of all people had more than an elementary school education; in 1961, the figure was 15 percent.[14] In the United Kingdom, a nation with an economic profile roughly comparable to the United States, approximately 17 percent of fifteen- to eighteen-year-olds were full-time students in 1955. In 1957, just 9 percent of British seventeen-year-olds were still in school.[15]

So it is unsurprising that global youth culture in the twentieth century was preponderantly American. The United States had a big head start, and the sectors of American industry that capitalized on it— notably fashion and music—enjoyed a competitive advantage internationally. Already formidable in 1945, this advantage was enhanced a decade later by rapid growth in another sector of the educational system, college. Between 1956 and 1969, college enrollment in the United States increased from 2.9 million to more than 8 million.[16] That increase *was* partly propelled by the baby boom (although the oldest boomer did not turn eighteen until 1964), but there were other factors, including increased state investment in education in response to the Soviet launch of Sputnik in October 1957 and the Selective Service's policy of granting draft deferments to college students, making college increasingly attractive to male students as the War in Vietnam escalated.* "Youth" turned from a four-year demographic into an eight-year one.

The growth in higher education was, again, unique to the United States. The United States was, after all, the only country with enough people in the pipeline to make it possible. In the school year 1960–1961, 6.3 percent of all Americans under twenty were in college; in West Germany and the United Kingdom, the figure was 1.4 percent.[17] "America used to be the big youth place in everybody's imagination," John Lennon said in 1966. "America had teen-agers and everywhere else just had people."[18] He was exactly right. Still, his remark raises an interesting question, which is why the most popular entertainers in the world in the 1960s were British.

2.

The Beatles started out playing American music. There was nothing unusual about that. It was what British musicians in the twentieth century had always done. Virtually every style of popular music recorded in the United States—jazz, blues, swing, Dixieland, country, folk—was picked up and performed in Britain.[19] Musical exchange between Britain and the United States was not entirely a one-way street, and there were indigenous British musical traditions (folk ballads and music-hall entertainment, for example). But the phonograph and recording technology were developed in the United States, and the American music industry dominated the world market. In 1958, despite quotas and other trade barriers, the United States enjoyed a 56 percent share of international record sales. Britain and Germany combined had 6 percent of the market, France 4 percent.[20]

There was also nothing exceptional about the Beatles' access to American music. They were from Liverpool, a port city where merchant seamen ("Cunard Yanks") brought back goods, including records, from the United States. Liverpool was also fifteen miles from the largest American military aircraft base in Europe, Burtonwood, an enormous complex comprising more than sixteen hundred buildings and a source for locals of American entertainment culture, including comic books

---

* Males were subject to a military draft in the United States from 1940 to 1973.

and music.[21] In fact, though, all the American music the Beatles performed could be bought in local record shops or heard on the radio—including Radio Luxembourg, which had the biggest transmitter in the world and, on Saturday and Sunday nights, broadcast prerecorded programs produced by American record companies and featuring American deejays. The Beatles were listening to what most people their age in Britain were listening to. In 1956, sixty-four of the top one hundred songs in Britain were American; in 1958, two thirds of the popular music broadcast on BBC radio was American.[22]

The Beatles all turned fifteen between 1955 and 1958, which coincided with the worldwide spread of rock 'n' roll. Rock 'n' roll was the first music specifically aimed at a teenage audience. "A frenzied teen-age music craze," *Life* called it in 1955.[23] Teenagers went to Frank Sinatra concerts, but so did adults; rock 'n' roll concerts were not for grown-ups. The first time Elvis Presley played in Las Vegas, at the New Frontier in 1956, he was a flop. He had never performed before an adult audience before.[24]

By 1958, American rock 'n' roll seemed to be everywhere. A series of Hollywood movies with rock 'n' roll soundtracks—*Blackboard Jungle*, released in 1955, followed by *The Girl Can't Help It*, *Don't Knock the Rock*, and *Rock Around the Clock*, all in 1956—had been sensations in Europe. There were rock 'n' roll cover bands in Britain, Italy, West Germany (where the music led to the adoption of the word "teenager"), and the Netherlands (where some bands were made up of Indonesian immigrants). Teenagers danced to rock 'n' roll in Canada, Argentina, Poland, Hungary, and Egypt, in Havana, Mexico City, Sydney, Jakarta, Bombay, and Karachi. In Tokyo, a nineteen-year-old Elvis imitator named Masaaki Hirao sang Presley's songs in English, a language neither he nor his fans understood. Pirated Presley recordings were sold on the black market in Leningrad.*

News reports on the phenomenon emphasized three things: rock 'n' roll was dance music for teenagers; it provoked varying degrees of adult anxiety and official disapproval; and it had all the look of a fad. Some people associated rock 'n' roll with antisocial behavior and juvenile delinquency; no one, except in Communist countries, considered it a form

---

* One place the music was slow to catch on was France. It was not until 1960 that a French singer named Jean-Philippe Léo Smet changed his name to Johnny Hallyday and, pretending to be American, performed in Presley's style—the first French rock 'n' roller.

of political protest, unless in Parsons's sense: "resistance to the pressure of adult expectations."[25]

But rock 'n' roll turned out to be more than a mass-market commodity. It survived the normal lifespan of a fad and became one of the cultural winners of the postwar era. Cultural winners are goods or styles that maintain market share through "generational" taste shifts—that is, through all the "the king is dead; long live the king" moments that mark the phases of cultural history for people living through it. This kind of survivability often depends on the good or style being available to do extra-cultural work. In the case of rock 'n' roll, the music became a way to tell a story about postwar American social history. That is why so much became invested in a certain version of rock 'n' roll's genealogy.

Where did rock 'n' roll come from? It seems to have been completely unplanned and unforeseen, the by-product of a number of unrelated developments in the American music business, the cumulative downstream effect of which was to open up a space for music for teenagers.

Before the Second World War, the American music business was oligopolistic and vertically integrated. In 1938, three record companies controlled the market: Decca, RCA Victor, and Columbia. Together, they had $32 million of that year's $33 million in record sales.* Broadcasting—that is, radio—was dominated by four national networks: NBC, which had two networks; CBS; and Mutual. The state of vertical integration is exemplified by RCA, which owned NBC, had its own record label, and manufactured phonographs. Rights to play music were controlled by the American Society of Composers, Authors, and Publishers (ASCAP), founded in 1914.[26]

As integrated as it was, the industry was highly volatile. A war between ASCAP and the broadcast companies had been going on since 1922, when ASCAP informed station owners that playing a record on the air constituted "performance for profit" and was an infringement of copyright. The broadcasters spent a decade contesting ASCAP's claim, but the courts were uncooperative, and in 1932, the broadcasters all signed licensing agreements with ASCAP. The fee was normally a percentage of a network's total income in return for rights to the entire ASCAP catalogue—by 1939, well over a million songs.

---

* If this seems oligopolistic, note that in 2020, just three companies—Sony BMG, Universal Music Group, and Warner Music Group—control some 90 percent of the market.

Then ASCAP overplayed its hand. It announced an increase of fees, and the broadcasters, anticipating this, rebelled. Their group, the National Association of Broadcasters, representing about six hundred radio stations, created its own licensing organization, Broadcast Music Incorporated (BMI). ASCAP responded by banning stations from playing ASCAP music. For almost a year, from January to October 1941, almost no ASCAP music was heard on the radio. People listened anyway, and in the end, ASCAP caved. The broadcasters agreed to a new licensing deal on better terms.[27]

But BMI did not disappear. Membership in ASCAP was restrictive. Every year, millions of dollars in royalties was shared among eleven hundred lyricists and composers and fewer than a hundred and fifty music publishers, thirteen of whom were owned by Hollywood studios. By offering more attractive terms, BMI was able to steal some of ASCAP's members. It also recruited composers, particularly "hillbilly" and Black songwriters, who were underrepresented in ASCAP. Unlike ASCAP, BMI collected royalties for plays on independent local radio stations (as opposed to network stations), which was where that kind of music tended to be broadcast. BMI's finger was therefore much closer to the pulse of popular music.[28]

The Justice Department, along with the Federal Communications Commission, was eager to increase media competition, and after the war, the FCC set out to license new radio stations. By 1950, there were 1,517 independent stations and 627 network affiliates broadcasting in the United States. There were 16.8 million record plays on network stations the next year, but 82.2 million plays on the independents. Most people who listened to the radio—and 95 percent of American households had at least one radio—listened to local independent stations.[29]

There were also changes in music delivery systems. By 1939, there were three hundred thousand jukeboxes in the United States. The jukebox made it possible for people to hear songs rarely played on the radio. Until 1948, jukeboxes could hold at most twenty-four records, but in 1949, Seeburg introduced a model, the M-100A, which held a hundred. By the early 1950s, there were machines that could hold two hundred records, which allowed for musical diversity.[30] In 1948, Columbia introduced the vinyl LP, which played at 33⅓ revolutions per minute: the album. Eight months later, RCA introduced the 45-rpm disk: the single. RCA also began manufacturing a plastic phonograph that sold for $12.95, played 45s, and was marketed to children. In 1952, six million such record players were sold. By then, more than half of new cars came with radios installed. The portable transistor radio went on the market in 1953. Finally (and this turned out to be significant), almost all the swing bands, led by musicians such as Benny Goodman, Count Basie, and Louis Jordan, bands whose music people went out to dance to, folded. By the end of the 1940s, the swing era was over.

It is a tenet of faith in the music business (and supported by multiple studies) that the more people hear a song, the more they feel the need to buy it.[31] These developments on the distribution side of the industry meant that more people were listening to more songs in more places, and one consequence was a huge jump in record sales. There were also more places to buy records. In 1954, there were 5,810 music stores in the country; by 1958, there were 7,974.[32] Eight million records were sold in 1946; in 1951, 186 million were sold, grossing $200 million. In 1955, sales grossed $227 million; in 1956, $331 million; in 1959, $603 million.[33] Popular music had moved much closer to the center of everyday life. And for teenagers, there were now many ways to listen to music outside the family living room: in diners, in the car, at school, in their bedrooms. A youth culture for music was financially viable.

Rock 'n' roll became defined as rhythm and blues—that is, music performed by Black artists for Black listeners—repurposed by mostly white artists for a mostly white audience. To some extent, this explanation is an artifact of the charting system used by the industry trade magazine *The Billboard* (as it originally called itself), which began charting songs in 1940. By 1949, it was publishing weekly charts of hits in three categories: pop, country and western (formerly "folk"), and, a term introduced in 1949, "rhythm and blues" (originally "Harlem Hit Parade," then "Race Records"). Separate charts listed the records most sold in shops, most requested in jukeboxes, and most played by disk jockeys; the magazine also published regional, or "territorial," charts. (All rankings were relative; actual sales figures were proprietary.)

The system was predicated on a segregated market. How did *Billboard* know that a song was a rhythm and blues hit and not a country or pop hit? Because its sales were reported by stores that catered to a Black clientele, its on-air plays were reported by stations that programmed for Black listeners, and its jukebox requests were made in venues with Black customers. Black artists could have pop hits. The Ink Spots, for example, a Black quartet, had fourteen songs in the top five on the pop charts between 1939 and 1947. That was because their music was marketed to white listeners.[34]

The proliferation of independent radio stations allowed the music audience to segment. A third of the population of Memphis, for example, was nonwhite. A local station there could make money programming for those listeners. In fact, the first station with all-Black programming in the United States (its owners were white) was in Memphis: WDIA, which began broadcasting, at 250 watts, in 1947, switched to an all-Black music format in 1949 and billed itself as "The Mother Station of the Negroes." B.B. King began his career there as a disk jockey and on-air performer.[35]

The recording industry segmented, too. The major record companies had mostly given up on "race music" in the 1930s, a financially tough decade for the industry. But *Billboard* charts showed that a market was still there, and a swarm of independent labels—the number is estimated to be between four hundred and six hundred—arose to make and sell rhythm and blues records: Specialty, Aladdin, Modern, Swingtime, and Imperial (all in Los Angeles, for a time, oddly, the capital of R&B), King (Cincinnati), Peacock (Houston), Chess (Chicago), Savoy (Newark), Atlantic (New York City), and many more. Those labels were all established between 1940 and 1950, and they dominated the market for R&B. Between 1949 and 1953, only 8 percent of R&B records were released on major labels.[36]

Rhythm and blues sales represented less than 10 percent of the music market—large enough for independent labels to serve profitably, but not large enough for the majors, whose production costs were higher.[37] What changed the business dynamic was the realization that not everyone buying R&B records or listening to R&B songs on jukeboxes or the radio was Black. *Billboard*'s charting system was not capturing the way popular music was actually consumed, and the narrative thus became one in which R&B was a music discovered by white people. This obscured the major component in R&B's success: the tastes of Black teenagers.

The fact that before *Brown v. Board of Education*, in 1954, public schools were racially segregated by law in seventeen states and the District of Columbia, with de facto segregation elsewhere, did not mean that Black teenagers were on a different educational trajectory from white teenagers. In 1953, when 86 percent of white teenagers between fourteen and seventeen were in high school, the figure for what the Census Bureau termed "Negro and other" teenagers was 82 percent.[38] Their lives had space for a youth culture, too. And it was nonwhite teenagers who discovered R&B.

One story that, because it illustrated what became the official genealogy, is standard in histories of rock 'n' roll is a visit by a disk jockey named Alan Freed to a record shop, the Record Rendezvous, in Cleveland, where he was supposedly astonished to see white teenagers eagerly purchasing R&B records, and decided to follow his "quality" (that is, classical) music show on WJW with a late-night program devoted to R&B. Freed adopted a frenetic on-air patter and used the handle "Moondog," and he was one of the first people to promote the term (though it had been around since the 1920s: it describes what Shakespeare called "the beast with two backs") "rock 'n' roll." Freed was also a concert promoter. In 1952, twenty thousand or more teenagers showed up for one of his shows at the Cleveland Arena, a venue that could accommodate half that number. There was some mayhem and a lot of press coverage.[39] The rock 'n' roll riot helped to put the music in the headlines.

But the record-shop story is a reconstruction. Freed was taken to the shop by its owner, Leo Mintz, who encouraged Freed to launch an R&B radio show in the hope of driving more business to his establishment. To that end, Mintz offered to pay the show's expenses, including Freed's salary. Freed did not see many, or possibly any, white teenagers buying records there that night; that was a detail he added in later retellings. The teenagers in the store, like the people who listened to the Moondog show, like the twenty-thousand-plus fans who showed up at the Cleveland Arena, were mostly Black.[40] It was those Black teenagers' dollars that made R&B popular in places with large Black populations, such as Cleveland and Memphis. In the Southwest, in Dallas, Houston, El Paso, and Los Angeles, the R&B market was driven by Latinos.[41]

Schools and neighborhoods might be segregated, but the radio dial was not. The demand from nonwhite teenagers drove up the number of radio plays, and the more radio plays the music got, the greater the number of white teenagers who heard it and wanted to buy it. By 1954, the industry was fully alive to the phenomenon. In April, *Billboard* published an article headlined "Teen-Agers Demand Music with a

Beat, Spur Rhythm-Blues," which reported that 20 to 30 percent of the radio audience for R&B programming and up to a third of the fans showing up at Freed's concerts were white: "The teen-age tide has swept down the old barriers which kept this music restricted to a segment of the population." Of course, white teenagers were listening because Black teenagers had made R&B a hot product. Freed was mentioned prominently in the article; a month later, he was hired at WINS in New York City. His rock 'n' roll radio show was now heard across the Northeast. Abbie Hoffman, who grew up in Worcester, Massachusetts, remembered listening to it as a teenager.[42]

A year later, Elvis Presley had his first national hits: "Baby Let's Play House," released in April 1955, and "Mystery Train," released in August. Presley recorded for Sun Records, a small Memphis outfit run by a producer named Sam Phillips. Less than two months after "Mystery Train" made the charts, Phillips sold Presley's contract to RCA Victor for $35,000. In the next 104 weeks, Presley had the No. 1 song for 55. The majors were now in on the action.

"The year 1955 was the year rhythm and blues virtually took over the pop field," *Billboard* announced.[43] The music got additional exposure in 1957, when the television show *American Bandstand*, hosted by Dick Clark and featuring pop acts and dancing teenagers, began broadcasting nationally. Within two years, *American Bandstand* had a weekly audience of twenty million. By the end of 1958, more than half the songs on the R&B charts were by white artists and 70 percent of the pop and R&B lists were identical.[44] Rock was the new pop.

What happened with rock 'n' roll is exactly what happened before the war with jazz and swing: a style of music identified with Black musicians and enjoyed by a racially mixed audience was taken up and eventually dominated by white performers and producers.[45] The big difference between rock 'n' roll and the earlier styles was the age groups they appealed to. Freed believed that what made R&B successful was the steady beat: it was music you could dance to. And *Billboard* reported that the dancing at a Freed concert in Manhattan was "reminiscent of the days when the kids were lindy-hopping in the aisles of the Paramount Theatre on Broadway when Benny Goodman and his orchestra were swinging there."[46] Rock moved into a social space vacated by swing, and populated it with a younger demographic.

Freed, Clark, and Phillips were key actors—more accurately, nodes—

in the production, performance, and dissemination of rock 'n' roll. They helped transform it from a niche commodity into a mass-market product, and they had a lot to do with giving it a sound, a look, and a level of energy. They were in the yolk of the egg. But they did not lay the egg. Like the rest of the industry, they were improvising to meet a demand that had arisen unexpectedly, and whose nature and extent they had to guess at on the fly.

3.

Offstage, Elvis Presley was the opposite of the type conventionally associated with the music of which he is universally considered the supreme exponent. He was not remotely rebellious, delinquent, or "animalistic" (a term used in denunciations of his performance style). He was shy and deferential and devoted to his parents. "Nice" is a word often used to describe him.

Presley had had no intention of becoming a rock 'n' roll singer and he never really considered himself one. He sang rock 'n' roll songs, but he sang all kinds of songs. He understood that pop music was a business in which a lot of money could be made; if rock 'n' roll made more of it, he was happy to sing rock 'n' roll. "I have to do what I can do best," as he said.[47] But he didn't sing only for the money. He sang because he was a singer, and his enormous popularity exposed people to genres of popular music they otherwise might not have paid attention to.

Presley was born in East Tupelo, Mississippi, in 1935. His father, Vernon, was a laborer who moved from job to job. The Presleys lived for a time in a Black neighborhood in Tupelo (though in a "white" house). They did not consider themselves, and there is no evidence that they were, racially intolerant.[48] Elvis was an only child—a twin brother was stillborn—and he was especially close to his mother, Gladys. Gladys was dynamic; people liked her. But the family was somewhat insular. In school, Elvis was a bit of an outsider and sometimes got picked on. He stood out not because of any special talent, but because, as a teenager, he dressed up: bolero jackets, a scarf worn as an ascot, dress pants with stripes down the sides. His demeanor remained reserved and respectful. In 1948, the family moved to Memphis, where Presley attended Humes High. (Schools were segregated by law in Tennessee.) The summer after he graduated, in 1953, he walked into the Memphis Recording Service to cut a record.[49]

The Memphis Recording Service was more than a recording facility. Its founder, Sam Phillips, had a vision. Like Presley, Phillips came to Memphis from the deeper South. He was born in 1923 in a small town in Alabama called Lovelace Community, near Florence. His father was a flagman on a railroad bridge over the Tennessee River. Phillips got his start in radio, working in Decatur and Nashville and finally, in 1945, making it to Memphis—in his mind what Paris was for Gertrude Stein and Ernest Hemingway. In 1950, he opened the Memphis Recording Service in a tiny space on Union Avenue a block away from Beale Street, the heart of the Memphis music scene.

"We record anything—anywhere—anytime" was the slogan. This meant a lot of church services, weddings, and funerals. But Phillips's dream, the reason he set the studio up, was to have a place any aspiring musician could walk into and try out, no questions asked. Phillips would listen and offer suggestions and encouragement. If he liked what he heard, he would record it. For a fee, the performer could cut his or her own record.

Phillips was patient with the musicians; he was adept with the technology; he was supportive. He thought that music is about self-expression. He liked blues songs especially, but he liked any song that sounded different. The pop sound in 1950 was smooth and harmonic; Phillips preferred imperfection. It made the music seem spontaneous and authentic, qualities that would become key attributes of rock 'n' roll. Word got around, and musicians no one else would record, many of them Black, turned up at the Memphis Recording Service. Phillips was the first to record Howlin' Wolf, Ike Turner, and B.B. King. A musical genre boils down to a certain kind of sound (which is why songs can be covered in different genres). As much as anyone, Phillips helped create the sound of rock 'n' roll.

To have his recordings pressed and distributed, Phillips relied on independent labels such as Modern Records and Chess. But he found the men who ran those outfits untrustworthy—he felt that they tried to poach his artists, or cheated him on royalties—and so in 1952, he started up his own label, Sun Records. That was relatively late in the history of independent labels.

Presley came in to make a record for his mother.* He paid $3.99 plus tax to record two songs, "My Happiness," which had been a hit for several artists, including Ella Fitzgerald, and "That's When Your Heartaches Begin," an Ink Spots song. Whether Phillips was in the booth that day or not later became a matter of dispute (he insisted that he was), but someone wrote next to Presley's name, "Good ballad singer. Hold." A year later, Phillips invited Presley back to try out a ballad he'd come across. The song didn't seem to work, and, per his standard operating procedure, Phillips had Presley run through all the material he knew, any song he could remember. After three hours, they gave up. Phillips decided to pursue the experiment, though, and he put Presley together with a couple of country musicians, Scotty Moore, an electric guitarist, and Bill Black, who played stand-up bass, and invited them to come into the studio, which, on July 5, 1954, they did.

They began the session with a Bing Crosby song, "Harbor Lights," then tried a ballad, then a country song. They did multiple takes; nothing seemed to click. Everyone was ready to quit for the night when, as Elvis told the story later, "this song popped into my mind that I had heard years ago and I started kidding around." The song was "That's All Right, Mama," an R&B number written and recorded by Arthur (Big Boy) Crudup. "Elvis just started singing this song, jumping around and acting the fool, and then Bill picked up his bass, and he started acting the fool, too, and I started playing with them," Moore said. Phillips stuck his head out of the booth and told them to start again from the beginning. After multiple takes, they had a record.[50] Phillips was friendly with a white disk jockey, Dewey Phillips (not related), who played some R&B on his show on WHBQ in Memphis. Sam gave the acetate to Dewey and Dewey played it repeatedly on his broadcast. It was an overnight sensation.

To have a record that people could buy, they needed a B-side. So Presley, Moore, and Black recorded an up-tempo cover of a bluegrass song, "Blue Moon of Kentucky," and in July 1954, Elvis Presley's first single came on the market. In his promotional campaign, Phillips emphasized the record's appeal to all listeners, pop, country, and rhythm and blues. "Operators have placed ["That's All Right"] on nearly all

---

* At least, that's the legend; according to a friend, the Presleys did not own a phonograph.

locations (white and colored) and are reporting plays seldom encountered on a record in recent years," he wrote in the press release. "According to local sales analysis, the apparent reason for its tremendous sales is because of its *appeal to all classes of record buyers*."

The trade press picked this up, for, three months after the *Billboard* article about R&B and white teenagers, it was exactly what the industry was primed to hear. "Presley is the potent new chanter who can sock a tune for either the country or the r. & b. markets," *Billboard* noted. ". . . A strong new talent."[51] (Crudup never got a dime from Presley or Sun, but as it happened, Crudup had borrowed much of the lyrics and music for "That's All Right, Mama" from a Big Joe Turner boogie-woogie number called "That's All Right, Baby," recorded in 1939 with Pete Johnson on piano.)[52]

Phillips was reported to have said, "If I could find a white man who had the Negro sound and the Negro feel, I could make a billion dollars." He denied it.[53] But it is clear that if he was looking for such a person, he did not pick Elvis Presley to be the one. Phillips called Presley in as a ballad singer, and that is what Presley believed he essentially was. Presley's favorite among his own songs was "It's Now or Never," which is neither bluesy nor rock 'n' roll, but Neapolitan.[54] Musically, "It's Now or Never" is a cover of "O Sole Mio."

"That's All Right, Mama" started as a joke. Moore and Black thought it was a joke, too. It worked, but it was completely unpremeditated. Presley later admitted that he had never sung like that before in his life.[55] It is interesting, though, that he remembered the song and that Moore and Black knew how to play it. They just never assumed it was a song that white artists performed. Rock 'n' roll was not "manufactured" by Phillips, Moore, Black, and Presley in Memphis any more (or any less) than the drip paintings were "manufactured" by Jackson Pollock, Lee Krasner, and Clement Greenberg on Long Island. They tried something out, and then they tried to figure out why it worked.

"That's All Right, Mama" was only a regional hit, and not even No. 1, in Memphis. "Blue Moon of Kentucky" was equally popular. Presley didn't make it onto the national charts for another year; by then, many white performers had stopped refurbishing R&B songs in a pop style and had started imitating them. In 1954, WDIA became a 50,000-watt station reaching the entire mid-South, and by 1955, more than six hundred stations in thirty-nine states programmed for Black listeners—which suggested that not only Black people were listening.[56] Producers could see where the sound was headed.

So when, for example, Pat Boone walked into Dot Records, in Gallatin, Tennessee, in the summer of 1955—before Presley had had a national hit—he was shocked to be asked to sing a rhythm and blues song. Like Presley, Boone saw himself as a ballad singer. But he recorded Fats Domino's "Ain't That a Shame" and it went to No. 1 on the pop chart. The same summer, Bill Haley's "Rock Around the Clock" went to No. 1 after it was heard in the movie *Blackboard Jungle*. Black performers began to benefit from the popularity of the new sound, too. In May 1955, Chuck Berry recorded "Maybellene" for Chess Records; Chess rushed the record to Alan Freed, and it went to No. 1 on the R&B chart and No. 5 on the pop chart. Little Richard's "Tutti Frutti" was released a few months later. By January, it had reached No. 17 on the pop chart. Boone and Presley both covered it. Boone's went to No. 12, Presley's to No. 20 as the B-side to "Blue Suede Shoes."[57]

Presley was therefore just one of a number of singers, Black and white, trying to meet the demand for songs with an R&B sound. And among those artists, Presley was originally identified not with rock 'n' roll, but with country, or "rockabilly," music. The first article about him in a national publication—in *Life* in April 1956—referred to him as a hillbilly singer.[58] What transformed him into a breakthrough figure in the evolution of pop music?

A big part of the answer is television. In 1948, 2 percent of American households had television sets. In 1952, it was about a third. But by 1955, 65 percent of households had television sets, and 86 percent had them by 1959. Prime time in those years was dominated by variety shows, hosted by people like Ed Sullivan, Steve Allen, Milton Berle, and Perry Como, that booked musical acts. Since most viewers received only three or four channels, the audience for each show was often enormous, in the tens of millions. Television exposure became the best way to sell a record.

On television, the performer's race is apparent. Many sponsors avoided mixed-race television shows, since they were advertising on national networks and did not want to alienate white viewers in certain regions of the country.* In the first years after it went national, *American*

---

* This was true to some extent for advertisers on broadcast radio as well, but there were hundreds more stations. Listeners need not feel trapped.

Bandstand did not book any Black acts.[59] There were few local television stations, and they did little programming. Television desegmented the media audience all over again. Radio had opened the door to music for different audiences; television closed it.

Presley was made for television, and not only because of his race. With a microphone and in front of an audience, he was transformed from a shy young man who tended to mumble into a gyrating fireball with an unbelievably sexy sneer. He made his first television appearance on Jimmy and Tommy Dorsey's *Stage Show* on CBS in January 1956, but his big break came in June, when he sang back-to-back versions of "Hound Dog," the second time as a slow-motion bump-and-grind routine, on *The Milton Berle Show*. Forty million people watched.* He sang "Hound Dog" the same way in September in his first appearance on *The Ed Sullivan Show*. Sixty million people watched that show—83 percent of all television viewers. By then, "Hound Dog," with its B-side, "Don't Be Cruel," had become the first single to top all three *Billboard* charts.

The same month, Presley's first LP, *Elvis Presley*, was released by RCA Victor; it went to No. 1 on the pop albums chart and stayed there for ten weeks. The song that introduced Europeans to Presley, "Heartbreak Hotel," entered the British pop charts in May 1956. In October, Presley's album was released in Britain on the HMV (His Master's Voice) label and went to No. 1 there as well. The revolution was accomplished.

On the level of reception, white performers were adopting a "Black sound." That is how the charts made things appear. On the level of production, it was a different story. For there is no such thing as a "Black sound" or a "white sound." "Hound Dog," which turned out to be one of Presley's biggest hits, was originally released on the Peacock label by a Black singer named Willie Mae (Big Mama) Thornton in 1953, when it went to No. 3 on the national R&B charts.[60] Thornton didn't write the song, however. It was written by two Jewish twenty-year-olds living in Los Angeles, Jerry Leiber and Mike Stoller, on commission from Thornton's producer at Peacock Records, Johnny Otis.† (Everyone believed that Johnny Otis was Black. In fact, he was Greek-American; his given name was Ioannis Veliotes. He used to say he considered himself "Black by persuasion.")[61]

---

* Berle later claimed he received 500,000 negative letters from viewers—and that is when he knew that Presley was a star. (www.youtube.com/watch?v=FjJr5Yimfeo)

† Peacock was based in Houston, as was Thornton, but the song was recoded in L.A.

As Leiber and Stoller tell the story, they wrote "Hound Dog" "in a matter of minutes."[62] They thought they had written a raunchy blues number, but when they brought it into the studio, Thornton insisted on crooning the lyrics. Leiber had to sing it for her so she could hear how it was supposed to sound. Otis sat in on the session and played the drums (he was also a musician), and took co-writing credit. If Thornton's singing on that record comes across as a parodic imitation of the blues style, that is why. She was copying a sound.

Leiber and Stoller would go on to write many standards of the rock 'n' roll era, including "Kansas City," "Jailhouse Rock," "Yakety Yak," and "Stand By Me." "Hound Dog" would be covered well over two hundred times, including in French, German, Spanish, and Portuguese.[63] Thornton's "Hound Dog" was covered by four country and western artists, and inspired a parody version, known as an "answer" record, called "Bear Cat," sung by Rufus Thomas, a Black R&B singer, and recorded on the Sun label by Sam Phillips.[64]

But Presley didn't cover Big Mama Thornton's version. He decided to add the song to his repertoire when, during his unsuccessful Las Vegas gig, he saw it performed at the Sands by an all-white Philadelphia act called Freddie Bell and the Bellboys, who recorded on the Teen label.[65] The group had rewritten Leiber and Stoller's lyrics to change it from a song about a lover who won't go away to a song about, actually, a dog. It was a gag number, in other words, and that's how Elvis performed it—in the goofing-around spirit in which he first sang "That's All Right, Mama." When he sang "Hound Dog" on the *Steve Allen Show*, a basset hound was brought onstage, and Presley sang to the dog.

Presley's bump-and-grind performances of the song on Berle's and Sullivan's shows were therefore tongue-in-cheek, a joke—because Freddie and the Bellboys' version of the song had erased any sexual content.[66] At that point, the song's chain of custody extended from the Jewish twenty-year-olds who wrote it for a fee, to the African American singer who had to be instructed how to sing it, to the white lounge act that spoofed it, to the hillbilly singer who performed it as a burlesque number. Presley's version of "Hound Dog" isn't inauthentic, because nothing about the song was ever authentic. Presley recorded "Hound Dog" in July 1956, in a session (which he directed) requiring thirty-one takes.[67] The B-side, "Don't Be Cruel," has a completely different, doo-woppy, country sound. "Don't Be Cruel" was written for Presley by Otis Blackwell, who would give him two more songs with the same sound, "Return to Sender" and "All Shook Up." Blackwell was Black.

Most musicians are much more eclectic than their fans. If he had nothing else to do, Presley sang gospel, as did Jerry Lee Lewis, Carl Perkins, and Johnny Cash, three other Sam Phillips discoveries. (A recording of the four of them jamming in the studio in 1956 was discovered and released several years after Presley's death.)[68] Muddy Waters sang "Red Sails in the Sunset." Robert Johnson sang "Yes, Sir, That's My Baby." James Brown liked Sinatra and disliked the blues. Leadbelly was a Gene Autry fan. Chuck Berry's "Maybellene" was a cover of a country and western song called "Ida Red," recorded in 1938 by a white band, Bob Wills and His Texas Playboys. Race had a lot to do with the music business in the United States. It had much less to do with the music.[69]

4.

John Lennon was much more a rock 'n' roll type than Elvis Presley was. Lennon was a big personality, and he could be charming, but he could also be caustic and irreverent, and he had an anti-establishment streak. The Beatles was his band, and he chose as his bandmates people who shared his wit and the attitude it clothed. "Fuckin' big bastards, that's what the Beatles were," he said in 1970. "You have to be a bastard to make it, that's a fact, and the Beatles were the biggest bastards on earth."[70]

Lennon was speaking a year after the band broke up, a time when he was in his "I don't believe in Beatles" phase. But he wasn't saying anything the other Beatles wouldn't or didn't say. "Although we didn't openly say, 'Fuck you!'," George Harrison said, "it was basically our thing. 'We'll show these fuckers.' And we walked right through London, the Palladium, and kept on going through Ed Sullivan and on to Hong Kong and the world."[71]

The Beatles were tough characters. They were happy to clown around in public, but they did not like being taken for fools, even a little, and in private, they didn't trouble to remove the barbs. "Nobody liked to be rounded upon by the four of then—in however jokey a way," said their press agent, Derek Taylor, a fellow Liverpudlian. "It was not pleasant for those four buggers to be at you. It was 'whoosh'—and all the fangs were in you at once. It didn't last, but it was very painful."[72]

Celebrity had nothing to do with it. In June 1962, after the Beatles had been turned down by virtually every record label in Britain, George Martin, at Parlophone, agreed to record them. Parlophone was owned by EMI, one of the two major British record companies (the other was Decca), and Martin was the director of the label, a trained musician, and the soul of professional courtesy and accommodation. When the Beatles turned up for their first session, Martin, to get them involved in the process, took them into the control room to listen to a playback. "If there's anything you don't like, tell me," he said. "Well, for a start," said George, "I don't like your tie." Martin rather liked his tie, and there was a beat before he laughed.[73] It was one of those moments when the universe is poised to plunge down a different path.

Martin went on to produce almost every song the Beatles recorded. He scored the music played on those songs by other musicians (none of the Beatles knew how to read or write music), he performed on almost a fifth of the songs himself, and he came up with many of the special effects that made albums such as *Sgt. Pepper's Lonely Hearts Club Band* sensations.[74] He thought that Lennon and McCartney were geniuses, and that he knew how to give them the sound they were after, but he was not under any illusion about where he stood in the band's affections. "[T]he Beatles were never ones for showing concern about, or gratitude towards, anyone else," he wrote in his autobiography. ". . . They had an independent, cussed streak about them, not giving a damn for anybody, which was one of the things I liked about them in the first place, and one of the factors which made me decide to sign them."[75]

The Beatles flourished in an era when "love" was a great totem before which the culture bowed down. They sang of love; they were loved by millions; "loveableness" was the essence of their appeal. But they loved only one another. The longer the band existed, the more exclusive their chemistry became. They came to feel that the only people in the world who did not think that the supreme joy of human life is to be touched by a Beatle were the Beatles.

Lennon was different from Presley—and every other American pop musician—in another way. He had gone to art college. Lennon was born in Liverpool in 1940. His father, Alfred, a steward on merchant ships, abandoned the family when John was six. John's mother, Julia, had already had a child by another man (a girl she put up for adoption and never saw again), and had then taken up with a sketchy character named John (Bobby) Dykins. She sent John to live with her sister, Mimi Smith, and Mimi's husband, George, who cleaned buses on the night shift. Mimi was strict, but she doted on John, and she was one of the few adults he respected. When John was fourteen, George Smith died of a hemorrhage. He was fifty-two. When John was seventeen, Julia, with whom he had reconnected and found a kindred spirit, was hit by a car driven by an off-duty policeman and killed.

John had formed a band, the Quarrymen, named after the local high school, Quarry Bank, a little more than a year earlier. Paul, who was a year and a half younger than John, joined the group in July 1957; George, who was a little less than a year younger than Paul, joined the following winter. Paul and George were still in high school when Lennon entered Liverpool College of Art in the fall of 1958.

At Quarry Bank, John had drawn cartoons and written punning sketches and humorous fables (James Thurber was an inspiration), which he self-published in an organ called *The Daily Howl*. He was a big fan of *The Goon Show*, broadcast on BBC radio from 1951 to 1960, starring Peter Sellers and Spike Milligan. Apart from music, he had no career ambitions, and he was completely lacking in a fundamental requirement for academic success: the ability to take schoolwork seriously.

This made him a good fit for the postwar British art college. Britain had more art colleges per capita than any nation in the world. The establishment of a National Diploma in Design, in 1944, lowered the bar for entry—probably all Lennon had to do was to submit to an interview and show a portfolio of his drawings—and this led to an academically permissive environment. (Requirements would be tightened up in 1961.) Many people went to art school because they had done poorly on their O-level exams (generally taken at sixteen) but showed some indication of creative talent. Ostensibly, art students were being trained for careers in fields like advertising, commercial art, and industrial design, but unlike in American art colleges—for example, the one Andy Warhol attended in Pittsburgh—the curriculum was not closely tied to the expectations of industry. There were few formal requirements (although there were some, which Lennon failed to meet) and the instructors sometimes had little artistic training or were otherwise undermotivated. They saw their job as letting the students create.

Postwar art college was therefore a place for gifted misfits to meet, and every British act that had a lasting impact on popular music in the

1960s had at least one member who attended art college: the Rolling Stones (Keith Richards and Charlie Watts), the Who (Pete Townsend), Cream (Eric Clapton and the lyricist Pete Brown), Led Zeppelin (Jimmy Page), the Kinks (Ray Davies), the Jeff Beck Group (Jeff Beck and Ron Wood, later with the Stones), the Animals (Eric Burdon), and Donovan.[76]

All those musicians entered art college at the moment when jazz, associated with intellectual seriousness and a bohemian look (beards, corduroys, sandals, and scarves), was being displaced by rock 'n' roll, which was associated with insouciance and a Teddy Boy look (leather jackets, drainpipe pants, brothel creeper and winklepicker shoes, pomaded hair). They therefore began their careers in an institutional setting in which questions about authenticity and the relation between art and entertainment were, however crudely or inexplicitly, in play. These were questions that few of their musical contemporaries in the United States had occasion to confront. British art students also came to think of art in general, and music in particular, as implying a set of related choices—as being part of a lifestyle.

Lennon was charismatic, and he attracted attention. It was in art college that he met Stuart Sutcliffe, a talented painter who read Kierkegaard, knew modern art, and was a fashion trendsetter. Sutcliffe gave some sophistication to Lennon's sense of style, and, to Paul's annoyance, he joined the band, playing, very badly, bass guitar.[77]

The Beatles galvanized, musically and personally, in Germany. They performed in Hamburg three times: in 1960 for three and a half months at the Indra Club and the Kaiserkeller on Grosse Freiheit and the Top Ten Club on the Reeperbahn; in 1961 for three months at the Top Ten Club; and in 1962 for a month and a half at the Star-Club on Grosse Freiheit. The drummer for those gigs, Pete Best, was neither a Lennon personality type nor an adequate drummer; he was replaced by Ringo Starr in 1962, when the Beatles began to record.

In Hamburg, the Beatles played almost around the clock. In their first seven weeks at the Indra, they spent more than two hundred hours onstage. On the second trip, their schedule was even more punishing. They performed mainly American music, songs by Elvis Presley, Buddy Holly and the Crickets, Gene Vincent, Carl Perkins, Little Richard, Eddie Cochran, the Coasters, Ray Charles, and Fats Domino.[78] Hamburg is a port city, and the crowd at the clubs included seamen, local gangsters, prostitutes, and off-duty strippers. There was a lot of drinking and fighting. The Beatles smoked and ate onstage; they wore leather pants and cowboy boots; they bantered with the audience and tried to avoid getting beaten up. The only job requirement was to *mach Schau*— make a show. Lennon once went onstage in his underwear with a toilet seat around his head.[79] The Hamburg clubs were censorship-free zones that the Beatles could treat as performance spaces. They brought the interactive stage style they had developed in Hamburg, along with their mastery of the rock 'n' roll songbook, back to Liverpool, and it was there, in the cellar club called the Cavern, that they became a phenomenon.

By then, Britain had started to develop its own teen culture. The British edition of the baby boom began earlier than the American one; it led to a 20 percent increase in the number of fifteen- to nineteen-year olds between 1956 and 1963.[80] British teen culture was driven by the same goods, like portable record players, that had helped launch American teen culture, and music was a big part of it: record sales in Britain increased from £9 million in 1955 to £14 million in 1957 and £22 million in 1963.[81] In 1957, 1.7 percent of British teenage spending went toward records, record players, and other music-related goods, but that was 44 percent of all spending on music.[82] Music in Britain was a youth market.

The Beatles played the Cavern 292 times. People lined up to see them during lunch hour and in the evening, and this attracted the attention of the operator of a Liverpool record store, Brian Epstein, who became the Beatles' manager, and who secured them their session with George Martin at Parlophone.[83] Martin was an ideal producer for the Beatles, not only because of his creativity with arrangements but also because, as the joke about the necktie demonstrated, he understood the Beatles' sense of humor. For Martin had built up the Parlophone label by recording comedy acts. He had made records with Peter Sellers, Peter Ustinov, Flanders and Swann, and the Goons, and he produced the cast album of *Beyond the Fringe*, the comedy revue written and performed by Dudley Moore, Peter Cook, Alan Bennett, and Jonathan Miller.[84] He was used to dealing with improvisation and the far-fetched.

Lennon and McCartney started writing songs together soon after they met, but the band rarely performed them. With Martin (who was skeptical at first: pop singers normally didn't write songs), they began recording them. "Love Me Do," the Beatles' first real single, was released in October 1962.* The Beatles' first album, *Please Please Me*, was released in March 1963 and went to No. 1 in Britain. In September, "She Loves You" became the fastest-selling single ever in Britain. Their second album, *With the Beatles*, was released on November 22 (the day John F. Kennedy was assassinated) and it also went to No. 1.

It wasn't only the sales that made people notice. It was also the fans. The term "Beatlemania" first appeared in October 1963 as a headline in the *Daily Mail*.[85] By then, the band was the hottest musical act in Europe. The American press started to pay attention, although it treated the group as a curiosity, and on February 7, 1964, the Beatles arrived in the United States. Two days later, their appearance on *The Ed Sullivan Show* was seen by 74 million people, the largest television audience ever to that point. Seventy million people watched them on the following week's *Ed Sullivan Show*, broadcast from Miami. "Can't Buy Me Love," released on March 20, had advance sales in the United States of 2.1 million. By April 4, twelve of the hundred bestselling songs in the United States, including the top five, were Beatles songs; by the end of the year, the Beatles had charted twenty-seven sides, six of them at No. 1, and eleven albums, with three at No. 1.[86] That summer, they went on a world tour (Presley never performed before a foreign audience in his life), then returned to the United States and played thirty concerts in twenty-three cities. That year, they were expected to take in $50 million from sales of licensed products, such as Beatle wigs.[87] They had become what every group dreamed of becoming: bigger than Elvis. They would dominate the popular music business for the next six years.

5.

Their success in the United States was the only thing that ever surprised the Beatles. A few British acts had charted songs in the American market, but none had broken through.[88] "They've got everything over there. What do they want *us* for?" McCartney is supposed to have complained on the flight over.[89] He meant that the Beatles had started out bringing American music to Europe and now found themselves doing something they quite reasonably considered absurd: bringing American music to America.

---

* They had, before Ringo, backed the British singer and guitarist Tony Sheridan on the standard "My Bonnie" in 1961—their first record on the British charts.

The speed and scale of the Beatles' impact in the United States can be partly explained by demographics. When they arrived, 40 percent of the population—78 million people—was under twenty. The infrastructure for youth culture that had been built up after the war was firmly in place: American business knew how to sell to teenagers. As in the case of Elvis Presley, the Beatles first became famous not because of their music but because of their fans. And as with Presley, those fans were virtually all female. There were 11 million teenage girls in the United States in 1964, and they bought more than half of all records sold. The Beatles had had male fans when they played clubs in Hamburg and Liverpool, but Beatlemania was a girl phenomenon. It was not until 1965 that boys began showing up at Beatles concerts in significant numbers.[90]

The band's longevity can be ascribed to sheer songwriting talent, which appeared to evolve as its fan base aged. The Beatles composed in an unusually wide range of styles. The White Album (officially *The Beatles*), which was released in November 1968 and was the work the band regarded as its last complete group effort, is a pastiche of nearly a dozen genres, from folk rock to blues, surf music, heavy metal, and ska. But the Beatles managed to make every song they played sound like a Beatles song.

Other factors were important, and one was the Beatles' skill at disarming the press. The press conference held after they landed at Kennedy Airport was an impromptu tour de force. Three thousand fans had turned out (before the visit, Capitol, the Beatles' American label, had put an unprecedented amount of money, probably around fifty thousand dollars, into promotion). There was screaming and mayhem as the Beatles were rushed off the plane and into an airport lounge, where they were confronted by two hundred reporters irritated by the harassed conditions of the assignment and armed with the customary professional cynicism.[91] Every question from the press was topped by a Beatle one-liner.

Q: Would you please sing something?
The Beatles (in unison): No!
Ringo: Sorry.

Q: There's some doubt that you *can* sing.
John: No. We need money first.

Q: How do you account for your success?

Beatle: We can't tell you.

Paul: Wish we knew.

John: Good press agent.

Q: What does excite them [fans] so much?

John: If we knew that, we'd form another group and be managers.

Paul: We have a message. [Expectant silence.] Our message is: buy more Beatle records!

One exchange was sublime.

Q: What do you think of Beethoven?

Ringo: Great. Especially his poems.

This was actually a running joke of Ringo's; he'd used it with reporters before.[92] If Elvis Presley had had a month to think about it, he couldn't have come up with that line.

"We have a press agent" is the perfect reply to a reporter who asks why you are successful, because that is pretty much what the reporter already thinks. The Beatles were show-business veterans. Lennon, McCartney, and Harrison had been together for six years and they had known Ringo almost as long: he had been in another Liverpool band, Rory Storm and the Hurricanes, which played on the same circuit as the Beatles, including the Hamburg clubs. The Beatles were accustomed to fan hysteria, and they had faced audiences far scarier than the New York press corps. Bantering was part of their act. They understood how the game was played. They did not think they had to pretend otherwise.

The press picked this up immediately. "The Beatle wit was contagious," *The New York Times* reported the next day. "Everyone guffawed. Photographers forgot about the pictures they wanted to take. The show was on." "What recommends the Beatles more than anything else," said *Time*, "is their bright and highly irreverent attitude toward themselves and their international magnitude. Reporters toss ticking questions at them, but it is generally the replies that explode."[93] This was not the style in which most American pop stars and their managers handled public relations.

Some of the Beatles' wit can be credited to the social style of working-class Liverpool life. Ringo, for instance, who was by far the least educated Beatle (childhood illnesses had kept him out of school for long periods), did not acquire his drollness with the mohair suit Brian Epstein accoutered him in. It was his natural manner of deflecting insults. The question about Beethoven was a genteel insult, and it is telling that he, the Beatle least likely to know much about Beethoven, should have had the quickest retort, and a retort to which no follow-up is possible.

And although the Beatles may have mystified grown-ups, they did not alarm them. Shortly after their appearance on Ed Sullivan, David Riesman was asked by *U.S. News & World Report* to compare the Beatles' reception with the craze for Elvis Presley. Presley, Riesman explained, "antagonized the older generation . . . [T]he Beatles have none of this somewhat sinister quality that Presley represented for adults. They don't have the quasi-sexual, quasi-aggressive note that was present in Presley." Consequently, he advised, Beatlemania was a fad, and would be short-lived.[94] Riesman was wrong about that, of course, but it was likely that it was precisely because the Beatles did not scare off adults that they were able to outlast Elvis. They were accepted as eternally beneficent household gods.

And finally, the Beatles had the advantage of arriving in the United States when the music that had inspired them was moribund. The people who predicted that rock 'n' roll was a fad and would burn itself out were not wrong right away. By 1964, almost all the American musicians whose songs the Beatles played in Hamburg and Liverpool were marginalized or dead. In March 1956, Carl Perkins broke his collarbone in a car accident in Delaware on his way to New York to appear on *The Perry Como Show*; he recovered, but he lost his chance at a television breakthrough, and this turned out to be a severe career setback. Two years later, Presley entered the U.S. Army as a private. He was stationed in Germany, and, although RCA had taken the precaution of recording a backlog of songs, he did not perform again for more than two years. When he was discharged, in 1960, he appeared on a television special with Frank Sinatra, then went to Hollywood and started making movies at the rate of two or three a year. The movies were panned, but the money was good.

In 1957, Little Richard quit rock 'n' roll to become a preacher. The same year, the news that Jerry Lee Lewis had married a thirteen-year-old cousin led to his banishment from radio and television. On February 3, 1959, Buddy Holly was killed in a plane crash in Iowa, along with

Ritchie Valens and J. R. Richardson, who performed as the Big Bopper. Later that year, Chuck Berry was charged under the Mann Act with transporting a woman—a fourteen-year-old hat-checker—across state lines for immoral purposes. He eventually served almost two years in prison. In 1960, Eddie Cochran, who had resisted flying to Britain for a tour because he was afraid of dying in a plane crash like Buddy Holly, died in a car accident in Wiltshire. Gene Vincent, who was in the car with him, was injured.

The survivors all went back to making records, but their careers were damaged, and their music was no longer in demand. When the Beatles arrived in New York, the pop charts had been dominated by singers like Bobby Vinton, Frankie Avalon, and Fabian—the "teen idols"—and groups like the Four Seasons. Presley had not had a No. 1 single since April 1962; he would not have another No. 1 in the United States until 1969.[95]

The cutting edge of popular music when the Beatles arrived was the folk revival, featuring artists such as Joan Baez, Bob Dylan, the Kingston Trio, and Peter, Paul, and Mary. In 1963, Baez became the first singer to sell out the Hollywood Bowl since Sinatra in 1944, and that year more than two hundred albums of folk music were released in the United States. Sales of acoustic guitars reached a million units a year.[96] Folk music was not party music. It did not have a backbeat, the dance propellant in rock 'n' roll. The sound was acoustic; the music was associated with progressive causes; and most of the performers were (as performers) sexless. Apart from Harry Belafonte, who sang calypso, and despite the fact that the movement maintained a curatorial respect for Black artists, such as Odetta, Sonny Terry, and Mississippi John Hurt, the hit-makers were all white. Folk was, so to speak, a "liberal" backlash against rock 'n' roll, as teen-idol pop was a "conservative" backlash. On February 9, the day the Beatles appeared on *Ed Sullivan*, the No. 1 album in the United States was *The Singing Nun*, recorded by an actual Belgian nun, Jeanne Paule Deckers, who accompanied herself on acoustic guitar—an act about as remote from "Hound Dog" in any of its renditions as can be imagined.*

But there was a post–rock 'n' roll sound close to the Beatles' sound. This was the music of Motown and of the so-called girl groups, a "Black sound" that was not rhythm and blues. Lennon discovered this music

---

* The Singing Nun's hit single, "Dominique," was sung in French.

in 1961, when he first heard songs such as "Angel Baby," by Rosie and the Originals, "Shop Around," by the Miracles, and "Will You Love Me Tomorrow," by the Shirelles—all Black groups—and added them to the Beatles' act. *The Beatles' Second Album*, released in March 1964, included covers of one girl-group song, "Devil in Her Heart," by the Donays, and three Motown songs: "You Really Got a Hold on Me," written and re-corded by Smokey Robinson; "Money," co-written by the founder of Mo-town, Berry Gordy, Jr., and recorded by Barret Strong; and "Please Mister Postman," by the Marvelettes.[97] Like the Beatles' own early songs, this was junior-high-prom music, much more pop than R&B.

It was not only bad luck and misadventure that had reduced the mar-ket for rock 'n' roll. Some of the wounds were self-inflicted by the indus-try, results of a war between ASCAP and BMI.[98] By 1952, 74 percent of No. 1 songs on *Variety*'s "Hit Parade" were BMI songs, as were 62 percent of the No. 2 and No. 3 songs.[99] In 1953, a group of ASCAP composers calling themselves the Songwriters of America sued BMI, the broadcasters, and the record companies those broadcasters owned, such as Columbia and RCA Victor. The plaintiffs charged collusion to prevent ASCAP-licensed songs from being recorded and broadcast. It was essentially an antitrust claim: BMI was the broadcasters' creature, so broadcasters had an interest in increasing the number of plays of BMI-licensed material. Though the merits of the claim were dubious and the lawsuit itself went nowhere (it was finally dismissed in 1971), ASCAP and its supporters did manage to incite three separate congres-sional investigations.

Apart from allowing members of Congress and pro-ASCAP wit-nesses to air their disdain for rock 'n' roll, the first two investigations did not yield much. But the third, conducted by the Legislative Oversight Subcommittee of the House Commerce Committee, shook up the busi-ness. The committee's remit was to examine the use of payola—the prac-tice of paying disk jockeys to play certain songs, hardly a novel practice in the industry. Two prominent targets of the hearings, held in 1960, were Alan Freed and Dick Clark. Freed was uncooperative, and he was fired by WABC (where he had moved in 1958), indicted, and fined. He died, broken and alcoholic, in 1965.

Clark was cleverer. His conflicts of interest were far more exten-sive than Freed's. He acknowledged a financial stake in more than a quarter of the songs he had played on his show between August 1957 and November 1959 (and that was probably a low estimate). But he escaped sanctions after selling his stake in several music publishers, a talent agency, a record-pressing plant, record companies, and other enterprises. He remained host of *American Bandstand* until 1987.[100]

But payola was how the independent labels that recorded R&B got their product on the air.[101] Leonard Chess used to drive to towns outside Chicago visiting deejays, with a car trunk full of alligator shoes. He would ask the deejay his shoe size and gift him a pair. Sometimes, Chess would simply hand over the recording he wanted the deejay to play with a fifty-dollar bill.[102] The issue could also be addressed by simple fraternizing. Sam Phillips's "friendship" with Dewey Phillips, which probably consisted of paying for his drinks, helped get Presley's first recording on the air.[103]

An anomaly in copyright law gave performers no rights to the songs they recorded. And when performers composed their own songs, it was often treated as work-for-hire, with rights retained by the publisher. (This is why Arthur Crudup did not see any royalties from Presley's cover of "That's All Right.") One of the first things Presley did after he signed with RCA Victor, therefore, was to create Elvis Presley Music, Inc., which held rights to the songs he recorded. When Epstein took over management of the Beatles, he created Northern Songs for the same purpose.

It was not uncommon for deejays to join the royalty stream. When Chess brought "Maybellene" to Freed at WINS, Freed was delighted to play the song, and took co-writing credit.[104] No one called this payola. It was just how the business worked. After all, Freed's career as a rock 'n' roll disk jockey and concert promoter in Cleveland had been started by a record-store owner who offered to subvent his radio show. Broadcasters played records in order to sell commercials, but from the music industry's point of view, records *are* commercials. They are advertisements for themselves. Why shouldn't the producers pay something for the exposure?

The payola scandal got an enormous amount of attention because it followed directly on the television quiz show scandal, which revealed that hugely popular shows such as *Twenty-One* and *The $64,000 Question* were rigged. And it changed the status of the disk jockey, who had been a key figure in the promotion of R&B and rock 'n' roll. To avoid suspicion of payoffs, radio stations began turning playlists over to program directors, who followed the charts. No one could get in trouble for playing a song listed in *Billboard*. This made it more difficult for nonmainstream music to get air play. Popularity became self-sustaining. The rich got richer.

Then, in November 1963, for reasons that have never been clear, *Billboard* stopped publishing an R&B chart. The proportion of songs on the *Billboard* charts performed by Black artists dropped from 42 percent in 1962 to 22 percent in 1966. In 1963, there were thirty-seven top-ten singles by Black artists; in 1964, there were twenty-one. The R&B chart did not come back until January 1965.[105] In between, the Beatles arrived.

To the extent that radio stations were basing playlists on the charts, therefore, less R&B was being broadcast when the Beatles entered the American music scene. Even luckier for them, one station that did not revert to chart-based programming was WINS. It replaced Freed (after a brief stint by Bruce Morrow, aka "Cousin Brucie") with Murray Kaufman, who, as Murray the K, became the Beatles' most energetic on-air cheerleader, a man known as the Fifth Beatle.[106] When disk jockeys who might have championed other groups were losing control over their playlists, the Beatles had their own man.

The negative coverage of the payola scandal was damaging because it led the media to treat rock 'n' roll as a commercial product pushed on teenagers by underhanded means. This is why, when the American press began to take note of the Beatles' success in Europe before the band went on *Ed Sullivan*, its first instinct was to attribute that success to anything but the music. "One reason for the Beatles' popularity," Edwin Newman reported from Britain on *The Huntley-Brinkley Report* on NBC in November 1963—the first televised footage of the Beatles ever seen in the United States—"may be that it's almost impossible to hear them."[107] And this is also why the Beatles' conquest of the press was both surprising (to the press) and important (to the music). The greatest service the band performed for American popular music in 1964 was to make it respectable.

All these developments in the music business opened competitive space for the Beatles, but there was a sense in which the Beatles weren't competing with anyone, and that was because American audiences didn't see them as imitation Americans. They saw them as Europeans. The key signifier of difference was the haircuts. These got started in

1961, when John and Paul were vacationing together in Paris and had their hair cut by a German friend, Jürgen Vollmer.[108] In the beginning, that they looked "like girls" was the common reaction, but there is no evidence that the Beatles thought of themselves as cross-dressers. On the other hand, Stuart Sutcliffe and his German girlfriend, Astrid Kirchherr, did like to cross-dress. "He was mad about my clothes," Kirchherr said.[109] Stuart wore his hair down over his forehead; Astrid sometimes wore hers swept back in an Elvis-like pompadour.[110] The Beatles adopted the Sutcliffe look.[111]

By the time they reached the United States, they were fashionable in what would later be called a metrosexual style. There were the trousers (Italian fabric and cut), the collarless jackets (inspired by Pierre Cardin and made in London, with the Beatles collaborating on the design), and the boots with Cuban heels (from Anello & Davide in Chelsea).[112] The Beatles were astonished when they arrived in the United States by the lack of sartorial style. "You were all walking around in fuckin' bermuda shorts, with Boston crew cuts and stuff on your teeth," Lennon said later. ". . . There was no conception of dress or any of that jazz. We just thought, 'what an ugly race,' looked just disgusting."[113] And then there was the Scouse accent—which, for Americans, was both exotic and ethnically indeterminate.

In performance, the Beatles did not snarl or gyrate. This was calculated. "[I]n the early days in England," as Lennon explained, "all the groups were like Elvis and a backing group, and the Beatles deliberately didn't move like Elvis. It was our policy because we found it stupid and bullshit."[114] Their lyrics lacked obvious sexual innuendo. (If "Please Please Me" is a song about oral sex, few people got it at the time.) Most important, they carried no ethnic baggage. As *Time* put it: "the Beatles made it all right to be white."[115] When white American musicians performed songs associated with Black artists, it seemed an act of appropriation; when British musicians did it—first the Beatles, then the Stones, the Animals, and Cream—it was regarded as an act of *hommage*. The British bands took race out of the equation.

6.

Originality is not at a premium in popular entertainment. The key to market entry is imitation-with-a-difference. It is understood that melodies, lyrics, sounds, and performance fashions work because they have worked before, and that audiences like what they are accustomed to liking. Many groups imitated the Beatles with a difference; the most commercially successful of them, the Monkees, was a deliberate Beatles knock-off.[116] But two acts in particular took inspiration from the Beatles and kept up with them musically (and long outlasted them): Bob Dylan and the Rolling Stones. Together, those three acts made possible something that would have been almost inconceivable before 1965. They made popular music that was not jazz or show tunes critically respectable.

Dylan and the Stones were the Beatles' contemporaries. Dylan was born in 1941, Brian Jones in 1942, Keith Richards and Mick Jagger in 1943. They all got started as musicians before the Beatles became famous, but for much of the 1960s, the Stones seemed to be if not copying, at least emulating the Beatles album by album. "Every fucking thing we did, Mick does exactly the same," Lennon complained.[117]

The Stones, too, were self-conscious about their look. Their manager, Andrew Oldham, saw what Epstein had accomplished by making the Beatles over from toughs into moptops, and he did the opposite with his artists. They were presented as toughs—even though their lyrics are far artier than the Beatles'. Oldham also pressured Jagger and Richards to write their own songs. Musically, the Stones laid claim to the bluesy, snarly part of rock 'n' roll, with Jagger, their front man, leaping about like Elvis—both styles that the Beatles had strategically forsworn. This allowed the bands to compete with each other without duplicating each other. It proved a highly profitable division of labor.[118]

Dylan first heard the Beatles' music in New York, but his revelation seems to have come while he was driving across the country to Berkeley with three male friends and, somewhere in Colorado, they began hearing Beatles songs played over and over on the car radio. It was February 1964; the Beatles had just performed on *Ed Sullivan* and their songs were climbing the charts. Dylan "practically jumped out of the car," one of his companions remembered. "Did you hear that?" he said.[119]

Dylan was uncomfortable being identified as a folk singer. He had changed his approach to his lyrics the summer before, after watching rehearsals of a show called *Brecht on Brecht* at the Sheridan Square Playhouse in the Village. (His girlfriend, Suze Rotolo, was assistant to the stage manager and set designer.) Dylan became obsessed with the Kurt

Weil song "Pirate Jenny" from *The Threepenny Opera*. "Woody [Woody Guthrie, Dylan's initial inspiration] had never written a song like that," Dylan wrote in his memoir. "It wasn't a protest or topical song and there was no love for people in it . . . This heavy song was a new stimulant for my senses, indeed very much like a folk song but a folk song from a different gallon jug in a different backyard."[120]

In the Beatles' music, Dylan heard a way out of folk. "They were doing things nobody was doing," as he described his reaction. "Their chords were outrageous, just outrageous . . . I knew they were pointing the direction of where music had to go . . . You see, there was a lot of hypocrisy all around, people saying it had to be either folk or rock. But I knew it didn't have to be like that. I dug what the Beatles were doing."[121] It was a two-way street: the Beatles had first heard Dylan's music earlier that year in Paris, and they played *The Freewheelin' Bob Dylan* over and over.[122]

The Beatles built their consumer base on singles—1964 was the peak year of singles sales in Britain: 80 percent of records sold were singles— but they extended it with albums.[123] And the album became the signature pop-music product. The Beatles started the trend with the cover of their second album, released in Britain as *With the Beatles*. Epstein hired the British photographer Robert Freeman, who shot the Beatles' faces in black and white against a black background. (Astrid Kirchherr had made photographic portraits of the Beatles in the same style.) Freeman and the Beatles pushed for a no-text cover for the album, but they were overruled by people at EMI, who liked the photograph itself little enough. The studio paid Freeman seventy-five pounds, triple the usual fee.

It was a good investment. The cover was a sensation, and sales were fantastic.[124] Freeman went on to do the covers for three more Beatles' albums—*Beatles for Sale*, *Help!*, and *Rubber Soul*. The *Sgt. Pepper's* cover was done by the Pop artist Peter Blake, *The Beatles* (the White Album) by the artist Richard Hamilton, who also designed the poster that came with it.* Jazz and classical albums used cover art (Andy Warhol did many album covers in the 1950s), but the pictures on pop albums had usually been blandly promotional. The Beatles made the album cover part of the message.

Dylan and the Stones quickly followed the example. Soon after

---

* Blake's wife, the artist Jann Haworth, contributed substantially to the design of the *Sgt. Pepper's* cover—in particular, the decision to create it as a set, rather than a collage of faces.

hearing the Beatles on the radio, Dylan switched to electric guitar and came up with what he called "that thin, that wild mercury sound," the sound on his next three albums.[125] He released *Bringing It All Back Home* in March 1965—the first of his records with an art cover: a photograph by Daniel Kramer, showing the singer in a set stocked with references to the music that had influenced him, including the 1955 album *Lotte Lenya Sings Berlin Theatre Songs by Kurt Weill.*

Bringing It All Back Home was the first in a rapid succession of major records coming out in the United States. In June, Dylan released "Like a Rolling Stone" and in July he gave his notorious electric performance of "Maggie's Farm" (possibly a goodbye to folk) at the Newport Folk Festival.[126] The same month, the Stones released *Out of Our Heads*, which included "(I Can't Get No) Satisfaction," their first No. 1 song. In August, Dylan released *Highway 61 Revisited* and the Beatles released *Help!* In September, Dylan released "Positively 4th Street," definitely a farewell to the Village folk scene, and in December, the Beatles' *Rubber Soul* and the Stones' *December's Children* came out. *Blonde on Blonde* (the title an echo of *Brecht on Brecht*) came out in May 1966, the Stones' *Aftermath* in June, *Revolver* in August. By the summer of 1967, when *Sgt. Pepper's Lonely Hearts Club Band* appeared—an album with cover art to top all cover art—those three acts had redefined pop music. They essentially created a new pop form. Songs like "Stuck Inside of Mobile," "Paint It Black," "A Day in the Life," "While My Guitar Gently Weeps," and "You Can't Always Get What You Want" were received as poetic statements about contemporary life. This was way beyond dance music, and way beyond "Hound Dog."

The development of the music coincided with the expansion of its consumer base, both in numbers, as the postwar cohort grew up and began buying records, and sociologically, as "youth" got extended past the teens and into the college years. But what allowed the music to persist beyond its market fundamentals and to transcend the normal lifespan of an entertainment taste was its critical reception. Rock criticism is what made rock 'n' roll a cultural winner.

Because the Beatles seemed to be as bemused by Beatlemania as everyone else was, the press could like them without taking them seriously. Reviews in American newspapers of their first performances were almost universally dismissive of the music. The band was treated as a fluke, four agreeable young men who had somehow struck it rich and who proposed to ride out their lucky streak. Wasn't that what a free society was all about? But this changed with the release of the first Beatles movie, *A Hard Day's Night*, in the summer of 1964.

The movie was in the works before the Beatles came to the United States. A loophole in their contract with Capitol gave them the rights to soundtrack albums, which Epstein quickly exploited to make a deal with United Artists to produce a movie and the accompanying album. It was the Beatles themselves who chose Richard Lester to direct *A Hard Day's Night*. Lester was from Philadelphia (the family name was Liebman) and he entered the University of Pennsylvania in 1947, when he was fifteen. He began working in television in 1950, then moved to England, where he met Peter Sellers and became involved with the Goons. In 1959, Lester and Sellers shot an eleven-minute, sixteen-millimeter short called *The Running, Jumping, and Standing Still Film*. The movie was released commercially in Britain, shown at a festival in Edinburgh, and nominated for an Academy Award. The Beatles loved it.[127]

Lester shot *A Hard Day's Night* in England in March and April 1964; the movie premiered in London on July 6.[128] It was filmed in a cinéma-vérité style, mixing fact and fiction, improvisation and script. The movie is effectively a staged "documentary" of a day in the life of the Beatles. Serious film critics, anticipating the kind of inexpensive exploitation film that Presley was making, were caught unprepared.

A Hard Day's Night arrived in theaters during a period of American fascination with new European cinema, and it rose on that tide of appreciation. Reviewers alluded to Godard, Antonioni, Fellini, and Truffaut.[129] In *The Village Voice*, Andrew Sarris called the movie "the 'Citizen Kane' of juke box musicals, the brilliant crystallization of such diverse cultural particles as the pop movie, rock 'n' roll, cinema-verite [*sic*], the nouvelle vague, free cinema, the affectedly handheld camera, frenzied cutting, the cult of the sexless sub-adolescent, the semi-documentary and studied spontaneity. So help me," he added, "I resisted the Beatles as long as I could."[130]

In his *Esquire* film column, Dwight Macdonald began by calling the Beatles "cult-fetishes of adolescent hysteria, exploiting (and being exploited by) the crass market for kitsch at its most primitive (and profitable)." Nevertheless, he had to admit, *A Hard Day's Night* was "as good cinema as I have seen for a long time," and "the Beatles are partly responsible."[131] The movie was nominated for a Grammy and two Oscars, including Best Score. (It lost to *My Fair Lady*, another artifact of

American fascination with the British.) Just as significantly, though, *A Hard Day's Night* is *not* an art film. It puts no strain on the intellect. It is a movie that grown-ups can enjoy. It was the first rock 'n' roll–related product to breach the adolescent-adult taste barrier.

The soundtrack album, which the Beatles began recording right after their first trip to the United States, did not get critical attention, because pop records were almost never reviewed in the United States outside of trade publications, but it indicated the direction the Beatles were about to take. For the first time, every track was a Beatles composition, and the startling opening chord of the title song announced a new attention to musicianship. That chord, played using all three guitars (Harrison's was a twelve-string), plus drums, with Martin on the piano, is usually identified as a G7 with an added ninth and a suspended fourth, but there is no consensus on exactly what notes are played on which instrument.[132] It is chromatically unresolved—not unlike the so-called *Tristan* chord that Wagner created for his overture.

This feature of the Beatles' music was identified very early. In December 1963, the music critic of the London *Times*, William Mann, referred to "pandiatonic clusters" in Beatles songs—meaning chords composed without classic harmonic restrictions. Mann also noted that the Aeolian cadence at the end of "Not a Second Time" is the same chord progression that closes Gustav Mahler's "Das Lied von der Erde."[133] Mann was laughed at; Lennon later called him a "bullshitter." "But," he added, "he made us credible with intellectuals."[134]

And after the release of *Rubber Soul*, *Revolver*, and *Sgt. Pepper's*, other writers began discussing the Beatles in the context of European art music. In 1968, *The New York Review of Books* ran an appreciation by the composer Ned Rorem, in which he compared the Beatles to Monteverdi, Schumann, and Poulenc. Rorem also mentioned McCartney's "leanings toward Stock-hausen [*sic*] and electronics."[135] Stockhausen's face is on the cover of *Sgt. Pepper's*, but his electronic music had a bigger influence on Lennon's songs. Rorem's mistake sprang from his assumption that, in the manner of Broadway show composers, Lennon wrote the lyrics and McCartney wrote the melodies. Nineteen sixty-eight was a little late to be getting this wrong.

A few months earlier, a similarly appreciative essay in *Partisan Review* by Richard Poirier, a literature professor at Rutgers, had compared *Sgt. Pepper's* to Alexander Pope and "A Day in the Life" to "The Waste

Land." The refrain "I'd love to turn you on," Poirier suggested, "has as much propriety to the fragmented life that precedes it in the song and in the whole work as does the 'Shantih, Shantih, Shantih' to the fragments of Eliot's poem."[136]

The motive for linking the Beatles to Poulenc and Eliot was to make them more interesting, but the association actually made them less interesting, because it detached them from the cultural stratum to which they belonged. The Beatles were not artists and never thought of themselves in those terms. They were entertainers; their product met a different appetite. It required a kind of critical attention that literature professors and art-music composers, however well disposed, were not equipped for. The Beatles' music needed the attention of someone who was as inward with the cultural realm it occupied as Poirier was with poetry and Rorem was with classical music. It needed, in other words, a fan. And one emerged.

By the circumstances of his birth, Jann Wenner could have been scripted to be the force behind the critical reception of rock 'n' roll. Wenner was born in New York City in the predawn of the postwar population explosion, January 7, 1946. The family moved to Northern California when Jann was an infant, and his father started a company that manufactured baby formula—a business with much room for growth in the ensuing decades. Wenner went to Berkeley. While there, he became a protégé of Ralph Gleason, a columnist who wrote about jazz and pop music for the *San Francisco Chronicle* (one of the few newspapers in the country with a pop music reviewer). In 1966, Wenner dropped out of college; a year later, he and Gleason started *Rolling Stone*. The first issue was dated November 9, 1967. John Lennon was on the cover.[137]

Wenner saw the magazine as something closer to a trade publication— "We're gonna be better than *Billboard*," he exhorted his staff—than an organ of traditional journalism.[138] That many of the writers and editors who worked for him felt differently worked to the magazine's advantage. *Rolling Stone* attracted readers who wanted a fan magazine; it also attracted readers who wanted a countercultural take on contemporary life.

Wenner is supposed to have said that he started the magazine in order to meet Lennon.[139] Whether this is true or not, Wenner loved the stars, and he believed that stars are what people want to read about. For him, the stars were the Beatles, Bob Dylan, and Mick Jagger. The name he gave to his magazine was an allusion to two of them. Three issues of *Rolling Stone* came out in 1967; the Beatles were on the covers of two. Twenty-one issues came out in 1968; the Beatles were on the covers of four, the Stones on two, and Dylan on one. The magazine's first anniversary issue, dated November 23, 1968, had a photograph on the cover of Lennon and Yoko Ono in the nude—the famous "two virgins" picture, provided, at Wenner's request, by Derek Taylor—and an interview with Lennon by Jonathan Cott. It was when that issue hit newsstands that sales of *Rolling Stone* took off.[140] After the Beatles officially broke up, in 1970, Wenner scored the first post-Beatles interview with Lennon—the "biggest bastards on earth" interview. It was, in effect, a payoff for his magazine's consistent support of Lennon, and one of the biggest entertainment scoops of the day.

Rolling Stone created the popular music canon, and it did this by calling songs such as "Lucy in the Sky with Diamonds," "Wild Horses," and "All Along the Watchtower" rock 'n' roll. The magazine transformed a term that was coined to name a teenage fad in dance music into a label for the music the magazine and its readers found affecting. This meant creating a continuous musical tradition from R&B to Woodstock, and the Beatles summed it up. "Although it is Bob Dylan who is the single most important figure in rock 'n' roll," Wenner wrote in 1968; "and although it is the Rolling Stones who are the embodiment of a rock 'n' roll band; it is nonetheless Our Boys, The Beatles, who are the perfect product and result of everything that rock 'n' roll means and encompasses."[141] The Beatles connected Presley with the present.

This interpretation was not inevitable. For people who were either too young or too old in 1964, the Beatles seemed to have nothing to do with Presley. Poirier, for example, expressed relief that the Beatles had overcome what he called their "tawdry enslavement to Elvis Presley."[142] For these listeners, Presley was a throwback, a down-market showman with the wrong hair. The Beatles may, in the spirit of good fun, have covered some rock 'n' roll hits on their first albums, but the band that produced *Rubber Soul* and *Revolver* belonged to a different category of entertainer. *Rolling Stone*, and the critical view it promoted, changed this.

It did so by looking back at Presley through the lens of the 1960s. The girls who screamed at Presley on *Milton Berle* were no more rebels or nonconformists than were the girls who screamed at the Beatles on *Ed Sullivan* eight years later. From the perspective of a later period, though, when liberation and protest were ascendant values in youth culture, Presley's tongue-in-cheek performance of "Hound Dog," once read nonproblematically by an audience still familiar with burlesque, could be interpreted as a challenge to the status quo.

The teenage girls therefore got written out of the story—as did the Black teenagers who could take credit for launching rock 'n' roll by buying the R&B music that the major labels declined to record. Black musicians were crucial to the official rock 'n' roll story, of course, and the significance of race was even exaggerated, since it sustained the conviction that rock 'n' roll was the music of outsiders, that it was authentic. The Black American experience (rather than, say, *The Goon Show*) was promoted as one of rock's roots. But the first generation of American popular music critics was almost entirely made up of white men. As late as 1990, *Rolling Stone* had not employed a single Black writer.[143]

Along with *Creem* and *Melody Maker* and a small number of other magazines devoted to popular music, *Rolling Stone* established the persona of the rock critic, as someone personally invested in the phenomenon, someone whose own subjectivity arises out of their immersion in the music. More specifically, the rock critic is someone who understands the music as part of a narrative of postwar social history. In the United States, rock 'n' roll became the story of the generational experience of white men. "Think of all the changes in the world that have occurred in the last five years," Wenner wrote, "and so many of them, especially for the young of my age, are attributable directly to the Beatles."[144]

In 1968 or 1969, Wenner hired Greil Marcus, a Berkeley graduate student, to be his first reviews editor. In 1969, Marcus published an anthology of essays called *Rock 'n' Roll Will Stand*. All seven contributors were white men.* "[R]ock 'n' roll was, is and will be a basic part of the experience, of the growing up years, of the present college and non-student generation," Marcus wrote in his contribution. ". . . But rock 'n' roll has existed only since about 1954, and it's a sad fact that most of those over thirty cannot be a part of it, and it cannot be a part of them."[145] Marcus was twenty-four. He had been at Berkeley during the Free Speech Movement in 1964, and for him, rock 'n' roll was anti-establishment

---

* Or appear to be. They are Marvin Garson, Mike Daly, Langston Winner, Stewart Kessler, Steve Strauss, Sandy Darlington, and Marcus.

music, "a reaction against a programmed, technological culture," he called it (which is the language of the Free Speech Movement).[146]

This way of thinking about the music helped transform it from an age-specific entertainment genre into a cultural form with political content. Talcott Parsons's "having a good time" became a mode of generational identity and solidarity; "recalcitrance to the pressure of adult expectations" became an oppositional or countercultural lifestyle.* Even the physical element of the music's performance, on this view, constituted a mode of resistance. "Rock and roll is still very much a dirty, raunchy, too physical and unrefined music," Wenner explained in 1968.[147] It is hard to match those words up with any song written by Dylan or the Beatles that is not a parody, but the claim is what linked two British bands and a folk singer from Minnesota to Elvis Presley, and, via Presley, to Arthur Crudup and Robert Johnson. In the 1950s, the United States exported a mass-market commercial product to Europe. In the 1960s, it got back a hip and smart popular art form. Americans were happy to believe that it was theirs all along.

---

* "For those of us who were ten or twelve when Elvis Presley came along, it was rock 'n' roll that named us as a generation." Todd Gitlin, *The Sixties: Years of Hope, Days of Rage* (New York: Bantam Books, 1987), 42. Gitlin, who was president of Students for a Democratic Society (SDS) in 1963–1964, was born in 1943.

10

CONCEPTS OF LIBERTY

John F. Kennedy in West Berlin, June 26, 1963. Standing in the car with Kennedy are Willy Brandt, the mayor of West Berlin, and Konrad Adenauer, Chancellor of the Federal Republic of Germany. Kennedy was unnerved by the frenzy of the crowds he attracted during his visit. Photograph by John Dominis. (*LIFE Picture Collection / Getty Images*)

1.

"All free men, wherever they may live, are citizens of Berlin," John F. Kennedy said before a huge crowd in the Rudolph Wilde Platz in West Berlin on June 26, 1963; "and, therefore, as a free man, I take pride in the words '*Ich bin ein Berliner.*'"[1] Kennedy knew something about Berlin. He had visited the city in August 1939, leaving just days before the German invasion of Poland, and again in July 1945, three months after the death of Hitler, when he was stunned by the devastation.[2] As president, he appreciated the generous political gift that was the *Antifaschistischer Schutzwall*—the Anti-Fascist Protective Wall, better known as *Die Berliner Mauer*, the Berlin Wall, ninety-six miles around—which had been erected to encircle West Berlin, at the instigation of Nikita Khrushchev, by the German Democratic Republic less than two years earlier.[3]

The Wall was an Iron Curtain within the Iron Curtain. Berlin was well inside Communist East Germany—it is less than an hour by car to the Polish border—and technically, it was West Berliners who were enclosed by the Wall, not East Berliners. But the Wall became overnight the symbol of the carceral character of Communist life. John le Carré's *The Spy Who Came In from the Cold*, whose final scene is a woman shot while climbing over the Wall, came out in September 1963, three months after Kennedy's speech. By then, thirty-five people had died trying to escape from East Berlin. When the Wall came down in November 1989, total dead, including seven East German soldiers, was a hundred and thirty-nine.[4]

There are 674 words in Kennedy's Berlin speech; 15 are "free" or "freedom." In his inaugural address, two and a half years before, fewer than 1,400 words, Kennedy had used "free," "freedom," and "liberty" ten times. Those were, of course, the slogans of the Western democracies, particularly United States, the leader of the Free World. In the geopolitical context, the words referred to free elections (as opposed to one-party dictatorships) and free markets (as opposed to state-run economies), but they promised something more, something existential.

For the feeling of freedom does not necessarily align with external conditions. That is what Jean-Paul Sartre meant when he wrote, "Never were we freer than under the German occupation."[5] It is what Arthur Koestler meant when he wrote about waiting to be executed in a fascist jail in Seville in 1937, "I feel that I have never been so *free* as I was then."[6] When the potential consequences are stark, life or death, every act can be experienced as a free, that is, genuine, choice. To use a banal example, many people feel free when they are driving a car, even though few everyday activities are more heavily regulated.

Autonomy, independence, and self-realization are correlates of "freedom," but they are all relative states within a regime—human life—that is heteronomous through and through. Freedom is not natural; it is carved out of a system of socialization and coercion, and it requires its own system of coercions to be maintained. As an absolute, freedom is the equivalent of arbitrariness and anarchy, and socially meaningless. So what politicians and writers meant when they used the word "freedom" was obvious in a rhetorical sense—people could be assumed to prefer freedom to whatever they imagined the alternative to be—but not at all obvious in a philosophical or legal sense. Given that freedoms are carve-outs, what are their proper limits? Does freedom bring other values, such as equality and social responsibility, along with it, or is it achieved at their expense? Can the state constrain individual liberties in the name of collective goods, such as community norms or national security?

Questions like those are as old as the concept of rights, but after 1945, the stakes were raised. Geopolitical tensions put pressure on the liberal democracies to expand the sphere of liberty, since it was liberty they claimed to stand for, but the same tensions made those nations anxious about jeopardizing national security and domestic stability. Harry S. Truman had no hesitation about giving national security priority over civil liberties, and for about ten years the American public appears to have approved the choice. But around 1956, the balance started to tip the other way. This wasn't because there was something inherently unsustainable about the degree of censorship exerted by officials (government agents), quasi-officials (ecclesiastical and educational authorities), and pseudo-officials (editorialists and ad hoc anti-Communist organizations) that prevailed after the war. Assuming some minimum, there is no "natural" level of liberty. The balance tipped because other priorities asserted themselves.

2.

Possibly the most influential essay on liberty in the first decades of the Cold War was written by a Russian émigré. Isaiah Berlin was born in 1909 to well-off Jewish parents in Riga, Livonia (now Latvia), then part of the Russian empire. In 1915, the family moved to Petrograd to escape the advancing German army, and in February 1917, Berlin witnessed the beginnings of the Russian Revolution—a mob running through the streets. Two months later, Lenin, after traveling through Germany from Zurich in a sealed train, arrived at the Finland Station in Petrograd and commandeered the revolution in the name of Bolshevism. After the October Revolution established the Bolsheviks in power, the Berlins tried to adjust, but they soon left Russia, abandoning everything, going first back to Riga (now the capital of an independent state), and then to England, which they reached in 1921. Isaiah was eleven.

Isaiah's father, Mendel, was a timber merchant, an industry in northern Europe engaged in by a large number of Jews.[7] He had done business with the British; he had money saved in a British bank; and he did not have difficulty finding work. When the family arrived, Isaiah knew virtually no English, but he became fluent, while retaining his fluency in Russian. He entered Oxford in 1928, and, apart from government work during the war, he never left it.[8]

Berlin was a charmer. Among people who knew him, he was famous almost as much for his talk as for his writing. He delivered formal lectures extemporaneously (and later sometimes had trouble writing them up) and he was an entertaining raconteur. He was, consistent with a thoroughly donnish presentation, socially effervescent (some thought flamboyant), a witty conversationalist and correspondent (some thought he could be catty), and a collector of friends and admirers (some thought he craved attention and was not always straightforward).[9]

After stabs at journalism and the law, he picked philosophy. When he started out, logical positivism, which had developed in Berlin and Vienna in the 1920s, was having an impact on British and American philosophy departments. This was partly because many German and Austrian philosophers immigrated to Britain and the United States after 1933, and partly because logical positivism's emphasis on empirical verifiability—a reaction against the phenomenology of Husserl and Heidegger—was compatible with much English-language philosophy since the seventeenth century. Along with his Oxford contemporaries A. J. Ayer and J. L. Austin, Berlin was at first excited by logical positivism and its rejection of "metaphysics." Berlin called himself an empiricist, and the British empiricists, John Stuart Mill especially, were always important thinkers for him. But he was uncomfortable with philosophy's pretensions to be a science of universal truths, and uncomfortable with certainty in general, and it took him more than a decade to find his way out of academic philosophy.

The first step took the unlikely form of a commission to write an intellectual biography of Karl Marx for the Home University Library of Modern Knowledge, a series for general readers. Berlin was not the publisher's first choice, possibly not even the second or third. He later said he had never read a word by Marx, but he calculated that Marx was a figure it was necessary to understand, and he regarded the book as an opportunity to do his homework (always a healthy motive for writing).[10]

He began work in 1933 by reading the continental thinkers logical positivism was trying to make obsolete: the French *philosophes*, German idealists, and Russian intellectuals.[11] *Karl Marx: His Life and*

Environment appeared in 1939, just after the start of the Second World War. Of the serious introductions to Marxism written in those years— Sidney Hook's *Towards the Understanding of Karl Marx* (1933), G. D. H. Cole's *What Marx Really Meant* (1934), E. H. Carr's *Karl Marx: A Study in Fanaticism* (1934), and Edmund Wilson's *To the Finland Station* (1940)—Berlin's had the longest shelf life.

Marx was an Enlightenment thinker. He believed that freedom, defined as self-mastery and self-understanding, is the goal of philosophy. He wanted a world that is rational and demystified, and in which human beings are liberated from the control of external forces. He thought that this happens when people grasp that forces they perceive to be external and inevitable are actually created by human beings and then reified as "the way things are" or "the way the universe works." For example, God. We created God, and then we pretended that God created us. We hypostatized our own concept and turned it into something "out there" whose commandments, which we also made up, we struggle to understand and obey. We are supplicants to our own fiction.

What made Marx different from his philosophical predecessors— most important, Hegel, from whose thought Marxist theory derives— was the belief that freedom cannot be achieved in an armchair. Freedom is a function of material conditions. That is what Marx and his collaborator Friedrich Engels meant when they compared German philosophers to someone who thinks you can save people from drowning by convincing them that gravity is an illusion.[12] And it is what Marx meant by the famous Eleventh Thesis on Feuerbach: "Philosophers have only *interpreted* the world in various ways; the point is to *change* it."[13] Philosophical problems arise out of real-life conditions, and they can be solved only by changing those conditions—by remaking the world.

For Marx, industrial capitalism was like religion. That is, it was a system created for good reasons—to increase productivity, something Marx acknowledged and even celebrated in *The Communist Manifesto*— but in which one class of human beings, the property owners, exploits another class, the workers. Property owners don't act this way because they are greedy or cruel—or, to put it the way Marx preferred, property owners *are* greedy and cruel, but the reason they are is because competition demands it. The system makes them do it, and the system is taken by everyone to be "the way things are." Industrial capitalism is a Frankenstein's monster: we created it, and now it is making us unhappy.

In such a world, all freedoms are "driving a car" freedoms. They are ideological constructs, self-delusions, not authentic states of being. Until capitalism collapses of its own contradictions and is replaced by a classless society, "freedom" is a mode of false consciousness. True freedom means understanding the real nature of social relations and grasping that one is the instrument of an economic system, which is the first step in de-instrumentalizing yourself. And that, in turn, requires understanding the logic of history, and seeing that the capitalist order is only a stage in a historical unfolding whose final end is communism, which Marx called "the riddle of history solved."[14]

The essence of communism is the (genuine) freedom to choose what to do with one's labor. In a communist society, Marx wrote, it will be possible "to hunt in the morning, fish in the afternoon, rear cattle in the evening, criticize after dinner . . . without ever becoming hunter, fisherman, shepherd, or critic."[15] This sounds fanciful, but it is the heart of Marx's thought. Human beings are naturally creative and sociable; an economic regime that alienates them from the product of their work and puts their interests at odds with the interests of their fellow human beings is inhumane.

Is there a problem with this? Berlin thought there was. The problem was Marxism's insistence that freedom requires something that is not freedom in order to come into being. When you tell people that they don't understand what freedom really is, that, whatever they may imagine, they are not free until *x* is the case, then you are on a path to coercion. You are compelling people to give up conceptions about themselves that *you* have decided are false in order to accept conditions that they would not otherwise have known how to choose.

There was much about Marx that Berlin admired. He thought Marx had basically invented modern social science—the analysis of social life as a product of material conditions. But he also thought that Marx subordinated everything to a deterministic theory of history, knowledge of which is the monopoly of a small group, and that this made him "among the great authoritarian founders of new faiths, ruthless subverters and innovators who interpret the world in terms of a single, clear, passionately held principle, denouncing and destroying all that conflicts with it. His faith . . . was of that boundless, absolute kind which puts an end to all questions and dissolves all difficulties."[16]

This is a caricature, although not an unfair one. Marx and Engels believed that communism would arrive by means of a violent revolution. That was not because they were violent men who had no respect for political process. It was because they thought that that is how history works. As it was for virtually everybody who wrote about politics in nineteenth-century Europe, their model for change was the French Revolution. Class struggle culminates in the violent overthrow of the existing regime; the entire ruling class (the aristocracy and the clergy in eighteenth-century France, the bourgeoisie—that is, property owners—in nineteenth-century Britain) is effectively wiped out. The reason that existing political processes are not followed is because those processes are designed to protect the interests of the ruling class. They are themselves part of the order to be overthrown. This is why for Marxists, "reformer" is a term of abuse.

Revolutions are therefore not things that have to be organized and carried out from scratch. Revolutions happen; they are the consequence of class conflict. They are endemic in the unfolding of history. The job of the professional revolutionary is to know when conditions are ripe, when history is ready to turn the page. For Berlin, what made Marx a fanatic was not that he believed capitalism was unjust or that private property should be abolished. It was not even that he believed these things should be accomplished by means of a revolution. That is a political position, subject to discussion and modification. What made Marx a fanatic was his adherence to a theory of history according to which a revolution of the kind he preferred is inevitable. It is in the script, and those who can read the script are justified in doing whatever is necessary to bring that revolution about.

3.

Berlin was disqualified from serving in the military because of a damaged left arm (injured during his birth), but he made his eagerness to join in the war effort known. In 1941, he was appointed to the British Press Office (later renamed the British Information Services) in New York, where he wrote reports on American public opinion and attempted to nurture support for American entry into the war. Berlin disliked New York. His dispatches were well received, however, and in 1942, he was transferred to the British embassy in Washington, where he was made head of the Political Survey Section, and, soon after, promoted to first secretary, a diplomatic post. He was much happier in Washington. He made friends with George Kennan and moved to Georgetown, where the columnist Joseph Alsop and a number of highly placed government officials lived, a cliquish community of well-educated people who were all in basically the same line of work, either running the government or writing about it (a lot like Oxford).[17]

In the fall of 1945, Berlin was seconded to the Moscow embassy at the behest of the British ambassador to the Soviet Union, Archibald Clark Kerr.[18] The assignment was to gather information and to report on the Soviet press. There, he was in touch again with Kennan, who had arrived a little more than a year earlier to serve as Averell Harriman's second-in-command. Kennan was impressed by Berlin; in his diary, he described Berlin as "undoubtedly the best informed and most intelligent foreigner in Moscow." They discussed Soviet intentions; Berlin argued what Kennan would argue: that the Soviets saw postwar conflict as inevitable, that they would do nothing to prevent it, and that they would blame it all on the West.[19] In November, Berlin made a visit to Leningrad, where, when it was Petrograd, he had lived as a boy. It was during that trip that he had his meeting with the poet Anna Akhmatova.

Though he alluded to it on various occasions, and, in the 1950s, even considered writing a piece about it for *The New Yorker*, Berlin did not make the story of that encounter public until 1980, in an essay he wrote for a collection called *Personal Impressions*.[20] As he explained it there, he had received permission to visit Leningrad, his childhood home, for two days, where he intended to buy old Russian books, which he heard could be had there more cheaply than in Moscow. He was accompanied by a representative of the British Council (an organization promoting educational and cultural opportunities) named Brenda Tripp. In Leningrad, Berlin wrote, he made his way to the Writers' Bookshop "of which I had been told," and was admitted into a back room reserved for "privileged persons," where he struck up a conversation with a fellow browser. The man turned out to be a prominent critic, Vladimir Orlov. They began discussing the fate of writers during the siege of Leningrad, which had lasted almost two and a half years, and Akhmatova's name came up.

She had been a prominent figure in a prerevolutionary literary group based in St. Petersburg known as the Acmeists, who adopted a post-symbolist aesthetic very like the one Ezra Pound was promoting in London at exactly the same time, Imagism. She had been a close friend of the poet Osip Mandelstam. But since 1925, her work had been largely suppressed. Berlin claimed that he was astounded to hear her name. "Is Akhmatova still alive?" he says he asked Orlov. Yes, Orlov said; in fact, she lives nearby. Would Berlin like to meet her? Berlin said he would. Orlov made a phone call and returned to report that a meeting was scheduled for three that afternoon.

Akhmatova lived in Fontanny Dom (Fountain House), once the palace of one of the wealthiest families in Russia, the Sheremetevs. Berlin and Orlov went to the building and were admitted into her third-floor apartment. She was, Berlin wrote, "immensely dignified, with unhurried gestures, a noble head, beautiful, somewhat severe features, an expression of immense sadness." Her first husband, Nikolay Gumilyov, a poet, had been arrested by the Cheka on trumped-up charges and executed in 1921; their son, Lev, was arrested in 1935, released after Akhmatova interceded with Stalin, and arrested again in 1938 and sent to the camps. Mandelstam had died in Siberia in 1938. Akhmatova's work had been suppressed, and she was living in near poverty. The apartment belonged to her former common-law husband Nikolai Punin, an art historian.

A friend of Akhmatova's was present, whom Berlin described as "an academic lady." The conversation was soon interrupted by someone shouting Berlin's name in the courtyard outside "like a tipsy undergraduate." This turned out to be Winston Churchill's son Randolph, in Leningrad working as a journalist and staying in the same hotel as Berlin, the Astoria. Churchill knew no Russian. Back at the hotel, according to Berlin, he had been able to get Tripp to order that his caviar be put on ice, then decided that Berlin would be a more able interpreter, and had come out to find him.

Horrified, Berlin went downstairs to escort Churchill back to the Astoria. But he returned at nine that evening and he and Akhmatova spent the night talking. He gave her news of exiles she had lost contact with; she told him about her life, about the fate of other Russian writers, about her friendship with Boris Pasternak, whom Berlin had met when he was in Moscow. (He would carry early manuscript chapters of *Dr. Zhivago* back to London with him.) She recited lines from Byron and from a poem-in-progress, "Requiem." Around 3 a.m., Lev came in. He had been released from the camps to serve in the army, and had just returned from Germany. The three shared a dish of boiled potatoes, then Lev went off to sleep and Berlin and Akhmatova talked until late morning. When Berlin left the Soviet Union, in January, he stopped in Leningrad to say goodbye. Akhmatova gave him a volume of her poems with a new poem, inspired by their conversation, written on the flyleaf. Berlin told Frank Roberts, a minister in the British embassy, that it was "the most thrilling thing that has ever, I think, happened to me."

The meeting did not immediately affect Akhmatova's career. On the contrary: in April, she read her poetry on a bill with Pasternak in Moscow, and in August, she gave a reading from the stage of the Bolshoi Dramatic Theatre in Leningrad. Both appearances were enthusiastically received. A volume of her poems was scheduled to be published that fall. But a week after the Leningrad reading, Zhdanov issued a proclamation condemning two literary journals, *Zvezda* and *Leningrad*, for publishing Akhmatova and another Leningrad writer, the satirist Mikhail Zoshchenko (whom Berlin had happened to meet in the back room of the Writers' Bookshop). Akhmatova's poetry, Zhdanov said, had "become ossified in a stance of bourgeois aristocratic aestheticism—of 'art for art's sake'—which refuses to follow in the footsteps of the people, is harmful to our youth and cannot be tolerated in Soviet literature."[21]

There was, however, a subtext. For one of the poems in the issue of *Leningrad* that Zhdanov referred to was about Berlin. The poem is "Cinque" ("Five"); each of its five sections is dated, November 26, 1945, to January 11, 1946. The first reads:

> As if on the rim of a cloud,
> I remember your words,
>
> And because of my words to you,
> Night becomes brighter than day.
>
> Thus, torn from the earth,
> We rose up, like stars.
>
> There was neither despair nor shame,
> Not now, not afterward, not at the time.
>
> But in real life, right now,
> You hear how I am calling you.
>
> And that door that you half opened,
> I don't have the strength to slam.[22]

It is not surprising that Stalin and Zhdanov—who knew, of course, all about her meeting with Berlin—read the line about the half-opened door as a provocation.

In September, in *Pravda*, Zhdanov repeated his condemnation. "She is neither a nun nor a fornicator," he wrote, "but really both of them, mixing fornication and prayer . . . Akhmatova's poetry is remote from the people."[23] Akhmatova was expelled from the Writers' Union, which meant that her work could not be published, and her book was pulped. In 1949, Punin and Lev Gumilyov were arrested. Gumilyov was sentenced to ten years; he was not released until 1956. Punin died in the Gulag. Akhmatova did not begin to resurface as a writer until after Stalin's death in 1953.[24]

In 1956, Berlin made a personal visit to Moscow. Akhmatova was in the city, and he telephoned her. He had married (something Akhmatova had already learned from Pasternak), and she told him she could not see him "for reasons which you will understand only too well," as Berlin reported the conversation. He said he took this to mean that she was worried for Lev, who had just been released, but the implication was that she believed that he had somehow betrayed their relationship by marrying.

Berlin did see Akhmatova one last time, in 1965, when she came to Oxford to receive an honorary degree. She gave a reading of her poems that included "Cinque."[25] She told Berlin that their encounter had started the Cold War. He thought that this "somewhat overestimated the effect of our meeting on the destinies of the world," but didn't say anything. Eight months later, on March 5, 1966, she died in Domodedovo, outside Moscow. March 5 was a date she had always commemorated. It was the anniversary of Stalin's death.[26]

Berlin's story has a magical quality that few have been able to resist.[27] In the back room of an old bookshop, a door is opened onto the vanished world of prerevolutionary St. Petersburg, and the protagonist is brought into the presence of a figure, part sibyl, part enchantress, who recites forbidden verses and summons up the spirits of the dead. It was unquestionably a moving experience. When Berlin returned to the Astoria the next morning, Tripp remembered that he collapsed on his bed. "I am in love," he said. "I am in love."[28]

But a good deal of the aura is created by alteration and elision.[29] The premise itself—a British diplomat, on a four-month appointment, goes on a holiday to revisit his childhood home and take advantage of cheaper book prices—is incredible. Berlin went to Leningrad on official business to gather information about Soviet writers and living conditions. He was there for eight days, not two, and he had known that Akhmatova was in Leningrad ever since he was stationed in Washington.[30]

The Leningrad trip was organized through Intourist, the Soviet travel agency, and the itinerary, which included visits to the theater and the Hermitage, was agreed upon in advance. The meeting with Akhmatova was prearranged by the proprietor of the Writers' Bookshop, Gennady Rakhlin, whom Berlin had almost certainly already met in Moscow and who was an agent of the NKVD. Berlin was a highly placed foreign diplomat traveling inside a totalitarian state run by a paranoid dictator who especially distrusted Churchill and the British. As Berlin knew perfectly well, nothing he did went unobserved or unreported.

Berlin already had Akhmatova's address, along with the addresses of Rakhlin and Orlov, inscribed in his journal before he left Moscow, so he could not have been surprised to learn that she was alive and nearby.[31] The meeting with Orlov was not by chance (nor, probably, was the encounter with Zoshchenko). The "friend" in Akhmatova's apartment was Antonia Oranzhireeva, an NKVD agent who had insinuated herself as a confidante into Akhmatova's life. She was present again, along with another confidante of Akhmatova's, possibly also an informant, Sofya Ostrovskaya, when Berlin returned that evening. Both women stayed until midnight.

The Kremlin could have had several motives for arranging the meeting. Berlin was in Leningrad to interview writers, so they supplied him with one. They might have wanted to generate favorable publicity about a famous poet, or they might have wanted to entrap her. But Berlin's motives for confecting the details are not hard to fathom. A duty to protect his own cover was presumably the least important. In 1980, when he first made the story public, Lev Gumilyov was still alive, and the Soviet Union was still a totalitarian state. Berlin felt guilty about having exposed Akhmatova to additional persecution, and he must have decided that the more fortuitous the whole affair could be made to sound, the safer everyone involved would be. Even the Randolph Churchill incident seems to have been cooked up, possibly to explain why Berlin stayed past the allotted time for the interview. Fontanny Dom housed a scientific agency, the Arctic Institute, whose work was classified, and Churchill could not have entered the courtyard without a permit. The caviar story (not inconsistent with Churchill's reputation) made it all seem harmless.

Berlin had gone to interview Akhmatova for professional reasons—he had actually never read a word of her poetry—and had fallen under a spell. The most intriguing elision in his account has to do with the number of visits he made to her apartment. He described the first, on the night of November 15, but the file on Akhmatova in the Leningrad office of the Ministry of State Security, dated August 15, 1946, records two subsequent visits: on November 17 from 10 p.m. until 7 a.m., and on November 18 or 19 starting at an unknown hour and ending at 4 a.m.[32] ("Even at 4am and 7:30am, I found all seats occupied" in Leningrad's trams, Berlin wrote in his official report to the embassy.[33] How would he have observed that?) Berlin left the city on the twentieth.

Akhmatova's beauty was legendary. She was married three times and had a number of liaisons. She was fifty-six when Berlin met her. He was thirty-six, unattached, and, so far as is known, sexually inexperienced.[34] Fires have been started from less promising materials. She was a seducer, but so, very much, was he. If he spent a night or two with her, it would explain "Cinque," which otherwise seems slightly deranged. (The title could refer to the number of their meetings, three in November and two, not one, in January.)

It also explains Berlin's guilt about exposing Akhmatova to persecution. He would not have felt guilty about a prearranged interview with informants present, which is otherwise all that took place. It explains the "fornicator" charge in Zhdanov's proclamation. And it explains the 1956 phone conversation. In the report Berlin filed soon after with the embassy, he wrote that many of the Leningrad writers he talked to were living in Fontanny Dom. This was untrue. The only residents there were Akhmatova and her ex-husband.[35] But the assertion would have provided an official rationale for visits to the building that were otherwise unaccountable.

4.

Berlin called his meeting with Akhmatova "one of the most memorable experiences—perhaps the most memorable experience of my life."[36] It personalized in a way that almost nothing else could have, since it triggered the emotions of a highly cultivated and temperamentally nostalgic Russian exile, the stakes for individuals in the geopolitical struggles on the periphery of which he had been working for the previous five years. Those two experiences—the wartime service and the glimpse of life under Stalin—inform Berlin's major essays, all of which were written in the 1950s (though he lived until 1997), and all of which are concerned with the human consequences of ideas: "The Hedgehog and the Fox" (published in 1951 under a different title, and as a book in 1953), "Historical Inevitability" (1953), "Herzen and Bakunin on Individual Liberty" (1955), and "Two Concepts of Liberty" (1958). If Berlin's reservations about academic philosophy had to do with its detachment from practical issues, he now found a genre that combined analysis with prescription, which could make the past speak to the present.

That genre was the history of ideas. The history of ideas is not the same thing as intellectual history. Intellectual history explains art and ideas by examining the conditions of their production and reception (as this book tries to do). Berlin did not think that ideas float free of material conditions, and he believed that historical conditions put pressure on ideas and cause them to morph over time. But he was not a historian or a sociologist. He took a "books talking to books" approach, which is the approach of the historian of ideas. He proposed to demonstrate, by lines of intellectual filiation, the connections between eighteenth- and nineteenth-century European social and political thought and twentieth-century totalitarianism.

Berlin's first essay in this genre, "Political Ideas in the Twentieth Century," appeared in 1950 in *Foreign Affairs*—a clear indication that Berlin did not conceive his audience to be academic philosophers. In that essay, he made the same argument that Lionel Trilling made in *The Liberal Imagination*, published the same year: the line separating liberalism from authoritarianism is much less bright than liberals assume. "No movement at first sight seems to differ more sharply from liberal reformism than does Marxism," Berlin wrote, "yet the central doctrines—human perfectibility, the possibility of creating a perfect society by a natural means, the belief in the compatibility (indeed the inseparability) of liberty and equality—are common to both."[37]

One interested reader was E. H. Carr, the realist author of *The Twenty Years' Crisis*, who attacked the essay as an example of what he called "the new skepticism." All Berlin was really saying, Carr wrote, was that any political program if carried to an extreme will have authoritarian consequences. And so, better to avoid politics. "Surtout, point de zèle," he concluded.[38] The phrase is Talleyrand's—"Above all, gentlemen, no zeal"—and though Berlin dismissed the criticism, he liked the phrase so much that he added it to his essay when he reprinted it, and "surtout, pas trop de zèle" became, for the rest of his life, his motto.[39]

A friendlier reader was Kennan. Totalitarianism, he wrote to Berlin, takes advantage of people's weakness; it manipulates "the irrational sides of their nature." What preserves us from being manipulated is the recognition that although we are imperfect, our problems are "susceptible to solution by rational processes, and should be so approached and solved."[40]

This was a telling misprision. Berlin agreed that people are imperfect—that was a constant theme in his work—but he did not think that rationality was the solution. He thought that rationality—trying to iron out the imperfections—was the problem. He began working out this theory in the spring of 1952, when he delivered six lectures at Bryn Mawr on "Political Ideas in the Romantic Age." That fall, he broadcast a version of them on the BBC as "Freedom and Its Betrayal." For several years, he struggled to make the talks into a book. He failed, but they served as the foundation for his writings for the next decade.[41]

The most widely known of those writings is "Two Concepts of Liberty," Berlin's inaugural lecture as Chichele Professor of Social and Political Theory at Oxford, delivered on October 31, 1958, and published in an expanded version the same year. One reason for the essay's influence is that it presents four linked but distinct philosophical ideas, each of which had political resonance in 1958. The first is the contrast between negative freedom and positive freedom—the "two concepts." Negative freedom is "freedom from" external forces of coercion, such as the state; positive freedom is "freedom to" reach particular ends, such as self-realization. The central argument of the essay is that all "freedoms to," no matter how appealing the ends in view, can become rationales for coercion.*

Take self-realization. Either we are realizing ourselves all the time, having no alternative, in which case we don't require freedom to do it, or else it is possible for us to realize a false self or an inferior self—say, our instinctual self rather than our rational self—in which case, we may

---

* The from/to distinction is, of course, not original with Berlin. Erich Fromm used it, for example, in *Escape from Freedom* (1941).

need an external force to guide us toward genuine self-realization. We may need someone who knows better than we do what is best for us.

"This monstrous impersonation," Berlin wrote, "which consists in equating what X would choose if he were something he is not, or at least not yet, with what X actually seeks and chooses, is at the heart of all political theories of self-realization."[42] Self-realization may be a good thing (Berlin obviously considered the notion rather empty), but it is not the same as liberty. Liberty is "freedom from," and the danger arises when people are persuaded that it is something else. "Everything is what it is," as Berlin put it in a later edition of the essay: "liberty is liberty, not equality or fairness or justice or culture, or human happiness or a quiet conscience."[43] "Every thing is what it is" is a famous phrase in British philosophy, and the essence of the empirical view.[44]*

The "two concepts" idea is connected to a second idea, which might be called the doctrine of the incommensurability of ultimate ends. The things we want in life are not perfectly compatible. If we want beauty, we may have to sacrifice truth, for example (despite what Keats's Grecian urn tells us). In the geopolitical context, the relevant choice in 1958, the choice everyone would have understood that Berlin was referring to, was liberty and equality. Liberal democracies might argue that what makes liberty *true* liberty is that everyone has an equal chance; socialist and Communist nations might argue that no one is free as long as there is inequality, such that one person's liberty rests on the exploitation of another. But the doctrine of incommensurability tells us that both arguments muddle concepts. To get more of one of those goods, we must give up some of the other. A world in which everyone is free *and* equal is a utopia. "The world that we encounter in ordinary experience," Berlin said, "is one in which we are faced with choices between ends equally ultimate, and claims equally absolute, the realization of some of which must inevitably involve the sacrifice of others."[45] Any other way of formulating the choice—as when Hegel argued that freedom consists in understanding one's place in the historical process—is metaphysics.

This leads to the third idea, pluralism. Given that different people value different ends, and given that those ends are not commensurable, and given that we do not want to coerce people into seeking ends they have not chosen, then pluralism is the social formation best suited to the

---

* Ludwig Wittgenstein considered using it as an epigraph for *Philosophical Investigations* (1953).

species. Pluralism, for Berlin, was the heart of liberalism. "I think that what I am pleading for is really what used to be called Liberalism," he had written six years earlier in a letter to the editor of *The Washington Post*, Herbert Elliston, "i. e. a society in which the largest number of persons are allowed to pursue the largest number of ends as freely as possible, in which these ends are themselves criticised as little as possible and the fervour with which such ends are held is not required to be bolstered up by some bogus rational or supernatural argument to prove the universal validity of the end."[46]

As a practical matter, pluralism describes a society not of individuals, but of groups, and this is addressed by the fourth idea, recognition. What groups want, Berlin argued, is not liberty. It is acknowledgment—as a "class or nation, or colour or race."[47] "Although I may not get 'negative' liberty at the hands of the members of my own society," as he explained it, "yet they are members of my own group; they understand me, as I understand them; and this understanding creates within me the sense of being somebody in the world."[48] The impetus for this statement may have been Berlin's Zionism, a lifelong commitment. But the argument about the human need for recognition was taken to be broadly relevant to decolonization and possibly a warning to the former imperial powers. Recognition might be more important than democracy.*

The four ideas are all propositions in political philosophy and can be debated as such. But Berlin placed them in a historical narrative. The narrative began with Socrates and the teaching that rational self-knowledge is a virtue. This doctrine, Berlin claimed, led to the belief that all rational ends are commensurable, that unhappiness is caused by the irrational or insufficiently rational, and that when everyone becomes rational and obeys rational laws, human beings will be free. Berlin called this view "the metaphysical heart of rationalism." "Socialized forms of it," he said, "widely disparate and opposed to each other as they are, are at the heart of many of the nationalist, communist, authoritarian, and totalitarian creeds of our day." And yet not one of that view's assumptions, he said, "is demonstrable, or, perhaps, even true."[49]

This was a (rather spectacular) amplification of what Berlin had said about Marx. Berlin was now arguing that the authoritarian ten-

---

* Recognition was also the theme of the seminar on Hegel run by Alexandre Kojève that Hannah Arendt attended in Paris before fleeing to the United States.

dencies of the faith in rationalism were not restricted to Marxism. "[A]ll forms of liberalism founded on a rationalist metaphysics," he said, "are less or more watered-down versions of this creed."[50] He saw totalitarianism not as anti-humanism but as humanism *in extremis*. Its seeds were everywhere.

"Two Concepts of Liberty" belongs on the same shelf as *The Liberal Imagination* and George Orwell's "Politics and the English Language." Berlin did with ideas what Orwell did with words and Trilling did with novels. He thought that philosophical ideas insinuate themselves into everyday discourse, and that we internalize them without examining them critically. Neglected for too long, these ideas may "acquire an unchecked momentum and an irresistible power over great multitudes of men that may grow too violent to be affected by rational criticism."[51]

Berlin's account of the origins of totalitarianism was exactly the kind of teleological narrative in which the protagonists are concepts that Hannah Arendt had deliberately avoided. Berlin met Arendt in 1942, not long after both arrived in the United States. He found her Zionism fanatical, and later on he developed a persistent distaste for her work. She "indulges in a kind of metaphysical free association which I am unable to follow except that the premises seem to me to be inaccurate and the conclusions unswallowable," he complained to William Phillips in 1963.[52] She was not a British empiricist. She was a Continental thinker.

The limitations of Berlin's method of historical explanation became evident in his attempt to answer the question, If the whole Western philosophical tradition is responsible for the rationalist metaphysics that underlies totalitarianism, where did pluralism come from? Berlin gave his answer in the A. W. Mellon lectures, delivered at the National Gallery of Art in Washington, D.C., in 1965 and broadcast on BBC radio the following year. As usual, he spoke extemporaneously, and as usual, his effort to turn the talks into a book failed. He had hoped it would be his major work; in the end, the book on Marx was his only monograph.[53]

What broke up the Enlightenment faith in reason, Berlin argued in the Mellon lectures, was the European Romanticism of the late eighteenth and early nineteenth centuries. Romanticism put an end to "the jigsaw-puzzle conception of life," the assumption that all questions can be answered, and the answers fitted together into a harmonious whole. It taught us "that there are many values, and that they are incompatible;

the whole notion of plurality, of inexhaustibility, of the imperfection of all human answers and arrangements; the notion that no single answer which claims to be perfect and true, whether in art or in life, can in principle be perfect or true."[54] Romanticism rejected the end of self-understanding and replaced it with the end of self-creation. Science, reason, and universalism, the values of Enlightenment thinkers, were replaced by a new set of values: sincerity, authenticity, toleration, variety. It is from this tradition, not the Socratic tradition, that liberal pluralism derives.

But, Berlin went on, it is also from this tradition that fascism derives. "The hysterical self-assertion and the nihilistic destruction of existing institutions because they confine the unlimited will . . . are a direct inheritance" from the Romanticist movement, he said.[55] It seems that same lineage produced completely disparate outcomes—liberal pluralism and fascism—which might suggest that intellectual genealogy is not the most reliable form of historical explanation.

There is no evidence that Trilling heard Berlin's lectures on Romanticism. He visited Oxford as Eastman Professor in 1964–1965 (his first trip to England; he was fifty-nine), but Berlin's lectures were not broadcast there until 1966 and were not published until after his death. Still, Berlin's theory that "a radical shift of values occurred in the latter half of the eighteenth century" is the thesis of Trilling's last book, *Sincerity and Authenticity* (1972), also a collection of talks, the Charles Eliot Norton lectures at Harvard, and also a book about books talking to books.[56]

Berlin's affinities with Trilling would seem natural, and they had a cordial relationship. Berlin was often in New York, and Trilling taught at Oxford twice during his career. Still, despite the similarity of their methods and outlooks, Berlin did not warm to Trilling. He found Trilling cautious, neurotic, and altogether not fun. "Diana goes screeching on about the iniquities of the Left," he complained to a friend, the sociologist Jean Floud, during a visit to New York in 1971: "Lionel sits there in a thin silvery light, smiling sadly at the irrationality and insensitiveness of friends, colleagues, mankind."[57] By then, though, it was a long way from 1950.

A criticism of Berlin might be that he embraced the position of *pas de zèle* with *trop de zèle*. Still, his reputation only grew after 1959. He came to stand for the principle of tolerance: allowing people to choose their own tastes and values and to pursue their own ends. But as an absolute, tolerance is no different from liberty or equality or the classless society. It is only another end, and it, too, needs values that cut against it. Should we be tolerant of intolerant people? That was the question people such as Hook and Trilling asked about Communists and fellow travelers (answering no). Should we be tolerant of expressions that many find hurtful or offensive? That question was at the heart of the obscenity cases that were about to change the legal and financial environment for the culture industries.

5.

Politically, a liberty is the flip side of a prohibition. It permits someone to do something by making it illegal for others to interfere. In the American system, liberties are constitutionally instantiated in the form of enumerated rights. These rights are anti-majoritarian: they are trump cards individuals can play when every other hand is against them. But they are not anti-democratic, because the Bill of Rights, and subsequent amendments to the Constitution, were enacted to strengthen, not compromise, democratic practices.

The right most symbolic of the geopolitical stakes in the decades after the war was the right denied to Anna Akhmatova and other victims of Zhdanovshchina, the right of free expression. The democratic rationale for that right is clear: unless all views are heard, the will of the majority will not have legitimacy. Narrowly interpreted, this can mean that the First Amendment applies only to political speech. But if you define "democracy" more expansively, or more existentially, as the name for a kind of society in which people feel that they are free to adopt and express beliefs and tastes and styles of life without fear of persecution, then the application of the First Amendment expands accordingly.[58] Something like this happened in the United States and Britain after 1956.

On October 2, 1953, President Dwight Eisenhower used a recess appointment to make Earl Warren chief justice of the United States Supreme Court. The Senate confirmed it in March. The politics of Eisenhower's choice—specifically, whether he had promised the position to Warren before a vacancy occurred—are debated; but it is agreed that Warren was considered a centrist in 1953.[59] He had been the Republican governor of California since 1943, and he had run for vice president on the ticket with Thomas E. Dewey in 1948.

Warren made his judicial debut on May 17, 1954, as the author of the Court's opinion in *Brown v. Board of Education*. Before Warren arrived, the Supreme Court had been almost dysfunctionally divided on that case, and six of the justices could be categorized as judicially conservative. But the decision in *Brown* overturned a fifty-eight-year-old precedent, *Plessy v. Ferguson*, and declared laws segregating education unconstitutional. And it was unanimous. The only opinion was Warren's; there were no concurrences. There was a new sheriff in town.

A year and a half later, Warren published an article called "Law and the Future" in *Fortune*. He began by calling the "struggle between Communism and freedom" the central political fact of the times. "Our legal system," he wrote, "is woven around the freedom and dignity of the individual. A Communist state ignores these values. Ours is the difficult task of defending and strengthening these values while also pursuing a goal that sometimes appears to be in conflict with them—namely, the physical security of our nation." But what might be constitutionally acceptable in one era, he went on, might not in another. Conditions change and law evolves. He ended with a warning: "In the present struggle between our world and Communism, the temptation to imitate totalitarian security methods is a subtle temptation that must be resisted day by day, for it will be with us as long as totalitarianism itself."[60]

This could have been taken as a hint that the Court was prepared to rebalance the trade-off between civil liberties and national security established during the Truman administration. And, soon after, it did. On June 17, 1957, the Court issued rulings in four cases: *Yates v. United States*, throwing out convictions under the Smith Act of members of the American Communist Party (CPUSA); *Watkins v. United States*, limiting the power of Congress to inquire about personal beliefs and associations; *Sweezy v. New Hampshire*, holding an investigation into the alleged subversive activities of a lecturer at the University of New Hampshire a violation the Fourteenth Amendment; and *Service v. Dulles*, reversing the dismissal of a State Department employee for disloyalty as a violation of procedural requirements.

The director of the FBI, J. Edgar Hoover, called June 17 "Red Monday." There was an effort in Congress to retaliate against the Court. But that failed, and the rulings slowed dramatically the official harassment and persecution of Communists and people suspected of Communist sympathies that had been under way, largely unchecked by the courts, for ten years. Government agencies continued surveillance of suspected Communists and subversives; those investigations were now mostly undercover.[61]

The Court was doing what Warren had predicted: it was acknowledging that conditions had changed. In the eighteen months before it issued those rulings, Nikita Khrushchev had denounced the crimes of Stalin in his so-called secret speech before the Twentieth Congress of the Communist Party of the Soviet Union; the Red Army's violent suppression of a revolt against the Communist government in Hungary had turned political opinion in Western Europe against the Soviet Union and had essentially ended the influence of the CPUSA; and Joseph McCarthy was dead. The threat of Communism did not disappear as a political issue—it was the issue that Kennedy ran on and that he devoted virtually his entire inaugural address to—but it no longer played a major role in domestic politics. Communism became a foreign-policy problem.

With the specter of a domestic threat more or less officially lifted, it was natural to imagine continuing to extend First Amendment protection to more "existential" freedoms—to literary and artistic freedom, for example. It took the Court several years to see its way to taking this step, and it finally did so not because of political pressure but because of changes inside the culture industries. Those industries found that they had created a market that they could not satisfactorily exploit.

6.

The so-called paperback revolution is misnamed. Paper book covers are almost as old as print. They date to the sixteenth century, and paper-backing has been the ordinary mode of book production in France, for instance, for centuries. The first edition of James Joyce's *Ulysses*, published in Paris in 1922, is a paperback. In the United States, paperback publishing was tried successfully on a major scale at least twice during the nineteenth century—in the 1830s, with an enterprise called the Library of Useful Knowledge, and after the Civil War, when, unfettered by international copyright agreements and, therefore, royalty obligations, American publishers brought out cheap paperbound editions of popular European novels.[62]

The twentieth-century paperback revolution was not a revolution in production. It was a revolution in distribution. Before the Second World War, the biggest problem in the book business was bookstores. There were not enough of them. Bookstores were clustered in big cities and college towns, and many were really gift shops with a few volumes for sale. Publishers sold much of their product by mail order and through book clubs, distribution systems that provide pretty much the opposite of what most people consider a fun shopping experience—browsing and impulse buying. Many book publishers had little interest in books as such. They were experts at merchandizing. "I sell books, I don't read them," Nelson Doubleday is supposed to have said.[63] Founded in 1897, by 1945, Doubleday was the largest publisher of magazines and books in the world. In the business, print runs were modest, and so, generally, were profits.

The "revolution" happened on June 19, 1939, when Robert de Graff launched Pocket Books. Pocket was the first American mass-market paperback line, and it transformed the industry. Neither the theory nor the practice of mass-market paperback publishing was original with de Graff. Credit is usually given to an Englishman, Allen Lane, the founder of Penguin Books. According to industry legend, Lane had his revelation while standing in a railway station in Devon, where he had been spending the weekend with the mystery writer Agatha Christie and her husband. He couldn't find anything worthwhile to buy to read on the train back to London, and so, in the summer of 1935, he launched Penguin Books with ten titles, including Christie's *Murder on the Links*. The books sold right from the start. It helped that Penguin had the whole British Commonwealth, a large chunk of the globe in 1935, as its market.[64]

The key to Lane's and de Graff's innovation was the system of distribution they devised. More than 180 million books were printed in the United States in 1939, the year de Graff introduced Pocket Books, but there were only 2,800 bookstores. There were, however, more than 7,000 newsstands, 18,000 cigar stores, 58,000 drugstores, and 62,000 lunch counters—not to mention train and bus stations.[65] De Graff saw that you could sell books in those places as easily as in a bookstore.

The mass-market paperback was designed to be displayed in wire racks that could be placed in virtually any retail space.* People who

---

* Mass-market paperback fiction can be distinguished from pulp fiction, stories in magazines that are printed on pulp paper, such as *Argosy, Black Mask, Spicy Detective Stories*, and *Western Story Magazine*.

didn't have a local bookstore, and even people who would never have entered a bookstore, could now browse the racks while filling a prescription or waiting for a train, and buy a book on impulse. Instead of using book wholesalers—"jobbers"—who distributed to bookstores, de Graff worked through magazine distributors. They handled paperbacks in the same way they handled magazines: periodically, they emptied the racks and installed a fresh supply.

Pocket Books were priced to sell for twenty-five cents. That was the hourly minimum wage in 1939, and de Graff is supposed to have come up with the figure after paying a quarter at a toll booth. Few people, he concluded, miss a quarter. Penguins sold for sixpence, the price of a pack of cigarettes. The theory was that people could spot a book they had always meant to read, or a book with an enticing cover, and pay for it with spare change. De Graff road-tested his idea by selling Pocket books at the start only in New York City, in subway newsstands and similar outlets. He launched with ten titles, including *Wuthering Heights* and an Agatha Christie mystery, *The Murder of Roger Ackroyd*. He knew he had a winner when 110 books were sold in a day and a half at a single cigar stand. By mid-August, after eight weeks and with distribution limited to the Northeast Corridor, de Graff had sold 325,000 books.[66]

He had discovered a market. In August, Penguin opened an American office. Others rushed to compete: Avon started up in 1941, Popular Library in 1942, Dell in 1943, Bantam in 1945, and after the war ended, half a dozen more, including, in 1948, New American Library (NAL), which published the Signet (fiction) and Mentor (nonfiction) imprints. The mass-market paperback era had begun. By 1950, paperbacks were selling in ninety thousand outlets.[67]

Paperbacks vastly expanded the book universe. The industry had got a taste of the possibilities during the war, when, encouraged by the success of Pocket and Penguin, publishers collaborated to produce Armed Services Editions of popular titles—paperbound double-columned books, trimmed to a size that slipped easily into the pocket of a uniform and could be thrown away after use. The books were distributed free of charge to the sixteen million men and women who served during the war. (Publishers also offered their own books for sale to the troops.) Eleven hundred and eighty titles were published in Armed Services

Editions, and an astonishing 123,535,305 books were distributed, at a cost to the government of just over six cents a copy.[68]

Servicemen and -women stationed overseas were a captive audience, but many came home having acquired a habit of reading for pleasure and a comfort with disposable paperbacks. In 1947, two years after the war ended, some 95 million mass-market paperback books were sold in the United States. Paperbacks changed the book business in the same way that jukeboxes, 45-rpm records, and transistor radios changed the music business. They got a lot of product cheaply to millions.

Paperbacks also transformed the culture of reading. De Graff was a high school dropout (Lane, too, left school when he was sixteen), and he seems not to have been much of a reader. He had no investment in the notion of books as uplifting. He thought of them as just another consumer product. "These new Pocket Books are designed to fit both the tempo of our times and the needs of New Yorkers," he announced in a full-page ad in the *Times* on the day his new line went on sale. (The copy was written by a Madison Avenue ad man.) "They're as handy as a pencil, as modern and convenient as a portable radio—and as good looking . . . Never again need you dawdle idly in reception rooms, fret on train or bus ride, sit vacantly staring at a restaurant table. The books you have always meant to read 'when you had time' will fill the waits with enjoyment."[69] Books were not like, say, classical music, a sophisticated pleasure for a coterie audience. Books were like ice cream. They were for everyone.

It was one thing to reprint classics, such as *Wuthering Heights* (a big seller for Pocket Books) or the tragedies of William Shakespeare (which de Graff regarded as a loss leader).[70] Selling books like those for a quarter was a way of democratizing culture, an impulse in American life since the days of the Library of Useful Knowledge and before. But alongside the classics and the reprints of hardcover bestsellers, there quickly blossomed on the racks a profusion of books with racy titles and lurid covers: *Scandals at a Nudist Colony*, by William Vaneer (Croydon), *Hitch-Hike Hussy*, by John B. Thompson and Jack Woodford (Beacon), *I Wake Up Screaming*, by Steve Fisher (Popular Library), and *The Daughter of Fu Manchu*, by Sax Rohmer (Avon), which carried the semantically challenging cover line "She flaunted an evil conspiracy for power and love."

There were also whodunits, such as the Perry Mason series, by Erle

Stanley Gardner (a huge seller for Pocket Books). But what the format seemed most readily to attract were iterations of the hard-boiled detective story. Raymond Chandler and Dashiell Hammett were paperbacked, and there were dozens of titles like *Exit for a Dame*, by Richard Ellington (Pocket), *Benny Muscles In*, by Peter Rabe (Gold Medal Books), *Lady, Don't Die on My Doorstep*, by Joseph Shallit (Avon), *Report for a Corpse*, by Henry Kane (Dell), and, starting with *I, the Jury* in 1948, the multimillion-selling Mike Hammer detective novels by Mickey Spillane (Signet). This product was not trying to pass itself off as serious literature. It was deliberately down-market, comic books for grown-ups.

You can't judge a book by its cover, but you can certainly sell one that way, and any title could be supplied with a titillating cover. In the same year that Signet published *I, the Jury*, it also published reprints of books by James Joyce, William Faulkner, Thomas Wolfe, and Arthur Koestler. Paperback publishers made no effort to distinguish classics from genre fiction. On the contrary: they commissioned covers for books like *Brave New World* and *The Catcher in the Rye* from the same artists who did the covers for *Strangler's Serenade* and *The Case of the Careless Kitten*. Avon, one of the most resolutely down-market of the major paperback imprints, used an image of Shakespeare's head as its colophon. "Millions of readers have found that this trademark expresses a high standard of reading entertainment," explained the blurb on back cover of Avon's *Amboy Dukes*, by Irving Shulman—a book captioned as "A novel of wayward youth in Brooklyn" and with a cover featuring two teenagers passionately entangled on the grass. (Not that Shakespeare would have objected.)

But spicing up the covers put paperback lines in competition with one another, and it quickly became a race to the bottom. Scantily clothed women and sexually suggestive poses, whether the author was Mary Shelley or John D. MacDonald, became almost a requirement of the format. If it was a hard-boiled detective novel or a mystery, the woman was in a state of undress, or wearing a peignoir and holding a gun.

The paperback reprint was therefore not only different physically from a hardcover; it had a different aura. The dust jacket for the American hardcover of *Nineteen Eighty-Four*, published by Harcourt, Brace in 1949, has a tasteful all-text design. The cover of the 1950 Signet reprint (the artist was Alan Harmon) features a sleeveless, and surprisingly toned, Winston Smith next to Julia, who wears an Anti-Sex League button pinned to a blouse whose neckline plunges to her hourglass midriff. O'Brien is figured in a black skullcap and bodice outfit, clutching what appears to be a whip. "Forbidden Love . . . Fear . . . Betrayal," says the cover line. "Complete and unabridged."

The practice of using that phrase, "complete and unabridged," began because de Graff worried that readers associated paperbacks with abridgements—books in the Armed Services Editions were often abridged to save on paper costs—but it became common on paperback reprints, since it suggested that you were getting a text previously available only in a censored form. Mass-market covers thereby managed to recapture the risqué, subversive aura of modernist writing, the reputation of the novels of Joyce and D. H. Lawrence. It put the frisson of scandal back into books, even old books.[71]

The use of cover art to pimp out titles produced some amusing anomalies. A classic case is the "nipple cover," attributed to a prolific pulp artist named Rudolph Belarski. It appeared on the 1948 Popular Library reprint of *The Private Life of Helen of Troy*, by John Erskine— Trilling's old teacher. Belarski claimed that he was told it didn't matter whether or not the scene depicted on his covers was in the novel. "The editors would say, 'Don't worry, we'll *write* it in! Just make sure to *make 'em round!*'"[72] His Helen is a blonde in what one takes to be the Mycenaean version of the peignoir, cinched at the waist and under the bust, and apparently with nothing on underneath. The cover line says: "Complete and unexpurgated."

In fact, there had been nothing to expurgate. There are no references in Erskine's book to nipples, breasts, or any other female body parts, except for a single mention of a "bosom." Most of the book is dialogue. The editors at Popular Library must have known the nipple cover would work, because Pocket Books had used a similar image on its 1941 reprint of Émile Zola's 1880 novel *Nana* and it proceeded to become one of the bestselling Pocket books among overseas troops during the war. Soldiers bought 586,374 copies, right behind *The Pocket Dictionary and Vocabulary Builder*.[73] (Popular Library at least had textual authority, since Nana is an actress who takes male Paris by storm after she appears onstage naked under a diaphanous sheath.)

Paperbacking could leverage a title with respectable revenue and decent word of mouth into the sales stratosphere, and often with significant knock-on effects. When Erskine Caldwell's *God's Little Acre*, a Gothic tale of lower-class white Southerners with plenty of illicit sex and generous overtones of incest, was published in hardcover by Viking in 1933, it sold a little over 8,000 copies. That was good enough for it to be reprinted by Modern Library in 1934, whose edition sold 66,000 copies. A Grosset & Dunlap reprint, in 1940, sold 150,000. Then, in 1946, the book became a Signet paperback, and in eighteen months, 3.5 million copies were sold.[74]

By 1961, Caldwell had sold 64 million copies of his books in paperback.[75] His success inspired a subgenre of Southern Gothic fiction, with titles like *Swamp Hoyden*, by Jack Woodford and John B. Thompson, and *The Sin Shouter of Cabin Road*, by John Faulkner. John Faulkner was not a nom de plume; John Faulkner was William Faulkner's brother. And it is likely that the popularity of Caldwell's novels helped sell William Faulkner's books as well. Between 1947 and 1951, Signet published six titles by Faulkner in mass-market format, with sales close to 3.3 million.[76] (It helped that Faulkner won the Nobel Prize in 1949.) One of the biggest sellers of the 1950s, Grace Metalious's *Peyton Place*, is essentially a Southern Gothic transplanted to New Hampshire. *Peyton Place* came out in 1956; it spent fifty-nine weeks at No. 1 on the *New York Times* bestseller list; it was turned into a movie and a television series; it sold 10 million copies.[77] It did not inspire a wave of New Hampshire Gothic.

Volume like this was unprecedented. Pocket Books didn't even go to press for fewer than a hundred thousand copies; Signet started at two hundred thousand, and Fawcett, the publisher of Gold Medal Books, had initial print runs of three hundred thousand. By contrast, *The Sun Also Rises* sold just over five thousand copies and *The Great Gatsby* a little over twenty thousand in their first printings.[78] Paperbacks increased the market for serious literature by a factor of a hundred. They increased the market for popular fiction by a factor of a thousand.

From the point of view of the hardcover publishers, although they tended to regard twenty-five-cent paperbacks as a bottom-feeding phenomenon, those books were eating into sales. The puzzle was how to get a piece of the new market without losing respectability or running afoul of the law. *Ulysses* had been declared not obscene by a federal judge, John Woolsey, in 1933, but by then the novel had been in print for eleven years and Joyce was one of the most famous writers in the world. American courts since had not been so permissive. In 1946, *Memoirs of Hecate County*, a collection of interlinked short stories by the *New Yorker* writer Edmund Wilson, was declared obscene by a New York court, despite testimony from Lionel Trilling, who suggested that in a story about sexuality (he was referring to the main story in the book, "The Princess with the Golden Hair"), a description of sex organs might be considered artistically necessary in the interests of "accuracy" and "precision."[79] The Supreme Court declined to overturn the verdict.*

There was political pressure on paperback publishers, though, as well. In 1952, the House of Representatives ordered investigations into the effect of radio and television programs on juvenile delinquency, morals, and crime, and into the effect of books, magazines, and comics on morals and behavior.[80] A major focus of the committee charged with the latter investigation was mass-market paperback fiction, and the star exhibit was *Women's Barracks*, by Tereska Torrès, a novelized account of the author's experience serving in London in the Free French Army during the war. To the annoyance of Torrès, who was not a lesbian, the book was marketed by Gold Medal Books, a Fawcett imprint that created the "paperback original," as lesbian fiction.[81]

The cover, by Baryé Phillips, a prolific cover artist who specialized in sex poses, has women undressing in a locker room with a butch-looking female officer looking on. But the steamiest passage in the book is this, from the only same-sex scene in the novel:

> How touching and amusing and exciting! Claude [an older woman] ventured still further in discovering the body of the child [in fact, a younger woman]. Then, so as not to frighten the little one, her hand waited while she gently whispered to her, "Ursula, my darling child, my little girl, how pretty you are!" The hand moved again.[82]

Women's Barracks had already sold a million copies. Thanks to the publicity surrounding the hearings, Fawcett sold a million more.[83]

In December, the committee published its report. "The so-called

---

* Wilson was furious because he counted Justice Felix Frankfurter a friend and Frankfurter recused himself. Wilson never forgave him.

pocket-sized books, which originally started out as cheap reprints of standard works, have largely degenerated into media for the dissemination of artful appeals to sensuality, immorality, filth, perversion, and degeneracy," it stated. The books constitute "a serious menace to the social structure of the Nation."[84] There was little the law could do, however. Mass-market paperback covers may have been arousing, but the descriptions of sex inside were usually periphrastic—"the hand moved again"—and they did not use obscene language. The committee's objection to *Women's Barracks* was simply an objection to homosexuality. Although Congress ignored the call for legislation, local efforts to ban certain mass-market books persisted around the country, and the controversy had a chilling effect on the paperback industry.[85]

Which was in trouble for other reasons, too. Mass-market paperbacking turned out not to be a stable business model. The hitch was the pricing. In a review of an early batch of Penguins in 1936, Orwell called the books "a splendid value" for readers but "a disaster" for publishers, booksellers, and authors.[86] Moving several hundred thousand units sounds impressive, but when the retail price is twenty-five cents, the revenue is not so impressive. De Graff paid his writers a 4 percent royalty—a penny a book (which is also what writers were paid for Armed Services Editions). Figuring in the retailer's cut, which was up to 40 percent, paper costs, and distribution, there was very little margin.

The plan was to recoup sunk costs as quickly as possible, but the break-even point was extremely high. This is why print runs were so enormous. Profitability started somewhere north of a hundred thousand copies. The result was that the market became flooded. In 1950, 214 million paperbacks were manufactured in the United States, generating $46 million in revenue.[87] But 14 million books went unsold—not a bad return rate, but a lot of books. By 1953, it was estimated that there was an industry-wide inventory of 175 million unsold books.[88] There were other developments: magazines began offering discount subscriptions, which reduced the traffic at newsstands, and the main magazine distribution company, the American News Company, lost an antitrust suit and went out of business. Although publishers continued to produce rack-sized editions, the mass-market phenomenon was over.[89]

But the format was reborn in an upscale incarnation. Jason Epstein was a product of the Columbia College Literature Humanities curriculum, the course that descended from Erskine's General Honors, and "the publishing business," as he later wrote, "became an extension of my undergraduate years."[90] After leaving Columbia in 1950, he went to work reading slush—unsolicited manuscripts—at Doubleday, the house where de Graff got his start. Doubleday was still being run by merchandizers who depended on revenue from the company's book clubs, notably the Literary Guild.

Epstein lived in the Village, and he hung out in the legendary Eighth Street Bookshop. He craved the new hardcover books he browsed there, but he couldn't afford them on his forty-five-dollars-a-week salary. He began to envision cheaper editions of the kind of books he had read at Columbia, and he discussed the idea of paperback reprints of classic and highbrow titles with the bookstore's owners, Ted and Eli Wilentz. In 1953, Epstein launched for Doubleday a line of paperbacks called Anchor Books.

Anchor's books were not aimed at a mass readership. Its first list included D. H. Lawrence's *Studies in Classic American Literature* and works by Joseph Conrad, André Gide, and Stendhal. The books were priced to break even at twenty thousand copies (not a small number in the book business) and sold from sixty-five cents to $1.25. The covers were arty, not cheesy. Many were by Edward Gorey. (Epstein found that these did well.)

The product became known as the "quality paperback"—to distinguish it from the other kind. But the books were rack-sized, and even Epstein found them a little tacky. After the Eighth Street Bookshop began stocking quality paperbacks, he considered the sight of them, as he later put it, "an affront to the store's serene dignity."[91] Still, by 1954, Anchor was selling six hundred thousand books a year—not Mickey Spillane territory, but a sustainable business model. In 1954, Knopf launched a quality paperback line, Vintage, and Beacon began one, too.

The model was also quickly followed by a publisher who was independently wealthy and who was rapidly acquiring some of the most advanced writers in the world, Barney Rosset, the owner of Grove Press. Rosset found a way for the publishing industry to expand its market and bring "sensuality, immorality, filth, perversion, and degeneracy," or sophisticated versions of those things, into the mainstream.[92]

7.

The road to expanded constitutional protection for books ran through France. There was a practical reason for this: after 1900, it was safer to publish English-language books in Paris than in London or New York. British and American obscenity laws were highly restrictive and aggressively enforced. In England and Wales, the Obscene Publications Act, passed in 1857, authorized the use of search warrants to seize pornographic materials; subsequent acts of Parliament made it illegal to advertise pornography, to send it through the mails, and to bring it in from abroad.

The Act was given judicial teeth by *Regina v. Hicklin*, decided in 1868, in which the court ruled on a pamphlet called "The Confessional Unmasked: Shewing the Depravity of the Romanish Priesthood, the Iniquity of the Confessional and the Questions Put to Females in Confession," distributed by an outfit called the Protestant Electoral Union.[93] The pamphlet would seem an unlikely aid to arousal, but the judge declared it in violation of the Act, and offered the following gloss: "the test of obscenity is this, whether the tendency of the matter is to deprave and corrupt those whose minds are open to such immoral influences and into whose hands a publication of this sort may fall."[94] This was interpreted to mean that the standard for obscenity is the moral effect something might have on a young woman. The test became known as the Hicklin Rule, and it was adopted by American courts in cases arising under the Act for the Suppression of Trade in, and Circulation of, Obscene Literature and Articles of Immoral Use, passed by Congress in 1873—legislation known as the Comstock Act.

In Britain, there was an immediate impact on the pornography business. For publishers, the new laws meant that their main worry was no longer the local constable or anti-vice society. The national government was on the case. The publishers responded by moving operations offshore. They set up shop first in Amsterdam, but by putting diplomatic pressure on the Dutch government, Britain managed to make life difficult for them there, so they relocated again, this time to Paris. By 1910, there were virtually no publishers of English-language pornography left in Britain. They were all in Paris.[95]

They soon found company there with another group of English-language houses, the publishers of modernist writers. These included

Sylvia Beach's Shakespeare and Company, which published *Ulysses*; Three Mountains Press, which published Ernest Hemingway, Ezra Pound, and Ford Madox Ford; Black Sun Press, run by the glamorous expatriates Harry and Caresse Crosby, which published Hart Crane and William Faulkner; Contact Editions, which published Gertrude Stein and William Carlos Williams; Black Manikin Press, which published D. H. Lawrence; and Hours Press, which published Samuel Beckett.[96] These presses were established partly because of the British and American writers and readers who were drawn to Paris by the cheap franc, and partly because, in some cases, their books were illegal in Britain or the United States.

In fact, obscenity was also illegal in France. But the relevant law, passed in 1881, in the early years of the Third Republic, to establish freedom of the press, stipulated that although expressions "contrary to good morals" remained criminal, books were to be given special treatment. A conviction for publishing an immoral book could be obtained only by a jury trial in the nation's highest court.[97] (The French may have felt some chagrin that in 1857, the government had prosecuted two of the country's most famous writers, Gustave Flaubert and Charles Baudelaire.) The French were also not terribly concerned about books written in English, since they were bought by tourists. Two English-language books besides *Ulysses* published in Paris between the wars would play key parts in the legal challenge to obscenity laws in Britain and the United States: Lawrence's *Lady Chatterley's Lover* and Henry Miller's *Tropic of Cancer*.

Tropic of Cancer is not a work to everyone's taste, but it made a deep impression on two people in a position to advance its fortunes. The first was Jack Kahane. Kahane was born in 1887 in Manchester, the son of Romanian Jews who had settled in England and had made, then lost, a fortune in the textile business. He was a Francophile; when the First World War broke out, he went off to France to fight for civilization. He was gassed and badly wounded in the trenches at Ypres. But he had fallen in love with a Frenchwoman, Marcelle Girodias, from a well-off family, and they married in 1917 and remained in France. In 1929, Kahane decided to go into the book business, and he founded Obelisk Press.[98]

Ulysses provided the formula for the kind of books Kahane wanted Obelisk to publish: high-prestige literature with a reputation for salacious bits. Thanks to British obscenity laws, he saw a ready market for his services. "I would start a publishing business that would exist for the convenience of those English writers, English and American, who had something to say that they could not conveniently say in their own countries," as he explained his thinking. "The next Lawrence or Joyce who came along would find the natural solution of his difficulties in Paris. And, of course, if any book that had reached publication . . . met with disaster, my publishing house would automatically publish it in France . . . [I]t seemed to be an impeccably logical conception."[99]

Kahane was correct that British laws were absurdly restrictive, and that prosecution made for good promotion. In 1929, he published *Sleeveless Errand*, by Norah James, a novel banned in Britain solely because its characters lead bohemian lives. He published it with a band around the cover—"Seized by the London Police: The Complete and Unexpurgated Text"—set the price at a hundred francs, and crossed his fingers. Sales were brisk.[100] There is no obscene language (apart from curses) or descriptions of sex in *Sleeveless Errand*. The characters just talk.

In 1933, Kahane published Radclyffe Hall's *The Well of Loneliness*, which had been banned in England in a notorious trial after its first Paris publisher, Pegasus, went out of business. (The two banned books inspired an anti-obscenity-law tract in the form of an illustrated children's book called *The Well of Sleevelessness*.) Knopf owned the American rights to Hall's book, but after the conviction in English courts, opted not to publish.[101] The most risqué words in *The Well of Loneliness* are: "and that night they were not divided."[102] The "they," however, are two women.

So Kahane got books like these on the rebound from publishers who had to eat their costs in Britain while he made a profit in France. But he yearned for a Joyce of his own, and in 1932, he found one, when William Bradley, an American literary agent based in Paris, approached him with the manuscript of *Tropic of Cancer*. Kahane had never heard of Henry Miller. Few people had. But he read the book in a day and was stunned. "I had read the most terrible, the most sordid, the most magnificent manuscript that had ever fallen into my hands," he recorded in his autobiography; "nothing I had yet received was comparable to it for the splendour of its writing, the fathomless depth of its despair, the savour of its portraiture, the boisterousness of its humor."[103] It was exactly the mix of the ambitious and the scandalous that he was looking for.

In September 1934, Obelisk Press published *Tropic of Cancer*. The book came with a wrap-around band stating "Must not be taken into Great Britain or U.S.A."—catnip to tourists. In subsequent printings,

Kahane added blurbs from T. S. Eliot ("a very remarkable book") and Ezra Pound ("at last an unprintable book that is fit to read"). The cover art was a crude rendering of a crab, drawn by Kahane's fifteen-year-old son, Maurice, whose services, as a family member, were pro bono.[104]

Miller wasn't crazy about the cover, but it was his first novel, he was thrilled finally to be in print (he was already in his forties), and he published several more books with Obelisk, including *Black Spring* and *Tropic of Capricorn*. By 1939, Obelisk had three thousand copies of *Tropic of Cancer* in print. Kahane died that year, a day after the start of the Second World War; nine months later, the Germans occupied Paris and censorship of a different kind went into effect. And that is when *Tropic of Cancer* found its second great champion, Barney Rosset.

In 1940, Rosset was a freshman at Swarthmore. He read about *Tropic of Cancer* in another Miller book, *The Cosmological Eye*, and took a train to New York City, where he bought a copy under the counter at the Gotham Book Mart—a store, incongruously located on West Forty-Seventh Street in the Diamond District, that was already legendary (it opened in 1920) as an outlet for avant-garde writing. Rosset said that he was sold the book by the store's founder and owner, Frances Steloff, and that his copy was stamped "Printed in Mexico." That was possibly an effort at misdirecting the authorities, but it also illustrated one of the problems with publishing banned books, which is that they are not copyrighted. Once there is a demand, anyone with a printing press can get in on the action.

Like Kahane, Rosset was knocked out by *Tropic of Cancer*. He found it "truly and beautifully anti-conformist," and he wrote a paper about it, called "Henry Miller vs. 'Our Way of Life,'" for his English class. His professor, Robert Spiller, gave it a B-minus.[105]* Rosset left Swarthmore after his freshman year, but he hung on to the paper. Many years later, when he was testifying in one of the *Tropic of Cancer* trials, he pulled the paper out of his pocket to show the judge that he was serious about the book.[106]

Acting on a tip from his ex-wife (he would marry five times in all), the painter Joan Mitchell, Rosset bought Grove Press, a Greenwich Village startup (named for Grove Street) with three titles to its name, for

---

* Spiller was the lead editor of the three-volume *Literary History of the United States*, which came out in 1948 and for many years was the standard text.

three thousand dollars in 1951. He did something with it that was fairly uncommon for American publishing houses, which tend to prefer a diversified portfolio: he made Grove into a brand. The formula was a better-capitalized version of the Obelisk formula: a combination of avant-garde literature, radical politics, and erotica. Rosset was not a merchandiser, and he was not looking to acquire bestsellers. He published what he liked.

He could afford to. He was born in Chicago in 1922; his father was Jewish and his mother was Irish. He identified with the Irish side. He saw himself as a scrappy underdog fighting the establishment, although, in fact, the family was quite wealthy. Rosset's father owned a bank, the Metropolitan Trust Company, and after he died, in 1954, Rosset (an only child) and his mother inherited the bank and merged it with Grove. Until Grove went public, in 1967, they owned the company.[107] This enabled Rosset to place long-term bets on writers. He had no investors to answer to.

He had bought his way in at the start of a boom time for the industry. In gross numbers: in 1947, receipts from book sales were $464 million; in 1967, they exceeded $2.1 billion.[108] Paperbacking had made the product affordable to millions, college enrollments were growing (and therefore the market for course books), and there wasn't much competition for leisure dollars from movies (which you could not watch at home) or television (which was programmed for the lowest common denominator). Rosset was a rebel, but he would not have been able to accomplish what he did at Grove if the whole industry wasn't riding high.

Rosset's first great accomplishment was to become Samuel Beckett's American publisher. Beckett was an elusive and problematic prize. He lived in Paris, where he had once been a member of Joyce's entourage; he wrote in French; and he was fanatical about the integrity of his art. His work had been "discovered" by Richard Seaver, a graduate of the University of North Carolina who was living in Paris writing a dissertation on Joyce and supported by, among other things, a job teaching English to Air France stewardesses. With friends—Alexander Trocchi, a Scot, and Jane Lougee, an American from Maine—he had helped to found *Merlin*, one of a number of English-language magazines in postwar Paris.

In 1952, Seaver happened to see two of Beckett's French-language novels, *Molloy* and *Malone meurt*, in the window of Éditions de Minuit—he recognized Beckett's name as a member of Joyce's circle—

and he bought them. He was thrilled. He then read Beckett's previous books, *More Pricks Than Kicks* and *Murphy*, both written in English and out of print, and wrote an essay on Beckett for *Merlin*. *Molly* and *Malone meurt*, he asserted, although "they defy all commentary, merit the attention of anyone interested in this century's literature."[109] *En attendant Godot* had not yet been produced, but Seaver had heard some of it read on the radio, and described the story in his essay. He got the issue of *Merlin* to Beckett via Beckett's publisher, Jérôme Lindon, and, by persistence, persuaded Beckett to show him the manuscript of his novel *Watt*, which he had written in English during the war, and to permit *Merlin* to publish it.[110]

According to Seaver, he got a letter from Rosset, in New York, saying that he (Rosset) had been intrigued by the essay in *Merlin* and asking whether a meeting with Beckett could be set up. Seaver put Rosset in touch with Lindon. In *his* memoir, though, Rosset claimed that Beckett was recommended to him by Joyce's publisher, Sylvia Beach, the owner of Shakespeare and Company.[111] However he got onto him, Rosset acquired the American rights to *Godot* before he and Beckett actually met, which happened in Paris in September 1953. Beckett and Rosset, much to the surprise of the former, hit it off.[112] Maybe it was the Irish ancestry.

It was also sound business sense. Rosset recognized Beckett's potential at a time when Beckett was barely a coterie author. Beckett would have been foolish to refuse his advances. Rosset must also have realized that he had a melodramatically self-abnegating prima donna on his hands, and he patiently walked Beckett through the steps necessary for his books to be published in the United States, starting with persuading him to translate them into English, which Beckett did only after making a tremendous fuss.

Rosset oversaw the American production of *Godot*, making sure that it met Beckett's standards. The play had opened in Paris to small audiences but positive notices in January 1953.[113] The first American production, in Miami Beach three years later, bombed, and a Broadway run, starring Bert Lahr, closed after sixty performances. By then, though, *Godot* had become a sensation in Europe. The reception there was warmer possibly because Europeans could read the tramps, Vladimir and Estragon, as wartime refugees, and the overbearing Pozzo, with his slave Lucky, as a Nazi overlord—allusions that were possibly remote for American audiences. There is a biographical basis for such a reading.

Beckett had been active in the Resistance, but his group was broken up by a double agent, and he had to flee from Paris with his partner, Suzanne Deschevaux-Dumesnil. They spent time on the road before ending up in a farmhouse in the Vaucluse, in southeastern France, and Didi and Gogo, the tramps in *Godot*, do behave like a quarrelsome couple.[114]

Rosset stuck with Beckett, and soon *Waiting for Godot* was an American sensation as well.* The Grove paperback came out in 1956 and eventually sold more than two million copies.[115] Between 1956 and 1969, *Waiting for Godot* was performed in every state except Arkansas and Alaska.[116] In its first five years, from 1953 to 1958, it was seen by more than a million people around the world.[117] In 1961, a Hungarian émigré living in England, Martin Esslin, named *Godot* as the prime example of what he called the Theatre of the Absurd, which, he explained, "strives to express its sense of the senselessness of the human condition."[118]

This confuses statelessness and homelessness, a political condition that the play arguably represents, with absurdity, a philosophical concept. It projects difficulties onto a simple text. The subject of *Godot* is the subject of all of Beckett's plays (apart from a few radio plays): happiness. And Beckett has only one thing to say about happiness: seize the day. "[O]ne day we were born, one day we shall die, the same day, the same second, is that not enough for you?" Pozzo says in his final speech.[119] It's true that Beckett approached the subject of happiness from the point of view of unhappiness. His characters (except for Winnie in *Happy Days*, who *should* be unhappy) are all unhappy, but that is not because Beckett thought that life is unhappy. It's because he thought what Charlie Chaplin and Buster Keaton and W. C. Fields thought, that unhappiness is funny.

Waiting for Godot is not static, as some people complained, and it is not about keeping alive the hope that one day, a Godot will appear. It is about the importance of realizing that Godot is only tomorrow's Pozzo. "He doesn't beat you?" Didi asks the Boy who comes with a message from Godot. "No Sir, not me," says the Boy. "Whom does he beat?" "He beats my brother, Sir."[120] There is no mystery to existence. It's here right now, we don't need to know why, and then it's over. Still, a play written in response to a specific violent disruption that was very

---

* During part of this period, Beckett was in a clandestine romantic relationship with Joan Mitchell, Rosset's ex-wife.

real to Beckett got made into an emblem of the human condition—as though that disruption was the norm, rather than a terrible exception to the norm, in human life. In any case, whatever *Godot* means, Grove had its Joyce.

8.

In 1954, Rosset received a letter from a Berkeley professor named Mark Schorer suggesting that Grove publish *Lady Chatterley's Lover*, then the most famous banned work of literature in the Western world. Lawrence had published the novel privately in Florence in 1928. He paid a personal visit to Beach in Paris to interest her in printing it, but she said she did not want to become known as a publisher of erotica.[121] Lawrence died in 1930. The novel was never copyrighted, and this made it instant carrion for offshore English-language publishers to feed on. Obelisk's edition, which came out in 1936, was the third *Lady Chatterley* published in Paris. In the United States, Knopf, with Lawrence's authorization, brought out an expurgated edition. (In this case, there was something to expurgate.)

Rosset actually disliked *Lady Chatterley*. The novel's class politics—it's the story of an English aristocrat's affair with her gamekeeper—didn't interest him, and he found descriptions of the hero talking to his penis, which he calls "John Thomas," silly. For his part, Lawrence hated pornography. His views on sex were far too high-minded for Rosset. But none of that mattered, because Rosset realized that *Lady Chatterley* could be the key to the liberation of *Tropic of Cancer*—"a Trojan horse for Grove," as he put it.[122]

The lack of copyright was a problem. The unexpurgated *Lady Chatterley* had always been banned in the United States and Britain. In order to publish it, Rosset needed a court to declare the book not obscene, and that would be expensive. If he won his case and the book was still not under copyright, every publisher could print it, and Grove would be powerless to stop them. So Rosset began an exhausting round of negotiations with Lawrence's widow, Frieda, and with Alfred Knopf, an irascible publishing titan who considered Rosset an upstart, and who pretended, on no legal grounds whatsoever, that his company owned the rights to any edition the courts might sanction.

Frieda died; Knopf blustered; Lawrence's British agent refused to cooperate. So finally, Rosset decided to go it alone. In 1959, Grove published an unexpurgated *Lady Chatterley* with a preface by Archibald MacLeish, a former Librarian of Congress, and an introduction by Schorer, plus blurbs from eminent persons of letters, and waited for the government to seize the book. It did, Rosset sued, and the game was on.

Rosset retained Ephraim London, a prominent First Amendment attorney, but London made the mistake of dismissing a suggestion from Rosset about how to handle the case and was fired on the spot. (That was characteristic. Rosset eventually rehired him, also characteristic.) Rosset knew two lawyers by acquaintance. He called one, and, by an incredible piece of luck, the man was not at home. For the second lawyer, whom Rosset knew only from tennis matches in the Hamptons, did pick up. He was Charles Rembar.[123]

Rembar had never tried a case before, and he was not an expert on the First Amendment.[124] He was Norman Mailer's cousin. He later claimed (probably inaccurately) to have come up with the nonword "fug" for Mailer to use as a legal substitute for "fuck" in his bestselling first novel, *The Naked and the Dead*.[125] But Rembar agreed to represent Grove in the legal battle over *Lady Chatterley*. He turned out to be a quick-witted courtroom tactician with a long-term legal strategy. The strategy was to rewrite the definition of obscenity using concepts to which the courts had already committed themselves.[126] He wanted to be able to say to the judges: Look, you've already said this is OK.

There was a major obstacle facing Grove in its suit against the Post Office, which had seized *Lady Chatterley*: a recent Supreme Court decision in *Roth v. United States*. Samuel Roth was an American Kahane who had the disadvantage of operating in a country where the obscenity laws were enforced. He was, at heart if not technically, a pirate, a bookaneer. He published and distributed unauthorized versions of modernist classics banned in the United States—one was *Lady Chatterley's Lover*—and he also sold pornography. One of the classics Roth pirated from was *Ulysses*; Joyce found out about it, and there was an international outcry.

Roth was frequently in trouble with the law and had even done jail time.[127] In 1957, his conviction for mailing obscene circulars and advertising an obscene book came before the Supreme Court. His case was joined with *Alberts v. California*, the appeal of a conviction for selling obscene books. The lawyers for both appellants placed their chips on a single argument: that obscenity statutes were unconstitutional. The Court held otherwise, and Roth went to prison for four years. The case was decided on June 24, 1957, and the majority opinion was written by William Brennan, an observant Catholic who had been appointed eight months earlier by Eisenhower and who would become one of the most liberal justices on the Warren Court. Brennan explained that courts had always carved out exceptions to the First Amendment protection of speech—for instance, libel—and that history showed obscenity to have been one of those exceptions. Brennan was not prepared to challenge that tradition, but he did offer what amounted to a new definition of obscenity, thus unintentionally initiating the almost total unraveling of obscenity jurisprudence.

The term "obscene" is a conundrum. Is an expression obscene because it's arousing or because it's gross? Is lust (a pleasurable feeling) the relevant affect, or is disgust (an unpleasant one)? Brennan tried to split the difference with a new term. "Obscene material is material which deals with sex in a manner appealing to prurient interest," he wrote. The Supreme Court had used "prurient" only once before in its history. That was in *Mutual v. Ohio* in 1915, when the Court held that motion pictures are not protected by the First Amendment. In *Mutual*, the Court noted that "a prurient interest may be excited and appealed to" by movies, but made no more of it.[128] Brennan cited *Mutual*, but he actually took the term from the American Law Institute's *Model Penal Code*.[129] He then saw fit to add definitions of "prurient" from other sources as well: a "tendency to excite lustful thoughts," a "shameful or morbid interest in nudity, sex, or excretion," and an expression "substantially beyond customary limits of candor."[130]

Possibly sensing that the scattershot nature of his definitions simply provided prosecutors with more weapons, Brennan tackled the problem from another direction. He defined what would *not* count as obscenity. "All ideas having even the slightest redeeming social importance—unorthodox ideas, controversial ideas, even ideas hateful to the prevailing climate of opinion—have the full protection of the guaranties," he wrote. "[I]mplicit in the history of the First Amendment is the rejection of obscenity as utterly without redeeming social importance."[131]

Roth was handed down on June 24, 1957. In a case handed down the same day, *Kingsley Books v. Brown*, the Court upheld a New York conviction for the sale of obscene materials. Both decisions were announced one week after the "Red Monday" opinions had staked out an expansive approach to the protection of political speech. It is possible that the Court did not want to be perceived to be putting all its First Amendment eggs in the same basket.

Looked at in one way, Brennan's opinion in *Roth* was a setback for anti-censorship forces. After all, it was the lead opinion in a decision that confirmed the conviction of a notorious pornographer. Whatever Brennan meant by his counterdefinition—"without redeeming social importance"—that criterion had been insufficient to protect Samuel Roth. Looked at another way, though, Brennan gave Grove a lot of language to work with. Rembar saw that the path to changing obscenity law was not to get Roth overruled. It was to get Brennan's opinion restated as an anti-censorship decision. This task took Rembar and the rest of the legal team at Grove seven years to accomplish.

The first move was easy. In Grove's case against the Post Office, Rembar got the United States District Court for the Southern District of New York to agree that *Lady Chatterley* was a serious work of literature. It was published by a reputable press with impressive scholarly accoutrements (and thus was not "pandering," the basis for the crime for which many pornographers were convicted). *Chatterley* easily met the "social importance" test. It fell into the *Ulysses* category: too eminent to suppress. The charge that the book offended contemporary standards—which is what the "customary limits of candor" test amounted to—was met by the fact that the Grove edition had been well received by the literary establishment.

By the time the opinion overturning the Post Office ban was released, in July 1959, the Grove *Lady Chatterley* had already sold more than a hundred thousand copies; by September, it was No. 2 on the *New York Times* bestseller list. It was still uncopyrighted. In the end, Knopf declined to enter the lists, but other publishers were not so punctilious. By the end of 1959, there were five paperback Chatterleys on the market. Only one, published by Dell, paid royalties to Grove. Altogether, six million copies of Lawrence's novel were sold.[132]

As Rembar could see, the *Chatterley* decision was not exactly a ringing call to end censorship. The court basically said, If it's good enough for Archibald MacLeish, it's good enough for the United States Constitution. Lawrence opened the door, but it was not obvious that Miller was going squeeze through it. *Tropic of Cancer* was a much harder case. There were several problems. The first was that Lawrence was a moralist and Miller was an anarchist. Miller didn't give a damn. "Social importance" was just the kind of cant he deplored. A second problem was that *Tropic of Cancer* and *Tropic of Capricorn* had been republished after the war in Paris by Kahane's son, Maurice Girodias.

During the Occupation, Maurice had taken his mother's Gentile name and started a press, Éditions du Chêne. He did not have trouble with the authorities. He published a pro-Pétain book by Georges Pelorson, a French collaborator (and once one of Beckett's closest friends), and a tract attacking the Jewish writer André Maurois with a cover illustration of Maurois as a vulture and Stars of David in the sky behind him.* After the Germans left, Girodias revived Obelisk, and brought out new editions of Miller's novels, looking to cash in on the GIs and the American tourists who came to Paris after the Liberation. He also published a French translation of *Tropic of Capricorn*, done by Pelorson under a pseudonym, and *Sexus*, the first (and sexiest) volume in Miller's Rosy Crucifixion trilogy.[133]

In 1951, in financial difficulties, Girodias lost control of Éditions du Chêne and Obelisk to Hachette, which thus acquired the Miller titles, but in 1953, he launched a new venture, Olympia Press. Olympia was a realization of Jack Kahane's vision: a Paris-based publisher specializing in English-language books that American and British houses would not touch, along with a long list of pornographic titles under the Traveler's Companion imprint. Girodias employed some of the *Merlin* editors to write the pornography.[134]

Olympia became a leader in the publication of legally challenged books. It published an English translation of *The Story of O* in 1953, written by Jean Paulhan's mistress, Anne Desclos, under the pseudonym Pauline Réage; *The Ginger Man*, by the Irish American writer J. P. Donleavy, in 1955; Vladimir Nabokov's *Lolita* in 1955; Terry Southern and Mason Hoffenberg's satire *Candy* in 1958, written under the *nom de plume* Maxwell Kenton; and three novels by William Burroughs: *Naked Lunch* (1959), *The Soft Machine* (1961), and *The Ticket That Exploded* (1962). Olympia also published translations of the Marquis de Sade.

---

* After the war, Pelorson changed his name to Georges Belmont and had a successful career as a writer and translator.

French law required companies operated by foreigners to have a French manager; Girodias offered his service in that capacity to the editors of *Merlin*, and thus became the publisher of *Watt* and of the English translations of Beckett's trilogy, *Molloy*, *Malone Dies*, and *The Unnamable* as well.[135]

What all this meant was that Grove and Olympia were in direct competition. To the extent that Grove could publish Olympia's authors legally in the United States, Rosset was taking business away from Girodias. Grove also was aggressive about acquiring English-language rights to avant-garde European writers, especially dramatists. In 1959, Rosset hired Seaver, and this became Seaver's arena. He translated more than fifty books from the French, including *The Story of O* (using a female pseudonym, Sabine d'Estrée).[136] Rosset essentially raided Girodias's list. He took over not only Miller, Burroughs, and Genet but also, later on, Sade and some of the erotica.[137]

Rosset was able to win this game because Girodias had the misfortune of reviving his father's business model just as French obscenity law was changing. On July 29, 1939, a month before the outbreak of the Second World War, the French government had issued a decree, "Code de la famille," designed to protect the country from foreign predators. The decree outlawed publication of material "contraires aux bonnes moeurs."[138] After the Liberation, the decree was supplemented by a law outlawing immoral books that fell into the hands of minors. A bull's-eye had been painted on English-language pornography. In 1946, Girodias was compelled to appear before a public prosecutor to defend his edition of *Tropic of Capricorn*. The prosecution provoked protests from French writers, who said it recalled the Nazi suppression of books, and after two years the case was dropped. The publicity helped Girodias sell a hundred thousand copies, but it was a taste of things to come. Between 1954 and 1963, fifty-five Olympia titles were banned, including *Lolita*.[139]

Someone tried to bring copies of the Paris edition of *Tropic of Cancer* into the United States. The books were seized and destroyed by Customs, and in 1953, a federal court upheld the seizure. "Practically everything that the world loosely regards as sin is detailed in the vivid, lurid, salacious language of smut, prostitution, and dirt," the judge observed of Miller's novel. "And all of it is related without the slightest expressed idea of its abandon."[140] It was *The Well of Loneliness* again: it wasn't that the acts were sinful. It was that the author so clearly approved.

The worst problem facing Grove, however, was that the Department of Justice advised Customs and the Post Office not to interfere with the distribution of *Tropic of Cancer*. Rosset had already published the book (it could not be banned in advance of publication because of the rule against prior restraint) and he had agreed to indemnify bookstores for their costs if they faced charges. This meant that the book was subject to any number of local prosecutions, and in the end, there were nearly sixty *Cancer* cases across the country. The word went out that all the police had to do was go into a store, pick up a copy, and turn to page five, where the words "I will ream out every wrinkle in your cunt" appear, and they could seize all copies.[141] Meanwhile, chances for a Supreme Court decision were looking remote. The American Civil Liberties Union supplied lawyers in some of the cases, but Grove was swamped. Rosset had to keep appealing losses in state courts and pray for a grant of certiorari to stop the bleeding.

Grove almost had a breakthrough in 1962, when the Supreme Judicial Court of Massachusetts, by a four-to-three vote, reversed a trial-court judgment against the book. But to Rembar's dismay, the state did not appeal, so he could not get a Supreme Court decision out of it. Litigation slogged on. Finally, and unexpectedly, in 1964, the Supreme Court, in *Grove v. Gerstein*, without an opinion, reversed a Florida judgment against Grove, and, on the same day, issued an opinion in *Jacobellis v. Ohio*, a case, argued by Ephraim London, that reversed the conviction of a theater manager in Cleveland Heights, Ohio, for showing a Louis Malle film called *Les Amants*. In his lead opinion, Brennan essentially restated what he had said in *Roth*, except this time, he reached an anti-censorship verdict.

Brennan explained that *Roth* held that a work cannot be proscribed "unless it is 'utterly' without social importance." *Les Amants*, and, by implication, *Tropic of Cancer*, clearly had social importance. As for "customary limits of candor," or "community standards," Brennan now said that he could not have meant the standards of local communities, such that each jurisdiction was free to impose its own bans. The Constitution is a national constitution; the First Amendment must be interpreted the same way everywhere. The standard must therefore be a "national standard."[142] By the time of *Jacobellis*, *Tropic of Cancer* had already sold more than two million copies. The justices must have sensed that the market had established that the standards test had been met.

Jacobellis retained obscenity as a category of unprotected speech but made it virtually impossible to censor serious books for their language or their subject matter. There were two more major tests of books and obscenity laws: *Naked Lunch* and *Memoirs of a Woman of Pleasure*, otherwise known as *Fanny Hill*, which had been the first book convicted of obscenity in the United States, back in 1821. (*Fanny Hill* is one of the most reprinted works of pornography in English. Girodias published it; so did Samuel Roth.) Rembar argued *Fanny Hill* before the Supreme Court.

You can say what you like about *Lady Chatterley*, but *Fanny Hill* just *is* pornography. Nevertheless, Rembar persuaded the justices that since various scholars and critics had already testified to its "social importance," they didn't even need to read it. It passed the test set out in *Roth*. Victories in those two cases sealed the deal. By the end of the decade, major American writers were publishing novels—Mailer's *An American Dream*, John Updike's *Couples*, Philip Roth's *Portnoy's Complaint*—that used words and described acts for which their publishers just ten years earlier would have faced jail. Through the efforts of literary critics, lawyers, and publishers, literary fiction had finally captured the terrain previously occupied by down-market publishers. Rosset liberated the industry.

He also picked up the tab. Once formerly taboo books could be sold without legal worries, the Obelisks, the Olympias, and the Groves were no longer necessary. The major houses, with their big advances, got into the act. Rosset's legal successes helped do him in. In the 1960s, Grove published many books that spoke to the historical moment, from *The Autobiography of Malcolm X* and Abbie Hoffman's *Steal This Book* (Rosset disliked Hoffman but felt he had to publish his book because Random House had refused it) to Frantz Fanon's *The Wretched of the Earth*, with an introduction by Jean-Paul Sartre.[143] And after the *Fanny Hill* decision, Rosset bought a collection of Victorian-era pornography and published titles such as *A Man with a Maid* and *Lashed into Lust*. Grove mainstreamed what used to be called "the underground."[144]

But the market had shifted. Rosset bought more than four hundred art films, including the sexually explicit Swedish film *I Am Curious (Yellow)*, but he had the same thing happen with those works that had happened with risqué books: the nation's art-movie houses switched to X-rated pornographic films and Rosset was left with no outlet. In 1970, Grove offices were occupied by feminists who accused Rosset of sexism. That incident was accompanied by an effort at unionization. Rosset found it all incredible—that a left-wing champion of underground writing should be a target for feminists and leftists. He was not the only nonconformist from the 1950s who found himself on the wrong side of change in the 1970s.

In 1985, after struggling for a decade to pay off its debts, Rosset sold Grove. The new owners, Ann Getty and George Weidenfeld, turned out to be no more financially prudent than Rosset. In 1986, they demoted him, and he quit. On hearing the news, Beckett, now a Nobel laureate, let it be known that he would never give another book to Grove. Although Rosset persevered with various small-scale publishing enterprises, he lacked the capital to compete for new books, and he died penniless, or close to it. He never got back on the big stage, and at the end, he was publishing mainly erotica at his outfit Blue Moon Books. Jason Epstein rendered a valediction: "He's altered the climate of publishing," Epstein said, "to everybody's advantage."[145]

11

CHILDREN OF A STORM

Anti-integrationists rioting in Clinton, Tennessee, September 1956. The family in the car was from Michigan and was driving through Clinton when they were attacked. The fight against integration in Clinton was led by the Tennessee Federation for Constitutional Government, chaired by Donald Davidson, an English professor at Vanderbilt and one of the founders of the New Criticism. John Kasper, a neo-Nazi and segregationist, was there, and was arrested four times for fomenting disorder. Kasper was a protégé of Ezra Pound; they had become friendly when Pound was confined in St. Elizabeths, an association that proved awkward for those seeking Pound's release. The photograph appeared along with other images of white people protesting school integration in the September 17, 1956, issue of *Life*, a week before the First Congress of Negro Writers and Artists in Paris. Photograph by Robert W. Kelley. (*LIFE Picture Collection / Getty Images*)

1.

Martin Luther King, Jr., used the word "equality" only once in his "I have a dream speech." He used the word "freedom" twenty times. Equality was the demand of an older generation of civil rights leaders, people like A. Philip Randolph of the Leadership Conference on Civil Rights, James Farmer of the Congress of Racial Equality, and Roy Wilkins and

Thurgood Marshall of the NAACP. King was as committed to equality as any of them, but he understood that the language of liberation had greater political force than the language of egalitarianism. Equality implies redistribution. Freedom implies individualism and is usually imagined as a non-zero-sum good. Freedom was a demand the federal government could get behind.

In fact, of course, freedoms are not zero-sum: a right for someone is a prohibition for someone else. And they are not rights at all unless all citizens enjoy them equally; otherwise, they are privileges. "The equal protection of the laws" is the right the Fourteenth Amendment enumerates. But casting the civil rights movement in the language of freedom was the smart choice in the era of the Cold War. It allowed the federal government to present itself as the liberator of an oppressed people, Southern Black people. The Mason-Dixon line could be figured as a North American Iron Curtain, and what had been a manifest failure of democratic government could be transformed into a triumph of democratic government.[1] Southern opponents of integration also—it was almost inevitable; the word was trumps—made their case in the name of freedom. "Let us rise to the call of freedom-loving blood that is within us and send our answer to the tyranny that clanks its chains upon the South," proclaimed Alabama governor George Wallace in his inaugural address in 1963. "I say . . . segregation now . . . segregation tomorrow . . . segregation forever."[2]*

Global politics made the civil rights revolution happen much faster than it otherwise might have. As a campaigner, John F. Kennedy was willing to align himself loosely with the civil rights movement, but ending racial segregation was not one of his priorities. In his inaugural address, Kennedy mentioned civil rights obliquely and only once, implied in a promise to uphold "those human rights to which this nation has always been committed, and to which we are committed today at home and around the world."[3] The last six words were added at the request of two aides, Harris Wofford and Louis Marin, who told Kennedy that he needed to make a gesture to the Black voters who had supported him.[4] Those voters had given Kennedy his margin of victory in five states— Texas, New Jersey, Michigan, Illinois, and South Carolina—that

---

* Wallace's speechwriter was Asa Earl Carter. Many years later, in 1976, under the name Forrest Carter, he published *The Education of Little Tree*, a fake memoir of growing up as a Cherokee.

Dwight Eisenhower carried in 1956.[5] "At home" is the only reference to domestic policy in the entire address.

But Kennedy quickly learned that racial discrimination in the United States was a foreign-policy issue, too, because it was a persistent theme in Soviet propaganda. Less than four months after his inauguration, on May 14, 1961, Mother's Day, a bus carrying an interracial group of Freedom Riders was firebombed outside Anniston, Alabama. The Freedom Riders were testing the effect of a recent Supreme Court decision outlawing segregated interstate bus terminals. (They were obliged to conclude that the effect was negligible.) Men had bombed the bus after pursuing it in cars when it left the Anniston station. They tried to prevent the Riders from escaping, but dispersed when a state patrol car arrived.

Photographs appeared in newspapers around the country, and this brought the incident to the attention of the White House. Kennedy had never heard of the Freedom Riders. He is supposed to have said to Wofford: "Can't you get your goddamned friends off those buses?" Kennedy had suffered an embarrassing setback less than a month earlier, when a CIA-directed invasion of Cuba was crushed by Cuban forces in the Bay of Pigs, and his first summit meeting with Nikita Khrushchev was scheduled to take place in Vienna in two weeks. He could imagine Khrushchev waving the photographs from Alabama in his face. (The summit did not go well for other reasons.)[6]

In July, the United Nations ambassador from the former French colony of Chad, Adam Malick Sow, was on his way from New York to Washington when he stopped for coffee at a diner in Maryland, the Bonnie Brae, and was refused service. Three other African diplomats had been refused service on the same road, Route 40, but Ambassador Sow complained to Kennedy himself, and the governor of Maryland, J. Millard Tawes, had to issue a public apology.[7] Kennedy had wanted to make the problem go away—"Can't you just tell the Africans not to drive on Route 40?" he asked Wofford. "Tell the ambassadors I wouldn't think of driving from New York to Washington." Kennedy, of course, took a plane.[8]

This was the context that gave the American civil rights movement political leverage. What Bayard Rustin, who had been a civil rights activist since the 1930s, called the "classical" phase of the movement began with the Supreme Court decision in *Brown* on May 17, 1954, and ended with the signing of the Voting Rights Act on August 6, 1965.[9] During those eleven years, thirty-three African countries gained independence, including Ghana, Sudan, Congo, Senegal, Nigeria, Uganda, Kenya, and Zambia.

Five days after President Lyndon Johnson signed the Voting Rights Act, rioting broke out in the Watts neighborhood of Los Angeles. It continued for six days; thirty-four people were killed. A change in legal status does not automatically bring changes in living conditions. As King realized when he joined the open-housing movement in Chicago in 1966, the absence of Jim Crow laws actually made the fight against discrimination much harder, since there was nothing to strike down. "Equality" was biting back. But all these events were covered in newspapers around the world, because, from the world's point of view, what was happening in the United States was part of something that was happening across the planet.

"The child of a storm," King called the 1964 Civil Rights Act.[10] Around the world, in a little more than a decade, a regime of racial domination that had been in place for centuries was knocked off its legal foundations. The result was a shift in social relations. At the macro level, nonwhite people improved their political and legal status at the expense of white people, who for five hundred years had enjoyed a near monopoly of power in most of the places they lived. At the micro, or individual, level, the new relations produced a change in consciousness, in identity. What it meant and how it felt to be a person of color changed after 1945. And so did what it meant to be a white person.

It was not self-evident how these new identities should be articulated. For most white people, racial equality meant integration and assimilation—"Now you can live like us." For many Black people, this meant assimilation to a culture that for hundreds of years had countenanced the subordination and enslavement of nonwhite people. What would joining that culture even mean for a nonwhite person? White supremacy was in its DNA. There was also the problem, obvious to many Black Americans but somehow not obvious to white Americans, that if a society has countenanced racism for centuries, that cannot be the only thing wrong with it. Such a society was not going to be cured with a simple nondiscrimination pill.

At the same time, complete separation seemed a denial of history. Most African Americans were born and raised in the United States;

native elites in French and British colonies spoke French and English, and many were educated in Europe. What added pain, anger, and frustration to the dilemma was that white people seemed to be uncomprehending. White people—and, because they trusted in their own fairness and tolerance, white liberals especially—didn't seem to get it. It was a psychologically vexed moment. Few people were as intimately attuned to it as James Baldwin.

2.

Identity was the obsession of Baldwin's life. Identity is a two-faced property: you shine one onto the world, and the world shines one onto you. Identity was therefore something Baldwin worked both to own and to escape. He was a role model whose message was, Don't let other people define you. In other words, Don't copy role models. Baldwin was a novelist whose essays are more psychologically clarifying than his fiction. He was an eloquent speaker who was committed to truth-telling—he wrote about resisting "the fearful pressures placed on one to lie about one's experience"—but whose positions were unpredictable, and who engaged in some myth-making about himself.[11] He was independent and he was hypersensitive—he wanted to be respected for making it clear that he did not need anyone's respect—but he was also charming, loved conversation, and made a lot of friends.

These inconsistencies and contradictions arose out of positions Baldwin had thought through. He was sensitive because he understood that your sense of self can't be separated from the way other people regard you. He sometimes exaggerated his past because he believed that what matters is less what happened than how it felt to a person like himself. And his fictional efforts seem indefinite because he was committed to an aesthetic that drew a bright line between literature and politics.

From 1948 to 1957, when French intellectuals were writing about race and prejudice, and France was engaged in wars of liberation in two of its colonies, Baldwin lived in Paris. He returned to the United States after the success of the Montgomery bus boycott, and he chose to become a public figure, and a spokesman (he preferred the term "witness") for the civil rights movement.[12] His third novel, *Another Country*, published in 1962, was on the *New York Times* bestseller list for twenty-three weeks. In 1963, the year he published *The Fire Next Time*, his face was on the cover of *Time*.

But Baldwin found himself riding a tiger. On the spectrum of civil rights politics, he kept getting pulled to the left. He was a defender of Martin Luther King, Jr., a defender of Malcolm X, a defender of Stokely Carmichael, a defender of Angela Davis, and a defender of Eldridge Cleaver and the Black Panthers. By the 1970s, he had lost most of his audience.[13]* He began spending a good deal of his time abroad, in Istanbul, where he had friends, and in the south of France, where he owned a house. His later works were critically disparaged, and he died in 1987. Many years after, when race relations in the United States were being talked about again in terms like those used in the 1950s and 1960s, his work enjoyed a revival.† But he had lived through a global change in thinking about racial identity.

Baldwin was born in Harlem in 1924. The 1920s was the era of the New Negro movement, a creative outburst in virtually all the arts, and many figures associated with the movement lived in Harlem: Langston Hughes, Claude McKay, Countee Cullen, W. E. B. Du Bois, Zora Neale Hurston. The New Negro movement became known as the Harlem Renaissance, and the name has cast a glamorous retrospective light on 1920s Harlem.[14]

The effect is misleading. Harlem became a predominately Black neighborhood in the early twentieth century. In 1905, 4,000 Black people were living above 125th Street, mostly in buildings settled by the middle class. Their arrival, though, drove out white people, and by 1930, there were almost 190,000 Black residents of Harlem, 70 percent of the population. (In 1960, 97 percent of people living in Harlem were Black.) Most of the new residents were migrants from the South and the Caribbean, and most were poor. In the 1920s, mortality and homicide rates in Harlem were 40 percent higher than in the rest of the city; the rates of infant mortality and stillbirths were twice as high; deaths from tuberculosis were three times as high.[15] The Depression made already bad conditions worse.

This was the Harlem Baldwin knew and hated. He was the oldest of nine children in the house. (He also had a stepbrother who was nine

---

* In 1973, *Time* turned down a piece based on interviews with Baldwin by Henry Louis Gates, Jr., on the grounds that Baldwin was "passé."
† Notably in Ta-Nehisi Coates, *Between the World and Me* (2015).

years older.) Both his parents were from the South. His mother, Berdis, cleaned houses. He never knew his biological father; his stepfather, David Baldwin, was a factory worker and Pentecostal preacher, a bitter and abusive man whose mother (Barbara, who lived with the family) had been a slave in Louisiana.[16] "He knew he was black," James later said, "but he did not know he was beautiful."[17]

"I hit the streets when I was seven," Baldwin said.[18] He seems to have meant that he ran errands and took odd jobs.[19] On other occasions, he described himself as the one at home responsible for his younger siblings.[20] He was precocious, and he read all the time. His favorite books were *Uncle Tom's Cabin* and *A Tale of Two Cities*. He said he read them over and over.[21] When he was fourteen, he became a preacher in a storefront church, the Fireside Pentecostal Assembly. Extemporaneous speaking was always one of his gifts. He went to middle school in Harlem, at Frederick Douglass Junior High, where the poet Countee Cullen was one of his teachers. Cullen was as close as Baldwin ever got to the Harlem Renaissance. He showed little interest in its literature or, until late in his career, admiration for its writers.[22]

Baldwin attended DeWitt Clinton High School in the Bronx, a mostly white school that Lionel Trilling and Irving Howe had also attended, and he made several friends there with whom he would be associated later on: the future photographer Richard Avedon and the future publishers Emile Capouya and Sol Stein. All four worked on the school's literary magazine, the *Magpie*.[23] Baldwin's English teacher was Abel Meeropol, who wrote the words for the anti-lynching song "Strange Fruit," recorded by Billie Holiday in 1939, and who, with his wife, Anne, adopted the two sons of Ethel and Julius Rosenberg after the Rosenbergs were executed for espionage in 1953.[24]

Influenced by a friend, Eugene Worth, Baldwin joined the Young People's Socialist League (YPSL), a Trotskyist organization, but he was always vague about what this entailed. He sometimes implied that he was never serious about organized politics; at other times, he claimed to have been a political activist. He also said that Worth committed suicide in 1946 by jumping off the George Washington Bridge, but there is no official record of the death.[25] It was partly through his connections with left-wing anti-Stalinist organizations that he was able to meet editors at the magazines where he began his writing career.[26]

High school was the end of Baldwin's formal education. When

he was nineteen, he moved to the Village, where he was introduced by Capouya to the painter Beauford Delaney, who became a lifelong friend—"the first walking, living proof for me that a black man could be an artist," Baldwin said.[27] With Delaney's help, he got a job as a waiter at Calypso, a Trinidadian restaurant on MacDougal Street.[28] Sometime in the spring of 1945, he met Richard Wright.

"I just knocked on his door out in Brooklyn! I introduced myself, and of course he'd no idea who I was," was Baldwin's version.[29] In fact, Wright had invited Baldwin to his house at the suggestion of the young white writer Esther Carlson, who had heard Baldwin read from a novel he was working on, then called "Cry Holy," and she probably went along with him. Wright knew exactly who Baldwin was. He liked to promote promising Black writers, and after the meeting, he recommended Baldwin for something called the Eugene F. Saxton Foundation Fellowship, which Baldwin went on to receive, a major break for him. Wright also introduced Baldwin to his own editors at Harper & Brothers, who took him to lunch at the San Remo, a popular Village bar and restaurant.[30] Baldwin was twenty.

The novel Baldwin was working on was based on his experiences in the Pentecostal church, and it was eventually rejected by Harper and not published until 1953, when it came out from Knopf as *Go Tell It on the Mountain*. By then, Baldwin had acquired a reputation as a writer for magazines of opinion. He began in 1947 with a piece for *The Nation* and went on to contribute regularly to *The New Leader*, *Commentary*, and *Partisan Review*—all organs of left-wing anti-Communism.

Baldwin was an ideal writer for these magazines because, through some combination of reading, reflection, emulation, and temperament, he had a pitch-perfect command of the critical voice of the anti-Communist left. He was allergic to agitprop and political reductionism, and he was a champion of moral realism. He saw the realist novel as a corrective to the fantasies and sentimentalism (terms he used frequently) of progressive thought. Although it took him a while to appreciate the work, the writer he came to admire most was Henry James.[31] Baldwin's definition of serious literature was Trilling's definition: "the human activity that takes fullest and most precise account of variousness, possibility, complexity, and difficulty."[32]

He called fiction with a political purpose "protest" literature. "The question forever posed by the existence of the protest novel," he wrote in

1948, "—a kind of writing becoming nearly as formalized as those delicate vignettes written for the women's magazines—is whether or not its power as a corrective social force is sufficient to override its deficiencies as literature . . . [I]s the 'great work' these novels are presumably doing in the world quite worth the torture they are to read?"[33] Trilling's criticism was directed at the simplifications of liberal thinking about politics, Baldwin's at the simplifications of liberal thinking about race. The line in both cases often boiled down to "reality is more complicated." Which is always a safe bet.

In November 1948, when he was twenty-four, Baldwin emigrated to Paris. By his own account, the destination was chosen virtually at random. "I didn't *come* to Paris in '48," he told an interviewer in 1970; "I simply *left* America."[34] He had reached a breaking point, he said later. "I knew what it meant to be white and I knew what it meant to [*sic*] a nigger, and I knew what was going to happen to me. My luck was running out." He had felt unwanted by political organizations because of his homosexuality; even in the Village, he had experienced discrimination and harassment because of his sexuality and his race. He worried, he said, that he would end up like his friend Eugene Worth.[35]

Baldwin's claim that he chose Paris at random is highly implausible. Paris was cheap, and it was known as a haven for Black writers and musicians. There were plenty of people there who spoke English—and Baldwin did not yet speak French. Paris was also a symbol of racial and sexual freedom. And, finally, Richard Wright was living there.

Wright was the most famous Black writer in the world. By 1948, his books had been translated into Bengali, Czech, Dutch, Finnish, French, German, Hebrew, Hungarian, Italian, Norwegian, Russian, Spanish, and Swedish.[36] He was born in a sharecropper's cabin in Mississippi and grew up in extreme poverty. In 1927, when he was nineteen, his family moved to Chicago, part of the "great migration" of Black Southerners to Northern cities. He became active in literary circles, and in 1933 was elected executive secretary of the Chicago branch of the John Reed Club. In 1937, he moved to New York City, where he became Harlem correspondent for the *Daily Worker*, and three years later, with the help of a Guggenheim fellowship, he published *Native Son*. The novel describes the asphyxiation, decapitation, and cremation of a white woman by a young Black man, Bigger Thomas, from the South Side of Chicago.

Thomas then tries and fails to extort money from the woman's wealthy parents, rapes and murders his Black girlfriend, gets caught in a manhunt, and is tried and sentenced to death. Nobody in America had ever published a story quite like that. Wright was thirty-one.[37]

Native Son was an immediate critical and financial success. It sold 215,000 copies in three weeks. Wright's autobiography, *Black Boy*, published in 1945, was also a hit, and sold 546,000 copies in its first year.[38] *Black Boy*'s intended subject is three systems of oppression: Southern racism, religious fundamentalism, and Communist Party doctrine, but the last part was dropped under pressure from the publisher and the selection committee of the Book-of-the-Month Club. Instead, Wright announced his break with Communism in a two-part article in *The Atlantic Monthly* in 1944, which was reprinted in 1949 in *The God That Failed*, a collection of essays by writers, including Arthur Koestler and André Gide, who had become disenchanted with Communism.[39]

Wright got to Paris through correspondence with the expatriate Gertrude Stein. In 1945, he reviewed Stein's memoir *Wars I Have Seen* and called it one of the best books on war he knew.[40] The review was duly shown to Stein, in Paris, who borrowed *Black Boy* from a U.S. Army library, read it, and had a friend write to inform Wright that she considered him "undeniably and self-evidently the most important writer in the States since herself."[41] Soon after, in an article for *The New York Times Magazine*, she mentioned Wright as someone who writes about Negroes "not as a Negro, but as a man."[42]

Wright was thrilled, because Stein's work, in particular, *Three Lives*, published in 1909, had been, along with Henry James and Joseph Conrad, one of his models when he started out.[43] He sent Stein more of his work; Stein continued to promote him. She told the *Chicago Defender*, a paper with a primarily Black readership, that Wright (in her words) "follows in the tradition of creative writers like Twain, Henry James, Howells, Walt Whitman and Gertrude Stein." "The theme is the Negro," she said, "but the treatment is that of a creative writer. The material is within him but he is outside of the material . . . With most Negro writers, the Negro is on top of the writer."[44] This is precisely what Trilling admired about Wright. "[T]he author," he wrote in his review of *Black Boy*, "does not wholly identify himself with his painful experience, does not, therefore, make himself a mere object of the reader's consciousness, does not make himself that different kind of human being, a 'sufferer.' He is not an object, he is a subject; he is the same kind of person as his reader, as complex, as free."[45]

In his letters to Stein, Wright expressed an interest in visiting Paris, and she encouraged him. With help from Claude Lévi-Strauss, then cultural attaché in the French consulate in New York, Wright secured a letter of invitation from the French government, which he needed to get a visa. And with his wife, Ellen, and their daughter, Julia, he arrived by boat at Le Havre on May 8, 1946. He took a train to Paris, where he was received as a celebrity.

Through a friend, Douglas Schneider, who was the American cultural attaché, Stein had arranged for the embassy to send two official limousines to pick up the Wrights and their luggage at the Gare Saint-Lazare. Though their train got in at 6:30 a.m., Stein was there as well. So were the critic Claude-Edmonde Magny and Maurice Nadeau, who was covering the arrival for *Combat*. Nadeau asked Wright whether the Black problem in the United States was close to a solution. "There is no black problem in the United States," Wright said, getting into the car. "There is a white problem."[46] He was echoing a principal thesis of the Swedish economist Gunnar Myrdal's two-volume analysis of American race relations, *An American Dilemma*, which had come out in 1944.[47]

The Wrights were driven down the Champs-Élysées and around the city, and over the next several weeks they were introduced to Parisian literary society. Richard paid a visit to Sylvia Beach, who had recommended *Native Son* to Simone de Beauvoir back in 1940. ("You like violent books," she told her; "well, here is a violent one.")[48] A reception was held in Wright's honor by the Ministry of Foreign Affairs; Gallimard hosted a party for him, where he met Maurice Merleau-Ponty, Jean Paulhan, and Marcel Duhamel, who would translate *Black Boy* into French.

Wright and Stein were an odd couple, and they quickly had a falling-out. Stein was ill with cancer; she died in July. But Wright continued to make his way. He saw Jean-Paul Sartre, whom he had already met during Sartre's visit to the United States in 1945; he met Beauvoir, Albert Camus, and André Gide. In October, he gave a talk at the Club Maintenant, where, exactly one year before, Sartre had delivered "Existentialisme est un humanisme."[49] The translation of *Black Boy* was serialized in *Les Temps Modernes* from January to June 1947, right alongside Sartre's major statement on writing and politics, "Qu'est-ce que la littérature?" After a brief return to the United States, where he showed Beauvoir around Harlem on her first American trip, Wright moved with his family to Paris, arriving in the summer of 1947. He lived there for the rest of his life.

"There is more freedom in one block of Paris than there is in the whole United States," Wright told a correspondent for the *Baltimore Afro-American*.[50] In an unpublished essay (the piece was turned down by *The Atlantic Monthly*), "I Choose Exile," he explained that he had tried to buy a house in Vermont and was refused when the owner discovered that his buyer, although wealthy and famous, was Black. But it was not only racism like this that had made him leave, he wrote. It was also because in the United States, "the desire for materialistic power dominates all."[51] Wright's critique of American racism, like Baldwin's, was always bound up with a judgment about the shallowness and spiritual poverty of American life.

About *his* trip to Paris, Baldwin said: "I was broke. I got to Paris with forty dollars in my pocket . . . I didn't know anyone and I didn't want to know anyone."[52] His circumstances were a little less dire. When he was living in the Village, he had met a photographer who worked with Avedon, Theodore Pelatowski, and they put together a book of prose and photographs of Harlem life. Baldwin was emulating a volume that Wright had created with Edwin Rosskum called *12 Million Black Voices*, published in 1941. But Baldwin and Pelatowski's project was turned down by publishers, and they abandoned it. Baldwin did get a grant for it, however, of fifteen hundred dollars from the Rosenwald Fellowship, and that was the money he used some of to buy a plane ticket to Paris. (A boat would have been a lot cheaper.) The forty dollars, or whatever the amount actually was, was what he had left.

And Baldwin's arrival was not unheralded. He had given his travel plans to at least one American friend there, and he was greeted at the train station in Paris by another American, Asa Benveniste, who rushed him off to the café Deux Magots on the Boulevard Saint-Germain, where Wright was sitting with yet another American, George Solomos. "Hey, boy," Wright is supposed to have said in greeting. Baldwin had landed on his feet. The Americans helped Baldwin find a room.[53] That night, or soon after, word having got around, a group of Americans woke him up and took him out for drinks. And virtually every account of Baldwin in Paris describes him in the company of American visitors and expatriates.[54] He had European friends as well, but—unlike

Wright, who shared a politics with the editors and writers at *Les Temps Modernes*—he had little use for French intellectuals and he did not socialize with them.

Benveniste and Solomos were meeting with Wright because they were starting up a magazine and wanted to get him to contribute.[55] Benveniste (who was from Brooklyn and was then calling himself Albert) and Solomos (who was from Detroit and had changed his name to Themistocles Hoetis) would both become friends of Baldwin's. The magazine they were planning was *Zero. Zero* published some important writers, and it lasted seven issues—not a bad showing, relatively. The first number appeared the following spring and included a short story by Wright, "The Man Who Killed a Shadow." Right after Wright's story was an essay by Baldwin, "Everybody's Protest Novel."

Baldwin chose a topic he had written about before, the protest novel, and a book he knew well, *Uncle Tom's Cabin.* (He seems to have started the essay while he was living in New York and to have promised it to *Partisan Review,* then rushed to complete it in time for the first issue of *Zero.*)[56] In his essay, Baldwin called Harriet Beecher Stowe's book the "cornerstone of American social protest fiction." Stowe created stock characters in order to enforce a political (or, he suggested, a theological) point about a social evil, slavery. That kind of fiction, he argued, produces stories that are "fantasies, connecting nowhere with reality, sentimental."[57] They are medieval in their morality—white and black, good and evil—and modern in their reduction of human beings to mechanical symbols.

The fantasy is the belief that people are what their social circumstances define them as, and this fails to recognize that circumstance is part of the dialectic of identity. "We take our shape, it is true, within and against that cage of reality bequeathed us at our birth," Baldwin explained;

> and yet it is precisely through our dependence on this reality that we are most endlessly betrayed. Society is held together by our need; we bind it together with legend, myth, coercion, fearing that without it we will be hurled into that void, within which, like the earth before the Word was spoken, the foundations of society are hidden. From this void—ourselves—it is the function of society to protect us; but it is only this void, our unknown selves, demanding, forever, a new act of creation, which can save us—"from

the evil that is in the world." With the same motion, at the same time, it is this toward which we endlessly struggle and from which, endlessly, we struggle to escape.[58]

Uncle Tom's Cabin locks its characters into the very dynamic, "whiteness" and goodness versus "blackness" and baseness, that the novel was ostensibly written to overcome: "The 'protest' novel, so far from being disturbing, is an accepted and comforting aspect of the American scene."[59] In the last paragraph, Baldwin argued that Wright had done the same thing in *Native Son*. Wright's novel, he argued, is "a continuation, a complement of that monstrous legend it was written to destroy. Bigger is Uncle Tom's descendant."[60]

Although it had recently been resuscitated by Edmund Wilson in *The New Yorker*, where he called it "a much more remarkable book than one had ever been allowed to suspect," *Uncle Tom's Cabin* had long ago become part of American popular culture, and its stereotypes were fair game.[61] *Native Son* was another matter. The argument that Bigger Thomas is a symptom rather than a person is made in the novel itself, by Thomas's pro bono Communist lawyer, Mr. Max, who delivers a lengthy speech at the trial in which he argues that industrial capitalism has created "mass man," a creature who is bombarded with images of consumerist bliss by movies and advertising, but is given no means for genuine fulfillment, and that the consequence is an inner condition of fear and rage which everyone shares, and for which Black men like Bigger Thomas are made the scapegoats.

Max's speech takes up twenty-three pages and is presented without irony. Wright probably believed much of it (although he supplied his own sociological analysis of his character in the pamphlet *How "Bigger" Was Born*, published the same year as *Native Son*). But the novel closes soon after with a broken conversation between Max and Thomas in the jail, in which Thomas insists in taking ownership of his actions. "I didn't know I was really alive in this world until I felt things hard enough to kill for 'em," he says.[62] Max reacts with horror, and the book ends. It is hard to see how this does not constitute an act of self-creation in the face of circumstance of the kind that Baldwin was calling for.

If Baldwin had second thoughts about publishing a criticism of Wright's novel in the pages of a magazine to whose editors Wright had introduced him, he did not dwell on them. In June, he republished

"Everybody's Protest Novel" in *Partisan Review*, which had a much larger and more influential readership than *Zero*. And in 1951, he published, also in *Partisan Review*, "Many Thousands Gone," an essay (written, oddly, as if from the point of view of a white person) that presented a much fuller critique of *Native Son*.*

Baldwin acknowledged that bitterness is a part of the psychology of Black Americans—"no American Negro exists who does not have his private Bigger Thomas living in the skull," he wrote—but it is only a part.[63] Black Americans also belong to a community, and *Native Son* fails to convey "any sense of Negro life as a continuing and complex group reality . . . Negroes are Americans and their destiny is the country's destiny. They have no other experience besides their experience on this continent and it is an experience which cannot be rejected, which yet remains to be embraced."[64] Baldwin's subtler point is what may have recommended his essay to the editors of *Partisan Review*. This was his characterization of *Native Son* as a relic of 1930s Popular Front ideology, in which the interests of Black Americans were identified with the interests of the working class. Mr. Max's speech, after all, is a Marxist condemnation of capitalism as a whole, and Baldwin called it "one of the most desperate performances in American fiction."[65]

The clash between Baldwin and Wright was overdetermined. Baldwin wanted to distinguish himself as a writer from Wright; Wright considered Baldwin an ambitious upstart. Baldwin distrusted Sartre and the *Temps Modernes* group and took the view *Partisan Review* did, which was that Wright was being used as a pawn by the French anti-American left.[66] Wright found homosexuality distasteful, and he could be mean and condescending; Baldwin no doubt grasped that, and he could be emotional and hypersensitive.[67]

Baldwin certainly did nothing to make the relationship easier. He later described coming late and somewhat drunk with a friend to a meeting of the Franco-American Friendship Group, an organization Wright had created.[68] He did not describe what he did there. According to the FBI report, however:

> On December 16, 1951, another Governmental agency conducting intelligence investigations reported that . . . Wright and his

---

* The title is from a folk song, "No More Auction Block," recorded by Paul Robeson in 1947.

group were the targets of attacks from one James Baldwin, a young Negro writer who was a student [*sic*] in Paris. Baldwin attacked the hatred themes of the [*sic*] Wright's writings and the attempt of the Franco-American Fellowship Group to Perpetuate [*sic*] "Uncle Tom Literature Methods."[69]

("Another Governmental agency" would have been the CIA—meaning that someone present was an informant, virtually a given in gatherings of American expatriates in postwar Paris.)

In 1953, Trilling selected "Many Thousands Gone" for the second issue, which he edited, of *Perspectives USA*, a journal started up by James Laughlin, the publisher of New Directions, and funded by the Ford Foundation. *Perspectives USA* was a nongovernmental exercise in cultural diplomacy, designed for distribution in Western Europe and published in French, Italian, and German as well as English. The contents emphasized American modernist writing and criticism—New Directions published Ezra Pound and William Carlos Williams—and it was sent to American embassies and consulates for free dissemination.[70]

Trilling paired Baldwin's essay with an essay by another Black expatriate, Richard Gibson, called "A No to Nothing," which had been first published in *The Kenyon Review*, on whose editorial board Trilling sat. Gibson argued that the reason there is not a single work by a Black American novelist that stands out as a masterpiece is because Black writers are pressured by what he called the "Professional Liberal" to write about "the Problem." That is all the Black writer is allowed to know. He referred to the "motley band of puerile imitators of Richard Wright—a doubtless sincere but defective thinker."[71] Trilling ran Baldwin's and Gibson's pieces together, under the title "Two Protests Against Protest"—duplicating, in an inverted way, the very typecasting that Gibson was complaining about. In the four years *Perspectives USA* came out, those two essays were the only writing it published by Black authors.[72]

In 1955, Baldwin reprinted both of his pieces on Wright as the opening chapters of *Notes of a Native Son*. That collection was the idea of Sol Stein, who put the essays together and arranged for the book to be published by Beacon Press as one of the first trade paperbacks—paperbound originals and reprints that were larger than the mass-market size of the Anchor paperbacks, a format that was Stein's innovation and an enormous commercial success.[73]

Notes of a Native Son is the book that made Baldwin's name as a public intellectual, and its appropriation of Wright's title makes explicit the claim that it is Baldwin's story, not Bigger Thomas's, that represents the reality of African American identity. In the title essay, Baldwin describes his realization, coming home from his father's funeral, that he shared the emotion that had crippled his father's life: hatred. And he recollects an encounter with a waitress who refused to serve him in a New Jersey diner. "I had been ready to commit murder," he wrote—his Bigger Thomas moment.[74] It is necessary, he now realizes, to accept life as it is, which means accepting that there is always injustice. It should also be possible to fight against injustice, but that fight begins in keeping one's heart "free of hatred and despair."[75]

Baldwin's criticism of *Native Son* belonged to a shift in the way writers and intellectuals thought about race after 1945, but it also played a part in revising Wright's reputation. Baldwin effectively repealed the critical verdict of white writers such as Stein and Trilling. He made Wright the victim of his own victimhood. When the French writer Michel Fabre came to the United States to do research for a biography of Wright in 1962, two years after Wright's death, he found that few people were interested in him. Among college students, he said, the "idol of the moment" was James Baldwin.[76]

3.

The boat on which Claude Lévi-Strauss, Victor Serge, and André Breton escaped from Europe in 1941, the *Capitaine Paul-Lemerle*, took them to the French colony of Martinique in the Lesser Antilles. Martinique was a transit point from which refugee passengers were expected to make their separate ways to their havens. For Serge, this was Mexico. For Lévi-Strauss and Breton, it was New York City, which Lévi-Strauss reached via Puerto Rico and Breton via the Dominican Republic.

The trip from Marseille took four weeks, and conditions on the boat were crowded and unhygienic. Serge called it "a sort of floating concentration camp."[77] When they arrived in Fort-de-France, the capital of Martinique, on April 20, all but three of the two hundred and twenty-two passengers were treated as prisoners, and either interned in a former leper colony called Le Lazaret—"one more concentration camp, scorching hot, without drinkable water, guarded by tall child-like Negroes, managed by thieves of policemen," Serge described it—or effectively placed under house arrest with their movements restricted and monitored.[78] Lévi-Strauss was one of the exceptions; he explained in *Tristes Tropiques* that this was because he knew the captain from an earlier voyage to Brazil. But Breton, his wife, Jacqueline, and their five-year-old daughter, Aube, were sent to Le Lazaret.[79]

The French had been in Martinique since 1635 running sugar plantations, the great source of wealth in the Caribbean archipelago. In 1664, the island was made a possession of the Crown and thus officially part of the Empire. During the Second World War, although it was blockaded by American destroyers, the island was governed by a Vichyite, Admiral Georges Robert, and the local authorities regarded the refugees as undesirables, and resented the decision of the French government to permit them to emigrate through Martinique.

That policy had been adopted not as a way of saving lives, but as a way of getting Jews, particularly German and Eastern European Jews who had fled to France after 1933, out of the country. It was a repatriation scheme, and it was humane only by contrast with what was to come. The policy went into effect in the winter of 1941, and the window stayed open just a short time. A combination of colonial resistance; pressure from the Americans, who worried about German spies getting through; and a change from a practice of allowing Jews to emigrate to one of transporting them to camps all led to the abandonment of the policy. By June, the Martinique route was closed.[80]

After a week in Le Lazaret, Breton and his family were allowed to take lodgings in Fort-de-France while they waited for their boat out. The family was assigned police escorts. (Breton was not a Jew, only a Surrealist poet, but he was assured that Surrealists were not wanted in Martinique, either.) One day, Breton walked into a local shop to buy a ribbon for his daughter and happened to see a magazine in the window. It was the first issue of a local literary journal, *Tropiques*. Breton began leafing through it and was stunned to find himself reading poetry that sounded like Rimbaud. The poem (later published as "Les Pur-Sang") was in fact prefaced with an epigraph from Rimbaud, and its author was one of the editors of *Tropiques*, Aimé Césaire.

The shopkeeper turned out to know Césaire. She arranged a meeting, and for the rest of the month Breton spent on the island, he and Césaire were regular companions. Césaire gave Breton a tour of Martinique, and they discussed Caribbean literature and folklore. Césaire later said that the time with Breton was "determinative. If I am what I am, I think it is largely because of this meeting with André Breton."[81]

Before Breton left, Césaire gave him a copy of a long poem he had published in 1939 in a Parisian journal called *Volontés*. The poem was "Cahier d'un retour au pays natal"—"Notebook of a Return to the Native Land." Breton admired it, and when he got to New York, he arranged for it to be translated. He also wrote an essay on Césaire, "Un Grand Poète Noir," which appeared as the preface to the English translation, published in 1947 in a bilingual edition, and to an edition published in Paris the same year.[82] The *Cahier* became a central text of the postwar anticolonial movement and a key articulation of the concept of *négritude*.

The term *négritude* originated in Paris in the 1930s. The French, like the British, had a practice of plucking out talented youth from their colonial populations and educating them in the metropole, with the goal of making them, in effect, nonwhite French persons. It is, looking back, an extraordinary example of the complacency of the imperialist mentality. The French and British somehow imagined that the most intelligent colonial subjects could be assimilated to a racist political and social system by giving them a Western education. What their educations enabled many of those subjects to see, of course, was the hypocrisy of European attitudes about race.

Césaire was plucked out of Martinique. He was born in Basse-Pointe, a small town in the north of the island. In school, he showed a gift for languages, and in 1931, when he was eighteen, he was sent to Paris to study at the Lycée Louis-le-Grand. He had been there only a week or two when he met Léopold Senghor, a student from Senegal. They became friends, and the first things they discussed, according to Césaire, were questions of identity: "Who am I? Who are we? Who are we in this white world?"[83]

Members of a Martinican family in Paris—three sisters, Jane, Paulette, and Andrée Nardal, and their cousins, the Achilles—hosted bilingual gatherings of Black writers and intellectuals, including many of the major figures of the Harlem Renaissance: Hughes, Cullen, Alain Locke, Jean Toomer, and the Jamaican writer Claude McKay. Césaire found these writers inspiring because they had affirmed their authorial identities without assimilating.[84] To a French colonial, this was a novel approach.

Césaire excelled at Louis-le-Grand and entered the École Normale Supérieure in 1935.[85] With Senghor and Léon Damas, who was from French Guinea and who, like Senghor, was studying at the Sorbonne, he founded a review, *L'Étudiant Noir*. The paper called for a revolution in race relations. The issue was not equality. The issue was freedom. "What does Black youth want?" Césaire wrote in the first issue. "To live. But to live truly, one must be grounded. The actor is the man who does not live truly . . . Black youth does not want to play any role. It wants to be grounded . . . It wants neither enslavement nor assimilation. It wants emancipation."[86] *Négritude* was a name for that ground. "To make the revolution," Césaire wrote, it was necessary "to seize within us the immediate negro, to plant our negritude like a beautiful tree until it bears its most authentic fruits."[87]

Négritude was therefore in the first instance a call for solidarity. Wherever they came from, Black students shared the experience of racialization and the experience of colonialism. The genius of the term was that it carried both associations: *nègre* means "black," but it is also used as a pejorative, like the n-word in English. ("Noir" would be the word corresponding to "Negro.") Césaire and his friends were reappropriating a slur from white French speakers, and in that enterprise, they were also playing off another meaning of *nègre*: "ghostwriter." "The word '*nègre*' had been thrown at us as an insult," Césaire later said, "and we picked it up and turned it into a positive concept."[88] (Césaire even wanted to call the review *L'Étudiant Nègre*, but he was unpersuasive.)[89]

Césaire spent the summer of 1936 in Martinique—the *retour* of his poem. He failed the *agrégation* but wrote a master's essay on African American poetry.[90] In 1939, after publishing his poem in France, he was back in Martinique teaching at the Lycée Schœlcher in Fort-de-France. (Victor Schœlcher was a nineteenth-century French abolitionist.) With his wife, Suzanne Roussy Césaire, and a friend, René Ménil—both had studied in Paris, and were now also teachers at the lycée—he founded *Tropiques*, the magazine that led to the meeting with Breton. (The owner of the shop Breton went into to buy the ribbon was Ménil's sister.) The magazine called for a cultural awakening in Martinique, but its literary model was European modernism. It was also anti-Vichy and was banned by Admiral Robert in 1943.[91]

When Césaire later spoke of that meeting as "TRÈS IMPOR-TANTE," he did not mean just that he was awed by Breton's poetic sensibility, although he was, or that Breton's patronage launched his career, although it did.[92] He meant that Breton confirmed the validity of a stylistic choice he had made.

The subject of *Cahier* is the cultural dislocation of a French-educated Black man from the islands. The poet finds himself between two worlds, belonging completely to neither, and the poem is the record of his struggle to recover his native identity. As a verbal artifact, it also enacts that problem, because the poet is someone who writes under the influence of nineteenth-century white French poets such as Rimbaud and Lautréamont. The poem's very title alludes unavoidably to one of the foundational texts of Western civilization, Homer's *Odyssey*.[93] The poet is embedded within the tradition he is trying to escape or overcome.

What Breton made Césaire realize was that he was producing Surrealism in the same way that (as Césaire put it) Monsieur Jourdain in Molière's play is producing prose—without being fully conscious of it.[94] Césaire of course knew about the Surrealists, but he had not thought of them as offering a solution to his identity problem. Breton encouraged him to see that Surrealism was subversive of classical style, was subversive of language itself. "It was like dynamite to the French language," as Césaire later explained it.

> I said to myself, "If I apply the surrealist approach to my particular situation, I can call up the forces of the unconscious." For me, this was the call to Africa. I told myself: "It is true that superficially we are French, we are marked by French customs. We are marked by Cartesianism, by French rhetoric, but if one breaks through this, if one descends to the depths, one can discover the fundamental African."[95]

What would "the fundamental African" look like? This became a key passage. In the first English translation:

> those who invented neither gunpowder nor compass
> those who tamed neither steam nor electricity
> those who explored neither the sea nor the sky

but those without whom the earth would not be the earth
gibbosity all the more beneficent, as the earth
of the desert is even more earth
silo where is ripened and preserved what is earthiest in earth

my niggerness [*négritude*] is not a stone, its deafness thrown against
    the clamor of the day
my niggerness is not a speck of dead water on the dead eye of earth
my niggerness is neither a tower nor a cathedral
it thrusts into the red flesh of the soil
it thrusts into the warm flesh of the sky
it digs under the opaque dejection of its rightful patience

Hurrah for the royal *Kailcedrat* [an African tree]!
Hurrah for those who invented nothing
for those who have never discovered
for those who have never conquered
but, in seizures, they deliver themselves to the essence of all things
ignorant of surfaces, but taken by the very movement of things
not caring to conquer, but playing the game of the world
truly the elder sons of the world
porous to all the breath of the world
fraternal space of all the breath of the world
bed without drain of all the waters in the world
spark of the ancient fire of the world
flesh or the flesh of the world
panting with the very movement of the world [96]

A nontechnological people. A people that has never invented or explored. A people whose identity is tied to the earth, and who relate to the world in a playful and erotic way. By harnessing this essence, a new Black culture could be formed. "It is not a question of going back, of the resurrection of an African past that we have come to know and respect," Suzanne Césaire explained in *Tropiques*; ". . . it is a question of becoming aware of the formidable cluster of diverse energies that we have hitherto locked up in ourselves . . . This earth, ours, can only be what we want it to be."[97]

But was this unlocked essence the product of race or of circumstance?

4.

Césaire's poem addresses a question that sits at the bottom of the problem of identity: Does it come from within or without? Within or without, *pour-soi* or *en-soi*, is also the fundamental choice in Sartrean existentialism. When Césaire wrote that "the actor is the man who does not live truly" because he is playing from a script written by someone else, he was defining inauthenticity in the way Sartre would define it in *L'Être et le néant*. When he described *négritude* as "the flesh of the world / panting with the very movement of the world," he was using the language of phenomenology: Blackness as a way of being. For that matter, when Baldwin wrote about the "void, our unknown selves, demanding, forever, a new act of creation," he was using a Sartrean formulation as well.

So it is not surprising that Sartre was drawn to the issues of racism and colonialism. In the fall of 1944, soon after the Liberation, but before knowledge of the death camps was widespread, Sartre wrote a book on anti-Semitism, published in 1946 under the title *Réflexions sur la question juive*. (The title weirdly evokes the German *Judenfrage*, the language of the Final Solution.) The book was severely criticized, and not just by Jewish writers, who found Sartre a little clueless about Judaism. But everything Sartre did in those years was an event, so the book was talked about.[98]

The sentence cited in virtually every review and commentary was: "The Jew is one whom other men consider a Jew."[99] Sartre offered his standard analysis of this predicament. As he had put it in *L'Être et le néant*: "there is freedom only in a situation, and there is a situation only through freedom. Human-reality everywhere encounters resistances and obstacles it has not created, but these resistances and obstacles have meaning only in and through the free choice which human-reality *is*."[100] In the case of the Jew, he "is in the situation of a Jew because he lives in the midst of a society that takes him for a Jew." The way to overcome this is not to deny it or erase it, but to own it. "Jewish authenticity consists in choosing oneself *as Jew*—that is, in realizing one's Jewish condition."[101] The ultimate goal of embracing Jewishness is to overcome it.

Sartre was quick to apply this argument to *négritude*. A year after *Réflexions sur la question juive*, he published a preface to *La Nouvelle Poésie nègre et malgache de langue française*. This anthology was edited by Léopold Senghor (Damas had published a similar anthology a year before, but it did not get much attention), and it included poets from

the Antilles, Madagascar, and French Africa. It was an attempt to identify a pan-African culture, Senghor's idea of *négritude*.

Sartre's preface was called "Orphée noire," and it is directed at the
white reader who stands on the brink of decolonization. "I want you to
feel, as I do, the shock of being seen," Sartre says.

> . . . For the white man has, for three thousand years, enjoyed the
> privilege of seeing without being seen. He was pure gaze . . .
> We, who were once divine-right Europeans, were already feeling
> our dignity crumbling beneath the gaze of the Americans and
> Soviets . . . At least we were hoping to recover a little of our gran-
> deur in the menial eyes of the Africans. But there are no menial
> eyes any longer: there are wild, free gazes that judge our earth.[102]

A Jew can deny being Jewish, he said, but a Black person cannot deny
being Black. The Black person is therefore "forced into authenticity."[103]

But this was all in order to enable Sartre to reach the conclusion that
négritude is only a stage—just as authentic Jewishness is only a stage.
Négritude may be an "anti-racism racism," he said, but it is a racism. It
can therefore be only a step on the path toward "the abolition of racial
differences."[104] In Hegelian terms, *négritude* is "the weaker upbeat in a
dialectical progression: the theoretical and practical affirmation of white
supremacy is the thesis, the position of negritude as the antithetical
value is the moment of negativity. But that negative movement is not sufficient in itself and the blacks who use it know this very well; they know
its aim is to prepare the synthesis or realization of the human in a society
without races. Thus negritude is bent upon self-destruction; it is transitional, not final; a means, not an end."[105] Sartre believed about ethnic identity what Clement Greenberg believed about abstraction: under socialism,
it would disappear. The writer who thought through the implications of
Sartre's writing on identity most fully was Frantz Fanon.

5.

Fanon, too, was from Martinique. He was twelve years younger than
Césaire; he had, in fact, been Césaire's student at the Lycée Schœlcher.
His route to the metropole was a little different, however. After Mar-
tinique was liberated from Vichy control, he fought in Europe and was

wounded in an engagement near Besançon. He was awarded the Croix de Guerre. As a veteran, he had the opportunity to continue his education in France. He decided to study medicine in Lyon (supposedly because he thought there were too many Black people in Paris).[106] He chose psychiatry as his specialty. He read literature and philosophy, and attended lectures by Maurice Merleau-Ponty, who taught at the Université de Lyon until 1948. (Fanon was too shy to introduce himself.) And he wrote his first book, *Peau noire, masques blancs* (*Black Skin, White Masks*).[107]

Fanon's title is another play on *nègre* as ghostwriter, a disguised author. Like Césaire's *Cahier d'un retour au pays natal*, the book is an analysis of Blackness as lived experience—*Erlebnis*, to use the phenomenological term. Fanon published a chapter in *Esprit*, a left-wing Catholic journal edited by Emmanuel Mounier. *Esprit* had connections with the publishing house Éditions du Seuil, and Fanon's manuscript ended up in the hands of an editor there, Francis Jeanson, who also happened to be the managing editor of *Les Temps Modernes*. The book came out in the summer of 1952 with a twenty-three-page preface by Jeanson and was largely ignored.[108] Its impact would come down the road.

Fanon wrote as a psychiatrist. He argued that conditions of racism and colonialism produced pathologies. He thought that psychoanalysis was an inappropriate method for understanding them, because psychoanalysis looks for psychic conflicts in early family life to explain neuroses, and for colonials, neuroses are the result of an *adult* experience of racism. "What I want to do," Fanon wrote, "is help the black man to free himself of the arsenal of complexes that has been developed by the colonial environment."[109]

The dominant culture was suffused with negative definitions of Blackness, from the association of Blackness with evil to representations in cultural products such as the Tarzan movies. Racial invidiousness could be found even in the well-meaning patronage of writers like Breton, who wrote of Césaire: "Here is a black man who handles the French language as no white man can today."[110] When Breton looked at Césaire, in other words, what he saw was a man with black skin. When a person with black skin is looked at by a person whose skin is white, Fanon argued, the Black person sees himself the way a white person sees him—what W. E. B. Du Bois called "double-consciousness." "*It is the racist who creates his inferior,*" Fanon wrote, citing Sartre.[111] He called this source of oppression *le regard blanc*—the white gaze.[112]

Still, Fanon thought that we are inescapably formed by the gaze of others. "Man is human only to the extent to which he tries to impose his existence on another man in order to be recognized by him," he wrote; the human world is "a world of reciprocal recognitions."[113]* What prevents true reciprocity is the damage caused to both parties by racism. Its victims are not in a position psychologically to participate in the act of recognition. In the end, Fanon's hope was irenic: it was for love to prevail. "[T]rue, authentic love," he wrote, "—wishing for others what one postulates for oneself, when that postulation unites the permanent values of human reality [that is, *Dasein*]—entails the mobilization of psychic drives basically free of unconscious conflicts."[114] On the last page of his book: "Superiority? Inferiority? Why not the quite simple attempt to touch the other, to feel the other, to explain the other to myself?"[115] This is exactly what Baldwin thought.

Fanon did disagree with Sartre about *négritude.* When he read the pages about *négritude* as racism in "Orphée noire," he wrote, "I felt that I had been robbed of my last chance . . . Help had been sought from a friend of the colored peoples, and that friend had found no better response than to point out the relativity of what they [the poets of *négritude*] were doing." And he put his finger on where Sartre's Marxism undercut his existentialism. If *négritude* is only a stage in the dialectic, he pointed out, then it is not an action *pour-soi*: "it is not I who make a meaning for myself, but it is the meaning that was already there, preexisting, waiting for me. It is not out of my bad nigger's misery, my bad nigger's teeth, my bad nigger's hunger that I will shape a torch with which to burn down the world, but it is the torch that was already there, waiting for that turn of history." Fanon refused to accept this. "I am not a potentiality of something," he said; "I am wholly what I am."[116]

Yet Fanon, too, saw that if the goal is color-blindness, *négritude* cannot be a permanent condition. *Peau noir, masques blancs* was written to liberate nonwhite people from being defined by the colonial situation,

---

* The first sentence is taken from Alexandre Kojève, *Introduction à la lecture de Hegel* (Paris: Gallimard, 1947), 19, based on Kojève's seminars. Kojève is glossing Hegel's *Phänomenologie des Geistes,* which Fanon cites. That work is also, of course, in the background of Sartre's *Réflexions sur la question juive.*

and *négritude* was, after all, dependent on that situation. Fanon agreed with Sartre that when colonialism disappeared, then race as a marker of identity would disappear along with it. But then where would identity come from?

6.

"My friends were Algerians and Africans," Baldwin said much later about his time in Paris. "They are the people who befriended me when I arrived here broke. In a sense, we saved each other, we lived together."[117] In fact, in an interview in 1959, after his return to the United States, Baldwin was explicit about the distance he felt from the Africans he met in Paris. "All discussions were on politics," he complained. "You could never get into anything else. They disgusted me, I think . . . They hated America, were full of racial stories, held their attitudes largely on racial grounds. Politically, they knew very little about it. Whenever I was with an African, we would both be uneasy. On what level to talk? The terms of our life were so different, we almost needed a dictionary."[118]

And shortly after arriving in France, he had written an essay, "The Negro in Paris," about how difficult it was for Black Americans to communicate with Africans. "They face each other, the Negro and the African, over a gulf of three hundred years—an alienation too vast to be conquered in an evening's good will, too heavy and too double-edged ever to be trapped in speech," he wrote.[119] He was echoing a poem by Countee Cullen:

> One three centuries removed
> From the scenes his father loved
> Spicy grove, cinnamon tree
> What is Africa to me?[120]

Richard Wright, on the other hand, did associate with French Black people. Not long after arriving in Paris, he met Césaire at the home of Léopold Senghor.[121] After he moved to France permanently, he joined with them in founding in 1947 the journal *Présence Africaine*. By then, the revolutionaries of *L'Étudiant Noir* had metamorphosed into statesmen. Césaire was the mayor of Fort-de-France, elected with Communist support (Fanon worked on the campaign), and he was in Paris serving in the National Assembly as the deputy from Martinique. Senghor was the deputy from Senegal. Léon Damas would be elected deputy from Guiana in 1948.

The figure behind *Présence Africaine*, however, was Alioune Diop, a Senegalese senator in the French Parliament. *Présence Africaine* had no ideology, Diop announced in the first issue. And, as the Comité de Patronage listed on the masthead indicated—the names included Sartre, Camus, Mounier, Gide, Césaire, Senghor, and Wright—it was not anti-European. It was cosmopolitan.[122] Its goal was, in Diop's words, to "define the African's creativity and hasten his integration into the modern world."[123]

In 1953, Wright was visited in Paris by two friends, Dorothy Pizer Padmore and George Padmore. He was from Trinidad; she was British, and they lived together, unmarried, in London. They had been encouraging Wright to visit Africa, and now Wright became convinced. George Padmore was a close adviser to Kwame Nkrumah, the prime minister of the Gold Coast, and he arranged for Nkrumah to write a "To whom it may concern letter" promising to look after Wright. Wright used the letter along with other documents with the Foreign Office in London, and after some delay he was granted permission to make the trip. He planned to stay four months; he lasted just two and a half.[124]

The Gold Coast had been an official colony of the United Kingdom since 1874. When Wright visited, from June to September 1953, it had attained limited self-government. Nkrumah was the leader of an independence party, the Convention People's Party (CPP), and in July, he delivered a speech (composed with advice from Padmore) before the legislature calling for full sovereignty. Nkrumah called it his "Motion of Destiny" speech. Wright was present as a spectator.

Nkrumah was educated in the United States in the 1930s. He had spent summers in Harlem, and in the speech, he predicted that independence for the Gold Coast would serve as an "inspiration" to Black Americans fighting segregation. His speech was the first step in the creation of the independent Republic of Ghana, which was proclaimed in 1957—the first sub-Saharan colony to achieve democratic self-government. Nkrumah was elected its first president in 1960.[125]

The book that came out of Wright's visit to the Gold Coast was *Black Power*—the first use of what would become a slogan in the United States after 1965. Like Wright's other nonfiction, it is an unstable mix of journalistic observation, first-person anecdote, and subjective reaction, and the reactions tend to color the observations.[126] Wright used lines from Cullen's poem asking "What is Africa to me?" as an epigraph, and that question dominates the book.

Wright was excited by African demands for independence. It was a sentiment he could get behind. "At a time when the Western world grew embarrassed at the sound of the word 'freedom,'" he wrote, "these people knew that it meant the right to shape their own destiny as they wished."[127] But when he got there, he found the Africans he interacted with either subservient and evasive—damaged, he concluded, by the experience of colonialism—or childlike and superstitious, mesmerized by concepts such as juju. He often found himself, in exasperation, behaving around Africans exactly like a British colonial.

He told Peter Abrahams, a Black South African writer who was in the Gold Coast doing research for his own piece, that there was too much casual sex in Africa.[128] The sight of boys dancing together made him uncomfortable: he wondered whether the British had brought male homosexuality to Africa.[129] He saw African women dancing, and he recognized the rhythms from his childhood in the South, but they meant nothing to him. "Never in my life had I been able to dance more than a few elementary steps," Wright confessed, "and the carrying of even the simplest tune had always been beyond me . . . [W]hat had bewildered me about Negro dance expression in the United States now bewildered me in the same way in Africa."[130] Virtually all of his encounters with African culture left him bewildered. "I had understood nothing," he wrote after seeing a funeral procession. "I was black and they were black, but my blackness did not help me."[131]

He doubted the capacity of Africans to govern themselves in the modern world. "[T]he tempo of progress of the West has qualitatively made the difference between the Western and non-Western world almost absolute," he thought. "The distance between tribal man and the West is greater than the distance between God and Western man of the sixteenth century."[132] "To think about Africa is to think about man's naïve attempt to understand and manipulate the universe of life in terms of magical religion," he decided, and he ended his book with a "letter" to Nkrumah. Africans, Wright informed him, were a primitive people. The only path to modernization for them was authoritarian rule.

Our people must be made to walk, forced draft, into the twentieth century! The direction of their lives, the duties that they must
perform to overcome the stagnancy of tribalism, the sacrifices that
must yet be made—all of this must be placed under firm social
discipline . . . AFRICAN LIFE MUST BE MILITARIZED![133]

A little Bolshevism was creeping back into Wright's thinking.

Later on, Nkrumah would find Wright's words congenial.[134] But in
1953, before Ghana had achieved independence, he was wary of Wright
and kept his distance. Wright, after all, had nothing at stake in African
politics, and Nkrumah was aware that almost as soon as he arrived,
Wright had made contact with officials in the United States Information Service in Accra, and that he often socialized with them. Officials
in the CPP, Nkrumah's party, presumably on instructions, would not
talk to Wright.

Wright felt snubbed. He was impressed by Nkrumah, a Black man
who commanded the world stage. Few Black men in the United States
had done that: Frederick Douglass in the nineteenth century, Du Bois
and Paul Robeson in the twentieth. But Wright found the frenzy that
Nkrumah aroused in his followers alarming, and he was not reassured
about what he considered Communist tendencies in the CPP. The day
before he left, he paid a visit to the American consul, William Cole, and
reported his suspicions, leaving behind a four-page memo that included
a description of the method George Padmore used to disguise his letters
to Nkrumah in order to evade government censorship in Britain. Once
he got back to Paris, Wright visited the American embassy and offered
further information about Padmore's secret role in Gold Coast politics,
along with evidence of covert Communist designs in the CPP.[135] Padmore was Wright's friend, the man who had made his trip to Ghana
possible.

On December 28, 1954, the Colombo Powers—India, Pakistan,
Ceylon, Burma, and Indonesia, so called because they initially met in
Colombo, the capital of Ceylon—announced a conference of Asian and
African nations to be held in Bandung on the island of Java, in Indonesia. Representatives came from twenty-nine nations, home to 1.3 billion
people. It was the first such gathering in history. By virtue of cultural
differences, isolationist policies, and ties to different Western imperial

powers, those nations had almost no history of alliances or collaboration. They now wished to ratify their decision to give their common
concerns priority in international relations. They did not wish to be client
states.[136] Wright was eager to witness the event, and he began looking
for funding. He ended up getting it from the CIA.

Wright approached the Paris office of the Congress for Cultural Freedom (CCF), an organization that promoted liberal anti-Communism.
Wright didn't know that the CCF was covertly funded by—in fact,
was entirely a creature of—the CIA, although he does appear to have
assumed that it had some sort of State Department sponsorship. In
exchange for travel funds and a stipend, he agreed to let the congress
publish any articles he wrote in the various European publications it
operated. He had already published a portion of *Black Power* in one of
them, *Preuves*, in France. He would publish excerpts from his Bandung
book in *Preuves* (two pieces) and three other CCF magazines: *Encounter*
in Britain, *Cuadernos* in Spain, and *Der Monat* in Germany.[137]

The Bandung conference began on April 17, 1955. The principal
common interest was independence from Western powers—"Asia for
Asians." The conference was anticipated with anxiety by some officials
in the U.S. government, who worried that it gave Communists an opportunity to commandeer the Third World stage. (The Soviet Union
was not invited, but the People's Republic of China, then an ally of the
Soviets, was—despite the fact that the PRC had recently invaded Ti-
bet.)[138] In the United States, there were allusions in the anti-Communist
press to a coming race war and the old fear of "the Yellow Peril."[139]

In the event, racial solidarity and nonalignment were not significant
themes of the conference. There were expressions of hostility to Communism, and considerable pro-Western sentiment. The new nations
understood that they needed mutual defense pacts with the Western
powers (some were already members of SEATO). And although there
were hopes of establishing economic agreements among themselves,
most nations were not sufficiently developed to form a trading bloc. But
the conference was a success both in negative terms—neither China nor
India, which had been expected to dominate the proceedings, did—
and positively as an assertion of political will on the part of what had
been named, just a few years before, the Third World.[140]

Still, the belief that Bandung stood for anti-white racial solidarity
with an anti-Western animus somehow survived the conference, and

Wright was one of the people responsible.[141] He spent three weeks in Indonesia. The CCF had arranged for a local journalist, Mochtar Lubis, the chief editor of the daily *Indonesia Raya*, to meet Wright at the airport in Jakarta, and Lubis helped him connect with local writers and political figures.[142] The book Wright produced, *The Color Curtain*, was published in 1956 with a preface by Gunnar Myrdal. The Cold War metaphor Wright adapted for his title suggested a global confrontation based on race rather than ideology, and that was how he interpreted Bandung. On the first day, he wrote, he was stunned to see a white journalist being given a hard time getting his credentials while he was waved through. This struck him as a display of pure racism, and he seems to have carried this impression with him throughout the visit.

The opening address at Bandung was delivered by Sukarno, the president of Indonesia, which had gained independence from the Netherlands only six years before. It was hardly anti-American. Sukarno informed the delegates that 180 years before, on April 18, 1775, Paul Revere had made his famous midnight ride, the start of "the first successful anti-colonial war in history."[143] If some Western observers saw racial homogeneity in the conference, Africans and Asians saw the opposite. For them, the potential for interstate discord was much more obvious than the potential for unity. And this was Sukarno's chief point. "Our ways of life are different," he said.

> Our national characters, or colours or motifs—call it what you will—are different. Our racial stock is different, and even the colour of our skin is different . . . All of us, I am certain, are united by more important things than those which superficially divide us. We are united, for instance, by a common detestation of colonialism . . . We are united by a common detestation of racialism. And we are united by a common determination to preserve and stabilise peace in the world.[144]

This was Wright's gloss of the speech:

> Sukarno was appealing to race and religion; they were the only realities in the lives of the men before him that he could appeal to. And, as I sat listening, I began to sense a deep and organic relation here in Bandung between race and religion, *two of the*

most powerful and irrational forces in human nature . . . [A] ra-
cial consciousness, evoked by the attitudes and practices of the
West, had slowly blended with a defensive religious feeling; here,
in Bandung, the two had combined into one: *a racial and religious*
system of identification manifesting itself in an emotional nationalism
which was now leaping state boundaries and melting and merging,
one into the other.[145]

As he had in the Gold Coast, Wright doubted the capacity of these
new nations for self-government. "ALL THE MEN THERE REPRE-
SENTED GOVERNMENTS THAT HAD ALREADY SEIZED
POWER AND THEY DID NOT KNOW WHAT TO DO WITH
IT," he concluded. It was the West's fault that "this unwieldy lump of
humanity" was now unified in tribal anger against it. The situation
was nothing like the situation in the United States. "I found that many
Asians hated the West with an absoluteness that no American Negro
could ever muster," Wright wrote. "Once his particular grievances were
redressed, the Negro reverted to a normal Western outlook."[146]

Wright thought he was seeing the postcolonial equivalent of mass
man. If modern technology was grafted onto these premodern societies, he warned, the outcome would be totalitarianism. Bandung was
"THE LAST CALL OF THE WESTERNIZED ASIANS TO THE
MORAL CONSCIENCE OF THE WEST!" If the West did not answer the call, "China then could walk as a fellow guest into an anti-
Western house built by reaction to colonialism and racialism . . . It was
a gift from the skies." The Chinese would exploit the Asian hatred of
colonialism, and they could count on the fact that people "will give
up their freedom to save their freedom."[147] This was not far from the
rationale for American intervention in Vietnam, already under way.

Wright was one of a number of commentators who had misunderstood the meaning of Bandung, as the *New York Times* Asia correspondent Tillman Durdin wrote in a review of *The Color Curtain*. "The
conference did not represent . . . the consolidation of an Asia-Africa
front against the West," Durdin pointed out. "It was not . . . a manifestation of the solidarity and resurgence of the colored peoples of the
world against the whites." Wright "overplays the color angle and attributes to Asians and Africans uniformity of attitude on color that does
not exist."[148]

After a portion of *The Color Curtain* was serialized in *Encounter* as "Indonesia Notebook," Wright's Indonesian host, Mochtar Lubis, sent a letter to the editor. "Mr. Wright wrote with great feeling and passion," he said, "but I am afraid while he was here in Indonesia he had been looking through 'coloured-glasses,' and he had sought behind every attitude he met colour and racial feelings." The people Wright interviewed and quoted, Lubis reported, "are all amazed to read Mr. Wright's Notebook in which Mr. Wright quotes them saying things which they never had said, or to which they did not put meaning as accepted by Mr. Wright."[149]

Whatever its meaning or its practical achievements, Bandung had international resonance, and it inspired the editors of *Présence Africaine* to mount a conference in Paris for Black writers and intellectuals. This took place in September 1956. Diop, Senghor, Césaire, Fanon, Abrahams, Wright, Hughes, and Baldwin were all there.

7.

The 1er Congrès des Écrivains et Artistes Noirs opened on the morning of September 19, 1956, in the Amphithéâtre Descartes at the Sorbonne, and lasted four days. Six hundred people, white and Black, attended the opening session. It was very hot inside the room.

Since 1919, there had been five Pan-African Congresses—in Paris, London (twice), New York, and Manchester. The Manchester Congress, in 1945, is where Padmore and Nkrumah first met. (Padmore was invited to the Paris Congress, but was ill, and did not attend.)[150] The main force behind those earlier congresses was W. E. B. Du Bois. The main force behind the Paris Congress was Alioune Diop. Diop had attended the Bandung conference as an observer, and he aspired to create a cultural Bandung in Paris. His idea was to produce a survey of Africanist literature and arts from around the world—a kind of inventory of the African's cultural capital. He thought that the emphasis on culture distinguished his congress from the earlier ones, where the focus had been politics.[151]

The sixty-three delegates who met in Paris came from twenty-four countries, including the United States; twenty-seven were scheduled to speak.[152] Wright was involved in the planning, and he proposed inviting a number of African American writers, although, in the end, none of them attended. He did inform the American embassy of his concerns about the Communist tendencies of some of the Americans whose names had been mentioned, and the U.S. government may have tried to affect the choice of representatives.[153]

Langston Hughes, who had been called before Joseph McCarthy's Senate subcommittee three years earlier, was not invited, but he was in the audience. Du Bois, who was not yet a Communist but who was pro-Soviet, was invited. In 1951, however, the U.S. government had charged a group called the Peace Information Center, of which Du Bois was chair, with failure to register as the agent of a foreign government—viz., the Soviet Union. Although the Justice Department lost the case, Du Bois's passport was revoked.[154]

Du Bois was eighty-eight. Along with others unable to attend, including Pablo Picasso and Claude Lévi-Strauss, he sent a message, which Diop read aloud on the first day of the congress. "I am not present at your meeting today because the United States government will not grant me a passport for travel abroad," he said. He added: "Any Negro-American who travels abroad today must either not discuss race conditions in the United States or say the sort of thing which our State Department wishes the world to believe."[155]

Du Bois's message was applauded, but not by the American delegates, who had reason to feel that their credibility had been rather summarily undercut. Wright, in particular, was displeased. "When my role [is] finished in this conference, I would appreciate it if you would tell me what governments paid me," he complained in the discussion period that followed the morning speeches.[156]

The difficulty the American delegates faced was the difficulty of manifesting solidarity with the delegates from other countries without sacrificing their conviction that their own history and conditions were distinct. They did not, as Black Americans, regard themselves as colonial subjects, and for them, freedom did not mean independence. It meant full citizenship in the existing political system. They were for integration, not separation. Separation they had. If the discussions at the Paris Congress had been political, the distinction between segregation and colonialism might have been made, but the subject was culture, and culture is a blob of mercury. Whenever you try to put a finger on it, it takes a different shape.

One of the central questions at the congress, therefore, even though it was probably not on the minds of most delegates, was what it meant to be an African American. What, exactly, is the "African" part of that identity? It made some sense to speak of a Black African culture distinct from a white European culture. Did it make sense to talk of an African American culture distinct from American culture? Senghor, Césaire, Fanon, and Wright all had different answers.

By the year of the congress, Senghor was heavily involved in Senegalese politics. In two months, he would be become the mayor of Thiès; in 1960, he would be elected the first president of Senegal. But he addressed the congress in his capacity as a poet, and his subject was *négritude*.[157] For Senghor, *négritude* referred to all the values of the African world, and it was an essentialist concept. People with African ancestry produced a different kind of cultural good because people with African ancestry experience the world differently. Senghor attributed this to what he called the "physio-psychology of the Negro."[158] The Negro had a particular way of being in the world, and it produced "another way of knowing," which he defined in opposition to white ways of knowing. "White reason is analytic through utilisation," he said; "Negro reason is intuitive through participation."[159] African thought is animistic: it sees objects as the expressions of a life force. Africanist culture reflects the African person: it is emotional, intuitive, holistic, and empathic. *Négritude*, therefore, extends throughout the diaspora, because it travels with the race. "The spirit of the African Negro civilisation, consciously or not, animates the best Negro artists and writers of to-day, whether they come from Africa or America," he said. "So far as they are conscious of African-Negro culture and are inspired by it they are elevated in the international scale; so far as they turn their backs on Africa the mother they degenerate and become feeble."[160]

Senghor had no compunctions about the racialist implications of his claim. He even cited Arthur Gobineau, whose work on the innate inequality of the races is a classic of nineteenth-century scientific race theory. Senghor *wanted* the races to be different. His goal was the liberation of Africanist culture as the culture of a race of people. Cultural liberation, he said, is the sine qua non of political liberation.

Senghor had erased colonialism completely from the concept of *négritude*. To Césaire, of course, the whole intention of the term was to capture the agonized position of the Black individual within a dominant racist culture. After his election to the National Assembly in 1945, he had played a key role in the "departmentalization" of Martinique. In

1946, the French Parliament passed a law making Martinique a department of France, meaning that its laws were the laws of France; there were no special colonial regulations. Césaire believed that strengthening the tie to France was the best way of securing the rights of Martinicans and of preserving Martinique as a republic.[161] Nevertheless, his hostility to colonialism was unabated. In 1950, he published *Discours sur le colonialisme*, a condemnation of European colonialism as naked exploitation. He called Europe a decadent civilization that had created and then failed to solve two problems: the problem of the proletariat and the problem of colonialism. "L'Europe," he declared, "est indéfendable."[162]

So for Césaire, all Black people confronted the same problem: colonialism. And this included African Americans. There is a non-Western Negro-African civilization, out of which the diversity of African cultures has arisen, and which extends into the diaspora. But this civilization must always be understood in the context of the colonial situation, because that is the global reality. The purpose of European imperialism, he said at the Congress, was not to raise up and enlighten the people of a premodern civilization. It was to destroy that civilization and put nothing in its place. "[A]ll colonization," he said, "leads in the longer or shorter run to the death of the civilisation of the conquered society." He dismissed as a transparent deception the promises of assimilation and integration—the promises of the system that had once taken him out of Basse-Pointe and transported him to Paris. He called them "snares and booby traps."[163]

Césaire dismissed as well the suggestion that contact with European culture adds to, rather than takes away from, indigenous culture. After all, who is the ultimate owner of the culture? The dialectic by which foreign elements are subsumed into indigenous cultures is denied to the colony. "Foreign elements are dumped on its soil, but remain foreign," Césaire argued. "White men's things. White men's ways. Things that sit alongside the indigenous people but over which the indigenous people has no power."[164] In these circumstances, it was impossible to predict what sort of culture might flourish in a postcolonial society—although, he said, "I refuse to believe that the future African culture could totally and brutally reject the old African culture." Political liberation, not cultural liberation, must come first, for "a civilization is living when the society in which it finds expression is free."[165]

Fanon took a harder line. He came to the congress from Algeria.

After getting his medical degree in Lyon, he worked at the Saint-Alban psychiatric hospital in Lozère, in south-central France, an institution committed to treatment based on a holistic assessment of the patient's condition. Under its founder, François Tosquelles, the hospital had played an important role in the Resistance.[166] While he was there, Fanon wrote a letter to Richard Wright, whose address he got from Alioune Diop. He expressed his admiration for Wright's work, listed the books of his he had read, and asked for the titles of any he might have missed. He mentioned *Peau noire, masques blancs* (in which he discusses *Native Son*), and told Wright that he was planning to write a study of "the human breadth" of Wright's works.[167]

It is not known whether Wright responded (and Fanon had not missed any titles). When they finally met, at the congress, Fanon was chief of staff in the psychiatric ward at Blida-Joinville hospital in northern Algeria. In 1954, a year after he arrived there, the Algerian War broke out, and he joined the revolutionary Front de Libération Nationale (FLN). By 1956, despite not knowing Arabic and despite internecine rivalries within the FLN, he had become involved in the anti-colonial struggle. This made his position at the congress a tricky one, since he risked arrest by French authorities if he spoke out in support of the FLN. His speech, delivered at the end of the first day, would turn out to be his last public address in France.[168]

For Fanon, the notion of a coherent Negro African culture within colonized territories was a mirage. He agreed with Césaire that colonization was culturally destructive, and deliberately so. "The undertaking of de-culturisation shows itself as the negative side of a more gigantic work of economic, and even biological, enslavement," he said. But the practice was even more nefarious, because the indigenous culture was not simply obliterated: "the end sought is the sustained death agony rather than the complete disappearance of the pre-existing culture. This culture, formerly full of life, and open to the future, becomes closed, fossilised in the colonial status, caught in the yoke of oppression."[169] Native culture persists, mummified.

This zombie culture is given official respect as the native people's "tradition." Fanon called this respect "tantamount to the most utter contempt, to the most elaborate sadism." He took his example from American culture: the blues. "[T]he blues 'plaint of the Negro slaves' is offered to the admiration of the oppressors," he argued. "It is a bit of stylised oppression which brings a profit to the exploiter and the racist. No oppression and no racism, no blues. The end of racism would sound the knell of the great Negro music."[170]

The "revival" of folk-art forms like the blues ensures that the subjugated people will remain isolated from the main currents of modern life. And it is the colonial elites, precisely the people who have been educated to see through it, who end up as the curators of this folk culture. He gave the example of Black intellectuals who consult a sorcerer before making a decision. The solution, Fanon said, was freedom from domination and, with freedom, an end to racism. Then "[t]he spasmodic and rigid culture of the occupying power, once liberated, is finally open to the culture of the people who have truly become brothers. The two cultures can stand side by side and enrich each other."[171] As long as one group is subaltern, no genuine culture can be produced.

Wright's position was not far from Fanon's, but he arrived at it by a completely different path. His speech was the last of the congress, and it is easy to imagine his impatience with the proceedings to that point. He would hardly have been sympathetic with Diop's original intention, which was to celebrate what Wright considered a backward culture. On the first day, following Senghor's speech, he had opened the discussion by asking what African culture had to do with him, a Black American raised in a modern civilization. "This is not hostility; this is not criticism," he insisted. "I am asking a question of *brothers*."[172] Senghor responded that if white Americans were taught Greek and Roman classics, then Black Americans could be taught the African tradition. This was not the answer Wright was looking for.

For his address two days later, Wright used a talk he had delivered already in Indonesia. It was called "Tradition and Industrialization," and the argument derived from the text he had written for *12 Million Black Voices*, back in 1941, when he was still a member of the Communist Party.[173] There, he argued that for Black Americans, African culture had died in the Middle Passage. Enslaved Africans in the United States developed a folk culture, along with a religious fundamentalism, that was primitive and repressive. The migration to Northern cities, which he had been part of, freed Black people from this premodern way of life, but racism was blocking their ability to profit from the benefits of modern society. Still, ultimately, the move north would be liberating for Black people, because entering the industrial economy would modernize them—which, for Wright, meant the freedom to make one's own choices. "The seasons of the plantations no longer dictate the lives of many of us," Wright had ended his book; "hundreds of thousands of us are moving into the sphere of conscious history."[174]

In Paris, Wright argued that the same was true for the colonial world. His message to the congress was: the future of Africa is Europe. The Western-educated African elites were the bridge to modern life. "[T]his elite in Asia and Africa constitutes islands of free men," he said, "the FREEST MEN IN ALL THE WORLD TODAY." They had "no weight of the dead past clounding [*sic*] their minds, no fears of foolish customs benumbing their consciousness."[175] Although it was not the intention, imperialism had smashed "the irrational ties of religion and custom and tradition" in the nonwhite world. "Today, a knowing black, brown, or yellow man can say: 'Thank you, Mr White Man, for freing [*sic*] me from the rot of my irrational traditions and customs, though you are still the victims of your own irrational customs and traditions." The "unspoken assumption in world history is 'WHAT IS GOOD FOR EUROPE IS GOOD FOR ALL MANKING [*sic*].' I say: So be it."[176] Europe had tried to modernize the Third World and had failed. Now Europe should give the African elite the tools they needed. "This conference, I feel must proceed to define the tools and the nature of finishing that job, and the strengthening of that elite," he ended. "Freedom is indivisible."[177]

American newspapers had published many stories about the Bandung conference, but there seems not to have been a single newspaper story about the meeting in Paris. There was one American reporter present, however, and that was James Baldwin. He sat with headphones on (though his French was now good) in the front of the hall with the rest of the press, and it was mainly via Baldwin that English-language readers learned what was said at the Congress of Black Writers and Artists.

Baldwin was on assignment from *Encounter*, where his piece, "Princes and Powers," was published in January 1957. It was reprinted in Baldwin's second essay collection, *Nobody Knows My Name*, in 1962, and it is one of his best essays, in part because his journalistic persona gave him some distance from the debates in the hall. He could zoom in and out, recount the impression individual speakers were making, and reflect on the larger issues in which they were heroically entangled.

Baldwin did write from a point of view, however—the point of view of an American. The main concern of the delegates at the conference was the future of the decolonizing world. For an American, the main concern was how that future might affect the global balance of power. "Hanging in the air," Baldwin wrote, "as real as the heat from which we suffered, were the great spectres of America and Russia, of the battle going on between them for the domination of the world. The ultimate resolution of this battle might very well depend on the earth's non-European population."[178]

When Baldwin's piece came out, Sol Stein complained about this characterization of the battle between the United States and the Soviets as a battle "for the domination of the world." Baldwin answered as a realist. "What else have nations ever battled for?" he answered Stein. ". . . [D]omination is one of the facts of life." He did not mean military domination, he added, like the Soviets had in Hungary. He meant the domination of an ideology. "In the case of America vs. Russia," he told Stein, "America is the last stronghold of the Western idea of personal liberty. And I certainly think that this idea *should* dominate the world." At the same time, he recognized the validity of the colonial world's claims. The men who spoke at the congress (as Wright pointed out in his remarks, there was not a single woman on the program) were only doing what European nations had done to them. "The European civilization overran and destroyed theirs, Europe's morals and aesthetics invalidated their own. This is the way, or one of the ways in which 'domination' works."[179]

Baldwin believed that in this war of ideas, Black Americans had a special role. The "American Negro," he wrote, "is possibly the only man of color who can speak of the West with real authority, whose experience, painful as it is, also proves the vitality of the so transgressed Western ideals." This is because Black Americans, unlike colonial Africans, have had the experience, however warped and stunted, of freedom.

> [W]e had been born in a society, which, in a way quite inconceivable for Africans, and no longer real for Europeans, was open, and, in a sense which has nothing to do with justice or injustice, was free . . . This results in a psychology very different—at its best and at its worst—from the psychology which is produced by a sense of having been invaded and overrun, the sense of having

no recourse whatever against oppression other than overthrowing the machinery of the oppressor . . . It had never been in our interest to overthrow it. It had been necessary to make the machinery work for our benefit and the possibility of its doing so had been, so to speak, built in.[180]

Black Americans did share with Africans, however, "the necessity to remake the world in their own image, to impose this image on the world, and no longer be controlled by the vision of the world, and of themselves, held by other people."

Césaire's account of the destructive power of colonialism was powerful, Baldwin said, but he left one thing out, and that was Césaire himself. Césaire had not been destroyed. His Europeanization was the source of his authority. "He had penetrated into the heart of the great wilderness which was Europe and stolen the sacred fire. And this, which was the promise of their freedom, was also the assurance of his power."[181] In the end, Baldwin agreed with Wright: the values that nonwhite people needed were right there in front of them. They were the values of Western civilization. All the nonwhite world had to do was own them. Africa was not the answer. Soon after the congress ended, Baldwin decided that it was time to end his exile and return to the United States.

12

CONSUMER SOVEREIGNTY

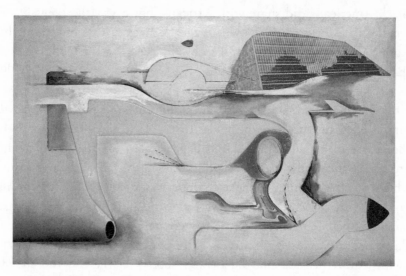

Richard Hamilton, *Hers Is a Lush Situation* (1958). Based on a magazine advertisement for a 1957 Cadillac; the title is from a review by Deborah Allen in the American trade journal *Industrial Design*: "The driver sits at the dead calm center of all this motion: hers is a lush situation." She was describing the 1957 Buick, a higher-priced General Motors car. Her review was quoted in an article by Reyner Banham, Hamilton's source. The tailpipe and front bumper are in the same perspective, Cubist-style. The background image in the reflection in the windscreen is the United Nations building in New York; the lips (top center) are from a photograph of Sophia Loren. The combination of elements was inspired by Duchamp's *Green Box*. High meets low: Pop Art. (*Pallant House Gallery, Chichester, UK [Wilson Gift through The Art Fund 2006] / © R. Hamilton, All Rights Reserved, DACS and ARS 2020*)

1.

Pop Art was an international phenomenon. It flourished, arising more or less independently and at more or less the same time, in countries around the world—the United Kingdom, Italy, France, Japan, Argentina, Cuba, Hungary, Brazil, and, of course, the United States. A number of art forms with affinities to Pop—performance art, Happenings,

Minimalism, Conceptual Art—began appearing around the same time, also globally and also more or less independently.[1] And there were hybrids. But what distinguished Pop Art from all other art forms was the ⸙ iconography.⸙

⸙ The iconography of Pop Art is "given" by the visual environment, ⸙ specifically, by commercial and entertainment culture: movies and television, newspaper and magazine photographs, advertisements, signage, and labeling and packaging. Pop Art is the representation of representations. And this makes it notoriously difficult to interpret. We know what these images signify in their original contexts. What do they signify in a work of art? Are they intended to be satirical? Celebratory? Deadpan? Are Pop artists hitching a ride on the advertising and entertainment industries, or are they exposing the banality and predictability of commercial culture and mass marketing? It Pop Art critical or is it complicit?

Right from the start, people found these questions unanswerable, and the artists themselves tended to be evasive and contradictory.[2] It was as though they had tapped into a current from outside the world of fine art, but had no settled idea what to make of it. The current they tapped into was generated by the extraordinary rate of economic growth after the war, and by the changes in social relations that came, seemingly pell-mell, along with it. Whatever art-historical and aesthetic interest Pop Art has (and it has a lot), Pop is the face of a moment.

Between 1950 and 1973, the world economy grew at the fastest rate in history. World GDP rose at an annual average rate of 4.91 percent. In the closest comparable periods, world annual growth rate averaged 3.01 percent from 1973 to 1998 and 2.11 percent from 1870 to 1913. Between 1500 and 1820, the world economy grew at an annual rate of just one third of 1 percent.[3] In Western Europe and the United States, the years from 1950 to 1973 also saw historically low levels of inequality in the distribution of capital ownership, i.e., wealth.[4]

Different regions prospered following different strategies. In Eastern Europe, growth was propelled by state investment in mining and industry; in much of Western Europe, it was propelled by a shift from predominately agricultural to industrial and service economies.[5] In some places, the years of high growth rates were given names: *les trentes glorieuses* in France; the *Wirtschaftswunder* in the Federal Republic of Germany; *il miracolo economico* or *boom economico* in Italy; *ogon no rokuju nendai* (the Golden Sixties) in Japan. But rapid growth was experienced everywhere—in historically poor countries such as Austria and Spain, as well as in former great powers like Germany and France. In Latin America, the annual average rate of growth was 5.38 percent; in Africa, 4.43 percent; in the Warsaw Pact countries, 4.86 percent; in China, 5.02 percent.[6]

At the time, it was natural to assume that these measures of prosperity were indices of economic normality: this was how the system (however you defined it) was supposed to function. But after 1973, the world's economies reverted to much more modest rates of growth and increasing inequalities of wealth and income.[7] National narratives of decline, or loss of "greatness," derive from that reversion. Various explanations have been proposed for the nature of economic conditions from 1950 to 1973, but they were probably the consequence of several things: unprecedented population growth, the downstream effects of unusually rapid technological innovation after 1870, government investment in science and technology, and a period of "catching up" following two world wars and a worldwide depression. Contributing to, and amplified by, these factors was an enormous increase in international travel, communications, trade, investment, and migration.[8] Technology and labor circulated internationally. So did goods. And so—along with and because of those things—did art and ideas.

In most economic respects, the nation that the rest of the world was catching up to was the United States. Fewer than half a million Americans died in the Second World War, and apart from a few fire balloons dropped by Japan in the Pacific Northwest and a harmless submarine bombardment off the coast of Santa Barbara, the United States mainland was not attacked. (Hawaii was a territory in 1941.) By contrast, more than 36 million Europeans died in the war, and many major cities, including Rotterdam, Le Havre, Hamburg, Coventry, Dresden, Minsk, Kiev, and Warsaw, along with large portions of London and Berlin, were destroyed. Twenty million Germans were left homeless. In Japan, 2.7 million died, sixty-six major cities were heavily bombed, and almost 9 million were left homeless. Allied attacks destroyed a quarter of Japan's wealth, including four fifths of its shipping, one third of its industrial machine tools, and a quarter of its rolling stock and motor vehicles.[9]

The war economy helped the United States reach full employment, and by the end of the 1940s, it had 7 percent of the world's population and 42 percent of its income. Half of the world's manufacturing output was American, including 57 percent of its steel, 43 percent of its electricity, 62 percent of its oil, and 82 percent of its cars. The United States housed three fifths of the world's capital stock and owned three quarters of the world's gold. Daily calorie consumption was 50 percent higher than in most of Western Europe.[10]

To a large extent, Europe benefited from a "follower's advantage." European countries could imitate American technologies and business strategies, avoiding the expense of inventing them. They also enjoyed an oversupply of labor, which reduced costs, and an undersupply of capital, which raised returns on investment.[11] Still, in many countries, postwar growth was made sustainable by American money. (Whether American money was *essential* to European recovery is a matter of debate.)[12] Between 1945 and 1955, the United States gave $53 billion in grants and loans to the rest of the world, including countries in South Asia, Africa, and Latin America.[13] In Western Europe, the European Recovery Program (ERP)—the Marshall Plan—contributed $13 billion to European nations, money that could be used not only to rebuild infrastructure but also to modernize their economies.

The Marshall Plan was announced in June 1947, but Congress did not appropiate the money until April 1948. Since the economic and political situation in Western Europe was alarming, by the time Marshall aid started flowing, the United States had already extended loans to Britain ($4.4 billion, not paid off until 2006), France ($1.9 billion), and other European countries, including Italy, Poland, Denmark, and Greece. When the ERP expired, in 1951, American military spending related to the NATO alliance replaced it as an economic stimulus and a source of dollars. And after 1956, private American investment in Europe took off. Between 1958 and 1963, a thousand American firms started doing business or created subsidiaries in Britain, six hundred in France, three hundred in Belgium. By 1960, American investments in the British economy exceeded a billion dollars.[14]

In negotiating these loans and grants, the U.S. government was naturally interested in opening markets to American goods. It forced the United Kingdom, for example, to end its system of imperial preferences, which set lower tariffs on goods traded inside British dominions. Later on, when historians began reconsidering the origins of the Cold War, this was sometimes treated as the hidden motive of American foreign policy.[15] But the motive was never a secret. Officials in both the United States and Western Europe believed that prosperity was an antidote to Communism, that productivity was the key to prosperity, and that nations that trade together do not go to war with one another.[16]

Lowering barriers to trade is why the United States supported the creation of the Organization for European Economic Cooperation (OEEC), the forerunner of the Common Market (the European Economic Community, formed in 1958) and the European Union (created in 1993), and it was the essence of the liberal internationalism that informed postwar foreign policy. Trade and freedom came together. The Act creating the ERP was explicit:

> The restoration or maintenance in European countries of principles of individual liberty, free institutions, and genuine independence rests largely upon the establishment of sound economic conditions, stable international economic relationships, and the achievement by the countries of Europe of a healthy economy independent of extraordinary outside assistance.[17]

The American presence in Europe gave rise to anxiety about "Americanization." The fear was not new. The term dates from the middle of the nineteenth century, and the belief that America represents Europe's future is even older. It is the premise of Alexis de Tocqueville's *Democracy in America*, published in 1835. The English journalist W. T. Stead published a book called *The Americanisation of the World* in 1901, and insofar as Americanization meant the adoption of American ways of doing business, that was happening well before the Second World War.[18] What made things different after 1945 was the sheer presence of American goods, American entertainment, American diplomatic and military personnel, and, simply, Americans. It looked like an invasion. Arthur Koestler called it "the coca-colonization of Western Europe."[19]

Economic policy in capitalist countries after 1945 was concentrated on maintaining a high level of demand. This was Keynesian orthodoxy: budget cuts and excess saving had prolonged the Depression; spending was the engine of full employment and economic growth. These policies had a cultural consequence: consumerism.

On the supply side, consumerism means a distribution system designed to enhance buyers' choice, what is known as "consumer sovereignty."

A dramatic case in Europe after the war is the self-service store—outlets, such as supermarkets, in which customers pick items off shelves rather than order them from someone behind a counter, such as a butcher or a baker. In 1950, there were 1,200 self-service stores in all of Europe; in 1960, there were 45,500. By 1965, there were 53,000 in West Germany alone.[20] On the demand side, consumerism means associating the acquisition of goods with social status and personal identity—the way people take pride in or identify themselves with a new-model car or a state-of-the-art kitchen. In the United States, consumerism can even be associated with a feeling of citizenship: buying stuff helps to sustain a free-market economy.[21]

The interface between these two aspects of consumerist culture, the way that sellers and buyers communicate, is marketing: styling, labeling, packaging, advertising. Product designs and advertisements are signaling systems. The signals (despite anxieties about subliminal messages: ice cubes that spell out "s-e-x," and so on) are not subtle. They have no time to be subtle. They flash attributes like "faster," "sexier," "classier," "easier to use," "more powerful," "more up-to-date."

The United States was a leader in marketing, too, and for many Europeans, "Americanization" described a radical change in the visual environment. The perceptual field was suddenly flooded with commercial iconography that was overwhelmingly American. Reactions to the change depended on the frictions latent in existing social and cultural dispensations, and one place that turned out to be particularly sensitive to it was the United Kingdom.

2.

The results of the British general election of 1945 were announced on July 26, just three months after the end of the war in Europe and while fighting in the Pacific was still under way, and they shocked many outside observers. Winston Churchill and the Conservative Party lost in a landslide. The Conservatives received 9,960,809 votes, opposition parties 15,018,140, with 11,992,292 going to Labour. In the United Kingdom, as in the United States in the 1948 presidential election—when Henry Wallace, running with the support of the CPUSA, received just 2.37 percent of the vote—the electoral impact of the Communist Party was negligible. Communists received 102,780 votes, or 0.4 percent of the total. When Churchill and the Conservatives were returned to power in 1951, Communists received just 21,000 votes.[22]

In retrospect, it is not hard to see why Churchill, an imperialist and anti-Bolshevist who had taken a notoriously hawkish position against the strikers in the British General Strike of 1926, was not the man for postwar times (although, as things turned out, he did have one act remaining). The election of 1945 was interpreted as a mandate for a welfare state. The form this would take had been signaled by the so-called Beveridge Report, named for William Beveridge, an economist who chaired a government committee charged with making recommendations about social insurance. The committee's report, *Social Insurance and Allied Services*, published in November 1942, became a bestseller and a popular image of a postwar Britain.[23] It proposed a national health care service—which in 1948, the Labour government created.

That government also invested in housing; it improved access to education; and it nationalized the Bank of England, transport services (railroads and airlines), and the coal, iron, steel, electricity, and gas industries.[24] Full employment was the priority of economic policy, and the policy was successful: unemployment in Britain was 2 percent or below until the mid-1960s.[25] But the annual growth rate averaged only 3 percent, against 4.6 percent in the other leading capitalist economies.[26]

The Labour government faced two difficulties. The first was that the country was effectively insolvent, with massive gold and dollar shortages. The United Kingdom had got through the war thanks to Lend-Lease, the program through which the United States donated matériel to the Allies (including the Soviet Union). Truman's abrupt termination of Lend-Lease immediately after the surrender of Japan—on August 17, three weeks after Labour came into office—was an enormous financial blow. Britain had lost a quarter of its wealth fighting Germany and Japan, and it was forced to use almost all of its Marshall Plan funds to pay off its debt rather than modernizing an aging industrial economic base.

The second liability was the Empire. After the war ended, Britain still deployed full naval fleets in the Atlantic, the Mediterranean, and the Indian Ocean; maintained a "China station"; deployed 120 Royal Air Force squadrons in bases around the world; and stationed troops in Hong Kong, Malaya, the Persian Gulf, North Africa, Trieste, Austria, West Germany, and the United Kingdom. Diplomatic and civil service personnel were posted across the globe.[27] The state was overextended. It could no longer exercise power in its traditional spheres of influence. One of those spheres was the Eastern Mediterranean, and it was Britain's notification of the American State Department that it would be terminating aid to Greece and Turkey that led to Truman's "alternative ways of life" speech in March 1947.[28]

Truman delivered that speech during the coldest winter in Britain since the 1890s. The bad weather, combined with damaged infrastructure, created shortages across northern Europe. An American visitor reported finding Europeans "abstracted and preoccupied . . . Every minute is dedicated to scrounging enough food, clothing and fuel to carry through the next 24 hours."[29] In Britain, blizzards prevented the delivery of coal and other heating supplies. The snow was followed by flooding, and the floods were followed by an exceptionally warm summer. That August was the hottest ever recorded in central England.[30] Four hundred and eighty-nine thousand British workers went out on strikes that year (some of them wildcat), and conditions were made worse by the extension of wartime rationing. Basic goods, including bread, meat, clothing, soap, petrol, sweets, and even potatoes were rationed.[31]

This was the year George Orwell was writing *Nineteen Eighty-Four*, and the novel's dystopia of shoddy goods, undernourishment, and rationing did not exaggerate by much living conditions in contemporary Britain. In 1947, Cyril Connolly, in his column in *Horizon*, tried to sum up the situation:

> The advantages which position, coal, skill and enterprise won for us in the nineteenth century have been liquidated and we go back to scratch as a barren, humid, raw, but densely over-populated group of islands with an obsolete industrial plant, hideous but inadequate housing, a variety of unhealthy jungle possessions, vast international commitments, a falling birth-rate and a large class of infertile rentiers or over-specialized middlemen and brokers as our main capital. Surrounded on all sides by an iron curtain of good eating, we yet suffer from undernourishment, lack of vitamins and sunshine, lack of hope, energy, leisure and spirit . . . [M]ost of us are not men or women but members of a vast, seedy, overworked, over-legislated, neuter class, with our drab clothes, our ration books and murder stories, our envious, stricken, old-world

apathies and resentments—a careworn people. And the symbol of this mood is London, now the largest, saddest and dirtiest of great cities with its miles of unpainted half-inhabited houses, its chopless chop-houses, its beerless pubs, its once vivid quarters losing all personality, its squares bereft of elegance, its dandies in exile, its antiques in America, its shops full of junk, bunk, and tomorrow, its crowds mooning round the stained wicker of the cafeterias in their shabby raincoats, under a sky permanently dull and lowering like a metal dish-cover.[32]

At the end of the column, he explained that there had been no March issue of *Horizon* "owing to fuel cuts."[33] The magazine folded three years later.

Some people associated austerity with a Labourite aversion to comfort beyond necessity, and this was not entirely unfair. "The great need at the moment," Orwell wrote in 1945, "is to make people aware of what is happening and why, and to persuade them that Socialism is a *better* way of life but not necessarily, in its first stages, a more comfortable one."[34] (One reason, he went on to say, was that colonialism was incompatible with socialism, and decolonization would mean a reduction in the British standard of living.)

But the return of the Conservatives to power in 1951 did not end austerity: food was rationed until 1954. In 1955, only 18 percent of British households had washing machines and 8 percent had refrigerators.[35] By then, 70 percent of American households had washing machines and more than 80 percent had refrigerators.[36] (The availability in the United States of labor-saving domestic appliances such as the washing machine may have helped sustain the postwar rise in the birth rate.)[37] Against this backdrop of economic hardship and commercial drabness, images of American consumerism were huge contrast-gainers. They projected pleasure, glamour, freedom from inhibition, freedom from want. The main vehicle for this imagery in postwar Britain was (besides Hollywood movies) American magazines.

The decades after the war was a boom time for general-interest magazines in the United States. Advertising dollars would eventually move to broadcast television (and advertising is also highly GDP-sensitive), but until 1970, the magazine industry was a growth sector in the American economy. Total magazine circulation grew from 83,235,720 in 1936 to 179,965,231 in 1955.[38] Revenues increased accordingly. In 1940, general-interest magazines carried $156 million worth of advertising; in 1946, $362 million; by 1960, $830 million.[39] Advertising income kept subscription prices low; low subscription prices increased circulation; increased circulation raised the base rates charged to advertisers—a virtuous circle.

The lack of a language barrier helped get American magazines into the British cultural mainstream, and so did the presence of the American military. One million GIs were stationed in Britain during the war, and the United States continued to maintain large bases, such as Burtonwood, outside Liverpool, after 1945. American soldiers brought American magazines, along with comic books and American popular music, into general circulation.

One reason that magazine advertisements jumped out at postwar readers was because advances in four-color offset lithography had made high-quality color advertising affordable. Another was because magazine ads reflected a revolution in product design. The products jumped out, too.[40] Britain, France, and Germany had a long history of attention to the artistic aspects of manufactured goods. Attention to design in American mass-market manufacturing began in the 1920s, led by men like Norman Bel Geddes, Henry Dreyfus, Walter Dorwin Teague, and Raymond Loewy.

Investment in product design might seem a luxury to be indulged in when sales are strong. But the design revolution began when the market for consumer goods was glutted, the mid-1920s, and it flourished during a period of weak demand, the 1930s.[41] And this is because one purpose of product design is to stimulate demand by inducing consumers to believe that they need to swap out their refrigerator or pencil sharpener before its shelf life has expired in order to get the "newer" model, even if what is new is only the envelope. It is getting people to want what they don't need. And how is the designed look sold to consumers? By picturing it in advertisements.

For people with left-wing (and right-wing) political views, advertising thus became the symbol of everything that was culturally debasing and ethically compromised about capitalism. Advertising manufactures needs; it sells appearances; it beguiles consumers with promises of what the British sociologist Richard Hoggart (referring to the content of weekly magazines, genre fiction, and pop songs) called "a candy-floss world."[42] It fools people into paying more than they should for things they need less than they imagine. The only people it profits are the businessmen.

In the United States, the adman became a stock figure of the sellout, criticized, as the financial consultant would be later on, as a parasite who makes money by helping other people make money. Madison Avenue types were recurring characters in Jules Feiffer's satirical comic strips in *The Village Voice* in the 1950s.[43] "One cannot defend production as satisfying wants if that production creates the wants," the economist John Kenneth Galbraith wrote in *The Affluent Society* in 1958.[44]

In Britain, advertising was attacked by Labour politicians, who threatened the industry with punitive taxation.[45] Aneurin Bevan, who, as minister of health, had led the creation of the National Health Service, called advertising "an evil machine which is doing great damage to modern society." He never watched television, he told a convention of advertising executives in 1953; from what he heard, he said, he was sure it was bad enough. But *sponsored* television—that is, television with commercials—was insupportable. "Why should we imitate always the worst features of other countries?" he asked.[46] "Other countries" meant the United States. (After intense debate, Parliament passed the Television Act of 1954, allowing commercial television in Britain, and ending the monopoly of the BBC.)[47] The British playwright and commentator J. B. Priestley coined a term for postwar consumerism: "admass." "Behind the Iron Curtain they have *Propmass*, official propaganda taking the place of advertising," he said, "but all with the same aims and objects."[48]

To some extent, the attack on advertising was part of a culture war waged by liberals and socialists against the pro-business parties in power in the United States (the Eisenhower administration, in office until 1961) and the United Kingdom (the Conservative Party, in office until 1964). Partisan culture wars like that can produce generalizations that outlive their political moments. Who called the 1950s a decade of materialism and conformity? Democrats and Labourites. But the attack on advertising was also part of the Cold War within the Cold War. Hoggart, in his book on the disappearance of traditional working-class culture in Britain, *The Uses of Literacy*, warned that the country "seems to be allowing cultural developments as dangerous in their own way as those we are shocked at in totalitarian society."[49]

Still, Hoggart recognized that a mass-market economy raised the standard of living for the average Briton. The Marxist cultural historian

Raymond Williams recognized this, too. Materialism is fine, he argued; people need affordable goods. But consumerism creates irrational wants. If we were sensible, he wrote, "we should find most advertising to be of an insane irrelevance . . . A washing-machine would be a useful machine to wash clothes, rather than an indication that we are forward-looking or an object of envy to our neighbours." What was needed, he said, was "to build an area of reality in which a whole range of significant choices can be freely made. This work . . . is a stage in the only revolution that matters: the creation of social forms in which men can live and choose for themselves."[50] That is, socialism.

The quasi-official aura of disapproval around consumerism was a clear invitation to generational reaction.[51] As politically progressive as the critics of consumerism were (Orwell included Priestley on a list of "crypto-Communists and fellow travelers" he sent to the Foreign Office in 1949), they were culturally rearguard.[52] Writers like Hoggart and Williams stood in a line of English criticism that went back to Matthew Arnold, no revolutionary. Younger artists and intellectuals had little taste for the provincialism of working-class culture, and they did not see consumerism as a blight. They saw it as a stimulus, a source of pleasure, an antidote to insularity—the future. One of the first British artists to promote this idea was Eduardo Paolozzi.

3.

Paolozzi was Italian Scottish, an identity a little less unusual than it might sound. His maternal grandparents emigrated from a tiny Italian village, Viticuso, around the turn of the century and settled in Leith, a working-class area of Edinburgh. On a trip to their hometown, their daughter, Carmella, met Paolozzi's future father, Rodolpho, and when they married, he came to Edinburgh, around 1920. The family ran a confectionary shop selling chocolate and homemade ice cream (a popular trade for Italians in Britain and Ireland: stores advertised "Neapolitan ice cream"), and apparently they did well.

Eduardo was born in 1924, a year before Benito Mussolini declared himself dictator of Italy.[53] Like many (but not all) Italian immigrants, the Paolozzis considered themselves *fascisti*. A picture of Mussolini hung in the back of their shop. Eduardo grew up bilingual and, effectively, bicultural. He spent summers at a fascist youth camp in Italy. "The Italians in Britain were considered strange and inferior," he said later, "but when you go to Italy you were a Prince."[54]

On June 10, 1940, Mussolini declared war on France (not a particularly valorous act, since France had just surrendered to Hitler), and that night, anti-Italian riots broke out across Britain. Edinburgh was the scene of some of the worst attacks.[55] The Paolozzis' shop was destroyed; Eduardo's father and grandfather were taken into custody, and he was interned in Saughton, an Edinburgh prison. He was sixteen.

The father and grandfather were selected for deportation to Canada. On July 1, they were packed along with more than fifteen hundred other men—Italians, Germans, Jews, and British servicemen—onto the *Arandora Star*, a former cruise vessel commandeered for service during the war. The next morning, the ship was struck by a torpedo fired by a German U-Boat and sank within thirty minutes. Four hundred and forty-six of the Italians on board drowned, including Paolozzi's father and grandfather.[56] Eduardo was released from prison fairly quickly, but in 1943, he was conscripted and assigned to the Royal Pioneer Corps, an army unit in which enemy aliens could serve. He spent most of the time bivouacked on a soccer field. After a year, he faked a mental disorder and was released. He seems not to have been embittered by his wartime experiences.

He had already attended classes at the Edinburgh College of Art; he now enrolled in the Slade, the art school of the University of London, which was relocated to Oxford during the war. In 1947, with the proceeds from a successful exhibition of his art, seventy-five pounds, he went to Paris, and he spent the next two years there. He became friendly with a number of artists, notably the Dadaist Tristan Tzara and the sculptor Alberto Giacometti. In 1952, after he left, his work was shown in the exhibition *Un Art autre*, organized by Michel Tapié, one of the first European exhibitions of Jackson Pollock's paintings.[57]

As a child in Edinburgh, Paolozzi had begun collecting pictures he cut out of magazines. When he lived in Paris, he got American magazines from ex-GIs and started making collages from images in them. He continued this after he returned to Britain, where it was easy to find American magazines, and he showed his collection to artist friends.[58] Then, on February 12, 1952, using an epidiascope—an opaque projector—he displayed some combination of images and collages to an audience of about thirty-five artists and critics at the Institute of Contemporary Arts (ICA) in London.

Many of the pictures were from ads; some were scientific images, images of food—whatever Paolozzi found dynamic or bizarre.[59] One of his collages, constructed from images that included a bodybuilder, an automobile, a drawing of an erect penis, a pinup, and a slice of blueberry pie, contained the word "BUNK!," and many years later, when Paolozzi finally exhibited the collages and gave them titles (this one was called *Evadne in Green Dimension*), the works became known as the Bunk collages.* His 1952 presentation at the ICA is standardly used to mark the first step toward Pop Art.

The ICA was created in 1947 as a nongovernmental venue for advanced art. Its founders had two models in mind: the Museum of Modern Art in New York and café society in Paris. As was the case in the United States, modernist art was too controversial for state agencies to be identified with.[60] The ICA, like MoMA, exhibited work that the government could not (although public money was quietly used to support some of its exhibitions).

It was also designed as a place to hang out, and the bar became a gathering spot for young artists, students, and teachers. In 1952, some of them requested permission to organize their own lecture and seminar series. Eventually, this group was given the name the Independent Group (IG)—to signify that its programming was independent of the ICA's.[61] (In fact, the group had full institutional support, particularly under the ICA's second director, Dorothy Moreland, and its members attended ICA-sponsored talks and participated in the mounting of ICA exhibitions.)

The IG was contemporaneous with the Club, the society for artists, musicians, and writers on Eighth Street in New York City, and it arose out of the same spirit: change was in the air. The members of the IG, like the members of the Club, thought of themselves as representing a moment rather than a movement. The name "Independent Group" did not even appear in print until 1955, when one of its members, Reyner Banham, referred to it in a footnote in an Italian publication. By then, it had ceased to meet.[62]

In the beginning, the IG was simply a collection of people who shared certain interests. Members included, besides Paolozzi, who was

---

* Evadne is a (female) name in Greek mythology that has also been used by fiction writers, such as Mary Shelley. It is not clear which character Paolozzi had in mind.

primarily a sculptor, and Banham, who was an architectural historian, Richard Hamilton and John McHale (visual artists), Nigel Henderson (photographer), Alison and Peter Smithson (architects), Lawrence Alloway (art critic), Frank Cordell (composer), and Toni del Renzio (writer and designer). These were bristly people. Discussions were described as "fiery."[63] Peter Smithson disliked Hamilton; Henderson was once Paolozzi's great friend but turned on him; Cordell's wife, Magda, left him for McHale; Hamilton and McHale had a falling-out whose after-effects persisted for decades.[64] Female spouses—besides Magda Cordell (a Hungarian refugee) and Alison Smithson, these included Mary Banham, Freda Paolozzi, and Terry Hamilton—were active as discussants, as art-making participants, and as artists themselves, but apart from Alison Smithson, they were almost entirely written out of the IG story.[65] A documentary about the IG created and narrated by Banham and produced in 1979 was entitled *Fathers of Pop*.

There was a fee to join the IG, and most events were by invitation; there seem to have been around fifty people on the mailing list, and twenty was a good turnout. The group hosted talks on helicopter design, Victorian and Edwardian decorative arts, microbiology, probability and information theory, advertising, Italian product design, fashion magazines, and the popular song business.[66] A. J. Ayer gave a lecture entitled "The Principle of Verification"; the *ARTnews* editor Thomas Hess gave a speech, "New Abstract Painters in America." A series of talks by IG members, "Aesthetic Problems of Contemporary Art," was open to the public.

What the talks had in common was subject matter and techniques then considered to be at best peripheral to the fine arts in Britain. In effect, the IG built up an alternative aesthetic and critical basis for arts practice. Much later, writers would argue that the IG was a retrospectively created myth, a back-formation from subsequent artistic developments.[67] It is certainly true that in the beginning, no one knew where discussions were headed. "We were just about stunned" by Paolozzi's Bunk images, Banham claimed in *Fathers of Pop*.[68] Which is an example of ex post facto myth-making, since it is not what Banham felt at the time.

"The I.C.A. last night was a flop," Alloway wrote to the artist Sylvia Sleigh (they would later marry) the day after Paolozzi's presentation. "Eduardo Paolozzi showed a collection of material—marine biology, early aeroplanes, and what have you—but the discussion never even got started. Reyner Banham spent most of the evening sniggering at Paolozzi's scrap book as it was flashed on the screen!"[69]* (Banham had not even been invited; he crashed the event.)[70] Alloway's account is backed up by the recollections of others, including Paolozzi himself. "[T]he reaction to my 'BUNK' lecture was one of disbelief and some hilarity," he wrote years later. "Material treated by all of us as interesting 'sources' of ideas was still regarded as banal." He remembered Banham giggling.[71]

Still, if there was a common starting point for the IG, it was a fascination, framed as un-British if not anti-British, with American culture, and that fascination was not ambivalent. The IG members were "bound together by our enthusiasm for the iconography of the New World," Paolozzi wrote. "The American magazine represented a catalogue of an exotic society, bountiful and generous, where the event of selling tinned pears was transformed into multi-coloured dreams, where sensuality and virility combined to form, in our view, an art form more subtle and fulfilling than the orthodox choice of either the Tate Gallery or the Royal Academy."[72] "It is important to realize," Banham wrote,

> how salutary a corrective to the sloppy provincialism of most London art of ten years ago US design could be. The gusto and professionalism of widescreen movies or Detroit car-styling was a constant reproach to the Moore-ish yokelry of British sculpture or the affected Piperish gloom of British painting. To anyone with a scrap of sensibility or an eye for technique, the average Playtex or Maidenform ad in American *Vogue* was an instant deflater of the reputations of most artists then in Arts Council vogue.[73]

The effect of the IG's programming was to shape this enthusiasm into an aesthetic, and one indication of the value of the IG discussions is that the manifesto-like publications its members produced were all written after the group disbanded. Those writings represented the outcome, not the premises, of IG activities. The IG was the hinge on which postwar British aesthetics turned.

The key IG writers were Banham, who served as the group's convener

---

* All the secondary literature on the IG dates Paolozzi's lecture to April 1952. The IG was formed in January 1952; Alloway's letter makes it clear that Paolozzi spoke on February 12, about a month later—which suggests that the organizers had him in mind from the start.

from 1952 to 1954, and Alloway, who, with McHale, replaced Banham in 1954. The last IG event, Frank Cordell on the popular music business, was held on July 15, 1955.[74] All three IG conveners later moved to the United States: Alloway in 1961, McHale in 1962, and Banham in 1976.

Banham was born in Norwich in 1922. His father was a gas-works engineer and the family was not well off. In 1939, he began training to become an engineer at the Bristol Aeroplane Company, and he worked there through the war. In 1949, he enrolled at the Courtauld Institute of Art in London, and he was a doctoral student there when he became involved with the IG. His dissertation, *Theory and Design in the First Machine Age*, a classic text, was published in 1960.

Banham was drawn to commercial imagery even before the IG came into existence. One of his first journalistic pieces, published in 1951, was on packaging, which he described as

> the all-intrusive agent of the western way of life, the transmitter of our visual vocabulary to the simple peasants of the world, who adorn their walls with the pretty labels of Dole pineapples, the bold fertility-symbol of Shell Oil, the august features of King C. Gillette. These are the symbols by which we are known, and of which the artists whom we most honour have contributed so little.[75]

Alloway was born in 1926 in the London suburb of Wimbledon, where his father ran a used-book store. He contracted tuberculosis when he was eleven, and missed two years of school. He then bounced around various educational institutions, but found success as a book reviewer. In 1943, he began taking extension courses at the University of London, and by this somewhat unorthodox means he learned art history and began a life of frenetic lecturing and reviewing. In 1955, he achieved some career stability by being appointed an assistant director of the ICA.

The IG aesthetic was, above all, nonhierarchical. There was a lot of stuff out there possessing aesthetic properties about which there was no way of talking critically. "We eagerly consume noisy ephemeridae, here with a bang today, gone without a whimper tomorrow—movies, beach-wear, pulp magazines, this morning's headlines and tomorrow's TV programmes," Banham wrote, "—yet we insist on aesthetic and moral standards hitched to permanency, durability, and perennity."[76] Alloway's term for nonhierarchical aesthetics was "the long front of culture." He argued that "unique oil paintings and highly personal poems as well as mass-distributed films and group-aimed magazines can be placed within a continuum rather than frozen layers in a pyramid."[77]

This position was to a large extent generational. Priestley was born in 1894; people born in the 1920s did not think of "admass" as an alien invasion. "We grew up with the mass media," as Alloway explained. ". . . The mass media were established as a natural environment by the time we could see them."[78] He thought that intellectuals from an older generation were trapped behind "the iron curtain of traditional aesthetics," what Banham called "the laws of Platonic aesthetics"— "objective, absolute, universal and eternally valid."[79] Those are not the laws of consumerism, where products are designed to meet a contemporary demand and then to become obsolete.

To Alloway, Clement Greenberg's "Avant-Garde and Kitsch" looked like a classic case of iron-curtain aesthetics. He thought that Greenberg could not grasp that avant-garde art and kitsch are just different areas of a single visual field. Greenberg's aesthetics, Alloway said, are "static, rigid, self-perpetuating. Sensitiveness to the variables of our life and economy enable the mass arts to accompany the changes in our life far more closely than the fine arts which are a repository of time-binding values."[80] In fact, of course, Greenberg's essay analyzes artistic form precisely as something that changes in terms of social conditions. But Alloway's argument was successful because it was made in the name of all the new cultural stimuli to which younger artists wanted access— the goods on the other side of the iron curtain. Banham put it this way: "To find the junior *avant-garde* admiring with equal fervour peasant houses on Santorini, and the chrome-work on Detroit cars; the *Cutty Sark*, Chiswick House, *Camels* cigarette packs, and Corbusier's chapel at Ronchamp; Pollock, Paolozzi and Volkswagens—all this sounds like the complete abandonment of standards. In fact it is nothing of the sort—it is the abandonment of stylistic prejudice."[81]

But the argument for the new aesthetic was not solely generational. There were class politics as well. The new aesthetic presented itself as democratic, a people's art. "[T]he élite," Alloway wrote, "accustomed to set aesthetics standards, has found that it no longer possesses the power to dominate all aspects of art. It is in this situation that we need to consider the arts of the mass media. It is impossible to see them clearly within a code of aesthetics associated with minorities with pastoral and upper-class ideas because mass art is urban and democratic."[82]

The reason mass-produced culture is democratic is because it gives consumers freedom of choice: "It is not the hand-craft culture which offers a wide choice of goods and services to everybody . . . but the industrialised one. As the market gets bigger consumer choice increases: shopping in London is more diverse than in Rome; shopping in New York more diverse than in London. General Motors mass-produces cars according to individual selections of extras and colours."[83] The "long front" conception of culture is not simply anthropological. The anthropological conception of culture does not have an aesthetic dimension, and the IG was all about understanding the aesthetic dimension of consumer culture.

The core of the difficulty lay in the term "aesthetics" itself. Although the word derives from ancient Greek, it originated as a critical term in the eighteenth century. Modern aesthetic theory begins with Shaftesbury's definition of the experience of beauty as disinterested pleasure.[84] There are multiple explanations for the rise of this way of conceiving of beauty: it was an answer to the strictures on art made by Plato in the *Republic*; it was needed to distinguish fine art from mass-produced and mass-circulated art after the emergence of print and other technologies of reproduction; it allowed writers and artists in Protestant countries, like Britain and Prussia, to appreciate religious art produced in Catholic countries, like Italy, by divorcing form from content. The classic formulation of the aesthetic was Immanuel Kant's *Kritik der Urteilskraft* (*Critique of Judgment*), published in 1790. He defined art as "purposiveness without purpose."

In the nineteenth century, this concept was used precisely for the purpose of establishing a hierarchy of art types, and it informed British art theory from Walter Pater's *The Renaissance* (1873) to Clive Bell's *Art* (1914), Roger Fry's *Vision and Design* (1920), and Herbert Read's *Art and Industry* (1934). (Read was a founder of the ICA.) The aesthetic was accompanied by the coinage of other terms designed to distinguish the pleasing and edifying from the mass of cultural products. "High art" was first used in Britain in 1817, "highbrow" in 1884, "lowbrow" (1906), "avant-garde" (1910), "middlebrow" (1924), and "kitsch" (1926).[85] The distinctions those terms represented were baked into the way the British talked about art. In 1952, this was a big ship to turn around.

4.

The United States was not, of course, the only country in which product design played a role in the postwar economy. Design is about sales, but it is also about product differentiation. In the brute mechanical sense, all passenger cars are more or less identical—engines on wheels. What differentiates automobile brands (after price) for most buyers is the look of the cabin. It was therefore desirable for that look to have a name. One of the features of postwar economic renewal in Europe was the rise of branding by nationality: Danish furniture, German cars, Belgian chocolates.[86] Countries became identified with a product line and a look.

This was especially true for Italy. Unlike France and Germany, which were recovering their prewar status as major economic powers after 1945, Italy was moving from the second tier of producers up to the first. Economic growth rates in Italy were higher than in most of Europe. Between 1951 and 1958, the domestic growth rate in Italy averaged 5.5 percent; between 1958 and 1963, 6.3 percent—the *boom economico*. Certain Italian products became internationally recognized brands: Fiat, Olivetti, Vespa. But the area where Italy built predominance was domestic appliances—"white goods," in particular, refrigerators and washing machines. (Demand for dishwashers was not high: middle-class Italians still employed kitchen help.)[87]

Before 1958, the market for these products was largely domestic, but after 1958, helped by the establishment of the Common Market (EEC), Italy became a major exporter. By the mid-1960s, Italy was the third-largest producer of refrigerators and washing machines in the world, behind the United States and Japan. Italian refrigerators were lower in cost, in part because they were smaller than American refrigerators. (A society in which people shop daily has different refrigeration needs from a society in which people shop once a week and consume large quantities of frozen food.) But those products also had—like the Vespa, the Lamborghini, and the Pavoni espresso machine—an Italian "look."[88]

Italian artists recognized the opportunity that industrial transformation and economic growth presented—new firms were hiring architects to design appliances such as clocks and radios—and a new design rationale was articulated at the X Triennale di Milano in 1954, an architectural and design exhibition.[89] The new idea was that industrial design is applied art. It brings art into everyday life and thereby gives artists a civic and social function.[90] "The object created by the machine is an integral part of the whole panorama of modern art," as Gillo Dorfles put it in a special congress held at the close of the Triennale.[91]

Dorfles was an artist as well as a critic, and one of the most prolific figures in postwar Italian culture. (He would write the essay on Jasper Johns that accompanied Leo Steinberg's in the art magazine *Metro* in 1962.) In the spring of 1955, the IG learned that Dorfles would be in London, accompanying an exhibition called *Modern Italian Design* at the Italian Institute, and that July, he came to the ICA to participate in an IG-sponsored conversation with Banham, "Aesthetics and Italian Product Design."[92]

According to McHale's notes, Dorfles argued for "an external standard of taste by which both objects of fine art and objects of good 'non-art' could be judged."[93] Afterward, Banham responded in an article, "Industrial Design e arte popolare," in the Italian journal *Civiltà delle Macchine*. Banham agreed with Dorfles to a point. Dorfles was taking a "long front" view of culture. But Banham thought that you cannot talk about product design and fine art using the same standards. Popular arts such as cars, movies, and comic books require their own aesthetic orientation. Traditional aesthetics had no relevance to what he called "throw-away" culture and McHale called "the expendable ikon."[*][94] Consumerist culture is not disinterested, as Kant said aesthetic experience must be. Consumerist culture is trying to sell you something. The question, Banham said, is always: "What *will* sell?"[95] You can't bracket that question for the purposes of aesthetic appreciation. It *is* the aesthetic.

This is why IG writers thought that communications theory was more relevant than Kant for understanding contemporary visual culture. Norbert Wiener's *The Human Use of Human Beings*, on cybernetics, published in 1950, and Wilbur Schramm's *The Process and Effects of Mass Communication*, an edited volume published in 1954, were discussed at IG meetings and were influences on Alloway in particular.[96] "Now when I write about art (published) and movies (unpublished), all kinds of messages are transmitted to every kind of audience along a

---

* The term may allude to William K. Wimsatt's *The Verbal Icon: Studies in the Meaning of Poetry* (1954). Wimsatt taught in the English Department at Yale, where McHale spent the academic year 1955–1956.

multitude of channels," he wrote in 1959. "Art is one part of the field; another is advertising."[97]

Dorfles actually agreed with this. "There can be no art without the purpose of establishing some kind of intersubjective communication," he wrote in an English-language art journal in 1957.[98] Understanding art as communication is also why the particular obsession of the IG group was magazine advertisements, the source of most of the images in Paolozzi's "Bunk" collages. For advertisements are pure signaling systems. There is no form for form's sake in an advertisement: everything is subordinate to the message, and the viewer "replies" by either purchasing the product or not. "The new role of the spectator or consumer, free to move in a society defined by symbols, is what I want to write about," Alloway said.[99]

One model for this kind of criticism was Marshall McLuhan's first book, *The Mechanical Bride: Folklore of Industrial Man*, published in 1951. The book consists of fifty-nine mini-essays on commercial-culture images—comics, mass-market paperback book covers, and advertisements. In 1951, McLuhan was an obscure English professor in Canada specializing in the poetry of Alfred Tennyson. *The Mechanical Bride* did not sell many copies.[100] But McHale admired it, probably because he had spent a year in the United States and saw it there, and it was discussed at IG meetings.[101]

But McLuhan was anti-admass. He considered advertising a mode of brainwashing. "To get inside in order to manipulate, exploit, control is the object," he said. ". . . To keep everybody in the helpless state engendered by prolonged mental rutting is the effect of many ads and much entertainment alike."[102] (Later on, he would change his tune.)

Roland Barthes's *Mythologies* is a French version of *The Mechanical Bride*—fifty-three essays pegged to everyday cultural material, mostly iconographic. Like McLuhan, Barthes was out to uncover an implicit ideology. But that is not what the IG writers were doing. McHale noted that *The Mechanical Bride*'s "strong moral overtones render many conclusions outmoded."[103] For IG members, removing moral, class, and political presuppositions was essential to being able to get access to the world of consumerism.

The Smithsons met as architecture students at the University of Durham, in the northeast of England. They married in 1949, and set up their practice a year later. They, too, found advertising a creative stimulus. Walter Gropius wrote a book on grain silos, they announced in 1956; "today we collect ads."[104] And they did: their kitchen wall was covered with advertisements clipped from magazines such as *Esquire* and *Ladies' Home Journal*.[105] They wanted to bring advertising's excitement and sense of immediacy into their work as architects. They wanted their buildings to function like an advertisement in the same sense that Gropius wanted his to function like a grain solo.

The Smithsons saw themselves fighting the same class war that Alloway was fighting. "We cannot ignore the fact that one of the traditional functions of fine art, the definition of what is fine and desirable for the ruling class was therefore ultimately that which is desired by all society, now had been taken over by the ad man," they wrote.

> [A]ds are packed with information—data of a way of life and a standard of living which they are simultaneously inventing and documenting . . . Mass production advertising is establishing our whole pattern of life—principles, morals, aims, aspirations, and standard of living. We must somehow get the measure of this intervention if we are to match its powerful and exciting impulses with our own.[106]

For some members of the IG, the most stimulating advertisements were the ones for American cars.

5.

Cars themselves had symbolic import in the postwar democracies. They stood for freedom, even if it was "driving a car" freedom. "Social and physical mobility, the feeling of a certain sort of freedom, is one of the things that keep our society together," the Smithsons wrote in 1958, "and the symbol of this freedom is the individually owned motor-car."[107] But Detroit cars in the 1950s were not just engines on wheels, like the Model T. They were metallic sculptures, stylized extravaganzas, loaded symbolic systems. It was the era of the tail fin.

In car design, streamlining (a style of product design associated with Raymond Loewy) came first. Automobiles are naturally amenable to streamlining, since streamlining is above all an aerodynamic look. A streamlined car looks fast, powerful, efficient. The tail fin, on the other hand, was a postwar phenomenon. The tail fin alludes to aerodynamics, too, but it also has the look, which streamlining does not, of excess. It does not make the car go faster. It's ornamental, a message without a function, "purposiveness without purpose" (except to sell cars).

The tail fin was invented by a designer at General Motors named Harley Earl, who was inspired by the Lockheed P-38 Lightning, a fighter plane that he saw in an airfield near Detroit in the spring of 1941. Nine months later, the United States was at war, and by government decree, the automobile industry shut down. From February 1942 to October 1945, no passenger cars were manufactured in the United States. The industry was converted to the production of matériel, from ammunition to tanks and planes. General Motors alone manufactured 2,300 products for the military, $12 billion worth.[108]

When the war ended, Earl introduced his new look. The first car with tail fins was the 1948 Cadillac (a General Motors brand). It entered a booming car market, the result of replacement demand and the needs of returning GIs. By the middle of 1953, though, those demands had been met and car sales plateaued. What now sold were new designs and annual model changes—goods people don't need, but can be persuaded to want.[109] An arms race ensued.

The industry term for tail fins, hood ornaments, oversized bumpers, protruding tailpipes, chrome detailing—nonfunctional design elements on cars—was "borax" (adjective: "borageous"). By 1955, cars had become so overloaded with borax that even Loewy objected. He called the new cars "jukeboxes on wheels," and thought they were damaging to the national interest. "Nothing about the appearance of the 1955 automobiles offsets the impression that Americans must be wasteful, swaggering, insensitive people," he warned. "Automotive borax offers gratuitous evidence to people everywhere that much of what they suspect about us may be true."[110]

But people *like* borax. And if the standard for design is "form follows function," then streamlining is borax, too. The streamlined toaster does not make better toast faster. It just looks like it does. Streamlining adheres to principles of classical sculpture and architecture, though: formally integrated, without excess. Tail-fin design, on the other hand, is all about ornament and appliqué. Some car models, for example, had faux air-intake vents on the sides.*

Banham was fascinated by borax. He gave a talk, "Borax, or the Thousand Horse-Power Mink," at the ICA in March 1955, before Dorfles's visit, and he followed it up with two articles, "Machine Aesthetic" and "Vehicles of Desire."[111] Banham called the Detroit automobile "a thick ripe stream of loaded symbols—that are apt to go off in the face of those who don't know how to handle them." The designer's "creative thumb-prints—finish, fantasy, punch, professionalism, swagger"—are signs of artistry. As the Smithsons said about ads, cars serve a function that art traditionally performed: they tell us something about life. As Banham put it: "Arbiter and interpreter between the industry and the consumer, the body stylist deploys, not a farrage of meaningless ornament, as fine-art critics insist, but a means of saying something of breathless, but unverbalisable, consequence to the live culture of the Technological Century."[112]

A few months after Banham's "Vehicles of Desire," Barthes published a very similar "reading" of the new Citroen model, the DS 19, an exaggeratedly streamlined car. "I believe that the automobile is, today, the almost exact equivalent of the great Gothic cathedrals," he wrote. "[T]he dashboard looks more like the worktable of a modern kitchen than a factory control room: the slender panes of matte rippled metal, the little levers with their white ball finials, the simplified dials, the very discreteness of the chromium, everything indicates a sort of control exerted over movement, henceforth conceived as comfort rather than performance." "DS," he pointed out, is pronounced *Déesse*—Goddess.[113]

The person who turned this way of thinking about advertisements and new-model cars into works of art was Richard Hamilton.

6.

Hamilton was born in London in 1922. His father drove a delivery van, and the family lived in council houses—public housing. His artistic talent got him admitted to the Royal Academy Schools. During the war, he worked as an engineering draftsman at EMI; in 1948, he was admitted

---

* The tail-fin era came to an abrupt end with the failure of Ford's Edsel in 1957–1958 (the year of a recession), followed by the first, and highly successful, American ad campaign for the Volkswagen Beetle, which has almost the opposite design look, in 1959.

to the Slade School, where he met Nigel Henderson. Along with other friends, they used to visit the American embassy so they could read magazines such as *Life*, *Esquire*, *Good Housekeeping*, and *Scientific American*.

Hamilton was involved with the ICA from early on. He was among the thirty or so who saw Paolozzi show the Bunk collages in 1952. Hamilton later said that the most influential IG discussions he participated in were on information theory, specifically, John von Neumann's *Theory of Games and Economic Behavior* (written with Oskar Morgenstern and published in 1944) and Claude Shannon's *The Mathematical Theory of Communication* (the book Jakobson sent to Lévi-Strauss).* Those books gave him the idea that "you can express everything with something as simple as ones and zeros, and that value judgments don't count—you can't say this is good and this is bad . . . You're really forced into wondering what makes sense and what doesn't."[114] This was a useful foundation for thinking about images as messaging systems—as McLuhan had done, and as Barthes was about to do. Then, in 1956, Hamilton participated in the exhibition that opened the ideas the IG had been talking about to a wider public, *This Is Tomorrow*.

This Is Tomorrow ran from August 9 to September 9 at the Whitechapel Gallery, a venue for advanced art in the East End. It was, by art-world measures, a blockbuster. Almost twenty thousand people visited; more than fourteen hundred catalogues were sold.[115] British Pathé made two television newsreels about the show. The tone of the voice-over was, a little bit, What will these darned artists come up with next? But the films do capture something of the intent.[116]

This Is Tomorrow was not actually an IG event. By then, the IG had stopped meeting. The exhibition emerged out of discussions among a large group vaguely headed by Theo Crosby, an architect and an editor at *Architectural Design*.[117] But IG figures, Alloway in particular, played a major role in framing the purpose. The format was design collaboration across art forms. Thirty-eight people—painters, sculptors, and architects—were divided into twelve groups, and each team was responsible for designing an environment.† Paolozzi, Henderson, and the

---

* The IG was addressed by a British expert on cybernetics, E. W. Meyer, who spoke on "Probability and Information Theory and Their Application to the Visual Arts," in March 1955.
† In some secondary literature, the number of artists is given as thirty-six, but this is a miscount. Group 1: Theo Crosby, William Turnbull, Germano Facetti, Edward Wright; Group

Smithsons were in one group. Hamilton was teamed with McHale and John Voelcker, an architect. Their exhibit was located right at the entry, so it was the environment visitors encountered first, and it seems to have been the most-photographed.

McHale and Hamilton agreed to use the occasion to represent the subjects the IG had been interested in. Their installation was in part a three-dimensional collage of advertising and entertainment images, including a blowup of a famous still of Marilyn Monroe in *The Seven Year Itch*; a giant inflatable Guinness bottle; a towering Robby the Robot, from the science fiction movie *Forbidden Planet*, carrying an unconscious, barely dressed woman, King Kong–style.* There was also a reproduction of Van Gogh's *Sunflowers*, said to be the most popular reproduction sold at the National Gallery.

The installation was also a sensorium. When visitors stepped on the floor, a strawberry freshener was emitted. People could select songs on a jukebox, which consequently seems to have played constantly while the exhibition was open. Visitors could also hear the tape-recorded voices of earlier visitors. Optical illusions were created; there was a projector and motorized simulacra of a piece by Marcel Duchamp. The whole installation was a fun-house experience that raised questions about perception—including, as collage does, the coherence, or not, of everyday sensory experience.

Hamilton's poster for the exhibition, *Just What Is It That Makes Today's Homes So Different, So Appealing?*, became a landmark in postwar art. The story of that work is complicated by disputes over who contributed what. McHale's year in the United States was spent at Yale, on a fellowship, where he studied with several artists, the most important of whom, for him, was Josef Albers. Albers relies, McHale wrote, "on psychophysical laws rather than aesthetic hypotheses."[118] This was IG-compatible.

Like Paolozzi, McHale was a collagist, and while he was in the

---

2: Richard Hamilton, John McHale, John Voelcker; Group 3: J. D. H. Catleugh, James Hull, Leslie Thornton; Group 4: Anthony Jackson, Sarah Jackson, Emilio Scanavino; Group 5: John Ernest, Anthony Hill, Denis Williams; Group 6: Eduardo Paolozzi, Alison and Peter Smithson, Nigel Henderson; Group 7: Victor Pasmore, Ernö Goldfinger, Helen Phillips; Group 8: James Stirling, Michael Pine, Richard Matthews; Group 9: Mary Martin, John Weeks, Kenneth Martin; Group 10: Robert Adams, Frank Newby, Peter Carter, Colin St. John Wilson; Group 11: Adrian Heath, John Weeks; Group 12: Lawrence Alloway, Geoffrey Holroyd, Tony del Renzio.
* *Forbidden Planet* was the first commercial movie with a completely electronic soundtrack. The music was by Bebe and Louis Barron, avant-garde composers who recorded the soundtrack in their studio on West Eighth Street in the Village. John Cage used the studio when he was making *Williams Mix*.

United States, he collected magazine ads, catalogue illustrations, copies of *Mad* magazine, Elvis Presley records, and similar items. Since he was abroad, his participation in the design of the installation for *This Is Tomorrow* was limited, much to Hamilton's annoyance. But Magda Cordell was having an affair with McHale, and she visited him in New Haven. When she returned, she brought McHale's collection with her, apparently in a black box.

Hamilton used McHale's material, along with magazines and comics that were available in the Cordells' flat, where he did the work, to construct his collage. He gave Magda Cordell and Terry, his wife, a list of topics—Man, Woman, Humanity, History, Food, Newspaper, Cinema, TV, Telephone, Comics, Words, Tape Recording, Cars, Domestic Appliances, Space—and they searched for corresponding images. Hamilton set out to produce a collage in the spirit of *Mad*, which was not available in Britain in 1956. It was in McHale's black box, though, and Hamilton must have recognized that *Mad* was a mass-culture satire on mass culture, a comic book about comic books.

What Makes Today's Homes So Different, So Appealing? presents an Adam and Eve in a consumerist paradise containing a full array of domestic appliances, popular entertainment, and reproduction technology. The living room is from an advertisement in *Ladies' Home Journal* for a flooring company, which is also the source of the title. The Adamic bodybuilder is Irwin (Zabo) Koszewski; his picture was clipped from a pocket-sized magazine called *Tomorrow's Man*, published in Chicago (and so must have been in McHale's stash). The phallic "Pop" is from an advertisement for Tootsie Roll Pops. Hamilton said he made the whole thing in an afternoon.[119] The original is 10.25 by 9.25 inches, the size of a sheet of paper. It was photocopied in black and white and blown up as a poster, which was placed near the entrance to the gallery. A copy also appeared in the catalogue.

This Is Tomorrow was a statement exhibition—arguably, three statements. The first was addressed to the critics of consumerism. Alloway had given a lecture at the ICA, "The Audience as Consumer: Independent Television and Audience Research."[120] The context was the introduction, less than two years earlier, of commercial television to Britain. Alloway's belief—the IG belief—was that watching a commercial is not the intellectual equivalent of being hit over the head with a brick. The commercial is part of an act of communication in which the viewer participates. Advertisement, design, packaging, and even entertainment goods, such as pop songs, are feedback loops. And this is what the catalogue for *This Is Tomorrow* informs visitors: "The elements of this exhibition are not only the concern of the artist," it says; "they are yours. We all share the same environment: we are all in the same boat." The philosophy of consumerism.

The exhibition's second and third statements addressed the futurism of its title. The exhibition seemed to be saying that, despite the rearguard efforts of British humanists, the future was being made by science and technology, and that art had to become part of that future, not its antagonist.* And finally, there is a prediction: What will the future look like? It will look like America.

The IG term for commercial culture, advertising, and product design was "popular art." Who first shortened this to "pop art" is unknown; the first appearance of "pop art" in print is in an article by the Smithsons in 1956.† They were referring to popular culture itself as a kind of art. In January 1957, Hamilton wrote the Smithsons a letter, evidently a follow-up to a conversation, in which he proposed to define pop art as:

Popular (designed for a mass audience)
Transient (short-term solution)
Expendable (easily forgotten)
Low cost
Mass produced
Young (aimed at youth)
Witty
Sexy
Gimmicky
Glamorous
Big business[121]

---

* C. P. Snow's "The Two Cultures," published a month after *This Is Tomorrow* closed, is an attack on British humanists as Luddites. Omitted from the book version (1959) was Snow's comment that scientific culture, as opposed to the humanities, is "steadily heterosexual . . . there is an absence—surprising to outsiders—of the feline and oblique." (*New Statesman and Nation* 52 [October 6, 1956], 413.)
† "The pop-art of today, the equivalent of the Dutch fruit and flower arrangement, the pictures of second rank of all the Renaissance schools, and the plates that first presented to the public the Wonder of the Machine Age and the New Territories, is to be found in today's glossies—bound up with the throw-away object." Alison Smithson and Peter Smithson, *Ark* (November 1956). The term also appears in the captions in Alloway's "The Arts and the Mass Media" (1958).

Peter Smithson said he never saw the letter because it never arrived; Hamilton published it in a collection of his writings in 1982.[122]

Hamilton's list is still a description of the popular arts, but it can be taken (and often is taken) as a recipe for fine art. And shortly after he wrote the letter, Hamilton produced a series of paintings that incorporate product-advertising imagery: *Hommage à Chrysler Corp.* (1957), *Hers Is a Lush Situation* (1958), *Toastuum* (1958), *$he* (1958–1961), and a series of four paintings titled *Towards a Definitive Statement on the Oncoming Trends in Menswear and Accessories* (1962). The process involved a Cubist rearrangement of details: "the main motif, the vehicle, breaks down into an anthology of presentation techniques," as he explained the shapes in *Hommage*.[123]

The question about these paintings is the question Pop Art always raises: Is the iconography of commercial culture being represented as imitation or critique? The question is a crux, insoluble, but the argument for critique was contradicted by Hamilton himself.[124] "Affirmation propounded as an avante [*sic*] garde aesthetic is rare," he wrote in 1961 for a little magazine for which Alloway was one the editors.

> The Pop-Fine-art mystique on the other hand—the expression of popular culture in fine art terms—is, like Futurism, fundamentally a statement of belief in the changing values of society. Pop-Fine-art is a profession of approbation of mass culture, therefore also antiartistic . . . [P]erhaps it is Mama—a cross-fertilization of Futurism and Dada which upholds a respect for the culture of the masses and a conviction that the artist in 20th century urban life is inevitably a consumer of mass culture and potentially a contributor to it.[125]

British Pop Art was an embrace of consumerism and free-market capitalism. That embrace was a critique, but it was a critique of the cultural politics of British humanism and the British left. It used the image of America to break the grip of the past on British art and thought. Of course, that past was rapidly receding for reasons having nothing to do with art. Like everyone else, the artists were along for the ride.

13

THE FREE PLAY OF THE MIND

Lawrence Ferlinghetti and Shigeyoshi (Shig) Murao at the *Howl* trial.
Photograph by Robert Lackenbach. (*LIFE Images Collection / Getty Images*)

1.

American higher education had two periods of explosive growth.[1] The first was between 1880 and 1920, when the modern research university came into being in the United States. Student enrollment in those years increased by 500 percent and the number of faculty increased by 400 percent.[2] The second period was between 1945 and 1975, when the number of institutions doubled, the number of undergraduates increased by almost 500 percent, and the number of graduate students increased by nearly 900 percent.[3] In the 1960s alone, undergraduate enrollments more than doubled; the number of doctorates awarded every year tripled; and more faculty positions were created than had been created in the entire 325-year history of American higher education prior to 1960.[4]

Both growth spurts were fueled by federal spending. The Morrill Acts, passed in 1862 and 1890, granted land to colleges and universities to enable them to provide education in "agriculture and the mechanic arts." The University of California was one of many public universities made possible by the first Morrill Act. It was created in 1868 by amalgamating the existing College of California with an institution endowed by land-grant revenues.[5]

After 1945, there were three major financial injections. The first was the G.I. Bill, which, among many provisions, paid tuition and living expenses for veterans attending institutions of higher education. By 1947, to almost everyone's surprise, almost half the students in American colleges and universities—1.15 million people—were on the G.I. Bill. It was a windfall for higher education. All colleges and universities had to do was add classroom seats and some dormitory beds, and the government paid full freight. In the end, 7.8 million veterans took advantage of the Act's benefits, 2 million of them enrolling in institutions of higher education.[6]*

The second stimulus was government funding for research, launched by a report organized by an MIT engineer and administrator with a long career in government, Vannevar Bush. The report, *Science—The Endless Frontier* (1945), became the standard argument for government subvention of basic science in peacetime. Key funding sources after 1945 included the National Institute of Mental Health, founded in 1949, and the National Science Foundation, founded in 1950. There was also funding from the Defense Department, NASA (later on), and other government agencies. Bush is the godfather of the system known as contract overhead—the practice of billing granting agencies for indirect costs, which allowed universities to spread the wealth across all of their activities.[7]

And the third stimulus was the National Defense Education Act of 1958 (NDEA), a response to Sputnik and the panic it induced about a "technology gap." The NDEA put the federal government for the first time in the business of subsidizing education directly rather than through contracts for research. The Act singled out certain areas for public investment: science, mathematics, and foreign languages. But

---

* Not every university welcomed the policy. The president of the University of Chicago, Robert Maynard Hutchins, predicted it would turn universities into "educational hobo jungles." James Conant, the president of Harvard, had similar concerns. In fact, G.I. Bill students were frequently at the top of their classes.

the NDEA, too, was a tide that lifted all boats. In 1946, federal grants to higher education amounted to $197 million; in 1970, it was $2.682 billion.[8] There was also substantial research support from private foundations, such as Rockefeller, Ford, Sloan, Pew, and Mellon.

The NDEA was passed just as the effects of the higher birth rate kicked in. Between 1955 and 1970, the number of eighteen-to-twenty-four-year-olds in the United States grew from 15 million to 24 million.[9] In 1955, there were 670,000 freshmen in American colleges; in 1970, there were more than 2 million.[10] Between 1954 and 1965, the University of California created four new campuses: Riverside, Irvine, Santa Cruz, and San Diego.[11]

The main idea, if not completely the reality, behind this second wave of expansion was meritocracy, the opening of opportunities to talent—or, in the language of the time, identifying aptitude in order to develop human capital. The Educational Testing Service was founded in 1948 for the purpose of administering the Scholastic Aptitude Test, which is essentially an IQ test designed to pick out the brightest members of each high school cohort, whatever their backgrounds and wherever they live, and funnel them into college.[12]

Meritocracy is a sorting mechanism, and it had an explicit national security rationale. In the words of the NDEA: "The security of the Nation requires the fullest development of the mental resources and technical skills of its young men and women . . . We must increase our efforts to identify and educate more of the talent of our Nation."[13] This was an echo of the report Harry S. Truman's Commission on Higher Education issued in 1947, which called for an end to barriers to educational opportunity based on race, religion, and class. (The commission seemed to feel that the situation for women was fine.)[14] If the purpose of education is to get the most out of a nation's human resources, it is irrational to exclude persons on the basis of attributes extraneous to aptitude, such as family income, religion, and skin color.

The concept of meritocracy extended to faculty—to a point. Before 1950, the professoriate was more than 70 percent Protestant; after 1950, the proportion of Catholic and Jewish professors increased significantly. On the other hand, the number of female and nonwhite faculty remained tiny. As late as 1969, 96 percent of professors were white and 81 percent were men.[15]

Expansion on that scale and involving those sums was bound to have an effect on cultural and intellectual life. In some areas, the university supplemented or replaced "Bohemia"—communities like Greenwich Village, Provincetown, and North Beach—as a space for independent art and thought. There was a boom in creative writing programs, for example, when universities realized that many G.I. Bill students wanted to write, and after the war it became a common practice for writers to be trained (and credentialed) in universities after taking courses taught by other writers who had been trained (and credentialed) in universities.[16]

The university also largely replaced the prewar world of little magazines and ad hoc political organizations, some of which had thrived because they supported people, Jews, for example, or political radicals, who faced obstacles to academic careers. If Clement Greenberg had been born ten years later, he would probably have become an art history professor.[17] Little magazines are hand-to-mouth affairs. Academic positions were attractive to the next generation of Greenbergs because of the institutional support they provided. Intellectuals did not have to work to create networks of like-minded people; they walked into fields already fully networked and with subsidized journals and presses.

What is striking about this spongelike development—absorption plus expansion—is that everything that got taken up into the academy ended up adopting a single discourse: the discourse of disinterestedness. Both periods of rapid growth in American higher education were periods of professionalization, and disinterestedness is a core value of professionalism. The professional does not pursue the work from self-interest—to promote a nonscholarly agenda or to make money. The professional academic's dedication is to knowledge, and knowledge production is what the institution rewards.[18] Academic freedom is designed to insulate scholars and researchers from political interference, and the standard of disinterestedness is, in effect, the pledge of the nonpolitical nature of academic inquiry. Many academics in the postwar years, particularly in the social sciences, cast themselves as post-ideological. One reason may have been a desire not to alienate their granting agencies.[19] But it was also the persona that their commitment to the profession required. Scholars in the 1950s who looked back on their prewar educations tended to be appalled by what they regarded as a lack of rigor and focus.[20]

And yet the American university did not become a factory for manufacturing experts. The distinctive feature of American education, the liberal arts and sciences college, was preserved and even flourished. In liberal educational systems, students do not "track" vocationally or professionally until they graduate. They pursue knowledge "for its own sake" across a range of fields. This is another meaning of "disinterestedness": an open mind, the freedom to think independent of "real-world" (familial, political, financial) constraints. It is the idea of *Bildung*, and it was part of Matthew Arnold's definition of culture. "And how is criticism to show disinterestedness?" he wrote in 1865.

> By keeping aloof from practice; by resolutely following the law of its own nature, which is to be a free play of the mind on all subjects which it touches; by steadily refusing to lend itself to any of those ulterior, political, practical considerations about ideas which plenty of people will be sure to attach to them.[21]

From 1955 to 1970, the proportion of liberal arts and sciences degrees among all bachelor's degrees awarded annually rose significantly for the first time in the century. And the evidence suggests that the students understood the mission. In 1967, 85.8 percent of freshmen listed "developing a meaningful philosophy of life" as a "very important" or "essential" personal goal. After 1970, as the proportion of degrees in the liberal arts and sciences began going down again, so did the percentage of freshmen giving high priority to developing a meaningful philosophy of life. By 2003, that number was 39.3 percent.[22]

In order to secure institutional legitimacy, though, even faculty in the liberal arts needed to present themselves as engaged in rigorous inquiry producing verifiable results. There had to be something there to investigate, and the investigation had to yield knowledge, not opinions. It was not immediately clear how literary criticism was going to qualify.

2.

The Modern Language Association (MLA), the professional organization for scholars of language and literature, was founded in 1883, during the first phase of academic professionalization. But it was not until 1951 that the MLA added "criticism" to its constitutional statement of purpose.[23] Before that, literary scholarship meant research: philology, bibliography, literary history, textual editing. "Criticism" meant appreciation, interpretation, and evaluation—subjective responses, not scholarship. Criticism is what magazines were for. To become an accepted academic practice, criticism needed to acquire some equivalent of the standard for scientific inquiry: verifiability.

This could not mean that interpretations of poems had to be reproducible, like the results of scientific experiments. It was impossible to require everyone to have the same understanding of Wordsworth's "A Slumber Did My Spirit Seal." What it did mean was that everyone had to have the same understanding of the protocols of interpretation, of what counted as a valid reading and what did not. A fence had to be built around the ballpark. The fence was erected by the New Criticism, the American name for an approach to literature that arose in two places in the 1920s: Vanderbilt University in Tennessee and the University of Cambridge in England. It was the first method of literary criticism to jump the gap between journalism and academia.

The New Criticism was a powerful and elegant paradigm. The power and elegance derived from the fact that it rules out of bounds many things people naturally think about when they read literature: the work as a reflection of the life of the author or the times in which it was written, the meanings the writer intended and the ideas they expressed, the way it makes us feel. The New Criticism set these often elusive and speculative questions aside and concentrated on the meanings generated by the words on the page. There was something bracing about this.

But can't anyone read the words on the page? The key claim of the New Criticism was that most people cannot. Literary language is figurative and polysemous, but people tend to read literature literally. They assume that the "I" in a text is the author, and that the work's meaning can be paraphrased. They think that the aesthetic or emotional effect on them is important to its worthiness as a poem or novel. The New Critics argued that these notions all lead to misreading. That it is hard for the untrained reader to abandon them was an excellent rationale for having English departments.

The figure behind the New Criticism in both its American and British instantiations was T. S. Eliot. Eliot belonged to a distinctive cultural type that flourished in the pre-academic era: he was a man of letters.[24] His influence is hugely disproportionate to both his position and his output. The poems and plays he published in his lifetime fill a single volume; his prose works are collections of talks and occasional journalism. He was dismissive of theories of literature, and he never held a regular academic appointment. During his most productive years as a writer, from 1917 to 1925, he worked in a bank.

Yet he was a true avant-gardist and he made a revolution. He changed the way poetry in English is written; he reset the paradigm for literary criticism; and (although this was never his intention) his work laid down the principles on which the modern English department is built. He is the most important figure in twentieth-century English-language literary culture.

He arrived in England in 1914, just after the war broke out, on a fellowship from the Harvard Philosophy Department, where he was a graduate student. Less than a year later, he had decided not to return to Cambridge. He had either come to England with a project in mind or devised one after meeting Ezra Pound, which happened about a month after he arrived. (Pound, a University of Pennsylvania graduate school dropout, had been in London since 1908.) The project was the professionalization of English letters.

Eliot and Pound argued, in the pages of little magazines in London, that the British confused literature with moral philosophy, social criticism, and religion. They were unprofessional, and "professionalism in art," as Eliot wrote in 1918, "is hard work on style with singleness of purpose."[25] The business of the poet is to make poems. Eliot's standard example of the poetry of mixed motives was the English Romantics—principally Blake, Wordsworth, Keats, and Shelley—and their Victorians heirs, principally Robert Browning, Tennyson, and Swinburne.

Eliot's principle was that "when we are considering poetry we must consider it primarily as poetry and not another thing."[26] What does that mean? It means seeing poems in the context of other poems. This is the argument of "Tradition and the Individual Talent," published in the little magazine *The Egoist* in 1919 (alongside excerpts from Joyce's *Ulysses*). "No poet, no artist of any art, has his complete meaning alone," Eliot wrote. "His significance, his appreciation is the appreciation of his relation to the dead poets and artists. You cannot value him alone; you must set him, for contrast and comparison, among the dead."[27] Only consciousness of the tradition makes it possible for a poet to produce something genuinely new.

Reading a poem as the expression of the writer's personality—or beliefs, or life history—is therefore uncritical. Poets may write poems under the stress of an emotion, he said, and poems may express emotions, but the two kinds of emotion are distinct. We are not interested in the poet. We are interested in the poem.

Eliot used this critical criterion to redefine the tradition. He introduced his first collection of critical essays, *The Sacred Wood*, in 1920, with an attack on the poetry and criticism of the nineteenth century, when, he thought, poets and critics had lost sight of what poetry should be. It was the seventeenth-century poets, in particular, the metaphysical poets—John Donne, Andrew Marvell, George Herbert—who were "in the direct current of English poetry," and they (along with the nineteenth-century French Symbolist poets) led to the modernist poetry that Eliot and Pound were writing.[28] Eliot's "tradition" required leaving out a lot of poetry.

Sales of Eliot's books at first were not robust. But he was taken up almost immediately by young British academics. The most influential of these was Ivor Armstrong Richards, who taught at Cambridge. Richards was excited by Eliot's second collection of poems, *Ara Vos Prec*, and he arranged to meet Eliot at Lloyds Bank in London, where Eliot was employed. "[A] figure stooping, very like a dark bird in a feeder," was Richards's first impression of Eliot standing at his worktable. He tried to talk Eliot into teaching at Cambridge; Eliot displayed no interest.[29] But Richards kept in touch, and they became friends.

Richards's field as an undergraduate had been moral science, a Cantabrigian combination of psychology and ethics, and he saw literature as an interesting problem in cognitive and affective reception. Richards thought that for most of us, poetry belongs in a "sphere of random beliefs and hopeful guesses," with similarly elusive subjects such as ethics, religion, justice, truth—subjects that are nevertheless "everything about which civilised man cares most."[30] He set out to get a handle on it. In 1925, he published *Principles of Literary Criticism*, a dense and abstract analysis of the aesthetic experience. In the same year, he began an experiment that would eventually produce a much more influential book, published in 1929, *Practical Criticism*.

The experiment involved handing students poems (in the end, Richards used thirteen) of varying quality, without titles, author names, or dates. Students were given time to study the poems—most read them four or more times—and then they submitted what Richards called "protocols," written evaluations. He collected around a thousand protocols.

He judged only thirty to be sound. All the rest—97 percent—displayed various types of misprision, and *Practical Criticism*, which quotes from 387 of the protocols, is essentially a taxonomy of the ways people misread poems: they make irrelevant associations, they have stock responses, they rely on "technical presuppositions," and so on. "The most disturbing and impressive fact brought out by this experiment," Richards wrote, "is that a large proportion of average-to-good (and in some cases, certainly, devoted) readers of poetry frequently and repeatedly *fail to understand it*."[31] The book was received as an empirical justification for teaching people how to read.

Richards was a charismatic lecturer, not because of his delivery, which was distinctly unhistrionic, but because he approached literature in a completely unbelletristic way. He treated it as a problem in psychology. "[H]e revealed to us, in a succession of astounding lightning flashes, the entire expanse of the Modern World," one undergraduate, Christopher Isherwood, remembered.

> . . . Poetry wasn't a holy flame, a fire-bird from the moon; it was a group of interrelated stimuli acting upon the ocular nerves, the semicircular canals, the brain, the solar-plexus, the digestive and sexual organs . . . In our conversation, we substituted the word "emotive" for the word beautiful; we learnt to condemn inferior work as a "failure in communication," or more crushing still, as "a private poem." We talked excitedly about "the phantom aesthetic state."[32]

Richards scientized the study of poetry. He made it a proper academic subject.*

Many people besides undergraduates showed up at Richards's lectures. Eliot himself filled out some protocols.[33] Marshall McLuhan studied with Richards when he was at Cambridge on a scholarship in the 1930s and learned from him techniques of close reading that he would apply to advertising copy in *The Mechanical Bride*.[34] Two Cambridge academics who would be leading figures in postwar literary

---

* Richards was not unique. Other literature professors were also treating the classroom as a place for experimentation—for example, Edith Rickert, at the University of Chicago. See Rachel Sagner Buurma and Laura Heffernan, *The Teaching Archive: A New History for Literary Study* (Chicago: University of Chicago Press, 2021), 66–106.

studies, F. R. Leavis and William Empson, were transformed by Richards's teaching. One critic who was inspired by hearing Richards's lecture was an American.

3.

Cleanth Brooks was born in Murray, Kentucky, in 1906. His father and grandfather were Methodist ministers and there was something self-consciously churchy about Brooks's approach to literature. The critical principle for which he is best known he called "the heresy of paraphrase." He did not mean the phrase ironically.

In 1924, he entered Vanderbilt, in Nashville. The university had recently severed ties with the Methodist Church and it did not have a strong national reputation, but it was probably the best university in the South and it attracted people who would become leading poets and critics: John Crowe Ransom, Donald Davidson, Allen Tate, and Robert Penn Warren. Ransom (also the son of a Methodist minister) and Davidson were from Tennessee; Tate and Warren, like Brooks, were from Kentucky.

These writers were modernists, but they were also men of letters in the nineteenth-century sense. Their poetry was dense and allusive but prosodically formal; they were not avant-gardists or vers-librists. They held a dual attitude toward the South. They were loyalists and critics, regionalists and cosmopolitans at the same time. The South may have been the backward place that Northern writers like H. L. Mencken described, but it stood for something, a traditional way of life, an alternative to industrial capitalism, and that was worth standing up for. They believed in something that Eliot, in "The Dry Salvages," a poem about his childhood in St. Louis and Cape Ann, in Massachusetts, called "the life of significant soil."[35]

Ransom, Davidson, Tate, and Warren published their poetry in a little magazine called *The Fugitive*, and they became known as the Fugitives.* The magazine lasted about three years, from 1922 to 1925, so by the time Brooks got to Nashville, the movement was near its end. Brooks wrote poetry, too. He took classes taught by Ransom, and he admired Davidson's criticism. His most important contact, though, was with Warren.[36]

---

* The origin and significance of the term are obscure; an association with the Fugitive Slave Act of 1850, one of the causes of the Civil War, was presumably unintended.

Warren, called Red, was a prodigy with a remarkable memory for literature. He entered Vanderbilt in 1921, when he was sixteen, intending to major in chemical engineering, but he got converted to poetry after taking classes with Ransom and Davidson. In the fall of his sophomore year, "The Waste Land" was published in the literary magazine *The Dial*, and Davidson loaned Warren a copy.[37] Warren and his friends memorized the poem and went around quoting from it; he drew a mural with crayons of scenes from the poem on the wall of a campus dormitory.[38]

Warren and Brooks became acquainted. After Brooks graduated from Vanderbilt, as class poet, he went to Tulane, in New Orleans, for graduate work. In 1929, he won a Rhodes Scholarship to study at Oxford. Warren was already there, at New College—he had won a Rhodes, too, after graduate work at Berkeley and Yale—and they began seeing each other nearly every day.[39] (Ransom had also had a Rhodes, in 1910–1913.)

During Brooks's first year at Oxford, Richards came to speak at his college, Exeter. Brooks had read *Principles of Literary Criticism* more than once, and although he was unpersuaded by the psychology, he was drawn by the attempt to think rigorously about the way poetry works. Richards's talk, he wrote later, was

> the first time I saw him and heard his voice. I had insisted that several of my friends attend the lecture with me, and to my surprise I found that, while I could follow clearly the argument, to my friends it was almost incomprehensible. They lacked the necessary preparation for what was a pioneering effort that broke with the literary training of the time—with the traditional British training as well as the American . . . [T]he practical effect of Richards's discussion of his thirteen selected poems was almost overpowering.[40]

While Brooks was at Oxford, Davidson began putting together a collection of essays. Ransom, Tate, and Warren agreed to contribute. There was a debate about what to call it. Tate and Warren wanted the title to be *Tracts Against Communism*.[41] Ransom and Davidson disagreed, and the book came out in 1930 as *I'll Take My Stand: The South and the Agrarian Tradition*, by Twelve Southerners. The use of a phrase from a song that had been popularized by blackface performers and served as the unofficial anthem of the Confederacy raised an issue the editors had actually hoped to finesse, the issue of Southern racism.

I'll Take My Stand is an all-out attack on the "North," by which the writers mean industrial capitalism, secularism, and social engineering—things that Warren and Tate apparently considered Communistic. "Agrarianism" was the authors' name for the alternative: a community-based, traditional society rooted in the land ("significant soil"). Warren's essay, "The Briar Patch," endorsed Booker T. Washington's agenda about race relations: "raising up" the African American race but maintaining racial separation. "[T]he Southern negro has always been a creature of the small town and farm," Warren explained. "That is where he chiefly belongs, by temperament and capacity; there he . . . is likely to find in agricultural and domestic pursuits the happiness that his good nature and easy ways incline him to as an ordinary function of his being."[42]

Even in the South, *I'll Take My Stand* was not well received.[43] Brooks, still in England, read it carefully, then sent a twelve-page letter to Davidson. On the "negro question," he wrote, "I don't think that we can afford to take a less liberal stand than Red Warren's." The real problem, though, was religious. What the regional question came down to was "maintaining or rebuilding a feudal society," and "a medieval-ism without religion is Hamlet played solely by hopelessly inadequate Rosencrantz's and Guildensterns' [*sic*]."[44]

In 1932, Eliot made his first visit to the United States since 1915 to deliver the Norton Lectures at Harvard. He stayed almost a year, and in April 1933, he gave the Page-Barbour Lectures at the University of Virginia. He began the lectures by expressing his interest in *I'll Take My Stand*. Although he had just arrived in the South, he said, his impressions had "strengthened my feeling of sympathy with [the book's] authors." (He did not mention that he was from Missouri, another border state with a history of slavery, like Tennessee and Kentucky.) He then proceeded to give a description of the ideal society that made the nature of his sympathy clear. Its population, he said, "should be homogeneous."

> [W]here two or more cultures exist in the same place they are likely either to be fiercely self-conscious or both to become adulterate. What is still more important is unity of religious background; and reasons of race and religion combine to make any

large number of free-thinking Jews undesirable . . . [E]xcessive tolerance is to be deprecated.[45]

Eliot published the lectures in 1934 as *After Strange Gods*. The subtitle was *A Primer of Modern Heresy*.

In 1936, a follow-up to *I'll Take My Stand* was published, edited by Tate and Herbert Agar, a journalist. This time, Brooks did contribute. His essay was "A Plea to the Protestant Churches." Liberal Protestantism, Brooks said, was in danger of becoming "merely a socio-political program." It placed its faith in science, and science can never be a source of values. Protestantism was "secularizing itself out of existence."[46]

In short, American New Criticism was founded by writers associated with a reactionary political and religious program, and under the aegis of a poet and critic, Eliot, who believed that modern society was, in his words, "worm-eaten with Liberalism."[47] They regarded the Enlightenment and the scientific revolution as misreadings of human nature. Eliot was a royalist. Tate was an anti-Semite who thought that liberalism and Marxism were Jewish.[48] Davidson was a white supremacist who would later lead an extralegal effort to prevent the integration of public schools in Tennessee.[49] The puzzle is obvious: How did the way these writers thought about literature became dominant in the postwar university, an institution that is the incarnation of the values of the modern liberal state? Meritocracy is precisely an attempt to counteract the undertow of region, tradition, and "orthodoxy."

Part of the answer is that, Davidson excepted, after 1936, they detached themselves from politics. Warren eventually changed his views on segregation, but there is not much evidence that the others changed theirs on anything. They just abstained from political associations. In this respect, the New Critics were following the pattern of Marxist intellectuals who, after 1936, began separating themselves from the Soviet Union, and by 1948 had largely shed or buried their political pasts.[50] "Literature and society" remained those intellectuals' rubric, with obvious links to Marxist thought, but the politics had disappeared. Did reactionary politics remain a subtext of the New Criticism?[51] Or was that politics translated into a posture of anti-modernity acceptable to critics with liberal or progressive views? Was there a point at which, with enough detail erased or ignored on both sides, the Southern critique of industrial capitalism intersected with, say, C. Wright Mills's or Allen Ginsberg's?

After 1936, the leading New Critics migrated north. Ransom moved to Kenyon College in 1937. Tate moved to Princeton in 1939 and the University of Minnesota in 1951. Warren moved from Louisiana State University (LSU) to the University of Minnesota in 1942, and in 1950, he went to Yale, where he rejoined Brooks, who had arrived there from LSU in 1947. Yale had already hired William K. Wimsatt in 1939 and René Wellek in 1946. Together, Brooks, Wellek, and Wimsatt put Yale at the forefront of academic literary studies. It would remain there for thirty years.

4.

This is the intellectual background of a critical approach that was widely adopted in the postwar university and that continues to constitute the bedrock of the discipline of literary studies in the twenty-first century. Wave after wave of anti-formalist assaults have battered the field since 1945, but "close reading," sometimes labeled "unpacking" or "thick description," has never been supplanted. You pull things out of texts. That is what it means to be a literature professor.

This is largely because the New Criticism validated academic criticism itself, replacing the man or woman of letters with the professor as the voice of critical authority. This was not accomplished by accident. The New Critics adapted to the university system self-consciously and programmatically. "Criticism," wrote Ransom in 1937, "must become scientific, or precise and systematic, and this means that it must be developed by the collective and sustained effort of learned persons—which means that its proper seat is in the universities."[52] The title of Ransom's essay was "Criticism, Inc." That later on such a phrase could have been meant only ironically shows how successful the New Critical program of professionalization was. For when professionals talk about their work in personal, not business, terms, when they mock the idea that they are somehow "incorporated," their socialization is complete.

The first rationale for justifying the professionalization of literary criticism—that there is a pedagogical need for it—had been addressed by Richards. Still, it was not obvious how the average literature professor was supposed to instruct the average college student. This need was met by one of the most successful textbooks ever produced, Brooks and Warren's *Understanding Poetry*, published in 1938.

The original plan was for Tate and Warren to do the book together, but Tate dropped out and invited Brooks to take his place.[53] Brooks and Warren were both then at LSU, where they had co-founded and were co-editing *The Southern Review*, a major venue for New Critical writing—along with *The Kenyon Review*, founded by Ransom in 1939, and *The Sewanee Review*, of which Tate became editor in 1944.* (These quarter-lies played the same role for New Critics that *Partisan Review*, *Commentary*, and *Dissent* did for Northern "literature and society" critics.)

Understanding Poetry is a 680-page book containing more than two hundred poems, accompanied by exegeses and classroom exercises. An introductory "Letter to the Teacher" echoes Eliot: "This book has been conceived on the assumption that if poetry is worth teaching at all it is worth teaching as poetry." And the authors warn against mistakes students make about poetry of the kind that Richards had identified in *Practical Criticism*: "message-hunting," "beautiful statements of some high truths," and so on.[54] The first edition reflected Eliot's canonical strictures. Shelley, in particular, was rudely treated.

There were four editions of *Understanding Poetry*, the last in 1976, but the second edition, published in 1950, had the greatest impact. It had 727 pages and added fifty-four poems by twentieth-century writers, including "The Waste Land," provided with a twenty-two-page interpretation. By 1954, that edition was being used in more than 250 institutions.[55]

In 1941, Ransom published *The New Criticism*, a study of Richards, Empson, Eliot, and Yvor Winters, who taught at Stanford. The book gave the New Criticism its name, even though Ransom's argument was that those critics were not "new" *enough*. He thought their analysis of poetry was adulterated by being mixed with psychology, history, and philosophy.

But then, the scope began to broaden. In 1939, Brooks had collected some of his own essays as *Modern Poetry and the Tradition*, and there, too, as the use of Eliot's term implied, the conception of the canon is highly selective. But Brooks's second collection, *The Well Wrought Urn*, which came out in 1947, presented close readings of ten poems from a range of historical periods, with the idea that *all* poems worth studying display certain formal features, specifically, paradox, irony, and

---

* Inexplicably, C. Wright Mills submitted his and Hans Gerth's essay on James Burnham, "A Marx for the Managers," to *The Southern Review*. Brooks turned it down.

ambiguity—devices that multiply and complicate meaning.* This had already been established as way of writing about seventeenth-century poets, such as Donne, and certain nineteenth-century poets deemed "non-Victorian," like Gerard Manley Hopkins and Thomas Hardy. Now Brooks was doing close readings of Milton, Wordsworth, Keats, and Tennyson—poets Eliot had sidelined from the tradition. He believed, he said, that he had discovered a "characteristic structure of poetry" per se.[56]

The treatment of the nineteenth-century poets was a little grudging, it's true. "Tennyson," Brooks wrote, "was not always successful in avoiding the ambiguous and the paradoxical; and indeed, in some of his poems his failure to avoid them becomes a saving grace."[57] But his inclusion of poets such as Tennyson and Wordsworth showed that close reading was applicable to all poetry, not just Eliot's canon. In 1951, in a special issue of *The Kenyon Review*, Brooks spelled out his formalist credo. He believed, he said, "[t]hat the primary concern of criticism is with the problem of unity—the kind of whole which the literary work forms or fails to form, and the relation of the various parts to each other in building up this whole . . . That form is meaning."[58] This is the principle of close reading.

Brooks's closest collaborator at Yale was Wimsatt, who was from Maryland, another border state, and he, too, was a defender of the old South. (He was also seven feet tall. Brooks was five-six; as a pair, they were the subject of commentary at Yale.)[59] With Monroe Beardsley, a philosopher, Wimsatt had published two key statements, both in *The Sewanee Review*: "The Intentional Fallacy" (1946), which argued that the meaning of a poem must be educed from internal evidence, and "The Affective Fallacy" (1949), which argued that a poem's effect on the reader is irrelevant to how well it functions as a poem. Wimsatt and Beardsley said that they were liberating literary criticism from "impressionism and relativism" and approaching an "objective criticism."[60] Both essays were republished in 1954 by the University Press of Kentucky in Wimsatt's *The Verbal Icon*, a title that captures the New Critical conception of the poem.

Still, academic criticism needed to present itself as not just a method but a discipline, a body of accumulated knowledge. This was the goal of

---

* Brooks's key statement on irony, "Irony and 'Ironic' Poetry," was published in the journal *College English* in 1948. He did not reprint the essay in a book.

Wimsatt and Brooks's *Literary Criticism: A Short History*, published in 1957, and René Wellek's *History of Modern Criticism*, the first volume of which appeared in 1955. Wellek was born in 1903 in Austria and educated in Prague, where he was involved in the linguistic circle that included Roman Jakobson. Like Jakobson, he fled Czechoslovakia in 1939 and, more quickly than Jakobson, made it to the United States. He taught at the University of Iowa before going to Yale in 1946. In 1949, with Austen Warren, a former Iowa colleague, he published *Theory of Literature*, a book that defined two types of criticism, "intrinsic" and "extrinsic." Intrinsic was the preferred mode.[61]

Though it covers only two hundred years, 1750–1950, Wellek's *History* turned into a massive undertaking. It is eight volumes in all, and the last two did not appear until 1992. The key stratagem in both histories, Wimsatt and Brooks's and Wellek's, is the incorporation of academic criticism into the pre-university tradition. Wellek's *History* begins with a chapter on Kant that leads, six volumes later, to a chapter on Wimsatt. This practice was followed in virtually every academic anthology of literary criticism: the literature professor is connected to pre-university poet-critics, like Coleridge and Horace, and philosophers, like Nietzsche and Kant. The one figure to whom the academic critic is not traced back, and who is almost always absent from these anthologies, is the turn-of-the-century man or woman of letters.

This explains the transformation of Eliot into a theorist and proto-academic.[62] Historically, Eliot stands between the first academic critics—Richards, Empson, Leavis, and the New Critics—and the whole sequence of poet-critics and philosophers stretching back to Kant, and from Kant back to Aristotle. In the academic critics' effort to situate themselves within a genealogy that extends prior to the formation of the modern university English department, Eliot was the link. Eliot the practicing poet and literary journalist disappears; he is replaced by a critic with a theory of poetry. Having a theory is what gets you into a history of criticism.

No doubt there were professors who sympathized with the assault Eliot mounted on modernity and who championed him for that reason. But there were many more who simply found Eliot ideally suited to the business of giving academic criticism a plausible prehistory, and who did not have a problem separating Eliot's literary concepts from his social criticism and political views. Either way, Eliot became a model figure in an academic discipline, literary criticism, that gradually but persistently turned inward-facing, becoming a field in which professors write only for other professors. This was almost certainly not a fate he had contemplated.

5.

Wellek's essay on Eliot appeared just as the New Criticism was losing its cutting-edge reputation. Eliot himself, in 1956, in a talk before an audience of fourteen thousand in a basketball stadium at the University of Minnesota (a measure of his celebrity), spoke disapprovingly of "the lemon-squeezer school of criticism," whose origins, he suspected, lay in "the classroom methods of Professor Richards."[63] (How many of the fourteen thousand Minnesotans would have had any idea who Professor Richards was is an interesting question.) But the New Criticism had accomplished its institutional mission. Literature was established as an autonomous field of inquiry, the exclusive subject of an academic discipline. The most substantive effort to establish an interdisciplinary approach was eventually spun off as a separate field: American Studies.[64]

The book standardly cited as marking the fresh direction in academic criticism is Northrop Frye's *Anatomy of Criticism*, published in 1957.[65] The claim is true as far as it goes: Frye's book was received as a rebuke to the New Criticism and it introduced a new method of interpretation, sometimes called myth and archetype criticism. But Frye's ambitions were no different from Ransom's and Wimsatt's. He wanted to make literary study more like a science. And his claims about literature were far more grandiose. If Richards is Locke, breaking down aesthetic response into its psychological components, Frye is Hegel. He built up a totalizing and leakproof system of literary forms.

As a person, Frye did not make a forceful first impression. He was shy and somewhat wan—"surprisingly colorless" is how M. H. Abrams, a professor at Cornell and Frye's exact contemporary, remembered him.[66]* As a teacher and a writer, on the other hand, Frye presented as a powerful intellect. He conveyed authority.

He was born in Quebec in 1912 and raised as a Methodist. He attended the University of Toronto, first at Victoria College, taking an

---

* Abrams was possibly provoked by hearing of Frye's description of *him* as a "rather undistinguished person in appearance" (Robert Denham, *Remembering Northrop Frye* [Jefferson, NC: McFarland and Co., 2010], 146).

undergraduate degree in philosophy (he never got a PhD), and then at Emmanuel College, a theology school. He was ordained a minister in the United Church of Canada, the largest Protestant church in the country, after which he spent two years at Merton College, Oxford. He returned to Canada on August 23, 1939, the day the Nonaggression Pact was signed.[67] He taught at Victoria for the rest of his career, serving as its chancellor from 1978 until his death in 1991.

The Christian commitments of the New Critics sometimes led people to look for underlying religious conceptions in their criticism. But in Frye's work, the religious conceptions are not hidden. His whole theory of literary meaning derives from religious thought. In college, Frye was obsessed with the modernist writers, Eliot in particular. But his politics were liberal. He read *After Strange Gods* with a sense of "personal outrage and betrayal," he said.[68] Not long after, he took a graduate class on William Blake and was assigned to write a paper on Blake's poem "Milton." Like students everywhere, he started the paper the night before it was due; as all students hope to but few do, he had a revelation. "About half-past three in the morning," he said, "some very funny things started happening in my mind, and I began to see dimensions of critical experience that I'd never dreamed existed before—a sudden expansion of the horizon. When I went out for breakfast—I remember it was a bitterly cold morning—I knew that I was to write a book on Blake."[69] (It is amusing to contrast Allen Ginsberg's Blakean revelation while masturbating in East Harlem.) It took him many years. The book was *Fearful Symmetry*, published in 1947.

Although Frye never mentions his name in it, his book is an answer to Eliot. In an essay first published in 1920, Eliot had made Blake stand for what was wrong with the Romantic poets. Blake had ideas, Eliot said, and that is not the poet's job. "We have the same respect for Blake's philosophy," he wrote, ". . . that we have for an ingenious piece of home-made furniture: we admire the man who has put it together out of the odds and ends about the house."[70] He contrasted Blake with Dante. It was Blake's misfortune to live in the intellectual confusion of modern times; Dante was lucky to have lived in the philosophically grounded world of medieval Christendom.

In an interview many years later, Frye called Eliot's essay "a most god-forsaken piece of nonsense." But he was not referring to what Eliot said about Blake. He was referring to what Eliot said about Dante. Frye thought that Dante constructed his own mythological universe—he created what Claude Lévi-Strauss called a *bricolage*—just like Blake did, and, in fact, just like Eliot did. *Bricolage*, as Lévi-Strauss defined it, "is about having a problem to solve. One has certain random elements available that bear no relation to the problem at hand. And then there is an effort of thought: how am I going to manage to resolve my particular problem."[71] In his poetry, Frye said, Eliot was constructing "the same kind of homemade philosophy that Blake was."[72] "I owe a great deal to this [Blake] essay," Frye wrote later, ". . . because I soon realized that Blake was a typical poet in this regard: he differed from Dante only in that Dante's *bricolage* was more widely accepted, and different from Eliot himself, in this respect, hardly at all."[73]

What was the revelation that Frye experienced reading Blake that winter night in 1935? He suddenly understood how to read Christian scripture. Blake "made sense of the background I was brought up in," he said. Blake "led me to see the shape in the Bible and the reasons why it's so central in our cultural tradition."[74]

Frye was not the only critic interested in Blake in the 1940s. Alfred Kazin, a son of Jewish immigrants, was infatuated with Blake and taught a class on him at Black Mountain College in 1945. (Kazin did not have much respect for Black Mountain as an educational institution.)[75] A year later, he published *The Portable William Blake*, with a fifty-five-page introduction. The same year, Mark Schorer, at Berkeley, published *Blake: The Politics of Vision*.

Frye reviewed these books with some condescension. "In general," he observed, "it may be said of Mr. Kazin, as to a lesser extent of Dr. Schorer, that his desire to explain Blake to the reader has not proved equal to his desire to have the reader overhear him making learned and acute comments about Blake."[76] Frye was interested in the reason Schorer's and Kazin's writing was so pretentious. It was the consequence, he decided, of a "defective method."[77] They didn't understand how to read Blake because they didn't understand how to read literature. So Frye dedicated himself to working out a scheme for literary criticism. This would become, ten years later, *Anatomy of Criticism*.

That book is largely an extension and elaboration of an article Frye published in 1951 in *The Kenyon Review*, called "The Archetypes of Literature." "[N]o one expects literature itself to behave like a science," he wrote, but "there is surely no reason why criticism, as a systematic and organized study, should not be, at least partly, a science."[78] The first step is to get rid of evaluation. For the New Critics, the whole point of developing an "objective" method of criticism was to be able to say which poems are good and which are not. Brooks thought that liberal education just *was* a normative enterprise. "The Humanities are in their present plight," he wrote in *The Well Wrought Urn*, "largely because their teachers have more and more ceased to raise normative questions, have refrained from evaluation."[79]

Frye thought that this way of thinking had no place in literature departments. "Casual value judgments belong not to criticism but to the history of taste," he wrote. "That wealthy investor Mr. Eliot, after dumping Milton on the market, is now buying him again; Donne has probably reached his peak and will begin to taper off; Tennyson may be in for a slight flutter but the Shelley stocks are still bearish. This sort of thing cannot be part of any systematic study."[80]

If criticism is to be systematic, literature has to be conceived of as a coherent system. Frye therefore treated all literature as what structuralist linguists called a *langue*, a language, of which individual works are instances of *parole*, the equivalent of individual speech acts. For another revelation in Frye's Blake all-nighter was the realization that Blake and Milton were using the same memes to tell versions of the same story. The critic's first task is to identify the memes. Once these are determined, all the other pieces of critical practice can operate on a common foundation.

In the *Anatomy*, Frye taxonomized literature into four major elements, each of which subsumed a set of variations. He called them modes, symbols, myths, and genres. Frye argued that these all derived from stories and rituals that date from the beginning of human societies and whose most powerful articulation is in scripture. Frye was not interested in religion per se—he called religious doctrines "ideology." He was interested in the myths and rituals behind religions, which he took to be the primordial basis for all culture.

Anatomy of Criticism is an erudite and complex book, and many reviewers were admiring but skeptical. In their response, Brooks and Wimsatt complained that Frye's system provides no way to distinguish a poem that is "alive" from "a document, wooden, dead, lifeless, a mere 'exhibit,' without literary merit."[81] (Frye's usual answer to this objection was that works it isn't rewarding to study won't be studied.) But the

Anatomy had an impact that was remarkably sustained. By the 1980s, it had sold more than a hundred thousand copies.[82]

One reason for its success was that the discipline was looking for a way to move on from close reading, and the *Anatomy* provided one. Another was Frye's "Tentative Conclusion," which assured readers that the baby was not being thrown out along with the New Critics. What is the goal of archetypal criticism? It gives students, Frye said,

> the ability to look at contemporary social values with the detachment of one who is able to compare them in some degree with the infinite vision of possibilities presented by culture. One who possesses such a standard of transvaluation is in a state of intellectual freedom. One who does not possess it is a creature of whatever social values get to him first: he has only the compulsions of habit, indoctrination, and prejudice.[83]

Which is the classic rationale for liberal education. It frees the mind.

One enthusiastic reviewer of the *Anatomy* was Harold Bloom, then a twenty-seven-year-old professor at Yale. Bloom was a son of Jewish immigrants and was brought up in an Orthodox home. He was a prodigy who could memorize long tracts of text. He went to Cornell, where he was a student of M. H. Abrams. Abrams's first book, *The Mirror and the Lamp: Romantic Theory and the Critical Tradition*, a critical landmark, came out in 1953. Bloom then went to Yale, where he received his PhD in 1955 with a dissertation on Shelley.

As all of this suggests, Bloom had little tolerance for the New Criticism and its canon. Many years later, he was asked what it had been like at Yale in the 1950s. "An Anglo-Catholic nightmare," he said.

> Everyone was on their knees to Mr T. S. Eliot and, no matter what you read or how you taught it or how you wrote, you were always supposed to gravely incline the head and genuflect to the spirit of Mr Thomas Stearns Eliot, God's vicar upon earth, the true custodian of Western tradition.[84]

Fearful Symmetry changed his life. "It ravished my heart away," he said. "I thought it was the best book I ever read about anything. I must have read it a hundred times between 1947 and 1950."[85] And when *Anatomy of*

Criticism came out, Bloom saw Frye as the answer to the New Criticism. "His very great book," he wrote, "which will be widely read and used, but mostly by critics under forty, will not much affect the dogmatism of the now Middle-aged Criticism."[86] This was an accurate prediction.

When he wrote the *Anatomy*, Frye had never heard of structuralism. Even later on, after he read Lévi-Strauss, he said that he had trouble seeing anything useful in it.[87] This is almost unbelievable. Frye's explication of the role of myths is almost exactly parallel to the one Lévi-Strauss published in 1955 in an English-language article in the *Journal of American Folklore*, a précis of his method. Lévi-Strauss's *Anthropologie structurale* appeared a year after *Anatomy of Criticism*. But since Lévi-Strauss's books were not translated into English until the 1960s, in a weird inversion of chronology, Frye's book prepared the way for Lévi-Strauss. It was Frye who itemized the deck of cards from which all literary hands are dealt.

Having spent almost twenty years on his first two books, Frye proceeded to publish thirty more. In 1965, Murray Krieger, a professor at Iowa, opened a conference on Frye's work by stating that Frye "has had an influence—indeed an absolute hold—on a generation of developing literary critics greater and more exclusive than that of any one theorist in recent critical history."[88] Nineteen sixty-five is also the year Eliot died. A year later, Jacques Derrida brought deconstruction to America.

6.

By then, the situation of academic literary studies had changed. As university enrollments boomed—from 3.6 million students in 1959 to 8 million in 1969—so did English departments. In 1950, when the New Criticism established itself, the MLA had 6,515 members; in 1970, it had 31,356 members, and 7.5 percent of all bachelor's degrees were awarded in English. (This turned out to be the high-water mark for university English departments: in 2012–2013, it was 2.8 percent, and the MLA had five thousand fewer members than it had in 1970.)[89]

English had become a big-tent discipline. Student demand was high, barriers to professional entry were low, and critical approaches proliferated. Professors quarreled, of course; it's a professional deformation. But there was no need to exclude anything because it was an expanding universe. The situation of poetry had changed, too. Poems resistant to New Critical reading, poems it made no sense to evaluate with New Critical criteria, had entered the publishing and academic mainstream. Their arrival was made dramatic by the outbreak of what became known as the Anthology Wars.*

The anthology is a common book genre for poetry. This is partly because single-author volumes don't sell very well. Between 1922 and 1932, even though it was probably the most famous twentieth-century poem in English, there were only two thousand copies of *The Waste Land* in print in the United States. Wallace Stevens's first book, *Harmonium* (1923), which contains many of his best-known poems, sold fewer than a hundred copies in its first year.[90] For buyers, anthologies have greater marginal utility, since they provide many poets for the cost of one.

The anthology is also an excellent way to promote a new school of poetry, as Pound did with *Des Imagistes* (1914), or to establish a canon, as William Butler Yeats tried to do with *The Oxford Book of Modern Verse* (1936). After the war, there was a flood of American poetry anthologies: F. O. Matthiessen's *Oxford Book of American Verse* (1950), Geoffrey Moore's *The Penguin Book of Modern American Verse* (1954), W. H. Auden's *The Criterion Book of Modern American Verse* (1956), and more. But the anthologies that came to stand for postwar poetry's before-and-after were *The New Poets of England and America* (1957), compiled by Donald Hall, Robert Pack, and Louis Simpson, and *The New American Poetry* (1960), edited by Donald M. Allen.[91]

Even though Hall, Pack, and Simpson were poets, *The New Poets* was received as an academic selection. Fifty-two poets are represented (including the editors), all under forty. Apart from a grumpy introduction by Robert Frost, who was eighty-three, there is no textual apparatus—no author biographies, no lists of books published, no statements on poetics. The editors' intention was to show "[t]hat poetry today is worthy of its inheritance," although they did not specify what this inheritance was.[92]

If they were referring to Eliot and Stevens, their choices suggested a

---

* The term seems to have been first used in *The Literary History of the United States*, 3rd edition (1963), edited by Robert Spiller (Barney Rosset's old teacher at Swarthmore). I am grateful to Jeffrey Careyva for this information.

severe attenuation of the early twentieth-century modernist impulse. The poems in *The New Poets* resembled the kind of verse that Eliot was ridiculing forty years earlier. Much of the imagery is stock pastoral props:

> The gaiety of three winds is a game of green
> Shining, of grey-and-gold play in the holly-bush
> Among the rocks on the hill-side, and if ever
> The earth was shaken, say a moment ago
> Or whenever it came to be, only the leaves and the spread
> Sea still betray it, trembling; and their tale betides
> The faintest of small voices, almost still.
> —W. S. Merwin, "White Goat, White Ram"

The diction has an arch literariness:

> On the enchanted lawn
> It sees the iron top of the flagpole
> Sublimed away and gone
> Into Parnassus regions beyond rust;
> And would undo the body to less than dust.
> —Anthony Hecht, "The Origin of Centaurs"

For some reason, dead dogs is a popular theme:

> My dog lay dead five days without a grave
> In the thick of summer, hid in a clump of pine
> And a jungle of grass and honeysuckle-vine.
> —Richard Wilbur, "The Pardon"

> Nightfall, that saw the morning-glories float
> Tendril and string against the crumbling wall,
> Nurses him now, his skeleton for grief,
> His locks for comfort curled among the leaf.
> —James Wright, "On the Skeleton of a Hound"[93]

The New Poets anthology came out in August 1957. That was one month before the Beat invasion.

7.

The concept of the Beat generation preceded Beat literature. The phrase appears to have been coined in a conversation between Jack Kerouac and John Clellon Holmes in Holmes's apartment on Lexington Avenue in November 1948. According to Holmes's later account, they were talking about "wild kids" and Times Square hipsters, and Holmes asked Kerouac why these people moved the way they did. "It's a sort of furtiveness," was Kerouac's answer.

> "Like we were a generation of furtives. You know, with an inner knowledge there's no use flaunting on that level, the level of the 'public,' a kind of beatness—I mean, being right down to it, to ourselves, because we all *really* know where we are—and a weariness with all the forms, all the conventions of the world. . . . So I guess you might say we're a *beat* generation," and he laughed a conspiratorial, the-Shadow-knows kind of laugh at his own words and the look on my face.[94]

Neither man recorded this conversation in his journals, though they were both obsessive journal keepers, since they used them as material for their novels. They did meet frequently in the fall of 1948, however, when Kerouac was taking classes at the New School with Kazin and Meyer Schapiro, and Kerouac wrote to another friend in December, "I want you to know that a new generation is existing, and rising, in America, and I call them 'The Beat.'"[95]

Holmes was working on a novel; after the conversation with Kerouac, he decided to call it "The Beat Generation." When the book came out, four years later, the title was changed to *Go*, a word used to shout encouragement to jazz soloists. *Go* is a semiautobiographical roman à clef. There is a Kerouac character, a Ginsberg character, a Cassady character, and so on, and many scenes are essentially transcriptions from Holmes's journals. The *New York Times*'s reviewer, Gilbert Millstein, was reading an advance copy of the novel when his eye caught the phrase "the Beat generation," and he telephoned Holmes and invited him to write a piece about it for the *Times Magazine*.

Holmes was thrilled. He was twenty-six and a virtual unknown. The essay he wrote, "'This Is the Beat Generation'"—the quotation marks acknowledging that the phrase was Kerouac's, whom Holmes duly credited—appeared on November 16, 1952. (Millstein's very brief review of *Go* had appeared a week before and was a pan. He explained to Holmes's agent that the positive bits had been cut by an editor when he was out of town. He was not the last reviewer to use that excuse.)[96]

Holmes's essay is not about a literary movement. It's about the postwar generation. Young people, Holmes explained, are obsessed with the question of how life should be lived. Some may seem like nihilists and hedonists, but they are really optimists, risk-takers, seekers. "[U]nlike the Lost Generation, which was occupied with the loss of faith," he wrote, "the Beat Generation is becoming more and more occupied with the need for it."[97]

The piece was taken by some readers as a defense of what *Time* magazine, a year earlier, had referred to as "the Silent Generation" (a term later adopted to characterize the entire decade, even though *Time* was referring only to the immediate postwar years), and it became a minor sensation.[98] Holmes got calls from publishers; he went on television; his picture appeared in *Glamour* with the caption reading in part: "a controversial new spokesman for today's youth. A veteran of World War II [Holmes was discharged from the navy for chronic migraines], his meteoric literary rise began with Scribner's publication of his first book, *Go* . . ."[99] As it happened, "'This Is the Beat Generation'" was the zenith of the Holmes meteor, but he had put Kerouac's phrase into play. When *On the Road* came out, five years later, the idea of the Beat generation was well established in the journalistic world.

The composition of *On the Road* is encrusted with myth, much of it created and curated by Kerouac himself. The story is that he typed the whole novel on a continuous roll of teletype paper in three weeks in April 1951 with the assistance of a lot of Benzedrine, after being inspired by a letter from Neal Cassady.[100] In fact, Kerouac began writing *On the Road* in 1947, before he had ever ridden in a car with Cassady. His whole purpose in befriending Cassady and making those cross-country trips (Kerouac was a bad driver and didn't like to drive) was to generate material for a book. Everything in Kerouac's life was material for a book. He kept journals on those trips, and these were the basis for *On the Road*. By the time he typed the scroll, his novel had already gone through several drafts and multiple titles. (One was "The Beat Generation"; another was "Shades of the Prison House," a line from Wordsworth's Immortality Ode, the subject of a major essay of Trilling's.)

Kerouac first tried writing a conventional novel, inventing fictional characters with backstories, but he became frustrated. The letter from Cassady credited for his breakthrough arrived in December 1950 and is known as the "Joan letter," because its ostensible subject is a girlfriend of Cassady's named Joan Anderson. It is nineteen single-spaced pages— sixteen thousand words. It took Cassady three days to write it.

The Joan letter is a manic, comic, uninhibited account of sexual misadventures, culminating in the writer's arrest for molesting a minor. It is written in Cassady's jokey faux-literary style. (This was how he talked, too. It also gives an idea of his approach to the subject of women.)

> Let me tell you, boy, there is nothing like a fine old mountain ballad, but when Mary Lou got drunk (nightly) and began "The Maple on the Hill" in yodeling screech, as her frosty blue eyes wept buckets, my cringing belly would curl into a genuine Gordion Knot. Not that she wasn't a lovely; blonde hair well bleached, smooth facial features, altho pancake madeup skin was much too dry, 5'2' figure, but the too-small breasts were more than compensated by the oversize ass so her weight, I judge, while just outside 123 3/4 lbs. did not yet, I suspect, approach 125 lbs., unless, of course, my hasty estimate is inaccurate, then, naturally, I allow, nay urge, that you draw your own conclusions about her avoir du pois. Amen, and may god rest ye merry gentlemen. Speaking of Miss Berle's behind I must say here that the one quality of it, indeed, the sole property by which I remember her whole body, was an exquisite overfleshiness that is not too often found. The tempting jelly of her physical self paralleled her entire spiritual being in that the excessive soft mass made for too much matter thru which to wade, and this adequate defense defeated my most wonderfully casual attack; since I was not a perfect fool. We became buddies with our guard up.[101]

Kerouac was knocked out. "I thought it ranked among the best things ever written in America," he wrote to Cassady.[102] The letter had the vernacular directness and narrative propulsion he was looking for, and the diegetic mode—"I did this, I did that"—became the mode of

On the Road. But Cassady's letter had been inspired in turn by a letter he had received a month earlier, in November 1950, from Holmes, which gave a similarly shaggy-dog account of sexual experiences. Cassady was attempting to imitate that model.

Two months after Cassady's letter arrived, in February 1951, Holmes finished *Go*, In March, he showed the final chapter to Kerouac. Kerouac must have felt a spur, possibly a competitive urge, from Holmes's manuscript, with its straightforward incorporation of incidents involving many of the people on whom the characters in *On the Road* are based. Meanwhile, Holmes was encouraging Kerouac to write without premeditation, and Kerouac's wife, Joan Haverty, was encouraging him to write his novel as though he was writing a letter. All this advice and inspiration led Kerouac to undertake his three-week typing binge. He did not use teletype paper; he typed on ten twelve-foot rolls of drawing paper, the kind architects use, that he found in the apartment he was staying in.* Kerouac was not on speed, only coffee. (Cassady *was* on speed when he wrote the Joan letter.)

In short, Kerouac was not making the novel up at the keyboard. He was basically copying from drafts and journals that sat next to his typewriter, adding riffs as he went along. And after he finished the scroll, he retyped the whole thing on single sheets and spent three weeks doing revisions. (He seems to have done these at Lucien Carr's apartment; soon after finishing the scroll, he and Joan broke up when she told him she was pregnant.) He would continue to make changes to the manuscript over the next six years.

Still, despite the exaggerations and elisions about its circumstances, there is a scroll. Because Kerouac and Ginsberg talked about spontaneity as a compositional principle, they fed the misperception that they wrote whatever came into their heads, that what they were doing was easy. As Truman Capote put it, in a phrase often quoted: "That's not writing. That's only typewriting."[103†] It's true that they had bursts of creativity, as all writers do, but they revised their bursts. The "Howl" manuscript shows that Ginsberg, too, made many changes.

---

* The apartment had belonged to a friend, Bill Cannastra, who was killed by sticking his head out of the window of a moving subway train, an incident that is the basis for the final chapter of *Go*. It is assumed that Cannastra was gay; Joan Haverty was his girlfriend at the time.
† Capote first used this phrase before *On the Road* came out in a *Paris Review* interview, where he was speaking generally about style.

More important, it is not easy to write a novel on a continuous roll of paper, just as it is not easy to make a painting by placing the canvas on the floor and throwing paint on it (and the Beats were often grouped with the "action painters").[104] The results may read as "spontaneous," but working that way is *hard*. Kerouac was forcing the narrative forward by preventing himself from going backward, as Pollock was forcing himself to respond to wherever the paint fell. In religious terms (and Kerouac was, deep down, a Catholic and a sufferer), the scroll was a collar. He did, after he finished, make changes. But first he had to submit to his discipline.

The Beat moment was created by the intersection of the fortunes of *On the Road* with the fortunes of "Howl," and a key player in that moment was the most mainstream news organ in the United States, *The New York Times*. Perhaps this made Trilling's point that the adversarial is a place the mainstream culture sees its own values reflected upside down in the exciting but essentially harmless guise of "rebellion." The Beats were the kind of rebels the straight world (or most of it) was comfortable with.

Howl and Other Poems was published by City Lights Books in October 1956, a year after Ginsberg debuted the poem at the Six Gallery. William Carlos Williams, although not in good health, contributed an introduction that ended with one of the great blurbs: "Hold back the edges of your gowns, Ladies, we are going through hell."[105]

City Lights was a tiny press and Ginsberg did a lot of the promotion himself (such as sending the mimeographed copies around). But the book got some breaks. The first was when *The New York Times Book Review* published a piece on the West Coast poetry scene by Richard Eberhart, an older poet and professor at Dartmouth who would shortly be named Poet Laureate. The idea for the piece had been given to Eberhart by Kenneth Rexroth, who, by virtue of his age and renown, was the dean of the San Francisco school of poetry and had been master of ceremonies at the Six Gallery reading. The editors at the *Book Review* regarded the piece as a "stunt."[106] When Eberhart was on the West Coast, "Howl" had not yet been published. He must have heard about the poem through Rexroth, and he contacted Ginsberg directly, who happily provided him not only with a copy of the poem but also with a twenty-page letter about his work.

"The West Coast is the liveliest spot in the country in poetry today," Eberhart wrote in his piece for the *Times*. He gave credit to Ruth Witt-Diamant, a professor who founded the Poetry Center at San Francisco

State College in 1954 as a gathering place for the writers of what was being called the San Francisco Renaissance. And he mentioned many West Coast poets, including Rexroth, Michael McClure, and Philip Whalen, all of whom read at the Six Gallery event. The "most remarkable poem" of the group, Eberhart said, was "Howl." "It is a howl against everything in our mechanistic civilization which kills the spirit," he wrote. ". . . It lays bare the nerves of suffering and spiritual struggle. Its positive force and energy come from a redemptive quality of love, although it destructively catalogues evils of our time from physical deprivation to madness."[107] The article was an unlikely boost in an establishment venue. When it came out, only one bookstore in New York City carried *Howl*.[108] That would change.

The second break came in June 1956, when the City Lights owner Lawrence Ferlinghetti and the manager of the bookstore, Shigeyoshi (Shig) Murao, were arrested for publishing and selling obscene literature, viz., *Howl and Other Poems*. Murao was a Japanese American who had been placed in a concentration camp for two years in Idaho during the war and had then joined the army as an interpreter. When he was arrested, he was thrown in the drunk tank, but he was released after the American Civil Liberties Union posted bail. (Ferlinghetti had taken the precaution of showing the book to the ACLU before publishing it, and they agreed to defend him in the event it was suppressed.) The charge against Murao would eventually be dropped, since the government decided that there was no way to prove he knew the contents of the books he sold (probably a racist assumption).[109]

The trial, in municipal court, began on August 16. The judge assigned to the case, Clayton Horn, was a Sunday school teacher who had recently sentenced a group of shoplifters to watch Cecil B. DeMille's movie *The Ten Commandments*.[110] But neither Ginsberg, who was out of the country, nor Ferlinghetti seems to have been seriously concerned. There were some obscene words in "Howl," but the poem was plainly not published with lewd intent, as California law required. Some nine writers and academics were happy to take the stand for the defense.

The star witness was Mark Schorer, now chairman of graduate studies in the English department at Berkeley.* The prosecution tried to

---

* Schorer had been Joan Didion's teacher at Berkeley, from which she graduated the prior spring. Didion was much influenced by his article "Technique as Discovery" (1948).

remind the judge of instances of obscene words in the poem by asking Schorer to justify them. They drew his attention, for example, to the line: "The world is holy! The soul is holy! The skin is holy! The nose is holy! The tongue and cock and hand and asshole holy!" What was the literary value of those words? That is not a tough question for an English professor. "I think he is saying every part of human life is holy," Schorer explained, "and he's not the first one who said it. William Blake, a great poet, said it in the eighteenth century."[111]

On the Road was published on September 4, 1957, while the *Howl* trial was under way. The *Times* reviewer was Gilbert Millstein—a fantastically lucky circumstance: the paper's regular daily reviewer, Orville Prescott, an outspoken traditionalist who thought that John P. Marquand was a superior novelist to William Faulkner, was on vacation.[112] Millstein saw Kerouac's book as the literary realization of what Holmes had written in his *Times Magazine* essay five years before (which he quoted), and he called it "a historic occasion." "It is possible," he wrote,

> that it will be condescended to by, or make uneasy, the neo-academicians and the "official" avant-garde critics . . . But the fact is that "On the Road" is the most beautifully executed, the clearest and the most important utterance yet made by the generation Kerouac himself named years ago as "beat," and whose principal avatar he is.
>
> Just as, more than any other novel of the Twenties, "The Sun Also Rises" came to be regarded as the testament of the "Lost Generation," so it seems certain that "On the Road" will come to be known as that of the "Beat Generation."[113]

Kerouac read the review at midnight standing on the corner of Sixty-Sixth Street and Broadway with his girlfriend, Joyce Johnson. When he woke up to the telephone ringing later that morning, he realized he had become a celebrity.[114] *On the Road* became a *Times* bestseller, on the list for five weeks, though never higher than No. 11. (The list was dominated by *Peyton Place*, by Grace Metalious. Like Kerouac's, Metalious's parents were French Canadian; like Kerouac, she drank herself to death.)

On October 4, a month after Millstein's review, Clayton Horn handed down his opinion in *California v. Ferlinghetti*. The judge turned out to be a staunch advocate of the First Amendment. His job was made easier by the fact that the Supreme Court had issued its opinion in *Roth* in June, just as the *Howl* case was going to trial. *Roth* provided an exception to obscenity law for works with social significance, and this was something the expert testimony had established in the case of Ginsberg's poems. "The people owe a duty to themselves and to each other," the judge concluded, "to preserve and protect their constitutional freedoms from any encroachment by government unless it appears that the allowable limits of such protection have been breached, and then to take only such action as will heal the breach."[115]

Although the *Howl* trial got a lot of attention in the San Francisco press, the *Times* never ran a story on it. But *Life* covered it with a picture essay ("Big Day for Bards at Bay"). Apart from pieces in *The Nation* and *The Village Voice*, most of the other reviews of *On the Road*, including one in the Sunday *Times Book Review*, were unfriendly. Yet through the trial and the favorable *Times* reviews, the Beat movement had gotten just enough exposure to become, almost overnight, a phenomenon. As sometimes happens in the publishing business, the author photo of Kerouac that accompanied Millstein's review might have tipped the balance by suggesting that whatever else one might say about the Beats, they were photogenic. In a golden era of photojournalism, this was a key to dissemination.

"Howl" and *On the Road* are about things that happened in the 1940s; by the time they came out, the United States was a different place. When Kerouac began his travels, for example, there were 37 million registered vehicles in the United States. When *On the Road* came out ten years later, there were 67 million.[116] The increase in car ownership reflected the growth in middle-class prosperity, and for many people this made the "beatness" that Ginsberg and Kerouac represented, which had been appropriate in the immediate postwar years, a period of social and economic uncertainty, seem an affectation, a lifestyle choice rather than a social condition.

"Howl" and *On the Road* were also hijacked by a social caricature that was already well developed by 1957: the (male) teenage delinquent and his older (also male) counterpart, the hipster—the silent generation's evil siblings. The type was the subject of studies by psychiatrists and social scientists and was promulgated by Hollywood movies such as *The Wild One* (1953), with Marlon Brando, and *Rebel Without a Cause* (1955), with James Dean, and in mass-market fiction like Irving

Shulman's *The Amboy Dukes*, about Brooklyn street gangs. (Shulman wrote the treatment for *Rebel Without a Cause*.) *West Side Story*, which opened on Broadway in 1957, is a playful inventory of bad-teenager tropes. The notion of a juvenile crime wave in the 1950s was mostly a myth. (A genuine crime wave would begin in 1963.)[117] But it gave writers who found Beat literature distasteful a context in which to place it and a vocabulary with which to characterize it.

In *Partisan Review*, the first notice of Beat writing, in early 1957, was a piece by John Hollander, an under-forty poet represented in *The New Poets of England and America*. He called *Howl* "a dreadful little volume."[118] Soon after *On the Road* came out, Norman Podhoretz, an editor at *Commentary*, published "The Know-Nothing Bohemians," also in *Partisan Review*. "[T]here is a suppressed cry in [Kerouac's] books," he wrote: "Kill the intellectuals who can talk coherently, kill the people who can sit still for five minutes at a time, kill those incomprehensible characters who are capable of getting seriously involved with a woman, a job, a cause."[119] A year later, in *Horizon*, Robert Brustein described Kerouac as "a man belligerently exalting in his own inarticulateness." With the Beat writers, Brustein said, "we are prepared for violence on every page . . . It is not so long a jump from the kick-seeking poet to the kick-seeking adolescent who, sinking his knife into the flesh of his victim, thanked him for the 'experience.'"[120]

A few months after that, in *Esquire*, Podhoretz repeated this analysis. "[W]hat juvenile delinquency is to life," he wrote, "the San Francisco writers are to literature—howling at random against they don't know what and making up aesthetic rules of their own that are a rough equivalent in literary terms of the rules of the street gang . . . Isn't the Beat Generation a conspiracy to overthrow civilization (which is created by men, not boys) and to replace it not by the State of Nature where we can all romp around in free-and-easy nakedness, but by the world of the adolescent street gang?"[121] Podhoretz, Brustein, and Hollander were all (like Ginsberg) former students of Lionel Trilling.

In February 1959, Ginsberg, Gregory Corso, and Peter Orlovsky gave a reading at Columbia University. For Ginsberg, now a celebrity, it was a kind of triumphal return. The room was packed. His father was in the audience. Also in attendance—their seats had been reserved— were Diana Trilling and some friends. (She referred to them all as "three wives from the English department.") Her report on the reading, "The Other Night at Columbia," appeared soon after in *Partisan Review*.

The essay is an exercise in pained condescension—"rather self-smug & bitchy & all balled up psychologically," as Ginsberg described it, not unfairly, in a letter to his father.[122] The poets' air of "disreputableness and rebellion," she decided, was an act. For they were really just children, "miserable children trying desperately to manage, asking desperately to be taken out of it all; there was nothing one could imagine except to bundle them home and feed them warm milk, promise them they need no longer call for mama and papa."[123] She mistakenly thought that one of the poems Ginsberg read, "The Lion for Real," was a love poem to her husband. He had, for the occasion, dedicated it to Lionel, but ironically. The poem has nothing to do with Trilling. It's about Ginsberg's William Blake vision. The lion is not Lionel. The lion is Blake.

Ginsberg enjoyed the arena. Kerouac did not, and Kerouac got by far the worst of it. He *looked* like a hip cat, and that is how his novel was marketed. "This is the bible of the 'beat generation'—the explosive bestseller that tells all about today's wild youth and their frenetic search for Experience and Sensation" was the cover copy on the Signet mass-market paperback in 1958. By the time of the fourteenth printing, it read: "The riotous odyssey of two American drop-outs, by the drop-out who started it all." On the back: "Jack Kerouac, Hippie Homer of the turned-on generation." Kerouac hated the hippies.

The constantly iterated claim that he and Ginsberg were rebels and hedonists, prone to crime and violence—or that they presented themselves as spokesmen for people like that—is such a crude misreading that it is hard not to speculate about why some people found the Beats and their books so threatening. The sadness that soaks through Kerouac's story comes from the certainty that the world of hoboes and migrant workers and joyriders—the world of Neal Cassady and his derelict father—is dying. But the sadness is not sentimentality, because many of the people in the book who inhabit that world would be happy to see it go. They do not share the literary man's *nostalgie de la boue*; they are restless, lonely—beat. "There ain't no flowers there," says a girl whom Sal Paradise, the Kerouac figure, tries to pick up in Cheyenne by suggesting a walk on the prairie among the flowers. "I want to go to New York. I'm sick and tired of this. Ain't no place to go but Cheyenne and ain't nothin in Cheyenne." "Ain't nothin in New York," Sal says. "Hell there ain't," she says.[124] She wants to get in the car, too.

Everyone has an irresistible urge to get to Denver or San Francisco or New York, because there will be jobs or friends or women. But once they arrive, hopes start to unravel, and it's back in the car again. The characters can't settle down. But they *want* to settle down. They are not sociopaths or rebels. Their crimes against the establishment consist of speeding, shoplifting, and a minor bout of car stealing (a little illegal drug use, too). They fear and dislike cops, as people without much money do; other than that, they are not especially antisocial. There is nothing like a critique of middle-class life in *On the Road*—or, for that matter, in "Howl."

The characters in *On the Road* are not hipsters, either, cats too cool for life in suits. There is nothing cool about Dean or Carlo Marx (the Ginsberg character: Karl converted into a Marx Brother). The characters marry and get legally divorced; they take jobs and quit them; they talk about Dostoyevsky and Hemingway and write novels and poems and hope for recognition. The narrator lives with his aunt, who sends him money when he needs a bus ticket home; otherwise, he draws on his GI benefits. The Beats weren't rebels. They were misfits. That is what the "best minds" section of "Howl" is saying. The book is not really about sexuality. It has a slightly different subject, which is masculinity.

There was no good cultural model in the period in which the story is set for the kind of men the characters are—as there was no good model for Kerouac and Ginsberg themselves. This was the reason Kerouac became embittered by the caricatures of the Beats: they played off stock conceptions of masculine types—the hip anarchist, the leotard-chasing jazz fiend, the swaggering barfly, the hot-rodder, the delinquent. Kerouac was none of these things. He was not a macho anti-aesthete. He was a poet and a failed mystic.

And this is the point at which the thematic preoccupations of *On the Road* meet the style of *On the Road*—the lyrical, gushing, excessive prose. Many novels about social dropouts and other disaffected types preceded *On the Road*. Those books are all written in the affectless, naturalist style of 1930s American fiction; they are grim and fatalistic. *Go* belongs to this genre. *On the Road* is completely different. It's exuberant, hopeful, sad, nostalgic; it is never naturalistic. Most of all, it is emotionally uninhibited. There is something risky about Kerouac's prose. It is sensitive and it is earnest, a performance of one of the most difficult emotions to express: male vulnerability. The Beats were men who wrote about their feelings.

8.

Until 1960, the Beats may have been selling books, but they were losing the battle for recognition. Donald Allen's anthology changed all that. The editors of *The New Poets* had made a point of excluding West Coast poets. It is not as though those writers were unpublished or unknown. Auden's *Criterion Book of Modern American Verse*, published a year before, includes nine poets born after 1916 and three are from California. This offered Allen an opening. He decided that his anthology would include *no* poets published in *The New Poets*, whom he called "the academic poets."[125] He also imposed no age limit. The result was a collection of writers whose poetics were distinctly un–New Critical—writers who, if you figured some (not all) of them into a genealogy, were descended not from Eliot and Stevens, but from Gertrude Stein, Williams, and Pound.

Allen was an Iowan. He received his BA and MA in English from the University of Iowa, served in the navy, where he studied Japanese, then did graduate study at Berkeley, where he met some of the local poets—Rexroth, Robert Duncan, Jack Spicer. He dropped out of Berkeley and moved to New York and, in 1951, attended on the G.I. Bill a Columbia class on book publishing. That is where he met Barney Rosset.

Rosset had just bought Grove, and he invited Allen to become an editor. After a few years, they had a disagreement, and Allen left to work at New Directions, but he was unhappy there and returned to Grove (the usual pattern with Rosset). He became the first editor, with Rosset, of the *Evergreen Review*, a quarterly designed to promote Grove authors that also became an influential literary magazine. The first issue, in 1956, had contributions from Sartre and Beckett.

Rosset read Eberhardt's *Times* piece on West Coast poetry and he asked Allen to investigate. Allen got in touch with his Bay Area friends, and the result was the second issue of the *Evergreen Review*, dedicated to the "San Francisco Scene."[126] It came out in July 1957, just as the *Howl* trial was about to get under way, and included work by Rexroth, Duncan, and Ferlinghetti, along with Henry Miller, who was living in Big Sur. Most important, it reprinted all of "Howl" (with a few elisions), giving it added exposure. Sales were brisk. That issue of the *Evergreen Review* was the only one ever to be reprinted, and it was reprinted more than once.[127] An LP of the poets reading their work was released by

Evergreen Records in 1958. The success of the "San Francisco Scene" issue led the way to *The New American Poetry*.

The editing of the anthology was a collaborative enterprise: Allen corresponded with, and sometimes consulted in person, a number of the poets he included, in particular, Ginsberg, Duncan, and Charles Olson. Olson turned out to be the headline poet in the anthology. The first poem in the book is his, "The Kingfishers," and the first and most ambitious in a set of "Statements on Poetics" is his essay "Projective Verse."

Olson was from Massachusetts. He was born in Worcester in 1910 and spent much of his life in Gloucester, an inspiration for his poetry. Politically, he was a Roosevelt liberal. He worked in Roosevelt's 1944 reelection campaign and came very close to taking a government job. He was living in Washington, D.C., when Ezra Pound arrived there in 1945 to be tried for treason.

Pound's infatuation with Mussolini, for whom he had already expressed his regard, dates from a concert given by Olga Rudge, a violinist who was Pound's longtime mistress, at Mussolini's home in 1927. That was when Pound came up with the idea of enlisting Mussolini as a patron of the avant-garde. Six years later, he had a private audience with Il Duce at the Palazzo Venezia in Rome, and presented him with a copy of *A Draft of XXX Cantos*, which Mussolini graciously acknowledged with the remark "Ma questo è divertente" ("How amusing"). Pound concluded that Mussolini had an intuitive grasp of the significance of his work.

In 1941, Pound began delivering broadcasts from the Rome studios of Ente Italiana Audizione Radio, attacking the Jews, Roosevelt, and American intervention in the war. The broadcasts continued through the Allied invasion of Italy in 1943. In 1945, he surrendered to American officials on a charge of treason and was imprisoned in an Army Disciplinary Training Center north of Pisa. After he was brought to the United States, thanks to the intercession of friends and of Dr. Winfred Overholser, the superintendent of St. Elizabeths Hospital in Washington, D.C., he was spared a trial on psychiatric grounds. He actually never received a diagnosis, but the American government did not want to find itself in the position of having to execute a poet.[128]

Pound was a lot like Ginsberg: a proselytizer, a promoter, a networker, a teacher. "Gertrude Stein liked him but did not find him amusing," is the famous description in *The Autobiography of Alice B. Toklas*. "She said he was a village explainer, excellent if you were a village, but if you were not, not."[129] By the time he was locked up in St. Elizabeths—he called it the Bughouse—Pound was a depressed and defeated but unrepentant man, given to ranting.

Many writers and critics visited him to listen. These included Eliot, Williams, Kathleen Raine, Louis Zukofsky, Allen Tate, Marianne Moore, Robert Lowell, John Berryman, James Dickey, Robert Duncan, Randall Jarrell, Archibald MacLeish, Elizabeth Bishop, W. S. Merwin, and (then a Harvard undergraduate) Frederick Seidel. Less distinguished visitors included a neo-Nazi segregationist named John Kasper, with whom Pound corresponded and may have collaborated.[130] One visitor was the Canadian critic Hugh Kenner, a student of McLuhan's at the University of Toronto and later a PhD student of Brooks's at Yale. Kenner would become Pound's academic champion, starting with *The Poetry of Ezra Pound* (1951) and culminating with *The Pound Era* (1971).

Being locked up was, in one sense anyway, an excellent career move. It made Pound highly visible, the object of ongoing efforts by eminent people to secure his release, and accessible. It also encouraged supporters to promote his work. While Pound was in St. Elizabeths, New Directions published *The Pisan Cantos* (1948), the first edition of the whole *Cantos* (1948), *Selected Poems* (1949), *Translations* (1953), and *The Literary Essays of Ezra Pound* (1954), with an introduction by Eliot, then at the peak of his cultural authority. As he had done in London before the First World War, Pound managed to influence a generation of poets.

One was Olson. Olson had gone to watch Pound in court, and although he hated Pound's politics and his anti-Semitism and believed that Pound was a traitor, he was fascinated by him. In 1946, he wrote a strange piece for *Partisan Review*, "This is Yeats Speaking," in which he proposed, somewhat elliptically and in the voice of Yeats (with whom Pound had worked during his first years in London), separating Pound the poet from Pound the fanatic. ("He was false . . . when he subordinated his critical intelligence to the objects of authority in others." A little like what Hannah Arendt would write about Martin Heidegger.)[131]

Partly Olson's interest in Pound was from pity, but partly it was from respect for Pound's knowledge and accomplishments. His visits began on January 4, 1946, when Pound had been confined for only thirteen days. Among other business matters, Olson helped Pound exchange manuscripts and proofs of *The Pisan Cantos* with New Directions, and he took time to copy down sections of the poems for himself. Olson's visits lasted, with growing infrequency, until February 1948, when he decided he had had enough. There were twenty-four in all.[132]

Olson wrote "The Kingfishers" in 1949 and "Projective Verse" in 1950. He also taught at Black Mountain College, ultimately becoming rector. Despite his dislike of Cage and Rauschenberg, he was a participant in *Theatre Piece No. 1*, in 1952, reading his own poetry. With Albers gone to Yale, the focus at Black Mountain shifted from the visual arts to poetry. Between 1952 and 1956, the poets Robert Creeley, Robert Duncan, Joel Oppenheimer, John Wieners, and Jonathan Williams spent time there. In 1954, Olson started up the *Black Mountain Review* with Creeley in order to promote the college and, he hoped, break the hold of the New Criticism on American poetry.[133] The review was edited by Creeley and printed in Mallorca, to save money. It folded in 1957, the year the college shut down. Olson stayed in North Carolina to oversee the closing of the college, then moved to the Fort Point neighborhood of Gloucester, where he would live for the rest of his life. This was where Allen visited him to consult on the anthology.

A well-wrought urn is an artifact perceived by the eye. A howl is a sound apprehended by the ear. Much of the meaning of the anthology wars lies in that distinction. The aesthetic of academic criticism, not only of the New Criticism but also of critics like Trilling, is cerebral. The aesthetic of the Beats and the Black Mountain poets is centered on biological energy. The word Olson used in "Projective Verse" was "kinetic," and the term he coined for the kind of poetry-making he advocated was "composition by field."

Olson divided poetry into "closed" (using traditional prosody) and "open," and he defined an open poem as "energy transferred from where the poet got it (he will have some several causations), by way of the poem itself to, all the way over to, the reader." This meant that "every element in an open poem (the syllable, the line, as well as the image, the sound, the sense) must be taken up as participants in the kinetic of the poem just as solidly as we are accustomed to take what we call the objects of reality."[134] No part of the poem takes time off. Eliot, Olson said, was "*not* projective" because "his root is the mind alone, and a scholastic mind at that." He failed to go "down through the workings of his own throat to that place where breath comes from, where breath has its beginnings."[135]

Allen set out to make Olson's terms his criteria for inclusion in the anthology. "My criteria for selecting poets are derived in part from

William Carlos Williams' essays . . . and Charles Olson's Projective Verse," he wrote to poets he was hoping to recruit. The first two criteria were "voice, and breathing" and "heat of the poem, energy, feeling."[136]

Olson's focus on the object derived from Williams's (poetic) motto: "No ideas but in things."[137] But most of his poetic derived from Pound. "The image is not an idea," Pound wrote in 1914. "It is a radiant node or cluster . . . a VORTEX, from which, and through which, and into which, ideas are constantly rushing."[138] The poem does not represent or mediate experience; the poem *is* an emotional and intellectual force field. It works by clusters and juxtapositions, not by exposition. This is how the *Cantos* are intended to be read: as blocks of text (or images) laid out on the page that stand in paratactic relation to one another, *without grammatical linkages*. Everything on the page is equally an image.

This can create interpretive problems. Here are the opening lines of "Canto IV":

> Palace in smoky light,
> Troy but a heap of smouldering boundary stones,
> ANAXIFORMINGES! Aurunculeia!
> Hear me. Cadmus of Golden Prows![139]

Apart from the reference to Troy, the rest is, well, Greek. What palace is "in smoky light"? "ANAXIFORMINGES" is from a poem by Pindar; "Aurunculeia" is from a poem by Catullus; Cadmus was the brother of Europa and the founder of Thebes. Even with the allusions identified, there remains the question of what to make of this particular "cluster." What about Troy, Cadmus, and so on makes for significance? No doubt the lines were composed with energy, but their effect on the reader is the opposite.

Olson's "The Kingfishers," though not an especially long poem, is ambitious on the scale of the *Cantos* and has the same subject matter: the rise and fall of civilizations.

> hear
> hear, where the dry blood talks
> where the old appetite walks
>
> la più saporita et migliore
> che si possa trovar al mondoù

where it hides, look
in the eye how it runs
in the flesh / chalk

but under these petals
in the emptiness
regard the light, contemplate
the flower

whence it arose[140]

The lines in Italian, disconnected from the rest by spacing so that they constitute an independent "image," are from Marco Polo's report of people he encountered in China and Japan who (he says) considered human flesh the most savory food in the world. The rest of the passage seems to refer to the remains of the Aztec civilization that was wiped out by the Spanish in the sixteenth century. Other lines in the poem are from Mao and Rimbaud. All these elements are associated, or can be construed that way, but whether Mao and Hernán Cortés represent similar or different instantiations of the force of historical change is unclear. The result is that "The Kingfishers" is a poem about whose meaning its commentators completely disagree.[141] There is nothing there to settle interpretation one way or another. To this extent, the poem is what Olson wanted it to be: an object.

A good deal of the work ordinarily done by grammar in a composition-by-field poem is done by typography, by spacing and line breaks, which are extensions of the standard poetic device of the caesura. Many of these are intended as vocal cues—where to pause, where to place the stress—and part of the effort to render the poem an aural, not a visual, artifact. "Ideally each line of 'Howl' is a single breath unit," Ginsberg wrote in 1959. "My breath is long—that's the Measure, one physical-mental inspiration of thought, contained in the elastic of a breath."[142] There are also typographical devices in open-form poetry that act as visual and vocal cues: all-capped words and lines, open parentheses and quotation marks, and so on.

When Pound died in 1972, Ginsberg called him the "[g]reatest poet of the age . . . The one poet who heard speech as spoken from the actual body."[143] Pound's anti-Semitism didn't bother him, he said. Although Pound did not say much about the breath himself, he read his own poetry in a highly theatrical voice, sometimes accompanying himself on a drum, drawing out the vowels and rolling the r's (sounding a lot like Tennyson in the recordings of him that we have, but that was also the way Yeats read). Many of the poems in *The New American Poetry* show the influence of Olson's essay—and therefore the influence of Pound and of Williams, who called "Projective Verse" a "seminal essay" and reprinted several pages of it in his autobiography in 1951.[144]* To put it baldly, those poems just *look* different from the formally regular poems in *The New Poets of England and America*. And that is because they are designed for the ear and the eye rather than the mind.

Allen essentially established the labels by which many of the poets in his anthology are still known: the Black Mountain poets, the San Francisco Renaissance, and the Beats. Allen placed some poets in a miscellaneous section, although a few could have been assigned to one of the groups—Gary Snyder with the San Francisco poets, LeRoi Jones (the only nonwhite poet) with the Beats.

Those three groups, however, were largely overlapping. They shared the same aesthetic, published in the same places. Allen's fourth group, the New York Poets—Frank O'Hara, John Ashbery, Barbara Guest, Kenneth Koch—had a completely different sensibility. They were ironic, playful, urbane, influenced by French poetry, not by Williams or Pound. They were most different from the others in being (or acting) somewhat unserious about poetry itself. One of Koch's poems, "Fresh Air," was an extended parody of the anthology wars.

> Who are the great poets of our time, and what are their names?
> Yeats of the baleful influence, Auden of the baleful influence, Eliot
>   of the baleful influence
> (Is Eliot a great poet? no one knows), Hardy, Stevens, Williams (is
>   Hardy of our time?),
> Hopkins (is Hopkins of our time?), Rilke (is Rilke of our time?),
>   Lorca (is Lorca of our time?), who is still of our time?

---

* It gives some idea of the long-term effects of the anthology wars that neither "projective verse" nor "composition by field" appeared in the first edition of *The Princeton Encyclopedia of Poetry and Poetics*, published in 1965, or in the "Enlarged Edition" of that work, in 1974. "Projective verse" finally made it into the 1994 edition, where it is described as "an influential 1950 essay." "Composition by field" only got in with the fourth edition, in 2012, where "Projective Verse" is now called, more than sixty years after it came out, "one of the most influential statements in American poetics since World War II."

Mallarmé, Valéry, Apollinaire, Éluard, Reverdy, French poets are still
of our time, Pasternak and Mayakovsky, is Jouve of our time?[145]

Absurdly, the *Times*'s reviewer of *The New American Poetry*, the poet
Harvey Shapiro, quoted this poem as an example of the objectionable
insouciance of the new poets.

From the start, the anthology wars were characterized as a duel between the academy and the avant-garde. His poets share "one common
characteristic," Allen wrote: "a total rejection of all those qualities typical of academic verse."[146] And this was how many of his poets saw themselves. "No avant garde American poet accepts the I. A. Richards-Valéry
thesis that a poem is an end in itself," Rexroth wrote in 1957. The San
Francisco Renaissance, he said, is "characterized by total rejection of the
official highbrow culture—where critics like John Crowe Ransom or Lionel Trilling, magazines like the Kenyon, Hudson and Partisan reviews,
are looked on as 'The Enemy'—the other side of the barricades."[147]

Yet *The New American Poetry* is designed for the classroom much better than the Hall, Pack, and Simpson volume. Allen has a section on poetics; he provides biographies of the poets; there is a bibliography. You can
teach from Allen. And that is exactly what he and Rosset had in mind:
they were aiming at the college market. Grove's list was already geared
toward college-age readers; the *New American Poetry* anthology, which included a number of poets published by Grove, helped push the product.

The New American Poetry also caught a dramatic shift in the market
for contemporary poetry. After 1960, the major publishing houses got
into the game. Poets who had appeared in little magazines like *Origin*,
published in Boston by the poet Cid Corman, and the *Black Mountain Review*, with circulations in the low hundreds, were suddenly able
to get their work into mainstream bookstores. In the 1950s, Creeley
was published by presses in editions of 200 to 600 copies; in 1962,
Scribner's published his *For Love* with a first printing of 6,000. And the
poetry audience kept growing. Between 1963 and 1964, the circulation
of *Poetry* magazine increased by almost 50 percent, to nearly 10,000.
Donald Allen's anthology sold 14,000 copies in its first year, 40,000 by
the mid-1960s, 112,500 by 1970.[148*]

---

* Allen edited two more anthologies: *Poetics of the New American Poetry* (1974), with Wayne
Tallman, and *The Postmoderns: The New American Poetry Revised* (1982), with George F.

The New Poets of England and America sold, too. Its *Second Selection*, edited by Hall and Pack and containing poets much like those in the first, came out in 1962. Its editors did not back down. "The problem of an audience . . . is inseparable from the question of the vitality of any art," Pack wrote in a rather polemical introduction. "In our time, the university, rather than the literary cliques, the poetry societies, the incestuous pages of little magazines, is capable of nurturing and supporting such an audience."[149] *The New Poets of England and America: Second Selection* went through six printings in its first year. Hall ventured a compromise with another anthology, published by Penguin, called *Contemporary American Poetry*. It came out in 1962 and contained a number of Allen's poets, including Duncan, Creeley, Snyder, Ashbery, and Denise Levertov, but pointedly excluded the Beats. By the end of the decade, Hall's anthology had been reprinted six times.

By then, the poetry anthology market had become irresistible to publishers. In three years, ten new anthologies came on the market.* Finally, in 1974, *The Norton Anthology of Modern Poetry*, edited by Richard Ellmann, appeared. It included virtually every poet from both *The New Poets* and *The New American Poetry*—a catholicity enabled by the expediency of making the volume 1,454 pages long and by the fact that there was now room for everyone. The university could accommodate everything.

9.

The notion that there is literature and then there is something that professors do with literature called "theory" is not really coherent. Literary theory dates from Aristotle, the first person we know who isolated literature as a field of inquiry. If you believe (as Aristotle did) that literature is different from other kinds of writing (such as philosophy and self-help

---

Butterick. Over all editions, the *New American Poets* and *New Poets* anthologies had only one poet in common.
* *Poems of Our Moment* (1968), edited by Hollander; *The Young American Poets* (1968), edited by Paul Carroll; *The Contemporary American Poets* (1969), edited by Mark Strand; *Twentieth-Century Poetry: American and British* (1969), edited by John Malcolm Brinnin; *Naked Poetry: Recent American Poetry in Open Forms* (1969), edited by Stephen Berg and Robert Mezey; *The Poets of the New York School* (1969), edited by John Bernard Myers; *31 New American Poets* (1969), edited by Ron Schreiber; *Black Poets: A Supplement to Anthologies Which Exclude Black Poets* (1969), edited by Dudley Randall; *Today's Negro Voices* (1970), edited by Beatrice Murphy; and *The Major Young Poets* (1971), edited by Al Lee.

books), and if you have ideas about what is relevant and what isn't for understanding it (biography or social history or just other poems), and if you have standards for judging whether a work is great or not so great (a pleasing style or a displeasing politics), then you have a theory of literature.

As Richards tried to show in *Practical Criticism*, everyone who reads literature operates from a set of assumptions about what it is, how it is supposed to work, and what makes it good or bad, even if those assumptions are unformulated and inchoate. The New Criticism arose as a way of making readers' assumptions explicit and consistent, and although it presents itself as just the natural way to read, it is a thoroughly theorized approach. Theorizing is not academicism. It's part of an inquiry into the role of art in human life. Works of art and literature are make-believe; "theory" is an effort to figure out why we create such things, what they mean, and why we care so much about them.

"Theory" in the post-1960 sense refers to a period when some of the influences on Anglo-American literary studies were coming from writers who were neither Anglo-American nor students of literature: principally, Jacques Derrida, a philosopher; Michel Foucault, a historian; and Jacques Lacan, a psychoanalyst. The relevance of what these writers were saying to literary criticism was obvious enough, but they were, so to speak, jumping the fence, and their academic training had no counterpart in American universities, which is one reason why some people felt their influence to be subversive or an assault on academic norms.

Deconstruction, the method of reading devised by Derrida, is a critique of structuralism. It does not displace or reject structuralism; it changes the structuralist model from within. Derrida was not a political radical; like most academics, he was a liberal with egalitarian social views. And deconstruction is not an attack on literature or literary studies or liberal education or academic knowledge production. On the contrary, it is a defense of literature based on a method of close reading, and it teaches students a way of grasping the contingency of present assumptions. It is therefore completely consistent with the paradigms of literary studies and the philosophy of liberal education. There is no better evidence that deconstruction was doing its pedagogical job than the fact that many people regarded it as a scandal to the way things are.

Deconstruction did not take English departments by storm. Institutionally, its progress outside of departments of French and Comparative

Literature was slow, mainly because translations of Derrida's work did not begin appearing until the mid-1970s.* Intellectually, deconstruction arrived as (to use a term that Derrida would problematize) an event, but the work of writers like Derrida required middlemen for it to be adapted to literary study in the United States. The key figure in his case was Paul de Man.

De Man was a Belgian émigré who taught in three American universities whose literature departments were industry leaders: Cornell (1960–1966), Johns Hopkins (1967–1970), and Yale, where he was a professor in the departments of French and Comparative Literature from 1970 until his death in 1983, at the age of sixty-four. Within the profession, de Man had a mystique. There were doubters and dissenters, but he was generally admired as a thinker, esteemed as a colleague, and idolized as a teacher.

Faculty found him erudite but ironic, cool but not aloof; students found him intimidating and charismatic. He had, M. H. Abrams later said, an air of "knowingness," an attribute that can take you a long way in a field like literary criticism in which expertise is hard to measure.[150] "Rigorous" is a word people used to describe the work; "austere" is one of the ways people described the man. Several of de Man's articles—he never published a monograph, which is unusual in literary studies, more normal in philosophy—became celebrated and much-studied texts, and a number of his graduate students went on to have distinguished careers at Yale and elsewhere.

When, in the spring of 1987, three and a half years after his death, it was learned that he had written during the war for two Belgian newspapers controlled by the Nazis, the discovery completely upended the image that students and colleagues had formed. The record showed that, for all intents and purposes, as a young man, de Man was a fascist. The paper for which he did most of his journalism, *Le Soir*, was the biggest daily in Belgium, with a quarter of a million readers. The Germans took it over almost immediately after occupying the country in May 1940 and staffed it with collaborationists. Anti-Semitic articles

---

* Apart from the paper he read at a conference at Johns Hopkins in 1966, which appeared in a collection in 1970, nothing by Derrida was available in English until 1973, when a translation of his book on Husserl was published. The work that had the greatest impact in the United States, *Of Grammatology*, appeared in 1976; the translator was Gayatri Chakravorty Spivak, an Indian émigré who had been a graduate student of Paul de Man's at Cornell.

became a front-page feature.* In his columns, de Man followed the Nazi line. He championed a Germanic aesthetic, denigrated French culture as effete, associated Jews with cultural degeneracy, praised pro-Nazi writers and intellectuals, and assured readers that the New Order had come to Europe. The war was over. It was time to join the winners.

The revelation of these wartime writings led to more discoveries about de Man's past, all of which suggested that, until he got to Cornell, in 1960, he had operated more or less outside the law.[151] He was a bigamist, didn't pay his bills, doctored his academic records, committed fraud as a businessman in Belgium, and lied about who he was. It is astonishing that someone with so much to hide chose to associate himself with a highly visible and controversial school of criticism. But he never got caught.

His first teaching job after he got to the United States after the war (fleeing a conviction for multiple acts of forgery and taking money under false pretenses as owner of a publishing house he had set up) was at Bard College. He was admitted to the PhD program in Comparative Literature at Harvard. (Since he never finished college, he doctored his transcript from the Free University of Brussels.) He nearly failed his PhD examinations and never completed one of the chapters of his dissertation, but he was awarded the degree. Through it all, he was writing criticism. An article called "The Intentional Structure of the Romantic Image" was published in France in 1960 and attracted interest. That fall, as faculty hiring was taking off, de Man got a job at Cornell. After that, he apparently got his life under control. Aside from financial delinquencies, there are no rumors of further misdeeds.

When he was a Harvard graduate student, he taught in a course, now semilegendary, called Humanities 6, directed by Reuben Brower, designed to instruct students in close reading. It turned out that this was something for which de Man had a genius. One of his students remembered how in class de Man would "sit in front of a text and just pluck magical things out of it."[152] That was the name of the game in literary criticism, and it was all that de Man ever did. He pulled things out of texts. His criticism was a demonstration of a way of reading. He used to warn his students not to confuse it with life.

----

* *The Adventures of Tintin* also appeared in *Le Soir* from 1940 to 1945; Tintin's creator, Hergé (Georges Remi), was for some period a convert to the New Order.

De Man's criticism—exactly like Brooks's and Frye's—tried to develop insights into the way literary language works. That's what "The Intentional Structure of the Romantic Image" was about: how the images in Romantic poems work. De Man found contradictions and paradoxes in the meaning that Romantic images are supposed to have, but that is what a New Critic would have been looking for, too.

Just before the article came out, de Man met Geoffrey Hartman at a Modern Language Association convention.* Hartman was a German refugee.[153] He had been in the *Kindertransport*, a program that evacuated Jewish children from Nazi Germany and resettled them in the United Kingdom. His parents were divorced. His father had fled to Argentina; his mother had already immigrated to the United States, getting out of Germany soon after *Kristallnacht*. Hartman did not see her again until he got there himself, in 1945. He attended Queens College in the City University of New York, majoring in comparative literature, and in 1949, he entered Yale as a graduate student and studied with Wellek. He was hired as an assistant professor in 1955, and became friendly with Bloom.

Hartman, too, was an admirer of Frye, and his dissertation, *The Unmediated Vision* (1954), was a study, influenced by phenomenology, of four poets marginal to the New Critical canon: Wordsworth, Hopkins, Rilke, and Valéry. His most important scholarly work, published in 1964, was *Wordsworth's Poetry, 1787–1841*. It followed Bloom's first two books, *Shelley's Mythmaking* (1959) and *The Visionary Company* (1961), a study of the six major English Romantic poets. The titles alone indicate how remote these studies were from New Critical values and concerns.

Hartman admired de Man's essay on the Romantic image and he showed it to Abrams. Abrams was by then dean of American Romanticists and a dominant figure in literary studies: he was founding editor of *The Norton Anthology of English Literature*, which would appear in 1962. Abrams made a Cornell appointment happen for de Man, and the career was launched. In 1964, without a book or, for that matter, a college degree, de Man was promoted to full professor. Two years later, the transformative event in de Man's academic life occurred when he met Derrida at a conference at Johns Hopkins.

---

* Hartman later said that the meeting was brief. In his memoir, he dates their friendship from 1965.

10.

The relation of Derrida's biography to his work presents a question of the kind Derrida loved: Was he inside or outside?[154] Derrida was a North African Jew. He was born in El Biar, outside Algiers, in 1930. His ancestors had emigrated from Spain before Algeria was colonized by, and eventually made a department of, France in the nineteenth century. His father was a wine salesman (as was Albert Camus's: wine was a major export industry). He was named Jackie, probably after the American actor Jackie Coogan. (He changed his name in 1959 on the occasion of his first public lecture.)

Algerian Jews—a small minority when Derrida was born, about thirty-five thousand—had been granted French citizenship in 1870. But in 1940, under the collaborationist Pétain regime, the decree was revoked, and in 1942, Derrida was expelled from his school, the Lycée Ben Aknoun. He later called this event an "earthquake," when "a little black and very Arab Jew who did not understand anything" was, without explanation, kicked out of school.[155]

In 1943, when Free French forces established themselves in Algiers, anti-Semitic measures were abolished and Derrida returned to school. He went on to the Lycée Émile-Félix-Gautier and then the Lycée Bugeaud, top schools in Algiers that prepared him for education in France. He arrived in Paris in the fall of 1949 and attended the Lycée Louis-le-Grande (the school Sartre, Senghor, Merleau-Ponty, and Césaire had all attended) to prepare for the entrance examination for the École Normale Supérieure. He failed the exam in 1951, but after his parents agreed to fund another year in Paris, he retook it and passed in 1952.

Derrida hated the ENS—"years of hell," he called his time there.[156] He failed the *agrégation*, passing on a second attempt with mediocre scores, then spent a year in Massachusetts in an exchange program with Harvard before returning to begin his teaching career in Koléa, not far from Algiers. In 1962, when the Algerian War ended and Algeria established its independence, Jews were deprived of legal rights and Derrida's parents had to flee.[157] Derrida helped them pack in somewhat scary conditions; after they left, their house was appropriated by the government. They never returned and ended up living in Nice.

Derrida was an anxious and occasionally depressive person, a writer and speaker of deceptive stamina who was uncomfortable taking a vacation. He found his early years in Paris close to unbearable because of homesickness and worry, and he dreaded going to the United States, even though he was accompanied by Marguerite Aucouturier, whom he would marry in Cambridge in 1957. There was a period in his career when he was afraid to fly. Like Camus, he was conflicted about his political allegiances: he sympathized with the Algerian independence movement but worried about the replacement of French colonialism with Arab nationalism.[158] His academic struggles made him hostile to the French educational system, and in many respects he made a better academic fit in the United States than in France, although in departments of literature, not philosophy.[159]

The background is important because a fundamental preoccupation of Derrida's writing—the word appears on the first page of his most important book, *De la grammatologie* (1967)—is ethnocentrism, by which he meant Eurocentrism. A Jew from a European colony who struggled to enter the French intellectual world might have not only an outsider's perspective but also an outsider's lived experience motivating his work. Or maybe it was that Derrida felt fully at home nowhere, not in the Jewish religion (his family was not particularly observant), or in independent Algeria, or in Paris, or in the United States.[160]

On the other hand, and despite all that, Derrida's entire career was on the inside track of French academic life: he did his *hypokâgne* at a top lycée; he did his *kâgne* at a leading Paris school; he was a *normalien*. He taught at the Sorbonne from 1960 to 1964 and the ENS from 1964 to 1984, when he left to become director of studies at the École des Hautes Études en Sciences Sociales. And he was a member of a distinctive generation of post-Sartrean French intellectuals, a group—many of whose members would become known years later (pejoratively and, in most cases, inaccurately) as the philosophers of *La Pensée 68*—that included Foucault, Lacan, Barthes, Gilles Deleuze, Julia Kristeva, Luce Irigaray, and Louis Althusser. Derrida's reputation profited from theirs and vice versa.[161]

Like Césaire and like Sartre, whom he admired when he was young, Derrida was a Republican. He did not want his choices or ideas attributed to accidents of birth. He almost never discussed his background until the 1990s, and, although his face would become a signifier of French cleverness and intellectual seduction, publicly available photographs of him before the late 1970s are almost nonexistent.

The Hopkins conference, which had the somewhat lost-in-translation title "The Languages of Criticism and the Sciences of Man," was a major enterprise. Funded by the Ford Foundation, it was organized by Richard Macksey, a Hopkins professor, and Eugenio Donato, an assistant professor and recent Hopkins PhD, under the auspices of the Hopkins Humanities Center, directed by René Girard, whose idea it seems to have originally been. There were more than a hundred participants from nine countries, headlined by fifteen "colloquists." Attendance was standing-room-only, and the conference was to be followed by two years of seminars and symposia. The goal was to introduce American academics to structuralism at a time when it was established in France but barely known to people who did not read French. The conference lasted for three days, October 18–21, 1966.

Derrida was a last-minute addition. An invited colloquist had to drop out, and Derrida was recommended by another participant, Jean Hippolyte, on the grounds that if asked, he was likely to come. Derrida was exhausted and under deadline pressure preparing several books for publication, but he seized the chance. He later claimed that he wrote his talk in ten days.[162] It was delivered on the final afternoon.

Derrida was virtually unknown in the United States in 1966. When he arrived at Hopkins, though, he had recently made a splash in France with the publication in the journal *Critique* of a two-part essay, called "De la grammatologie," which would become the first chapter in his book *De la grammatologie* in 1967. Foucault, who, along with Barthes, was on the editorial board of *Critique*, told Derrida that his article was the most radical text he had ever read.[163]

That article is where Derrida first used in print the term "deconstruction," a neologism he initially spelled *dé-construction* and defined as "not demolition but de-sedimentation."[164] The word was both lucky and unlucky. Meant to suggest a variation on a Heideggerian term, *Destruktion*, "deconstruction" was taken by many people to mean simply "exposing the hidden meaning" or "demolishing," which is not what Derrida intended. But the idea of exposing and demolishing is a lot of what gave deconstruction appeal, and the word passed into popular usage, where it often means simply "disassembled," such that you can now order a Deconstructed Caesar Salad. Even writers hostile to deconstruction, or what they understand to be deconstruction, used (and still use) the term in their own writing. Deconstruction is what

Derrida presented at Hopkins. His paper was called "Structure, Sign, and Play in the Discourse of the Human Sciences," and it landed like a bomb.

Deconstruction is difficult to explain in a manner consistent with deconstruction. This is what accounts for the notorious wordplay and circularity in Derrida's prose. Derrida's essay in a widely discussed book called *Deconstruction and Criticism*, for example, a collection of essays by Yale professors published in 1979, has a hundred-page footnote. We could say that deconstruction is an attempt to go through the looking glass, to get beyond or behind language, but a deconstructionist would have to begin by explaining that the concepts "beyond" and "behind" are themselves effects of language. Deconstruction is all about interrogating apparently unproblematic terms in a medium, language, that bases its claim to determinate meaning on a fiction. It's like digging a hole in the middle of the ocean with a shovel made of water.

Because Derrida had to do it fast, and because it had to be (by Derrida's standards) succinct, the Hopkins paper is the most cogent and accessible statement of his position that he ever composed. He used Lévi-Strauss as the exemplar of the structuralist approach, and he did so by the (very French) tactic of crediting Lévi-Strauss with recognizing the fatal flaw within his own thought and then accusing him of evading or obfuscating it.

This is an important feature of deconstruction: the philosophers and poets whose texts are deconstructed *already know* the game they are playing. Deconstruction is not about exposing authorial naïveté. It's about seeing how writers handle the contradictions or aporias their own use of language has got them into. When Derrida published a version of his critique of Lévi-Strauss in France the following year, Lévi-Strauss responded indignantly that he was not writing philosophy—the text in question was *Tristes Tropiques*—and so had no obligation to be rigorous. But that is exactly what Derrida meant: Lévi-Strauss knew the dice were loaded. He rolled them anyway.[165]

In the Hopkins paper, Derrida begins by pointing out an incoherence in the concept of structure as it is used by linguists and anthropologists. Jakobson and Lévi-Strauss describe cultures—languages, kinship systems, myths—as systems of relation. Meaning is a function difference; it is not anchored to some nonsignifying reality. And so everything within the system—phonemes, morphemes, mythemes, kinship roles—is subject to substitutions and transformations, to what Derrida calls *jeu*, meaning "play" or "game."

But this describes a flux, not a structure. A structure must have a center, a fixed point, something that cannot be substituted for or relativized and whose significance is not a function of difference. The history of Western thought, Derrida argues, is the history of efforts to name such a fixed point, from Plato's *eidos* (form or idea) and Aristotle's *energeia* (actuality) to Augustine's God, Descartes's consciousness, and Heidegger's Being. And the fact that this "center"—what Derrida calls the "transcendental signified"—has a history shows that it, too, is subject to substitution, and that it, too, is a term whose meaning is a function of its relation to the other terms in a given system of signification.[166] In a scientific worldview, for example, the name for the fixed point is "truth." Science requires such a concept, but the concept is "inside" science, not before it or above it.

Derrida thinks the same contradiction is present in the binaries that underwrite Western thought, starting with the binary speech/writing. He tries to show that writers from Plato to Rousseau and Saussure privilege speech over writing. Speech is figured as prior, originary, and unmediated, and writing as derivative, dependent, and supplementary. All binaries work this way, with one term primary and the other derivative, but when we put pressure on them, they break down.

Take Derrida's epic footnote: we think of a footnote (or a preface or an appendix) as paratextual, supplementary, not essential. But for something to be a text there has already to be something that is a paratext. Meaning ("this is a text") is never freestanding; it depends on difference ("this is not a text"). The sentence in *De la grammatologie* that is translated as "there is nothing outside of the text" reads, in French, "il n'y a pas de hors-texte."[167] It's a pun: *hors* is "outside," but *hors-texte* is a noun denoting a preface, bookplate, insert. So that the sentence means (or it also means) "there is no paratext." Transposed into the language of Plato's allegory: there is no outside-the-cave. Philosophy itself is work with shadows.

In the Hopkins talk, Derrida put pressure on two binaries used by Lévi-Strauss. The first is nature/culture. Anthropologically, nature refers to the essentially—that is, biologically and universally—human, and culture refers to particular forms or systems that particular groups have created. But virtually the first time he applies this distinction in *Les Structures élémentaires de la parenté*, Lévi-Strauss runs into a problem with an indispensable concept in his argument: the incest prohibition. The incest prohibition is cultural (because man-made, not required by biology), but it is also universal, present in every kinship system, and hence on the "nature" side of the binary. This is a scandal, Derrida says, but only in a system that sanctions a nature/culture distinction in the first place.

The other binary arises from Lévi-Strauss's use of the term *bricoleur*. A *bricoleur* is someone who puts together from bits and pieces that were produced for other reasons an instrument to serve a provisional purpose. This is what Lévi-Strauss claimed he was doing with philosophical terms when he responded to Derrida's criticism of *Tristes Tropiques*, and it is what Frye thought all poets are doing. Lévi-Strauss contrasts the *bricoleur* with someone who is the originator of a coherent instrument or system, someone who creates ex nihilo: the engineer. But if *bricolage* refers to "the necessity of borrowing one's concepts from the text of a heritage which is more or less coherent or ruined," Derrida says, then "it must be said that every discourse is *bricoleur*," and that therefore "the engineer is a myth produced by the *bricoleur*."[168]

Derrida's ideas about binaries and the transcendental signified had a widespread effect on academic literary criticism, even among scholars who did not practice deconstructionist readings or consider their work theoretically motivated. Derrida taught critics to regard terms such as "essence," "origin," "telos," "substance," "presence," "plenitude," "truth" as always dependent on the exclusion or repression of something else, a something that is labeled as derivative, secondary, imperfect, mediated. As he put it in an interview in 1971:

> In a classic philosophical opposition we have, not a peaceful co-existence of facing terms, but a violent hierarchy. One of the two terms dominates the other (axiologically, logically, etc.), occupies the commanding position. To deconstruct the opposition is first of all, at a given moment, to reverse the hierarchy.[169]

The term that Derrida became mostly closely associated with is one he came to regret: "freeplay." The word he used in "Structure, Sign, and

Play" is *jeu*, which Macksey translated sometimes as "freeplay," sometimes as "game" or "stake." The function of the center, Derrida wrote, is "not only to orient, balance, and organize the structure—one cannot in fact conceive of an unorganized structure—but above all to make sure that the organizing principle of the structure limits what we might call the *freeplay* [*jeu*] of the structure."[170] Another way to put it, in the context of literary criticism, is to say that the center is what an interpretation is answerable to. By decentering the center, by turning it into a metaphor, Derrida was, in effect, removing the gyroscope from the system and opening up an unending play of interpretation.

It's true that deconstruction made theoretically conceivable what de Man, referring to his own mode of reading, called "vertiginous possibilities of referential aberration."[171] Barthes, in particular, interpreted Derrida as liberating the reader from the intentions of the author. "Derrida was one of those who helped me to understand what was at stake (philosophically, ideologically) in my own work," he said: "he disequilibriated the structure, he opened up the sign: he is, for us, *the one who unpicked the end of the chain [qui a décroché le bout de la chaîne]*."[172]

But Derrida did not mean by *jeu* that "anything goes." "Free" would hardly have been an unproblematic term for him. "Greatly overestimated in my texts in the United States," he complained later, "this notion of 'freeplay' is an inadequate translation of the lexical network connected to the word *jeu*."[173] There is a difference between indeterminacy (a term he did not use) and undecidability. When the meaning is undecidable, it is undecidable among determinate positions. Derrida only meant that whatever constrains or controls our interpretation, whatever makes those positions determinate for us, is itself a function of interpretation. As he acknowledged in the Hopkins talk, the position is Nietzschean: it's interpretation all the way down.*

---

* "The causes of a thing's origin and its eventual uses, the manner of its incorporation into a system of purposes, are worlds apart. Everything that exists, no matter what its origin, is again and again interpreted anew, requisitioned anew, transformed and rearranged for a new use by a power superior to it . . . The whole history of a thing, an organ, a tradition becomes a continuous chain of reinterpretations and rearrangements, which need not be causally connected among themselves, which may simply follow one another at random. The development of a thing, a custom, an organ is not its progress toward a goal, let alone the most logical and shortest progress, requiring the least energy and expenditure. Rather, it is a sequence of more or less profound, more or less independent processes of appropriation, including the resistances used in each instance, the attempted transformations for purposes of defense or reaction, as well as the results of successful counterattacks. The form is fluid, the 'meaning' even more so." (*The Genealogy of Morals*, 1887.)

It is true, Derrida says, that the "absence of the transcendental signified extends the domain and the interplay [*jeu*] of signification *ad infinitum*." But there is no way out of the system: "*There is no sense* in doing without the concepts of metaphysics in order to attack metaphysics. We have no language—no syntax and no lexicon—which is alien to this history; we cannot utter a single destructive proposition which has not already slipped into the form, the logic, the implicit postulations of precisely what it seeks to contest."[174] In the discussion following his paper, he explained that deconstruction "is simply a question of . . . being alert to the implications, to the historical sedimentations of the language we use." Derrida meant to make interpretation more rigorous, not less.

De Man was a designated commentator at the Hopkins conference. He had already read Derrida's article in *Critique*, and he realized that they were both trying to do similar things. Their professional obsessions were beautifully complementary: Derrida's was writing; De Man's was reading. They had breakfast together at Hopkins, and when *De la grammatologie* came out, the following year, de Man wrote to say how thrilled and interested he was, and how he expected it to help in the clarification of his own thinking.[175]

J. Hillis Miller was present for Derrida's talk as well. Miller was a professor at Hopkins, and like de Man, he had read the article in *Critique* and was excited by it. When Derrida returned to Hopkins in 1968, he and Miller became friends.

In 1972, Miller moved to Yale, and de Man arranged a regular visiting appointment for Derrida, who taught there every year until de Man's death. Along with Shoshana Felman, who joined the faculty in 1970, these were the literature professors most closely associated with Derrida and deconstruction. By 1975, a new "Yale School" had replaced the school of Brooks, Warren, Wellek, and Wimsatt.[176]

De Man's binary was grammar/rhetoric, and he called his method "rhetorical reading." The idea is that we organize—we stabilize—language as we read it. We bring to a text mental habits that fix the meaning of the words, and then we attribute that meaning to the words. We say, "That's what the text really says." De Man's point was that often, and almost always in the case of literature, it is in fact not what the text really says. He wanted to get the reader's mental habits out of the act of reading.

One of the things that makes literature different from philosophy and self-help books is that in nonliterary texts, tropes, rhetorical devices, and figures of speech are incidental to the meaning, and in literary texts, metaphors, symbols, allegories, all the forms and styles of fiction, are sources of meaning. We don't read literature literally. We assume that what is meant is more than, or other than, what the words literally say. This is the belief that de Man complicated (as he also complicated the belief that philosophical writing is fundamentally *not* figurative and rhetorical).

The best-known illustration of the de Manian method involves the line that ends William Butler Yeats's poem "Among School Children": "How can we know the dancer from the dance?" We naturally read that line rhetorically, to mean: "We cannot know the difference." But, de Man pointed out, grammatically, the sentence is a question, and it means: "Please tell me, how *can* I know the dancer from the dance?" The meanings are contradictory, but there is nothing in "what the text really says" that tells us which one is correct.[177] This observation doesn't debunk the poem, or prove that language is "inherently false," or reduce Yeats to incoherence. On the contrary, it complicates lines that are usually read as a celebration of Romantic symbolism, lines about the union of sign and referent, word and thing, and turns the poem into a reflection on its own (to use a de Manian phrase) aesthetic ideology.

De Man believed that he was defending literature. He argued that literature is the only kind of writing that is aware of the instability of the distinction between the literal and the figurative, between grammatical and rhetorical modes of meaning. "For the crucial statement that the structuralists make about language, namely that sign and meaning can never coincide, is what is precisely taken for granted in the kind of language we call literary," he wrote in 1967. ". . . Literature, unlike everyday language, begins on the far side of this knowledge; it is the only form of language free from the fallacy of unmediated expression."[178] And, in one of his most widely read essays, "Semiology and Rhetoric," published in 1973:

> The deconstruction is not something we have added to the text but it constituted the text in the first place. A literary text simultaneously asserts and denies the authority of its own rhetorical mode and, by reading the text as we did, we were only trying to come closer to being as rigorous a reader as the author had to be in order

to write the sentence in the first place. Poetic writing is the most advanced and refined mode of deconstruction.[179]

For some people, this kind of criticism might be narrow or uninteresting, but it is hard to see anything scandalous about it.

Yale-school criticism of the 1970s had the same appeal and shortcomings as the New Criticism. It generated intellectual power by bracketing off most of what might be called the real-life aspects of literature—that literature is written by people, that it affects people, that it is a report on experience. Asked what deconstruction might have to say to readers looking for those things, one of de Man's former students, Barbara Johnson, who later taught at Harvard, said: "[I]f it is indeed the case that people approach literature with the desire to learn something about the world, and if it is indeed the case that the literary medium is not transparent, then a study of its non-transparency is crucial in order to deal with the desire one has to know something about the world by reading literature."[180] That might not quite satisfy the skeptic.

Still, it was exciting to get inside the atom. "[W]e knew we were at the *center* of intellectual life," Alice Kaplan, another former student of de Man's, wrote. "We were sharpening our minds like razors, because we were the carriers of a new way of reading: the most advanced, thoroughgoing, questioning reading that had ever been done on a text."[181] It was a fantastically limited approach, she admitted, but everything that happened since seemed to her unworthy by comparison.

Deconstruction is a *via negativa*. It's good for getting down to what de Man called the mechanical level of language. But it can't bring anything substantive back, because anything substantive is subject to the rigors of deconstruction all over again. Deconstruction started to run into the sands when it got used to interpret texts in conformance with the political views of the interpreter (a type of self-fulfilling prophecy that afflicts many schools of criticism). Deconstruction is not a train you can get off at the most convenient station.

That this anti-foundationalism did not have much effect outside university literature departments (with the exception of some kinds of arts practice) contributed to, though it was hardly the cause of, a rift between academic and journalistic criticism after the 1960s. In many respects, deconstruction realized the dream of Ransom and Richards of a purely professional mode of literary analysis. It was something only professors did. And it "solved" the problem of literary criticism's status in a university system organized around the production of knowledge by making the interrogation of what counts as knowledge into a topic of inquiry.

Hartman, too, always saw deconstruction as "a defense of literature," as he wrote in an essay in which he tried to come to terms with the revelations about de Man's wartime writings.[182] But he could see that for de Man, there was something else in its appeal. He called de Man "a connoisseur of nothingness."[183] De Man took the train to the end of the line. It may be that he was able to write what he did, both the chillingly unpardonable things and the chillingly inspiring ones, because he believed in nothing.

"[T]ruth grows up inside of all the finite experiences," as another anti-foundationalist, William James, put it. "They lean on each other, but the whole of them, if such a whole there be, leans on nothing. All 'homes' are in finite experience; finite experience as such is homeless. Nothing outside of the flux secures the issue of it."[184] Deconstructionists used the same term for this "nothing" that Trilling did in "On the Teaching of Modern Literature": *abîme*—the abyss. The idea, of course, is that, having looked into it, students will find their way back, enlightened, ready to do society's work.

And this is what liberal education is designed to do—to have students see not that the domain of human values is illusional, for it's as real as it could be, but that it is founded on nothing. That is what Arnold thought criticism could do. It is what Richards thought poetry could do. Many liberal educators worried that deconstruction was destabilizing. It was. So is liberal education. It is meant to enable students to see that the world they were born into is not natural or inevitable. Deconstruction simply added language to the list of the things we should not take for granted. It reminds us that the ice we walk on is never not thin.

14

COMMONISM

Andy Warhol filming Marcel Duchamp at the Cordier & Eckstrom Gallery, 978 Madison Avenue, New York City, February 7, 1966. The man immediately to Warhol's right, turned away, is the photographer Stephen Shore, who was a discovery of Edward Steichen and who frequented the Factory. The partly hidden woman in the patterned dress is the model Benedetta Barzini, who would be briefly engaged to Warhol's assistant Gerard Malanga. The exhibition was a group show to benefit the Marcel Duchamp Fund of the American Chess Foundation, and included works by Robert Rauschenberg, James Rosenquist, and Jasper Johns. It was titled *Hommage à Caïssa*, the goddess of chess. Photograph by Nat Finkelstein. (*Nat Finkelstein Estate*)

1.

Andy Warhol's parents came from a village in the Carpathian Mountains in what is now Slovakia. They immigrated to Pittsburgh, where, in 1928, Andy was born, the youngest of three boys.* Warhol's father worked in construction, and he died, of peritonitis, when Andy was

---

* The year of Warhol's birth was long a matter of uncertainty. Warhol lied about it, even to his doctor, and his parents failed to register for a birth certificate.

thirteen, but he had saved money for his son to go to college, since it was obvious that Andy was an unusual and talented child.[1]

Warhol's mother, like Jackson Pollock's mother, encouraged art-making at home, and Warhol entered the Carnegie Institute of Technology (now Carnegie Mellon University) when he was seventeen, majoring in painting and design. He struggled at first. He was younger than most of the students, a number of whom were veterans attending on the G.I. Bill. But he eventually became an admired and occasionally controversial figure. A classmate described him as like "an angel in the sky," which is consistent with the reaction many people had to him before he became famous.[2] After he graduated, in June 1949, he moved to New York City, where he quickly found work as an illustrator.

By 1960, Warhol was one of the most successful commercial artists in New York. He drew, with a distinctive and recognizable line, called the "blotted line," magazine illustrations, advertisements, book jackets, and album covers. He made $70,000 a year and owned a four-story town house on the Upper East Side, where he lived with his mother, Julia, who spoke to him in Rusyn, the language of her home country. But he always had fine-art aspirations. He had several shows of stylistically conventional work (though with explicitly gay subject matter) in minor venues, none attracting much in the way of critical attention or buyers. His break came in July 1962, when he had a one-man exhibition at the Ferus Gallery on La Cienega Boulevard in Los Angeles. This was *32 Campbell's Soup Cans*—thirty-two paintings of soup cans, each a different flavor. A New York show followed in September. It sold out. And, for the next five and a half years, Warhol was on the cutting edge of the avant-garde.

He began making movies in 1963, eventually devoting most of his time to them. He also produced the Velvet Underground and "wrote," using a tape recorder, a novel, entitled *a*. In the mid-1960s, his studio on East Forty-Seventh Street, known as the Factory, was a center of social mingling. Virtually everyone fashionable in the worlds of art, ideas, and entertainment passed through it, from Judy Garland and Bob Dylan to Susan Sontag and John Ashbery.

Then, in 1968, shortly after moving his studio to a space on Union Square, Warhol was shot and nearly killed by a paranoid schizophrenic named Valerie Solanas, and the attitudes he represented, to the press and the public, went out of fashion almost overnight. Although he returned to painting and to the social life of a celebrity, his work had lost its place on the leading edge of the contemporary arts. He died in New York Hospital after an operation in 1987. He was fifty-eight. As sometimes happens, his death helped to revive his reputation, and eventually his work became a source of techniques and ideas for other artists. Its value also appreciated fantastically.

The essence of Warhol's genius was to eliminate the one aspect of a thing without which that thing would, to conventional ways of thinking, cease to be itself, and then to see what happened. He made movies of things that never moved; he used actors who could not act; he made art that did not look like art. He wrote a novel without doing any writing. He sent an actor, Allen Midgette, to impersonate him on a lecture tour. He had other people make his paintings, or pretended that he did. He systematically lied in interviews.

And he demonstrated, every time he did this, that it didn't make any difference. His Brillo boxes were received as art, and his eight-hour movie of the Empire State Building was received as a movie. The people who saw someone pretending to be Andy Warhol believed that they had seen Andy Warhol. And what he made up in interviews was quoted to explain his intentions. Warhol wasn't hiding anything, and he wasn't out to trick anyone. He was only changing one rule, the most basic rule, of the game. He found that people keep on playing.

For a critic, Warhol poses two meta-problems. One has to do with the man and the other with the work. It should be a rule when writing about Warhol never to take anything he said seriously, and it would be a rule, probably, if there were not always one or two bits that suit the writer's purpose. From the beginning, Warhol postured and prevaricated. He made it a game to see if he could get through an interview answering only *yes* or *no*. "Basically he's a liar when he's being interviewed," his principal assistant, Gerard Malanga, explained.[3]

The sources of several of Warhol's most apparently considered remarks— a 1963 interview in *ARTnews* by Gene Swenson and a 1966 interview in *The East Village Other* by Gretchen Berg—were doctored.* Berg referred to her piece as a "word collage," and in the *ARTnews* interview, Warhol is made to refer to an article in *The Hudson Review*, a publication that

---

* When the Swenson interview was reprinted in *Pop Art Redefined* (1969), an editing mistake added seven paragraphs that were actually from another interview, also in *ARTnews*, with Tom Wesselmann.

was about as far outside his orbit as the *Proceedings of the Modern Language Association*.⁴

He was often perfectly frank about this. In 1969, he was interviewed by the *New Yorker* writer Calvin Tomkins, a friend of Rauschenberg and Johns who was cool to Warhol's art. "Warhol wasn't anything like what I had expected," Tompkins wrote later. "Instead of a barely articulate, slightly sinister manipulator of troubled souls . . . he came across as playful, sly, funny, and very alert." Tomkins was an experienced interviewer, but Warhol took charge. He asked the first question—"Do you have a big cock?"—and he ended the interview with: "Have I lied enough?"⁵

The aperçus for which Warhol is known—"I'd like to be a machine, wouldn't you?" and so on—were either deliberately provocative or ad-libbed.⁶ Asked a routine question, he gave the most blasé or perverse answer he could think of. More often than not, these were received as insights into his personality and his art—or, like the saying "In the future everybody will be world-famous for fifteen minutes," which is obviously inane, as penetrating critiques of contemporary life.⁷

Warhol's books—*The Philosophy of Andy Warhol* (1975), *Popism: The Warhol 60s* (1980), and *The Andy Warhol Diaries* (1989)—are no less disingenuous. *The Philosophy of Andy Warhol*, for example, was written partly by Bob Colacello, the editor of Warhol's magazine, *Interview*. Colacello gave the pages of each chapter to Warhol, who read them over the phone to his friend Brigid Berlin, taping her reactions, and then gave everything to his writer, Pat Hackett, who revised the manuscript and sent it to the publisher. Warhol never set figurative pen to paper.⁸

Warhol loved gossip. He spent hours every day on the phone keeping up with the scene, and he populated his world with men and women who shared his taste. Quite a few of these later produced memoirs: Malanga, who was Warhol's assistant from 1963 to 1968; John Giorno, the star of Warhol's first film, *Sleep* (1963); Mary Woronov, who performed with the Velvet Underground and acted in some of the films; and the so-called superstars Sue Hoffman (aka Viva) and Isabelle Collin-Dufresne (aka Ultra Violet). Other associates—Billy Linich (aka Billy Name), who was de facto chief of operations at the Factory; Berlin, a Fifth Avenue heiress and connoisseur of amphetamines, the Factory drug of choice; and the underground movie actor Taylor Mead—were interviewed repeatedly over the years.

So were art-world figures who were associated with Warhol in the early stages of his career, particularly Emile de Antonio (the friend and supporter of John Cage) and Henry Geldzahler, a curator of American art at the Metropolitan Museum of Art, both of whom introduced Warhol to artists, dealers, and collectors. Ivan Karp, who worked at the Leo Castelli Gallery and discovered many of the Pop artists, gave a number of interviews, as did Robert Scull, the taxi tycoon and art collector whose first wife was the subject of one of Warhol's earliest and most famous portrait paintings, *Ethel Scull 36 Times* (1963), and Irving Blum, who ran the Ferus Gallery and who bought *32 Campbell's Soup Cans* from Warhol for a thousand dollars. (In 1995, he sold it to the Museum of Modern Art for $14.5 million.)

These sources have handle-with-care stamped all over them. On the art-world side, the subjects have a professional or financial stake in Warhol's reputation (as well as their own). And even on the personal side, people tend to become invested in their own stories. Life at the Factory involved a lot of jockeying for Warhol's attention, a state of affairs that Warhol encouraged and that continued in spirit long after the life was over.* These people were all caught up in a system whose sole reward—Warhol paid his assistants little and his actors nothing in the Factory years—was proximity to the artist. In memorializing their experiences, disinterestedness was about the last concern they had. The culture around Warhol was a culture of high artifice—its icon, eventually, was the drag queen—and the gossip, the posing, and the pretense were part of that. They do not make a firm basis for history.

The work is similarly inscrutable because it poses squarely the fundamental Pop conundrum: celebration or critique? Soup cans, Coca-Cola bottles, grocery cartons, movie stars, newspaper photos—did Warhol paint this stuff because he thought it was great or because he thought it was junk? Is his work a commentary on the shallowness, repetitiveness, and commercialism of consumer culture, or is it a celebration of supermarkets and Hollywood, a romp with the vulgar—a commentary, instead, on the highbrow Puritanism of the fine-art tradition? Even the silkscreens of electric chairs and car crashes are impossible to interpret. Why did he produce those images? To magnify the horror or to aestheticize it? These were questions the British Pop artists could answer,

---

* The Factory habitués' nickname for Warhol, invented either by Robert Olivo (aka Ondine) or Dorothy Dean, one of the few Black people in Warhol's circle, was Drella—a mash-up of Cinderella and Dracula.

because for them consumerist imagery was exotic and their work was an implicit rebuke to postwar British culture. For American artists like Warhol, it *was* the culture.

These are questions about which, needless to say, Warhol was exceedingly coy. This was his version, in *Popism*, of how he got to Pop:

> At five o'clock one particular afternoon the doorbell rang and De [Emile de Antonio] came in and sat down. I poured Scotch for us, and then I went over to where two paintings I'd done, each about six feet high and three feet wide, were propped, facing the wall. I turned them around and placed them side by side against the wall and then I backed away to take a look at them myself. One of them was a Coke bottle with Abstract Expressionist hash marks halfway up the side. The second one was just a stark, outlined Coke bottle in black and white. I didn't say a thing to De. I didn't have to—he knew what I wanted to know.
>
> "Well, look, Andy," he said after staring at them for a couple of minutes. "One of these is a piece of shit, simply a little bit of everything. The other is remarkable—it's our society, it's who we are, it's absolutely beautiful and naked, and you ought to destroy the first one and show the other.
>
> That afternoon was an important one for me.[9]

Ingenuous? Disingenuous? Who can tell? The account itself is probably entirely from de Antonio, transcribed into Warhol's voice by his "co-writer" on *Popism*, Pat Hackett.[10] And Warhol seems to have staged the same demonstration for more than one visitor. Ivan Karp is on record with an identical story.[11] That is because Warhol liked to give the impression that he let other people make his artistic decisions for him.

A standard way of cutting the interpretive knot is to say that Warhol was a mirror of the times. But as with any mirror, Warhol reflected back whoever was looking. In this respect, he was like Bob Dylan, another enigma of the day onto whom people projected all sorts of views. Dylan actually had nothing particularly interesting to say about American life, and neither did Warhol.* Dylan is a songwriter. Warhol was an artist.

---

* "If I wasn't Bob Dylan, I'd probably think that Bob Dylan has a lot of answers," he once said. (*Playboy* 25 [March 1978], 90.)

That was something he did his best to obscure. No one did more than Warhol himself to promote the perception that he was a naïve interloper in the art world. But his life was devoted to art. Art is pretty much all he did. He collected it: by 1961, he owned work by Toulouse-Lautrec, Georges Braque, René Magritte, Joan Miró, Paul Klee, Jasper Johns, Roberto Matta, Ellsworth Kelly, Frank Stella, Jim Dine, and Ray Johnson. He attended openings, screenings, and performances in every kind of venue, from Times Square movie theaters to Judson Church avant-garde dance recitals in the Village. He had a subscription to the Metropolitan Opera.

He knew most of the major figures in the New York art world, not only artists and dealers but also poets, filmmakers, dancers, musicians, and critics. He almost never took a vacation. "[A] very single-minded person," James Rosenquist said, "he had this drive to work, work, work."[12] Leo Castelli called him "the least casual artist that I know."[13] Between 1962 and 1964 alone, he created two thousand works of art. Over the course of his career, he made five hundred movies.

Rauschenberg liked to pretend that he was just doing what came naturally, but he also liked to talk about his work, and he did not make it difficult to understand in an art-world context. Warhol did make it difficult. He constantly denied having artistic intentions; that is what most of the persiflage was about. He got people caught up in wondering whether he really liked Elizabeth Taylor, or whether he was piercing through the official façade in order to expose the real America as a place of executions, car crashes, and poisoned tuna.

Malanga was not without an agenda, but as Warhol's chief assistant in the Factory years, he was involved in virtually every creative activity Warhol engaged in. Although he tended to take credit for many of Warhol's ideas and innovations (he is not the only person to do this, and Warhol wouldn't have minded), he was privy to whatever Warhol chose to share about his intentions, and it's clear from the many interviews Malanga gave, as well as from his own writings, that for Warhol, all decisions were purely artistic decisions.

"I've always considered Andy a Conceptual artist in that he was really a spiritual child of Duchamp," Malanga wrote shortly after Warhol's death. "Andy revitalized the notion of *concept* by activating it into an end result, always keeping in mind that the idea was very much the content of whatever it was he would depict in painting or film or gesture . . . Andy's paintings are really a documentation or comment on the tradition of art."[14] Which is what Clement Greenberg said avant-garde art should be.

2.

It took the Abstract Expressionists almost ten years to achieve both critical and commercial success. It took the American Pop artists about ten months. This is because by 1962, the year Pop burst on the scene, an art-world infrastructure was finally in place—the galleries, dealers, collectors, curators, museum officials and trustees, critics, and a public audience for contemporary art.

The idea that Abstract Expressionism dominated the art world either domestically or internationally is a myth produced by a Cold-War-within-the-Cold-War argument about American cultural imperialism. When the Abstract Expressionists came onto the scene around 1950, the Museum of Modern Art was still committed to European modernism and was wary of contemporary American art. It demonstrated no special interest in Abstract Expressionism.[15] Even after Jackson Pollock's breakthrough show in 1949, MoMA turned down a chance to buy *Autumn Rhythm* for ten thousand dollars. Its reluctance to purchase art by the American Abstract Expressionists was so well known that in 1952 seven of them wrote a letter to the museum accusing it of having no appreciation for avant-garde painting.[16]

The Abstract Expressionists themselves did not think of their art as "American." They were perfectly aware of its European roots, and preferred to think of themselves in cosmopolitan, not parochial, terms.[17] Nor was Abstract Expressionism a very visible presence in Europe. Pollock had shows in 1950 in Venice and Milan of works from Peggy Guggenheim's collection, all of them pre-drip. His abstract work was featured in two gallery shows in Paris—*Véhémences confrontées* (1951) and *Un Art autre* (1952)—organized by the critic Michel Tapié with the idea of setting up a conversation between European and American painting.[18] *Véhémences confrontées* traveled (as *Opposing Forces*) to the Institute of Contemporary Arts in London in 1953—the first time a Pollock had been seen in Britain. His work was important for the Independent Group artists, but popular response was hostile. No American museum, dealer, or government agency sponsored those shows: Tapié borrowed the canvases from Pollock's friend Alfonso Ossorio.[19] He told Pollock he hoped to get European collectors interested in buying a painting, and it seems that a few did.[20]

Except for work by American artists living in Paris and Rome, almost all the contemporary American art seen by Europeans in the 1950s was on loan to a museum. And although European museums displayed American art, they did not buy it. In 1958, there was not a single painting by Willem de Kooning, Franz Kline, Robert Motherwell, or Mark Rothko in a European museum. There were two Pollocks; both were in the Stedelijk in Amsterdam, a museum that, under the direction of Willem Sandberg, was dedicated to avant-garde art, and both were gifts of Peggy Guggenheim.* In an exhibition of more than a hundred works by American artists that toured Europe in 1956, *Modern Art in the United States*, by far the most popular painting was Andrew Wyeth's hyperrealist *Christina's World* (purchased by MoMA in 1949). Although the Pollocks made a big impression on London audiences, much of it was negative.[21]

No European museum purchased a Pollock until 1961, when the Tate bought *Number 23* (1948). By contrast, in 1960, American museums owned thirteen works by the Russian-born French painter Nicolas de Staël, Pollock's contemporary.[22] Mark Rothko did not have a solo exhibition in Europe until 1961. Willem de Kooning did not have one until 1967. By then, Warhol had had ten European exhibitions and Rauschenberg had had fifteen.[23]

And it is not the case that Pollock's work, or Abstract Expressionism generally, received special support from the government or American museums.[24] The "message" of art exhibitions sent abroad was that there was not one American style of painting; on the contrary, the United States was a place where a diversity of styles could flourish. So, for example, although Pollock had four works in a show called *Twelve Contemporary American Painters and Sculptors*, which was organized by MoMA and traveled to Paris, Zurich, Düsseldorf, Stockholm, Helsinki, and Oslo in 1953–1954, the emphasis was on diversity: the other artists included Ben Shahn, Edward Hopper, Alexander Calder, John Marin, and Stuart Davis.[25]

---

* Only one, *Reflection of the Big Dipper* (1947), was a drip painting; the other was a pre-drip abstraction, *The Water Bull* (1945).

An exhibition devoted exclusively to Abstract Expressionism did finally come to Europe in 1958. This was *The New American Painting*, assembled by Dorothy Miller at the request of European museums for the Museum of Modern Art. It contained works by sixteen artists, including Pollock, Rothko, Kline, de Kooning, Arshile Gorky, Grace Hartigan, Barnett Newman, and Clyfford Still. The exhibition was produced by MoMA's International Program of Circulating Exhibitions, but the idea came from Arnold Rüdlinger, the director of the Kunsthalle in Basel.[26]* A Pollock retrospective, also organized by MoMA, toured Europe at same time on a somewhat different itinerary.†

Reaction to *The New American Painting* was mixed. Newspaper critics were mostly hostile. "It is not new. It is not painting. It is not American," wrote a reviewer in Milan.[27]‡ European artists were impressed by Pollock, whose paintings contradicted his reputation as a wild man. But they were not shocked. They had been making abstract art since the 1910s, and abstract expressionist art since the 1940s.[28] *The New American Painting* was no longer new in the United States, either. Johns and Rauschenberg had already had their shows at the Castelli Gallery. Pollock was dead. The Abstract Expressionist moment was over.

In the United States in those years, there were few places to buy contemporary American art of any kind. In 1945, by a conservative calculation, there were seventy-three art galleries in New York City.[29] (Art was also sold by dealers unaffiliated with a gallery.) Only a handful showed contemporary American art. Annual sales of European and American painting and sculpture in New York was about $6 million in 1945, less than half the average annual art sales in Paris before the war (about $15 million), and Paris sales were much higher after the war. Half of the

---

* It is not the case (as claimed in Frances Stonor Saunders, *The Cultural Cold War* [New York: New Press, 2001], 267) that MoMA's founding director, Alfred Barr, ever referred to Abstract Expressionism as "benevolent propaganda for foreign intelligentsia." That phrase was used many years later by a *critic* of the museum's policies, Max Kozloff ("American Painting During the Cold War," *Artforum* 11 [May 1973], 44). Nor did Barr refer to it, in the letter to Henry Luce about *Time/Life*'s coverage in 1949, as "artistic free enterprise" (Saunders, 267). Those words were inserted into the letter by Nelson Rockefeller—a capitalist speaking to a capitalist. There is no evidence that Barr ever thought of art in those terms. (See "Nelson's draft," Microfilm roll 1271, 175, Alfred Barr Papers, Museum of Modern Art Archives.)

† The museum had connections to government agencies within the State Department, notably the United States Information Agency. Evidence of a connection to the CIA is thin. Foundations (such as the Farfield) that operated as CIA cutouts for other purposes also helped subvent exhibitions like these, but the catalogues for the touring exhibitions emphasized Abstract Expressionism's European roots. The goal was to promote European unification. It was not to establish a cultural imperium.

‡ A Rome paper, *Avanti!*, did call Pollock "Il Presley della pittura."

$6 million was for work by Old Masters and Impressionist painters, just 15 percent for contemporary American art. American artists were vastly outsold by European artists.[30]

In 1953, Eleanor Ward, the founder of the Stable Gallery, had a show that included all the major Abstract Expressionists except Rothko and Still, who were then turning down group shows. It included Jackson Pollock's *Blue Poles* (1952), the last of the drip paintings, and works by de Kooning and Kline. Not a single painting sold.[31] In 1955, when an arts journalist asked gallery owners whether they thought it likely that "the center of the international art world will shift from Paris to New York," none said it already had, and most doubted it would.[32]

The Abstract Expressionists did not enjoy robust sales until 1956, the year of Pollock's death—which primed the market, since it meant that the number of Pollocks in the world was now finite. In 1957, the Metropolitan Museum of Art purchased *Autumn Rhythm* for thirty thousand dollars. In 1958, *Time* reported a surge in prices for Abstract Expressionist works—though it noted that many of the buyers were Europeans.[33] The stabilization of the franc in 1959 helped the American market, since it was no longer cheaper to buy in Paris.

By then, a domestic art market had come into being. In 1955, there were 123 art galleries in New York; in 1960, there were 154. There was also a boom in museum attendance.[34] The opening of Frank Lloyd Wright's Guggenheim building on Fifth Avenue in October 1959 was mobbed. In 1960, the Metropolitan Museum of Art had 4,005,490 visitors; in 1961, it had 5,088,764, over a million more. (Attendance at the Louvre that year was 1.5 million.)[35] By 1965, there were 246 art galleries in New York City.[36]

One reason Pop Art had immediate buyers is that the timing was lucky. In 1962, there was an economic downturn in the United States, and Warhols and Lichtensteins were cheaper than Pollocks and Rothkos.[37] Buyers of Pop Art may have been drawn to the buzz, but many were serious collectors, such as Burton and Emily Tremaine, who had been buying modern art since 1945. A few, like the Sculls, were portrayed as arrivistes—both were described as "brash"; he owned a taxi fleet—but the Tremaine money was from business, too. Tremaine started his career as president of the Superior Screw and Bolt Company of Cleveland.[38] These people saw a bargain, and they capitalized.

In 1962 and 1963, there were Pop Art exhibitions at the Pasadena

Art Museum, the Guggenheim Museum, the Mary Atkins Museum of Fine Arts in Kansas City, the Contemporary Arts Museum in Houston, the Washington Gallery of Modern Art, the Oakland Art Museum, and the Albright-Knox Art Gallery in Buffalo.[39] The Abstract Expressionists had never had that kind of exposure.

What Pop Art did not have at first was a critical voice. It was received with bemusement, skepticism, dismissal, and outrage. In places like *Time* and *Life*, it was treated as a fad. In this respect, the quick sales worked against Pop Art's critical reputation, since it was easy to ascribe its proliferation to what *Time* called "profit-minded galleries [as opposed to profit-minded magazines] and collectors of whatever's new [as opposed to publishers of the same]."[40]

In the magazines whose artistic preferences had been shaped by Greenberg, Pop was not so far beneath contempt that it could be ignored completely, but almost. In *The Nation*, Hilton Kramer called Pop "the usual attempt to disguise an essentially conformist and Philistine response to modern experience under a banner of audacity and innovation."[41] In *Partisan Review*, Peter Selz wrote:

> The Abstract Expressionists dedicated their lives to art and made a point of doing so . . . But the Pop painters, because of their lack of stance, their lack of involvement, are producing works that strike the uninfatuated viewer as slick, effete, and chic. They share with all academic art—including, by the way, Nazi and Soviet art—the refusal to question their complacent acquiescence to the values of the culture. And most ironic of all is the fact that this art of abject conformity, this extension of Madison Avenue, is presented as *avant garde*.[42]

Selz was the curator of painting and sculpture at MoMA.

Greenberg himself never wrote about Pop Art, although in interviews he made it plain that his view was Selz's. Pop Art "used academic means to illustrate unconventional things," he said in a documentary; the artists "come more than halfway to meet your taste." It was "scene art," he said, academic, minor: "It's easy stuff."[43] In his private journal, he speculated that Pop was a "revolt of the collectors against late Abst. Exp. One of those curious rebellions in which what's rebelled against deserves to be rebelled against, but where the rebellion itself is on behalf of something ultimately less worthy. A lowering of level. The collectors are middlebrows, after all, and Pop art is middlebrow."[44]

For reviewers, the art presented two problems more basic than even how to interpret it: what to call it, and where it came from. A number of labels were tried, most of them based on the idea that this was art that represented everyday things: Commonists, Factualists, Popular Realists, OK Art, and (not meant as a compliment) the New Vulgarians.* In 1962, a show of Pop Art at the Pasadena Art Museum was called *New Painting of Common Objects*. Even Lawrence Alloway, who had left London to take a position of curator at the Guggenheim Museum, called his show of Warhol, Rauschenberg, Roy Lichtenstein, Jim Dine, Jasper Johns, and James Rosenquist, mounted from March to June 1963, *Six Painters and the Object*.†

The breakthrough show for Pop Art was at the Janis Gallery in midtown from October 31 to December 1, 1962. It was called *The New Realists: An Exhibition of Factual Paintings and Sculpture from France, England, Italy, Sweden, and the United States*.‡ John Ashbery wrote the foreword to the catalogue. "The New Realism," he explained, "is the European term for the art of today which in one way or another makes use of the qualities of manufactured objects."[45] Which seems a little off the mark.

The New Realists was an enormous show. Janis brought together twenty-nine American and European artists. He had to rent a second space on Fifty-Seventh Street to accommodate them. The show was a sensation in part because Janis represented many of the leading Abstract Expressionists and a number quit in protest.§ "[T]he new New Realism hit the New York art world with the force of an earthquake," Harold Rosenberg wrote in *The New Yorker*.[46] "With this show, 'pop' art is officially here," announced the *Times*'s art critic Brian O'Doherty.[47] Although his first New York show, at the Stable, had not even opened,

---

* Warhol may have been the first to call Pop Art "commonism"; see the caption to his car drawings, "Deus ex Machina," in *Harper's Bazaar* (November 1962). The word is not listed in the *OED*. Ivan Karp is also said to have used the term early on.
† This is one of the few points of intersection between the Independent Group and American Pop artists. In 1964, a student of Richard Hamilton's, Mark Lancaster, worked briefly as Warhol's assistant and appeared in some of his movies. He went on to design sets for Merce Cunningham.
‡ Janis was adapting the term used in France, *Nouveau réalisme*.
§ Mark Rothko, Adolph Gottlieb, Philip Guston, and Robert Motherwell quit the gallery. Willem de Kooning, contrary to legend, did not, although the show does seem to have precipitated the de Koonings' move out of the city to Long Island.

Warhol was featured in the *Newsweek* story on the Janis show. Asked what he thought of Abstract Expressionism, Warhol said: "I love the New York School, but I never did any abstract expressionism—I don't know why, it's so easy."[48]

The term "New Realism" repeated the representationalist theory of the new art. But the *Times*'s reviewer thought the term was philosophically pretentious, and preferred "Pop."[49] The matter was settled when, on December 13, 1962, two weeks after *The New Realists* closed, Selz convened "A Symposium on Pop Art" at MoMA. (Most of his panelists were unsympathetic.) And Pop Art became the name that stuck.* When Warhol was asked, in 1963, where the name came from, he said, "It came from Alloway, I guess."[50]

But where did Pop Art come from? People had been educated by figures like Alfred Barr and Clement Greenberg to think of modern art as a story with a single narrative whose stages developed internally to the practice. Painters X did this, which led painters Y to do that: Impressionism, Cubism, Surrealism, Abstraction. This is why the charge that Pop Art was a market-driven phenomenon had bite: the marketplace does not figure in internalist accounts. What drives art is art.

Very quickly, two explanations were proposed, sometimes by the same observer. The first was that Pop Art was a reaction against Abstract Expressionism. This was an easy case to make because it fit the single-narrative model, and because the contrasts extended beyond the obvious abstract/representational difference to the whole ethos of the styles. Abstract Expressionism was associated with the unconscious, the symbolic, originality, and anxiety (also jazz, alcohol, and heterosexuality), Pop Art with the mechanical, the literal, impersonality, and pleasure (also rock 'n' roll, amphetamines, and sexual indifference or queerness). In a caricatural nutshell: Jackson Pollock versus Andy Warhol.

The other explanation was that Pop Art was anti-art, a revival of Dada. That theory proved to have more purchase. But it also suggested that the art genealogy that leads to Warhol was not the one Barr and Greenberg had plotted out. His art has nothing to do with Impressionism, Cubism, and Surrealism. It flowered on a different branch, one that

---

* "Pop" is usually taken as short for "popular," as in "pop culture"; but it also derives from "soda pop," and some of the earliest Pop and proto-Pop works featured Coca-Cola bottles.

includes industrial design, Bauhaus, and Dada. There is no one genealogy of modern art.

3.

When Marcel Duchamp died, in 1968, he had only one work in a public collection in France. In *Le Figaro*, his death was reported in the chess column. Duchamp's brother, the painter Jacques Villon, was far better known. In the United States, on the other hand, Duchamp's death made the front page of *The New York Times*, and hundreds of his works were either committed to or already in American museums. Duchamp is one of those figures, like Jacques Derrida, who seem to many Americans quintessentially French, but whose reputations are largely due to their reception in the United States.[51]

Duchamp was a product of the pre–First World War European avant-garde, the cultural moment that produced Eliot and Joyce, Picasso and Stein, Proust and Satie, Rilke and Akhmatova, Igor Stravinsky and Richard Strauss, a movement of art and letters that the First World War, the rise of fascism, and the Bolshevik Revolution would break apart. He was born in Normandy in 1887.[52] His father was a notary; his maternal grandfather was an artist, and three of Marcel's siblings became artists. He studied at the Académie Julian, the Paris art school that Rauschenberg attended many years later, but he failed the entrance examination for the École des Beaux-Arts and got a job in a print shop in Rouen, where he learned etching, engraving, and typesetting.

Duchamp's early paintings are in the Post-Impressionist styles of the times, Fauvism and Cubism, but he quickly developed an impulse to push the limits of painterly form. He pushed so hard he went right through the envelope, and, when you do that, it looks like a negation. It is so *not*-art that it's read as *anti*-art. Is *Nude Descending a Staircase, No. 2*, which Duchamp made in January 1912, a representation of motion in the formal language of Cubism? Or is it a send-up of Cubist style?

In the summer of 1912, Duchamp spent two months in Munich.*

---

* T. S. Eliot lived in Munich the previous summer and finished "The Love Song of J. Alfred Prufrock" there, a poem that reflects Eliot's infatuation with the French poet Jules Laforgue—who was also an infatuation of Duchamp's: *Nude Descending a Staircase* began as an illustration of a Laforgue poem, "Encore à cet astre." The Blaue Reiter group of artists was formed in Munich in 1911, and Wassily Kandinsky, who was a member, made the move to total abstraction there in 1911 or 1912. Duchamp does not seem to have had contacts with the group.

His stay there is something of a mystery, but the break with conventional ideas of art seems to date from that visit. It was in Munich that he began his major work, *La Mariée mise à nu par ses célibataires, même (The Bride Stripped Bare by Her Bachelors, Even)*, also known as the *Large Glass*.

In 1913, back in Paris, Duchamp "created" the first of what he called his "readymades."[53] This was the bicycle wheel, which he mounted upside down on a stool. The bicycle wheel was followed by the bottle rack, the snow shovel (acquired in New York City), and the upside-down urinal, *Fountain*. A found object that he added something to, like the postcard of the Mona Lisa to which he added a mustache and goatee, *L.H.O.O.Q.* (1919), Duchamp called an "aided" or "assisted" readymade. He later explained that his principle of selection was his indifference to the readymade as an aesthetic object. He added, slyly, that "since the tubes of paint used by the artist are manufactured and readymade products, we must conclude that all the paintings in the world are 'Readymades Aided.'"[54]

In 1923, he abandoned work on the *Large Glass*. That was also the year (he claimed) that he stopped making art. For the next ten years, he devoted himself mainly to chess, apparently in the hope, unrealized, of winning tournaments. This was later taken as the ultimate anti-art gesture, but it was probably because, after an exceptionally creative period, he had run out of ideas. It does not seem to have bothered him.

Very little bothered Duchamp. He possessed an extraordinary serenity. "When I met Marcel Duchamp in New York in 1916 he was twenty-nine years old and wore a halo," wrote his friend Henri-Pierre Roché.

> What was that halo made up of? It was his outward calm, his easygoing nature, his keenness of intellect, his lack of selfishness, his receptiveness to whatever was new, his spontaneity and audacity. Just being with him was a pleasure and a privilege that he seemed unaware of, even while his circle of disciples was constantly growing . . . [His] reputation in New York as a Frenchman was equalled only by Napoleon and Sarah Bernhardt. He could have had his choice of heiresses, but he preferred to play chess and live on the proceeds of the exclusive French lessons he gave for two dollars an hour. He was an enigma, contrary to all tradition, and he won everybody's heart.[55]

Duchamp had arrived in New York in 1915. He was already famous because of the *Nude*, which had been the *succès de scandale* of the New York Armory Show of 1913. He doubled his renown with *Fountain*, which was removed from an exhibition sponsored by the Society of Independent Artists in 1917. And he charmed several Americans who would become patrons and collectors, most important of whom were Katherine Dreier and Walter Arensberg. Duchamp moved back to France in 1923 and lived there, with sporadic trips to New York, until he emigrated in 1942. In 1943, he moved to an apartment on West Fourteenth street, where he lived for the next twenty-two years.

When he painted the *Nude*, Duchamp realized that he was not interested in representing movement. He was interested in representing the *idea* of movement.[56] His break with conventional notions of art began there, with a rejection of its sensory aspects, in particular, what he called "the retinal." "Since Courbet," he said later (one of many times he explained himself),

> it's been believed that painting is addressed to the retina. That was everyone's error. The retinal shudder! Before, painting had other functions: it could be religious, philosophical, moral. If I had the chance to take an antiretinal attitude, it unfortunately hasn't changed much; our whole century is completely retinal . . . It's absolutely ridiculous. It has to change; it hasn't always been like this.[57]

Rejecting the sensory aspect of painting turned out to lead to the rejection of virtually everything associated with nineteenth-century ideas of art: originality, style, intention, seriousness, taste. Duchamp set out to strip all traces of artistry from his art. "I unlearned to draw," he said.[58] He was fascinated by two apparently incongruous states: the mechanical and the erotic. That's what the *Large Glass* is, sexual desire figured as an exercise in hydraulics. A more playful case is *L.H.O.O.Q.* The title is two puns: in French, *Elle a chaud au cul* (She has a hot ass); in English, *LOOK*. Look: adding a mustache and goatee turns an iconic image of femininity into an androgyne! Duchamp went to extraordinary lengths to eliminate the "artist's touch"; he also created a female alter ego, Rrose Sélavy (pronounced in French: *Eros, c'est la vie*), and had himself photographed in drag.

Duchamp's ideas about art were obviously orthogonal to the main tendency in postwar American painting. Abstract Expressionism "seems to have reached the apex of this retinal approach" he said in 1960. It belonged to "the worn-out cult of the hand."[59] Greenberg mentions Duchamp just four times in passing in his criticism, first in 1943 and not again until 1967. He understood what Duchamp was up to, but he considered it an experiment that had produced no interesting results.

Still, Duchamp was a postwar presence in New York. Although he cultivated an indifference to galleries, museums, collectors, dealers—to the social apparatus of arts practice—he happily sold his own art, and he worked as a dealer on behalf of collectors such as Arensberg, taking a commission. That was how he made his living. He figured prominently in Robert Motherwell's influential anthology *The Dada Painters and Poets*, published in 1952. In 1953, he organized a historical exhibition of international Dada for the Janis Gallery and was written up in *Life*. In 1957, the Guggenheim mounted a show of the works of Duchamp and his brother Jacques. In 1959, the publication of Robert Lebel's *Marcel Duchamp*, which included the first catalogue raisonné, was celebrated with a show at Janis. In 1961, Duchamp was featured in *The Art of Assemblage* at MoMA. And, every year from 1945 to his death, his works appeared in group shows in New York City and around the country.

For obvious reasons—the use of chance, the fascination with the mechanical, the disparagement of taste—he was a hero to Cage. Cage was so awed, in fact, that he was unable to figure out a way to talk to Duchamp, so he decided to visit him to play chess. They did this happily for several years. They never discussed art. Duchamp was also probably an inspiration for Rauschenberg's *Erased de Kooning Drawing* in 1953: Rauschenberg had seen the exhibition of Dada art at the Janis Gallery that spring, which included *L.H.O.O.Q.* (The catalogue, designed by Duchamp, was printed on pieces of tissue paper and wadded into balls that were mailed to invitees and made available in wastebaskets at the entrance.) Rauschenberg took Johns to the Philadelphia Museum of Art to see the newly installed collection of Duchamp's work, donated by Arensberg.[60] But Rauschenberg always had to fight the impression that his own art was neo-Dada. "It's not a negation," he said of the erased de Kooning; "it's a celebration."[61] He insisted that he was never Dada. "Dada was anti," he said in 1961; "I am pro."[62]

Duchamp was not anti, either. Even though it incorporates an icon-oclastic gesture (defacement of a work of art), *L.H.O.O.Q.* is not an iconoclasm. It's an artistic transformation. It just takes an image as its object. *L.H.O.O.Q.* does not debunk Leonardo's painting; it queers it (an allusion to Leonardo's reputed sexuality?) and thus disenchants it. To demystify is not to debunk. "Did you, or do you, really want to destroy art?" Duchamp was asked at a MoMA symposium in 1961. "I don't want to destroy art for anybody else but for myself, that's all," was his answer. (The audience applauded.)[63]

With the arrival of Pop Art, Duchamp was back in style. In 1963, the Pasadena Art Museum mounted a major Duchamp retrospective. Du-champ and his wife, Alexina (Teeny) Duchamp, were accompanied on the flight out to California by Richard Hamilton, who had been introduced to Duchamp in 1952 when he saw Duchamp's work in a show at the Tate. Hamilton's friend and fellow IG member, the photographer Nigel Hen-derson, loaned him a copy of the *Green Box*, a collection of notes and drawings about the *Large Glass*.* Hamilton became a devoted follower. In 1960, with the help of George Heard Hamilton (no relation) and with Du-champ's approval, he published an English translation of the *Green Box*.

Apart from the show at the Tate, Hamilton had seen few of Du-champ's works before the Pasadena retrospective. After it, he recorded his reaction. "Suddenly the image is destroyed," he wrote.

> "Marcel Duchamp Anti-Artist" is revealed as a fake and it only took his work to do it. He simply changed the terms by which paint-ing had lived for centuries. In changing the rules, in re-inventing art as though it had never existed, he re-opened the possibility of working. The new rules were these: Art is conceptual—that is to say it has nothing to do with the visual stimuli external to the art-ist's mind . . . At the same time, art (Duchamp's in particular) was in danger of taking itself too seriously, so that the new art must be "hilarious."[64]

This is the Duchamp of whom Malanga thought Warhol was the spir-itual child.

---

* Henderson knew Duchamp because his mother, Wyn Henderson, managed Peggy Guggen-heim's London gallery, Guggenheim Jeune.

4.

Warhol was also the heir of the Bauhaus. Warhol's teacher in his upperclass years at Carnegie Tech, Robert Lepper, taught both industrial design and pictorial design students. Lepper remembered Warhol. "Andy was the baby of the class," he said; "the other students all looked after him. He was a tiny, undernourished little guy."[65] On a trip in 1938 or 1939, Lepper had stopped at Black Mountain unannounced to meet Josef Albers.[66] And although he did not teach Bauhaus ideas to his pictorial design students, they were discussed in his industrial design classes, and one of Warhol's classmates remembered discussing Lázsló Moholy-Nagy's *Vision in Motion* with him, and said that Warhol spoke about it enthusiastically.[67]

Moholy-Nagy was committed to the Bauhaus slogan "Art and Technology—A New Unity," and in his writings he criticized the elevation of fine or handmade art over mechanical and mass-produced design. "I was not at all afraid of losing the 'personal touch,' so highly valued in previous painting," he wrote.

> On the contrary, I even gave up signing my paintings. I put numbers and letters with the necessary data on the back of the canvas, as if they were cars, airplanes, or other industrial products. I could not find any argument against the wide distribution of works of art, even if turned out by mass production . . . In an industrial age, the distinction between art and non-art, between manual craftsmanship and mechanical technology is no longer an absolute one.[68]

He described ordering a painting from a sign factory over the telephone.

In industrial art, the distinctive feature of machine form, against painterly form, is precision, the precision of lines (in drawings) and geometrical planes (on the equipment). This feature of American Pop Art was noticed right away by reviewers—in Lichtenstein's paintings of comic strip panels, Warhol's soup cans, Robert Indiana's and Ed Ruscha's signs, James Rosenquist's adaptations of billboard art. The artists were sometimes referred to as the hard-edge school. When Warhol switched to Pop, he abandoned the individualized blotted-line look and switched to machine form, too.

Warhol began making his early Pop works soon after he moved into the house on Lexington Avenue, in September 1960.[69] By then, he had spent eleven years observing the New York art scene. That scene did not all revolve around the Museum of Modern Art and the midtown galleries. Much of the new art was happening below Fourteenth Street and could be inspected in the spaces that sprouted up to exhibit it. And almost all of the downtown art was post-abstraction. Found-object art, performance art, poster art, conceptual art, political art, minimalist art, Pop Art, Fluxus, Happenings, feminist art—virtually every style that would become mainstream in the 1960s could be seen, sometimes in embryonic form, downtown.[70] Johns's and Rauschenberg's shows at Castelli in 1957 brought word of this new art uptown.

Warhol saw their shows and became obsessed with the two of them. He angled for a way to meet them, for a long time without success. He was told that they considered him too "swish."[71] In 1961, Warhol went into the Castelli Gallery and bought a Johns painting, *Light Bulb*, for $450.[72] A week later, he came in again and got into a conversation with Ivan Karp, who showed him some of Lichtenstein's work, which was in storage while Castelli decided whether and when to do a show. Warhol was distraught. He told Karp that he had been doing the same kind of paintings, based on comic strips and advertisements, and he could see that Lichtenstein's were better. Warhol's works were smudged and dripped on—painterly. Lichtenstein's were clean and literal, mechanical.

Karp had had no idea that Warhol was an artist, and he arranged to visit his studio in the Lexington Avenue house. When he arrived, he was astonished to see that Warhol's was the only name on the bell. Karp later said that while he was there, Warhol played, over and over at top volume, a pop single called "I Saw Linda Yesterday." (The memory is erroneous: the single was released in 1962, but other early visitors reported having the same experience with other pop songs.[73] It was an act, as were the piles of fan magazines Warhol left all over the floor.)

What Warhol hoped, of course, was to become one of Castelli's artists. Castelli visited the studio with Karp, but he found Warhol off-putting. (Karp said Warhol was wearing a theatrical mask and offered one for Castelli to wear.) Castelli also was already representing Lichtenstein, and he thought that Pop Art would make a bigger splash if several galleries exhibited Pop artists simultaneously. His business instincts, in this as in most cases, turned out to be right.

Karp referred people to Warhol, so did Geldzahler, and Warhol sold some paintings out of his studio.[74] But he still had trouble finding a gallery. Several New York gallerists turned him down. Irving Blum, who was the director of the Ferus Gallery in Los Angeles, came to New York once a year to visit artists' studios, and on his 1961 visit, two friends—Geldzahler and Richard Bellamy, who ran the Green Gallery, which had just opened—recommended Warhol. Blum paid a visit, but he was unimpressed by the comic strip figures Warhol was painting.

On his next New York trip, five months later, Blum stopped in at Castelli, and Karp showed him transparencies of Lichtenstein's paintings, which had still not been exhibited. Blum was intrigued; the hard-edged style reminded him of Léger. When he told Karp he'd like to show them at the Ferus, Karp explained that Castelli was planning a show. Blum could see which way the wind was blowing, and he immediately arranged another visit to Warhol's studio. Having seen Lichtenstein's work himself, Warhol had abandoned the comic strip pieces and had started painting soup cans and Coke bottles. Blum saw a few soup can canvases—hard-edge paintings, like Lichtenstein's but different enough—and he offered Warhol a show.

Warhol seems to have expressed reluctance about having his first major solo show in Los Angeles, so Blum told him that movie stars came to the Ferus.* Whether this was true or not, it was a good effort, and Warhol must have appreciated it as such. The show opened in July and closed on August 4, the day Marilyn Monroe committed suicide. There was no formal opening; Warhol didn't even go out. Blum displayed the thirty-two canvases on a rail he installed in the gallery because he had trouble lining them up symmetrically. So the supermarket-shelf effect, although it became a standard way of analyzing the exhibition, was unintended.[75] The paintings were sold separately and priced at two hundred dollars apiece. (Blum's commission was 50 percent.)

As works of fine art, the soup can paintings are a scandal, but a scandal of a different kind from atonal music or chance compositions. Cage's works do pose the question, Is this music? But they also engage the listener in a complex sonic experience, just as Rauschenberg's combines engage the viewer in complex visual experiences. The soup cans

---

* The first Pop piece by Warhol exhibited in a gallery was *200 One Dollar Bills* in a group show at the Green Gallery, June 12–July 21, 1962. Other artists included Yayoi Kusama, Robert Morris, and James Rosenquist.

do not engage you in any kind of visual experience. They give nothing back to the gaze. As Warhol's friend Frank Stella put it (referring to his own geometrical abstractions): "What you see is what you see."[76]* The soup cans do raise a conceptual question, though, and one person who got this, not surprisingly, was Duchamp. Duchamp thought that Warhol had restored the concept to painting. "If you take a Campbell's soup can and repeat it fifty times," he said, "you are not interested in the retinal image. What interests you is the concept that wants to put fifty Campbell's soup cans on a canvas."[77]

What is that concept? In 1966, Balcomb Greene, a Carnegie Tech teacher who, back in 1949, had helped Warhol get settled in New York, published an essay called "A Thing of Beauty." At Carnegie, Greene was a cutting-edge figure with a Bauhaus aesthetic. But he hated Pop. Greene's argument was that once, a work of art had permanence. "A thing of beauty is a joy forever," as Keats wrote in "Endymion." But, Greene said,

> [t]his view of permanence has lately been disputed by a theory of contemporaneousness, and by the appearance of new art works which seem to support it. The most startling was the display in an art gallery, in place of the Grecian urn, "That still unravished bride of quietness"—the display of a painting of twenty-four [*sic*] identical cans of Campbell's tomato [*sic*] soup, lined up exactly as a grocer might attempt it . . . With a sense of melancholy . . . I contemplate my intellectual affinity with John Keats, who is dead.[78]

But the Campbell's soup can was not an image of contemporaneity in 1962. The product dates from the nineteenth century; by 1962, Campbell's cans had carried the same design for more than fifty years.[79] Campbell's came over, as it were, on the consumerist *Mayflower*. It's an image from modernity's antiquity, the Grecian urn of mass-market societies. And functionally, a tin soup can *is* an urn. Warhol's painting is a painting about the nature of painting. It represents the idea that a soup can is a commodity, and so is a painting of a soup can. You can buy the real soup can for thirty-three cents; you can buy a painting of it for two

---

* Stella had painted a series of Benjamin Moore paint cans. Warhol asked him to produce six miniature versions, which he bought in the spring of 1961—possibly an influence on the soup cans. Stella was one of Castelli's artists.

hundred dollars. There is a marketplace for everything. This collapse of the fine art–commerce distinction seems banal today, but in 1962, it tied people in knots.

Warhol still did not have a New York gallery. There are conflicting accounts of how he ended up at Eleanor Ward's Stable Gallery, which she had moved from West Fifty-Eighth Street (the block was being razed for a new apartment building) to a space in her town house on East Seventy-Fourth Street just off Madison Avenue. One thing that does seem true is that Ward had a falling-out with one of her artists, leaving an opening in her fall schedule.[80] She called Warhol from her summer house in Connecticut and offered him the spot. She probably did this without enthusiasm.*

It was a lucky break, and Warhol needed it. Rosenquist had had a one-man show at the Green Gallery in January; Lichtenstein's show at Castelli had opened in February and sold out. Janis's *New Realists* show was scheduled for November. Warhol was the last of the Pop artists to have a major New York show.† There is no sense in asking whether Pop Art would have happened without Warhol. It did happen without him.

That first Stable show, in the fall of 1962, was one of the few Warhol shows that was not an installation. He exhibited a variety of pieces, including *Marilyn* silkscreens and two of his *Dance Diagram* paintings— blowups of instructions from two how-to books, *Lindy Made Easy (with Charleston)* and *Fox Trot Made Easy*, works that recall the well-known photographs of Pollock in his studio: Pollock's dance as a mechanical routine.[81] (Warhol also made some works he called "piss paintings"— drips—around the same time, though these have been lost.) The Stable show was a success; everything sold. Warhol had made his New York bones.

Warhol's second Stable show opened on April 21, 1964, in an atmosphere that had been electrified by (in addition to the Beatles' arrival in February) a cultural crackdown by the New York City Department of Licenses. In the Village, the café Le Metro was closed for staging poetry readings by Allen Ginsberg and other Beat writers, on the grounds that

---

* Ironically, considering the role she played in Warhol's career, Ward quit the business in 1970 because she thought that art had become too commercialized.
† One of the ways Pop was anointed was the publication in *Life* in 1964 of an article about Lichtenstein entitled "Is He the Worst Artist in the United States?" The author was Dorothy Seiberling, the person behind the *Life* article "Jackson Pollock: Is He the Greatest Living Painter in the United States?" in 1949.

it was not licensed as a coffee shop. On February 17, the Pocket Theatre, on Thirteenth Street, and the Gramercy Arts, on Twenty-Seventh Street, were closed by the authorities. On March 3, police raided the New Bowery Theatre on St. Mark's Place and arrested four people for screening the movie *Flaming Creatures*. On April 3, Lenny Bruce was arrested on obscenity charges at the Cafe au Go Go on Bleecker Street.* Then, on April 14, Warhol's mural *Thirteen Most Wanted Men* caused a ruckus.

The crackdown appears to have been part of the city's effort to clean up its act for the World's Fair, to be held in Queens.[82] Warhol was one of a number of artists who had been invited by Philip Johnson to create a work to be displayed on the outside of the New York Pavilion there. (The others included Lichtenstein, Indiana, Rosenquist, and Rauschenberg.) Using a fifteen-page police department booklet provided by a gay city policeman named Jim O'Neill, Warhol silkscreened blown-up mug shots of thirteen accused felons.

As soon as it went up, the mural attracted attention in the press. Jimmy Breslin wrote a column making fun of it. Johnson had to explain that the piece was "a comment on the sociological factor in American life."[83] (It is not clear what meaning of "sociological" he had in mind.) After a week, though, Johnson announced that the piece was coming down. It seemed that Warhol didn't like the way it had been mounted and would submit another piece. Eleanor Ward felt obliged to defend her artist. "Andy just didn't like the way it looked," she told the *Herald Tribune*, "and I think it's wonderful of Mr. Johnson to let him make another one on such short notice." Johnson assured the reporter, "There is no question about any official complaint."[84]

Much later, Johnson claimed that, in fact, the directive to remove the mural had come from the governor, Nelson Rockefeller. Seven of the thirteen men had Italian names; according to Johnson, Rockefeller was afraid of alienating Italian American voters.[85] This was probably another tall tale. It may simply have been that the state's lawyers saw litigation on the horizon.[86] Warhol told a reporter that he had received legal threats from one of the men. The man had been pardoned—"so the mural wasn't valid any more."[87] Warhol proposed substituting a

---

* Bruce's warm-up act was Tiny Tim, who would achieve his own celebrity after appearing on the television show *Rowan and Martin's Laugh-In* in 1968.

portrait of Robert Moses, the urban developer who was president of the World's Fair. When this was judged unacceptable, he simply had *Thirteen Most Wanted Men* (the title is a homoerotic pun) painted over with silver paint—a visible erasure, and a statement about censorship.

The Stable show opened just as the World Fair incident was playing out in the press. On the first night, people lined up on the sidewalk waiting to get in. The exhibition consisted of four hundred sculptures designed to look like cartons of Heinz ketchup, Del Monte peaches, Campbell's tomato juice, Mott's apple juice, Kellogg's cornflakes, and Brillo soap pads. The pieces were stacked in piles in both rooms of the gallery, requiring viewers to navigate the aisles cautiously (part of the reason for the crush outside).

One of the visitors at the opening was Arthur Danto, a professor of philosophy at Columbia. He was from Detroit. After serving in North Africa, he went to Wayne University, then to graduate school in philosophy at Columbia on the G.I. Bill. Danto had really come to New York because he wanted to be an artist, but, somewhat unexpectedly, he became a professor instead.

He went to the Stable show with his wife, Barbara Westman, a painter, and he was transfixed by the Brillo box. "It was a transformative experience for me," he said. "It turned me into a philosopher of art."[88] When a speaker had to pull out of a panel on aesthetics at the American Philosophical Association meeting in Boston that October, Danto was invited to take his place. The paper he delivered was called "The Artworld." It was published in *The Journal of Philosophy* in December, and soon was widely anthologized.[89]

"The Artworld" is an attempt to answer the question: Why is something that is visually indistinguishable from a Brillo box a work of art but a Brillo box is not? Danto's theory was that in order to answer that question, you need a theory. As he put it: "To see something as art requires something the eye cannot decry [*sic*]—an atmosphere of artistic theory, a knowledge of the history of art: an artworld."[90] Someone who knew nothing about the history of art would never be able to see Warhol's Brillo box as anything but either a Brillo box or a prank. Only someone who understood why it was that, for example, in 1961 a painting of a Coke bottle with hash marks counted as art could also understand why a painting of a Coke bottle without hash marks might also count as art.

Danto was a Greenbergian: he saw the history of painting, from representational art through Impressionism, Cubism, and abstraction, as a series of manipulations of the relationship between art and reality. A wooden box painted to look like a grocery carton was just one more turn of that screw. His most important insight, though, and where he differed from Greenberg, was to see the history of art as driven by sublation. Styles do not all push in the same direction; the emergence of one style of painting creates the conditions for the possibility of the "opposite" style. Pop Art makes sense as a dialectical negation of abstraction. Warhol's dance steps and piss paintings both subvert and preserve an aspect of the Abstract Expressionist conception of art-making. This works because the suppressed elements in Abstract Expressionism—say, representationalism and commercialism—are still present within, are in fact constitutive of, that artistic paradigm, and they account for, precisely, the aesthetic impact of Pop.

To Danto, therefore, Pop Art was not a frivolous repudiation of Abstract Expressionism. It was what Greenberg said it should be, the next step in art's investigation of its own nature. And it brought that investigation to an end. Pop Art showed that the only difference between art, such as a sculpture that looks like a grocery carton, and reality, such as a grocery carton, is that the first is received as art and the second is not. At that moment, art could be anything it wanted. The illusion/reality barrier had been broken. A term that would later be adopted for this state of affairs is "postmodernism."

The obvious objection to Danto's argument about the Brillo box is that Duchamp had already broken through the illusion/reality barrier with the readymades. Hadn't he raised the philosophical issues that Danto ascribed to Warhol's 1964 Stable show? The answer to this, somewhat less obvious, is that the boxes in the Stable show are not readymades. They are not even "assisted readymades." Warhol had the boxes manufactured by a cabinetmaker near York Avenue; Malanga and Billy Name painted them; and then Warhol and Malanga silkscreened the designs onto the sides. Only five sides, in most cases, were painted. (The "I want to be a machine" remark, invoked endlessly, is just more Warhol persiflage. His art-making was always highly artisanal. It was probably while the boxes were being made that the studio started being called the Factory, a name Warhol is said to have disliked.)[91]

Everything was done to make the boxes look like the real thing, but

Warhol was not simply copying Duchamp.[92] He was responding to Duchamp's readymades by creating objects that only look like readymades. Warhol's box sculptures are trompe l'oeil: they are lifelike illusions, but not illusions of something natural, like the painted grapes of Zeuxis that the birds pecked at. They are illusions of a type of art that presents itself as art without illusions. The Brillo box imitates the kind of art object in which the element of imitation has been eliminated. Warhol turned the screw one rotation further than Danto realized. The Brillo boxes did not break the illusion/reality barrier at all. They were just one more move in the game.

"[H]e has destroyed Art with a capital A," the *Times* exclaimed about the Stable show.[93] That was not quite the motivation. Warhol's art was not a critique of artistic convention, or of traditional ideas about mimesis and creativity, or even of Abstract Expressionism and the Greenbergian aesthetic. Nor was it a continuation of the Dada and Bauhaus avant-garde. His art was a critique of the avant-garde itself.

Warhol spent more than a decade studying the avant-garde closely. His efforts to break into it were continually repudiated, so he seems to have decided: if you can't join them, beat them. Warhol's art was a provocation directed not to the high-low art police, people like Greenberg and Kramer, but to the very artists who had apparently solved the high-low problem. Warhol's work made art that was once considered daring, such as Rauschenberg's *Monogram* and Johns's *Flag* series, seem fussy and recondite, art-world in-jokes.[94] For Warhol saw that people like Claes Oldenburg, Rauschenberg, and Johns were still doing high-art things with low-art materials, and that this was true of Lichtenstein and Rosenquist as well. None of those artists could have taken on a subject like Marilyn Monroe, Elizabeth Taylor, or Jackie Kennedy, the faces on famous Warhol silkscreens, without twisting every which way to avoid the appearance of sentimentality. They were all operating safely behind the ramparts of highbrow taste.

So Johns made a work called *Flag on Orange Field*, and Warhol made *Marilyn on a Gold Field*. Oldenburg made sculptures of consumer goods, and Warhol produced multiple identical sculptures of the cartons those goods come in. Rauschenberg silkscreened bits and pieces from magazines and newspapers, and Warhol silkscreened money. Warhol looked at the cards on the table of the New York avant-garde, and he raised the ante.

This is true as well of Warhol's movies, to which he devoted most of his time between 1965, when he announced his retirement from painting, and 1968. Formally, *Sleep* and *Empire* are programmatically the opposite of the poetic, dreamy, phantasmagorical underground movies being made in New York at the time. Warhol saw that the more that underground filmmakers strove to undermine cinematic convention, the more cinematic their movies became. Warhol made movies that eliminated (along with the acting and the drama) the cinematic. He found that people who could sit through them experienced them as cinema.

After the shooting in 1968, everything changed. The experience quite naturally terrified Warhol. He had just moved to a new studio on Union Square (two floors upstairs from Communist Party offices), and he quickly dispensed with what remained in his entourage of Factory-era crazies. But the culture had changed, too. Two days after Warhol was shot, Robert Kennedy was assassinated in Los Angeles. After Kennedy's death, a profile of Warhol that had been scheduled for the cover of *Life* was killed. The Warhol sixties were over. (The shooter, Solanas, got three years.* Warhol was always afraid she would strike again.)

The first works Warhol made after he recovered, in August 1968, were a portrait of Happy Rockefeller and an advertisement for Schrafft's. Warhol had never made much money in the Factory years—total net income at Warhol Enterprises, Inc., in 1965 was $112.77—but he now began churning out celebrity portraits on commission.[95] By 1979, he was making from $1 million to $2 million a year on the portraits. He announced that he had embarked on a new kind of art, business art. This is the Warhol from whom figures like Jeff Koons and Damien Hirst are descended.

Warhol also created some powerful silkscreens in the post-Factory years—the Mao portraits, the sunsets that look like mushroom clouds and/or Rothkos, the Ladies and Gentlemen series, the Last Suppers. But the aura of wealth and celebrity that he ostentatiously cultivated, hanging out with the hotelier Ian Schrager and the Shah of Iran, and that he celebrated in his magazine, *Interview*, complicated his reception. When he was quoted as saying things like, "Being good in Business is

---

* There is a story that Solanas may have originally staked out the publisher Maurice Girodias, who she believed had cheated her on a book deal and whose office was on Gramercy Park. Warhol's studio was nearby, on Union Square.

the most fascinating kind of art," it made him seem like everyone else in the 1980s, a time when the financial sector in New York was taking off.

Barbara Rose became friends with Warhol in the 1960s, when she was a graduate student and was married to Frank Stella. She knew Warhol well: he took her to the opera and he bought her a present when her first child was born. Rose became an art historian, and sometime in the 1970s, she began writing a book on Warhol. She never finished it, but the manuscript survives.

Rose believed she understood what the subject matter of Warhol's art really was. "He was using the classic tactic of the avant-garde—subversion—to annihilate the avant-garde itself," she said. "Propelled by the insistent if repressed fury of an outsider at the banquet of vanguard culture to which he was not invited, he steadily and successfully cleared that table in a revolutionary gesture . . . He is both the last representative of the traditional avant-garde, as well as its self-appointed assassin." His final act, as the creator of "business art," was "the last outrage the middle-class and the intellectuals who form taste could register: he publicly assumed the role of the corrupt artist."[96]

Of course, Warhol didn't kill the avant-garde. He was only making a move in the endless game that is literary and artistic modernism, which is the game of trying to find out what art would look like if we had no illusions about it, what art would be if all the conventional markers of the artwork were exposed and stripped away, if art were reduced to its purely transactional status as a product for sale or an asset for investment, if the artist was revealed to be what artists really are, businesspeople. In 1919, Max Weber described modern life as the *Entzauberung der Welt*—the disenchantment of the world.[97] That description does not apply to everything—there is still plenty of magical thinking around—but it does apply to modern art. And what does a completely demystified art object look like? It looks like a work of art. That's the thing about the disenchantment of the world. It's so enchanting.

15

VERS LA LIBÉRATION

Charlotte Moorman being taken to a paddy wagon after her arrest for indecent exposure during a performance of Nam June Paik's *Opera Sextronique,* 125 West Forty-First Street, New York City, February 9, 1967. On May 9, after a three-day trial, Moorman was convicted of a misdemeanor. On October 17, the musical *Hair,* which includes a brief nude scene, opened at the Public Theater; it would run for 1,750 performances on Broadway. On June 21, 1969, *Oh! Calcutta,* which has many nude scenes, opened; it had 5,959 Broadway performances. Photograph by Hy Rothman. (*NY Daily News / Getty Images*)

1.

The book you have been reading so far reflects the period it covers: it is mostly about men. Stories of postwar art and thought from the point of view of women artists, writers, and intellectuals would read very differently. This is not just because women were underrepresented in those fields. It is also because after 1945, women confronted a deeply entrenched ideology of gender difference. They saw an underside of the postwar artistic and intellectual regime that was largely invisible to white men.

Why that ideology was so powerful and its effects so widespread, why men of every political view and in every walk of life seem to have subscribed to it, is one of the enigmas of postwar American history. One explanation is that the relegation of women to the domestic sphere was a response to threats like Communism and nuclear war. The home was figured as a kind of haven requiring someone's full-time commitment.[1] But a Cold War explanation doesn't make complete sense. The doctrine of containment specifically prescribed building up the strength of the democracies, and from that point of view, discrimination that keeps half the population from full participation in the workforce and public life is irrational.

Yet by many measures, American women were worse off in 1963 than they had been in 1945 or even in 1920. In 1920, 20 percent of PhDs were awarded to women; in 1963, it was 11 percent. Forty-seven percent of college students were women in 1920; in 1963, 38 percent. The median age at first marriage was dropping; almost half of all women who got married in 1963 were teenagers. Between 1940 and 1960, the birth rate for fourth children tripled.[2*]

Demographically, it looked like a snowball effect. When 16 million veterans, 98 percent of whom were men, came home in 1945, two predictable things happened. The proportion of men in the workforce increased as men returned to, or were given, jobs that had been done by women during the war. By early 1946, 2.25 million women had quit their jobs and 1 million had been laid off.[3] And there was a spike in the birth rate.

But what should have been a correction became a trend. Fifteen years later, the birth rate was still high—families didn't stop having children after one or two—and although millions of women returned to the workforce in the 1950s and the military draft drew men out of the workforce, gender discrimination in employment was even more pervasive than racial discrimination. By the late 1950s, 75 percent of women

---

* The rise of the divorce rate in the 1970s, sometimes interpreted as an index of national decline, was possibly in part the result of too-early marriages made during a period of economic prosperity.

who worked were in female-only, mainly service jobs.[4] Classified job ads in *The New York Times* were segregated by gender until 1968.

Analytically, there were three pieces to the regime of subordination. The first was patriarchy. Society was ruled by men. Apart from the Nineteenth Amendment, giving women the right to vote, there were no laws against gender discrimination as such. It could be practiced with impunity. Women were virtually absent in the high-status professions and in public life. In 1963, more than 80 percent of college faculty were men (a higher percentage than in 1920); 95 percent of physicians were men; 97 percent of lawyers were men; more than 97 percent of United States senators, members of Congress, and ambassadors were men. There had been only two women cabinet members and only three women ambassadors in American history.* In 1963, of 78 federal judgeships, none was held by a woman; of 307 federal district court judges, two were women. Of approximately 9,400 state legislators, 341 (4 percent) were women. Three states (Alabama, Mississippi, and South Carolina) did not allow women to serve on juries.[5]

Almost every priest, rabbi, and minister in the United States was a man. Male-only institutions, from Harvard and Yale to the Junior Chamber of Commerce and the National Press Club, where female guests had to sit in the balcony and were not allowed to ask questions, were prevalent.[6] This was not just an establishment practice. Women in progressive organizations such as the Student Non-Violent Co-ordinating Committee (SNCC) and Students for a Democratic Society (SDS) complained of a caste system that "uses and exploits women."[7] No woman held a national office in SDS until 1966, when Helen Garvey was elected an assistant national secretary.[8]

The popular understanding was that the only reason for a marriage-able woman to go to college or take a job was to find a husband. If that was why women went to college or worked, it made economic sense: the gender disparity in pay—in 1963, women's pay was 59 percent of men's (less than in 1951)—and career opportunities meant that virtu-ally the only way a woman could improve her economic position was by marrying.[9]

There was widespread consensus that for women with children, this

---

* The first woman cabinet member, Frances Perkins, Franklin Roosevelt's secretary of labor, opposed giving women equal pay for equal work.

was for the best. "The important thing for a mother to realize," Benjamin Spock advised in *The Common Sense Book of Baby and Child Care*, which sold 18.5 million copies between 1946 and 1964, the years of the baby boom, "is that the younger the child the more necessary it is for him to have a steady loving person taking care of him . . . If a mother realizes clearly how vital this kind of care is to a small child, it may make it easier for her to decide that the extra money she might earn, or the satisfaction she might receive from an outside job, is not so important after all."[10]*

Men performed contortions to come up with a rationale for this dispensation that could be squared with the national interest. "You may be hitched to one of these creatures we call 'Western man,'" Adlai Stevenson told the Smith College class of 1955, "and I think part of your job is to keep him Western, to keep him truly purposeful, to keep him whole." He had, he jovially confessed, "very little experience as a wife or mother." But he believed that this

> assignment for you, as wives and mothers, has great advantages. In the first place, it is home work—you can do it in the living-room with a baby in your lap or in the kitchen with a can opener in your hand. If you're really clever, maybe you can even practice your saving arts on that unsuspecting man while he's watching television! And, secondly, it is important work worthy of you, whoever you are, or your education, whatever it is, because we will defeat totalitarian, authoritarian ideas only by better ideas.[11]

Even presidents of women's colleges preached this line. The president of Radcliffe (a man, Wilbur K. Jordan) is reported to have welcomed entering classes in the 1950s by telling the women that if they were lucky, they might marry a Harvard man.[12] Jordan's successor, Mary Bunting—someone committed to higher education for women—warned that "our goal should not be to equip and encourage women to compete with

---

* Even in 1970, after the women's liberation movement had made an impact on popular thought, Spock's views were unreconstructed. "Women are usually more patient in working at unexciting, repetitive tasks," he wrote. ". . . I believe women are designed in their deeper instincts to get more pleasure out of life—not only sexually, but socially, occupationally, maternally—when they are not aggressive. To put it another way, I think that when women are encouraged to be competitive too many of them become disagreeable." (*Decent and Indecent* [New York: McCall, 1970], 32.)

men . . . Women, because they are not generally the principal breadwinners, can perhaps be most useful as the trail breakers, working along the bypaths, doing the unusual job that men cannot afford to gamble on."[13] It seems like a kind of magical thinking that caused people to believe that keeping capable, highly educated citizens at home—actually de-incentivizing them from entering the workforce—was a good way to win the Cold War.

In the theoretically more enlightened world of art and ideas, the pattern was no different. In 1956, Jacques Barzun's face was on the cover of *Time*. The cover line read: "America and the Intellectual: The Reconciliation," and inside were photographic portraits, by Alfred Eisenstadt, of fifteen intellectuals, including Lionel Trilling, Reinhold Niebuhr, Sidney Hook, and J. Robert Oppenheimer—all white men with lots of gray matter, often shown pondering a book. In the lengthy accompanying article, not a single woman is mentioned except Barzun's wife, who is identified only as "the former Mariana Lowell of Boston."[14]

Although key roles in the development and promotion of postwar American art were played by women—the gallerists Peggy Guggenheim, Betty Parsons, Martha Jackson, Edith Halpert, and Eleanor Ward; the curator Dorothy Miller; the editor Dorothy Seiberling—when MoMA sent *The New American Painting* on its European tour in 1958–1959, only one of the seventeen painters was a woman (Grace Hartigan), even though Helen Frankenthaler, Joan Mitchell, Lee Krasner, Mary Abbott, and Elaine de Kooning all had substantial bodies of work. Dorothy Miller's quadrennial exhibitions at MoMA, leading showcases for new American artists, had three women in its first edition, *Fourteen Americans* (1946). There were no women in *Fifteen Americans* (1952), one woman in *Twelve Americans* (1956), and two women in *Sixteen Americans* (1959).

Just one of the twenty-nine artists in Sidney Janis's *New Realists* exhibition, the show that launched Pop Art in 1962, was a woman (Marisol), and when, after the show, downtown artists began moving to uptown galleries, most of the women remained below Fourteenth Street.[15] In Irving Sandler's three-hundred-page history of Abstract Expressionism, *The Triumph of American Painting*, published in 1970, only two women artists are (briefly) mentioned, Ethel Schwabacher, an Abstract Expressionist, and Elaine de Kooning, who is quoted commenting on the work of a man, Arshile Gorky, and is identified as "herself a painter."[16] The

New York Philharmonic did not have a permanent woman member until 1966, when Orin O'Brien joined. Announcing the appointment, *The New York Times* reported her to be "as comely a colleen as any orchestra could wish to have in its ranks."[17]

The Great Books of the Western World, launched in 1952 by Robert Hutchins, former president of the University of Chicago, and Mortimer Adler, who had taught philosophy there, was a fifty-four-volume set containing 434 works by seventy-six authors and comprising 32,000 pages, or 25 million words. Every word was written by a white man. The first edition of *The Norton Anthology of English Literature* was published 1962 and would become a standard teaching anthology in college English courses. All the editors were men. The two-volume set has 3,394 pages of texts. Thirty-three of those pages contain writing by women.* Harcourt Brace's two-volume anthology *Major British Writers*, published in an enlarged edition in 1959, has 1,841 pages. No women are represented.

Not a single writer in Richard Macksey and Eugenio Donato's *The Languages of Criticism and the Sciences of Man*, the proceedings of the 1966 Johns Hopkins conference on structuralism, was a woman. Of the fifty-two poets in *The New Poets of England and America* in 1957, six were women; in the *Second Selection* (1962), out of sixty-two poets, seven were women. Of the forty-four poets in *The New American Poetry* in 1960, four were women. Of the twenty-five poets in Donald Hall's Penguin anthology *Contemporary American Poetry* (1962), two were women. A. Alvarez's Penguin anthology *The New Poetry* (also 1962) had nineteen poets; zero were women. (And Alvarez was a friend of Sylvia Plath. She and Adrienne Rich did make it into the 1966 edition.)

The editors of the leading women's magazines—*Redbook, McCall's, Good Housekeeping, Ladies' Home Journal*—were all men. Only one of the top sixteen editorial positions at *Life* in 1956 was held by a woman— "Chief of Research." None of *Life's* staff writers was a woman; two of ten associate editors and eight of thirty-four assistant editors were women. The magazine had eight copy readers, however, and all were women. *The New York Times* did not even hire its first female copy reader until 1956 (Betsy Wade). Almost every other woman at the paper was assigned to

---

* More than half are devoted to a short story by the New Zealand writer Katherine Mansfield. The other women represented are Ann Radcliffe (1 p.), Elizabeth Barrett Browning (2 pp.), Emily Brontë (4 pp.), Christina Rossetti (4 pp.), and Virginia Woolf (5 pp.).

the women's section, "Food, Fashions, Family, Furnishings," whose office was separate from the newsroom. As late as 1972, not one of the paper's twenty-two national correspondents was a woman; there were no women on the editorial board; and the paper had no woman columnist.[18]

Ivy League faculties took many decades even to approach gender balance.* Princeton did not appoint its first tenured woman until 1968, a year before the college began admitting women. (She was Suzanne Keller in sociology.) When Yale College began admitting women, also in 1969, it had two tenured women on the faculty. Harvard awarded its first honorary degree in 1692 (Increase Mather); it awarded its first honorary degree to a woman in 1955 (Helen Keller). Women were not allowed to walk through the front door of the Harvard Faculty Club until 1968. In 1972, only 14 of the 752 professors at all of Harvard's schools were women; 7 of them were in the schools of Public Health and Education.[19]

Harvard College finally started admitting women in 1977, when it "merged" with Radcliffe. (Male and female students were still segregated. The complete absorption of Radcliffe into Harvard did not happen until 1999.) Harvard did not have a full-time tenured woman in the English department until 1981 (Marjorie Garber). It did not tenure a woman from within the English department until 2003 (Leah Price). Harvard did not have a tenured woman in the Philosophy department until 1989 (Gisela Striker). It did not tenure a woman from within the Philosophy department until 2002 (Alison Simmons).[20]

The second piece of the regime of subordination was sexism. Women were assumed to be innately different from men, not designed for creative, intellectual, or entrepreneurial work. This is obvious enough from the statistics of women in the professoriate and the professions, and there is anecdotal evidence almost everywhere you dip a toe in the period. "He felt that women just weren't that good writers," Michael Rumaker, who studied writing at Black Mountain College, said of Charles Olson. "It was man's business to write, to be involved in the

---

* In 1976, women made up 3 percent of the arts and sciences faculty at Harvard, 1.6 percent at Yale, and 1 percent at Princeton. Even at Berkeley, co-ed since 1871, women made up just 5.6 percent of the faculty. The Graduate Center of the City University of New York was founded in 1961; in 1972, there were 55 women on the faculty and 566 men. Every department chair was a man.

arts, making, creating. And women—they could make children, that was their world."[21]

Women like Diana Trilling who carved out successful careers as critics were aware that they were venturing on territory marked "male." "If you weren't a known person, if you weren't a name," she said about the parties she attended with New York writers and editors, "then the only way as a woman that you could be justified in being there was to be somebody for sexual conquest. And if you were neither a name nor sexually available, you should have stayed at home, because it was just misery. Unless a man in the intellectual community was bent on sexual conquest, he was never interested in women. He wanted to be with the men."[22]

Lee Krasner remembered Hans Hofmann remarking about a painting, "This is so good you would not believe it was done by a woman."[23] "Clem got on his kick of 'women painters,'" Grace Hartigan wrote in her journal after a dinner party in 1951. "Same thing—too easily satisfied, 'finish' pictures, polish, 'candy' . . . He said he wants to be the contemporary of the first great woman painter. What shit—he'd be the first to attack." Clem was Clement Greenberg; Lee Krasner was also at the dinner.[24] "Women novelists lack executive force," Susan Sontag recorded the Columbia English professor Steven Marcus declaring in 1963.[25]

"Paul said there are no women artists because a woman is too much concerned with her own body," Judith Malina, co-founder of the Living Theatre, wrote in her diary in 1952.[26] Paul was Paul Goodman, whose book *Growing Up Absurd* (1960) became an honored text for the New Left. "I say the 'young men and boys' rather than the 'young people,'" he explains in that book's introduction, "because the problems I want to discuss in this book belong primarily, in our society, to the boys: how to be useful and make something of oneself. A girl does not *have* to, she is not expected to, 'make something' of herself. Her career does not have to be self-justifying, for she will have children, which is absolutely self-justifying, like any other natural or creative act."[27]

"'I don't believe in women directors,' said Sarris the other day. And he was right." Sarris was Andrew Sarris, who would become one of the most influential movie critics of the period, and the remark was reported by Jonas Mekas, his mentor, who was the movie critic for *The Village Voice* and the leading voice in avant-garde cinema. Mekas added, "I mean, he was right until now."[28] The year was 1963.

And then there was the misogyny.

2.

Without question the most widely disseminated source of images of violence to women in the 1940s and early 1950s was a commercial product consumed almost exclusively by children: comic books. The launch of the anti-comics crusade is customarily credited to a column called "A National Disgrace" in the *Chicago Daily News* in 1940, alerting readers to "a poisonous mushroom growth of the last two years."[29] After that, the evils of comic books became a constant in cultural commentary. In 1944, for example, William Marston, the creator of Wonder Woman, got into an exchange about comic books with Cleanth Brooks and two of his colleagues in the pages of *The American Scholar*, the journal of the Phi Beta Kappa Society.[30] (Brooks was against them.)

During the war, comic books were huge informal exports, distributed around the world by American soldiers, and after the war, the industry boomed. Data vary, but by every account the numbers were enormous. By 1952, it is estimated that more than twenty publishers were putting out close to 650 titles a month, 80 million to 100 million comic books were sold every week, and the average issue was passed along to six or more readers. It is likely that comic books were reaching more people in 1952 than magazines, radio, or television did.[31]

There were two schools of criticism. One regarded comic books as a danger to literacy, a bad way for children to learn, or not learn, how to read. (This is the school to which Brooks belonged.) The other regarded them as a danger to society and believed that they turned children into juvenile delinquents. Fredric Wertham was (mostly) of the second school.

Wertham was a German-born psychiatrist (his name was shortened from Wertheimer) who had come to the United States in 1922 to teach at Johns Hopkins, where he eventually became chief resident in charge of psychiatry. In 1934, he moved to New York City to serve as the head of the Court of General Sessions psychiatric clinic. He worked at Bellevue, and then at Queens Hospital Center as director of psychiatric services. In 1946, with the support of Richard Wright and Ralph Ellison, he opened the Lafargue Clinic in Harlem, where patients were charged twenty-five cents if they could afford it—the first effectively free psychiatric facility in the United States for people of color.* In 1947, he started the Quaker Emergency Service Readjustment Center, devoted in part to the treatment of sex offenders.[32]

Wertham began his campaign against comic books on June 7, 1948, when he delivered a broadcast on the CBS radio network, and his prime example of the perniciousness of comic books was their prolific portrayal of violence against women. "[T]here has been no other literature for adults or for children in the history of the world, at any period or in any nation," he told listeners, "that showed in pictures and in words, over and over again, half-nude girls in all positions being branded, burned, bound, tied to wheels, blinded, pressed between spikes, thrown to snakes and wild animals, crushed with rocks, slowly drowned or smothered, or having their veins punctured and their blood drawn off. Do I have to prove that this is not good for children?"[33]

The comic-book industry operated below regulatory radar. The Association of Comics Magazine Publishers, founded in 1948 in response to criticism by figures like Wertham and complaints by religious and parents' organizations, was toothless; its editorial guidelines were ignored. And not surprisingly, for the natural tendency of the comic book is toward the outré. Exaggeration—studlier heroes, bloodier killings, pointier breasts—is in the DNA of the medium. It's what comic-book art is good at. And the chance to work in a permissive and lucrative enterprise drew talent into the field. Imagination was rewarded, nothing was censored, kids lived for the product, and most grown-ups found comic books beneath contempt and therefore beneath notice.

Wertham had assurance and an imperious manner—*The New Yorker* described him as "easily . . . one of the most peppery and intemperate personalities of our time"—and his writings and speeches attracted the attention of citizens' groups and public officials, who consulted him, and comic-book publishers, who reportedly hired private investigators to look into his past.[34] Wertham's major work on the comics, *Seduction of the Innocent*, was a Book-of-the-Month Club alternate selection and was excerpted in *Ladies' Home Journal*. It came out on April 19, 1954.

Seduction of the Innocent is based in part on Wertham's interviews

---

* The children of Julius and Ethel Rosenberg were Wertham's patients at Lafargue for several years after their parents were executed, in 1953. The clinic was named for Paul Lafargue, Marx's son-in-law.

with children who were identified as delinquents, and several of those discussions are about sadism. An adolescent tells him:

> When you see a girl and you see her headlights [breasts] and she is beaten up, that makes you hot and bothered! If she will take a beating from a man she will take anything from him.

A twelve-year old boy:

> In the comic books sometimes the men threaten the girls. They beat them with their hands. They tie them around to a chair and then they beat them. When I read such a book I get sexually excited. They don't get me sexually excited all the time, only when they tie them up.[35]

Wertham's book received a lot of attention, and most of it was positive. Two days after it came out, he testified in televised hearings convened by a subcommittee of the Senate Judiciary Committee charged with investigating the causes of juvenile crime, held at the Foley Square U.S. Courthouse (now the Thurgood Marshall Courthouse) in New York City. The committee's authority was enhanced by the presence of Senator Estes Kefauver, whose hearings on organized crime, in 1950–1951, also televised, had made him a national figure.* Wertham testified on the first day. "It is my opinion," he told the senators and the cameras, "without any reasonable doubt and without any reservation, that comic books are an important contributing factor in many cases of juvenile delinquency."[36]

He gave the committee examples of stories in which a girl's tongue is ripped out; in which a girl is hit with a gun; in which a man poisons his wife; in which a police captain kills his wife; in which a girl is whipped; in which a girl is beaten to death; and in which a woman kills a man and then serves his organs as a meal.[37] Comic books not only teach sadism, he said; they also teach racism. "Hitler was a beginner compared to the comic-book industry," he said. "They get the children much younger. They teach them race hatred at the age of four."[38]

---

* Kefauver ran for president in the Democratic primaries in 1952 and received 3.1 million votes, about 3 million more than the eventual nominee, Adlai Stevenson.

The hearings went on for another two days, and some witnesses questioned Wertham's methods, but he had scored his point. According to a Gallup poll in November 1954, 70 percent of Americans believed that comic books were a cause of juvenile crime. From the fall of 1954 through the summer of 1955, laws restricting the sale of comic books were passed in more than a dozen states, and there were public comic-book burnings.

Most of the laws would be annulled by the courts as an unconstitutional state exercise of prior restraint. But in 1954, the Comics Magazine Association of America (CMAA) was formed, and it imposed a code of standards of almost incredible restrictiveness. Five censors working full-time vetted new comics. Even Betty and Veronica in the Archie comics were ordered to appear in less tight-fitting blouses in accordance with the requirement that "females shall be drawn realistically without exaggeration of any physical qualities."[39] The Code put most comic titles out of business: between 1954 and 1956, the industry went from publishing almost 650 titles a year to publishing around 250, and more than eight hundred artists, writers, and other comic-book makers left the business.[40] Though it had no legal force, the Code was effective because distributors refused to stock comic books that did not have CMAA approval.[41]

The comic-book inquisition is usually read in the context of American social anxieties, but the same sequence of events happened at almost exactly the same time in France and Britain. The United Kingdom had been flooded with comic books brought over by American soldiers during and after the war, and a campaign to regulate them started up around 1949, the same time that Wertham began his crusade. By 1954, to avoid restrictions on imports, British publishers were getting matrices for crime and horror comics from companies such as EC and printing the books in Britain. This led to a swift response by the Conservative government, and in 1955, Parliament passed the Children and Young Persons (Harmful Publications) Act, which stopped the production of undesirable comic books.

Events in France followed the same timeline. American comic books came to France in 1934 with the publication of *Journal de Mickey*. They offered a perfect political target—for the Communists, who attacked American culture; for the Catholics, who deplored lax morals and explicit drawings; and for businessmen, who wanted to protect French industry. In January 1949, a comic-book bill prepared by the Communists and the Catholic Mouvement Republicaine Populaire was introduced in the National Assembly.

In May, *Les Temps Modernes* published a translation of an anti-comics article that had appeared a year earlier in the American magazine *Neurotica* called "The Psychopathology of the Comics," by Gershon Legman. Legman was not a prude. *Neurotica* was a Beat journal; John Clellon Holmes, Jack Kerouac, Carl Solomon, and Allen Ginsberg were contributors.* Legman's argument was that comic books depict sadism, and the reason is because they cannot legally depict sex. The result, as he put it, "is the hypocrisy that can examine all these thousands of pictures in comic books showing half-naked women being tortured to death, and complain only that they're half naked."[42][†] In July, by a vote of 422 to 181, the French National Assembly passed the *Loi de 16 juillet 1949 sur les publications destinées à la jeunesse*, which established a commission to oversee publications for children and adolescents—a censorship board. By 1955, it had purged comic books sold in France of sexually suggestive and racially offensive imagery.[43]

From a latter-day perspective, these comic-book inquisitions can seem an attempt to suppress an edgy, provocative, satirical popular art form, and to dictate to people what they should read. In this view, a big, powerful, established social entity (consisting of psychiatrists and government officials) was squashing a bunch of little, powerless entities (consisting of comic-book artists and vote-less readers).

But the psychiatrists and the officials almost certainly saw things the other way around. At the time of the hearings where Wertham testified, comic books were a hundred-million-dollar-a-year business. And many contemporaries thought that Wertham was right. "All parents should be grateful to Dr. Fredric Wertham for having written 'Seduction of the Innocent,'" said the review in the *Times*.[44] The reviewer was C. Wright Mills. *The New Yorker* concluded that although *Seduction of the Innocent* was in many ways "an absurd and alarmful book . . . the concrete evidence it offers of a real crime against the children seems to be practically unanswerable."[45] Robert Warshow, whose essays on

---

* Legman was one of several people who took credit for coining the phrase "Make love, not war."
† Frantz Fanon quoted Legman's article in *Black Skin, White Masks*. Fanon's take: "The magazines are put together by white men for little white men," 146.

popular culture were unusual in the period for their nuance and appreciation, wrote an essay for *Commentary* in which he worried about the effect of horror comics on his eleven-year-old son, Paul. Warshow did not much admire Wertham's book but he accepted its verdict. "I myself would not like to live surrounded by the kind of culture Dr. Wertham could thoroughly approve of," he wrote, "and what I would not like for myself I would hardly desire for Paul. The children must take their chances like the rest of us. But when Dr. Wertham is dealing with the worst of the comic books he is on strong ground; some kind of regulation seems necessary."[46]

The depiction of women in comics books was continuous with a large swath of adult fiction, which was, of course, much harder to regulate. Sexualized violence is a standard image on mass-market paperback covers. Even the cover of the Signet edition of *On the Road* includes a drawing of a man beating a woman who has fallen to the ground at his feet—a scene that corresponds to nothing in the text itself.

Often a woman's death is the climax of the story. Here is the ending of *I, the Jury*, the first Mike Hammer novel, by Mickey Spillane:

> The roar of the .45 shook the room. Charlotte staggered back a step. Her eyes were a symphony of incredulity, an unbelieving witness to truth. Slowly, she looked down at the ugly swelling in her naked belly where the bullet went in. A trickle of blood welled out . . . Her eyes had pain in them now, the pain preceding death. Pain and unbelief.
>
> "How c-could you?" she gasped.
>
> I had only a moment before talking to a corpse, but I got it in.
>
> "It was easy," I said.[47]

The covers for every Mike Hammer novel published in the 1950s— *My Gun Is Quick* (1950), *Vengeance Is Mine!* (1950), *One Lonely Night* (1951), *The Big Kill* (1951), and *Kiss Me, Deadly* (1952)—depict a sexy woman either pointing a gun, being threatened by a man with a gun, or dead.

Here is the last line of *Casino Royale*, the first James Bond novel, by Ian Fleming.

> "The bitch is dead now."[48]

The book came out in the United States in 1953 and a Popular Library paperback came out one year later. The cover of the paperback shows "the bitch" (her name is Vesper) partly undressed; the cover line reads: "She Played A Man's Game With A Woman's Weapons." The title was changed to *You Asked for It*.[49]

In Grace Metalious's *Peyton Place*, the central love relationship, between Tomas (described as "a massively boned man with muscles that seemed to quiver every time he moved") and Constance, begins when he rapes her, in a scene written as though rape were an especially effective form of courtship:

> He carried her, struggling, up the dark stairway, and when he reached the second floor, he kicked open the door of her room with his foot.
>
> "I'll have you arrested," she stammered. "I'll have you arrested and put in jail for breaking and entering and rape—"
>
> He stood her on the floor beside the bed and slapped her a stunning blow across the mouth with the back of his hand.
>
> "Don't open your mouth again," he said quietly. "Just keep your mouth shut."
>
> He bent over her and ripped the still wet bathing suit from her body, and in the dark, she heard the sound of his zipper opening as he took off his trunks.
>
> "Now," he said. "Now."
>
> It was like a nightmare from which she could not wake until, at last, when the blackness at her window began to thin to pale gray, she felt the first red gush of shamed pleasure that lifted her, lifted her, lifted her and then dropped her down into unconsciousness.[50]

Not a single reviewer of the novel mentioned the date rape, which Metalious had added at the request of her publisher (a woman, Kathryn Messner).[51] The figure of the male sexual assaulter was so unexceptionable as a protagonist that it must have seemed natural for the screenwriters on MGM's *The Beat Generation* (1959) to make the beatnik character, Stan Hess, a serial rapist.

It is not, of course, that most people thought violence against women was acceptable in real life (although spousal rape was not a crime anywhere in the United States until 1975).[52] It is that many people thought that sexual violence was perfectly acceptable as fantasy. Even for sophisticated people, the suffering of the female victim could seem beside the point.

Norman Mailer's stabbing of his second wife, Adele, took place in the early morning of November 20, 1960. After more than a decade of frustration, Mailer had reached a positive inflection point in his career. His war novel, *The Naked and the Dead*, published in 1948, was based partly on his own experiences and partly on stories he heard from soldiers in the army unit he joined, the 112th Cavalry, about a patrol behind enemy lines in Leyte, an island in the Philippines. The book's success—sixty-two weeks on the *Times* bestseller list—had made Mailer a rich man.

But his next two novels, *Barbary Shore* (1951) and *The Deer Park* (1955), were critical flops. He had resurrected himself by adopting a first-person style and by turning to reportage, a medium better suited than literary fiction not only to his talents (Mailer had trouble making up stories) but also to his ambitions as a writer and thinker. He had published his breakthrough book, *Advertisements for Myself*, in 1959; just before the stabbing, *Esquire* had published the first of his major journalistic pieces, "Superman Comes to the Supermarket," on the nomination of John F. Kennedy at the Democratic National Convention that summer.

Mailer had planned a party in anticipation of an announcement that he was running for mayor of New York City, and about two hundred or so guests showed up at the Mailers' apartment on West Ninety-Fourth Street. The mood was sour from the start. Mailer wore a bullfighter's shirt, got drunk, and kept going outside to pick fights on the street. His wife, Adele, shut herself in the bathroom with a friend to complain about her marriage. Allen Ginsberg got into an argument with Norman Podhoretz and called him a "big dumb fuckhead." By the time the stabbing occurred, most of the guests had left.

According to both his and her recollections, Adele taunted Mailer and called him a faggot, and he stabbed her twice with a penknife, in the back and in the abdomen. The second wound pierced her pericardium, the membrane around the heart. According to Adele, someone tried to help her after she was stabbed, but Mailer kicked her. "Get away from her," he said. "Let the bitch die." The remaining guests got her to a hospital, where she underwent a six-hour operation.

Adele said that in the hospital, some of Mailer's friends presented her with a petition asking her to refuse to allow doctors to administer shock treatment to her husband, on the grounds that it might damage his creative genius. Mailer's mother came to see her to insist that she tell the police that she had got her injuries by falling on a broken bottle.[53] Mailer told her to lie to the grand jury. The incident was widely reported, from the stabbing to the sentencing, which finally happened, after a year of legal proceedings, when Mailer pled guilty and was given a suspended sentence. "Norman Mailer Goes Free in Knifing Case" was the headline in the *Times*.[54]*

Nearly everyone who knew the Mailers and whose reflections have been reported blamed Adele. "People felt it was a tragedy, that a man had been driven to do something that he didn't really want or intend to do, that he'd lost control," Irving Howe said later. "Among the 'uptown intellectuals' there was this feeling of shock and dismay, and I don't remember anyone judging him . . . He was seen as a victim."[55]

In the literary world, the act was interpreted by the lights of the modernist ideology of the artist. (Or else treated as another round in the eternal War between Men and Women. "I see your namesake has got himself in trouble by stabbing his wife," the political journalist and *Commentary* editor George Lichtheim is supposed to have said to Podhoretz. "I didn't know this was illegal in New York.")[56] James Baldwin explained that by trying to kill his wife, Mailer was hoping to rescue the writer in himself from the spiritual prison he had created with his fantasies of becoming a politician: "[I]t is like burning down the house in order, at last, to be free of it," he wrote in *Esquire*.[57] Lionel Trilling told Diana that the stabbing was "a Dostoevskian ploy": Mailer was testing the limits of evil in himself.[58]

Midge Decter, Podhoretz's wife—both were close friends of the Mailers—wrote to a British friend that

> the whole business with Mailer turned me so sick with literature, with "insight," with Columbia University, that I couldn't bear to do anything but go to the movies. Everyone in New York came alive with sex and titillation. And in this whole God-forsaken city

---

* Adele's father was a linotype operator at the New York *Daily News* and had to set the headline for the stabbing.

of 8,000,000 there could not be found one healthy philistine to say—the man is a thug, or a criminal. It's all nothing but experience, experience, experience.[59]

She was one of the few people who held Mailer accountable.* Her husband, on the other hand, escorted Mailer to the police station when he turned himself in. (It is only noting the obvious to contrast this display of empathy and concern with Podhoretz's attacks on the Beats as killers.)

The stabbing seems to have enhanced Mailer's social and literary cachet. A month after it was reported, Baldwin, Podhoretz, Jason Epstein, Alfred Kazin, William Phillips, Lillian Hellman, Robert Lowell, and Lionel Trilling published a letter in *Time* announcing: "Many critics and fellow writers feel that Mailer's work is of continuing significance and brilliance."[60] Two years later, Mailer published a book of poems with the title *Deaths for the Ladies (And Other Disasters)*. His next novel, *An American Dream*, was published in March 1965. In the novel, the protagonist strangles his wife, has sex with her maid, throws the wife's body out the window of her apartment building, has sex again with the maid (in case the point was missed that violence against women is a turn-on), and in the end gets away with it.

The book was reviewed in *Life*, the *Atlantic*, *Partisan Review* (twice), *National Review* (by Joan Didion), the *New Republic* (by Joseph Epstein), *The New York Times* (twice), *The New York Review of Books* (by Philip Rahv), and *Commentary* (by Richard Poirier). About half of the reviewers called the book powerful and compelling; the rest called it a disaster—pretty much the normal distribution for Mailer's fiction. Not one of them mentioned that this story about a man who kills his wife and gets away with it was written by a man who had nearly killed his wife and had gotten away with it.† To the extent that the incident was alluded to at all, it was subsumed under the category of what Poirier called Mailer's "acts of self-debasement."[61] The act of spousal abuse was turned into a dark night of the soul. Mailer's soul.

---

* In 1968, Decter was the editor, at *Harper's*, on the first half of Mailer's *The Armies of the Night*, for which he won his first Pulitzer Prize. Another friend who blamed Mailer was Dashiell Hammett, who prevented Lillian Hellman from lending him bail money.
† The reviewer for *Time* did note the fact of the stabbing.

3.

Bettye Naomi Goldstein was from Peoria. She graduated from Smith College in 1942, then went to Berkeley as a doctoral student in psychology. She dropped out after a year and moved to Manhattan. Active politically in college, she began working as a labor journalist for Federated Press, a left-wing news service. In 1947, now Betty, she married Carl Friedan (he had changed the name from Friedman), a Second World War veteran who worked in theater. They lived in a basement apartment on West Eighty-Sixth Street, but after their first child, Daniel, was born, in 1948, they moved to a garden apartment in Queens and Carl stopped his theater work and started up a public relations and advertising firm.

In 1952, when Betty was pregnant with her second child, Jonathan, she either lost or left her job as a writer for the *UE News*, an organ of the United Electrical Radio & Machine Workers Union. Its leadership had once included some members of the Communist Party, but by 1952, the Communist presence was mostly eliminated, and the union was in decline, with a falling membership.[62] Friedan soon resumed her career as a freelance magazine writer, contributing articles mostly to women's magazines.

She entered the field at a time when the woman's magazine was a very big business. In 1955, the circulation of *Good Housekeeping* was 3,535,542; *Ladies' Home Journal*'s was 4,893,897; *Women's Home Companion*'s was 4,146,401. Those numbers are comparable to the circulations of general interest titles like *Life* (5,603,875), *Look* (4,069,221), and *Time* (1,935,946), and they are far higher than men's magazines like *Esquire* (752,591), *Sports Illustrated* (597,363), and *Popular Mechanics* (1,343,618). If you add in pass-alongs, readers in places like waiting rooms and beauty parlors, that in most cases doubled circulation numbers. In 1953, a year when the average family earned $4,200, a four-color one-page ad in *Ladies' Home Journal* cost $20,000.[63]

In 1956, after the birth of their third child, Emily, the Friedans moved to Rockland County, living first in Snedens Landing and then, with financial help from the G.I. Bill, in Grand View-on-Hudson in an eleven-room house on an acre of land overlooking the river. Betty had household help three and a half to four days a week; Carl commuted into the city. Their annual income was between fifteen and twenty thousand dollars, putting them in the top 2 percent of earners. (Median income was now five thousand dollars.)[64]

Around that time, Betty joined two Smith classmates, Anne Mathers Montero and Marion Ingersoll, in devising a detailed questionnaire for their fifteenth reunion. The alumnae were asked questions about personal and sexual fulfillment, their experiences with pregnancy and childbirth, whether they felt frustrated as housewives, and other matters, such as "Do you put the milk bottle on the table?" Two hundred grads responded in time for their reunion in the spring of 1957.[65] That reunion led to the book that launched the women's liberation movement, also known as second-wave feminism, *The Feminine Mystique*. It came out in February 1963.

Two stories grew up around Friedan and her book. The first, which Friedan promoted, is that the book arose out of her dissatisfaction with life as a suburban housewife and after she read the results of the Smith questionnaire.[66] "If I hadn't wasted a whole year, 1956–57, doing an alumnae questionnaire of inappropriate and unnecessary depth on the experiences and feelings of my Smith college classmates fifteen years after graduation," she wrote in 1976,

> . . . if their answers had not raised such strange questions about that role we were all then embracing . . . I might never have written that book, *The Feminine Mystique*.[67]

The other narrative, which Friedan renounced, is that the reason she encouraged the first narrative was to play down her radical past, and that her book was carefully hedged to disguise her political history and views.[68]

Neither account is accurate. It is true that Friedan was an activist. After *The Feminine Mystique* was published, she went on to become one of the most powerful figures in the women's movement. From 1966 to 1970, she served as the first president of the National Organization for Women (NOW). In 1970, she conceived the highly effective Women's Strike for Equality. In 1971, together with Bella Abzug, Gloria Steinem, Shirley Chisholm, and others, she founded the National Women's Political Caucus. But she was not a radical. She did not want to end capitalism or overthrow the social order. She only wanted to level the playing field for women. It was on this issue that she broke with NOW in 1970.[69] In many ways, Friedan was always a first-wave feminist.*

And although her marriage was rocky and she was insecure about her writing career, Friedan was not unhappy as a woman, and neither were the majority of her Smith classmates. She wrote her book because she thought that *younger* women were victims of the feminine mystique. She was not trying to liberate herself. She was trying to free young women from a bad self-conception. She eventually saw that sexism had limited her own opportunities, too, but that was not the reason she wrote *The Feminine Mystique*.

Friedan's magazine work does not suggest a subversive intention. In 1952, after her tenth Smith reunion, Friedan drafted an article called "Was Their Education UnAmerican?" She pointed out that the Smith she attended from 1938 to 1942 exposed students to a range of social and political views, including left-wing views, and yet 66 percent of the Smith class of 1942 supported Eisenhower for president, 11 percent supported Robert Taft, and only 8 percent were Stevenson supporters. Smith graduates were conservative, and they were loyal. This did not mean that their educations had been meaningless. It meant that "education under academic freedom produces the best kind of American citizens."[70]

Three years later, Friedan published a piece in *Charm: The Magazine for Women Who Work*, called "I Went Back to Work." She quit her job when her child was born, she said, and had felt conflicted about going back to work.† But then she realized she could maintain a balance between home and career, because "[e]ven though I work at an outside job, I now feel that having children and raising a family is the main stream of my life as much as it is of theirs."[71] In 1956, she wrote the text for a photo-essay in *Cosmopolitan* called "Millionaire's Wife." The subject was Marjorie Steele, the second wife of Huntington Hartford II, heir to the A&P fortune and one of the world's richest people.‡ Steele was having what turned out to be a brief career as an

---

* The terms "first-" and "second-wave feminism" date from an article by Martha Weinman Lear in *The New York Times Magazine*, March 10, 1968.
† Many years later, Friedan claimed she was fired because she was pregnant, but this can't be verified.
‡ By the time he died, in 2008, at the age of ninety-seven, he had spent almost all of his money.

actress and had appeared on Broadway in *Cat on a Hot Tin Roof.* The Hartfords owned an eleven-room duplex on Beekman Place, a fifty-acre farm in New Jersey, and a house in Palm Beach. "When you have as much money as she," Freidan wrote, "it can take hard work just to be a person, just to be yourself. Marjorie knows that she is lucky: she has always had the joyous hard work of an actress to give her own life a mainspring."[72] (In fact, *Cat on a Hot Tin Roof* was Steele's last role. She gave up acting to raise her family. She and Huntington were divorced in 1960.)

The same year in *McCall's*, Friedan published "I Was Afraid to Have a Baby," an as-told-to piece by the actress Julie Harris. "All my life I have wanted to be truly creative, as an artist, as an actress," Harris "told" Friedan. "I have thought that the creative experience is the greatest one can have. It is. But acting on the stage offers only glimpses of creation. Motherhood is the experience of pure creation itself."[73] Adlai Stevenson and Dr. Spock would have approved of these pieces.

It was around this time that Friedan and her Smith classmates began putting together their alumni questionnaire for the 1957 reunion. That May an article appeared in *Ladies' Home Journal* called "Is College Education Wasted on Women?" The author was Nevitt Sanford, who had been one of Friedan's professors in the psychology department at Berkeley. Sanford had been retained by Vassar College to do a study of its students. His team compared current Vassar students with graduates from twenty years and fifty years before. A chief finding was that student culture had changed.[74]

"Not only is feminism dead," Sanford reported; "we have passed into a phase of antifeminism." Current Vassar students believed that the values they were taught in college would be out of place in the social world they expected to inhabit. "[E]xcept for a minority," Sanford reported, "the philosophy and aims of the college are not the major influences in the formation of values and habits of life."[75] Sanford suggested that colleges needed to reform their curricula to meet women students where they lived.

This is exactly what Friedan discovered at her fifteenth reunion. "[A]s the weekend wore on, a strange Alice in Wonderland feeling grew in us," she wrote about her and her classmates' experience. "We could not see our former selves in the pretty girls of '58, '59, '60. To us, college had been 'the pursuit of truth and knowledge.' To these girls, as one said to me, 'it's an arrangement.'" Friedan interviewed some of the students.* "I guess everybody wants to graduate with a diamond ring on her finger, that's the important thing," one told her. A sophomore explained that she had decided not to major in science because "I intend to get married and have four children and live in a nice suburb. My husband will probably be drawing a good salary from a big company. What good will it do me to study physics? Boys would think I was odd. Besides, it's too time-consuming. I can't leave early for football weekends. Science is something you can't do on the train."

Friedan learned that there was an unwritten rule not to talk shop, meaning schoolwork, in the dorms. She reported, "In the coffee dive where we used to sit for hours, in passionate bull sessions about what-is-truth, art-for-art's sake, religion, sex, war, and peace, Freud and Marx and what's-wrong-with-the-world, a senior said: 'We never waste time like that. I guess we don't have bull sessions about abstract things. Mostly we talk about our dates.'"

Friedan thought that these students would live to regret not taking advantage of their education, because they would have no resources for pursuing work or other activities outside the home. "Perhaps the girls might listen to 200 women who are leading the very lives they want to lead—the women of my own Smith generation," she concluded her article. "We could tell the pretty girls of Smith '59 and '60—and all the other girls on all the other campuses who are wasting their time in college today—that they have it all wrong . . . I think it's high time someone questioned the truth of this picture that is making the girls waste time in college."[76] It's not hard to see why this article was rejected by *McCall's, Ladies' Home Journal,* and *Redbook*.† Friedan was not saying that suburban housewives were frustrated. She was saying that contemporary women college students were mindless. She was attacking the next generation of subscribers.

---

* One Smith graduate she missed was Gloria Steinem, who was class of 1956. Steinem was torn between marriage and career. She abandoned her fiancé—literally leaving him her engagement ring and a note—to go to India on a scholarship as a kind of goodwill ambassador, an experience that launched her career as a journalist and activist. Steinem and Friedan would have a contentious relationship.

† Correspondence related to these submissions does not survive. Some communications seem to have been made through Friedan's agent, Marie Rodell.

In the Smith alumnae magazine, Friedan reported that, based on the questionnaire, the education she and her classmates received had not prevented them from achieving sexual fulfillment or enjoying motherhood. A majority of her respondents reported that they were "not frustrated" as housewives; 74 percent said they had "satisfying interests beyond our homes or within ourselves—the serious interests our education gave us." Their only regret was that they had not worked harder in college.[77] By the time that article appeared, the manuscript of *The Feminine Mystique* was almost finished.

Friedan originally had a very different book in mind. It was to be called "The Togetherness Woman," and was designed as an attack on this product of what she called "the sexual counter-revolution." The term "togetherness" derived from *McCall's*, which in 1954 started calling itself "the magazine of togetherness." Editorially, the idea was that *McCall's* would be a magazine for the nuclear family as a whole, not just the housewife. This was, of course, a strategy to attract advertisers by providing a wider readership base. Friedan thought that the term captured the trap she saw Smith students entering. In a book proposal, she explained that "The Togetherness Woman" would make "the heretical suggestion that 'togetherness' is a form of revenge—women making their husbands share the meaningless tasks of their role."[78]

It's easy to see what was happening. At her reunion, Friedan had been confronted with young women who identified self-fulfillment as "togetherness" and who saw their education as a way station to marriage. What shocked her was that these women were not being coerced into an unfulfilling life. They *wanted* that life. They had a very clear picture of what it would be like, including the probability that it would require some pretense of subordination to their husbands, and they were actively choosing it.

Friedan was worried about these women, but she plainly didn't like them, and she was on the verge of writing a book that blamed them for their own oppression. She needed a way to explain why women were not at fault for the situation into which they were gladly inserting themselves. She really did regard it as a puzzle, and she began doing extensive research, reading studies and interviewing women and social-science experts. She finally got over the hurdle. One of the books that got her there was *The Second Sex*.

4.

Simone de Beauvoir began *Le Deuxième sexe* in October 1946 and finished it in June 1949. During that time, she also spent four months in the United States and six months writing *L'Amérique au jour le jour* (*America Day by Day*).[79] That left not a lot of time to write a book that is 978 pages long. But the circumstances were unusual. Beauvoir wrote her book during the only major crisis in the history of the pact, as she and Sartre called their relationship.[80]

Sartre met Dolorès Vanetti Ehrenreich during his first trip to New York, in 1945, and they became lovers during his second trip, in 1946. According to the pact, such affairs were supposed to be "contingent," but Sartre apparently proposed marriage to Vanetti and considered moving to New York and taking an academic position at Columbia. Beauvoir responded (to the end of their lives, their affairs were mostly copycat) by starting an affair with the novelist Nelson Algren during *her* first trip to the United States, in 1947. Both affairs went on for some time, but Vanetti and Algren were not interested in an open marriage, and the relationships had ended by 1950.[81] By then, *Le Deuxième sexe* had appeared.

Beauvoir later said she had set out to write a book about herself and realized that the first thing she needed to explain about herself was that she was a woman. There are no traces of autobiography in *Le Deuxième sexe*, but it is likely that one motivation was the threat Beauvoir felt Vanetti posed to her relationship with Sartre and the uncertain basis of her relationship with Algren. This made her think (if only hypothetically, putting herself in the shoes of a less talented woman, perhaps) about the possibility that she might lose both men. What would her life prospects be then, as a single woman in her forties?

In defining the identity "woman," Beauvoir used the terms Sartre used in *Réflexions sur la question juive* and "Orphée noire." Humans are beings that have no essence. Yet every man imagines he knows what woman's essential nature is. What provides woman with her essence is that she is man's Other: her nature is the product of the male gaze. But this binary is not easily undone. As Beauvoir explained, citing Lévi-Strauss's work on kinship systems, binaries are inescapable. Dualities, alternatives, contrasts, symmetries: this is how humans make sense of the world. "[W]oman is the Other, in a totality of which the two components are necessary to one another," as she put it.[82]

When a woman accepts this situation, however, she becomes an *être-en-soi*, unfree, a being whose actions are determined by others. She can become independent only by acting as an *être-pour-soi*, a being who consciously chooses for herself. What makes this hard to do? Not nature, not social relations, but culture. *Le Deuxième sexe* is an enormous inventory of the many ways cultures reflect and reinforce sexism and patriarchy.

In the first volume (the two volumes were published separately in France), Beauvoir demystifies the biology of sexual difference, criticizes Freudian psychoanalysis and Marxian historical materialism, and analyzes the representation of women in five major writers, including D. H. Lawrence and André Breton.* In the second volume, *L'Expérience vécue* (*Lived Experience*), she describes women's life stages and the social roles available to them. The last part, "Vers la libération," is a chapter called "La Femme indépendente," in which Beauvoir said what Virginia Woolf had said twenty years earlier in *A Room of One's Own*: economic independence comes first.

The English translation of Beauvoir's book came out in 1953. The translator, Howard Parshley, was a zoology professor at Smith, where he may have been one of Friedan's teachers.[83] Friedan later said that she read the book in "the early Fifties," but this is probably misremembered.[84] On the other hand, she almost certainly read "Femininity: The Trap," a short article Beauvoir published in *Vogue* during her trip to the United States in 1947. (Vanetti was then in Paris with Sartre). The *Vogue* piece is almost a précis of *La Deuxième sexe*. (Beauvoir was identified in an Editor's Note as "[a] woman who thinks like a man."[85])

If Friedan did read the translation of *The Second Sex* when it first came out, then she reread it, probably in 1960, in the Frederick Allen Reading Room of the New York Public Library on Forty-Second Street, where she did her research for *The Feminine Mystique*.[86] She seems to have read the entire English book (732 pages in Parshley's abridgement), for she took more than seventy pages of notes: on childbirth, menopause, nursing, mother-daughter relations, motherhood, aging, sexuality, and housekeeping.

In the final chapter, on the independent woman, Beauvoir addressed

---

* This would be a model for Kate Millett's *Sexual Politics*, originally her Columbia University doctoral dissertation, published in 1970.

Friedan's problem: why women seem to choose willingly a subordinate position. "It must be admitted that the males find in woman more complicity than the oppressor usually finds in the oppressed," Beauvoir wrote.

> And in bad faith they take authorization from this to declare that she has *desired* the destiny they have imposed on her . . . Society in general—beginning with her respected parents—lies to her by praising the lofty values of love, devotion, the gift of herself . . . She cheerfully believes these lies because they invite her to follow the easy slope: in this others commit their worst crime against her; throughout her life from childhood on, they damage and corrupt her by designating as her true vocation this submission, which is the temptation of every existent in the anxiety of liberty . . . She does wrong in yielding to the temptation; but man is in no position to blame her.[87]

Friedan noted the number of the page this passage appears on, and next to it, she wrote:

> "Mystique of femininity"
> —Why women believe it[88]

Le Deuxième sexe is clearly a model for *The Feminine Mystique*. Friedan does not ascribe women's subordination to social or political forces. She analyzes it as an effect of culture. She, too, argues that there is no such thing as women's essential nature—the fundamental tenet of second-wave feminism. The belief that women are biologically destined for domesticity, she says, is just a construct created by psychologists and social scientists and used as an ex-post-facto justification for inequality. The popularized version of this bad science, the stuff that gets said at commencement exercises and on television sitcoms and around the water cooler about the way women really are, is the "mystique." In her final chapter, "A New Life Plan for Women," Friedan echoed Beauvoir. "It is easier to live through someone else than to become complete yourself," she wrote. "The freedom to lead and plan your own life is frightening if you have never faced it before."[89]

Friedan was skittish about associating her book with Beauvoir's.[90]

Contrary to what is sometimes written, *The Second Sex* had a fairly welcome reception in the United States.[91] It is true that Dwight Macdonald called it "a feminist polemic posing as a scholarly survey" and complained about "the unremitting whine of her special pleading."[92] But the English translation was reviewed with admiration in the *Times Book Review* by one of the most prestigious social scientists in the country, Clyde Kluckhohn, who called it "a truly magnificent book."[93] (Kluckhohn thought Beauvoir put too much emphasis on culture, which is interesting, since he was a cultural anthropologist.) *The Second Sex* was named one of the year's best books by the *Times*'s Orville Prescott (no iconoclast), who called it "[p]robably the most-talked-about book, and often by people who had not read it."[94] It spent five weeks on the bestseller list, almost as long as *The Feminine Mystique* did ten years later. The reception, particularly of the second volume, was much less friendly in France.

Still, in the United States, Beauvoir's book was received as, in Prescott's words, "very French." Kluckhohn said something that might have meant the same thing: "too intellectualistic." *The Second Sex* did not speak to American women in the personal way that Friedan's book did.* Of course, Beauvoir was one half of a world-famous open relationship, and by 1963, when Friedan's book came out, her and Sartre's anti-Americanism was notorious. She was therefore not a likely model for most American women. Friedan must have taken this into account when she undertook to present herself as an ordinary overeducated suburban housewife, "one of us."

The Feminine Mystique had a much less propitious launch. It came out in the middle of a four-month newspaper strike in New York City and had to get the public's attention at first without the benefits of newspaper advertisements or reviews. But the book was excerpted in *McCall's* and *Ladies' Home Journal* (though a number of magazines also turned it down), and its publisher, W. W. Norton, was astute enough to sense that it might have a blockbuster on its hands. It hired a publicist who arranged a book tour (then an unusual promotional tool), and gave the book a dust jacket the color of a fire truck.[95] The cover blurb, by the writer and television personality Virgilia Peterson, promised

---

* It didn't help that one of Parshley's mistranslations made Beauvoir seem anti-motherhood, something Kluckhohn (who praised the translation) then criticized her about.

that the book is "far and away more real, truer, and more moving than Simone de Beauvoir's *The Second Sex.*" *The Feminine Mystique* ended up spending six weeks on the *Times* bestseller list. The first paperback printing sold 1.3 million copies. By the time of Friedan's death, in 2006, more than 3 million copies had been sold.

Later on, Friedan would be criticized for ignoring working-class and nonwhite women, and for slighting the contributions of previous books on the subject, including (besides *The Second Sex*) Elizabeth Hawes's *Why Women Cry* (1943), Mirra Komarovsky's *Women in the Modern World* (1953), and Alva Myrdal and Viola Klein's *Women's Two Roles* (1956)—all of them well known to Friedan. She was also accused of exaggerating the sexism in the stories in women's magazines she analyzed.[96] But those things didn't matter. What mattered was that she touched the lives of ordinary readers.

She accomplished this by doing something Beauvoir and Myrdal did not do (though Komarovsky, an academic sociologist, did): she put women's voices in her book. She drew on her fifteen years of experience as a reporter to find and interview eighty women of different ages, and what she found complicated the picture she had formed at her 1957 reunion and changed the argument she had outlined in her proposal for "The Togetherness Woman."[97] It turned out that her Smith classmates were not the norm. Many women told her how frustrated and depressed their lives were making them. She listened to their stories, and she quoted them in her book.

For the core of that book's appeal is personal: this is what it feels like to be a white, middle-class housewife in 1963. Why it feels that way, what forces trapped women inside what Friedan called (in an uncharacteristically extreme analogy) "the comfortable concentration camp," might be debated.[98] But an enormous number of women recognized themselves in Friedan's pages—or, since *The Feminine Mystique*, too, was a book more talked about than read, an enormous number of women experienced the title with a shock of recognition. Hundreds wrote her letters.[99]

Was Friedan pushing on an open, or at least an unlatched, door? In an article she published in *Good Housekeeping* three years before the book came out, she described a "strange stirring," the beginnings of a backlash against the culture of "togetherness woman."[100] By the time *The Feminine Mystique* appeared, there was evidence that the postwar model of domesticity was no longer sustainable. Since 1950, the number of women enrolled in college had nearly doubled, and the employment rate for women had risen four times faster than for men. At some point, the growing number of women in the educational and vocational pipelines would have produced pressure to get rid of gender discrimination, at least in the extreme form it had taken. It also seems to have dawned on public officials after the Soviets launched Sputnik in 1957 that limiting career opportunities for half the population was not a prudent use of human resources. The country was about to shift from a manufacturing economy to a service and information economy, from work based on brawn to work based on brains. It made no sense to keep educated people at home. And by the end of 1964, the baby boom would be over.

Friedan's publisher was even worried that the discontent of middle-class housewives was already an old story in 1963. In 1962, Helen Gurley Brown, then an advertising copywriter, soon the editor of *Cosmopolitan*, published *Sex and the Single Girl*, which ended with this advice:

> You may marry or you may not. In today's world that is no longer the big question for women. Those who glom onto men so that they can collapse with relief, spend the rest of their days shining up their status symbol and figure they never have to reach, stretch, learn, grow, face dragons or make a living again are the ones to be pitied. They, in my opinion are the unfulfilled ones.
>
> You, my friend, if you work at it, can be envied the rich, full life possible for the single woman today. It's a good show . . . enjoy it from wherever you are, whether it's two in the balcony or one on the aisle—don't miss *any* of it.[101]

This does not sound like a Smith graduate.

And deliberately so. "I write for the girl who doesn't have anything going for her," Brown told Joan Didion (who thought that people who disparaged Brown's book were snobs). "The girl who's not pretty, who maybe didn't go to college, who may not even have a decent family background."[102] *Sex and the Single Girl* sold two million copies in three weeks and stayed on the bestseller list over a year, far longer than *The Second Sex* or *The Feminine Mystique*.[103]

In December 1961, toward the end of his first year as president—and six weeks after fifty thousand women walked off their jobs in the Women's Strike for Peace—John F. Kennedy appointed a Commission on the Status of Women. In his executive order, he gave, among other reasons, a national security rationale the opposite of Stevenson's: "It is in the national interest to promote the economy, security, and national defense through the most efficient and effective utilization of the skills of all persons."[104]

Kennedy's commission issued its report two years later, and it was far more progressive than Friedan's book. The commission gave attention to the situation of nonwhite women, a group Friedan had ignored, and it issued a number of recommendations to change the legal structure that limited women's rights, including a law mandating that women be paid the same as men for doing the same work, which Congress promptly passed in the form of the Equal Pay Act of 1963.

That act helped pave the way for the Civil Rights Act of 1964, legislation on which virtually all the gains of the movement to secure women's rights would be based for many years. The women's movement, like the civil rights movement, was in what geopolitically obsessed politicians like Kennedy perceived to be the national interest. Those movements were perfectly consistent with both a commitment to strengthen the democracies and with liberal ideology.[105] Legally permitted discrimination may have had domestic political uses, but in the realm of geopolitics, it was an albatross.

5.

"We are incompetent to solve the times," Emerson wrote in 1860.[106] If Susan Sontag ever read those words—and there was very little she did not read—she ignored them.* Her career was her life, and her life was an unceasing effort to figure out what was happening and bring the news to her readers.

When Sontag burst onto the intellectual scene, in the early 1960s, there was no one like her. She had been educated at Berkeley, Chicago, Harvard, and Oxford, and had lived in Los Angeles, San Francisco, Paris, and New York. She knew the salons and the bars, the *monde* and the

---

* Sontag once said she "loved" Emerson and called him "the first true great American writer" (*Revista de Occidente*, no. 79 [December 1987], 111. "Me encantan Emerson, el verdadero primer gran escritor norteamericano.")

demimonde. She had a command of the Western literary, philosophical, and classical music canon; she was up to date on Continental thought; she was a dedicated cinéaste who often saw two or three movies a day; and she followed the avant-garde. She wrote for *Partisan Review, Film Quarterly,* and *Mademoiselle.* She posed for an Andy Warhol "screen test" at the Factory, and she had an affair with Jasper Johns. She also wrote experimental fiction. Every other American critic of the period looks provincial by comparison.

Sontag came to stand for a moment when a bright-line distinction between high art and commercial culture stopped making sense to educated audiences, and she would be attacked—sneered at, really—by writers like Irving Howe for critical permissiveness and the abandonment of standards. This was a misreading. Sontag wasn't merely an elitist. She was a snob. She was the kind of person who does not own a television.[107] Her standards were highbrow standards. She just wanted to be on the cutting edge of cultural awareness.

Sontag saw that her social world was going through a taste shift. Grown-ups were listening to the Supremes; academics were watching French and Italian movies; she and her friends were going to Happenings. Sontag had no desire to discard the canon. She admired Lionel Trilling, and believed that the kind of contemporary art and thought she was interested in belonged to the tradition he had devoted his career to, art whose task was "to strengthen the adversarial consciousness."[108]

But Trilling was a stranger to the *demimonde.* He disliked poetry readings, rarely went to the theater, and never went to the movies, even to see European imports.[109] People like Trilling—or Macdonald, or Howe—didn't know what to make of a film that featured a polysexual orgy, or a performance by a woman playing classical cello with her top off. In two famous essays written within a few weeks of each other in 1964, Sontag expressed, for many readers, the significance of this shift. Those essays would quickly become outmoded, but they put Sontag where she wanted to be, in the forefront of American letters.

Sontag was born in New York City in 1933. Her father, Jack Rosenblatt, was a fur trader who died of tuberculosis on a trip to China when Susan was five. Susan was asthmatic, so in 1943 her mother, Mildred, moved with her and her sister, Judith, to Tucson for the climate. Two years later, Mildred married Nathan Sontag, a decorated war pilot who was in the business of selling clocks; soon after, the family moved to Sherman Oaks, in the San Fernando Valley area of Los Angeles. Susan attended North Hollywood High School.[110]

Sontag later called her childhood "that long prison sentence."

> I felt I was slumming, in my own life. My task was to ward off the drivel (I felt I was drowning in drivel)—the jovial claptrap of classmates and teachers, the maddening bromides I heard at home. And the weekly comedy shows festooned with canned laughter, the treacly Hit Parade, the hysterical narratings of baseball games and prize fights—radio, whose racket filled the living room on weekday evenings and much of Saturday and Sunday, was an endless torment. I ground my teeth, I twirled my hair, I gnawed at my nails, I was polite. Though untempted by the new, tribal delights of suburban childhood that had quickly absorbed my sister, I didn't think of myself as a misfit, for I assumed my casing of affability was being accepted at face value. (Here the fact that I was a girl seeps through.) What other people thought of me remained a dim consideration, since other people seemed to me astonishingly unseeing as well as uncurious, while I longed to learn everything: the exasperating difference between me and everyone I'd met—so far.[111]

Sontag could overdramatize, but this is a fair summary of her lifelong attitude toward American middle-class life and its pleasures.

Sontag's refuge was reading. To say she was precocious would be almost understating the case. "Basically, I believe Schopenhauer to be wrong," she wrote in her journal. "In making this statement I am considering only the most elemental portion of his philosophy: the inevitable barrenness of existence."[112] She was fourteen. At fifteen:

> Immersed myself in Gide all afternoon and listened to the Busch (Glyndebourne festival) recording of *Don Giovanni*. Several arias (such soul-stretching sweetness!) I played over and over again . . . Wasted the evening with Nat. He gave me a driving lesson and then I accompanied him and pretended to enjoy a Technicolor blood-and-thunder movie.[113]

Which captures both the obsessive nature of her intellectual passions and her humorlessness. A list, later that year, of "books and plays and stories I have to read" runs to over a hundred titles.[114]

Sontag had friends her age who shared her tastes. She hung out in a newsstand on the corner of Hollywood Boulevard and Las Palmas where *Partisan Review* was sold; at Pickwick Bookstore, where she bought Thomas Mann's *Magic Mountain* (but was caught shoplifting other books); at the Laurel Theatre, where she saw foreign movies; and at the Highland Record Store, where she listened to classical music. She and her friends debated (she later claimed) questions like, How many extra years of life for Stravinsky would justify our dying on the spot?[115]

When she was fifteen, she entered Berkeley, where she met her first serious love interest, Harriet Sohmers. Sohmers was five years older than Sontag, a New Yorker who had spent a summer at Black Mountain College, where she met John Cage and Merce Cunningham and had her first lesbian affair, with Peggy Tolk-Watkins, later owner of a celebrated lesbian bar, the Tin Angel, on the Embarcadero in San Francisco. Sohmers introduced Sontag to that scene, and sex and sexuality became, and would remain, among Sontag's private preoccupations. As with everything else, she racked up the numbers. When she was seventeen, she made a list ("The Bi's Progress") of the men and women she had had sex with. It had thirty-six names.[116]

In 1949, Sontag transferred to the University of Chicago, where, in November 1950, she met Philip Rieff, then a twenty-eight-year-old sociology instructor. After a week, he proposed; in January, they married. Their son, David, was born in 1952. The relationship was emotionally and intellectually co-dependent. Sontag seems to have written some of Rieff's book reviews for him, and she had a major hand in—possibly wrote much of—the book that established his career, *Freud: The Mind of the Moralist*.[117] By the time it came out, in 1959, the marriage had come to an end. Sontag called Rieff "an emotional totalitarian," but domineering partners seem to have been, all her life, her type.[118]

Sontag graduated from Chicago at nineteen and enrolled as a graduate student in English at Harvard.* She hated the English department

---

* Rieff was teaching at Brandeis. They became good friends with E. H. Carr and his common-law wife, Joyce Marion Stock Forde. Carr had been invited to teach at Brandeis by Herbert Marcuse and was a visiting scholar at the Russian Research Center at Harvard. Harvard holds Leon Trotsky's exile papers.

and switched to philosophy, then got a fellowship from the American Association of University Women to go to Oxford to work on "the metaphysical presuppositions of ethics." She arrived in September 1957, leaving David behind. In December, she quit Oxford and went to Paris, hoping to reconnect with Sohmers, who had been living there since 1950 working off and on for the *New York Herald Tribune* and translating Sade's *Justine* for Maurice Girodias.[119] Sontag never returned to school. She had decided to end her marriage and her academic career in the same year. She was just turning twenty-five.

When Sontag arrived in Paris, she knew very little French and associated mainly with Americans. But France became her cultural base. Although she once described herself as a "self-Europeanized American," Europe for her was principally France.[120] She is buried there, in Montparnasse Cemetery.[121]

The reunion with Sohmers did not go well. "I am sure I've never been in such an absurd situation," Sohmers wrote in her journal soon after Sontag moved in, "living with someone I neither desire sexually nor feel strongly about."[122] Sontag clung to Sohmers, though, and they traveled in Europe. In September, she returned to the United States and to her son, and in January 1959, took an apartment in New York on the Upper West Side and started an editorial job at *Commentary*. Sohmers returned from Paris soon after and started living with Susan and David. But then, Sontag met María Irene Fornés.

Fornés was a crucial figure in Sontag's development. She was born in 1930 in Havana and had little formal schooling. Her father died when she was a teenager; in 1945, she and her mother and sister moved to New York City. She went to St. Joseph's Academy on Washington Place in the Village, where she learned English, and worked at various low-skilled jobs, which she claimed to enjoy. She later said she met Norman Mailer at a folk dance at the New School in 1947. She studied painting with Hans Hofmann, and it was probably in his class or at the New School that she became friends with Adele Morales, Mailer's second wife.*

In 1953, she met Harriet Sohmers. They became lovers, and Fornés moved to Europe to be around her. She saw *Waiting for Godot*, in the original Roger Blin production, and *Endgame* in Paris. "It turned my

---

* Morales, too, was born in Cuba; her mother was Spanish and her father was Peruvian. There is no certain basis for the assertion that she, Fornés, and Mailer had a ménage à trois (cf. Benjamin Moser, *Sontag* [New York: Ecco, 2019], 174).

life upside down," she said of *Godot*.[123] Around this time, she gave up painting. In 1957, just before Sontag arrived in Paris from Oxford, Fornés returned to New York.[124] And that is where, in 1960, Sontag met her, at a birthday party she was throwing for Sohmers. At first, she and Irene kept their affair a secret, but eventually, Fornés told Sohmers to move out.[125] Sohmers said that the episode ended her interest in female lovers.[126]

It was Fornés who got Sontag to focus on her writing. The story that she and Sontag told was that they were sitting in Le Figaro, a café in the West Village, probably in 1960, and Sontag was complaining about the difficulty she was having starting a novel. Fornés said, How hard can it be? Let's go home right now and start writing. They had not even been served their drinks. Unexpectedly (since they had just moved to New York and knew only a few people), an acquaintance came over to the table and invited them to a party. Sontag wanted to go; Fornés said no, they were going home. So they did. They sat at the kitchen table and Sontag began writing her first novel, *The Benefactor*. This became their practice.

Fornés was dyslexic, and she had not only never written anything in her life, she had hardly read anything. She got out a cookbook, opened it to a random page, copied the first words she saw, and began writing. When she ran out of inspiration, she found another sentence in the cookbook and copied some words from that.[127] It was the literal beginning of her career. She would become one the most celebrated dramatists of the Off-Broadway theater, winning eleven Obie awards, more than any other playwright.[128] When she taught, she used the kitchen-table format in her drama writing workshop, working right alongside her students.[129]

And Sontag would become Susan Sontag. Her essays soon began appearing in *Partisan Review*, where she was made theater critic (once Mary McCarthy's job), and *The New York Review of Books*. By 1963, when *The Benefactor*, which she dedicated to Fornés, came out, she had become a figure. Then she wrote "Notes on Camp" and became a celebrity.

It's significant that both women were still telling the story of the kitchen table years after. It was unusual for Sontag to turn down an invitation to a party, that's true, but she would have become a writer no matter what. That was why she left an academic world in which she was a rising star. The kitchen table story seems to stand for something for which there was no convenient anecdote, and this was the effect that having Fornés in her life had on Sontag's sensibility.[130]

Fornés was not untutored—Hofmann's class exposed her to advanced ideas about the visual arts, and she later adapted his push-pull theory of composition to dramatic form—but she was not an intellectual. Her response to art was unmediated by academic training. The contrast with Sontag can hardly have been greater. Sontag was not just one of the most cerebral of critics; she was one of the most cerebral of human beings. "My greatest unhappiness: the agonized dichotomy between the body and the mind," she wrote in her journal when she was sixteen, and that dichotomy tormented her throughout her life. It is one of the sources of her insecurity (startling to people who knew, from the public image, only the vanity).

Sontag's trouble connecting with things sensually was a source of frustration for her and for those who knew her. "Sexually it was a dud," Sohmers said about their relationship years later. "She was beautiful, but she was not sexual."[131] Even at the time of their affair, Sohmers found Sontag unstimulating. "I dislike so much about her," she wrote in her journal, ". . . the way she sings, girlish and off key, the way she dances, rhythmless and fake sexy." In another entry, after a visit to the Prado, in Madrid: "Susan drives me mad with her long scholarly explanations of things one only needs the eyes and ears of someone like Irene to see . . . I find these textbook dissertations of hers unbearable!"[132] It was the difference between Black Mountain and the University of Chicago.

Sontag made sense of life by reading about it. She forbade her son to look out the window when they rode in a train: he needed to read about a place if he wanted to understand it. She never looked out the window herself. Friends were struck by her unresponsiveness to painting and music.[133] Her experience was always intellectualized, disembodied. This is true even of her prose, which has many virtues but is not stylish or (except in a self-consciously learned way) witty. She is never funny, and she hated irony, which she saw as an evasion of seriousness (as sometimes it is).[134]

Sontag got satisfaction from writing, but she took little pleasure in it, and it shows. "Her prose," a New York Times reviewer remarked, "sometimes reads as if translated from the Polish."[135] Her fiction—even the commercially successful novels she published toward the end of her life, The Volcano Lover (1992), which was a New York Times bestseller, and *In America* (1999), which won a National Book Award—is weirdly lifeless. How she came to write two manifestos against seriousness and intellectualizing, "Notes on Camp" and "Against Interpretation," is kind of a mystery.

The subjects had been kicking around in Sontag's head for a long time. She started making notes about interpretation in 1956, possibly when she was working on the chapter on interpretation in *Freud: The Mind of the Moralist*. And she had taken an almost anthropological fascination, not entirely sympathetic, with gay subcultures ever since her year in San Francisco. "Notes on Camp" may have originated in 1958 as an unpublished essay called "Notes on Homosexuality."[136]

But the essays she wrote in 1964 were almost certainly inspired by her encounters with the New York art scene, and in particular, with Jack Smith's underground movie *Flaming Creatures*.

6.

Jack Smith was born in Columbus, Ohio, in 1932. His father drowned in a boating accident when Jack was young, and the family moved to Houston, at one point too poor even to live in a trailer park. After Smith's mother remarried, twice, they ended up in Wisconsin. Smith was discontented as a child (and somewhat paranoid as an adult). He moved to New York City around 1953, and in 1957, opened the Hyperbole Photography Studio in a storefront on Eighth Street, where he shot tableaus of people posed in exotic clothing, as though they were in film stills. (He scavenged clothes and fabrics discarded from Manhattan department stores.)[137] In the late summer and fall of 1962, over the course of eight or so afternoons, he shot his forty-two-minute film *Flaming Creatures*.

It was a good time for independent filmmakers and a bad time. The good part was a growing "cinema world": film societies, distribution outfits, and exhibition spaces—the infrastructure needed to get finished movies before a film-educated public. This had begun to emerge in the United States after the war with the founding of the University Film Producers' Association (later the University Film and Video Association), which rented movies to colleges (eventually a very big market), and with organizations like the Art in Cinema series, at the San Francisco Museum of Modern Art, and Cinema 16, in New York City, which provided venues for exhibition and discussion and served as a distribution service. By 1955, there were three hundred film societies in the United States. But by the 1960s, there were four thousand.[138] And the number of first-run art houses—theaters dedicated to new, mostly foreign films—rose from around 80 in 1950 to 450 in 1963.[139]

Film is a high-cap art form, and financing is always an issue. In 1955, the filmmaker Maya Deren founded the Creative Film Foundation, which secured grants for independent filmmakers. The army's prolific distribution of 16mm handheld cameras, such as the Bolex, used to make documentary and propaganda films, created a postwar surplus, and starting filmmakers were able to get equipment cheaply. And in 1962, the Film-Makers' Cooperative, a for-profit distribution center, was founded in New York City.[140]

One of the figures behind the Cooperative was Jonas Mekas, a man with whom the fortunes of *Flaming Creatures* would, much to Smith's annoyance, forever be tied. Mekas was from Lithuania, where he was born in a tiny farming town in 1922. When the Second World War broke out, Stalin, in accordance with a secret protocol in the Nonaggression Pact, annexed Lithuania. After Germany invaded the Soviet Union, less than two years later, and occupied Lithuania, Mekas seems to have been among those who welcomed the Nazis as liberators.

He worked on two weekly newspapers, *Naujosios Biržų zinios* (*New Biržai News*) and *Panėvėžio Apygardos Balsas* (*Panėvėžys Region Voice*), that published anti-Semitic articles and German propaganda. There is no evidence that Mekas himself wrote anti-Semitic material (the family was Protestant). Or that he had any involvement with the genocide of Lithuanian Jews. (Almost all of the country's two hundred thousand Jews were massacred with the assistance of the local population.) But in his postwar memoirs and reminiscences, he was vague about his wartime activities. The evidence suggests that he was a nationalist whose principal interest was poetry.[141]

Attempting to flee Lithuania, Jonas and his younger brother Adolfas ended up in a forced labor camp in Germany, where they spent eight months. Then, after the war ended, they spent four years in camps for displaced persons, finally immigrating to the United States in 1949. They were headed to Chicago, where a friend had arranged jobs for them, but when their ship pulled into New York harbor at ten o'clock at night and they saw the lights of Times Square, they decided they had to stay.[142]

Jonas borrowed three hundred dollars and bought a Bolex, and he began shooting a documentary of Williamsburg, where they were living. In 1955, with very little money, he and Adolfas started up the quarterly *Film Culture*, and in 1958, Jonas began a column, "Movie Journal," in *The Village Voice*.[143] He was the *Voice*'s first regular movie critic. Readers bombarded the paper with angry letters about the column, and 20th Century Fox removed it from its press mailing list, but that was exactly the kind of attention the *Voice* thrived on.[144]

At first, Mekas was hostile to the cinema avant-garde. He called avant-garde movies "film poems," and he criticized them as adolescent, creatively uninspired, technically crude, and thematically narrow. He also objected to what he called, somewhat opaquely, "the conspiracy of homosexuality." He wanted films that provided "a deeper insight into the human soul, emotions, experiences, as related to the whole rather than to exceptional abnormalities."[145] By 1962, though, he had undergone what he later called a Saint Augustine conversion, and *Film Culture* had become the leading journal of a kind of cinema that acquired various names: "underground cinema," "visionary film," or (Mekas's term for it) the New American Cinema. These movies were "abnormal" and poetic in exactly the style he had deplored seven years before.[146]

Flaming Creatures is nothing if not abnormal in Mekas's sense. Smith shot it with a three-lens Bolex on film stock that he stole from the outdated film bin at Camera Barn. The choice of stock, some of which was of exotic make, accounts for what is visually the most striking feature of the movie, the changing patina of the image—that is, the "filminess" of the film.[147] The movie was shot on the roof of the Windsor Theatre (then defunct) on the Lower East Side.

Flaming Creatures was very much Smith's project. The scenes and costumes all alluded to movies he was obsessed with, particularly Josef von Sternberg's films with Marlene Dietrich, such as *The Devil Is a Woman*, in which Dietrich is dressed in exotic guises, and the Technicolor dramas of the Universal star Maria Montez, such as *Cobra Woman* and *Ali Baba and the Forty Thieves*. The appeal of these movies was their shameless and tacky glamour, a quality Smith called "moldiness." By dispensing with serious acting and dialogue, or by treating them as jokes, they somehow got to what he thought of as the essence of cinematic pleasure.

Flaming Creatures is a string of loosely connected episodes: close-ups of men applying lipstick, for example, and a transvestite vampire looking like Marilyn Monroe or Veronica Lake emerging from a casket. The central episode is what appears to be a rape, interrupted by what appears to be an earthquake, which turns into what appears to be an orgy. It is often difficult to distinguish the men, most of whom are in drag, from the women; there is no dialogue apart from a few voice-overs; genitals are shown, though detumescent. The effect is dreamy and polymorphous, erotic but not quite pornographic. Total costs are said to have been three hundred dollars, most of it spent on the rental of the coffin.

Although the vision was Smith's, a number of figures in the downtown arts scene were involved: Cage and Cunningham's friend Ray Johnson; the screenwriter Ron Tavel, who would later work on Andy Warhol's films; Irving Rosenthal, the founder of *Big Table*, the first issue of which was impounded in 1958 for including an excerpt from William Burroughs's *Naked Lunch*; the musician La Monte Young, an influence on (among other things) the "drone" sound of the Velvet Underground; and the artist, composer, and filmmaker Tony Conrad.*

Conrad was, by happenstance, Smith's roommate. He had come to New York as a Cage disciple in 1962, after graduating from Harvard, and at first he thought Smith's work was just pornography.† But he helped create the soundtrack for *Flaming Creatures*, which was assembled on ¼-inch magnetic tape and featured an eclectic mix that included a Béla Bartók concerto for solo violin and the country and western song "It Wasn't God Who Made Honky-Tonk Angels," sung by Kitty Kallen, along with excerpts from the soundtracks of *Ali Baba and the Forty Thieves* and *The Devil Is a Woman*.[148]

Smith held screenings for friends in the winter of 1963. The movie's first semipublic exhibition was on March 9, at a benefit hosted by a fellow filmmaker, Piero Heliczer, and that is where Jonas Mekas saw it. He was entranced, and made it the subject of one of his *Voice* columns, where he called it "a most luxurious outpouring of imagination, of imagery, of poetry, of movie artistry—comparable only to the work of the greatest, like Von Sternberg."[149] On April 29, 1963, Mekas

---

* Young's influence on the Velvet Underground was via a Welsh classically trained musician, John Cale, who came to the United States in 1963 in part because of his fascination with Cage. Cale met Lou Reed, then a songwriter who would become front man for the group, in 1964; Reed was already developing a drone sound. Warhol became the band's manager in 1965.
† Conrad was later startled to realize that he had been a classmate and acquaintance of Ted Kaczynski—the Unabomber. They both majored in mathematics.

exhibited *Flaming Creatures* in a series he was running called Underground Midnight at the Bleecker Street Cinema. And that is where the troubles began.[150]

The reason it was a bad time to make an independent film was because of New York City's crackdown on risqué, even merely outré, entertainment—the crackdown that Andy Warhol's commissioned piece for the World's Fair, *Thirteen Most Wanted Men*, got caught up in. After *Flaming Creatures* was screened, the Bleecker Cinema shut down the Underground Midnight series on the grounds that it was illegal to exhibit a movie that did not have a license. Mekas promptly inaugurated a new series, the Filmmakers' Showcase, at the Gramercy Arts Theatre. He got around the licensing problem by taking donations rather than charging admission. *Flaming Creatures* was screened at the Gramercy twice in August, attracting large audiences. It became well enough known to receive a notice in the *Saturday Review*, where the movie critic, Arthur Knight, called it "a faggoty stag reel . . . defiling at once both sex and cinema."[151] (Knight would go on to write *Playboy*'s popular series Sex in Cinema.)

In December, *Film Culture* named Smith the winner of its fifth annual Independent Film Award. (Previous winners were John Cassavetes, Robert Frank, Ricky Leacock, and Stan Brakhage.) A screening scheduled as part of the award presentation was canceled when the theater, the Tivoli, locked its doors after receiving a phone call from the city bureau of licenses. Mekas climbed onto the roof of a car parked outside on Eighth Avenue and conducted the ceremony from there.[152] Not long after that fiasco, *Flaming Creatures* was banned from the Third International Experimental Film Competition in Knokke-Le-Zoute, Belgium. Mekas was on the jury, and he resigned in protest. He screened the movie in his hotel room, however, where it was seen by a number of European directors, including Jean-Luc Godard, Agnès Varda, and Roman Polanski. (Varda found it repulsive.) It was never formally exhibited at the festival, but it was given a special *film maudit* prize.*

The Knokke-Le-Zoute affair got attention within the industry—it made the front page of *Variety*—and *The New York Times* ran a story.[153] In April, *Flaming Creatures* was banned from a film festival at the

---

* "Cursed film." The term derives from Mallarmé's phrase *poète maudit*; it was adapted in 1949 by the French film critic André Bazin for his annual Festival du Film Maudit at Biarritz.

Moderna Museet in Stockholm after the director, Pontus Hultén, one of the most advanced museum directors in Europe, was told by the police that action could be taken if the movie was shown.[154] This, too, got written up in the trades. The industry naturally had an interest in knowing where the lines were being drawn.

Mekas wrote these controversies up in his *Voice* column, and his efforts got the movie attention—which, of course, was the idea. But not all of it was the good kind. On March 3, 1964, two undercover police officers stopped a showing of *Flaming Creatures* at the New Bowery Cinema on St. Mark's Place and arrested the projectionist (Ken Jacobs), the ticket seller (Florence Karpf), and the usher (Gerald Sims). Someone (it was the poet Diane di Prima) phoned Mekas, who rushed over and demanded to be arrested, too. The authorities saw no reason not to oblige him. Mekas saw the arrests as the occasion for a stand against film censorship, and the following week, he invited some New York writers to a private screening in hopes of enlisting them in his campaign.[155] This was very likely when Susan Sontag saw *Flaming Creatures* for the first time.

While he was finishing *Flaming Creatures*, Smith had published an essay called "The Perfect Filmic Appositeness of Maria Montez" in *Film Culture*. It is hard to imagine that Sontag did not read it. Even if she was not a regular reader of *Film Culture*, it makes sense to believe that Mekas gave copies of the issue to the people he was recruiting to testify at the trial so they would have a way to describe what Smith was up to. In the essay, Smith tried to explain how it is that we can enjoy art, like the Maria Montez costume dramas, that is bad in every conventional respect—stilted dialogue, hammy acting, thoroughly fake. "Why do we object to not being convinced—why can't we enjoy phoniness?" he asked.

> The primitive allure of movies is a thing of light and shadows. A bad film is one which doesn't flicker and shift and move through lights and shadows, contrasts, textures by way of light. If I have these I don't mind phoniness (or the sincerity of clever actors), simple minded plots (or novelistic "good" plots), nonsense or seriousness (I don't feel nonsense in movies as a threat to my mind since I don't go to movies for the ideas that arise from sensibleness of ideas.)[156]

Sontag was plainly struck by *Flaming Creatures*. Shortly after seeing it, she wrote a piece about it for *The Nation*, which had already run an editorial condemning the censorship of the movie.[157] "Art is, always, the sphere of freedom," Sontag wrote.

> In those difficult works of art, works which we now call *avant-garde*, the artist consciously exercises his freedom. And as the price the *avant-garde* artist pays for the freedom to be outrageous is the small numbers of his audience, the least of his rewards should be freedom from meddling censorship by the philistine, the prudish and the blind . . . Smith's film, involving as it does certain esoteric assumptions about experience and beauty, is obscure, precious, intimate. It would be as lost on today's mass audience as a puppet theatre is on a huge stage.[158]

This is not exactly a stand for the freedom of speech. It is a stand for the special privileges of the artist. In fact, the censorship issue didn't really interest Sontag. It only proved the public's obtuseness. What she responded to was the critical challenge the movie presented. It resisted intellect.

"The film is built out of a complex web of ambiguities and ambivalences, whose primary image is the confusion of male and female flesh," she wrote. "The shaken breast and the shaken penis become interchangeable with each other." She could see that it would be a mistake to try to translate this experience into the critical language ordinarily used to come to terms with serious art (which is what Smith was saying in his *Film Culture* essay). *Flaming Creatures* was somehow both serious and unserious. The images are spoofy; the effect is real.

"*Flaming Creatures*," Sontag concluded, "is a triumphant example of an aesthetic vision of the world."

> . . . The space in which *Flaming Creatures* moves is not the space of moral ideas, which is where American critics have traditionally located art. What I am urging is that there is not only a moral space, by whose laws *Flaming Creatures* would indeed come off badly; there is also aesthetic space, the space of pleasure. Here Smith's film moves and has its being.[159]

Mekas continued to play up the upcoming trial, at one point accepting an invitation to be interviewed along with Smith by Mike Wallace for his television program. Wallace began by asking Smith a question in which he suggested that *Flaming Creatures* was obscene. Smith stood up, cursed Wallace out, and left the studio. The program was never aired.[160]

And Smith hated the publicity that surrounded his movie. He believed that Mekas was using his film to promote himself and his idea of a New American Cinema. He began calling him Uncle Fishhook. He even came to resent Sontag. He thought that she, too, was using his work to promote herself and her critical agenda. He did not want to be appropriated.[161] He was not the only person to accuse Mekas of manipulation. "There are really two Jonases," Amos Vogel, co-founder with his wife, Marcia, of Cinema 16, told a journalist, "—one very dedicated, the other a Machiavellian maneuverer, a history rewriter, an attempted pope. He has two passions: film and power."[162]

For beneath the underground in the New York art world, there was a deeper underground. It included people like Tony Conrad, La Monte Young, Henry Flynt (another Harvard graduate and classmate of the Unabomber), and the Lithuanian émigré George Maciunas—artists and musicians associated with the movement called Fluxus. The Abstract Expressionists had wanted institutional recognition and the worldly goods (renown, sales) that came with it. So had Johns and Rauschenberg. John Cage remembered a conversation with de Kooning: "You and I are very different," de Kooning told him. "I want to be a great artist."[163] But the Fluxus artists were anti-capitalist, anti-imperialist, anti-racist, anti-hierarchical, anti-art. Their heroes were Cage and Duchamp.[164] They picketed Karlheinz Stockhausen. For them, people like Mekas and Sontag were hopelessly compromised figures.

The trial of Mekas et al. was held on June 2, 1964, before a three-judge panel that included a former New York City mayor, Vincent Impellitteri. Mekas had at first retained Ephraim London, the man who had argued *Burstyn v. Wilson*, the 1952 case in which the Supreme Court ruled that movies are protected by the First Amendment, and was involved in the Grove Press cases.[165] By the time the *Flaming Creatures* trial came around, though, Mekas and his co-defendants were represented by a lawyer who specialized in civil rights cases, and who had the fitting name Emile Zola Berman. (Four years later, Berman would represent Robert F. Kennedy's assassin, Sirhan Sirhan.)

The movie was shown in court as the judges watched impassively, two of them chewing on cigars.[166] They left little doubt about whether they found it obscene, but they allowed the defense to call a few of the many witnesses it had scheduled. Allen Ginsberg was one (the judges asked him if he was married); Sontag was another. Asked to give an example of pornography, she suggested posters outside movie theaters in Times Square that use sadistic imagery to advertise war movies.[167] This was Gershon Legman's position on comic books, and it was not likely to help the accused in this courtroom. The judges convicted Mekas, Jacobs, and Karpf, but acquitted Sims, on the grounds that he had been hired at the last minute, so was not witting. In August, Mekas and Jacobs were sentenced by another judicial panel to sixty days in the city workhouse. The sentences were suspended.*

In between the trial and the sentencing, Mekas served as cameraman for Andy Warhol's eight-hour movie of the Empire State Building, *Empire*. Warhol had been a regular at Mekas's screenings, and he was infatuated with Jack Smith. His six-hour *Sleep* (1963) is an answer to *Flaming Creatures*: if you want to film a dream, this is what the camera really sees. Mekas loved Warhol's work anyway. Mekas was on the side of whatever was far out. And he could sit through anything.

Sontag's first piece of writing after the *Flaming Creatures* trial was a review of a book by Eugène Ionesco. She didn't think much of Ionesco's plays, but she had a theory about them. "It has been said that Ionesco's early plays are 'about' meaninglessness, or 'about' non-communication," she explained. "But this misses the important fact that in much of modern art one can no longer really speak of subject matter in the old sense. Rather, the subject matter is the technique."[168] This is the position—the radical marginalization of content—that she would elaborate in the next two essays she wrote, "Notes on Camp" and "Against Interpretation," and that would become the statement she intended to make with her first critical book, *Against Interpretation*, a book she called "a theory of my own sensibility."[169]

---

* That was hardly the end of the saga. In 1967, the case, *Jacobs v. New York*, reached the United States Supreme Court, where the appeal was dismissed as moot since the period of the suspended sentences had expired. But Justice Abe Fortas voted to reverse the conviction. This would return to haunt him when, in 1968, Lyndon Johnson nominated him to replace the retiring Earl Warren as chief justice. Senators opposed to Fortas, led by Strom Thurmond, made an issue of the fact that he had voted to allow obscene movies to be exhibited, and *Flaming Creatures* was screened at least a dozen times for senators in the Capitol building. The nomination was defeated when a cloture vote failed. The next chief justice, Warren Burger, was appointed by Richard Nixon.

Sontag wrote "Notes on Camp" in Paris, where she spent about a month in August and September 1964.[170] The main part of the essay is dedicated to Oscar Wilde. Sontag had taken an interest in a long piece about Wilde in *The New Yorker* by W. H. Auden that was mostly concerned with Wilde's relationship with Lord Alfred Douglas and his trial for sodomy.[171] Sontag was therefore paying homage to Wilde's martyrdom, but she was also proposing to emulate his talent for the epigram. Her essay is a sequence of numbered sections—the "notes"—modeled on Wilde's preface to *The Picture of Dorian Gray*. (Unlike Wilde's preface, however, "Notes on Camp" does not rely on paradox and chiasmus, and it is not witty.)

Before she wrote "Notes on Camp," Sontag had discussions about publishing it in a glossy large-format magazine called *Show*, owned and edited by Huntington Hartford, the A&P heir. *Show* was by no means a mass-market or show-biz publication. It published writers like Jack Kerouac and James Baldwin (both with essays on Shakespeare); Arthur Schlesinger, Jr., was the movie critic. Sontag's interest may have been piqued by an article by Russell Lynes in the December 1963 issue of *Show* called "Bad Taste, Good Taste, Distaste," which touched on her topic. But the *Show* deal didn't happen (it may have fallen through because the magazine was being sold, Hartford having lost $5 million on it), and "Notes on Camp" appeared in the fall 1964 issue of a very different sort of magazine, *Partisan Review*.

Years later, William Phillips claimed that he had to fight his co-editor Philip Rahv to get the piece accepted.[172] Rahv was dead when Phillips said this, but if it is true, then Rahv was exercising uncharacteristically poor editorial judgment. "Notes on Camp" has sensation written all over it. It led to stories in *Time* (where Sontag was described as "one of Manhattan's brightest young intellectuals") and *The New York Times Magazine* (where she was referred to as "the Sir Isaac Newton of Camp").[173] The title itself was repurposed endlessly (as in Victor Navasky's "Notes on Cult; or, How to Join the Intellectual Establishment," published in *The New York Times Magazine* soon after *Against Interpretation* came out). Andy Warhol made a seventy-minute movie called *Camp*, starring Jack Smith. Sontag had put the word on everyone's lips. And "Notes on Camp" is the most famous piece she ever wrote. Later in life, she would react with cold fury when people asked her about it.[174] This was probably because she resented being known as a person who transformed an insider, "downtown" term into an uptown parlor game. But it was also because she had changed her own critical position.

The appearance in print of the word "camp" dates back to the beginning of the twentieth century, and it was generally associated with the tastes of male homosexuals. Sontag acknowledged this: "[H]omosexuals, by and large, constitute the vanguard—and the most articulate audience—of Camp," she explained.[175] But the point of her essay—its originality, really—was to liberate camp from its subcultural origins and make it available to everyone.

Camp is a taste for the exaggerated and outlandish, the artificial and mannered—the queer. But you do not have to identify as queer to indulge it. Sontag called it "a certain mode of estheticism. It is *one* way of seeing the world as an esthetic phenomenon." Camp is a vacation from morality and content. "[O]ne cheats oneself, as a human being" she wrote, "if one has respect only for the style of high culture, whatever else one may do or feel on the sly."[176]

Sontag overloaded the essay with references, and this produced a basic confusion. Is camp an attribute of certain things (Tiffany lamps, say)? Or is it a way of responding to anything, on the theory that all things can be read as parodies of themselves? Many of Sontag's examples—Aubrey Beardsley, *The Devil Is a Woman*, Bette Davis, Ronald Firbank—suggested the former, but some suggested the latter: *The Maltese Falcon* ("among the greatest Camp movies ever made"), "much of Mozart," Henry James's *The Wings of the Dove*, "[t]he public manner and rhetoric of [Charles] de Gaulle."[177] These (to most readers) riddling examples helped re-create the sense of camp as a coterie taste: you're either in on the joke or you're not.

And it gave Sontag's classification a popular appeal, much like Russell Lynes's article "Highbrow, Middlebrow, Lowbrow," published in *Harper's* in 1949, and the English sociolinguist Alan S. C. Ross's article on U and non-U (*U* meaning "upper class") speech, popularized by Nancy Mitford in *Encounter* in 1954. These labels were invitations to readers to draw up their own lists. You can get sucked down these rabbit holes very quickly. *Flaming Creatures* reflects camp tastes (Dietrich movies, Kitty Kallen). But does that make *Flaming Creatures* itself camp? Not only could much commercial culture seem to have camp potential; so could much avant-garde art. The opportunities for debate were endless.

"Against Interpretation" appeared in the December 1964 issue of the *Evergreen Review*. In the world of little magazines, the *Evergreen Review* was big. Grove had just relaunched it that spring with a larger trim size and a glossy format. Circulation rose to around fifty thousand, more than twice the circulation of *Partisan Review*.[178] The essay has two epigraphs. One is by Wilde, which was appropriate since Sontag's essay is consistent with, though by no means a copy of, Wilde's essay "The Critic as Artist" (1891). The other is by Willem de Kooning, who, interviewed by the British art critic David Sylvester, said: "Content is a glimpse of something, an encounter like a flash. It's very tiny— very tiny, content."[179]* De Kooning meant that all he needed to make a painting was a pictorial idea (the content); he could then play with it formally in multiple ways. This was very much to Sontag's point. Content is an occasion for form.

Her choice of a painter was telling, because music and the visual arts are the least "interpretable" in the sense Sontag meant. In a way, her essay was an attack on contemporary fiction and drama for lagging behind in formal experimentation, for insisting on having a message. "Most American novelists and playwrights are really either journalists or gentleman sociologists and psychologists," she complained. "They are writing the literary equivalent of program music."[180]

Her chief target was the search for hidden meanings, in particular, criticism that derived from Freud and Marx. "[I]nterpretation," she said, "is the revenge of the intellect upon art." This was a way of saying that people who interpret are people who can't handle the experience. "Interpretation makes art manageable, conformable," she said. What is needed is "to recover our senses . . . In place of hermeneutics we need an erotics of art."[181] This can be read as the lesson she learned from Irene Fornés, and from another friend, the artist Paul Thek, who is supposed to have ended conversations about art by saying "I'm against interpretation."[182] Sontag dedicated her book to him.

In "Notes on Camp," Sontag had written that camp "blocks out content," that it "incarnates a victory of 'style' over 'content,' of 'esthetics'

---

* The interview was published in 1963 in the first issue of *Location*, a little magazine founded by Harold Rosenberg and Thomas Hess and edited by Donald Barthelme. Its second issue, Summer 1964, would be its last.

over 'morality.'"[183] This implied that there remained a content-centered kind of art. But in "Against Interpretation," she collapsed that distinction. Now all critical response should be a response to form. She made this the message of her book.

In "Notes on Camp," the formalist aesthetic is still in the "vacation from seriousness" mode. But when formalism was expanded into a principle of all criticism, it resulted in claims like the one Sontag made about Leni Riefenstahl's Nazi films *Triumph of the Will* and *Olympia*. Those movies, she wrote, "transcend the categories of propaganda or even reportage . . . Through Riefenstahl's genius as a filmmaker, the 'content' has—let us even assume, against her intentions—come to play a purely formal role."[184]

The final essay in *Against Interpretation*, "One Culture and the New Sensibility," first appeared in *Mademoiselle*. (*Mademoiselle* had given Sontag a "merit award" in 1963, which gives us an idea of the nature of Sontag's celebrity.) She argued that contemporary artists—she mentions, among others, Morton Feldman, Frank Stella, and Merce Cunningham— make work that is technically complex and that requires as much training to understand as science does. But she then went on to describe a "new sensibility." The "Matthew Arnold idea of culture" is no longer tenable, she says.

> From the vantage point of this new sensibility, the beauty of a machine or of the solution to a mathematical problem, of a painting by Jasper Johns, of a film by Jean-Luc Godard, and of the personalities and music of the Beatles is equally accessible.[185]

This, too, was not news in New York City in 1965. As usual, the fashion magazines were way ahead of the academy. The April 1965 issue of *Harper's Bazaar*, edited by Richard Avedon, mixed photographic portraits of Johns and Rauschenberg with pictures of Ringo Starr, Bob Dylan, and fashion models, all rendered in the same playful style.

But it was the final sentence in *Against Interpretation*, and it branded Sontag as popular culture enthusiast and critical relativist. Howe complained that she "employs the dialectical skills and accumulated knowledge of intellectual life in order to bless the new sensibility as a dispensation of pleasure, beyond the grubby reach of interpretation and thereby, it would seem, beyond the tight voice of judgment."[186] Sontag came to stand for permissiveness, for leveling, for an art of "anything goes." "One of the mid-sixties free-swinging ladies," *The New York Times* called her.[187] In *The New Republic*, she was "the Camp girl, who burns for 'style' and 'sensibility' while consigning content and ethical involvement to the fire."[188]

But Sontag was not a permissivist or a leveler. She was not saying that the Beatles are as good as Thomas Mann. She was saying that the fine arts can be approached with the same openness and lack of pretension that people bring to pop songs and Hollywood movies. And she wasn't thinking of the kind of critic she wanted Irving Howe to be. She was thinking of the kind of critic she wanted to be.

7.

Sontag's promotion of the aesthetic may have seemed dangerous to writers like Howe who saw literature as a site of moral instruction, but there was nothing radical about it. She was using the term as it was used when it was first applied to the arts in the eighteenth century. An aesthetic appreciation precisely allows you to bracket content. In eighteenth-century Britain, this might be Catholic iconography; for Sontag, it turned out to be Nazi ideology.

How radical was this? It's true that there were Freudian and Marxist interpreters around in 1964, and the myth-and-archetype school of literary criticism that descended from Northrop Frye included symbol hunters of the kind Sontag ridiculed.* But no sophisticated student of literature and the arts would have found her attack on moralizing and hidden meanings exceptionable. Sontag's strictures on paraphrase repeat what the New Critics had been saying since the 1940s. Her remarks about Riefenstahl duplicate the argument for awarding Ezra Pound the Bollingen Prize for his elegy for fascism, the *Pisan Cantos*, in 1948. Greenberg's art criticism is pure formalism. Meyer Schapiro, in his article "Nature of Abstract Art" in 1937 (the article he thought Greenberg had cribbed from), had argued that with abstraction, "the pure form once masked by an extraneous content was liberated."[189] In fact, Sontag

---

* Psychoanalytic criticism as an academic school does not really begin until 1966, the year of Frederick Crews's *The Sins of the Father: Hawthorne's Psychological Themes* and Norman Holland's *Psychoanalysis and Shakespeare*.

had made a point of looking up Schapiro's article when she was writing "Against Interpretation."[190]

And what was replacing the New Criticism was equally anti-interpretative. Finding meanings is the practice that free play subverts. When Sontag was putting her book together in France in 1965, she met Jacques Derrida, and after *Against Interpretation* came out, she sent him a copy. Derrida read it, he told her, "with rapture," and he promised to send her his own essay "against interpretation." This was the two-part article in *Critique*, "De la grammatologie"—the article that introduced deconstruction to the world.[191]

What *was* new in Sontag's essay, and what was responsive to her cultural moment, was not the attack on interpretation. It was the phrase "an erotics of art." It is not completely obvious what this means. Sontag's only gloss is: "The function of criticism should be to show *how it is what it is*, even *that it is what it is*, rather than to show *what it means*."[192] Whatever this is, it does not sound like an "erotics."

Sontag seems to have been picking up on two things. One had to do with the censorship situation. The standard legal defense of works of art and literature charged with obscenity was that the artist or writer needed to use taboo words or images to achieve a truer representation or a more pointed social commentary. At Mekas's trial, for example, his lawyer told the court that *Flaming Creatures* was a "satire on our general culture's use of sex to the point that it is an anti-sex film."[193] A spokesman for Mekas's Film-Makers' Cooperative explained that the movie was a "fantastic lampoon of commercialized sex and sexual mores." An instructor from the New School testified that it was "full of symbolic motifs."[194] These people were all interpreting, and they were using interpretation as a signal that they were being serious. If you can interpret something, it must have value.

But this was all a distraction from the simple fact that *Flaming Creatures* is, mildly but ineluctably, sexually arousing. That is why some people wanted to see it and why other people wanted to prevent them from seeing it. Arousal has always been something that art and literature trigger and feed. There are genitalia in the cave paintings. But arousal was not a legal defense. It took someone to say that the erotic is a legitimate feature of art, independent of the demands of representation or social commentary. It is strange that Sontag was the person to say this, but she was.

The other thing she was picking up on was a new emphasis in the contemporary arts. "[I]t is eyesight alone," Greenberg had written in 1958.[195] He meant that by getting rid of figural representation, abstraction had freed the eye, and painting and even sculpture could be contemplated in purely visual terms. The same bias was behind Trilling's queasy avoidance of poetry readings and theater as substitutes for the solitary reading experience, and behind the New Critics' indifference to "breath." For these men, aesthetic experience was disembodied.

The new emphasis when Sontag was writing was not on the body as a subject of the artwork. It was on the body of the artist as part of the artwork—in performance art, in New Music concerts, in poetry readings. Sontag was familiar with quite a few artists who were involved in these developments. One was Allan Kaprow, the "inventor" of the Happening (an offhand term that stuck). Kaprow took Pollock as a model. "I am convinced that to grasp a Pollock's impact properly," he wrote in 1958, "one must be something of an acrobat, constantly vacillating between an identification with the hands and body that flung the paint and stood 'in' the canvas, and allowing the markings to entangle and assault one into submitting to their permanent and objective character."[196]

Sontag collaborated with Kaprow on an article on Happenings in 1965 in a little magazine called *Second Coming*. Her editor there was another friend, Carolee Schneemann, who had in 1963 begun making work in which her own, usually nude, body was an extension of the painting with *Eye Body: 36 Transformative Actions for Camera*. The following year, Schneemann produced *Meat Joy*, a piece that had, as she described it, "the character of an erotic rite."[197] Eight bikini-clad men and women perform choreographed routines in which, for over an hour, they cover themselves with paint, writhe on the floor with raw fish, chickens, and sausages (not unlike the orgy sequence in *Flaming Creatures*), and shine flashlights, to the accompaniment of a soundtrack of pop songs and random sounds. *Meat Joy* was performed in the Festival de la Libre Expression at the American Center in Paris in May 1964, then in London that June, and finally at Judson Memorial Church in New York City in November.[198] Schneemann, too, saw her work as an extension of Pollock's integration of the body into the act of painting.[199]

Sontag also knew about Yoko Ono's work; she mentioned her in the article on Happenings. Ono's father was a banker, and the family moved to New York from Tokyo after the war. She attended Sarah Lawrence

College in Bronxville, but in 1956, she dropped out and moved to the Village with her husband, the composer Toshi Ichiyanagi. (They had met in the music library at Juilliard.) Ichiyanagi attended Cage's 1958 Town Hall concert and became fascinated by his work, and he and Ono took a loft on Chambers Street and, in 1960 and 1961, staged a well-attended concert series there. Maciunas came to some of these, and that is how Ono became associated with Fluxus.

Ono's first solo concert, *Works by Yoko Ono*, took place at the Carnegie Recital Hall in November 1961. It involved some twenty artists and musicians (Jonas Mekas was a participant) performing various acts—eating, breaking dishes, throwing bits of newspaper. Someone offstage flushed a toilet at designated intervals. A man was positioned in the back of the darkened auditorium to give the audience a sense of foreboding. The piece finished, according to the account in *The Village Voice*, with the artist's own amplified "sighs, breathing, gasping, retching, screaming—many tones of pain and pleasure mixed with a jibberish of foreign-sounding language that was no language at all."[200] *The New York Times* reported that the hall was "packed."[201]

Ono spent the next two years in Japan, but she returned to perform *Cut Piece* at Carnegie Recital Hall in March 1965. This is a work in which audience members are invited to come onstage and cut off pieces of the artist's clothing. She also performed *Bag Piece*, in which two performers get inside a bag, remove their clothes, put them on again, and emerge from the bag.[202]*

Listed on the concert program as "personal mgr. for Miss Ono" was Charlotte Moorman, from Arkansas, a classical cellist who had studied at Juilliard but realized she was bored playing classical music. Her involvement in the New Music scene came through a Juilliard classmate, Kenji Kobayashi, who introduced her to Ichiyanagi and Ono. She began performing pieces by Cage and Young, and made her solo debut playing experimental music in a downtown loft in 1963.[203]

The same year, she turned herself into an impresario, and she ended up running, more or less annually, a Festival of the Avant Garde that lasted fifteen incarnations. Moorman hated the term "avant-garde": she was performing in the present tense—how could she be ahead of

---

* Ono met John Lennon in London in 1966. Their relationship began in 1968; they married in Gibraltar ("near Spain") in 1969.

her time? But she added the term to the name of her festivals to warn visitors—"just so everyone would know that the festivals are not composed of works by Mozart."[204] The festivals got an enormous amount of attention, even if some of it was bemused or mocking. The first one, in 1963, was written up for Huntington Hartford's *Show* by Gloria Steinem, in a piece accompanied by portrait photos of Moorman, Cage and Tudor, Earle Brown, the percussionist Max Neuhaus, and Morton Feldman. Steinem was skeptical of the New Music, but the photographs made the musicians look like movie stars.[205]

Moorman met Nam June Paik in 1964, when she was putting together her second festival, to be held at Judson Hall, across from Carnegie Hall on Fifty-Seventh Street. Paik was born in Seoul. His family left the country in 1950, when he was eighteen, and he was educated in Japan and Germany. He listened to Schoenberg and Stravinsky when he was in high school in Korea, and although he went to Germany ostensibly to study philosophy, he became involved in the New Music scene there, performing antic pieces of his own composition, some of which involved destroying his instruments. In 1958, he met Cage in Darmstadt and became friends with Stockhausen.

Stockhausen was in New York when Moorman was putting together her 1964 festival, and she asked his permission to stage a piece he had written in 1961 in collaboration with his partner, later wife, Mary Bauermeister, called *Originale* (*Originals*). It had been performed in Cologne, where Paik was in the cast.

Originale is a complex work of musical theater, scored to run for ninety-four minutes, with eighteen scenes and twenty-one performers. The format is the same as Cage's Black Mountain *Theatre Piece No. 1*: the performers are doing unrelated things simultaneously, but each action is precisely timed. Each performer has a set of instructions, and each is cast to play himself or herself (hence "originals"): a Director, a Poet, Painters, and so on, including Stagehands, who go about their business as usual. Stockhausen told Moorman that she had his permission, so long as she used Nam June Paik. Moorman had never heard of Paik, but by chance, Paik had just arrived in New York, and they met. Their collaboration would last for decades.[206]

Originals was performed for five nights at the festival. Maciunas and other Fluxus artists picketed the event, carrying signs with slogans such as "Fight the Art of the Social Climbers" and "Action Against

Cultural Imperialism." One of their targets was Moorman, who Maciunas seems to have regarded as a competitor; another was Stockhausen. Henry Flynt had heard him give a talk at Harvard in which he seemed to disparage jazz. Music like jazz and the blues, associated with Black musicians, was important to Fluxus figures like Flynt and Conrad, and Stockhausen was branded as a cultural imperialist.[207] These antagonisms were less meaningful than they appeared, though. They were the consequence of many artists all fundamentally engaged in pushing the boundaries, and all wanting attention. They therefore made boundaries of one another.

Inside Judson Hall, the audience's seats were clustered facing in different directions. Props included German shepherds, hens, a chimpanzee, saxophonists, percussionists, a piano, a ladder, a movie screen, and a large clock. The actors threw rotten apples at the audience (or vice versa: perceptions differed). Women posing as models (Olga Kluver and Letty Eisenhauer) stripped to their underwear. Allen Ginsberg recited a poem that included a reference to John Foster Dulles. Moorman played the cello (she had her choice of music each performance) while sitting on a balcony railing above the stage. Kaprow, who helped recruit the cast, played the part of the Director.[208] Paik's performance was recollected by one audience member as follows:

> Standing on a chair, fully dressed, Paik sprayed his head and upper body with shaving lather, dowsed himself with rice, and then plunged into a washtub. He scooped up some of the soapy water into his shoe and gargled with it.[209]

The spectacle, outside and inside the hall, attracted attention. All five evenings were sold out, and people were turned away at the door. *The New York Times* and the *New York Herald Tribune* ran two stories each on the production; *The Village Voice* ran three; it was covered in *Time*. Moorman was invited to appear on *The Tonight Show*—which she did, performing a piece by Cage.[210]

Schneemann had a small part in *Originals*, and helped with costumes and props. During a rehearsal, when Moorman was having trouble with her gown, Schneemann suggested she wear a sheet. Moorman tried, but it fell off when she climbed to the balcony. She played anyway and told Schneemann she liked the way it felt.[211] In the performance, she did not perform naked, but she did wear, one night, a tightly wrapped gauze dress with, as the audience could plainly see, nothing on underneath.

This seems to have been what led to Moorman's nude performances, the first of which was of Paik's *Cello Sonata No. 1 for Adults Only* at the New School in January 1965. As she played, she removed her clothing one item at a time, and ended up lying naked on the stage holding her cello on top of her.[212] Finally, on February 9, 1967, Moorman was arrested by undercover police officers during a performance of Paik's *Opera Sextronique* at a Times Square theater leased by the Film-Makers' Cooperative. Mekas had offered them the space rent free.

In the third "aria" of the *Opera*, when Moorman came onstage topless, she was arrested and thrown into a paddy wagon. She spent the night in jail and was convicted of a misdemeanor for indecent exposure. Two months later, the governor, Nelson Rockefeller, signed a law banning topless waitresses that nevertheless provided an exemption for women who exposed their breasts while entertaining.[213] Ten years after that, when Paik and Moorman staged a re-creation of *Opera Sextronique*, the two policemen who had arrested her in 1967 performed as actors.[214]

Although they felt bound to discretion by a shared commitment to experimentation, Cage, Cunningham, and Johns hated Paik and Moorman's work.[215] It was the same problem they had had with Rauschenberg when he broke with the dance company: they made themselves the center of the artwork. The work was no longer about sound and movement. It was about bodies, and sexualized bodies are a distraction.

But that was exactly Paik and Moorman's intent. The naked body in their pieces was intended to arouse. "Sex has been a main theme in art and literature," Paik explained to a journalist later. "Why not in music?" In Germany, he said, he had wanted to stage a performance of the Moonlight Sonata by a nude woman. "I thought it would be very beautiful to do this in Germany. But I couldn't find anyone to do it . . . In my 'Etude for Pianoforte,' I wanted to have a girl who would take off many pairs of panties. I even tried to get prostitutes, but none of them would agree."[216] Meeting Moorman was a gift from the gods.

Schneemann, too, was ostracized. Maciunas "excommunicated" her from Fluxus, she said. "[I]t had to do with too much sensuality, too much self expression, basically overt physicality and the explicit body."[217] *Cut Piece* arouses more dangerous urges, but it, too, is plainly sexual. Next to these artists and the extremes they were willing to go to, Sontag's "erotics of art" seems almost timid.*

Against Interpretation was an owl that flew at dusk. Before 1966, when the book came out, Sontag showed no interest in politics. In all the time she lived in Paris, she never mentioned French politics in her notebooks, or even the Algerian War—even though that was the chief preoccupation of French intellectuals.[218] A good deal of the appeal of camp, as she explained, is that it is "disengaged, depoliticized—or at least apolitical."[219] And, as passages like the one on Riefenstahl and her dismissal of Marx suggest, the aesthetic view she was proposing required ignoring politics.

But then several things happened to make this position outmoded. Two of those things, the women's movement and gay liberation, Sontag had almost nothing to do with. She disliked being thought of as a woman writer, and she was secretive about her own sexuality. In letters to her sister, she referred to Irene as Carlos; Judith did not learn that Sontag had female lovers until just before Susan's death.[220] Even during the AIDS crisis, when many of her friends were dying (Paul Thek was one), she did not come out. But those social movements, with their refocused attention on the politics of representation—what Beauvoir and Friedan had critiqued—did bring interpretation back with a vengeance.

And then the American Pop movement ended. Pop Art had established itself internationally in 1964, with Rauschenberg's triumph at the Venice Biennale—even though Rauschenberg was not himself a Pop artist. But then, in the United States and Britain, Pop lost its edge. If Pop Art can be understood as consumerist iconography jumping the barrier into fine art, the end of Pop can be described as fine art jumping the barrier back to consumerism. By 1965, Pop was a fashion, a design style. Pop Art was talked about right alongside popular entertainment and commercial goods as though there was no distinction. This might look like the consummation of Sontag's idea of "one sensibility," but

---

* Many other works in the period Sontag was writing were body-centered: Yayoi Kusama's *Accumulation No. 1* (a chair covered with fabric penises) at the Green Gallery in 1962; Paul Thek's *Meat* pieces (wax sculptures made to look like raw meat with clumps of hair attached) at the Stable Gallery in 1964; Robert Delford Brown's *Meat Show* (a display of 3,600 pounds of raw meat) in the Manhattan meat-packing district in 1964; Shigeko Kubota's *Vagina Painting* at the Cinematheque in 1965. The ordinary body was the central theme of Judson Dance Theater and its leading choreographer and dancer, Yvonne Rainer. Sontag attended the dance concerts there.

what it really meant was that an art created by appropriating packaging had been appropriated back by packaging.[221]

This was also the moment when liberal attacks on commercial culture virtually disappeared, when the vices of popular culture became a largely conservative obsession. Why this happened when it happened is mysterious, but it may have been as simple as the fact that with the Beatles, youth culture penetrated the adult market, and the Beatles were followed a few years later by Hollywood movies that also appealed to educated adults. In Sontag's case, however, her interest went elsewhere because of an event with which she did become powerfully engaged. This was the War in Vietnam.

16

FREEDOM IS THE FIRE

James Baldwin on the steps of the capitol in Montgomery, Alabama, where Martin Luther King, Jr., delivered his "How long? Not long!" speech, March 25, 1965, the conclusion of the march for voting rights that started in Selma. Behind Baldwin is Walter Reuther, president of the United Auto Workers. To Baldwin's left is Bayard Rustin, and next to Rustin is A. Philip Randolph, founder of the Leadership Conference on Civil Rights and president of the Brotherhood of Sleeping Car Porters. Photograph by Stephen F. Somerstein. (*Getty Images*)

1.

James Baldwin and Norman Mailer, both New Yorkers, met in Paris. This was not unusual, for after the war, Paris continued to play the same role in transatlantic culture it had played since the nineteenth century: it was the crossroads, the place people came to paint, write, and perform. Most of the expatriate writers and artists who had been displaced by the German invasion returned as soon as the city was liberated: Samuel Beckett, Gertrude Stein, Alberto Giacometti, almost all of the Surrealists. And new visitors flooded the city. More than three hundred American artists worked in Paris after the war, including Ed Clark, Romare Bearden, Richard Serra, Robert Rauschenberg, Joan Mitchell, Larry Rivers, Al Held, Ellsworth Kelly, Sam Francis, Kenneth Noland, and Jules Olitski. Noland, Kelly, and Olitski, who became leading painters in the second major avant-garde movement championed by Clement Greenberg, color-field abstraction, had their first shows in Paris.[1] Joan Mitchell and the publisher Barney Rosset were married in Paris. She had her studio there. John Cage lived there for most of 1949, when he met and became friends with Pierre Boulez. Philip Glass spent two years in Paris studying music. The painter Beauford Delaney moved there in 1953 and stayed. The art critic Annette Michelson began her career in Paris, where she lived for sixteen years.*

Saul Bellow began *The Adventures of Augie March* in Paris.† Allen Ginsberg began his poem "Kaddish" in a Paris café. James Jones wrote *The Thin Red Line* in Paris. Paris was where Chester Himes, who moved there in 1953, created the Harlem police detectives of his thrillers, Gravedigger Jones and Coffin Ed Johnson. Lawrence Ferlinghetti lived there for three years. John Ashbery lived there for ten years and wrote his second book of poems, *The Tennis Court Oath*, there. William Burrough's *Naked Lunch* and Vladimir Nabokov's *Lolita* were first published in Paris.

There were so many English-language speakers in Paris after the war that half a dozen literary magazines started up to serve them: *Zero*, *Points*, *Merlin*, *New-Story*, *Locus Solus*, *Id*, *Janus*, *Transition* (not the interwar *transition*, edited by Maria McDonald and Eugène Jolas), and *The Paris Review*, coedited by George Plimpton and then, after Plimpton moved the main office to New York, by Robert Silvers, who, in 1963, became co-founder and -editor of *The New York Review of Books*.[2] There were English-language bookstores, notably Gaït's English Bookshop and Le Mistral, later renamed Shakespeare and Company. (The

---

* Roy Lichtenstein was in Paris briefly intending to study at the Sorbonne, but he had to return to the United States when his father became ill.
† Much of *Augie March* was written in Europe—in Paris, Salzburg, and Rome. Bellow liked to boast that he did not write a single word of it in Chicago, his hometown (he was born in Canada and moved to Chicago when he was nine) and the city in which the novel is set.

Germans had forced Sylvia Beach to close the original store, where she had published *Ulysses*.)

Jazz was always popular in Paris, and many American musicians moved there after the war. Some of them played with Sidney Bechet, who began performing in Paris in 1925 and moved there permanently in 1951, and some with Dizzy Gillespie, whose 1948 tour introduced bebop to Europe.[3] Miles Davis played in Paris and fell in love with the Left Bank chanteuse Juliette Gréco. Hundreds more American culture-makers and culture-consumers passed through the city, for a week or a month or a season, part of a tourism boom that took off in the summer of 1949 and lasted a decade. In 1950, 264,000 Americans visited France. This was still well below prewar volume—in 1925, France had 400,000 American tourists—but the numbers increased steadily. In 1960, 792,000 Americans visited France.[4]

The reason bad economic conditions didn't prevent Americans from coming to Paris and even from moving there was that although those conditions made life hard for people with francs, they made life very inexpensive for people with dollars. The people with dollars didn't have more comforts than the people with francs did. They also, right after the war, had to stand in line at food shops and, for long after that, share communal water closets. But everything was cheaper for them. From the Treaty of Versailles to the reascendance of de Gaulle and the birth of the Fifth Republic in 1958, the key to the attraction of Paris was the exchange rate. It's a lot easier for a city to become the capital of the modern when it's cheap for foreigners to live there.

This was especially true for the Americans and the British. Before the First World War, the value and exchange rates of the currencies of the United Kingdom, France, and the United States were stabilized by the gold standard. From 1815 to 1914, the rate of inflation in Britain and France was virtually zero. The war—that is, the amount of money and debt governments issued to pay for the war—changed that. Britain, France, and Germany all abandoned the gold standard, explicitly or in practice. After the war, the inflationary effects were greater in Germany and France than in America and Britain, which were better off financially.[5] This was reflected in exchange rates. In 1919, a dollar was worth 5.45 francs; in 1928, it was worth 25 francs, and a pound was worth between 120 and 125 francs.[6] In 1925, Britain imposed severe austerity in order to reestablish gold convertibility at the prewar exchange rate of around five dollars to the pound. France did not. When the franc stabilized briefly, in 1929, it stood at roughly 20 percent of its 1914 value in dollars.[7]

The problem after the Second World War was not only debt; it was also bad policy and widespread destruction of the country's capital stock.[8] In the postwar years, inflation soared. From 1945 to 1948, the rate of inflation in France was 50 percent a year. In 1945, prices rose 61 percent, and the franc lost 38 percent of its purchasing power. In 1946, prices rose 80 percent; they rose 58 percent in 1947 and 36 percent in 1948.[9] The steady devaluation of the franc raised the exchange value of the dollar and the pound. Two months after the Liberation, in November 1944, a dollar bought 49.62 francs and a pound bought 200. Thirteen months later, in December 1945, a dollar was worth 119.10 francs and a pound was worth 480. In January 1948, the rate was 214.39 francs to a dollar and 865 to a pound.[10] Those were the official exchange rates. On the black market, Americans could get twice as many francs for their dollars.[11]

No wonder tourist numbers jumped. And they continued to rise as the French currency continued to slide. By 1958, when a dollar was worth 493.70 francs and a pound was worth 1,382, the franc had lost 99 percent of its pre–First World War value.[12] Finally, on December 27, 1958, under a second de Gaulle government, the country issued the "new franc," valued at one hundred times the old franc. Along with other economic reforms, this produced a relatively stable currency for the first time since 1919. Inflation had essentially wiped out the debt that France had incurred during and immediately after the war, which had a positive effect on postwar reconstruction (although it also wiped out the savings of millions of people).[13] Paris suddenly became rather expensive for foreigners. This is when American tourists started complaining about French rudeness.[14] It is also when American artists and writers stopped deciding that it was important to live in Paris.

2.

Mailer first came to Paris with his first wife, Bea—both were on the G.I. Bill—in 1947, soon after completing *The Naked and the Dead*. He had nurtured the traditional American writer's fascination with the city. "I'd dreamed of it all through the war, and I'd dreamed of it in college," he said later. "In those days, my idea of heaven was to be an expatriate in Paris." In the event, the Mailers did not have a happy experience. "I knew everything about what it was to be an expatriate in Paris, so I also knew that we did not fit the description," as Mailer put it. They lived in what he called "a grim little apartment" on the rue Bréa, in Montparnasse, near the Luxembourg Gardens. (To middle-class Americans, most Paris apartments would have seemed grim.) They hung out largely with other Americans. They signally failed to transform themselves into cosmopolitans.

"I probably have never been as much of an American as I was in Paris during that year," Mailer said. "I became fully aware of all that I liked about my country, and I found myself defending America constantly in conversations with French people."[15] This sense of anticlimax was not uncommon among American writers and artists who came to Paris after the war. They had grown up, after all, with tales of Hemingway and Fitzgerald. Bellow, who arrived in Paris on a Guggenheim fellowship three months after Mailer left, had the same reaction. "*Gay Paris?*" he wrote after he got back. "Gay, my foot! Mere advertising. Paris is one of the grimmest cities in the world."[16]

But Mailer did get one thing out of his Paris year. He met Jean Malaquais, a man who would become his lifelong political guru. More than fifty years later, Mailer would still be able to write: "Jean Malaquais was not only my good friend, perhaps even my best friend, but my mentor, more—he had more influence upon my mind than anyone I ever knew."[17]

Malaquais was one of the stateless people. His real name was Wladimir Jan Pavel Israël Pinkus Malacki and he was born in 1908 in Muranów, a Jewish section of Warsaw. Although he eventually became an American citizen and a college teacher, he always preferred to think of himself as *apatride* and a *tâcheron*, a nomad and a hack, a man without country or profession. He elected a fate that millions had thrust upon them in the aftermath of the First World War.

Malaquais's parents were nonobservant Jews, and both probably died in the death camps, but Malaquais left Poland long before that.[18] In 1926, when he was seventeen, and after traveling through Central Europe, Palestine, and North Africa.[19] he took a boat to Marseille. Like many Poles—Joseph Conrad is a famous example—Malaquais hated Russia and idealized France. "In my young man's imagination," he said near the end of his life, "France was *the* country one must live in, *the* country where one must study. It was the French Revolution, the Commune, the country of welcome, and so on and so on."[20]

His enthusiasm was quickly chastened when he discovered that France was not immune to xenophobia. He later claimed that he held fifty-two jobs, including as a miner in Provence, where stateless people could work without questions asked; a deckhand in the merchant marine; and a porter in Les Halles, the Paris food market.[21] But he did retain an attachment to the language, one of many he spoke and read. "It was a love match, one of the few marriages that did not become unhappy," he said.[22]

It was in Paris that Malaquais began to demonstrate his exceptional knack for making connections, relationships with influential people that seemed to have been both genuine friendships and sources of patronage. One of these was André Gide. Malaquais had joined the French Army in 1939. When the Germans invaded, he was taken prisoner, but managed, daringly, to escape and to make his way back to Paris.[23] He ended up in Marseille looking for a visa, along with his partner Galina (Galy) Yurkevitch, a Russian émigré who had found her way to Paris via Yugoslavia.[24]

Varian Fry and the Emergency Rescue Committee had been given Malaquais's name by Justin O'Brien, a professor of French at Columbia University and the future translator of Gide's *Journals*. But he had trouble securing a visa for him. It was not until September 1942, long after Fry left France, that Malaquais and Galina, now his wife, in possession, again with Gide's help, of Mexican visas, were able to get out.[25]

Once he arrived in New York, Malaquais expanded his circle of useful acquaintances. He finished his second novel, *Planète sans visa*, and in the spring of 1947, he returned to Paris to help launch it, carrying with him a letter from Clement Greenberg identifying him as *Commentary*'s "accredited correspondent in Western Europe."[26] It was sometime the next year that Malaquais met Mailer at a party. They got into an argument about Henry Wallace. Malaquais thought Mailer was naïve.

In the fall, Malaquais returned to New York to teach at the New School and met Mailer again. Mailer was not entirely happy to see Malaquais; he remembered the Paris meeting as a disaster. This time, however, they bonded.[27] Malaquais became Mailer's political tutor. Mailer's first assignment was to read the transcripts of the Moscow trials. And Mailer asked Malaquais to undertake the French translation of *The Naked and the Dead*.

It was a singular friendship. In their letters, Mailer referred to Malaquais as his "dear older brother"; Malaquais called Mailer "my younger brother."[28] But each thought that the other was a terrible writer. Each criticized the other's books (until Malaquais stopped writing them) with sometimes bruising frankness. And no one around Mailer could abide Malaquais. "He lived on everybody, a sponger," Mailer's mother said. "He does nothing but blow his horn . . . My idea of Malaquais as a man is mud."[29] "[A]n egotistical opportunist and a user," Adele Mailer described him.[30] Despite Mailer's admiration for his dialectical skills, Malaquais did not have much of a reputation as a political thinker, either. Irving Howe, who shared Malaquais's left-wing anti-Communist politics and who liked his books, called him "opinionated, cocksure, and dogmatic."[31]

What Mailer and Malaquais quickly came to agree on was the view that the Soviet Union was a totalitarian instantiation of state capitalism. What they differed on was the extent to which the United States was an insidious version of the same thing—"a soft totalitarian straitjacket," as Malaquais described it in a letter to Gide.[32] This dispute seems to have formed the core of their long intellectual friendship. Sometimes, Mailer thought that the United States was drifting into totalitarianism; at other times, he thought it was the best hope for defeating it. For the rest of his career, "totalitarian" was his term for social and political tendencies he feared and abhorred, among them, feminism.

3.

The meeting between Baldwin and Mailer took place in the late spring or early summer of 1956 in Malaquais's Montparnasse apartment. (Malaquais had returned to Paris to write a dissertation on Kierkegaard.) Baldwin and Mailer were almost the same age, and they were too much in the same place professionally not to pretend to admire each other, and too much alike temperamentally for much trust to develop between them. Both writers, and increasingly as their careers progressed, used their personalities as part of the literary proffer. They were on show all the time. That makes for vulnerability.

"They were very competitive as writers," Malaquais said about that first meeting, "and I had the feeling that Baldwin was a confounded snob. He would throw names around, he was more 'elegant' than Norman, more 'European' . . . They were drinking a lot, two bottles of whiskey, arguing, I remember, and the meeting lasted until two or three in the morning, when they left together. It was a love-hate relationship from the start."[33] "The toughest kid on the block was meeting the toughest kid on the block," is how Baldwin later described it.[34] The relationship would always be uneasy.

When they met, Baldwin's second novel, *Giovanni's Room*, about a love affair between two men, an American expatriate and an Italian in Paris, had recently been turned down by Knopf because of the homosexuality. The book would be published by Dial in the fall, and Baldwin was anxious about the reception (which would be largely positive, and the book sold well, six thousand copies in six weeks).[35]

And Mailer was still in a bad patch in his career. When he returned to New York, he collaborated (by providing the capital) with Dan Wolf (whom he met through Malaquais at the New School), and Edwin Fancher, a psychiatrist, in founding *The Village Voice*. Mailer was not involved in editorial work, but he wrote a column, which he called "*QUICKLY*: A Column for Slow Readers." The name was adapted from a phrase of André Gide's, which Mailer presumably got through Malaquais, and which he adopted permanently: "Do not understand me too quickly."

The *Voice* columns certainly read as though they were written quickly. But they offered Mailer a low-risk venue for experimentation. Since he was a part owner, he did not have to worry about a publisher censoring him. And exposure was limited. When he started the column, *Voice* circulation was 3,000, little-magazine territory. The personal and argumentative nature of the columns led to the personal and argumentative nature of *Advertisements for Myself*, published in 1959, in which all or part of every *Voice* column is reprinted, with commentary. What Mailer learned at the *Voice* was the literary value of leading with your personality. He never forgot it.

The *Voice* column also gave Mailer space to formulate his philosophy of hip, which he called "an American existentialism."[36] He soon renamed the column "The Hip and the Square." (The pun, based on the Village neighborhood Washington Square, was not original: John Wilcock's long-running *Voice* column was called "The Village Square.") And Mailer hardly invented the concept of hip. It had been around since the rise of bebop in the 1940s; the writer Anatole Broyard had criticized hip for its inauthenticity in *Partisan Review* in 1948. It was also part of Beat vocabulary. Ginsberg refers to "angelheaded hipsters" in the opening lines of *Howl*.[37] But Mailer turned it into a metaphor for race-crossing.

He performed this feat in "The White Negro," an expanded version of the *Voice* columns that he published in a special New York issue of Irving Howe's magazine *Dissent* in 1957. Its argumentative structure follows Sartre's in "Existentialisme est un humanisme." Sartre began with a world without God and asked, So how should we act? Mailer began with the prospect of meaningless death—"instant death by atomic war, relatively quick death by the State as *l'univers concentrationnaire*, or . . . a slow death by conformity with every creative and rebellious instinct stifled"—and asked the same question: How should we act?

It is, of course, an ancient question. If life is all there is, why do we have such a hard time knowing how to live it? Mailer's answer was modeled on his understanding of Black American experience, that is, the experience of Black men in America. Black men had already been living in the world that white people now found themselves in, he claimed. "Any Negro who wishes to live must live with danger from his first day," he wrote, "and no experience can ever be casual to him, no Negro can saunter down a street with any real certainty that violence will not visit him on his walk." The Black man therefore

> kept for his survival the art of the primitive, he lived in the enormous present, he subsisted for his Saturday night kicks, relinquishing the pleasures of the mind for the more obligatory pleasures of the body, and in his music he gave voice to the character and quality of his existence, to his rage and the infinite variations of joy, lust, languor, growl, cramp, pinch, scream and despair of his orgasm.

Mailer's "hipster" was the white man who has "absorbed the existentialist synapses of the Negro, and for practical purposes could be considered a white Negro."[38] "The only Hip morality," Mailer wrote, ". . . is to do what one feels whenever and wherever it is possible." And the measure of one's success is the quality of one's orgasm.

The hip philosophy also embraced, sometimes, violence.

It can of course be suggested that it takes little courage for two strong eighteen-year old hoodlums, let us say, to beat in the brains of a candy-store keeper, and indeed the act—even by the logic of the psychopath—is not likely to prove very therapeutic for the victim is not an immediate equal. Still, courage of a sort is necessary, for one murders not only a weak fifty-year old man but an institution as well, one violates private property, one enters into a new relation with the police and introduces a dangerous element into one's life. The hoodlum is therefore daring the unknown, and so no matter how brutal the act it is not altogether cowardly.[39]

The *Dissent* editorial board had no problem accepting "The White Negro" for publication. Howe wrote to Mailer to tell him that Meyer Schapiro "with gleaming eyes grabbed me at the end of the meeting to say: Hipsterism is Hasidism Without God."[40] The essay was a coup for Howe's little magazine. The issue sold 14,000 copies, triple the normal circulation. The essay was published as a pamphlet by Lawrence Ferlinghetti's City Lights Books in 1959, and that edition that went through five printings.[41]

Even taken as a conceit, Mailer's central claim is incomprehensible. Are male orgasms, which typically last less than ten seconds, really qualitatively distinguishable? Or even interesting?* "One squirt and done," as Ruth says to Harry Angstrom in John Updike's *Rabbit, Run* (1960), a novel that has a satire of Beat philosophy as a subtext.[42] Still, "The White Negro" did manage to make a prescriptive statement out of a variety of preoccupations that were, by 1957, commonplace: nuclear annihilation, juvenile delinquency, social conformity, and sexual norms.

The fascination of white American men with Blackness, the complicated desire to "be Black" or "act Black," dates back to the abolitionists and the blackface minstrels of the antebellum period.[43] And entertainment was usually the sphere in which white-to-Black race-crossing was enacted, since entertainment is where most white Americans take their image of Blackness from, and since entertainment just *is* acting. Offstage, the skin can be removed. You can ride home in the front of the bus.

---

* As were a number of men in his circles, from Jack Kerouac to Dwight Macdonald, Mailer was influenced by the renegade psychoanalyst Wilhelm Reich's *The Function of the Orgasm*, published in English in 1942. It "was like a Pandora's box to me," he later said. (Christopher Turner, *Adventures in the Orgasmatron* [New York: Farrar, Straus and Giroux, 2011], 429 [interview with Mailer].)

The main entertainment-world examples to hand in 1957 were rock 'n' roll and jazz, quasi-integrated popular sounds, a few of whose white performers even considered themselves to be "voluntarily" Black.[44] Mailer had no interest in rock 'n' roll, but white people like Mailer took jazz—the music, the fashion, the argot—extremely seriously. They considered it to be authentically Black because it is improvised and spontaneous, a corollary to the idea that jazz and the blues are untutored musical expressions descended from the field holler.

A jazz style was adapted by white performers in several forms. Poets in neighborhoods like the Village and North Beach read their work to live jazz accompaniment. And the cutting-edge stand-ups of the period, like Lenny Bruce, performed in a cool, riffy, "spontaneous" mode.[45] In the case of Richard Buckley, a white comic from California who outfitted himself like an English aristocrat (he sometimes wore a pith helmet) and performed as Lord Buckley, much of the act consisted of talking jive. His famous schtick "The Nazz" is a jive retelling of the Christ story: "I'm gonna put a cat on you, was the sweetest, gonest, wailin'est cat that ever stomped on this sweet swingin' sphere. And they called dis here cat . . . Da Nazz!"[46] Buckley's album *Hipsters, Flipsters and Finger Poppin' Daddies Knock Me Your Lobes* was released in 1955.* The title is a jive rendition of Marc Antony's speech in Shakespeare's *Julius Caesar*. Hip was very much part of the scene.

The pushback argument was that although jazz *is* a genuine expression of Black experience, the only part of that experience that white people wanted to adopt was the hedonic part. They didn't want to actually live like Black Americans. Three months after "The White Negro" came out, the Village writer Seymour Krim informed *Voice* readers that they were ignoring the real life of Black people, which he described as a life of debt, drink, and wife-beating. "The next time we act *hip* and *dig* the joys of jazz expression, musical or verbal," he warned, "we could do worse than pause and ask ourselves if we are prepared to accept the price and implications of this way of life."[47]

From the Black American perspective, this was all a colossal misreading. Jazz musicians knew that soulfulness and spontaneity are the product of discipline and responsibility. Their social values were

---

* Buckley died of a stroke in 1960 shortly after his "cabaret card," needed to perform in New York City, was lifted. Lenny Bruce died of an overdose in 1966 after being essentially blackballed in the entertainment industry.

often the same as those of middle-class white people, and they saw the depiction of Black musicians as transgressive outsiders as a way of keeping them in their place.[48] Nineteen fifties jazz, the kind of nightclub jazz that Mailer listened to, was highbrow, even coterie music. Bebop, the style formed in the 1940s, and free jazz, a response to bebop, were both self-conscious attempts to make the music *harder* to perform and to appreciate.[49]

Many successful Black artists did not come from the world Krim described; there was certainly no correlation between the background and the music. The least, to white people, "Black" (or sexualized) popular jazz musician, Louis Armstrong, came from a broken home and grew up in a violent New Orleans neighborhood known as the Battlefield. The musician who seemed to white people, attitudinally, the most "Black" (and sexualized), Miles Davis, came from an affluent family in Illinois and went to Juilliard. Black artists did suffer from segregation, discrimination, and racism; most of them would not have said that those things were inspirations for their music. Hip, jive, and jazz are all elaborately constructed idioms. Doing the dozens, like playing bebop or, later on, rapping, is something very few people can do, let alone do well. The very origin of "hip" in "hep," meaning "in the know," is enough to make this clear. Hip was an act. Authenticity had nothing to do with it.

That was what Broyard had tried to explain to *Partisan Review* readers in 1948, nine years before Mailer's essay.* White people had been taken in by a pose, he said. The hipster had become a "there but for the grip of my superego go I."

> He was received in the Village as an oracle; his language was *the revolution of the word, the personal idiom.* He was the great instinctual man, an ambassador from the Id. He was asked to read things, look at things, feel things, taste things, and report. What was it? Was it *in there*? Was it *gone*? Was it *fine*? He was an interpreter for the blind, the deaf, the dumb, the insensible, the impotent.[50]

And the Beats, although they were many people's idea of hipsters, thought that "The White Negro" was ridiculous. "I thought the essay

---

* Broyard, who was from New Orleans, was legally Black, a fact he concealed for most of his career, including from his daughter.

was very square," Ginsberg said, ". . . Kerouac's take on 'The White Negro' was that it was well intentioned but poisonous."[51] The association of Beatness with hoodlums was the last thing those writers wanted.

Howe later said that it had been "unprincipled" of him to accept "The White Negro" without removing the sentences condoning the murder of a candy store owner.[52] He does not seem to have had second thoughts about Mailer's characterization of Black men. Nor did Mailer. He always regarded the essay as a key work in his canon. He called it "one of the best things I have done" when he reprinted it in *Advertisements for Myself*. Thirty years later, he described it as the place he had marked out his "frontier" as a writer.[53]

4.

Baldwin said that it was while he was covering the Congress of Black Writers and Artists in September 1956, a few months after meeting Mailer, that he decided to return to the United States. "One bright afternoon," he wrote,

> several of us, including the late Richard Wright, were meandering up the Boulevard St.-Germain, on the way to lunch. Much, if not most of the group was African, and all of us (though some only legally) were black. Facing us, on every newspaper kiosk on that wide, tree-shaded boulevard were photographs of fifteen-year-old Dorothy Counts being reviled and spat upon by the mob as she was making her way to school in Charlotte, North Carolina . . . It made me furious, it filled me with both hatred and pity, and it made me ashamed. Some one of us should have been there with her! I dawdled in Europe for nearly yet another year . . . but it was on that bright afternoon that I knew I was leaving France . . . Everybody else was paying their dues, and it was time I went home and paid mine.[54]

Baldwin wanted to suggest that the pictures of Dorothy Counts woke him up to the irrelevance of the debates about African culture taking place in the Amphithéâtre Descartes. But Dorothy Counts did not try to integrate Charlotte schools until September 1957, a year later. By then, Baldwin was back in the United States.

On the other hand, there would have been plenty of reminders on Paris newsstands that fall of what was happening in the South. The *New York Herald Tribune* ran front-page stories and photographs about resistance to school integration in Clinton, Tennessee ("Racist Rioting Spreads in Eastern Tennessee"), Sturgis, Kentucky ("Near-Riot"), and Texarkana, Texas ("Mobs Bar Negroes from 2 South Schools").[55] *Life* ran a three-part series, from September 3 to 17, on "Segregation," with photographs of violent white opposition to school integration. The American civil rights movement was no longer a regional affair.

As Baldwin admitted, it was not until almost a year later that he left France. This was partly because of a romantic relationship with a musician named Arnold, whom he had met on a visit to the United States in 1955 and who had moved to Paris. During the breakup, Baldwin seems to have attempted suicide.[56] The delay was also because he needed magazine assignments that would pay his way to go to the South. He secured these from *Partisan Review* and *Harper's* and took a boat to New York in July.

One of the first people he met after he got there was Kenneth Clark.[57] Clark had heard of Baldwin as a promising writer from Elliott Cohen in the early 1950s, when Baldwin was still in Paris, and when he found out that Baldwin was back in New York, he invited him to dinner.[58] They got together several times after that.[59] Clark had just returned from a fact-finding trip to the South, so Baldwin, who was nervous at the prospect, would have been eager to get his advice. Still, the friendship is a little unexpected, because Clark was an experimental psychologist and Baldwin usually had an allergy to social science. But Clark was different.

Clark was born in 1914 in the Panama Canal Zone (his mother was Jamaican), grew up in Harlem, and attended Howard University, where he majored in political science, got a master's degree in psychology, and met his wife, Mamie Phipps, who was from Arkansas. She was a math major, but he persuaded her to switch to psychology. They both got their PhDs in psychology at Columbia, the first African Americans to do so.

When she was a master's student at Howard, Mamie had written a thesis on the effects of race on the self-image of nursery schoolchildren in Washington, D.C. Kenneth found the results intriguing, and they began collaborating. They published their first paper on the subject in 1939.[60] When Baldwin met them, she was director of the Northside

Center for Child Development in Harlem, a psychiatric clinic for children that the Clarks had founded in 1946; he was an assistant professor at the City College of New York.

For their most important experiment, whose results were published in 1950, the Clarks bought four fifty-cent dolls at a five-and-ten on 125th Street, two pink dolls and two brown dolls. They asked Black children to point to the doll they thought was "nice," the one they thought was "bad," and the one they thought was most like themselves. They found that children who attended segregated schools were more likely to choose the pink doll as the "nice" doll and the brown doll as the "bad" one, and that many of the children picked the "white" doll as the one most like themselves. (Fredric Wertham, who had also done studies of the psychological damage caused by segregation, dismissed the Clarks' work as "insignificant dolls play.")[61]

The Clarks' work was discovered by an NAACP lawyer named Robert Carter, who suggested using it in the argument for overturning *Plessy v. Ferguson*, the 1896 case that held segregation ("equal but separate") to be constitutional. In *Plessy*, the Court had said: "We consider the underlying fallacy of the plaintiff's argument to consist in the assumption that the enforced separation of the two races stamps the colored race with a badge of inferiority. If this be so, it is not by reason of anything found in the act, but solely because the colored race chooses to put that construction upon it."[62] The Clarks' study seemed to show that the psychological damage of segregation was real and immediate, not a "construction." No one had persuaded those children that white people were "nicer." They had already internalized white supremacy. Although some of the lawyers brought in to consult with the NAACP found the idea of introducing the doll study as a legal argument risible, Thurgood Marshall decided to use it.[63]

Marshall was the man tasked with masterminding the NAACP's assault on *Plessy*. School integration was the great cause of his life. He had grown up in Baltimore, and although the public law school of his own state university was only a few blocks from where he lived, he could not attend it because it did not admit Black students. After graduating from Lincoln, a historically Black university in Pennsylvania, he went to Howard for his law degree. In 1938, he became the lead attorney for the NAACP and pursued a perilous career waging legal war against discrimination in cases across the South.

Marshall believed that schools were the key to ending segregation, partly because he thought that education was the path to social advancement for Black people, and partly because he thought that if people mix together as children they will be less susceptible to racial prejudice as adults. Marshall traveled around the South inspecting the conditions of segregated schools and found (not to anyone's surprise) that schools for Black children were drastically inferior. In 1948–1949, the average investment per student in Atlanta public schools was $570 for white children and $228.05 for Black children, and similar disparities existed across the South.[64]

This suggested a legal strategy Marshall called "Jim Crow Deluxe": accept separation, but demand genuine equality. The reasoning was that it would be so expensive for Southern school districts to maintain dual school systems if they were equal in quality that they would be forced to integrate. The strategy had support within the NAACP, but Marshall eventually rejected it and began finding and litigating the cases that would be consolidated in *Brown*.[65] He was committed to getting a court to declare that separate facilities are inherently unequal.

This is where the Clarks' study proved useful. When *Brown* was finally decided, in 1954, it gave Earl Warren the inch of ground he needed to stand on in order to move aside the obstacle of *Plessy*. "To separate [Black schoolchildren] from others of similar age and qualifications solely because of their race," Warren said, "generates a feeling of inferiority as to their status in the community that may affect their hearts and minds in a way unlikely ever to be undone."[66] Possibly the state of psychological knowledge in 1896 had been inadequate for the Court to realize this, he suggested, but it is "amply supported by modern authority."[67] And he cited, in footnote 11, seven sociological and psychological studies; the Clarks' was the first. Warren dismissed criticism of his reference to the Clarks and other social scientists ("It's a *footnote*," he said), but the citation was important, because it supported a conclusion, which the Court was not obliged to reach, that for education to be "equal," it has to be integrated.

The Clarks' findings intersected nicely with Baldwin's preoccupation. They were studying empirically what he had been writing about from the beginning of his career: the self-image Black people and white people both derive from conditions of white supremacy. And as Baldwin became involved with the civil rights movement, even identified with it in the public eye (despite the fact that most of the leaders of the movement kept him at arm's length), this became his theme. Making Black Americans equal to white Americans was not the goal. The goal had to be the transformation of the whole society.

Baldwin was engaged with the movement even before he left Paris. On March 12, 1956, 101 congressmen and senators—one fifth of the United States Congress—issued a manifesto protesting the Supreme Court decision in *Brown*. "This unwarranted exercise of power by the Court," the signatories proclaimed, ". . . is destroying the amicable relations between the white and Negro races that have been created through 90 years of patient effort by the good people of both races. It has planted hatred and suspicion where there has been heretofore friendship and understanding."[68]* The same week, *Life* published a "Letter to the North" by William Faulkner. "Go slow" was Faulkner's advice. Both documents contained an implicit threat of white violence. Faulkner's "Letter" was reprinted in *Reader's Digest*, one of the largest mass-circulation magazines in the world.

After he won the Nobel Prize in 1949, Faulkner had become, following decades of neglect and poor sales, an American literary icon. In what could be considered compensatory gestures, he was awarded a Pulitzer Prize in 1955 and two National Book Awards, in 1951 and 1955. After his novel *Intruder in the Dust*, published in 1948, was adapted into a movie, its sales outstripped all of Faulkner's previous work, and Random House embarked on a project to bring all of his books back into print.[69] For many Northern white people, Faulkner was a man of broad humanist sympathies who understood the Southern point of view. He spoke with authority on race relations.

Three weeks after the *Life* piece, in an interview in the *Reporter*, Faulkner expanded on his thinking. He was asked whether he thought the Montgomery bus boycott, which had been under way for a little more than four months (it would last another eight), was a good idea. As long as it wasn't carried too far, Faulkner said. And then he added:

> But I don't like enforced integration any more than I like enforced segregation. If I had to choose between the United States gov-

---

* It is not as though Southern "massive resistance" to school desegregation was not effective. In 1962, eight years after Brown, not a single Black schoolchild in Mississippi, Alabama, or South Carolima attended a school with white students.

ernment and Mississippi, then I'll choose Mississippi . . . As long
as there's a middle road, all right, I'll be on it. But if it came to
fighting I'd fight for Mississippi against the United States even if it
meant going out in the streets and shooting Negroes. After all, I'm
not going out to shoot Mississippians.[70]

There had been no organized Black violence in the South in 1956;
Faulkner was speaking in the context of a bus boycott, which does not
even count as civil disobedience, since it breaks no laws. The remarks
about shooting Negroes (who were apparently not Mississippians) got
attention. *The New York Times* reported them; there was a story in *Time*.
Faulkner tried to retract them, hinting that he had been drunk (certainly a possibility). But the damage was done.

Four months later, in July, *Life* ran a piece by Robert Penn Warren
called "Divided South Searches Its Soul." Warren was possibly the second-
greatest literary authority on Southern race relations among Northern
white people. His novel *All the King's Men* came out in 1946, won a Pulitzer Prize, and was made into a movie that won the 1950 Academy Award
for Best Picture. He was a bona fide Southerner who taught at Yale.

Warren had come around on the question of integration, and he
traveled through the South for *Life* interviewing Black and white Southerners. The general idea of his article is that integration is a dilemma.
What the testimony of the white Southerners he quotes seemed to show
(though Warren did not say this) was the incoherence of the Southern
defense of Jim Crow. The rationale seemed to be that this was the way
things had been for seventy years (Jim Crow laws date from around
1890), and that disturbing them would result in social disorder. There
was sometimes a threat of a replay of the Civil War.

For there is only one logical defense of segregation, and it was made
by a Northerner. "The central question," wrote William F. Buckley in
the *National Review* in 1957, ". . . is whether the White community
in the South is entitled to take such measures as are necessary to prevail, politically and culturally, in areas in which it does not predominate
numerically. The sobering answer is *Yes*—the White community is so
entitled because, for the time being, it is the advanced race." This was,
Buckley said, the position of his magazine.[71]

Most of Warren's white interlocutors avoided this degree of candor
(most of his Black interview subjects were evasive), and Warren ended

his article by announcing that he was himself in favor of integration. He presented his opinion, however, in the form of a dialogue, pro and con, to suggest that the issue had compelling arguments on either side.

These occasions were almost too perfect, and Baldwin responded to them in *Partisan Review*. He mentioned Warren noncommittally a few times—he may have liked Warren's framing of the issue as a painful moral one for white people—but he unloaded on Faulkner. Faulkner is "so plaintive concerning this 'middle of the road' from which 'extremist' elements of both races are driving him," he wrote, "that it does not seem unfair to ask just what he has been doing there until now . . . Why—and how—does one move from the middle of the road where one was aiding Negroes into the streets—to shoot them?" "The time Faulkner asks for does not exist," he said, "—and he is not the only Southerner who knows it."[72] Baldwin was still in Paris, but he had inserted himself into the civil rights movement.

Baldwin went south in September 1957. He traveled first to Charlotte (though he does not seem to have met, nor did he write about, Dorothy Counts), then to Atlanta, where he met, briefly, Martin Luther King, Jr. Baldwin knew the world of Black preachers from his youth, and he was amazed to find in King a minister who was genuine. But Baldwin had also spent his entire professional life to that point in the company of writers, artists, musicians, and intellectuals, people for whom posing and conniving are just part of business. He had never had the occasion to meet a man like King.

5.

It is natural to imagine King and Marshall as political brothers, twin giants of the spirit of integration. They did agree on that much, but in most other respects, they came from different planets. Marshall was a pragmatist. When he traveled in the South, he sat in the back of the bus ("I have a back problem," he used to explain; "there's a big yellow streak running down it"), and he was famous for his ability to schmooze Southern sheriffs.[73] His faith was entirely in the law. He spent years before his triumph in *Brown* amassing a series of narrow rulings in segregation cases so that he would have a body of case law at his disposal when he finally got to argue the big one. Marshall was idealistic only in the extent to which he believed that a clean win in the Supreme Court would translate into genuine social change. His reverence for the Constitution may have made him blind to the fact that most Americans speak a different moral language. And that was the language King spoke.

King had had no ambition to become the leader of a movement. When Rosa Parks was arrested for refusing to give up her seat to a white passenger on a Montgomery city bus on December 1, 1955, King was a twenty-six-year-old minister just a year into his job at the Dexter Avenue Baptist Church in Montgomery. He imagined that he might one day become a professor. The boycott that followed Parks's arrest was not King's idea, and when he was informed of the plan, he did not immediately endorse it. He did after some reflection, though, and offered a room in the basement of his church for the organizers to meet.

On December 5, a mass meeting was called, to be held in the building of another Black congregation, the Holt Street Baptist Church. That afternoon, the boycott organizers met in King's church basement and voted to call themselves the Montgomery Improvement Association. Then, to his surprise, and probably because no one else was eager to accept the risk of white reprisal, King was elected the group's president. It was after six o'clock. The mass meeting was scheduled for seven. King rushed home to tell his wife, Coretta, and to write a speech.

It normally took King fifteen hours to write a sermon. For this address, the first political speech he ever gave, he had twenty minutes to prepare. He spent five of those twenty minutes having a panic attack. Fifteen minutes later, he was picked up and driven to the Holt Street Church. The car ran into a traffic jam five blocks from the church, and he had to fight his way through a crowd of people to get inside. Five thousand or more Black citizens of Montgomery had turned out. And at seven thirty, after the singing of "Onward Christian Soldiers," with only a few notes in his hand, King got up to deliver one of the greatest speeches of his career.[74]

What had given King pause about endorsing the boycott was a concern that it might be unethical and un-Christian. The boycott might be unethical because if it shut down Montgomery buses, it would deprive other riders of a service they depended on, and deprive bus drivers of the way they made a living. It might be un-Christian because it was a response to an injury by inflicting an injury. It was revenge, and revenge belongs to the Lord. King felt that he had to work through these worries about the movement before he could lead it. "I came to see," he wrote, "that what we were really doing was withdrawing our cooperation from an evil system, rather than merely withdrawing our support from the bus company. The bus company, being an external expression of the system, would naturally suffer, but the basic aim was to refuse to cooperate with evil."[75]

The Holt Street Church speech was thus an exercise in ethical reasoning in the mode of a pep rally. King was a call-and-response preacher. As he spoke, he probed the mood of the room, trying out lines until he found a rhythm with the audience. The famous passages in the "I have a dream" speech, delivered on the Washington Mall in 1963, were extemporized. He had realized part of the way through his prepared speech that he was losing the crowd and, prompted by Mahalia Jackson, who was standing behind him on the rostrum, he switched to the "dream" conceit, which he had used in speeches before.

The climax of the Holt Street speech is a series of calls answered by louder and louder cries and applause in response.

> We are not wrong in what we are doing.
> (*Well.*)
> If we are wrong, the Supreme Court of this nation is wrong.
> (*Yes, sir!*)
> If we are wrong, the Constitution of the United States is wrong.
> (*Yes!*)
> If we are wrong, God Almighty is wrong.
> (*That's right!*)
> If we are wrong, Jesus of Nazareth was merely a utopian dreamer
>   that never came down to earth.
> (*Yes!*)
> If we are wrong, justice is a lie.
> (*Yes!*)
> Love has no meaning. And we are determined here in Montgomery
>   to work and fight until justice runs down like water (*Yes!*) and
>   righteousness like a mighty stream.[76] *

This is not pragmatic, and it is a very high standard of justice. But most of the Black people who sustained the boycott knew the New

---

* That last line, one of King's favorites, from Amos 5:24, is inscribed on Maya Lin's Civil Rights Memorial at the Southern Poverty Law Center, in Montgomery, a block from King's old church on Dexter Avenue.

Testament a lot more intimately than they knew the Fourteenth Amendment. King's language appealed as well to many white Americans who held the federal government and its courts in conspicuous disregard, but who were susceptible to a moral appeal based on Scripture. Marshall had a strategy, but King had a dream. Marshall changed the law; King changed the country in places that the law does not touch. Without his crusade, the ruling in *Brown* might never have been enforced.

King inspired not just his listeners that day. He inspired himself. He must have realized, when he stepped down from the pulpit, that he had found his calling. He must also have known that he would one day meet a fate that was already in the cards, and that was virtually guaranteed by his speech. It was not the speech, though, but the moment of indecision before it, when he asked himself what the ethical implications were of what he was about to do, that made King a leader. Baldwin seemed to get that about him.

King and Baldwin also shared a vision of what the moment needed. Love was their solution. Marshall was not interested in love. He thought that direct action such as sit-ins and boycotts was street theater. He resented King's assumption that he was accomplishing something by breaking the law in order to make a symbolic point. He resented as well the time and money that the NAACP was obliged to expend every time King's nonviolent resisters got hauled off to jail. "I think he was great, as a leader," he said of King. "As an organizer he wasn't worth shit . . . All he did was to dump all his legal work on us, including the bills."[77]

Baldwin had little interest in constitutional law, just as he had little interest in social and economic programs designed to lift Black Americans out of poverty—the kind of solutions white liberals embraced. Baldwin wanted a moral revolution. He was chiliastic—like King, and like Malcolm X. "Human freedom is a complex, difficult—and private—thing," he wrote after his first trip to the South. "If we can liken life for a moment to a furnace, then freedom is the fire which burns away illusion. Any honest examination of the national life proves how far we are from the standard of human freedom with which we began."[78] This was raising the bar much higher than most white Americans wanted, or believed it was necessary, to jump.

Baldwin published his second essay collection, *Nobody Knows My Name*, in July 1961. It included his response to Mailer, "The Black Boy

Looks at the White Boy," which had first appeared in *Esquire*. He could make no sense, Baldwin said, of "The White Negro." He dismissed Mailer's idea as a resurrection of archaic Black stereotypes, and said he thought Mailer was trying to imitate writers like Kerouac, who Baldwin could not take seriously. As for the jazz musicians he and Mailer had sometimes hung out with, he said that they "did not for an instant consider him as being even remotely 'hip.' . . . He never broke through to them, at least not as far as I know; and they were far too 'hip,' if that is the word I want, even to consider breaking through to him. They thought he was a real sweet ofay cat, but a little frantic."[79]

Soon after, *The New Yorker* sent Baldwin to Africa, a place he did not much want to visit. "I think of the poor Negroes of the US who identify themselves with Africa, or imagine that they identify themselves with Africa—and on what basis?" he wrote to his friend William Cole from Israel.[80] In the end, he got only as far as Turkey.

Nobody Knows My Name was a bestseller. So was Baldwin's third novel, *Another Country*, which came out in June 1962. *The New York Times* compared it to "The Waste Land." Soon after, Norman Podhoretz, who had become editor of *Commentary* after Elliot Cohen's suicide in 1959, suggested to Baldwin that he write a piece about the Nation of Islam, a subject of interest partly because of the growing separatist influence of Malcolm X but mainly because of the recent conversion to Islam, under Malcolm's guidance, of Cassius Clay, who had changed his name to Muhammad Ali.

Baldwin went to Chicago and met, in his house, the leader of the Nation of Islam, Elijah Muhammed. He found the whole setup alienating, and he was disgusted by Elijah Muhammed's talk of "white devils." He returned and wrote his piece, then proceeded to sell it (much to Podhoretz's annoyance) to *The New Yorker*. Baldwin may have felt he owed the magazine something after the Africa debacle. He also received a much higher fee. The piece was handled by the editor in chief, William Shawn, himself, and it appeared in the November 17, 1962, issue under the very *New Yorker* headline "Letter from a Region in My Mind." It took up almost the entire magazine.

Baldwin's account of his encounter with Elijah Muhammed must have been fascinating to *New Yorker* readers. In the reflective sections of his article, he stressed the two themes central to his views on race relations. The first was the power of love; the second was the need for white

Americans to remake themselves before Black Americans could be liberated. "I do not know many Negroes who are eager to be 'accepted' by white people, still less to be loved by them," he wrote;

> they, the blacks, simply don't wish to be beaten over the head by whites every instant of our brief passage on this planet. White people in this country will have quite enough to do in learning how to accept and love themselves and each other, and when they have achieved this—which will not be tomorrow and may very well be never—the Negro problem will no longer exist, for it will no longer be needed.[81]

The ultimate question, he said, was: "Do I really *want* to be integrated into a burning house?"[82]

The *New Yorker* article, along with "The Dungeon Shook: Letter to My Nephew," published the following month in *The Progressive*, came out in January 1963 as *The Fire Next Time*. The publisher, Dell, bought paperback rights for $65,000. The house knew what it was doing. Don Fine, the editor in chief, called the book "an almost over-elegant, altogether polished exposition of black-white relations that white Americans could embrace without discomfort, and which really was considerably less fiery than its biblical title."[83] Five months later, Baldwin's face was on the cover of *Time*. He had become what he (or part of himself) dreaded and what he was (and knew himself to be) temperamentally ill-equipped to be: a public figure.

At first, from a sense of confidence or fatalism or both, he seems to have embraced the role. On May 3, in Kelly Ingram Park in Birmingham, police, under the director of the public safety commissioner, Eugene (Bull) Connor, trained fire hoses and sicced German shepherds on peaceful demonstrators, most of whom were teenagers. The city did not try to disguise what it was doing, and photographs appeared everywhere.* "The eyes of the world are on Birmingham," King told his followers at a church meeting that night.[84]

---

* *Life* ran a two-page photo spread. Andy Warhol silkscreened three of the photographs, by Charles Moore, for a series called *Race Riots*, part of what is known as his "Death and Disaster" paintings, which include car crashes, electric chairs, and suicides. It has proved tempting to read these works as social commentary, but there is no evidence that that is what Warhol had in mind. It seems more likely that the subject of the "Death and Disaster" works is scopophilia:

On May 11, a day after Baldwin's appearance on the cover of *Time*, the home of King's brother and a motel where King had stayed in Birmingham were bombed. Baldwin sent a telegram to Robert Kennedy, the attorney general, accusing the president of failing to exercise moral leadership. Because Baldwin was now himself part of any story he was involved in, the telegram was reported by AP. The headline in the *Times*: "Kennedy Blamed by Baldwin."

The Kennedys were not new to this business, and they did the politic thing. Baldwin was invited to meet Robert Kennedy at his house in Hickory Hills, Virginia. They had breakfast, and the idea came up of having Baldwin set up a meeting between Kennedy and a group of Black people. Baldwin arranged it, and the meeting was held on the afternoon of May 24 in Kennedy's New York apartment at 24 Central Park South, next to the Plaza Hotel. Kennedy brought along the leader of the Justice Department's Civil Rights Division, Burke Marshall.

It is unclear who Kennedy expected to meet, but Baldwin had assembled a group mostly from the world of entertainment and the arts: the singers Lena Horne and Harry Belafonte (who was close to King), the playwright Lorraine Hansberry, the white actor Rip Torn, and Baldwin's brother David, also an actor. Baldwin also invited his lawyer, Clarence Jones; his agent, Robert Mills; and Kenneth Clark. Jones had worked with King, but the only leader from a civil rights organization present was Edwin Berry, executive secretary of the Chicago Urban League. (Baldwin invited King, who could not attend.) The guest who turned out to be the key figure as things unfolded was not a celebrity. He was Jerome Smith, a Black Freedom Rider who had been beaten in McComb, Mississippi, a year and a half before. He was still scarred and walked with a limp.[85]

What happened is what usually happens whenever Hollywood and Broadway try to talk to Washington. "There was no communication," as Clark put it afterward. "I think we might as well have been talking different languages."[86] The feeling was mutual. "They didn't know anything," Kennedy reported to Arthur Schlesinger, Jr. "They don't know what the laws are—they don't know what the facts are—they don't know what we've been doing or what we're trying to do."[87]

these are images you can't stop looking at, like the photograph of a lynching that was removed from *The Family of Man* because visitors stopped to stare at it. Warhol categorized the race riots works as "Mongomerty [*sic*] dog Negro."

Kennedy wanted policy ideas. He was there to get answers to the question, What do Negroes need? The celebrities, of course, knew more about Black poverty than Kennedy did, but they were not, or they were no longer, poor, and they did not know anything about policy. They wanted moral leadership. The president should personally escort a Black student into a Southern school, they suggested. Kennedy thought this would be phony.

His position was that the administration had already done a lot for civil rights and for Black people in general. As he began to realize that no one there seemed to know or care about that, he became increasingly angry.* He tried the argument that his family were once poor Irish immigrants and now one of them was president. In forty years, he said, a Black man will be president. Under the circumstances and in front of that audience, this was not a helpful thing to say (although, as things turned out, Kennedy was off by only five years).

The breaking point was reached when Kennedy got into an exchange with Jerome Smith. Smith described what it was like to campaign for voter registration in Mississippi. When he was finished, Kennedy leaned forward. "We've all had hard times," he said. For the celebrities, this was too much. They saw Smith as the walking emblem of what Black Americans were suffering. Hansberry called him "the voice of twenty-two million people." If Kennedy could not understand what Jerome Smith had gone through, she said, she had no hopes for the administration.

By then, Kennedy was no longer listening. "It really was one of the most violent, emotional verbal assaults and attacks that I had ever witnessed," Clark said later. "Bobby became more silent and tense, and he sat immobile in the chair. He no longer continued to defend himself. He just sat, and you could see the tension and the pressure building in him."[88]

Baldwin had tipped off the press about a "secret meeting," thereby ensuring that it would not be, and *The New York Times* ran front-page stories about it for three days. "A source close to Kennedy" (meaning, probably, Kennedy) was quoted as calling the meeting "unfortunate." Elsewhere, it was described as a "flop." Nevertheless, on June 11, in Tuscaloosa, officials from the Justice Department confronted George Wallace in order to allow Vivian Malone and James Hood to register at the University

---

* Belafonte, for one, knew, but he seems to have felt trapped between the Black people at the meeting and Kennedy and Marshall.

of Alabama—the "stand in the schoolhouse door"—and that evening, President Kennedy delivered a televised address from the Oval Office on civil rights. "It is not enough to pin the blame on others," Kennedy said, "to say this is a problem of one section of the country or another, or deplore the facts that we face . . . Those who do nothing are inviting shame as well as violence. Those who act boldly are recognizing right as well as reality." The president was now on the record.

That night, Medgar Evers, the NAACP's field secretary for Mississippi, was shot and killed by a member of the White Citizens Council, Byron De La Beckwith, in Evers's own driveway. His wife and their three little children, who had stayed up to watch Kennedy's speech, saw him die. Baldwin had met Evers, and they were friends. The following week, Evers was buried in Arlington National Cemetery and the administration sent a civil rights bill to Congress. In August, Kennedy welcomed the leaders of the March on Washington to the White House. Three months later, he would be dead. Kennedy was not a martyr for racial equality. "He didn't even have the satisfaction of being killed for civil rights," Jackie Kennedy is supposed to have said. "It had to be some silly little Communist."[89] But his televised White House speech made it politically possible for his successor, Lyndon Johnson, to get the Civil Rights Bill passed.

Baldwin's name was prominent in all the stories about the Kennedy meeting. Baldwin had insisted on the meeting; he had invited the participants; they were Baldwin's friends, his "clan."[90] Right after the meeting, Baldwin and Clark, both rattled by the encounter, went off to tape a television interview on the public station WNDT. When it aired, a few days later, the *Times* reviewed it. "Challenge on Racism: James Baldwin Puts Problem Squarely in the Laps of All Americans" was the headline.[91]

In becoming a spokesman, Baldwin must now have realized that he had also made himself a target. Civil rights leaders were not happy with reports of the Kennedy meeting. They felt the same way Baldwin and his friends did—that the administration was not exercising leadership. King had made that complaint himself.[92] But they could not see the benefit of having a group of people they regarded as unrepresentative of the movement and of Black people in general pissing off the attorney general and his brother the president. Whitney Young, the executive secretary of the National Urban League, told a reporter, "[I]t would have been more appropriate for those present to have discussed the questions of race discrimination in the entertainment and literary world. These people themselves make no claims of expertness in the large areas of deep and complex racial problems . . . It's like asking Gregory Peck and Frank Sinatra to go to Washington to discuss foreign policy."[93]

Baldwin found himself attacked not by segregationists but by Northern liberals. The reaction had already started with the *New Yorker* piece. "Dear Mr. Baldwin," Hannah Arendt wrote to him just a few days after "Letter from a Region in My Mind" came out:

> What frightened me in your essay was the gospel of love which you begin to preach at the end. In politics, love is a stranger, and when it intrudes upon it nothing is being achieved except hypocrisy. All the characteristics you stress in the Negro people: their beauty, their capacity for joy, their warmth, and their humanity, are well-known characteristics of all oppressed people. They grow out of suffering and they are the proudest possession of all pariahs. Unfortunately, they have never survived the hour of liberation by even five minutes. Hatred and love belong together, and they are both destructive; you can afford them only in the [*sic*] private and, as a people, only so long as you are not free.[94]

Arendt had already weighed in on the question of integration in a piece that Howe solicited for *Dissent* after it had been turned down by *Commentary*. Her essay was a response to the Little Rock school integration crisis in September 1957, when nine Black students tried to enroll in Central High School and were blocked by a mob of white people.* President Eisenhower, who had commanded segregated armed forces in the Second World War and was no friend to school integration, had had to federalize the Arkansas National Guard and send in the 101st Airborne Division. The governor of Arkansas, Orville Faubus, responded by closing the public high schools in Little Rock for a year.

Arendt chose this occasion to cash out her theory of the social. Equality, she explained, is a *political* right. It cannot be made a *social* right. "[W]ithout discrimination of some sort," she said, "society would

---

* The "Little Rock Nine" were Ernest Green, Elizabeth Eckford, Jefferson Thomas, Terrence Roberts, Carlotta LaNier, Minnijean Brown, Gloria Ray Karlmark, Thelma Mothershed, and Melba Pattillo Beals.

simply cease to exist and very important possibilities of free association and group formation would disappear." This was a special danger in the United States, she believed, because mass society "blurs lines of discrimination and levels group distinctions . . . [T]he government has no right to interfere with the prejudices and discriminatory practices of society."[95]

The very first piece on the front page of the very first issue of *The New York Review of Books*, February 1, 1963, was a review of *The Fire Next Time* by F. W. Dupee of the Columbia English department. Dupee took exception to Baldwin's apocalyptic tone. "Do I really *want* to be integrated into a burning house?" Baldwin had written. The answer, Dupee wrote, is that "[s]ince you have no other, yes; and the better-disposed firemen will welcome your assistance."

Baldwin had abandoned criticism for prophecy and prescription for provocation, Dupee said. He was goading white racists, who were in a better position to cause trouble than Black people were, "and it is unclear to me how *The Fire Next Time*, in its madder moments, can do nothing except inflame the former and confuse the latter."[96] The point was repeated by Kenneth Rexroth in the *San Francisco Examiner*. *The Fire Next Time*, he wrote, "is designed to make white liberals feel terribly guilty and to scare white reactionaries into running and barking fits."[97]

White liberals who identified with the Kennedys resented being told they were not "getting it." But even white liberals who may have considered themselves politically purer of heart expressed impatience. With Baldwin, Susan Sontag wrote in *The New York Review of Books* a few months after the Kennedy meeting, "passion seemed to transmute itself too readily into stately language, into an inexhaustible self-perpetuating oratory.[98]

At the end of the year, Podhoretz persuaded Baldwin to participate in a *Commentary* symposium, "Liberalism and the Negro." Baldwin's fellow symposiasts were Gunnar Myrdal, Nathan Glazer, and Sidney Hook, the epitome of liberal integrationist opinion. It became a war almost from the start, and Baldwin's most persistent antagonist was Glazer. This was not surprising. Unlike the others, Glazer had worked in the American government. He served in the Housing and Home Finance Agency, precursor to the Department of Housing and Urban Development (HUD), when Kennedy was president, and he had just published, with Daniel Patrick Moynihan, *Beyond the Melting Pot*. Glazer had written most of the book, which was based on research into

630 | THE FREE WORLD

the conditions of ethnic groups in New York City. He must have felt entitled to believe that he had a better grasp of government programs and of the facts on the ground than Baldwin did.

The argument of *Beyond the Melting Pot* is that many Americans retain their ethnic identities regardless of the degree of their assimilation in other respects, and from this it followed that Black Americans should do the same—that is, they should become like other ethnic groups. The trouble, Glazer said, is that the Negro "insists that the white world deal with his problems because, since he is so much the product of America, they are not *his* problems, but everyone's."[99] But once he becomes willing to accept that he is a member of a group, he will be able to take responsibility for himself and other members of his community.

Baldwin knew what he was in for, and he set the stakes early on. "[T]o my mind, you see," he said, "before one can really talk about the Negro problem in this country, one has got to talk about the white people's problem . . . There is a sense," he went on, "in which one can say that the history of this country was built on my back." To the suggestion that he become a member of one of the ethnic groups competing for their share of the pie, his answer was: "What pie are you talking about? From my own point of view, my personal point of view, there is much in that American pie that isn't worth eating."[100]

Glazer thought that Baldwin was making the same mistake that he and Riesman thought people like Burnham and Mills made. Baldwin believed that power is more rational and concrete than it is. Glazer argued that it's not prejudice that slows racial progress as much as ignorance, incompetence, and bureaucratic inefficiency. "[T]he problems are a product of the kind of unwieldy institutions we have," he told Baldwin, "the kind of feudal country we have, the kind of recalcitrant special interests that have developed—among them Negro interests. And so we all fight it out."

To this kind of argument Baldwin's response was "if you don't know what Ray Charles is singing about, then it is entirely possible that you can't help me."[101] It is a good bet that none of the white men sitting around the table had ever willingly listened to Ray Charles. But they all wanted to help Black people, and they were being told that this was the reason they probably couldn't. They reacted the way Robert Kennedy did when he was told that he didn't understand the lived experience of Jerome Smith: *Erlebnis* is not a policy.

The *Commentary* symposium was published in March. In August, *Esquire* ran a profile of Baldwin that had been commissioned by the magazine's editor, Harold Hayes, who thought that Baldwin's war on white liberals was absurd.[102] (Hayes was from North Carolina.) The writer, Marvin Elkoff, dutifully portrayed Baldwin as mercurial and high-strung, and quoted him calling the white liberal "blinder, more innocent and ignorant than the segregationist," and saying things like: "If you don't realize that the same people who killed Kennedy also killed Medgar Evers, then you don't understand what is going on in the world." In the end, Elkoff concluded, "everybody was playing his [Baldwin's] game, and of course not nearly as well . . . At bottom he is disaffiliated, a medium of emotion."[103]

At Christmastime, Baldwin published a deluxe boxed coffee table book of photographs with his high school friend Richard Avedon, now a successful fashion photographer. The collaboration was Avedon's idea, and Avedon spent a long time trying to get Baldwin to finish his accompanying essay. The Avedon photographs are an inchoate assortment that includes Allen Ginsberg, George Wallace, the Everly Brothers, members of SNCC, Martin Luther King, Jr.'s, son, and Marilyn Monroe, along with pictures of people at the beach and inmates in a mental hospital outside Baton Rouge (who had not been told they were being photographed). Many of the subjects look as reptilian and papier-mâché as possible, an effect Avedon had a gift for. Baldwin's essay is a cri de coeur on the banality of American life. It begins with despairing reflections on the artificiality of actors in television commercials and descends into musings like: "When a civilization treats its poets with the disdain with which we treat ours, it cannot be far from disaster; it cannot be far from the slaughter of the innocents."[104]

There is a way in which this boutique item, which does not present itself as a book about race, brings the precariousness of Baldwin's position into focus. When he said things like "the history of this country was built on my back" or, in a widely publicized debate with William F. Buckley at the Cambridge Union, "I picked cotton, I carried it to the market, I built the railroads under someone else's whip," he was using an established conceit of group autobiography (as Malcolm X did in his autobiography, published in 1965.)[105] The understanding is that if these things did not happen to the author, they happened to somebody like the author. The "I" stands for the group.

White people don't write group autobiographies, however. It was not that people did not believe that when Baldwin lived in the United States, he had encountered racism and discrimination. It was that professionally, he had suffered no more, and arguably less, from efforts to censor him than, for instance, Norman Mailer or Henry Miller had. From the very beginning, he had been supported and promoted by powerful writers and editors, Black and white. He had written bestsellers: the only book that sold more copies than *Another Country* in 1963 was William Golding's *Lord of the Flies*. He wrote for *Partisan Review* and *The New Yorker*. He had been on the cover of *Time*. He hung around with celebrities; he was rich; he had an entourage. And on top of all that, he had been living in Paris for eight years, and when the Montgomery bus boycott turned out to be a success, he turned up on the scene and started telling everyone what it was like to be Black in America.

The New York Review of Books was ready for *Nothing Personal*. The headline was "Everybody Knows My Name," and the reviewer was Robert Brustein, who was soon to become dean of the Yale School of Drama. It was a time, Brustein began, of "show-biz moralists."

> Now comes Richard Avedon, high-fashion photographer for *Harper's Bazaar*, to join these other outrage exploiters, giving the suburban clubwoman a titillating peek into the obscene and ugly faces of the mad, the dispossessed, and the great and neargreat [*sic*]—with James Baldwin interrupting from time to time, like a punchy and pugnacious drunk awakening from a boozy doze during a stag movie, to introduce his garrulous, irrelevant, and by now predictable comments on how to live, how to love, and how to build Jerusalem.

"[L]ending himself to such an enterprise," Brustein concluded, "Baldwin reveals that he is now part and parcel of the very things he is criticizing.[106] Baldwin was one of a handful of Black writers who had a white audience in 1963, and he lost it.

Another white intellectual who found it necessary to call Baldwin out was Irving Howe. But this time, Baldwin ducked, and Howe's shot struck a different target.

6.

Ralph Waldo Ellison was named after the Transcendentalist philosopher. This conferred on him an aspiration that turned out to be one that he not only embraced but, after his own fashion, also fulfilled. "I could suppress the name of my namesake out of respect for the achievements of its original bearer," he said, "but I cannot escape the obligation of attempting to achieve some of the things which he asked of the American writer."[107] He entered the contemporary canon, something he cared about in a much more palpable way than most of his peers did, and he articulated a view of American culture that had wide appeal. But when he was born, in 1913 in Oklahoma City, those accomplishments would have seemed fantastic.

Oklahoma had been a state for six years when Ellison was born. Statehood had led to the imposition of Jim Crow laws, and, as in the rest of the South, those laws became increasingly numerous and increasingly strict. It was as though Southern legislatures could not stop finding new things to segregate. Ellison's educational and employment prospects were therefore limited, and his family was poor. His father died when Ralph was two, and he and his brother, Herbert, were supported by their mother, Ida, who worked as a maid and a janitor.

Ellison's first passion was music. He wanted to attend the Tuskegee Institute, in Alabama, the all-Black college founded by Booker T. Washington. After several aborted attempts, he finally arrived there after hoboing from Oklahoma in 1933. Many colleges with all-Black student bodies did not have Black faculty, but the faculty at Tuskegee was Black as well.[108] Ellison played the trumpet in the school orchestra—that seems to be why he was admitted—but he also discovered the institute's library. He later said he was turned on to literature by reading "The Waste Land," and then searching out and reading the texts cited in the poem's notes.[109]

From the beginning, Ellison, like Richard Wright, decided to "own" the white literary tradition. And like T. S. Eliot, he had, or he came to have, after passing through a political phase, a belief in literature as an autonomous artistic realm. This did not mean that literature has nothing to do with politics or the conduct of life, only that the "literary" is a value in itself. Ellison was also, like most American writers of the time with learning and ambition, a culture snob.

Ellison's finances made it a struggle for him to stay at Tuskegee—he could not afford to go home for vacations, and he had trouble paying the tuition. In 1936, without graduating, he moved to New York City and began his career as a writer. Almost as soon as he arrived, he met Alain Locke, the impresario of the Harlem Renaissance, and Langston Hughes, and Hughes introduced him to Richard Wright. Ellison and Wright had a close friendship, which continued even after Wright moved to Paris. Each was a witness at the other's wedding; Ellison read *Native Son* as Wright was working on it.

Ellison became involved with Communist Party publications, an association that lasted past the period of the Popular Front. He was probably a Party member, and he defended the Moscow Trials. He broke with the Party in 1942, rather late, and for the rest of his life he played down the association.[110] (When the Communist Party appears, as the Brotherhood, in *Invisible Man*, it is savagely satirized.) A few years after leaving the Party, in a farmhouse in Vermont, he began writing *Invisible Man*.

The novel was published in April 1952. Ellison's work was already known in literary circles, and almost all the reviews were positive. It was not a big seller right away, but its importance was established when it won the 1953 National Book Award for fiction, beating out Ernest Hemingway's *The Old Man and the Sea* (one of Hemingway's worst books, but very popular, and it won a Pulitzer). This immediately put Ellison in a class with Wright. It also credentialed him, and he would always enjoy the favor of the literary and artistic establishment. Ellison was the kind of person for whom admission to membership in the Century Club is a big deal.

Howe's attack on Baldwin appeared in *Dissent* in September 1963, in the wake of the Kennedy debacle, under the unfortunate title "Black Boys and Native Sons." Howe's essay was a response to Baldwin's criticism of Wright in "Everybody's Protest Novel," "Many Thousands Gone," and an essay he wrote after Wright's death, "Alas Poor Richard."

Howe took Baldwin to be arguing against the literature of protest as a genre, and to be presenting himself as a novelist who could not be put in a box labeled "Negro writer." This seemed to Howe a delusional aspiration. "How could a Negro put pen to paper," he asked, "how he could he so much as think or breathe, without some impulse to protest?"[111] Baldwin was trying to rescue literature from sociology, but writers, or, Howe seemed to be saying, Black writers, at least, cannot escape sociology. They can only try to turn it to literary account. Howe reviewed all of Baldwin's fiction. Only in *Another Country*, he thought, was Baldwin finally grappling with the subject of *Native Son*: the experience of race in America.

Baldwin seems to have ignored Howe's essay. He was not at a point in his life where he had time for quarrels in little magazines. But Howe did get an answer from his other "black boy," Ralph Ellison. "The Negro writer who has come closest to satisfying Baldwin's program is not Baldwin himself," Howe had written, "but Ralph Ellison, whose novel *Invisible Man* is a brilliant though flawed achievement, standing with *Native Son* as the major fiction thus far composed by American Negroes." What was astonishing about *Invisible Man*, he said, "is the apparent freedom it displays from the ideological and emotional penalties suffered by Negroes in this country," and he went through the book, assessing its strengths and weaknesses. He particularly objected to "the sudden, unprepared and implausible assertion of unconditioned freedom with which the novel ends."[112]

Ellison took exception, as any writer would, to the patronizing tone of the essay. Still, he and Howe were not enemies. Howe had been on the jury that chose *Invisible Man* for the National Book Award, and he had reviewed it, in terms not very different from those in the *Dissent* essay. Howe had sent Ellison his piece on Wright and Baldwin before it came out with an invitation to respond. Ellison declined, but he was persuaded by the editor of *The New Leader* to write a response for his magazine.[113] The venue was attractive because *The New Leader* was where King's "Letter from a Birmingham Jail" had appeared, in June 1963. Its civil rights bona fides were established. It put Ellison on the right side of the movement.

Ellison's response to Howe, "The World and the Jug," would become, when it appeared in longer form in Ellison's collection *Shadow and Act* (1964), probably his most cited essay. He notes at the start that Howe's piece is written with "something of the Olympian authority that characterized Hannah Arendt's 'Reflections on Little Rock'" (also, of course, published in *Dissent*).[114] But then, he says, Howe appears in blackface, explaining to Black Americans not only what their experience is but also how they feel about it. What this reveals, Ellison said, is the "Northern white liberal version of the white Southern myth of absolute separation of the races."

> Howe seems to see segregation as an opaque steel jug with the
> Negroes inside waiting for some black messiah to come along and
> blow the cork . . . But if we are in a jug it is transparent, not
> opaque, and one is allowed not only to see outside but to read of
> what is going on out there . . . So in Macon County, Alabama, I
> read Marx, Freud, T. S. Eliot, Pound, Gertrude Stein and Hem-
> ingway. Books which seldom, if ever, mentioned Negroes were to
> release me from whatever "segregated" idea I might have had of
> my human possibilities.[115]

He suggested that Howe's prescription for Black authors was no different from the line laid down by the Communist Party. "I fear the social
order which it [Howe's essay] forecasts more than I do that of Mississippi," he wrote. "Ironically, during the 1940s it [the Party] was one of
the main sources of Wright's rage and frustration."[116]

Ellison sent Howe a letter assuring him that he meant nothing personal, and the two men agreed to another round. Howe replied to Ellison in *The New Leader*, pointing out that he had also said some positive
things about Ellison's and Baldwin's work and some negative things
about Wright's. The aspersion about Stalinism he addressed by suggesting that Ellison had got carried away and could not really have meant
it, or he would have regarded it as a slur. Ellison then replied to Howe's
reply to his reply, and the affair came to an end.

Apart from the condescension, what is notable about "Black Boys and
Native Sons" is Howe's apparent inability to understand *Invisible Man*.
This may have been because he was comfortable with Wright's natural-
ism, and saw the quasi-surrealist style of Ellison's novel as aestheticism.
But it is hard to understand how anyone could read the book as not a
novel of protest. *Invisible Man* is a catalogue of every irony inherent in the
concept of Emancipation. Every style of response to that moment in
American history, every stereotype that haunts its failure, every doomed
quest to recover its promise or revenge its betrayal, seems to be recorded
in Ellison's book. "The protest is there," he told Howe, "not because I was
helpless before my racial condition, but because I *put* it there."[117]

Invisible Man is not, for the most part, about white people. It is about
the self-deceptions that Black people have been forced to rely on, the
makeshift identities they have had to devise, to cope with that disaster—
from Booker T. Washington's philosophy of Black self-help to the Black

nationalism of Marcus Garvey. Unlike Wright, who invented a character who was not like himself—"Wright could imagine Bigger, but Bigger could not possibly imagine Richard Wright," as Ellison put it—the invisible man of Ellison's novel is Ellison. This is his own story, through a kind of kaleidoscopic lens. To Howe's complaint that the final pages express an unearned affirmation of American life, Ellison must have laughed. Those words of affirmation are spoken by a Black man living in a coal cellar.

It may have been the first time in American history that a Black writer had gone up against a white critic and won the battle.[118] Ellison thought that white and Black people needed to accept the fact that, despite segregation, American culture is a mixed-race culture. They also needed to realize that art and literature is a commons. Once a book or a painting or piece of music is out there, it is public property. Those who do not take ownership of what they need are only depriving themselves. That was not the only position one could take, but it was, in 1963, not an unreasonable position. It would be overtaken by events.

7.

The Civil Rights Act was signed into law on July 2, 1964. Johnson was unhappy when he learned that King had been among the two hundred people present for the signing. "I'm sorry he was there," he complained to his press secretary, George Reedy. "It was very unfortunate he was there."[119] Johnson, like the Kennedys, did not want to appear to be dancing to a tune played by Black Americans. He wanted the Civil Rights Act to be seen as the moral and political doing of white people coming to the rescue of an oppressed group. It would not do to have it appear as though the members of that group had too much agency. They were *oppressed*.

The Civil Rights Act desegregated public accommodations: hotels, restaurants, stores, and movie theaters. In Title VII, the law also barred discrimination in employment—and, although it was never intended this way, Title VII turned out to be a legislative triumph for the women's movement.

For the problem confronting the women's movement, still in a nascent stage in 1964, was the problem the civil rights movement had been facing forever: the lack of legal leverage. Marshall had the Fourteenth Amendment's equal protection clause, and that proved ultimately to be a winning card. But no one read the Fourteenth Amendment as covering women. When it was ratified, women were still fifty-two years away from getting the vote.

During the debate over the Civil Rights Bill, Howard Smith, a congressman from Virginia, introduced an amendment adding the word "sex" to the list of classes protected under Title VII. Smith was an opponent of the bill, a conservative politician responsible for the Alien Registration Act of 1940, known as the Smith Act, which made it a crime to be a member of any organization that advocated the overthrow of the government, and for the War Labor Dispute Act of 1943, which curbed the power of labor unions.

It was commonly assumed that Smith's sex amendment was a poison pill designed to make it harder for liberals to support the bill. But it seems that Smith was responding to a request from the National Woman's Party (NWP), a tiny women's group made up mostly of wealthy white women that had been founded in 1916 by the suffragist Alice Paul. The NWP was not interested in racial equality.[120] It was concerned that under the new law, Black men and Black women would be protected under the category of race, leaving one group with no protection at all: white women.

Although the Senate debate over the Civil Rights Bill was one of the longest in history, Smith's insertion of "sex" into Title VII survived. Title VII created the Equal Employment Opportunity Commission (EEOC), which was charged with overseeing compliance. The commission began its work in July 1965, and it quickly became clear that it regarded the "sex" provision as a fluke. It was stunned when of the 8,854 complaints received in its first year, almost a third charged gender discrimination.

Feminists such as Betty Friedan could see that the EEOC, even though it was empowered only to recommend, not to sanction, was the only governmental body in a position to act on their behalf. When, after a year, it was clear that the commission was reluctant to deal with gender complaints, a group of women decided that they needed an organization that would do for them what the NAACP was doing for Black Americans, and in the summer of 1966, the National Organization for Women (NOW) was founded by a group that included Friedan and Pauli Murray, a lawyer and veteran of the civil rights movement.

Friedan and Murray wrote the organization's statement of purpose, and Friedan was named its president.* By the time of the Nixon administration, the EOOC was aggressively exercising the power of the federal government on behalf of equal opportunity, leading to the creation of affirmative action criteria for hiring. White women would be the main beneficiaries.[121]

A major area relatively untouched by the Act was voting rights, and this led to the final chapter in the classical phase of the civil rights movement, the struggle to pass the Voting Rights Act, a struggle that climaxed in the march from Selma to Montgomery, Alabama, in March 1965. Baldwin was one of the marchers, and he sat on the steps of the state capitol in Montgomery when King delivered an oration to a crowd of twenty thousand. King spoke just a few yards from where, a little more than two years before, George Wallace had pledged himself to "segregation now . . . segregation tomorrow . . . segregation forever." The Voting Rights Act was signed into law by Johnson on August 6.

And then the focus shifted. The War in Vietnam sucked the attention of white politicians and intellectuals away from race, and almost everything else, for the next five years. And the concept of Black identity changed. The figure who came to symbolize this change was the third of the three principal Black leaders of the era, Malcolm X. Until just before he was killed, Malcolm was not an integrationist, and he rejected King's method of nonviolence. His message was simple. What Americans of African descent were demanding was a revolution, and there is historically no such thing as a nonviolent revolution. Revolutions are about independence, Malcolm said, and they are therefore about land.

As he put it in what is perhaps his most important speech, known as the Message to the Grassroots, on November 10, 1963, in the King Solomon Baptist Church in Detroit:

> I cite these various revolutions, brothers and sisters, to show you that you don't have a peaceful revolution. You don't have a turn-the-other-cheek revolution. There's no such *thing* as a nonviolent revolution. The only kind of revolution that's nonviolent is the

---

* Murray had worked for Friedan as a freelance typist when Friedan was writing *The Feminine Mystique*.

Negro revolution. The only revolution in which the goal is loving your enemy is the Negro revolution. It's the only revolution
in which the goal is a desegregated lunch counter, a desegregated
theater, a desegregated park, and a desegregated public toilet; you
can sit down next to white folks—on the toilet. That's no revolution. Revolution is based on land. Land is the basis of all independence. Land is the basis of freedom, justice, and equality.[122]

Toward the end of his life, Malcolm moderated his views. He also
broke with the Nation of Islam, and formed his own pan-Africanist
group, the Organization of Afro-American Unity (OAAU). And it was
at a meeting of the OAAU in the Audubon Ballroom on Broadway and
165th Street in Washington Heights that he was assassinated by agents
of the Nation of Islam. The date was February 21, 1965, a month before
the march to Montgomery. But the spirit of Malcolm survived, given
momentum by the publication by Grove that October of *The Autobiography of Malcolm X*, co-authored with Alex Haley (later the author of
Roots). By 1968, more than half a million copies had been sold.[123] And
that spirit manifested itself in two new movements, one political and the
other cultural.

The political movement was Black Power. The phrase had been used
by Wright back in 1954 for the title of his book about his trip to the
Gold Coast, but it owed its currency to Stokely Carmichael, who was
born in Trinidad and Tobago in 1941 and moved with his family to the
United States when he was eleven. He had become active in the civil
rights movement in 1961 as a twenty-year-old Freedom Rider. In 1964,
he was a field organizer for SNCC in Mississippi, helping to coordinate
the voter-registering campaign in what was known as Freedom Summer.
He became chairman of SNCC in 1966, taking over from John Lewis.

That year, James Meredith set out on a 220-mile solo march from
Memphis to Jackson, Mississippi. Meredith had been the student who,
in 1962, integrated the University of Mississippi after Robert Kennedy
had five hundred federal marshals sent in to back him up. He was
marching to Jackson to mobilize support for voter registration under the
new Voting Rights Act. He called it the March Against Fear. It received
moderate press coverage until, on June 6, outside Hernando, Mississippi, Meredith was shot by a forty-year-old unemployed hardware contractor named Aubrey Norvell. Meredith survived, but reporters were

on the scene, and an AP photograph of him crying out as he lay in the road went around the world.

King and SNCC workers took up the march from the place Meredith had fallen. Eventually there would be fifteen thousand marchers. Carmichael was one of the leaders, and one night, when they were stopped near Greenwood, before a crowd of about six hundred, he gave a speech in which he shouted five times, "We want Black Power." The crowd chanted it back.[124] This was a rejection of the integrationist aspiration of King's "I Have a Dream" speech. It was also a rejection of nonviolence. In 1967, Carmichael wrote a book with Charles V. Hamilton called *Black Power*. "Integration," they said, "is a subterfuge for the maintenance of white supremacy." In 1968, Carmichael became honorary prime minister of the Black Panther Party.

The key figure in the cultural change was LeRoi Jones, who was born in Newark in 1934. His father was a postal supervisor and his mother was a social worker, and this put them in the Black middle class, a class that Jones would spend his career accusing of selling out to the white world. In 1954, Jones flunked out of Howard University, where he had been regarded as a troublemaker, and joined the air force (not the obvious choice for troublemakers). He left the service in 1957, moved to the Village, and, in 1958, married Hettie Cohen, who was the circulation manager of *Partisan Review*. They had two daughters and started a poetry magazine, *Yugen*, in which they published many of the Beats.[125] He first came to somewhat wider attention when he published a long letter in *Partisan Review* defending the Beats against Podhoretz's attack on them in "The Know-Nothing Bohemians."

Jones is the only Black poet in Donald Allen's *The New American Poetry*. In "How You Sound," published in the "Poetics" section of that anthology, he named "the 'Projective Verse' of Olson" as the method of his own poetry, a poetry of pure self-expression. "There cannot be anything I must *fit* into the poem," he wrote. "Everything must be made to fit into the poem. There must not be any preconceived notion of *design* for what the poem *ought* to be." He named as the most influential poets on him Lorca, Williams, Pound, Olson, and Eliot, and among his contemporaries, Philip Whalen, Gary Snyder, Michael McClure, Frank O'Hara, John Wieners, Robert Creeley, Allen Ginsberg, "&c. &c. &c."[126] All of the contemporaries were in Allen's anthology. None on either list was Black.

By 1963, Jones's sense of identity had become more race-conscious and his conception of race increasingly strident. In his work, there started to be a "with us or against us" tone. He published a book, *Blues People*, in which he argued that the blues and jazz was a Black music expressive of the reality of Black life in the United States. Ellison reviewed the book in *The New York Review of Books*, and attacked Jones for ignoring "the intricate network of connection which binds Negroes to the larger society" and "the fact that the creators of the style were seeking, whatever their musical intentions . . . a fresh form of entertainment which would allow them their fair share of the entertainment market."[127] Jones was crushing the music with a burden of sociology, he said.

The same year, Jones published, in the little magazine *Kulchur*, a piece called "Brief Reflections on Two Hot Shots." The hot shots were the South African writer Peter Abrahams (the man Wright had met in Ghana) and Baldwin, who Jones called the "Joan of Arc of the cocktail party." Baldwin and Abrahams, he said, "will not even open their mouths to say anything but that they are well-dressed, educated and have feelings that are easily hurt." They "want the hopeless filth of enforced ignorance to be stopped only because they are sometimes confused with the sufferers." The message that people should love one another, he said, "has very little meaning to the world at large . . . [P]erhaps the rest of us can get to the work at hand. Cutting throats!"[128]

When he heard that Malcolm X had been killed, Jones left his wife and children, changed his name to Amiri Baraka, and moved to Harlem to establish the Black Arts Repertory Theatre/School, the beginning of the Black Arts Movement. "Implicit in the Black Arts Movement," wrote Larry Neal, with Baraka one of its intellectual leaders, "is the idea that Black people, however dispersed, constitute a *nation* within the belly of white America."[129] "The Negro artist who is not a nationalist at this late date," wrote Baraka in 1969, "is a white artist."[130]

In 1966, the New Left magazine *Ramparts* published a piece by Eldridge Cleaver, who, the magazine explained, was imprisoned in Soledad, California, for "assault with intent to murder" (leaving out the other charge on which he had been sentenced, which was rape). "There is in James Baldwin," Cleaver wrote, "the most grueling, agonizing, total hatred of the blacks, particularly of himself, and the most shameful, fanatical, fawning, sycophantic love of the whites that one can find in any black American writer of note." He suggested that Black homosexuals like Baldwin "are outraged and frustrated because in their sickness they are unable to have a baby by a white man."[131] When Cleaver was released, he became minister of information for the Black Panther Party. The piece on Baldwin was reprinted in Cleaver's collection *Soul on Ice*, which *The New York Times*, in a positive review by Charlayne Hunter, called "highly readable and often witty."[132] In 1961, when she was nineteen, Charlayne Hunter, along with Hamilton Holmes, had integrated the University of Georgia. She mentioned Cleaver's Baldwin essay only in passing.

By then, Baldwin had long since abdicated his role as a spokesperson. He had spent most of the previous four years in Turkey. The Black Arts Movement did not last long; neither did the Panthers, their demise violently accelerated by the FBI's campaign to destroy them. But those movements were succeeded by a series of efforts to reformulate the concept of Black identity, both by Black politicians seeking to work "within the system" and by Black artists and intellectuals hoping to preserve some independence from it. These efforts were made frustrating and sometimes heartbreaking by the fact that most white liberals were no longer paying attention. Having given Black people legal equality and assuring them the vote, they could not see the need to devote more public resources to Black Americans as a group. In 1995, when Kenneth Clark was eighty-one, he was asked by a *New York Times* reporter what he thought Black people should call themselves. "White" was what he said.[133]

17

HOLLYWOOD—PARIS—HOLLYWOOD

Pauline Kael, May 11, 1966, the month she was fired from *McCall's*.
Photograph by Anthony Calvacca. (*New York Post Archives / NYP
Holdings, Inc. / Getty Images*)

1.

The word "cinema" is French, and in many respects the cinema is a
French invention. A French scientist, Étienne-Jules Marey, developed
the technology. French manufacturers, Louis and Auguste Lumière,
produced the first commercial movies and, in 1895, opened the first
movie theater. A French businessman, Charles Pathé, turned moviemaking into a mass-market industry by integrating all aspects of the
business: production, distribution, and exhibition. In 1910, two thirds
of the movies shown in the world were made in France. American audiences watched Westerns imported from France in which the Indians
wore mustaches.[1] The story of how, over the next sixty years, the United

States came to dominate world cinema is largely the story of its rivalry with France.[2]

The cinema is not only a business. It is also an art. (The first person to say so, naturally, was a Frenchman, Edmond Benoît-Lévy, in 1907.) For many years, Hollywood moviemakers insisted that movies were just a business (which is legally how they were regarded), and they amassed a fortune. For the most part, talk about "the artistic possibilities of the medium" did not interest them. But after the Second World War, Hollywood was obliged to reinvent its product. This turned out to be an undertaking that required some attention to the artistic possibilities of the medium, and that was a subject to which the French had given serious thought. French movie culture changed American cinema. It helped make Hollywood the world capital of film. It also disposed, once and for all, of France as a cinematic rival.

Nations protect their film industries in multiple ways: by establishing import quotas on films, by limiting the amount of revenue foreign movie companies can repatriate, by subsidizing movie production. Yet within a nation's film industry, there are competing interests. If you are a European movie producer, you want to restrict the number of Hollywood films coming into your country, since they are likely to suck exhibition revenue away from your own pictures. But if you are the owner of a European movie theater, you want more Hollywood imports, because people will pay to see them.

The degree of leverage a government has to regulate movies is a function of its general financial position and of geopolitics. After 1945, Hollywood could take advantage of the relative weakness of European states to pry open markets. In the former Axis powers, the United States basically dumped celluloid. Six hundred American films were released in Italy in 1946, against only 65 Italian films. In 1948, 668 American films were released in Italy, and only 54 Italian films. In the American zone of Germany, by 1949, 70 percent of the movies people saw were made in Hollywood.[3]

The governments of Britain and France had some bargaining power, but not much. After the war, Britain was faced with a balance-of-payments crisis and Hollywood studios were taking $70 million a year in rentals out of the country. So in 1947, the Labour government imposed a 75 percent ad valorem customs duty (75 percent of a movie's expected earnings paid up front) on foreign films. Hollywood responded with a boycott. The government encountered pressure from British theater owners and the tax was replaced by an agreement that American companies could take only $17 million a year out of the United Kingdom, plus a sum equal to the earnings of British films released in the United States. (The remaining money could be used for domestic film production, good for the British economy, but damaging to the independence of British film companies, since they became dependent on American studios for financing.) In 1949, 392 American movies were released in Britain and only 131 British movies. In 1951, 424 American movies were released and 114 British movies.[4]

France had instituted a quota system before the war, and when the French market opened up again after 1944, Hollywood was eager to chip away at it. "Hollywood" meant the Motion Picture Export Association (MPEA), a marketing arm of the Motion Picture Association of America (MPAA), which is, basically, a lobby. Hollywood needed a lobby because the industry's profits depended on foreign rentals, and it wanted the government to exert pressure to keep foreign screens open. In 1946, for example, 45 percent of Hollywood's income came from overseas—$125 million, roughly half the net profit of the industry as a whole.[5]

So the industry promoted the line that Hollywood movies were advertisements for the American way of life, and that restrictions on imports were motivated by anti-American ideology. "We, the industry, recognize the need for informing people in foreign lands about the things that have made America a great country," the president of Paramount, Barney Balaban, told *The New York Times* in 1946, "and we think we know how to put across the message of our democracy . . . The reason we are fighting against State and semi-State control abroad is that the terms which we accept now will determine the pattern for the future."[6] "Free trade and free communications cannot be separated in the case of motion pictures," wrote the president of the MPAA, Eric Johnston, in his annual report for 1946. "There may be as yet no satisfactory monetary medium for world trade in goods, but the motion picture does provide an adequate medium for world trade in ideas. Not to use it as such is to squander one of the best resources for world peace."[7]

Government officials repeated this rationale. "Totalitarian or near-totalitarian influence has spread to such a point," the chief of the motion picture division in the Commerce Department warned in 1948, that, in many countries falling within its orbit, nationalization of industry is being enforced and trade in commodities is under complete government control, while in other areas disciples of this ideology hold high government positions and bring strong deterrent influences (highly troublesome to U.S. interests) to bear within those countries. It is therefore easy to understand why the American motion picture is under heavy attack, for it is unquestionably an excellent means of expressing to the European peoples the American way of life.[8]

As with much postwar foreign policy, government interests coincided with business interests even though the motivations were not the same. The United States was against protectionism and nationalization because it believed that free trade and open markets made Western Europe a safer place. The American movie industry wanted free trade and open markets because it had a competitive product and believed that on a level playing field, Hollywood movies would beat European movies at the box office.

For a time, they were right. On May 28, 1946, the United States and France signed an agreement—known as the Blum-Byrnes Agreement, after the U.S. secretary of state, James Byrnes, and the French special envoy, the former prime minister Léon Blum—specifying the terms of American financial assistance to France.[9] (This aid was prior to and separate from the Marshall Plan.) In a two-page side agreement, France modified its quota system for movies and required exhibitors to reserve four weeks out of every thirteen for French-made movies, the other nine weeks to be open to competition.* A limit was also imposed on the amount of revenue American companies could repatriate.

"Open competition" meant, effectively, American movies. They were cheaper to rent—having already recouped their costs in the United States, Hollywood studios could underprice the competition—and the French public was eager to see them.† For demand had built up during

* The actual French negotiator was the economist and diplomat Jean Monnet, whose goal was the modernization (meaning, essentially, the Americanization) of the French economy. Monnet was later a leader in the establishment of the European Union. The side agreement concerning movies was negotiated by Monnet's colleague Pierre Baraduc.
† There were already hundreds of American movies unlicensed for theatrical exhibition circulating in France courtesy of the U.S. Office of War Information and the army's Psychological Warfare Division. These would presumably have been available to Parisian film societies.

the war. Since 1940, new American films had been banned in France. Under German control, the French film industry had produced 219 movies, but in roughly the same period, 1939 to 1944, Hollywood had produced 2,212 movies, more than ten times as many.[10] These movies were now poised to descend onto French screens.

The agreement went into effect on July 1, 1946. That month, twenty-six Hollywood movies opened in Paris, including *The Invisible Man Returns* (1940), *How Green Was My Valley* (1941), *Citizen Kane* (1941), *The Maltese Falcon* (1941), *Stormy Weather* (1943), and *Laura* (1944).[11] Over the next year and a half, 1,576 American movies were licensed for exhibition in France, against 553 movies made in other foreign countries and 233 movies made in France.[12] When those American movies arrived, a French film culture was ready to meet them.

2.

Postwar French movie culture was created largely by two men who never worked together and who did not particularly like each other: Henri Langlois and André Bazin. Langlois was a collector, a schemer, and an unkempt whirling dervish. He was born to French parents in 1914 in Turkey, where his father worked as a journalist. In 1922, the family had to flee when one of the treaties carving up Europe after the First World War assigned Smyrna, where they were living, to Greece. They got out on a French battleship as the city was burning behind them, and they ended up in Paris.[13]

Langlois did not finish his baccalaureate degree; there is a story that he failed a written exam by arguing that Charlie Chaplin was superior to Molière.[14] He loved silent movies, and it seems to have been in part in order to preserve them in the sound era that in 1936, he and a friend, Georges Franju, started a society dedicated to the exhibition and preservation of film: the Cinémathèque Française.* Langlois thought that people who consider only some movies worth saving are idiots, and he devoted his life to the pursuit and capture of every piece of film ever shot, along with posters, costumes, set designs—anything connected to the movies. He worked around the clock, traveled everywhere in search

---

* The Museum of Modern Art's film library, curated by Iris Barry, a British émigré once part of Ezra Pound's circle in London, performed the same function as Langlois's Cinémathèque; it was started in 1932.

of films, helped set up film libraries around the world, and, in later life, grew quite fat.

Bazin, on the other hand, was an intellectual and a man of saintly disposition. He was born in Angers, a medieval city southwest of Paris, in 1918. As a young man, he was an enthusiast of *le style américain*—the novels in French translation of Faulkner, Dos Passos, and Hemingway. But the great influence on his thought was Emmanuel Mounier, the founder of the journal *Esprit* and an exponent of personalism, a kind of spiritual alternative to existentialism, in which inner experience counts as more real than external facts, intuition more meaningful than analysis, feelings truer than concepts.

Bazin had hoped to become a teacher, but he failed the oral portion of the *agrégation*, at least in part because of a bad stutter, and in 1941, with a Sorbonne philosophy student named Jean-Pierre Chartier, he started a film club and discovered a vocation.[15] Bazin suffered from tuberculosis and, for the last four years of his life, leukemia. He died at the age of forty. But until the end, he wrote, lectured, and organized film discussion groups incessantly.

Running film societies in Paris in 1941 could be a risky business. Joseph Goebbels, the Nazi minister of propaganda, was obsessed with movies (as was Adolf Hitler); he considered them weapons in the war of mass psychology. When the Germans occupied Paris, Goebbels set about confiscating prints, purging the French film industry of Jews, closing down film clubs, and flooding French screens with German movies—mostly knock-offs of Hollywood productions, which he had encouraged German filmmakers to imitate. But Langlois and Bazin both survived.

Before the war, Langlois had made friends with the director of the Reichsfilmarchiv, Frank Hensel, who showed up in Paris in 1940 as the director of cinema for the German army. Hensel provided protection to the Cinémathèque and got Langlois movies the Germans were supposed to have confiscated. Langlois had to run screenings in places like his mother's apartment, and he had the actress Simone Signoret transport film canisters in a baby carriage to avert suspicion. But he kept going.[16]

Bazin's film club was allowed to continue because it was housed in a center that had been modeled on fascist youth groups in Germany. Chartier, Bazin's partner, refused to watch German movies, and in 1943 he left to join Resistance fighters in the French Alps. But Bazin did go to see German movies, and he even screened films by G. W. Pabst and Fritz Lang for his club. Though he was anti-fascist, he refused to join the Resistance.[17] His heart belonged to the cinema.

After the Liberation, Bazin developed a philosophy of cinema derived from personalism. It was a rather beautiful enlacement of individualism and detachment. The mission of the cinema, Bazin argued, is to represent the world, but the world as it is seen under the pressure of a personal vision. The moviemaker is not supposed to slice, dice, and resplice reality by the usual cinematic techniques, however. That's not what "vision" means. The world we see in the movie is the world we see in all its completeness; the camera does not make its presence felt. What is conveyed by the organization and the sequence of shots, the mise-en-scène, is the spirit—the inner life, intuition, feeling—of the person who made it.

It was a view that led Bazin to attack a technique long taken to be almost definitive of the medium, montage. In the Odessa Steps sequence in Sergei Eisenstein's *Battleship Potemkin* (1925), for example, the illusion of a woman's face being slashed is created by splicing together two separate shots, the first of a sword poised to be swung, the second of the woman's bloody face.* That the sword could have been swung on Tuesday and the face filmed on Wednesday doesn't matter; on the screen, the events appear to be contiguous. Eisenstein was not only a pioneering practitioner of montage; he was also montage's leading theorist, arguing in a work called *Film Form*, published in English in 1949, that montage is dialectical in the tradition of Marx and Engels. "Montage," he said, "has been established by the Soviet film as the nerve of cinema."[18] He used stills of the sword and the slashed face in *Potemkin* as an illustration of the technique.

In real life, though, no one sees this way. What we see is a single action from one point of view, the point of view of the individual spectator. Bazin therefore became a champion of Jean Renoir, whose long, nonjudgmental takes in movies like *La Règle du jeu* (*The Rules of the Game*) seem to open the world to our gaze, and of Orson Welles, whose use in *Citizen Kane* and *The Magnificent Ambersons* of deep focus (or depth of field, *la profondeur de champ*)—shots that maintain the

---

* Although the movie presents itself as a reenactment of the 1905 mutiny on the *Potemkin*, the Odessa Steps massacre is fictional.

foreground, middle distance, and far distance in continuous focus— allow actions and reactions to unfold without the conventional shot- reverse-shot editing.

Bazin argued that montage and conventional cutting force an inter- pretation on the viewer, while deep focus confers agency. As he put it: "depth of focus brings the spectator into a relation with the image closer to that which he enjoys with reality . . . It implies, consequently, both a more active mental attitude on the part of the spectator and a more pos- itive contribution on his part to the action in progress . . . It is from his attention and his will that the meaning of the image in part derives."[19] There is obviously a slight discrepancy between the demand for a per- sonal vision and the demand for audience agency, but that presumably would be a tension the director negotiates.

Bazin became a regular at the weekly screenings at the Cinémathèque, which was becoming the premier film society in a city that, after 1944, was suddenly bursting with film societies and obsessed with the mov- ies.[20] In 1948, Langlois moved the Cinémathèque from the Avenue d'Iena to a slightly larger screening room on the Avenue de Messine, and this became the place cinephiles gathered to see movies of all types and from all periods.

Langlois didn't have a theory of cinema; he had a theory of pro- gramming. He showed silent films without music and foreign films without subtitles. He designed triple bills based on unobvious similari- ties among movies of different genres, periods, and nationalities. He did not introduce films or suggest to viewers what to look for. The effect was to train people to concentrate on the visual elements—lighting, camera angles, editing, and so on—and it taught them to rate those things above the dialogue, the story, and the "message."[21]

What Langlois and Bazin were doing, in their different spheres, was resuscitating an old dream about movies: that cinema is a universal art form. For some people, that dream had died with the advent of sound. Sound erected language barriers, and turned movies into filmed theater. But Bazin didn't think so. He thought that the goal of cinema is the ever-more-complete representation of reality, an asymptotic relation al- ways falling short of what he called "the myth of total cinema." Sound was therefore just one more technical advance, as 3-D images might be in the future. By making the mise-en-scène the essence of cinema,

Langlois and Bazin reconstituted the movies as what the Italian movie theorist (he lived in France) Ricciotto Canudo called "the seventh art."

In the beginning, French Communists had been as excited as everyone else by the return of American movies, and they were generally cooperative in the effort to rebuild the French economy with American loans. But that was because Communists were in a working coalition with the governing Socialists. In May 1947, the Socialist premier, Paul Ramadier, kicked the Communist ministers out of the government and the Party (the PCF) responded by calling for France to align itself with the Soviet Union and by attacking the Blum-Byrnes Agreement, which it portrayed as a sell-out to American interests and a betrayal of French filmmakers. (The PCF also launched a campaign against Coca-Cola, claiming that it contained toxic ingredients and was bad for French wine growers.[22]* They were, of course, following the policy switch dictated by Andrei Zhdanov at the first meeting of the Comintern, in September 1947.)

The PCF was not large—in 1946, it had about 400,000 members—but it commanded enormous cultural authority. A Committee for the Defense of French Cinema was mounted; street demonstrations were organized. The French right, anti-American for different reasons, was also hostile to Hollywood (and to Coca-Cola). In 1948, the government renegotiated the film agreement, reserving an extra week each quarter for French movies, and in 1949, a government agency, the Centre National de la Cinématographie (CNC), began subsidizing French movie production.[23]

In fact, the Hollywood invasion did less damage to the French film industry than the Communists claimed. There was a short-term drop in production and some job loss, but even during the height of the American import boom, from 1946 to 1949, French movies had almost twice as many viewers as American movies in France. This may have been because French moviegoers preferred to see the kinds of films to which they were habituated—particularly comedies, which don't translate well—or because there was a mismatch between the worldview of the midcentury American and the worldview of the midcentury Frenchperson. What amused or titillated one was offensive or mystifying to the other. Reviews of *The Maltese Falcon* in the popular press (*Libération*,

---

* Probably no brand was more globalized by the Second World War than Coca-Cola. It is estimated that American soldiers consumed ten billion bottles of it.

Le Figaro, L'Étoile du Soir), for example, complained that the story was impossible to follow. And because the screen-time quotas were widely ignored by exhibitors, France was quickly swamped with inferior American product, and Hollywood movies started getting a bad name. By 1950, the French film industry had recovered.[24]

Still, the critical reception of American movies split along political lines.* *Citizen Kane* was a particular bone of contention, with Jean-Paul Sartre and the Communist press on one side (critical) and Bazin on the other (admiring).[25] In 1949, one of the periodicals to which Bazin contributed regularly, *L'Écran Français*, was taken over by the PCF, and he lost his job. His apolitical approach was no longer tolerable, and the outbreak of the Korean War soon after increased the level of anti-Americanism among French intellectuals.[26] Bazin made the break an open one by publishing in *Esprit* an article called "Le Cinéma soviétique et le mythe de Stalin," in which he attacked the doctrine of socialist realism and declared his preference for the myth of Tarzan. A year later, along with the critics Jacques Doniol-Valcroze and Lo Duca, he became a founding editor of *Cahiers du Cinéma*. And that is where the New Wave was born.

3.

The German Occupation had a somewhat paradoxical effect on French cinema. The Germans not only allowed filmmaking to continue; in some cases, they also raised the level of production values, craftsmanship, and technical expertise. After the war, this led to a photographically perfected studio look, *le glacis de la lumière*, and the industry product came to be known as the Tradition of Quality.[27]

But the price of continuing to produce movies was to renounce the politics of resistance—to become, if only in a passive sense, collaborationist. In the *épuration*, the film industry took its share of hits. The director Henri-Georges Clouzot was charged with committing an "indignity to France" for his nasty portrayal of a provincial village in *Le Corbeau* and was banned from the industry for life. (The ban was

---

* Almost immediately, the French defined one American film genre as "film noir"—a cinematic style brought to Hollywood by German and Austrian émigré directors, composers, and cinematographers, and wedded to American hard-boiled fiction. By 1955, there was a French book on the genre, Raymond Borde and Etienne Chaumeton's *Panorama du film noir américain, 1941–1953*, but the term was not used by American movie critics until the 1970s.

lifted, but *Le Corbeau* could not be seen again in France until 1969.) The star of *Les Enfants du paradis*, Arletty, was imprisoned for "horizontal collaboration" with an officer in the Luftwaffe. (Arletty had a memorable way of expressing her lack of repentance. "My heart belongs to France," she said, "but my ass belongs to the whole world.") The director Jean Mamy and the film historian Robert Brasillach were executed.[28] A shadow therefore fell over not only French movies made during the Occupation but also French film in general. This context is part of what gave François Truffaut's article "Une certain tendance du cinéma français" ("A Certain Tendency in French Cinema"), published in *Cahiers du Cinéma* in 1954, its polemical force.

For people whose image of Truffaut is based on his alter ego in his first feature film, *Les Quatre cents coups* (*The 400 Blows*), the sweet delinquent Antoine Doinel, or on the beatific scientist he plays in Steven Spielberg's *Close Encounters of the Third Kind*, the truth about his personality can be a little startling. Before he became a director, he was regarded as the most vicious critic in France. Truffaut was not the most original thinker in the New Wave group; Éric Rohmer and Jacques Rivette were its intellectual leaders. He was not, as a filmmaker, as iconoclastic as his friend Jean-Luc Godard. But he was the New Wave's *enfant terrible*. His attacks on other people's movies were so over-the-top that in 1958 he was denied a press pass for the Cannes Film Festival.

Truffaut was the discovery, protégé, and surrogate son of André Bazin. Truffaut's relations with his own family were vexed. He was an illegitimate child and was raised by a grandmother; when his parents finally took him in, they often left him by himself in Paris while they went mountain-climbing (his father's obsession). The cinema became Truffaut's surrogate home. He would skip school to go to the movies.[29] One day, when he was nine or ten, his aunt took him to see a film that he had already seen earlier that day. He couldn't tell her that, because he had been playing hooky, but watching the movie again, he started attending to the choices the director had made and he became intrigued by technique.[30] This led him to see movies multiple times. He saw *Le Corbeau* thirteen times; he saw *Les Enfants du paradis* nine times.[31] He discovered Langlois's approach on his own.

Truffaut and Bazin met in 1948, when Truffaut was sixteen. A week later, Truffaut's father had him thrown in jail for stealing a typewriter (Truffaut needed money for his film club), and he spent the next year and a half in reform schools. When he got out, Bazin hired him as his personal secretary. In 1950, Truffaut enlisted in the French Army. He was posted to Saigon, but he had second thoughts, and when he failed to show up for training exercises, he was arrested for desertion. He served several months in military prisons, one of them in the French Zone of occupied Germany. After he got out, he moved in with Bazin and his wife, and in 1953, he was made an editor at *Cahiers du Cinéma*.

Truffaut had been working on the article "Une certain tendance du cinéma français" since his time in military prison, but Bazin and his co-editors were reluctant to print it. They made Truffaut revise it extensively, and when it finally came out, in January 1954, they ran an editorial apologizing for his tone. But the piece caused a sensation. It made Truffaut a celebrity among cineastes. He would go on to write hundreds of film reviews.

The reaction may be a little hard to understand today. Truffaut's article was an attack on the Tradition of Quality, but it bristles with the names of filmmakers and films that are almost completely forgotten, and a large portion is devoted to analyzing the work of two screenwriters, Jean Aurenche and Pierre Bost, who specialized in literary adaptations. Truffaut's audience would have consisted of the small number of readers who were as obsessed with movies as he was. Like many landmark polemics, it was essentially inside baseball.

Still, two points stood out. First, Truffaut attacked French movies for their left-wing cant. In the name of what he called "psychological realism," he said, French movies represented policemen and priests as corrupt, expressed anti-military sentiments, used obscenities, and in general represented life cynically. They were giving the French public what the French public had come to expect: "smut, non-conformity, and facile audacity." The content may have seemed hardheaded, but the style was formulaic and predictable. The Tradition of Quality was "an anti-bourgeois cinema made by the bourgeois for the bourgeois."

Truffaut's other point was that these were screenwriter's movies, not director's movies. The director, as he put it, was only "the gentleman who puts the frame" around someone else's words, and the screenplays were themselves doctored translations of literary originals. French movies were filmed stories; their directors were *metteurs en scène*, not *auteurs*. "I do not believe," Truffaut announced (in Cold War language), "in the peaceful coexistence of the *Tradition of Quality* and an *auteur's cinema*."[32]

"Une certaine tendance" is often cited as the place that introduced the term *la politique des auteurs*, but Truffaut did not use that phrase in his article.* He used *auteur* in the way Bazin used it: as a praise word for directors like Orson Welles. And the idea of the director of a movie as like the author of a book had been articulated in 1948 by Alexandre Astruc, in an article called "Naissance d'une nouvelle avant-garde: la caméra-stylo"—the camera-pen. Truffaut simply used a distinction that had been around since 1918, when the director Louis Delluc distinguished between *auteurs* (filmmakers who write their own screenplays) and *metteurs en scène* (filmmakers who adapt other people's work).[33]

It was a year later, in a review of *Ali Baba et les quarante voleurs*, that Truffaut introduced the phrase *politique des auteurs*.[†] He was defending *Ali Baba*, he wrote, "by virtue of the *Politique des Auteurs* that my fellow critics and I practice. All based on the beautiful formula of Giraudoux: 'there are no works, there are only authors.'"[34] Auteurism was now a "policy": individual movies were understood in the context of a directorial vision expressed across a body of work. The (deliberate) analogy was with literature. There is *Bleak House*, and then there is "the Dickens novel." The former is a specific representation of nineteenth-century English society; the latter is the spirit (or personality or point of view or formal approach) informing that representation. The *Cahiers* critics wanted people to talk about movies the same way, as a "Hitchcock movie" or a "Hawks movie." Although the phrase was translated as "auteur theory," it is not really a theory (or a politics). *Politique* means "policy." It is a critical starting point.

By 1955, *Cahiers du Cinéma* had come to stand for three things: contempt for contemporary French cinema, veneration of Hollywood, and the *politique des auteurs*. These might look like the principles of an enlightened avant-garde; in fact, the *Cahiers* critics were attacking French cinema culture from the right. This wasn't just because of their taste for American movies. The film journal *Positif*, launched a year after *Cahiers*, was also pro-Hollywood and auteurist. But the politics of *Positif* were left-wing. That magazine referred to Truffaut as "the fascist."[35]

Cahiers's emphasis on movie form made it seem to intellectuals who

---

* Truffaut is also said to have referred to the Tradition of Quality as *le cinéma du papa*, but he seems never to have used that expression.
† A French adaptation directed by Jacques Becker, not the 1944 Maria Montez vehicle used as an intertext in Jack Smith's *Flaming Creatures*.

were influenced by Sartre a bastion of reactionary aestheticism, and its praise of American movies bled into an uncritical praise of America.[36] "The most beautiful American films that I have seen," Rohmer wrote in *Cahiers* in 1955,

> have more than anything else aroused violent envy, and sorrow that France should have given up the pursuit of a claim to universality that it once—not long ago—affirmed so strongly, that we should have let the torch of a certain idea of man be extinguished in order for it to be re-lit across the seas—in short, that we had to admit defeat on ground to which we have rightful claim . . . [T]he California coast is not, for the gifted and ardent cineaste, the hell that some have pretended. It is rather the chosen land, the haven that Florence was for painters of the Quattrocento or Vienna for musicians in the nineteenth century.[37]

The *Cahiers* critics saw in American movies what the British artists at the ICA saw in American advertising: a hopeful contrast with the living conditions and moral disillusionment of postwar Europe.

The *Cahiers* crusade against the French film industry was not based entirely on aesthetic grounds. Most of its critics didn't want to be critics; they wanted to be filmmakers. The film industry in France was notoriously a closed shop, heavily regulated by the CNC. A work card had to be earned through a process of apprenticeship to be allowed to direct a movie.[38] Truffaut's attack on the Tradition of Quality burned a bridge with the industry. It took several years for him and his friends to build a new one. But they did.

4.

Truffaut and Godard probably met in a screening room somewhere (Truffaut seems to have belonged to every film club in Paris), and they had become friends by the summer of 1949. Godard was a year older than Truffaut, and his background was quite different. He was born in Paris in 1930 and was raised in Switzerland, where his father, a doctor, ran a clinic. His mother, Odile Monod, was from one of the most distinguished Protestant families in France; her father was a founder of the Banque Paribas (today the eighth-largest bank in the world).

When he was sixteen, Godard went to Paris to attend the Lycée Buffon, intending to become an engineer. Family connections were useful. He accompanied André Gide to Antonin Artaud's performance at the Théâtre du Vieux-Colombier in 1947 (the event Carl Solomon ran across when he was AWOL in Paris). In 1949, he entered the Sorbonne to study anthropology, and heard Lévi-Strauss lecture. But he had already become a habitué of the Cinémathèque. Like Truffaut, though with less reason, he was in the habit of stealing. He was not a kleptomaniac; he generally stole only the amounts he needed. But his victims included his own family—he sold first editions of Paul Valéry that he removed from his grandfather's library—and by 1954, the family had cut him off.[39] He therefore found himself in the same position as Truffaut: looking for financing so he could make movies.

The breakthrough movie for the *Cahiers* group was Truffaut's *Les Quatre cents coups*. It was financed by Truffaut's father-in-law, Ignace Morgenstern, a film distributor. (Other New Wave directors, such as Claude Chabrol and Jacques Rivette, had had to finance their first films themselves.) Filming on *Les Quatre cents coups* began on November 10, 1958. That night, Bazin died. Truffaut was present at the end, and he dedicated his movie to Bazin.

Les Quatre cents coups was selected to represent France at Cannes, a choice approved by André Malraux, de Gaulle's minister of culture, who, faced with falling movie attendance, was hoping to revivify the industry. Truffaut won the award for best director (a year after he had been banned from the same festival), and the term "New Wave," already in circulation, went global.* Truffaut's victory was covered abroad, and his movie's foreign distribution sales alone amounted to double its budget. As always when a low-budget film makes serious money, producers started looking for more of the same, in this case, new young directors, and over the next four years, almost 170 French directors made their first films. Truffaut had finally succeeded in disrupting the industry.[40]

Les Quatre cents coups opened in Paris on June 6, 1959. On August 17, Godard began shooting *À bout de souffle* (*Breathless*). The story, about a French car thief named Michel (played by Jean-Paul Belmondo) with an American girlfriend named Patricia (Jean Seberg), was taken

---

* The phrase *nouvelle vague* was first used in 1957 in stories in *L'Express* (later in a book) by the journalist Françoise Giroud about the postwar generation. She did not have cinema in mind.

from an idea Godard heard from Truffaut in 1956. That idea was based on a story that had been all over French tabloids in 1952, about a man named Michel Portail who killed a motorcycle policeman and was turned in to the police by his American girlfriend. In real life, Michel Portail was sentenced to life in prison. In Truffaut's treatment, he runs away. In Godard's movie, he is shot and killed by the police.

When Godard found someone willing to produce a movie, Georges Beauregard, a man of right-wing views attracted to risky projects, he asked Truffaut to send him a treatment of his Portail movie. Truffaut wrote up four pages, Godard showed them to Beauregard, and Beauregard agreed to finance the picture. The budget was small, 510,000 francs, and most of it was spent to buy the American actress Jean Seberg from Columbia. That was about a third of the cost of the average French production. The profit amounted to something like fifty times the investment.[41]

Allegorically, À bout de souffle is a love affair between France and America in which things end badly for France. The girl who seems the promise of freedom proves, in the end, to be the friend of authority. Generically, the movie is a crime-couple picture. Models for Godard included Fritz Lang's *Thieves Like Us* (1939), *Gun Crazy* (aka *Deadly Is the Female*; 1949), directed by Joseph L. Lewis, and Nicholas Ray's *They Live by Night* (1949). Godard knew them all; Lang and Ray were two of his favorite directors. But unlike those movies, À bout de souffle is shot in a quasi-documentary style. Godard hired as his cameraman Raoul Coutard, who had spent eleven years in Indochina, five as a soldier and six as a photographer, and who was expert with documentary techniques.

Much of À bout de souffle was shot with a handheld camera, a Cameflex, and fast film stock, allowing Godard to use almost no artificial lighting. The movie was shot in four weeks. Godard would write the script at breakfast and rehearsed the actors briefly before the camera rolled. (All the sound was post-synchronized.) Godard was indifferent to continuity—he kept the "script girl" away from the shooting as much as possible—and he broke the rules about camera angles and cutting. The result is a jazzy film with a *verité*, improvised feel to it.

And yet À bout de souffle is one of the most self-consciously intertextual movies ever made. It contains references to more than a dozen other movies, as well as to poetry, music, and novels, from William Faulkner's *The Wild Palms* to Dashiell Hammett's *The Glass Key*. Michel imagines himself as an American movie hero, specifically, Humphrey Bogart, whose gestures he practices, and one of whose lines ("I always fall for the wrong dames," from *The Maltese Falcon*) he recites. His speech is filled with slang, something that had been absent from French movies before Jean-Pierre Melville's *Bob le flambeur* (1955). To use slang was to sound American.[42] As a tip of the hat, Godard has a character refer to "Bob the gambler," and Melville himself makes an appearance in the role of a celebrity writer named Parvulesco, who is given the best line in the film. "Quelle est votre plus grand ambition dans la vie?" Patricia asks Parvulesco at an airport press conference she is covering as a reporter. "Devenir immortel," he answers, "et puis, mourir." "To become immortal, and then, to die," in other words, to be a movie star.

Many scenes in *À bout de souffle* are quotations from Hollywood movies. A restroom mugging is from a Bogart movie called *The Enforcer* (1951); a shot of a character through a rolled-up poster is from Sam Fuller's *Forty Guns* (1957). Michel drinking from a milk bottle is from Ray's *Rebel Without a Cause* (1955); his dance of death at the end of the movie is from Anthony Mann's *Man of the West* (1958). There are references to Robert Aldrich's *Ten Seconds to Hell* (1959), Budd Boetticher's *Westbound* (1959), Mark Robson's *The Harder They Fall* (1956), and Otto Preminger's *Whirlpool* (1950), which Patricia watches in a movie theater. (That allusion is also self-reflexive: Preminger was the man who discovered Seberg when he made her the star of his *Joan of Arc*.)

There are even film theory commentaries embedded in the film. The turning point in all crime-couple movies is the killing of a policeman or some other official. In *À bout de souffle*, the victim is a motorcycle cop who tries to pull Michel over when he is driving a stolen car. The car stalls and Michel grabs a gun from the glove compartment (it belongs to the American army officer from whom he stole the car) and shoots the policeman. Godard pans slowly from Belmondo's face to his hand as he pulls the trigger, then cuts to a shot of the policeman falling. But in the first shot, the gun is fired from left to right, and in the second, the man falls from right to left. It is what the French call a *faux raccord*— a failure of continuity.

The failure is deliberate. Godard is performing two critiques at once. On the one hand, he is thumbing his nose at Bazin. Back in 1953, Bazin published an article in *Cahiers du Cinema* called "Montage Interdit" ("Montage Forbidden"); in the same issue, Godard published "Montage, mon beau souci" ("Montage, My Beautiful Concern"). Godard argued that Bazin's interdiction against montage in favor of techniques like deep focus privileged the treatment of space at the expense of the treatment of time. Movies are not restricted to clock time (as theater fundamentally is); movies can represent time as it is experienced by the subject. At the same time, Godard was thumbing his nose at cinematic technique. The scene in which Michel shoots the policeman is a montage: cause (gun firing) and effect (man falling), temporally continuous but spatially discontinuous. Godard shows what a montage literally is: independent shots that the mind connects. He deconstructs montage.

By breaking the rules, Godard wrote a new rulebook. He cleverly used the press to play up the unconventionality of his methods, so that when the movie came out in France, people had heard as much about Godard as they had about the film. And what was the point of all the rule breaking? "I need a certain freedom," Godard explained to a reporter. "I get it by blurring the lines a little. By fooling around with the usual ways. The producer thinks that I improvise when I'm only adapting myself to his conditions in order to create a greater possibility of invention."[43]

After the war, when European movies began getting a foothold in the American market, French movies were actually late in line, and the movie that started it was not *The 400 Blows* or *Breathless*. It was Roger Vadim's . . . *And God Created Woman*, released in the United States in 1957. That film has only one interest, and it is not primarily cinematic.

Vadim (né Roger Vladimir Plemiannikov) met Brigitte Bardot in 1949, when she was fifteen and already a cover girl for *Elle*. He married her in 1952, and set about making her a star. *Et Dieu . . . créa la femme* was not Bardot's first movie—she had created a small sensation in a movie called *La Lumière d'en face* (*The Light Across the Street*) in 1955— but Vadim made certain it would not be her last. She is completely naked in her first scene. She is sunbathing; an older man, a friend, surprises her. He says he has a car for her—and he hands her, as a joke, a toy car. In the story (written by Vadim), Bardot plays a sexual free agent. She sleeps with whom she pleases, behavior that is brought to an end when her new husband (played by Jean-Louis Trintignant) slaps her around a little.

Cahiers critics adored the film. It was the utter naturalness of Bardot's sexuality that got them. "It is pointless to compliment Vadim for being ahead of his time, because all that has happened is that everyone else is behind while he is up to date," Godard wrote.[44] Truffaut named *Et Dieu . . . créa la femme* one of the "great films" of 1956. He defended Bardot against charges of sexploitation. "[A]fter seeing three thousand movies in ten years," he wrote, "I can no longer stand the cutesy and false love scenes of Hollywood cinema and the dirty, licentious, and no less fake love scenes of French cinema." Vadim showed his wife's body because he loved her, and because people go to the movies to see movie stars. That is the problem with critics, Truffaut said: "films made from the love of actors are judged by people who don't like actors."[45]

Simone de Beauvoir agreed. Bardot, she explained, was a free human being, an *être-pour-soi*. "She cares not a rap for other people's opinion," Beauvoir said. "B.B. does not try to scandalize. She has no demands to make; she is no more conscious of her rights than she is of her duties. She follows her inclinations. She eats when she is hungry and makes love with the same unceremonious simplicity." Vadim's "debunking of love and eroticism is an undertaking that has wider implications than one might think. As soon as a single myth is touched, all myths are in danger."[46] Beauvoir's essay was published in *Esquire* accompanied by several pages of cheesecake shots of Bardot. Beauvoir later said it was her favorite essay.

The appeal of . . . *And God Created Woman* was in no way damaged by the Vatican's decision to denounce it, and when it was brought to the United States, it made $4 million in rentals, shattering the record for European imports. Bardot became the popular symbol of the new cinema. Her ass belonged to the whole world. She was the hips that launched a thousand faces. One of them was Faye Dunaway's.

5.

Bonnie and Clyde was written for François Truffaut.[47] The movie was the brainchild of Robert Benton and David Newman, who worked at *Esquire* in the early 1960s when the magazine was going through its transformation, under the editorship of Harold Hayes and Clay Felker, into the flagship of the literary and (often) first-person style of reporting that became known as the New Journalism.[48]

Newman was an outspoken New Yorker, Benton a gentle Texan, and they became best friends and creative partners. They worked on some of the satirical features for which *Esquire* is known, including the Dubious

Achievement Awards, and Newman became a caption and headline doctor. He wrote the headline for Tom Wolfe's first piece of New Journalism, in 1963: "There goes (VAROOM! VAROOM!) that Kandy Kolored (THPHHHHHH!) tangerine-flake streamline baby (RAHGHHHH!) around the bend (BRUMMMMMMMMMMMMMMMMMM . . .)."

In 1964, they published a photo-essay in *Esquire* called "The New Sentimentality," in which they tried to do what Susan Sontag was doing with the essays she would soon collect in *Against Interpretation*: define the taste shift that seemed to be taking place among sophisticated New Yorkers. Their phrase, "the new sentimentality," didn't catch on, but the piece was popular in Europe, no doubt because part of the taste shift they were describing was an enthusiasm for European movies.

European movies needed American exhibitors, and these were the first-run art house theaters. In 1950, there were only about eighty of them in the United States, but the number grew quickly: there were 226 in 1954, 399 in 1960, 450 in 1963. Art houses pitched their movies either as highbrow entertainment (for people who disdained Hollywood and television) or as purveying risqué subject matter. In the interest of the former, art houses would have cafés rather than concession stands, and would distribute printed programs. In the interest of the latter, they would play up the fact that foreign movies were not subject to the MPAA's Production Code. So that a Chicago theater advertised Roberto Rossellini's *Open City* in 1946 as "Adults Only: Savage Orgy of Lust." A poster at a Forty-Ninth Street theater in New York advertised Vittorio De Sica's neorealist *The Bicycle Thief* in 1949 as "the uncensored version!" even though the scene in question was a little boy pissing on a wall.

These were movies for adults, but they did not have "adult content." The movie that led to the Supreme Court decision that movies were protected by the First Amendment, *Burstyn v. Wilson* (1952), Rossellini's short *The Miracle*, has no graphic content at all. It is a very unsexy movie. The complaint was that it was sacrilegious, not that it was obscene. But while the case was in court, the movie played to standing-room audiences at the Paris Theater in New York City.[49] People were not lining up to see *The Miracle* for the blasphemy. They were hoping for a little more. One reason . . . *And God Created Woman* was a box-office hit was that it was a European movie that was actually sexy.

At bottom, the appeal of foreign films to American exhibitors was commercial. The federal government's antitrust action against the studios, begun in 1938 but not completed until the Supreme Court's decision in *Paramount v. U.S.* in 1948, found the studios in violation of antitrust law. Hollywood was vertically integrated: production, distribution, and exhibition were all controlled by the studios. After *Paramount*, the studios had to divest themselves of the theaters they owned, and this opened the exhibition market to competition. One consequence was that new Hollywood releases played longer at first-run movie houses (which could now control the number of weeks they were exhibited), and when they reached so-called sub-run theaters, audiences were smaller. And a drop in overseas rentals after 1950, now that Hollywood could no longer dump its product in foreign markets, drove up the cost of studio films. All these things made imports attractive to smaller theaters.

So for about twenty years after the war, a kind of shadow film industry grew up, with independent distributors renting movies by foreign producers to niche exhibition spaces usually located in big cities and college towns. As happened with rhythm and blues in the same period, this shadow industry came to an end when the studios decided to get in on the act and began producing (sometimes with frozen overseas income) and distributing foreign movies themselves. By 1969, the studios had hired most of the big-name foreign directors, and, although foreign films continued to be shown in repertory theaters, the first-run art house had virtually disappeared. Some (as Barney Rosset learned the hard way) would switch to pornography.[50]

Newman and Benton were enthusiasts of this new European cinema and subscribers to auteur theory. "We lived and died by it," Newman said.[51] So with this transplanted French film culture in their heads, they decided to make their own movies. They figured that the best way to break into the business was by writing a screenplay.[52] The idea to do the story of Clyde Barrow and Bonnie Parker came from a book about gangsters of the John Dillinger era that Newman and Benton had both happened to read. Benton already knew about Bonnie and Clyde, because they were folk heroes in the part of East Texas he came from; his father had attended their funeral.[53]

The movie they imagined was an amalgam of two New Wave types. They wanted a witty gangster picture featuring cool antiheroes, in the manner of Belmondo in *Breathless* and Charles Aznavour in Truffaut's *Shoot the Piano Player*, together with a romantic situation that would be a little *outré*, in the manner of *Jules and Jim*, a particular favorite of both men. That movie came out when Benton was ending a relationship with Gloria Steinem; he saw it, for purposes of consolation, eight times. Newman named his daughter Catherine, after the character played by Jeanne Moreau.[54] So they wrote a gangster story with a ménage à trois: they put Bonnie and Clyde into a sexual threesome with the character who became C. W. Moss (played in the movie by Michael Pollard). Then they set about trying to get the treatment to Truffaut.

They were helped by an unusual woman named Helen Scott. Scott was born in New York but raised in Paris, where her father was a correspondent for the Associated Press. She was a Communist organizer in the 1930s; during the war, she did broadcasts for the Free French from Brazzaville, in the Congo. She served as press attaché for Chief Justice Robert Jackson at the Nuremberg trials, was blacklisted in the McCarthy era, and in 1959, became director of public relations for the French Film Office in New York City. She met Truffaut in 1960, when he came for the American distribution of *The 400 Blows*, and they became, despite the differences in their political outlooks, friends. She assisted him in putting together a series of interviews he did with Hitchcock, published as *Hitchcock/Truffaut* in 1966.[55]

Benton and Newman knew Scott from their *Esquire* work: she had provided them with stills of French movies to use in the magazine. The three got together in Benton's apartment on East Eighty-Second Street, and Newman read the treatment to her.[56] Scott liked it and agreed to send it to Truffaut, who, after he had it translated, let it be known that he was interested. He already knew the Bonnie and Clyde story. It had been the subject of a comic strip, "Ménage de Gangsters," by Paul Gordeaux in the newspaper *France-Soir* in 1962, and Truffaut had clipped it.

At the time, Truffaut was trying to put together a deal to direct *Fahrenheit 451* for Universal, but he could see the appeal of a small-budget project, particularly since his English was nonexistent, and he agreed to a meeting. In 1964, the three met at the Drake Hotel with Scott translating, and Truffaut went over the treatment, showing Benton and Newman how to block the movie out and making a series of suggestions. Interestingly, most of his advice was to make the movie less New Wavey and more Hollywood. And he screened for them Lewis's *Gun Crazy* (1949), also the story of a couple who rob banks, in order to point out how the ending, in which the couple dies in a shootout with the police, had been mishandled. When the lights came up, Newman and Benton saw that Godard was sitting in the screening room with them.[57]

But Truffaut decided to make *Fahrenheit 451*, and he handed the *Bonnie and Clyde* screenplay to Godard. Godard flew back to New York to discuss the project. In order to finance their research, Newman and Benton had sold an option on the movie (retaining the right of director approval) to a brother-and-sister producing team, Elinor and Norton Wright. The Wrights were relatively untested—Norton was an assistant producer on the television show *Captain Kangaroo*. They were not prepared for Godard, and Godard was not prepared for them. The concept of "the package" was beyond his grasp. He thought that the producer was the person who wrote the checks, which was the way it worked in France. He did not understand that the Wrights would have to go to a studio for the money, and he grew increasingly exasperated during their meeting. He could start shooting in three weeks, he told them. The weather would be bad in Texas, the producers explained. "We can make this picture anywhere," Godard replied. "We can make it in Tokyo." The producers called Texas for a weather report. Godard stood up. "I'm talking cinema, and you're talking meteorology," he exclaimed, and walked out.* Later, he called Newman and Benton from the airport. "Your producers are amateurs," he told them. "Give me a call when the option expires."

The option did expire, and the man who picked it up was Warren Beatty. Truffaut happened to loathe Beatty. He and Brando and a few others, Truffaut confided to the Wrights, were on a list of people it would be better not to make films at all than work with.[58] But they met in France, where Beatty was making *Kaleidoscope*, and Truffaut recommended Benton and Newman's screenplay to him. Beatty looked them up when he was back in New York, and he signed on to produce the picture.

Beatty had made a movie with Arthur Penn in 1965, *Mickey One*, a noirish picture in which he had been somewhat miscast as a stand-up comic, and he approached Penn to direct. Penn was a sophisticated theater person. He had attended Black Mountain College on the G.I. Bill, had studied method acting at the Actor's Studio, and had returned to Black Mountain to teach theater, working with John Cage on the production of Erik Satie's play *The Ruse of Medusa*.[59] He was an adviser to

---

* Accounts of the meeting differ. Godard's exit may have been less dramatic. See Mark Harris, *Pictures at a Revolution* (New York: Penguin, 2008), 66–67.

John F. Kennedy in the television debates with Richard Nixon in 1960 and an established director for television and Broadway.

But his Hollywood projects had been frustrating. *The Left-Handed Gun*, with Paul Newman, was not well reviewed; he was fired from *The Train* by the movie's star, Burt Lancaster; and *The Chase*, with Robert Redford, was edited by the producer, Sam Spiegel, without his approval.[60] But Penn knew what the New Wave was all about. He was stunned by *The 400 Blows*; he said it reminded him of his own childhood. And he regarded *Mickey One* as an American New Wave film. (Alexandra Stewart, Truffaut's girlfriend at the time, was the movie's co-star.) He let Beatty persuade him to make *Bonnie and Clyde*.

Beatty had never produced before. His career had been in a slump since his debut in *Splendor in the Grass* (1961), but the studios were in a slump, too. In 1965, Adolph Zukor, who was ninety-two, and Barney Balaban, who was seventy-eight, were still on the board at Paramount; Jack Warner at Warner Bros. was seventy-three; Darryl Zanuck at 20th Century Fox was sixty-three. These men were not attuned to the New Sentimentality. The studios had no idea what the 1960s were about, and they had pretty much forgotten what movies were about, too—a fact epitomized by Fox's farcical miscalculation (described by John Gregory Dunne in a classic report, *The Studio*) with *Doctor Dolittle*, starring Rex Harrison.

Attendance had been in free fall since 1946. Average weekly attendance that year was 90 million. In 1950, it was 60 million; in 1960, 40 million.[61] Movie tickets dropped from 12.3 percent of Americans' recreational expenditures in 1950 to 5.2 percent in 1960 and 3.3 percent in 1965.[62] During the Depression, the music business had declined and the studios had prospered. Now, in a growing economy, music was winning. The Hollywood product was no longer competitive.

The decline in attendance was overdetermined.[63] The baby boom, which made people stay home more; television; the chilling effect on the industry of the investigation by the House Un-American Activities Committee of Communists in Hollywood—there seems to be no single cause, and the same thing was happening in Britain and France without social changes on the same scale.* Hollywood tried all sorts of gimmicks to make moviegoing attractive—manufacturing blockbusters

---

* U.S. annual movie attendance in 1946 was 4.1 billion; in 1965, it was 228 million. British figures are slightly better, but still dramatic: 1.6 billion in 1946, 326 million in 1965.

(movies accompanied by large-scale advertising campaigns and product tie-ins), using Cinemascope and 3-D projection (making movies more like a theatrical experience, sometimes with musical overtures and intermissions), and generally overproducing. These experiments led to a series of whale-sized flops: *Cleopatra*, *The Greatest Story Ever Told*, *Doctor Dolittle*, *Mutiny on the Bounty*, *The Bible*, *Waterloo*.[64]

Even Hollywood winners like Fred Zinnemann, who made *High Noon* (1952), *From Here to Eternity* (1953), and *The Sundowners* (1960)—movies that received a total of twenty-five Academy Award nominations—thought that Hollywood was running on empty. "If you go to France nowadays," he told *The New York Times*, "you can get into an argument about a movie very easily. You are constantly involved in passionate discussions about the creative side of movie making . . . [Y]ou feel that the movie-makers are dealing with the world of today and the problems of today. Here in Hollywood we are going in circles."[65] In 1963, *Life* put out a special double issue on the movies. They were mostly foreign. "While the whole film world has been buzzing with new excitement," it commented, "Hollywood has felt like Charlie Chaplin standing outside the millionaire's door—wistful and forsaken."[66]

All this uncertainty probably made it easier for Beatty to make his case for financing to Warner Bros. He managed to persuade Jack Warner, who had no taste for the project, to put up $1.6 million. Beatty took 40 percent of the gross. It turned out to be a very good deal. The movie cost $3 million to make and returned almost $23 million in its first year and a half. It ultimately grossed $125 million.

Most of the movie was shot on location in Texas (much to the annoyance of Warner, who didn't see why they couldn't make it on the lot). Newman and Benton's screenplay really did achieve the unsettling contrast of comedy and violence they intended—farce (Pollard in the getaway car unable not to take advantage of a parking spot that has just opened up) followed by terror (the close-up shooting of the bank manager who has run after the car). It's bluegrass (played by Flatt and Scruggs, the duo who recorded the theme song for the massively popular CBS show *The Beverly Hillbillies*) and blood.* It was also brilliantly cast: Gene Hackman and Estelle Parsons as Clyde's brother and sister-in-law,

---

* Weekly audience for *The Beverly Hillbillies* was 57 million. That is more than four times the size of the television audience for the 2019 World Series.

foils to the glamorous hicks Beatty and Dunaway; Gene Wilder (Penn knew him from the Actors Studio) in his movie debut as the man who mistakenly reveals, in a moment of giddiness after he realizes that the gangsters who have kidnapped him are fun-loving folks, that he is an undertaker; and as the fifth member of the bank-robbing gang, Pollard (an old friend of Beatty's: they worked together on the television series *The Many Loves of Dobie Gillis*). Newman and Benton had imagined a farm-boy stud in the part, in keeping with the idea of a ménage à trois. But by the time the filming started, the ménage idea, always a sticking point for Penn and the actors, who thought it would distract audiences, had been dropped. It is hard to imagine that the movie would have been as popular if it had kept that kink.

Popularity was not immediate. Warner hated the film. "What the fuck is this?" was his comment after Beatty screened the finished picture for him. Beatty suggested that *Bonnie and Clyde* might be thought of as "an homage" to the Warner gangster movies of the 1930s, like *Scarface* and *Public Enemy*. "What the fuck's an homage?" Warner said.[67] The studio opened the picture small in the late summer of 1967. And that was when New Wave crashed into the Old Wave.

The leading antagonist was the *New York Times* movie critic Bosley Crowther. Crowther was an enemy of "gratuitous sex and violence": he thought that *The Jungle Book* (1942) was too violent. On top of that, Beatty had committed an uncharacteristic faux pas and insulted Crowther one night at Sardi's restaurant. For whatever reasons, Crowther made *Bonnie and Clyde* a cause. He reviewed it three times and called it

> a cheap piece of bald-faced slapstick comedy that treats the hideous depredations of that sleazy, moronic pair as though they were as full of fun and frolic as the jazz-age cut-ups in "Thoroughly Modern Millie" . . . This blending of farce with brutal killings is as pointless as it is lacking in taste, since it makes no valid commentary upon the already travestied truth. And it leaves an astonished critic wondering just what purpose Mr. Penn and Mr. Beatty think they serve with this strangely antique, sentimental claptrap.[68]

He compared sympathy for Bonnie and Clyde to sympathy for Lee Harvey Oswald and Hitler. The movie was similarly panned in *Life*, *Saturday Review*, and *The New Republic*. *Time* called it "a strange and purposeless mingling of fact and claptrap that teeters uneasily on the brink of burlesque . . . sheer, tasteless aimlessness." Joe Morgenstern, in *Newsweek*, called it "stomach-turning," "a squalid shoot-'em-up for the moron trade."[69]

There were some early revisionist indications. The week his review came out, Morgenstern took his wife, the actress Piper Laurie, to see *Bonnie and Clyde* in New York, and this time, feeling the audience's excitement, he was swept away. He asked *Newsweek* for space to publish a retraction, which appeared the following week. He had been wrong, he said. It was, he now saw, the combination of "gratuitous crudities with scene after scene of dazzling artistry" that made the movie important.[70]

Morgenstern was a friend of Pauline Kael's—they lived two blocks from each other on the Upper West Side—and it has been suggested that Kael put him up to the retraction. But Morgenstern had already written it before they discussed the movie. Then Kael herself weighed in, with a seven-thousand-word essay in *The New Yorker*. It has sometimes been said that with that piece, Pauline Kael saved *Bonnie and Clyde*. That is not what happened. What happened is that *Bonnie and Clyde* saved Pauline Kael.

6.

In 1967, Kael was a forty-eight-year-old freelancer. She had written for just about every well-known magazine in America, including *The New Republic*, *Partisan Review*, the *Atlantic*, *Mademoiselle*, *Holiday*, *Vogue*, *Life*, and *McCall's*. Before moving to New York, in 1963, she had made weekly radio broadcasts about movies on KPFA in San Francisco, and she had been contributing regularly to journals like *Film Quarterly* and *Sight and Sound* since 1954. A collection of her pieces, *I Lost It at the Movies*, was published in 1965 and became a bestseller.

But she had acquired a reputation as a person who was difficult to work with. At KPFA, she had resigned on the air, much to the annoyance of the station manager. In February 1966, after *I Lost It at the Movies* came out, she signed a contract to write a movie column for *McCall's*, a magazine with 8.5 million readers. She proceeded to pan *Born Free* ("a tear-jerking account of a trembling, stiff-upper-lipped, emotionally frustrated woman's obsession") and *The Sound of Music* ("the sugar-coated lie that people seem to want to eat") and was fired in May.[71] "I knew that she was extremely critical when I hired her," the editor, Robert Stein, explained. "But her reviews became more and more uniformly unfavorable—not only to all films, but questioning the motives of the people who made the films . . . The experiment did not work out."[72] In October, Kael replaced Stanley Kauffmann as movie critic for *The New Republic*. She lasted less than a year.

The problem was partly personality, but it was mostly that Kael did not like the kind of movies that were being made. She liked smart entertainment, and she thought that most foreign films were not entertaining and most Hollywood movies were not smart. *Bonnie and Clyde is* smart entertainment, and it marks the moment when a different kind of American movie began to be made. Kael just barely managed to get on board that train. But she got herself into the front car.

There are two peculiarities about Kael's background. The first is that she grew up in the Bay Area in the middle of the San Francisco Renaissance but disliked most art films. And the second is that although she became a director's critic herself, she made her name by attacking auteur theory.

Kael was born in 1919 in Petaluma, California, where her parents, Jewish immigrants from Poland, ran a chicken farm. (Chicken farming was apparently a business that attracted Jewish immigrants.)[73] She entered Berkeley on a scholarship and majored in philosophy, but dropped out several credits shy of graduation for reasons that are unclear. She may have run out of money, or she may have been bored with academic life. She got involved with a filmmaker named James Broughton; they were introduced by the poet Robert Duncan, with whom Kael was close. They never married (Broughton was gay), but they had a child together, a girl named Gina James. Broughton made avant-garde films, which Kael hated. "She deplored little theater, little magazines, little films," Broughton said. "She valued the big time, the big number, the big screen."[74] This was not the Bay Area aesthetic circa 1950.

Kael started out writing plays, but one day in 1952, she was sitting with a friend in a coffeehouse in Berkeley talking about Charlie Chaplin's *Limelight*. The discussion was overheard by Peter Martin, who was the co-founder, with Lawrence Ferlinghetti, of City Lights Pocket Book Shop. Martin also edited a movie magazine called *City Lights*. He invited Kael to write up her views on Chaplin. She did.

Because of his politics, Chaplin was almost a god among progressive filmgoers in 1952, and progressive filmgoers were precisely the kind of people who were likely to be reading *City Lights*, a journal named, of course, for a Chaplin movie. Kael thought that *Limelight* was the height of pomposity and self-importance. "The Chaplin of *Limelight* is no irreverent little clown," she wrote;

> his reverence for his own ideas would be astonishing even if the ideas were worth consideration. They are not—and the context of the film exposes them at every turn. The exhortations in the directions of life, courage, consciousness, and "truth" are set in a story line of the most self-pitying and self-glorifying daydream variety . . . [T]his is surely the richest hunk of self-gratification since Huck and Tom attended their own funeral.[75]

She had entered the arena with a splash. She was thirty-three.

The success or notoriety of the *City Lights* article led to her own show about movies on KPFA, Pacifica public radio. She also became the manager of the Cinema Guild and Studio, a twin-screen art house in Berkeley, where she wrote the program notes and married the owner, a Viennese émigré named Edward Landberg. The marriage lasted about a year. ("She was also very bossy," Landberg said. "I soon found out that I couldn't stand this woman.")[76]

Kael began writing about movies for *Sight and Sound* and *Partisan Review*. She stayed on at the Cinema Guild after the divorce, but in 1962, she and Landberg quarreled, and she quit. Her reputation had by then made it impossible for her to get a job as a reviewer in San Francisco. That is when she wrote her attack on auteur theory, "Circles and Squares." The essay was also an attack on the movie critic of *The Village Voice*. It is possible she imagined that this was not the worst career move for a person in her predicament.

The *Voice* critic was Andrew Sarris. Sarris was a protégé of Jonas Mekas. He was born in Brooklyn in 1929 and went to Columbia College, where he was an indifferent student.[77] After graduating in 1951, he spent some time in the army, then entered graduate school in English with the thought of becoming a theater director. It was at Columbia that he met Mekas, who was sitting in on a class there. Mekas had just started *Film Culture*, and he invited Sarris to join as an unpaid editor and contributor. Sarris was on board by the time the second issue came out, in 1955.

In 1958, a friend of Sarris's, Eugene Archer, went to Paris on a Fulbright, and his letters home introduced Sarris to the French movie scene. Sarris went to Paris himself in 1961, where he was converted, he said, to "the sacred importance of the cinema."[78] When he returned, Mekas arranged for him to cover movies for the *Voice*. Mekas kept his own column, which he devoted to promoting the New American Cinema, and Sarris, who had little interest in experimental cinema (he and Mekas made an odd couple in that regard), reviewed mostly commercial productions.

By 1962, seven years after it was founded, the *Voice* had lost sixty thousand dollars. Circulation was seventeen thousand. Then, lightning struck. On December 7, 1962, the New York Typographical Union went out on strike and shut down every daily paper in the city. They did not strike the *Voice*, however, and by the time the strike ended, one hundred and fourteen days later, *The New York Review of Books* had come into being and *The Village Voice* had more than doubled its circulation. On newsstands in New York City, the *Voice* was outselling *Time*, *Newsweek*, and *The New Yorker*.[79] Suddenly, being the *Voice* movie critic was a big deal. Much to his astonishment, Sarris was well known.

Kael's attack on him appeared that year in the pages of *Film Quarterly*. She was ostensibly responding to an article Sarris had published the year before in *Film Culture* called "Notes on the Auteur Theory in 1962." By 1962, everyone who read *Film Culture* knew what an auteur was. Sarris was responding to some objections to auteur theory that had been raised by Bazin himself five years earlier, in a piece in *Cahiers*. Sarris's defense of the theory was not theoretical, or not very theoretical; it was essentially pragmatic. He was trying to explain why the assumptions of auteurism helped critics understand and evaluate movies. "At the very least," he said, "I would like to grant the condemned system a hearing before its execution . . . What follows is consequently less a manifesto than a credo, a somewhat disorganized credo, to be sure, expressed in formless notes rather than in formal brief."[80] He would soon wish that he had taken a little more trouble with the form.

A great deal of the sensation made by Kael's attack on Sarris was owed to its ad hominem character. She made fun of Sarris's prose, of his brains, and of his taste, and at the end she suggested that auteur theory was "an attempt by adult males to justify staying inside the small range of experience of their boyhood and adolescence—that period when masculinity looked so great and important, but art was something talked about by poseurs and phonies and sensitive-feminine types."[81] It is not clear how this is an argument against *la politique des auteurs*.

Kael did score some points against auteurism: it ignored the collaborative nature of moviemaking, and it led to excessive attention to minor work in search of what Sarris had clumsily called the "interior meaning," a hidden or implicit meaning that auteurists attribute to the director. "[The] ideal auteur," as Kael summed up the theory, "is the man who signs a long-term contract, directs any script that's handed to him, and expresses himself by shoving bits of style up the crevasses of the plots."[82]

Sarris never really recovered. "I was completely amazed that I would be attacked that way. I was flabbergasted. And I wish I had had my essay reprinted after hers, because I think what happened was that more people read her piece than ever read mine," he later said.[83] Kael had asked the editor of *Film Quarterly*, Ernest Callenbach, to send an advance copy of her piece to Sarris with the suggestion that he might care to reply in the same issue. Sarris passed on the invitation, although he did publish a response in a subsequent issue, an essay called "The Auteur Theory and the Perils of Pauline." In that article, he did not mention "Circles and Squares" once.

Sarris and Kael did meet, at her invitation, in 1964. He came into the city from Queens, where he was living with his mother, and met Kael with her daughter and a friend at a restaurant. He found the evening uncomfortable. "I wasn't as worldly and aggressive as she was about sex," he said later. "About who was gay and who wasn't. I wasn't an expert on such things."[84] He always felt that Kael was somehow impugning his sexuality—even though, as he knew, she had been close to homosexuals (like Duncan and Broughton) in San Francisco, and even though he was not gay.[85] Thirty years later, this was still bothering him.[86]

At the same time that Kael's piece appeared, Sarris published a sixty-eight-page piece on American directors in a special issue of *Film Culture*, in which he ranked American directors in multiple categories of his own invention, from Pantheon Directors (Chaplin, Hawks, Welles, etc.) to Fallen Idols (John Huston, Elia Kazan, Billy Wilder) and Minor

Disappointments (John Frankenheimer, Stanley Kubrick). This act of critical taxonomy presented a big target to skeptics of auteurism. Kael used it to attack Sarris in *Film Quarterly* all over again. She called the piece "a big shell game of distinctions, theories, judgments, terminologies, comparisons . . . The more Sarris writes of 'systematic reappraisal' the more confusion piles up around him. This Hercules fills his own Augean Stables, and types up little lists to clean them out."[87]

Film Quarterly had a circulation of 5,500, but the contretemps got picked up and commented on in other magazines, though most of these were film journals, like *Sight and Sound, Film Comment,* and *Cinéaste.* The only more general interest magazines that covered it were *Commentary* and the *Saturday Review.* Still, the attention no doubt helped Kael win a Guggenheim, which she used to put together *I Lost It at the Movies.*

So when *Bonnie and Clyde* opened in the summer of 1967, Kael was without a job. She wrote a seven-thousand-word defense of the movie and submitted it to *The New Republic,* but the magazine said it was too long. So she had her agent offer it to a magazine where space was never a problem, *The New Yorker.* Unexpectedly, since *The New Yorker* had already published a favorable review of *Bonnie and Clyde,* William Shawn bought it.[88] By the time Kael's piece came out, on October 14, 1967, the movie had already closed.

7.

In 1967, *The New Yorker* was the most successful magazine in America. Two years before, it had carried 6,092 pages of advertising. Its closest competitor, *Business Week,* had 4,808 pages. And *The New Yorker* had turned down $750,000 worth of ads for firms, such as Sears, Roebuck, whose products it considered beneath the taste level of its audience. In 1966, *The New Yorker* ran 6,143 pages of ads.[89]

The magazine's business plan was niche marketing. Circulation was under five hundred thousand, and there were no efforts to increase it, because *The New Yorker* wanted to be able to tell advertisers that it was delivering an upper-quintile demographic, consisting of readers who could afford the jewelry, fur coats, and expensive scotches advertised in its pages, and that the target audience for these goods matched its circulation base. In other words, advertising dollars were not being wasted on people who could not afford the product. The magazine turned down ads for Sears because it had ads for Bergdorf and Bonwit Teller. *The New Yorker* was a general-interest commercial magazine for people who disliked commercialism and who rarely subscribed to general-interest magazines—a magazine, essentially, for people who didn't read magazines. There was no better way, if you were selling an upscale product in 1965, to reach them.

The purpose of a magazine's editorial content is the same as the purpose of a television show's entertainment content: it is to pick out a demographic for advertisers. And in the postwar period, a literate and unstuffy anti-commercialism was a cherished ingredient of upper-middle-class taste. *The New Yorker* reached this audience with an editorial product rigorously manufactured to avoid any semblance of the sensational, the prurient, or the merely topical—any semblance, that is, of the things educated people could be assumed to associate with commercial media.[90]

It also avoided, less famously but with equal diligence, anything that hinted at cultural pretension, and this policy, too, was based on a genuine insight into the psychology of its audience. For *New Yorker* readers, though proud of their education and their taste, were culturally insecure. They did not need to be told who Proust and Freud and Stravinsky were, but they were glad, at the same time, not to be expected to know anything terribly specific about them. They were intelligent people who were extremely wary of being out-browed. They were eager not to like the wrong things, or to like the right things for the wrong reasons.

The New Yorker was enormously attentive to this insecurity. It pruned from its pieces anything that might come across as allusive or knowing, and it promoted, in its writing and cartoons, a sensibility that took urbanity to be perfectly compatible with a certain kind of naïveté. *The New Yorker* made it possible to feel that being an anti-sophisticate was the mark of true sophistication, and that any culture worth having could be had without special aesthetic equipment or intellectual gymnastics.

Kael made it possible for people to feel this way about the movies. She was hired by *The New Yorker* soon after the *Bonnie and Clyde* piece was published. She started in January 1968, replacing Brendan Gill, and split her duties with Penelope Gilliatt, a situation she complained about constantly. Gilliatt finally stopped her column in 1979. Kael retired in

1991. By then, she had raised a band of critical disciples and taught a generation how to respond not just to movies but to popular entertainment generally.* This was cultural work that needed to be done.

The New Yorker was the perfect place to do it because it required disarming both of the phobias in the sensibility the magazine had so successfully identified: the fear of too low and the fear of too high. It meant overcoming the intelligent person's resistance to the pulpiness, the corniness, and the general moral and aesthetic schmaltz of Hollywood movies, but without refining those things away by some type of critical alchemy, as Kael accused Sarris of trying to do. *The New Yorker*'s readers did not want an invitation to slum. But they didn't want to be told that appreciating movies was something that called for a command of *la politique des auteurs*, either. They needed to believe that it was possible to enjoy the movies without becoming either of the two things *New Yorker* readers would sooner have died than be taken for: idiots or snobs.

This was precisely the approach that Kael had devoted her pre–*New Yorker* career to perfecting. She aimed at people who did not want to sit through either *The Sound of Music* or *Hiroshima Mon Amour* (which she called "a woman's picture—in the most derogatory sense of the term").[91] "Object to the Hollywood film and you're an intellectual snob," she had written in 1956; "object to the avant-garde film and you're a Philistine."[92] Educated people were afraid to enjoy movies—even though, as she pointed out, the advantage movies have over poetry and classical music is: "We go to the movies because we want to."[93] That was always the starting point of her criticism.

The critic she singled out in her attack on *Hiroshima Mon Amour* as falling for the movie's mystique was Dwight Macdonald. Her criticism of people like Macdonald was that their Eurocentrism made them unable to understand American movies and why Americans liked them. "What you're not willing to do," she lectured Macdonald and the critic John Simon in a panel discussion at the Donnell Library in midtown in 1963, "is to accept the enthusiasm an *American* feels for the *American* experience when it's handled on the screen."[94]

---

* Kael's, mostly male, disciples, known as the Paulettes, covered many popular culture fields: Greil Marcus (music), Tom Shales and James Wolcott (television), Terrence Rafferty, David Denby, Hal Hinson, Michael Sragow, Elvis Mitchell, David Edelstein, John Powers, and Peter Rainer (movies), Lloyd Rose (theater), and Allen Barra (sports). No other postwar critic exerted as much influence as Kael. The troops were kept in line through the awareness that at any moment, she might turn on them, as she did, for example, with Rafferty and Denby.

By 1965, Macdonald had written himself into a difficult place. He had become the scourge of the middlebrow. He had helped Clement Greenberg produce "Avant-Garde and Kitsch," back in 1939, and he adopted Greenberg's high-low scheme. "Folk Art was the people's own institution, their private little kitchen-garden," Macdonald wrote in 1953, shortly after he joined *The New Yorker* as a staff writer. ". . . But Mass Culture breaks down the wall, integrating the masses into a debased form of High Culture and thus becoming an instrument of political domination." A more insidious development, however, was what he called *l'avant-garde pompier*, phony avant-gardism. "There is nothing more vulgar," he declared, "than sophisticated *kitsch*."[95]

This "indeterminate specimen" Macdonald would name Midcult, the culture of middlebrow aspiration. Mass culture could be left to the masses; the real enemy was the literature, music, theater, art, and criticism of middle-class high-mindedness. And over the next ten years, Macdonald devoted much of his critical zeal to the job of identifying Midcult, exposing its calculated banalities, and persuading readers of its meretriciousness.

One of his first long pieces for *The New Yorker* was a demolition job on the Encyclopedia Britannica's fifty-four-volume edition, with Syntopicon (a two-volume index of topics), of the Great Books, and on the enterprise's Aristotle, Mortimer J. Adler.* Shawn was pleased with the piece, and he encouraged Macdonald to find more monuments to demolish. Macdonald was happy to do so. He took on the Revised Standard Version of the King James Bible (in 1953), the young British writer Colin Wilson's work of popular philosophy, *The Outsider* (1956), and Webster's Third International Dictionary (1962).

It is not hard to guess why Shawn was pleased with Macdonald's takedowns of middlebrow enterprises like Adler's Great Books. The subjects made for witty, intelligent journalism; readers loved the pieces and wrote letters saying so; and they attracted attention. But there might have been another reason lurking in the shadows. Shawn was an enigmatic figure. It's impossible to know (as it's impossible to know in the case of most successful magazine editors) how much of his editorial

---

* Adler had taught in John Erskine's General Honors, the course Trilling would take over, before going to the University of Chicago.

policy was calculation based on a canny insight into his magazine's readership and how much was simply a reflection of what he unaffectedly liked and didn't like. But he must have seen that Macdonald's pieces put just the inch and a half of distance he needed between his glossy and carefully crafted product and the genteel fakery of wannabes and rivals. Macdonald's attacks on middlebrowism inoculated *The New Yorker* against the charge of being middlebrow.

Those attacks on middlebrow were directed as much at the cultural establishment as they were at buyers and readers. Macdonald thought that people were being tricked into purchasing these goods by being told that they ought to like them, or that the stuff was good for them. Just like kitsch, Midcult was a marketing phenomenon. It was culture manufactured for the aspiring sophisticate. In the case of kitsch, no one was being fooled. What alarmed Macdonald was that in the case of Midcult, *everyone* seemed to be fooled—not only the readers but also the writers, the editors, the publishers, and the reviewers. They had all become convinced of their own high-mindedness. They believed that they were engaged in an uplifting enterprise of human betterment—even as they raked in the profits. "No promotion" was their means of promotion, and readers who aspired to something superior to simple pleasure and diversion fell for it. It was funny that he could not see that the magazine he wrote his pieces for had perfected this formula to a point where it had become nearly invisible.

But this is exactly what Kael was calling Macdonald out on in the case of *Hiroshima Mon Amour*. He had fallen for a sales pitch. The movie is arty, it's European, it's about love and death. It can even be hard to sit through, a real test of seriousness. Kael thought that Macdonald was being forced to pretend to like something he could not possibly have really liked. But since he had written off mass culture entertainment, and now had written off Broadway theater and literary fiction, he had browed himself into a corner.

Kael didn't persuade *New Yorker* readers to go to Hollywood movies; they were already going. That wasn't the problem. The problem was teaching them how to think intelligently about them. One way to think intelligently is to have a theory, and Kael hated theories. "[M]ovies are a medium in which it's possible to respond in an infinity of ways to an infinity of material without forming precise or definite attitudes, or

making conscious judgments, or referring to values of any kind beyond 'cinema,'" she wrote in 1966. ". . . Turning the movies into an
official academic 'art' can be a way of stripping them of relevance to
our lives."[96]

"Isn't it clear that trying to find out what cinema 'really' is, is derived from a mad Platonic and metaphorical view of the universe," she
said at a film conference at Dartmouth in 1965, "—as if ideal, pure
cinema were some pre-existent entity that we had to find? Cinema is not
to be found; but movies are continuously being made."[97] In an essay reprinted in *I Lost It at the Movies*, "Is There a Cure for Movie Criticism?":
"We want to see, to feel, to understand, to respond in a new way. Why
should pedants be allowed to spoil the game?"[98]

Her way of responding to movies was not very different from Susan
Sontag's idea about an erotics of interpretation. "If a lady says, 'That
man don't pleasure me,'" she explained to the readers of *Holiday* in
1966, "that's it. There are some areas in which we can decide for ourselves."[99] Male critics at first didn't know what she was talking about.
The *New York Times* reviewer, the film historian Richard Schickel, began his review of *I Lost It at the Movies* by saying, "I am not certain just
what Miss Kael thinks she lost at the movies." "[W]hat *did* she lose at
the movies?" Macdonald asked in his review.[100] If there was any doubt,
Kael's titles for subsequent collections cleared it up: *Kiss Kiss Bang Bang,
Going Steady, Deeper into Movies, When the Lights Go Down, Taking It
All In.*

Kael's contention that serious movies should meet the same standard as pulp—that they should be entertaining—turned out to be an
extremely useful and widely adopted critical principle. For it rests on
an empirically solid proposition, which is that although people sometimes have a hard time deciding whether or not something is art, they
are rarely fooled into thinking they are being entertained when they are
not. It was Kael's therapeutic advice to the overcultivated that if they
just concentrated on responding to the stimulus, the aesthetics would
take care of themselves.

8.

Kael understood what Newman and Benton were trying to do with
Bonnie and Clyde because before she wrote her piece about the movie,

she took them to lunch. She was therefore able to explain that *Bonnie and Clyde* combined comedy and horror because "the young French directors discovered the poetry of crime in American life (from our movies) and showed the Americans how to put it on the screen in a new, 'existential' way." She was also able to "guess" that Newman and Benton, "whose Bonnie seems to owe so much to Catherine in 'Jules and Jim,' had more interesting ideas about Bonnie's and Clyde's (and maybe C. W.'s) sex lives."[101] Amazing. How did she know that?

Neither Kael's reconsideration nor Morgenstern's retraction brought *Bonnie and Clyde* back from the dead, however. That happened because in December, *Time* ran a Robert Rauschenberg collage of images from *Bonnie and Clyde* on the cover. The story inside (unsigned, but by Stefan Kanfer) was titled "The Shock of Freedom in Films." Kanfer called *Bonnie and Clyde* "not only the sleeper film of the decade but also, to a growing consensus of audiences and critics, the best movie of the year." (There had certainly been no such consensus.) "Hollywood has at long last become part of what the French film journal *Cahiers du Cinéma* calls 'the furious springtime of world cinema,'" he declared. *Bonnie and Clyde* "has proved to the industry that the 'new movie' and 'popular success' are not antithetical terms."[102] The article enabled Beatty to persuade Warner's to rerelease the film. The day it reopened, it received ten Academy Award nominations.*

Casting Bonnie was a challenge. The role was turned down by Tuesday Weld, Natalie Wood, Carol Lynley, and Jane Fonda.[103] Newman and Benton had Jean Seberg in mind for the part.[104] Penn imagined Bardot. But he found Dunaway (who, in an odd coincidence, was also coming off an Otto Preminger picture, *Hurry Sundown*).

Benton and Newman's treatment begins with Bonnie sauntering down the street, trailed by Clyde. The opening of the movie is completely different. Dunaway is naked on her bed, her hair dyed blond, her lips made up in a pout, exhibitionistic, sexually restless: it's the opening of . . . *And God Created Woman* transported from '50s St. Tropez to '30s Texas, complete with the car. The thin shift she throws on after she sees

---

* It won two: Estelle Parsons, for Best Supporting Actress, and Burnett Guffey, for Cinematography. Mike Nichols won Best Director for *The Graduate*; Best Picture was *In the Heat of the Night*.

Clyde out the window, casing her mother's car, and runs downstairs to confront him is like the shifts Bardot sashays around in in Vadim's movie. When Dunaway stroked Clyde's pistol and sucked on her Coke bottle, the New Wave had truly come to America.

Dunaway thought that the essence of the character was sexual freedom. "I was finally liberated from that damn push-up bra," she said. ". . . Bonnie was a creature who wanted freedom, and a bra just didn't fit. That she wasn't wearing any underwear in the opening scene belonged to the sexuality of the woman."[105] What Beauvoir had said about B.B.

Most of the controversy around *Bonnie and Clyde* was about the violence, and this reflects Penn's contribution. Penn knew that he had a chance to do something new because Mike Nichols's *Who's Afraid of Virginia Woolf?* (1966)—in which he was forced to change the play's "Screw you!" to "Goddamn you!"—had shown the old Production Code to be a dinosaur. The Code was in limbo in 1967 (in 1968, it would be replaced by the ratings system), and Penn seized the opportunity.

The Code had been interpreted to forbid a director from showing a gun firing and a person being hit in the same shot. Until 1951, when an exception was made for scenes "absolutely necessary" for the plot, it had specifically banned showing law-enforcing officers, including private detectives and bank guards, dying at the hands of criminals. This explains the shock that audiences felt when they saw Clyde shoot a bank manager clinging to the running board of the getaway car, and, in the same shot, blood pouring down the man's face. No one had ever seen that effect before.*

That scene is, of course, a generic convention: the crime couple's capers are played for laughs until somebody gets killed. But Penn filmed the scene as though in direct response to Godard's montage in *Breathless*. Godard had made the montage visible. Penn eliminated it entirely. And just to underline the point, he imitated the famous last shot of the Odessa Steps sequence in *Battleship Potemkin*. It is as though he had Eisenstein's *Film Form* open in front of him when he did the scene.

---

* The special effects in *Bonnie and Clyde* were by Danny Lee.

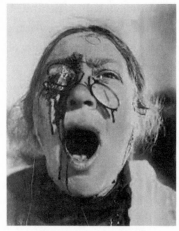

Sergei Eisenstein, dir.,
Battleship Potemkin (1925).

Arthur Penn, dir.,
Bonnie and Clyde (1967).

In their treatment, Benton and Newman specified that the massacre of Bonnie and Clyde at the end of the movie "takes just seconds." "*At no point* in the gun-fight do we see Bonnie and Clyde in motion. We never see Bonnie and Clyde dead."[106] That was consistent with Code restrictions. But Penn thought it was too abrupt, and he so contrived his celebrated ending, a ballet of death with Bonnie's and Clyde's bodies twitching spastically as the bullets mow them down.

Penn used four cameras filming at different speeds, and spliced the sequence with real-time sound.[107] The scene recalls, of course, Belmondo's similarly extended dance of death as he staggers down a Paris street before collapsing and dying while the *flics* stare contemptuously down at him. Since the Code had not allowed the camera to rest on a dead body, Penn's ending caused a sensation, and his technique has been used in Hollywood ever since. Just to make the allusion clear, as Clyde and Bonnie drive up to the scene of the ambush, he is wearing a pair of sunglasses with a lens missing. That is an allusion to the penultimate scene of *Breathless*, when Michel, too tired and bored to run any longer, sits and waits for the police to arrive, wearing a pair of sunglasses with a lens missing. The screenwriters insisted on the quotation.[108]

Dunaway became the symbol not only of the movie but also of what the movie stood for in the New Hollywood—just as Bardot had come to symbolize the New Wave. She was on the cover of *Life* (January 12, 1968) and the cover of *Newsweek* (March 4, 1968). Bardot took the compliment. On New Year's Eve, 1967, she and her new boyfriend, the composer Serge Gainsbourg, performed "Bonnie and Clyde" (written by Gainsbourg) on French television. Bardot was wearing the kind of clothes (designed by Theodora Van Runkle, who was nominated for an Oscar) the movie had made popular. A month later, *Bonnie and Clyde* opened in Paris to enormous attention. The stars rode to the premiere in antique cars; the mannequins in the shop windows they passed were all wearing Bonnie and Clyde outfits—1930s pin-striped suits, midi skirts, berets. The movie is said to have revived the French beret industry. Production went from 1,500 to 20,000 hats a week.

The British opening was also a smash. The Warner Theatre in Leicester Square reported the biggest one-day box office in its thirty-three-year history. In six months, four million tickets were sold.[109] Later that winter, Penn and Beatty were sitting in a restaurant in London when Penn thought he recognized Dunaway sitting at another table. The woman was wearing a beret and a Bonnie Parker blouse. She turned out to be Brigitte Bardot.[110]

Reception in France was more mixed. *Bonnie and Clyde* was a hit, but, except for fashion, it did not really affect French culture, in part because the appeal the movie enjoyed in the United States—outlaw family against the System—didn't mean much to the French, who had not yet been touched by the counterculture. But it was also because cinematically, the French had already been there. *Cahiers du Cinéma* ran an interview with Penn in December before the movie opened, but it panned the movie in March. "The era (roaring twenties) is just a cunning pretext for unleashing a violence that is as aseptic as it is profitable," wrote its critic, Michel Delahaye, not bothering even to get the decade right. ". . . The director has such contempt for his characters that he treats them as though they were retarded."[111]* Godard, too, did not have much use for what Penn had done. He called Newman and Benton. "Now that we have Penn's version," he said, "it's time to do ours." Truffaut was disgusted by the decision to eliminate the ménage à trois. He thought Beatty had censored the script out of fear of being ridiculed.

A month after *Bonnie and Clyde* opened in Paris, Malraux had Langlois fired from the leadership of the Cinémathèque. There were protests

---

* On the other hand, *Positif* called it a "film sublime." As in the United States, most general-interest reviews in France focused on the violence.

and fights in the streets (Helen Scott was knocked down in one), until, in April, Langlois was reinstated. A week later, the riots of May '68 broke out. The counterculture had come to France. Godard became a Maoist, *Cahiers* became Marxist, and French movie culture never recovered. Today, European cinema in the United States has almost disappeared. In the 1960s European films accounted for 5 percent of the American box office and American films for 35 percent of the European box office. By the mid-1990s, European films accounted for 0.5 percent of the box office in the United States and Hollywood movies generated 80 percent of movie revenue in Europe. Only the subsidy system keeps French cinema alive.

Bonnie and Clyde is not really a New Wave movie, any more than *À bout de souffle* is a gangster movie. ("It belongs . . . with 'Alice in Wonderland,'" Godard later said of his movie. "I thought it was 'Scarface.'")[112] *Bonnie and Clyde* is a Hollywood movie. Beatty is an entertainer, and it's his movie. But it is serious entertainment made by people who knew something about the medium. And it changed American movie culture. Three months after his review of *Bonnie and Clyde* was published, the *Times* announced Crowther's retirement. He had been at the paper since 1940. He was replaced in January by Renata Adler, who was twenty-nine years old. The same month, Kael began at *The New Yorker*, where she would preside over the Hollywood New Wave—the period, from 1968 to 1980, of Francis Ford Coppola, Martin Scorsese, Robert Altman, Stanley Kubrick, Paul Mazursky, Peter Bogdanovich, Hal Ashby. Those directors' films did not "save Hollywood"; Hollywood was saved by *The Exorcist* and *The Towering Inferno* and *Jaws*. But they restored its credibility. They brought the cinema back to America.

18

THIS IS THE END

U.S. marines landing at Red Beach Two, ten miles north of Da Nang, on the morning of March 8, 1965—the first American combat troops deployed in Vietnam. By 1968, 536,100 American soldiers would be stationed there. (*Bettmann / Getty Images*)

1.

For almost thirty years, by means financial, military, and diplomatic, the United States tried to prevent Vietnam from becoming a Communist state. Millions died in that struggle. By the time active American military engagement ended, the United States had dropped three times as many tons of bombs on North Vietnam, a country the size of Illinois, as were dropped by the Allies in all of the Second World War. In matériel and lost aircraft, the United States spent ten dollars for every dollar of damage its bombs inflicted.[1] Three million Americans served in Vietnam; 58,000 died there. The United States got nothing for it.

There were really two wars against the Communists in Vietnam. The first was an anti-colonial war between Communist nationalists and France, which, except for a few months in 1945 when the Japanese took over, had ruled the country since 1884. This was the War in Indochina. It lasted from 1946 to 1954, when the French lost a battle at Dien Bien Phu and negotiated a settlement, the Geneva accords, that partitioned the country at the seventeenth parallel. The United States had funded France's military failure to the tune of $2.5 billion, more money than France received under the Marshall Plan.[2] The second war was a civil war between the two "states" created at Geneva: North Vietnam, governed by Communists, and South Vietnam, backed by American aid and, eventually, American troops. That war lasted from 1954 (or 1955 or 1959, depending on one's definition of an "act of war") to 1975, when Communist forces entered Saigon and unified the country. This second war was the War in Vietnam.*

Geopolitics helps to account for the U.S. government's concerns about the future of Indochina in the 1940s and 1950s, a time when relations with the Soviet Union and China were hostile and Southeast Asia and the Korean peninsula were in political turmoil. But paying for France, a nearly bankrupt power, to reclaim its colony just as the world was about to experience a wave of decolonization was a dubious undertaking. By 1963, "peaceful co-existence" was the policy of the American and Soviet governments, Korea had been successfully partitioned, and the Sino-Soviet split made the threat of a global Communist movement no longer seem a pressing concern. And yet that was when the United States gave its blessing to a coup in which the president of South Vietnam, Ngo Dinh Diem, was assassinated, and embarked, soon after, on a policy of military escalation. In 1963, there were sixteen thousand American advisers in South Vietnam; by 1968, more than half a million American troops were deployed there.

The American military mission was catastrophic on many dimensions. The average age of American GIs in Vietnam was nineteen. (In the Second World War, it was twenty-six.) In 1970, some sixty thousand of them were on drugs, opium or heroin, and more than eight hundred incidents of fragging—officers wounded or killed by their own troops—were reported. Half a million veterans would suffer from post-traumatic stress disorder (PTSD), a higher proportion than for either of

---

* A third war, in 1979, between China and Vietnam was the bloodiest in terms of casualties per day, but by then most of the rest of the world was not taking notice.

the two world wars.[3] In fact, that term originated as a way of diagnosing Vietnam veterans.

It is not the case that Western opinion leaders turned against the war only after U.S. marines waded ashore at Da Nang in 1965 and the body count began to rise. Intervention in Southeast Asia will be "an endless entanglement," France's president, Charles de Gaulle, told President Kennedy when the Kennedys made their brilliant visit to Paris in 1961. The United States, he said, would find itself in a "bottomless military and political quagmire, however much you spend in men and money."[4] Jawaharlal Nehru, the prime minister of India, said that sending American troops would be a disastrous decision. Walter Lippmann, the dean of American political commentators back when political commentary had such titles, warned in 1963 that "the price of a military victory in the Vietnamese war is higher than American vital interests can justify."[5]

De Gaulle and Nehru had reasons of their own for wanting the United States to keep out of Southeast Asia. But Kennedy himself was keenly aware of the risks of entrapment, and so was his successor. "There ain't no daylight in Vietnam, there's not a bit," Lyndon Johnson said in 1965.[6] Three years later, he was forced to withdraw from his own reelection campaign, his political career destroyed by his inability to end the war. The first time someone claimed to see "the light at the end of the tunnel" in Vietnam was in 1953. People were still using that expression in 1967. By then, a large percentage of American public opinion and much of the media had turned against the war. Yet the United States continued to send men to fight there for six more years.

Johnson had no experience in foreign policy. Much as Harry S. Truman had, he allowed the generals and the policy hawks to convince him of a central fallacy of Cold War thinking: that America's standing was at stake in every regime change around the world. But it is doubtful that the country's standing was ever dependent on its commitment to South Vietnam. France had lost a war of colonial liberation. That could have been the end of it. Instead, a war of nation-building turned into a war of attrition. After American troops began arriving, the policy was to kill as many of the enemy as possible. "The Oriental doesn't put the same high price on life as the Westerner," explained William Westmoreland, commander of American forces from 1964 to 1968. "Life is plentiful, life is cheap in the Orient. And as a philosophy of the Orient expresses it, life is not important."[7]

American presidents who pursued a policy of engagement in Vietnam were not imperialists. They genuinely wanted a free and independent South Vietnam, and the gap between that aspiration and the reality of the military and political situation in-country turned out to be unbridgeable. Political terms are short, and so politics is short-term. The main consideration that seems to have presented itself to those presidents, from Truman to Nixon, who insisted on staying the course was domestic politics—the fear of being blamed by voters for losing Southeast Asia to Communism. If Southeast Asia was going to be lost, they preferred that it be on some other president's head.

Vietnam was obviously a crisis in foreign policy. Did it affect electoral politics? Voters wanted the United States out of Vietnam, but many also wanted the United States to win first. In 1968, when Vietnam was the central issue in Democratic presidential politics, 20 percent of Northern Democrats favored withdrawal and 35 percent favored escalation.[8] There was a bolus of discontent, in other words, but it did not translate into clear-cut political realignment. Vietnam had a smaller effect on the fortunes of the Democratic Party than the 1964 Civil Rights Act did.[9] Race relations reconfigured American politics, not foreign policy.*

But Vietnam was a huge cultural inflection point. Much as the First World War did for European modernism, the War in Vietnam disrupted the artistic and critical avant-garde of its time. Preoccupations changed from formal and aesthetic questions to political questions. Susan Sontag's transformation is emblematic. She went from political indifference to the barricades almost overnight. *Against Interpretation*, a book as nonpolitical as *Understanding Poetry*, came out in January 1966; a month later, on February 20, Sontag joined Norman Mailer, Robert Lowell, and other writers in an antiwar "Read-In" at Town Hall. It was the first political protest of her life.[10] The next winter, she was calling the United States "the arch-imperium of the planet, holding man's biological as well as his historical future in its King Kong paws . . . American power is indecent in its scale." The United States, she said, was "founded on a genocide"; it is "the culmination of Western white civilization," and "the white race *is* the cancer of human history."[11]

---

* Crudely: the Democratic Party lost white voters. In 1968, Hubert Humphrey got 38 percent of the white vote. George McGovern got 32 percent in 1972; Jimmy Carter, a Southerner, got 36 percent running against Ronald Reagan in 1980; Hillary Clinton got 37 percent in 2016 running against a man almost no one thought could win. Race was a subtext in all those elections.

In that article, Sontag identified with young antiwar protestors, distancing herself from an older generation of leftists, like Irving Howe and Philip Rahv, who dismissed youth culture and youth activism as naïve and irresponsible. Sontag was *almost* a young person in 1967. She was thirty-four. Howe was forty-seven; Rahv was fifty-nine. But Sontag was right: Vietnam split liberals along generational lines. This is largely because it intersected with a backlash against the postwar university.

2.

There have been student political organizations since the beginning of the twentieth century. The Intercollegiate Socialist Society was founded by the writer Upton Sinclair in 1905 as the campus wing of the Socialist Party of America. Student political organizations in the 1960s, however, were distinctive. For one thing, they were committed to direct action—marches, boycotts, sit-ins, strikes.* They were not simply recruiting devices for electoral politics. Student activists were (usually) radical democrats, but they had little interest in electoral politics. Most of them rejected the two major parties. Many of them rejected the whole idea of parties.

And a chief target of their protests was the university itself. This was new. People in an older generation for whom higher education had been the golden door out of working-class life or ethnic provincialism could not understand why students would want to shut down the universities. They were tearing up their own tickets. When, in 1968, Lionel Trilling heard that Columbia students had occupied Hamilton Hall and were holding the dean, Henry Coleman, hostage, he thought at first that it might be "a rather friendly hoax."[12] He could not get his head around the idea that college students had political agendas. Nineteen sixty-eight was a little late to be picking up on this, but presidents of major universities—Columbia, Harvard, Berkeley, Cornell—lost their jobs because they failed to grasp that student activists were not motivated by regard for their institutions.

Most distinctive and least definable was the "rush" that many student activists later recalled, a kind of "new dawn" sensation, a feeling of personal liberation achieved through political solidarity. This feeling is

---

* Students in other countries engaged in direct action before American students started doing it, including in Turkey, South Korea, and Japan.

what Americans who were in college then usually mean by "the Sixties": a largely illusory but nevertheless genuinely moving sense of agency, a sense that the world was turning under their marching feet. Like any social affect, there is a story behind it.

The new type of student organization emerged independently at two universities that were major educational success stories: the University of Michigan and the University of California at Berkeley. Those schools were great postwar knowledge factories. More than a third of their students were in graduate or professional school. Michigan had more contracts with the National Aeronautics and Space Administration (NASA) than any other university in the country. Berkeley was the main federal contractor for nuclear research, and had more Nobel laureates on its faculty than any other university in the world.[13]

Michigan was the birthplace of the largest and best-known student political organization of the decade (and probably ever), Students for a Democratic Society (SDS).[14] SDS was descended from the Student League for Industrial Democracy (SLID), which was a subsidiary of the League for Industrial Democracy (LID), which was a successor to Sinclair's Intercollegiate Socialist Society of 1905. SLID had been limping along until, in 1960, it was renamed SDS—on the grounds that, as the first president of SDS, Alan Haber, put it, SLID was an embarrassing acronym for an outfit in decline.[15]

Haber entered the University of Michigan in 1954 (and did not receive his BA until 1965). His first name was Robert, after the Progressive senator Robert La Follette of Wisconsin, and his parents approved of SLID and their son's politics. Haber was known at Michigan as the campus radical, but he was not a fire-eater. If SDS had been associated only with people like him, it would almost certainly have failed to attract recruits. To do that, it needed a charismatic person who came from the place most students at big public universities in the Midwest in the 1950s came from, the shores of the American mainstream. Tom Hayden was such a person.

Hayden was born in Royal Oak, a suburb of Detroit, in 1939. His parents were Catholic—he was named for Saint Thomas Aquinas—who, unusually, got divorced, and Hayden was raised principally by his mother in somewhat straitened circumstances. But he had a normal childhood and he did well in school. He entered Michigan in 1957 and became a reporter on the student paper, *The Michigan Daily*.

Hayden had no political ambitions. In his coursework, he was drawn to the existentialists. Walter Kaufmann, whose anthology *Existentialism from Dostoevsky to Sartre* came out in 1956 and was popular among college students, taught at Michigan as a visitor, and Hayden took a class with him. But in 1960, there was an uptick in student activism, and Hayden, a twenty-one-year-old college junior, independent and professionally uncommitted, was perfectly positioned to be caught up in it. "I didn't get political," as he put it. "Things got political."[16]

The inspiration for the Northern student movement was a Southern student movement.[17] On February 1, 1960, four first-year students from the all-Black North Carolina Agricultural and Technical State University sat down at a whites-only lunch counter in the Woolworth's department store in downtown Greensboro. The waitress (an African American) refused to serve them, so they sat there all day. The next day, nineteen additional students showed up to sit at the lunch counter. The day after, it was eighty-five. By the end of the week, there were four hundred. Sit-ins quickly spread across the state and beyond.[18]* Within six weeks, the movement had led to the formation, under the leadership of a civil rights veteran, Ella Baker, of the Student Non-Violent Coordinating Committee (SNCC), which would become the major activist organization of the civil rights movement.† James Baldwin, on his second trip to the South, met with activist students at Florida A&M, in Tallahassee. "They are not the first Negroes to face mobs," he wrote in *Mademoiselle*; "they are merely the first Negroes to frighten the mob more than the mob frightens them . . . It seems to me they are the only people in this country now who really believe in freedom."[19]

In March, Haber came to Hayden's office at the *Daily*. He told him that Michigan students were picketing Ann Arbor stores as a show of sympathy for the Southern students, and suggested that he cover it. Hayden went out to report on the picketers, and he wrote some stories. He had little impulse to join them. Around the same time, though, he read *On the Road*. As it did for many readers, the book inspired him to

---

* There had been sit-ins in at least a dozen cities before Greensboro but none had caught on. It is estimated that seventy thousand people participated in sit-ins after Greensboro, many of which were successful in desegregating lunch counters in places, like Woolworth's, that had a lot of Black customers.

† Among the organizers were John Lewis (later a congressman), Julian Bond (later a state legislator), Marion Barry (later mayor of Washington, D.C.), Diane Nash (a longtime Chicago activist), and James Bevel (later vice presidential candidate on a ticket with Lyndon LaRouche).

hitchhike to California, and there, he got a quick course in politics. In Berkeley, he met with students who had demonstrated at an appearance in San Francisco of the House Un-American Activities Committee, which had subpoenaed a Berkeley student, and who had had the police disperse them with fire hoses. In Delano, he met labor organizers for Chicano farmworkers. In Los Angeles, at the Democratic National Convention that nominated John F. Kennedy for president, he interviewed Martin Luther King, Jr.

And he spoke at a student conference near Monterey sponsored by a Berkeley group called SLATE. Founded in 1957, the name came from a "slate" of anti-discrimination candidates for election to the student government, then dominated by the fraternities and sororities. Hayden's talk was on "value stimulation." The spirit of self-determination, he said, "has bowed to the vast industrial and organizational expansion of the last 75 years. As a result, the majority of students feel helpless to chart their society's direction. The purpose of the student movements is at once simple and profound: to prove human beings are still the measure."[20]

His final stop, in August, was the annual conference of the National Student Association (NSA), being held at the University of Minnesota. About twenty-five members of SNCC had been invited, and Hayden was thrilled to meet them. "They lived on a fuller level of feeling than any people I'd ever seen," he wrote later, "partly because they were making modern history in a very personal way, and partly because by risking death they came to know the value of living each moment to the fullest. Looking back, this was a key turning point, the moment my political identity began to take shape."[21]

The NSA convention was debating whether to adopt a statement of support for the sit-ins. The issue was controversial for some delegates because it meant endorsing illegal actions. One of the speakers in favor of a statement of support was a white graduate student from the University of Texas named Sandra (Casey) Cason.[22] Cason was from Victoria, Texas. Her parents were divorced, and she was raised mainly by her mother.[23] She learned about legal segregation when she read *Brown* in a class in school. She took segregation "as a personal affront," she later said, "viewing it as a restriction on my freedom."[24]

Even before Greensboro, Cason had participated in sit-ins in Austin, where she was active in the Young Women's Christian Association. The

University of Texas, pursuant to *Brown*, had started admitting Black undergraduates in 1956, but only one dormitory was desegregated, the Christian Faith and Life Community. That is where Cason lived. She got interested in existentialism, and began reading Camus. In the summer of 1959, after getting her BA, she taught Bible school in Harlem, and read James Baldwin.

"If I had known that not a single lunch counter would open as a result of my action, I could not have done differently than I did," she said in her speech to the NSA delegates in Minneapolis.

> I am thankful for the sit-ins if for no other reason than that they provided me with an opportunity for making a slogan into a reality by making a decision an action. It seems to me that this is what life is all about. While I would hope that the NSA Congress will pass a strong sit-in resolution, I am more concerned that all of us, Negro and white, realize the possibility of becoming less inhuman humans through commitment and action with all their frightening complexities.
>
> When Thoreau was jailed for refusing to pay taxes to a government which supported slavery, Emerson went to visit him. "Henry David," said Emerson, "what are you doing in there?" Thoreau looked at him and replied, "Ralph Waldo, what are *you* doing out *there?*"

She paused, and then she repeated the last line.[25] There was an ovation. The convention endorsed the sit-ins by a vote of 305 to 37. Hayden was stunned. In almost any earlier left-wing political organization, Cason's speech would have been written off as an expression of bourgeois individualism. But she was saying exactly what Hayden had been saying in Monterey. She was telling the students that this was about *them*.

It is doubtful that Black demonstrators being taunted, fire-hosed, beaten, and arrested felt that they were coming to know "the value of living each moment to the fullest," just as it is doubtful that living in fear of vigilante violence enables Black men to have better orgasms. People like Cason and Hayden cared about injustice, of course; but the fundamental appeal of politics for them was existential. Direct action was not just about liberating oppressed people. It was about becoming an *être-en-soi*. That was the rush. "[W]e were alike . . . in our sense of moral adventure," Hayden wrote about meeting Cason, "our existential sensibility, our love of poetic action, and our feeling of romantic involvement."[26] Hayden was now ready to join SDS.

Hayden courted Cason by sending her boxes of books, including Herman Hesse's *Siddhartha*, which he had madly underlined. He also saw her on several trips to the South. One was to McComb, Mississippi, where he helped Black citizens register to vote in a drive organized by Bob Moses of SNCC (Hayden called him "a Socratic existentialist"), and where he was attacked and knocked to the sidewalk.[27] Tom and Casey got married in 1961.* They moved to New York City, and it was there, in a railroad flat on West Twenty-Second Street, that Hayden wrote the first draft of what would be known as the Port Huron Statement.

"I was influenced deeply by *The Power Elite*," Hayden said, and the effect is obvious.[28] The Port Huron Statement says that the Cold War had made the military the dominant power in what Hayden called (after Mills) "the triangular relations of the business, military, and political arenas." Domestic needs, from housing and health care to minority rights, were all subordinated "to the primary objective of the 'military and economic strength of the Free World.'"[29] The Cold War was making the United States undemocratic.

But who could be agents of change in the regime that Mills and Hayden described? The working class is the agent of change in leftist theory, a theory to which organizations like LID remained true. But history had taken a different turn. In the 1910s and 1920s, when the Socialist Party in the United States had its greatest support—its leader, Eugene Debs, got almost a million votes in the 1920 presidential election even though he was running from prison—between 45 and 50 percent of national income went to the top decile of income earners. In the 1950s, though, the top decile was taking less than 35 percent, and real income growth was roughly the same for the top 10 percent and the bottom 90 percent of earners. GDP growth was also exceptionally high: 2.58 percent per year in the United States between 1949 and 1972, versus only 1.11 percent per year between 1917 and 1948.[30] The class dichotomy of property-owning plutocrats versus exploited proletarians, appropriate in Britain in 1848 when Marx and Engels wrote *The*

---

* The marriage fell apart because Hayden had an affair. They divorced in 1965. Hayden remarried twice, both times to actresses, Jane Fonda and Barbara Williams.

Communist Manifesto, was anachronistic in postwar America. In impressionistic terms: bankers and business executives in the 1950s mostly lived in the same kind of houses, ate the same kind of food, and drove the same kind of cars as the (white) people who worked for them.[31]

For his part, Mills was contemptuous of organized labor. Labor leaders not only sat at the table with the rest of the power elite, he said; they also played no real role in elite decision making. Faith in the revolutionary mission of the working class belonged to what he called the "labor metaphysic," a Victorian relic.[32] Mills was not really interested in wealth and income inequality anyway. He was interested in democracy and power inequality. But he had no candidate for a change agent.

In the fall of 1956, after *The Power Elite* came out, Mills went to Europe on a Fulbright teaching fellowship. He was posted to the University of Copenhagen, but he traveled around (sometimes on a BMW motorcycle he purchased in Munich), and in 1957, he gave a talk at the London School of Economics. That visit was his introduction to the intellectual left in Britain, and he and his hosts hit it off. Mills had been disappointed by the reception of *The Power Elite* in the United States; in Britain, he found people who thought the way he did. "I was much heartened by the way my kind of stuff is taken up there," he wrote to an American friend.[33] When he returned to the United States, he met Irving Howe for lunch and raved nonstop about his discovery of a new intellectual revolutionary cadre. Howe thought Mills was having a manic episode.[34]

The British intellectuals to whom Mills found himself drawn—among them, the cultural theorist Stuart Hall, the historian E. P. Thompson, and the sociologist Ralph Miliband—were calling themselves the New Left.[35]* They were more traditionally Marxist than Mills, but they believed that culture and ideology had become as important as class in determining the course of history. Mills returned to the LSE in 1959 to speak on just that topic, giving three lectures entitled "Culture and Politics." ("A huge, alarming Texan has just been lecturing to the London School of Economics," reported *The Observer*.)[36] In 1960, Mills wrote an article for the British left's journal, *New Left Review*. The article was

---

* "New Left" originated in France, where it dates from 1954 or earlier. André Malraux was using the term *nouvelle gauche* in 1955.

called "Letter to the New Left," and in it Mills announced a new agent of change.

"I have been studying, for several years now, the cultural apparatus, the intellectuals—as a possible, immediate, radical agency of change," he wrote. "For a long time, I was not much happier with this idea than were many of you; but it turns out, in the spring of 1960, that it may be a very relevant idea indeed." He had despaired of finding this kind of intellectual in the United States.[37] But traveling abroad, he had come to believe that young intellectuals were "real live agencies of historical change." They had restored his faith in the ability of intellectuals to enlighten the democratic public. "The Age of Complacency is ending," he concluded. "Let the old women complain wisely about 'the end of ideology.' We are beginning to move again."[38]

Mills's "Letter" was mocked by Daniel Bell, his Columbia colleague and one of the "old women" to whom Mills was referring. Bell called Mills "a kind of faculty adviser to the 'young angries' and 'would-be angries' of the Western world," and said that "what James Burnham once did for 'the managers,' Mills may now be trying to do for the intellectuals."[39] But the "Letter" was immediately taken up by SDS, which circulated copies among its members and reprinted it in a journal, *Studies on the Left*, launched by graduate students at the University of Wisconsin. "He seemed to be speaking to us directly," Hayden wrote about the "Letter"; ". . . [Mills] identified ourselves, the young and the intellectuals, as the new vanguard."[40] This was a wishful misreading. Mills did not have Americans in mind at all. He was responding to developments in Britain, in Eastern Bloc countries such as Poland and Hungary, and above all in Latin America. His next book, *Listen, Yankee*, would be a defense of Castro's revolution.[41] Those were the young intellectuals he was referring to.

Nevertheless, Hayden was inspired to compose his own "Letter to the New (Young) Left," published in *The Activist*, a journal out of Oberlin College. In *his* "Letter," Hayden complained about the "endless repressions of free speech and thought" on campus and "the stifling paternalism that infects the student's whole perception of what is real and possible." Students needed to organize, he said. They could draw on "what remains of the adult labor, academic and political communities," but it was to be a student movement. Student is what "young" meant.

What was needed was not a political program, Hayden said. What was needed was a radical *style*. "[R]adicalism of style," he wrote, "demands that we oppose delusions and be free. It demands that we change our life."[42] Not having a program put the activist out there over the abyss. The American New Left's rejection of programs would turn out to have consequences. Direct actions, like sit-ins, undertaken for one cause (for example, abolishing ROTC), would find themselves being piggybacked by other, often heterogeneous causes (for example, university expansion into Black neighborhoods, as happened at Columbia in 1968 and Harvard in 1969). Demands kept multiplying. This was not because events got out of the organizers' control. It was because that is the way the New Left was designed to work.

It is either ironic or fitting that the SDS convention at which its statement was adopted was held at an educational camp in Port Huron, Michigan, that had been loaned to SDS by the United Auto Workers. For the Port Huron Statement represents the American left's farewell to the labor movement.* The SDS statement did end up containing a section supporting unions, but that was added at the demand of the students' LID sponsors. Some critical remarks about the Soviet Union were added for the same reason. But those preoccupations—the working class and Stalinism—were precisely what the students wanted to be rid of. "[D]ead issues," Casey Hayden called the concern about Communism. "I didn't know any communists, only their children, who were just part of our gang."[43] The students did not think of themselves as pro-Communist. They thought of themselves as anti-anti-Communist. To older left-wing intellectuals, though, that amounted to the same thing. Hence the New Left slogan (coined by Jack Weinberg, at Berkeley) "Don't trust anyone over thirty." It meant, "Don't trust an old socialist."

The Port Huron convention began on June 11, 1962, with fifty-nine registered participants. (SDS then had eleven chapters; there would eventually be more than three hundred.) In the spirit of the document's key concept, "participatory democracy," the delegates debated Hayden's forty-nine-page draft, going through it section by section.[44]

---

* The title of the document may reflect the fact that two years earlier, a conservative student group, the Young Americans for Freedom (YAF), had issued the Sharon Statement, named for the Connecticut town in which William F. Buckley lived. Hayden was much concerned with the YAF. A YAF Rally for World Liberation from Communism at Madison Square Garden in 1962 drew 18,500 people.

Participatory democracy—"democracy is in the streets"—and authenticity were its core principles. "The goal of man and society," the statement says, "should be human independence: a concern not with the image of popularity but with finding a meaning in life that is personally authentic." And since pure democracy and genuine authenticity are conditions that can only be reached asymptotically, it was a formula (like Sartre's) for lifelong recommitment.

The statement begins and ends with the university. "Our professors and administrators," it says,

> sacrifice controversy to public relations; their curriculums change more slowly than the living events of the world; their skills and silence are purchased by investors in the arms race; passion is called unscholastic. The questions we might want raised—what is really important? Can we live in a different and better way? If we wanted to change society, how would we do it?—are not thought to be questions of a "fruitful, empirical nature," and thus are brushed aside.[45]

The university is a mechanism of social reproduction. It "'prepares' the student for 'citizenship' through perpetual rehearsals and, usually, through emasculation of what creative spirit there is in the individual . . . That which is studied, the social reality, is 'objectified' to sterility, dividing the student from life." Academic research serves the power elite. "Many social and physical scientists," the statement says, "neglecting the liberating heritage of higher learning, develop 'human relations' or 'morale-producing' techniques for the corporate economy, while others exercise their intellectual skills to accelerate the arms race."[46] These functions are all masked by the ideology of disinterestedness.

At the end of the statement, the university reappears, but now transformed into a site of radical change. "We believe that the universities are an overlooked seat of influence," it says. They constitute "a potential base and agency in a movement of social change." Academics can perform the role that Mills accused American intellectuals of abandoning: enlightening the public. For this to happen, students and faculty, in alliance, "must wrest control of the educational process from the administrative bureaucracy . . . They must make debate and controversy, not dull pedantic cant, the common style for educational life."[47]

The Port Huron deliberations lasted three days. They ended at dawn.

Hayden was elected president of SDS (Haber was happy to return to being an undergraduate), and the delegates walked together to the shore of Lake Huron, where they stood in silence, holding hands. "It was exalting," one of them, Sharon Jeffrey, said later. "We felt that we were different, that we were going to do things differently. We thought that we knew what had to be done, and that we were going to do it. It felt like the dawn of a new age."[48]

3.

Tom Hayden's charisma was the cool kind. He was lucid and unflappable. Mario Savio's charisma was hot. Savio was a speaker, not a negotiator. He channeled anger. Like Hayden, Savio was raised a Catholic, and like Hayden, his politics were a kind of existentialist anti-politics. "I am not a political person," he said in 1965, a few months after he had become famous as the face of the Berkeley Free Speech Movement, something most people would have called political. ". . . What was it Kierkegaard said about free acts? They're the ones that, looking back, you realize you couldn't help doing."[49]

Savio was born in New York City in 1942. His parents were Italian immigrants, and Italian was his first language. When he learned English, he developed a fairly severe speech impediment, which may have helped make possible his later renown as the greatest orator of the American New Left, since he had to concentrate on his enunciation. Savio entered Christian Brothers Manhattan College in 1960, then transferred to Queens College. When his parents moved to California, he transferred again, this time to Berkeley. He was already socially involved: he worked for a Catholic relief organization in Mexico the summer before coming to Berkeley, and the campus appealed to him in part because he had heard about the student protests against the House Un-American Activities Committee that had been broken up by police. He entered as a junior and majored in philosophy.

His first campus political activity was attending meetings of the University Friends of SNCC. He worked for civil rights in the Bay Area, and in 1964, he went to Mississippi to participate in Freedom Summer. Soon after he returned to Berkeley, the Free Speech Movement (FSM) began.[50]

The Free Speech Movement seemed to erupt spontaneously. That was part of its appeal and part of its mystique: no one planned it, and no one ran it. It had no connection to SDS or any other national political group. But the reason for that is that the FSM was a parochial affair. It was not a war for social justice. It was a war against the university administration. And the fuse had been lit long before 1964.

Tensions between administrators and students dated back to the founding of SLATE in 1957. Tensions between administrators and faculty dated back to the controversy over loyalty oaths in 1949. The administration was hostile to political activism on campus for two reasons. The first had to do with the principle of disinterestedness, which calls for partisan politics to be kept out of the classroom and scholarship. But there was a more pragmatic reason as well. U.C. administrators were wary of the system's Board of Regents, many of whom were conservative businessmen. Joseph McCarthy was dead, but the House Un-American Activities Committee, though increasingly zombie-like, was not. So political activity on campus was banned or tightly regulated—not only student organizations, leafleting, and the like but also outside political speakers. It wasn't that administrators did not want dissent. It was that they did not want trouble.

Until the fall semester in 1964, however, students had been allowed to set up tables representing political causes on a twenty-six-foot strip of sidewalk just outside campus on the corner of Telegraph Avenue and Bancroft Way. One day, a vice chancellor (his name was Alex C. Sherriffs) whose office was in Sproul Hall, one side of which faces the area with the tables, decided that the spectacle was a bad look for the university. He conveyed his concern to his colleagues, and on September 16, the university announced a ban on tables and political activities in general on the corner of Telegraph and Bancroft.

Representatives of student organizations appealed the ban and met with administrators, but the students found the response unsatisfactory and began picketing. On September 30, in violation of the ban, organizations set up tables at Sather Gate, on the Berkeley campus. University officials took the names of students who were manning tables and informed them they would be disciplined. Students responded by staging a brief sit-in outside the dean's office. The next day, tables were set up again on campus, and this time, at 11:45 a.m., university police arrested Jack Weinberg for trespassing. Weinberg was a former Berkeley mathematics major who had been soliciting funds for the Congress of Racial Equality (CORE) at the foot of the steps to Sproul Hall. When he was arrested, he went limp, so officers placed him in a police car that had been driven into the middle of Sproul Plaza. He would remain sitting in that car until 7:30 the next evening.

Students immediately surrounded the car; eventually there were more than seven thousand people in the plaza. Some of them climbed onto the roof, with Jack Weinberg still inside, to make speeches. That roof was where Savio made his oratorical debut. Student leaders met with administrators, now led by the president of the entire U.C. system, Clark Kerr, and negotiated an agreement for handling Weinberg, the students who had been disciplined for violating the ban on tables earlier, and the students who were preventing the police from moving the car, and for revisiting the rules for on-campus political activities.

Given what was at stake, Kerr was the perfect antagonist for Savio and the FSM, because he had literally written the book on the postwar university. This was *The Uses of the University*, published in 1963, a text that would become a bible for educators, revised and reprinted five times, the last time in 2001. *The Uses of the University* is short and non-academic; it basically transcribes three lectures Kerr had given at Harvard, in which he described the transformations in higher education that led to what he called "the multiversity" or "the federal grant university." Savio called Kerr "the foremost ideologist of [the] 'Brave New World' conception of education."[51]

As his book's title suggests, Kerr's view of the university was instrumental. The institution could grow and become all things to all people because it was intertwined with the state. It operated as a factory for the production of knowledge and of future knowledge producers. Undergraduate enrollments were growing rapidly in the 1960s, but the number of graduate students was growing much faster. These were the experts society needed. The president of a modern university, Kerr argued, is therefore not a leader, someone with a vision, but a mediator.

"Mediator" was a term Kerr would later regret using, for it exposed exactly the weakness Hayden and Savio had identified in higher education: the absence of values, the soullessness of the institution.[52] Kerr was not unmindful of this grievance. The transformation of the university had done undergraduates "little good," he admitted. ". . . The students find themselves under a blanket of impersonal rules for admissions, for scholarships, for examinations, for degrees. It is interesting to watch how a faculty intent on few rules for itself can fashion such a plethora of them for the students." "Interesting to watch" is mediator talk. Kerr even had a premonition of how the problem might play out. "If federal grants for research brought a major revolution," he wrote, "then the resultant student sense of neglect may bring a minor counterrevolt, although the target of the revolt is a most elusive one."[53] Unless, of course, the university *gives* the students the target. A ban on tables was such a target.

The students involved in the Sproul Plaza "stand-in" didn't trust Kerr. They suspected he would manipulate the processes he had agreed to in order to ensure that discipline would be imposed on the students and that restrictions on political activity would remain. They probably were right: Kerr seems to have underestimated the strength of student support for the activists all along. So the activists continued to strategize, and, sometime in the early morning of October 5, they came up with a name for their movement.

It was a brilliant choice. The students didn't really want free speech, or only free speech. They wanted institutional and social change. But they decided to play a long game, the end of which was the co-optation of the faculty. The faculty had good reasons for caution about associating themselves with controversial political positions, but there was nothing controversial about free speech. Free speech was what the United States stood for. It was the banner carried into the battles against McCarthyism and loyalty oaths, a cause no liberal could in good conscience resist. The other way to gain faculty support was to get the administration to call in the police. No faculty wants campus disputes resolved by state force. At Berkeley, this was especially true for émigré professors, who knew what it was like to live in a police state. Astonishingly, the administration walked right into the trap.

The FSM continued to hold rallies in Sproul Plaza, using the university's own sound equipment. And since most students walked through the plaza at some point, coming or going, the rallies attracted large crowds. Tables reappeared on campus, and the organizers were sometimes summoned for disciplinary action and sometimes not. On November 20, three thousand people marched from Sather Gate to University Hall, where a meeting of the regents was taking place. The students were not allowed inside.

Then Kerr overplayed his hand. On November 28, disciplinary action was announced against Savio and another student, Arthur Goldberg, for the entrapment of the police car on October 1, among other malfeasances. On December 1, the FSM issued demands that the charges against Savio and Goldberg be dropped, that restrictions on political speech be abolished, and that the administration refrain from further disciplining of students for political activity. If these demands were not met, the group promised to take "direct action."

The demands were not met. A huge rally was held in Sproul Plaza the next day, leading to the occupation of Sproul Hall by a thousand people. Before they entered the building, Savio gave his famous speech, recorded and broadcast by KPFA, in Berkeley. "We have an autocracy which runs this university," Savio said.

> It's managed . . . Well, I ask you to consider: If this is a firm, and if the board of regents are the board of directors; and if President Kerr in fact is the manager; then I'll tell you something. The faculty are a bunch of employees, and we're the raw material! But we're a bunch of raw materials that don't mean to be—have any process upon us. Don't mean to be made into any product. Don't mean . . . Don't mean to end up being bought by some clients of the University, be they the government, be they industry, be they organized labor, be they anyone! We're human beings!
>
> There's a time when the operation of the machine becomes so odious, makes you so sick at heart, that you can't take part! You can't even passively take part! And you've got to put your bodies upon the gears and upon the wheels . . . upon the levers, upon all the apparatus, and you've got to make it stop! And you've got to indicate to the people who run it, to the people who own it, that unless you're free, the machine will be prevented from working at all![54]

The transformation of students at elite universities into a new working class (with an echo of Charlie Chaplin in *Modern Times*) was complete.

To Joan Baez singing "We Shall Overcome" (a civil rights anthem, but originally a song of the labor movement), the students proceeded to occupy the four floors of Sproul Hall. Shortly after three o'clock the following morning, 367 police officers stormed the building and arrested 773 persons, the largest mass arrest in California history.* Protestors

---

* The mass arrests were instigated and supervised by an assistant county prosecutor named Edwin Meese III, who would become Ronald Reagan's attorney general. Meese also played a role in escalating the confrontation with police that led to the riots around People's Park in Berkeley

passively resisted; police responded by throwing the men down the stairs. It was not until 4 p.m. that the last protestor was removed.

Kerr had done what the FSM had hoped he would do: he had radicalized the faculty. Nathan Glazer had joined the faculty in 1963. He initially supported the students, but he also gave a speech on the roof of the commandeered car against civil disobedience, and he eventually found the FSM's tactics alarming. He thought they had been clever but disingenuous in making the issue one of free speech when it really boiled down to an issue of institutional authority.[55] However, at a meeting of more than eight hundred professors and instructors, presided over by Glazer, the faculty voted by an overwhelming margin to support the students' demands. On January 2, the regents announced a liberal policy on political activity and the replacement of the school's chancellor, a clear signal of capitulation. Unrest at Berkeley was by no means at an end. The War in Vietnam would see to that. Nor were the repercussions over. In 1967, Savio served four months in prison for his role in the Sproul Hall sit-in.[56] But the point had mostly been won.

To the extent that the FSM was about the federal grant university, the picture that Mills, Hayden, and Savio painted was hardly shocking. Their concerns were shared by the presiding political figure of the period, Dwight D. Eisenhower. "Today, the solitary inventor, tinkering in his shop, has been overshadowed by task forces of scientists in laboratories and testing fields," Eisenhower said in his farewell address, broadcast on January 17, 1961.

> In the same fashion, the free university, historically the fountainhead of free ideas and scientific discovery, has experienced a revolution in the conduct of research. Partly because of the huge costs involved, a government contract becomes virtually a substitute for intellectual curiosity. For every old blackboard there are now hundreds of new electronic computers.
>
> The prospect of domination of the nation's scholars by Federal employment, project allocations, and the power of money is ever present and is gravely to be regarded.

---

in May 1969, where a student, James Rector, was shot and killed and more than a hundred law enforcement officials, students, and Berkeley residents were injured.

> Yet, in holding scientific research and discovery in respect, as we should, we must also be alert to the equal and opposite danger that public policy could itself become the captive of a scientific-technological elite.[57]

He might almost have been reading Mills.

In one respect, though, the events at Berkeley in 1964, like the experience at Port Huron two and a half years earlier, belonged to a generation (or a narrow demographic slice of a generation) and a moment. "What can I call it: the existential amazement of being at The Edge, where reality breaks open into the true Chaos before it is reformed?" one of the FSM leaders, Michael Rossman, wrote ten years after.

> I have never found words to describe what is still my most vivid feeling from the FSM: the sense that the surface of reality had somehow fallen away altogether . . . Nothing was any longer what it had seemed. Objects, encounters, events, all became mysterious, pregnant with unnamable implications, capable of astounding metamorphosis.[58]

Greil Marcus, the future *Rolling Stone* music critic, was a Berkeley undergraduate in 1964. He described the experience of rallies and mass meetings this way:

> Your own history was lying in pieces on the ground, and you had the choice of picking up the pieces or passing them by. Nothing was trivial, nothing incidental. Everything connected to a totality, and the totality was how you wanted to live: as a subject or as an object of history . . . As the conversation expanded, institutional, historical power dissolved. People did and said things that made their lives of a few weeks before seem unreal—they did and said things that, not long after, would seem ever more so.[59]

The "fled is that music" tone in these reminiscences is partly because the War in Vietnam would eclipse almost everything in American public life, and make political activism much more dangerous. But it is also because faith in a progressive vanguard of students and intellectuals was about to suffer serious damage.

4.

As Warren Hinckle III remembered it, he and Michael Wood met one afternoon in December 1966 in the semi-deserted dining room of the Algonquin Hotel on West Forty-Fourth Street. Hinckle was the editor of *Ramparts*, a West Coast magazine that, although only four years old, had become a slick muckraker with a New Left slant and a rapidly growing circulation. Wood was there because of Marc Stone, a public relations man (and the brother of the investigative journalist I. F. Stone), whom he had met at a conference. Stone represented *Ramparts*, and when Wood told him that he had a story to tell, Stone set him up with Hinckle.[60]

Hinckle was a swashbuckler (with an eyepatch). He had a gift for promotion and for spending money not his own. When he was in New York, he hung out at the Algonquin, whose bar and dining room had been long patronized by *New Yorker* writers and editors. He ordered Wood a slice of chocolate cake, and Wood spilled his beans. He told Hinckle that the National Student Association—the organization at whose convention Tom Hayden met Casey Cason, and which represented more than a million students at four hundred American colleges—was funded by the CIA.

Having been approached before by anxious informants promising blockbuster stories, Hinckle was skeptical. The stuff seemed too good to be true. He asked Wood what would happen to him if the CIA found out he had told this to a journalist. Wood said that he had never signed a secrecy agreement with the Agency, so he couldn't be prosecuted, but he had heard that the CIA could doctor his medical records to show that he had psychiatric problems. He was plainly in distress. Hinckle ordered him another piece of cake and charged it to the magazine.[61]

Wood had brought copies of the NSA's financial records with him. He turned them over to Hinckle, and Hinckle gave them to his staff and ordered them to check Wood's story out. There were difficulties getting people to talk at first, but by February *Ramparts* had material for an article. They scheduled it for the March 1967 issue—exactly twenty years after Truman's "alternative ways of life" speech. The story turned out to be a stick of dynamite, and when it went off, it exposed a vast web of Agency involvement in supposedly nongovernmental groups and activities. It helped to mark the end of the "culture war" phase of the Cold

War. As Hinckle later summed it up: "It is a rare thing in this business when you say bang and somebody says I'm dead."[62]

The NSA and the CIA were both born a few months after Truman's speech.[63] The CIA had its eye on the NSA from the start, and the relationship gained steadily in strength and intimacy until the day the secret became public. The NSA was a liberal organization. As the invitation to SNCC leaders to attend the 1960 convention indicates, civil rights was part of the agenda early on. The NSA's second president (1948–1949), James (Ted) Harris, was Black. Its fourth president (1950–1951) was the future civil rights and antiwar activist Allard Lowenstein. And the NSA's politics were typical of most of the organizations the CIA covertly supported: they were socially progressive, anti-colonialist, and sometimes even socialist. The important thing was that they were also anti-Communist.

A standard explanation for this is that the people who ran covert operations at the CIA from 1947 to 1967 were not right-wing jingoists. They were liberal anti-Communists, veterans of Roosevelt's Office of Strategic Services (OSS), the forerunner of the CIA. They were good guys who despised the Soviet Union as a traitor to progressive principles. If people held this belief about the CIA, the Agency exploited it. CIA officials used to tell NSA students who were in the know about the covert arrangement—the Agency's term for them was "witty"—that while the State Department was supporting authoritarian dictatorships, the CIA supported foreign students involved in democratic resistance and national liberation movements. This was supposed to make the NSA students feel that they had bargained with the right devil.

The students were misled. The CIA is part of the executive branch. Its director reports to the president; its operations and expenditures are subject to congressional oversight. The director of the CIA during the 1950s, Allen Dulles, was the secretary of state's brother. The notion that the CIA was running its own foreign policy, or that it was a "rogue elephant," as one senator later called it, is absurd.[64]* Two wide-ranging investigations of CIA activities, by a presidential committee in 1967 and by Congress in 1975, concluded that although the Agency did many illegal things, it did them with the explicit or tacit approval of the administrations it worked for.

---

* The senator was Frank Church. After he learned of the level of presidential involvement in CIA activities, he retracted the remark.

The question about all of the organizations the CIA funded covertly, from the NSA to the Congress for Cultural Freedom and, possibly, *Partisan Review*, was how much the Agency called the tune and what it hoped to gain.[65] In the case of the NSA, only a few members of the organization knew of the CIA connection. These were the top officials, and they were sworn to secrecy. The penalty for disclosure was twenty years. The CIA seems to have intervened with the Selective Service System to keep key NSA members from being drafted. It also held budgetary approval over the NSA's international programs.[66]

The NSA was not used for political warfare—that is, operations designed to disrupt Soviet-backed events. The CIA did create a front organization called the Independent Research Service (inventing titles that are as meaningless as possible is part of the spy game) for the purpose of recruiting American students to disrupt Soviet-controlled World Youth Festivals in Vienna in 1959 and Helsinki in 1962. (Among other tactics, stink bombs were used. These were college students.) The person in charge of IRS recruiting was Gloria Steinem, who knew perfectly well where the money was coming from, and who never regretted taking it.* "If I had a choice I would do it again," she said after the CIA connection was revealed.[67]

Nor was the NSA primarily used to promote American principles abroad. The Agency did embed agents in the NSA, and it worked behind the scenes to ensure that pliable students got elected to run the association, and that the desired policy positions got adopted. (Vietnam became a serious issue: as an agency of the executive branch, the CIA could not allow the NSA to take an antiwar position. The president wouldn't like that use of taxpayer money.) But essentially, the NSA functioned as a glove that concealed the American government's hand, and allowed it to do business with people who would never knowingly have done business with the American government. These people thought that they were dealing with an independent student group. They had no idea that the NSA was a front.

What did this permit the CIA to do? First, the NSA was used as a cutout. The CIA funneled financial support to favored foreign student groups by means of grants ostensibly coming from the NSA. Second, the NSA was a recruitment device. It enabled the Agency to identify

---

* Steinem attempted to recruit Hayden for the Helsinki conference. They met twice.

potential recruits—that is, potential intelligence sources—among student leaders in other countries. And, third, NSA members who attended international conferences filed written reports or were debriefed afterward, giving the CIA a large database of information. The CIA did not buy into the adage that the student leader of today is tomorrow's student leader. It calculated that the heads of national student organizations were likely someday to become important figures in their countries' governments. When that happened (and it often did), the U.S. government had a file on them.

In fact, debriefing was a widespread Agency practice with Americans who went overseas. Major news organizations, including *Time*, CBS, and *The New York Times*, cooperated with the CIA for many years, in some instances providing cover jobs for CIA agents.[68] And the Agency planted agents in overseas organizations, and not only in the journals, such as *Encounter*, published by the Congress for Cultural Freedom. *The Paris Review* was founded in 1953 as a cover for its coeditor, Peter Matthiessen, who was a CIA agent.[69] He could report back on what he heard in Paris.

This may seem benign enough—collecting information is an intelligence service's job—but there was a problem. It had to do with the "State bad guys, CIA good guys" routine. The State Department deals with nations with which the United States has diplomatic relations. Having diplomatic relations with a foreign government prohibits you from negotiating with, or acknowledging the legitimacy of, groups committed to that government's overthrow. This is why it's convenient to have a government agency that operates clandestinely. The CIA could cultivate relations with oppositional groups secretly, and this permitted the U.S. government to work both sides of the street. Whether information the CIA gathered about students who were political opponents of a regime ever ended up in the hands of that regime, which could then have used the information to arrest and execute its enemies, is unknown.[70] The nature of the operation certainly makes it possible.

Looking back, it is odd that the relationship remained secret as long as it did. The NSA was just one of many organizations funded by the CIA, and by no means the largest. And over the life of that relationship, dozens of people were in the know. But until Michael Wood told Warren Hinckle over chocolate cake in the Algonquin, no one ever spoke up publicly. This is a testament to something—the naïveté of the students, the arrogance of the grown-ups (at the CIA, NSA students were referred to as "the kiddies"), or the power of anti-Communism to overcome every scruple.

One thing it is not a testament to is the CIA's tradecraft. The evidence of the Agency's covert funding system was hidden in plain sight. In 1962, a writer named Ernst Henri published a piece called "Who Finances Anti-Communism?" that revealed the interlocked nature of the funding mechanisms for American overseas propaganda and cultural diplomacy.[71] He basically opened the door onto the CIA connection for anyone who wanted to follow him. No one did, because his article was published in the *World Marxist Review*, which was the name of the English-language edition of the Communist journal *Problemy mira i sotsializma* (*Problems of Peace and Socialism*), published in Prague. Ernst Henri was a pseudonym for a Soviet writer who posed as a German émigré.

Americans got a peek in 1964, when a House of Representatives subcommittee ran an investigation into the tax-exempt status of philanthropic foundations. When the committee had trouble getting information from the IRS about a certain New York–based charitable foundation called the J. M. Kaplan Fund, the chair, a Texas congressman named Wright Patman, surmised that the reason the IRS was not cooperating was because the CIA was preventing it. Patman didn't appreciate the disrespect; in retaliation, he made public a list of eight foundations that between 1961 and 1963 had given almost a million dollars to the J. M. Kaplan Fund. "Patman Attacks 'Secret' CIA Link: Says Agency Gave Money to Private Group Acting as Its Sub-Rosa Conduit" was the headline in the *Times*, which published the names of the eight conduit foundations. After a closed-door meeting with representatives from the CIA and the IRS, Patman emerged to announce that he was dropping the matter.[72]

Still, the cat was partway out of the bag. As their transparently invented names suggest—the Gotham Foundation, the Borden Trust, the Andrew Hamilton Fund, and so on—those eight foundations were CIA cutouts. The Agency had approached wealthy people it knew to be sympathetic and asked them to head dummy foundations. Those people were then put on a masthead, a name for their foundation was invented, sometimes an office was rented to provide an address, and a conduit came into being. The members of these phony boards even held annual meetings, at which "business" was discussed, expenses paid by the Agency.

The dummy foundations were used to channel money to groups the Agency wanted to support. Sometimes the CIA passed funds through the dummies to legitimate charitable foundations, like the Kaplan Fund, which in turn passed them along to groups like the National Student Association. Sometimes the cutouts simply gave the money directly to the CIA's beneficiaries. The CIA's name did not appear anywhere.

The *Times* published an editorial saying that "the practice ought to stop . . . The use of Government intelligence funds to get foundations to underwrite institutions, organizations, magazines and newspapers abroad is a distortion of CIA's mission on gathering and evaluating information."[73] (It actually *was* serving the intelligence-gathering function, of course.) And in 1966, the paper ran a series of articles on the CIA's spying operations in which it revealed that the CIA was funding the Congress for Cultural Freedom and its European-based magazines. The paper also reported that the Agency had funded some American academics when they traveled abroad.[74] The Agency seems to have done nothing in response to these stories, and nothing came of them.

This is when Wood made his appearance. Wood was from the Coachella Valley in Southern California. His father was a farmer. After graduating from high school in 1960, he went to Berkeley, then transferred to Pomona College at the end of his freshmen year. At Pomona, he put together a three-day conference on equality; in 1964, he dropped out to work as a civil rights organizer in the Watts neighborhood of Los Angeles. His work there attracted the attention of the NSA, which offered him a job.[75]

Wood was quickly promoted to the position of director of development—fundraising. Then he discovered something strange. No one at the NSA seemed terribly interested in raising money. Grant proposals were perfunctory, and Wood learned that the president of the NSA, Philip Sherburne, the man who had hired him, was negotiating for donations on his own. Wood confronted Sherburne and told him that unless he was given control of all fundraising activities, he would have to resign. Sherburne invited him to lunch.

They met in Washington, D.C., where the NSA had just moved its headquarters (to adjoining four-story town houses off Dupont Circle, made available by the CIA), in a restaurant on Connecticut Avenue called the Sirloin and Saddle. Sherburne was a first-generation college student from Oregon. He had grown up on a dairy farm in a town, Rainier, with a population of one hundred. He became renowned at the University of Oregon, in Eugene, for his probity. Wood liked him. Sherburne told Wood that the reason there was so little concern about raising money at the NSA was because the organization was funded largely by the CIA. In the years since the relationship began, Sherburne said, maybe a hundred NSA members had known this, and those people had been informed only after the CIA had run background checks on them. Obviously, Wood had not passed his background check. Sherburne was violating the terms of his own secrecy agreement by telling Wood about the CIA connection, but he was doing it, he said, because he was trying to terminate the relationship. He asked Wood to keep their conversation secret.

Wood didn't know what to do. He counted Sherburne a friend, and he knew that if he revealed the contents of their conversation, Sherburne could go to jail. But he hated the thought that the CIA had financial leverage over the NSA. He finally decided to betray the confidence, and approached Marc Stone. When *Ramparts* started checking Wood's claims, its researchers discovered records showing that some of the eight dummy foundations named by Congressman Patman two years before were donors to the NSA. The CIA had not even bothered to change their names. By February 1967, the magazine had a story ready to go.

But the CIA had got wind of Wood's defection, and it gathered twelve past presidents of the NSA and scheduled a news conference at which they would admit having received CIA funding but swear that the Agency had never influenced NSA policy. Hinckle, in turn, learned of the CIA's plan to scoop him. He immediately took out ads in *The New York Times* and *The Washington Post* to announce: "In its March issue, *Ramparts* magazine will document how the CIA has infiltrated and subverted the world of American student leaders."[76] Placing the ad tipped off the *Times* and the *Post*, whose reporters naturally called the CIA for comment. And so, on the same day that the ads appeared, February 14, 1967, both newspapers ran stories reporting that for fifteen years, the National Student Association had been taking money from the CIA. Circulation for the March issue of *Ramparts* was close to a quarter of a million.

Once the NSA thread had been pulled, a whole tapestry of CIA covert operations started to unravel. The story was covered in newspapers and magazines across the country. Wood went on ABC's *Issues and Answers*, where he was asked whether he thought that he had destroyed the CIA as an effective instrument in the Cold War. CBS News broadcast an hour-long program hosted by Mike Wallace called "In the Pay of the CIA." President Johnson asked his undersecretary of state, Nicholas Katzenbach, what was going on. The CIA, Katzenbach reported, "did not act on its own initiative but in accordance with national policies established by the National Security Council in 1952 through 1954. Throughout it acted with the approval of senior interdepartmental review committees, including the Secretaries of State and Defense or their representatives. These policies have, therefore, been in effect under four Presidents."[77]

In the middle of this public storm, Tom Braden entered the picture. Braden was a California newspaper publisher. (Much later on, he would have a career as Pat Buchanan's punching bag on the first edition of CNN's *Crossfire*.) He had gone to Dartmouth, then, in 1940, enlisted in the British Eighth Army and fought in North Africa. When the United States entered the war, he joined the Office of Strategic Services. After the war, he briefly taught English at Dartmouth, then spent two years as executive secretary of the Museum of Modern Art. In 1950, he joined the CIA.[78] At the CIA, Braden created a program designed to combat Communist front organizations in Europe. It was run through the International Organizations Division, of which he was director. Among other things, his division channeled money into organizations with international agendas—organizations like the NSA—that the CIA wanted to support. Braden left the Agency in 1954, and he had not been named in any of the reporting on the NSA story, but he responded anyway in an article for *The Saturday Evening Post* with the title "I'm Glad the CIA Is 'Immoral.'"

Braden's article was essentially the straight version of *Mad* magazine's Cold War satire "Spy vs. Spy." The CIA's system of covert funding, Braden wrote, was "a vast and secret operation whose death has been brought about by small-minded and resentful men."[79] It had been a perfectly legitimate way to fight the Soviet Union's practice of operating through front organizations. The International Union of Students, an organization founded in Prague in 1946, was a front. The Kremlin was its puppet master. In the looking-glass war that was the Cold War, it was legitimate—it was, politically, "moral"—for the CIA to respond by secretly supporting the NSA so that it could compete with the IUS for the political sympathies of foreign students. Braden's article blew the cover off many CIA operations. He named names, including officials in the American labor movement who had received CIA funds to bribe Communist unions in Europe. He revealed that the CIA had an agent in the Congress for Cultural Freedom, and that an editor of *Encounter* was a CIA agent.

As the story grew, it became clear that the CIA's tentacles had been everywhere. The Agency gave money to the National Council of Churches, the United Auto Workers, the International Commission of Jurists, the International Marketing Institute, the American Friends of the Middle East, the Pan American Foundation, the American Newspaper Guild, the National Education Association, the Communications Workers of America, and the Synod of Bishops of the Russian Church Outside Russia. Some of these groups, such as an outfit called the American Society of African Culture, were creations of the Agency; others had CIA agents planted in them. The Socialist Norman Thomas, unwittingly, took money from the CIA. Operations such as Radio Free Europe and the Free Russia Fund, which regularly appealed to the public for contributions, turned out to have been funded by the CIA. Of the 700 grants of more than ten thousand dollars made between 1963 and 1966 by foundations other than Ford, Carnegie, and Rockefeller, the CIA was involved in 108. It was behind half of all grants for international activities.[80]

The money trail wound through some twenty-six CIA-created dummy foundations and twenty legitimate foundations and reached almost a hundred organizations.[81] The CIA owned or subsidized more than fifty newspapers, news services, radio stations, and periodicals, most of them abroad. American publishing houses, including G. P. Putnam's, Ballantine, and Doubleday, unknowingly published books that had CIA involvement.[82] The CIA seems to have funneled money to the Iowa Writers' Workshop.[83]

The revelations about the Agency's involvement with the Congress for Cultural Freedom and journals like *Encounter* led to a large-scale disaffiliation of Western intellectuals from American foreign policy.*

---

* Among American writers who published in *Encounter*: Harold Rosenberg, Clement Greenberg, Barbara Rose, Dwight Macdonald, Lionel Trilling, Diana Trilling, Richard Wright, James Baldwin, Edmund Wilson, F. W. Dupee, Jack Kerouac, Meyer Schapiro, Nathan Glazer,

An effort to curry the allegiance of foreign elites ended up alienating them almost completely. After 1967, every official and unofficial venture in American cultural diplomacy became suspect. One reaction of writers who were surprised to learn that the CIA had been subventing their work was: No one ever told us what to write. But that was exactly the point. They did not need to be told. They were already saying the things the CIA—that is, the U.S. government—wanted the world to hear.

After *The New York Times* outed the Congress for Cultural Freedom as a creature of the Agency, an august group of citizens—the former ambassador to India John Kenneth Galbraith; the physicist J. Robert Oppenheimer; the Kennedy confidant Arthur Schlesinger, Jr.; and George Kennan—wrote a letter to the editor. "An examination of the record of the congress," they explained, "its magazines and other activities will, we believe, convince the most skeptical that the congress has had no loyalty except an unwavering commitment to cultural freedom—and that in terms of this standard it has freely criticized actions and policies of all nations, including the United States."[84]

It was not true that no negative opinions about the United States were ever censored, but the important point is that *of course* the CIA sponsored writers critical of U.S. policies. The Agency believed, not unreasonably, that the fact that dissent was tolerated in the United States was a major Cold War selling point. "American artists and writers are not pawns of the state" was the message in these state-sponsored publications and exhibitions. The CIA's belief in the propaganda value of dissent called the bluff on American intellectuals. It meant that writers who imagined themselves as having a critical distance from American policy, or a skeptical relation to capitalism or consumerism or militarism or vulgar anti-Communism, were actually talking the party line. They did not need to be bought out because they had been on board all along.

"Both as symptom and as source, the campaign for 'cultural freedom' revealed the degree to which the values held by intellectuals had become indistinguishable from the interests of the modern state—interests which the intellectuals now served even while they maintained the illusion of detachment," wrote Christopher Lasch, then a young historian at the University of Iowa, after the *Ramparts* story broke. ". . . The American

---

Daniel Bell, David Riesman, and Irving Howe. Among British writers: Reyner Banham, J. B. Priestley, Lawrence Alloway, Richard Hoggart, and Raymond Williams.

press is free, but it censors itself. The university is free, but it has purged itself of ideas. The literary intellectuals are free, but they use their freedom to propagandize for the state. The freedom of American intellectuals as a professional class blinds them to their un-freedom."[85] Those writers and students who were imagined to constitute the vanguard of social change turned out, as a class, to be doing the work of the state.

The final irony of the whole American cultural diplomacy effort after 1945 is that what the CIA, the State Department, the museums, and the foundations tried to do—sell American art and ideas to other countries—was accomplished by other means and with little state involvement, apart from the admittedly crucial role of keeping markets open. It is true that when conditions inside the Soviet bloc relaxed, during the "thaw" in the early 1960s, debates about Communism among American intellectuals stimulated dissident writers in those nations.[86] But the world was not colonized by *Partisan Review* or the Museum of Modern Art. It was colonized by Pop Art and Hollywood. Modernist literature did not provide moral sustenance to dissidents in Eastern Bloc countries. Beat literature did.[87] Very few people knew who Lionel Trilling was. Everyone had heard of Elvis Presley.

5.

The revelations about the CIA's covert network exposed the hidden logic of containment. As George Kennan had defined it in the X Article, containment was a policy "designed to confront the Russians with unalterable counterforce at every point where they show signs of encroaching upon the interests of a peaceful and stable world."[88] In Kennan's original conception, American responses might be asymmetrical, but in practice, things were often tit for tat. This was simple enough when it involved ordinary cultural diplomacy. If the Soviet Union sent the Bolshoi Ballet on a world tour, the State Department could (and did) send Louis Armstrong on a world tour. It was less simple when the Soviet Union or China provided military support to a national liberation movement, as in Vietnam. Containment meant that the United States should support the country's anti-Communist regime. The goal was equipoise, maintaining the status quo circa 1947.

But the first type of action—sending Armstrong around the world and propping up the Diem regime in South Vietnam—was consistent with the principles of a democratic superpower. They were (more or less, since the CIA was involved in South Vietnamese politics from the start) public and aboveboard. The hard cases had to do with things like fronts and political warfare. Braden's argument in "I'm Glad the CIA Is 'Immoral'" was that the theory of containment mandated the creation of American fronts, like the NSA, to operate as a "counterforce" to Soviet fronts, like the International Union of Students. And when Communists tried to subvert elections in Western Europe, the United States was obliged to mount its own covert (or semi-covert) campaign—as it did, successfully, in the Italian elections in 1948.[89]*

The Italian operation was the result of a recommendation by George Kennan. Kennan had begun his job as director of the State Department's Policy Planning Staff (PPS) in May 1947. His resources were small at first—the office had only three people when it opened—and his remit was huge. Right away, he had to make recommendations about the implementation of the Marshall Plan. By November, his office had prepared thirteen formal reports, and he had given the secretary of state, George Marshall, a comprehensive statement of postwar grand strategy.[90]

Kennan seems to have come to the conclusion early on that for containment to work, the United States needed the capacity to undertake what he called "political warfare," including covert action.[91] In May 1948, the PPS issued a memorandum calling for a "range from such overt actions as political alliances, economic measures (as ERP [the Marshall Plan]), and 'white' propaganda to such covert operations as clandestine support of 'friendly' foreign elements, 'black' psychological warfare and even encouragement of underground resistance in hostile states."[92] It recommended the creation of the position of director of special studies, within the National Security Council, to run political warfare. The NSC adopted the proposal, and this led to the formation of the Office of Policy Coordination (OPC) as a unit of the CIA.

The man appointed to run the OPC was also recommended by Kennan. He was Frank Wisner, a friend from Kennan's Georgetown circle (though Kennan pretended he barely knew him). Wisner was a driven man. "By hard work and brilliance, and by reaching widely for similarly activist OSS alumni," wrote a later CIA director, William

---

* There is debate about whether and how much the CIA's efforts made a difference to the outcome in those elections.

Colby, "he started [the OPC] operating in the atmosphere of an order of Knights Templar, to save Western freedom from Communist darkness—and from war."[93] James Burnham worked in the OPC from 1949 to 1953. Like Burnham, Wisner didn't believe in containment. He believed in liberation.

Through Wisner's office, the CIA carried out black ops all over the world, dropping agents behind the Iron Curtain into countries like Albania and Poland to foster insurgencies. Most of them were immediately captured or killed (some killed themselves when they were discovered). It turned out that the Soviets knew in advance of every operation, because they had spies inside the recruiting system, and because the British intelligence officer privy to the missions was a double agent, Kim Philby.[94]

The OPC's budget was partly concealed by an arrangement that allowed the Agency to siphon off 5 percent of Marshall Plan funds from deposits in overseas banks. This came to some $685 million.[95] In 1949, Wisner's first full year as its head, the OPC had 302 employees and a budget of $5 million; by 1952, it had more than 2,800 employees, more than 3,000 overseas contractors, and a budget of $82 million. Clandestine intelligence collection and covert action accounted for 74 percent of the Agency's budget and 60 percent of its personnel strength.[96]

But there was something almost deliberately amateur and ineffectual about a lot of the OPC's activities. Even if a rebellion had got off the ground in Albania or Poland, the United States government would never have intervened to support it. In fact, there were plenty of opportunities after 1948 to support revolts in Iron Curtain countries, and the United States did nothing. Strikes and protests in East Germany in 1953 and Poland in 1956 were violently suppressed, and, although the strikers had hoped otherwise, the United States did not get involved.[97] Protests in Hungary in 1956 turned into a full-scale revolution, and the Soviet-backed government was overthrown. The Red Army invaded. More than two thousand Hungarians were killed, two hundred thousand fled the country, and the leader of the new government, the reform-minded Communist Imre Nagy, was arrested, tried in secret, and hanged as an example to other deviationists. The Hungarians, too, had expected help from the West, but help never came. When it was pointed out that Radio Free Europe had been urging Hungarians to resist Soviet domination for years, the administration's position was that the United States had never advocated *violent* resistance.[98]

In realist terms, the situation was simple. The United States had no national interest in going to war in a nuclear age over the self-determination of Hungary. Talk of "liberation" was mostly just talk, just as Soviet talk of "peace" was mostly just talk. In 1958, during a symposium held under the auspices of the Congress for Cultural Freedom in Paris, Raymond Aron suggested that the division of the European continent was a solution less dangerous than any other, because it meant that what happened on the other side of the wall stayed on the other side of the wall.[99] Few officials in the West really wanted to see the Iron Curtain lifted as long as the Soviet Union existed. At a minimum, the existence of an Iron Curtain—and it was a real border that ran down the middle of the continent, marked and fortified—was a permanent advertisement for the coercive nature of Communism.

So the United States did nothing to stop construction of the wall that encircled West Berlin in 1961. In August 1968, when 500,000 Warsaw Pact troops invaded Czechoslovakia and overthrew the reformist government of Alexander Dubček, no Western power interfered. Nor did the United States play a significant role beyond cheerleading in the Velvet Revolution in 1989, which led to the overthrow of Communist regimes in Eastern Europe and the collapse of the Soviet empire. For forty-five years, the Soviets had been allowed to have their way there, a state of affairs that was largely officially ignored and sometimes even officially denied. In 1976, President Gerald Ford, who had been in Washington for twenty-seven years, asserted in a debate with Jimmy Carter that "there is no Soviet domination of Eastern Europe."[100] (He later clarified this by saying that Eastern Europeans did not *feel* dominated.)

Frank Wisner was an identifiable government type, a Cold War maximalist. The mystery is what Kennan, an anti-maximalist, ever saw in him. In 1975, in testimony before a Senate committee looking into abuses by the CIA and other government agencies, Kennan told the senators that the OPC "did not work out at all the way I had conceived it . . . We had thought that this would be a facility which could be used when and if an occasion arose when it might be needed. There might be years when we wouldn't have to do anything like this."[101] He later told his biographer that his failure to oversee Wisner's activities was "probably the worst mistake I ever made in government."[102] This was all disingenuous. Kennan met weekly with Wisner in the beginning (they were also seeing each other socially, of course), and he supported Wisner's projects.[103] But the enormous octopus of domestic and foreign manipulation and subterfuge that Wisner created was an embarrassment to the policy of containment. In Kennan's memoirs, there is no mention of the OPC.

Vietnam, on the other hand, *was* a crisis for containment. Under the Truman Doctrine, the United States was committed to preventing a Communist state (North Vietnam) from taking over a non-Communist one. But as was obvious from the moment they were created at Geneva in 1954, those states were fictions. And from the Vietnamese point of view, the war was not about political ideology at all. It was a war of independence. Vietnam is where the two dominant geopolitical phenomena of the postwar period, the Cold War and decolonization, intersected. Vietnam was a duck and a rabbit.

Was American intervention in Vietnam true to the containment doctrine that had guided American policy since 1947, or was it a catastrophic misinterpretation? That question was clearly on the table when Averell Harriman, Dean Acheson, Robert Lovett, John McCloy, and Charles Bohlen were invited to the White House to consult with Johnson on the war, in July 1965.

The situation had grown dire rapidly. Aerial bombardment of the North, Operation Rolling Thunder, began on February 24. On February 27, the State Department released a White Paper blaming the conflict on "foreign aggression" (Vietnamese who lived above the seventeenth parallel being the foreigners). And on March 8, marines landed near Da Nang, the first American combat troops in Southeast Asia.

Reaction was swift. The first antiwar teach-in was held at the University of Michigan on March 24, followed by one at Berkeley (thirty thousand people attending an event that lasted thirty-six hours), and then more across the country. On April 17, a march of twenty thousand people organized by SDS took place in Washington.[104] Johnson was panicked.

The Wise Men, as they were called, semi-facetiously, by Johnson's national security adviser, McGeorge Bundy, were not happy with Johnson's war. They were not all that thrilled with Johnson, either. They were East Coast lawyers and bankers, Ivy Leaguers—men who did not descend to partisan wrangling. When they ran policy back in the day—*Present at the Creation* was the modest title Acheson gave his memoirs—Southern Democrats were a type they avoided. But they found themselves in an awkward place. The War in Vietnam was being fought in the name of checking Communist aggression, and checking Communist aggression was the very face of the policy they had put in place. When they came to the White House, on July 8, they were briefed on the progress of the war, then met with Johnson, who began complaining about how mean to him his critics were being.

The Wise Men were appalled. This was not how you discussed policy. As Acheson described the scene in a letter two days later to Truman (whom he addressed as "Dear Boss"):

> I got thinking about you and General Marshall and how we never wasted time "fighting the problem," or endlessly reconsidering decisions, or feeling sorry for ourselves.
>
> Finally I blew my top and said that he [Johnson] was wholly right in the Dominican Republic [where the United States had sent troops three months earlier] and Vietnam, that he had no choice except to press on, that explanations were not as important as successful action . . . With this lead my colleagues came thundering in like the charge of the Scots Greys at Waterloo.[105]

Johnson was momentarily fortified. The feeling would not last.

The realists saw things differently. Hans Morgenthau, whose book *Politics Among Nations* had made the case for international-relations realism, registered his opposition to American policy in Vietnam very early.[106] In 1955, he traveled there as a Defense Department observer and interviewed Diem. He could see that Diem was no liberal democrat. When he returned, he published a four-part article that amounted to an unqualified condemnation of American policy in Asia. This was long before the militarization of American involvement (although not before the CIA's orchestration of South Vietnamese politics).

At first, Morgenthau's position was the hardheaded realist position. "It is ideologically consistent, but politically and militarily foolish, to oppose a Communist government for no other reason than that it is Communist," he wrote in 1964.[107] The United States was confusing principles with power. He made his opposition known to a wider public in an article in *The New York Times Magazine* in 1965, six weeks after the marines landed. The reason the United States was in Vietnam, he explained, was because of "a basic principle of our foreign policy that was implicit in the Truman Doctrine of 1947 . . . This principle is the military containment of Communism." But that principle was misapplied in Asia. "The United States can no more contain Chinese influence in Asia by arming South Vietnam and Thailand than China could contain American influence in the Western Hemisphere by arming, say, Nicaragua and Costa Rica," he said.[108]

The *Times* piece was called "We Are Deluding Ourselves in Vietnam," and it got the attention of the White House. Morgenthau was fired from his consulting job at the Defense Department. Johnson expressed his displeasure, and Bundy seems to have decided to find a way to please the boss.

Although he had private concerns, Bundy was officially a believer in Johnson's policy. For he was himself a fruit of the liberal internationalist tree. His father, Harvey Bundy (Hackley, Yale, Harvard Law), had served under Henry Stimson in the Hoover and Roosevelt administrations. McGeorge himself (Groton, Yale) was co-author of Stimson's autobiography. His brother William (Groton, Yale, Covington & Burling) was Johnson's assistant secretary of state for Far Eastern Affairs and was married to Mary Eleanor Acheson, Dean Acheson's daughter.

McGeorge's academic field was government, and he had taught foreign policy at Harvard before becoming dean there. So he knew all about Morgenthau. And on June 21, they debated on a panel in Georgetown in an event broadcast nationally. The CBS News commentator Eric Sevareid moderated. The debate began over the definition of "national interest"—was or was it not being served in Vietnam? But at the end of the hour, Morgenthau charged that "the Government lives in a different factual world from the factual world in which its critics live." This was the card Bundy was waiting to see on the table, and he pounced. He had brought with him a list of remarks Morgenthau had published, dating to 1956, in which his analysis of various things had turned out to be wrong. He started to read from the list. Sevareid intervened. "Since this has become something of a personal confrontation," he said, "I think Professor Morgenthau should have a small chance at least to answer Mr. Bundy." "I admire the efficiency of Mr. Bundy's office . . ." Morgenthau began. Bundy interrupted. "I do my own work," he said.[109]

The evening was awarded to Bundy. "Debate Is Dominated by McGeorge Bundy," *The New York Times* reported.[110] Nevertheless, the show catapulted Morgenthau into visibility as a leading antiwar figure.

He was later named by intellectuals as the second greatest influence, after Noam Chomsky, on their thinking about Vietnam.[111] He also received hate mail, and he claimed that the White House had undertaken an operation called "Project Morgenthau" to discredit him.[112]

Morgenthau was a blunt and caustic character, but the experience shook him.[113] It is difficult to defend, on live television, your own quotations taken out of context. Bundy knew that, and Morgenthau knew that he knew it, and it infuriated him. He tried to respond in a piece in *The New York Review of Books* that September. "These officials are under a compulsion to protect their imaginary world at all costs, intellectual and moral, from contact with the real one," he wrote of the administration. ". . . We are here in the presence of an issue not of foreign policy or military strategy, but of psychopathology."

The crisis was not a crisis of *Realpolitik*, however—a refusal to face facts. It was a crisis of something that was not supposed to weigh in the making of foreign policy: moral authority. "[T]his nation, alone among the nations of the world," Morgenthau wrote, "was created for a particular purpose: to achieve equality in freedom at home, and thereby set an example for the world to emulate."[114] Some nations *are* better than others. Within a year, Morgenthau had broadened his indictment to cover American intellectuals generally. "The intellectuals of America have indeed been raped," he declared in *The New Republic*; "but many of them have looked forward to the experience and are enjoying it."[115] The realist had become a moralist.

Kennan's position was more diplomatic, and it was complicated by his distaste for many of the war's opponents and their manner of protest. He thought that student demonstrators bore "a disconcerting resemblance to phenomena we have witnessed within our own time in the origins of totalitarianism," an opinion he unwisely published in *The New York Times*.[116] Kennan had supported Kennedy's handling of the situation in Vietnam even after he was no longer in the government. He waited to express his reservations publicly until December 1965, well after the bombing campaign was under way and troops were on the ground.

"The young Americans who march around with Vietcong flags or profess to favor a Vietcong victory are choosing a very strange way to demonstrate an attachment to the cause of either independence or freedom, if this is indeed what they are interested in," he wrote in *The

Washington Post. Still, the rationale for military intervention was the wrong one. The government repeatedly invoked "our commitments." That was the kind of language Kennan despised. "Commitments to whom?" he asked. "To some South Vietnamese government? . . . If, in short, what we are actually fighting over is the preservation of some balance of power in that part of the world, which is something about which we have every right to be concerned, let us then discuss the problem in those terms and not try to drape our actions in legalisms and moralisms."[117] (This is a prime example of Kennan's detachment from retail politics: presidents cannot ask voters to send their children to war in the name of the balance of power.)

Two months later, on February 10, 1966, Kennan appeared before the Senate Foreign Relations Committee and testified for almost a full day. He had been distressed by Johnson's refusal to stop the bombing, and he came to lecture the committee not on the geopolitical damage the war was doing but, like Morgenthau, on the moral damage. "Our motives are widely misinterpreted," he said in a prepared statement,

> and the spectacle emphasized and reproduced in thousands of press photographs and stories that appear in the press of the world, the spectacle of America inflicting grievous injury on the lives of a poor and helpless people, and particularly a people of different race and color, no matter how warranted by military necessity or by the excesses of the adversary, produces reactions among millions of people throughout the world profoundly detrimental to the image we would like them to hold of this country. I am not saying that this is just or right. I am saying that this is so.[118]

He was asked, of course, What about containment? Isn't that what resisting North Vietnamese aggression is? "I did not mean to convey, in the article I wrote at that time, the belief that we could necessarily stop communism at every point on the world's surface," Kennan explained. "There were things I failed to say, I must admit, in that article, which should have been said, and one of them was that certain areas of the world are more important than others; that one had to concentrate on the areas that were vital to us."[119]

Senator Frank Church of Idaho, an early skeptic on the War, saw this as a promising line. "Would it be your judgment," he asked, "that, in these areas of the world, the people may be less concerned or less fearful or less opposed to communism, as such, than they are to imperialism and colonialism?" "Oh, yes," Kennan replied. ". . . And not only that, but the Europeans have things to lose by communism, by a Communist form of rule, which the Asians are not conscious of having to lose." "They [the Europeans] have freedom to lose, do they not, Mr. Ambassador?" Church asked. "Precisely," Kennan said. He pointed out that the Chinese do not have a word for freedom.[120] Kennan's testimony was televised live.* Kennan was not an academic hothead. Millions heard him, and his appearance marked the point at which what was regarded as "establishment" opinion began to turn against the war.

Still, the war ground on for another nine years. And the longer it lasted, the greater the damage to the reputation of the United States. Morgenthau and Kennan were right. Vietnam not only shattered the image of American invincibility. It meant that a whole generation grew up looking on the United States as an imperialist, militarist, and racist power. The political capital the nation accumulated by leading the alliance against fascism in the Second World War and helping rebuild Japan and Western Europe it burned through in Southeast Asia.

The English writer James Fenton was in Saigon working as a journalist when Viet Cong and North Vietnamese Army troops arrived there in 1975. He managed, more or less by accident, to be sitting in the first tank that entered the courtyard of the presidential palace where Diem had once presided over a nation about to descend into chaos. Like many Westerners of his education and generation, Fenton had hoped for a Viet Cong victory, and he was impressed by the Viet Cong and by the North Vietnamese Army soldiers when they marched into the city soon after. But he stayed around long enough to see the shape the postwar era would take.

The Vietnamese Communists did what totalitarian regimes do: they took over the schools and universities; they shut down the press; they pursued programs of enforced relocation and reeducation; they imprisoned, tortured, and executed their former enemies. Saigon was renamed Ho Chi Minh City and Ho's body, like Lenin's, was installed in a mausoleum for public viewing. Agriculture was collectivized and a five-year

---

* CBS aired instead a fifth rerun of an episode of *I Love Lucy*, a series that had been off the air since 1957. The president of CBS News, Fred Friendly, the man who had produced Edward R. Murrow's programs attacking Joseph McCarthy, resigned.

plan of modernization was instituted with disastrous results. Between 1975 and 1995, 839,228 Vietnamese fled the country, many on boats launched into the South China Sea. Two hundred thousand of them are estimated to have died there.[121] Those people may or may not have known the meaning of the word "freedom," but they knew the meaning of oppression. "The victory of the Vietnamese," Fenton concluded, "was a victory for Stalinism."[122]

NOTES

Statue of Liberty in New York Harbor, 1961. Photograph by Peter J. Eckel
(*LIFE Picture Collection / Getty Images*)

PREFACE

1. A number of writers have been drawn to this period for reasons like mine, notably: W. T. Lhamon, *Deliberate Speed: The Origins of a Cultural Style in the American 1950s* (Washington, DC: Smithsonian University Press, 1990); Thomas Crow, *The Rise of the Sixties: American and European Art in the Age of Dissent, 1955–1969* (London: Weidenfeld and Nicolson, 1996); Daniel Belgrad, *The Culture of Spontaneity: Improvisation and the Arts in Postwar America* (Chicago: University of Chicago Press, 1998); Morris Dickstein, *Leopards in the Temple: The Transformation of American Fiction, 1945–1970* (Cambridge, MA: Harvard University Press, 2002); Fred Kaplan, *1959: The Year Everything Changed* (Hoboken, NJ: J. Wiley and Sons, 2009); Clive Bush, *The Century's Midnight: Dissenting European and American Writers in the Era of the Second World War* (Oxford: Peter Lang, 2010); Daniel Horowitz,

Consuming Pleasures: Intellectuals and Popular Culture in the Postwar World (Philadelphia: University of Pennsylvania Press, 2012); Mark Greif, *The Age of the Crisis of Man: Thought and Fiction in America, 1933–1973* (Princeton: Princeton University Press, 2015); Peter Bacon Hales, *Outside the Gates of Eden: The Dream of America from Hiroshima to Now* (Chicago: University of Chicago Press, 2014); and George Cotkin, *Feast of Excess: A Cultural History of the New Sensibility* (New York: Oxford University Press, 2016).

INTRODUCTION: WHAT THE COLD WAR MEANT

1. David Reynolds, *From World War to Cold War: Churchill, Roosevelt, and the International History of the 1940s* (Oxford: Oxford University Press, 2006), 235–36.

2. Robert E. Sherwood, *Roosevelt and Hopkins: An Intimate History* (New York: Harper and

Brothers, 1948), 922–23; Cordell Hull, *The Memoirs of Cordell Hull*, vol. 2, *1451–71* (New York: Macmillan, 1948); Edward R. Stettinius, *Roosevelt and the Russians: The Yalta Conference* (Garden City, NY: Doubleday, 1949), 3–26; Herbert Feis, *Churchill, Roosevelt, Stalin: The War They Waged and the Peace They Sought* (Princeton: Princeton University Press, 1957), 596–600; Arthur Schlesinger, Jr., "Origins of the Cold War," *Foreign Affairs* 46 (1967): 22–52; John Lewis Gaddis, *The United States and the Origins of the Cold War, 1941–1947* (New York: Columbia University Press, 1972), 6–7, 34–62; Wilson D. Miscamble, *George F. Kennan and the Making of American Foreign Policy, 1947–1950* (Princeton: Princeton University Press, 1992), 4.

3. "Special Message to the Congress on Greece and Turkey: The Truman Doctrine," in *Public Papers of the Presidents of the United States: Harry S. Truman, January 1 to December 31, 1947* (Washington, DC: U.S. Government Printing Office, 1963), 178–79.

4. See Odd Arne Westad, "The Cold War and the International History of the Twentieth Century," in Melvyn P. Leffler and Odd Arne Westad, eds., *The Cambridge History of the Cold War*, vol. 1, *Origins* (Cambridge: Cambridge University Press, 2010), 17.

5. Harry S. Truman, *Memoirs*, vol. 2, *Years of Trial and Hope* (Garden City, NY: Doubleday, 1956), 106; Deborah Welch Larson, *Origins of Containment: A Psychological Explanation* (Princeton: Princeton University Press, 1985), 316–17.

6. Table 3.1—Outlays by superfunction and function, 1940–2017, ll. 45–55, Office of Management and Budget, "Historical Tables" (U.S. Government Printing Office, Washington, DC, 2010). See www.whitehouse.gov/omb/historical -tables/.

7. See John Lewis Gaddis, *The Long Peace: Inquiries into the History of the Cold War* (New York: Oxford University Press, 1987), 36.

1. AN EMPTY SKY

1. George F. Kennan, "The View from Russia," in Thomas T. Hammond, ed., *Witnesses to the Origins of the Cold War* (Seattle: University of Washington Press, 1982), 28.

2. George F. Kennan, "The Soviet Union as a Problem for the West" [1951], Box 245, Folder 2, George F. Kennan Papers, Seeley G. Mudd Manuscript Library, Princeton University.

3. Godfrey Hodgson, *America in Our Time* (New York: Random House, 1976), 111–33; Walter Isaacson and Evan Thomas, *The Wise Men: Six Friends and the World They Made* (New York: Simon and Schuster, 1986), 26–30, 644.

4. George F. Kennan, *Memoirs 1925–1950* (Boston: Little, Brown, 1967), 77.

5. David Mayers, *George Kennan and the Dilemmas of U.S. Foreign Policy* (New York: Oxford University Press, 1988), 49–58; John Lewis Gaddis, *George F. Kennan: An American Life* (New York: Penguin, 2011), 114–19.

6. Gaddis, *George F. Kennan*, 117; Anders Stephanson, *Kennan and the Art of Foreign Policy* (Cambridge, MA: Harvard University Press, 1989), 25.

7. George F. Kennan, "Morality and Foreign Policy," *Foreign Affairs* 64 (1985): 211–12.

8. George F. Kennan, *Memoirs 1950–1963* (Boston: Little, Brown, 1972), 116.

9. Gaddis, *George F. Kennan*, 204.

10. Kennan, *Memoirs 1950–1963*, 129–30.

11. Gaddis, *George F. Kennan*, 538.

12. Ibid., 675, quoting diary of George Kennan, October 8, 1990.

13. Nicholas Thompson, *The Hawk and the Dove: Paul Nitze, George Kennan, and the History of the Cold War* (New York: Henry Holt, 2009), 24.

14. Kennan, *Memoirs 1925–1950*, 13.

15. Thompson, *The Hawk and the Dove*, 26.

16. Kennan, *Memoirs 1925–1950*, 8–9, 24–34; Gaddis, *George F. Kennan*, 11, 48–49.

17. Frederic L. Propas, "Creating a Hard Line Toward Russia: The Training of State Department Soviet Experts, 1927–1937," *Diplomatic History* 8 (1984): 210–11; David Mayers, *The Ambassadors and America's Soviet Policy* (New York: Oxford University Press, 1995), 98–99.

18. Charles E. Bohlen, *Witness to History, 1929–1969* (New York: W. W. Norton, 1973), 39; Michael Hughes, "The Virtues of Specialization: British and American Diplomatic Reporting on Russia, 1921–39," *Diplomacy and Statecraft* 11 (2000): 89–90.

19. Robert Kelley, "Soviet Policy on the European Border," *Foreign Affairs* 3 (September 15, 1924): 90–98; Mayers, *The Ambassadors*, 101–103; H. W. Brands, *Inside the Cold War: Loy Henderson and the Rise of the American Empire, 1918–1961* (New York: Oxford University Press, 1991), 24–25; Bohlen, *Witness to History*, 39.

20. Loy Henderson, *A Question of Trust: The Origins of U.S.-Soviet Diplomatic Relations: The Memoirs of Loy Henderson*, ed. George W. Baer (Stanford: Hoover Institution Press, 1986), 147–48.

21. Foy D. Kohler and Mose L. Harvey, eds., *The Soviet Union, Yesterday, Today, Tomorrow: A Colloquy of American Long Timers in Moscow* (Coral Gables: Center for Advanced International Studies, University of Miami, 1975), 166.

22. Donald E. Davis and Eugene P. Trani, *Distorted Mirrors: Americans and Their Relations with Russia*

and China in the Twentieth Century (Columbia: University of Missouri Press, 2009), 38.

23. George Kennan to Hans Morgenthau, August 17, 1948, Box 33, Folder 7, Hans Morgenthau Papers, Library of Congress.

24. Isaacson and Thomas, *The Wise Men*, 147–48; Kennan, *Memoirs 1925–1950*, 33–34.

25. Kohler and Harvey, *The Soviet Union*, 167.

26. Kennan, *Memoirs 1925–1950*, 33.

27. Daniel F. Harrington, "Kennan, Bohlen, and the Riga Axioms," *Diplomatic History* 2 (1978): 423–37; cf. Daniel Yergin, *Shattered Peace: The Origins of the Cold War and the National Security State* (Boston: Houghton Mifflin, 1977), 17–41, and Davis and Trani, *Distorted Mirrors*, 33–44.

28. George F. Kennan to Walt Ferris, January 12, 1931, quoted in Isaacson and Thomas, *The Wise Men*, 149.

29. Isaacson and Thomas, *The Wise Men*, 148.

30. Kennan, *Memoirs 1925–1950*, 57.

31. Natalie Grant, "The Russia Section: A Window on the Soviet Union," *Diplomatic History* 2 (1978): 107–10.

32. Gaddis, *George F. Kennan*, 72–84.

33. Dennis J. Dunn, *Caught Between Roosevelt and Stalin: America's Ambassadors to Moscow* (Lexington: University Press of Kentucky, 1998), 40–41, 57–58, 79–81.

34. Kennan, *Memoirs 1925–1950*, 87–88.

35. Ibid., 108–109.

36. Ibid., 136.

37. Gaddis, *George F. Kennan*, 166–69.

38. Bohlen, *Witness to History*, 160.

39. Averell Harriman and Elie Abel, *Special Envoy to Churchill and Stalin, 1941–1946* (New York: Random House, 1975), 48.

40. Dmitri Volkogonov, *Stalin: Triumph and Tragedy*, ed. and trans. Harold Shukman (London: Weidenfeld and Nicolson, 1991), 352; Svetlana Alliluyeva, *Only One Year*, trans. Paul Chavchavadze (New York: Harper and Row, 1969), 392; Simon Sebag Montefiore, *Stalin: The Court of the Red Tsar* (New York: Knopf, 2003), 307; David E. Murphy, *What Stalin Knew: The Enigma of Barbarossa* (New Haven: Yale University Press, 2005), 245–51.

41. John Erickson, *Stalin's War with Germany*, vol. 1, *The Road to Stalingrad* (New York: Harper and Row, 1975), 220; Alan Bullock, *Hitler and Stalin: Parallel Lives*, 2nd rev. ed. (New York: Vintage, 1993), 728.

42. G. F. Krivosheev, ed., *Soviet Casualties and Combat Losses in the Twentieth Century* (London: Greenhill Books, 1997), 118–21.

43. John Keegan, *The Second World War* (New York: Penguin, 1989), 192–208, 227, 237, 462–71; Gerhard L. Weinberg, *A World at Arms: A Global History of World War II*, 2nd ed. (Cambridge: Cambridge University Press,

2005), 272; Murphy, *What Stalin Knew*, 232–33; Chris Bellamy, *Absolute War: Soviet Russia in the Second World War* (New York: Knopf, 2007), 8–9.

44. Erickson, *The Road to Stalingrad*, 394–472; Keegan, *The Second World War*, 462–81; Weinberg, *A World at Arms*, 454.

45. George F. Kennan, *Sketches from a Life* (New York: Pantheon, 1989), 83–84.

46. Manfred Messerschmidt, "Foreign Policy and Preparation for War," in Militärgeschichtliches Forschungsamt, ed., *Germany and the Second World War*, vol. 1, *The Build-Up of German Aggression*, trans. P. S. Falla, Dean S. McMurry, and Ewald Osers (New York: Oxford University Press, 1990), 543–54; Bullock, *Hitler and Stalin*, 692–97.

47. Walter Laqueur, *Russia and Germany: A Century of Conflict* (London: Weidenfeld and Nicolson, 1965), 23–24; Bullock, *Hitler and Stalin*, 747–56; Keegan, *The Second World War*, 186–87; Bellamy, *Absolute War*, 25–31; Timothy Snyder, *Bloodlands: Europe Between Hitler and Stalin* (New York: Basic Books, 2010), 155–312.

48. Bellamy, *Absolute War*, 13–15; Vladimir O. Pechatnov, "The Soviet Union and the World, 1944–1953," in Leffler and Westad, *The Cambridge History of the Cold War*, vol. 1, 90.

49. See John Lewis Gaddis, *Strategies of Containment: A Critical Appraisal of Postwar American National Security Policy During the Cold War*, rev. ed. (New York: Oxford University Press, 2005), 3.

50. Herbert Feis, *Churchill, Roosevelt, Stalin: The War They Waged and the Peace They Sought* (Princeton: Princeton University Press, 1957), 6–18; Harriman and Abel, *Special Envoy*, 84–101.

51. Milovan Djilas, *Conversations with Stalin*, trans. Michael B. Petrovich (New York: Harcourt, Brace and World, 1962), 114.

52. Keegan, *The Second World War*, 46–47; Bellamy, *Absolute War*, 87–88; Deborah Welch Larson, *Origins of Containment: A Psychological Explanation* (Princeton: Princeton University Press, 1985), 95–106; John Erickson, *Stalin's War with Germany*, vol. 2, *The Road to Berlin* (London: Weidenfeld and Nicolson, 1983), 247–90; Norman Davies, *Rising '44: The Battle for Warsaw* (New York: Viking, 2004), 153–65.

53. George F. Kennan, Diary, Thursday, July 27, 1944, Box 231, Folder 12, Kennan Papers.

54. Erickson, *The Road to Berlin*, 274–90; Bullock, *Hitler and Stalin*, 849–50; Jonathan Walker, *Poland Alone: Britain, SOE, and the Collapse of the Polish Resistance, 1944* (Stroud, UK: History Press, 2008), 204–30, 235–58.

55. Joseph Stalin to Winston Churchill, August 16, 1944, *Correspondence Between the Chairman of the Council of Ministers of the U.S.S.R.*

and the Presidents of the U.S.A. and the Prime Ministers of Great Britain during the Great Patriotic War of 1941–1945, vol. 1, Correspondence with Winston S. Churchill and Clement R. Attlee (Moscow: Foreign Languages Publishing House, 1957), 254.

56. Feis, Churchill, Roosevelt, Stalin, 382–89; Harriman and Abel, Special Envoy, 339–41.

57. The Ambassador in the Soviet Union (Harriman) to the Secretary of State, August 15, 1944, Foreign Relations of the United States: Diplomatic Papers, 1944, vol. 3, The British Commonwealth and Europe (1944) (Washington, DC: U.S. Government Printing Office, 1965), 1376.

58. Geir Lundestad, The American Non-Policy Toward Eastern Europe, 1943–1947: Universalism in an Area Not of Essential Interest to the United States (New York: Humanities Press, 1975), 183–92; Larson, Origins of Containment, 100.

59. Erickson, The Road to Berlin, 288; cf. Larson, Origins of Containment, 105.

60. Antony Beevor, The Second World War (London: Weidenfeld and Nicolson, 2012), 615–16.

61. Shachar Pinsker, A Rich Brew: How Cafés Created Modern Jewish Culture (New York: New York University Press, 2018), 55.

62. Erickson, The Road to Berlin, 289–90; Bullock, Hitler and Stalin, 849–50.

63. Jan M. Ciechanowski, The Warsaw Rising of 1944 (Cambridge: Cambridge University Press, 1974), 243; Anne Applebaum, Iron Curtain: The Crushing of Eastern Europe, 1944–1956 (New York: Doubleday, 2012), 102–103.

64. Weinberg, A World at Arms, 1095n98; Harriman and Abel, Special Envoy, 337.

65. Winston S. Churchill, The Second World War, vol. 6, Triumph and Tragedy (Boston: Houghton Mifflin, 1953), 144.

66. Kennan, Memoirs 1925–1950, 210–11.

67. Ibid.; George F. Kennan, American Diplomacy 1900–1950 (Chicago: University of Chicago Press, 1951), 86–87; George F. Kennan, Russia and the West Under Lenin and Stalin (Boston: Little, Brown, 1961), 365–66; George F. Kennan to John Lukacs, January 18, 1995, in George F. Kennan and the Origins of Containment, 1944–1946: The Kennan-Lukacs Correspondence, ed. John Lukacs (Columbia: University of Missouri Press, 1997), 31; Kennan interview, CNN, The Cold War, Disc 1, Comrades 1917–1945 (Turner Original Productions DVD, 1998).

68. Isaacson and Thomas, The Wise Men, 240–41; cf. Gaddis, George F. Kennan, 184–87.

69. Gaddis, George F. Kennan, 174.

70. Bohlen, Witness to History, 174–76.

71. Joseph Stalin, "New Five-Year Plan for Russia: Election Address," Vital Speeches of the Day 12 (1946): 300; "Stalin Sets a Huge Output Near

Ours in 5-Year Plan, Expects to Lead in Science," New York Times, February 10, 1946, 1.

72. The Chargé in the Soviet Union (Kennan) to the Secretary of State, February 12, 1946, Foreign Relations of the United States, 1946, vol. 6, Eastern Europe, the Soviet Union (1946) (Washington, DC: U.S. Government Printing Office, 1969), 695. Syntax is telegramese.

73. Kennan, Memoirs 1925–1950, 293.

74. The Chargé in the Soviet Union (Kennan) to the Secretary of State, February 22, 1946, Foreign Relations of the United States, 1946, vol. 6, 700.

75. Ibid., 707.

76. Gaddis, George F. Kennan, 218–19; Lloyd C. Gardner, Architects of Illusion: Men and Ideas in American Foreign Policy, 1941–1949 (Chicago: Quadrangle Books, 1970), 279–300.

77. Arnold A. Rogow, James Forrestal: A Study of Personality, Politics, and Policy (New York: Macmillan, 1963), 122–26; Isaacson and Thomas, The Wise Men, 382–84.

78. Issacson and Thomas, The Wise Men, 350.

79. James Forrestal, The Forrestal Diaries, ed. Walter Millis (New York: Viking, 1951), 134.

80. Townsend Hoopes and Douglas Brinkley, Driven Patriot: The Life and Times of James Forrestal (New York: Knopf, 1992), 272–73; cf. Gaddis, George F. Kennan, 230–31, and Yergin, Shattered Peace, 170–71.

81. George F. Kennan to Jeanette Kennan Hotchkiss, December 25, 1946, quoted in Gaddis, George F. Kennan, 246.

82. David McCullough, Truman (New York: Simon and Schuster, 1992), 418–19; John Lewis Gaddis, "The Insecurities of Victory: The United States and the Perception of the Soviet Threat after World War II," in Michael J. Lacey, ed., The Truman Presidency (Cambridge: Cambridge University Press, 1989), 250–51.

83. Tony Judt, Postwar: A History of Europe Since 1945 (New York: Penguin, 2005), 108.

84. David Caute, The Great Fear: The Anti-Communist Purge Under Truman and Eisenhower (New York: Simon and Schuster, 1978), 55; James T. Patterson, Grand Expectations: The United States, 1945–1974 (New York: Oxford University Press, 1996), 113.

85. Yurii N. Zhukov, Stalin: tainy vlasti (Moscow: Vagrius, 2005), 334. I am grateful to Olga Voronina for this source.

86. George F. Kennan, "Psychological Background of Soviet Foreign Policy," Box 251, Folder 5, Kennan Papers.

87. Gaddis, George F. Kennan, 258–59; Hoopes and Brinkley, Driven Patriot, 273–81; Arnold A. Offner, Another Such Victory: President Truman and the Cold War, 1945–1953 (Stanford: Stanford University Press, 2002), 127–28.

88. X [George F. Kennan], "The Sources of Soviet Conduct," *Foreign Affairs* 25 (1947): 567.

89. Ibid., 575.

90. "The Story Behind Our Russian Policy," *Newsweek* 30 (July 21, 1947), 15–16.

91. Walter Lippmann, *The Cold War: A Study in U.S. Foreign Policy* (New York: Harper and Brothers, 1947), 18.

92. Gaddis, *Strategies of Containment*, 59–61.

93. Kennan, *Memoirs 1925–1950*, 360–61.

94. James Chace, *Acheson: The Secretary of State Who Created the American World* (New York: Simon and Schuster, 1998), 167; Kennan, *Memoirs 1925–1950*, 314–15.

95. Policy with Respect to American Aid to Western Europe, PPS/1, May 23, 1947, *State Department Policy Planning Staff Papers, 1947–1949*, vol. 1, *1947* (New York: Garland, 1983), 11.

96. Patterson, *Grand Expectations*, 113–36; Gaddis, *George F. Kennan*, 694.

97. Offner, *Another Such Victory*, 202.

98. Ira Katznelson, *Fear Itself: The New Deal and the Origins of Our Time* (New York: Liveright, 2013), 460; David K. Johnson, *The Lavender Scare: The Cold War Persecution of Gays and Lesbians in the Federal Government* (Chicago: University of Chicago Press, 2004). See also Landon R. Y. Storrs, *The Second Red Scare and the Unmaking of the New Deal Left* (Princeton: Princeton University Press, 2013), 1–3, which gives a higher number of terminations.

99. Gaddis, *George F. Kennan*, 264–70; Policy with Respect to American Aid to Western Europe, *State Department Policy Planning Staff Papers*, vol. 1, 3–11.

100. www.marshallfoundation.org/marshall/the-marshall-plan/marshall-plan-speech/.

101. Gaddis, *George F. Kennan*, 264–70.

102. Quoted in Jonathan Haslam, *Russia's Cold War: From the October Revolution to the Fall of the Wall* (New Haven: Yale University Press, 2011), 89.

103. A. Zhdanov, "The International Situation," *For a Lasting Peace, for a People's Democracy* [Belgrade] 1 (November 10, 1947), 2. This was the official paper of the Cominform.

104. Geoffrey Roberts, *Stalin's Wars: From World War to Cold War, 1939–1953* (New Haven: Yale University Press, 2006), 317–20, 333–36; R. Craig Nation, *Black Earth, Red Star: A History of Soviet Security Policy, 1917–1991* (Ithaca: Cornell University Press, 1992), 174–75.

105. Steven Long, *The CIA and the Soviet Bloc: Political Warfare, the Origins of the CIA, and Countering Communism in Europe* (London: I. B. Tauris, 2014), 24–45.

106. Thompson, *The Hawk and the Dove*, 63.

107. Laura Fermi, *Illustrious Immigrants: The Intellectual Migration from Europe, 1930–1941*, 2nd ed. (Chicago: University of Chicago Press, 1971), 28–29; Cristoph Frei, *Hans J. Morgenthau: An Intellectual Biography* (Baton Rouge: Louisiana State University Press, 2001), 44–60.

108. Frei, *Hans J. Morgenthau*, 62–73; Oliver Jütersonke, *Morgenthau, Law, and Realism* (New York: Cambridge University Press, 2010), 21–26.

109. William E. Scheuerman, *Hans Morgenthau: Realism and Beyond* (Cambridge: Polity, 2009), 101–102.

110. Hans J. Morgenthau, "The Escape from Power in the Western World," in *Conflicts of Power in Modern Culture: Seventh Symposium*, ed. Lyman Bryson, Louis Finkelstein, and R. M. MacIver (New York: Harper and Brothers, 1947), 1–2.

111. Hans J. Morgenthau, *Politics Among Nations: The Struggle for Power and Peace* (New York: Knopf, 1948), 16–17.

112. Hans J. Morgenthau, "Another 'Great Debate': The National Interest of the United States," *American Political Science Review* 46 (1952): 961–88; Peter Wilson, "The Myth of the 'First Great Debate,'" *Review of International Studies* 24 (1998): 1–15.

113. Alfred Grosser, "L'étude des relations internationales, spécialité américaine?," *Revue Française de Science Politique* 6 (1956): 634–51; William T. R. Fox and Annette Baker Fox, "The Teaching of International Relations in the United States," *World Politics* 13 (1961): 339–59; Stanley Hoffmann, "An American Social Science: International Relations," *Daedalus* 106 (1977): 41–60; Steve Smith, "Paradigm Dominance in International Relations: The Development of International Relations as a Social Science," in Hugh C. Dyer and Leon Mangasarian, eds., *The Study of International Relations: The State of the Art* (London: Macmillan, 1989), 15–27.

114. Arnold Wolfers, introduction to Arnold Wolfers and Laurence W. Martin, eds., *The Anglo-American Tradition in Foreign Affairs: Readings from Thomas More to Woodrow Wilson* (New Haven: Yale University Press, 1956), xxvi.

115. David Callahan, *Between Two Worlds: Realism, Idealism, and American Foreign Policy After the Cold War* (New York: HarperCollins, 1994), 39–41.

116. Stephanson, *Kennan and the Art of Foreign Policy*, 5; Isaacson and Thomas, *The Wise Men*, 147.

117. George Kennan to Hans Morgenthau, May 27, 1949, Box 33, Folder 7, Morgenthau Papers; Wilson D. Miscamble, *George F. Kennan and the Making of American Foreign Policy, 1947–1950* (Princeton: Princeton University Press, 1992), 283–84.

118. Morgenthau, *Politics Among Nations*, 196.

119. Hans J. Morgenthau, "Views on Nuremberg," *America* 76 (December 7, 1946), 266–67.

120. Ibid., 267.

121. Kennan, *Memoirs 1925–1950*, 175.

122. Hans J. Morgenthau, "The Political Science of E. H. Carr," *World Politics* 1 (1948): 134.

123. Hans J. Morgenthau, *In Defense of the National Interest: A Critical Examination of American Foreign Policy* (New York: Knopf, 1951), 33–37.

124. George Orwell, "Comment on Robert Duvall's 'Whitehall's Road to Mandalay,'" in *The Complete Works of George Orwell*, ed. Peter Davison, vol. 15, *Two Wasted Years* (London: Secker and Warburg, 1998), 48.

125. John Adams to Thomas Jefferson, February 2, 1816, in *The Adams-Jefferson Letters: The Complete Correspondence Between Thomas Jefferson and Abigail and John Adams*, ed. Lester J. Cappon (Chapel Hill: University of North Carolina Press, 1959), 463.

2. THE OBJECT OF POWER

1. Fred R. Shapiro, ed., *The Yale Book of Quotations* (New Haven: Yale University Press, 2006), 569.

2. George Orwell, "Toward European Unity," in *The Complete Works of George Orwell*, ed. Peter Davison, vol. 19, *It Is What I Think, 1947–1948* (London: Secker and Warburg, 1998), 163–67.

3. John Rodden, *George Orwell: The Politics of Literary Reputation*, rev. ed. (New Brunswick: Transaction, 2002), 21–29.

4. Thomas R. Maddux, "Red Fascism, Brown Bolshevism: The American Image of Totalitarianism in the 1930s," *Historian* 40 (November 1977), 85–103.

5. Carl J. Friedrich, "The Problem of Totalitarianism—An Introduction," in *Totalitarianism: Proceedings of a Conference Held at the American Academy of Arts and Sciences, March 1953*, ed. Carl J. Friedrich (Cambridge, MA: Harvard University Press, 1954), 2n3; Benjamin L. Alpers, *Dictators, Democracy, and American Public Culture: Envisioning the Totalitarian Enemy, 1920s–1950s* (Chapel Hill: University of North Carolina Press, 2003), 12.

6. The President's Special Conference with the Association of Radio News Analysts, May 13, 1947, *Public Papers of the Presidents of the United States: Harry S. Truman, 1947, Containing the Public Messages, Speeches, and Statements of the President, January 1 to December 31, 1947* (Washington, DC: U.S. Government Printing Office, 1963), 238.

7. Les K. Adler and Thomas G. Paterson, "Red Fascism: The Merger of Nazi Germany and Soviet Russia in the American Image of Totalitarianism, 1930s–1950s," *American Historical Review* 75 (1970): 1046–48.

8. Abbott Gleason, *Totalitarianism: The Inner History of the Cold War* (New York: Oxford University Press, 1995), 39–50, 143–66.

9. The Chargé in the Soviet Union (Kennan) to the Secretary of State, February 22, 1946, *Foreign Relations of the United States, 1946*, vol. 6, *Eastern Europe, the Soviet Union (1946)* (Washington, DC: U.S. Government Printing Office, 1969), 708.

10. Rodden, *Orwell*, 46, 49; Jeffrey Meyers, *Orwell: Wintry Conscience of a Generation* (New York: W. W. Norton, 2000), 290.

11. Michael Shelden, *Orwell: The Authorised Biography* (London: Heinemann, 1991), 463.

12. George Orwell, *The Road to Wigan Pier*, in *Works*, vol. 5, 169.

13. Meyers, *Orwell*, 86.

14. "Notes from Orwell's Last Literary Notebook," in *Works*, vol. 20, *Our Job Is to Make Life Worth Living, 1949–1950*, 204.

15. Meyers, *Orwell*, 8–12, 28–45, 73–81.

16. Shelden, *Orwell*, 275.

17. Meyers, *Orwell*, 176.

18. Ibid., 214.

19. Ibid., 224–59.

20. Ibid., 214.

21. Orwell, *The Road to Wigan Pier*, 148.

22. George Orwell, "My Country Right or Left," in *Works*, vol. 12, *A Patriot After All, 1940–1941*, 272.

23. George Orwell, *The Lion and the Unicorn: Socialism and the English Genius*, in *Works*, vol. 12, 415.

24. Ibid., 409–10.

25. Ibid., 391.

26. George Orwell, "London Letter," in *Works*, vol. 18, *Smothered Under Journalism, 1946*, 286.

27. George Orwell, "As I Please," in *Works*, vol. 16, *I Have Tried to Tell the Truth, 1943–1944*, 365.

28. See James Burnham and Max Shachtman, "Intellectuals in Retreat," *New International* 5 (1939): 3–22; James Burnham, *The Struggle for the World* (New York: John Day, 1947), 136–43, 242–48.

29. Daniel Kelly, *James Burnham and the Struggle for the World: A Life* (Wilmington, DE: ISI Books, 2002), 149–52, 189–93; Hugh Wilford, *The Mighty Wurlitzer: How The C.I.A. Played America* (Cambridge, MA: Harvard University Press, 2008), 74–76; Peter Grose, *Operation Rollback: America's Secret War Behind the Iron Curtain* (Boston: Houghton Mifflin, 2000), 103–104; John Lewis Gaddis, *George F. Kennan: An American Life* (New York: Penguin Press, 2011), 316–17.

30. William F. Buckley, "James Burnham 1905–1987," *National Review* 39 (September 11, 1987), 31; Kelly, *James Burnham*, 218–21.

31. Quoted in Kelly, *James Burnham*, 382n21.

32. Kelly, *James Burnham*, 97.

33. John West [James Burnham], "The Roosevelt 'Security' Program," *New International* 2 (1935): 42.

34. James Burnham, *The Managerial Revolution: What Is Happening in the World* (New York: John Day, 1941), 58, 152–54.

35. Ibid., 175–76.

36. Ibid., 178–79.

37. James Burnham, *The Machiavellians: Defenders of Freedom* (New York: John Day, 1943), 246.

38. Kelly, *James Burnham*, 110.

39. George Orwell, in *Works*, vol. 20, 19n3.

40. George Orwell, "As I Please," in *Works*, vol. 16, *I Have Tried to Tell the Truth, 1943–44,* 61.

41. Isaac Deutscher, "*1984*—The Mysticism of Cruelty," in *Heretics and Renegades and Other Essays* (London: Jonathan Cape, 1955), 48n1.

42. George Orwell, "As I Please," in *Works*, vol. 17, *I Belong to the Left, 1945,* 39.

43. George Orwell, "You and the Atom Bomb," in *Works*, vol. 17, 320–21.

44. George Orwell, "Second Thoughts on James Burnham," in *Works*, vol. 18, 278, 283.

45. Orwell, "Toward European Unity," 163.

46. George Orwell, "Orwell's Statement on *Nineteen Eighty-Four*," in *Works*, vol. 20, 135.

47. George Orwell, *Nineteen Eighty-Four*, in *Works*, vol. 9, 192–93, 194, 213.

48. Ibid., 208, 209.

49. Ibid., 274–76.

50. Ibid., 280. See also William Steinhoff, *George Orwell and the Origins of "1984"* (Ann Arbor: University of Michigan Press, 1975), 200–204; cf. Richard Rorty, *Contingency, Irony, and Solidarity* (Cambridge: Cambridge University Press, 1989), 183.

51. Arthur M. Schlesinger, Jr., *The Vital Center: The Politics of Freedom* (Boston: Houghton Mifflin, 1949), 250.

52. "The Year in Books," *Time* 38 (December 15, 1941), 110.

53. See Theodor W. Adorno, Betty Ruth Aron, Else Frenkel-Brunswick, Daniel J. Levinson, Maria Hertz Levinson, William R. Morrow, and R. Nevitt Sanford, *The Authoritarian Personality* (New York: Harper and Brothers, 1950); Erich Fromm, *Escape from Freedom* (New York: Rinehart, 1941); Rollo May, *The Meaning of Anxiety* (New York: Ronald Press, 1950); Schlesinger, *The Vital Center*, 243–44.

54. H. H. Gerth and C. Wright Mills, "A Marx for the Managers," *Ethics* 52 (1942): 201.

55. Guy Oakes and Arthur J. Vidich, *Collaboration, Reputation, and the Ethics of American Academic Life: Hans H. Gerth and C. Wright Mills* (Urbana: University of Illinois Press, 1999), 2–14.

56. Irving Louis Horowitz, *C. Wright Mills: An American Utopian* (New York: Free Press, 1983), 13–39.

57. C. Wright Mills, *The Power Elite* (New York: Oxford University Press, 1956), 28.

58. Daniel Bell, "*The Power Elite*—Reconsidered," *American Journal of Sociology* 64 (1958): 250.

59. Mills, *The Power Elite*, 297.

60. Ibid., 3.

61. Ibid., 304.

3. FREEDOM AND NOTHINGNESS

1. Michael Neiberg, *The Blood of Free Men: The Liberation of Paris, 1944* (New York: Basic Books, 2012), 55–59; Antony Beevor, *The Second World War* (London: Weidenfeld and Nicolson, 2012), 613.

2. Charles de Gaulle, *The Complete War Memoirs of Charles de Gaulle*, vol. 2, *Unity: 1942–1944*, trans. Richard Howard (New York: Simon and Schuster, 1964), 324–33; Jean-Pierre Azéma, *From Munich to the Liberation, 1938–1944*, trans. Janet Lloyd (Cambridge: Cambridge University Press, 1984), 180–82; John Keegan, *The Second World War* (New York: Penguin, 1990), 411–14; Antony Beevor and Artemis Cooper, *Paris After the Liberation, 1944–1949*, rev. ed. (London: Penguin, 2004), 93.

3. Robert O. Paxton, *Vichy France: Old Guard and New Order, 1940–1944* (New York: Columbia University Press, 1972), 38; Robert Gildea, *Marianne in Chains: Daily Life in the Heart of France During the German Occupation* (New York: Henry Holt, 2002), 323–24.

4. Jacques Fauvet, *Histoire du parti communiste français*, vol. 2, *Vingt-cinq ans de drames, 1939–1965* (Paris: Fayard, 1965), 139.

5. Gertrude Stein, *Paris, France* (New York: Charles Scribner's Sons, 1940), 11.

6. Harold Rosenberg, "On the Fall of Paris," *Partisan Review* 7 (1940): 440.

7. Warren Irving Susman, "Pilgrimage to Paris: The Backgrounds of American Expatriation, 1920–1934," PhD dissertation, University of Wisconsin, 1957, 166.

8. Rosenberg, "On the Fall of Paris," 441–42.

9. David Pryce-Jones, *Paris in the Third Reich: A History of the German Occupation, 1940–1944* (London: Collins, 1981), 197.

10. Olivier Wieviorka, *Normandy: The Landings to the Liberation of Paris*, trans. M. B. DeBevoise (Cambridge, MA: Harvard University Press, 2008), 314–15; Raphael Minder, "Rafeal Gómez Nieto, Last Member of Unit That Helped Liberate Paris, Dies at 99," *New York Times*, April 5, 2020, D6.

11. Charles de Gaulle, "Discours prononcé a l'Hôtel de Ville de Paris," in *Discours et messages*, vol. 1, *Pendant la guerre, juin 1940–janvier 1946* (Paris: Plon, 1970), 440.

12. Karl Marx, "The Civil War in France: Address of the General Council of the International Working-Men's Association," in Karl Marx and

Frederick Engels, *Collected Works*, vol. 22, *Marx and Engels, 1870–71*, ed. Yevgenia Dakhina (London: Lawrence and Wishart, 1986), 341. First published, in English, in London.

13. Neiberg, *The Blood of Free Men*, 85, 201–38; Beevor, *The Second World War*, 614–15; Keegan, *The Second World War*, 414.

14. "Editorial: Paris," *Life* 17 (September 4, 1944), 26.

15. "Paris Is Free Again!," *Life* 17 (September 11, 1944), 25.

16. Charles Wertenbaker, "The Streets and the People," *Life* 17 (September 11, 1944), 38; and see "Paris Is Free!," *Time* 44 (September 4, 1944), 34–36.

17. A. J. Liebling, "Letter from Paris," *New Yorker* 20 (September 9, 1944), 44, 46.

18. Lansing Warren, "General Who Held Paris in War Backs Abetz," *New York Times*, July 21, 1949, 16.

19. Paul Webster and Nicholas Powell, *Saint-Germain-des-Prés* (London: Constable, 1984), 18; Alan Riding, *And the Show Went On: Cultural Life in Occupied Paris* (New York: Knopf, 2010), 229; Glenn Myrent and Georges P. Langlois, *Henri Langlois: First Citizen of Cinema*, trans. Lisa Nesselson (New York: Twayne, 1995), 73–74.

20. Beevor and Cooper, *Paris After the Liberation*, 136.

21. Richard Ellmann, *James Joyce*, rev. ed. (New York: Oxford University Press, 1982), 736.

22. Henri Michel, *Paris Résistant* (Paris: Albin Michel, 1982), 112.

23. Ibid., 332.

24. Tony Judt, *Postwar: A History of Europe Since 1945* (New York: Penguin, 2005), 33; Allan Mitchell, *Nazi Paris: The History of an Occupation* (New York: Berghahn Books, 2008), 160; Robert O. Paxton, "The Truth About the Resistance," *New York Review of Books* 63 (February 25, 2016) (online).

25. Keegan, *The Second World War*, 490; Judt, *Postwar*, 39.

26. Serge Klarsfeld, *Memorials to the Jews Deported from France, 1942–1944* (New York: Beate Klarsfeld Foundation, 1983), xvi; Julian Jackson, *France: The Dark Years, 1940–1944* (Oxford: Oxford University Press, 2001), 362.

27. Pryce-Jones, *Paris in the Third Reich*, 19–31; Mitchell, *Nazi Paris*, 34; Dominique Veillon, *Fashion Under the Occupation*, trans. Miriam Kochan (Oxford: Berg, 2002), 107–24; Jackson, *France: The Dark Years*, 300–318. And see Patrick Buisson, *1940–1945, Années érotiques: L'Occupation intime* (Paris: Albin Michel, 2011).

28. Pascal Fouché, *L'Édition française sous l'Occupation, 1940–1944* (Paris: Bibliothèque de Littérature Française Contemporaine de Uni-versité Paris 7, 1987); and see André Schiffrin, *The Business of Books: How International Conglomerates Took Over Publishing and Changed the Way We Read* (London: Verso, 2000), 17–18.

29. Pierre Assouline, *Gaston Gallimard: A Half-Century of French Publishing*, trans. Harold J. Salemson (San Diego: Harcourt Brace Jovanovich, 1988), 213–19; Webster and Powell, *Saint-Germain-des-Prés*, 32–34; Riding, *And the Show Went On*, 64–65, 113–14; Beevor and Cooper, *Paris After the Liberation*, 143.

30. Webster and Powell, *Saint-Germain-des-Prés*, 52.

31. Jackson, *France: The Dark Years*, 313–14; Ronald Aronson, *Camus and Sartre: The Story of a Friendship and the Quarrel That Ended It* (Chicago: University of Chicago Press, 2004), 36; Fouché, *L'Édition française sous l'Occupation*, 80.

32. Olivier Corpet and Claire Paulhan, *Collaboration and Resistance: French Literary Life Under the Nazi Occupation* (New York: Five Ties, 2009); Laurence Bertrand Dorléac, *Art of the Defeat: France 1940–1944*, trans. Jane Marie Todd (Los Angeles: Getty Research Institute, 2008); Michel, *Paris Résistant*, 129–31.

33. Riding, *And the Show Went On*, 94–99, 150, 291; Olivier Todd, *Albert Camus: A Life*, trans. Benjamin Ivry (New York: Carroll and Graf, 1997), 136–37; Alex Ross, *The Rest Is Noise: Listening to the Twentieth Century* (New York: Farrar, Straus and Giroux, 2007), 358–59.

34. Simone de Beauvoir, *The Prime of Life*, trans. Peter Green (New York: Harper and Row, 1976), 211–12. ("Les prétentions politiques des intellectuels de gauche lui faisaient hausser les épaules . . . Palabrer, déclamer, manifester, prêcher: quelle vaine agitation!" Simone de Beauvoir, *La Force de l'âge* [Paris: Gallimard, 1960], 272–73.)

35. Marc Bloch, *Strange Defeat: A Statement of Evidence Written in 1940*, trans. Gerard Hopkins (London: Oxford University Press, 1949); Ernest R. May, *Strange Victory: Hitler's Conquest of France* (New York: Hill and Wang, 2000); Julian Jackson, *The Fall of France: The Nazi Invasion of 1940* (Oxford: Oxford University Press, 2003).

36. Jean-Pierre Azéma and François Bédarida, eds., *1938–1948, les années de tourmente: de Munich à Prague; dictionnaire critique* (Paris: Flammarion, 1995), 693–97; Éric Conan and Henry Rousso, *Vichy: An Ever-Present Past*, trans. Nathan Bracher (Hanover: University Press of New England, 1998), 129.

37. Marius Perrin, *Avec Sartre au Stalag 12 D* (Paris: Jean-Pierre Delarge, 1980), 114–16; Ronald Hayman, *Sartre: A Life* (New York: Simon and Schuster, 1987), 178.

38. Beauvoir, *The Prime of Life*, 342. ("Sartre pensait beaucoup à l'après-guerre: il était bien

décidé à ne plus se tenir à l'écart de la vie politique. Sa nouvelle morale, basée sur la notion
d'authenticité, et qu'il s'efforçait de mettre en
pratique, exigeait que l'homme 'assumât'
sa 'situation'; et la seule manière de la faire
c'était de la dépasser en s'engageant dans une
action: toute autre attitude était une fuit, une
prétention vide, une mascarade fondées sur la
mauvaise foi. On voit qu'un sérieux change-
ment s'était produit en lui." Beauvoir, *La Force
de l'âge*, 442.)

39. Olivier Todd, *Malraux: A Life*, trans. Joseph
West (New York: Knopf, 2005), 61, 285–88.

40. Jean-Paul Sartre, "Merleau-Ponty vivant," *Temps
Modernes* 17 (1961): 184–85 ("Née dans l'en-
thousiasme, notre petite unité prit la fièvre et
mourut un an plus tard faute de savoir que
faire"); Annie Cohen-Solal, *Jean-Paul Sartre:
A Life*, trans. Anna Cancogni, ed. Norman
MacAfee (New York: Pantheon, 1987), 170–75.

41. Ingrid Galster, *Sartre, Vichy, et les intellectuels*
(Paris: L'Harmattan, 2001), 79–94; Jonathan
Judaken, *Jean-Paul Sartre and the Jewish Question: Anti-antisemitism and the Politics of the
French Intellectual* (Lincoln: University of Nebraska Press, 2006), 49–105; Carole Seymour-
Jones, *A Dangerous Liaison: Simone de Beauvoir
and Jean-Paul Sartre* (London: Century, 2008),
263–67.

42. Gilbert Joseph, *Une si douce Occupation: Simone de Beauvoir, Jean-Paul Sartre, 1940–1944*
(Paris: Albin Michel, 1991), 161–74; cf. Bernard Henri-Lévy, *Sartre: The Philosopher of
the Twentieth Century*, trans. Andrew Brown
(Cambridge: Polity, 2003), 280–84.

43. Jean-Paul Sartre, "Paris Alive: The Republic
of Silence," trans. Lincoln Kirstein, *Atlantic
Monthly* 174 (December 1944), 39.

44. Jean-Paul Sartre, "The New Writing in France,"
Vogue 106 (July 1945), 85.

45. Susan Rubin Suleiman, *Crises of Memory and
the Second World War* (Cambridge, MA: Harvard University Press, 2006), 30–35.

46. Bernard Frizell, "Existentialism: Amid Left
Bank Revels, Postwar Paris Enthrones a Bleak
Philosophy of Pessimism Derived by a French
Atheist from a Danish Mystic," *Life* 20 (June
17, 1946), 60.

47. Simone de Beauvoir, "Jean-Paul Sartre: Strictly
Personal" [trans. Malcolm Cowley], *Harper's
Bazaar* (January 1946), 158.

48. Simone de Beauvoir, *Philosophical Writings*, ed.
Margaret A. Simons (Urbana: University of Illinois Press, 2004), 234.

49. Jean-Paul Sartre, "Victoire de Gaullisme," *Le
Figaro* 119 (January 26, 1945), 2.

50. Jean-Paul Sartre, "The Republic of Silence,"
in *The Aftermath of War (Situations III)*, trans.
Chris Turner (London: Seagull, 2008), 6. ("Et
le choix que chacun faisait de lui-même était

authentique puisqu'il se faisait en présence de
la mort, puisqu'il aurait toujours pu s'exprimer
sous la forme 'Plutôt la mort que . . .' . . . Ainsi,
dans l'ombre et dans le sang, la plus forte des
Républiques s'est constituée. Chacun de ses ci-
toyens savait qu'il se devait à tous et qu'il ne
pouvait compter que sur lui-même; chacun
d'eux réalisait, dans le délaissement le plus total, son rôle historiques. Chacun d'eux, contre
les oppresseurs, entreprenait d'être lui-même,
irrémédiablement et en se choisissant lui-même
dans sa liberté, choisissait la liberté de tous."
Jean-Paul Sartre, "La République du silence,"
in *Situations III* [Paris: Gallimard, 1949], 12,
14.)

51. Jean-Paul Sartre, "The Liberation of Paris: An
Apocalyptic Week," in *The Writings of Jean-
Paul Sartre*, vol. 2, *Selected Prose*, ed. Michel
Contat and Michel Rybalka, trans. Richard
McCleary (Evanston: Northwestern University
Press, 1974), 162. ("Il ne dépendait pas d'eux
que les divisions en retraite ne se rabattissent
sur Paris et ne fissent de notre ville un nouveau Varsovie. Mais ce qui dépendait d'eux
c'était de témoigner par leurs actes—et quelle
que fût l'issue de la lutte inégale qu'ils avaient
entreprise—de la volonté française . . . Aussi
l'autre aspect de l'insurrection parisienne,
c'est cet air de fête qu'elle n'a pas quitté. Des
quartiers entiers s'étaient endimanchés. Et, si
je me demande ce qu'on fêtait ainsi, je vois que
c'était l'homme et ses pouvoirs." Jean-Paul Sartre, "Une semaine d'Apocalypse: la libération
de Paris," *Clartés*, no. 9 [August 24, 1945], 1.)

52. John Gerassi, *Jean-Paul Sartre: Hated Conscience of His Century*, vol. 1, *Protestant or Protestor?* (Chicago: University of Chicago Press,
1989), 120.

53. Toril Moi, *Simone de Beauvoir: The Making of
an Intellectual Woman*, 2nd ed. (New York: Oxford University Press, 2008), 70.

54. Raymond Aron, *Memoirs: Fifty Years of Po-
litical Reflection*, trans. George Holoch (New
York: Holmes and Meier, 1990), 22–23;
Deidre Bair, *Simone de Beauvoir: A Biography*
(New York: Simon and Schuster, 1990), 127–
46; Hayman, *Sartre*, 31–33, 51; Beauvoir, *The
Prime of Life*, 198, 324; Cohen-Solal, *Jean-Paul
Sartre*, 489–90.

55. See Jean-Paul Sartre, *Sartre by Himself: A Film
Directed by Alexandre Astruc and Michel Con-
tat*, trans. Richard Seaver (New York: Outback
Press, 1978), 91; Madeleine Gobeil, "Sartre
Talks of Beauvoir," *Vogue* 146 (July 1965), 72.

56. Beauvoir, *The Prime of Life*, 26. ("A quoi bon,
par exemple, habiter sous un même toit quand
le monde était notre propriété commune? et
pourquoi craindre de mettre entre nous des
distances qui ne pouvaient jamais nous séparer?
Un seul projet nous animait: tout embrasser,

et témoigner de tout; il nous commandait de suivre, à l'occasion, des chemins divergents, sans nous dérober l'un à l'autre la moindre de nos trouvailles; ensemble, nous nous pliions a ses exigences, si bien qu'au moment même où nous nous divisions, nos volontés se confondaient. C'est se qui nous liait qui nous déliait; et par ce déliement nous nous retrouvions liés au plus profond de nous." Beauvoir, *La Force de l'âge*, 30.)

57. Beauvoir, *The Prime of Life*, 24. ("'Entre nous . . . il s'agit d'un amour nécessaire: il convient que nous connaissions aussi des amours contingentes.'" Beauvoir, *La Force de l'âge*, 26–27.)

58. Bair, *Simone de Beauvoir*, 89–92; Simone de Beauvoir, *Memoirs of a Dutiful Daughter*, trans. James Kirkup (Cleveland: World Publishing, 1959), 128. ("Simone a un cerveau d'homme. Simone est un homme." Simone de Beauvoir, *Mémoires d'une jeune fille rangée* [Paris: Gallimard, 1958], 169.)

59. Bair, *Simone de Beauvoir*, 145–46.

60. Hayman, *Sartre*, 73, 75.

61. Beauvoir, *The Prime of Life*, 112. ("'Tu vois, mon petit camarade, si tu es phénoménologue, tu peux parler de ce cocktail, et c'est de la philosophie!' Sartre en pâlit d'émotion." Beauvoir, *La Force de l'âge*, 141); Aron, *Memoirs*, 60.

62. Ethan Kleinberg, *Generation Existential: Heidegger's Philosophy in France, 1927–1961* (Ithaca: Cornell University Press, 2005), 116.

63. Sartre, *Sartre by Himself*, 26.

64. Aron, *Memoirs*, 48.

65. Elisabeth Young-Bruehl, *Hannah Arendt: For Love of the World* (New Haven: Yale University Press, 1982), 104.

66. Tom Rockmore, *Heidegger and French Philosophy: Humanism, Antihumanism, and Being* (London: Routledge, 1995), 74.

67. Jean-Paul Sartre, *War Diaries: Notebooks from a Phony War, November 1939–March 1940*, trans. Quintin Hoare (London: Verso, 1984), 182–83.

68. Kleinberg, *Generation Existential*, 129–33.

69. Martin Heidegger, *Being and Time*, trans. John Macquarrie and Edward Robinson (New York: Harper and Row, 1962), 68. ("Das Seiende, dem es in seinem Sein um dieses selbst geht, verhält sich zu seinem Sein als seiner eigensten Möglichkeit." Martin Heidegger, *Gesamtausgabe*, vol. 2, *Sein und Zeit*, ed. Friedrich-Wilhelm W. von Herrmann [Frankfurt: Vittorio Klostermann, 1977], 57.)

70. Kleinberg, *Generation Existential*, 70–71; John Haugeland, "Reading Brandom Reading Heidegger," *European Journal of Philosophy* 13 (2005): 423.

71. Rüdiger Safranski, *Martin Heidegger: Between*

Good and Evil, trans. Ewald Osers (Cambridge, MA: Harvard University Press, 1998), 94–95.

72. Martin Heidegger, "What Is Metaphysics?," in *Basic Writings: From "Being and Time" (1927) to "The Task of Thinking" (1964)*, ed. David Farrell Krell, rev. ed. (San Francisco: HarperCollins, 1993), 110. ("Für diesen Einsprung ist entscheidend: einmal das Raumgeben für das Seiende im Ganzen; sodann das Sichloslassen in das Nichts, d. h. das Freiwerden von den Götzen, die jeder hat und zu denen er sich wegzuschleichen pflegt." Martin Heidegger, "Was Ist Metaphysik?," in *Gesamtausgabe*, vol. 9, *Wegmarken*, ed. Friedrich-Wilhelm von Hermann [Frankfurt: Vittorio Kloestermann, 1976], 122.)

73. Heidegger, "What Is Metaphysics?," 102. ("Das Nichts enthüllt sich in der Angst." Heidegger, "Was Ist Metaphysik?," in *Gesamtausgabe*, vol. 9, 113.)

74. Heidegger, "What Is Metaphysics?," 109. ("[D]ie volle Befremdlichkeit des Seienden." Heidegger, "Was Ist Metaphysik?," in *Gesamtausgabe*, vol. 9, 121.)

75. Heidegger, "What Is Metaphysics?," 109. ("Das menschliche Dasein kann sich nur zum Seienden verhalten, wenn es sich in das Nichts hineinhält." Heidegger, "Was Ist Metaphysik?," in *Gesamtausgabe*, vol. 9, 121.)

76. Heidegger, "What Is Metaphysics?," in *Basic Writings*, 103. ("Ohne ursprüngliche Offenbarkeit des Nichts kein Selbstsein und keine Freiheit." Heidegger, "Was Ist Metaphysik?," in *Gesamtausgabe*, vol. 9, 115.)

77. Heidegger, *Being and Time*, 67. ("Das 'Wesen' des Daseins liegt in seiner Existenz." Heidegger, in *Gesamtausgabe*, vol. 2, 56.) Italics in the original.

78. Jean-Paul Sartre, *Being and Nothingness: An Essay on Phenomenological Ontology*, trans. Hazel E. Barnes (New York: Philosophical Library, 1956), 25. ("L'homme n'est point *d'abord* pour être libre *ensuite*, mais il n'y a pas de différence entre l'être de l'homme et son *'être-libre.'*" Jean-Paul Sartre, *L'Être et le néant: Essai d'ontologie phénoménologique* [Paris: Gallimard, 1943], 61.)

79. Sartre, *Being and Nothingness*, 38. ("[M]a liberté est l'unique fondement des valeurs et . . . *rien*, absolument rien, ne me justifie d'adopter telle ou telle valeur, telle ou telle échelle de valeurs. En tant qu'être par qui les valeurs existent je suis injustifiable. Et ma liberté s'angoisse d'être le fondement sans fondement des valeurs." Sartre, *L'Être et le néant*, 76.)

80. Sartre, *Being and Nothingness*, 439. ("Je suis condamné à exister pour toujours par delà mon essence, par delà les mobiles et les motifs de mon acte: je suis condamné à être libre." Sartre, *L'Être et le néant*, 515.)

81. Sartre, *Being and Nothingness*, 439–40. ("Dans la mesure où le pour-soi veut se masquer son propre néant et s'incorporer l'en-soi comme son véritable mode d'être, il tente aussi de se masquer sa liberté . . . C'est parce que la réalité-humaine *n'est pas assez* qu'elle est libre . . . La liberté, c'est précisément le néant qui *est été* au cœur de l'homme et qui contraint la réalité-humaine à *se faire*, au lieu *d'être* . . . [P]our la réalité-humaine, être c'est *se choisir.*" Sartre, *L'Être et le néant*, 515–16.)

82. Martin Heidegger, *Gelassenheit* (Pfullingen, West Germany: Neske, 1959).

83. See Pascale Casanova, *The World Republic of Letters*, trans. M. B. DeBevoise (Cambridge, MA: Harvard University Press, 2004), 130–31, 336–45.

84. Maurice-Edgar Coindreau, *The Time of William Faulkner: A French View of Modern American Fiction*, ed. and trans. George McMillan Reeves (Columbia: South Carolina University Press, 1971), xv–xxi; Maurice-Edgar Coindreau, *Mémoires d'un traducteur: entretiens avec Christian Guidicelli* (Paris: Gallimard, 1974), 33–34.

85. Humphrey Ambler and E. Aldrich Kniffin, "The Undergraduate Week," *Princeton Alumni Weekly* 27 (November 5, 1926), 180.

86. See Stephen Koch, *The Breaking Point: Hemingway, Dos Passos, and the Murder of José Robles* (New York: Counterpoint, 2005).

87. Coindreau, *Mémoires d'un traducteur*, 37.

88. Maurice-Edgar Coindreau, "From Bill Cody to Bill Faulkner," *Princeton University Library Chronicle* 17 (1956): 188–89; Thelma M. Smith and Ward L. Miner, *Transatlantic Migration: The Contemporary American Novel in France* (Durham: Duke University Press, 1955), 89–90.

89. Coindreau, *Mémoires d'un traducteur*, 33–42; Assouline, *Gaston Gallimard*, 133–34.

90. David M. Earle, *Re-covering Modernism: Pulps, Paperbacks, and the Prejudice of Form* (Burlington, VT: Ashgate, 2009), 168.

91. Joseph Blotner, *Faulkner: A Biography*, vol. 1 (New York: Random House, 1974), 729–30; Maurice-Edgar Coindreau, "William Faulkner: Prix Nobel de Littérature," *France-Amérique* 17 (November 26, 1950), 9; cf. Coindreau, *Mémoires d'un traducteur*, 11–12.

92. James Burnham, "Trying to Say," *Symposium* 2 (1931): 51.

93. Coindreau, *Mémoires d'un traducteur*, 10–12; Blotner, *Faulkner*, vol. 1, 684–87.

94. Maurice-Edgar Coindreau, "William Faulkner in France," *Yale French Studies* 10 (1952): 86–88.

95. Morvan Lebesque, "William Faulkner: prix Nobel de littérature," *Carrefour*, November 14, 1950, 9; Casanova, *The World Republic of Letters*, 131.

96. Coindreau, *Mémoires d'un traducteur*, 46.

97. Smith and Miner, *Transatlantic Migration*, 18.

98. Ibid., 61–68; Casanova, *The World Republic of Letters*, 152–53; cf. Lawrence H. Schwartz, *Creating Faulkner's Reputation: The Politics of Modern Literary Criticism* (Knoxville: University of Tennessee Press, 1988).

99. Simone de Beauvoir, "An American Renaissance in France," *New York Times Book Review*, June 22, 1947, 7f.

100. Jean-Paul Sartre, "American Novelists in French Eyes," *Atlantic Monthly* 178 (August 1946), 114.

101. Jean-Marc Gouanvic, "Panorama de la traduction-importation de la littérature américaine en France (1820–1960)," in Ton Naaijkens, ed., *Event or Incident: On the Role of Translation in the Dynamics of Cultural Exchange* (Bern: Peter Lang, 2010), 165–66.

102. Maurice-Edgar Coindreau, "On Translating Faulkner," *Princeton Alumni Weekly* 61 (April 29, 1960), 3–4.

103. Maurice-Edgar Coindreau, "William Faulkner," *Nouvelle Revue Française* 36 (1931): 927. ("Mais dans les œuvres de William Faulkner, le sujet n'est qu'un prétexte au déploiement d'une technique . . . Pour être juste envers Faulkner il faut oublier ses thèmes et ne s'occuper que le façon dont il les traite.")

104. Valery Larbaud, preface to William Faulkner, *Tandis que j'agonise*, trans. Maurice-Edgar Coindreau (Paris: Gallimard, 1934), vi. ("Ce patois peut être curieux pour le lecteur de langue anglaise . . . mais ce n'est guère qu'un anglais dégradé, entaché de négligence et de mauvaises habitudes, qui nous a paru plus difficile que savoureux.")

105. See Stanley D. Woodworth, *William Faulkner en France: panorama critique (1931–1952)* (Paris: M. Minard, 1959), 33; cf. Félix Ansermoz-Dubois, *L'Interprétation française de la littérature américaine d'entre-deux-guerres (1919–1930): Essai de bibliographie* (Lausanne: Imprimerie La Concorde, 1944), 115.

106. Woodworth, *William Faulkner en France*, 2–36; François Pitavy, "The Making of a French Faulkner: A Reflection on Translation," *Faulkner Journal* 24 (Fall 2008), 89–95.

107. Beauvoir, *The Prime of Life*, 190. ("Faulkner avait su donner une durée à son histoire tout en annulant le temps." Beauvoir, *La Force d'âge*, 244.)

108. Maurice-Edgar Coindreau, preface to William Faulkner, *Lumière d'août* (Paris: Gallimard, 1935), xiii. ("[N]'est qu'une illusion commode de notre cerveau.")

109. Maurice Le Breton, "Technique et Psychologie chez William Faulkner," *Études Anglaises* 1 (1937): 425. ("[L]a multiplicité hétéroclite des sensations élémentaires du moi.")

110. Sartre, "American Novelists in French Eyes," 117.

111. See Louis Menand, "The Promise of Freedom, the Friend of Authority: American Culture in Postwar France," in Michael Kazin and Joseph A. McCartin, eds., *Americanism: New Perspectives on the History of an Ideal* (Chapel Hill: University of North Carolina Press, 2006), 205–20.

112. See Jean-Pierre Morel, "Jules Romaines et Dos Passos: Remarques," in Dominique Viart, ed., *Jules Romaines et les écritures de la simultanéité: Galsworthy, Musil, Döblin, Dos Passos, Valéry, Simon, Butor, Peeters, Plissart* (Villeneuve d'Ascq, France: Presses Universitaires du Septentrion, 1996), 223–36.

113. Beauvoir, *The Prime of Life*, 253, 274, 114.

114. Albert Camus, "Que pensez-vous de la littérature américaine?," *Combat*, January 17, 1947, 2; Jean-Paul Sartre, "*The Outsider* Explained," in *Critical Essays*, 167–69, originally published in *Cahiers du Sud* 29 (1943): 189–206; Jean-Paul Sartre, "'Vous nous embêtez avec Faulkner le vieux,' disent les Américains," *Combat*, January 3, 1947, 2.

115. Jean-Paul Sartre, "On *The Sound and the Fury*: Temporality in Faulkner," in *Critical Essays*, 119. ("J'aime son art, je ne crois pas à sa métaphysique." Jean-Paul Sartre, "À propos de *Le Bruit et le Fureur*: La Temporalité chez Faulkner," *Situations I* [Paris: Gallimard, 1947], 80.)

116. Jean-Paul Sartre, "On John Dos Passos and *1919*," in *Critical Essays*, 30. ("Je tiens Dos Passos pour le plus grand écrivain de notre temps." Jean-Paul Sartre, "À propos de John Dos Passos et de *1919*," *Situations I*, 25.)

117. Perry Miller, "Europe's Faith in American Fiction," *Atlantic Monthly* 188 (December 1951), 53.

118. Camus, "Que pensez-vous de la littérature américaine?," 2.

119. Sartre, "American Novelists in French Eyes," 118.

120. James B. Meriwether and Michael Millgate, eds., *Lion in the Garden: Interviews with William Faulkner, 1926–1962* (New York: Random House, 1968), 70.

121. Claude-Edmonde Magny, *The Age of the American Novel: The Film Aesthetic of Fiction Between the Two Wars*, trans. Eleanor Hochman (New York: Frederick Ungar, 1972), published as *L'Âge du roman américain* (Paris: Éditions du Seuil, 1948). Other studies include Ansermoz-Dubois, *L'Interprétation française de la littérature américaine d'entre-deux-guerres*; Albert Baiwir, *Abrégé de l'histoire du roman américain* (1946); Pierre Brodin, *Les écrivains américains de l'entre-deux-guerres* (1946); Charly Guyot, *Les romanciers américains d'aujourd'hui* (1948); Jean Simon, *Le roman américain au XXe siècle* (1950); Nelly Vaucher-Zananiri,

Voix d'amérique: études sur la littérature américaine d'aujourd'hui (1945). Magazine special issues on American fiction are listed in Smith and Miner, *Transatlantic Migration*, 202–204.

122. Magny, *The Age of the American Novel*, 3–33.

123. Beauvoir, *The Prime of Life*, 114–15, 197. ("La vie intérieure, je l'ai dit, nous détestons ça." Beauvoir, *La Force de l'âge*, 253.)

124. Sartre, *War Diaries*, 273–74. ("[Q]ui eût été beau, hésitant, obscur, lent et probe dans ses pensées, qui n'eût pas eu de grâce acquise mais une grâce sourde et spontanée; je ne sais pourquoi je le voyais ouvrier et vagabond dans l'Est américain. Comme j'eusse aimé sentir se former en moi, lentement, patiemment, des idées incertaines, comme j'eusse aimé bouillir de grandes colères obscures, défaillir de grandes tendresses sans cause. Tout cela, mon ouvrier américain [il ressemblait à Gary Cooper], pouvait le faire et le sentir. Je le voyais assis sur un talus du chemin de fer, las et poussiéreux; il attendait le wagon à bestiaux où il sauterait sans se faire voir, et j'aurais aimé être *lui* . . . qui pensait peu, parlait peu et faisait toujours ce qu'il fallait." Jean-Paul Sartre, *Carnets de la drôle de guerre: Septembre 1939–Mars 1940*, nouvelle édition, ed. Arlette Elkaïm-Sartre [Paris: Gallimard, 1995], 515.) I owe much in this discussion to Holly Hutton, "Imported from France: American Adaptations of Existentialist Ideas and Literature," PhD dissertation, Graduate Center of the City University of New York, 2004.

125. Beevor and Cooper, *Paris After the Liberation*, 170, 200.

126. Jean-Paul Sartre, "À propos de l'existentialisme: mise au point," *Action*, no. 17, December 29, 1944, 11–12. ("Vos attaques me paraissent inspirées par la mauvaise foi et l'ignorance"; "Marx n'accepterait-il pas, en effet, *cette devise de l'homme qui est la nôtre: faire et en faisant se faire et n'être rien que ce qu'il s'est fait*"; "il peut choisir d'être l'homme qui refuse que la misère soit le lot des hommes.")

127. Michael Scriven, *Sartre and the Media* (New York: St. Martin's 1993), 32–40; Cohen-Solal, *Jean-Paul Sartre*, 233–43.

128. Beevor and Cooper, *Paris After the Liberation*, 147–49.

129. Simone de Beauvoir, *Force of Circumstance*, trans. Richard Howard (New York: G. P. Putnam's Sons, 1965), 32. ("[N]ous découvrîmes que nous n'avions rien su . . . j'eus honte de vivre." Simone de Beauvoir, *La Force des choses* [Paris: Gallimard, 1963], 44–45.)

130. Cohen-Solal, *Jean-Paul Sartre*, 188; Marcel Merleau-Ponty, "La querelle de l'existentialisme," *Temps Modernes* 1 (1945): 344–56.

131. Dominique Janicaud, *Heidegger en France*, vol. 1, *Récit* (Paris: Albin Michel, 2001), 52–97.

132. Henri Lefebvre, "'Existentialisme' et marxisme: réponse à une mise au point," *Action*, no. 40, June 8, 1945, 8 ("une machine de guerre théorique contre le marxisme").

133. Jean Beaufret, "À propos de l'existentialisme," *Confluences* 1 (1945): 192–99, 307–18, 415–22, 531–38, 637–42, 764–71. See also Kleinberg, *Generation Existential*, 158–62.

134. A. J. Ayer, "Novelist-Philosophers: V—Jean-Paul Sartre," *Horizon* 12 (1945): 12–26, 101–10.

135. Ibid., 25.

136. H. J. Kaplan, "Paris Letter," *Partisan Review* 12 (1945): 366, 476–80.

137. Albert Guérard, "French and American Pessimism," *Harper's Magazine* 191 (September 1945), 267–72.

138. Sartre, "The New Writing in France," 84–85; Jean-Paul Sartre, "The Case for Responsible Literature," *Horizon* 11 (1945): 307–12; Jean-Paul Sartre, "The Case for Responsible Literature," *Partisan Review* 12 (1945): 304–308.

139. Vercors, "La Responsabilité de l'écrivain," *Carrefour* 2 (February 10, 1945), 1. ("Comparer l'industriel à l'écrivain, c'est comparer Caïn et le diable. Le crime de Caïn s'arrête à Abel. Le péril du diable est sans limite.")

140. Beauvoir, *La Force des choses*, 50.

141. M[aurice] N[adeau], "Trop de monde pour écouter Jean-Paul Sartre," *Combat*, October 30, 1945, 1.

142. Cohen-Solal, *Jean-Paul Sartre*, 251–52.

143. A[drien] J[ans], "Jean-Paul Sartre à Bruxelles," *Le Quotidien*, October 26, 1945, 1.

144. Gabriel Marcel, "Le Phénomène Sartre," *Temps Présent*, November 10, 1945, 5.

145. Cohen-Solal, *Jean-Paul Sartre*, 249, 285.

146. Sartre, in *Writings*, vol. 1, 132–33.

147. Jean-Paul Sartre, *Existentialism*, trans. Bernard Frechtman (New York: Philosophical Library, 1947), 60–61, 27. ("L'existentialisme n'est pas autre chose qu'un effort pour tirer toutes les conséquences d'une position athée cohérente"; "C'est là le point de départ de l'existentialisme . . . nous n'avons ni derrière nous, ni devant nous, dans le domaine lumineux des valeurs, des justifications ou des excuses. Nous sommes seuls, sans excuses." Jean-Paul Sartre, *L'Existentialisme est un humanisme* [Paris: Les Éditions Nagel, 1946], 94, 36–37.)

148. See Yi-Ping Ong, *The Art of Being: Poetics of the Novel and Existentialist Philosophy* (Cambridge, MA: Harvard University Press, 2018).

149. Sartre, *Existentialism*, 33. ("[J]e n'avais qu'une réponse à faire: vous êtes libre, choisissez, c'est-à-dire inventez. Aucune morale générale ne peut vous indiquer ce qu'il y a à faire; il n'y a pas de signe dans le monde." Sartre, *L'Existentialisme est un humanisme*, 47.)

150. Sartre, "À propos de l'existentialisme," 11.

151. See Vincent Descombes, *Modern French Philosophy* (Cambridge: Cambridge University Press, 1980), 17–20.

152. Dominique Aury, "Qu'est-ce que l'existentialisme?," *Lettres Françaises*, December 1, 1945, 4.

153. Nancy Jachec, *The Philosophy and Politics of Abstract Expressionism* (Cambridge: Cambridge University Press, 2000), 81–85.

154. George Cotkin, *Existential America* (Baltimore: Johns Hopkins University Press, 2003), 91–133; Mark Poster, *Existential Marxism in Postwar France: From Sartre to Althusser* (Princeton: Princeton University Press, 1975), 109–60; Jeannette Colombel, *Jean-Paul Sartre: un homme en situations* (Paris: Librairie Générale Française, 1985), 212–25; Michel Surya, *La Révolution rêvée: pour une histoire des intellectuels et des oeuvres révolutionnaires, 1944–1954* (Paris: Fayard, 2004), 301–10.

155. Georg Lukács, *Existentialisme ou marxisme?*, trans. E. Kelemen (Paris: Les Éditions Nagel, 1948), 84. ("[U]ne sorte de carnaval permanent de l'intériorité fétichisée.")

156. A. Fadeyev, "La Science et la culture dans la lutte pour la paix, le progrès, et la démocratie," in *Congrès Mondial des Intellectuels pour la paix, Wroclaw, Pologne, 25–28 Août 1948* (Warsaw, 1949), 25. ("[L]es chacals pouvaient à taper à la machine . . . les hyènes savaient manier le stylo.")

157. Sartre, in *Writings*, vol. 1, 15.

158. William Barrett, *What Is Existentialism?* (New York: Partisan Review, 1947), 7.

159. Simone de Beauvoir, *The Mandarins*, trans. Leonard M. Friedman (Cleveland: World Publishing, 1956), 173. ("La Ville Lumière s'était éteinte. Si un jour elle brillait de nouveau, la splendeur de Paris serait celle des capitales déchues: Venise, Prague, Bruges la Morte. Pas les mêmes rues, pas la même ville, pas le même monde." Simone de Beauvoir, *Les Mandarins* [Paris: Gallimard, 1954], 157–58.)

160. Beauvoir, *Force of Circumstance*, 39. ("[D]evenue une puissance de second ordre, la France se défendait en exaltant, à des fins d'exportation, les produits de son terroir: haute couture et littérature . . . [L]es pays étrangers s'émouvaient avec bienveillance de ce vacarme et l'amplifiaient." Beauvoir, *La Force des choses*, 51.)

161. Stanley Garfinkel, "Le Théâtre de la Mode: naissance et renaissance," trans. Marianne Véron, in Edmonde Charles-Roux, Herbert R. Lottman, Stanley Garfinkel, and Nadine Gasc, *Le Théâtre de la Mode* (Paris: Du May, 1990), 61–80.

162. Penelope Rowlands, *Carmel Snow and Her Life in Fashion, Art, and Letters* (New York: Atria Books, 2005), 365; Marie-France Pochna, *Christian Dior: The Man Who Made the World Look New*, trans. Joanna Savill (New York: Arcade, 1996), 131–37.

163. Jean-Paul Sartre, "The Quest for the Absolute," in *The Aftermath of War (Situations III)*, 334. ("Ce n'est qu'une longue silhouette indistincte qui marche à l'horizon." Jean-Paul Sartre, "La Recherche de l'absolu," in *Situations III*, 289–90.)

164. See Mark Greif, *The Age of the Crisis of Man: Thought and Fiction in America, 1933–1973* (Princeton: Princeton University Press, 2015), esp. 61–99.

4. OUTSIDE THE LAW

1. Robert Bideleux and Ian Jeffries, *A History of Eastern Europe: Crisis and Change*, 2nd ed. (New York: Routledge, 2007), 321–32.

2. Doreen Warriner, *Revolution in Eastern Europe* (London: Turnstile Press, 1950), 64–78; Bideleux and Jeffries, *A History of Eastern Europe*, 327.

3. T. S. Eliot, *The Waste Land* (New York: Boni and Liveright, 1922), 44.

4. T. S. Eliot, *The Waste Land: A Facsimile and Transcript of the Original Drafts Including the Annotations of Ezra Pound*, ed. Valerie Eliot (New York: Harcourt Brace Jovanovich, 1971), 74–75.

5. Eliot, *The Waste Land* (1922), 62.

6. Elisabeth Young-Bruehl, *Hannah Arendt: For Love of the World* (New Haven: Yale University Press, 1982), 21.

7. Ibid., 32–36; Rüdiger Safranski, *Martin Heidegger: Between Good and Evil*, trans. Ewald Osers (Cambridge, MA: Harvard University Press, 1998), 137–38.

8. Hannah Arendt, "Martin Heidegger at Eighty," trans. Albert Hofstadter, *New York Review of Books* 17 (October 21, 1971), 50. ("Das Gerücht vom heimlichen König." Hannah Arendt, "Martin Heidegger ist achtzig Jahre alt," *Merkur* 23 [1969]: 893.)

9. Karl Löwith, *My Life in Germany Before and After 1933: A Report*, trans. Elizabeth King (Urbana: University of Illinois Press, 1994), 28; and see 44–47.

10. Safranski, *Martin Heidegger*, 94, 100, 121; Arendt, "Martin Heidegger at Eighty," 50–51.

11. Martin Heidegger to Hannah Arendt, February 10, 1925, in *Letters, 1925–1975: Hannah Arendt and Martin Heidegger*, ed. Ursula Ludz, trans. Andrew Shields (Orlando, FL: Harcourt, 2004), 3. ("Ich werde Sie nie besitzen dürfen, aber Sie werden fortan in mein Leben gehören, und es soll an Ihnen wachsen." *Hannah Arendt/Martin Heidegger Briefe 1925 bis 1975, und andere Zeugnisse* [Frankfurt: Vittorio Klostermann, 1999], 11.) See also Elżbieta Ettinger, *Hannah Arendt/Martin Heidegger* (New Haven: Yale University Press, 1995), 14–16.

12. Hannah Arendt to Martin Heidegger, April

22, 1928, in *Letters, 1925–1975*, 50. ("Ich liebe Dich wie am ersten Tag—das weißt Du, und das habe ich immer . . . gewußt . . . Ich hätte mein Recht zum Leben verloren, wenn ich meine Liebe zu Dir verlieren würde, aber ich würde diese Liebe verlieren und ihre *Realität*, wenn ich mich der Aufgabe entzöge, zu der sie mich zwingt." *Hannah Arendt/Martin Heidegger Briefe*, 65–66.) See also Ettinger, *Hannah Arendt*, 26–30; Young-Bruehl, *Hannah Arendt*, 46–70.

13. Young-Bruehl, *Hannah Arendt*, 61–62.

14. Safranski, *Martin Heidegger*, 248–63; Ulrich Sieg, "Die 'Verjudung des deutschen Geistes,'" *Die Zeit* 52 (December 29, 1989), 19; Ettinger, *Hannah Arendt/Martin Heidegger*, 37, 47. See also Victor Farías, *Heidegger and Nazism*, ed. Joseph Margolis and Tom Rockmore, trans. Paul Burrell and Gabriel R. Ricci (Philadelphia: Temple University Press, 1989); Hugo Ott, *Martin Heidegger: A Political Life*, trans. Allan Blunden (London: HarperCollins, 1993), 133–260; Jennifer Schuessler, "Heidegger's Notebooks Renew Focus on Anti-Semitism," *New York Times*, March 31, 2014, C1.

15. Martin Heidegger to Hannah Arendt [Winter 1932/33], in *Letters, 1925–1975*, 52–53.

16. Young-Bruehl, *Hannah Arendt*, 246–48; Ettinger, *Hannah Arendt*, 66–82.

17. Martin Heidegger to Hannah Arendt, February 10, 1925, in *Letters, 1925–1975*, 3; Martin Heidegger to Hannah Arendt, February 21, 1925, in *Letters, 1925–1975*, 5. ("Und einmal werden Sie verstehen und dankbar sein—nicht mir—daß der Besuch in der 'Sprechstunde' der entscheidende Schritt war, zurück aus der Bahn in die furchtbare Einsamkeit wissenschaftlichen Forschens, die nur der Mann aushält." *Hannah Arendt/ Martin Heidegger Briefe*, 11; "Männliches Fragen lerne Ehrfurcht an schlichter Hingabe; einseitige Beschäftigung lerne Weltweite an der ursprünglichen Ganzheit fraulichen Seins." *Hannah Arendt/Martin Heidegger Briefe*, 13.)

18. Young-Bruehl, *Hannah Arendt*, 77–80; cf. Hannah Arendt to Karl Jaspers, June 13, 1929, in *Hannah Arendt/Karl Jaspers Correspondence, 1926–1969*, ed. Lotte Kohler and Hans Saner, trans. Robert and Rita Kimber (New York: Harcourt Brace Jovanovich, 1992), 5.

19. Jean-Michel Palmier, *Weimar in Exile: The Anti-Fascist Emigration in Europe and America*, trans. David Fernbach (London: Verso, 2006), 85–95.

20. Hannah Arendt, interview with Günter Gaus, ZDF-TV (Germany), October 28, 1964, trans. Joan Stambaugh, in Hannah Arendt, *Hannah Arendt: The Last Interview and Other Conversations* (New York: Melville House, 2013), 8.

21. Debórah Dwork and Robert Jan van Pelt, *Flight from the Reich: Refugee Jews, 1933–1946* (New York: W. W. Norton, 2009), 1–13.

22. Malcolm J. Proudfoot, *European Refugees, 1939–52: A Study in Forced Population Movement* (Evanston: Northwestern University Press, 1956), 27.

23. Young-Bruehl, *Hannah Arendt*, 115–52.

24. Julian Jackson, *France: The Dark Years, 1940–1944* (Oxford: Oxford University Press, 2001), 217–19.

25. Ian Ousby, *Occupation: The Ordeal of France, 1940–1944* (London: John Murray, 1997), 187.

26. Hannah Arendt, letter to the editor, *Midstream* 8 (September 1962): 87; Daniel Maier-Katkin, *Stranger from Abroad: Hannah Arendt, Martin Heidegger, Friendship and Forgiveness* (New York: W. W. Norton, 2010), 111–13.

27. See Raymond Aron, *Memoirs: Fifty Years of Political Reflection*, trans. George Holoch (New York: Holmes and Meier, 1990), 122–23; Maier-Katkin, *Stranger from Abroad*, 113.

28. See Palmier, *Weimar in Exile*, 256–66.

29. Hannah Arendt to Karl Jaspers, May 30, 1946, in *Hannah Arendt/Karl Jaspers Briefwechsel, 1926–1969*, ed. Lotte Köhler and Hans Saner (Munich: Piper 1985), 77 ("unser bester Freund").

30. Young-Bruehl, *Hannah Arendt*, 155–63.

31. Hannah Arendt, "Reflections: Walter Benjamin," trans. Harry Zohn, *New Yorker* 44 (October 19, 1968), 95–98; Howard Eiland and Michael W. Jennings, *Walter Benjamin: A Critical Life* (Cambridge, MA: Harvard University Press, 2014), 674–75; Arthur Koestler, *Scum of the Earth* (New York: Macmillan, 1941), 278.

32. Eiland and Jennings, *Walter Benjamin*, 664.

33. "Ich habe es gesehen . . . : Erster Bericht von den Deportations-Tagen in Gurs, aus dem Tagebuch eines französischen Geistlichen," *Aufbau* 8 (December 18, 1942), 1, 4, 23; Ousby, *Occupation*, 190; Young-Bruehl, *Hannah Arendt*, 162–63.

34. Arendt, *The Last Interview*, 23.

35. Raymond Aron, "The Essence of Totalitarianism According to Hannah Arendt," trans. Marc LePain with Daniel Mahoney, in *In Defense of Political Reason: Essays by Raymond Aron*, ed. Daniel J. Mahoney (Lanham, MD: Rowman and Littlefield, 1994), 98. ("Le mélange de métaphysique allemande, de sociologie subtile, de vitupérations morales aboutit à exagérer qualités et défauts des hommes et des régimes totalitaire . . . à substituer à l'histoire réelle une histoire à chaque instant ironique ou tragique." Raymond Aron, "L'Essence du totalitarianisme," *Critique* 80 [1954]: 53.)

36. Hannah Arendt to Mary B. Underwood, September 24, 1946, Speeches and Writings File: Outlines and research memoranda–1946, Folder 1, 1–8, Hannah Arendt Papers, Library of

Congress; see Hannah Arendt to Gary Kornblith, April 2, 1973, Correspondence File: General–Ki-Ko, 55–56, Arendt Papers. See also Roy T. Tsao, "The Three Phases of Arendt's Theory of Totalitarianism," *Social Research* 69 (2002): 579–619.

37. Hannah Arendt to Karl Jaspers, September 4, 1947, in *Hannah Arendt/Karl Jaspers Correspondence*, 133–36. See also Margaret Canovan, *Hannah Arendt: A Reinterpretation of Her Political Thought* (Cambridge: Cambridge University Press, 1992), 18–22; Young-Bruehl, *Hannah Arendt*, 203.

38. Hannah Arendt, *The Origins of Totalitarianism* (New York: Harcourt, Brace, 1951), 312–16. See also Robert Burrowes, "Totalitarianism: The Revised Standard Version," *World Politics* 21 (1969): 272–94.

39. E. H. Carr, "The Ultimate Denial," *New York Times Book Review*, March 25, 1951, 3.

40. Walter Benjamin, "Theses on the Philosophy of History," in *Illuminations*, ed. Hannah Arendt, trans. Harry Zohn (New York: Harcourt Brace and World, 1968), 257. ("Vergangenes historisch artikulieren heißt nicht, es erkennen 'wie es denn eigentlich gewesen ist.' Es heißt, sich einer Erinnerung bemächtigen, wie sie im Augenblick einer Gefahr aufblitzt." Walter Benjamin, "Über den Begriff der Geschichte," in *Gesammelte Werke*, vol. 2 [Frankfurt: Zweitausendeins, 2011], 959.)

41. Benjamin, "Theses on the Philosophy of History," 265. ("Der Historismus begnügt sich damit, einen Kausalnexus von verschiedenen Momenten der Geschichte zu etablieren. Aber kein Tatbestand ist als Ursache eben darum bereits ein historischer. Er ward das, posthum, durch Begebenheiten, die durch Jahrtausende von ihm getrennt sein mögen. Der Historiker, der davon ausgeht, hört auf, sich die Abfolge von Begebenheiten durch die Finger laufen zu lassen wie einen Rosenkranz. Er erfaßt die Konstellation, in die seine eigene Epoche mit einer ganz bestimmten früheren getreten ist." Benjamin, "Über den Begriff der Geschichte," 966.)

42. Hannah Arendt, Appendix: "Totalitarianism," in *The Origins of Totalitarianism* (New York: Schocken Books, 2004), 617–18.

43. Hannah Arendt, "On Hannah Arendt," in Melvyn A. Hill, ed., *Hannah Arendt: The Recovery of the Public World* (New York: St. Martin's Press, 1979), 308.

44. Arendt, "Reflections: Walter Benjamin," 156. See also David Luban, "Explaining Dark Times: Hannah Arendt's Theory of Theory," *Social Research* 50 (1983): 215–48; Seyla Benhabib, *The Reluctant Modernism of Hannah Arendt* (Thousand Oaks, CA: Sage, 1996), 91–95; Eva de Valk, "The Pearl Divers: Hannah

Arendt, Walter Benjamin, and the Demands of History," *Krisis*, no. 1 (2010), 36–47. Cf. Leonard Krieger, "The Historical Hannah Arendt," *Journal of Modern History* 48 (1976): 672–84; Judith N. Shklar, "Hannah Arendt as Pariah," *Partisan Review* 50 (1983): 69–70.

45. Hannah Arendt to Mary B. Underwood, September 24, 1946, Arendt Papers.

46. Philip Rieff, "The Theology of Politics: Reflections on Totalitarianism as the Burden of Our Time," *Journal of Religion* 32 (1952): 119.

47. Arendt, *The Origins of Totalitarianism* (1951), 434.

48. Hannah Arendt, "The Concentration Camps," *Partisan Review* 15 (1948): 747.

49. Arendt, *The Origins of Totalitarianism* (1951), [vii]; Karl Jaspers, *Von der Wahrheit* (Munich: R. Piper, 1947), 25.

50. Hannah Arendt to Mary B. Underwood, September 24, 1946, Arendt Papers.

51. Arendt, *The Origins of Totalitarianism* (1951), 275–76.

52. Ibid., 266.

53. Hannah Arendt, "We Refugees," *Menorah Journal* 31 (1943): 76.

54. Arendt, *The Origins of Totalitarianism* (1951), 308–309.

55. Ibid., 316–17.

56. Ibid., 430.

57. Ibid., 6.

58. Ibid., 428.

59. Ibid., 429.

60. Hannah Arendt to Alfred Kazin, July 7, 1951, in "The Correspondence between Hannah Arendt and Alfred Kazin," ed. Helgard Mahrdt, *Samtiden* [Oslo] 1 (2005): 127.

61. Alfred Kazin, *A Lifetime Burning in Every Moment: From the Journals of Alfred Kazin* (New York: HarperCollins, 1996), 128–29; Richard M. Cook, *Alfred Kazin: A Biography* (New Haven: Yale University Press, 2007), 150–52.

62. Abbott Gleason, *Totalitarianism: The Inner History of the Cold War* (New York: Oxford University Press, 1995), 13–20.

63. See Palmier, *Weimar in Exile*, 609–12; Gleason, *Totalitarianism*, 31–38.

64. See Martin Jay, "The Political Existentialism of Hannah Arendt," in *Permanent Exiles: Essays on the Intellectual Migration from Germany to America* (New York: Columbia University Press, 1985), 237–56.

65. Albert Gates [Albert Glotzer], "Judgment of an Era: An Examination of the Totalitarian System," *New International* 17 (1951): 315–23, and 18 (1952), 20–31, 74–89.

66. Benjamin L. Alpers, *Dictators, Democracy, and American Public Culture: Envisioning the Totalitarian Enemy, 1920s–1950s* (Chapel Hill: University of North Carolina Press, 2003), 292–94. Cf., e.g., Alexander Bloom, *Prodigal Sons: The*

New York Intellectuals and Their World (New York: Oxford University Press, 1986), 219–20.

67. See Hannah Arendt, "Philosophy and Politics," *Social Research* 57 (1990): 73–103 (from a typescript composed in 1954); Canovan, *Hannah Arendt*, 253–74.

68. Hannah Arendt, *The Origins of Totalitarianism*, rev. ed. (New York: Meridian, 1958), 469.

69. Arendt, "Martin Heidegger at Eighty," 53–54.

70. Arendt, *The Last Interview*, 10, 19.

71. Ibid., 3.

72. Arendt, "Martin Heidegger at Eighty," 54.

73. Hannah Arendt, *The Human Condition* (Chicago: University of Chicago Press, 1958), 22–78. See also Hanna Fenichel Pitkin, *The Attack of the Blob: Hannah Arendt's Concept of the Social* (Chicago: University of Chicago Press, 1998); Canovan, *Hannah Arendt*, 116–22.

74. Arendt, *The Human Condition*, 175–76.

75. Ibid., 77.

76. Hannah Arendt, "'The Rights of Man': What Are They?," *Modern Review* 3 (1949): 30.

77. See, inter alia, Walter Laqueur, "The Arendt Cult: Hannah Arendt as Political Commentator," *Journal of Contemporary History* 33 (1998): 483–96; Amos Elon, "The Case of Hannah Arendt," *New York Review of Books* 44 (November 6, 1997), 25–29; Bernard Wasserstein, "Blame the Victim—Hannah Arendt Among the Nazis: The Historian and Her Sources," *Times Literary Supplement*, October 30, 2009, 13–15; David Nirenberg, *Anti-Judaism: The Western Tradition* (New York: W. W. Norton, 2013), 461–65.

78. Young-Bruehl, *Hannah Arendt*, 165–66.

79. Ibid., 213; cf. Suzanne Kirkbright, *Karl Jaspers, a Biography: Navigations in Truth* (New Haven: Yale University Press, 2004), 183.

80. Hannah Arendt to Karl Jaspers, January 29, 1946, in *Hannah Arendt/Karl Jaspers Correspondence*, 30–31. ("Über Amerika wäre überhaupt viel zu sagen. Es gibt hier wirklich so etwas wie Freiheit und ein starkes Gefühl bei vielen Menschen, daß man ohne Freiheit nicht leben kann. Die Republik ist kein leerer Wahn . . . Dazu kommt, daß die Menschen sich hier in einem Maße mitverantwortlich für öffentliches Leben fühlen, wie ich es aus keinem europäischen Lande kenne . . . Der Grundwiderspruch des Landes ist politische Freiheit bei gesellschaftlicher Knechtschaft." *Hannah Arendt/Karl Jaspers Briefwechsel*, 66–67.)

81. Table 1: Reported Book Sales, through 1995, Herbert J. Gans, "Best-Sellers by American Sociologists," in Dan Clawson, *Required Reading: Sociology's Most Influential Books* (Amherst: University of Massachusetts Press, 1998), 24. Erving Goffman's widely read and influential *The Presentation of Self in Everyday Life* was published in 1956. Goffman was Canadian.

82. See, inter alia, Wilfred M. McClay, "David Riesman and *The Lonely Crowd*," *Society* 46 (2009): 21–28; Daniel Horowitz, *Consuming Pleasures: Intellectuals and Popular Culture in the Postwar World* (Philadelphia: University of Pennsylvania Press, 2012), 125–31; Eugene Lunn, "Beyond 'Mass Culture': *The Lonely Crowd*, the Uses of Literacy, and the Postwar Era," *Theory and Society* 19 (1990): 63–86.

83. David Riesman to Reuel Denney, April 27, 1949, Box 6, Folder 2, Papers of David Riesman, Harvard University Archives. And see David Riesman, *The Lonely Crowd: A Study of the Changing American Character* (New Haven: Yale University Press, 1950), 271.

84. Lionel Trilling to David Riesman, August 24, 1949, Box 50, Folder Tr-Ts, 1947–1970, Riesman Papers.

85. David Riesman, "On Discovering and Teaching Sociology: A Memoir," *Annual Review of Sociology* 14 (1988): 3.

86. David Barboza, "An Interview with David Riesman," *Partisan Review* 61 (1994): 575, 584; Horowitz, *Consuming Pleasures*, 124–25; Lawrence J. Friedman, *The Lives of Erich Fromm: Love's Prophet* (New York: Columbia University Press, 2013), 132–33.

87. Friedman, *The Lives of Erich Fromm*, 4–46.

88. Erich Fromm, *Man for Himself: An Inquiry into the Psychology of Ethics* (New York: Henry Holt, 1947), 70.

89. See David Riesman to Hannah Arendt, February 27, 1947, Arendt Papers; Peter Baehr, *Hannah Arendt, Totalitarianism, and the Social Sciences* (Stanford: Stanford University Press, 2010), 36–38.

90. David Riesman to Hannah Arendt, November 11, 1948, Arendt Papers.

91. David Riesman to Hannah Arendt, February 28, 1949, Arendt Papers.

92. David Riesman to Hannah Arendt, June 7, 1949, Arendt Papers.

93. David Riesman to Hannah Arendt, June 13, 1949, Arendt Papers.

94. David Riesman to Hannah Arendt, September 22, 1949, Arendt Papers.

95. David Riesman to Hannah Arendt, June 7 and 27, 1949, Arendt Papers.

96. David Riesman, "A Personal Memoir: My Political Journey," in Walter W. Powell and Richard Robbins, eds., *Conflict and Consensus: A Festschrift in Honor of Lewis A. Coser* (New York: Free Press, 1984), 332.

97. David Riesman, "The Path to Total Terror," *Commentary* 11 (1951): 392–93, 397–98.

98. Barboza, "An Interview with David Riesman," 575. And see Riesman, *The Lonely Crowd*, 235–55.

99. Carl J. Friedrich to David Riesman, December

28, 1950, Box 13, Folder: Glazer, Nathan, Riesman Papers.

100. "David Riesman, Sociologist Whose 'Lonely Crowd' Became a Bestseller, Dies at 92," *New York Times*, May 11, 2002, A18.

101. David Riesman, *The Lonely Crowd: A Study of the Changing American Character*, rev. ed. (New York: Anchor Books, 1953), 17.

102. Ibid., 15, 22.

103. Leo Löwenthal, "Biographies in Popular Magazines," in Paul Lazarsfeld and Frank Stanton, eds., *Radio Research, 1942–1943* (New York: Duell, Sloan and Pearce, 1944), 516–18.

104. Riesman, *The Lonely Crowd* (1950), 294.

105. Ibid., 349–50.

106. Hannah Arendt, *Culture for the Millions? Mass Media in Modern Society*, ed. Norman Jacobs (Princeton: D. Van Nostrand, 1961), 51.

5. THE ICE BREAKERS

1. Clement Greenberg, "Pollock," TS memoir, Box 34, Folder 2, Clement Greenberg Papers, Getty Research Institute; Jeffrey Potter, *To a Violent Grave: An Oral Biography of Jackson Pollock* (New York: G. P. Putnam's Sons, 1975), 66; Steven Naifeh and Gregory White Smith, *Jackson Pollock: An American Saga* (New York: Clarkson N. Potter, 1989), 398. Cf. Naifeh and Smith, *Jackson Pollock*, 857n; Rosalind Krauss, *The Optical Unconscious* (Cambridge, MA: MIT Press, 1993), 244.

2. Lee Krasner, untitled essay on Pollock, Box 2, Folder 41, Jackson Pollock and Lee Krasner Papers, Archives of American Art, Smithsonian Institution; Gail Levin, *Lee Krasner: A Biography* (New York: William Morrow, 2011), 164–66; Naifeh and Smith, *Jackson Pollock*, 298.

3. Levin, *Lee Krasner*, 76–77, 90–91, 128; Florence Rubenfeld, *Clement Greenberg: A Life* (Minneapolis: University of Minnesota Press, 1997), 44.

4. Clement Greenberg interview transcript, 1968, Box 2, Folder 63, Pollock and Krasner Papers.

5. Naifeh and Smith, *Jackson Pollock*, 598; Irving Sandler, *The New York School: The Painters and Sculptors of the Fifties* (New York: Harper and Row, 1978), 44n28. See also Vivien Raynor, "Jackson Pollock in Retrospect—'He Broke the Ice,'" *New York Times Magazine*, April 2, 1967, 50ff; Dore Ashton, *The New York School: A Cultural Reckoning* (New York: Viking, 1973), 152.

6. Irving Sandler, *The Triumph of American Painting: A History of Abstract Expressionism* (New York: Praeger, 1970).

7. See Serge Guilbaut, *How New York Stole the Idea of Modern Art: Abstract Expressionism, Freedom, and the Cold War*, trans. Arthur Goldhammer (Chicago: University of Chicago Press, 1983), 49–99.

8. Max Kozloff, "American Painting During the Cold War," *Artforum* 11 (May 1973), 43–54; Eva Cockroft, "Abstract Expressionism, Weapon of the Cold War," *Artforum* 12 (June 1974), 39–41; David Shapiro and Cecile Shapiro, "Abstact Expressionism: The Politics of Apolitical Painting," *Prospects* 3 (1977): 175–214; Guilbaut, *How New York Stole the Idea of Modern Art*, 168–74; Frances Stonor Saunders, *The Cultural Cold War: The CIA and the World of Arts and Letters* (New York: New Press, 1999), 255–78. Cf. Michael Kimmelman, "Revisiting the Revisionists: The Modern, Its Critics, and the Cold War," *Studies in Modern Art* 4 (1994): 39–55; Robert Burstow, "The Limits of Modernist Art as a 'Weapon in the Cold War': Reassessing the Unknown Patron of the Monument to the Unknown Political Prisoner," *Oxford Art Journal* 20 (1997): 68–80; David Caute, *The Dancer Defects: The Struggle for Cultural Supremacy During the Cold War* (Oxford: Oxford University Press, 2003), 539–67; Irving Sandler, "Abstract Expressionism and the Cold War," *Art in America* 96 (June/July 2008), 65–74.

9. See Jean-Michel Palmier, *Weimar in Exile: The Antifascist Emigration in Europe and America*, trans. David Fernbach (London: Verso, 2006), 368–69.

10. Arpad Kadarkay, *Georg Lukács: Life, Thought, and Politics* (Oxford: Blackwell, 1991), 312; see also Georg Lukács, *Record of a Life: An Autobiographical Sketch*, ed. István Eörsi, trans. Rodney Livingstone (London: Verso, 1983), 70–111.

11. Rubenfeld, *Clement Greenberg*, 49; Alice Goldfarb Marquis, *Art Czar: The Rise and Fall of Clement Greenberg* (Boston: MFA Publications, 2006), 48–49.

12. Rubenfeld, *Clement Greenberg*, 60.

13. "Clement Greenberg," in Stanley Kunitz, ed., *Twentieth-Century Authors: First Supplement: A Biographical Dictionary of Modern Literature* (New York: Wilson, 1955), 386–87; Rubenfeld, *Clement Greenberg*, 40–44; Clement Greenberg, "Chronology to 1949," in *The Collected Essays and Criticism*, ed. John O'Brian, vol. 1, *Perceptions and Judgments, 1939–1944* (Chicago: University of Chicago Press, 1986), 253–54.

14. See Clement Greenberg, "New York Painting Only Yesterday," in *Essays and Criticism*, vol. 4, *Modernism with a Vengeance, 1957–1969* (Chicago: University of Chicago Press, 1986), 20, and, e.g., Clement Greenberg to Harold Lazarus, September 27, 1937, and June 2, 1938, in Clement Greenberg, *The Harold Letters, 1928–1943: The Making of an American Intellectual*, ed. Janice Van Horne (Washington, DC: Counterpoint, 2000), 177, 182.

15. Clement Greenberg to Harold Lazarus, January 16, 1939, in Greenberg, *The Harold Letters*, 191–92.

16. Michael Wreszin, *A Rebel in Defense of Tradition: The Life and Politics of Dwight Macdonald* (New York: Basic Books, 1994), 4.

17. Dwight Macdonald, "The Soviet Cinema: 1930–1938," *Partisan Review* 5 (1938): 37.

18. Dwight Macdonald, "Soviet Society and Its Cinema," *Partisan Review* 6 (1939): 80.

19. Clement Greenberg to Dwight Macdonald, February 6, 1939, Box 3, Folder 2, Greenberg Papers. Carbon TS with added written changes by Greenberg.

20. Clement Greenberg to Harold Lazarus, April 18, 1939, in Greenberg, *The Harold Letters*, 200.

21. Rubenfeld, *Clement Greenberg*, 52 (interview with Greenberg).

22. Clement Greenberg to Harold Lazarus, June 27, 1939, in Greenberg, *The Harold Letters*, 203.

23. Clement Greenberg to Harold Lazarus, August 28, 1940, in Greenberg, *The Harold Letters*, 222.

24. Diana Trilling, "An Interview with Dwight Macdonald," *Partisan Review* 51 (1984): 806. The Frankenstein remark appears in the republished version, in *Interviews with Dwight Macdonald*, ed. Michael Wreszin (Jackson: University Press of Mississippi, 2003), 126. It had evidently been edited out at *Partisan Review*.

25. Clement Greenberg, Journal 1947, Box 15, Folder 1, Greenberg Papers.

26. David McLellan, *Karl Marx: A Biography*, 4th ed. (New York: Palgrave Macmillan, 2006), 92–93.

27. Georg Lukács, "Heinrich Heine as National Poet," in *German Realists in the Nineteenth Century*, trans. Jeremy Gaines and Paul Keast (Cambridge, MA: MIT Press, 1993), 151, 153. ("*Grenzerscheinung* zwischen der Periode des ideologischen Aufstiegs und ideologischen Niedergangs der Bourgeoisie." Georg Lukács, "Heinrich Heine als Nationaler Dichter," *Internationale Literatur/Deutsche Blätter* 10 [1938]: 125; "voller historischer Gerechtigkeit," 124.)

28. Clement Greenberg, "Avant-Garde and Kitsch," in *Essays and Criticism*, vol. 1, 5–10. The "imitation of imitating" is in the *Partisan Review* version of the essay (*Partisan Review* 6 [1939]: 37).

29. Greenberg, "Avant-Garde and Kitsch," in *Essays and Criticism*, vol. 1, 11–22.

30. Clement Greenberg, Dark Green Diary, 1935, 1936, 1939, Box 14, Folder 7, Greenberg Papers.

31. Clement Greenberg to Harold Lazarus, November 29, 1939, in Greenberg, *The Harold Letters*, 211.

32. Marquis, *Art Czar*, 62; Rubenfeld, *Clement Greenberg*, 58.

33. Clement Greenberg, "Towards a Newer Laocoon," *Partisan Review* 7 (1940): 305.

34. Rubenfeld, *Clement Greenberg*, 63–73.

35. Clement Greenberg to Dwight Macdonald, June 15, 1943, Box 20, Folder 494, Dwight Macdonald Papers, Sterling Memorial Library, Yale University.

36. Quoted in Marquis, *Art Czar*, 77. Unmailed letter discovered by Greenberg's widow, Janice Van Horne.

37. Clement Greenberg to Dwight Macdonald, August 26, 1943, Macdonald Papers.

38. Mark Polizzotti, *Revolution of the Mind: The Life of André Breton* (New York: Farrar, Straus and Giroux, 1995), 50–54.

39. André Breton, "Manifeste du surréalisme," *Œuvres complètes*, vol. 1 (Paris: Gallimard, 1988), 316 ("le règne de la logique"), 328 ("le fonctionnement réel de la pensée"), 346 ("Le surréalisme est le 'rayon invisible' qui nous permettra un jour de l'emporter sur nos adversaires").

40. Polizzotti, *Revolution of the Mind*, 246–56, 399–400, 456.

41. Mary V. Dearborn, *Mistress of Modernism: The Life of Peggy Guggenheim* (Boston: Houghton Mifflin, 2004), 32–43.

42. Anton Gill, *Art Lover: A Biography of Peggy Guggenheim* (New York: HarperCollins, 2002), 115.

43. Ibid., 213–55.

44. Peggy Guggenheim, *Confessions of an Art Addict* (London: André Deutsch, 1960), 74.

45. Calvin Tomkins, *Marcel Duchamp: A Biography* (New York: Henry Holt, 1996), 318.

46. Ibid., 314–18.

47. Bruce Altshuler, *The Avant-Garde Exhibition: New Art in the Twentieth Century* (New York: Harry N. Abrams, 1994), 136.

48. U.S. Census Bureau, Population, No. 5, "Immigration: 1900 to 2001," *Statistical Abstract of the United States, 2003* (Washington, DC: U.S. Government Printing Office, 2003).

49. Herbert A. Strauss, ed., *Jewish Immigrants of the Nazi Period in the U.S.A.*, vol. 1, *Archival Resources* (New York: K. G. Saur, 1978), xx.

50. Maurice R. Davie, *Refugees in America: Report of the Committee for the Study of Recent Immigration from Europe* (New York: Harper and Brothers, 1947), 15–34. See also Henry L. Feingold, *The Politics of Rescue: The Roosevelt Administration and the Holocaust, 1938–1945* (New Brunswick: Rutgers University Press, 1970), 3–21; Saul S. Friedman, *No Haven for the Oppressed: United States Policy toward Jewish Refugees, 1938–1945* (Detroit: Wayne State University Press, 1973), 17–36; Michael L. Krenn, *Fall-Out Shelters for the Human Spirit: American Art and the Cold War* (Chapel Hill: University of North Carolina Press, 2005), 67–83; Richard Breitman and Allan J. Lichtman, *FDR and the Jews* (Cambridge, MA: Harvard University Press, 2013), 69–83.

51. Feingold, *The Politics of Rescue*, 160–61.

52. Sheila Isenberg, *A Hero of Our Own: The Story of Varian Fry* (New York: Random House, 2001), 54–65.

53. Andy Marino, *A Quiet American: The Secret War of Varian Fry* (New York: St. Martin's, 1999), 145.

54. Colin W. Nettelbeck, *Forever French: Exile in the United States, 1939–1945* (New York: Berg, 1991), 2.

55. See *Varian Fry et les candidats à l'exil: Marseille, 1940–1941* (Arles: Actes Sud, 1999).

56. Martica Sawin, *Surrealism in Exile and the Beginning of the New York School* (Cambridge, MA: MIT Press, 1995), 116–43; Tomkins, *Marcel Duchamp*, 325–28.

57. Marion F. Deshmukh, "Cultural Migration: Artists and Visual Representation Between Americans and Germans During the 1930s and 1940s," in David E. Barclay and Elisabeth Glaser-Schmidt, eds., *Transatlantic Images and Perceptions: Germany and America Since 1776* (Cambridge: Cambridge University Press, 1997), 266.

58. David Kerr, dir., *Varian Fry: The Artist's Schindler* (Home Vision Arts DVD, 1997), 40:20.

59. Sybil Gordon Kantor, *Alfred H. Barr, Jr., and the Intellectual Origins of the Museum of Modern Art* (Cambridge, MA: MIT Press, 2002), 317–41; Tomkins, *Marcel Duchamp*, 309–10; Naifeh and Smith, *Jackson Pollock*, 414.

60. Naifeh and Smith, *Jackson Pollock*, 445.

61. Ibid., 450–51.

62. Peggy Guggenheim, *Out of This Century: Confessions of an Art Addict* (New York: Universe Books, 1979), 315.

63. Quoted in Naifeh and Smith, *Jackson Pollock*, 338 (interview by a *Life* reporter, 1959).

64. Clement Greenberg, memories of Pollock dictated to Cleve Gray, Box 34, Folder 1, Greenberg Papers.

65. Ibid.

66. Laura de Coppet and Alan Jones, *The Art Dealers: The Powers Behind the Scenes Tell How the Art World Really Works* (New York: Clarkson N. Potter, 1984), 84 (interview with Castelli).

67. Quoted in Naifeh and Smith, *Jackson Pollock*, 338. Their interview.

68. Ibid., 106.

69. Thomas Hart Benton, "The Mechanics of Form Organization in Painting," *Arts* 10 (1926): 285–89, 340–42; *Arts* 11 (1927): 43–44, 95–96, 145–48; see also Justin Wolff, *Thomas Hart Benton: A Life* (New York: Farrar, Straus and Giroux, 2012), 46, 168–69.

70. See Naifeh and Smith, *Jackson Pollock*, 152, 298; B. H. Friedman, *Jackson Pollock: Energy Made Visible* (New York: McGraw-Hill, 1972), 10–11.

71. See Naifeh and Smith, *Jackson Pollock*, 342–49.

72. John Graham, *System and Dialectics of Art* (New York: Delphic Studios, 1937), 15.

73. Ibid., 55. Emphasis in the original.
74. Irving Sandler, "John D. Graham: The Painter as Esthetician and Connoisseur," *Artforum* 7 (October 1968), 50–53; Mark Stevens and Annalyn Swan, *De Kooning: An American Master* (New York: Knopf, 2004), 96; cf. Dorothy Dehner, "John Graham: A Memoir," *Leonardo* 2 (1969): 287–93; Natalie Edgar, ed., *Club Without Walls: Selections from the Journals of Philip Pavia* (New York: Midmarch Arts Press, 2007), 30–37.
75. Naifeh and Smith, *Jackson Pollock*, 349.
76. "Jackson Pollock," *Art and Architecture* [Los Angeles] 61 (February 1944), 14. See also Solomon, *Jackson Pollock*, 146; Naifeh and Smith, *Jackson Pollock*, 867n.
77. Naifeh and Smith, *Jackson Pollock*, 326–34, 361–63.
78. Ibid., 333.
79. See Judith Wolfe, "Jungian Aspects of Pollock's Imagery," *Artforum* 11 (November 1972), 65–73; Sue Taylor, "The Artist and the Analyst: Jackson Pollock's 'Stenographic Figure,'" *American Art* 17 (Autumn 2003): 52–71. Cf. William Rubin, "Pollock as Jungian Illustrator: The Limits of Psychological Criticism," *Art in America* 67 (November 1979), 104–23 (December 1979), 72–91.
80. Breton, "Manifeste du surréalisme," 328. ("SURRÉALISME, n. m. Automatisme physique pur par lequel on se propose d'exprimer, soit verbalement, soit par écrit, soit de toute autre manière, le fonctionnement réel de la pensée.")
81. See Max Kozloff, "An Interview with Robert Motherwell," *Artforum* 4 (September 1965), 33–37.
82. See transcriptions of conversations with Sidney Janis, tape recorded by Helen Franc, June 15, 1967, Special Collections, Museum of Modern Art Library; Friedman, *Jackson Pollock*, 62–63; Naifeh and Smith, *Jackson Pollock*, 467–68; Potter, *To a Violent Grave*, 75.
83. Guggenheim, *Out of This Century*, 295–96; Naifeh and Smith, *Jackson Pollock*, 468–69.
84. Jackson Pollock to Charles Pollock, July 29, 1943, in *American Letters, 1927–1947: Jackson Pollock & Family*, ed. Sylvia Winter Pollock (New York: Polity, 2011), 186.
85. Francis V. O'Connor, "Jackson Pollock's Mural for Peggy Guggenheim: Its Legend, Documentation, and Redefinition of Wall Painting," in Susan Davidson and Philip Rylands, eds., *Peggy Guggenheim and Frederick Kiesler: The Story of Art of This Century* (New York: Guggenheim Museum, 2004), 150–69; Yvonne Szafran, Laura Rivers, Alan Phenix, Tom Learner, Ellen G. Landau, and Steve Martin, *Jackson Pollock's Mural: The Transitional Moment* (Los Angeles: J. Paul Getty Museum, 2014), esp. 31–89; Carol C. Mancusi-Ungaro, "Jackson Pollock:

Response as Dialogue," in Kirk Varnedoe and Pepe Karmel, eds., *Jackson Pollock: New Approaches* (New York: Museum of Modern Art, 1999), 117–18.
86. Jean Connolly, "Art," *Nation* 156 (1943), 786.
87. Dearborn, *Mistress of Modernism*, 209–12.
88. Rubenfeld, *Clement Greenberg*, 72–73; Naifeh and Smith, *Jackson Pollock*, 467; Greenberg, "Pollock," 8–9, Greenberg Papers.
89. Potter, *To a Violent Grave*, 76.
90. Naifeh and Smith, *Jackson Pollock*, 472; Greenberg, "Pollock," Greenberg Papers. See also Rubenfeld, *Clement Greenberg*, 75.
91. I owe this insight to Caroline Jones. See Jones, *Eyesight Alone: Clement Greenberg's Modernism and the Bureaucratization of the Senses* (Chicago: University of Chicago Press, 2005), 216–34.
92. Clement Greenberg, "Review of Exhibitions of Mondrian, Kandinsky, and Pollock," in *The Collected Essays and Criticism*, ed. John O'Brian, vol. 2, *Arrogant Purpose, 1945–1949* (Chicago: University of Chicago Press, 1986), 16.
93. Clement Greenberg to Harold Lazarus, December 12, 1939, in Greenberg, *The Harold Letters*, 212.
94. Helen Epstein, "Meyer Schapiro: 'A Passion to Know and Make Known,'" *ARTnews* 82 (May 1983), 60–85 (Summer 1983), 84–95; Robert A. McCaughey, *Stand, Columbia: A History of Columbia University in the City of New York, 1754–2004* (New York: Columbia University Press, 2003), 264.
95. Meyer Schapiro, "The Social Bases of Art," *Proceedings of the American Artists' Congress* 1 (1936): 37.
96. Meyer Schapiro, "Public Use of Art," *Art Front* 2 (November 1936), 6.
97. See Patricia Hill, "1936: Meyer Schapiro, *Art Front*, and the Popular Front," *Oxford Art Journal* 17 (1994): 30–41; Fred Orton, "Action, Revolution and Painting," *Oxford Art Journal* 14 (1991): 3–17; Ashton, *The New York School*, 56–61.
98. Meyer Schapiro, "Nature of Abstract Art," *Marxist Quarterly* 1 (1937): 77.
99. Clement Greenberg, "The Late Thirties in New York," in *Art and Culture: Critical Essays* (Boston: Beacon Press, 1961), 230.
100. See Ashton, *The New York School*, 78–84.
101. Graham, *System and Dialectics of Art*, 23.
102. Ibid., 15.
103. See Axel Horn, "Jackson Pollock: The Hollow and the Bump," *Carleton Miscellany* 7 (Summer 1966): 80–87; Stephen Polcari, "Jackson Pollock and Thomas Hart Benton," *Arts Magazine* 53 (March 1979), 120–24; Henry Adams, *Tom and Jack: The Intertwined Lives of Thomas Hart Benton and Jackson Pollock* (New York: Bloomsbury, 2009), 270–76.

104. Nicolas Calas, *Confound the Wise* (New York: Arrow Editions, 1942), 244.

105. Naifeh and Smith, *Jackson Pollock*, 579.

106. Oral history interview with Lee Krasner, November 2, 1964–April 11, 1968, Archives of American Art, Smithsonian Institution.

107. Barbara Rose, "Jackson Pollock at Work: An Interview with Lee Krasner," *Partisan Review* 47 (1980): 83–85; Naifeh and Smith, *Jackson Pollock*, 533–42.

108. John Hay Whitney and Nelson Rockefeller to Henry Luce, March 24, 1949, Microfilm roll 1277, p. 172, Alfred Barr Papers, Museum Archives, Museum of Modern Art. The letter was drafted by Barr, but Rockefeller made changes.

109. Bonnie Wertheim, "Dorothy Seiberling, Influential Arts Editor, Dies at 97," *New York Times*, November 26, 2019, B10.

110. See Bradford R. Collins, "*Life* Magazine and the Abstract Expressionists, 1948–51: A Historiographic Study of a Late Bohemian Enterprise," *Art Bulletin* 73 (1991): 283–308.

111. "Jackson Pollock: Is He the Greatest Living Painter in the United States?," *Life* 27 (August 8, 1949), 42.

112. Naifeh and Smith, *Jackson Pollock*, 597–600.

113. Kozloff, "An Interview with Robert Motherwell," 33.

114. Robert Goldwater, "Reflections on the New York School," *Quadrum* 8 (1960): 17–36.

115. Clement Greenberg, "L'Art américain au XX siècle," trans. Catherine Le Guet, *Temps Modernes* 2 (1946): 349. ("[L]e stimulant que leur présence, sinon leur art, a apporté à un certain nombre de peintres abstraits.")

116. James E. B. Breslin, *Mark Rothko: A Biography* (Chicago: University of Chicago Press, 1993), 232–54; Stevens and Swan, *De Kooning*, 280–97.

117. Naifeh and Smith, *Jackson Pollock*, 649–50.

118. Hans Namuth, "Photographing Pollock," Box 2, Folder 4, Pollock and Krasner Papers.

119. See Pepe Karmel, "Pollock at Work: The Films and Photographs of Hans Namuth," in Kirk Varnedoe, *Jackson Pollock* (New York: Museum of Modern Art, 1998), 87–137; Barbara Rose, "Hans Namuth's Photographs and the Jackson Pollock Myth: Part Two: 'Number 29, 1950,'" *Arts Magazine* 53 (March 1979), 117–19.

120. Krauss, *The Optical Unconscious*, 301.

121. Naifeh and Smith, *Jackson Pollock*, 648–53.

122. Ibid., 656.

123. Correspondence in Box 53, Folders 665, 666, Alfonso Ossorio Papers, Harvard University Art Museums Archives.

124. Naifeh and Smith, *Jackson Pollock*, 671–73.

125. Max Kozloff, "Art," *Nation* 198 (1964), 151–52.

126. Donald Judd, "Jackson Pollock," *Arts Magazine* 41 (April 1967), 32–35.

127. Donald Kuspit, "To Interpret or Not to Interpret Jackson Pollock," *Arts Magazine* 53 (March 1979), 125–27.

128. Michael Fried, "Jackson Pollock," *Artforum* 4 (September 1965), 14–17.

129. [Berton Roueché], "Unframed Space," *New Yorker* 26 (August 5, 1950), 16.

130. Alan Kaprow, "The Legacy of Jackson Pollock," *ARTnews* 57 (October 1958), 55–57. See also Catherine M. Soussloff, "Jackson Pollock's Post-Ritual Performance: Memories Arrested in Space," *TDR* 48 (2004): 60–78.

131. T. J. Clark, *Farewell to an Idea: Episodes from a History of Modernism* (New Haven: Yale University Press, 1999), 299–304.

132. Naifeh and Smith, *Jackson Pollock*, 633 (interview with May Tabak Rosenberg); Rubenfeld, *Clement Greenberg*, 166–68.

133. Harold Rosenberg, "The American Action Painters," in *The Tradition of the New* (New York: Horizon Press, 1959), 25, 27–28.

134. Clyfford Still to Jackson Pollock, December 14, 1952, Box 2, Folder 16, Pollock and Krasner Papers.

135. Clyfford Still to Harold Rosenberg, December 14, 1952, verso, Box 1, Folder 7, Harold Rosenberg Papers, Getty Research Institute.

136. Rosenberg, *The Tradition of the New*, 32.

137. Thomas B. Hess, *Abstract Painting: Background and American Phase* (New York: Viking, 1951), 103.

138. See Elaine de Kooning, "Hans Hofmann Paints a Picture," *ARTnews* 48 (February 1949), 38–41, 58–59.

139. Oral history interview with Harold Rosenberg, December 17, 1970–January 28, 1973, Archives of American Art, Smithsonian Institution.

140. See Debra Bricker Balken, "Harold Rosenberg and the American Action Painters," in Norman L. Kleeblatt, ed., *Action/Abstraction: Pollock, de Kooning, and American Art, 1940–1976* (New Haven: Yale University Press, 2008), 205–13.

141. Simone de Beauvoir to Jean-Paul Sartre, in Simone de Beauvoir, *Letters to Sartre*, ed. and trans. Quintin Hoare (New York: Arcade, 1993), 422.

142. Harold Rosenberg to Simone de Beauvoir, March 25, 1952, Box 1, Folder 9, Rosenberg Papers.

143. Peggy Guggenheim to Lester Longman, October 3, 1948; Frank Seiberling to André Emmerich, October 13, 1961; Willard L. Boyd to Ulfert Wilke, March 25, 1974, Pollock Correspondence, University of Iowa Stanley Museum of Art. See also Eileen Kinsella, "Iowa Drops Plans for Possible Pollock Sale," *ARTnews*, October 14, 2008 (online); Mary Abbe, "Iowa Debates Selling $150 Million Pollock Painting," *Star Tribune* (Minneapolis, MN), February 21, 2011 (online).

6. THE BEST MINDS

1. Lionel Trilling, Journal, 1934–1936, Box 2, Folder 10, Lionel Trilling Papers, Rare Book and Manuscript Library, Columbia University. See also Lionel Trilling, "From the Notebooks of Lionel Trilling," *Partisan Review* 51 (1984): 498–503; Diana Trilling, *The Beginning of the Journey: The Marriage of Diana and Lionel Trilling* (New York: Harcourt Brace, 1993), 273–80.

2. Robert A. McCaughey, *Stand, Columbia: A History of Columbia University in the City of New York, 1754–2004* (New York: Columbia University Press, 2003), 256–76.

3. Zachary Leader, *The Life of Saul Bellow: To Fame and Fortune, 1915–1964* (New York: Knopf, 2015), 196 (quoting an interview with Bellow).

4. Mark Van Doren, "Jewish Students I Have Known," *Menorah Journal* 13 (1927): 267–68. ("F." is Trilling: see Van Doren, *The Autobiography of Mark Van Doren* [New York: Harcourt, Brace, 1958], 130.)

5. Meyer Schapiro to Lionel Trilling, October 15, 1939, Box 9, Folder 1, Trilling Papers.

6. Sidney Hook, *Out of Step: An Unquiet Life in the Twentieth Century* (New York: Harper and Row, 1987), 212–15.

7. Nicholas Murray Butler to Lionel Trilling, June 2, 1939, Box 5, Folder 9, Trilling Papers.

8. Diana Trilling, "Lionel Trilling, a Jew at Columbia," *Commentary* 67 (March 1979), 46.

9. Nicholas Lemann, *The Big Test: The Secret History of the American Meritocracy* (New York: Farrar, Straus and Giroux, 1999), 114–54, 166; Edward S. Shapiro, "The Friendly University: Jews in Academia Since World War II," *Judaism* 46 (1997): 365–74; E. Digby Baltzell, *The Protestant Establishment: Aristocracy and Caste in America* (New York: Random House, 1964), 336–39; Marcia Graham Synnott, "Anti-Semitism and American Universities: Did Quotas Follow Jews?," in David A. Gerber, ed., *Anti-Semitism in American History* (Urbana: University of Illinois Press, 1986), 233–71.

10. Dan A. Oren, *Joining the Club: A History of Jews and Yale*, 2nd ed. (New Haven: Yale University Press, 2000), 281–82.

11. Lionel Trilling, "Under Forty: A Symposium on American Literature and the Younger Generation of American Jews," *Contemporary Jewish Record* 7 (1944): 15.

12. Trilling, *The Beginning of the Journey*, 18.

13. Ibid., 12–40.

14. Jerome Karabel, *The Chosen: The Hidden History of Admission and Exclusion at Harvard, Yale, and Princeton* (Boston: Houghton Mifflin, 2005), 77–136; Michael Rosenthal, *Nicholas Miraculous: The Amazing Career of the Redoutable*

Dr. Nicholas Murray Butler (New York: Farrar, Straus and Giroux, 2006), 332–52.

15. Frederick Paul Keppel, *Columbia* (New York: Oxford University Press, 1914), 180; McCaughey, *Stand, Columbia*, 262.

16. Marcia Graham Synnott, *The Half-Opened Door: Discrimination and Admissions at Harvard, Yale, and Princeton, 1900–1970* (Westport, CT: Greenwood Press, 1979), 3–25; Harold S. Weschler, *The Qualified Student: A History of Selective College Admissions in America* (New York: John Wiley and Sons, 1977), 131–85; "Frosh Statistics Show Religious Preferences," *Columbia Spectator* 5 (October 27, 1921), 4; "May Jews Go to College?," *Nation* 114 (1922), 708.

17. "Professional Tendencies Among Jewish Students in Colleges, Universities, and Professional Schools," *American Jewish Year Book* 22 (1920): 383–93.

18. C. Morris Horowitz and Lawrence J. Kaplan, *The Jewish Population of the New York Area, 1900–1975* (New York: Federation of Jewish Philanthropies of New York, 1959), 15; Paul Ritterband, "Counting the Jews of New York, 1900–1991: An Essay in Substance and Method," *Papers in Jewish Demography 1997* (2001): 199–228; Ira Rosenwaike, *Population History of New York City* (Syracuse: Syracuse University Press, 1972), 125–29.

19. Benjamin Balint, *Running Commentary: The Contentious Magazine That Transformed the Jewish Left into the Neoconservative Right* (New York: PublicAffairs, 2010), 4.

20. Deborah Dash Moore, *At Home in America: Second Generation New York Jews* (New York: Columbia University Press, 1981), 3–17.

21. See Alexander Bloom, *Prodigal Sons: The New York Intellectuals and Their World* (New York: Oxford University Press, 1986), 11–27; Terry A. Cooney, *The Rise of the New York Intellectuals: Partisan Review and Its Circle, 1934–1945* (Madison: University of Wisconsin Press, 1986), 43–44; Hugh Wilford, *The New York Intellectuals: From Vanguard to Institution* (Manchester: Manchester University Press, 1995), 2–8; Joseph Dorman, *Arguing the World: The New York Intellectuals in Their Own Words* (New York: Free Press, 2000), 9–11. Cf. Russell Jacoby, *The Last Intellectuals: American Culture in the Age of Academe* (New York: Basic Books, 1987), 72–111. See also Norman Podhoretz, *Making It* (New York: Random House, 1967), 116–25.

22. See "Under Forty: A Symposium on American Literature and the Younger Generation of American Jews," 3–36; Irving Howe, *World of Our Fathers: The Journey of the East European Jews to America and the Life They Found and Made* (New York: Harcourt Brace Jovanovich, 1986), 598–602.

23. McCaughey, *Stand, Columbia*, 288.

24. See Joan Shelley Rubin, *The Making of Middle-brow Culture* (Chapel Hill: University of North Carolina Press, 1992), 176–77.

25. Katherine Elise Chaddock, *The Multi-Talented Mr. Erskine: Shaping Mass Culture Through Great Books and Fine Music* (New York: Palgrave Macmillan, 2012), 81–100; Rubin, *The Making of Middlebrow Culture*, 148–97; McCaughey, *Stand, Columbia*, 288–90; Alex Beam, *A Great Idea at the Time: The Rise, Fall, and Curious Afterlife of the Great Books* (New York: Public Affairs, 2008), 16–18; Lionel Trilling, "Some Notes for an Autobiographical Lecture," in *The Last Decade: Essays and Reviews, 1965–1975*, ed. Diana Trilling (New York: Harcourt Brace Jovanovich, 1979), 232–35.

26. Lionel Trilling, "A Personal Memoir," in Dora B. Weiner and William R. Keylor, eds., *From Parnassus: Essays in Honor of Jacques Barzun* (New York: Harper and Row, 1976), xv–xxii.

27. See Laurence Vesey, *The Emergence of the American University* (Chicago: University of Chicago Press, 1965), 180–251, and Gerald Graff, *Professing Literature: An Institutional History* (Chicago: University of Chicago Press, 1987), 81–97.

28. See John Erskine, *My Life as a Teacher* (Philadelphia: J. B. Lippincott, 1948), 165–71.

29. John Erskine, *The Memory of Certain Persons* (Philadelphia: J. B. Lippincott, 1947), 342–43; Lionel Trilling, "The Van Amringe and Keppel Eras," in Dwight C. Miner, ed., *A History of Columbia College on Morningside* (New York: Columbia University Press, 1954), 44.

30. Jacques Barzun, "Remembering Lionel Trilling," *Encounter* 47 (October 1976): 83; Trilling, *The Last Decade*, 238–39.

31. Alan M. Wald, *The New York Intellectuals: The Rise and Decline of the Anti-Stalinist Left from the 1930s to the 1980s* (Chapel Hill: North Carolina University Press, 1987), 31.

32. Mark Krupnick, "The *Menorah Journal* Group and the Origins of Modern Jewish-American Radicalism," *Studies in American Jewish Literature* 5 (1979): 56–67; Trilling, *The Beginning of the Journey*, 137–45. See also Elinor Grumet, "The Apprenticeship of Lionel Trilling," *Prooftexts* 4 (1984): 153–73.

33. Lionel Trilling, "Young in the Thirties," *Commentary* 41 (May 1966), 47.

34. Ibid.

35. "An Address to Jewish Students," Box 34, Folder 1, Trilling Papers.

36. Trilling, Journal, 1952–1955, Box 2, Folder 7, Trilling Papers. See also Trilling, *The Beginning of the Journey*, 84.

37. Lionel Trilling, "On the Death of a Friend," *Commentary* 29 (February 1960), 93.

38. Trilling, *The Beginning of the Journey*, 178–

96; Wald, *The New York Intellectuals*, 56–60; Malcolm Cowley, *The Dream of the Golden Mountains: Remembering the 1930s* (New York: Viking, 1980), 55–58.

39. Lionel Trilling to Eric Bentley, March 7, 1946, Box 5, Folder 8, Trilling Papers.

40. Lionel Trilling to Eric Bentley, May 12, 1946, Box 5, Folder 8, Trilling Papers.

41. Edmund Wilson, "Uncle Matthew," *New Republic* 98 (March 20, 1939), 199.

42. Robert Penn Warren, "Arnold vs. the 19th Century," *Kenyon Review* 1 (1939): 217.

43. [John Middleton Murry], "Matthew Arnold To-Day," *Times Literary Supplement*, March 11, 1939, 148.

44. Trilling, *The Beginning of the Journey*, 397–98.

45. "Forster and the Human Fact," *Time* 42 (August 9, 1943), 102.

46. Lionel Trilling, *E. M. Forster* (Norfolk, CT: New Directions, 1943), 11; Lionel Trilling, "The Princess Casamassima," in *The Liberal Imagination: Essays on Literature and Society* (New York: Viking, 1950), 89.

47. Whittaker Chambers, *Witness* (New York: Random House, 1952), 25–88; Sam Tanenhaus, *Whittaker Chambers: A Biography* (New York: Random House, 1997), 123–36.

48. Trilling, *The Beginning of the Journey*, 216–17; see also Lionel Trilling, *The Middle of the Journey* (New York: Viking, 1947), 149–51.

49. Lionel Trilling to Eric Bentley, November 28, 1947, Box 5, Folder 8, Trilling Papers.

50. Orville Prescott, "Books of the Times," *New York Times*, December 8, 1947, 23.

51. See Lionel Trilling, *The Journey Abandoned: The Unfinished Novel*, ed. Geraldine Murphy (New York: Columbia University Press, 2008).

52. Trilling, *The Beginning of the Journey*, 387–90.

53. John Rodden, ed., *Lionel Trilling and the Critics: Opposing Selves* (Lincoln: University of Nebraska Press, 1999), 24n29.

54. Lionel Trilling, preface to *The Liberal Imagination*, ix.

55. Ibid., x, xv.

56. Ibid., x–xi.

57. Trilling, *E. M. Forster*, 13.

58. Lionel Trilling, "Art and Fortune," in *The Liberal Imagination*, 275–76.

59. Lionel Trilling, "The Function of the Little Magazine," in *The Liberal Imagination*, 100.

60. Lionel Trilling, "Reality in America," in *The Liberal Imagination*, 11–12.

61. Lionel Trilling, "On the Modern Element in Modern Literature," *Partisan Review* 28 (1961): 19.

62. Lionel Trilling, "The Meaning of a Literary Idea," in *The Liberal Imagination*, 301.

63. Michael Schumacher, *Dharma Lion: A Biography of Allen Ginsberg* (New York: St. Martin's, 1992), 25 (interview with Ginsberg).

64. Barry Miles, *Allen Ginsberg: A Biography* (New York: Simon and Schuster, 1989), 4–32. See also Allen Ginsberg, "Kaddish," in *Collected Poems, 1947–1997* (New York: HarperCollins, 2006), 222 ("newly in love with R—my high school mind hero, jewish boy who came a doctor later—then silent neat kid— / I later laying down life for him, moved to Manhattan—followed him to college").

65. See Alfred Kazin, *New York Jew* (New York: Knopf, 1978), 42–43.

66. Trilling, Journal, 1952–1955, June 18 [1955], Box 2, Folder 7, Trilling Papers. See also Trilling, *The Beginning of the Journey*, 368–73; James Trilling, "My Father and the Weak-Eyed Devils," *American Scholar* 68 (Spring 1999): 17–41.

67. Trilling, Journal, September 1948–April 1952, Box 2, Folder 6, Trilling Papers.

68. Trilling, Journal, 1952–1955, June 18 [1955], Box 2, Folder 7, Trilling Papers.

69. Edie Kerouac-Parker, *You'll Be Okay: My Life with Jack Kerouac* (San Francisco: City Lights Books, 2007), 122.

70. Barry Miles, *Call Me Burroughs: A Life* (New York: Twelve, 2013), 60–98.

71. Barry Gifford and Lawrence Lee, *Jack's Book: An Oral Biography of Jack Kerouac* (New York: St. Martin's, 1978), 3–34; Paul Maher, Jr., *Kerouac: The Definitive Biography* (Lanham, MD: Taylor Trade Publishing, 2004), 72–119; Steven Watson, *The Birth of the Beat Generation: Visionaries, Rebels, and Hipsters, 1944–1960* (New York: Pantheon, 1995), 34–38.

72. Frank S. Adams, "Columbia Student Kills Friend and Sinks Body in Hudson River," *New York Times*, August 17, 1944, 1; "Student Is Indicted in 2d-Degree Murder," *New York Times*, August 25, 1944, 15; Ted Morgan, *Literary Outlaw: The Life and Times of William Burroughs* (New York: Henry Holt, 1988), 104; Maher, *Kerouac*, 122–23; Watson, *The Birth of the Beat Generation*, 44–48.

73. Adams, "Columbia Student Kills Friend and Sinks Body in Hudson River," 13.

74. "Student Is Held without Bail in Slaying of Man," *New York Herald Tribune*, August 18, 1944, 13a.

75. Eric Homberger, "Lucien Carr, Muse and Journalist, 1925–2005," *Globe and Mail* [Toronto], February 16, 2005, S9.

76. "Kammerer's Parents Prominent," *New York Times*, August 17, 1944, 13.

77. See Pamela Harrison, "Who Really Gave Birth to the Beats?," *New York* 9 (June 7, 1976), 12–13; Homberger, "Lucien Carr"; James Grauerholz, afterword to Jack Kerouac and William S. Burroughs, *And the Hippos Were Boiled in Their Tanks* (New York: Grove, 2008), 188–92; Dustin Griffin, "The St. Louis Clique: Burroughs, Kammerer, and Carr," *Journal of Beat Studies* 3 (2014): 1–45. Cf. Kerouac-Parker, *You'll Be Okay*, 130.

78. Allen Ginsberg, *The Book of Martyrdom and Artifice: First Journals and Poems, 1937–1952*, ed. Juanita Liebermann-Plimpton and Bill Morgan (Cambridge, MA: Da Capo, 2006), 86–115.

79. See Véronique Lane, "The Parting of Burroughs and Kerouac: The French Backstory to the First Beat Novel, from Rimbaud to Poetic Realist Cinema," *Comparative American Studies* 11 (2013): 265–79.

80. Joyce Johnson, *The Voice Is All: The Lonely Victory of Jack Kerouac* (New York: Viking, 2012), 204–205.

81. Miles, *Call Me Burroughs*, 119–20.

82. Louis Ginsberg to Hannah Litzky, January 16, 1945, in Allen Ginsberg and Louis Ginsberg, *Family Business: Selected Letters between a Father and Son*, ed. Michael Schumacher (New York: Bloomsbury, 2001), 5.

83. Louis Ginsberg to Lionel Trilling, in Ginsberg and Ginsberg, *Family Business*, 5–6.

84. Miles, *Allen Ginsberg*, 57–59; Schumacher, *Dharma Lion*, 54–57.

85. Allen Ginsberg to Lionel Trilling, July 1945, Box 6, Folder 6, Trilling Papers.

86. Lionel Trilling to Allen Ginsberg, August 9, 1945, Box 14, Folder 16, Allen Ginsberg Papers, Rare Book and Manuscript Library, Columbia University.

87. Jack Kerouac to Allen Ginsberg, September 6, 1945, in *Jack Kerouac and Allen Ginsberg: The Letters*, ed. Bill Morgan and David Stanford (New York: Viking, 2010), 21, 25.

88. Allen Ginsberg to Lionel Trilling, August 27, 1945 [unsent], Box 9, Folder 13, Ginsberg Papers. This is a draft of the September 4 letter.

89. Delmore Schwartz, introduction to Arthur Rimbaud, *A Season in Hell*, trans. Delmore Schwartz (Norfolk, CT: New Directions, 1939), iii–xiii. See also James Atlas, *Delmore Schwartz: The Life of an American Poet* (New York: Farrar, Straus and Giroux, 1977), 169–71. William Barrett helped Schwartz produce a revised translation, published in 1940, which may be the edition Ginsberg read.

90. Allen Ginsberg to Lionel Trilling, September 4, 1945, Box 6, Folder 6, Trilling Papers.

91. Lionel Trilling to Allen Ginsberg, September 11, 1945, Box 14, Folder 16, Trilling Papers.

92. Lionel Trilling, preface to *Beyond Culture: Essays on Literature and Learning* (New York: Viking, 1965), ix–xviii.

93. Allen Ginsberg to Lionel Trilling, September 4, 1945, Box 6, Folder 6, Trilling Papers.

94. Allen Ginsberg, "The Art of Poetry VIII: Allen Ginsberg, an Interview," *Paris Review* 10 (Spring 1966), 38.

95. Allen Ginsberg, *Howl and Other Poems* (San Francisco: City Lights Books, 1956), 12.

96. Maher, *Kerouac*, 182.

97. John Clellon Holmes, Journal, November 10, 1948, Box 20, Binder 1948, John Clellon Holmes Papers, Howard Gottlieb Archival Research Center, Boston University.

98. Gifford and Lee, *Jack's Book*, 127 (interview with Holmes).

99. John Clellon Holmes to Alan Harrington, April 28, 1949, Box 20, Binder 1949, Holmes Papers.

100. Gina Berriault, "Neal's Ashes," *Rolling Stone* (October 12, 1972), 34 (interview with Carolyn Cassady).

101. David Sandison and Graham Vickers, *Neal Cassady: The Fast Life of a Beat Hero* (Chicago: Chicago Review Press, 2006), 1–10.

102. Berriault, "Neal's Ashes," 32–36 (interview with Carolyn Cassady); Gerald Nicosia and Anne Marie Santos, *One and Only: The Untold Story of "On the Road,"* (Berkeley: Cleis Press, 2011), 81; Sandison and Vickers, *Neal Cassady*, 138; Ann Charters and Samuel Charters, *Brother-Souls: John Clellon Holmes, Jack Kerouac, and the Beat Generation* (Jackson: University Press of Mississippi, 2010), 102; Ginsberg, *Howl and Other Poems*, 12; Holmes, Journal, January 19, 1949, Box 20, Binder 1949, Holmes Papers.

103. Gifford and Lee, *Jack's Book,* 129 (interview with Holmes).

104. Allen Ginsberg to Lionel Trilling, August 1947, Box 6, Folder 6, Trilling Papers.

105. Lionel Trilling to Allen Ginsberg, October 26, 1947, Box 14, Folder 16, Ginsberg Papers.

106. "Wrong-Way Turn Clears Up Robbery," *New York Times*, April 23, 1949, 30.

107. Allen Ginsberg to Lionel Trilling, April 1949, Box 6, Folder 6, Trilling Papers.

108. Allen Ginsberg to Jack Kerouac, ca. early May 1949, in *Jack Kerouac and Allen Ginsberg: The Letters*, 69.

109. Chambers, *Witness*, 193–94; Tanenhaus, *Whittaker Chambers*, 35.

110. Schumacher, *Dharma Lion*, 112–13; Miles, *Allen Ginsberg*, 118–19.

111. Louis Ginsberg to Lionel Trilling, June 29, 1949, Box 6, Folder 6, Trilling Papers.

112. Herbert Huncke, *Guilty of Everything: The Autobiography of Herbert Huncke* (New York: Paragon House, 1990), 108; Hilary Holladay, *American Hipster: A Life of Herbert Huncke* (New York: Magnus Books, 2013), 162–69.

113. Allen Ginsberg to Jack Kerouac, July 13, 1949, in *Jack Kerouac and Allen Ginsberg: The Letters*, 99.

114. Carl Solomon, *More Mishaps* (San Francisco: City Lights Books, 1968), 51.

115. Allen Ginsberg to Jack Kerouac, February 24, 1949 [1950], in *Jack Kerouac and Allen Ginsberg: The Letters*, 121.

116. Allen Ginsberg to Neal Cassady, Summer 1950, in *As Ever: The Collected Correspondence of Allen Ginsberg and Neal Cassady*, ed. Barry Gifford (Berkeley: Creative Arts, 1977), 70. Bill Morgan has them sleeping together in November 1948 (Bill Morgan, *The Typewriter Is Holy: The Complete, Uncensored History of the Beat Generation* [New York: Free Press, 2010], 37).

117. Watson, *The Birth of the Beat Generation*, 34.

118. Trilling, Journal, September 1948–April 1952, Box 2, Folder 6, Trilling Papers.

119. Trilling, Journal, January 23, 1951, September 1948–April 1952, Box 2, Folder 6, Trilling Papers.

120. Trilling, Journal, 1970–1974, Box 5, Folder 1, Trilling Papers.

121. Trilling, *The Beginning of the Journey*, 223–56.

122. Uwe Henrik Peters, *Psychiatrie im Exil: Die Emigration der Dynamischen Psychiatrie aus Deutschland 1933–1939* (Düsseldorf: Kupka Verlag, 1992), 16; Eli Zaretsky, *Secrets of the Soul: A Social and Cultural History of Psychoanalysis* (New York: Knopf, 2004), 280–81.

123. Nathan Hale, Jr., *The Rise and Crisis of Psychoanalysis: Freud and the Americans, 1917–1985* (New York: Oxford University Press, 1995), 246. See also Dorothy Ross, "Freud and the Vicissitudes of Modernism in America, 1940–1980," in John Burnham, ed., *After Freud Left: A Century of Psychoanalysis in America* (Chicago: University of Chicago Press, 2012), 163–88.

124. Edward Shorter, *A History of Psychiatry: From the Era of the Asylum to the Age of Prozac* (New York: John Wiley and Sons, 1977), 166–81; Zaretsky, *Secrets of the Soul*, 280–81; Joel Paris, *The Fall of an Icon: Psychoanalysis and Academic Psychiatry* (Toronto: University of Toronto Press, 2005), 26.

125. Élisabeth Roudinesco, *Jacques Lacan & Co.: A History of Psychoanalysis in France*, trans. Jeffrey Mehlman (Chicago: University of Chicago Press, 1990), 116–22.

126. Trilling, *The Beginning of the Journey*, 252.

127. Hale, *The Rise and Crisis of Psychoanalysis*, 242; H. Stuart Hughes, *The Sea Change: The Migration of Social Thought, 1930–1965* (New York: Harper and Row, 1975), 189–239; Paul Roazen, *Freud and His Followers* (New York: Knopf, 1975), 517–20.

128. See Bruno Bettelheim, *Freud and Man's Soul* (New York: Knopf, 1983), and Zaretsky, *Secrets of the Soul*, 295–96.

129. Sigmund Freud, *The Standard Edition of the Complete Psychological Works of Sigmund Freud*, ed. and trans. James Strachey (London: Hogarth Press and the Institute of Psycho-Analysis,

1953–1974), vol. 18, *Beyond the Pleasure Principle*, 39. ("[D]es Organismus nur auf seine Weise sterben will." Sigmund Freud, *Gesammelte Werke: Chronologisch Geordnet*, ed. Anna Freud et al., vol. 13, *Jenseits des Lustprinzips* [London: Imago, 1940–1968], 41.)

130. Freud, "The Economic Problem of Masochism," in *Standard Edition*, vol. 19, *The Ego and the Id and Other Works*, 163. ("Er heiße dann Destruktionstrieb, Bemächtigungstrieb, Wille zur Macht." Freud, "Das Ökonomische Problem des Masochismus," *Gesammelte Werke*, vol. 13, 376.)

131. William McDougall, *Psycho-Analysis and Social Psychology* (London: Methuen, 1936), 64.

132. See Ernest Jones, *Life and Work of Sigmund Freud*, vol. 3, *The Last Phase, 1919–1939* (New York: Basic Books, 1957), 272–78. Cf. Frank Sulloway, *Freud, Biologist of the Mind: Beyond the Psychoanalytic Legend* (New York: Basic Books, 1979), 393–415.

133. Freud, *Civilization and Its Discontents*, in *Standard Edition*, vol. 21, 145. ("'[H]immlischen Mächte.'" Freud, *Gesammelte Werke*, vol. 14, *Das Unbehagen in der Kultur*, 506.)

134. Freud, *Civilization and Its Discontents*, 112–14. ("Die Kommunisten glauben den Weg zur Erlösung vom Übel gefunden zu haben. Der Mensch ist eindeutig gut, seinem Nächsten wohlgesinnt, aber die Einrichtung des privaten Eigentums hat seine Natur verdorben. Besitz an privaten Gütern gibt dem einen die Macht und damit die Versuchung, den Nächsten zu mißhandeln; der vom Besitz Ausgeschlossene muß sich in Feindseligkeit gegen den Unterdrücker auflehnen . . . Ich habe nichts mit der wirtschaftlichen Kritik des kommunistischen Systems zu tun, ich kann nicht untersuchen, ob die Abschaffung des privaten Eigentums zweckdienlich und vorteilhalf ist. Aber seine psychologische Voraussetzung vermag ich als haltlose Illusion zu erkennen . . . Sie ist nicht durch das Eigentum geschaffen worden, herrschte fast uneingeschränkt in Urzeiten . . . bildet den Bodensatz aller zärtlichen und Liebesbeziehungen unter den Menschen . . . Befreiung des Sexuallebens, beseitigt also die Familie, die Keimzelle der Kultur, so läßt sich zwar nicht vorhersehen, welche neuen Wege die Kulturentwicklung einschlagen kann, aber eines darf man erwarten, daß der unzerstörbare Zug der menschlichen Natur ihr auch dorthin folgen wird." Freud, *Gesammelte Werke*, vol. 14, 472–75.)

135. Sidney Hook, *Heresy, Yes—Conspiracy, No!* (New York: John Day, 1953), 35.

136. *Congressional Record* 100 (March 31, 1956), 4280–94.

137. Will Lissner, "Columbia Is Dropping Dr. Weltfish, Leftist," *New York Times*, April 1,

1953, 1, 19; Ellen W. Schrecker, *No Ivory Tower: McCarthyism and the Universities* (New York: Oxford University Press, 1986), 255–57; McCaughey, *Stand, Columbia*, 345. See also Ralph S. Brown, Jr., *Loyalty and Security: Employment Tests in the United States* (New Haven: Yale University Press, 1958), 122–34.

138. "Educators Attack Congress Inquiries," *New York Times*, November 18, 1953, 28.

139. Lionel Trilling, letter to the editor, *New York Times*, November 26, 1954, 30.

140. Louis Menand, "The Limits of Academic Freedom," in Louis Menand, ed., *The Future of Academic Freedom* (Chicago: University of Chicago Press, 1996), 3–20.

141. David Caute, *The Great Fear: The Anti-Communist Purge Under Truman and Eisenhower* (New York: Simon and Schuster, 1978), 422–47; Schrecker, *No Ivory Tower*, 17–23; Diane Ravitch, *The Troubled Crusade: American Education, 1945–1980* (New York: Basic Books, 1983), 98–99.

142. Caute, *The Great Fear*, 406.

143. *Statistical Abstract of the United States 1956* (Washington, DC: U.S. Government Printing Office, 1956), 115, 125; *Biennial Survey of Education in the United States, 1954–56* (Washington, DC: U.S. Government Printing Office, 1960), ch. 4, sec. 1, 10.

144. Paul F. Lazarsfeld and Wagner Thielens, *The Academic Mind: Social Scientists in a Time of Crisis* (Glencoe, IL: Free Press, 1958), 95.

145. Group for the Advancement of Psychiatry, *Considerations Regarding the Loyalty Oath as a Manifestation of Current Social Tension and Anxiety* (Topeka: Group for the Advancement of Psychiatry, 1954), 1, 5–6.

146. Lionel Trilling, *Freud and the Crisis of Our Culture* (Boston: Beacon Press, 1955), 46.

147. Ibid., 48.

148. Ibid.

149. Ibid., 52–54.

150. William L. Shirer, *The Rise and Fall of the Third Reich: A History of Nazi Germany* (New York: Simon and Schuster, 1960), 350–53; Alan Bullock, *Hitler and Stalin: Parallel Lives*, 2nd rev. ed. (New York: Vintage, 1993), 360–61; A. M. Sperber, *Murrow: His Life and Times* (New York: Fordham University Press, 1998), 119–22.

151. Peter Gay, *Freud: A Life for Our Time* (New York: W. W. Norton, 1998), 625–29.

152. Martin Freud, *Glory Reflected: Sigmund Freud, Man and Father* (London: Angus and Robertson, 1957), 16; Élisabeth Roudinesco, *Freud in His Time and Ours*, trans. Catherine Porter (Cambridge, MA: Harvard University Press, 2016), 560.

153. Schumacher, *Dharma Lion*, 183.

154. Allen Ginsberg, *The Gay Sunshine Interview* (Bolinas, CA: Grey Fox Press, 1974), 22. Cf.

Jane Kramer, *Allen Ginsberg in America* (New York: Random House, 1969), 42–43.

155. Schumacher, *Dharma Lion*, 188–89; Ginsberg, *The Gay Sunshine Interview*, 20–23.

156. Schumacher, *Dharma Lion*, 214–16; Miles, *Allen Ginsberg*, 192–94.

157. Michael McClure, *Scratching the Beat Surface* (San Francisco: North Point Press, 1981), 13. See also Peter Manso, *Mailer: His Life and Times* (New York: Simon and Schuster, 1985), 261 (interview with McClure).

158. Al Aronowitz, "The Beat Generation—XII," *New York Post*, March 22, 1959, M5.

159. Larry Smith, *Lawrence Ferlinghetti: Poet-at-Large* (Carbondale: Southern Illinois University Press, 1983), 6–24; Neeli Cherkovski, *Ferlinghetti: A Biography* (Garden City, NY: Doubleday, 1979), 45.

160. Lawrence Ferlinghetti to Allen Ginsberg, October 13, 1955, quoted in Miles, *Allen Ginsberg*, 194.

161. Allen Ginsberg to Lionel Trilling, undated, Box 6, Folder 6, Trilling Papers.

162. Lionel Trilling to Allen Ginsberg, May 29, 1956 (carbon), Box 6, Folder 6, Trilling Papers.

163. Louis Ginsberg to Allen Ginsberg, May 27, 1956, in Ginsberg and Ginsberg, *Family Business*, 46.

7. THE HUMAN SCIENCE

1. Mary Evelyn Townsend, *European Colonial Expansion since 1871* (Chicago: J. B. Lippincott, 1941), 19; Muriel E. Chamberlain, *The Longman Companion to European Decolonisation in the Twentieth Century* (London: Longman, 1998), 3–12.

2. David B. Abernethy, *The Dynamics of Global Dominance: European Overseas Empires, 1415–1980* (New Haven: Yale University Press, 2000), 133; Eric Hobsbawm, *Age of Extremes: The Short Twentieth Century, 1914–1991* (London: Michael Joseph, 1994), 222.

3. Odd Arne Westad, *The Global Cold War: Third World Interventions and the Making of Our Time* (Cambridge: Cambridge University Press, 2005), 396–407; Leslie James and Elisabeth Leake, *Decolonization and the Cold War: Negotiating Independence* (London: Bloomsbury, 2015); Mark Philip Bradley, "Decolonization, the Global South, and the Cold War, 1919–1962," in Melvyn P. Leffler and Odd Arne Westad, eds., *The Cambridge History of the Cold War*, vol. 1, *Origins* (Cambridge: Cambridge University Press, 2010), 464–85. Cf. Anders Stephanson, "Cold War Degree Zero," in Joel Isaac and Duncan Bell, eds., *Uncertain Empire: American History and the Idea of the Cold War* (New York: Oxford University Press, 2010), 19–49.

4. Westad, *The Global Cold War*, 8–72.

5. Alfred Sauvy, "Trois Mondes, Une Planète," *L'Observateur*, August 14, 1952, 14.

6. Townsend, *European Colonial Expansion since 1871*, 23; E. J. Hobsbawm, *The Age of Empire, 1875–1914* (New York: Pantheon, 1987), 66–74. See also D. K. Fieldhouse, *Economics and Empire, 1830–1914* (London: Macmillan, 1984), 463–77.

7. Wm. Roger Louis, "The European Colonial Empires," in Michael Howard and Wm. Roger Louis, eds., *The Oxford History of the Twentieth Century* (New York: Oxford University Press, 1998), 93.

8. Thomas Piketty, *Capital in the Twenty-First Century*, trans. Arthur Goldhammer (Cambridge, MA: Harvard University Press, 2014), 120–22.

9. Hobsbawm, *The Age of Empire*, 59.

10. Ibid., 79.

11. On Lévi-Strauss's life, see Emmanuelle Loyer, *Lévi-Strauss: A Biography*, trans. Ninon Vinsonneau and Jonathan Magidoff (Cambridge: Polity, 2018).

12. Simone de Beauvoir, *Mémoires d'une jeune fille rangée* (Paris: Gallimard, 1958), 294 ("[Lévi-Strauss] m'intimidait par son flegme"); Alfred Métraux, *Itinéraires 1 (1935–1953): Carnet de notes et journaux de voyage*, ed. André-Marcel d'An (Paris: Payot, 1978), 42 ("Je trouve froid, compassé, très universitaire français"); Annie Cohen-Solal, "'Claude L. Strauss' aux États-Unis," *Critique* 55 (1999): 18 (interview with Dolorès Vanetti) ("Il parlait peu mais, quand il parlait, il était drôle, précis, pince-sans-rire et parfois même glacial"); Patrick Waldberg, "Au fil du souvenir," in Jean Pouillon and Pierre Maranda, eds., *Échanges et communications: mélanges offerts à Claude Lévi-Strauss à l'occasion de son 60ème anniversaire*, vol. 1 (The Hague: Mouton, 1970), 583 ("son abord pouvait être difficile et parfois même glaçant").

13. Patrick Wilcken, *Claude Lévi-Strauss: The Poet in the Laboratory* (New York: Penguin, 2010), 29–47.

14. Claude Lévi-Strauss, *Œuvres* (Paris: Gallimard, 2008), xlv–xlvi.

15. Edmund Leach, *Claude Lévi-Strauss* (New York: Viking, 1970), 11; Wilcken, *Claude Lévi-Strauss*, 358n65.

16. Claude Singer, *Vichy, l'Université, et les Juifs* (Paris: Belles-Lettres, 1992), 145.

17. See James Clifford, *The Predicament of Culture: Twentieth-Century Ethnography, Literature, and Art* (Cambridge, MA: Harvard University Press, 1988), 117–51.

18. Claude Lévi-Strauss and Didier Eribon, *Conversations with Claude Lévi-Strauss*, trans. Paula Wissing (Chicago: University of Chicago Press, 1991), 28.

19. Wilcken, *Claude Lévi-Strauss*, 115–39.

20. See Melville J. Herskovits, *Franz Boas: The Science of Man in the Making* (New York: Scribner,

1953), 1–24; George W. Stocking, Jr., "Franz Boas and the Culture Concept in Historical Perspective," in *Race, Culture, and Evolution: Essays in the History of Anthropology* (New York: Free Press, 1968), 195–233; Louis Menand, *The Metaphysical Club* (New York: Farrar, Straus and Giroux, 2001), 383–87; Charles King, *Gods of the Upper Air: How a Circle of Renegade Anthropologists Reinvented Race, Sex, and Gender in the Twentieth Century* (New York: Doubleday, 2019). Cf. Adam Kuper, *Culture: The Anthropologists' Account* (Cambridge, MA: Harvard University Press, 1999), 56–62.

21. Lévi-Strauss and Eribon, *Conversations*, 37–38.

22. Wilcken, *Claude Lévi-Strauss*, 151.

23. Claude Lévi-Strauss, "New York in 1941," in *The View from Afar*, trans. Joachim Neugroschel and Phoebe Hoss (Chicago: University of Chicago Press, 1985), 261–62.

24. Lévi-Strauss and Eribon, *Conversations*, 43. ("Ce que je sais d'ethnologie, c'est pendant ces années-là que je l'ai appris." Claude Lévi-Strauss and Didier Eribon, *De Près et de Loin* [Paris: Éditions Odile Jacob, 1988], 65.)

25. See François Chaubet and Emmanuelle Loyer, "L'école libre des hautes études de New York: exil et résistance intellectuel (1942–1946)," *Revue Historique* 302 (2000): 939–72.

26. Loyer, *Lévi-Strauss*, 227.

27. Roman Jakobson, "Réponses," *Poétique* 57–60 (1984): 3–25 (interview by Tzvetan Todorov); Roman Jakobson, preface to Tzvetan Todorov, ed. and trans., *Théorie de la littérature: Textes des formalistes russes réunis* (Paris: Éditions du Seuil, 1965), 9–13. And see Roman Jakobson, *My Futurist Years*, ed. Bengt Jangfeldt and Stephen Rudy, trans. Stephen Rudy (New York: Marsilio, 1997).

28. N. S. Trubetzkoy, *Principles of Phonology*, trans. Christiane A. M. Baltaxe (Berkeley: University of California Press, 1969), 323.

29. Bengt Jangfeldt, "Roman Jakobson in Sweden 1940–41," *Cahiers de l'ILSL* 9 (1997): 149–57; Andrew Lass, "Poetry and Reality," in Christopher Benfey and Karen Remmler, eds., *Artists, Intellectuals, and World War II: The Pontigny Encounters at Mount Holyoke College* (Amherst: University of Massachusetts Press, 2006), 177–79.

30. Lévi-Strauss and Eribon, *Conversations*, 41; Roman Jakobson, "Entretien," in *Jakobson* (Lausanne: Éditions l'Age d'Homme, 1978), 17.

31. Roman Jakobson, *Six leçons sur le son et les sens* (Paris: Éditions de Minuit, 1976), 2. See also Roman Jakobson, *Six Lectures on Sound and Meaning*, trans. John Mepham (Hassocks, UK: Harvester Press, 1978), 10.

32. Claude Lévi-Strauss, preface to Jakobson, *Six leçons*, 7.

33. Lévi-Strauss and Eribon, *Conversations*, 42. ("Ses cours étaient un éblouissement . . . Il avait surtout un don dramatique sans égal; il transportait ses auditeurs auxquels il donnait le sentiment justifié de vivre un moment décisif dans l'histoire de la pensée." Lévi-Strauss and Eribon, *De Près et de Loin*, 64.)

34. Claude Lévi-Strauss to Emma and Raymond Lévi-Strauss, September 13, 1942, in *"Chers tous deux": Lettres à ses parents, 1931–1942*, ed. Monique Lévi-Strauss (Paris: Éditions du Seuil, 2015), 559. ("[U]n remarquable cours de linguistique d'un de mes collègues qui m'apporte, dans ce domaine, des connaissances indispensables à mon travail.")

35. Roman Jakobson, "Romantické Všeslovanství—Nová Slavistika," *Čin* 1 (1929): 11. See also François Dosse, *History of Structuralism*, vol. 1, *The Rising Sign, 1945–1966*, trans. Deborah Glassman (Minneapolis: University of Minnesota Press, 1997), 45.

36. Jakobson, *Six Lectures*, 66. ("Un phonème signifie autre chose qu'un autre phonème dans la même position; c'est son unique valeur." Jakobson, *Six leçons*, 78.)

37. Roman Jakobson, C. Gunnar M. Fant, and Morris Halle, *Preliminaries to Speech Analysis: The Distinctive Features and Their Correlates* (Cambridge, MA: Acoustics Laboratory, Massachusetts Institute of Technology, 1952), 40. See also Roman Jakobson and Morris Halle, *Fundamentals of Language* (The Hague: Mouton, 1956), 28–32.

38. Claude Lévi-Strauss, "Structural Analysis in Linguistics and Anthropology," in *Structural Anthropology*, trans. Claire Jacobson and Brooke Grundfest Schoepf (New York: Basic Books, 1963), 33. ("La phonologie ne peut manquer de jouer, vis-à-vis des sciences sociales, le même rôle rénovateur que la physique nucléaire, par exemple, a joué pour l'ensemble des sciences exactes." Claude Lévi-Strauss, "L'Analyse structurale en linguistique et en anthropologie," *Word* 1 [1945]: 35.)

39. Lévi-Strauss, *Structural Anthropology*, 34. ("[D]ans un *autre ordre de réalité*, les phénomènes de parenté sont des phénomènes du *même type* que les phénomènes linguistiques." Lévi-Strauss, "L'Analyse structurale," 36.)

40. Lévi-Strauss, *Structural Anthropology*, 46. ("Le caractère primitif et irréductible de l'élément de parenté tel que nous l'avons défini résulte en effet, de façon immédiate, de l'existence universelle de la prohibition de l'inceste. Celle-ci équivaut à dire que, dans la société humaine, un homme ne peut obtenir une femme que d'un autre homme, qui la lui cède sous forme de fille ou de sœur." Lévi-Strauss, "L'Analyse structurale," 48.)

41. Claude Lévi-Strauss, *The Elementary Structures of Kinship*, rev. ed., trans. James Harle Bell,

John Richard von Sturmer, and Rodney Needham, ed. Rodney Needham (Boston: Beacon Press, 1969), 493. ("[L]inguistes et sociologues n'appliquent pas seulement les mêmes méthodes, mais [ils] s'attachent à l'étude du même objet." Claude Lévi-Strauss, *Les Structures élémentaires de la parenté* [Paris: Presses Universitaires de France, 1949], 612.)

42. Sol Tax, Loren C. Eiseley, Irving Rouse, and Carl F. Voegelin, eds., *An Appraisal of Anthropology Today* (Chicago: University of Chicago Press, 1953), 321.

43. Claude Lévi-Strauss, *Tristes Tropiques*, trans. John Weightman and Doreen Weightman (New York: Atheneum, 1975), 178. ("L'ensemble des coutumes d'un peuple est toujours marqué par un style; elles forment des systèmes. Je suis persuadé que ses systèmes n'existent pas en nombre illimité, et que les sociétés humaines . . . ne créent jamais de façon absolue, mais se bornent à choisir certaines combinaisons dans un répertoire idéal qu'il serait possible de reconstituer." Lévi-Strauss, *Œuvres*, 167.)

44. Tax et al., eds., *An Appraisal of Anthropology Today*, 293–94.

45. See Leach, *Claude Lévi-Strauss*, 15–32, 121–30; Howard Gardner, *The Quest for Mind: Piaget, Lévi-Strauss, and the Structuralist Movement*, 2nd ed. (Chicago: University of Chicago Press, 1981), 111–247; Christopher Johnson, *Claude Lévi-Strauss: The Formative Years* (Cambridge: Cambridge University Press, 2003), 88–103.

46. Brigitte Mazon, *Aux Origines de l'école des hautes études en sciences sociales: le rôle du mécénat américain (1920–1960)* (Paris: Éditions du Cerf, 1988), 72–73; Aristide R. Zolberg, "The École Libre at the New School," *Social Research* 65 (1998): 944–47; Wilcken, *Claude Lévi-Strauss*, 153–54; Denis Bertholet, *Claude Lévi-Strauss* (Paris: Plon, 2003), 161–64.

47. Lévi-Strauss and Eribon, *Conversations*, 47–49.

48. Simone de Beauvoir, Review of *Les Structures élémentaires de la parenté*, by Claude Lévi-Strauss, *Temps Modernes* 5 (1949–1950): 943, 949 ("un éclatant réveil").

49. Robert F. Murphy, "Connaissez-Vous Lévi-Strauss?," *Saturday Review* 52 (May 17, 1969), 52–53.

50. Wilcken, *Claude Lévi-Strauss*, 186 (interview with Lévi-Strauss).

51. Mark Mazower, *Governing the World: The History of an Idea* (New York: Penguin, 2012), 191–213; Oona Hathaway and Scott J. Shapiro, *The Internationalists: How a Radical Plan to Outlaw War Remade the World* (New York: Simon and Schuster, 2017), 193–201, 209–14.

52. Stephen C. Schlesinger, *Act of Creation: The Founding of the United Nations* (Boulder: West-

view, 2003), 193–225; Mazower, *Governing the World*, 245.

53. See Jean-Marie Benoist, "Claude Lévi-Strauss Reconsiders," *Encounter* 53 (July 1979): 19 (interview with Lévi-Strauss); Lévi-Strauss and Eribon, *Conversations*, 60–61.

54. "A Statement by Experts on Race Problems," *International Social Science Bulletin* 2 (1950): 393.

55. Claude Lévi-Strauss, *Race and History* (Paris: UNESCO, 1952), 14.

56. Ibid., 43, 46.

57. Claude Lévi-Strauss, "Le Coucher de soleil: entretien avec Boris Wiseman," *Temps Modernes* 59 (2004), 2. ("J'ai écrit ce livre dans une sorte de rage et d'impatience. J'éprouvais aussi un certain remords. Je pensais que j'aurais mieux fait d'écrire autre chose.")

58. Lévi-Strauss and Eribon, *Conversations*, 58. ("Je pensais pécher contre la science." Lévi-Strauss and Eribon, *De Près et de Loin*, 86–87.) On *Tristes Tropiques*, see Loyer, *Lévi-Strauss*, 322–35.

59. Wilcken, *Claude Lévi-Strauss*, 116, 206–16.

60. Lévi-Strauss, *Tristes Tropiques*, 17. ("Je hais les voyages et les explorateurs." "Eh quoi? Faut-il narrer par le menus tant de détails insipides, d'événements insignifiants?" Lévi-Strauss, *Œuvres*, 3.)

61. Lévi-Strauss, *Tristes Tropiques*, 385–86. ("Il faudra admettre que, dans la gamme des possibilités ouvertes aux sociétés humaines, chacune a fait un certain choix, et que ces choix sont incomparable entre eux: il se valent." Lévi-Strauss, *Œuvres*, 413.)

62. Lévi-Strauss, *Tristes Tropiques*, 389. ("On a dit parfois que la société occidentale était la seule à avoir produit des ethnographes; que c'était là sa grandeur"; "son existence même est incompréhensible, sinon comme une tentative de rachat: il est le symbole de l'expiation." Lévi-Strauss, *Œuvres*, 417.)

63. Lévi-Strauss, *Tristes Tropiques*, 326. ("[E]lles ont été foudroyées par ce monstrueux et incompréhensible cataclysme que fut, pour une si large et si innocente fraction de l'humanité, le développment de la civilisation occidentale." Lévi-Strauss, *Œuvres*, 342.)

64. Lévi-Strauss, *Tristes Tropiques*, 413–14. ("Le monde a commencé sans l'homme et il s'achèvera sans lui . . . [E]lles se confondront au désordre dès qu'il aura disparu. Si bien que la civilisation, prise dans son ensemble, peut être décrite comme un mécanisme prodigieusement complexe où nous serions tentés de voir la chance qu'a notre univers de survivre, si sa fonction n'était de fabriquer ce que les physiciens appellent entropie, c'est-à-dire de l'inertie. Chaque parole échangée, chaque ligne imprimée, établissent une communication

entre deux interlocuteurs, rendant étale un niveau qui se caractérisait auparavant par un écart d'information, donc une organisation plus grande. Plutôt qu'anthropologie, il faudrait écrire 'entropologie' le nom d'une discipline vouée à étudier dans ses manifestations les plus haute ce processus de désintégration." Lévi-Strauss, *Œuvres*, 443–44.)

65. James Gleick, *The Information: A History, a Theory, a Flood* (New York: Pantheon, 2011), 269–86.

66. Claude Lévi-Strauss to Roman Jakobson, March 27, 1950, Box 43, Folder 34, Roman Jakobson Papers, Institute Archives and Special Collections, Massachusetts Institute of Technology. ("[J]'ai littéralement dévoré la 'Mathematical theory,' etc. . . ."; "l'immense intérêt du livre est précisément de donner une théorie de la pensée du point de vue de la machine, c'est à dire, pour le première fois me semble-t-il, considérée comme un objet.")

67. Claude E. Shannon and Warren Weaver, *The Mathematical Theory of Communication* (Urbana: University of Illinois Press, 1949), 103–106.

68. Norbert Wiener, *Cybernetics, or Control and Communication in the Animal and the Machine* (New York: John Wiley and Sons, 1948), 19.

69. Claude Lévi-Strauss, *The Naked Man*, trans. John Weightman and Doreen Weightman (New York: Harper and Row, 1981), 694. ("[V]aste et complexe édifice, lui aussi irisé de mille teintes, qui se déploie sous le regard de l'analyste, s'épanouit lentement et se referme pour s'abîmer au loin comme s'il n'avait jamais existé." Claude Lévi-Strauss, *L'Homme Nu* [Paris: Plon, 1971], 620.)

70. Benoist, "Claude Lévi-Strauss Reconsiders," 26.

71. *The Family of Man: The Greatest Photographic Exhibition of All Time* (New York: Museum of Modern Art, 1955), 4.

72. John Szarkowski, "*The Family of Man*," *Studies in Modern Art* 4 (1994): 13–21.

73. Thomas L. Alexander to Edward Steichen, October 22, 1958, Edward Steichen Archive, Museum of Modern Art.

74. Eric J. Sandeen, *Picturing an Exhibition: "The Family of Man" and 1950s America* (Albuquerque: University of New Mexico Press, 1995), 39–42; Katherine Hoffman, "*The Family of Man*: An Introduction," *History of Photography* 29 (2005): 317–19.

75. Szarkowski, "*The Family of Man*," 13.

76. A. D. Coleman, "Steichen Then, Now, and Again: Legacies of an Icon," in Todd Brandow and William A. Ewing, eds., *Edward Steichen: Lives in Photography* (New York: W. W. Norton, 2008), 275–89; Oliver Lugan, "Edward Steichen as Exhibition Designer," in Brandow and Ewing, *Edward Steichen*, 267–73; Phoebe Lou

Adams, "Through a Lens Darkly," *Atlantic Monthly* 195 (April 1955), 72.

77. Minor White, "The Controversial *Family of Man*," *Aperture* 3 (1955): 8–27.

78. Hilton Kramer, "The New American Painting," *Partisan Review* 20 (1953): 423.

79. Hilton Kramer, "Exhibiting the Family of Man," *Commentary* 20 (1955): 364.

80. Augusta Strong, "'Family of Man'—A Stirring Ode to All the Earth's People," *Worker*, April 17, 1955, 8. See also "'Family of Man' at the Philadelphia Museum of Art," *Daily Worker*, April 1, 1956, 16; David Platt, "Movies, TV, and . . . ," *Daily Worker*, June 10, 1955, 6; David Platt, "Places to Take the Kids This Easter Season," *Worker*, April 10, 1955, 9; Joseph North, "A Day Is More Than Roses," *Worker*, May 8, 1955, 1; "'Family of Man' Exhibit Tours Country in June," *Daily Worker*, May 25, 1955, 6.

81. Rollie McKenna, "Photography," *New Republic* 123 (March 14, 1955), 30; Martin S. Dworkin, "'The Family of Man,'" *Progressive* 19 (August 1955), 25–26.

82. "UAW–CIO and The Family of Man," *Ammunition* 13 (March 1955).

83. Samuel Lachize, "Une bouleversante exposition de photos du monde entier; 'La grande famille des hommes,'" *L'Humanité*, January 25, 1956, 1. ("Il est réconfortant de savoir que cette collection unique, qui fait la tour du monde, nous vient des États-Unis, tant elle exprime l'amour des hommes, la fraternité de cette grande famille qu'ils forment autour de la terre . . . Une grande exposition qu'il faut avoir vue.")

84. Eric J. Sandeen, "The International Reception of *The Family of Man*," *History of Photography* 29 (2005): 353.

85. Marcel Cornu, "Un Art qui crie la vérité," *Lettres Françaises*, January 26, 1956, 1. ("[U]ne extraordinaire exposition de photographies"; "une marmelade de paroles sucrées et fades"; "ces images à vif et parfois explosives"; "une merveille.")

86. "Transcript of the President's News Conference on Foreign and Domestic Matters," *New York Times*, July 2, 1959, 10.

87. Alvin Shuster, "U.S. Exhibit Adds Traditional Art," *New York Times*, July 8, 1959, 31; Marilyn S. Kushner, "Exhibiting Art at the American National Exhibition in Moscow, 1959: Domestic Politics and Cultural Diplomacy," *Journal of Cold War Studies* 4 (Winter 2002): 6–26; Edith G. Halpert, "Moscow Greeting: American Art Rouses Lively Response," *New York Times*, August 2, 1959, 15.

88. Ralph K. White, "Soviet Reactions to Our Moscow Exhibit: Voting Machines and Comment Books," *Public Opinion Quarterly* 23 (1959): 461–70.

89. Walter L. Hixson, *Parting the Curtain: Propa-*

ganda, Culture, and the Cold War (New York: St. Martin's Griffin, 1998), 161–83; Kenneth Osgood, *Total Cold War: Eisenhower's Secret Propaganda Battle at Home and Abroad* (Lawrence: University Press of Kansas, 2006), 90–93.

90. See John O'Brian, "The Nuclear Family of Man," *Asia-Pacific Journal* 6 (July 2008): 1–13.

91. Fred Turner, "The Family of Man and the Politics of Attention in Cold War America," *Public Culture* 24 (2012): 83.

92. Cyril Bibby, "The Power of Words," *UNESCO Courier* 9 (February 1956), 24.

93. See Samuel Beckett to Maurice Nadeau, April 12, 1951, and September 5, 1953, in *The Letters of Samuel Beckett*, ed. George Craig, Martha Dow Fehsenfeld, Dan Gunn, and Lois More Overbeck, vol. 2, *1941–1956* (Cambridge: Cambridge University Press, 2011), 238–39, 399.

94. Roland Barthes, "La Grande Famille des Hommes," *Lettres Nouvelles* 4 (1956): 476. ("[O]u à l'étudiante noire d'Alabama.")

95. Jean-Marc Dreyfus, "Censorship and Approval: The Reception of *Nuit et Brouillard* in France," in Ewout van der Knaap, ed., *Uncovering the Holocaust: The International Reception of "Night and Fog"* (London: Wallflower Press, 2006), 37; Richard Raskin, *Nuit et Brouillard, by Alain Resnais* (Aarhus [Denmark]: Aarhus University Press, 1987), 34–44.

96. Adams, "Through a Lens Darkly," 69.

97. See David Damrosch, *Meetings of the Mind* (Princeton: Princeton University Press, 2000), 57–59.

98. Roland Barthes, "The Great Family of Man," in *Mythologies*, trans. Richard Howard and Annette Lavers (New York: Hill and Wang, 2012), 197. ("[U]ne très vieille mystification, qui consiste toujours à placer la Nature au fond de l'Histoire"; "supprimer le poids déterminant de l'Histoire"; "cette zone ultérieure des conduites humaines, là où l'aliénation historique introduit de ces 'différences' que nous appellerons tout simplement ici des 'injustices.'" Roland Barthes, "La Grande Famille des Hommes," in *Mythologies* [Paris: Editions du Seuil, 1957], 196.)

99. Claude Lévi-Strauss, *The Savage Mind* (Chicago: University of Chicago Press, 1966), 262. ("[R]écuser l'équivalence entre la notion d'histoire et celle d'humanité, qu'on prétend nous imposer dans le but inavoué de faire de l'historicité l'ultime refuge d'humanisme transcendantal." Lévi-Strauss, *Œuvres*, 841.)

100. Louis-Jean Calvet, *Roland Barthes: A Biography*, trans. Sarah Wykes (Bloomington: Indiana University Press, 1995), 129–34. See also Claude Lévi-Strauss to Roman Jakobson, August 8 [no year], Box 43, Folder 33, Jakobson Papers.

101. See Lévi-Strauss and Eribon, *Conversations*, 73.

8. THE EMANCIPATION OF DISSONANCE

1. Peyton Boswell, "Defense on Two Fronts," *Art Digest* 16 (December 15, 1941), 3.

2. Sidney Janis, "School of Paris Comes to U.S.," *Decision* 2 (November–December 1941), 95.

3. Daniel-Henry Kahnweiler, "The State of Painting in Paris: 1945 Assessment," trans. Douglas Cooper, *Horizon* 12 (1945): 338.

4. John Bernard Myers, *Tracking the Marvelous: A Life in the New York Art World* (New York: Random House, 1981), 66.

5. I am following an argument made by Kathryn Anne Boyer, "Political Promotion and Institutional Patronage: How New York Displaced Paris as the Center of Contemporary Art, ca. 1935–1968," PhD dissertation, University of Kansas, 1994; Hiroko Ikegami, *The Great Migrator: Robert Rauschenberg and the Global Rise of American Art* (Cambridge, MA: MIT Press, 2010); and Catherine Dossin, *The Rise and Fall of American Art, 1940s–1980s: The Geopolitics of Western Art Worlds* (Burlington, VT: Ashgate, 2015).

6. Richard Kostelanetz, "A Conversation with Robert Rauschenberg," *Partisan Review* 35 (1968): 94.

7. Barbara Rose, *Rauschenberg* (New York: Vintage, 1987), 50 (interview with Rauschenberg).

8. William Seitz, *The Art of Assemblage* (New York: Museum of Modern Art, 1961); Alan R. Solomon, *Robert Rauschenberg* (New York: Jewish Museum, 1963); Leo Steinberg, *Encounters with Rauschenberg: A Lavishly Illustrated Lecture* (Chicago: University of Chicago Press, 2000).

9. Rose, *Rauschenberg*, 20 (interview with Rauschenberg).

10. Calvin Tomkins, *Off the Wall: Robert Rauschenberg and the Art World of Our Time* (Garden City, NY: Doubleday, 1980), 14–25; Reminiscences of Susan Weil, 2014, 1:4, Rauschenberg Oral History Project, Rauschenberg Foundation Archives.

11. John Andrew Rice, *I Came Out of the Eighteenth Century* (New York: Harper and Brothers, 1942), 328.

12. Martin Duberman, *Black Mountain: An Exploration in Community* (Evanston: Northwestern University Press, 1972), 1–39; Ruth Erikson, "A Progressive Education," in Helen Molesworth, ed., *Leap Before You Look: Black Mountain College, 1933–1957* (Boston: Institute of Contemporary Art, 2015), 77–80.

13. See [John Andrew Rice], "A Misadventure in Education, by an Ousted Professor," Black Mountain College Museum and Arts Center Collection, Special Collections and University Archives, D. H. Ramsey Library, University of North Carolina at Asheville.

14. Nicholas Fox Weber, *The Drawings of Josef Albers* (New Haven: Yale University Press,

1984), 2–3; Frederick A. Horowitz and Brenda Danilowitz, *Josef Albers: To Open Eyes; The Bauhaus, Black Mountain College, and Yale* (London: Phaidon, 2006), 1–11.

15. Stefan Bittner, "German Readers of Dewey— Before 1933 and After 1945," in Jürgen Oelkers and Heinz Rhyn, eds., *Dewey and European Education: General Problems and Case Studies* (Dordrecht, Netherlands: Kluwer Academic Publishers, 2000), 83–108.

16. Horowitz and Danilowitz, *Josef Albers*, 16.

17. Neil Welliver, "Albers on Albers," *ARTnews* 64 (January 1966), 48 (interview with Albers).

18. Achim Borchardt-Hume, "Two Bauhaus Histories," in Achim Borchardt-Hume, ed., *Albers and Moholy-Nagy: From Bauhaus to the New World* (London: Tate Publishing, 2006), 67.

19. Nicholas Fox Weber, *The Bauhaus Group: Six Masters of Modernism* (New York: Knopf, 2009), 356.

20. See William H. Jordy, "The Aftermath of the Bauhaus in America: Gropius, Mies, and Breuer," in Donald Fleming and Bernard Bailyn, eds., *The Intellectual Migration: Europe and America, 1930–1960* (Cambridge, MA: Harvard University Press, 1969), 485–543. Cf. Kathleen James-Chakraborty, "From Isolationism to Internationalism: American Acceptance of the Bauhaus," in Kathleen James-Chakraborty, ed., *Bauhaus Culture: From Weimar to the Cold War* (Minneapolis: University of Minnesota Press, 2006), 53–70.

21. Weber, *The Bauhaus Group*, 360 (quoting Anni Albers).

22. Welliver, "Albers on Albers," 51 (interview with Albers).

23. Hans M. Wingler, *The Bauhaus: Weimar, Dessau, Berlin, Chicago*, trans. Wolfgang Jabs and Basil Gilbert (Cambridge, MA: MIT Press, 1969), 9.

24. Nicholas Fox Weber, *Patron Saints: Five Rebels Who Opened America to a New Art, 1928–1942* (New York: Knopf, 1992), 194–204; Katherine Chaddick Reynolds, *Visions and Vanities: John Andrew Rice and Black Mountain College* (Baton Rouge: Louisiana State University Press, 1998), 107–108; Weber, *The Bauhaus Group*, 410–13.

25. Anni and Josef Albers to Wassily and Nina Kandinsky, December 3, 1933, in *Josef Albers and Wassily Kandinsky: Friends in Exile: A Decade of Correspondence, 1929–1940*, ed. Nicholas Fox Weber and Jessica Boisel (Manchester, VT: Hudson Hill Press, 2010), 21. ("[U]nd amerika muss unglaublich gross sein. was wir davon sahen, ist wirklich interessant, besonders die amerikaner. sehr freundlich. wir erleben soviel herzlichkeit wie lange nicht. und soviel jugend u. leben und—kulturinteresse.")

26. See Christopher Benfey, *Red Brick, Black Mountain, White Clay* (New York: Penguin, 2012), 112–41.

27. Weber, *The Bauhaus Group*, 304, 378.

28. Jeffrey Saletnik, "Bauhaus in America," in Molesworth, *Leap Before You Look*, 102–105.

29. Kenneth Silverman, *Begin Again: A Biography of John Cage* (New York: Knopf, 2010), 172.

30. Carl Goldstein, *Teaching Art: Academics and Schools from Vasari to Albers* (Cambridge: Cambridge University Press, 1996), 253–83.

31. Walter Gropius, "Programm des Staatlichen Bauhauses in Weimar," Weimar, [April] 1919.

32. Reginald R. Isaacs, *Walter Gropius: der Mensch und sein Werk*, vol. 1 (Berlin: Mann, 1983), 297–98.

33. See Éva Forgács, "Reinventing the Bauhaus: The 1923 Bauhaus Exhibition as a Turning Point in the Direction of the School," in *Bauhaus: Art as Life* (London: Koenig Books, 2012), 77–82.

34. Duberman, *Black Mountain*, 46.

35. Ibid., 52.

36. See T'ai Smith, *Bauhaus Weaving Theory: From Feminine Craft to Mode of Design* (Minneapolis: University of Minnesota Press, 2014).

37. Julia Brown Turrell, *Rauschenberg Sculpture* (Fort Worth: Modern Art Museum of Fort Worth, 1995), 58–61 (interview with Rauschenberg).

38. "On Rauschenberg" (TS), John Cage Personal Library, John Cage Trust, Red Hook, New York.

39. Andy Oates interview with Karen Thomas, June 5, 2011, Rauschenberg Oral History Project, Rauschenberg Foundation Archives.

40. Tomkins, *Off the Wall*, 32.

41. Reminiscences of Susan Weil, 1:31, 1:33.

42. See Walter Hopps, *Robert Rauschenberg: The Early 1950s* (Houston: Houston Fine Arts Press, 1991), 22–23, 34–37.

43. Reminiscences of Susan Weil, 3:150, 1:45.

44. Hopps, *Robert Rauschenberg*, 44–58.

45. Tom Darter, "John Cage," *Keyboard* 8 (September 1982), 21–22 (interview with Cage).

46. John Cage, *For the Birds* (Boston: Marion Boyars, 1981), 157; Tomkins, *Off the Wall*, 9 (quoting Cage).

47. Tomkins, *Off the Wall*, 70.

48. Turrell, *Rauschenberg Sculpture*, 62 (interview with Rauschenberg). See also Rose, *Rauschenberg*, 48, 34 (interview with Rauschenberg).

49. Silverman, *Begin Again*, 6.

50. Thomas S. Hines, "'Then Not Yet "Cage"': The Los Angeles Years, 1912–1938," in Marjorie Perloff and Charles Junkerman, eds., *John Cage: Composed in America* (Chicago: University of Chicago Press, 1994), 78–81; Christopher Shultis, "Cage and Europe," in David Nicholls, ed., *The Cambridge Companion to John Cage* (Cambridge: Cambridge University

Press, 2002), 20–23; Nigel Warburton, *Ernö Goldfinger: The Life of an Architect* (New York: Routledge, 2004), 1–4.

51. Calvin Tomkins, *Duchamp: A Biography* (New York: Henry Holt, 1996), 148, 181.

52. David Revill, *The Roaring Silence: John Cage, A Life* (New York: Arcade, 1992), 37–49; Kay Larson, *Where the Heart Beats: John Cage, Zen Buddhism, and the Inner Life of Artists* (New York: Penguin, 2012), 39–43.

53. Maurice R. Davie, *Refugees in America: Report of the Committee for the Study of Recent Immigration from Europe* (New York: Harper and Brothers, 1947), 24, 41.

54. Laura Fermi, *Illustrious Immigrants: The Intellectual Migration from Europe, 1930–1941* (Chicago: University of Chicago Press, 1968), 215–33; Anthony Heilbut, *Exiled in Paradise: German Refugee Artists and Intellectuals in America from the 1930s to the Present* (New York: Viking, 1983), 146–59; Jarrell C. Jackman, "German Émigrés in Southern California," in Jarrell C. Jackman and Carla M. Borden, eds., *The Muses Flee Hitler: Cultural Transfer and Adaptation, 1930–1945* (Washington, DC: Smithsonian Institution Press, 1983), 95–110; Dorothy Lamb Crawford, *A Windfall of Musicians: Hitler's Émigrés and Exiles in Southern California* (New Haven: Yale University Press, 2009).

55. Roger Sessions, "Vienna—Vale, Ave," *Modern Music* 15 (1938): 207.

56. Arnold Schoenberg, "Gesinnung oder Erkenntnis?," in Hans W. Heinsheimer and Paul Stefan, eds., *25 Jahre neue Musik, Jahrbuch 1926 der Universal-edition* (Vienna: Universal-Edition, 1926), 30.

57. See Charles Rosen, *Arnold Schoenberg* (New York: Viking, 1975), 23–62.

58. Arnold Schoenberg, *Harmonielehre* (Vienna: Universal-Edition, 1911), 487–88n.

59. Alex Ross, *The Rest Is Noise: Listening to the Twentieth Century* (New York: Farrar, Straus and Giroux, 2007), 53–55, 74–76.

60. Reinhold Brinkmann, *Arnold Schönberg: Drei Klavierstücke Op. 11* (Wiesbaden: Franz Steiner Verlag, 1969), 40. And see Rosen, *Arnold Schoenberg*, 72.

61. John Cage and David Tudor, *Indeterminacy: New Aspect of Form in Instrumental and Electronic Music* (Folkways LP, 1959). Text in John Cage, *Silence* (Middletown: Wesleyan University Press, 1961), 260–73. See also John Cage, "Mosaic," *Kenyon Review* 27 (1965): 535–40.

62. Severine Neff, "Point/Counterpoint: John Cage Studies with Arnold Schoenberg," *Contemporary Music Review* 33 (2014): 451–82; David W. Bernstein, "John Cage, Arnold Schoenberg, and the Musical Idea," in David W. Patterson, ed., *John Cage: Music, Philosophy, and Intention,*

1933–1950 (New York: Routledge, 2002), 15–23; Michael Hicks, "John Cage's Studies with Schoenberg," *American Music* 8 (1990): 125–40; Revill, *The Roaring Silence*, 47–48.

63. Jeff Goldberg, "John Cage," *Transatlantic Review*, nos. 55/56 (May 1976), 104 (interview with Cage).

64. Hicks, "John Cage's Studies with Schoenberg," 128.

65. Arnold Schoenberg, *Theory of Harmony*, 3rd ed., trans. Roy E. Carter (Berkeley: University of California Press, 1978), 2. ("Nur die Bewegung bringt hervor, was man wirklich Bildung nennen könnte . . . Von ihm selbst muss die Bewegung ausgehen, seine Unrast muss sich auf die Schüler übertragen. Dann werden sie suchen wie er." Arnold Schoenberg, *Harmonielehre*, 3rd ed. [Vienna: Universal-Edition, 1922], vii.)

66. Alan P. Lessem, "Teaching Americans Music: Some Emigré Composer Viewpoints, ca. 1930–1955," *Journal of the Arnold Schoenberg Institute* 11 (1988): 13–14.

67. Calvin Tomkins, *The Bride and the Bachelors: Five Masters of the Avant-Garde* (New York: Viking, 1965), 85 (quoting Cage).

68. John Cage, "The Future of Music: Credo," in *Silence*, 5 (original all capitals). Excerpt published in John Cage, *Twenty-Five Year Retrospective Concert of the Music of John Cage* (G. Avakian LP, 1959). Both texts were misdated by Cage; see also David Nicholls, *John Cage* (Urbana: University of Illinois Press, 2006), 21–22.

69. John Cage, "Forerunners of Modern Music," *Tiger's Eye* 7 (March 1949): 52–56.

70. Merce Cunningham, *The Dancer and the Dance* (New York: Marion Boyars, 1985), 33.

71. Merce Cunningham, "The Function of a Technique for Dance," in Walter Sorell, ed., *The Dance Has Many Faces* (Cleveland: World Publishing, 1951), 254.

72. Carolyn Brown, *Chance and Circumstance: Twenty Years with Cage and Cunningham* (New York: Knopf, 2007), 4.

73. Silverman, *Begin Again*, 21.

74. Revill, *The Roaring Silence*, 69–71.

75. Janet Mansfield Soares, "Martha Hill—'With the Future in Mind,'" *Juilliard Journal* (April 1987), 4 (interview with Hill).

76. David Vaughan, *Merce Cunningham: Fifty Years*, ed. Melissa Harris (New York: Aperture, 1997), 20–22.

77. Krisztina Passuth, *Moholy-Nagy*, trans. Éva Grusz, Judy Szöllösy, and László Baránszky (New York: Thames and Hudson, 1985), 69–71.

78. Bill Womack, "The Music of Contingency: An Interview," *Zero* 3 (1979): 69 (interview with Cage).

79. Franz Schulze, *Philip Johnson: Life and Work* (New York: Knopf, 1994), 97; Hines, "'Then

Not Yet "Cage,"'" 84–89; Larson, *Where the Heart Beats*, 30–33.

80. Hines, "'Then Not Yet "Cage,"'" 99n60.

81. Anton Gill, *Art Lover: A Biography of Peggy Guggenheim* (New York: HarperColllins, 2002), 300.

82. Silverman, *Begin Again*, 22–23; Revill, *The Roaring Silence*, 84–89.

83. Womack, "The Music of Contingency," 69.

84. Richard Kostelanetz, "Conversation with John Cage," in Richard Kostelanetz, *John Cage: An Anthology* (New York: Praeger, 1970), 23.

85. David W. Patterson, "Cage and Asia: History and Sources," in Nicholls, *The Cambridge Companion to John Cage*, 48–49.

86. John Cage, "List No. 2," in *John Cage: An Anthology*, 138–39.

87. Larson, *Where the Heart Beats*, 163–66; Patterson, "Cage and Asia," 53.

88. Elliot Caplan, dir., *Cage/Cunningham* (Kultur DVD, 1991); A. Irwin Switzer, *D. T. Suzuki: A Biography*, ed. John Snelling (London: Buddhist Society, 1985), 41–47.

89. Peter Yates, *Twentieth Century Music: Its Evolution from the End of the Harmonic Era into the Present Era of Sound* (New York: Pantheon, 1967), 309; Revill, *The Roaring Silence*, 138–39.

90. Van Meter Ames, "Current Western Interest in Zen," *Philosophy East and West* 10 (1960): 25. See also "Zen: Beat & Square," *Time* 72 (July 21, 1958), 49; Stephen Mahoney, "The Prevalence of Zen," *Nation* 187 (1958), 311–15; Richard Hughes Seager, *Buddhism in America*, rev. ed. (New York: Columbia University Press, 2012), 46–50.

91. Kenneth Slawenski, *J. D. Salinger: A Life* (New York: Random House, 2010), 190; Bernice Goldstein and Sanford Goldstein, "Zen and Nine Stories," *Renascence: Essays on Values in Literature* 22 (1970): 171–82.

92. Rick Fields, *How the Swans Came to the Lake: A Narrative History of Buddhism in America*, 3rd ed. (Boston: Shambhala, 1992), 268–72; Michael Goldberg, dir., *D. T. Suzuki: A Zen Life* (Japan Interculture Foundation DVD, 2005).

93. D. T. Suzuki, *Essays in Zen Buddhism* (London: Ryder, 1949), 26.

94. Richard Kostelanetz, ed., *Conversing with Cage* (New York: Limelight, 1994), 59 (transcript from taped interview with Cage by Lars Gunnar Bodin and Bengt Emil Johnson, for "John Cage: Musical Pleasure," *Ord och Bild* [Stockholm] 74 [January 1, 1965], 142–49); Tomkins, *The Bride and the Bachelors*, 97.

95. Interview with John Cage by Irving Sandler, May 6, 1966, quoted in Richard Kostelanetz, "The Aesthetics of John Cage: A Composite Interview," *Kenyon Review*, n.s., 9 (Autumn 1987): 108.

96. Arnold Schoenberg, *Style and Idea* (New York: Philosophical Library, 1950), 46.

97. Michael Hicks and Christian Asplund, *Christian Wolff* (Urbana: University of Illinois Press, 2012), 5–12; David Patterson, "Cage and Beyond: An Annotated Interview with Christian Wolff," *Perspectives of New Music* 32 (1994): 56–59, 63; Christian Wolff, interview with Ev Grimes, December 30 and 31, 1985, Oral History of American Music, Yale University Library; Cage, *For the Birds*, 43–44; Revill, *The Roaring Silence*, 129–31.

98. James Pritchett, *The Music of John Cage* (Cambridge: Cambridge University Press, 1993), 74–104.

99. Ibid., 78–79; Tomkins, *The Bride and the Bachelors*, 111–12; Revill, *The Roaring Silence*, 134.

100. Merce Cunningham, *Changes: Notes on Choreography*, ed. Frances Starr (New York: Something Else Press, 1968), [64].

101. John Cage, "Goal: New Music, New Dance," *Dance Observer* 9 (1939): 297.

102. "Relation of Arts to Modern Audience," *Vassar Miscellany* 32 (March 3, 1948), 5.

103. Merce Cunningham, "The Impermanent Art," *Seven Arts*, no. 3 (1955): 70.

104. Tomkins, *The Bride and the Bachelors*, 246 (quoting Cunningham).

105. Oral history interview with John Cage, May 2, 1974, Archives of American Art, Smithsonian Institution.

106. Duberman, *Black Mountain*, 300 (quoting Cage).

107. See, e.g., Grace Glueck, "Each Day, Another Albers Pancake," *New York Times*, December 5, 1971, sec. 2, 24.

108. Duberman, *Black Mountain*, 292–98.

109. John Cage, "Defense of Satie," in *John Cage: An Anthology*, 81–82 (probably an abridged compilation of the Black Mountain talks).

110. Duberman, *Black Mountain*, 302 (quoting Penn).

111. Tomkins, *Off the Wall*, 66; Reminiscences of Susan Weil, 1:15–16.

112. Francine du Plessix Gray, "Black Mountain, an American Place," *New York Times Book Review*, July 31, 1977, 3.

113. Charles Olson to Robert Creeley, January 29, 1952, in *The Complete Correspondence of Charles Olson and Robert Creeley*, vol. 9, ed. Richard Blevins (Santa Rosa, CA: Black Sparrow Press, 1990), 63; Duberman, *Black Mountain*, 354–55, 402–403.

114. Amy C. Beal, *New Music, New Allies: American Experimental Music in West Germany from the Zero Hour to Reunification* (Berkeley: University of California Press, 2006), 82–83; John Holzaepfel, "Cage and Tudor," in Nicholls, *The Cambridge Companion to John*

Cage, 169–72; John Holzaepfel, "Reminiscences of a Twentieth-Century Pianist: An Interview with David Tudor," *Musical Quarterly* 78 (1994): 630; David Tudor interview with Teddy Hultberg, May 17 and 18, 1988, davidtudor.org/Articles/hultberg.html-Tudor /Cage.

115. Harold C. Schonberg, "The Far-Out Pianist," *Harper's Magazine* 221 (June 1960), 49–50.

116. See John Cage to David Tudor, ca. January 1951, in John Cage and David Tudor, *Correspondence on Interpretation and Performance*, ed. Martin Iddon (Cambridge: Cambridge University Press, 2013), 7–8.

117. Florence Rubenfeld, *Clement Greenberg: A Life* (Minneapolis: University of Minnesota Press, 1997), 145–46.

118. Cage and Tudor, *Correspondence on Interpretation and Performance*, 13n22.

119. Mary Caroline Richards, "The Theater of Antonin Artaud," *Ararat* 7 (Autumn 1966): 7.

120. Antonin Artaud, *The Theater and Its Double*, trans. Mary Caroline Richards (New York: Grove, 1958), 146, 86, 51. ("[C]ar le théâtre qui ouvre un champ physique demande qu'on remplisse ce champ, qu'on en meuble l'espace avec des gestes, qu'on fasse vivre cet espace en lui-même et magiquement, qu'on y dégage une volière de sons, qu'on trouve des rapports nouveau entre le son, le geste et la voix." Antonin Artaud, *Œuvres complètes*, vol. 4 [Paris: Gallimard, 1955–], 170. "[U]ne anarchie qui s'organise," 62. "[U]ne idée du spectacle total," 104.)

121. Ruth Erikson, "Chance Encounters: Theater Piece No. 1 and Its Prehistory," in Molesworth, *Leap Before You Look*, 298–301; David Patterson, "Two Cages, One College: Cage at Black Mountain College, 1948 and 1952," *Journal of Black Mountain Studies* 4 (Spring 2013), www .blackmountainstudiesjournal.org/wp/?page_id =1866; Lucy Bradnock, "White Noise at Black Mountain," in Kaira M. Cabañas, ed., *Spectres of Artaud: Language and the Arts in the 1950s* (Madrid: Museo Nacional Centro de Arte Reina Sofía, 2012), 64–80; William Fetterman, *John Cage's Theatre Pieces: Notations and Performances* (Amsterdam: Harwood Academic Publishers, 1996), 97–104; Mary Emma Harris, *The Arts at Black Mountain College* (Cambridge, MA: MIT Press, 1987), 226–28; Duberman, *Black Mountain*, 368–79.

122. Michael Kirby and Richard Schechner, "An Interview with John Cage," *Tulane Drama Review* 10 (Winter 1965): 52–53.

123. John Cage, "Juilliard Lecture," *A Year from Monday: New Lectures and Writings* (Middletown: Wesleyan University Press, 1967), 109: Cage, foreword to *Silence*, x.

124. "Projector," JBP 94–24, Folder 172, John Cage Music Manuscript Collection, Performing Arts Research Collections, New York Public Library.

125. David Tudor, "From Piano to Electronics," *Music and Musicians* 20 (1972): 24–26.

126. Klaus Wildenhahn, dir., *John Cage* [1966] (Absolut Medien GmbH DVD, 2010) (Cunningham speaking).

127. Kirby and Schechner, "An Interview with John Cage," 53.

128. Robert Rauschenberg to Betty Parsons, October 18, 1951, reproduced in Hopps, *Robert Rauschenberg*, 230.

129. Kostelanetz, "A Conversation with Robert Rauschenberg," 94.

130. Rose, *Rauschenberg*, 45 (interview with Rauschenberg).

131. John Cage, "On Robert Rauschenberg, Artist, and His Work," *Metro* 4/5 (1961): 43, 38.

132. John Kobler, "'Everything We Do Is Music,'" *Saturday Evening Post* 241 (October 19, 1968), 92 (interview with Cage).

133. Allan Miller and Paul Smaczny, dirs., *John Cage: Journeys in Sound* (Accentus Music DVD, 2012) (Tudor speaking).

134. Kyle Gann, *No Such Thing as Silence: John Cage's 4′ 33″* (New Haven: Yale University Press, 2010), 215–17; "John Cage Uncaged: A Weekend of Musical Mayhem," BBC Press Office, January 12, 2004, www.bbc.co.uk /pressoffice/pressreleases/stories/2004/01 _january/12/john_cage.shtml.

135. Fetterman, *John Cage's Theatre Pieces*, 69–76 (interview with Cage); Gann, *No Such Thing as Silence*, 167–78.

136. John Cage, "The Changing Audience for the Changing Arts: Panel," in Associated Councils for the Arts, *The Arts: Planning for Change* (New York, 1966), 47–48.

137. Cunningham, *The Dancer and the Dance*, 106.

138. Patterson, "Cage and Beyond: An Annotated Interview with Christian Wolff," 57–58.

139. "John Cage's Studio Home," *Junior Bazaar* 2 (June 1946).

140. Brown, *Chance and Circumstance*, 104.

141. Morton Feldman, "Autobiography," in *Essays*, ed. Walter Zimmerman (Kerpen, West Germany: Beginner Press, 1985), 38.

142. Schonberg, "The Far-Out Pianist," 52 (quoting Feldman).

143. Richard Dufallo, *Tracking: Composers Speak with Richard Dufallo* (New York: Oxford University Press, 1989), 109 (interview with Brown).

144. Interview with John Cage by Irving Sandler, May 6, 1966, quoted in Kostelanetz, *Conversing with Cage*, 177.

145. Kostelanetz, *Conversing with Cage*, 176, 178 (transcripts from interview with Cage by Irving Sandler, May 6, 1966, and from tape recording of interview with Cage by Bodin and Johnson, 1965, for "John Cage").

146. Rose, *Rauschenberg*, 49 (interview with Rauschenberg).

147. Tomkins, *Off the Wall*, 84.

148. Ibid., 77 (quoting Ward); Paul Gardner, "The Stable Wasn't 'Just a Gallery,'" *ARTnews* 81 (May 1982), 112; Emily Grenauer, "Musings on Miscellany," *New York Herald Tribune*, December 27, 1953, D6; Harold Rosenberg, "Icon Maker: Barnett Newman," in *The De-Definition of Art: Action Art to Pop to Earthworks* (New York: Horizon, 1972), 91 (quoting Newman).

149. Natalie Edgar, ed., *Club Without Walls: Selections from the Journals of Philip Pavia* (New York: Midmarch Arts Press, 2007), 72.

150. Tomkins, *Off the Wall*, 96–97.

151. Mark Stevens and Annalyn Swan, *De Kooning: An American Master* (New York: Knopf, 2004), 360.

152. Brown, *Chance and Circumstance*, 86.

153. Peter Fuller, "Jasper Johns Interviewed Part II," *Art Monthly*, no. 19 (September 1, 1978), 7.

154. Grace Glueck, "'Once Established,' Says Jasper Johns, 'Ideas Can Be Discarded,'" *New York Times*, October 16, 1977, sec. 2, 31.

155. Subseries IV, C, Folder 14, Calvin Tomkins Papers, Museum of Modern Art (interview with Rosenthal).

156. Lilian Tone, "Chronology," in Kirk Varnedoe, *Jasper Johns: A Retrospective* (New York: Museum of Modern Art, 1996), 118–25; Joan Young and Susan Davidson, "Chronology," in Walter Hopps and Susan Davidson, *Robert Rauschenberg: A Retrospective* (New York: Guggenheim Museum, 1997), 553–55; Barbaralee Diamonstein, *Inside the Art World: Conversations with Barbaralee Diamonstein* (New York: Rizzoli, 1994), 114–20 (interview with Johns); Mark Stevens, "Super Artist: Jasper Johns, Today's Master," *Newsweek* 90 (October 24, 1977), 66–79; Tomkins, *Off the Wall*, 109–19; Interview with Rachel Rosenthal by Karen Thomas, July 26, 2011, Robert Rauschenberg Oral History Project; Oral history interview with Rachel Rosenthal, September 2–3, 1989, Archives of American Art, Smithsonian Institution.

157. Calvin Tomkins, "Everything in Sight: Robert Rauschenberg's New Life," *New Yorker* 81 (May 23, 2005), 76.

158. Rose, *Rauschenberg*, 858 (interview with Rauschenberg); Hopps and Davidson, *Robert Rauschenberg*, 109.

159. Robert Rauschenberg, "Random Order," *Location* 1 (Spring 1963): 27–31.

160. Ann Hindry, "Conversation with Jasper Johns," *Artstudio* [Paris] 12 (Spring 1989), 7.

161. Roberta Bernstein, "Interview with Jasper Johns," *Fragments: Incompletion and Discontinuity* (New York: New York Literary Forum, 1981), 287.

162. David Sylvester, *Interviews with American Artists* (New Haven: Yale University Press, 2001), 134 (transcript of interview with Rauschenberg, August 1964).

163. "His Heart Belongs to Dada," *Time* 73 (May 4, 1959), 58.

164. Yoshiaki Tono, "I Want Images to Free Themselves from Me," *Geijutsu Shincho* [Tokyo] 15 (August 1964), 54–57; interview with Johns, translated from the Japanese by Tadatoshi Higashizono, in Jasper Johns, *Writings, Sketchbook Notes, Interviews*, ed. Kirk Varnedoe (New York: Museum of Modern Art, 1996), 100.

165. André Parinaud, "Un 'misfit' de la peinture New-Yorkaise se confesse," *Arts* [Paris], no. 821 (May 10, 1961), 18. ("Dans cette toile, l'arbre, le rocher, la Vierge ont, tout même importance en même temps. Il n'y a pas de hiérarchie. C'est de qui m'intéresse.")

166. Rose, *Rauschenberg*, 64 (interview with Rauschenberg).

167. Sylvester, *Interviews with American Artists*, 137.

168. Dorothy Gees Seckler, "The Artist Speaks: Robert Rauschenberg," *Art in America* 54 (September–October 1966), 76.

169. Rose, *Rauschenberg*, 60 (interview with Rauschenberg).

170. Tomkins, *Off the Wall*, 135–36.

171. Calvin Tomkins, "A Good Eye and a Good Ear," *New Yorker* 56 (May 26, 1980), 42–47.

172. Oral history interview with Leo Castelli, July 1969, Archives of American Art, Smithsonian Institution.

173. Diamonstein, *Inside the Art World*, 116–17 (interview with Johns).

174. Oral history interview with Leo Castelli, May 14, 1969–June 8, 1973, Archives of American Art, Smithsonian Institution; Tomkins, "A Good Eye and a Good Ear," 52.

175. Oral history interview with Leo Castelli, May 14, 1969–June 8, 1973; Tomkins, *Off the Wall*, 141–42.

176. Rubenfeld, *Clement Greenberg*, 211 (interview with Kramer).

177. Grace Glueck, "Castelli Gives Major Work to the Modern," *New York Times*, May 10, 1989, C15.

178. Tomkins, *Off the Wall*, 142–45; Oral history interview with Leo Castelli, May 14, 1969–June 8, 1973.

179. Silverman, *Begin Again*, 121–22; Revill, *The Roaring Silence*, 144, 179–80.

180. Douglas Kellner and Dan Streible, "Emile de Antonio: Documenting the Life of a Radical Filmmaker," in *Emile de Antonio: A Reader* (Minneapolis: University of Minnesota Press,

2000), 7–10; Revill, *The Roaring Silence*, 190–92; John Cage, *Musicage: Cage Muses on Words, Art, Music*, ed. Joan Rettalack (Middletown: Wesleyan University Press, 2011), 89–90.

181. Richard Kostelanetz and John Cage, "A Conversation About Radio in Twelve Parts," *Bucknell Review* 32, no. 2 (1989), 281–83; Tomkins, *The Bride and the Bachelors*, 127–29; Ross Parmenter, "Music: Experimenter," *New York Times*, May 16, 1958, 20.

182. Martin Iddon, *New Music at Darmstadt: Nono, Stockhausen, Cage, and Boulez* (Cambridge: Cambridge University Press, 2013), 2; Christopher Fox, "Music After Zero Hour," *Contemporary Music Review* 26 (2007): 9.

183. Friedrich Hommel, "How the Province Became International: Early Days of the New Music in Darmstadt," trans. Asa Eldh, *Sonus* 10 (Fall 1989), 73–74.

184. Wolf Lepenies, *The Seduction of Culture in German History* (Princeton: Princeton University Press, 2006), 128–45.

185. JCS 1779, Directive to Commander in Chief of the U.S. Forces of Occupation Regarding the Military Government of Germany, July 11, 1947, Department of State Office of Public Affairs, *Germany, 1947–1949: The Story in Documents* (Washington, DC: U.S. Government Printing Office, 1950), 40. See also Richard J. Aldrich, "OSS, CIA, and European Unity: The American Committee on United Europe, 1948–60," *Diplomacy and Statecraft* 8 (1997): 184–227.

186. Ross, *The Rest Is Noise*, 343–54; David Monod, *Settling Scores: German Music, Denazification, and the Americans, 1945–1953* (Chapel Hill: University of North Carolina Press, 2005); Toby Thacker, "'Playing Beethoven Like an Indian': American Music and Reorientation in Germany, 1945–1955," in Dominik Geppert, ed., *The Postwar Challenge: Cultural, Social, and Political Change in Western Europe, 1945–58* (Oxford: Oxford University Press, 2003), 365–86; Fox, "Music After Zero Hour," 7–9; Iddon, *New Music at Darmstadt*, 11–14.

187. Duberman, *Black Mountain*, 45–46; Amy C. Beal, "Negotiating Cultural Allies: American Music in Darmstadt, 1946–1956," *Journal of the American Musicological Society* 53 (2000): 110–16. Cf. Frances Stonor Saunders, *The Cultural Cold War: The CIA and the World of Arts and Letters* (New York: New Press, 1999), 23–24, where the Darmstadt school is incorrectly referred to as "a bold initiative of the American government."

188. Beal, *New Music, New Allies*, 78–86.

189. Stefan Wolpe, "On New (and Not-so-New) Music in America," trans. Austin Clarkson, *Journal of Music Theory* 28 (1984): 8. ("Alles ist möglich. Alles liegt offen. Das ist die geschichtliche Situation." Wolpe, Appendix to "On New [and Not-So-New] Music in America," 31.)

190. Joan Peyser, *To Boulez and Beyond*, rev. ed. (Lanham, MD: Scarecrow Press, 2008), 188–89.

191. Luigi Nono, "Die Entwicklung der Reihentechnik," *Darmstädter Beiträge zur Neuen Musik* 1 (1958): 34. ("[D]ie man etwa die 'Schule von Darmstadt' nennen könnte und das man im Bereich der bildenden Kunst etwa mit dem vergleichen könnte, was seinerzeit im 'Bauhaus' in Weimar und Dessau geleistet wurde.") See also Luigi Nono, *Scritti e colloqui*, vol. 1, ed. Angela Ida De Benedictis and Veniero Rizzardi (Milan: Ricordi, 2001), 34.

192. Christopher Fox, "Luigi Nono and the Darmstadt School: Form and Meaning in the Early Works (1950–1959)," *Contemporary Music Review* 18 (1999): 111–30.

193. Beal, *New Music, New Allies*, 5, 74–104.

194. John Cage, "Composition as Process," in *Silence*, 36.

195. Cage, "Composition as Process," 53 (all capitals in the original).

196. John Cage, "On the History of Experimental Music in the United States," in *Silence*, 75; see also John Cage, "Zur Geschichte der experimentellen Musik in den Vereinigten Staaten," trans. Heinz-Klaus Metzger, *Darmstädter Beiträge* 2 (1959): 46–53.

197. William Duckworth, *Talking Music: Conversations with John Cage, Philip Glass, Laurie Anderson, and Five Generations of American Experimental Composers* (New York: Schirmer Books, 1995), 197.

198. Luigi Nono, "The Historical Reality of Music Today," *Score* 27 (July 1960), 42, 44, 45. See also Nono, *Scritti e colloqui*, vol. 1, 46–53.

199. See Angela Ida De Benedictus, "Open Form in the United States and Europe: Freedom from Control vs. Control of Freedom," in Felix Meyer, Carol J. Oja, Wolfgang Rathers, and Anne C. Shreffler, eds., *Crosscurrents: American and European Music in Interaction, 1900–2000* (Woodbridge, UK: Boydell Press, 2014), 411–24.

200. Paul van Emmerik, ed., *A John Cage Companion*, cagecomp.home.xs4all.nl/.

201. Revill, *The Roaring Silence*, 194–96; Silverman, *Begin Again*, 166–68.

202. See Lynn Zelevansky, "Dorothy Miller's 'Americans,' 1942–63," *Studies in Modern Art* 4 (1994): 57–93.

203. Dorothy Miller, ed., *Sixteen Americans* (New York: Museum of Modern Art, 1959), n.p.

204. Paul Taylor, "Interview with Robert Rauschenberg," *Interview* 20 (December 1990), 147.

205. Annie Cohen-Solal, *Leo and His Circle: The Life of Leo Castelli*, trans. Mark Polizzotti with the author (New York: Knopf, 2011), 254–55.

206. Ikegami, *The Great Migrator*, 19.
207. K. G. Hultén, *4 Amerikanare: Jasper Johns, Alfred Leslie, Robert Rauschenberg, Richard Stankiewicz* (Stockholm: Moderna Museet, 1962), 5. ("[M]an har kort sagt farit till Paris för att lära sig måla, och sedan aldrig helt kommit därifrån. Men nu är det inte längre så, det är som om en uppdämd flod sluppit lös . . . Efter andra världskriget har de största äventyren i bildkonsten utspelat sig i Amerika, det intressantaste måleriet tilldrar sig i New York.")
208. Tomkins, *Off the Wall*, 189–90; Ikegami, *The Great Migrator*, 107–11; Dossin, *The Rise and Fall of American Art*, 165–69.
209. See James English, *The Economy of Prestige: Prizes, Awards, and the Circulation of Cultural Value* (Cambridge, MA: Harvard University Press, 2005), 249–63.
210. See Dossin, *The Rise and Fall of American Art*, 21–25; Nancy Jachec, *Politics and Painting at the Venice Biennale, 1948–64: Italy and the Idea of Europe* (Manchester, UK: Manchester University Press, 2007); Adrian R. Duran, *Painting, Politics, and the New Front of Cold War Italy* (Farnham, UK: Ashgate, 2014).
211. Donald Sassoon, *Contemporary Italy: Politics, Economy, and Society Since 1945* (London: Longman, 1986), 31; Paul Ginsborg, *A History of Contemporary Italy: Society and Politics, 1943–1988* (New York: Palgrave Macmillan, 2003), 239–53.
212. "Seven New Shows: Subtle . . . Simple . . . Sure . . . Surprising," *Newsweek* 61 (February 18, 1963), 65.
213. Cage, "On Robert Rauschenberg," 37.
214. Steven Naifeh and Gregory White Smith, *Jackson Pollock: An American Saga* (New York: Clarkson N. Potter, 1989), 605–606; "Chaos, Damn It!," *Time* 56 (November 20, 1950), 72.
215. Leo Castelli to Bruno Alfieri, January 13 and 28, 1961, Alfieri to Castelli, January 17, 1961, Box 1, Folder 15, Leo Castelli Gallery Records, Archives of American Art, Smithsonian Institution.
216. Ken Johnson, "Leo Steinberg, Art Historian, Dies at 90," *New York Times*, March 14, 2011, B19.
217. Hopps, *Robert Rauschenberg* 161 (interview with Steinberg).
218. Leo Steinberg, "Back Talk from Leo Steinberg," in Susan Brundage, ed., *Jasper Johns, 35 Years: Leo Castelli* (New York: Harry N. Abrams, 1993), n.p. See also Steinberg's note in Box 9, Folder 6, Leo Steinberg Research Papers, Getty Research Institute.
219. Josh Greenfeld, "Sort of the Svengali of Pop," *New York Times Magazine*, May 8, 1966, 45–46.
220. Leo Steinberg to Leo Castelli, July 21, 1962, Box 20, Folder 39, Leo Castelli Gallery Records; Invoice dated November 8, 1962, Box 20, Folder 39, Leo Castelli Gallery Records.
221. Gillo Dorflès, "Jasper Johns and the Hand-made Ready-made Object," *Metro* 4/5 (1962): 81.
222. Leo Steinberg, "Jasper Johns," *Metro* 4/5 (1962): 92, 100.
223. April Bernard and Mimi Thompson, "Johns on . . . ," *Vanity Fair* 47 (February 1984), 65.
224. Philip Rylands and Enzo Di Martino, *Flying the Flag for Art: The United States and the Venice Biennale, 1895–1991* (Richmond, VA: Wyldbore and Wolferstan, 1993), 139.
225. Oral history interview with Lois A. Bingham, April 16, 1981, Archives of American Art, Smithsonian Institution.
226. Alan Solomon to Leo Castelli, November 25, 1963, Box 20, Folder 14, Leo Castelli Gallery Records. See also Cohen-Solal, *Leo and His Circle*, 271–72.
227. Clement Greenberg, "Louis and Noland," in *Collected Essays and Criticism*, vol. 4, *Modernism with a Vengeance, 1957–1969*, ed. John O'Brian (Chicago: University of Chicago Press, 1993), 94–100.
228. Alan R. Solomon, "Americans in Venice at the Biennale," *Art Gallery* 7 (June 1964), 14.
229. See Alan Solomon to Leo Castelli, August 3, 1964, Box 20, Folder 14, Leo Castelli Gallery Records.
230. Kirk Varnedoe, *Cy Twombly: A Retrospective* (New York: Museum of Modern Art, 1994), 25–31; Dossin, *The Rise and Fall of American Art*, 69–70.
231. Alan Solomon to Mario Labroca, n.d. [1963], draft, Alan R. Solomon Papers, Archives of American Art, Smithsonian Institution.
232. Greenfeld, "Sort of the Svengali of Pop," 40; Brown, *Chance and Circumstance*, 384–85; Calvin Tomkins, "The Big Show in Venice," *Harper's Magazine* 229 (April 1965), 98–104; Ikegami, *The Great Migrator*, 69–94; Cohen-Solal, *Leo and His Circle*, 286–304; Laurie J. Monahan, "Cultural Cartography: American Designs at the 1964 Venice Biennale," in Serge Guilbaut, ed., *Reconstructing Modernism: Art in New York, Paris, and Montreal, 1945–1964* (Cambridge, MA: MIT Press, 1990), 369–407.
233. Ikegami, *The Great Migrator*, 94–101.
234. See Alan Solomon to Leo Castelli, August 3, 1964, Solomon Papers.
235. Rosalind Constable, "Art Pops In: Europe Explodes as American Takes the Prize," *Life* 57 (July 10, 1964), 65–68.
236. Tomkins, "A Good Eye and a Good Ear," 67. See also Burt Chernow, *Christo and Jean-Claude: An Authorized Biography* (New York: St. Martin's Griffin, 2000), 138 (interview with Kramer).
237. Alan Solomon to Leo Castelli, August 3, 1964, Box 20, Folder 14, Leo Castelli Papers, Archives of American Art, Smithsonian Institution.

238. Alan Solomon to Lois Bingham, n.d. [1964], Solomon Papers.

239. Subseries IV, C, Folder 1, Tomkins Papers (interview with Solomon).

240. Cohen-Solal, *Leo and His Circle*, 295. I do not have independent confirmation of these meetings.

241. See Monahan, "Cultural Cartography," 406–407.

242. Daniel Cordier, letter to the editor, *Arts Magazine* 38 (September 1964), 7.

243. Pierre Cabanne, *Dialogues with Marcel Duchamp*, trans. Ron Padgett (New York: Viking, 1971), 96.

244. Michel Ragon, "Rauschenberg: La vedette de l'école de New York," *Arts* [Paris], no. 1011 (June 23–July 6, 1965), 4.

245. Silverman, *Begin Again*, 182–85.

246. Merce Cunningham, "*Story*: Tale of a Dance and a Tour," *Dance Ink* 6 (Spring 1995): 16–21 (Summer 1995), 19–22 (Fall 1995), 32–36; Brown, *Chance and Circumstance*, 375–446; Vaughan, *Merce Cunningham*, 134–46.

247. Cunningham, "*Story*," 36.

248. Alain Jouffroy, "R. Rauschenberg," *L'Oeil*, no. 113 (May 1964), 34.

249. P. C. [Pierre Cabanne], "Les Plus grands artistes revelés depuis 20 ans," *Arts* [Paris], no. 1011 (June 23–July 6, 1965), 1–3.

9. NORTHERN SONGS

1. Talcott Parsons, "Age and Sex in the Social Structure of the United States," *American Sociological Review* 7 (1942): 606–607.

2. Elliot E. Cohen, "A 'Teen-Age Bill of Rights,'" *New York Times Magazine*, January 7, 1945, 16, 54; Kelly Schrum, *Some Wore Bobby Sox: The Emergence of Teenage Girls' Culture, 1920–1945* (New York: Palgrave Macmillan, 2004), 2; Jon Savage, *Teenage: The Creation of Youth Culture* (New York: Viking, 2007), 448–53; Grace Palladino, *Teenagers: An American History* (New York: Basic Books, 1996), 96–115; Lizabeth Cohen, *A Consumer's Republic: The Politics of Mass Consumption in Postwar America* (New York: Knopf, 2003), 318–19; Dwight Macdonald, "A Caste, a Culture, a Marketplace," *New Yorker* 34 (November 22, 1958), 57–94, and (November 29, 1958), 57–107; Louis Kraar, "Teenage Customers: Merchants Seek Teens' Dollars, Influence Now, Brand Loyalty Later," *Wall Street Journal*, December 6, 1956, 1. See also *OED*, "Teen-age, 2. Pertaining to, suitable for, or characteristic of a young person in his or her teens."

3. J. Milton Yinger, "Contraculture and Subculture," *American Sociological Review* 25 (1960): 625–35; Talcott Parsons, *The Social System* (Glencoe, IL: Free Press, 1951), 522; James S. Coleman, *The Adolescent: The Social Life of the Teenager and Its Impact on Education* (New York: Free Press of Glencoe, 1961), 329.

4. Cf., e. g., Landon Y. Jones, *Great Expectations: America and the Baby Boom Generation* (New York: Coward, McCann, and Geoghegan, 1980).

5. Based on "Live births, deaths, marriages, and divorces: 1909–1970," U.S. Bureau of the Census, *Historical Statistics of the United States: Colonial Times to 1970*, vol. 1 (Washington, DC: U.S. Government Printing Office, 1975), 49. See also Louis Menand, "You Say It's Your Birthday," *New Republic* 198 (April 18, 1988), 34–40; Richard Pells, *War Babies: The Generation That Changed America* (n.p.: Cultural History Press, 2014).

6. Judy Clavir and John Spitzer, eds., *The Conspiracy Trial* (Indianapolis: Bobbs-Merrill, 1970), 344 (transcript of trial proceedings in *United States v. Dellinger et al.*).

7. Schrum, *Some Wore Bobby Sox*, 1–6; Elaine Tyler May, *Homeward Bound: American Families in the Cold War Era*, rev. ed. (New York: Basic Books, 1999), 148–49; Macdonald, "A Caste, a Culture, a Marketplace," 73–74, 82–83; Karal Ann Marling, *As Seen on TV: The Visual Culture of Everyday Life in the 1950s* (Cambridge, MA: Harvard University Press, 1994), 158. I am indebted to Kaitlin Terry, "The Origins of Teenage Culture: Girls, Style, and Consumerism in the American High School, 1945–1956," senior thesis, Harvard College, 2012.

8. Schrum, *Some Wore Bobby Sox*, 122–26; Joel Williamson, *Elvis Presley: A Southern Life* (New York: Oxford University Press, 2015), xviii–xx, 39–40.

9. Table 9: Enrollment in regular public and private elementary schools, by grade level: 1869–70 to fall 1992, National Center for Education Statistics, *120 Years of American Education: A Statistical Portrait*, ed. Thomas D. Snyder (Washington, DC: NCES, 1993), 37.

10. See Claudia Goldin and Lawrence F. Katz, *The Race Between Education and Technology* (Cambridge, MA: Harvard University Press, 2008), 163–246.

11. Martin Trow, "The Second Transformation of American Secondary Education," *International Journal of Comparative Sociology* 2 (1961): 144–66; Claudia Goldin, "Labor Markets in the Twentieth Century," in Stanley L. Engerman and Robert E. Gallman, eds., *The Cambridge Economic History of the United States*, vol. 3, *The Twentieth Century* (New York: Cambridge University Press, 2000), 560 (figures are rounded).

12. Persons enrolled in school by single years of age from five to twenty, by sex: 1920 to 1950, *Statistical Abstract of the United States, 1954* (Washington, DC: U.S. Government Printing Office, 1954), 115 (figures are rounded).

13. Claudia Goldin, "America's Graduation from High School: The Evolution and Spread of Secondary Schooling in the Twentieth Century," *Journal of Economic History* 58 (1998): 345–74.

14. Table 22: Education Qualification of Italians Over Six Years of Age, Paul Ginsborg, *A History of Contemporary Italy: Society and Politics, 1943–1988* (New York: Palgrave Macmillan, 2003), 440.

15. Table 2: Comparative Education Data for Youth 14 to 18 Years Old: Great Britain and the United States, Claudia Goldin and Lawrence F. Katz, "Why the United States Led in Education: Lessons from Secondary School Expansion, 1910 to 1940," National Bureau of Economic Research Working Paper No. 6144, August, 1997; Pupils enrolled in school as percentage of age group by level of education and country, about 1955, J. Frederic Dewhurst, John O. Coppock, and P. Lamartine Yates, *Europe's Needs and Resources: Trends and Prospects in Eighteen Countries* (New York: Twentieth Century Fund, 1961), 315. See also A. M. Carr-Saunders, D. Caradog Jones, and C. A. Moser, *A Survey of Social Conditions in England and Wales* (Oxford: Clarendon Press, 1958), 57–58. (All figures are rounded.)

16. Roger Geiger, "The Ten Generations of American Higher Education," in Philip G. Altbach, Robert O. Berdahl, and Patricia J. Gumport, eds., *American Higher Education in the Twenty-First Century: Social, Political, and Economic Challenges* (Baltimore: Johns Hopkins University Press, 1999), 61–63; Total fall enrollment in degree-granting postsecondary institutions, by attendance status, sex of student, and control of institution: selected years, 1947 through 2023, U.S. Department of Education, Digest of Education Statistics, nces.ed.gov/programs /digest/d13/tables/dt13_303.10.asp (figures are rounded).

17. Table 5.1: Educational enrollment rates per 1,000 population under age 20, 1950–2000, Mary Mahony, "Employment, Education, and Human Capital," in Roderick Floud and Paul Johnson, eds., *The Cambridge Economic History of Modern Britain*, vol. 3, *Structural Change and Growth, 1939–2000* (Cambridge: Cambridge University Press, 2004), 119.

18. Leonard Gross, "John Lennon: Beatle on His Own," *Look* 30 (December 13, 1966), 66 (interview with Lennon).

19. Simon Frith et al., *The History of Live Music in Britain*, vol. 1, *1950–1967* (London: Routledge, 2016), 8, 94.

20. Andrew Blake, "Americanisation and Popular Music in Britain," in Neil Campbell, Jude Davies, and George McKay, eds., *Issues in Americanisation and Culture* (Edinburgh: Edinburgh

University Press, 2004), 147–62; Roberta Freund Schwartz, *How Britain Got the Blues: The Transmission and Reception of American Blues Style in the United Kingdom* (Burlington, VT: Ashgate, 2007), 1–71; Russell Sanjek, *Pennies from Heaven: The American Popular Music Business in the Twentieth Century* (New York: Da Capo, 1996), 379–80.

21. Daniel Immerwahr, *How to Hide an Empire: A History of the Greater United States* (New York: Farrar, Straus and Giroux, 2018), 357–58.

22. Bill Harry, *Bigger Than the Beatles* (Liverpool: Trinity Mirror NW, 2009), 42–58; Spencer Leigh, *The Best of Fellas: The Story of Bob Wooler, Liverpool's First D.J.* (Liverpool: Drivegreen Publications, 2002), 123–29; Mark Lewisohn, *All These Years*, vol. 1, *Tune In* (London: Little, Brown 2013), 482n; Sanjek, *Pennies from Heaven*, 379; André Millard, *Beatlemania: Technology, Business, and Teen Culture in Cold War America* (Baltimore: Johns Hopkins University Press, 2012), 72–77, 87–102.

23. "Rock 'n' Roll," *Life* 38 (April 18, 1955), 166.

24. Peter Guralnick, *Last Train to Memphis: The Rise of Elvis Presley* (Boston: Little, Brown, 1994), 271–72. Cf. "The Elvis Presley Story: He's Making Monkeys out of Singers," *Variety*, May 9, 1956, 1, 63.

25. Lutgard Mutsaers, "Indorock: An Early Euro-rock Style," *Popular Music* 9 (1990): 307–20; Franco Minganti, "Jukebox Boys: Postwar Italian Music and the Culture of Covering," in Heide Fehrenbach and Uta G. Poiger, *Transactions, Transgressions, Transformations: American Culture in Western Europe and Japan* (New York: Berghahn Books, 2000), 153–54; Uta G. Poiger, *Jazz, Rock, and Rebels: Cold War Politics and American Culture in a Divided Germany* (Berkeley: University of California Press, 2000), 168–205; "Rock 'n' Roll Exported to 4 Corners of Globe," *New York Times*, February 23, 1957, 12; "Global Report on Rock 'n' Roll," *New York Times Magazine*, April 20, 1958, 25, 56, 58–61; Linda Martin and Kerry Segrave, *Anti-Rock: The Opposition to Rock 'n' Roll* (Hamden, CT: Archon Books, 1988); Timothy W. Ryback, *Rock Around the Bloc: A History of Rock Music in Eastern Europe and the Soviet Union* (New York: Oxford University Press, 1990), 20–24. See also Gertrude Samuels, "Why They Rock 'n' Roll—And Should They?," *New York Times Magazine*, January 12, 1958, 17, 19.

26. Philip H. Ennis, *The Seventh Stream: The Emergence of Rocknroll in American Popular Music* (Hanover: Wesleyan University Press, 1992), 46, 52–54, 58–61; Sanjek, *Pennies from Heaven*, 38.

27. Donald Clarke, *The Rise and Fall of Popular Music* (New York: St. Martin's, 1995), 253–55.

28. André Millard, *America on Record: A History of Recorded Sound* (New York: Cambridge University Press, 1995), 158–75; Nat Shapiro, ed., *Popular Music: An Annotated Index of American Popular Songs*, vol. 2, *1940–1949* (New York: Adrian Press, 1965), 5–7; John Ryan, *The Production of Culture in the Music Industry: The ASCAP–BMI Controversy* (Lanham, MD: University Press of America, 1985), 53–100; Ennis, *The Seventh Stream*, 63–64, 106.

29. Clarke, *The Rise and Fall of Popular Music*, 256; Ennis, *The Seventh Stream*, 135–37, 167.

30. Tyler Cowen, *In Praise of Commercial Culture* (Cambridge, MA: Harvard University Press, 1998), 164; Vincent Lynch and Bill Henkin, *Jukebox: The Golden Age* (Berkeley: Lancaster-Miller, 1981), 10, 19, 110.

31. See Robert Bornstein, "Exposure and Affect: Overview and Meta-analysis of Research, 1968–1987," *Psychological Bulletin* 106 (1989): 265–89.

32. *Statistical Abstract of the United States, 1964* (Washington, DC: U.S. Government Printing Office, 1964), 826.

33. Richard James Burgess, *The History of Music Production* (New York: Oxford University Press, 2014), 67–69; Cowen, *In Praise of Commercial Culture*, 164–65; Sanjek, *Pennies from Heaven*, 234, 245–46, 343; Ennis, *The Seventh Stream*, 101–102, 113–18, 132–33, 164, 229; Charlie Gillett, *The Sound of the City: The Rise of Rock and Roll*, rev. ed. (New York: Pantheon, 1983), 39.

34. Richard Crawford, *America's Musical Life: A History* (New York: W. W. Norton, 2001), 721–34; Peter Guralnick, *Sam Phillips: The Man Who Invented Rock 'n' Roll* (New York: Little, Brown, 2015), 178.

35. Ennis, *The Seventh Stream*, 173–74; Guralnick, *Sam Phillips*, 60–62; Guralnick, *Last Train to Memphis*, 39; Louis Cantor, *Dewey and Elvis: The Life and Times of a Rock 'n' Roll Deejay* (Urbana: University of Illinois Press, 2005), 64–67.

36. Gillett, *The Sound of the City*, 7–11; Burgess, *The History of Music Production*, 58–60; Ennis, *The Seventh Stream*, 176.

37. Gillett, *The Sound of the City*, 14.

38. School enrollment, by age, race, and sex, 1953 to 1970, and by age and sex, 1940 to 1952, United States Bureau of the Census, *Historical Statistics of the United States*, vol. 1, 371.

39. James Miller, *Flowers in the Dustbin: The Rise of Rock and Roll, 1947–1977* (New York: Simon and Schuster, 1999), 57–61.

40. John A. Jackson, *Big Beat Heat: Alan Freed and the Early Years of Rock & Roll* (New York: Schirmer, 1991), 1–3, 32–36; Palladino, *Teenagers*, 121–23.

41. See George Lipsitz, "Land of a Thousand Dances: Youth, Minorities, and the Rise of Rock and Roll," in Lary May, ed., *Recasting America: Culture and Politics in the Age of the Cold War* (Chicago: University of Chicago Press, 1989), 267–301.

42. Jackson, *Big Beat Heat*, 64–71; Bob Rolontz and Joel Friedman, "Teen-Agers Demand Music with a Beat, Spur Rhythm-Blues," *Billboard* 66 (April 24, 1954), 1, 18, 50; Abbie Hoffman, *Woodstock Nation: A Talk-Rock Album* (New York: Random House, 1969), 24, corroborated in Jonah Raskin, *For the Hell of It: The Life and Times of Abbie Hoffman* (Berkeley: University of California Press, 1996), 16.

43. "1955: The Year R&B Took Over Pop Field," *Billboard* 67 (November 12, 1955), 126; Gillett, *The Sound of the City*, 53–54.

44. Clarke, *The Rise and Fall of Popular Music*, 419; Guralnick, *Sam Phillips*, 257–72; Elijah Wald, *How the Beatles Destroyed Rock 'n' Roll: An Alternative History of American Popular Music* (New York: Oxford University Press, 2009), 180.

45. See Larry Starr and Christopher Waterman, *American Popular Music: From Minstrelsy to MTV* (New York: Oxford University Press, 2003), 122–26.

46. Herm Schoenfeld, "R&B Big Beat in Pop Music: Teenagers Like 'Hot Rod' Tempo," *Variety*, January 19, 1955, 54.

47. Elvis Presley, Memphis press conference, February 25, 1961, www.youtube.com/watch?v=Fxpz-qv0-7E, 1:38.

48. See Louie Robinson, "The Truth About That Elvis Presley Rumor: 'The Pelvis' Gives His Views on Vicious Anti-Negro Slur," *Jet* 12 (August 1, 1957), 60.

49. Guralnick, *Last Train to Memphis*, 11–91.

50. Guralnick, *Sam Phillips*, 212 (interview with Moore); Lee Cotton, *All Shook Up: Elvis Day by Day, 1954–1977*, 2nd ed. (Ann Arbor, MI: Popular Culture, Ink, 1998), 29–30. There are numerous variants. Cf. Colin Escott with Martin Hawkins, *Good Rockin' Tonight: Sun Records and the Birth of Rock 'n' Roll* (New York: St. Martin's, 1991), 63–65; Jerry Hopkins, *Elvis: A Biography* (New York: Warner Books, 1971), 61–63; Kevin Crouch and Tanja Crouch, *Sun King: The Life and Times of Sam Phillips, the Man Behind Sun Records* (London: Platkus, 2008), 71–74; Scotty Moore and James L. Dickerson, *Scotty and Elvis: Aboard the Mystery Train* (Jackson: University Press of Mississippi, 2013), 53–56.

51. Guralnick, *Sam Phillips*, 214–17; "Talent: Elvis Presley," *Billboard* 66 (August 7, 1954), 39.

52. Clarke, *The Rise and Fall of Popular Music*, 388–89. I am grateful to Jerry Zolten for pointing out the Big Joe Turner connection.

53. Guralnick, *Sam Phillips*, 207.

54. Presley, Memphis press conference, 2:30.

55. Robinson, "The Truth About That Elvis Presley Rumor," 60.

56. Ennis, *The Seventh Stream*, 174–76.

57. Ibid., 225, 227; Clarke, *The Rise and Fall of Popular Music*, 374–79.

58. "A Howling Hillbilly Success," *Life* 40 (April 30, 1956), 64.

59. Sanjek, *Pennies from Heaven*, 444.

60. Ed Ward, Geoffrey Stokes, and Ken Tucker, *Rock of Ages: The Rolling Stone History of Rock 'n' Roll* (New York: Rolling Stone Press, 1986), 75.

61. George Lipsitz, *Midnight at the Barrelhouse: The Johnny Otis Story* (Minneapolis: University of Minnesota Press, 2010), xviii (interview with Otis).

62. Jerry Leiber and Mike Stoller, *Hound Dog: The Leiber and Stoller Autobiography* (New York: Simon and Schuster, 2009), 61–62.

63. "Discography," www.leiberstoller.com/Discography.html.

64. Ward et al., *Rock of Ages*, 75.

65. Cotton, *All Shook Up*, 90.

66. Miller, *Flowers in the Dustbin*, 129–37.

67. Peter Guralnick and Ernst Jorgensen, *Elvis Day by Day* (New York: Ballantine, 1999), 77–78.

68. Elvis Presley, Carl Perkins, Jerry Lee Lewis, and Johnny Cash, *The Complete Million Dollar Quartet* (RCA/Sony BMG CD, 2006).

69. Elijah Wald, *Escaping the Delta: Robert Johnson and the Invention of the Blues* (New York: HarperCollins, 2004), 58, 118, 218, 233; Clarke, *The Rise and Fall of Popular Music*, 374, 378. See also Philip Tagg, "Open Letter: 'Black Music,' 'Afro-American Music,' and 'European Music,'" *Popular Music* 8 (1989): 79–84, 285–98; Reebee Garofalo, "Crossing Over: 1939–1989," in Jannette L. Dates and William Barlow, eds., *Split Image: African Americans in the Mass Media* (Washington, DC: Howard University Press, 1990), esp. 73–90; Simon Frith, *Performing Rites: On the Value of Popular Music* (Cambridge, MA: Harvard University Press, 1996), 123–44; Karl Hagstrom Miller, *Segregating Sound: Inventing Folk and Pop Music in the Age of Jim Crow* (Durham: Duke University Press, 2010); Jack Hamilton, *Just Around Midnight: Rock and Roll and the Racial Imagination* (Cambridge, MA: Harvard University Press, 2016).

70. Jann Wenner, "The *Rolling Stone* Interview: John Lennon, Part One: The Working Class Hero," *Rolling Stone*, no. 74 (January 7, 1971), 40.

71. *The Beatles Anthology* (San Francisco: Chronicle Books, 2000), 103 (Harrison).

72. *The Beatles Anthology*, 266 (Taylor).

73. Lewisohn, *All These Years*, 670–71; *The Beatles Anthology*, 70 (Harrison). Cf. Philip Norman, *Shout! The Beatles in Their Generation* (New York: Simon and Schuster, 1981), 165; George

Martin with Jeremy Hornsby, *All You Need Is Ears* (New York: St. Martin's, 1979), 126.

74. Guilbert Gates, "A Song-by-Song Look at What Made George Martin the Fifth Beatle," *New York Times*, March 15, 2016 (online).

75. Martin, *All You Need Is Ears*, 166.

76. Clive Ashwin, *A Century of Art Education, 1882–1982* (Middlesex Polytechnic, 1982), 35–41; Simon Frith and Howard Horne, *Art into Pop* (London: Methuen, 1987), 39–41, 71–94; George Melly, *Revolt into Style: The Pop Arts* (Oxford: Oxford University Press, 1989), 146; Simon Frith, *Sound Effects: Youth, Leisure, and the Politics of Rock 'n' Roll* (New York: Pantheon, 1981), 75–76; Stuart Macdonald, *The History and Philosophy of Art Education* (London: University of London Press, 1970), 261; Robert Hewison, *Too Much: Art and Society in the Sixties, 1960–75* (New York: Oxford University Press, 1987), 62–64.

77. Mike Evans, *The Art of the Beatles* (New York: Beech Tree Books, 1984), 10–17; Alan Clayson and Pauline Sutcliffe, *Backbeat: Stuart Sutcliffe, The Lost Beatle* (London: Pan Books, 1994), 34–55; Bob Spitz, *The Beatles: The Biography* (Boston: Little Brown, 2005), 105–108.

78. Lewisohn, *All These Years*, 378, 365.

79. Ibid., 652.

80. Nigel Whiteley, "Toward a Throw-Away Culture: Consumerism, Style Obsolescence, and Cultural Theory in the 1950s and 1960s," *Oxford Art Journal* 10, no. 2 (1987), 20.

81. Dominic Sandbrook, *Never Had It So Good: A History of Britain from Suez to the Beatles* (London: Little, Brown, 2005), 384–453; Millard, *Beatlemania*, 138–39.

82. Table 1: Expenditure by Teenagers, 1957, Mark Abrams, *The Teenage Consumer* (London: London Press Exchange, 1959), 10.

83. Dave Laing, "Six Boys, Six Beatles: The Formative Years, 1950–1962," in Kenneth Womack, ed., *The Cambridge Companion to the Beatles* (Cambridge: Cambridge University Press, 2009), 24–26.

84. Martin, *All You Need Is Ears*, 53–55, 85–100.

85. "Beatlemania!," *Daily Mail*, October 21, 1963, 3.

86. Mark Lewisohn, *The Complete Beatles Chronicle* (London: Pyramid Books, 1992), 136–39; Dave McAleer, *The All Music Book of Hit Singles* (San Francisco: Miller Freeman Books, 1996), 93; Jonathan Gould, *Can't Buy Me Love: The Beatles, Britain, and America* (New York: Harmony Books, 2007), 3–6; Sanjek, *Pennies from Heaven*, 382–83.

87. Clarence Newman, "The Beatles Craze Threatens Big Dent in Parents' Wallets," *Wall Street Journal*, February 12, 1964, 1.

88. Bill Harry, *The British Invasion: How the Beatles*

and Other U.K. Bands Conquered America (New Malden, UK: Chrome Dreams, 2004), 12–20.

89. Norman, *Shout!*, 220.

90. Millard, *Beatlemania*, 124–26; Gould, *Can't Buy Me Love*, 106.

91. Millard, *Beatlemania*, 19. See www.youtube .com/watch?v=hgU6foVr-wY (an abridgement).

92. Alan Clayson, *Ringo Starr* (London: Sanctuary, 2003), 124, and see www.beatlesinterviews.org /db1964.0205.beatles.html.

93. Albert Maysles, David Maysles, Kathy Dougherty, and Susan Froemke, dirs., *What's Happening! The Beatles in the U.S.A.* (1964), rereleased in an edited version as *The Beatles: The First U.S. Visit* (Apple DVD, 1991); Paul Gardner, "The Beatles Invade, Complete with Long Hair and Screaming Fans," *New York Times*, February 8, 1964, 59; "The Unbarbershopped Quartet," *Time* 83 (February 21, 1964), 47. Variants abound: e.g., Geoffrey Giuliano and Brenda Giuliano, *The Lost Beatles Interviews* (London: Virgin Books, 1994), 13–14; Hunter Davies, *The Beatles*, 2nd ed. (New York: McGraw Hill, 1985), 195–96; Norman, *Shout!*, 221; Spitz, *The Beatles*, 460.

94. "What the Beatles Prove about Teenagers," *U.S. News & World Report* 56 (February 24, 1964), 88 (interview with Riesman).

95. Ian Inglis, "'The Beatles Are Coming!': Conjecture and Conviction in the Myth of Kennedy, America, and the Beatles," *Popular Music and Society* 24 (2000): 95–97; Steve Chapple and Reebee Garofolo, *Rock 'n' Roll Is Here to Pay* (Chicago: Nelson-Hall, 1977), 49–52; Paul Friedlander, *Rock and Roll: A Social History* (Boulder: Westview, 1996), 42–66; Clarke, *The Rise and Fall of Popular Music*, 401.

96. Ronald D. Cohen, *Rainbow Quest: The Folk Music Revival and American Society, 1940–1970* (Amherst: University of Massachusetts Press, 2002), 125–228; David Hajdu, *Positively 4th Street: The Lives and Times of Joan Baez, Bob Dylan, Mimi Baez Fariña, and Richard Fariña* (New York: Farrar, Straus and Giroux, 2001), 190, 192.

97. Lewisohn, *All These Years*, 419–23; Hamilton, *Just Around Midnight*, 123–45.

98. See, generally, Jack Gould, "Discordant Notes: Long Standing Dispute Between B.M.I. and Songwriters Flares Anew," *New York Times*, October 7, 1956, sec. 2, 11; Marya Mannes, "Who Decides What Songs Are Hits?," *Reporter* (January 10, 1957), 36–38; Russell Sanjek, "The War on Rock," *Down Beat Music '72 Yearbook* (Chicago: Maher Publications, 1972), 17–19, 58–66; Ryan, *The Production of Culture in the Music Industry*; Sanjek, *Pennies from Heaven*, 401–90; Chapple and Garofalo,

Rock 'n' Roll Is Here to Pay, 64–68; Ennis, *The Seventh Stream*, 165–68; Martin and Segrave, *Anti-Rock*, 85–102.

99. Ryan, *The Production of Culture in the Music Industry*, 112–13.

100. Ennis, *The Seventh Stream*, 259–65, 315, 324; Miller, *Flowers in the Dustbin*, 163–68; Jackson, *Big Beat Heat*, 244–96; Thomas Doherty, *Teenagers and Teenpics: The Juvenilization of American Movies in the 1950s* (Philadelphia: Temple University Press, 2002), 184–85. See also R. H. Coase, "Payola in Radio and Television Broadcasting," *Journal of Law and Economics* 22 (1979): 269–328; Sanjek, *Pennies from Heaven*, 447–48.

101. Jackson, *Big Beat Heat*, 244–45.

102. Wald, *How the Beatles Destroyed Rock 'n' Roll*, 174; Richard Cohen, *The Record Men: The Chess Brothers and the Birth of Rock 'n' Roll* (New York: W. W. Norton, 2004), 132.

103. Guralnick, *Sam Phillips*, 80–84, 214.

104. Garofalo, "Crossing Over: 1939–1989," 74.

105. David Brackett, "The Politics and Practice of 'Cross-over' in American Popular Music, 1963 to 1965," *Musical Quarterly* 78 (1994): 778–79; Clarke, *The Rise and Fall of Popular Music*, 467; Gillett, *The Sound of the City*, 233–34.

106. Michael R. Frontani, *The Beatles: Image and the Media* (Jackson: University Press of Mississippi, 2007), 65–67.

107. *The Huntley-Brinkley Show*, November 18, 1963, www.nbcnews.com/video/nightly-news /53567852/#5356785218 (audio only).

108. Lewisohn, *All These Years*, 505–506.

109. Colin Fallows, "Interview with Astrid Kirchherr," in Matthew H. Clough and Colin Fallows, eds., *Stuart Sutcliffe: A Retrospective* (Liverpool: Liverpool University Press, 2009), 51.

110. Clayson and Sutcliffe, *Backbeat*, 143–44.

111. Lewisohn, *All These Years*, 421, 485.

112. Millard, *Beatlemania*, 104–106.

113. Jann Wenner, "The *Rolling Stone* Interview: John Lennon, Part Two; Life with the Lions," *Rolling Stone*, no. 75 (February 4, 1971), 37.

114. Wenner, "The *Rolling Stone* Interview: John Lennon, Part One," 33.

115. "The Sound of the Sixties," *Time* 85 (May 21, 1965), 86.

116. Ward et al., *Rock of Ages*, 321–22.

117. Wenner, "The *Rolling Stone* Interview: John Lennon, Part One," 40. See also Bill Wyman, *Stone Alone: The Story of a Rock 'n' Roll Band* (New York: Viking, 1990), 127–29.

118. See John McMillian, *Beatles vs. Stones* (New York: Simon and Schuster, 2013).

119. Hajdu, *Positively 4th Street*, 196–97 (interview with Victor Maymudes); a slightly different version is in Anthony Scaduto, *Bob Dylan* (New York: Grosset and Dunlap, 1971), 175 (interview with Dylan).

120. Suze Rotolo, *A Freewheelin' Time: A Memoir of Greenwich Village in the Sixties* (New York: Broadway Books, 2008), 233–35; Bob Dylan, *Chronicles: Volume One* (New York: Simon and Schuster, 2004), 272–75.

121. Scaduto, *Bob Dylan*, 175 (interview with Dylan).

122. See David Hajdu, *Love for Sale: Pop Music in America* (New York: Farrar, Straus and Giroux, 2016), 135–149.

123. Millard, *Beatlemania*, 140.

124. Robert Freeman, *The Beatles: A Private View*, 2nd ed. (Big Tent Entertainment, 2003), 56. Freeman's story is somewhat embellished from the first edition, 1990.

125. Ron Rosenbaum, "Playboy Interview with Bob Dylan," *Playboy* 25 (March 1978), 69.

126. Hajdu, *Positively 4th Street*, 258–63; Elijah Wald, *Dylan Goes Electric! Newport, Seeger, Dylan, and the Night That Split the Sixties* (New York: Dey Street Books, 2015), 247–78.

127. Sam Kashner, "Making Beatlemania: *A Hard Day's Night* at 50," *Vanity Fair* (July 2, 2014) (online).

128. Stephen Glynn, *A Hard Day's Night* (London: I. B. Tauris, 2005), 9–30.

129. See Bernard Gendron, *Between Montmartre and the Mudd Club: Popular Music and the Avant-Garde* (Chicago: University of Chicago Press, 2002), 168–70. I follow, generally, Gendron's account on 161–204.

130. Andrew Sarris, "Bravo Beatles!," *Village Voice*, August 27, 1964, 13.

131. Dwight Macdonald, "Films," *Esquire* 62 (January 1965), 116–17.

132. Tim Riley, *Tell Me Why: A Beatles Commentary* (New York: Knopf, 1988), 99–100; Jason I. Brown, "Mathematics, Physics, and *A Hard Day's Night*," *CMS Notes* 36 (October 2004), 4–8. Cf. [Wayne of Uranus], sites.google.com /site/ahdnchord/home.

133. [William Mann], "What Songs the Beatles Sang . . . ," *Times* [London], December 27, 1963, 4.

134. Wenner, "The *Rolling Stone* Interview: John Lennon, Part One," 39.

135. Ned Rorem, "The Music of the Beatles," *New York Review of Books* 10 (January 18, 1968), 26.

136. Richard Poirier, "Learning from the Beatles," *Partisan Review* 34 (1967): 545.

137. Robert Draper, *Rolling Stone Magazine: The Uncensored History* (New York: Doubleday, 1990), 35–61. See, generally, Frontani, *The Beatles: Image and the Media*, 178–214.

138. Draper, *Rolling Stone*, 131.

139. Ibid., 71.

140. Ibid., 80–81.

141. Jann Wenner, "Beatles, Beatles, Beatles," *Rolling Stone*, no. 24 (December 21, 1968), 10.

142. Poirier, "Learning from the Beatles," 532.

143. See Evelyn McDonnell, "The Feminine Critique," in Evelyn McDonnell and Ann Powers, eds., *Rock She Wrote* (London: Plexus, 1995), 5–23; Draper, *Rolling Stone*, 20.

144. Jann Wenner, "Books: The Beatles," *Rolling Stone*, no. 20 (October 26, 1968), 17.

145. Draper, *Rolling Stone*, 85–87, 131–32; Greil Marcus, "Who Put the Bomp in the Bomp De-Bomp De-Bomp?," in Greil Marcus, ed., *Rock 'n' Roll Will Stand* (Boston: Beacon Press, 1969), 8.

146. Marcus, "Who Put the Bomp in the Bomp De-Bomp De-Bomp?," 24.

147. Wenner, "Books: The Beatles," 15.

10. CONCEPTS OF LIBERTY

1. "Remarks in the Rudolph Wilde Platz, Berlin, June 26, 1963," *Public Papers of the Presidents of the United States: John F. Kennedy, January 1, 1963, to November 22, 1963* (Washington, DC: U.S. Government Printing Office, 1964), 525.

2. Nigel Hamilton, *JFK: Reckless Youth* (New York: Random House, 1992), 271–72, 718–19. See also John F. Kennedy, *Prelude to Leadership: The European Diary of John F. Kennedy, Summer 1945* (Washington, DC: Regnery, 1995), 49–50.

3. "Das Gespräch zwischen Ulbricht und Chruschtschow," *Welt*, May 30, 2009, www.welt.de /politik/article3828831/Das-Gespraech-zwischen -Ulbricht-und-Chruschtschow.html.

4. "The Victims at the Berlin Wall, 1961–1989," Zentrum für Zeithistorische Forschung, Potsdam, November 2016, www.berliner-mauer -gedenkstaette.de/en/todesopfer-240.html.

5. Jean-Paul Sartre, "Paris Alive: The Republic of Silence," trans. Lincoln Kirstein, *Atlantic Monthly* 174 (December 1944), 39.

6. Arthur Koestler, *Dialogue with Death*, trans. Trevor Blewitt and Phyllis Blewitt (New York: Macmillan, 1942), 203.

7. See Bryan Diamond, "Isaac Diamond and the Jews in the Timber Trade in the East End," *Jewish Historical Studies* 35 (1996–1998): 255–75.

8. Michael Ignatieff, *Isaiah Berlin: A Life* (New York: Metropolitan Books, 1998), 10–61.

9. See Alan Ryan, "Isaiah Berlin: The History of Ideas as Psychodrama," *European Journal of Political Theory* 12 (2012): 61–73; Ignatieff, *Isaiah Berlin*, 1–9.

10. Isaiah Berlin, "In Conversation with Steven Lukes," *Salmagundi*, no. 120 (Fall 1998), 70.

11. Isaiah Berlin, *Flourishing: Letters, 1928–1946*, ed. Henry Hardy (London: Chatto and Windus, 2004), 67–68 (interview with Berlin); Ramin Jahanbegloo, *Conversations with Isaiah Berlin* (London: Peter Halban, 1992), 10–14.

12. See Karl Marx and Frederick Engels, *The German Ideology*, in Karl Marx and Frederick Engels, *Collected Works*, vol. 5 (London: Lawrence and Wishart, 1975–2004), 24.

13. Karl Marx, "Theses on Feuerbach," in Marx and Engels, *Collected Works*, vol. 5, 5. ("Die Philosophen haben die Welt nur verschieden interpretiert, es kommt drauf an, sie zu verändern." Karl Marx, "Thesen über Feuerbach," in Karl Marx and Friedrich Engels, *Werke*, vol. 3, ed. Institut für Marxismus-Leninismus beim Zentralkomitee der Kommunistischen Partei der Sowjetunion und Institut für Geschichte der Arbeiterbewegung Berlin [Berlin: Dietz, 1957–], 7.)

14. Karl Marx, "Economic and Philosophical Manuscripts of 1844," in Marx and Engels, *Collected Works*, vol. 3, 297. ("[D]as aufgelöste Rätsel der Geschichte." Karl Marx, "Ökonomisch-philosophische Manuskripte," in Karl Marx and Friedrich Engels, *Gesamtausgabe*, vol. 1/2 [Berlin: Dietz, Akademie, 1975–], 263.) See also Isaiah Berlin, *Karl Marx: His Life and Environment* (London: T. Butterworth, 1939), 121–44; Peter Singer, *Karl Marx: A Very Short Introduction* (Oxford: Oxford University Press, 1980), 16–22, 32–58; Gareth Stedman Jones, *Karl Marx: Greatness and Illusion* (Cambridge, MA: Harvard University Press, 2016), 375–431.

15. Marx and Engels, *The German Ideology*, 47. ("[M]orgens zu jagen, nachmittags zu fischen, abends Viehzucht zu treiben, nach dem Essen zu kritisieren, wie ich gerade Lust habe, ohne je Jäger, Fischer, Hirte oder Kritiker zu werden." Marx and Engels, *Werke*, vol. 3, 33.)

16. Berlin, *Karl Marx*, 25–26.

17. See Gregg Herken, *The Georgetown Set: Friends and Rivals in Cold War Washington* (New York: Knopf, 2014).

18. Ignatieff, *Isaiah Berlin*, 97–147; "Chronology 1906–1946," in Berlin, *Flourishing*, 699–701. See also Anne Deighton, "Don and Diplomat: Isaiah Berlin and Britain's Early Cold War," *Cold War History* 13 (2013): 525–40.

19. George F. Kennan, *The Kennan Diaries*, ed. Frank Costigliola (New York: W. W. Norton, 2014), 191, entry for December 17, 1945.

20. Isaiah Berlin to John Lehmann, January 12, 1955, in Isaiah Berlin, *Enlightening: Letters 1946–1960*, ed. Henry Hardy and Jennifer Holmes (London: Chatto and Windus, 2009), 472.

21. Andrei Zhdanov, "Report of Comrade Zhdanov on the Journals *Zvezda* and *Leningrad*," in *The Central Committee Resolution and Zhdanov's Speech on the Journals Zvezda and Leningrad/Doklad t. Zhdanova o zhurnalakh Zvezda i Leningrad*, English trans. Felicity Ashbee and Irina Tidmarsh (Royal Oak, MI: Strathcona Publishing, 1978), 42.

22. Anna Akhmatova, *The Complete Poems of Anna Akhmatova*, vol. 2, trans. Judith Hemschemeyer, ed. Roberta Reeder (Somerville, MA: Zephyr Press, 1990), 235.

23. Zhdanov, "Report of Comrade Zhdanov on the Journals *Zvezda* and *Leningrad*," 53.

24. Amanda Haight, *Anna Akhmatova: A Poetic Pilgrimage* (New York: Oxford University Press, 1990), 159–61.

25. Audio at podcasts.ox.ac.uk/anna-akhmatova-reading-her-poems-about-isaiah-berlin-oxford-1965.

26. Isaiah Berlin, "Meetings with Russian Writers in 1945 and 1956," in *Personal Impressions*, ed. Henry Hardy (New York: Viking, 1980), 189–208; Isaiah Berlin to Frank Roberts, February 20, 1946, in *Flourishing*, 619. See also Ignatieff, *Isaiah Berlin*, 148–69; Isaiah Berlin, "A Visit to Leningrad," *Times Literary Supplement*, March 23, 2001, 13–15; Haight, *Anna Akhmatova*, 189–93.

27. See György Dalos, *The Guest from the Future: Anna Akhmatova and Isaiah Berlin*, trans. Antony Wood (New York: Farrar, Straus and Giroux, 1996).

28. Ignatieff, *Isaiah Berlin*, 161 (interview with Tripp).

29. I follow L. Kopylov, T. Pozdniakova, and N. Popova, *"I éto bylo tak": Anna Akhmatova i Isaiia Berlin* (St. Petersburg: Anna Akhmatova Museum at the Fontany House, 2009). I am indebted to Claire Atwood for her redactions. See also Olga Voronina, "'We Started the Cold War': A Hidden Message Behind Stalin's Attack on Anna Akhmatova," in Annette Vowinckel, Marcus M. Payk, and Thomas Lindenberger, eds., *Cold War Cultures: Perspectives on Eastern and Western European Societies* (New York: Berghahn Books, 2012), 55–75; Isaiah Berlin, *Personal Impressions*, 3rd ed., ed. Henry Hardy (Princeton: Princeton University Press, 2014), 398n1; Josephine von Zitzewitz, "That's How It Was: New Theories about Anna Akhmatova and Isaiah Berlin, Her 'Guest from the Future,'" *Times Literary Supplement*, September 9, 2011, 14–15; Sophie Kazimirovna Ostrovskaya, *Memoirs of Anna Akhmatova's Years 1944–1950*, trans. Jessie Davies (Liverpool: Lincoln Davies, 1988).

30. See Isaiah Berlin to Maurice Bowra, June 7, 1945, in *Flourishing*, 574 ("Akhmatova lives in Leningrad"), and 599–612.

31. See Berlin, *Personal Impressions*, 3rd ed., 400.

32. Published in translation in Dalos, *The Guest from the Future*, 211–13.

33. Berlin, "A Visit to Leningrad," 13.

34. See Ignatieff, *Isaiah Berlin*, 208–211.

35. Isaiah Berlin, "A Visit to Leningrad," in Isaiah Berlin, *The Soviet Mind: Russian Culture Under Communism*, ed. Henry Hardy (Washington, DC: Brookings Institution Press, 2004), 38n.

36. Jahanbegloo, *Conversations with Isaiah Berlin*, 15 (interview with Berlin).

37. Isaiah Berlin, "Political Ideas in the Twentieth Century," *Foreign Affairs* 28 (1950): 364.

38. E. H. Carr, "The New Skepticism," *Times Literary Supplement*, June 9, 1950, 357.

39. See Berlin, *Flourishing*, [vi] n3.

40. George Kennan to Isaiah Berlin, April 26, 1950, Box 5, Folder 5, George F. Kennan Papers, Seeley G. Mudd Manuscript Library, Princeton University.

41. See Isaiah Berlin, *Freedom and Its Betrayal*, 2nd ed., ed. Henry Hardy (Princeton: Princeton University Press, 2014); Isaiah Berlin, *Political Ideas in the Romantic Age*, 2nd ed., ed. Henry Hardy (Princeton: Princeton University Press, 2014).

42. Isaiah Berlin, *Two Concepts of Liberty* (Oxford: Oxford University Press, 1958), 18.

43. Isaiah Berlin, "Two Concepts of Liberty," in *Four Essays on Liberty* (New York: Oxford University Press, 1969), 125.

44. See George Edward Moore, *Principia Ethica* (Cambridge: Cambridge University Press, 1903), title page; quoting Joseph Butler, *Fifteen Sermons Preached at the Rolls Chapel*, 2nd ed. (London: W. Botham, for James and John Knapton, 1729), xxix.

45. Berlin, "Two Concepts of Liberty," 168.

46. Isaiah Berlin to Herbert Elliston, December 30, 1952, in *Enlightening*, 350.

47. Berlin, *Two Concepts of Liberty*, 41.

48. Ibid., 42.

49. Berlin, "Two Concepts of Liberty," 144. In the original version, Berlin had "Marxist" for "communist."

50. Berlin, *Two Concepts of Liberty*, 33–34.

51. Ibid., 4.

52. Isaiah Berlin to William Phillips, May 7, 1963, in *Enlightening*, 430n2.

53. Ignatieff, *Isaiah Berlin*, 275–76.

54. Isaiah Berlin, *The Roots of Romanticism*, ed. Henry Hardy (Princeton: Princeton University Press, 1999), 146–47.

55. Ibid., 145.

56. Ibid., xii.

57. Isaiah Berlin to Noel Annan, May 1, 1964, and Isaiah Berlin to Jean Floud, March 15, 1971, in Isaiah Berlin, *Building: Letters 1960–1975*, ed. Henry Hardy and Mark Pottle (London: Chatto and Windus, 2013), 191, 445.

58. See Morton J. Horwitz, *The Warren Court and the Pursuit of Justice* (New York: Hill and Wang, 1998), 99–111; Marjorie Heins, *Not in Front of the Children: "Indecency," Censorship,*

and the Innocence of Youth (New York: Hill and Wang, 2001), 62, 63.

59. See G. Edward White, *Earl Warren: A Public Life* (New York: Oxford University Press, 1982), 128–55.

60. Earl Warren, "The Law and the Future," *Fortune* 18 (November 1955), 106, 230.

61. Michal R. Belknap, *Cold War Political Justice: The Smith Act, the Communist Party, and American Civil Liberties* (Westport, CT: Greenwood, 1977), 236–58; Arthur J. Sabin, *In Calmer Times: The Supreme Court and Red Monday* (Philadelphia: University of Pennsylvania Press, 1999), 1–13; Barry Friedman, *The Will of the People: How Public Opinion Has Influenced the Supreme Court and Shaped the Meaning of the Constitution* (New York: Farrar, Straus and Giroux, 2009), 250–58. See also Eric A. Posner and Adrian Vermeule, *Terror in the Balance: Security, Liberty, and the Courts* (New York: Oxford University Press, 2007), 230–34.

62. John Tebbel, *A History of Book Publishing in the United States*, vol. 1, *The Creation of an Industry, 1630–1865* (New York: R. R. Bowker, 1972), 240–51; vol. 2, *The Expansion of an Industry, 1865–1919* (New York: R. R. Bowker, 1975), 481–88.

63. See Charles A. Madison, *Book Publishing in America* (New York: McGraw-Hill, 1966), 461. See also Jason Epstein, *Book Business: Publishing Past Present and Future* (New York: W. W. Norton, 2001), 39–41.

64. Jeremy Lewis, *Penguin Special: The Life and Times of Allen Lane* (London: Viking, 2005), 71–100; Kenneth C. Davis, *Two-Bit Culture: The Paperbacking of America* (Boston: Houghton Mifflin, 1984), 26–28.

65. John Tebbel, *A History of Book Publishing in the United States*, vol. 3, *The Golden Age Between Two Wars, 1920–1940* (New York: R. R. Bowker, 1978), 662; *Statistical Abstract of the United States, 1944–45* (Washington, DC: U.S. Government Printing Office, 1945), 873–75.

66. "Currents in the Trade," *Publisher's Weekly* 136 (August 19, 1939), 25; Tebbel, *A History of Book Publishing*, vol. 3, 508–11.

67. Tebbel, *A History of Book Publishing*, vol. 3, 7; Beth Luey, "The Organization of the Book Publishing Industry," in David Paul Nord, Joan Shelley Rubin, and Michael Schudson, eds., *A History of the Book in America*, vol. 5, *The Enduring Book: 1945–1995* (Chapel Hill: University of North Carolina Press, 2009), 43.

68. Paula Rabinowitz, *American Pulp: How Paperbacks Brought Modernism to Main Street* (Princeton: Princeton University Press, 2014), 112–16.

69. *New York Times*, June 19, 1939, 34.

70. Tebbel, *A History of Book Publishing*, vol. 3, 509.

71. See David M. Earle, *Re-covering Modernism: Pulps, Paperbacks, and the Prejudice of Form* (Burlington, VT: Ashgate, 2009).

72. Lee Server, *Over My Dead Body: The Sensational Age of the American Paperback, 1945–1955* (San Francisco: Chronicle Books, 1994), 64.

73. Davis, *Two-Bit Culture*, 65–80.

74. Earle, *Re-covering Modernism*, 167.

75. Davis, *Two-Bit Culture*, 123.

76. Rabinowitz, *American Pulp*, 272.

77. Davis, *Two-Bit Culture*, 258.

78. Earle, *Re-covering Modernism*, 168.

79. Transcript of record, *Doubleday & Company v. New York*, 335 U.S. 848 (1948), at 35.

80. "House Votes Inquiries on Elections, Crime on Radio-TV, Immoral Books," *New York Times*, May 13, 1952, 1.

81. John Lichfield, "Tereska Torres: The Reluctant Queen of Lesbian Literature," *Independent*, February 5, 2010 (online).

82. Tereska Torres, *Women's Barracks* (New York: Fawcett, 1950), 46. Torrès did not use the diacritical mark on her byline.

83. Rabinowitz, *American Pulp*, 280. See also Yvonne Keller, "Was It Right to Love Her Brother's Wife So Passionately? Lesbian Pulp Novels and U.S. Lesbian Identity, 1950–1965," *American Quarterly* 57 (2005): 388–89.

84. *Report of the Select Committee on Current Pornographic Materials, House of Representatives, Eighty-Second Congress* (Washington, DC: U.S. Government Printing Office, 1952), 3–4.

85. Davis, *Two-Bit Culture*, 220–37.

86. George Orwell, Review of *Esther Waters*, by George Moore [et al.], in *The Complete Works of George Orwell*, ed. Peter Davison, vol. 10, *A Kind of Compulsion, 1903–1936* (London: Secker and Warburg, 1998), 445.

87. Davis, *Two-Bit Culture*, 146–47.

88. Rabinowitz, *American Pulp*, 242.

89. Davis, *Two-Bit Culture*, 250–55.

90. Epstein, *Book Business*, 56.

91. Ibid., 64.

92. Loren Glass, *Counterculture Colophon: Grove Press, the* Evergreen Review, *and the Incorporation of the Avant-Garde* (Stanford: Stanford University Press, 2013), 22–32.

93. Walter Kendrick, *The Secret Museum: Pornography in Modern Culture* (New York: Viking, 1987), 119–22.

94. *Regina v. Hicklin*, L.R. 3 Q.B. 360 (1868), at 371.

95. Colette Colligan, *A Publisher's Paradise: Expatriate Literary Culture in Paris, 1890–1960* (Amherst: University of Massachusetts Press, 2014), 19–29.

96. See Hugh Ford, *Published in Paris: American and British Writers, Printers, and Publishers in Paris, 1920–1939* (New York: Macmillan, 1975).

97. Colligan, *A Publishers' Paradise*, 28–29.

98. Neil Pearson, *Obelisk: A History of Jack Kahane and the Obelisk Press* (Liverpool: Liverpool University Press, 2007), 7–13, 28–38, 58–62.

99. Jack Kahane, *Memoirs of a Booklegger* (London: Michael Joseph, 1939), 227–28. See also Sylvia Beach, *Shakespeare and Company* (New York: Harcourt, Brace, 1959), 132–33.

100. Colligan, *A Publishers' Paradise*, 177; Pearson, *Obelisk*, 63–67, 79–80.

101. John de St. Jorre, *Venus Bound: The Erotic Voyage of the Olympia Press and Its Writers* (New York: Random House, 1994), 14–17.

102. Radclyffe Hall, *The Well of Loneliness* (Paris: Pegasus Press, 1928), 365.

103. Kahane, *Memoirs of a Booklegger*, 260.

104. St. Jorre, *Venus Bound*, 23–27; Pearson, *Obelisk*, 171–73.

105. Barney Rosset, *Rosset: My Life in Publishing and How I Fought Censorship* (New York: OR Books, 2016), 35.

106. Barney Rosset, "The Art of Publishing II," *Paris Review* 39 (Winter 1997), 175; Gerald Jonas, "The Story of Grove," *New York Times Magazine*, January 21, 1968, 47 (interview with Rosset).

107. Glass, *Counterculture Colophon*, 4–5.

108. Laura J. Miller and David Paul Nord, "Reading the Data on Books, Newspapers, and Magazines: A Statistical Appendix," in Nord, Rubin, and Schudson, *A History of the Book in America*, vol. 5, 509.

109. Richard Seaver, "Samuel Beckett: An Introduction," *Merlin* 1 (1952): 73.

110. Richard Seaver, *The Tender Hour of Twilight: Paris in the '50s, New York in the '60s: A Memoir of Publishing's Golden Age*, ed. Jeannette Seaver (New York: Farrar, Straus and Giroux, 2012), 12, 21–22, 61–67; James Knowlson, *Damned to Fame: The Life of Samuel Beckett* (London: Bloomsbury, 1996), 394–95; St. Jorre, *Venus Bound*, 54–57.

111. Seaver, *The Tender Hour of Twilight*, 245–48; Rosset, *Rosset*, 109–110; and see Jonas, "The Story of Grove," 49.

112. See Samuel Beckett to Pamela Mitchell, September 26, 1953, *The Letters of Samuel Beckett*, ed. George Craig, Martha Dow Fehsenfeld, Dan Gunn, and Lois More Overbeck, vol. 2, *1941–1956* (Cambridge: Cambridge University Press, 2011), 406.

113. See Ruby Cohn, *From Desire to Godot: Pocket Theater of Postwar Paris* (Berkeley: University of California Press, 1987), 155, 159–70.

114. See Knowlson, *Damned to Fame*, 314–19.

115. Glass, *Counterculture Colophon*, 65.

116. Henry S. Sommerville, "Commerce and Culture in the Career of the Permanent Innovative

Press: New Directions, Grove Press, and George Braziller Inc.," PhD dissertation, University of Rochester, 2009, 288.

117. Martin Esslin, *The Theater of the Absurd* (New York: Doubleday Anchor, 1961), 10.

118. Esslin, *The Theater of the Absurd*, xix.

119. Samuel Beckett, *Waiting for Godot* (New York: Grove, 1954), 58.

120. Ibid., 34.

121. Beach, *Shakespeare and Company*, 92–94.

122. Rosset, *Rosset*, 148.

123. Ibid., 158–60.

124. Charles Rembar, *The End of Obscenity: The Trails of Lady Chatterley, Tropic of Cancer, and Fanny Hill* (New York: Random House, 1968), 61.

125. Peter Manso, *Mailer: His Life and Times* (New York: Simon and Schuster, 1985), 105–106 (interviews with Rembar and Mailer).

126. Rembar, *The End of Obscenity*, 23–26.

127. See Leo Hamilton, "The Secret Careers of Samuel Roth," *Journal of Popular Culture* 1 (1968): 317–38; Jay A. Gertzman, *Samuel Roth: Infamous Modernist* (Gainesville: University Press of Florida, 2013), 258–63.

128. *Mutual v. Ohio*, 236 U.S. 230 (1914), at 242.

129. William B. Lockart and Robert C. McClure, "Censorship of Obscenity: The Developing Constitutional Standards," *Minnesota Law Review* 45 (1960–1961): 56.

130. *Roth v. United States*, 354 U.S. 476 (1957), at 477, 487.

131. *Roth v. United States*, at 484.

132. Seaver, *The Tender Hour of Twilight*, 266.

133. St. Jorre, *Venus Bound*, 42–51.

134. Seaver, *The Tender Hour of Twilight*, 196–99.

135. See Patrick Kearney, *The Paris Olympia Press*, rev. ed., ed. Angus Carroll (Liverpool: Liverpool University Press, 2007).

136. Seaver, *The Tender Hour of Twilight*, 245–48; Rosset, *Rosset*, 97–98.

137. I follow the argument in Glass, *Counterculture Colophon*, 20, 131.

138. *Décret-loi du 29 Juillet 1939 relatif à la famille et à la natalité françaises, dit: Code de la famille* (Paris: Centre d'information interprofessionel, 1946), 38.

139. Seaver, *The Tender Hour of Twilight*, 184; Kearney, *The Paris Olympia Press*, 333–35.

140. *Besig v. United States*, 208 F. 2d 143 (1953), at 145.

141. Henry Miller, *Tropic of Cancer* (New York: Grove, 1961), 5.

142. *Jacobellis v. Ohio*, 378 U.S. 184 (1964), at 191, 195.

143. Rosset, "The Art of Publishing II," 208–209.

144. Glass, *Counterculture Colophon*, 103, 129.

145. Martin Mayer, "How to Publish 'Dirty Books' for Fun and Profit," *Saturday Evening Post* 242 (January 25, 1969), 33 (interview with Epstein).

See also John Marchese, "The Bustling Days and Rum-and-Coke Nights of Barney Rosset," *7 Days* 2 (September 6, 1989), 21.

11. CHILDREN OF A STORM

1. I follow the argument of Mary L. Dudziak, *Cold War Civil Rights: Race and the Image of American Democracy* (Princeton: Princeton University Press, 2000). See also John David Skrentny, "The Effect of the Cold War on African American Civil Rights: America and the World Audience, 1945–1968," *Theory and Society* 27 (1998): 237–285; Thomas Borstelmann, *The Cold War and the Color Line: American Race Relations in the Global Arena* (Cambridge, MA: Harvard University Press, 2001); Brenda Gayle Plummer, *Rising Wind: Black Americans and U.S. Foreign Affairs* (Chapel Hill: University of North Carolina Press, 1996), 167–297; Brenda Gayle Plummer, *In Search of Power: African Americans in the Era of Decolonization, 1956–1974* (Cambridge: Cambridge University Press, 2013); Paul Gordon Lauren, "Seen from the Outside: The International Perspective on America's Dilemma," in Brenda Gayle Plummer, ed., *Window on Freedom: Race, Civil Rights, and Foreign Affairs, 1945–1988* (Chapel Hill: University of North Carolina Press, 2003), 21–43.

2. The Inaugural Address of Governor George Wallace, Administrative Files, Alabama Department of Archives and History, Montgomery, Alabama.

3. Inaugural Address, *Public Papers of the Presidents of the United States: John F. Kennedy*, vol. 1, *January 20–December 31, 1961* (Washington, DC: U.S. Government Printing Office, 1962), 1.

4. Thurston Clarke, *Ask Not: The Inauguration of John F. Kennedy and the Speech That Changed America* (New York: Henry Holt, 2004), 135–36.

5. Steven F. Lawson, *Black Ballots: Voting Rights in the South, 1944–1969* (New York: Columbia University Press, 1976), 256–57.

6. Richard Reeves, *President Kennedy: Profile of Power* (New York: Simon and Schuster, 1993), 122–25, 156–71. See also "Bi-Racial Buses Attacked, Riders Beaten in Alabama," *New York Times*, May 15, 1961, 1, 22.

7. "Maryland Apologizes to Four African Envoys," *New York Times*, July 12, 1961, 13. See also Michael Krenn, "The Unwelcome Mat: African Diplomats in Washington, D.C., During the Kennedy Years," in Plummer, *Window on Freedom*, 163–80.

8. Reeves, *President Kennedy*, 60 (interview with Wofford).

9. Bayard Rustin, "From Protest to Politics: The Future of the Civil Rights Movement," in *Down the Line: The Collected Writings of Bayard*

Rustin (Chicago: Quadrangle Books, 1971), 111. (Rustin's chronology ends in 1964.)

10. Martin Luther King, Jr., "Hammer of Civil Rights," *Nation* 198 (1964), 231.

11. James Baldwin, "A Word from Writer Directly to Readers," in Herbert Gold, ed., *Fiction of the Fifties: A Decade of American Writing* (Garden City, NY: Doubleday, 1959), 19. See also James Campbell, *Talking at the Gates: A Life of James Baldwin* (New York: Viking, 1991), 3.

12. Julius Lester, "James Baldwin—Reflections of a Maverick," *New York Times Book Review*, May 27, 1984, 22 (interview with Baldwin).

13. See, e.g., Henry Louis Gates, Jr., "The Fire Last Time: What James Baldwin Can and Can't Teach America," *New Republic* 206 (June 1, 1992), 37–43.

14. See David Levering Lewis, *When Harlem Was in Vogue* (New York: Knopf, 1981).

15. Cheryl Lynn Greenberg, *"Or Does It Explode?": Black Harlem in the Great Depression* (New York: Oxford University Press, 1991), 13–34; Jonathan Gill, *Harlem: The Four Hundred Year History from Dutch Village to Capital of Black America* (New York: Grove, 2011), 282–87.

16. James Baldwin, "Me and My House," *Harper's Magazine* 211 (November 1955), 54; Campbell, *Talking at the Gates*, 3–5.

17. Bryant Rollins, "James Baldwin, Author Extraordinary: Boy Preacher at 14—and Still Preaching," *Boston Globe*, April 14, 1963, A56 (interview with Baldwin).

18. James Baldwin, "Dark Days," *Esquire* 94 (October 1980), 42–46.

19. See James Baldwin, "Freaks and the American Ideal of Manhood," *Playboy* 32 (January 1985), 192.

20. See James Baldwin, "A Conversation with James Baldwin," *Freedomways* 3 (Summer 1963): 362.

21. James Baldwin, "Autobiographical Notes," in *Notes of a Native Son* (New York: Beacon Press, 1955), 4.

22. Herb Boyd, *Baldwin's Harlem: A Biography of James Baldwin* (New York: Atria Books, 2008), 7–10; Campbell, *Talking at the Gates*, 10, 20. See also Baldwin, "Dark Days," 42–46.

23. Campbell, *Talking at the Gates*, 14.

24. See James Baldwin to Abel Meeropol, September 29, 1974, Box 3b, Folder 2, James Baldwin Papers, Schomburg Center for Research in Black Culture.

25. David Leeming, *James Baldwin: A Biography* (New York: Knopf, 1994), 46; James Baldwin, "The Art of Fiction LXXVIII: James Baldwin, an Interview," *Paris Review* 26 (Spring 1984), 57; James Baldwin, "The New Lost Generation," *Esquire* 56 (July 1961), 113; Douglas Field, *All Those Strangers: The Art and Lives of James Baldwin* (New York: Oxford University Press, 2015), 153n13.

26. James Baldwin, "Introduction: The Price of the Ticket," in *The Price of the Ticket: Collected Nonfiction, 1948–1985* (New York: St. Martin's/Marek, 1985), xii–xiii.

27. Baldwin, "Introduction: The Price of the Ticket," ix.

28. Campbell, *Talking at the Gates*, 20.

29. Baldwin, "The Art of Fiction LXXVIII," 71. See also Leeming, *James Baldwin*, 49.

30. Lesley Conger, "Jimmy on East 15th Street," *African American Review* 29 (1995): 564–65. See also Leeming, *James Baldwin*, 49–50; Hazel Rowley, *Richard Wright: The Life and Times* (New York: Henry Holt, 2001), 315–16. Michel Fabre, *The Unfinished Quest of Richard Wright* (New York: William Morrow, 1973), 290, has a different version.

31. See David Adams Leeming, "An Interview with James Baldwin on Henry James," *Henry James Review* 8 (1986): 47–56.

32. Lionel Trilling, preface to *The Liberal Imagination* (New York: Viking, 1950), xv. See also Field, *All Those Strangers*, 12–33.

33. James Baldwin, "Five Problem Novels," *Commentary* 5 (April 1948), 378.

34. James Baldwin, "Conversation: Ida Lewis and James Baldwin," *Essence* 1 (October 1970), 22.

35. Baldwin, "The Art of Fiction LXXVIII," 50.

36. Charles T. Davis and Michel Fabre, *Richard Wright: A Primary Bibliography* (Boston: G. K. Hall, 1982), 195–212.

37. See Louis Menand, "Richard Wright: The Hammer and the Nail," in *American Studies* (New York: Farrar, Straus and Giroux, 2002), 76–90.

38. Fabre, *The Unfinished Quest of Richard Wright*, 180; Rowley, *Richard Wright*, 321; Arnold Rampersad, *Ralph Ellison: A Biography* (New York: Knopf, 2007), 130; Lawrence P. Jackson, *The Indignant Generation: A Narrative History of African American Writers and Critics, 1934–1960* (Princeton: Princeton University Press, 2011), 200.

39. Richard Wright, "I Tried to Be a Communist," *Atlantic Monthly* 174 (August 1944), 61–70 (September 1944), 48–56; Richard Crossman, ed., *The God That Failed* (New York: Harper, 1950); Rowley, *Richard Wright*, 284–91.

40. Richard Wright, "Gertrude Stein's Story Is Drenched in Hitler's Horrors," *PM*, March 11, 1945, 15; Fabre, *The Unfinished Quest of Richard Wright*, 112.

41. Joseph Barry to Richard Wright, April 26, 1945, Box 106, Folder 1619, Richard Wright Papers, Beinecke Rare Book and Manuscript Library, Yale University.

42. Gertrude Stein, "The New Hope of Our 'Sad Young Men,'" *New York Times Magazine*, June 3, 1945, 38.

43. Richard Wright, lecture on writing, notes, 1941(?), Box 3, Folder 40, Wright Papers.

44. Ben Burns, "Double-Talk Prose; Common Sense Talk," *Chicago Defender*, October 27, 1945, 11 (interview with Stein).

45. Lionel Trilling, "A Tragic Situation," *Nation* 160 (1945): 391.

46. Fabre, *The Unfinished Quest of Richard Wright*, 302–303; Rowley, *Richard Wright*, 331–32; Maurice Nadeau, "Pas de problème noir aux U.S.A.," *Combat*, May 11, 1946, 1.

47. Gunnar Myrdal, *An American Dilemma: The Negro Problem and American Democracy* (New York: Harper and Brothers, 1943), 1: xlvii–li.

48. Michel Fabre, "An Interview with Simone de Beauvoir," *Studies in Black Literature* 1 (Fall 1970), 3.

49. John L. Brown, "A Report from Paris," *New York Times*, July 7, 1946, 20; Fabre, *The Unfinished Quest of Richard Wright*, 297–306; Rowley, *Richard Wright*, 328–43.

50. Richard Dier, "One Block of Paris Has More Freedom Than Whole U.S.," *Baltimore Afro-American*, February 22, 1947, M–11D (interview with Wright).

51. Richard Wright, "I Choose Exile" (1951), Box 6, Folder 110, Wright Papers; Carol Polsgrove, *Divided Minds: Intellectuals and the Civil Rights Movement* (New York: W. W. Norton, 2001), 80–81.

52. Baldwin, "The Art of Fiction LXXVIII," 50–51.

53. W. J. Weatherby, *James Baldwin: Artist on Fire* (New York: Donald I. Fine, 1989), 65–66. There are varying accounts of who was where during Baldwin's arrival. Leeming, *James Baldwin*, 56–57, has Sartre present at the Deux Magots as well.

54. Otto Friedrich, *The Grave of Alice B. Toklas and Other Reports from the Past* (New York: Henry Holt, 1989), 334–80. See also Stanley Karnow, *Paris in the Fifties* (New York: Times Books, 1997), 22, and, generally, Weatherby, *James Baldwin*, 65–88.

55. See James Campbell, "George Solomos Obituary," *Guardian*, December 13, 2010 (online).

56. See James Campbell, *Exiled in Paris: Richard Wright, James Baldwin, Samuel Beckett, and Others on the Left Bank* (New York: Scribner, 1995), 28; Field, *All Those Strangers*, 29–30.

57. James Baldwin, "Everybody's Protest Novel," *Zero*, no. 1 (Spring 1949), 54, 57.

58. Ibid., 57.

59. Ibid.

60. Ibid., 58.

61. Edmund Wilson, "'No! No! No! My Soul An't Yours, Mas'r!'," *New Yorker* 24 (November 27, 1948), 134. See also Jackson, *The Indignant Generation*, 283–90; Adena Spingarn, *Uncle Tom: From Martyr to Traitor* (Stanford: Stanford University Press, 2018).

62. Richard Wright, *Native Son* (New York: Harper and Brothers, 1940), 358.

63. James Baldwin, "Many Thousands Gone," *Partisan Review* 18 (1951): 676, 678.

64. Ibid., 678.

65. Ibid., 677.

66. See Sidney Hook, "Report on the International Day Against Dictatorship and War," *Partisan Review* 16 (1949): 732n.

67. See Chester Himes, *The Quality of Hurt: The Autobiography of Chester Himes*, vol. 1 (Garden City, NY: Doubleday, 1972), 199–201; Richard Wright, "The Position of the Negro Artist and Intellectual in American Society" (1960), Box 3, Folder 41, Wright Papers.

68. James Baldwin, "Alas Poor Richard," in *Nobody Knows My Name: More Notes of a Native Son* (New York: Dial, 1961), 207–10.

69. Richard Nathaniel Wright, Part 2 of 2, FBI Records: The Vault, July 27, 1955, 49. vault.fbi.gov/Richard%20Nathaniel%20Wright/Richard%20Nathaniel%20Wright%20Part%202%20of%202/view.

70. Greg Barnhisel, *Cold War Modernists: Art, Literature, and American Cultural Diplomacy* (New York: Columbia University Press, 2015), 193–94. See also Matthew Corcoran, "'Pure Child of a Wavering Mother': *Perspectives USA*, 1952–1956," ALM thesis, Harvard University, 2012.

71. Richard Gibson, "A No to Nothing," *Kenyon Review* 13 (1951): 253–54.

72. Elspeth Egerton Healey, "Writing, Communities, Aesthetics, Politics, and Late Modernist Literary Consolidation," PhD dissertation, University of Michigan, 2008, 215n56. See also Jackson, *The Indignant Generation*, 350–51.

73. James Baldwin and Sol Stein, *Native Sons: A Friendship That Created One of the Greatest Works of the Twentieth Century: "Notes of a Native Son"* (New York: One World, 2004), 27–30.

74. James Baldwin, "Notes of a Native Son," in *Notes of a Native Son*, 97.

75. Ibid., 114.

76. Fabre, *The Unfinished Quest of Richard Wright*, v.

77. Victor Serge, *Mémoires d'un révolutionnaire, 1901–1941* (Paris: Éditions du Seuil, 1951), 401. ("[U]ne sort de camp de concentration flottant.")

78. Serge, *Mémoires d'un révolutionnaire*, 402. ("[U]n camp de concentration de plus, torride, sans eau potable, gardé par de grands enfants noirs, administré par des gendarmes qui sont des filous.")

79. Claude Lévi-Strauss, *Tristes Tropiques*, in *Œuvres* (Paris: Gallimard, 2008), 11–24; André Breton, *Martinique, Charmeuse de serpents*, in *Œuvres complètes*, vol. 3 (Paris: Gallimard, 1999), 367–410; Mark Polizzotti, *Revolution of the Mind: The Life of André Breton* (New

York: Farrar, Straus and Giroux, 1995), 496–98; Emmanuelle Loyer, *Lévi-Strauss: A Biography*, trans. Ninon Vinsonneau and Jonathan Magidoff (Cambridge: Polity, 2018), 198–204.

80. Eric Jennings, "Last Exit from Vichy France: The Martinique Escape Route and the Ambiguities of Emigration," *Journal of Modern History* 74 (2002): 289–324.

81. Alain Virmaux and Odette Virmaux, *André Breton: Qui êtes-vous?* (Lyon: La Manufacture, 1987), 103–104 (interview with Césaire, 1966). ("[U]ne époque tout à fait cruciale, déterminante. Si je suis ce que je suis, je crois que c'est en grande partie à cause de cette rencontre avec André Breton.")

82. See Thomas A. Hale, "Two Decades, Four Versions: The Evolution of Aimé Césaire's *Cahier d'un retour au pays natal*," in Carolyn A. Parker and Stephen H. Arnold, eds., *When the Drumbeat Changes* (Washington, DC: Three Continents Press, 1981), 186–95; "Note sur le texte," in Breton, *Œuvres complètes*, vol. 3, 1262.

83. Aimé Césaire, *Nègre je suis, nègre je resterai: Entretiens avec Françoise Vergès* (Paris: Albin Michel, 2005), 23.

84. Janet G. Vaillant, *Black, French, and African: A Life of Léopold Sédar Senghor* (Cambridge, MA: Harvard University Press, 1990), 90–92; Lilyan Kesteloot, *Black Writers in French: A Literary History of Negritude*, trans. Conroy Kennedy (Washington, DC: Howard University Press, 1991), 56–57; Césaire, *Nègre je suis*, 25–26.

85. Gregson Davis, *Aimé Césaire* (Cambridge: Cambridge University Press, 1997), 4–6; D. H. Figuerdo and Frank Argote-Freyre, *A Brief History of the Caribbean* (New York: Facts on File, 2008), 193–94.

86. Aimé Césaire, "Jeunesse Noir et Assimilation," *L'Étudiant noir* 1 (March 1935), 3. ("Que veut la jeunesse Noire? Vivre. Mais pour vivre vraiment, il faut rester sol. L'acteur est l'homme qui ne vit pas vraiment . . . La jeunesse Noire ne veut jouer aucun rôle; elle veut être sol . . . Les jeunes nègres d'aujourd'hui ne veulent ni asservissement ni assimilation, ils veulent émancipation.")

87. Aimé Césaire, "Conscience Raciale et Révolution Sociale," *L'Étudiant Noir* 1 (May–June 1935), 1–2. ("[P]our faire la révolution . . . saisir en nous le nègre immédiate, planter notre négritude comme un bel arbre jusqu'a ce qu'il porte ses fruits les plus authentiques.")

88. Bennetta Jules-Rosette, *Black Paris: The African Writers' Landscape* (Urbana: University of Illinois Press, 1998), 34 (transcription from audiotape of presentation at Maison Helvétique, 1967).

89. Aimé Césaire, "Truer Than Biography: Aimé Césaire Interviewed by René Depestre," trans. Lloyd King, *Savacou*, no. 5 (June 1971), 77.

90. Gary Wilder, *Freedom Time: Negritude, Decolonization, and the Future of the World* (Durham: Duke University Press, 2015), 22.

91. Alice Cherki, *Frantz Fanon: A Portrait*, trans. Nadia Benabid (Ithaca: Cornell University Press, 2006), 10.

92. Aimé Césaire, "Entretien avec Aimé Césaire, par Jacqueline Leiner," in *Tropiques* (Paris: Éditions Jean-Michel Place, 1978), vi.

93. See Davis, *Aimé Césaire*, 22.

94. Césaire, "Entretien avec Aimé Césaire," vi.

95. Césaire, "Truer than Biography."

96. Aimé Césaire, *Cahier d'un retour au pays natal*, trans. Lionel Abel and Ivan Goll (New York: Brentano's, 1947), 113–15. ("[C]eux qui n'ont inventé ni la poudre ni la boussole / ceux qui n'ont jamais su dompter la vapeur ni l'électricité / ceux qui n'ont exploré ni les mers ni le ciel / mais ceux sans qui la terre ne serait pas la terre / gibbosité d'autant plus bienfaisante que la terre déserte davantage la terre / silo où se préserve et mûrit ce que la terre a de plus terre / ma négritude n'est pas une pierre, sa surdité ruée contre la clameur du jour / ma négritude n'est pas une taie d'eau morte sur l'œil mort de la terre / ma négritude n'est ni une tour ni une cathédrale // elle plonge dans la chair rouge du sol / elle plonge dans la chair ardente du ciel / elle troue l'accablement opaque de sa droite patience // Eia pour le Kaïlcédrat royal! / Eia pour ceux qui n'ont jamais rien inventé / pour ceux qui n'ont jamais rien exploré / pour ceux qui n'ont jamais rien dompté // mais ils s'abandonnent, saisis, à l'essence de toute chose / ignorants des surfaces mais saisis par le mouvement de toute chose / insoucieux de dompter, mais jouant le jeu du monde / véritablement les fils aînés du monde / poreux à tous les souffles du monde / aire fraternelle de tous les souffles du monde / lit sans drain de toutes les eaux du monde / étincelle du feu sacré du monde / chair de la chair du monde palpitant du mouvement même du monde!" Aimé Césaire, "Cahier d'un retour au pays natal," *Volontés*, no. 20 [August 1939], 40–41.)

97. Suzanne Césaire, "Malaise d'une civilisation," *Tropiques*, no. 5 (April 1942), 48–49. ("Il ne s'agit point d'un retour en arrière, de la résurrection d'un passé africain que nous avons appris à connaître et à respecter. Il s'agit, au contraire, d'une mobilisation de toutes les forces vives mêlées sur cette terre où la race est le résultat du brassage le plus continu; il s'agit de prendre conscience du formidable amas d'énergies diverses que avons jusqu'ici enfermées en nous-mêmes . . . Cette terre, la nôtre, ne peut être que ce que vous voulons qu'elle soit.")

98. Michel Rybalka, "Publication and Reception of 'Anti-Semite and Jew,'" *October* 87 (Winter 1999), 161–82.

99. Jean-Paul Sartre, *Anti-Semite and Jew*, trans. George J. Becker (New York: Schocken Books, 1948), 69. ("Le Juif est un homme que les autres hommes tiennent pour Juif." Jean-Paul Sartre, *Réflexions sur la question juive* [Paris: Paul Morihien, 1946], 88.)

100. Jean-Paul Sartre, *Being and Nothingness*, 489. ("[I]l n'y a de liberté qu'en *situation* et il n'y a de situation que par la liberté. La réalité-humaine rencontre partout des résistances et des obstacles qu'elle n'a pas créés; mais ces résistances et ces obstacles n'ont de sens que dans et par le libre choix que la réalité-humaine *est*." Jean-Paul Sartre, *L'Être et le néant: Essai d'ontologie phénoménonolgique* (Paris: Gallimard, 1943), 569–70.)

101. Sartre, *Anti-Semite and Jew*, 71, 136. ("[L]e Juif est en situation de Juif parce qu'il vit au sein d'une collectivité qui le tient pour Juif"; "L'authenticité juive consiste à se choisir comme juif, c'est-à-dire à réaliser sa condition juive." Sartre, *Réflexions sur la question juive*, 93, 178.)

102. Jean-Paul Sartre, "Black Orpheus," in *The Aftermath of War (Situations III)*, trans. Chris Turner (London: Seagull, 2008), 259. ("[J]e vous souhaite de ressentir comme moi le saisissement d'être vus. Car le blanc a joui trois mille ans du privilège de voir sans qu'on le voie; il était regard pur . . . Jadis Européens de droit divin, nous sentions depuis quelques temps notre dignité s'effriter sous les regards américains ou soviétiques . . . Au moins espérions-nous retrouver un peu de notre grandeur dans les yeux domestiques des Africains. Mais il n'y a plus d'yeux domestiques: il y a les regards sauvages et libres qui jugent notre terre." Jean-Paul Sartre, "Orphée noire," in Léopold Sédar Senghor, ed., *La Nouvelle Poésie nègre et malgache de langue française* [Paris: Presses Universitaires de France, 1948], ix–x.)

103. Sartre, "Black Orpheus," 268. ("Ainsi est-il acculé à l'authenticité." Sartre, "Orphée noire," xiv.)

104. Sartre, "Black Orpheus," 268. ("[C]e racisme anti-raciste est le seul chemin qui puisse mener à l'abolition des différences de race." Sartre, "Orphée noire," xiv.)

105. Sartre, "Black Orpheus," 320. ("En fait, la Négritude apparaît comme le temps faible d'une progression dialectique: l'affirmation théorique et pratique de la suprématie du blanc est la thèse; la position de la Négritude comme valeur antithétique est le moment de la négativité. Mais ce moment négatif n'a pas de suffisance par lui-même et les noirs qui en usent le savent fort bien; ils savent qu'il vise à préparer la synthèse ou réalisation de l'humain dans une société sans race. Ainsi la Négritude est pour se détruire, elle est passage et non aboutissement, moyen et non fin dernière." Sartre, "Orphée noire," xli.)

106. Irene L. Gendzier, *Frantz Fanon: A Critical Study* (New York: Patheon, 1973), 14–16.

107. David Macey, *Frantz Fanon: A Biography* (London: Verso, 2012), 127.

108. Ibid., 152–60.

109. Frantz Fanon, *Black Skin, White Masks*, trans. Charles Lam Markmann (New York: Grove, 1967), 30. ("[C]e que nous voulons, c'est aider le Noir à se libérer de l'arsenal complexuel qui a germé au sein de la situation coloniale." Frantz Fanon, *Peau noire, masques blancs* [Paris: Éditions du Seuil, 1952], 24.)

110. Quoted in Fanon, *Black Skin, White Masks*, 39.

111. Ibid., 90. ("[C]'est le raciste qui crée l'infériorisé." Fanon, *Peau noire*, 75.)

112. Fanon, *Peau noire*, 93 ("le regard blanc").

113. Fanon, *Black Skin, White Masks*, 216, 218. ("L'homme n'est humain que dans la mesure où il s'impose à un autre homme, afin de se faire reconnaître par lui"; "un monde de reconnaissances réciproques." Fanon, *Peau noire*, 175–76, 177.)

114. Fanon, *Black Skin, White Masks*, 41. ("[L]'amour vrai, réel,—vouloir pour les autres ce que l'on postule pour soi, quand cette postulation intègre les valeurs permanentes de la réalité humaine,—requiert la mobilisation d'instances psychiques fondamentalement libérées des conflits inconscients." Fanon, *Peau noire*, 33.)

115. Fanon, *Black Skin, White Masks*, 231. ("Supériorité? Infériorité? Pourquoi tout simplement ne pas essayer de toucher l'autre, de sentir l'autre, de me révéler l'autre?" Fanon, *Peau noire*, 188.)

116. Fanon, *Black Skin, White Masks*, 133–35. ("Quand je lus cette page, je sentis qu'on me volait ma dernière chance . . . On avait fait appel à un ami des peuples de couleur, et cet ami n'avait rien trouvé de mieux que de montrer la relativité de leur action"; "ce n'est pas moi qui me crée un sens, mais c'est le sens qui était là, pré-existant, m'attendant. Ce n'est pas avec ma misère de mauvais nègre, mes dents de mauvais nègre, ma faim de mauvais nègre, que je modèle un flambeau pour y foutre le feu afin d'incendier ce monde, mais c'est le flambeau qui était là, attendant cette chance historique"; "Je ne suis ce pas une potentialité de quelque chose, je suis pleinement ce que je suis." Fanon, *Peau noire*, 108–109.)

117. Baldwin, "Conversation: Ida Lewis and James Baldwin," 24.

118. Harold R. Isaacs, "Five Writers and Their African Ancestors," *Phylon* 21 (1960): 324.

119. James Baldwin, "The Negro in Paris," *Reporter* 2 (June 6, 1950), 36.

120. Countee Cullen, "Heritage," in *Color* (New York: Harper and Brothers, 1925), 36.

121. Léopold Senghor to Richard Wright, June 24, 1946, Box 106, Folder 1606, Wright Papers; Fabre, *The Unfinished Quest of Richard Wright*, 317.

122. See Cedric Tolliver, "Making Cultural Capital: *Présence Africaine* and Diasporic Modernity in Post–World War II Paris," in Jeremy Braddock and Jonathan P. Eburne, eds., *Paris, Capital of the Black Atlantic* (Baltimore: Johns Hopkins University Press, 2013), 200–22.

123. Alioune Diop, "Niam n'goura, ou les raisons d'être de Présence Africaine," *Présence Africaine*, no. 1 (November–December 1947), 7. ("[À] définir l'originalité africaine et de hâter son insertion dans le monde moderne.") See also Kesteloot, *Black Writers in French*, 279–87.

124. Toru Kiuchi and Yoshinobu Hakutani, *Richard Wright: A Documented Chronology, 1908–1960* (Jefferson, NC: McFarland), 284–88; Rowley, *Richard Wright*, 416–34.

125. John D. Hargreaves, *Decolonization in Africa*, 2nd ed. (London: Longman, 1996), 123–31; Leslie James, *George Padmore and Decolonization from Below: Pan-Africanism, the Cold War, and the End of Empire* (New York: Palgrave Macmillan, 2015), 134; Kwame Anthony Appiah, "What Was Africa to Them?," *New York Review of Books*, September 27, 2007 (online).

126. See Kwame Anthony Appiah, "A Long Way from Home: Wright in the Gold Coast," in Harold Bloom, ed., *Richard Wright: Modern Critical Views* (New York: Chelsea House, 1987), 173–90.

127. Richard Wright, *Black Power: A Record of Reactions in the Land of Pathos* (New York: Harper and Brothers, 1954), 54.

128. Peter Abrahams, "The Blacks," *Holiday* 25 (April 1959), 75.

129. See Wright, *Black Power*, 139–41.

130. Ibid., 57.

131. Ibid., 127.

132. Ibid., 117.

133. Ibid., 334, 345–47.

134. See Kwame Nkrumah to June Milne, September 30, 1967, in *Kwame Nkrumah: The Conakry Years, His Life and Letters*, comp. June Milne (London: Panaf, 1990), 183–84.

135. Rowley, *Richard Wright*, 436–37; Carol Polsgrove, *Ending British Rule in Africa: Writers in a Common Cause* (Manchester, UK: Manchester University Press, 2009), 124–29; Brian Russell Roberts and Keith Foulcher, eds., *Indonesian Notebook: A Sourcebook on Richard Wright and the Bandung Conference* (Durham: Duke University Press, 2016), 17–18.

136. See Peggy Durdin, "Behind the Façade of Asian Unity," *New York Times Magazine*, April 17, 1955, 9ff.

137. Peter Coleman, *The Liberal Conspiracy: The Congress for Cultural Freedom and the Struggle for the Mind of Postwar Europe* (New York: Free Press, 1989), 59–102; Rowley, *Richard Wright*, 459.

138. See Cary Fraser, "An American Dilemma: Race and Realpolitik in the American Response to the Bandung Conference, 1955," in Plummer, *Window on Freedom*, 115–40; Kweku Ampiah, *The Political and Moral Imperatives of the Bandung Conference of 1955: The Reactions of the U.S., U.K., and Japan* (Folkestone, UK: Global Oriental, 2007), 63–165; Jason C. Parker, "Small Victory, Missed Chance: The Eisenhower Administration, the Bandung Conference, and the Turning of the Cold War," in Kathryn C. Statler and Andrew L. Johns, eds., *The Eisenhower Administration, the Third World, and the Globalization of the Cold War* (Lanham, MD: Rowman and Littlefield, 2006), 153–74.

139. See, e.g., George Sokolsky, "Conference at Bandung Is Conference of Race," *Washington Post*, April 21, 1955, 17; "Asia: Can the West Hold Back the Tide?," *Newsweek* 45 (January 17, 1955), 32–33.

140. See George McTurnan Kahin, *The Asian-African Conference, Bandung, Indonesia, April 1955* (Ithaca: Cornell University Press, 1956), 32–38; Elie Abel, "U.S. Forebodings Eased by the Trend at Banding," *New York Times*, April 23, 1955, 1; Tillman Durdin, "U.S. Finds Support among Afro-Asians," *New York Times*, April 24, 1955, 5; Odd Arne Westad, *The Global Cold War: Third World Interventions and the Making of Our Times* (Cambridge: Cambridge University Press, 2005), 99–104.

141. See Robert Vitalis, "The Midnight Ride of Kwame Nkrumah and Other Fables of Bandung (Ban-doong)," *Humanity* 4 (2013): 261–88.

142. Roberts and Foulcher, *Indonesian Notebook*, 13–17; Brian Russell Roberts, *Artistic Ambassadors: Literary and International Representation of the New Negro Era* (Charlottesville: University of Virginia Press, 2013), 146–72.

143. "Speech by President Sukarno of Indonesia at the Opening of the Conference," *Asia-Africa Speaks from Bandung* (Jakarta: Ministry of Foreign Affairs, Republic of Indonesia, 1955), 23.

144. Ibid., 22.

145. Richard Wright, *The Color Curtain: A Report on the Bandung Conference* (Cleveland: World Publishing, 1956), 139–40.

146. Ibid., 25–26, 207, 209,

147. Ibid., 164, 202, 220.

148. Tillman Durdin, "Richard Wright Examines the Meaning of Bandung," *New York Times Book Review*, March 18, 1956, 1, 33.

149. Mochtar Lubis, "Through Coloured Glasses?," *Encounter* 6 (March 1956): 73.

150. James R. Hooker, *Black Revolutionary: George Padmore's Path from Communism to Pan-Africanism* (New York: Prager, 1967), 91, 127.

151. Richard H. King, *Race, Culture, and the Intellectuals, 1940–1970* (Washington, DC: Woodrow Wilson Center Press, 2004), 208–15; Bob Swaim, dir., *Lumières Noires* (Entreacte Productions, France 2 TV DVD, 2007); Macey,

Frantz Fanon, 174–76, 276–89; Penny M. Von Eschen, *Race Against Empire: Black Americans and Anticolonialism, 1937–1957* (Ithaca: Cornell University Press, 1997), 167–84.

152. Macey, *Frantz Fanon*, 276–77.

153. Rowley, *Richard Wright*, 474.

154. David Levering Lewis, *W. E. B. Du Bois: The Fight for Equality and the American Century, 1919–1963* (New York: Henry Holt, 2000), 546–54.

155. W. E. B. Du Bois, "To the Congrès des Écrivains et Artistes Noires," *Présence Africaine*, n.s., nos. 8–9–10 (June–November 1956), 383 (French edition. Issues were published in separate English and French editions).

156. "Débats," *Présence Africaine*, n.s., nos. 8–9–10 (June–November 1956), 67 (French edition).

157. See Vaillant, *Black, French, and African*, 252–71.

158. Léopold Sédar Senghor, "The Spirit of Civilisation or the Laws of African Negro Culture," *Présence Africaine*, n.s., nos. 8–9–10 (June–November 1956), 53 (English edition). ("[P]hysiopsychologie du Nègre." French edition, 53.)

159. Senghor, "The Spirit of Civilisation," 52 (English edition). ("La raison blanche est analytique par utilisation, la raison nègre, intuitive par participation." French edition, 52.)

160. Senghor, "The Spirit of Civilisation," 64 (English edition). ("L'esprit de la civilisation négro-africaine anime, consciemment ou non, les meilleurs des artistes et écrivains nègres d'aujourd'hui, qu'ils soient d'Afrique ou d'Amérique. Dans la mesure où ils en ont conscience et s'inspirent de la culture négro-africaine, il se haussent au rang international; dans la mesure où ils tournent le dos à l'Afrique-mère, ils dégénèrent et s'affadissent." French edition, 65.)

161. Wilder, *Freedom Time*, 106–12.

162. Amié Césaire, *Discours sur le colonialisme* (Paris: Éditions Réclame, 1950), 9.

163. Aimé Césaire, "Culture and Colonization," *Présence Africaine*, n.s., nos. 8–9–10 (June–November 1956), 199, 200 (English edition). ("[T]oute colonisation se traduit à délai plus ou moins long par la mort de la civilisation de la société colonisée." "[U]n leurre et un attrape-nigaud." French edition, 196, 198.) See also Aimé Césaire, "Culture and Colonization," trans. Brent Hayes Edwards, *Social Text* 28 (Summer 2010): 127–44.

164. Césaire, "Culture and Colonization," 204 (English edition), 139–41 ("Les éléments étrangers sont posés sur son sol, mais lui restent étrangers. Choses de blancs. Manières de blancs. Choses qui côtoie le peuple indigène mais sur lesquelles le peuple indigènes n'a pas puissance." French edition, 202.)

165. Césaire, "Culture and Colonization," 197, 206 (English edition). ("Je refuse de croire que la future culture africaine puisse opposer une fin de non-recevoir totale et brutale à l'ancienne culture africaine." French edition, 204.)

166. Macey, *Frantz Fanon*, 142–47.

167. Frantz Fanon to Richard Wright, January 6, 1953, Box 97, Folder 1324, Wright Papers. ("[L]a portée humaine de vos ouvrages.") See also Michel Fabre, "Frantz Fanon et Richard Wright," in Elo Dacy, ed., *L'Actualité de Frantz Fanon: Actes du colloque de Brazzaville (12–16 décembre 1984)* (Paris: Éditions Karthala, 1986), 169–77.

168. Macey, *Frantz Fanon*, 276–87.

169. Frantz Fanon, "Racism and culture," *Présence Africaine*, n.s., nos. 8–9–10 (June–November 1956), 122, 124 (English edition). ("L'entreprise de déculturation se trouve être le negatif d'un plus gigantesque travail d'asservissement économique, voire biologique." "[L]e but recherché est davantage une agonie continuée qu'une disparation totale de la culture préexistante." French edition, 122, 124.) See also Frantz Fanon, "Racism and Culture," in *Toward the African Revolution*, trans. Haakon Chevalier (New York: Monthly Review Press, 1967), 31–44.

170. Fanon, "Racism and Culture," 126 (English edition). ("C'est ainsi que le blues 'plainte des esclaves noirs' est présenté a l'admiration des oppresseurs. C'est un peu d'oppression stylisée qui revient à l'exploitant et au raciste. Sans oppression et sans racisme pas de blues. La fin du racisme sonnerait le glas de la grande musique noire." French edition, 126.)

171. Fanon, "Racism and Culture," 131 (English edition). ("La culture spasmée et rigide de l'occupant, libérée s'ouvre enfin à la culture du peuple devenu réellement frère. Les deux cultures peuvent s'affronter, s'enrichir." French edition, 131.)

172. "Débats," *Présence Africaine*, n.s., nos. 8–9–10 (June–November 1956), 67 (French edition).

173. See Tommie Shelby, "Richard Wright: Realizing the Promise of the West" (paper in my possession).

174. Richard Wright and Edwin Rosskam, *12 Million Black Voices: A Folk History of the Negro in the United States* (New York: Viking, 1941), 147.

175. Richard Wright, "Tradition and Industrialization," *Présence Africaine*, n.s., nos. 8–9–10 (June–November 1956), 356.

176. Ibid., 354–57.

177. Ibid., 360.

178. James Baldwin, "Princes and Powers," *Encounter* 8 (January 1957): 52.

179. James Baldwin to Sol Stein, undated, Baldwin Papers.

180. Baldwin, "Princes and Powers," 53.
181. Baldwin, "Princes and Powers," in *Nobody Knows My Name*, 41. These words are not in the original *Encounter* essay.

12. CONSUMER SOVEREIGNTY

1. See Okwui Enwezor, Katy Siegel, and Ulrich Wilmes, eds., *Postwar: Art Between the Pacific and the Atlantic, 1945–1965* (Munich, Germany: Haus der Kunst; New York: Prestel, 2016); Darsie Alexander, with Bartholomew Ryan, eds., *International Pop* (Minneapolis: Walker Art Center, 2015); Jessica Morgan and Flavia Frigeri, *The World Goes Pop* (New Haven: Yale University Press, 2015); Julia Robinson, ed., *New Realisms: 1957–1962: Object Strategies Between Readymade and Sculpture* (Madrid: Museo Nacional Centro de Arte Reina Sofía, 2010); Philomena Mariana, ed., *Global Conceptualism: Points of Origin, 1950s–1980s* (Flushing, NY: Queens Museum of Art, 1999).
2. See, e.g., Peter Selz, ed., "A Symposium on Pop Art," *Arts Magazine* 38 (April 1963), 36–45; Bruce Glaser, "Oldenburg Lichtenstein Warhol," *Artforum* 4 (February 1966), 21–24. Also Hal Foster, *The First Pop Age: Painting and Subjectivity in the Art of Hamilton, Lichtenstein, Warhol, Richter, and Ruscha* (Princeton: Princeton University Press, 2012), 7–14; Daniel Horowitz, *Consuming Pleasures: Intellectuals and Popular Culture in the Postwar World* (Philadelphia: University of Pennsylvania Press, 2012), 229.
3. Table 3-1a: Growth of Per Capita GDP, Population, and GDP: World and Major Regions, 1000–1998, Angus Maddison, *The World Economy: A Millennial Perspective* (Paris: Development Centre of the Organisation for Economic Co-Operation and Development, 2001), 126.
4. Thomas Piketty, *Capital in the Twenty-First Century*, trans. Arthur Goldhammer (Cambridge, MA: Harvard University Press, 2014), 336–76.
5. Tony Judt, *Postwar: A History of Europe Since 1945* (New York: Penguin Press, 2005), 327–28.
6. Table 8b: Rate of Growth of World GDP, 20 Countries and Regional Totals, 1–2001 AD, Maddison, *The World Economy*, 640.
7. Figure 2.2: Growth Rate of World Population, Antiquity to 2100, Piketty, *Capital in the Twenty-First Century*, 80, 304–76; Robert J. Gordon, *The Rise and Fall of American Growth: The U.S. Standard of Living Since the Civil War* (Princeton: Princeton University Press, 2016), 319–28.
8. Maddison, *The World Economy*, 125; Herman Van der Wee, *Prosperity and Upheaval: The World Economy, 1945–1980*, trans. Robin Hogg and Max R. Hall (New York: Viking, 1986), 345–78; Gordon, *The Rise and Fall of American Growth*, 1–13 and passim.

9. Judt, *Postwar*, 16–18; John W. Dower, *Embracing Defeat: Japan in the Wake of World War II* (New York: W. W. Norton, 1999), 45–48.
10. James T. Patterson, *Grand Expectations: The United States, 1945–1974* (New York: Oxford University Press, 1996), 61–62; Judt, *Postwar*, 350.
11. See Gianni Toniolo, "Europe's Golden Age, 1950–1973: Speculations from a Long-Run Perspective," *Economic History Review*, n.s., 51 (1998): 252–67.
12. See Alan S. Milward, *The Reconstruction of Western Europe, 1945–1951* (London: Methuen, 1984), 90–125; cf. Judt, *Postwar*, 89–99.
13. Table 1112: U.S. Government Foreign Grants and Credits by Country, *Statistical Abstract of the United States, 1956* (Washington, DC: U.S. Government Printing Office, 1956), 893–94.
14. Judt, *Postwar*, 89–99, 151–52, 350–5l; Richard Pells, *Not Like Us: How Europeans Have Loved, Hated, and Transformed American Culture Since World War II* (New York: Basic Books, 1997), 188–90; Francis Williams, *The American Invasion* (New York: Crown, 1962), 16.
15. Starting with William Appleman Williams, *The Tragedy of American Diplomacy* (Cleveland: World Publishing, 1959).
16. See Charles Maier, "The Politics of Productivity: Foundations of American International Economic Policy After World War II," in *In Search of Stability: Explorations in Historical Political Economy* (Cambridge: Cambridge University Press, 1987), 121–52.
17. House of Representatives, *Foreign Assistance Act of 1948*, Title 1, sec. 102: Findings and Declaration of Policy (Washington, DC: U.S. Government Printing Office, 1948), 1–2.
18. See Marie-Laure Djelic, *Exporting the American Model: The Postwar Transformation of European Business* (New York: Oxford University Press, 1998); Victoria de Grazia, *Irresistible Empire: America's Advance through Twentieth-Century Europe* (Cambridge, MA: Harvard University Press, 2005).
19. Arthur Koestler, *The Lotus and the Robot* (London: Hutchinson, 1960), 277.
20. Victoria de Grazia, "Changing Consumption Regimes in Europe, 1930–1970: Comparative Perspectives on the Distribution Problem," in Susan Strasser, Charles McGovern, and Matthias Judt, eds., *Getting and Spending: European and American Consumer Societies in the Twentieth Century* (Cambridge: Cambridge University Press, 1998), 77–79.
21. Lizabeth Cohen, *A Consumer's Republic: The Politics of Mass Consumption in Postwar America* (New York: Knopf, 2003), esp. 112–54.
22. David Childs, *Britain Since 1945: A Political History*, 7th ed. (London: Routledge, 2012), 2–3; Judt, *Postwar*, 205.

23. Paul Johnson, "The Welfare State, Income, and Living Standards," in Roderick Floud and Paul Johnson, eds., *The Cambridge Economic History of Modern Britain*, vol. 3, *Structural Change and Growth, 1939–2000* (Cambridge: Cambridge University Press, 2004), 217–18.

24. Childs, *Britain Since 1945*, 14.

25. Mary O'Mahony, "Employment, Education, and Human Capital," in Floud and Johnson, *The Cambridge Economic History of Modern Britain*, vol. 3, 116.

26. Table 1: Output growth of the world capitalist countries and the UK, 1870–1989 (annual % growth rates), Michael Kitson, "The Comparative Weakness of the UK Economy," in Philip Arestis, Gabriel Palma, and Malcolm Sawyer, eds., *Markets, Unemployment, and Economic Policy: Essays in Honour of Geoff Harcourt*, vol. 2 (London: Routledge, 1997), 134. See also N. F. R. Crafts, "Economic Growth," in N. F. R. Crafts and N. W. C. Woodward, eds., *The British Economy Since 1945* (Oxford: Oxford University Press, 1991), 261–90.

27. Judt, *Postwar*, 160–62. Cf. Derek Leebaert, *Grand Improvisation: America Confronts the British Superpower, 1945–1957* (New York: Farrar, Straus and Giroux, 2018).

28. Dean Acheson, *Present at the Creation: My Years in the State Department* (New York: W. W. Norton, 1969), 217–19.

29. Hamilton Fish Armstrong, "Europe Revisited," *Foreign Affairs* 25 (1947): 537.

30. Gordon Manley, "Central England Temperatures: Monthly Means, 1659 to 1973," *Quarterly Journal of the Royal Meteorological Society* 100 (1974): 393–98; Alex J. Robertson, *The Bleak Midwinter 1947* (Manchester, UK: Manchester University Press, 1987).

31. Judt, *Postwar*, 161–63; Table 2.2: Workers directly involved in strikes in all industries and services, 1944–53, Childs, *Britain Since 1945*, 22.

32. Cyril Connolly, "Comment," *Horizon* 15 (1947): 151.

33. Ibid., 154.

34. George Orwell, "London Letter," in *The Complete Works of George Orwell*, vol. 17, *I Belong to the Left, 1945*, ed. Peter Davison (London: Secker and Warburg, 1998), 248.

35. James Obelkevich, "Consumption," in James Obelkevich and Peter Catterall, eds., *Understanding Postwar British Society* (London: Routledge, 1994), 145; Paul Addison, *No Turning Back: The Peacetime Revolutions of Postwar Britain* (Oxford: Oxford University Press, 2010), 20–75.

36. Table 20: Homes with Electrical Applicances, 1932–1971, Stanley Lebergott, *The American Economy* (Princeton: Princeton University Press, 1975), 288. (Data from 1953.)

37. See Martha J. Bailey and William J. Collins, "Did Improvements in Household Technology Cause the Baby Boom? Evidence from Electrification, Appliance Diffusion, and the Amish," *American Economic Journal: Macroeconomics* 3 (2011): 189–217.

38. Association of National Advertisers, *Magazine Circulation and Rate Trends* (New York: National Association of Advertisers, 1956), 1. Numbers are for ABC (Audit Bureau of Circulation) audited titles.

39. Table 1: Gross National Advertising in General and Farm Magazines, 1915–63, Theodore Peterson, *Magazines in the Twentieth Century* (Urbana: University of Illinois Press, 1956), 26.

40. David Reed, *The Popular Magazine in Britain and the United States, 1880–1960* (Toronto: University of Toronto Press, 1997), 194–95; Peterson, *Magazines in the Twentieth Century*, 35; and, generally, Clifford L. Helbert, ed., *Printing Progress: A Mid-Century Report* (Cincinnati: International Association of Printing House Craftsmen, 1959).

41. Arthur J. Pulos, *American Design Ethic: A History of Industrial Design* (Cambridge, MA: MIT Press, 1983), 336–419.

42. Richard Hoggart, *The Uses of Literacy: Aspects of Working-Class Life, with Special Reference to Publications and Entertainments* (London: Chatto and Windus, 1957), 171.

43. See Jules Feiffer, *The Explainers* (New York: McGraw Hill, 1960).

44. John Kenneth Galbraith, *The Affluent Society* (Boston: Houghton Mifflin, 1958), 153.

45. Lawrence Black, *The Political Culture of the Left in Affluent Britain: Old Labour, New Britain?* (New York: Palgrave Macmillan, 2003), 94–123; Stefan Schwarzkopf, "They Do It with Mirrors: Advertising and British Cold War Consumer Politics," *Contemporary British History* 19 (2005): 135–37.

46. "Role of Advertising in Commerce," *Times* [London], May 2, 1953, 3.

47. Asa Briggs, *The History of Broadcasting in Britain*, vol. 4, *Sound and Vision* (Oxford: Oxford University Press, 1979), 885–1024; Bernard Sendall, *Independent Television in Britain*, vol. 1, *Origin and Foundation, 1946–62* (London: Macmillan, 1982), 3–55.

48. J. B. Priestley and Jacquetta Hawkes, *Journey Down a Rainbow* (New York: Harper and Brothers, 1955), 50.

49. Hoggart, *The Uses of Literacy*, 281.

50. Raymond Williams, "The Magic System," *New Left Review*, no. 4 (July–August 1960), 32.

51. See Black, *The Political Culture of the Left in Affluent Britain*, 188–94.

52. George Orwell, "Lists of Names of Crypto-Communists and Fellow-Travelers Sent to Information Research Department 2 May 1949,"

in *The Unknown Orwell: Being a Supplement to the Complete Works of George Orwell*, comp. Peter Davison (London: Timewell Press, 2006), 147.

53. Terri Colpi, *The Italian Factor: The Italian Community in Great Britain* (Edinburgh: Mainstream Publishing, 1991), 48–49; Eduardo Paolozzi interview with Frank Whitford, May 4, 1994, National Life Stories, C466/17, British Library; Robin Spencer, ed., *Eduardo Paolozzi: Writings and Interviews* (Oxford: Oxford University Press, 2000), 5. See, generally, Thomas Lawson, "Bunk: Eduardo Paolozzi and the Legacy of the Independent Group," in Institute of Contemporary Arts, *Modern Dreams: The Rise and Fall of Pop* (Cambridge, MA: MIT Press, 1988), 18–29; Robin Spencer, "Sir Eduardo Luigi Paolozzi," in *Oxford Dictionary of National Biography* (Oxford: Oxford University Press, 2013).

54. Eduardo Paolozzi, "Wonderful World," in Stefano de Martino and Alex Wall, comps., *Cities of Childhood: Italian Colonies of the 1930s* (London: Architectural Association, 1988), 10.

55. Colpi, *The Italian Factor*, 105–108.

56. Ibid., 115–21.

57. Paolozzi interview with Whitford, May 4, 1994, National Life Stories.

58. Eduardo Paolozzi, "Retrospective Statement," in David Robbins, ed., *The Independent Group: Postwar Britain and the Aesthetics of Plenty* (Cambridge, MA: MIT Press, 1990), 192.

59. Graham Whitman, "Chronology," in Robbins, *The Independent Group*, 20; Paolozzi interview with Whitford, National Life Stories; John-Paul Stonard, "The 'Bunk' Collages of Eduardo Paolozzi," *Burlington Magazine* 150 (2008): 238–41.

60. Anne Massey, *The Independent Group: Modernism and Mass Culture in Britain, 1945–59* (Manchester, UK: Manchester University Press, 1995), 25.

61. Nanette Aldred, "Art in Postwar Britain: A Short History of the ICA," in Alistair Davies and Alan Sinfield, eds., *British Culture of the Postwar: An Introduction to Literature and Society, 1945–1999* (London: Routledge, 2000), 148; Julian Cooper, dir., *Fathers of Pop* (Arts Council of England DVD, 1979) (interview with Hamilton).

62. Reyner Banham, "Industrial Design e arte popolare," *Civiltà delle macchine* 3 (November/December 1955), 15n21.

63. Mary Banham interview with Corinne Julius, January 18, 2002, C467/67, National Life Stories.

64. See Stonard, "The 'Bunk' Collages of Eduardo Paolozzi," 242; Beatriz Colomina and Peter Smithson, "Friends of the Future: A Conversation with Peter Smithson," *October*

94 (Autumn 2000), 5; Hans-Ulrich Obrist, "Pop Daddy," *Tate: The Art Magazine*, no. 4 (March/April 2003), 62 (interview with Hamilton); Richard Hamilton, "A Statement by RichardHamilton,"www.warholstars.org/articles/richardhamilton/richardhamilton.html.

65. Mary Banham, "Retrospective Statement," in Robbins, *The Independent Group*, 187–88.

66. Brian Wallis, "Tomorrow and Tomorrow and Tomorrow: The Independent Group and Popular Culture," in Institute of Contemporary Arts, *Modern Dreams*, 14–16; Whitman, "Chronology," 18–31.

67. See Wallis, "Tomorrow and Tomorrow and Tomorrow," 8–17; Christopher Finch, "London Pop Recollected," in David E. Brauer, Jim Edwards, Christopher Finch, and Walter Hopps, eds., *Pop Art: U.S./U.K. Connections, 1956–1966* (Houston: Menil Collection, 2001), 20–41; Nigel Whiteley, *Reyner Banham: Historian of the Immediate Future* (Cambridge, MA: MIT Press, 2002), 425n3; Anne Massey, *Out of the Ivory Tower: The Independent Group and Popular Culture* (Manchester, UK: Manchester University Press, 2013), 10–36; Massey, *The Independent Group*, 109–27.

68. Cooper, dir., *Fathers of Pop* (interview with Banham).

69. Lawrence Alloway to Sylvia Sleigh, February 13, 1952, Box 5, Folder 2, Lawrence Alloway Papers, Getty Research Institute.

70. Whitman, "Chronology," 20.

71. Paolozzi, "Retrospective Statement," 192; Stonard, "The 'Bunk' Collages of Eduardo Paolozzi," 240.

72. Paolozzi, "Retrospective Statement," 192.

73. Reyner Banham, "Representations in Protest," *New Society* 13 (May 8, 1969), 718.

74. Massey, *The Independent Group*, 139–44.

75. Reyner Banham, "Packaging," *Art News and Review* 3 (February 24, 1951), 6.

76. Reyner Banham, "Vehicles of Desire," *Art* 1 (September 1, 1955), 3.

77. Lawrence Alloway, "The Long Front of Culture," *Cambridge Opinion*, no. 17 (1959), 25.

78. Lawrence Alloway, "Personal Statement," *Ark*, no. 19 (Spring 1959), 28.

79. Ibid., 28; Reyner Banham, "Industrial Design and Popular Art," *Industrial Design* 7 (March 1960), 62.

80. Lawrence Alloway, "The Arts and the Mass Media," *Architectural Design* 28 (February 1958), 84.

81. Reyner Banham, "Machine Aesthetes," *New Statesman* 56 (August 16, 1958), 193.

82. Alloway, "The Arts and the Mass Media," 84.

83. Alloway, "The Long Front of Culture," 25.

84. See Jerome Stolnitz, "On the Significance of Lord Shaftesbury in Modern Aesthetic Theory," *Philosophical Quarterly* 11 (1961): 97–113;

Larry Shiner, *The Invention of Art: A Cultural History* (Chicago: University of Chicago Press, 2001), 130–51; Paul Guyer, *A History of Modern Aesthetics*, vol. 1, *The Eighteenth Century* (Cambridge: Cambridge University Press, 2014), 30.

85. *Oxford English Dictionary* (online).

86. Judt, *Postwar*, 442.

87. Giangiacomo Nardozzi, "The Italian 'Economic Miracle,'" *Rivista di Storia Economica*, 19 (2003): 139–41; Paul Ginsborg, *A History of Contemporary Italy: Society and Politics, 1943–1988* (New York: Palgrave Macmillan, 2003), 214.

88. Ivan Paris, "Domestic Appliances and Industrial Design: The Italian White-Goods Industry During the 1950s and 1960s," *Technology and Culture* 57 (2016): 617; Ginsborg, *A History of Contemporary Italy*, 214; Ivan Paris, "White Goods in Italy during a Golden Age (1948–1973)," *Journal of Interdisciplinary History* 44 (2013): 97.

89. Giovanni Albera and Nicolas Monti, *Italian Modern: A Design Heritage* (New York: Rizzoli, 1989), 23–25.

90. See Kjetil Fallan, "Annus Mirabilis: 1954, Alberto Rosselli and the Institutionalisation of Design Mediation," in Grace Lees-Maffei and Kjetil Fallan, eds., *Made in Italy: Rethinking a Century of Italian Design* (London: Bloomsbury, 2014), 262–67; Luisa J. Orto, "Design as Art: *il Design* and Italian National Identity," PhD dissertation, New York University, 1995, 126–71.

91. *La memoria e il futuro: I Congresso Internazionale dell'Industrial Design, Triennale di Milano, 1954* (Milan: Skira, 2001), 32. ("[L]'oggetto creato dalla macchina fa parte integrante di tutto il panorama dell'arte moderna.")

92. Whitman, "Chronology," 30–31.

93. Appendix: "Notes on the Independent Group Session of 1955," in Robbins, *The Independent Group*, 249.

94. John McHale, "The Expendable Ikon 1 and 2," *Architectural Design* 29 (February/March 1959), 82–83, 116–117.

95. Banham, "Industrial Design and Popular Art," 65 (English version of "Industrial Design e arte popolare").

96. Nigel Whiteley, *Art and Pluralism: Lawrence Alloway's Cultural Criticism* (Liverpool: Liverpool University Press, 2012), 53.

97. Alloway, "Personal Statement," 28.

98. Gillo Dorfles, "Communication and Symbol in the Work of Art," *Journal of Aesthetics and Art Criticism* 15 (1957): 289.

99. Alloway, "Personal Statement," 28.

100. Philip Marchand, *Marshall McLuhan: The Medium and the Messenger* (New York: Ticknor and Fields, 1989), 110.

101. "Richard Hamilton in Conversation with Michael Craig-Martin," in Hal Foster and Alex Bacon, eds., *Richard Hamilton* (Cambridge, MA: MIT Press, 2010), 6.

102. Herbert Marshall McLuhan, *The Mechanical Bride: Folklore of Industrial Man* (New York: Vanguard, 1951), v.

103. McHale, "The Expendable Ikon 1 and 2," 82.

104. Alison Smithson and Peter Smithson, "Personal Statement," *Ark*, no. 18 (Fall 1956), 49.

105. Mary Banham interview with Corinne Julius, National Life Stories; Robbins, *The Independent Group*, 195n2.

106. Smithson and Smithson, "Personal Statement," 49–50.

107. Smithson and Smithson, "Mobility: Road Systems," *Architectural Review* 128 (October 1958), 385.

108. William Knoedelseder, *Fins: Harley Earl, the Rise of General Motors, and the Glory Days of Detroit* (New York: Harper, 2018), 153–58, 173.

109. Thomas Hine, *Populuxe* (New York: Knopf, 1986), 83–94. See also David Gartman, *Auto Opium: A Social History of American Automobile Design* (London: Routledge, 1994), 136–81.

110. Raymond Loewy, "Jukebox on Wheels," *Atlantic Monthly* 195 (April 1955), 38.

111. Appendix: "Notes on the Independent Group Session of 1955," in Robbins, *The Independent Group*, 248.

112. Banham, "Vehicles of Desire," 3.

113. Roland Barthes, "The New Citroën," in *Mythologies*, trans. Richard Howard and Annette Lavers (New York: Hill and Wang, 2012), 169, 171. ("Je crois que l'automobile est aujourd'hui l'équivalent assez exact des grandes Cathédrales gothiques"; "le tableau de bord ressemble d'avantage à l'établi d'une cuisine moderne qu'à la centrale d'une usine: les minces volets de tôle mate, ondulée, les petits leviers à boule blanche, les voyants très simples, la discrétion même de la nickelerie, tout cela signifie une sorte de contrôle exercé sur le mouvement conçu comme confort plus que comme performance." Roland Barthes, "La Nouvelle Citroën," *Lettres Nouvelles* 34 [1955]: 825–26.)

114. "Richard Hamilton in Conversation with Michael Craig-Martin," 3–6.

115. Masey, *The Independent Group*, 97. See also Horowitz, *Consuming Pleasures*, 209–13; Lynne Cooke, "The Independent Group: British and American Pop Art, A 'Palimpcestuous' Legacy," in Kirk Varnedoe and Adam Gopnik, eds., *Modern Art and Popular Culture: Readings in High and Low* (New York: Museum of Modern Art, 1990), 193–95; David E. Brauer, "British Pop Art: 1956–1966, A Documentary Essay," in Brauer et al., *Pop Art* 62; Graham

Whitham, "This Is Tomorrow: Genesis of an Exhibition," in Institute of Contemporary Arts, *Modern Dreams*, 34–39.

116. See www.britishpathe.com/video/this-is-tomorrow-aka-this-is-tomorrow/.

117. Theo Crosby, "Night Thoughts of a Faded Utopia," in Robbins, *The Independent Group*, 197–98.

118. John McHale, "Josef Albers," *Architectural Design* 26 (1956): 205.

119. I rely on John-Paul Stonard, "Pop in the Age of Boom: Richard Hamilton's 'Just What Is It that Makes Today's Homes So Different, So Appealing?'," *Burlington Magazine* 149 (2007): 612–20. See also Obrist, "Pop Daddy," 62.

120. Massey, *The Independent Group*, 96.

121. Richard Hamilton to Alison and Peter Smithson, January 16, 1957, in Richard Hamilton, *Collected Words, 1953–1982* (London: Thames and Hudson, 2001), 28.

122. Colomina and Smithson, "Friends of the Future," 5.

123. R. H., "Hommage à Chrysler Corp.," *Architectural Design* 28 (March 1958), 120.

124. See, e.g., Foster, *The First Pop Age*, 52–53; Benjamin H. D. Buchloh, "Among Americans: Richard Hamilton," in Mark Godfrey, Paul Schimmel, and Vicente Todoli, *Richard Hamilton* (London: Tate, 2014), 93–106.

125. Richard Hamilton, "For the Finest Art Try—POP," *Gazette*, no. 1 (1961), 3.

13. THE FREE PLAY OF THE MIND

1. See Roger L. Geiger, *American Higher Education since World War II: A History* (Princeton: Princeton University Press, 2019), 91–175. Portions of this section are drawn from Louis Menand, *The Marketplace of Ideas: Reform and Resistance in the American University* (New York: W. W. Norton, 2010).

2. Series H 689–699: Institutions of Higher Education—Number and Faculty: 1870–1970, and Series H 700–715: Institutions of Higher Education—Degree-Credit Enrollment: 1870–1970, U.S. Bureau of the Census, *Historical Statistics of the United States: Colonial Times to 1970* vol. 1 (Washington, DC: U.S. Government Printing Office, 1975), 382–83.

3. Roger L. Geiger, "The Ten Generations of American Higher Education," in Philip G. Altbach, Robert O. Berdahl, and Patricia J. Gumport, eds., *American Higher Education in the Twenty-First Century: Social, Political, and Economic Challenges* (Baltimore: Johns Hopkins University Press, 1999), 61–64.

4. U.S. Bureau of the Census, *Historical Statistics of the United States*, vol. 1, 382, 383, 387; Walter P. Metzger, "The Academic Profession in the United States," in Burton R. Clark, ed., *The Academic Profession: National, Disciplinary, and Institutional Settings* (Berkeley: University of California Press, 1987), 124.

5. Louis Menand, Paul Reitter, and Chad Wellmon, eds., *The Rise of the Research University: A Sourcebook* (Chicago: University of Chicago Press, 2017), 165–66.

6. Glenn Altschuler and Stuart M. Blumin, *The G.I. Bill: A New Deal for Veterans* (New York: Oxford University Press, 2009), 86; Roger L. Geiger, *Research and Relevant Knowledge: American Research Universities Since World War II* (New York: Oxford University Press, 1993), 40–41; Suzanne Mettler, *Soldiers to Citizens: The G.I. Bill and the Making of the Greatest Generation* (New York: Oxford University Press, 2005), 7.

7. U.S. Office of Scientific Research and Development, *Science—The Endless Frontier* (Washington, DC: U.S. Government Printing Office, 1945). See also Geiger, *Research and Relevant Knowledge*, 157–97; Hugh Davis Graham and Nancy Diamond, *The Rise of American Research Universities: Elites and Challenges in the Postwar Era* (Baltimore: Johns Hopkins University Press, 1997), 26–50.

8. Series H 716–727: Institutions of Higher Education: Current Income: 1890–1970, U.S. Bureau of the Census, *Historical Statistics of the United States*, vol. 1, 384.

9. Elizabeth A. Duffy and Idana Goldberg, *Crafting a Class: College Admissions and Financial Aid, 1955–1994* (Princeton: Princeton University Press, 1998), 4.

10. College enrollment of recent high school graduates: 1960 to 1994, U.S. Bureau of the Census, *Statistical Abstract of the United States, 1996* (Washington, DC: U.S. Government Printing Office, 1996), 180; Table 165: Total First-Time Freshmen Enrolled in Institutions of Higher Education, National Center for Education Statistics, *Digest of Education Statistics, 1990* (Washington, DC: U.S. Government Printing Office, 1991), 176.

11. Verne A. Stadtman, *The University of California, 1868–1968* (New York: McGraw-Hill, 1970), 400–24.

12. Nicholas Lemann, *The Big Test: The Secret History of the American Meritocracy* (New York: Farrar, Straus and Giroux, 1999), 53–69.

13. National Defense Education Act, Public Law 85-864, *United States Statutes at Large* 72 (1958), 1581. See also Gary S. Becker, *Human Capital: A Theoretical and Empirical Analysis, with Special Reference to Education* (New York: National Bureau of Economic Research, 1964); Theodore William Schultz, *The Economic Value of Education* (New York: Columbia University Press, 1963).

14. President's Commission on Higher Education, *Higher Education for American Democracy*, 6 vols. (Washington, DC: U.S. Government Printing Office, 1947).

15. Everett Carll Ladd, Jr., and Seymour Martin Lipset, *The Divided Academy: Professors and Politics* (New York: W. W. Norton, 1975), 170–71; Alan E. Bayer, *College and University Faculty: A Statistical Description* (Washington, DC: American Council on Education, 1970), 12.

16. See Mark McGurl, *The Program Era: Postwar Fiction and the Rise of Creative Writing* (Cambridge, MA: Harvard University Press, 2009).

17. See Russell Jacoby, *The Last Intellectuals: American Culture in the Age of Academe* (New York: Basic Books, 1987).

18. See Menand, *The Marketplace of Ideas*, 95–125.

19. Thomas Bender, "Politics, Intellect, and the American University, 1945–1995," in Thomas Bender and Carol E. Schorske, eds., *American Academic Culture in Transformation: Fifty Years, Four Disciplines* (Princeton: Princeton University Press, 1997), 17–54.

20. See Bender and Schorske, *American Academic Culture in Transformation*, esp. 309–29.

21. Matthew Arnold, *Essays in Criticism: First Series* (London: Macmillan, 1865), 18–19.

22. Joan Gilbert, "The Liberal Arts College: Is It Really an Endangered Species?," *Change* 27 (September/October 1995), 36–43; John H. Pryor et al., *The American Freshman: Forty Year Trends, 1966–2006* (Los Angeles: Higher Education Research Institute, Graduate School of Education and Information Studies, University of California, Los Angeles, 2007), 31–34.

23. Gerald Graff, *Professing Literature: An Institutional History* (Chicago: University of Chicago Press, 1987), 283.

24. See John Gross, *The Rise and Fall of the Man of Letters: A Study of the Idiosyncratic and the Humane in Modern Letters* (New York: Macmillan, 1969).

25. Apteryx [T. S. Eliot], "Professional, Or . . .," *Egoist* 5 (1918): 61.

26. T. S. Eliot, *The Sacred Wood: Essays on Poetry and Criticism*, 2nd ed. (London: Methuen, 1928), viii.

27. T. S. Eliot, "Tradition and the Individual Talent," *Egoist* 6 (1919): 55.

28. T. S. Eliot, "The Metaphysical Poets," *Times Literary Supplement*, October 20, 1921, 670. The French poets were labeled "Symbolist" by an English critic, Arthur Symons.

29. I. A. Richards, "On TSE," in Allen Tate, ed., *T. S. Eliot: The Man and His Work* (New York: Delacorte, 1966), 2–4; *The Letters of T. S. Eliot*, ed. Valerie Eliot and Hugh Haughton, vol. 2, *1923–1925* (New Haven: Yale University Press, 2011), 387n3.

30. I. A. Richards, *Practical Criticism: A Study of Literary Judgment* (New York: Harcourt, Brace, 1929), 6.

31. John Paul Russo, *I. A. Richards: His Life and Work* (Baltimore: Johns Hopkins University Press, 1989), 298–99; Richards, *Practical Criticism*, 13.

32. Christopher Isherwood, *Lions and Shadows: An Education in the Twenties* (Norfolk, CT: New Directions, 1947), 121–22.

33. See T. S. Eliot to I. A. Richards, November 20, 1927, in *The Letters of T. S. Eliot*, vol. 3, *1926–1927*, ed. Valerie Eliot and Hugh Haughton (New Haven: Yale University Press, 2012), 834–35, 834n2.

34. W. Terrence Gordon, *Marshall McLuhan: Escape into Understanding; A Biography* (New York: Basic Books, 1997), 45, 48–49.

35. T. S. Eliot, "The Dry Salvages," *New English Weekly* 18 (February 27, 1941), 220.

36. Mark Royden Winchell, *Cleanth Brooks and the Rise of Modern Criticism* (Charlottesville: University of Virginia Press, 1996), 20–27.

37. Joseph Blotner, *Robert Penn Warren: A Biography* (New York: Random House, 1997), 30–35.

38. Ruth Fisher, "A Conversation with Robert Penn Warren," *Four Quarters* 21 (May 1972), 11; Robert Penn Warren, "My Cup Ran Over," *Reckon* 1 (1995): 126.

39. Cleanth Brooks, "Life on the High Seas," *Reckon* 1 (1995): 122–23; Blotner, *Robert Penn Warren*, 99–100.

40. Cleanth Brooks, "I. A. Richards and Practical Criticism," in George Core, ed., *The Critics Who Made Us* (Columbia: University of Missouri Press, 1993), 35–36.

41. Blotner, *Robert Penn Warren*, 113; Winchell, *Cleanth Brooks*, 44.

42. Robert Penn Warren, "The Briar Patch," in Twelve Southerners, *I'll Take My Stand: The South and the Agrarian Tradition* (New York: Harper and Brothers, 1930), 260–61.

43. Paul V. Murphy, *The Rebuke of History: The Southern Agrarians and American Conservative Thought* (Chapel Hill: University of North Carolina Press, 2001), 63–67.

44. Cleanth Brooks to Donald Davidson, March 18 [1931], Box 4, Folder 38, Donald Davidson Papers, Vanderbilt University Special Collections.

45. T. S. Eliot, *After Strange Gods: A Primer of Modern Heresy* (New York: Harcourt, Brace, 1934), 16, 20, 67.

46. Cleanth Brooks, "A Plea to the Protestant Churches," in Herbert Agar and Allen Tate, eds., *Who Owns America? A New Declaration of Independence* (Boston: Houghton Mifflin, 1936), 325, 331.

47. Eliot, *After Strange Gods*, 12.

48. Thomas A. Underwood, *Allen Tate: Orphan of the South* (Princeton: Princeton University Press, 2000), 205–206.

49. Murphy, *The Rebuke of History*, 202–203; Benjamin Houston, "Donald Davidson and the Segregationist Intellect," in Lisa Tendrich Frank and Daniel Kilbride, eds., *Southern Character: Essays in Honor of Bertram Wyatt-Brown* (Gainesville: University Press of Florida, 2011), 160–77.

50. See Alan M. Wald, *The New York Intellectuals: The Rise and Decline of the Anti-Stalinist Left from the 1930s to the 1950s* (Chapel Hill: University of North Carolina Press, 1987), 3–24.

51. See Grant Webster, *The Republic of Letters: A History of Postwar American Literary Opinion* (Baltimore: Johns Hopkins University Press, 1979); Mark Jancovich, *The Cultural Politics of the New Criticism* (Cambridge: Cambridge University Press, 1993); Graff, *Professing Literature*, 183–208.

52. John Crowe Ransom, "Criticism, Inc.," *Virginia Quarterly Review* 13 (1937): 587.

53. Underwood, *Allen Tate*, 233–34.

54. Cleanth Brooks and Robert Penn Warren, *Understanding Poetry: An Anthology for College Students* (New York: Henry Holt, 1938), iv, 10–18.

55. Alan Golding, *From Outlaw to Classic: Canons in American Poetry* (Madison: University of Wisconsin Press, 1995), 105–109.

56. Cleanth Brooks, *The Well Wrought Urn: Studies in the Structure of Poetry* (New York: Reynal and Hitchcock, 1947), ix.

57. Ibid., 153.

58. Cleanth Brooks, "My Credo V," *Kenyon Review* 13 (1951): 72.

59. Winchell, *Cleanth Brooks*, 252.

60. W. K. Wimsatt, Jr., and Monroe Beardsley, "The Affective Fallacy," *Sewanee Review* 57 (1949): 31.

61. Webster, *The Republic of Letters*, 364–65.

62. See Louis Menand, "T. S. Eliot and Modernity," *New England Quarterly* 69 (1996): 554–79.

63. T. S. Eliot, "The Frontiers of Criticism," *Sewanee Review* 64 (1956): 537.

64. See Graff, *Professing Literature*, 209–25; Kermit Vanderbilt, *American Literature and the Academy: The Roots, Growth, and Maturity of a Profession* (Philadelphia: University of Pennsylvania Press, 1986), 489–96.

65. See Art Berman, *From the New Criticism to Deconstruction: The Reception of Structuralism and Post-Structuralism* (Urbana: University of Illinois Press, 1988), 96–101; Frank Lentricchia, *After the New Criticism* (Chicago: University of Chicago Press, 1980), 3–26. Both note that Frye's approach was not as abrupt a departure from the New Criticism as some readers have assumed.

66. M. H. Abrams to Robert D. Denham, April 20, 1994, in Denham, ed., *Remembering Northrop Frye: Recollections by His Students and Others in the 1940s and 1950s* (Jefferson, NC: McFarland, 2011), 147.

67. John Ayre, *Northrop Frye: A Biography* (Toronto: Random House, 1989), 21–27, 53–160.

68. Northrop Frye, "The Search for Acceptable Words" (1973), in *Collected Works of Northrop Frye*, vol. 27, *The Critical Path and Other Writings on Critical Theory, 1963–1975*, ed. Jean O'Grady and Eva Kushner (Toronto: University of Toronto Press, 2009), 320.

69. Northrop Frye, "Music in My Life" (1985), in *Collected Works of Northrop Frye*, vol. 24, *Interviews with Northrop Frye*, ed. Jean O'Grady (Toronto: University of Toronto Press, 2008), 739.

70. T. S. Eliot, *The Sacred Wood: Essays on Poetry and Criticism* (London: Methuen, 1920), 142–43.

71. "Claude Lévi-Strauss, le dernier géant de la pensée française," *Le Figaro*, July 26, 1993, 9.

72. Northrop Frye, "Imprint Interview" (1990), in *Works*, vol. 24, 1058.

73. Northrop Frye, *Collected Works of Northrop Frye*, vol. 19, *The Great Code: The Bible and Literature*, ed. Alvin A. Lee (Toronto: University of Toronto Press, 2006), 15.

74. Northrop Frye, "Northrop Frye in Conversation" (1989), in *Works*, vol. 24, 930.

75. Richard M. Cook, *Alfred Kazin: A Biography* (New Haven: Yale University Press, 2007), 97–98.

76. Northrop Frye, "Blake on Trial Again" (1947), in *Collected Works of Northrop Frye*, vol. 16, *Northrop Frye on Milton and Blake*, ed. Angela Esterhammer (Toronto: University of Toronto Press, 2005), 188.

77. Ibid.

78. Northrop Frye, "Archetypes of Literature" (1951), in *Collected Works of Northrop Frye*, vol. 21, *The Educated Imagination and Other Writings on Critical Theory, 1933–1963*, ed. Germaine Warkentin (Toronto: University of Toronto Press, 2006), 122.

79. Brooks, *The Well Wrought Urn*, 212.

80. Frye, "Archetypes of Literature," 123.

81. William K. Wimsatt and Cleanth Brooks, *Literary Criticism: A Short History*, vol. 2, *Romantic and Modern Criticism* (Chicago: University of Chicago Press, 1957), 711.

82. Ayre, *Northrop Frye*, 262.

83. Northrop Frye, *The Collected Works of Northrop Frye*, vol. 22, *Anatomy of Criticism: Four Essays*, ed. Robert D. Denham (Toronto: University of Toronto Press, 2006), 324.

84. Imre Salusinszky, *Criticism in Society* (New York: Methuen, 1987), 61 (interview with Bloom).

85. Ibid., 62 (interview with Bloom).

86. Harold Bloom, "A New Poetics," *Yale Review* 47 (1957): 133.

87. See Northrop Frye, *Selected Letters, 1934–1991*, ed. Robert D. Denham (Jefferson, NC: McFarland, 2009), 321n567.

88. Murray Krieger, "Northrop Frye and Contemporary Criticism: Ariel and the Spirit of Gravity," in Murray Krieger, ed., *Northrop Frye in Modern Criticism: Selected Papers from the English Institute* (New York: Columbia University Press, 1966). 1.

89. www.mla.org/Membership/Our-Members/Membership-Statistics; National Center for Education Statistics, Table 157.10: Total fall enrollment in institutions of higher education, by attendance status, sex of student, and control of institution: Fall 1947 to fall 1988; NCES, Table 322.10, Bachelor's degrees conferred by postsecondary institutions, by field of study: selected years, 1970–71 through 2012–13.

90. Robert von Hallberg, *American Poetry and Culture 1945–1980* (Cambridge, MA: Harvard University Press, 1985), 12.

91. Golding, *From Outlaw to Classic*, 22; Jed Rasula, *The American Poetry Wax Museum: Reality Effects, 1940–1990* (Urbana: National Council of Teachers of English, 1996), Appendix 1, 486–87. I rely on these and Alan Golding, "*The New American Poetry* Revisited, Again," *Contemporary Literature* 39 (1998): 180–211; Rasula, *The American Poetry Wax Museum*, 225–305; and Jeffrey Careyva, "'The War of the Anthologies: Academic Ambitions and Frustrations," Harvard GSAS, 2019 (in my possession).

92. Donald Hall, Robert Pack, and Louis Simpson, eds., *New Poets of England and America: An Anthology* (New York: Meridian, 1957), 9.

93. Ibid., 223, 119, 324, 341.

94. John Clellon Holmes, *Nothing More to Declare* (New York: E. P. Dutton, 1967), 107. Kerouac gives a slightly different account in Al Aronowitz, "St. Jack (A Famous Interview with Jack Kerouac)," in *The Blacklisted Masterpieces of Al Aronowitz* (Bearsville, NY: The Author, 1981), 31–32.

95. Jack Kerouac, "Notes from a Letter to [Allan] Temko, Dec. 13, '48," Box 4, Folder 70, Jack Kerouac Papers, Berg Collection, New York Public Library.

96. John Clellon Holmes to Phyllis Jackson, November 17, 1952, Box 20, Binder 1952, John Clellon Holmes Papers, Howard Gottlieb Archival Research Center, Boston University.

97. Clellon Holmes, "'This Is the Beat Generation,'" *New York Times Magazine*, November 16, 1952, 19.

98. "The Younger Generation," *Time* 58 (November 5, 1951), 46.

99. Ann Charters and Samuel Charters, *Brother-Souls: John Clellon Holmes, Jack Kerouac, and the Beat Generation* (Jackson: University Press of Mississippi, 2010), 43, 221; Clellon Holmes, "The Young American Hope," *Glamour* (April 1953), 142.

100. See, for the following, Charters and Charters, *Brother-Souls*, 173–95; Howard Cunnell, "Fast This Time," in Jack Kerouac, *On the Road: The Original Scroll* (New York: Penguin, 2007), 1–52; Isaac Gewirtz, *Beatific Soul: Jack Kerouac on the Road* (New York: New York Public Library, 2007), 72–147; and Joan Haverty Kerouac, *Nobody's Wife: The Smart Aleck and the King of the Beats* (Berkeley: Creative Arts, 1995), 201–203.

101. Neal Cassady to Jack Kerouac, December 17, 1950, Box 2, Folder 9, Jack Kerouac Collection, 1950–1978, Stuart A. Rose Manuscript, Archives, and Rare Book Library, Emory University.

102. Jack Kerouac, "Letter from Jack," *Notes from Underground* [Berkeley] 1 (1964): 23.

103. Leonard Lyons, "Lyons Den," *Daily Defender*, January 27, 1959, 29. Quoting Capote on the television program *Open End*, hosted by David Susskind. See also Norman Mailer, "Of a Small and Modest Malignancy, Wicked and Bristling with Dots," *Esquire* 88 (November 1977), 133–35.

104. Cf. Daniel Belgrad, *The Culture of Spontaneity: Improvisation and the Arts in Postwar America* (Chicago: University of Chicago Press, 1998), 204–10.

105. William Carlos Williams, "Howl for Carl Solomon," in Allen Ginsberg, *Howl and Other Poems* (San Francisco: City Lights Books, 1956), 8.

106. Harvey Breit to Richard Eberhart, July 6, 1956, Box 34, Folder 16, Richard Eberhart Papers, Rauner Special Collections Library, Dartmouth College.

107. Richard Eberhart, "West Coast Rhythms," *New York Times*, September 2, 1956, 7, 18.

108. Michael Schumacher, *Dharma Lion: A Biography of Allen Ginsberg* (New York: St. Martin's, 1992), 244.

109. Barry Silesky, *Ferlinghetti: The Artist in His Time* (New York: Warner Books, 1990), 57, 69, 72; Jonah Raskin, *American Scream: Allen Ginsberg's Howl and the Making of the Beat Generation* (Berkeley: University of California Press, 2004), 215–16; Shigeyoshi Murao, "Footnotes to My Arrest for Selling Howl," in Allen Ginsberg, *Howl: Original Draft Facsimile, Transcript, and Various Versions Fully Annotated by Author*, ed. Barry Miles (New York: Harper and Row, 1986), 170–71; Patricia Wakida, "Shig Murao, San Francisco Book Legend from Seattle," *North American Post* (2004) 64 (August 12, 2009), 1, 3.

110. Schumacher, *Dharma Lion*, 259.

111. J. W. Ehrlich, ed., *Howl of the Censor* (San Carlos, CA: Nourse Publishing, 1961), 34. The book is a transcript of the *Howl* trial.

112. Dennis McNally, *Desolate Angel: Jack Kerouac, the Beat Generation, and America* (New York: Random House, 1979), 239.

113. Gilbert Millstein, "Books of the Times," *New York Times*, September 5, 1957, 27.

114. Joyce Johnson, *Minor Characters: A Beat Memoir* (Boston: Houghton Mifflin, 1983), 180–85.

115. Ehrlich, *Howl of the Censor*, 127.

116. No. 568: Existing rural road mileage, and No. 572: Motor vehicles, U.S. Bureau of the Census, *Statistical Abstract of the United States, 1949* (Washington, DC: U.S. Government Printing Office, 1949), 522, 526; No. 694: Existing road mileage, and No. 709: Motor-vehicle registrations, U.S. Bureau of the Census, *Statistical Abstract of the United States, 1958* (Washington, DC: U.S. Government Printing Office, 1958), 546, 557.

117. Daniel Bell, "The Myth of Crime Waves," in *The End of Ideology: On the Exhaustion of Political Ideas in the Fifties* (Glencoe, IL: Free Press, 1960), 137–58; James Gilbert, *A Cycle of Outrage: America's Reaction to the Juvenile Delinquent in the 1950s* (New York: Oxford University Press, 1986), 63–142; Francis Fukuyama, *The Great Disruption: Human Nature and the Reconstitution of Social Order* (New York: Simon and Schuster, 1999), 27–36.

118. John Hollander, "Poetry Chronicle," *Partisan Review* 24 (1957): 297.

119. Norman Podhoretz, "The Know-Nothing Bohemians," *Partisan Review* 25 (1958): 318.

120. Robert Brustein, "The Cult of Unthink," *Horizon* 1 (September 1958): 38, 41–42.

121. Norman Podhoretz, "Where Is the Beat Generation Going?," *Esquire* 50 (December 1958), 150.

122. Allen Ginsberg to Louis Ginsberg, May 12, 1959, in Allen Ginsberg and Louis Ginsberg, *Family Business: Selected Letters between a Father and Son*, ed. Michael Schumacher (New York: Bloomsbury, 2001), 117.

123. Diana Trilling, "The Other Night at Columbia," *Partisan Review* 26 (1959): 226.

124. Jack Kerouac, *On the Road* (New York: Viking, 1957), 35.

125. Donald Allen to Charles Olson, September 24, 1958, in *Poet to Publisher: Charles Olson's Correspondence with Donald Allen*, ed. Ralph Maud (Vancouver: Talonbooks, 2003), 47. Quoted from letter Allen sent to all potential contributors.

126. S. E. Gontarski, "Don Allen: Grove's First Editor," *Review of Contemporary Fiction* 10 (Fall 1990): 132–34.

127. Barney Rosset, *Rosset: My Life in Publishing and How I Fought Censorship* (New York: OR Books, 2016), 220.

128. Noel Stock, *The Life of Ezra Pound*, expanded ed. (San Francisco: North Point Press, 1982), 266, 306–307, 390–420.

129. Gertrude Stein, *The Autobiography of Alice B. Toklas* (New York: Harcourt Brace, 1933), 246.

130. Daniel Swift, *The Bughouse: The Poetry, Politics, and Madness of Ezra Pound* (New York: Farrar, Straus and Giroux, 2017), 11–12, 26, 110–11, 198–204.

131. Charles Olson, "This Is Yeats Speaking," *Partisan Review* 13 (1946): 140.

132. Ralph Maud, *Charles Olson's Reading: A Biography* (Carbondale: Southern Illinois University Press, 1996), 63–69; Charles Olson, *Charles Olson and Ezra Pound: An Encounter at St. Elizabeths*, ed. Catherine Seelye (New York: Viking, 1975); Burton Hatlen, "Pound's *Pisan Cantos* and the Origins of Projective Verse," in *Ezra Pound and Poetic Influence: The Official Proceedings of the 17th International Ezra Pound Conference Held at Castle Brunnenburg Tirolo di Merano* (Amsterdam: Rodopi, 2000), 130–53. See, generally, Peter Grant, "Charles Olson's Life and Work—A Chronology," charlesolson .org/Files/chronology1.htm.

133. Martin Duberman, *Black Mountain: An Exploration in Community* (Evanston: Northwestern University Press, 1972), 409–17.

134. Charles Olson, "Projective Verse vs the Non-Projective," *Poetry New York*, no. 3 (1950), 13, 17.

135. Ibid., 21–22.

136. Donald Allen to Charles Olson, September 24, 1958, in Olson and Allen, *Poet to Publisher*, 47.

137. William Carlos Williams, "A Sort of a Song" (1944), in *The Collected Poems of William Carlos Williams*, vol. 2, *1939–1962*, ed. Christopher MacGowan (New York: New Directions, 1988), 55. The phrase is better known from Williams's later poem "Paterson."

138. Ezra Pound, "Vorticism," *Fortnightly Review*, n.s., 96 (1914): 469.

139. Ezra Pound, *The Cantos of Ezra Pound* (New York: New Directions, 1970), 13.

140. Charles Olson, *The Collected Poems of Charles Olson*, ed. George F. Butterick (Berkeley: University of California Press, 1987), 91.

141. See Burton Hatlen, "Kinesis and Meaning: Charles Olson's 'The Kingfishers' and the Critics," *Contemporary Literature* 30 (1989): 546–72.

142. Allen Ginsberg, Liner notes, *Allen Ginsberg Reads "Howl" and Other Poems* (Fantasy 7006 LP, 1959).

143. Allen Ginsberg, *Allen Verbatim: Lectures on Poetry, Politics, Consciousness*, ed. Gordon Ball (New York: McGraw-Hill, 1974), 180. Transcript of an interview on KDNA, St. Louis, November 1, 1972.

144. William Carlos Williams, *Autobiography* (New York: Random House, 1951), 329.

145. Kenneth Koch, "Fresh Air," in Donald M. Allen, ed., *The New American Poetry* (New York: Grove, 1960), 231–32.

146. Donald M. Allen, preface to *The New American Poetry*, xi.

147. Kenneth Rexroth, "Disengagement: The Art of the Beat Generation," *New World Writing*, no. 11 (1957), 39–40.

148. Von Hallberg, *American Poetry and Culture*, 13–14.

149. Robert Pack, introduction to Donald Hall and Pack, eds., *New Poets of England and America: Second Selection* (Cleveland: Meridian Books, 1962), 182.

150. Evelyn Barish, *The Double Life of Paul de Man* (New York: Liveright, 2014), 14 (interview with Abrams).

151. David Lehman, *Signs of the Times: Deconstruction and the Fall of Paul de Man* (New York: Poseidon, 1991); Barish, *The Double Life of Paul de Man*. Neither book is sympathetic to its subject or reliable about his work. See also Louis Menand, "The Politics of Deconstruction," *New York Review of Books* 38 (November 21, 1991), 39–44.

152. Barish, *The Double Life of Paul de Man*, 344 (interview with Brooks).

153. Geoffrey Hartman, *A Scholar's Tale: Intellectual Journey of a Misplaced Child of Europe* (New York: Fordham University Press, 2007); Salusinszky, *Criticism in Society*, 75–96 (interview with Hartman).

154. See, for the following, Benoît Peeters, *Derrida: A Biography*, trans. Andrew Brown (New York: Polity, 2012) 9–79; Edward Baring, *The Young Derrida and French Philosophy, 1945–1968* (Cambridge: Cambridge University Press, 2011), 15–20; Michèle Lamont, "How to Become a Dominant French Philosopher: The Case of Jacques Derrida," *American Journal of Sociology* 93 (1987): 584–622.

155. Jacques Derrida and Geoff Bennington, *Jacques Derrida* (Paris: Éditions du Seuil, 1991), 57 ("un petit Juif noir et très arabe qui n'y comprenait rien"). See also Jacques Derrida and Elisabeth Roudinesco, *De quoi demain . . .* (Paris: Fayard/Galilée, 2001), 179–82; Jacques Derrida, *Sur parole: instantanés philosophiques* (La Tour d'Aigues: Éditions de l'Aube, 1999), 12–14.

156. Derrida, *Sur parole*, 30 ("des années infernales pour moi").

157. David Mikics, *Who Was Jacques Derrida? An Intellectual Biography* (New Haven: Yale University Press, 2009), 16–17, 22, 24, 48.

158. Edward Baring, "Liberalism and the Algerian War: The Case of Jacques Derrida," *Critical Inquiry* 36 (2010): 239–61.

159. Lamont, "How to Become a Dominant French Philosopher," 602–14.

160. See, for example, François Dosse, *History of Structuralism*, vol. 2, *The Sign Sets, 1967–Present*, trans. Deborah Glassman (Minneapolis: University of Minnesota Press, 1997), 17–18.

161. Lamont, "How to Become a Dominant French

Philosopher," 600. See also Luc Ferry and Alain Renaut, *La Pensée 68: essai sur l'anti-humanisme contemporain* (Paris: Gallimard, 1985).

162. Peeters, *Derrida*, 165–66; Bret McCabe, "Structuralism's Samson," *Johns Hopkins Magazine* 64 (Fall 2012) (online); François Cusset, *French Theory: How Foucault, Derrida, Deleuze, and Co. Transformed the Intellectual Life of the United States*, trans. Jeff Fort (Minneapolis: University of Minnesota Press, 2008), 28–33.

163. Peeters, *Derrida*, 161 (quoting a letter from Foucault to Derrida, December 21, 1965).

164. Jacques Derrida, "De la grammatologie," *Critique* 21 (1965): 1023 ("non pas la démolition mais la dé-sédimentation").

165. Claude Lévi-Strauss, "Une lettre à propos de 'Lévi-Strauss dans le dix-huitième siècle,'" *Cahiers pour l'Analyse* 8 (October 1967), 89–90.

166. Jacques Derrida, "Structure, Sign, and Play in the Discourse of the Human Sciences," trans. Richard Macksey, in Richard Macksey and Eugenio Donato, eds., *The Languages of Criticism and the Sciences of Man: The Structuralist Controversy* (Baltimore: Johns Hopkins University Press, 1970), 249. Reprinted in an abridged edition titled *The Structuralist Controversy* (1972). "Structure, Sign, and Play" was published in French in Jacques Derrida, *L'Écriture et la différence* (Paris: Éditions du seuil, 1967), 409–28. The printed version is evidently not identical to the lecture.

167. Jacques Derrida, *De la grammatologie* (Paris: Éditions de Minuit, 1967), 227; Jacques Derrida, *Of Grammatology*, trans. Gayatri Chakravorty Spivak, rev. ed. (Baltimore: Johns Hopkins University Press, 2016), 172.

168. Derrida, "Structure, Sign, and Play," 255–56.

169. Jacques Derrida, "Positions: Entretien avec Jean-Louis Houdebine et Guy Scarpetta," *Promesse*, nos. 30–31 (Fall–Winter 1971), 9. ("Faire droit à cette nécessité, c'est reconnaître que dans une opposition philosophique classique, nous n'avons pas affaire à la coexistence pacifique d'un *vis-à-vis*, mais à une hiérarchie violente. Un des deux termes commande l'autre [axiologiquement, logiquement, etc.], occupe la hauteur. Déconstruire l'opposition c'est d'abord, à un moment donné, renverser la hiérarchie.")

170. Derrida, "Structure, Sign, and Play," 247–48.

171. Paul de Man, "Semiology and Rhetoric," *Diacritics* 3 (Fall 1973), 30.

172. Roland Barthes to [Jean] Ristat, *Lettres Françaises*, March 29, 1972, 3. ("Derrida a été de ceux qui m'ont aidé à comprendre quel était l'enjeu [philosophique, idéologique] de mon propre travail: il a déséquilibré la structure, il a ouvert le signe: il est pour nous *celui qui a décroché le bout de la chaîne*.")

173. Jacques Derrida, "Afterword: Toward an Ethic of Discussion," trans. Samuel Weber, in *Limited*

Inc (Evanston: Northwestern University Press, 1988), 115–16.

174. Derrida, "Structure, Sign, and Play," 249–50.

175. Peeters, *Derrida*, 161 (quoting a letter from de Man to Derrida, October 6, 1967).

176. Salusinszky, *Criticism in Society*, 230–31 (interview with Miller); Marc Redfield, *Theory at Yale: The Strange Case of Deconstruction in America* (New York: Fordham University Press, 2016), 19–61; Wallace Martin, introduction to Jonathan Arac, Wlad Godzich, and Wallace Martin, eds., *The Yale Critics: Deconstruction in America* (Minneapolis: University of Minnesota Press, 1983), xv–xxxvii.

177. De Man, "Semiology and Rhetoric," 30.

178. Paul de Man, "The Crisis of Contemporary Criticism," *Arion* 6 (Spring 1967), 53–54.

179. De Man, "Semiology and Rhetoric," 32.

180. Salusinszky, *Criticism in Society*, 166 (interview with Johnson).

181. Alice Kaplan, *French Lessons: A Memoir* (Chicago: University of Chicago Press, 1993), 171–72.

182. Geoffrey Hartman, "Blindness and Insight," *New Republic* 198 (March 7, 1988), 29.

183. Hartman, *A Scholar's Tale*, 86.

184. William James, *Pragmatism*, in *The Works of William James*, ed. Frederick H. Burkhardt (Cambridge, MA: Harvard University Press, 1975), 125.

14. COMMONISM

1. On Warhol's life: Blake Gopnik, *Warhol* (New York: Ecco, 2020); Patrick S. Smith, *Andy Warhol's Art and Films* (Ann Arbor: UMI Research Press, 1986); David Bourdon, *Warhol* (New York: Abrams, 1989); Victor Bockris, *Warhol* (London: Frederick Muller, 1989); Steven Watson, *Factory Made: Warhol and the Sixties* (New York: Pantheon, 2003); Tony Scherman and David Dalton, *Pop: The Genius of Andy Warhol* (New York: HarperCollins, 2009); John Wilcock, *The Autobiography and Sex Life of Andy Warhol*, ed. Christopher Trela (New York: Trela Media, 2010).

2. Rainer Crone, *Andy Warhol: A Picture Show by the Artist* (New York: Rizzoli, 1987), 38 (interview with Philip Pearlstein).

3. Wilcock, *The Autobiography and Sex Life of Andy Warhol*, 123 (interview with Malanga).

4. G. R. Swenson, "What Is Pop Art? Answers from 8 Painters, Part 1," *ARTnews* 62 (November 1963), 26, 60–61; see also Jennifer Sichel, "'Do You Think Pop Art's Queer?' Gene Swenson and Andy Warhol," *Oxford Art Journal* 41 (2018): 59–83; Gretchen Berg, "Andy Warhol: My True Story," *East Village Other* 1 (November 1–15, 1966), 9–10, reprinted in 1967 in the *Los Angeles Free Press* and *Cahiers du Cinéma*. Berg quotation from interview by Kenneth

Goldsmith, in Kenneth Goldsmith, ed., *I'll Be Your Mirror: The Selected Andy Warhol Interviews, 1962–1987* (New York: Carroll and Graf, 2004), 86.

5. Calvin Tomkins, "The Fame Factory," *New Yorker* 73 (December 1, 1997), 97.

6. "Pop Art—Cult of the Commonplace," *Time* 81 (May 3, 1963), 72 (interview with Warhol). Repeated in the 1963 *ARTnews* interview and elsewhere.

7. First publication appears to be *Andy Warhol* (Stockholm: n.p., 1968), a catalogue published on the occasion of a Warhol exhibition in Stockholm at the Moderna Museet, February–March 1968. Blake Gopnik doubts Warhol ever said it at all: "In the future, everyone will be world-famous for 15 minutes," warholiana .com., February 6, 2019.

8. Bob Colacello, *Holy Terror: Andy Warhol Close Up* (New York: HarperCollins, 1990), 207–208.

9. Andy Warhol and Pat Hackett, *Popism: The Warhol '60s* (New York: Harcourt Brace Jovanovich, 1980), 5–6.

10. Information from Blake Gopnik.

11. Jean Stein, *Edie: An American Biography* (New York: Knopf, 1982), 194–95 (interview with Karp); Wilcock, *The Autobiography and Sex Life of Andy Warhol*, 93–94 (interview with Karp); Oral history interview with Ivan C. Karp, March 12, 1969, Archives of American Art, Smithsonian Institution.

12. James Rosenquist, *Painting Below Zero: Notes on a Life in Art* (New York: Knopf, 2009), 128.

13. Wilcock, *The Autobiography and Sex Life of Andy Warhol*, 49.

14. Gerard Malanga, "Working with Warhol," *Village Voice* 32, May 5, 1987, Art Supplement, 4–7.

15. Lynn Zelevansky, "Dorothy Miller's 'Americans,' 1942–63," *Studies in Modern Art* 4 (1994): 61–67. Cf. Frances Stonor Saunders, *The Cultural Cold War: The CIA and the World of Arts and Letters* (New York: New Press, 1999), 266, where Zelevansky's meaning is inverted.

16. "Metropolitan Hit by 7 Modernists," *New York Times*, June 30, 1952, 21.

17. See the essays in Joan Marter, ed., *Abstract Expressionism: The International Context* (New Brunswick: Rutgers University Press, 2007).

18. Michel Tapié, *Véhémences confrontées* (Paris: Galerie Nina Dausset, 1951); Michel Tapié, "Jackson Pollock avec nous," in *Jackson Pollock* (Paris: Studio Paul Facchetti, 1952).

19. Jeremy Lewison, "Jackson Pollock and the Americanization of Europe," in Kirk Varnedoe and Pepe Karmel, eds., *Jackson Pollock: New Approaches* (New York: Museum of Modern Art, 1999), 206–207; Catherine Dossin, *The*

Rise and Fall of American Art, 1940s–1980s: The Geopolitics of Western Art Worlds (Burlington, VT: Ashgate, 2015), 64–65.

20. Michel Tapié to Jackson Pollock, February 29, 1952, Jackson Pollock and Lee Krasner Papers, Archives of American Art, Smithsonian Institution; Alfonso Ossorio to Lee Krasner and Jackson Pollock, March 22, 1952, Pollock and Krasner Papers.

21. Patrick Heron, "Americans at the Tate Gallery," *Arts* [New York] 30 (March 1956), 15–17.

22. Dossin, *The Rise and Fall of American Art*, 54, 88–89.

23. Dieter Honisch and Jens Christian Jensen, *Amerikanische Kunst von 1945 bis heute* (Cologne: DuMont, 1974), 224–307.

24. See Stacy Tenenbaum, "The Triumph of 'The New American Painting': MoMA and Cold War Cultural Diplomacy," in Margaret Garlake, ed., *Artists and Patrons in Post-War Britain* (Aldershot, UK: Ashgate, 2001), 125–53; Nancy Jachec, "Transatlantic Cultural Politics in the Late 1950s: The Leaders and Specialists Grant Program," *Art History* 26 (2003): 533–55; Sigrid Ruby, "The Give and Take of American Painting in Postwar Western Europe," *Cahiers Charles V* 28 (2000): 171–95; David Caute, *The Dancer Defects: The Struggle for Cultural Supremacy During the Cold War* (Oxford: Oxford University Press, 2003), 553–55; Robert Burstow, "The Limits of Modernist Art as a 'Weapon in the Cold War': Reassessing the Unknown Patron of the Monument to the Unknown Political Prisoner," *Oxford Art Journal* 20 (1997): 68–70; Michael Kimmelman, "Revisiting the Revisionists: The Modern, Its Critics, and the Cold War," *Studies in Modern Art* 4 (1994): 39–55; Museum of Modern Art, *The New American Painting: As Shown in Eight European Countries, 1958–1959* (New York: Museum of Modern Art, 1959).

25. "American Painting and Sculpture Show to Inaugurate Museum's International Program in Paris Opening on April 24," n.d., Press Release Archives, 1927–1999, Museum of Modern Art. Cf. Saunders, *The Cultural Cold War*, where the exhibition is incorrectly described as "exclusively devoted to the New York School" (269).

26. See Jachec, "Transatlantic Cultural Politics in the Late 1950s," 533–55.

27. Leonardo Borgese, *Corriera della Sera* [Milan], June 8, 1958, quoted in Museum of Modern Art, *The New American Painting*, 8.

28. See Kenneth Rexroth, "Americans Seen Abroad," *ARTnews* 58 (June, July, August 1959), 30ff.

29. Steven W. Naifeh, *Culture Making: Money,*

Success, and the New York Art World (Princeton: History Department of Princeton University, 1976), 81.

30. "57th Street," *Fortune* 34 (September 1946), 145–48.

31. Les Levine, "The Golden Years: A Portrait of Eleanor Ward," *Arts Magazine* 48 (April 1974), 42. See also Laura de Coppet and Alan Jones, *The Art Dealers: The Powers Behind the Scene Tell How the Art World Really Works* (New York: Clarkson N. Potter, 1984), 38–39 (interview with Sidney Janis).

32. Dorothy Gees Seckler, "Gallery Notes," *Art in America* 43 (October 1955), 46.

33. "Boom on Canvas," *Time* 71 (April 7, 1958), 82.

34. Dore Ashton, *The New York School: A Cultural Reckoning* (New York: Viking, 1973), 229; Naifeh, *Culture*, 81–82; A. Deirdre Robson, *Prestige, Profit, and Pleasure: The Market for Modern Art in New York in the 1940s and 1950s* (New York: Garland, 1995), 255; Marvin Elkoff, "The American Painter as a Blue Chip," *Esquire* 63 (January 1965), 38; "Best Show in Town," *Time* 80 (November 16, 1962), 50–55; McCandlish Phillips, "Attendance Soars at Museums Here," *New York Times*, November 27, 1961, 1, 32. There does not seem to be an official count of galleries in the city.

35. Roland L. Redmond and James J. Rorimer, "Review of the Year 1961–1962: Report of the President and of the Director," *Metropolitan Museum of Art Bulletin*, n.s., 21 (October 1962), 38–39; G. W. [Georges Wildenstein], "La Chronique des arts," *Gazette des Beaux-arts*, nos. 1110–11 (July–August 1961), 2.

36. Naifeh, *Culture Making*, 81–82.

37. See "State of the Market," *Time* 81 (June 21, 1963), 62; "Sold Out Art," *Life* 55 (September 20, 1963), 125–29.

38. Glenn Fowler, "Burton G. Tremaine, Executive, 89, Dies; a Collector of Art," *New York Times*, March 27, 1991, D23.

39. Dossin, *The Rise and Fall of American Art*, 158–64. See also "Pop Pop," *Time* 82 (August 30, 1963), 54.

40. "Pop Art—Cult of the Commonplace," 70.

41. Hilton Kramer, "Art," *Nation* 195 (1962): 335.

42. Peter Selz, "Pop Goes the Artist," *Partisan Review* 30 (1963): 315.

43. Emile de Antonio, dir., *Painters Painting: A Candid History of the New York Art Scene, 1940–1970* (Arthouse Films DVD, 1972) (interview with Greenberg).

44. Clement Greenberg, June 1, 1963, Journal #21, 1960–1977, Clement Greenberg Papers, Getty Research Institute.

45. John Ashbery, foreword to *The New Realists* (New York: Sidney Janis, 1962), n.p.

46. Harold Rosenberg, "The Game of Illusion," *New Yorker* 88 (November 24, 1962), 162.

47. Brian O'Doherty, "Art: Avant-Garde Revolt," *New York Times*, October 31, 1962, 41.

48. "Products," *Newsweek* 60 (November 12, 1962), 94.

49. O'Doherty, "Art: Avant-Garde Revolt."

50. Jennifer Sichel, "'What Is Pop Art?': A Revised Transcript of Gene Swenson's 1963 Interview with Andy Warhol," *Oxford Art Journal* 41 (2018): 89.

51. Calvin Tomkins, *Duchamp: A Biography* (New York: Henry Holt, 1996), 16, 380–81, 450.

52. On Duchamp's life: Tomkins, *Duchamp*; Pontus Hultén, ed., *Marcel Duchamp: Work and Life* (Cambridge, MA: MIT Press, 1993); Robert Lebel, *Marcel Duchamp* (New York: Grove, 1959).

53. The term first appears in Marcel Duchamp to Suzanne Duchamp, ca. January 5, 1916, in Jean Crotti, "Affectueusement, Marcel: Ten Letters from Marcel Duchamp to Suzanne Duchamp," *Archives of American Art Journal* 22, no. 4 (1982), 5.

54. "The Art of Assemblage: A Symposium," *Studies in Modern Art* 2 (1992): 136.

55. H. P. Roché, "Souvenirs of Marcel Duchamp," trans. William N. Copley, in Lebel, *Marcel Duchamp*, 79. Roché was the author of *Jules et Jim* (1952), which François Truffaut adapted for his 1962 movie.

56. See James Johnson Sweeney, "Eleven Europeans in America," *Bulletin of the Museum of Modern Art* 13, no. 4/5 (1946), 19–21 (interview with Duchamp).

57. Pierre Cabanne, *Dialogues with Marcel Duchamp*, trans. Ron Padgett (New York: Viking, 1971), 43.

58. Tomkins, *Duchamp*, 34 (interview with Duchamp).

59. Katharine Kuh, *The Artist's Voice: Talks with Sixteen Artists* (New York: Harper and Row, 1962), 89–90.

60. Barbaralee Diamonstein, *Inside the Art World: Conversations with Barbaralee Diamonstein* (New York: Rizzoli, 1994), 117 (interview with Johns).

61. Robert Rauschenberg, San Francisco Museum of Modern Art, October 1999, www.sfmoma.org/watch/robert-rauschenberg-to-john-cage-be-careful-and-drive-straight/.

62. Françoise Choay, "Dada, Néo-Dada, et Rauschenberg," *Art International* [Lugano] 5 (October 20, 1961), 85 ("Dada était anti, je suis pro").

63. "The Art of Assemblage: A Symposium," 150.

64. Richard Hamilton, "Duchamp," *Art International* 7 (January 18, 1964), 25.

65. Bockris, *Warhol*, 61 (interview with Lepper).

66. Robert Lepper to Rainer Crone, January 1974, Box 1, Folder 1, Robert L. Lepper Papers, Carnegie Mellon University Archives.

67. Smith, *Andy Warhol's Art and Films*, 110 (interview with Jack Wilson).

68. László Moholy-Nagy, *The New Vision and Abstract of an Artist* (New York: Wittenborn, 1947), 79.

69. George Frei and Neil Printz, eds., *The Andy Warhol Catalogue Raisonné*, vol. 1, *Paintings and Sculpture, 1961–1963* (New York: Phaidon, 2002), 18.

70. See Russell Ferguson, ed., *Hand-Painted Pop: American Art in Transition, 1955–62* (Los Angeles: Museum of Contemporary Art, 1992); Pepe Karmel, ed., *New York Cool: Painting and Sculpture from the NYU Art Collection* (New York: Grey Art Gallery, 2008); Melissa Rachleff, *Inventing Downtown: Artist-Run Galleries in New York City, 1952–1965* (New York: Grey Art Gallery, 2017); Jed Perl, *New Art City* (New York: Knopf, 2005).

71. Warhol and Hackett, *Popism*, 11–12.

72. Receipts in the Warhol Archives, Andy Warhol Museum, Pittsburgh. Stories that Warhol bargained down the price seem to be mistaken.

73. I am grateful to Blake Gopnik for this information.

74. Oral history interview with Ivan C. Karp, March 12, 1969, Archives of American Art, Smithsonian Institution; de Coppet and Jones, *The Art Dealers*, 138–39 (interview with Karp).

75. Irving Blum interview with Jeanmarie Theobads, Museum of Modern Art Oral History Program; Stein, *Edie*, 192–95 (interviews with Hopps and Blum). Blum gives a somewhat different account in Kirk Varnedoe, "Campbell's Soup Cans, 1962," in *Ferus* (New York: Rizzoli, 2002), 45–52.

76. Bruce Glaser, "Questions for Stella and Judd," ed. Lucy Lippard, *ARTnews* 65 (September 1966), 59. Transcript of an interview on WBAI-FM, February 1964.

77. Rosalind Constable, "New York's Avant Garde and How It Got There," *New York Herald Tribune*, May 17, 1964, *New York* magazine insert, 10.

78. Balcomb Greene, "A Thing of Beauty," *Art Journal* 25 (1966): 364.

79. Kirk Varnedoe and Adam Gopnik, *High & Low: Modern Art Popular Culture* (New York: Museum of Modern Art, 1991), 345.

80. Scherman and Dalton, *Pop*, 116–18.

81. See Benjamin H. D. Buchloh, "Andy Warhol's One-Dimensional Art: 1956–1966," in Annette Michelson, ed., *Andy Warhol* (Cambridge, MA: MIT Press, 2001), 14.

82. Stephanie Garvis Harrington, "City Puts Bomb Under Off-Beat Culture Scene," *Village*

Voice, March 26, 1964, 1, 14; J. Hoberman and Jonathan Rosenbaum, *Midnight Movies* (New York: Harper and Row, 1983), 59–60.

83. Richard Barr and Cyril Egan, Jr., "Mural Is Something Yegg-stra," *New York Journal American*, April 15, 1964, 1.

84. Emily Grenauer, "Fair Mural Taken Off, Artist to Do Another," *New York Herald Tribune*, April 18, 1965, 11. Grenauer noted that Duchamp had once displayed a wanted poster with his own face on it. Warhol would have seen the piece at the Pasadena retrospective.

85. Scherman and Dalton, *Pop*, 220–22; Mark Lamster, *The Man in the Glass House: Philip Johnson, Architect of the Modern Century* (New York: Little, Brown, 2018), 304.

86. Robert A. M. Stern, Thomas Mellins, and David Fishman, *New York 1960: Architecture and Urbanism Between the Second World War and the Bicentennial* (New York: Monacelli Press, 1995), 1036.

87. Grace Glueck, "In Britain, What's a Government Budget Without Art?," *New York Times*, July 19, 1964, X12.

88. Arthur C. Danto, "My Life as a Philosopher," in *The Philosophy of Arthur C. Danto*, ed. Randall E. Auxier and Lewis Edwin Hahn (Chicago: Open Court, 2013), 3–28; Arthur C. Danto, *Andy Warhol* (New Haven: Yale University Press, 2009), xiii. See also Arthur C. Danto, *After the End of Art: Contemporary Art and the Pale of History* (Princeton: Princeton University Press, 1997), 122–24.

89. Danto, "My Life as a Philosopher," 26–27.

90. Arthur C. Danto, "The Artworld," *Journal of Philosophy* 61 (1964): 580.

91. Gerard Malanga, *Archiving Warhol: An Illustrated History* (n.p.: Creation Books, 2002), 147–48; George Frei and Neil Printz, eds., *The Andy Warhol Catalogue Raisonné*, vol. 2, *Paintings and Sculpture, 1964–1969* (New York: Phaidon, 2004), 18; Glenn O'Brien, "Andy," *Parkett*, no. 12 (1987), 60 ("for years Andy was trying unsuccessfully to get the people who worked for him to stop saying 'The Factory'").

92. I follow Bertrand Rougé, "Just Figuring: Or, the Endless End of Art—Readymades, Trompe l'Oeil, Metaphors, and Other Meta-Indiscernibles," in Danto, *The Philosophy of Arthur C. Danto*, 279–305.

93. Stuart Preston, "Old and New Ways of Seeing Things," *New York Times*, April 25, 1964, X21.

94. See Buchloch, "Andy Warhol's One-Dimensional Art: 1956–1966."

95. Scherman and Dalton, *Pop*, 259.

96. Barbara Rose, "Andy Warhol: A Study in the Sociology and Aesthetics of the Sixties," Box 2, Folder 20, Barbara Rose Papers, Getty Research Institute.

97. Max Weber, "Wissenschaft als Beruf" (1919), in *Gesamtausgabe*, vol. 17, ed. Horst Baier et al. (Tübingen: J. C. B. Mohr, 1984–2018), 109.

15. VERS LA LIBÉRATION

1. William H. Chafe, *The Paradox of Change: American Women in the 20th Century* (New York: Oxford University Press, 1991), 187–88; Elaine Tyler May, *Homeward Bound: American Families in the Cold War Era*, rev. ed. (New York: Basic Books, 1999). Cf. Linda Eisenmann, *Higher Education for Women in Postwar America, 1945–1965* (Baltimore: Johns Hopkins University Press, 2007).

2. Patricia Albjerg Graham, "Expansion and Exclusion: A History of Women in American Higher Education," *Signs* 3 (1978): 766; Stephanie Coontz, *A Strange Stirring: The Feminine Mystique and American Women at the Dawn of the 1960s* (New York: Basic Books, 2011), 51, 106–11.

3. James Patterson, *Grand Expectations: The United States, 1945–1974* (New York: Oxford University Press, 1996), 33.

4. Chafe, *The Paradox of* Change, 160–61; Patterson, *Grand Expectations*, 33.

5. *Report of the Committee on Civil and Political Rights to the President's Commission on the Status of Women* (Washington, DC: U.S. Government Printing Office, 1963), 3, 13, 20–21.

6. Coontz, *A Strange Stirring*, 1–18.

7. Casey Hayden and Mary King, "Sex and Caste," *Liberation* 11 (April 1966), 35–36. See also Sara Evans, *Personal Politics: The Roots of Women's Liberation in the Civil Rights Movement and the New Left* (New York: Knopf, 1979); Kathryn Kish Sklar, ed., *How and Why Did Women in SNCC (the Student Non-Violent Coordinating Committee) Author a Pathbreaking Feminist Manifesto, 1964–1965?* (Alexandria, VA: Alexander Street Press, 2015) (online).

8. Evans, *Personal Politics*, 112.

9. Coontz, *A Strange Stirring*, 62.

10. Benjamin Spock, *The Common Sense Book of Baby and Child Care* (New York: Duell, Sloan and Pearce, 1946), 484.

11. Adlai E. Stevenson, "A Purpose for Modern Woman," *Women's Home Companion* 77 (September 1955), 30.

12. Barbara Miller Solomon, *In the Company of Educated Women: A History of Women and Higher Education in America* (New Haven: Yale University Press, 1985), 192. Her source was "several Radcliffe Alumnae."

13. Mary I. Bunting, "The Radcliffe Institute for Independent Study," *Educational Record* 42 (1961): 281.

14. "Parnassus, Coast to Coast," *Time* 67 (June 11, 1956), 70.

15. Melissa Rachleff, *Inventing Downtown: Artist-Run Galleries in New York City, 1952–1965* (New York: Grey Art Gallery, 2017), 229–31.

16. Irving Sandler, *The Triumph of American Painting: A History of Abstract Expressionism* (New York: Praeger, 1970), 54.

17. Allen Hughes, "One Is Avant-Garde, the Other No Gentleman," *New York Times*, September 4, 1966, D11.

18. Nan Robertson, *The Girls in the Balcony: Women, Men, and* The New York Times (New York: Random House, 1992), 7, 84; Amanda Svachula, "When the *Times* Kept Female Reporters Upstairs," *New York Times*, September 20, 2018 (online).

19. hwpi.harvard.edu/files/faculty-diversity/files/timeline-final_32.pdf.

20. faculty.harvard.edu/first-tenured-women.

21. Martin Duberman, *Black Mountain: An Exploration in Community* (Evanston: Northwestern University Press, 1972), 402–403 (interview with Michael Rumaker).

22. Joseph Dorman, *Arguing the World: The New York Intellectuals in Their Own Words* (New York: Free Press, 2000), 102 (interview with Trilling); and see Diana Trilling, *The Beginning of the Journey: The Marriage of Diana and Lionel Trilling* (New York: Harcourt, Brace, 1993), 330–31.

23. Oral history interview with Lee Krasner, 1972, Archives of American Art, Smithsonian Institution.

24. Grace Hartigan, Journal, December 3, 1951, Box 31, Grace Hartigan Papers, Special Collections Research Center, University Archives, Syracuse University.

25. Susan Sontag, *Reborn: Journals and Notebooks, 1947–1963*, ed. David Rieff (New York: Farrar, Straus and Giroux, 2008), 310.

26. Judith Malina, *The Diaries of Judith Malina* (New York: Grove, 1984), 248 (entry for October 11, 1952).

27. Paul Goodman, *Growing Up Absurd: Problems of Youth in the Organized System* (New York: Random House, 1960), 13.

28. Jonas Mekas, "Movie Journal," *Village Voice*, July 25, 1963, 14.

29. Sterling North, "A National Disgrace," *Chicago Daily News*, May 8, 1940, 21.

30. William Moulton Marston, "Why 100,000,000 Americans Read Comics," *American Scholar* 13 (1944): 35–44; Harold C. Field, Cleanth Brooks, and Robert B. Heilman, "On 'Why 100,000,000 Americans Read Comics," *American Scholar* 13 (1944): 247–52.

31. David Hajdu, *The Ten-Cent Plague: The Great Comic-Book Scare and How It Changed America* (New York: Farrar, Straus and Giroux, 2008), 5.

32. Bart Beaty, *Fredric Wertham and the Critique of Mass Culture* (Jackson: University Press of Mississippi, 2005), 16–17.

33. Frederic [*sic*] Wertham, "Are Comic Books Harmful to Children?," *Friends Intelligencer* 105 (1948): 396.

34. Wolcott Gibbs, "'Keep Those Paws to Yourself, Space-Rat!'," *New Yorker* 30 (May 8, 1954), 134; Beaty, *Fredric Wertham*, 146.

35. Fredric Wertham, *Seduction of the Innocent* (New York: Rhinehart, 1954), 178, 183.

36. *Hearings Before the Subcommittee to Investigate Juvenile Delinquency of the Committee on the Judiciary, United States Senate* (Washington, DC: U.S. Government Printing Office, 1954), 83.

37. Ibid., 82, 84, 86, 87, 88, 95.

38. Ibid., 95.

39. "Code of the Comics Magazine Association of America, Inc.," *Catholic Lawyer* 1 (1955): 60–61.

40. Hajdu, *The Ten-Cent Plague*, 274–95, 337–51.

41. Amy Kiste Nyberg, *Seal of Approval: The History of the Comics Code* (Jackson: University Press of Mississippi, 1998), 117–28.

42. G. Legman, "The Psychopathology of the Comics," *Neurotica*, no. 3 (Autumn 1948), 21.

43. Thierry Crépin, *"Haro sur le ganster": La moralisation de la presse enfantine, 1934–1954* (Paris: CNRS Éditions, 2001); Richard I. Jobs, "Tarzan under Attack: Youth, Comics, and Cultural Reconstruction in Postwar France," *French Historical Studies* 26 (2003): 687–725.

44. C. Wright Mills, "Nothing to Laugh At," *New York Times Book Review*, April 25, 1954, 20.

45. Gibbs, "Keep Those Paws to Yourself, Space-Rat!'," 141.

46. Robert Warshow, "Paul, the Horror Comics, and Dr. Wertham," *Commentary* 17 (1954): 604.

47. Mickey Spillane, *I, the Jury* (New York: E. P. Dutton, 1947), 217–18.

48. Ian Fleming, *Casino Royale* (London: Jonathan Cape, 1953), 218.

49. See Raymond Benson, *The James Bond Bedside Companion* (New York: Dodd, Mead, 1984), 9.

50. Grace Metalious, *Peyton Place* (New York: Julian Messner, 1956), 100, 150.

51. Ardis Cameron, *Unbuttoning America: A Biography of Peyton Place* (Ithaca: Cornell University Press, 2015), 3, 142.

52. Elizabeth Pleck, *Domestic Tyranny: The Making of American Social Policy Against Family Violence from Colonial Times to the Present*, 2nd ed. (Urbana: University of Illinois Press, 2004), 182.

53. Adele Mailer, *The Last Party: Scenes from My Life with Norman Mailer* (New York: Barricade Books, 1997), 347–63; J. Michael Lennon, *Norman Mailer: A Double Life* (New York: Simon and Schuster, 2013), 281–86.

54. *New York Times*, November 14, 1961, 45.

55. Peter Manso, *Mailer: His Life and Times* (New York: Simon and Schuster, 1985), 327 (interview with Howe).

56. Thomas L. Jeffers, *Norman Podhoretz: A Biography* (New York: Cambridge University Press, 2010), 82.

57. James Baldwin, "The Black Boy Looks at the White Boy," *Esquire* 55 (May 1961), 106.

58. Manso, *Mailer*, 331 (interview with Diana Trilling).

59. Midge Decter to Jacqueline Wheldon, February 24, 1961. Courtesy of Wynn Wheldon.

60. James Baldwin et al., "Norman Mailer," *Time* 76 (December 26, 1960), 2.

61. Richard Poirier, "Morbid-Mindedness," *Commentary* 39 (June 1965), 91.

62. Ronald W. Schatz, *The Electrical Workers: A History of Labor at General Electric and Westinghouse, 1932–1960* (Urbana: University of Illinois Press, 1983), 82–83, 232.

63. Association of National Advertisers, *Magazine Circulation and Rate Trends* (New York: National Association of Advertisers, 1956), 12–92.

64. Daniel Horowitz, *Betty Friedan and the Making of* The Feminine Mystique: *The American Left, the Cold War, and Modern Feminism* (Amherst: University of Massachusetts Press, 1998), 88–132, 165–71; U.S. Department of Commerce, "Income of Families and Persons in the United States: 1957," in *Current Population Reports* (Washington, DC: U.S. Government Printing Office, 1958), 1.

65. Betty Goldstein Friedan, "If One Generation Can Ever Tell Another," *Smith Alumnae Quarterly* 52 (1961): 68–70.

66. See, e.g., Patterson, *Grand Expectations*, 643; Jessica Weiss, *To Have and To Hold: Marriage, the Baby Boom, and Social Change* (Chicago: University of Chicago Press, 2000), 6; Judith Hennessee, *Betty Friedan: Her Life* (New York: Random House, 1999), 70–71; Stephanie Coontz, *The Way We Never Were: American Families and the Nostalgia Trap* (New York: Basic Books, 1992), 164; James West Davidson and Mark Hamilton Lytle, *After the Fact: The Art of Historical Detection*, 2nd ed. (New York: Knopf, 1986), 364–67 (interestingly, given its inaccuracies in this case, a book about historical method).

67. Betty Friedan, *It Changed My Life: Writings on the Women's Movement* (New York: Random House, 1976), 17. Ellipses in the original. See also Betty Friedan, "Up from the Kitchen Floor," *New York Times Magazine*, March 4, 1973, 8.

68. Coontz, *A Strange Stirring*, 139–43; Horowitz, *Betty Friedan*, 5, 197–99.

69. Horowitz, *Betty Friedan*, 231.

70. Betty Friedan, "Was Their Education Un-American?," M-575, Box 31, Folder 415, Papers of Betty Friedan, Schlesinger Library, Radcliffe Institute for Advanced Study. File is misdated 1957.

71. Betty Friedan, "Why I Went Back to Work," *Charm*, April 1955, 145.

72. Betty Friedan, "Millionaire's Wife," *Cosmopolitan* 141 (September 1956), 81.

73. Betty Friedan, "I Was Afraid to Have a Baby, by Julie Harris as told to Betty Friedan," *McCall's* 84 (December 1956), 74.

74. See Nevitt Sanford, "Personality Development During the College Years," *Journal of Social Issues* 12 (1956): 3–12.

75. Nevitt Sanford, "Is College Education Wasted on Women?," *Ladies' Home Journal* 74 (May 1957), 79, 198.

76. "Are Women Wasting Their Time in College?," Box 32, Folder 429, Friedan Papers. (Quotations taken from multiple drafts of the essay.) See also Marcia Cohen, *The Sisterhood: The True Story of the Women Who Changed the World* (New York: Simon and Schuster, 1988), 84 (quoting Friedan). See Betty Friedan, *The Feminine Mystique* (New York: W. W. Norton, 1963), 152–56.

77. Friedan, "If One Generation Can Ever Tell Another," 68–70.

78. "Early abstract," Box 42, Folder 551, Friedan Papers.

79. Simone de Beauvoir, *La Force des choses* (Paris: Gallimard, 1963), 204n.

80. See Toril Moi, *Simone de Beauvoir: The Making of an Intellectual Woman*, 2nd ed. (New York: Oxford University Press, 2008), 235–69.

81. Hazel Rowley, *Tête-à-Tête: Simone de Beauvoir and Jean-Paul Sartre* (New York: HarperCollins, 2005), 149–202.

82. Simone de Beauvoir, *Le Deuxième sexe*, vol. 1, *Les Faits et les mythes* (Paris: Gallimard, 1949), 22 ("elle est l'Autre au cœur d'une totalité dont les deux termes sont nécessaires l'un à l'autre").

83. Horowitz, *Betty Friedan*, 313n7.

84. Betty Friedan, "No Gods, No Goddesses," *Saturday Review* 2 (June 14, 1975), 16.

85. Simone de Beauvoir, "Femininity, the Trap—a French View," *Vogue* 129 (March 15, 1947), 234. See Moi, *Simone de Beauvoir*, 235–69.

86. Date based on a library call slip in "BF Notes re SdeB," Box 86, Folder 985, Friedan Papers.

87. Simone de Beauvoir, *The Second Sex*, trans. and ed. H. M. Parshley (New York: Knopf, 1953), 721. ("Le fait que les hommes rencontrent chez leur compagne plus de complicité que l'oppresseur n'en trouve habituellement chez l'opprimé; et ils s'en autorisent avec mauvaise foi pour déclarer qu'elle a *voulu* la destinée qu'ils lui ont imposée . . . [L]a société entière—à commencer par ses parents respectés—lui ment en exaltant la haute valeur de l'amour, du

dévouement, du don de soi et en lui dissimulant que ni l'amant, ni le mari, ni les enfants ne seront disposés à en supporter la charge encombrante . . . Elle accepte allégrement ces mensonges parce qu'ils l'invitent à suivre la pente de la facilité: et c'est là le pire crime que l'on commet contre elle; dès son enfance et tout au long de sa vie on la gâte, on la corrompt en lui désignant comme sa vocation cette démission qui tente tout existant angoissé de sa liberté . . . Elle a tort de céder à la tentation; mais l'homme est mal venu de le lui reprocher." Simone de Beauvoir, *Le Deuxième sexe*, vol. 2, *L'Expérience vécue* [Paris: Gallimard, 1949], 565–66.)

88. "BF Notes re SdeB," Friedan Papers.

89. Friedan, *The Feminine Mystique*, 338.

90. See Sandra Dijkstra, "Simone de Beauvoir and Betty Friedan: The Politics of Omission," *Feminist Studies* 6 (1980): 290–303.

91. See Coontz, *A Strange Stirring*, 143; Horowitz, *Betty Friedan*, 313n7.

92. Dwight Macdonald, "The Lady Doth Protest," *Reporter* 14 (April 1953), 36.

93. Clyde Kluckhohn, "The Female of Our Species," *New York Times Book Review*, October 6, 1953, 3.

94. Orville Prescott, "In My Opinion, These Are the Year's Best," *New York Times Book Review*, June 7, 1953, 3.

95. Hennessee, *Betty Friedan*, 75–77.

96. Joanne Meyerowitz, "Beyond the Feminine Mystique," in Joanne Meyerowitz, ed., *Not June Cleaver: Women and Gender in Postwar America, 1945–1960* (Philadelphia: Temple University Press, 1994), 229–62.

97. Susan Oliver, *Betty Friedan: The Personal Is Political* (New York: Pearson Longman, 2008), 65–66.

98. Friedan, *The Feminine Mystique*, 309.

99. May, *Homeward Bound*, 186–95.

100. Betty Friedan, "Women Are People Too!," *Good Housekeeping* 151 (September 1960), 161.

101. Helen Gurley Brown, *Sex and the Single Girl* (New York: Bernard J. Geis, 1962), 267.

102. Joan Didion, "Bosses Make Lousy Lovers," *Saturday Evening Post* 237 (January 30, 1965), 36.

103. Laurie Ouelette, "Inventing the Cosmo Girl: Class Identity and Girl-Style American Dreams," *Media, Culture & Society* 21 (1999): 361.

104. Executive Order 10980, Establishing the President's Commission on the Status of Women, 26 *Federal Register* 12059.

105. See Joanne Meyerowitz, "Sex, Gender, and the Cold War Language of Reform," in Peter Kuznick and James Gilbert, eds., *Rethinking Cold War Culture* (Washington, DC: Smithsonian Institution Press, 2001), 106–23; G. Calvin Makenzie and Robert Weisbrot, *The Liberal Hour: Washington and the Politics of Change in the 1960s* (New York: Penguin, 2008), 134–83.

106. Ralph Waldo Emerson, *The Conduct of Life* (Boston: Ticknor and Fields, 1960), 1.

107. Franklin Foer, "Susan Superstar," *New York* 38 (January 31, 2005) (online).

108. Susan Sontag, "The Art of Fiction No. CXLIII," *Paris Review* 37 (Winter 1995), 193.

109. See Trilling's essays in Arthur Krystal, ed., *A Company of Readers: Uncollected Writings of W. H. Auden, Jacques Barzun, and Lionel Trilling from the Readers' Subscription and Mid-Century Book Clubs* (New York: Free Press, 2001).

110. Benjamin Moser, *Sontag: Her Life and Work* (New York: HarperCollins, 2019), 20–65.

111. Susan Sontag, "Pilgrimage," *New Yorker* 63 (December 21, 1987), 38.

112. Susan Sontag, Journals 1948–1950, 1954–2003, March 7, 1947, Box 123, Folder 1, Sontag Papers, Library Special Collections, Charles E. Young Research Library, University of California at Los Angeles.

113. Sontag, *Reborn*, 7.

114. Ibid., 8–9.

115. Moser, *Sontag*, 60–65; Sontag, "Pilgrimage," 39–41.

116. Moser, *Sontag*, 84–91.

117. Ibid., 98–129.

118. Sontag, *Reborn*, 140.

119. Alice Kaplan, *Dreaming in French: The Paris Years of Jacqueline Bouvier Kennedy, Susan Sontag, and Angela Davis* (Chicago: University of Chicago Press, 2012), 98–99.

120. Susan Sontag, "He Landed Among Us Like a Missile," in Valentina Polukhina, ed., *Brodsky Through the Eyes of His Contemporaries*, vol. 2 (Boston: Academic Studies Press, 2008), 327; Kaplan, *Dreaming in French*, 97.

121. Kaplan, *Dreaming in French*, 140.

122. Harriet Sohmers Zwerling, *Abroad: An Expatriate's Diaries, 1950–1950* (New York: Spuyten Duyvil, 2014), 268.

123. Ross Wetzsteon, "Irene Fornés: The Elements of Style," *Village Voice*, April 29, 1986, 45.

124. Stephanie Harrington, "Irene Fornés, Playwright: Alice and the Red Queen," *Village Voice*, April 21, 1966, 1, 33–34; Bruce Weber, "María Irene Fornés, 88, Playwright Who, to Her Peers, Was a Genius," *New York Times*, October 31, 2018, B14. See also Manso, *Mailer*, 165–66 (interview with Fornés).

125. Carl Rollyson and Lisa Paddock, *Susan Sontag: The Making of an Icon*, rev. ed. (Jackson: University Press of Mississippi, 2016), 63–66; Moser, *Sontag*, 173–78.

126. Zwerling, *Abroad*, 304.

127. Irene Fornés, "Maria Irene Fornés Discusses Forty Years in Theatre with Maria M. Delgado" [1997], in Maria M. Delgado and Caridad Svich, eds., *Conducting a Life: Reflections on*

the *Theatre of Maria Irene Fornes* (Lyme, NH: Smith and Kraus, 1999), 255–56; Marithelma Costa and Adelaida López, "Susan Sontag o la pasión por las palabras," *Revista de Occidente*, no. 79 (December 1987), 115 (interview with Sontag); Wetzsteon, "Irene Fornés," 43. Minor details differ.

128. Moser, *Sontag*, 734n49. The Obies website lists nine (www.obieawards.com/events/2010s/).

129. Marc Robinson, introduction to *The Theater of Maria Irene Fornés* (Baltimore: Johns Hopkins University Press, 1999), 19.

130. See Moser, *Sontag*, 173–75.

131. Ibid., 87 (interview with Harriet Sohmers Zwerling).

132. Zwerling, *Abroad*, 265 (ellipsis in original), 271.

133. Moser, *Sontag*, 162 (interview with Joanna Robertson), 728–29n25 (interviews with Ted Mooney, Leon Wieseltier, and Stephen Koch).

134. See David Rieff, preface to Sontag, *Reborn*, xi–xii.

135. Eliot Fremont-Smith, "After the Ticker Tape Parade," *New York Times*, January 31, 1966, 37.

136. Sontag, *Reborn*, 94; Moser, *Sontag*, 230.

137. Edward Leffingwell, Carole Kismarc, and Marvin Heiferman, eds., *Jack Smith, Flaming Creature: His Amazing Life and Times* (Long Island City, NY: Institute for Contemporary Art, P.S. 1 Museum, 1997), 71; Mary Jordan, dir., *Jack Smith and the Destruction of Atlantis* (Arthouse Films DVD, 2007).

138. Greg Taylor, *Artists in the Audience: Cult, Camp, and American Film Criticism* (Princeton: Princeton University Press, 1999), 75.

139. Barbara Wilinsky, *Sure Seaters: The Emergence of Art House Cinema* (Minneapolis: University of Minnesota Press, 2001), 132.

140. Greg S. Faller, "'Unquiet Years': Experimental Cinema in the 1950s," in Peter Lev, ed., *History of American Cinema*, vol. 7, *Transforming the Screen, 1950–1959*, by Peter Lev (New York: Scribner, 2003), 280–85; Robert Sklar, *Movie-Made America: A Cultural History of American Movies*, rev. ed. (New York: Vintage, 1994), 306.

141. Timothy Snyder, *Bloodlands: Europe Between Hitler and Stalin* (New York: Basic Books, 2010), 190–92; Michael Casper, "I Was There," *New York Review of Books* 65 (June 7, 2018) (online).

142. Jonas Mekas, *I Had Nowhere to Go* (New York: Black Thistle Press, 1991), 293–94.

143. Bruce Weber, "Jonas Mekas, 'Godfather' of American Avant-Garde Film, Is Dead at 96," *New York Times*, January 24, 2019, A24.

144. Kevin Michael McAuliffe, *The Great American Newspaper: The Rise and Fall of the* Village Voice (New York: Scribner, 1978), 56–57.

145. Jonas Mekas, "The Experimental Film in America," *Film Culture* 1 (May–June 1955), 15, 17, 18.

146. Jonas Mekas, "The Experimental Film in America," in P. Adams Sitney, ed., *Film Culture Reader* (New York: Praeger, 1970), 26. See also Stan Vanderbeek, "The Cinema Delimina: Films from the Underground," *Film Quarterly* 14 (Summer 1961), 5–15; P. Adams Sitney, *Visionary Film: The American Avant-Garde* (New York: Oxford University Press, 1974); Jonas Mekas, *Movie Journal: The Rise of the New American Cinema, 1959–1971* (New York: Macmillan, 1972).

147. David E. James, introduction to *To Free the Cinema: Jonas Mekas and the New York Underground* (Princeton: Princeton University Press, 1992), 9–11; J. Hoberman, *On Jack Smith's* Flaming Creatures *(and Other Secret-Flix of Cinemaroc)* (New York: Hips Road, 2001), 27.

148. David Riesman, "In the Grip of the Lobster: Jack Smith Remembered," *Millennium Film Journal* 23–24 (Winter 1990–1991), 63–69 (interview with Conrad); Branden W. Joseph, *Beyond the Dream Syndicate: Tony Conrad and the Arts after Cage (A "Minor" History)* (New York: Zone Books, 2008), 229–69; Hoberman, *On Jack Smith's* Flaming Creatures, 8, 20–33.

149. Jonas Mekas, "Movie Journal," *Village Voice*, April 18, 1963, 13.

150. On the following, see, generally, Hoberman, *On Jack Smith's* Flaming Creatures, 36–51; Brian L. Frye, "The Dialectics of Obscenity," *Hamline Law Review* 35 (2012): 236–75.

151. Arthur Knight, "New American Cinema?," *Saturday Review* 46 (November 2, 1963), 41.

152. J. Hoberman and Jonathan Rosenbaum, *Midnight Movies* (New York: Harper and Row, 1983), 59.

153. Elliott Stein, "Fog at Knokke," *Sight and Sound* 33 (Spring 1964), 88–89; "'Film Underground' Explosion: Belgians Balk N.Y. 'Creatures,'" *Variety*, January 15, 1964, 1, 15; "German Experimental Film Wins at Festival in Belgium," *New York Times*, January 2, 1964, 31.

154. "Cancel 'Flaming' as Entry in Stockholm's 'New American' Series," *Variety*, April 15, 1964, 25.

155. "Cops Raid Homo Films Again: Mekas Risking Jail Sentence," *Variety*, March 18, 1964, 5.

156. Jack Smith, "The Perfect Filmic Appositeness of Maria Montez," *Film Culture* 27 (1962), 31.

157. "Flaming Censorship," *Nation* 198 (1964): 311.

158. Susan Sontag, "A Feast for Open Eyes," *Nation* 198 (1964): 374.

159. Ibid., 376.

160. Jonas Mekas, *A Dance with Fred Astaire* (New York: Anthology Editions, 2017), 11.

161. Jack Smith, "Uncle Fishhook and the Sacred Baby Poo-Poo of Art," *Semiotext(e)* 3:2 (1978): 192–203.

162. Calvin Tomkins, "All Pockets Open," *New Yorker* 48 (January 6, 1973), 37 (interview with Vogel).

163. Richard Kostelanetz, ed., *Conversing with Cage* (New York: Limelight, 1994), 13 (interview with Cage by Gwen Deely, 1976).

164. See the chart in George Maciunas, *Diagram of Historical Development of Fluxus and Other 4 Dimensional, Aural, Optic, Olfactory, Epithelial and Tactile Art Forms (Incomplete)* (Ahus, Sweden: Kalejdoskop, 1978).

165. See Mekas, *A Dance with Fred Astaire*, 265.

166. Paul Hoffman, "A Movie Show—in Criminal Court," *New York Post*, June 3, 1964, 16.

167. Stephanie Garvis Harrington, "Pornography Is Undefined at Film-Critic Mekas' Trial," *Village Voice*, January 9, 1964, 13.

168. Susan Sontag, "Ionesco: The Theatre of the Banal," *New York Review of Books* 2 (July 9, 1964) (online).

169. Susan Sontag, *Against Interpretation and Other Essays* (New York: Farrar, Straus and Giroux, 1966), viii.

170. Moser, *Sontag*, 228.

171. W. H. Auden, "An Improbable Life," *New Yorker* 39 (March 9, 1963), 155–77; Edward Field, *The Man Who Would Marry Susan Sontag: And Other Intimate Literary Portraits of the Bohemian Era* (Madison: University of Wisconsin Press, 2005), 164.

172. Rollyson and Paddock, *Susan Sontag*, 90; William Phillips, letter to the editor, *New York Times Magazine*, August 23, 1992, 10–12. See also Moser, *Sontag*, 228 (interview with Norman Podhoretz).

173. "Camp," *Time* 84 (December 11, 1964), 75; Thomas Meehan, "Not Good Taste, Not Bad Taste—It's 'Camp,'" *New York Times Magazine*, March 21, 1965, 30.

174. See Terry Castle, "Some Notes on Camp," in Barbara Ching and Jennifer A. Wagner-Lawlor, eds., *The Scandal of Susan Sontag* (New York: Columbia University Press, 2009), 21–31.

175. Susan Sontag, "Notes on Camp," *Partisan Review* 31 (1964): 529.

176. Ibid., 516, 526.

177. Ibid., 517, 520, 521, 523, 526.

178. Loren Glass, *Counterculture Colophon: Grove Press, the* Evergreen Review, *and the Incorporation of the Avant-Garde* (Stanford: Stanford University Press, 2013), 120–21.

179. Willem de Kooning, "Content Is a Glimpse . . . ," *Location*, Spring 1963, 47.

180. Susan Sontag, "Against Interpretation," *Evergreen Review*, no. 34 (December 1964), 79.

181. Sontag, "Against Interpretation," 78, 80, 93.

182. Daniel Schreiber, *Susan Sontag: A Biography*, trans. David Dollenmayer (Evanston: Northwestern University Press, 2014), 98.

183. Sontag, "Notes on Camp," 520, 526.

184. Susan Sontag, "On Style," in *Against Interpretation*, 26. The sentences on Riefenstahl do not appear in the original essay, in *Partisan Review*. They may have been cut by the editors.

185. Sontag, *Against Interpretation*, 302, 304.

186. Irving Howe, "The New York Intellectuals: A Chronicle and a Critique," *Commentary* 46 (October 1968), 49.

187. "New and Recommended," *New York Times*, February 20, 1966, 107.

188. Elisabeth Stevens, "Miss Camp Herself," *New Republic* 154 (February 19, 1966), 24.

189. Meyer Schapiro, "Nature of Abstract Art," *Marxist Quarterly* 1 (1937): 77.

190. Susan Sontag, *As Consciousness Is Harnessed to Flesh: Journals and Notebooks, 1964–1980*, ed. David Rieff (New York: Farrar, Straus and Giroux, 2012), 53.

191. Jacques Derrida to Susan Sontag, February 12, 1966, Box 84, Folder 43, Sontag Papers ("avec ravissement"; "Je vous envoie aujourd'hui mes deux derniers articles de Critique contre l'interprétation"). Derrida misdated the letter 1965.

192. Sontag, "Against Interpretation," 93.

193. Emile Berman as reported in Harrington, "Pornography Is Undefined at Film-Critic Mekas' Trial," 9.

194. Stephanie Garvis Harrington, "City Sleuths Douse 'Flaming Creatures,'" *Village Voice*, March 12, 1964, 3, 13.

195. Clement Greenberg, "Sculpture in Our Time," in *The Collected Essays and Criticism*, vol. 4, *Modernism with a Vengeance, 1957–1969*, ed. John O'Brian (Chicago: University of Chicago Press, 1986), 59.

196. Allan Kaprow, "The Legacy of Jackson Pollock," *ARTnews* 57 (October 1958), 25.

197. Carolee Schneemann, *More Than Meat Joy: Performance Works and Selected Writings*, 2nd ed. (Kingston, NY: McPherson, 1997), 63.

198. See Carolee Schneemann, *Kinetic Painting*, ed. Sabine Breitwieser (Munich: Prestelk, 2015), 130; Carolee Schneemann, *Correspondence Course: An Epistolary History of Carolee Schneemann and Her Circle*, ed. Kristine Stiles (Durham: Duke University Press, 2010), 55n158.

199. See Carolee Schneemann, "Up to and Including Her Limits," Museum of Modern Art, www.moma.org/learn/moma_learning/carolee-schneemann-up-to-and-including-her-limits-1973-76/.

200. Jill Johnston, "Life and Art," *Village Voice*, December 7, 1961, 10.

201. A[lan] R[ich], "Far-Out Music Is Played at Carnegie," *New York Times*, November 25, 1961, 27.

202. Midori Yoshimoto, *Into Performance: Japanese Women Artists in New York* (New Brunswick: Rutgers University Press, 2005), 79–114; Luciana Galliano, "Toshi Uchiyanagi: Japanese Composer and 'Fluxus,'" *Perspectives of New*

Music 44 (2006): 250–61; Klaus Biesenbach and Christophe Cherix, *Yoko Ono: One Woman Show, 1960–1971* (New York: Museum of Modern Art), 43–113.

203. Joan Rothfuss, *Topless Cellist: The Improbable Life of Charlotte Moorman* (Cambridge, MA: MIT Press, 2014), 43–51.

204. Stephen Varble, "Interview with Charlotte Moorman on the Avant-Garde Festivals," in Geoffrey Hendricks, ed., *Critical Mass: Happenings, Fluxus, Performance, Intermedia and Rutgers University, 1958–1972* (New Brunswick: Rutgers University Press, 2003), 173.

205. Gloria Steinem, "Music Music Music Music: On the Heels of the Avant-Garde," *Show* 4 (January 1964), 57–60.

206. Calvin Tomkins, "Video Visionary," *New Yorker* 51 (May 5, 1975), 46–61.

207. Joseph, *Beyond the Dream Syndicate*, 193–202; Benjamin Piekut, *Experimentalism Otherwise: The New York Avant-Garde and Its Limits* (Berkeley: University of California Press, 2011), 65–101.

208. Faubion Bowers, "A Feast of Astonishments," *Nation* 199 (1964): 172–75; Alan Rich, "Stockhausen's 'Originale,'" *New York Herald Tribune*, September 9, 1964; Harold Schonberg, "Music: Stockhausen's 'Originale' Given at Judson," *New York Times*, September 9, 1964, 46; Rothfuss, *Topless Cellist*, 96–105; Piekut, *Experimentalism Otherwise*, 140–42; Mark Bloch, *Meat, Maps, and Militant Metaphysics: Robert Delford Brown* (Wilmington, NC: Cameron Art Museum, 2008), 38–40; Peter Moore, dir., *Stockhausen's Originale: Doubletakes* (1964), ubu.com/film/stockhausen_originale.html.

209. David Bourdon, "A Letter to Charlotte Moorman," *Art in America* 88 (June 2000), 83.

210. Rothfuss, *Topless Cellist*, 105.

211. Tomkins, "Video Visionary," 58; Rothfuss, *Topless Cellist*, 102 (interview with Schneemann).

212. Rothfuss, *Topless Cellist*, 110.

213. See Sophie Landres, "Indecent and Uncanny: The Case Against Charlotte Moorman," *Art Journal* 76 (Spring 2017), 48–69; Rothfuss, *Topless Cellist*, 175–205.

214. Glenn Collins, "Charlotte Moorman, 58, Is Dead; a Cellist in Avant-Garde Works," *New York Times*, November 9, 1991, 12.

215. Piekut, *Experimentalism Otherwise*, 162–68.

216. Tomkins, "Video Visionary," 58 (interview with Paik).

217. "An Evening with Fluxus Women: A Roundtable Discussion," *Women & Performance* 19 (2009): 373.

218. See Kaplan, *Dreaming in French*, 108–11.

219. Sontag, "Notes on Camp," 517.

220. Moser, *Sontag*, 186.

221. See Blake Gopnik, *Warhol* (New York: Ecco, 2020), 398–400.

16. FREEDOM IS THE FIRE

1. Alfred Pacquement, "Jean Dubuffet à New York, Américains à Paris dans les années 50," in Pontus Hultén, ed., *Paris/New York: 1908–1968* (Paris: Centre Pompidou/Gallimard, 1991), 679–80; Peter Selz, "Amerikaner im Ausland," in Christos M. Joachimides and Norman Rosenthal, pubs., David Anfam and Gerti Fietze, eds., *Amerikanische Kunst im 20. Jahrhundert: Malerei und Plastik, 1913–1993* (Munich: Prestel-Verlag, 1993), 205; Elisa Capdevila, *Les Américains à Paris: Artistes et bohèmes dans la France de l'après-guerre* (Malakoff, France: Armand Colin, 2017), 16–66.

2. Thomas Barbour, "Little Magazines in Paris," *Hudson Review* 4 (1951): 278–83; Christopher Sawyer-Lauçanno, *The Continual Pilgrimage: American Writers in Paris* (New York: Grove, 1992), 125–61.

3. Bill Moody, *The Jazz Exiles: American Musicians Abroad* (Reno: University of Nevada Press, 1993), 173–74; Tyler Stovall, *Paris Noir: African Americans in the City of Light* (Boston: Houghton Mifflin, 1996), 163–81; Colin Nettelbeck, *Dancing with de Beauvoir: Jazz and the French* (Melbourne: Melbourne University Press, 2004), 53–75.

4. Brooke L. Blower, *Becoming Americans in Paris: Transatlantic Politics and Culture Between the World Wars* (New York: Oxford University Press, 2011), 22; Christopher Endy, *Cold War Holidays: American Tourism in France* (Chapel Hill: University of North Carolina Press, 2004), 8; Antony Beevor and Artemis Cooper, *Paris After the Liberation, 1944–1949*, rev. ed. (London: Penguin, 2004), 361.

5. Thomas Piketty, *Capital in the Twenty-First Century*, trans. Arthur Goldhammer (Cambridge, MA: Harvard University Press, 2014), 131–32, 103–109.

6. Eugen Weber, *The Hollow Years: France in the 1930s* (New York: W. W. Norton, 1994), 26–27.

7. Benjamin F. Martin, *France and the Après Guerre, 1918–1924: Illusions and Disillusionment* (Baton Rouge: Louisiana State University Press, 1999), 256.

8. Martin Wolfe, *The French Franc Between the Wars, 1919–1939* (New York: Columbia University Press, 1951), 207–209; Melchior Palyi, *A Lesson in French—Inflation* (New York: Economists' National Committee on Monetary Policy, 1959).

9. J. G. Mérigot and P. Coulbois, *Le Franc, 1938–1950* (Paris: R. Pichon and R. Durand-Auzias, 1950), 86–87.

10. Jean-Pierre Dormois, *The French Economy in the Twentieth Century* (Cambridge: Cambridge University Press, 2004), 54.

11. See Stanley Karnow, *Paris in the Fifties* (New

York: Times Books, 1997), 5; Eugene Walter, in George Plimpton et al., "The Paris Review Sketchbook," *Paris Review* 23 (Spring 1981), 333.

12. Dormois, *The French Economy in the Twentieth Century*, 54; Lawrence H. Officer, "Exchange Rates Between the United States Dollar and Forty-One Currencies," *MeasuringWorth*, 2015, www.measuringworth.com/exchangeglobal/.

13. Serge Berstein, *The Republic of de Gaulle, 1958–1969*, trans. Peter Morris (Cambridge: Cambridge University Press, 1993), 103–105; Piketty, *Capital in the Twenty-First Century*, 133, 546. Cf. Walter Laqueur, *Europe Since Hitler* (Harmondsworth, UK: Penguin, 1972), 214.

14. Endy, *Cold War Holidays*, 150–81.

15. Norman Mailer and Richard Wilbur, "Postwar Paris: Chronicles of Literary Life," *Paris Review* 41 (Spring 1999), 282. Cf. Peter Manso, *Mailer: His Life and Times* (New York: Simon and Schuster, 1985), 115–16.

16. Saul Bellow, foreword to Fyodor M. Dostoevsky, *Winter Notes on Summer Impressions*, trans. Richard Lee Renfield (New York: Criterion Books, 1955), 15. See also Zachary Leader, *The Life of Saul Bellow: To Fame and Fortune, 1915–1964* (New York: Knopf, 2015), 346–54.

17. Norman Mailer, "Un Hommage à Jean Malaquais," trans. Katia Holmes, in Jean Malaquais, *Planète sans visa* (Paris: Éditions Phébus, 1999), 17. ("Jean Malaquais n'était pas seulement mon meilleur ami, il était mon mentor. Il a exercé sur moi plus d'influence que jamais quiconque.") Dated March 1999; adapted from Norman Mailer, "A Preface to *The Joker*," in Jean Malaquais, *The Joker*, trans. Herma Briffault (New York: Warner Books, 1974), 11–25.

18. Geneviève Nakach, *Malaquais rebelle* (Paris: Le Cherche Midi, 2011), 16; James Kirkup, "Obituary: Jean Malaquais," *Independent*, January 6, 1999 (online).

19. Interview with Élisabeth Malaquais by James McAuley, Paris, July 9, 2011.

20. Nakach, *Malaquais rebelle*, 43. ("[L]a France était, dans mon [?] imagination de jeune homme de ces pays-là, LE pays où il faut vivre, LE pays où il faut étudier. C'était la Révolution française, la Commune, le pays d'accueil, ainsi de suite, ainsi de suite.")

21. Interview with Élisabeth Malaquais; Kirkup, "Obituary."

22. A. Roubé-Jansky, "Les Conrad Français," *Les Nouvelles Littéraires artistiques et scientifiques*, April 6, 1940, 4. ("Ce fut un mariage d'amour; un des rares mariages qui ne soient point malheureux.")

23. Jean Malaquais, *Jean Malaquais' War Diary*, trans. Peter Grant (Garden City, NY: Doubleday, Doran, 1944), 198–246.

24. Norman Mailer and Jean Malaquais, *Correspondance, 1949–1986*, ed. Élisabeth Malaquais and Geneviève Nakach, trans. Hélène Ancel (Paris: Le Cherche Midi, 2008), 13n2.

25. Nakach, *Malaquais rebelle*, 149–57, 174–78.

26. Ibid., 240–47; Clement Greenberg to Whom It May Concern, June 24, 1947, Jean Malaquais Papers, Harry Ransom Center, University of Texas at Austin.

27. Nakach, *Malaquais rebelle*, 265.

28. See, e.g., Norman Mailer to Jean Malaquais, August 8, 1957, and Malaquais to Mailer, May 27, 1957, Norman Mailer Papers, Harry Ransom Center, University of Texas at Austin.

29. Manso, *Mailer*, 148 (interview with Fanny Mailer).

30. Adele Mailer, *The Last Party: Scenes from My Life with Norman Mailer* (New York: Barricade Books, 1997), 227.

31. Manso, *Mailer*, 129 (interview with Howe).

32. Jean Malaquais to André Gide, September 29, 1950, in Mailer and Malaquais, *Correspondance*, 211. ("[T]out doux le carcan totalitaire.")

33. Manso, *Mailer*, 233–34 (interview with Malaquais).

34. James Baldwin, "The Black Boy Looks at the White Boy," *Esquire* 55 (May 1961), 102.

35. David Leeming, *James Baldwin: A Biography* (New York: Knopf, 1994), 133.

36. Norman Mailer, "Column Sixteen," in *Advertisements for Myself* (New York: G. P. Putnam's Sons, 1959), 314.

37. Allen Ginsberg, *Howl and Other Poems* (San Francisco: City Lights Books, 1956), 9.

38. Norman Mailer, "The White Negro: Superficial Reflections on the Hipster," *Dissent* 4 (1957): 277, 278, 279.

39. Ibid., 280, 290, 284.

40. Irving Howe to Norman Mailer [May 10, 1957], Series II, Container 527.23, Mailer Papers. See also Gerald Sorin, *Irving Howe: A Life of Passionate Dissent* (New York: New York University Press, 2002), 144.

41. J. Michael Lennon, *Norman Mailer: A Double Life* (New York: Simon and Schuster, 2013), 813n.

42. John Updike, *Rabbit, Run* (New York: Knopf, 1960), 76.

43. See John Stauffer, *The Black Hearts of Men: Radical Abolitionists and the Transformation of Race* (Cambridge, MA: Harvard University Press, 2002); Eric Lott, *Love and Theft: Blackface Minstrelsy and the American Working Class* (New York: Oxford University Press, 1993).

44. See Baz Dreisinger, *Near Black: White-to-Black Passing in American Culture* (Amherst: University of Massachusetts Press, 2008), 93–120.

45. Andrew Ross, *No Respect: Intellectuals and Popular Culture* (New York: Routledge, 1989), 89–92.

46. Lord Buckley, *Euphoria* (Vaya Records LP, 1955).

47. Seymour Krim, "Anti-Jazz: A Question of Self-Identity," *Village Voice*, October 30, 1957, 16.

48. Ingrid Monsen, "The Problem with Hipness: Race, Gender, and Cultural Conceptions in Jazz Historical Discourse," *Journal of the American Musicological Society* 48 (1995): 420–22.

49. Fred Kaplan, *1959: The Year Everything Changed* (Hoboken, NJ: Wiley, 2009), 84–93.

50. Anatole Broyard, "A Portrait of the Hipster," *Partisan Review* 15 (1948): 726.

51. Manso, *Mailer*, 258–60 (interview with Ginsberg).

52. Irving Howe, *A Margin of Hope: An Intellectual Autobiography* (San Diego: Harcourt Brace Jovanovich, 1982), 240. See also Manso, *Mailer*, 253–54 (interview with Howe).

53. Manso, *Mailer*, 254 (interview with Mailer).

54. James Baldwin, *No Name in the Street* (New York: Dial, 1972), 50.

55. *New York Herald Tribune*, September 5, 7, 12, 1956.

56. Leeming, *James Baldwin*, 119–20.

57. Most of the exchanges that follow are covered in Carol Polsgrove, *Divided Minds: Intellectuals and the Civil Rights Movement* (New York: W. W. Norton, 2001), and Lawrence P. Jackson, *The Indignant Generation: A Narrative History of African American Writers and Critics, 1934–1960* (Princeton: Princeton University Press, 2011), 411–509.

58. W. J. Weatherby, *James Baldwin: Artist on Fire* (New York: Donald I. Fine, 1989), 87–88.

59. Weatherby, *James Baldwin*, 135.

60. Kenneth Clark and Mamie Clark, "The Development of Consciousness of Self and the Emergence of Racial Identification in Negro Preschool Children," *Journal of Social Psychology* 10 (1939): 591–99.

61. James E. Reibman, "Ralph Ellison, Fredric Wertham, M.D., and the LaFargue Clinic: Civil Rights and Psychiatric Services in Harlem," *Oklahoma City Law Review* 26 (2001): 1050.

62. *Plessy v. Ferguson*, 163 U.S. 537 (1896), at 537, 551.

63. Richard Kluger, *Simple Justice: The History of Brown v. Board of Education and Black America's Struggle for Equality* (New York: Knopf, 1976), 316–21.

64. James T. Patterson, Brown v. Board of Education: *A Civil Rights Milestone and Its Troubled Legacy* (New York: Oxford University Press), 11.

65. Juan Williams, *Thurgood Marshall: American Revolutionary* (New York: Times Books, 1998), 182.

66. *Brown v. Board of Education*, 347 U.S. 483 (1954), at 494.

67. Ibid.

68. "The Decision of the Supreme Court in the School Cases: Declaration of Constitutional Principles," *Congressional Record*, 84th Congress Second Session, vol. 102 (Washington, DC: U.S. Government Printing Office, 1956), 4459–60.

69. David Wyatt, "Faulkner's Hundred," *Southern Review* 33 (1997): 197–98.

70. Russell Warren Howe, "A Talk with William Faulkner," *Reporter* 14 (March 22, 1956), 19. The interview was recycled by Howe from a piece he had already published in the London *Sunday Times*.

71. "Why the South Must Prevail," *National Review* 4 (1957): 149.

72. James Baldwin, "Faulkner and Desegregation," *Partisan Review* 23 (1956): 570, 573.

73. Kluger, *Simple Justice*, 325–26.

74. See Martin Luther King, Jr., *The Autobiography of Martin Luther King, Jr.*, ed. Clayborne Carson (New York: Grand Central Publishing, 1998), 58–61; Taylor Branch, *America in the King Years*, vol. 1, *Parting the Waters, 1954–63* (New York: Simon and Schuster, 1988), 133–42.

75. James Melvin Washington, ed., *A Testament of Hope: The Essential Writings of Martin Luther King, Jr.* (San Francisco: Harper and Row, 1986), 429.

76. Martin Luther King, Jr. "Montgomery Bus Boycott," December 5, 1955, www.digitalhistory.uh.edu/disp_textbook.cfm?smtid=3&psid=3625.

77. Williams, *Thurgood Marshall*, 341.

78. James Baldwin, "Letter from the South: Nobody Knows My Name," *Partisan Review* 26 (1959): 82.

79. Baldwin, "The Black Boy Looks at the White Boy," 104.

80. James Baldwin to William Cole, October 5, 1961, in James Baldwin, "Letters from a Journey," *Harper's Magazine* 226 (May 1963), 49.

81. James Baldwin, "Letter from a Region of My Mind," *New Yorker* 38 (November 17, 1962), 60.

82. Ibid., 137.

83. Weatherby, *James Baldwin*, 207 (interview with Fine).

84. Foster Hailey, "Dogs and Hoses Repulse Negroes at Birmingham," *New York Times*, May 4, 1963, 1; "Dogs, Kids, and Clubs," *Time* 81 (May 10, 1963), 19.

85. James Baldwin, "On the Bobby Kennedy Meeting," October 24, 1979, Box 43, Folder 33, James Baldwin Papers, Schomburg Center for Research in Black Culture; Layhmond Robinson, "Robert Kennedy Fails to Sway Negroes at Secret Talks Here," *New York Times*, May 26, 1963, 1; Polsgrove, *Divided Minds*, 176–87; Jean Stein, *American Journey: The Times of Robert Kennedy*, ed. George Plimpton (New York: Harcourt Brace Jovanovich, 1970),

118–22. There are multiple accounts; unusually, for a verbal exchange with so many witnesses, they do not conflict substantially.

86. "Baldwin Clan Flops in Meet with 'RFK,'" *Pittsburgh Courier*, June 8, 1963, 2.

87. Arthur M. Schlesinger, Jr., *A Thousand Days: John F. Kennedy in the White House* (Boston: Houghton Mifflin, 1965), 963 (conversation with Kennedy).

88. Stein, *American Journey*, 120 (interview with Kenneth Clark).

89. William Manchester, *Death of a President: November 20–25, 1963* (New York: Harper and Row, 1967), 407.

90. Anthony Lewis, "Robert Kennedy Confers Today with Theater Men on Race Issue," *New York Times*, May 27, 1963, 1; "Baldwin Clan Flops in Meet with 'RFK.'"

91. Jack Gould, "TV: Challenge on Racism," *New York Times*, May 30, 1963, 29.

92. Martin Luther King, Jr., "Bold Design for the New South," *Nation* 196 (1963): 259–62.

93. Evelyn Cunningham, "It's Now Official: Bobby Kennedy Goofed on 'Secret' Rights Parley," *Pittsburgh Courier*, June 1, 1963, 1.

94. Hannah Arendt to James Baldwin, November 21, 1962, Correspondence, BA, Hannah Arendt Papers, Library of Congress.

95. Hannah Arendt, "Reflections on Little Rock," *Dissent* 6 (1959): 51, 53.

96. F. W. Dupee, "James Baldwin and the 'Man," *New York Review of Books* 1 (February 1, 1963) (online).

97. Kenneth Rexroth, "Baldwin's Scare Story of Race Relations," *San Francisco Examiner*, February 3, 1963, 17.

98. Susan Sontag, "The Ideal Husband," *New York Review of Books* 1 (September 26, 1963) (online).

99. Nathan Glazer and Daniel Patrick Moynihan, *Beyond the Melting Pot: The Negroes, Puerto Ricans, Jews, Italians, and Irish of New York City* (Cambridge, MA: MIT and Harvard University Press, 1963), 53.

100. "Liberalism and the Negro: A Roundtable Discussion," *Commentary* 37 (March 1964), 27, 35.

101. Ibid., 37, 40.

102. Carol Polsgrove, *It Wasn't Pretty, Folks, but Didn't We Have Fun? "Esquire" in the Sixties* (New York: W. W. Norton, 1995), 116–17.

103. Marvin Elkoff, "Everybody Knows His Name," *Esquire* 62 (August 1964), 64, 121–22.

104. Richard Avedon and James Baldwin, *Nothing Personal* (New York: Atheneum, 1964), n.p.

105. "The American Dream and the American Negro," *New York Times Magazine*, March 7, 1965, 33.

106. Robert Brustein, "Everybody Knows My Name," *New York Review of Books* 2 (December 17, 1964) (online).

107. Ralph Ellison, "Hidden Name and Complex Fake," *Shadow and Act* (New York: Random House, 1964), 166.

108. Arnold Rampersad, *Ralph Ellison: A Biography* (New York: Random House, 2007), 3–51.

109. Ralph Ellison, *Shadow and Act* (New York: Random House, 1964), 161.

110. Rampersad, *Ralph Ellison*, 93–154.

111. Irving Howe, "Black Boys and Native Sons," *Dissent* 10 (1963): 354.

112. Ibid., 362–64.

113. See Rampersad, *Ralph Ellison*, 400–402.

114. Ralph Ellison, "The World and the Jug," *New Leader* 46 (December 9, 1963), 23.

115. Ibid., 25.

116. Ibid., 26.

117. Ralph Ellison, "A Rejoinder," *New Leader* 47 (February 3, 1964), 21.

118. Rampersad, *Ralph Ellison*, 402.

119. Todd Purdum, *An Idea Whose Time Has Come: Two Presidents, Two Parties, and the Battle for the Civil Rights Act of 1964* (New York: Henry Holt, 2014), 327.

120. See Michael Gold, "A Tale of Two Amendments: The Reasons Congress Added Sex to Title VII and Their Implication for the Issue of Comparable Worth," *Duquesne Law Review* 19 (1981): 453–77; Robert C. Bird, "More Than a Congressional Joke: A Fresh Look at the Legislative History of Sex Discrimination of the 1964 Civil Rights Act," *William and Mary Law Review* 3 (1997): 137–61; Jo Freeman, "How 'Sex' Got Into Title VII: Persistent Opportunism as a Maker of Public Policy," *Law and Inequality* 9 (1991): 163–84; Cynthia Dietch, "Gender, Race, and Class Politics and the Inclusion of Women in Title VII of the 1964 Civil Rights Act," *Gender and Society* 7 (1993): 183–203; Louis Menand, "The Sex Amendment," *New Yorker* 90 (July 21, 2014), 74–81.

121. Melvin I. Urofsky, *The Affirmative Action Puzzle: A Living History from Reconstruction to Today* (New York: Pantheon, 2020), 377.

122. Malcolm X, "Message to the Grassroots," in *Malcolm X Speaks: Selected Speeches and Statements* (New York: Merit, 1965), 9.

123. Mel Watkins, "Black Is Marketable," *New York Times Book Review*, February 16, 1969, 3.

124. Taylor Branch, *America in the King Years*, vol. 3, *At Canaan's Edge, 1965–68* (New York: Simon and Schuster, 2006), 453–86.

125. Jackson, *The Indignant Generation*, 424–26.

126. LeRoi Jones, "How You Sound?," in Donald M. Allen, ed., *The New American Poetry* (New York: Grove, 1960), 424–25.

127. Ralph Ellison, "The Blues," *New York Review of Books* 2 (February 6, 1964) (online).

128. LeRoi Jones, "Brief Reflections on Two Hot Shots," *Kulchur* 3 (Winter 1963), 2–4.

129. Larry Neal, "The Black Arts Movement," *Drama Review: TDR* 12 (Summer 1968), 39.

130. Amiri Baraka, "Rays Race Raise Raze," in *Rays Race Raise Raze: Essays Since 1965* (New York: Random House, 1971), 98.

131. Eldridge Cleaver, "Notes on a Native Son," *Ramparts* 5 (June 1966), 52, 54.

132. Charlayne Hunter, "To Mr. and Mrs. Yesterday," *New York Times Book Review*, March 24, 1968, 3.

133. Sam Roberts, "An Integrationist to This Day, Believing All Else Has Failed," *New York Times*, May 7, 1995, sec. 4, 7.

17. HOLLYWOOD—PARIS—HOLLYWOOD

1. Rémi Fournier Lanzoni, *French Cinema: From Its Beginnings to the Present* (New York: Continuum, 2002), 23–39; Robert Sklar, *Movie-Made America: A Cultural History of American Movies*, rev. ed. (New York: Vintage, 1994), 5–10; David Puttnam, *Movies and Money* (New York: Knopf, 1998), 35–55.

2. See Jens Ulff-Møller, *Hollywood's Film Wars with France: Film-Trade Diplomacy and the Emergence of the French Film Quota Policy* (Rochester: University of Rochester Press, 2001).

3. Victoria de Grazia, "Mass Culture and Sovereignty: The American Challenge to European Cinemas, 1920–1960," *Journal of Modern History* 61 (March 1989): 82; Victoria de Grazia, *Irresistible Empire: America's Advance Through Twentieth-Century Europe* (Cambridge, MA: Harvard University Press, 2005), 335.

4. Puttnam, *Movies and Money*, 162–64; Table 7: United Kingdom: Nationality of Films Registered for Distribution, Thomas H. Guback, *The International Film Industry: Western Europe and America Since 1945* (Bloomington: Indiana University Press, 1969), 44–45; Charles Harpole, ed., *History of the American Cinema*, vol. 6, *Boom and Bust: American Cinema in the 1940s*, by Thomas Schatz (New York: Charles Scribner's Sons, 1997), 297–300.

5. Schatz, *Boom and Bust*, 297; "Film Biz Revenue Up 15% in '45," *Variety*, May 7, 1947, 11.

6. Thomas M. Pryor, "Mission of the Movies Abroad," *New York Times*, March 24, 1946, sec. 2, X3.

7. Eric Johnston, *The Motion Picture on the Threshold of a Decisive Decade* (New York: Motion Picture Association of America, 1946), 8.

8. Nathan D. Golden, "Future of U.S. Pix Abroad Grave as Curbs Pile Up," *Variety*, January 7, 1948, 157. I am grateful to Andrew Koenig for this reference.

9. Frank Costigliola, *France and the United States: The Cold Alliance Since World War II* (New York: Twayne, 1992), 55.

10. Serge Guilbaut, *How New York Stole the Idea of Modern Art: Abstract Expressionism, Freedom, and the Cold War*, trans. Arthur Goldhammer (Chicago: University of Chicago Press, 1983), 137.

11. Evelyn Ehrlich, *Cinema of Paradox: French Filmmaking Under the German Occupation* (New York: Columbia University Press, 1985), 193; Ulff-Møller, *Hollywood's Film Wars with France*, 146–47.

12. Visas de censure délivrée en France de 1946 à 1953 pour les films de long métrage, Patricia Hubert-Lacombe, *Le Cinéma français dans la guerre froide, 1946–1956* (Paris: Éditions L'Harmattan, 1996), 180.

13. Glenn Myrent and Georges P. Langlois, *Henri Langlois: First Citizen of Cinema*, trans. Lisa Nesselson (New York: Twayne, 1995), 8; Richard Roud, *A Passion for Films: Henri Langlois and the Cinémathèque Française* (Baltimore: Johns Hopkins University Press, 1983), 3–6.

14. David Thomson, *The New Biographical Dictionary of Film* (New York: Knopf, 2004), 507.

15. Dudley Andrew, *André Bazin* (New York: Oxford University Press, 1978), 9–60.

16. Roud, *A Passion for Films*, 49–50; Jacques Richard, dir., *Henri Langlois: Phantom of the Cinémathèque* (Kino DVD, 2005).

17. Andrew, *André Bazin*, 48–60.

18. Sergei Eisenstein, *Film Form: Essays in Film Theory*, trans. Jay Leyda (New York: Harcourt, Brace and World, 1949), 46.

19. André Bazin, "L'Évolution du langage cinématographique," in *Qu'est-ce que le cinéma?*, vol. 1, *Ontologie et langage* (Paris: Les Éditions du Cerf, 1958), 143. ("[L]a profondeur de champ place le spectateur dans un rapport avec l'image plus proche de celui qu'il entretient avec la réalité . . . qu'elle implique par conséquent une attitude mentale plus active et même une contribution positive du spectateur à la mise en scène . . . De son attention et de sa volonté dépend en partie le fait que l'image ait un sens.")

20. Dudley Andrew, "Bazin before *Cahiers*: Cinematic Politics in Postwar France," *Cineaste* 12, no. 1 (1982), 14.

21. Jean Douchet, *French New Wave*, trans. Robert Bonnono (New York: D.A.P., 1999), 50–53.

22. J. C. Louis and Harvey Z. Yazijian, *The Cola Wars* (New York: Everest House, 1980), 77–78.

23. Irwin M. Wall, *The United States and the Making of Postwar France, 1945–1954* (Cambridge: Cambridge University Press, 1991), 113–26; Jacques Portes, "Les Origines de la légende noire des accords Blum-Byrnes sur le cinéma," *Revue d'Histoire Moderne et Contemporaine* 33 (1986): 314–29; Jean-Pierre Jeancolas, "From

the Blum-Byrne Agreement to the GATT Affair," in Geoffrey Nowell-Smith and Steven Ricci, eds., *Hollywood and Europe: Economics, Culture, National Identity: 1945–95* (London: BFI, 1998), 47–52; Richard Kuisel, "The Fernandel Factor: The Rivalry Between the French and American Cinema in the 1950s," *Yale French Studies*, no. 98 (2000), 119–34.

24. Hubert-Lacombe, *Le Cinéma français dans la guerre froide*, 154; Portes, "Les Origines de la légende noire des accords Blum-Byrnes sur le cinéma," 327–29. See also "Dikes Open on U.S. Pix Flood," *Variety*, March 10, 1948, 3f.; Costigliola, *France and the United States*, 55–57.

25. See Jean-Paul Sartre, "Quand Hollywood veut faire penser . . . Citizen Kane, film d'Orson Welles," *L'Écran Français*, no. 5 (August 1, 1945), 3ff.; Georges Sadoul, "Hypertrophie du cerveau," *Lettres Françaises*, July 5, 1946, 9; André Bazin, "La Technique de *Citizen Kane*," *Temps Modernes* 2 (1947): 943–49.

26. Olivier Barrot, *L'Écran Français, 1943–1953: histoire d'un journal et d'une époque* (Paris: Éditeurs Français Reunis, 1979), 318–19.

27. See Erlich, *Cinema of Paradox*; Jill Forbes, "The French Nouvelle Vague," in *The Oxford Guide to Film Studies*, ed. John Hill and Pamela Church Gibson (New York: Oxford University Press, 1998), 462. See also Colin Crisp, *The Classic French Cinema, 1930–1960* (Bloomington: Indiana University Press, 1993), 43–63; Alan Williams, *Republic of Images: A History of French Filmmaking* (Cambridge, MA: Harvard University Press, 1992), 245–71; Lanzoni, *French Cinema*, 103–42.

28. Williams, *Republic of Images*, 272–76; Lanzoni, *French Cinema*, 136–39; Alan Riding, *And the Show Went On: Cultural Life in Occupied Paris* (New York: Knopf, 2010), 331–34.

29. Antoine de Baecque and Serge Toubiana, *Truffaut*, trans. Catherine Temerson (Berkeley: University of California Press, 1999), 3–43.

30. François Truffaut, *Les Films de ma vie* (Paris: Flammarion, 1975), 14.

31. De Baecque and Toubiana, *Truffaut*, 22.

32. François Truffaut, "Une certaine tendance du cinéma français," *Cahiers du Cinéma* 6 (January 1954), 21, 27, 25, 26. ("[D]e noirceur, de non-conformisme, de facile audace . . . *un cinéma anti-bourgeois fait par des bourgeois, pour les bourgeois* . . . le monsieur qui met des cadrages là-dessus . . . Eh bien je ne puis croire à la co-existence pacifique de la *Tradition de la Qualité* et d'un *cinéma d' auteurs*.")

33. See Richard Abel, *French Cinema: The First Wave, 1915–1929* (Princeton: Princeton University Press, 1984), 284.

34. François Truffaut, "Ali Baba et la 'Politique des auteurs,'" *Cahiers du Cinéma* 8 (February 1955), 47. ("[E]n vertu de la *Politique des Auteurs* que mes congénères en critique et moi-même pratiquons. Toute basée sur la belle formule de Giraudoux: 'il n'y a pas d'œuvre, il n'y a que des auteurs.'")

35. De Baecque and Toubiana, *Truffaut*, 84.

36. See Antoine de Baecque, *Cahiers du Cinéma: histoire d'une revue*, vol. 1, *À l'assaut du cinéma* (Paris: Cahiers du Cinema, 1991), 89–125.

37. Éric Rohmer, "Redécouvrir l'Amérique," *Cahiers du Cinéma* 11 (Christmas 1955), 11. ("Les plus beaux films américains qu'il m'a été donné de voir ont, avant toute chose, excité en moi une violente envie, éveillé ce regret que la France ait renoncé à poursuivie une prétention à l'universalité qu'elle affirma, jadis et naguère, avec tant de force, qu'elle ait laisse le flambeau d'une certaine idée de l'homme éteindre pour se rallumer au-delà des mers, bref qu'elle doive s'avouer battue sur un terrain dont elle est légitime propriétaire . . . [L]a côte californienne n'est pas, pour le cinéaste doué et fervent, cet enfer que d'aucuns prétendent, mais bien cette terre d'élection, cette patrie que fut Florence au *quattrocento* pour les peintres, ou Vienne au XIXe pour les musiciens.")

38. Douchet, *French New Wave*, 77–78.

39. Richard Brody, *Everything Is Cinema: The Working Life of Jean-Luc Godard* (New York: Metropolitan Books, 2008), 4–19; Colin Mac-Cabe, *Godard: A Portrait of the Artist at Seventy* (New York: Farrar, Straus and Giroux, 2003), 17–54.

40. Douchet, *French New Wave*, 167–68.

41. MacCabe, *Godard*, 110; Brody, *Everything Is Cinema*, 72.

42. See Jill Forbes, "The '*Série Noire*,'" in Brian Rigby and Nicholas Hewitt, eds., *France and the Mass Media* (Basingstoke, UK: Macmillan, 1991), 94–95.

43. Marc Pierret, "Carnet de bord d'un apprenti cinéaste," *France Observateur*, no. 495 (October 29, 1959), 15. ("Il me faut une certaine liberté. Je la trouve en brouillant un peu les pistes. En rusant avec les lieux communs. Le producteur croit que j'improvise, alors que simplement je m'adapte à ses conditions pour créer une plus grande possibilité d'invention.")

44. Jean-Luc Godard, "Des épreuves suffisantes," *Cahiers du Cinéma* 13 (July 1957), 35. ("[I]nutile de féliciter Vadim d'être en avance car il se trouve seulement que si tous les autres sont en retard, lui, en revanche, est à l'heure juste.")

45. François Truffaut, "B.B. est victime d'une cabal," *Arts* 597 (December 12–18, 1956), 3. ("Pour ma part, après avoir vu trois mille films en dix ans, je ne puis plus supporter les scènes d'amour, mièvres et mensongères du cinéma hollywoodien,

crasseuses, grivoises et non moins truquées des films français"; "C'est ainsi que des films faits par amour des acteurs sont jugés par des gens qui n'aiment pas les acteurs.")

46. Simone de Beauvoir, "Brigitte Bardot and the Lolita Syndrome," trans. Bernard Frechtman, *Esquire* 52 (August 1959), 34, 38.

47. See, generally, Peter Biskind, *Easy Riders, Raging Bulls: How the Sex-Drugs-and-Rock'n'Roll Generation Saved Hollywood* (New York: Simon and Schuster, 1998), 26–41; Louis Menand, "Paris, Texas," *New Yorker* 78 (February 17 and 24, 2003), 169–77; Mark Harris, *Pictures at a Revolution: Five Movies and the Birth of the New Hollywood* (New York: Penguin, 2008), passim.

48. See Carol Polsgrove, *It Wasn't Pretty, Folks, but Didn't We Have Fun? "Esquire" in the Sixties* (New York: W. W. Norton, 1995).

49. Barbara Wilinsky, *Sure Seaters: The Emergence of Art House Cinema* (Minneapolis: University of Minnesota Press, 2001), 140n13.

50. Ibid., 67–70, 126–29, 132–33.

51. Interview with David Newman by Marina Harss and the author, January 15, 2003.

52. David Newman and Robert Benton, "Lightning in a Bottle," in Sandra Wake and Nicola Hayden, eds., *Bonnie and Clyde* (London: Lorrimer, 1972), 13–15.

53. Patrick Goldstein, "Blasts from the Past," *Los Angeles Times*, August 24, 1997, 78 (interview with Benton).

54. Goldstein, "Blasts from the Past," 78 (interview with Newman).

55. Vincent Canby, "Helen Scott's Death Grieves Film World," *Chicago Tribune*, December 3, 1987, 10A; "Helen G. Scott, 72, Writer for Truffaut and Other Directors," *New York Times*, November 24, 1987, B11.

56. Interview with Robert Benton by the author, January 11, 2003.

57. Matthew Bernstein, "Perfecting the New Gangster: Writing *Bonnie and Clyde*," *Film Quarterly* 53 (Summer 2000): 16–31; Newman and Benton, "Lightning in a Bottle," 21.

58. De Baecque and Toubiana, *Truffaut*, 212.

59. Martin Duberman, *Black Mountain: An Exploration in Community* (Evanston: Northwestern University Press, 1972), 260, 302.

60. Nat Segaloff, *Arthur Penn: American Director* (Lexington: University Press of Kentucky, 2011), 45, 60–140; Dave Kehr, "Arthur Penn: Rebel Whose Signature Was 'Bonnie and Clyde,'" *New York Times*, September 30, 2010, A1f.

61. Series H 862–877: Participation in Selected Recreational Activities: 1896–1970, U.S. Bureau of the Census, *Historical Statistics of the United States, Colonial Times to 1970*, vol. 1 (Washington, DC: U.S. Government Printing Office, 1975), 400.

62. Charles Harpole, ed., *History of the American Cinema*, vol. 7, *The Fifties: Transforming the Screen, 1950–1959*, by Peter Lev (New York: Scribner, 2003), Appendix 3: "Motion Picture Box Office Receipts in the United States," 304; Charles Harpole, ed., *History of the American Cinema*, vol. 8, *The Sixties, 1960–1969*, by Paul Monaco (New York: Scribner, 2003), Appendix 5: "Motion Picture Box Office Receipts in the United States," 271.

63. See Michelle Pautz, "The Decline in Average Weekly Cinema Attendance: 1930–2000," *Issues in Political Economy* 11 (2002) (online).

64. David Thomson, *The Whole Equation: A History of Hollywood* (New York: Knopf, 2005), 319–21.

65. Murray Schumach, "Movie Creativity in Europe Hailed," *New York Times*, April 13, 1961, 31.

66. John Dominis, "Meanwhile Back in Hollywood, Efficiency Takes Over," *Life* 55 (December 20, 1963), 46.

67. Arthur Penn, "Making Waves: The Directing of Bonnie and Clyde," in Lester D. Friedman, ed., *Bonnie and Clyde* (London: British Film Institute, 2000), 29. Penn has "hell"; Biskind (35) has "fuck," based on interviews with Penn and Beatty.

68. Bosley Crowther, "Screen: Bonnie and Clyde Arrives," *New York Times*, August 14, 1967, 36. See also Bosley Crowther, "Run, Bonnie and Clyde," *New York Times*, September 3, 1967, sec. 2, 10.

69. "Low-Down Hoedown," *Time* 90 (August 25, 1967), 78; J. M. [Joseph Morgenstern], "Two for a Tommy Gun," *Newsweek* 70 (August 21, 1967), 65.

70. Joseph Morgenstern, "The Thin Red Line," *Newsweek* 70 (August 28, 1967), 82.

71. Quoted in "Perils of Pauline," *Newsweek* 67 (May 30, 1966), 80.

72. Ibid. (interview with Stein).

73. On Kael's life: Brian Kellow, *Pauline Kael: A Life in the Dark* (New York: Viking, 2011); Phillip Lopate, "Lady in the Dark," *New York Woman* 4 (November 1989), 100–107.

74. James Broughton, *Coming Unbuttoned: A Memoir* (San Francisco: City Lights Books, 1993), 68.

75. Pauline Kael, "Some Notes on Chaplin's *Limelight*," *City Lights*, no. 3 (Spring 1953), 56–57.

76. Kellow, *Pauline Kael*, 54 (interview with Landberg).

77. David E. James, ed., *To Free the Cinema: Jonas Mekas and the New York Underground* (Princeton: Princeton University Press, 1992), 62–69 (interview with Sarris). See also George Hickenlooper, *Reel Conversations: Candid Interviews with Film's Foremost Directors and Critics* (New York: Citadel, 1991), 3–16 (interview with Sarris); Raymond J. Haberski, Jr., *It's Only a Movie! Films and Critics in American Culture* (Lexington: University Press of Kentucky, 2001), 122–27.

78. Andrew Sarris, *Confessions of a Cultist: On the Cinema, 1955–1969* (New York: Simon and Schuster, 1970), 15.

79. Kevin Michael McAuliffe, *The Great American Newspaper: The Rise and Fall of the* Village Voice (New York: Scribner, 1978), 121–30, 134.

80. Andrew Sarris, "Notes on the Auteur Theory in 1962," *Film Culture* 27 (Winter 1962–63), 1.

81. Pauline Kael, "Circles and Squares," *Film Quarterly* 16 (Spring 1963), 26.

82. Ibid., 17.

83. Hickenlooper, *Reel Conversations*, 9 (interview with Sarris).

84. Kellow, *Pauline Kael*, 78 (interview with Sarris).

85. See James, *To Free the Cinema*, 77 (interview with Sarris).

86. See Andrew Sarris, "Notes of an Accidental Auteurist," *Film History* 7 (1995): 358–61.

87. Pauline Kael, "Criticism and Kids' Games," *Film Quarterly* 17 (Autumn 1963), 62–63.

88. Kellow, *Pauline Kael*, 100–102.

89. Gigi Mahon, *The Last Days of* The New Yorker (New York: McGraw Hill, 1988), 61–62.

90. I draw in what follows on Louis Menand, "A Friend Writes," *New Republic* 202 (February 26, 1990), 27–34.

91. Pauline Kael, "Fantasies of the Art House Audience," *Sight and Sound* 31 (Winter 1961), 6.

92. Pauline Kael, "Movies, the Desperate Art," in William Phillips and Philip Rahv, eds., *The Berkley Book of Modern Writing*, no. 3 (New York: Berkley Publishing Corp., 1956), 205.

93. Pauline Kael, "Incredible Shrinking Hollywood," *Holiday* 39 (March 1966), 86.

94. "War of the Critics," broadcast December 12, 1963, CD, Pacifica Radio Archives.

95. Macdonald, "A Theory of Mass Culture," *Diogenes* 1 (Summer 1953): 2–3, 7, 14, 16, 17.

96. Kael, "Incredible Shrinking Hollywood," 88.

97. Pauline Kael, "It's Only a Movie," in David C. Steward, ed., *Film Study in Higher Education* (Washington, DC: American Council on Education, 1966), 143–44.

98. Pauline Kael, *I Lost It at the Movies: Film Writings 1954–1965* (Boston: Little Brown, 1965), 292.

99. Kael, "Incredible Shrinking Hollywood," 86.

100. Richard Schickel, "A Way of Seeing a Picture," *New York Times*, March 14, 1965, sec. 7, 6; Dwight Macdonald, "Films," *Esquire* 64 (August 1965), 27.

101. Pauline Kael, "*Bonnie and Clyde*," *New Yorker* 43 (October 21, 1967), 160.

102. "The Shock of Freedom in Films," *Time* 90 (December 8, 1967), 66, 76.

103. Ellis Amburn, *The Sexiest Man Alive: A Biography of Warren Beatty* (New York: HarperCollins, 2002), 97.

104. Interview with David Newman by Marina Harss and the author, January 15, 2003.

105. Faye Dunaway, *Looking for Gatsby: My Life* (New York: Simon and Schuster, 1995), 127.

106. David Newman and Robert Benton, treatment for *Bonnie and Clyde*, in my possession.

107. Jean-Louis Comolli and André S. Labarthe, "Off-Hollywood: entretien avec Arthur Penn," *Cahiers du Cinéma*, no. 196 (December 1967), 35.

108. Interview with Arthur Penn by Marina Harss and the author, January 22, 2003.

109. Allan Hunter, *Faye Dunaway* (New York: St. Martin's, 1986), 52–53.

110. [Mel Gussow], "Faye Dunaway: Star, Symbol, Style," *Newsweek* 71 (March 4, 1968), 42.

111. M[ichel] D[elahaye], "*Bonnie and Clyde*," *Cahiers du Cinéma*, no. 199 (March 1968), 71–72. ("L'époque [roaring twenties] est simple et roublard prétexte au déchaînement d'une violence aussi aseptisée que rentable . . . Par ailleurs, le réalisateur méprise ses personnages qu'il traite comme des demeurés.")

112. "Trois entretiens: Jean-Luc Godard," *Cahiers du Cinéma*, no. 138 (December 1962), 23. ("[J]e le situe du côté où on doit le situer: celui d'*Alice au pays merveilles*. Moi, je croyais que c'était *Scarface*.")

18. THIS IS THE END

1. Stanley Karnow, *Vietnam: A History*, rev. ed. (New York: Viking Penguin, 1991), 517.

2. Ibid., 148.

3. Ibid., 33–34, 646–47.

4. Charles de Gaulle, *Mémoires d'espoir: Le renouveau, 1958–1962* (Paris: Plon, 1970), 268–69. ("[L]'intervention dans cette région sera un engrenage sans fin . . . Je vous prédis que vous irez vous en lisant pas à pas dans un bourbier militaire et politique sans fond, malgré les pertes et les dépenses que vous pourrez y prodiguer"). Note that de Gaulle is "remembering" this from the perspective of 1970.

5. Fredrik Logevall, *Choosing War: The Lost Chance for Peace and the Escalation of War in Vietnam* (Berkeley: University of California Press, 1999), 27; Walter Lippmann, "The Nettle of Viet-Nam," *Washington Post*, September 3, 1963, A13.

6. Lyndon Johnson to Richard Russell, March 6, 1965, in Michael Bechloss, *Reaching for Glory: Lyndon Johnson's Secret White House Tapes, 1964–1965* (New York: Simon and Schuster, 2001), 213.

7. Peter Davis, dir., *Hearts and Minds* (1974) (Criterion DVD, 2002) (interview with Westmoreland).

8. Philip E. Converse, Warren E. Miller, Jerrold G. Rusk, and Arthur C. Wolfe, "Continuity and Change in American Politics: Parties and Issues in the 1968 Election," *American Political Science Review* 63 (1969): 1086.

9. See Everett Carll Ladd, Jr., "Liberalism Upside Down: The Inversion of the New Deal Order," *Political Science Quarterly* 91 (1976–1977): 577–600; Doug McAdam and Karina Kloos, *Deeply Divided: Racial Politics and Social Movements in Postwar America* (New York: Oxford University Press, 2014).

10. Benjamin Moser, *Sontag: Her Life and Work* (New York: HarperCollins, 2019), 273.

11. Susan Sontag, "What's Happening to America?," *Partisan Review* 34 (1967): 51–52, 57–58.

12. Columbia Crisis: Lionel Trilling (1970), Oral History Research Archives, Rare Book and Manuscript Library, Columbia University.

13. Ruth Bordin, *The University of Michigan: A Pictorial History* (Ann Arbor: University of Michigan Press, 1967), 129; W. J. Rorabaugh, *Berkeley at War: The 1960s* (New York: Oxford University Press, 1989), 10.

14. On what follows: James Miller *"Democracy Is in the Streets": From Port Huron to the Siege of Chicago* (New York: Simon and Schuster, 1987), 21–140; Maurice Isserman, *If I Had a Hammer . . . The Death of the Old Left and the Birth of the New Left* (New York: Basic Books, 1987), 173–219; Paul Berman, *A Tale of Two Utopias: The Political Journey of the Generation of 1968* (New York: W. W. Norton, 1996), 21–62; Todd Gitlin, *The Sixties: Years of Hope, Days of Rage* (New York: Bantam, 1987), 110–16; Milton Viorst, *Fire in the Streets: America in the 1960s* (New York: Simon and Schuster, 1979), 163–96.

15. Miller *"Democracy Is in the Streets,"* 38 (interview with Haber).

16. Steven V. Roberts, "Will Tom Hayden Overcome?," *Esquire* 70 (December 1968), 179 (interview with Hayden).

17. See Grace Elizabeth Hale, *A Nation of Outsiders: How the White Middle Class Fell in Love with Rebellion in Postwar America* (New York: Oxford University Press, 2011), 163–203. On the white student movement and progressive politics generally, see Van Gosse, *Rethinking the New Left: An Interpretive History* (New York: Palgrave Macmillan, 2005).

18. Taylor Branch, *America in the King Years*, vol. 1, *Parting the Waters, 1954–63* (New York: Simon and Schuster, 1988), 271–75.

19. James Baldwin, "They Can't Turn Back," *Mademoiselle* 51 (August 1960), 358.

20. Thomas Hayden, "American Student Requires Value Stimulation," *Michigan Daily*, August 5, 1960, 2.

21. Tom Hayden, *Reunion: A Memoir* (New York: Random House, 1988), 39–40.

22. See Harold L. Smith, "Casey Hayden: Gender and the Origins of SNCC, SDS, and the Women's Liberation Movement," in Elizabeth Hayes Turner, Stephanie Cole, and Rebecca Sharpless, eds., *Texas Women: Their Histories, Their Lives* (Athens: University of Georgia Press, 2015), 359–88.

23. Casey Hayden, "Fields of Blue," in Constance Curry et al., eds., *Deep in Our Hearts: Nine White Women in the Freedom Movement* (Athens: University of Georgia Press, 2000), 335–75.

24. Hayden, "Fields of Blue," 337.

25. Casey Hayden, "August 1960, National Student Association Convention, Minneapolis, Minnesota," in Davis W. Houck and David E. Dixon, *Women and the Civil Rights Movement, 1954–1965* (Jackson: University Press of Mississippi, 2009), 138.

26. Hayden, *Reunion*, 48.

27. Tom Hayden, "The Dream of Port Huron," in Tom Hayden, ed., *Inspiring Participatory Democracy: Student Movements from Port Huron to Today* (Boulder: Paradigm, 2013), 4.

28. Hayden, *Reunion*, 78.

29. Students for a Democratic Society, *The Port Huron Statement* (New York: Students for a Democratic Society, 1962), 18, 25. This is the first print edition. Earlier copies were mimeographed.

30. Thomas Piketty, *Capital in the Twenty-First Century*, trans. Arthur Goldhammer (Cambridge, MA: Harvard University Press, 2014), 23–24; Robert J. Gordon, *The Rise and Fall of American Growth: The U.S. Standard of Living since the Civil War* (Princeton: Princeton University Press, 2016), 608–10.

31. See Daniel Markovits, *The Meritocracy Trap: How America's Foundational Myth Feeds Inequality, Dismantles the Middle Class, and Devours the Elite* (New York: Penguin Press, 2019), 197–201.

32. C. Wright Mills, "Letter to the New Left," *New Left Review*, no. 5 (September–October 1960), 22. See also C. Wright Mills, *The Power Elite* (New York: Oxford University Press, 1956), 262–65.

33. C. Wright Mills to Lewis Coser, April 4, 1957, in *C. Wright Mills: Letters and Autobiographical Writings*, ed. Kathryn Mills (Berkeley: University of California Press, 2000), 234.

34. Irving Howe, *A Margin of Hope: An Intellectual Autobiography* (San Diego: Harcourt Brace Jovanovich, 1982), 244.

35. Daniel Geary, "'Becoming International Again': C. Wright Mills and the Emergence of a Global New Left, 1956–1962," *Journal of American History* 95 (2008): 710–36.

36. Pendennis, "Texas Elite," *Observer*, January 25, 1959, 9.

37. C. Wright Mills, "On Knowledge and Power," *Dissent* 2 (1955): 201–12.

38. Mills, "Letter to the New Left," 23.

39. Daniel Bell, "'Vulgar Sociology,'" *Encounter* 15 (December 1960), 54, 55.

40. Hayden, *Reunion*, 80. See also Miller, *"Democracy Is in the Streets,"* 86–87.

41. See Thomas Rosteck, "Giving Voice to a Movement: Mills's 'Letter to the New Left' and the Potential of History," in Sharon McKenzie Stevens and Patricia Malesh, eds., *Active Voices: Composing a Rhetoric of Social Movements* (Albany: SUNY Press, 2009), 118.

42. Tom Hayden, "A Letter to the New (Young) Left," *Activist* 2 (Winter 1961), 4–7.

43. Hayden, "Fields of Blue," 348.

44. Isserman, *If I Had a Hammer . . .* , 209–10; Miller, *"Democracy Is in the Streets,"* 110–25.

45. Students for a Democratic Society, *The Port Huron Statement*, 5.

46. Ibid., 10.

47. Ibid., 61–63.

48. Miller, *"Democracy Is in the Streets,"* 125 (interview with Jeffrey).

49. Jack Fincher, "'The University Has Become a Factory,'" *Life* 58 (February 26, 1965), 100 (interview with Savio).

50. On what follows: "Chronology of Events: Three Months of Crisis," *California Monthly* 75 (February 1965), 34–75; Rorabaugh, *Berkeley at War*, 8–47; Robert Cohen, *Freedom's Orator: Mario Savio and the Radical Legacy of the 1960s* (New York: Oxford University Press, 2009), 75–228.

51. Mario Savio, "Berkeley Fall," in Mario Savio, Eugene Walker, and Raya Dunayevskaya, *The Free Speech Movement and the Negro Revolution* (Detroit: News and Letters, 1965), 17.

52. Clark Kerr, *The Uses of the University*, 4th ed. (Cambridge, MA: Harvard University Press, 1995), 107–108.

53. Clark Kerr, *The Uses of the University* (Cambridge, MA: Harvard University Press, 1963), 103, 104.

54. www.americanrhetoric.com/speeches/mariosavio sproulhallsitin.html. See also Max Heirich, *The Spiral of Conflict: Berkeley 1964* (New York: Columbia University Press, 1971), 271–72. Heirich was present for the speech and occupation.

55. Nathan Glazer, "What Happened at Berkeley," *Commentary* 39 (February 1965), 39–47; Joseph Dorman, *Arguing the World: The New York Intellectuals in Their Own Words* (New York: Free Press, 2000), 144–47 (interview with Glazer).

56. Cohen, *Freedom's Orator*, 254.

57. Dwight D. Eisenhower, Farewell Radio and Television Address to the American People, January 17, 1961, *Public Papers of the Presidents of the United States, Dwight D. Eisenhower, 1960–61* (Washington, DC: Superintendent of Documents, 1961), 1038–39.

58. Michael Rossman, "Inside the FSM," *California Monthly* 84 (December 1974), 10.

59. Greil Marcus, *Lipstick Traces: A Secret History of the Twentieth Century* (Cambridge, MA: Harvard University Press, 1989), 444.

60. James Ridgeway, "The *Ramparts* Story: . . . Um, Very Interesting," *New York Times Magazine*, April 20, 1969, 37.

61. Warren Hinckle III, *If You Have a Lemon, Make Lemonade* (New York: W. W. Norton, 1974), 172–73; Peter Richardson, *A Bomb in Every Issue: How the Short, Unruly Life of Ramparts Magazine Changed America* (New York: New Press, 2009), 74–75.

62. Hinckle, *If You Have a Lemon, Make Lemonade*, 180.

63. For what follows: Karen M. Paget, *Patriotic Betrayal: The Inside Story of the CIA's Secret Campaign to Enroll American Students in the Crusade against Communism* (New Haven: Yale University Press, 2015); Hugh Wilford, *The Mighty Wurlitzer: How The C.I.A. Played America* (Cambridge, MA: Harvard University Press, 2008), 129–48, 237–48.

64. Nicholas M. Horrock, "An Awesome Question: Was Murder U.S. Policy?," *New York Times*, December 7, 1975, sec. 4, 4.

65. "Foundations, Private Organizations Linked to CIA," *Congressional Quarterly* 25 (February 24, 1967), 271–72. On *Partisan Review*, see Wilford, *The Mighty Wurlitzer*, 104, and William Phillips and Frances Stonor Saunders, "'PR' and Its Funding," *London Review of Books* 22 (March 2, 2000) (online).

66. Testimony of Philip Sherburne, Hearing Held before the Committee on Foreign Relations, U.S. Senate, March 16, 1967, 52–120.

67. "The CIA and 'the Kiddies,'" *Newsweek* 69 (February 27, 1967), 27 (interview with Steinem).

68. Carl Bernstein, "The CIA and the Media," *Rolling Stone*, no. 250 (October 20, 1977), 55–67; Harrison E. Salisbury, *Without Fear or Favor: The New York Times and Its Times* (New York: Times Books, 1980), 567–84; "The CIA's 3-Decade Effort to Mold the World's Views," *New York Times*, December 25, 1977, 1f.

69. Immy Humes, dir., *Doc* (The Doc Tank Inc. DVD, 2011) (interview with Matthiessen); Joel Whitney, "Exclusive: The Paris Review, the Cold War, and the CIA," *Salon*, May 27, 2012 (online).

70. See Paget, *Patriotic Betrayal*, 288, 399–402.

71. Ernst Henri, "Who Finances Anti-Communism?," *World Marxist Review* 5 (February 1962), 46–54.

72. "Patman Attacks 'Secret' CIA Link," *New York Times*, September 1, 1964, 1f; "CIA Issue Dropped," *New York Times*, September 1, 1964, 19.

73. "Misusing CIA Money," *New York Times*, September 4, 1964, 28.

74. "CIA Spies from 100 Miles Up; Satellites Probe Secrets of Soviet," *New York Times*, April 27, 1966, 1f.

75. Testimony of Michael Wood, Hearing Held before the Committee on Foreign Relations, March 16, 1967, 3; "Pomona College May Quit NSA over CIA Involvement," *Los Angeles Times*, February 19, 1967, A1.

76. *New York Times*, February 14, 1967, 32.

77. "CIA Support to Private Organizations," *American Foreign Policy: Current Documents, 1967* (Washington, DC: U.S. Government Printing Office, 1969), 1214.

78. "CIA Man Who Told," *New York Times*, May 8, 1967, 37.

79. Thomas W. Braden, "I'm Glad the CIA Is 'Immoral,'" *Saturday Evening Post* 240 (May 20, 1967), 10.

80. Michael Warner, "Sophisticated Spies: CIA's Links to Liberal Anti-Communists, 1949–1967," *Journal of Intelligence and Counterintelligence* 9 (1996): 428.

81. "Foundations, Private Organizations Linked to CIA," 271–72; "How to Care for the CIA Orphans," *Time* 89 (May 19, 1967), 62.

82. "The CIA's 3-Decade Effort to Mold the World's Views," 1f.

83. Eric Bennett, *Workshops of Empire: Stegner, Engle, and American Creative Writing during the Cold War* (Iowa City: University of Iowa Press, 2015), 112.

84. John Kenneth Galbraith et al., letter to the editor, *New York Times*, May 9, 1966, 38.

85. Christopher Lasch, "The Cultural Cold War," *Nation* 205 (1967): 198, 208.

86. I am grateful for a communication on this point from Norman Birnbaum.

87. See Brian Goodman, *Cold War Bohemia* (Cambridge, MA: Harvard University Press, forthcoming).

88. X [George F. Kennan], "Sources of Soviet Conduct," *Foreign Affairs* 25 (1947): 581.

89. See James E. Miller, "Taking Off the Gloves: The United States and the Italian Elections of 1948," *Diplomatic History* 7 (1983): 35–56; Brogi Alessandro, *Confronting America: The Cold War between the United States and the Communists in France and Italy* (Chapel Hill: University of North Carolina Press, 2011), 101–10.

90. John Lewis Gaddis, *George F. Kennan: An American Life* (New York: Penguin Press, 2011), 270–88.

91. See Stephen Long, *The CIA and the Soviet Bloc: Political Warfare, the Origins of the CIA and Countering Communism in Europe* (London: I. B. Tauris, 2014), 46–94; David F. Rudgers, "The Origins of Covert Action," *Journal of Contemporary History* 35 (2000): 249–62; Michael Warner, "The CIA's Office of Policy Coordina-

tion: From NSC 10/2 to NSC 68," *International Journal of Intelligence and Counterintelligence* 11 (1998): 211–20; Sarah-Jane Corke, *U.S. Covert Operations and Cold War Strategy: Truman, Secret Warfare, and the CIA, 1945–1953* (New York: Routledge, 2008), 45–63.

92. Policy Planning Staff Memorandum, May 4, 1948, C. Thomas Thorne, Jr., and David S. Patterson, eds., *Foreign Relations of the United States: The Emergence of the Intelligence Establishment* (Washington, DC: U.S. Government Printing Office, 1996), 668–69.

93. William Colby, *Honorable Men: My Life in the CIA* (New York: Simon and Schuster, 1978), 73.

94. Gregg Herken, *The Georgetown Set: Friends and Rivals in Cold War Washington* (New York: Knopf, 2014), 108–13, 121–22, 141–47; Tim Weiner, *Legacy of Ashes: The History of the CIA* (New York: Random House, 2007), 51–52.

95. Weiner, *Legacy of Ashes*, 31–33.

96. U.S. Senate, *Final Report of the Select Committee to Study Governmental Operations with Respect to Intelligence Activities*, vol. 4 (Washington, DC: U.S. Government Printing Office, 1976), 31, 41.

97. Anne Applebaum, *Iron Curtain: The Crushing of Eastern Europe, 1945–1956* (New York: Doubleday, 2012), 438–46, 456–57.

98. Stephen E. Ambrose, *Eisenhower*, vol. 2, *The President* (New York: Simon and Schuster, 1984), 372.

99. George F. Kennan, *Memoirs 1950–1963* (New York: Pantheon, 1972), 253.

100. Bernard Gwertzman, "Ford Denies Moscow Dominates East Europe; Carter Rebuts Him," *New York Times*, October 7, 1976, 1.

101. U.S. Senate, *Final Report of the Select Committee to Study Governmental Operations with Respect to Intelligence Activities*, vol. 4, 31.

102. Gaddis, *George F. Kennan*, 318 (interview with Kennan). The source for these (or similar) words is sometimes given as Kennan's Church Committee testimony (n96 above); they do not appear in the printed record.

103. Scott Lucas and Kaeten Mistry, "Illusions of Coherence: George F. Kennan, U.S. Strategy and Political Warfare in the Early Cold War, 1946–1950," *Diplomatic History* 33 (2009): 59; Gaddis, *George F. Kennan*, 355.

104. Tom Wells, *The War Within: America's Battle Over Vietnam* (Berkeley: University of California Press, 1994), 24–26.

105. Dean Acheson to Harry S. Truman, July 10, 1965, in *Among Friends: Personal Letters of Dean Acheson*, ed. David S. McLellan and David C. Acheson (New York: Dodd, Mead, 1980), 273.

106. See Jennifer W. See, "Prophet Without Honor: Hans Morgenthau and the War in Vietnam, 1955–1963," *Pacific Historical Review* 70 (2001): 419–48.

107. Hans J. Morgenthau, "Realities of Containment," *New Leader* 47 (June 8, 1964), 3.

108. Hans J. Morgenthau, "'We Are Deluding Ourselves in Vietnam,'" *New York Times Magazine*, April 18, 1965, 25.

109. Louis Menashe and Ronald Radosh, eds., *Teach-Ins U.S.A.: Reports, Opinions, Documents* (New York: Frederick A. Praeger, 1967), 205–206 (transcript of program). "Work" is in brackets.

110. Jack Gould, "TV: Vietnam Forum a Forward Step," *New York Times*, June 23, 1965, 83.

111. Charles Kadushin, *The American Intellectual Elite* (Boston: Little, Brown, 1974), 188.

112. "Bernard Johnson's Interview with Professor J. Morgenthau," in Kenneth Thompson and Robert J. Myers, eds., *Truth and Tragedy: A Tribute to Hans J. Morgenthau* (New Brunswick: Transaction, 1984), 382–83. See also Lorenzo Zambernardi, "The Impotence of Power: Morgenthau's Critique of American Intervention in Vietnam," *Review of International Studies* 37 (2011): 1352n87.

113. I follow Ellen Glaser Rafshoon, "A Realist's Moral Opposition to War: Hans J. Morgenthau and Vietnam," *Peace and Change* 26 (2001): 55–77, and Zambernardi, "The Impotence of Power," 1335–56.

114. Hans J. Morgenthau, "Vietnam: Shadow and Substance," *New York Review of Books* 3 (September 16, 1965), 5.

115. Hans J. Morgenthau, "Truth and Power," *New Republic* 155 (November 26, 1966), 13–14.

116. George F. Kennan, "Rebels Without a Program," *New York Times Magazine*, January 21, 1968, 70.

117. George F. Kennan, "Our Push-Pull Dilemma in Vietnam," *Washington Post and Times-Herald*, December 12, 1965, E1, E4. And see Gaddis, *George F. Kennan*, 590–94.

118. U.S. Senate, *Hearings Before the Committee on Foreign Relations*, January 28, February 4, 8, 10, 17, and 18, 1966, 334.

119. Ibid., 350.

120. Ibid., 357.

121. Max Boot, *The Road Not Taken: Edward Lansdale and the American Tragedy in Vietnam* (New York: Liveright, 2018), 571–72; Mark Philip Bradley, *Vietnam at War* (New York: Oxford University Press, 2009), 175–77; Christopher Goscha, *Vietnam: A New History* (Boulder: Basic Books, 2016), 386. And see Nghia M. Vo, *The Vietnamese Boat People, 1954 and 1975–1992* (Jefferson, NC: McFarland, 2006).

122. James Fenton, "The Fall of Saigon," *Granta*, no. 15 (Spring 1985), 112.

A complete list of works cited can be found on www.louismenand.com.

ACKNOWLEDGMENTS

I wrote this book in an office in the stacks in Widener Library at Harvard, and my heartfelt thanks go to the librarians, staff, maintenance crew, and guards who work every day to make Widener, along with the Harvard Library's special collections, one of the great scholarly resources in the world. I could not have written the book you might read, or are reading, or have read without them.

Harvard students are amazing as well. I had help with research and fact-checking from Lauren Schuker, James McAuley, Lena Bae, Victoria Baena, Marshall Bradlee, Marissa Grunes, Olga Yurievna Voronina, Brian Goodman, Claire Atwood, Mycah Margaret Brazelton-Braxton, Caroline Engelmayer, Grazie Christie, Luke Xu, Richard Yarrow, and Thayer Anderson. Thanks to those brilliant people. And thanks for advice and information to Mark Stevens, Amanda Claybaugh, Christian Schlegel, Tyler Haddow, Werner Sollors, Dale Fisher, Pepe Karmel, David Alworth, Yi-Ping Ong, Eric Sandeen, Jerry Zolten, Jodi Hauptman, David Dyzenhaus, Peter Gordon, Nicholas Donofrio, Suzanne Goldberg, Barbara Stack, Thomas Jeffers, Duncan White, Odile Harter, Donna Bergen, Nathan Glazer, Susan Halpert, Tyler Cabot, Jeffrey Careyva, Tommie Shelby, Philip Gefter, Mark Lamster, Andy Koenig, Mark Greif, Anna MacDonald, Alan Wald, Evan Brier, Susan Lively, Paul Fry, Penelope Laurans, John Wilcock, Bill Geerhart, Maggie Gram, Michael O'Connell, Cody Kommers, Christina Davis, Charles Rosenberg, Brian Goodman, Roger Stoddard, Norman Birnbaum, and Maggie Doherty. Rebecca Panovka helped me with everything, from the citations to the shape of the book. I'm very thankful for her commitment.

I am grateful to the students in English 170a and English 278p for their enthusiasm. And my thanks to the wonderful students in English

U751.00 at the CUNY Graduate Center, spring 1999—the place where this all began.

I am grateful to Anne T. Bass, Robert M. Bass, Miyoung Lee, and Neil Simpkins for supporting my work at Harvard. At *The New Yorker*, thanks to my editors, David Remnick, Henry Finder, Ann Goldstein, and Peter Canby, and to my collaborator, Marina Harss. At FSG, thanks to Jonathan Galassi, Alex Star, and Ian Van Wye. Thanks as always to Andrew Wylie.

I am grateful to Alex Rehding, Lanier Anderson, Blake Gopnik, Lev Menand, and Jesse McCarthy for casting expert eyes on some of these pages. My friends Martin Puchner and Tod Lippy read the whole manuscript (which was a lot longer than this book) and gave me welcome advice and support. So did Alison Simmons, my ball of fire.

INDEX

Page numbers in *italics* refer to illustrations.

A NOTE ABOUT THE AUTHOR

Louis Menand is Professor of English at Harvard University and a staff writer at *The New Yorker*. His book *The Metaphysical Club* won the Pulitzer Prize in History and the Francis Parkman Prize from the Society of American Historians. In 2016, he was awarded a National Humanities Medal by President Barack Obama.